Cryptocurrencies in National Laws

Ius Comparatum

VOLUME 8

The titles published in this series are listed at *brill.com/iacl*

Cryptocurrencies in National Laws

A Global Survey

Edited by

Matthias Lehmann
Tetsuo Morishita

BRILL | NIJHOFF

LEIDEN | BOSTON

Library of Congress Cataloging-in-Publication Data

Names: Lehmann, Matthias, 1972- editor | Morishita, Tetsuo, 1966- editor
Title: Cryptocurrencies in national laws : a global survey / edited by Matthias Lehmann and Tetsuo Morishita.
Description: Boston, Massachusetts : Brill, 2025. | Series: Iacl, 2214-6881 | Includes bibliographical references and index. | Summary: "Did you ever wonder whether cryptocurrencies are allowed in Egypt? Or which rights token holders have in case of an insolvency under US law? Or what is the tax treatment of Bitcoin in France? This is the first book to address these questions and others in a comprehensive manner. Twenty-six reporters describe the rules of their national law as applying to the new phenomena, from regulatory to private law, including conflict of laws. The findings are then summarised by two experts. The wide array of information provided in this book will help the reader navigate the global labyrinth of blockchain laws"– Provided by publisher.
Identifiers: LCCN 2024056559 (print) | LCCN 202405 (ebook) | ISBN 9789004722491 (hardback) | ISBN 9789004722507 (ebook)
Classification: LCC K4433 .C795 2025 (print) | LCC K4433 (ebook) | DDC 343/.032–dc23/eng/20241122
LC record available at https://lccn.loc.gov/2024056559
LC ebook record available at https://lccn.loc.gov/2024056560

Typeface for the Latin, Greek, and Cyrillic scripts: "Brill". See and download: brill.com/brill-typeface.

ISSN 2214-6881
ISBN 978-90-04-72249-1 (hardback)
ISBN 978-90-04-72250-7 (e-book)
DOI 10.1163/9789004722507

This book is printed on acid-free paper and produced in a sustainable manner.

Contents

General Report at the IACL Annual Conference in Asunción (Paraguay)

Matthias Lehmann and Tetsuo Morishita

1 Introduction

Cryptocurrencies are among the most remarkable, but also the most disputed, innovations of our time. Some celebrate them as a possible replacement for state-issued or "fiat" currencies, whereas others loathe them as objects of speculation without any inherent value. While only time will tell which of these opinions is correct, states are increasingly introducing new legal rules to police these phenomena. However, only some of these rules are based on suggestions by global fora and institutions, focusing in particular to combat anti-money laundering and safeguard financial stability.[1] The thrust of the law is domestic law, idiosyncratic in both form and content, which creates a fragmented legal environment.

The submission of cryptocurrencies to different national laws may seem antithetical, given that they were conceived as global transfer mechanisms operating outside the law and beyond national borders.[2] Nevertheless, the application of a fragmented regime is a reality today, and as such merits study. Comparing and juxtaposing the different national regulations may have several benefits. First, it gives participants in crypto markets an overview of the various rules they must obey. Second, it may serve legislators as a source of inspiration which regulation to adopt or how to amend their existing one. Third, it could stimulate global regulators to become active by identifying gaps or contradictions in the national regulations and trying to harmonise them. These are the aims of this General Report.

The term "cryptocurrencies" is understood here in a broad sense to cover units transferred on a blockchain that are intended to be used for payments

1 On anti-money laundering issues see Financial Action Task Force, 'Virtual Currencies – Key Definitions and Potential AML/CFT Risks' (2014), available at: http://www.fatf-gafi.org/media/fatf/documents/reports/Virtual-currency-key-definitions-and-potential-aml-cft-risks.pdf (accessed 27 March 2022); on financial stability issues, see e.g. Financial Stability Board, 'Assessment of Risks to Financial Stability from Crypto-Assets' (2022), available at https://www.fsb.org/2022/02/assessment-of-risks-to-financial-stability-from-crypto-assets (accessed 14 April 2022).

2 See the original Bitcoin white paper by Satoshi Nakamoto, 'Bitcoin: A Peer-to-Peer Electronic Cash System' (2008), available at: https://bitcoin.org/bitcoin.pdf (accessed 20 June 2022).

 | DOI:10.1163/9789004722507_002

or as a store of value. Besides Bitcoin as the original and best known, there are many others, which differ from each other in a number of respects, e.g. their volume, the method for their creation, the existence of parties to manage or monitor the system on which they are recorded, the level of anonymity, or the backing by real-world assets (for a taxonomy of cryptocurrencies, see below 1.2).

The structure of this report is as follows: in the rest of this introduction, we will briefly explain the technology underlying cryptocurrencies (A), provide a taxonomy (B), and discuss their possible benefits (C), but also their dangers (D). In the second part, we will compare regulatory rules on cryptocurrencies intended to safeguard public interests, such as preventing financial and other crimes, securing financial stability, and ensuring investor protection. The third part will analyse and compare private law issues, such as the rules governing the protection and transfer of cryptocurrencies. A final part concludes.

1.1 *The Underlying Technology*

The idea behind cryptocurrencies was to privatise and globalise money. To this end, a private global payment transfer mechanism has been invented, which allows direct electronic transfers (peer to peer) of digital assets without the need of both the state and intermediaries. An obstacle on the way towards "private money" was the double-spending problem, i.e. the danger that an asset transferred once would be transferred again by the same person. This issue is critical because money should be exclusive to the holder and be spent only once, whereas digital information is non-exclusive and can generally be freely copied. At the same time, the standard solution to avoid double-spending, a centralised ledger, was unavailable as there is no worldwide institution that could be trusted to keep it.

The answer to this dilemma is called Distributed Ledger Technology (DLT). Essentially, the information will be stored on an electronic ledger that is kept on computers ("nodes") which are constantly updated and synchronised so that the information on the ledger is identical. Moreover, the nodes are independent of each other and dispersed around the world. This makes the network not only resistant to any attack, but also shields it against national authorities.

Any changes to the ledger, such as a transfer of assets, require a consensus of the nodes, which need to agree on the legitimacy and the authenticity of the transfer. To this end, they consult the ledger in order to verify whether the transfer is covered by enough assets. Public-private key cryptography is used to check that the right holder has authorised the transfer. This allows the parties to remain anonymous, or rather pseudonymous, because they are known by their public address, which operates similarly to an email address.

Any transferor must sign the transfer with her private key, which is privy to her and resembles a password. The transfer will be submitted to a process called "hashing", which results in a new code that can be easily traced back to its origins. This works like a one-way trap in that it allows the nodes to easily verify that the correct private key has been used without disclosing the content of the private key to them.

Information about transfers is constantly broadcast to the network of nodes, which verify them and assemble the legitimate and authorised ones into "blocks" of data. These blocks are then broadcasted to other nodes, which check their correctness, again by the use of "hashing". In order to avoid the dominance of malicious nodes in the network that could falsify the ledger, specific "proof" is required from them, which may either consist in the performance of some computing task ("proof of work") or in pledging some native crypto-assets the nodes stand to lose in case of malicious behaviour or inactivity ("proof of stake"). Nodes will be compensated for their efforts by newly minted units of the native cryptocurrency as well as transaction fees ("gas fees") paid by the users.

Once a block is accepted by the other nodes, it will be added to the existing chain of blocks on the ledger (therefore the expression "blockchain"). Through hashing, the blocks in the blockchain will be connected in such a way that it is impossible to change or tamper with the information. In other words, the blockchain is "immutable", safe for creating a separate chain and the dying out of the other one in a "hard fork". The latter however requires consensus by a majority of the nodes, which is difficult to obtain, and therefore remains a rare event.

The result is a distributed, irreversible and tamper-proof record of transactions that is kept in identical form on computers all over the globe. This has a number of benefits, but also downsides, as we will show below (sub 1.3 and 1.4).

1.2 *Taxonomy*

In this General Report, we adopt a very wide notion of cryptocurrencies, which shall encompass both coins and tokens. Coins are units that exist on a dedicated network, typically have no issuer, and do not represent any value outside the blockchain (therefore, they are also called "native assets"). Tokens, on the other hand, build on a pre-existing network and have an issuer that is often known. Tokens may embody a right, for instance a share, a bond, or a claim, or a real-world asset, such as a piece of land or a commodity. In this case, they are called "non-native assets".

Coins, such as Bitcoin, are the most likely to have payment functions. On the other hand, tokens may also serve as a means of payment. Generally, one distinguishes between investment tokens, payment tokens and utility tokens. Most tokens, however, are hybrid ones that mix these functions.[3] Tokens may be further categorised into fungible or non-fungible tokens. The latter (known as NFT) do not lend themselves to financial operations and thus are excluded from this report.

One may also distinguish cryptocurrencies according to their level of programmability. Some are mere records of transfers and can only execute simple functions, such as Bitcoin. The second generation of cryptocurrencies, epitomised by Ether, offers an additional layer on which more complex operations can be executed, for instance smart contracts.

One particular form of token are so-called stablecoins (the terminology is confusing, because stablecoins are in reality tokens). Stablecoins are designed to overcome the volatility typical for virtual assets, making them more attractive as an investment product and a more likely contender for fiat currencies. To this end, they are often backed by another asset or a portfolio of other assets, which may consist, for instance, of a number of fiat currencies or a portfolio of sovereign bonds. The stability may also be obtained by the reference to an index or by an algorithm that buys or sells the coins to smoothen out changes in demand and supply; in this case, one speaks of "synthetic stablecoins".

Central banks, while being sceptical about private cryptocurrencies, have opened up to the idea of issuing digital currencies themselves. These so-called Central Bank Digital Currencies (CBDC) will raise a number of interesting problems, such as the law applicable to them, the possibility of their exchange or their potential for interoperability. Yet CBDC are still in the project stage and therefore will not be studied in this General Report.

1.3 *Benefits*

Cryptocurrencies hail great promises. By allowing transfers between individuals on different points of the planet, they could become the world's genuinely first global payment system. Existing services, such as credit cards, money remittances, or wire transfers, are never truly global. Instead, they are an aggregation of national services or a national provider with a worldwide presence and customer base. Moreover, these services rely on intermediaries.

3 See on the taxonomy International Securities Services Association (ISSA), 'Infrastructure for Crypto-Assets: A Review by Infrastructure Providers' (October 2018), available at: https://www.issanet.org/e/pdf/2018-10_ISSA_report_Infrastructure_for_Crypto-Assets.pdf (accessed 13 March 2020); European Securities Markets Authority (ESMA), 'Advice on Initial Coin Offerings and Crypto-Assets' (9 January 2019), p. 8 para. 19; Philipp Hacker and Chris Thomale, 'Crypto-Securities Regulation: ICOs, Token Sales and Cryptocurrencies under EU Financial Law' (2018) 15(4) European Company and Financial Law Review 645–696.

Cryptocurrencies, on the contrary, work autonomously without the need for an intermediary. They function 365 days a year, 24 hours a day and are accessible from any location in the world. They are independent of state borders and immune to government interruptions, such as capital controls.

Cryptocurrencies thus aspired to become the dominant means of payment worldwide. But reality has developed differently. Cryptocurrency transfers are too slow, too expensive, and lack – at least at this moment – the scalability to compete with fiat currencies as a means of payment. Their prime function is presently another one: as stores of value. Large sums of capital have been invested in them, and they convey immense spending power.[4] This can be explained, in part, by the search for an alternative investment asset, particularly after central banks have inundated markets with liquidity in the wake of the Global Financial Crisis of 2008. Now that this era is coming to an end and central banks are tightening the supply of fiat money and raising interest rates, the value of cryptocurrencies has suffered tremendously. But their independence of governments and central banks may make them attractive again should states' monetary policy loosen once more.

In assessing the possible benefits of cryptocurrencies, one must also remember the many people in the world who have no access to bank accounts and other financial services. For these so-called "unbanked", cryptocurrencies offer the prospect of being able to store the fruits of their labour and obtain finance for their ventures even though they live in countries with an underdeveloped or non-existent financial industry or are discriminated against as bank customers. Many people are also looking for a means of payment or store of value that is independent of the interventions by malign governments or corrupt central bankers. These people may consider cryptocurrencies, regardless of their shortcomings, as progress.

1.4 *Dangers*

As is well known, cryptocurrencies also entail significant risks. Many of them lend themselves to abuse for criminal purposes. An illustration was the "Silk Road", a platform of the so-called "dark net" where arms and drugs were traded.[5] In fairness, one must add that most illegal transactions are still conducted in fiat currencies, which has never caused calls for their prohibition. Also, it must be highlighted that the blockchain may greatly help law enforcement since

4 The value of Bitcoin, as of 1 June 2023, stood at US$ 527,742,880,987, available at: https://coinmarketcap.com (accessed 1 June 2023).

5 Lawrence Trautman, 'Virtual Currencies: Bitcoin & What Now after Liberty Reserve, Silk Road, and Mt. Gox' (2013) 20(1) Richmond Journal of Law & Technology 56.

it provides a perfect record of all transfers. But the condition for such use is that the identity of the holders can be revealed, which is challenging because of the pseudonymity that comes with the public-private key cryptography. Cryptocurrencies provide a useful means to transfer value to an undisclosed location, which blackmailers appreciate as much as tax evaders and sanctions violators.

The investment function of cryptocurrencies also comes with stark risks. Given the pseudonymity and the limited regulation and supervision, misinformation, lies and outright fraud are rampant. As a matter of fact, most of the tokens that are issued via "Initial Coin Offerings" (ICO) do not serve to fund start-ups, but are mere Ponzi schemes. At the same time, the very volatile values of the crypto market entice speculation. Much of the market resembles waging and betting more than serious investment.

The environmental effects of cryptocurrencies are also the subject of debate. It is especially criticised that the proof-of-work mechanism contributes to global warming and climate change. This may not be entirely accurate given that many nodes use sustainable energy forms, such as waterpower. But it remains that the proof-of-work mechanism consumes vast amounts of energy that could be used more efficiently for other purposes. The setting is about to change as networks increasingly replace it with the proof-of-stake mechanism, which is much less energy-intensive. Yet many of the existing networks still use proof of work, and it will be hard to transition them into a more sustainable mode of operation.

Finally, cryptocurrencies are also doubtful from a macroeconomic viewpoint. They reduce the power of monetary policy to avert crises. Should they crowd out fiat currencies, central banks will lose the possibility of influencing the economy by injecting or taking out market liquidity. Theoretically, they could also buy and sell crypto-assets, but this will be much harder than providing fiat currency, which can be "printed" or produced at will. In fact, with the advent of cryptocurrencies, the fate of the monetary system could be transferred from the hands of humans to algorithms. While this may come with benefits in terms of predictability, it dramatically reduces flexibility, particularly the possibility of responding to unexpected events.

2 Regulation and Supervision

So far, only a few countries have adopted regulations specifically targeting cryptocurrencies, except in the context of the fight against money laundering and terrorist financing. However, this does not mean that countries have left cryptocurrency transactions unregulated and without supervision. Rather, many countries are using their existing regulatory frameworks for banking, payments, financial instruments etc. to regulate and take necessary supervisory measures for cryptocurrency transfers that have the same features and risks as traditional financial transactions. In addition, the increase in the volume of cryptocurrency transactions and the growing risks of cryptocurrencies will likely spur the enactment of new, dedicated statutes on cryptocurrencies by other states and bodies. The EU Regulation on Markets in Crypto-Assets (MiCAR), which was adopted on 16 May 2023 and applies in its entirely since 30 December 2024, is an example of such statute.

2.1 *Challenges in the Regulation and Supervision of Cryptocurrencies*

The regulation and supervision of cryptocurrencies encounter several obstacles that either do not arise in the traditional financial context or are substantially greater than those posed by traditional financial transactions.[6]

2.1.1 Variety of Usages and Risks

There are many different types of cryptocurrencies that have a wide variety of usages. Although these are all classified under the broad term "cryptocurrencies", in fact, there are few examples of them serving as a "currency" in the sense of legal tender. The well-known case is El Salvador, which recognises Bitcoin as legal tender (alongside the US$).[7]

The question of whether proposed or existing regulatory requirements are appropriate depends on the functions, actual usage and risks of the new assets. In this respect, crypto-assets are often categorised into three types: "exchange/payment tokens" (used as a means of payment), "security/asset tokens" (representing shares, bonds, or other financial instruments), and "utility tokens" (representing claims to receive certain goods or services).[8] A crypto-asset,

---

6 For example, SEC listed following four difficulties in supervision of ICOs, which are equally applied to cryptocurrencies: (1) tracing money is more difficult because traditional institutes such as banks are not involved, (2) obtaining information is more difficult because the trans actions and uses span the globe, (3) it is difficult to get information because there is no one central authority, and (4) it is difficult to freeze assets or detain assets because virtual currency wallets are encrypted, and virtual currencies are not held by a third-party custodian. (SEC, 'Investor Bulletin: Initial Coin Offering' (25 July 2017)).

7 See El Salvador, Decreto n° 57 'Ley Bitcoin' 9 June 2021 (D.O. 110 vol. 431).

8 UK Cryptoassets Taskforce, 'final report' (2018) 11; Swiss, 'FINMA ICO Guidelines of February 2018'. MiCAR categorises crypto-assets it covers into 'utility tokens', 'asset-referenced tokens' and 'e-money tokens'(Recital 9).

however, may serve more than one function. For example, Bitcoin is used both for investment and payment purposes.

The risks arising from the product design of individual crypto-assets are also relevant. For example, some crypto-assets are susceptible to being used for money laundering and other illegal activities, as records of transfers in these assets are not made public.[9]

This reality poses challenges, such as how to categorise a given cryptocurrency, how to handle cryptocurrencies that may fall into multiple categories, and how to structure regulation and supervision in line with the different risks of individual cryptocurrencies. It is unclear what kind of regulation and supervision can adequately respond to these challenges.

2.1.2 The Ever-Changing Usage

The use of cryptocurrencies is constantly evolving. While many crypto-assets are still used for investment or speculation, an increasing number of them – such as stablecoins – are used for payment purposes. In addition, cryptocurrencies are increasingly employed by automated mechanisms, such as in Decentralized Autonomous Organizations (DAO) and Decentralized Finance (DeFi).[10] It is expected that the functions of cryptocurrencies will continue to change even more rapidly and drastically in the future as technology advances further. This leads to the difficult question of the most appropriate regulatory and supervisory method in responding to this changing picture. Statutory regulations based on detailed legal and regulatory definitions may, in some cases, make it difficult to quickly respond to new use cases arising from novel technological developments or other factors. These include the purposes for which cryptocurrencies are employed or the way in which they are distributed or marketed.[11]

---

9 This concern was expressed in Study Group on Virtual Currency Exchange Services at Japan Financial Services Agency, 'Report from the Study Group on Virtual Currency Exchange Services' (21 December 2018) 9, available at: https://www.fsa.go.jp/en/refer/councils/virtual-currency/20181221-1.pdf (accessed 23 July 2024).

10 IOSCO, 'Decentralized Finance Report' (OR01/2022, March 2022) 10.

11 The Swiss Federal Council has expressed its view on the ideal regulation of DLT by enumerating the following points: (1) Regulations should promote innovation as much as possible, but the market and society should decide which technology will survive; (2) There is no need to make major changes to current laws and regulations, but when necessary due to deficiencies or obstacles, specific necessary adjustments should be made quickly; (3) Principles-based and technology-neutral regulations should be maintained, but exceptions should be allowed when necessary; (4) The rules should be clear and legally certain, and attempts to circumvent regulations through fraudulent practices or the use of new technologies should not be tolerated; (5) Authorities should have an open attitude toward new technologies and innovation, and should value regular dialogue with

2.1.3 Unclear Future Benefits and Risks

It is not clear whether cryptocurrencies will bring new and substantial value to future societies, or whether they will increase financial disorder, facilitate crime, and cause harm to investors. It is also unclear whether the use of cryptocurrencies will remain a phenomenon limited to certain circles of society, or whether they will become so prevalent that social activities in global society will not run smoothly without them. No country wants to fall behind by hindering the development of the key innovations of the future. On the other hand, legislators and regulators also want to prevent the negative effects of new technologies. Thus, authorities in each country face the difficult task of striking the right balance between openness to innovation and prevention of harm.[12]

These conflicting goals form the background of the diverging attitudes of countries, which ultimately render legal harmonisation and cooperative regulatory efforts more difficult.

2.1.4 New Players, Missing Players

The cryptocurrency sector is dominated by players that are different from those that are at the focus of traditional financial regulation, e.g. banks, securities firms, and insurance companies. Actors in the cryptocurrency sector have an unconventional type of corporate culture and are typically unfamiliar with conventional financial regulation. Regulators therefore face challenges in how to properly interact with and effectively regulate these new players. In addition, for completely decentralised networks like Bitcoin, which have no issuer and can be held and transferred without any intermediaries, finding an entity to regulate and supervise is in itself a problem.[13] Further challenges arise from DAO and DeFi, which raise the question of how transactions that are fully

---

industry. See Swiss Federal Council, 'Federal Council report on the Legal framework for distributed ledger technology and blockchain in Switzerland: An overview with a focus on the financial sector'(December 2018) 12 et seq.

12 The FSB, 'Statement on International Regulation and Supervision of Crypto-asset Activities' (11 July 2022) 1 expresses this concern by saying "An effective regulatory framework must ensure that crypto-asset activities posing risks similar to traditional financial activities are subject to the same regulatory outcomes, while taking account of novel features of crypto-assets and harnessing potential benefits of the technology behind them."

13 Primavera De Filippi and Aaron Wright, *Blockchain and the Law* (Harvard University Press 2018) 173 et seq. discuss various possible alternate regulation addressees. The consultation paper of FSB also states, "The extensive use of distributed ledger technology as well as the decentralized nature of operations and/or governance have contributed to opaqueness and lack of accountability in governance of both stablecoin arrangements and other crypto-assets. It can be difficult to identify the entities or natural persons that should be held accountable for good governance and regulatory compliance", Financial

automated and conducted without human intervention can be properly regulated and supervised.

2.1.5 Cross-Border Nature

Most cryptocurrency transactions using DLT are completed online and span several states.[14] In this respect, the Financial Stability Board (FSB) demands that, "[c]rypto-assets and markets must be subject to effective regulation and oversight commensurate to the risks they pose, both at the domestic and international level", and "[a]ny persons and entities operating in crypto-asset markets must be aware that they should meet all applicable regulatory, supervisory and oversight requirements of a particular jurisdiction before commencing any operations."[15] However, achieving such an ideal "awareness" and compliance with all applicable regulatory and supervisory regimes is not easy.

First, the regulatory attitude towards cryptocurrencies differs widely from one country to another. This allows crypto-asset providers to base themselves in less-regulated countries and do business all over the world. By doing so, such providers might escape from effective regulation and oversight when a country has tightened its regulatory regime.

Second, in the world of cryptocurrencies, where the entire transaction may be completed on the internet, it is easy for foreign business operators to provide services to residents of a country where they are not permitted to do so under the laws of that country. In this case, even if the regulations of that country purport to apply extraterritorially and the authorities attempt to exercise their supervisory powers over the foreign operator, but the foreign operator ignores the applicability of those regulations and does not submit to this supervision, there is nothing that can be done.

Third, if parties involved in a transaction are located in more than one country, authorities in multiple countries need to work together to address the case. However, such cooperation may be difficult when the regulatory policies of the relevant countries differ.

Stability Board, 'International Regulation of Crypto-asset Activities: A proposed framework – questions for consultation' (11 October 2022) 3.

14 For example, in China, though foreign business providers are explicitly prohibited from providing services to Chinese residents and the Chinese Internet firewall system blocks the web-sites of offshore exchange platforms, there are still some people who use private VPNs to access offshore exchange platforms to buy and sell cryptocurrencies (China, sub 3.3).

15 FSB, 'Statement on International Regulation and Supervision of Crypto-asset Activities' (11 July 2022).

2.1.6 Relationship between Technology and Law

Cryptocurrencies are underpinned by technologies such as distributed ledger technology and public key cryptography. The extent to which these technologies are reliable and can be used safely has a direct correlation with the risks associated with cryptocurrency transactions. However, these technologies are still new and the risks are not yet fully known. On the other hand, if technology can reduce risk in general and prevent illegal or inappropriate transactions, it may be possible to use these technologies to fulfil some of the roles that laws and regulations have played. The challenge is striking the appropriate balance between the roles to be played by law and by technology.

2.2 *National and International Landscape in Regulations of Cryptocurrencies*

2.2.1 General Attitudes of Governments

Attitudes towards cryptocurrencies differ widely. While Bitcoin is currently legal tender in one country, El Salvador,[16] there are countries that substantially restrict its usage. Some of the countries for which we have received reports illustrate this. China prohibits the issuance of cryptocurrencies for business or financing purposes related to cryptocurrencies; though even in China, individuals are not prohibited from simply holding crypto-assets.[17] Kazakhstan prohibits the issuance and circulation of unsecured digital assets, including cryptocurrencies, within its territory, save for exceptional cases.[18]

Most countries take an intermediate position between these two extremes: they do not give cryptocurrencies the status of legal tender, but they also do not prohibit the circulation of cryptocurrencies nor crypto-related business. Most of these countries agree that cryptocurrencies should be subject to some form of regulation; consensus is particularly strong in the area of anti-money laundering and countering terrorism finance. However, there are various differences in the content of national laws regarding (1) which cryptocurrencies are subject to regulation and supervision, (2) for which purposes and goals, (3) under which legal framework, and (4) which specific matters need to be regulated. In addition, the fiscal treatment of cryptocurrencies differs widely; with some countries taxing the income derived from cryptocurrency trading,

---

16 The Central African Republic has briefly declared Bitcoin to be legal tender but thereafter withdrawn this decision.

17 China, sub 1.

18 Kazakhstan, sub 2.

while others market themselves as "crypto-tax havens" and try to lure crypto-businesses onto their territory with low or no taxes.[19]

One can indeed take different views on the need for regulation. Some countries emphasise primarily the risks associated with cryptocurrencies, while others adopt especially lenient policies in a bid to become a global centre of crypto-related business. The differing realities across countries also must be borne in mind: in some countries, cryptocurrencies have become a popular subject of investment and speculation, while in others their use is still negligible. The diverging level of regulation and supervision reflects these differences in governmental views, political strategies, as well as local circumstances.

2.2.1 International Organisations

Various initiatives regarding cryptocurrencies have been undertaken at the international level. For example, in July 2023, the FSB published a "Global Regulatory Framework for Crypto-Asset Activities". This framework stresses "same activity, same risk, same regulation", "high level and flexibility" and "technology neutrality" as fundamental policy principles and consists of two sets of recommendations: (1) high-level recommendations for the regulation, supervision and oversight of crypto-asset activities and markets and (2) revised high-level recommendations for the regulation, supervision, and oversight of "global stablecoin" arrangements. The former consists of nine recommendations and the latter of ten. Both do not comprehensively cover cryptocurrency issues, but focus on financial stability.[20] The Financial Action Task Force (FATF) has led the worldwide initiatives on AML/CTF. It published a "Guidance for a Risk-Based Approach, Virtual Currencies" (June 2015), which was updated in 2018 and 2019. Also, the FATF published "Updated Guidance for a Risk-based Approach: Virtual Assets and Virtual Asset Service Providers" (2021), containing guidance on the application of a "travel-rule" to cryptocurrencies. These global initiatives, especially those of the FATF, have been influential in many countries.

2.3 *Regulatory Definitions and Categories of "Cryptocurrency"*

Before addressing the content of regulations, we first consider how countries define cryptocurrencies therein.

---

19 Werner Vermaak, 'Where Are the World's Crypto Tax Havens in 2021?' (2022), available at: https://coinmarketcap.com/alexandria/article/where-are-the-worlds-crypto-tax-havens-in-2021 (accessed 23 July 2024). On tax law, see *infra* 5.

20 FSB, 'Global Regulatory Framework for Crypto-asset Activities' (17 July 2023).

Many countries do not have any special regulations on cryptocurrencies, other than the AML/CFT ones. In such countries, definitions in the AML/CFT regulations are the only definitions of cryptocurrencies. These AML/CFT regulations are often in line with FATF guidance and European directives.[21] Although these definitions differ in wording, their essence is the same: they focus on functions conventionally thought of as currency functions, such as a medium of exchange and store of value.[22]

However, to regulate cryptocurrencies appropriately according to their different functions, a single definition of cryptocurrencies or crypto-assets may not suffice. Countries with special laws and regulations for crypto-assets have multiple categories and/or definitions as to regulate different types of crypto-assets in different ways. For example, the EU Regulation on Markets in Crypto-Assets (MiCAR) defines "crypto-asset" as a "digital representation of a value or a right which may be transferred and stored electronically, using distributed ledger technology or similar technology"; however, it has three further specific categories, namely "asset-referenced token", "electronic money token", and "utility token". Similarly, Japan has multiple definitions for virtual assets such as "crypto-asset" (e.g. tokens that may be used for payment), "electronically recorded transferable right" (e.g. tokens that may be used for investment), and "electronic payment instrument" (some types of stablecoins).[23]

Of these types of crypto-assets, utility tokens are probably the farthest away from conventional financial transactions and products. For this reason, even those countries that submit exchange/payment tokens and security/asset tokens to financial regulation do not regulate utility tokens.[24] A significant exception is the EU, which addresses utility and other tokens in its MiCAR. However, the focus of the Regulation is on stablecoins (dubbed "asset-referenced tokens" and "e-money tokens"), which are submitted to the most stringent conditions, and even are capped in volume when they become so significant

21 Directive (EU) 2018/843 of the European Parliament and of the Council of 30 May 2018 amending Directive (EU) 2015/849 on the prevention of the use of the financial system for the purposes of money laundering or terrorist financing, and amending Directives 2009/138/EC and 2013/36/EU [2018] OJ L 156/43.

22 For example, in line with the European directive, the Danish Money Laundering Act provides the following definition: "Virtual currency: A digital expression of value that is not issued or guaranteed by a central bank or a public authority, is not necessarily tied to a legally created currency and does not have the same legal status as currency or money, but is accepted by physical and legal entities as a means of exchange, which can be transferred, stored and traded electronically".

23 Japan, sub. 1.2.

24 For example, Japanese regulations on crypto-assets are not applied to utility tokens.

that they could endanger fiat currencies.[25] This shows that stablecoins are an entirely different category from the three others and raise special concerns.

2.4 *Regulation of AML/CFT*

Most countries for which national reports were submitted subject cryptocurrencies to AML/CFT rules. However, there are some differences between the respective regulations. In addition to conventional rules, such as imposing on cryptocurrency exchanges the obligation to report suspicious transactions to the relevant authorities, some countries have legislated or intend to legislate a so-called "travel rule". This rule requires crypto-asset exchanges that send virtual currency at the request of users to disclose certain information about the sender and recipient of the virtual currency to the recipient's exchange.[26]

2.5 *Four Types of Regulatory Responses to Cryptocurrencies*

In other areas than AML/CFT, the regulation of cryptocurrencies in the countries where a national report was submitted can be broadly divided into four main categories:

1. Countries that severely restrict cryptocurrency transactions through special laws and regulations or administrative measures;
2. Countries that do not have special laws and regulations for cryptocurrencies, but regulate them by applying existing regulations on payments, financial instruments, or the like, depending on the function of the cryptocurrency;
3. Countries that have enacted special laws regulating those who engage in businesses involving cryptocurrencies and transactions in cryptocurrencies, and that allow transactions to be conducted in accordance with those regulations;
4. Countries that have not enacted special laws and regulations for cryptocurrencies, nor submit them to legal restrictions, but rather allow for them to be freely traded.

25 See on the last point Art 23 MiCAR.

26 In Japan, the travel rule has entered into force in April 2022. In the EU, the European Commission, 'Regulation 2023/1113 of the European Parliament and of the Council on the information accompanying transfers of funds and certain crypto-assets' (OJ L.150/1, 9.6.2023) applies the travel rule to crypto-assets service providers, and the European Banking Authority issued the Guidelines on information requirements in relation to transfers of funds and certain crypto-assets transfers under Regulation (EU) 2023/1113 on 4 July 2024.

The following provides an overview of the status of each category. Please note that the description of countries belonging to the EU was made prior to the implementation of MiCAR.[27]

2.5.1 Countries that Severely Restrict Cryptocurrencies

As mentioned earlier, China, Kazakhstan, and Egypt have substantial restrictions on activities related to cryptocurrencies. However, these are not the only countries with such restrictions.

In Macao, despite there being no legislation that prohibits cryptocurrency transactions, the Monetary Authority explicitly requires, since 2018, all banks and payment services institutions in the Special Administrative Region "not to participate in or provide, directly or indirectly, any financial services that involve the use of virtual currencies or virtual commodities as the means of payment". According to the national report, such administrative actions by the Authority discourage all types of activities involving cryptocurrencies and make the operation of crypto intermediary services practically impossible in Macao.[28]

In Turkey, the Central Bank has issued a regulation prohibiting the use of crypto-assets in payments for goods and services. According to the National Report, "Turkish lawmakers do not want cryptocurrencies to be an alternative payment instrument to the Turkish Lira. Therefore, they intentionally refrain from using the phrase 'cryptocurrency'". With this regulation, services that enable direct or indirect use of crypto-assets in payments are prohibited. Moreover, payment and electronic money institutions cannot act as intermediaries for platforms that offer trading, custody, transfer, or issue services related to crypto-assets; nor can they assist fund transfers made on these platforms. However, investment in crypto-assets is not prohibited in Turkey.[29]

2.5.2 Countries Using Existing Regulatory Frameworks without Special Laws Targeting Cryptocurrencies

Using the existing rules for other financial products or services is the most popular approach to cryptocurrency regulation and supervision so far. The United States is a typical example: cryptocurrencies tend to be subject to the general regulations at the level of federal law, e.g. the Securities Act 1933 and the Securities Exchange Act 1934, because most cryptocurrencies are

---

27 Regarding the impact of MiCAR on the national legal framework, see for example, Sweden, sub 3.3, Hungary, sub 13.1, France, sub 1.1.3, sub 2.1.2, sub 2.2.5 and sub 2.7.

28 Macao, sub 3.

29 Turkey, sub 3.1.

considered to be "securities". Bitcoin and Ether are two notable exceptions; they are considered to be "commodities" under the Commodity Exchange Act.[30] Some federal states, such as the State of New York, have enacted additional laws for crypto services.[31]

In Singapore, whether a digital asset is subject to the existing regulatory framework depends on its function. Where the asset serves the same function as a security, the Securities and Futures Act (SFA) may apply. Where it has the characteristics of a digital payment token, it will be governed by the Payment Services Act. Finally, where a digital asset is backed by commodities, it may fall under the Commodity and Trading Act (CTA).[32]

The UK also regulates crypto-assets in line with traditional categories. Depending on their function, they may be classified as (1) "specified investments" under the Financial Services and Markets Act 2000 (FSMA 2000) and the associated "Regulated Activities Order 2001" (RAO 2001); (2) "financial instruments" under the old but maintained MiFID regime; (3) "e-money" under the Electronic Money Regulations 2011 (EMR 2011); or (4) activities falling within the scope of the Payment Services Regulations 2017 (PSR 2017).[33] It should be noted that the UK government took actions for future regulatory framework of cryptocurrencies, and published the response to the consultation and the plan for the regulation of fiat-based stablecoin in October 2023.[34]

The Australian Securities and Investments Commission (ASIC) states that it "currently regulates crypto-assets and related products and services to the extent they fall within the existing regulatory perimeter of 'financial products and services.'"[35] If the activities of an entity concerning cryptocurrencies and crypto-assets fall into the category of providing financial services or issuing, distributing or dealing in financial products under the Corporations Act, the entity will need to apply to ASIC for an Australian Financial Services (AFS) License and will be subject to the various obligations imposed on AFS licensees.[36]

30 US, sub 2 and 3.

31 US, sub III 2.

32 Singapore, sub 2.1.

33 UK, sub 2.1.1.

34 HM Treasury, "Response to the consultation and call for evidence" (October 2023), and HM Treasury, "Update on Plans for the Regulation of Fiat-backed Stablecoins" (October 2023).

35 The Senate (Australia), Select Committee on Australia as a Technology and Financial Centre, Final Report (October 2021), [2.36].

36 Australia, sub 2.1.

Germany also has used the existing regulatory framework to regulate cryptocurrencies, particularly the Banking Act (KWG). One of the features of German regulatory law is that a new definition of "crypto value" (Kryptowert) has been added to the KWG. The KWG expressly provides that "crypto values" are a "financial instrument", with the consequence that a person providing services related to 'crypto values' requires a licence as a financial services institution under the Act.[37]

Denmark does not have special legislation for cryptocurrencies, but all marketing and advertisement of cryptocurrencies are subject to the Danish Marketing Act (2017).[38] In addition, if a cryptocurrency represents a claim against an issuer which is used as a means of payment, that cryptocurrency may be subject to the regulation of electronic money under the Payment Act.[39]

In Italy, the majority view is that cryptocurrencies are not "financial instruments" within the meaning of the Italian Act that implements the EU MiFID regime.[40] However, through a regulation issued in 2022 by the Ministry of Economics and Finance, exchanges and e-wallet (custody) service providers fall within the existing framework for professional currency-exchange service providers. Provision of such services is reserved for registered firms, and abusive practices and activities in this context are subject to a pecuniary fine.[41]

Sweden is a further country that addresses cryptocurrencies with existing legislation. Depending on the nature of the crypto-asset, it may be subject to the Electronic Money Act (2011:755) and/or the Financial Instruments Trading Act (1991:980).[42]

In New Zealand, the Financial Market Authority, which exercises supervisory functions, has expressed the view that if activities relating to cryptocurrencies involve the provision of "financial services" to persons in New Zealand; such activities may be regulated under the Financial Service Providers Act, which requires service providers to be registered. Similarly, if activities involving cryptocurrencies are considered to be activities involving financial products (debt securities, equity securities, managed investment products, and derivatives), such activities will fall under the Financial Market Conduct Act.[43]

In Taiwan, the Financial Supervisory Commission has issued an order declaring that cryptocurrencies with the features of "securities" (i.e. typically

37 Germany, sub 2.2.
38 Denmark, sub 4.
39 Denmark, sub 2.
40 Italy, sub 2.
41 Italy, sub 3.
42 Sweden, sub 3.2.
43 New Zealand, sub 3.1 and 3.2.

issued with the purpose of fund-raising from the public) will be treated as a kind of "securities" under the Securities Exchange Act.[44] In addition, issuing cryptocurrencies in exchange for accepting deposit without banking license or soliciting money from the public in a Ponzi scheme will be a breach of the Banking Act.[45]

In Austria, crypto-related businesses may be subject to the regulations on banking or financial instruments, depending on the purpose and function of the business. For example, issuing cryptocurrencies in exchange for money that is repayable may be considered as a deposit business. Also, issuing crypto-assets such as payment tokens may be regulated as the issuance and management of payment instruments.[46] Although the prevailing view is that cryptocurrencies, such as Bitcoin, are not financial instruments, security tokens will be regulated as securities under the existing regulatory framework.[47]

In Switzerland, the supervisory authority, FINMA, published 2018 the FINMA ICO Guidelines relating to token issuance, which classifies tokens into three categories.[48] However, as there are no laws specifically enacted for cryptocurrencies, according to the National Report, "cryptocurrencies are neither explicitly authorised nor prohibited."[49] In September 2020, the Swiss Federal Act on the Adaptation of Federal Laws to Developments in Distributed Electronic Register Technology (DLT Act) was adopted. It mainly addresses DLT securities, DLT trading venues and the segregation of DLT assets in insolvency proceedings. The striking feature of the DLT Act is that it adapted ten relevant laws to reflect the nature of tokens, focusing on their economic function. Through such adaptation, Swiss laws were made flexible and capable of responding to innovative business models, which FINMA assesses on a case-by-case basis by applying the principle "same risks, same rules". For example, the DLT Act amended the Banking Act so that any person who accepts certain types of crypto-assets must obtain a licence because accepting crypto-assets is considered to have some similarities to accepting bank deposits.[50]

44 Taiwan, sub 3.2.
45 Taiwan, sub 3.3.
46 Austria, sub 2.2.
47 Austria, sub 2.3.
48 Switzerland, sub 2.2.
49 Switzerland, sub 3.1.
50 Switzerland, sub 3.2–3.6.

2.5.3 Countries that have Enacted Special Laws and Regulations on Cryptocurrencies

Some countries have enacted special laws for cryptocurrencies, though the substantive content and scope of such special regimes differ.

For example, Finland enacted the Act on Virtual Currency Providers in 2019 to address money laundering and protect consumers.[51] The Act targets "virtual currency providers", such as virtual currency issuers, virtual currency exchanges, and wallet service providers.[52] The Act imposes an obligation to register, preserve service-related documents and information, safeguard and hold client assets, as well as duties relating to marketing, customer due diligence, and risk management systems.[53]

In France, the PACTE law[54] introduced two regulatory frameworks specifically for crypto-assets. The first is a regime addressing public offerings of tokens, which provides for an optional visa issued by the financial supervisor (Autorité des Marchés Financiers – AMF). This intends to encourage the development of ICO, and applies to tokens that have the quality of digital assets that are subject to the regulation of public offering of securities (with the exception of security tokens). To obtain the optional visa from the AMF for a public offering of tokens, the issuer must (1) be incorporated as a legal entity established or registered in France; (2) produce a white paper in compliance with the regulations and instructions of the AMF; (3) set up a process for the monitoring and safeguarding of the assets invested by token-holders in compliance with the regulations and instructions of the AMF; (4) set up a system to combat money laundering and terrorism financing.[55] In addition, the PACTE law introduced regulations for digital asset service providers. Registration is mandatory to provide one of the following businesses or services: (1) custody of digital assets; (2) purchase or sale of digital assets for legal tender; (3) exchange of digital assets for other digital assets; and (4) operating a trading platform for digital assets. This regulation applies when a digital asset service is provided in France, which is deemed to be the case when the service is provided by a service provider with facilities in France, or when it is provided at the initiative of the service provider to customers residing or established in France. According to the AMF, the service is considered to be provided in France when the provider addresses a

51 Finland, sub 2.2.1.

52 Finland, sub 3.2.4.

53 Finland, sub 3.2.5.

54 Loi n° 2019-486 du 22 mai 2019 relative à la croissance et la transformation des entreprises.

55 France, sub 1.1.4.

promotional communication, regardless of the medium, to customers residing or established in France or when the provider has a postal address or telephone number in France.[56] From January 2024, the requirements for mandatory registration have been enhanced by introducing requirements similar to MiCAR to address the collapse of FTX.[57]

Japan amended its Payment Services Act in 2016 and introduced a new chapter on cryptocurrencies in response to the insolvency of Mt. Gox. The main purpose of the amendment was customer protection. Following serious hacking cases involving cryptocurrency exchanges and the challenge of dealing with ICOs, the Japanese Payment Services Act and Financial Instruments and Exchange Act were further amended in 2019: (1) the term "virtual currencies" used in the Payment Services Act was changed to "crypto-assets"; (2) the regulation of crypto-asset exchanges was strengthened; (3) a new regulation on crypto-asset custodians was introduced; (4) a new regulation on issuers and intermediaries of securities tokens was introduced; (5) crypto-asset derivatives and margin transactions have been made subject to the securities regulation and margin regulation; and (6) the rules on unfair transactions, such as market manipulation, have become applicable to crypto-assets. In addition, the Payment Services Act and Banking Act were amended in 2022 to develop a regulatory framework for stablecoins. This amendment clarified the rules on issuing stablecoins and introduced a regulatory framework for intermediaries dealing with stablecoins.[58]

Korea enacted the Act for Protection of Virtual Asset Users in July 2023, which has entered into force on July 19, 2024. The Act is designed to regulate the virtual asset service industry from consumer/investor protection perspectives by introducing express rules on segregation of customers' assets and on measures to address computer hacking or network crash. The Act also regulates unfair transactions in virtual asset markets.[59] In addition to the Act, the Financial Investment Services and Capital Markets Act may be applied to security-type tokens and the Foreign Exchange Transaction Law may be applied to stablecoins that grant a right to certain fiat currencies.[60]

In the EU, the special regulatory framework targeting cryptocurrencies, MiCAR, is remarkable in the breadth of its scope, the strictness of its regulations,

---

56 France, sub 1.2.1.

57 France, sub 1.2.3.

58 Japan sub 2.

59 Financial Services Commission, Press Release: Government to Ensure Virtual Asset User Protection, Transaction Transparency and Market Discipline, June 30, 2023 (https://www.fsc.go.kr/eng/pr010101/80317).

60 Korea, sub 1.2.1.

and the number of countries involved. It is a comprehensive regulatory framework for crypto-assets, with special rules for asset-referenced tokens and electronic money tokens. It imposes a number of duties on crypto-asset service providers (CASP), which are defined as those who engage in services relating to crypto-assets such as (1) custody and administration; (2) operating trading platforms; (3) exchanging crypto-asset for funds; (4) exchanging crypto-assets for other crypto-assets; (5) executing orders on behalf of third parties; (6) placing crypto-assets; (7) providing transfer services on behalf of third parties; (8) receiving and transmitting orders on behalf of third parties; (9) providing advice; and (10) providing portfolio management. Regarding the regulation of asset-referenced tokens, no issuer can offer tokens to the public without authorisation and issuers must satisfy various requirements such as robust governance and sufficient own funds. White papers providing information listed in the regulation must be published. Issuers have to maintain a reserve of assets and ensure that the reserve assets are segregated from the issuers' own assets. Issuers shall ensure that holders of tokens have a direct claim and redemption right against the issuer and on the reserve fund.[61] E-money tokens may be offered to public only by credit institutions or e-money institutions, and issuers must notify a crypto-asset white paper to the competent authority and publish that crypto-asset white paper before the offering.[62] CASPs need an authorisation from the competent authority of the Member State, and shall be registered by ESMA. They must meet prudential requirements and make adequate arrangements to safeguard the ownership rights of clients, especially in the event of the crypto-asset service providers' insolvency. When providing custody and administration of crypto-assets on behalf of third parties, CASPs must segregate customers' assets from their own assets, and will be liable to their customers for the loss of crypto-assets resulting from malfunctions or hacks up to the market value of the crypto-assets.[63]

2.5.4 Countries that Do Not Regulate Cryptocurrencies Either under Special or Existing Legislation

Some countries do not regulate cryptocurrencies, either under special laws targeting cryptocurrencies or existing legislation.

For example, Croatia does not have any special legislation on cryptocurrencies. The Croatian National Bank has expressly concluded that cryptocurrency transactions do not represent payment transactions and that trading and

61 Title III of MiCAR contains rules for asset-referenced tokens.

62 Title IV of MiCAR contains rules for e-money tokens.

63 Title V of MiCAR contains rules for CASPs.

payment in cryptocurrencies cannot be considered a payment service under the Payment Transactions Act. Consequently, cryptocurrencies in Croatia are not regulated except for anti-money laundering purposes.[64] The Polish National Report explains that "it can be concluded that trading in cryptocurrencies has generally been allowed in Poland from the very beginning. Still, there are no specific laws dealing with the regulation of cryptocurrencies in Polish legal system."[65] The situation in these countries will change with the entry into force of MiCAR.

However, the fact that there is no regulation on cryptocurrencies does not automatically mean that these countries actively support cryptocurrencies. Rather, it seems that the countries listed here are taking a "wait-and-see" approach because the scale of cryptocurrency transactions remains small and has not yet reached the stage where it has a major social impact.[66]

2.5.5 Observation

At this stage, there is no correct or incorrect approach as to how to regulate cryptocurrencies. There is a certain rationale underpinning all of the policy decisions we have identified from the national reports. It seems that it will take a little more time before the most appropriate way to regulate the phenomenon of cryptocurrencies becomes clear.

Because of their variety, the determination of whether a specific cryptocurrency is subject to an existing law or regulation remains unclear; this tends to be determined on a case-by-case basis, even in countries that intend to extend their existing regime to the new phenomena. On the other hand, enacting new laws and regulations specifically for cryptocurrencies will not necessarily solve all the problems they have created. In particular, it is difficult to establish a definition that appropriately encompasses various cryptocurrencies according to their functions. Once, however, a definition is established, technological and business developments may make the definition obsolete. In this case, the actual situation would no longer be adequately captured by the definition, and phenomena that should be regulated may be left out of the scope of the regulation.

---

64 Croatia, sub 2.

65 Poland, sub 3.1.

66 The national report of the Netherlands calls such regulatory attitude as "regulatory sand-box".

2.6 *The Possibility and Content of Special Regulations for Cryptocurrencies*

Several arguments may be raised in support of special regulatory laws and regulations specifically targeting cryptocurrencies. First, even if the content of such laws and regulations were the same as those for other financial transactions, express reference to cryptocurrencies would make the application of such regulations to cryptocurrencies more transparent and more predictable for all parties concerned. Second, as was intended by Switzerland's DLT Act, some modifications to existing laws and regulations may improve their application to cryptocurrencies, thereby making the same regulations work more efficiently and effectively. Third, risks specific to cryptocurrencies, or those that are more significant for cryptocurrencies than for other payment or financial instruments, could be specifically addressed through tailored rules.

Assuming that a new comprehensive regulatory framework is, thus, desirable, it remains difficult to decide what and how to regulate.

2.6.1 Parties to be Regulated

As with traditional financial regulation, issuers, intermediaries, exchanges, or investors could be subject to regulation, depending on the type of activities they engage in. For example, MiCAR regulates issuers of tokens and intermediaries who will provide various services to their customers. Also, to maintain the fairness of the crypto market, anti-competitive behaviour by individual investors in the crypto context – such as market manipulation and insider trading – could be subject to regulation.[67]

For cryptocurrencies without an issuer, such as Bitcoin, regulating individual users could be an option. However, the current regulations mainly target intermediaries and focus on AML/CFT and customer protection; probably because it is not yet considered sufficiently necessary to regulate the use of Bitcoin *per se*, and because most Bitcoin users employ intermediaries such as cryptocurrency exchanges. However, if cryptocurrencies without an issuer and/or direct holdings without intermediaries become more prevalent in the future, the question of who and how to regulate them will likely become a difficult issue.

Finally, the environmental impact of mining is an issue unique to cryptocurrencies that has also been discussed in various national reports.[68]

---

67 Both MiCAR and Japanese law have specific provisions that prohibit wrongful behaviour of individuals in relation to crypto-assets.

68 Concerns from environmental aspects are mentioned in some national reports, such as Finland, sub 8, Sweden sub 3.3, Kazakhstan, sub 5 & 7.4, and USA, sub 2 (fn 76).

2.6.2 Types of Cryptocurrencies

The risks associated with cryptocurrencies can vary widely, depending on the function and nature of the individual cryptocurrency itself. For this reason, a possible regulatory approach could be for authorities to check the nature of the cryptocurrencies intended for use and allow only those considered suitable from a risk perspective. This is the approach taken in Japan: in the application for registration, the types of crypto-assets that an applicant plans to handle are to be specified; the Japanese Financial Services Authority then checks if the listed crypto-assets are appropriate from the perspective of AML/CFT, the protection of customers, and the proper execution of services.[69]

The question of how to regulate stablecoins is also an important issue, and regulators across the world have demonstrated considerable caution in relation to global stablecoins. First, the relationship and potential competition with national currencies issued by a sovereign authority is a serious matter. For example, Turkey does not allow cryptocurrencies to be used for payments;[70] and it is possible that other countries will adopt similar policies if the volume of payments in cryptocurrencies increases. Second, if users expect cryptocurrencies to function in the same way as fiat currencies with stable value, it is essential to ensure that such users' legitimate expectations are met. To this end, regulatory measures to be considered could include: allowing only those with a high degree of trustworthiness to act as issuers;[71] providing holders of stablecoins with rights to claim redemption at par value;[72] or imposing strict requirements that the crypto-assets are securely backed.[73] Finally, considering the various incidents of hacking, and the fact that some technologies are insufficiently mature for use as a long-term alternative to fiat currencies, it remains an open question as to whether it is technically possible to create a cryptocurrency that is as stable as legal tender.

2.6.3 Protecting Customers

Customer protection is one of most important concerns of financial regulation. To protect customers who use cryptocurrencies, certain unique measures need to be considered.

69 Japan, sub 2.2.2.

70 Turkey, sub 3.1.

71 MiCAR allows the issuance of electronic money token by credit institutions and e-money institutions (Article 43, 1).

72 Article 44 MiCAR. Given the importance of granting such redemption rights, the next question arises as to whether to require that the assets backing the redemption rights be secured in the country.

73 Japan, sub 4.2.

One such measure concerns the information to be disclosed by issuers. In this regard, the MiCAR requires crypto-asset issuers to publish a white paper, with a mandatory minimum content.[74] In addition, crypto-asset service providers are required to act fairly and professionally, and provide sufficient and accurate information including various risks of crypto-assets.[75]

Protecting customers' assets from hacking is also an important issue. Japan provides a salient example: after experiencing several cases involving exchanges being hacked, Japan adopted strict rules regarding the protection and management of customers' assets. Under Japanese law, customers' crypto-assets must be managed in a separate wallet from that in which the crypto-assets of the crypto exchanges/custodians themselves are managed; and the customers' crypto-assets must be managed in media that are not constantly connected to the internet (i.e., not in hot wallets), except to the minimum extent necessary for the smooth operation of the business (at most 5% of the total value). To protect customers from the risk of hacking, a crypto-asset exchange is further required to hold crypto-assets of the same type and to the same volume as the customers' crypto-assets in a medium that is constantly connected to the internet (i.e., in a hot wallet) but separately from the exchange's own crypto-assets. These are called 'performance-guarantee crypto-assets', because they are used to ensure the performance by crypto-asset exchanges of their obligations to customers in the event that crypto-assets in a hot wallet are stolen by hackers. Customers have a lien (a right to receive payment from the assets in preference over other creditors) over the crypto-assets that are separately kept from the asset of the crypt-assets exchange and the performance guarantee crypto-assets kept by the crypto-asset exchange.[76]

2.7 *Cross-Border Aspects of Regulations and Supervision*

Given that cryptocurrency transactions easily transcend borders, the question of how to regulate such cross-border transactions is another difficult issue.

For example, the Finish Act on Cryptocurrency Service Providers is considered to apply to both (1) domestic and foreign virtual currency providers that provide services in Finland, and (2) domestic virtual currency providers, even if they provide services only abroad and not in Finland.[77] In Japan, the supervisory authority has expressed the view that posting advertisements for crypto-asset exchange services on a website constitutes the solicitation of services to

74 For example, Article 4 (1), 5 MiCAR and Article 24 MiCAR.

75 Article 59 and 73 MiCAR; Japan, sub 2.2.2. and 4.3.

76 Japan, sub 2.2.2.

77 Finland, sub 2.2.3.

persons in Japan, unless the website clearly states that the service will not be provided to persons in Japan, or the service provider takes necessary measures to avoid transacting with persons on Japanese soil, e.g., by checking the location of its customers.[78] The MiCAR has similar provisions prohibiting foreign entities from providing crypto-asset services within the EU without authorisation.[79] However, where a client in the EU initiates transactions with a service provider in a third country purely at its own initiative, no such authorisation is required.[80]

Even where the relevant legislation expressly stipulates that the provision of services by foreign entities without the requisite authorisation/registration is illegal, such regulation remains difficult to enforce. For example, the Japanese FSA has issued warnings to fifteen foreign businesses for having offered crypto-asset exchange services to Japanese residents via the internet without due registration; however, to the best of the Japanese reporter's knowledge, there has not been any response from these foreign entities.[81] Cooperation amongst countries is critical to the effective regulation of cross-border trade. However, countries differ in their responses to cryptocurrencies; and companies offering crypto-services globally are often based in countries where cryptocurrencies are less heavily regulated. As a result, cooperation amongst countries is also difficult to achieve. Furthermore, investors based in a country where cryptocurrency businesses are severely restricted may prefer to invest in other countries.[82]

2.8 *Summary*

The regulation of cryptocurrencies presents a variety of difficult challenges and remains at a developing stage. In addition, there are considerable differences between countries regarding what and how to regulate.

One could argue that cryptocurrencies are in themselves incompatible with state regulation; in part because the technology underpinning cryptocurrencies was originally conceived of as a departure from state regulation. However, appropriate regulatory intervention by states is necessary if cryptocurrencies are to be used by a large number of people in a secure manner, as well as to bring value to society; rather than being used only by a limited circle of

78 Japan, sub 2.2.2, Japan Financial Services Agency, 'Administrative Guideline for Financial Companies', Chapter for Crypto-Asset Exchange Service Providers, II-5-2.

79 Article 59 MiCAR.

80 Article 61 MiCAR.

81 Japan, sub 2.2.2.

82 China, sub 6.1.

crypto-enthusiasts. In order to properly regulate cryptocurrency transactions that easily cross borders and promote the security of legitimate transactions, it is important to deepen the discussion in a global forum involving many countries, not just developed countries.

3 Private Law

Cryptocurrencies are important assets with enormous market value. It is therefore unsurprising to see litigation over them starting in some jurisdictions, which may be a harbinger of things still to come.[83] Front and centre of such disputes are questions of private law, for instance who "owns" cryptocurrencies, how they can be transferred, or how they will be treated in insolvency. The responses by national laws vary widely. Hardly ever before has the international community been so divided about the appropriate rules to govern what is factually an object of trade and commerce.

To some extent, the private law problems seem to depend on regulatory treatment. Where cryptocurrencies are prohibited under regulatory law, it appears futile to debate their treatment under the private law of bilateral relations. However, even those countries that opt for an outright prohibition of "virtual" currencies cannot avoid providing some rules of private law in relation to these assets. The Chinese example is instructive: Despite various agencies of the People's Republic having continuously tightened the regulatory vices almost to the point of a complete ban on cryptocurrencies, the Chinese debate about the effect of cryptocurrencies, whether previously or newly acquired, on private rights is ongoing.[84] A special category to cover these new assets was even introduced into the People's Republic's Civil Code: "virtual network property."[85]

The Chinese example shows that a legal system can hardly avoid answering the emerging private law problems regarding cryptocurrencies, given that citizens cannot be completely prevented from holding digital assets, which they may have acquired prior to a ban or abroad. Moreover, private law questions will inevitably resurface once digital assets are issued by central banks.

---

83 See e.g. France, sub 1.1.1.1; Netherlands, sub 3; Singapore, sub 3; Sweden, sub 4.5; Turkey, sub 2; UK (England), sub 6.1.

84 See China, sub 4.1.2.

85 See Article 127 Chinese Civil Code and China, sub 4.1.1.

3.1 *In Search for the Appropriate Category*

A crucial challenge all countries are facing is how to characterise cryptocurrencies. Are they money? Or are they securities in the sense of financial instruments? Are they perhaps negotiable instruments, similar to dematerialised cheques, bills of exchange or letters of credit? Or are they simply claims? Could they perhaps even be compared to intellectual property?

The question of whether cryptocurrencies can be shoehorned in one of these traditional categories, and if so, which, is significant because it will often determine which set of the existing private law rules govern cryptocurrencies. This concerns a wide range of questions, from their protection against attacks to their treatment in insolvency or the rules applicable to their transfer. Also, more unexpected problems may surface. An example is a Dutch case, in which a court had to categorise bitcoins in order to calculate damages claim for their non-delivery.[86] Another example is Turkey, where there has been debate as to whether capital contributions to commercial companies can be made in cryptocurrencies.[87] These examples illustrate how the question of proper characterisation can become critical in virtually any area of private law.

To a large extent, the problem of putting cryptocurrencies into the traditional categories of private law is a direct consequence of the ambiguous nature of these assets themselves. As a matter of fact, these assets resemble legal chameleons: they were designed as means of payment, yet they are not issued by a state; they are used as store of value, yet many of them do not represent a real-world asset; they consist of data, yet the information they provide has no intrinsic value; they are transferred through a register, yet this register does not give the public any detail regarding the holder's identity. So what are they?

In order to answer this question, one may be tempted to draw an analogy to the debate in the regulatory field, where the proper characterisation of crypto-assets has long been discussed.[88] Yet it is important to highlight that regulatory law and private law serve very different purposes: whereas the first is concerned with the commonweal, the second deals with rights and obligations of individuals. To achieve these different goals, both fields have developed specific concepts, principles and rules; while the terms they use may sometimes seem similar or identical, they are often mere homonyms. For these reasons,

---

86 Netherlands, sub 1.3.

87 Turkey, sub 8.1.

88 For instance, the fear that cryptocurrencies may become competitors of state-issued money and threaten the regalian power of the central bank may lead to a characterisation as money rather than as a financial instrument, see Egypt, sub 4.

the categorisation used under regulatory law should not be seen as determinative for private law.

3.1.1 Money

Legal systems are quite unanimous in refusing to consider cryptocurrencies as "money."[89] This may come as a surprise given that the first of them, Bitcoin, was intended to be a form of "private money".

One reason for this attitude may be the regulatory objective of protecting the sovereign power of states to coin money, which in some jurisdictions has led to hardening the stance against any assimilation of cryptocurrencies with money. An illustration is provided by Egypt, where the characterisation as money is categorically rejected precisely because they are seen as competing with state-issued currency.[90] Yet as has been mentioned before, the regulatory categories should not predetermine private law, given the differences in both purpose and content.[91]

There must therefore be other reasons for the almost universal rejection of the categorisation as "money". One could point to the indeterminacy of this notion itself. Specifically, money can be either "fiat currency", i.e. coins and notes, on the one hand, or "scriptural money" ("book money"), i.e. money held in an account with a bank, on the other.[92] These two forms of money have a very different nature in private law and are subject to very different rules. While the first can be seen as an object of property rights in some contexts, and therefore subject to the rules on the transfer of movables, the second is typically considered as a claim against the depositing institution, i.e. the bank.

Cryptocurrencies are certainly not "fiat currencies", because they are not a means of payment issued by a state. It is also reasonably clear that – with the exception of El Salvador[93] – they are not "legal tender", because there is no legal obligation of creditors to accept them to discharge the debt. This point is made in numerous national reports.[94]

89 See e.g. Australia, sub 1.1; Canada (Québec), sub 2; Croatia sub 1, Czech Republic, sub 2; Hungary, sub 5.

90 See Egypt, sub 4.

91 See *infra* 3.1.

92 See Charles Proctor, *Mann on the Legal Aspect of Money* (7th edn, Oxford University Press 2012) 42, para 1.70.

93 See *supra* 2.1.1.

94 See e.g. Australia, sub 1.1; Canada (Québec), sub 2; Croatia sub 1; Czech Republic, sub 2; South Korea, sub 4.1; Turkey, sub 1.

Cryptocurrencies are also not "scriptural money", or "book money", in the sense of a claim against the depositing institution.[95] While most of them are held with intermediaries such as crypto-exchanges and wallet providers,[96] they can also be held directly by the owner and be transferred without the intervention of any intermediary. This even corresponds to their primary design.

While the rejection of the money characterisation is almost universal, many legal systems consider cryptocurrencies as "payment" or "consideration" for sales and other contracts.[97] It also bears mentioning that many countries follow the money characterisation in the context of insolvency proceedings.[98] The position is thus far from being coherent or uniform.

Ultimately, it may not matter whether cryptocurrencies are to be properly called "money" or not. After all, this notion is merely a legal metaphor and not a panacea for the many private law issues surrounding the new assets. Instead, it should be acknowledged that the blockchain, as a digital, private mechanism to store and transfer value, is new and cannot be compared with existing phenomena because it will likely lead to very different problems. The implications for private law, such as the rules that apply to their protection and their transfer, still remain to be worked out.

3.1.2 Securities (Financial Instruments)

One may ponder over the characterisation as "securities" or "financial instruments" also in the area of private law.[99] After all, many cryptocurrencies serve investment purposes, and shares and bonds are frequently issued in tokenised form. This has led many regulators to consider them as securities or financial instruments. Though regulatory law and private law are in principle independent from each other, this does not exclude the possibility that the same categorisation might occasionally work.

The consequences of characterisation as a security are however not clear. On the one hand, this approach could offer far-reaching protection for crypto holders, as many countries consider holders of securities to be "owners" of such securities, even where they are held with an intermediary. On the other hand, this is not universally the case, as the example of the U.S. teaches, where

95 Netherlands, sub 1.3.

96 See *infra* 3.1.2.

97 See *infra* 3.3.1.1.

98 See *infra* 3.2.1.1.

99 E.g. France, sub 2.1; Hungary, sub 5.1 (the latter report ultimately rejects this characterisation).

the holder merely has a "securities entitlement."[100] Still, the securities categorisation affords a comparatively well-protected status to the investor.

The most important argument against the securities characterisation, though, is that only very few cryptocurrencies confer rights against an issuer. Many of them are, in substance, simply "digital" assets that do not embody a participation in a company or the obligation of a debtor. In addition, it would be problematic to transpose the rules on the acquisition of securities, which are geared towards intermediation, to crypto-assets, which are designed for peer-to-peer transfer.[101] This may explain why only very few countries follow the securities characterisation.

3.1.3 Negotiable Instruments

Instead of opting for a characterisation as a security or financial instrument, it is also possible to consider cryptocurrencies as negotiable instruments. This may seem justified to the extent that they are designed for direct (peer-to-peer) transfer without the intervention of intermediaries and, in this respect, resemble cheques and bills of exchange more than securities, such as shares and bonds, which are mainly traded via exchanges and brokers.

An analogy with negotiable instruments is therefore at least plausible. How this might play out is suggested in the Croatian report. It notes that the transfer of cryptocurrencies has characteristics similar to a transfer by endorsement, i.e. the signature – usually positioned on the back – of a negotiable instrument, and compares the blockchain with the uninterrupted chain of endorsement necessary to prove the right of the person in possession of the negotiable instrument.[102] The analogy opens the way for piggybacking the rules for negotiable instruments, which have the advantage of being well-established and partly uniformised at the international level.[103]

Yet, most other legal systems do not follow this characterisation. The major reason seems to be that traditional negotiable instruments are very different from cryptocurrencies in real terms. The authorisation of a Bitcoin transfer via private key is hardly comparable to the signature on a paper from an empirical viewpoint, but it also has very different legal effects; for instance, it does not

100 See § 8:501 Uniform Commercial Code (UCC).

101 See *supra* 1.1.

102 Croatia, sub 4.2.

103 See in particular the Geneva Conventions on Bills of Exchange (Convention providing a Uniform Law for Bills of Exchange and Promissory Notes, signed at Geneva (7 June 1930, League of Nations Treaty Series 143 (1933–34), No 3313) 257) and on Cheques (Convention providing a Uniform Law for Cheques, signed at Geneva (9 March 1931, League of Nations Treaty Series, 143 (1933–34), No 3316) 355).

lead – at least not according to the intention of the parties – to a liability of the transferor, such as that legally provided for in the case of transfers of cheques and bills of ladings.[104] Furthermore, the rules regarding the transfer of paper documents do not correspond to the digital reality, in particular the recording of the holder on a distributed ledger, and consequently are not apt to solve the legal questions arising from it.[105]

This does not mean that some of the rules for negotiable instruments would not be helpful for cryptocurrencies, such as those on the protection of the good faith acquirer or the inapplicability of the exception for stolen assets. However, these rules cannot be applied to the blockchain world without modification. They can serve as a source of inspiration rather than as a directly applicable legal framework.

3.1.4 Claims

Because cryptocurrencies are intangible, generally have value, and are transferred peer to peer, they are likely candidates for the category "claims". This characterisation is especially attractive for those legal systems that strictly distinguish between corporeal and incorporeal objects and do not recognise property rights in the latter.

An example is South Korea. The reporters for this jurisdiction highlight that some crypto-assets, especially utility tokens, provide the holder with certain rights, and could be classified as "nominative claims."[106] However, they ultimately reject this characterisation because it precludes the protection of the innocent acquirer.[107] The Croatian report also toys with the characterisation as claims, yet ultimately dismisses it in light of the unsuitability of the rules on assignment.[108] Indeed, these rules seem an ill-fit on several accounts, as will be discussed later.[109]

More fundamentally still, cryptocurrencies do not necessarily confer a right against the issuer or another person. It is entirely possible, and in fact quite common, that they do not embody any rights at all. Many coins and tokens are merely "intrinsic" and do not represent any extrinsic value, the prime

---

104 See Article 15 Geneva Convention on Bills of Exchanges and Promissory Notes; Article 18 Geneva Convention on Cheques.

105 See also *infra* 3.3.2.2. on the requirements for transfer.

106 South Korea, sub 3.1.

107 *Ibid.*

108 Croatia, sub 4.2.

109 See *infra* sub 3.3.2.2.

examples being Bitcoin and Ether.[110] This alone makes it difficult to treat these new assets as "claims".

3.1.5 Intellectual Property

Given the incorporeal nature of cryptocurrencies and the typical lack of a debtor, they could perhaps be compared to intellectual property. This characterisation has for instance been suggested in the Canadian, Dutch, and Turkish literature.[111] The idea is to see cryptocurrencies as virtual objects, which would allow the existence of a right *in rem* concerning them.

There are, however, several reasons to question this parallel. First, intellectual property rights are subject to the principle of *numerus clausus*, and (rights in) cryptocurrencies are not mentioned as being among them.[112] Second, most crypto-assets lack the innovative character required by intellectual property law as a pre-condition for protection. Third, the threats to them are quite different from those to intellectual property, for which the risk of copying an innovation is dominant, whereas in the case of cryptocurrencies it is more the risk of hacking, theft or insolvency of an intermediary, which is absent in the case of intellectual property.

3.1.6 Data

At their core, cryptocurrencies essentially are information that is stored on a ledger. It therefore seems not entirely far-fetched to characterise them as data, or "data-based res", as some reports suggest.[113] Though this characterisation is possible, not much is gained by it. One reason is that the civil law rules governing data have yet to be developed. Even more relevant is another point: "data" can usually be copied freely and are not subject to control by one person, i.e. they are non-rivalrous and non-exclusive, which explains most of the problems in the creation of property rights regarding them. Cryptocurrencies, in contrast, are different: their value diminishes when they are used and they can be controlled; in other words, they are rivalrous and exclusive. Therefore, it can already be foreseen that the private law rules governing data, even if fully developed, will not be perfectly fitted to cryptocurrencies.

---

110 See South Korea, sub 7.1.

111 Canada (Québec), sub 2.1; Netherlands, sub 5.3; Turkey, sub 6.1. See also Poland, sub 5.6.

112 Switzerland, sub 5.2 (using the term "DLT-Wertrecht").

113 Hungary, sub 2.3; UK (England), sub 4.1.1.

3.1.7 Separate Category

In light of these difficulties in characterising cryptocurrencies, some jurisdictions have chosen to create a special category for them.

One example is Switzerland, where the concept of "register value right" (*Registerwertrecht, droit valeur inscrit, diritto valore registrato*) has been introduced.[114] This is defined as a right that can be invoked and transferred only via a register on which it is recorded.[115] It does not cover cryptocurrencies such as Bitcoin and Ether, since they do not embody any right.[116] It can however cover stablecoins or utility tokens.

Another example is Kazakhstan, where the term "digital assets" has been introduced into the Civil Code and the Law on Informatisation.[117] Kazak law distinguishes between digital assets that are "secured" and "unsecured", with the first being protected by law, while the second are not. The idea underpinning the Kazak law seems to be to provide a legally certain framework for permitted uses of blockchain technology while simultaneously creating legal disincentives for the use of prohibited private cryptocurrencies.

Introducing a special category would allow to overcome the difficulties of characterisation, and to create tailor-made rules for cryptocurrencies. On the other hand, it may render the law more complex and cause novel characterisation issues, especially when the technology moves on to the next level. It is therefore vital to devise the new rules as openly as possible and to grasp the essential characteristics that distinguish cryptocurrencies or other digital assets from traditional objects of commerce. This can be done only after a thorough analysis of the rules applying to them, on which we will focus now.

3.2 *Protection of Cryptocurrency Holders*

3.2.1 Protection in General

Legal systems are lightyears apart when it comes to the protection of cryptocurrency holders. A word of clarification: As such "holders", we understand here those persons who have factual "control" over the asset, because they have the private key necessary to dispose of a crypto-asset registered on a blockchain, as well as those for whom others – usually an intermediary – exercises

---

114 Swiss Federal Act on the Adaptation of Federal Law to Developments of Distributed Ledger Technology (*Bundesgesetz zur Anpassung des Bundesrechts an Entwicklungen der Technik verteilter elektronischer Register*).

115 Art. 973d(1) Swiss Code of Obligations (*Obligationenrecht*).

116 Switzerland, sub 5.2.

117 Kazakhstan, sub 1.

control on their behalf.[118] Regarding their protection, an abyss exists between countries on the one extreme that do not recognise any private rights at all, and those on the other that offer very stringent protection for them.

3.2.1.1 *Application of Property Law*

The highest standard of protection is generally provided by property law. Therefore, it is crucial to know whether cryptocurrencies can be the object of property rights or not in a given legal system. This is very different to the preceding discussion regarding the proper category for cryptocurrencies themselves, e.g. money, a claim, or some other legal concept: The question now is no longer what a cryptocurrency *is*, but whether it can be the *object* of something, more specifically of a property right. This changes the perspective significantly, given that simple objects, such as commodities or animals, can be subject to property rights.

Many legal systems struggle to include digital assets within their taxonomies for property rights and their possible objects. In this respect, the dichotomy between tangible and intangible objects, which many legal systems retain, creates significant problems. Interestingly, this distinction features in both Civil and Common law systems, although with different effects.

Within the Civil law tradition, some legal systems restrict property rights to tangible or "corporeal" objects. A typical example is Swiss law, which limits property law to "impersonal, three-dimensional, demarcated, existing, and physically tangible objects that can be subjected to human possession."[119] Similar restrictions exist in Croatia, Germany, Hungary, Japan, and South Korea.[120] In these systems, property rights in intangible, or "incorporeal", objects exist only exceptionally, for instance, for manageable natural resources or other intangibles specifically mentioned by the law.[121] Under these systems, cryptocurrencies cannot be the object of property rights. Due to the lack of physicality and the lack of a specific statutory basis, they would be neither things in the legal sense nor equivalent legal objects.[122] This has resulted in

118 See in this respect the definition of "control" by the UNIDROIT Principles on Digital Assets and Private Law, Principle 6(1).

119 Switzerland, sub 5.2.

120 Croatia, sub 4.1; Germany, sub 2.3.2; Hungary, sub 5.1; Japan, sub 5.1.2; South Korea, sub 7.1. See also Turkey, sub 6.1. and Poland, sub 2.3, where the charactersation as a "thing" is disputed.

121 See Croatia, id.; South Korea, id.

122 Switzerland, sub 5.2. However the Swiss legislator has introduced a new, special category of "register value rights", which captures many tokens, but not coins, see *supra* 3.1.7.

some doctrinal contortions, such as the suggestion of an analogous application of the rules of property law.[123]

This contrasts with other Civil law systems that have a much broader understanding of the scope of property law, such as Austria, the Czech Republic, France, Italy, Macao, the Netherlands or Sweden. These systems define the objects of property rights e.g. as "all tangible and intangible objects belonging to a person",[124] "goods"[125] or all "patrimonial rights."[126] A particularly striking example is Swedish law, which considers that intangibles can be the object of property rights if they are recognised as such "by the parties and in general."[127] These systems have considerably fewer difficulties in accepting those who control the private keys of cryptocurrencies as the latter's owners. This does not exclude frequent and significant uncertainty whether local courts will indeed accept property rights in crypto-assets, as several reports highlight.[128]

In the Common law, several courts have affirmed that cryptocurrencies can be the subject of property rights.[129] However, the legal basis for such recognition is not entirely clear. Historically, the Common law recognised two objects of personal property: "things in possession" and "things in action."[130] Cryptocurrencies do not straightforwardly qualify for either category, as they cannot be physically "possessed" nor are they recoverable by taking legal "action" against an obligee. Hence, it seems the Common law needs to undergo some evolution before it can capture the reality of the new phenomena without internal contradictions.[131]

Fundamentally, the difficulties of inserting cryptocurrencies into the existing property framework are due to the fact that most cryptocurrencies lack any point of reference, such as a tangible object, a claim against a person, or some other right. At their core, they are merely digitally recorded information. The real novelty is that technology prevents the multiplication of this information through copying and any other manipulation, thereby solving the

---

123 See Poland, sub 2.3; see also Switzerland sub 5.2 (for coins).

124 Austria, sub 3.1; Czech Republic, sub 3; see also Macau, sub 3.2 (stating that the Macau Civil Code does not require "things" to be corporeal).

125 Canada (Québec), sub 2.1; Italy, sub 4.1.

126 Netherlands, sub 5.3. Whether crypto-assets can be the object of property rights under Dutch law is nevertheless debated, see id., sub 3.

127 Sweden, sub 4.2.

128 France, sub 1.1.1.1; Macau, sub 4; Netherlands, sub 1.3 and 3; Taiwan, sub 4.2.1.

129 Singapore, sub 4.1; UK, sub 6.1.

130 UK, sub 4.1.1.

131 See also UK Law Commission, 'Digital Assets: Final Report'(June 2023) 49, para 3.49 (concluding that the Common law "should remain free to develop, where appropriate, legal principles specific to third category things …").

"double-spending problem". This has been achieved by the use of public-private key encryption, the decentralised validation of transactions through consensus mechanisms, and the immutability of the ledger on which such transactions are recorded. By combining these techniques, a digital object has for the first time become rivalrous and exclusive. This is fundamental from a legal point of view, because it makes cryptocurrencies somewhat similar to tangible assets. In the social reality that is the subject of private law, both tangible and digital assets raise similar problems surrounding attribution and protection.

In light of the new reality of virtual assets, the requirement of corporeality as a precondition of transfer rules and property protection looks increasingly obsolete. The question is what takes its place. The Polish report notes the "favorable factual situation" of the person in actual control of the cryptocurrency unit, which would consist "in the possibility of disposing over it."[132] In the same vein, some reports refer to the spending power inherent in cryptocurrencies as worthy of protection.[133] This may indeed be considered an asset in itself, similar to the spending power inherent in other objects like fiat money or negotiable instruments, where the tangible object merely acts to support and embody a much more valuable, intangible asset. But it goes beyond the remit of this report to take sides in this debate. Whatever the substance of the crypto-asset, it certainly needs protection against the whole world, or *erga omnes*. Admittedly, this may not be easy, but the social reality of digital assets calls for such protection. In this context, a reconsideration of fundamental notions of national private law may be required.

3.2.2 Protection against Attacks

Given their spectacular value, it is not surprising that crypto-assets are frequently the object of attacks. Their intangible nature and the pseudonymous way of holding and transferring them make them a particularly attractive target for tortfeasors and criminals. Interesting cases relayed in the national reports illustrate how hackers try to gain and have gained access to private keys, and fraudsters try to get and have gotten control over the data stored on computers through phishing attacks.[134] Many of these cases play out in a cross-border setting. Therefore, a comparison of the ways in which legal systems protect the victims against such attacks is in order.

132 Poland, sub 5.6.

133 Italy, sub 4.1; Netherlands, sub 5.6 (referring to J. L. Snijders and Y.C. Tonino, 'Goederenrechtelijke status van bitcoin (kapitaalkracht)' (2018) 6 *Financiering, Zekerheden & Insolventierechtpraktijk* 46, 49–50).

134 See UK (England), sub 6.1 and the cases reported there.

There is one preliminary point to note regarding the practical relevance of these claims. Many reports underline the difficulties of enforcing a claim regarding crypto-assets against a fraudster, hacker or a third party.[135] In particular, they point to the intangible nature and the pseudonymous way of holding and transferring them, making it hard, if not impossible, to find the asset and identify the proper defendant. However, numerous cases brought in several jurisdictions against hackers and other criminals demonstrate that these practical difficulties are not insurmountable.[136] In any event, one point should not be overlooked: facts must be distinguished from law, and practical problems of enforcement do not spare to provide a clear legal answer to the question of the appropriate remedy in case the facts lie on the table.

3.2.2.1 *Tort Law*

Most countries provide a remedy in tort against attacks on cryptocurrency holdings. An obvious case is where such assets are protected as property, which results in imposing liability on those causing damage to them.[137] Yet even in the Civil law systems that limit property rights to tangible (corporeal) objects, loss of cryptocurrencies through hacking or fraud may lead to a tort claim, for instance, on the ground of causing unlawful damage or having committed an illegal act.[138] The Common law makes further grounds of action available, such as misrepresentation, fraud, or breach of confidence.[139] There could also lie a claim for conversion in some Common law jurisdictions, provided cryptocurrencies could be characterised as *physical* property.[140] And, of course, where the digital asset is stored on a physical object, such as a piece of paper, a USB key or a hard drive, an action against the misappropriation of the physical object is also available.[141]

3.2.2.2 *Vindication*

In systems recognising property rights over intangibles, the "dispossessed" former holder has in addition a claim based on his ownership.[142] This is the time-honoured *rei vindicatio* of Roman law. In connection with the principle *nemo dat quod non habet* (also known as *nemo plus iuris transferre posset quam*

135 See e.g. Croatia, sub 4.9; South Korea, sub 7.4.
136 See the cases in the UK, sub 6.1. See also Hungary, sub 5.8.
137 See e.g. Austria, sub 3.8; France, sub 2.9.2.
138 Hungary sub 5.8; South Korea, sub 7.4; Turkey, sub 7.2.
139 UK (England), sub 4.9.1 and sub 6.1.8.
140 Australia, sub 3.9; UK (England), sub 6.1.9.
141 Australia, sub 3.9.
142 See e.g. Austria, sub 3.8.

ipse habet), it also works against third parties.[143] In case of hacking, this claim may even be brought against innocent acquirers because good faith acquisition is usually excluded for stolen goods.[144]

3.2.2.3 *Unjust Enrichment*

Where a party has received crypto-assets without any legal basis, she may be subject to a claim of unjust enrichment.[145] This possibility exists in most legal systems, but is specifically important for countries not recognising property rights in intangibles.[146]

The Croatian report, for instance, highlights that a third person to whom the hacker has sold and transferred cryptocurrencies may be subject to an action for unjust enrichment by the "legitimate holder."[147] As a consequence, such a person would have to return the assets and, where this is not possible, give compensation for its value.[148]

The South Korean report takes a similar view. It specifically highlights that the third person would not be protected by the innocent acquirer rule, given that intangible assets do not qualify as objects of property rights under South Korean law.[149] It furthermore mentions that the third person may have a contractual remedy against the hacker who sold the cryptocurrency.[150]

3.2.2.4 *Claim against Custodian*

In light of the practical difficulties in identifying the recipient of the digital asset, it may be easier to bring a – contractual or non-contractual – claim against the wallet provider or some other intermediary.[151] Some legal systems provide for strict liability of the custodian.[152] Most legal systems, however, require some form of negligence on its part.[153]

Also, liability might be excluded in the general terms and conditions of the latter. Some courts accept these uncritically.[154] Others, however, subject them

143 UK (England), sub 4.9.1. See also Australia, sub 3.9.
144 See in more detail *infra* 3.3.2.3.
145 See Croatia, sub 4.9; Italy, sub 4.7; South Korea, sub 7.4; New Zealand, sub 4.
146 See *supra* 3.2.1.1.
147 Croatia, sub 4.9.
148 Croatia, sub 4.9; Italy, sub 4.7.
149 South Korea, sub 7.4.
150 *Ibid.*
151 Turkey, sub 7.2.
152 See e.g. Italy, sub 4.7.
153 See e.g. Denmark, sub 9; France, sub 2.9.1; Japan, sub 5.1.7; Turkey, sub 7.2.
154 See Japan, sub 5.1.7 and the decision of the Tokyo District Court, February 4, 2019, Kinyu Homujijo No. 2128 cited there.

to the rules of unfair terms control.[155] Regulatory law may also impose special duties on the intermediary, including liability in case of their violation.[156] These may also lead to compensation for the customer.

3.2.2.5 *Intermediate Summary*

The protections offered by tort law and the law of unjust enrichment are important. However, they are relatively weak when the crypto-assets have been transferred to a third party, in particular where the latter is insolvent. In this case, the strongest protection is still provided by the property categorisation, as will be seen in the following.

3.2.3 Protection in Case of Insolvency

There are substantial differences across legal systems regarding the proprietary protection of cryptocurrencies in the case of insolvency.

3.2.3.1 *General Protection*

The protection of the holder of cryptocurrencies in insolvency depends on how such assets are generally treated. In this context, the consequences of the different characterisations come to the fore.

One approach would be to see cryptocurrencies as "money" for the purposes of insolvency law, even though they are not recognised as legal tender.[157] This method results in the holder of the assets having merely the status of a creditor, who must register her claim with the insolvency court or administrator. As a consequence, she will compete with the other creditors under the *pari passu* principle – and is therefore likely to recover only a fraction of her investment. Those countries that do not recognise any specific right of the person in control of cryptocurrencies come to a similar result; still, some of them protect the client via a special procedural segregation right in insolvency.[158]

Other countries see cryptocurrencies, despite their intangible and non-possessory nature, as possible objects of property rights in an insolvency. They will not consider them as part of the insolvency estate. Instead, they allow

---

155 France, sub 2.9.1.

156 This is the case in France, see *id.*

157 See Japan, sub 5.1.1 and the judgment of Tokyo District Court, 31 January 2018, Hanrei Jiho No. 2387 (Mt Gox) cited there. Generally, Japanese courts hesitate over the proper characterisation, see *id.* and sub 5.1.2 for the opinion of the report's author.

158 Germany, sub 4.2.2 (pointing to a new provision that protects the customer in the event of the custodian's insolvency); a similar right exists in Switzerland, see Article 242a Swiss Federal Act on Debt Enforcement and Bankruptcy.

the holder to reclaim or gain immediate control over them.[159] This result is obtained without special provisions or legal reform, simply by considering cryptocurrencies as objects of proprietary rights.

3.2.3.2 *Insolvency of an Intermediary* (*Wallet Provider or Crypto-Exchange*)

The most relevant case in practice is the insolvency of an intermediary that has acquired or manages crypto-assets for its customers. In this case, it becomes crucial to determine the rights of the client. They do not only depend on the conceptualisation of crypto-assets and the rights in them,[160] but also on the particulars of the relationship between the intermediary and the customer.[161] In this regard, one must distinguish between different types of wallets.

Non-custodial wallets merely protect the customer's private keys without having any power of disposal over the crypto-assets themselves.[162] In their case, the client can be established relatively easily as the owner, provided that the legal system in question recognises proprietary rights in crypto-assets at all.

Matters are more complicated for custodial wallets, i.e. those where the intermediary has full control over the crypto-assets.[163] Few legal systems consider this analogous to a bank account, recognising a mere personal claim on the part of the holder to be brought in the insolvency proceedings together with all other creditors.[164] Instead, most legal systems consider the customer to be the owner on the grounds that the intermediary exercises control in the customer's interest, on his behalf or for his benefit.[165] Some laws require, in addition, that the assets are traceable or identifiable as belonging to the customer,[166] or are at least segregated from those of the intermediary (even if

159 See South Korea, sub 7.2.3 (though indicating some uncertainty in this regard); UK (England), sub 4.1.6.

160 See *supra* 3.2.3.1.

161 See Austria, sub 4; Denmark, sub 8; Finland, sub 5.6; Macau, sub 3.8; UK (England), sub 4.1.6.

162 A typical example of a non-custodial (or "self-custodial") wallet is Metamask, see https://metamask.io (accessed 4 June 2023).

163 A typical example of a custodial wallet is Coinbase, see https://www.coinbase.com (accessed 4 June 2023).

164 France, sub 2.1.1 and 2.6 (although the reporter defends a different solution, he admits that the question remains open); Turkey, sub 9.3. See also Sweden, sub 4.2.

165 See Austria, sub 4 (but depending on the terms of the custody agreement); Finland, sub 5.6 (on the condition that the customer's assets have been held separately from those of the custodian); Macau, sub 3.8; Italy, sub 4.4; New Zealand, sub 1.3 (assuming the custodian held the assets as a trustee). See also Sweden, sub 4.3.

166 Denmark, sub 8; Italy, sub 4.7. See also Macau, sub 3.8 (excluding ownership of clients over crypto-assets held in a single account by the intermediary).

mixed with those of other customers).[167] When these conditions are fulfilled, the customer will be protected as the owner in the event of the intermediary's insolvency. Still, this protection may be insufficient where there is a shortfall of assets, e.g., because the intermediary did not acquire enough crypto-assets or has in the meantime disposed of them.[168]

An ingenious way to deal with the latter problem has been developed in Croatian law, which assumes that, following an unauthorised disposal by the intermediary to a third party, the client has a right to request an assignment of the intermediary's counterclaim against that third party.[169] The practical exercise of this right, however, presupposes that the intermediary has acquired enough assets for all of its customers in the first place. It does not solve the problem where this is not the case, nor does it offer much help if the counterclaim has already been fulfilled by the third party, or if it cannot be enforced against the third party.

Overall, the client's position would be considerably better if she were considered the owner of the crypto-assets, whether by direct holding or through a custody arrangement.

3.2.3.3 *Insolvency of the Cryptocurrency Holder*

Where the holder of cryptocurrencies becomes insolvent, it is generally agreed that the crypto-assets become part of its insolvency estate.[170] This is true even under those laws that generally do not recognise property rights in crypto-assets.[171] There may be practical issues for the insolvency administrator in obtaining the necessary private keys, but these are not insurmountable. For instance, the insolvency administrator could use its right to information conferred under insolvency legislation to obtain them.[172]

3.2.3.4 *Insolvency of the Cryptocurrency Issuer*

A very different problem is the insolvency of a cryptocurrency issuer. This situation is unfortunate but particularly likely given the general absence of regulation and the frequent lack of substantive capital on the part of issuers. However, the legal questions created by such an insolvency are virtually identical to those that occur in the insolvency of any other issuer, e.g. of financial

167 Finland, sub 5.6.
168 See Australia, sub 3.4 (in the context of a trust).
169 Croatia, sub 4.6.
170 See e.g. Austria, sub 4; Germany, sub 4.2.2.
171 See e.g. Germany, sub 4.2.2.
172 *Ibid.*

instruments. There is nothing inherent in the characteristics of cryptocurrencies that fundamentally alters the situation.

3.2.3.5 *Intermediate Summary*

Insolvency law is in many ways the testing ground for the proprietary protection of cryptocurrencies. The demise of a major intermediary, such as a wallet provider or a crypto-exchange, could lead to severe and wide-ranging individual losses. It may seem contradictory for a state to allow its citizens to invest in such assets on the one hand, but renege on their protection in insolvency on the other. At any rate, states are well-advised to clarify the position a cryptocurrency holder has in their law.

3.3 *Trading in Cryptocurrencies*

Cryptocurrencies are tradable assets and frequently change hands. This gives rise to a number of legal questions.

3.3.1 Transactions over Cryptocurrencies

Many of these questions concern contract law or what could be called more generally "transactions law". For instance, if a token is exchanged against a good or a service, the question may arise on what legal basis the transfer of the token may be demanded. There may also be more intricate questions, e.g. the consequences of the delivery of the wrong token.

In many legal systems, the answers depend on the type of contract in question. For instance, Civil law systems typically feature a code that provides for several transaction regimes, e.g. "sales", "donations", "leases", etc. The application of one or another of these regimes depends on the characteristics of the objects of the transaction. But also under some Common law systems, it may be necessary to decide on the nature of the contract, for instance when deciding on the applicability of a specific statute.[173]

3.3.1.1 *Sale or Barter*

Very few systems have qualms about treating the exchange of a good or service against Bitcoin as a "sale", despite generally not considering cryptocurrencies as legal tender or even "money."[174] The justification for this in Civil law systems is that a sale merely requires some form of "payment" and, in the real world,

173 See Australia, sub 3.2 (on the Australian Sale of Goods legislation).

174 See e.g. Austria, sub 3.3; Czech Republic, sub 3; Denmark, sub 8.1; Finland, sub 5.2.3. Some problems seem to exist in Switzerland, where the rules on sales are however applied *mutatis mutandis*, see Switzerland, sub 5.2. In Québec and in Hungary, transactions over

cryptocurrencies can serve as such means of "payment."[175] In the Common law, they can serve as the requisite consideration for the formation of a contract under the general law of contract.[176] At the same time, the acquisition of a cryptocurrency against fiat currency is also frequently characterised as a "sale", although in this case, the cryptocurrency features as the "object" and the fiat currency as the "payment" of the transaction.[177] The Taiwanese report explains this with a vivid image by suggesting one could sell crypto-coins to another as if selling rice or other fungible goods.[178]

If two cryptocurrencies are exchanged against each other, this is often characterised as a "barter"[179] or as a contract of "exchange."[180] Some systems generally prefer to speak of an "exchange" even where cryptocurrencies are transferred as a remuneration for other goods and services.[181]

The function of the cryptocurrency may thus vary between a means of payment, an object of a sale, or a barter. In the end, though, it may not matter much which of these transaction types is considered the more apposite, since in many systems, sales and barters are governed by the same rules. Moreover, under the principle of freedom of contract, these rules can be amended anyway to fit the parties' needs.[182]

3.3.1.2 *Donation*

Donations may seem an odd topic in the crypto-context, yet their relevance is highlighted by the Hungarian report, which cites the case of a Hungarian resident who created a fund to gather donations of cryptocurrencies.[183] Legal systems have no qualms about allowing the "donation" of cryptocurrencies, independent of whether they consider them as objects of property rights or not.[184]

---

cryptocurrencies are generally considered to be exchange contracts, see Canada (Québec), sub 2.3; Hungary, sub 5.3.

175 See Czech Republic, *id.*

176 UK (England), sub 4.1.2.

177 See e.g. Denmark, sub 8.2; France, sub 2.2.4; Taiwan, sub 4.2.2. For an analogous application of the rules of sale Poland, sub 5.4; Turkey, sub 7.1.

178 Taiwan, sub 4.2.1.

179 Austria, sub 3.3; Denmark, sub 8.2; Hungary, sub 5.3; Taiwan, sub 4.2.2. See also Finland, sub 5.2.3 ("either sale or exchange").

180 France, sub 2.2.3; Macau, sub 3.3.

181 Croatia, sub 4.2.

182 See also Croatia, sub 4.2.

183 Hungary, sub 5.3.

184 Austria, sub 3.2–3.3; Croatia, sub 4.2; Czech Republic, sub 3; Denmark, sub 8.1; Finland, sub 5.2.1; France, sub 2.2.1; Italy, sub 4.3; Macau, sub 3.3; Poland, sub 5.6; Sweden, sub 4.2; Taiwan, sub 4.2.2; Turkey, sub 7.4.1.

This can hardly be surprising since basically any object or right can be transferred for free. Another question is when a gift is fulfilled, which is of particular relevance for systems not considering the promise of a gift to be binding.[185] As a general rule, the obligation arising from a contract of donation is fulfilled when the recipient of the gift has become its owner. When this is the case depends on the rules applicable to transfer.[186]

3.3.1.3 *Loan*

The vast majority of legal systems recognises the possibility of lending crypto-assets.[187] In most countries, it suffices for the borrower to return assets of the same type, quantity and quality as those that have been lent.[188] This is illustrated by a French judgment about a loan over Bitcoin.[189] The court ruled that the cryptocurrency is "consumable and fungible". Consequently, the defendant was ordered to reimburse an amount of coins equivalent to those borrowed, and any benefits accruing from them were held to belong to the borrower.

A special case is English law, which seems to require the restitution of the very same asset ("*in specie*") in case of a loan, except where the object lent is money.[190] The fact that Bitcoin and other cryptocurrencies are not considered as money thus seems to preclude this type of operation. Yet practice seems to have found an alternative arrangement in the form of a sale and buyback, which achieves the same goals.[191]

Interest, as consideration for granting the loan, usually has to be paid in legal tender. Yet freedom of contract may also allow parties to stipulate other goods as remuneration.[192] Where usury laws exist, their application to interest paid in cryptocurrency may be questionable. One may deny that usury laws apply in this context on the grounds that the latter does not qualify as "money."[193] However, others may find this overly formalistic because, from a policy perspective, the borrower deserves the protections afforded by usury laws, regardless of whether she has to pay interest in fiat money or crypto-assets.

185 See Turkey, sub 7.4.1.

186 See *infra* 3.3.2.

187 See e.g. Austria, sub 3.5; Denmark, sub 8.7; Hungary, sub 5.6; Macau, sub 3.4. For application of the rules on loans "at least by analogy" Poland, sub 5.4.

188 See e.g. Hungary, sub 5.6; Turkey, sub 7.6.

189 France, sub 1.1.1.1. On this case, see also *infra* 3.3.2.1.3.

190 See UK (England), sub 4.1.8.

191 *Ibid* (referring to *Wang v Darby*).

192 See Italy, sub 4.6.

193 Turkey, sub 7.6.

If a specific type of cryptocurrency has been lent, then the same has to be returned. A different type only counts as performance where the creditor has agreed to accept it. Legal systems are fairly unanimous on this point.[194] This also applies where the new asset to be returned results from a hard fork, like Bitcoin Cash.[195] If the borrowed asset is no longer available due to the hard fork, the rules on impossibility or supervening circumstances may apply.[196] They may result in the borrower's obligation to pay the market price of the borrowed crypto-asset in fiat money.[197]

3.3.1.4 *Other Transactions*

As cryptocurrencies are considered in many Civil law systems as "payments", they can also function as the counter-performance in other types of contractual relationships, such as contracts for the performance of specific work or specific services, as well as, e.g., mandate, lease, rental or transport contracts.[198] In Common law systems, they can be the "consideration" for any counter-performance and the engagement to provide them will generally be enforceable under the general law of contracts.[199]

3.3.2 Acquisition and Transfer of Cryptocurrencies

A salient problem in private law is how cryptocurrencies are acquired and transferred. Both the conditions and timing of acquisition and transfer are subject to considerable uncertainty.

3.3.2.1 *Original Acquisition*

Cryptocurrencies may be acquired at the moment of their creation. This is the so-called "original acquisition". It plays an especially prominent role in the crypto-world because crypto-assets may be created from nothing.

3.3.2.1.1 ICO

One way of original acquisition is by subscribing to an ICO or otherwise participating in the first distribution of new assets. There seem to be no rules on how this acquisition is to be legally constructed. Perhaps it is still too early to debate this question in legal detail.

194 See Hungary, sub 5.6; Macau, sub 3.4; Turkey, sub 7.6.
195 Turkey, sub 7.6.
196 Italy, sub 4.6.
197 Italy, sub 4.6.
198 See Croatia, sub 4.2.
199 UK (England), sub 4.1.2.

3.3.2.1.2 Mining

A frequent way of acquisition is through "mining", i.e. as a reward for validating a new block that is added to a blockchain. In the legal systems reviewed, there seem to be no specific rules on this, and theoretical legal analysis is also rare. A Dutch author has suggested that a miner has a claim for its efforts against the other participants in the network, which would morph into a bearer claim in the exact moment of mining or "one legal Planck-second later."[200] The Finnish report mentions mining as a case of "original acquisition", without giving further information.[201]

Apparently, this type of original acquisition is accepted in all countries where mining is legal. A particular case is Kazakhstan, where mining is not prohibited, but the resulting crypto-assets can only be circulated to a limited extent.[202] This renders mining significantly less attractive and may stall mining activities in the country.

3.3.2.1.3 Hard Forks and Airdrops

In the strange world of cryptocurrencies, special situations may occur in which crypto-assets miraculously double or seem to fall from heaven. The first of these situations is the so-called hard fork, in which the network participants cannot agree on the correct version of the blockchain, resulting in the emergence of two (or more) competing versions of the ledger and causing a multiplication of the assets.[203] The second situation is a so-called "airdrop", in which new crypto-assets are distributed for free to crypto-wallet holders, e.g. to promote a new type of asset.[204]

Legal systems have yet to decide how to treat such situations. Those that rely on a proprietary characterisation could fall back on the existing rules on the acquisition of fruits.[205] It has also been suggested to apply the rules on the occupation of movable things[206] or to qualify the airdropped assets as gifts.[207]

200 Netherlands, sub 5.7.

201 Finland, sub 5.1.

202 Kazakhstan, sub 2. Mining is also specially taxed under Kazak law, see *infra* 5.

203 See Andreas M. Antonopoulos, *Mastering Bitcoin* (2nd edn, O'Reilly 2017) 589–592.

204 Brooke Becher, 'What Is a Crypto Airdrop?', available at https://builtin.com/blockchain/crypto-airdrop (accessed 4 June 2023).

205 See Austria, sub 3.2 (for hard forks); Czech Republic, sub 3; Finland, sub 5.1; Hungary, sub 5.2; Macau, sub 3.2; South Korea, sub 7.2.1.

206 Italy, sub 4.3; Macau, sub 3.2.

207 Austria, sub 3.2 (for airdrops); South Korea, sub 7.2.1.

A French court has taken the position that new coins acquired during the loan belong to the borrower and must not be returned to the lender.[208]

Where the original crypto-assets are held with an intermediary, it seems the intermediary and the client can agree by contract on the distribution of the new cryptocurrency units.[209] If the original crypto-assets held for the customer in custody are not individually identifiable, the customer may merely have a claim for an amount equal to the new assets created via hard fork or airdrop against the custodian.[210] However, a Japanese court has ruled against the customer of a crypto-exchange in such a situation.[211]

3.3.2.2 *Derivative Acquisition* (*Transfer*)

Many complex problems concern the transfer of cryptocurrencies. In this regard, the new technology collides frequently with the received conceptions, principles and rules of private law.

Technologically, the "transfer" is complete when the block, including the information about it, has been validated. The recipient becomes the holder, and this position is immutable unless the recipient chooses to send the assets to another. From a legal point of view, however, it is more than doubtful whether the confirmation of the block and its addition to the chain alone can be considered sufficient to effect the transfer. It suffices to think of the possibilities of transfers induced by mistake, extortion or fraud to lose faith in the statement "code is law". Obviously, there need to be exceptions to reliance on technology.

The question is how these exceptions should be reflected in the law. Usually, the legal system does not consider a mere fact, such as a change in possession, as sufficient to transfer an asset.[212] There has to be something more, like a contract or a special agreement about the transfer between the parties. The trouble is what exactly shall be demanded as a condition of the transfer. Much depends in this regard on how a legal system characterises cryptocurrency as such.

For instance, countries that see the new type of assets as claims would have to apply the rules on assignment.[213] However, these rules are unsuitable for the transfer of cryptocurrencies. The South Korean report highlights that they do

208 France, sub 1.1.1.1.
209 Finland, sub 5.1; Macau, sub 3.2.
210 Denmark, sub 8.
211 Japan, sub 5.1.1.
212 See Italy, sub 4.2.
213 See *supra* 3.1.4.

not include any protection for the innocent acquirer.[214] The Croatian report criticises the requirement of notifying the debtor of the transfer.[215]

Others have suggested using the rules on the transfer of negotiable instruments, specifically the requirement of endorsement, for the crypto-world.[216] Yet, as has already been mentioned, the use of a private key on the internet can hardly be equated with the signature of a physical document.[217] It is unnecessary for the acquirer of crypto-assets to verify the existence of an uninterrupted chain of endorsements, as the blockchain technology itself ensures that the transferor has obtained his position from the previous holder. This is a remarkable difference from negotiable instruments, which leads to entirely different legal issues.

Those who draw a parallel between crypto-assets and modern financial instruments, such as intermediated shares and bonds, tend to use the rules on the transfer of intermediated securities.[218] Yet these rules do not lend themselves to digital assets either. Most of them are modelled on centralised holding systems, e.g. via a chain of banks. Cryptocurrencies, on the contrary, are founded on the idea of a peer-to-peer transfer via a distributed ledger. Even though they are frequently held with an intermediary, their transfer depends on the recording on a distributed ledger. The conditions for a change of ownership are thus quite different from those that apply in the world of intermediated securities.

The money characterisation does not yield much certainty about the applicable transfer rules either.[219] It seems hardly fathomable, for instance, to transplant the rules on wire transfers, which are built on a complex interaction between banks, to the crypto-world. This would not only deprive clients of property protection but could also lead to a multiplication and, ultimately, an inflation of crypto-assets, which is antithetical to the intentions behind Bitcoin.[220] A parallel with tangible money, i.e. coins and notes, leads to the more general question of whether cryptocurrencies can be transferred under the same rules as tangible objects. Two different sets of rules are available in this regard: those for movables and those for immovables.

---

214 South Korea, sub 7.1.

215 Croatia, sub 4.2.

216 Croatia, sub 4.2.

217 See *supra* 3.1.3.

218 See *supra* 3.1.2. For the analogous application of rules relating to cash and bearer securities Turkey, sub 7.3.

219 See *supra* 3.1.1.

220 See Satoshi Nakamoto, *supra* note 2, 1 (stating that the Bitcoin peer-to-peer electronic cash system is intended to prevent double-spending).

If one were to apply the rules for the transfer of movables, this would require in most systems a transfer of "possession."[221] Yet because of cryptocurrencies' intangible nature, it seems impossible to exercise possession over them. Still, one could use "control", as defined above,[222] as a functional equivalent to "possession" in the digital world. In most legal systems, however, this would not be possible without some tweaking of the rules on property transfer of movables.

Another possibility is to follow the rules on immovables, which, in many countries, require the recording of the transfer in a register. The blockchain could be analogised to a land register, even though it is distributed and hence fundamentally different from the centralised land register.[223] Such an approach could at least explain why the recordings on the blockchain have legal value. However, it has to overcome significant hurdles because entries on the blockchain are pseudonymous and thus do not reveal the holder's identity, in contrast to the generally available information in public registers.

Independently of which rules are used to conceptualise the transfer, one may reasonably quarrel about the legal conditions necessary for achieving a change of ownership or title to the transferred crypto-assets. Must the transferor have legal capacity to contract? Where an agent is involved in the transfer, is authority required? How should transfers influenced by mistake, fraud, or coercion be dealt with?

It is highly likely that the legal systems will follow their general rules on this subject. However, significant legal uncertainty surrounds the determination of their territorial or personal reach.[224] This compounds the tremendous uncertainty regarding the applicable rules within the domestic legal system.

3.3.2.3 *Good Faith Acquisition*

The difficulties in construing the transfer are somewhat mitigated through the protection of the innocent acquirer. Most countries know this protection in one form or another, e.g. via a rule on "good faith acquisition", on "the bona fide purchaser" or on the "innocent purchaser". These rules could be extended to the blockchain context.

This route is barred, though, for the countries that do not recognise property rights in intangible goods. As a consequence of this fundamental principle,

221 See e.g. Austria, 3.2; Italy, sub 4.3; South Korea, sub 7.2.1.

222 See *supra* 3.2.1.

223 This approach is followed by the German Act on Electronic Securities (*Gesetz über elektronische Wertpapiere* – eWpG), see its § 25.

224 See on the conflict-of-laws rules *infra* 3.5.

they cannot protect the innocent acquirer against the claim of the holder.[225] This throws a spanner in the works of blockchain networks, which rely on the free transferability or negotiability of crypto-assets. One reporter from such a legal system – Hungary – therefore suggests introducing protection for the bona fide purchaser of a crypto-asset as the best way to serve the interests of the participants of the market.[226] A report from another country – Turkey – wants to apply the rules for the protection of good faith acquirers of cash and bearer securities by analogy.[227]

Legal systems following the property characterisation fare much better in this respect. They can apply the rule on good faith acquisition without major obstacles.[228] Yet even they do not protect the innocent purchaser comprehensively. In particular, there is an exception for stolen or otherwise illegitimately appropriated goods, which may become relevant in the case of hacking.[229] As a consequence, the victim could successfully sue the innocent acquirer.

This result poses problems similar to a complete rejection of good faith acquisition of cryptocurrencies. A way out could be offered by the counter-exception for money, because even stolen money can be acquired in good faith.[230] Yet this would presuppose characterising crypto-assets as money, which is not easily justifiable and may contradict the characterisation adopted in other contexts. Another possibility would be to simply apply the counter-exception for stolen money by analogy to stolen or otherwise illegitimately appropriated cryptocurrencies. In this way, cryptocurrencies could become "super-negotiable", as is often said in the U.S.[231] But it must not be forgotten that, by the same token, the protection of the current holder would be diminished.

225 See South Korea, sub 7.4.

226 Hungary, sub 5.8.

227 Turkey, sub 7.3.

228 See e.g. Croatia, sub 4.2; Denmark, sub 8.4. See also Italy, sub 4.7. But see Austria, sub 3.8 (describing the possibility of good faith acquisition as unclear); Sweden, sub 4.4 (excluding the protection of the bona fide purchaser because cryptocurrencies are not chattels nor promissory notes).

229 See France, sub 2.9.3; New Zealand, sub 4.

230 New Zealand, sub 4.

231 See e.g. Norman I. Silber, 'Substance Abuse at UCC Drafting Sessions Symposium: Consumer Protection and the Uniform Commercial Code' (1997) 75 Washington University Law Quarterly 225, 230.

3.3.2.4 *Intermediate Conclusion*

In order to function, the market requires certainty over the acquisition of crypto-assets and the protection from adverse claims by previous holders. At the same time, victims of fraud or coercion require protection as well. The correct solution seems to be to allow such victims a claim against the perpetrators, but exclude any claims they may have against subsequent bona fide purchasers. This solution resembles that adopted in most legal systems regarding fiat currency, i.e. state-issued coins and banknotes.

3.3.3 Creation of Special Rights in Cryptocurrencies

Cryptocurrencies can also be the subject of rights effective against third parties but with a more limited content than property rights. These rights can be created by special declarations or transactions. Two of them will be discussed in the following: collateral rights and trust.

3.3.3.1 *Collateral Rights* (*in Particular: Pledge*)

There are various ways in which a security right in an asset can be created. A typical way is a pledge. In most systems, a pledge is possible only for movable property. This creates a problem for those systems that do not recognise cryptocurrencies as objects of property rights: Many of them also tend to exclude the pledge for such assets.[232]

There are special operations available for creating collateral rights over intangibles. A very common one is the assignment of claims as a security. Yet its application to cryptocurrencies requires that the latter can be characterised as claims, which is subject to doubt.[233] An alternative way is the pledge of rights or intangible objects, which is possible in some systems.[234]

For those countries that accept crypto-assets as possible objects of pledges, the question arises as to how the pledge can be perfected. There seems to be a general agreement that this requires depriving the pledgor of the possibility to dispose of the asset, or making the public aware of the existence of the collateral right. The mere transfer of the private key may not suffice because it does not exclude that the pledgor has kept a copy.[235] The Hungarian report identifies three ways to perfect a pledge: (1) by depositing the asset with the creditor,

---

232 See e.g. Germany, sub 4.1.2.2; Japan, sub 5.1.4 (describing the validity of such pledges as unclear under Japanese law).

233 See *supra* 3.1.4.

234 See e.g. France, sub 2.7; Macau, sub 4; South Korea, sub 7.2.2; Taiwan, sub 4.2.5; Turkey, sub 7.5.

235 Austria, sub 3.4.

(2) by registration, and (3) by depositing the asset with a custodian and making the pledgor's right of retrieval subject to the performance of his obligations.[236] Implementing these ways in the crypto-context may, however, prove difficult in practice. For instance, it needs to be clarified how and where a security right in cryptocurrencies can be registered: On the blockchain itself? Or in a separate register? It seems this issue cannot be solved without any intervention of the legislator.

3.3.3.2 *Trust*

The question of whether cryptocurrencies can be the subject of a trust, or become trust property, is answered differently.

Consensus does not even exist within the Common law, where the trust has originated. In New Zealand, it is clear that crypto-assets can be held on trust since the seminal judgment by the High Court in *Ruscoe v Cryptopia*.[237] This decision is also accepted as authoritative in Australia.[238] Trusts over cryptocurrencies can also be established under the law of Singapore, provided there is certainty as to the settlor's intention, the subject matter of the trust, and its objects.[239] The situation in England seems much more uncertain, with decisions for and against the possibility of creating a trust over cryptocurrencies.[240] However, also English law recognises the possibility of an intermediary holding of cryptocurrencies for its customers in trust.[241]

Some Civil law systems today know either the trust[242] or similar legal institutions, such as the "private foundation" in Austrian law,[243] the "trust fund" in Czech law,[244] the "fiducie" in French law,[245] or the "fiduciary asset management contract" in Hungarian law.[246] It seems relatively uncontested that these entities or constructs can have cryptocurrencies as assets.[247]

The consequence of a trust over crypto-assets generally is that the trustee is considered the legal owner of these assets, but that the trustee's creditors

236 Hungary, sub 5.7.
237 New Zealand, sub 1.3.
238 Australia, sub 3.4.
239 Singapore, sub 4.
240 UK (England), sub 4.1.4.
241 UK (England), sub 4.1.1.
242 See Japan, sub 5.1.3; Taiwan, sub 4.2.4.
243 Austria, sub 3.7.
244 See e.g. Czech Republic, sub 3 ("trust fund").
245 France, sub 2.4.
246 Hungary, sub 5.5.
247 See Austria, sub 3.7; Czech Republic, sub 3; France, sub 2.4; Japan, sub 5.1.3; Taiwan, sub 4.2.4.

cannot seize them, and that the trust beneficiary has an interest in them protected under equity. This is not always sure, though. The Taiwanese report notes, for instance, that it is "perhaps possible to argue" that the crypto-coins in a segregated trust account would not be the property of a wallet operator.[248] Where such uncertainty exists, the whole trust construction is in doubt. In addition, it has to be borne in mind that a beneficiary's interest has limited reach; in particular, it is not effective against the *bona fide* purchaser for value without notice of the beneficiary's interest. In this sense, a parallel to the "good faith" or "innocent acquirer" exception exists also in trust law.

3.3.4 Inheritance of Cryptocurrencies

Almost all of the reported jurisdictions accept the possibility of inheriting cryptocurrencies.[249] This is true also for those countries that do not recognise property rights in intangibles.[250] Even in China, where the law takes a rather restrictive position on cryptocurrencies, they can be legally inherited.[251] This seems quite logical since the heir steps into the shoes of the *de cujus* with regard to all assets, rights and relationships. As a consequence, all legal positions or interests of the deceased are transferred, regardless of their legal nature.

Inheritance of cryptocurrencies is possible both testate and intestate.[252] The Italian report underlines that the conferral of a password or other credentials does not necessarily amount to a legacy regarding the protected digital assets, but can also be meant as a mandate to perform a task for the deceased after his death (*mandatum post mortem exequendum*).[253] In this case, no transfer happens at the moment of death. The same is true in those legal systems in which legacies do not have a direct transfer effect but merely create an obligation of the heir to give the object to the legatee.

Several reports highlight the practical conundrums cryptocurrencies pose for inheritance.[254] In particular, it may be difficult for the heirs to get information about the crypto-assets held by the deceased and/or to obtain the private

248 Taiwan, sub 4.2.6.

249 See e.g. Australia, sub 3.3; Austria, sub 3.6; China, sub 4.2.6; Croatia, sub 4.3; Czech Republic, sub 3; Denmark, sub 8.3; Finland, sub 5.3; France, sub 2.3; Germany, sub 4.1.3; Japan, 5.1.6; Kazakhstan, sub 4; Macau, sub 4; Poland, sub 5.6; South Korea, sub 7.3.3; Sweden, sub 4.2; Taiwan, sub 4.2.3; UK (Scotland), sub 4.3.2. Under Kazak law, the situation is described as unclear, see Kazakhstan, sub 4.

250 Croatia, sub 4.3.

251 China, sub 4.2.6.

252 See e.g. Czech Republic, sub 3; Denmark, sub 8.3; Finland, sub 5.3; South Korea, sub 7.3.3.

253 Italy, sub 4.3.

254 See e.g. Croatia, sub 4.3; Czech Republic, sub 3; Macau, sub 3.9.

keys necessary to dispose of them. For this reason, the Czech report recommends that cryptocurrency holders keep a record of their digital assets.[255] The Turkish report suggests, quite innovatively, either keeping the private key in a closed will with a notary or transferring the assets via a smart contract upon the owner's death.[256] However, as the Finnish report notes, these are solutions to practical, rather than legal, problems.[257]

Access may seem particularly complicated when the assets are held with an intermediary. However, as noted by a number of reports, the heir also succeeds in the contract the deceased had with the intermediary.[258] This position will usually afford her a right to information about the holdings. Thus, holding through an intermediary facilitates rather than complicates their inheritance, as the Finnish report remarks.[259] This, of course, presupposes that the heir knows with which intermediary the cryptocurrencies were held. Also, she may find it difficult to prove her right to the cryptocurrencies. These hurdles resemble those that have arisen with access to other digital assets of a deceased, such as social media accounts. Introducing a statutory right of information against intermediaries may remedy this problem.[260]

3.4 *Enforcement against Cryptocurrencies*

A number of puzzling problems are also caused by the enforcement of judgments or claims against cryptocurrencies. Two are: First, can cryptocurrencies be seized or attached to enforce a money claim? Second, how is a claim for the delivery of cryptocurrencies enforced?

3.4.1 Cryptocurrencies as Enforcement Assets

The question of how money claims can be enforced against crypto-assets is pivotal. Their considerable market value, fungibility, and easy transferability make them an ideal object of enforcement proceedings for a debt. Yet the relevant existing rules on enforcement are ill-suited for them.

A good illustration of the difficulties arising is provided by German law, which provides two categories of assets as possible objects of enforcement proceedings: "things", understood as tangible objects, and "claims and other property rights."[261] Cryptocurrencies do not appear to fall in either of them.

---

255 Czech Republic, sub 3.
256 Turkey, sub 7.4.2.
257 Finland, sub 5.3.
258 Australia, sub 3.3; Finland, sub 4.3; Germany, sub 4.1.3; Italy, sub 4.3.
259 Finland, sub 5.3.
260 See also the proposition in Czech Republic, sub 3.
261 Germany, sub 4.2.1.

The German literature has discussed the analogous application of the rules on enforcement against "other property rights."[262] Yet this would not allow to obtain the relevant keys from the debtor, which are indispensable to realise the value of the assets. One can thus understand why the German reporter calls for a fundamental overhaul of the law.[263]

Austria has reacted by adopting an explicit rule under which cryptocurrencies are possible objects of enforcement.[264] But as noted by the Austrian reporter, the rule does not specify how enforcement shall be done in practice.[265] A possible model could be provided by Croatian law, under which the creditor can seek a court order prohibiting the debtor from alienating or transferring the crypto-assets.[266] But, as the Croatian reporter notes, this presupposes that the creditor knows about such assets in the first place.[267] The same problem arises in France, which has a special procedure for the seizure of rights in incorporeal objects,[268] and in Japan, where the rules on the enforcement in other rights are applied.[269] Enforcement may be easier where the crypto-assets are held with an intermediary, because in this case, a request for information and an order for seizure could be sent to such intermediary. The Polish report describes a case in which a bailiff conducted such a procedure against a crypto-exchange.[270] However, this approach will generally only be possible in the country in which the intermediary is located, i.e., where it has its seat or other establishment.[271] This limits the possibilities of creditors, and creates the need for more frequent cross-border enforcement.

3.4.2 Enforcement of Claims for Cryptocurrencies

The other case is where a claim for specific cryptocurrencies is to be enforced, e.g. because they have been sold but not delivered. This situation may be rarer than the previously discussed enforcement of money judgments against a crypto-asset, yet is no less intricate.

In this regard, Turkish law provides a specific avenue, because it allows the court to order the debtor to transfer the appropriate number of cryptocurrencies

262 *Ibid.*
263 *Ibid.*
264 Austria, sub 4.
265 *Ibid.*
266 See Croatia, sub 4.5.
267 See Croatia, sub 4.5.
268 France, sub 2.5.
269 Japan, sub 5.1.5.
270 Poland, sub 5.8.
271 See Croatia, sub 4.5.

to satisfy the creditor's claim.[272] Some quite draconian sanctions are threatened in case of default, such as three months of imprisonment.[273] It also seems possible to attach and sell the crypto-assets, although no information is provided on how this will be practically done.[274] Finally, the creditor can also obtain cryptocurrencies of the same kind from a third person on the debtor's charge.[275]

3.4.3 Intermediate Summary

Creditors face considerable difficulties when trying to attach crypto-assets or enforce claims for the delivery of specific crypto-assets. Most of them are related to the intangible nature of the assets and the pseudonymous functioning of the blockchain. These are incommensurable with the traditional modes of enforcement. Countries need to start modernising their laws in order to meet the new challenges. Otherwise, some of the debtor's most valuable assets may be immune to enforcement.

3.5 *Private International Law*

The application of any solution to the previously discussed problems must be preceded by a private international law or "conflict of laws" analysis. This discipline serves to identify the applicable law to any private law issue.

3.5.1 Applicable Inheritance Law

There are some issues for which identifying the applicable law is a relatively straightforward exercise, even in the digital context. These are the issues for which the relevant criteria of private international law are independent of the blockchain. An illustration is inheritance law, which mostly uses personal criteria as connecting factors, particularly the nationality or the last habitual residence of the deceased. These criteria create hardly any specific problems in the blockchain context.[276] It is true that the location of assets may be relevant for the inheritance of immovable assets, yet cryptocurrencies are rarely considered as such.

---

272 Turkey, sub 9.1.2.

273 *Ibid.*

274 *Ibid.*

275 *Ibid.*

276 See e.g. Switzerland, sub 5.4.

3.5.2 Applicable Insolvency Law

Insolvency law is another example where conflict-of-laws issues can be solved relatively easily. Like in inheritance law, the applicable law here depends mostly on personal criteria, in particular the centre of main interests of the debtor. Because the determination of the governing insolvency law is thus also independent of the location of any assets in the insolvency estate, no specific problems arise in a blockchain context.[277]

Exceptions may apply, e.g. in case of Article 8 European Insolvency Regulation (Recast),[278] which protects rights *in rem* of creditors or third parties in assets of the debtor "which are situated within the territory of another Member State at the time of the opening of proceedings." It could be argued that this provision encompasses crypto-assets, which would require their localisation in a specific state. There is currently no information available on how this could be done.

3.5.3 Applicable Transaction Law

The applicable transaction law can be identified without major difficulties. Most legal systems recognise the parties' choice of the applicable law. In the absence of a choice, they refer to personal criteria to determine the applicable law, such as the habitual residence of the seller or – in case of a consumer contract – that of the buyer.[279] Since these criteria are independent of the blockchain, no major issues arise.

3.5.4 Applicable Tort Law

Things are more complicated when it comes to determining the applicable law to torts. The problems are still manageable for legal systems referring to the law of the place of the tortious conduct or of the act causing the damage.[280] These systems have no more issues than usual when identifying the applicable tort law. Of course, identifying the place where the tortfeasor acted may create headaches in practice. But at least when litigation is started in a court, the defendant and the damaging act are typically known.

More problems occur in systems relying on the place where the damage occurred to determine the applicable tort law.[281] Courts in these countries

---

277 See e.g. Finland, sub 5.6.

278 Regulation (EU) 2015/848 of 20 May 2015 on insolvency proceedings [2015] OJ L 141/19.

279 See e.g. Hungary, sub 5.3.

280 See e.g. Article 133(2) Swiss Federal Act on Private International Law.

281 See e.g. the EU Member States, Article 4(1) Rome II Regulation; Japan, sub 5.1.11; UK, sub 4.2.

may first have to locate the cryptocurrency before determining the law applicable to the tortious interference with it.[282] Locating digital assets is however notoriously difficult, given the distributed nature of the blockchain, as will be discussed in more detail now.

3.5.5 Applicable Property Law

The hardest of all private international law riddles concerns the identification of the property law that governs blockchain assets. The national reports document considerable perplexity surrounding this topic. The Czech report, for instance, notes that

> the issue of collision norms for cryptocurrencies in the private international law is complex and to a large part no definitive provisions or interpretations are currently established even in other jurisdictions.[283]

Traditionally, the question of ownership in tangible things is submitted to the law of the place where they are located (*lex rei sitae*). However, as the UK report notes, cryptocurrencies have no such geographical location.[284] The High Court of England and Wales has opted for the place of domicile of the cryptocurrency's owner.[285] This of course begs the question of how the "owner" of the cryptocurrencies can be identified, which would require as a first step a determination of the applicable law to ownership. The circularity of the reasoning underpinning these decisions is thus clearly exposed.[286] Efforts are underway to define a "digital location,"[287] but this may be a misnomer, because the point is to determine the law applicable to such cryptocurrencies, not their location as such.

The Hungarian reporter suggests referring to the law of the place of destination, as is done for goods to be transferred.[288] This rule is however tailored to goods in transit. It does not work particularly well in the crypto context, in which both the locations of the sender and the recipient are often secret. The Finnish report suggests applying domestic law to any "global decentralised cryptocurrency", such as Bitcoin or Ether, where the transferor, the transferee, and any

---

282 UK, sub 4.2.
283 Czech Republic, sub 3.
284 UK, sub 4.2.
285 See UK, sub 4.2. See also the suggestion in the report for Japan, sub 5.1.11.
286 See also UK, sub 4.2.
287 See UK, sub 4.2.
288 Hungary, sub 5.3 (noting that under Hungarian law, the parties also have the right to select the law of destination for goods in transit).

relevant third parties have their habitual residence in the same country.[289] This, of course, requires that (1) the location of such parties is known, which is not always a given, and (2) that all interested third parties live in the same country, which is practically impossible given the global nature of crypto-assets.

Against this background, it may be better to forget about location altogether and follow special conflict-of-laws rules for intangibles. In this line, the South Korean report suggests using the conflicts rules governing claims for utility tokens.[290] Yet even this characterisation is not without problems, as is shown by the case of hybrid tokens.[291] The existing conflicts rules for intellectual property rights or dematerialised securities are also of no avail. Therefore, one cannot but agree with the Finnish report when it notes that no conflicts rules exist for cryptocurrencies and similar digital objects.[292]

Uniform law may provide an answer. The South Korean report suggests following drafts by the UNIDROIT Working Group on Digital Assets and applying the law of the current private key holder or the law of the blockchain system.[293] However, in the final version of the UNIDROIT Principles on Digital Assets and Private Law, the reference to the place of the current private key holder has been dropped.[294] Under the final rules, the law of the blockchain system can be chosen, but in practice, such a choice is extremely rare. Much more important in practice are the other connecting factors used by UNIDROIT, in particular the statutory seat of the issuer and the law governing a custody agreement.

3.6 *Summary on Private Law*

All in all, one cannot escape the conclusion that the private law governing cryptocurrencies is highly fragmented and uncertain. Many legal systems have not developed any special rules, nor have they decided which general rules shall apply. The effects of such uncertainty concerns particularly the question of how crypto-asset holders are protected against attacks or in the insolvency of an intermediary, as well as the rules governing transfer. This uncertainty at the substantive law level is compounded by significant doubts as to the identification of the applicable law.

As a result, it is not exaggerated to say that cryptocurrency holdings, from a private law viewpoint, are in a legal limbo. This situation urgently calls for

---

289 Finland, sub 4.1.

290 South Korea, sub 7.6.1.

291 See *supra* 1.2.

292 Finland, sub 5.1.

293 South Korea, sub 7.6.1.

294 UNIDROIT Principles on Digital Assets and Private Law (2023), available at https://www.unidroit.org/wp-content/uploads/2023/04/C.D.-102-6-Principles-on-Digital-Assets-and-Private-Law.pdf (accessed 2 June 2023).

global harmonisation or, even better, uniformisation of national law, both in the area of substantive private law and conflict-of-laws rules. UNIDROIT has made the first step by publishing the "Principles on Digital Assets and Private Law". A project on the law applicable to "Digital Tokens" is currently being studied by the Hague Conference on Private International Law. Hopefully, these efforts will improve the situation and lead to more uniformity in the private (international) law of cryptocurrencies.

4 Criminal Law

4.1 *Money Laundering, Financing Terrorism and Other Finance-Related Crimes*

The first and most important criminal law concern raised by cryptocurrencies is the fight against money laundering and terrorism finance. Cryptocurrencies lend themselves to both types of criminal activity due to the pseudonomity of their holders and the fact that they can be easily used across borders without intermediaries such as financial institutions. Nevertheless, a tight regulatory AML/CFT framework for cryptocurrencies has been established in many states,[295] which goes back to the activities of the FATF at the global level. These frameworks are further buttressed by strong criminal sanctions.

Other criminal activities typically financed via cryptocurrencies are equally subject to criminal sanctions. These include the sale or purchase of illegal drugs, weapons, or child pornography using cryptocurrencies; or blackmail ransoms paid with cryptocurrencies.[296] In all of these areas, the capacities of law enforcement must be improved to meet the challenges of the blockchain age.

4.2 *Criminal Offenses Relating to Cryptocurrency Businesses*

Some countries criminalise the engagement with cryptocurrencies as such. In Kazakhstan, the circulation of cryptocurrencies is prohibited, and any violation of this prohibition may result in criminal prosecution.[297] In other states, activities relating to cryptocurrencies require a prior registration or authorisation; in these countries, conducting such activities without registration or authorisation constitutes a criminal offence.[298]

295 See supra 2.4.
296 France, sub 2.9.4.
297 Kazakhstan sub 6.
298 For example, Australia, sub 2.4; Egypt, sub 2.2.

4.3 *Hacking and Theft of Cryptocurrencies*

A vast number of countries do not have criminal laws specifically for cryptocurrencies.[299] The question therefore is whether existing criminal laws apply to acts relating to crypto-assets.[300] In some countries, the definition of theft is limited to tangible things and money, and therefore does not cover the hacking or stealing of cryptocurrencies. Nevertheless, hacking or theft of cryptocurrencies may be criminally punished using other statutes, for instance the prohibition of fraud, if the focus is on the value of the cryptocurrency;[301] or the prohibition of computer fraud, if the focus is on the illegal manipulation of computers via hacking.[302] In France, it seems that hacking can simultaneously constitute theft and computer fraud.[303] The examples go a long way to show that cryptocurrencies are not totally unregulated even in countries with no specific crypto laws.

4.4 *Forfeiture/Confiscation of Cryptocurrencies*

An important question concerns the sanction of crimes involving cryptos. There are some cases where cryptocurrencies were forfeited on the basis that they were stolen or constituted proceeds of crime. For example, in the Czech Republic, Bitcoin held by a criminal was forfeited and publicly auctioned because it had been proved that they were proceeds of crime.[304]

Some countries clarify this possibility explicitly in their law. The Hungarian Criminal Procedure Act includes a provision on the confiscation of digital data used for payments, and provides that digital data can be confiscated by excluding the holder from the right of disposal over the confiscated asset. This provision is intended to allow for the confiscation of cryptocurrencies.[305] It may be unnecessary in other countries where the existing law can be interpreted to allow this possibility.

299 For example, Croatia, sub 2;; Denmark, sub 5; Finland, sub 2.3; Poland, sub 3.4; South Korea, sub 4.1; Switzerland, sub 3.7; UK, sub 2.3.

300 For example, in Sweden and Switzerland, hacking is criminal offense and hacking of cryptocurrencies will be penalized (Sweden, sub 4.4.; Switzerland, sub 3.7).

301 Hungary, sub 13.2; Taiwan, sub 4.2.1; Turkey sub 4.

302 Japan, sub 6.2; Poland, sub 3.4.

303 France, sub 2.9.2.

304 Czech Republic, sub 5.

305 Hungary, sub 13.2. Also, in UK, sub 2.3.

5 Tax Law

Given their considerable value, cryptocurrencies present a growing interest from a fiscal point of view. The tax rules on crypto-assets are complex and diverge considerably from country to country. Therefore, we focus on taxable events, rather than on the type and name of the taxes.

5.1 *Buying and Selling Cryptocurrencies against Fiat Money*

Almost all countries impose tax on gains obtained through the sale of cryptocurrencies.[306] This type of tax applies irrespective of whether the gain is made through professional or non-professional activities.[307] The tax can be levied as a wealth/capital gains tax or income tax, or both, in relation to natural persons; or as corporate tax in relation to legal persons.

If gains obtained through crypto-investments are taxed, it is only logical to allow a tax deduction for losses and the costs of acquisition. This practice is widespread;[308] however, the exact extent to which deductions can be made often depends on the circumstances, e.g. between professional and non-professional activities.[309] Sometimes, crypto-losses are not fully deductible.[310]

A few countries exempt low levels of gains derived from crypto-transactions, e.g. by defining a certain *de minimus* threshold.[311] Others do not tax crypto-gains if the asset has been held for a specified length of time.[312]

The buying and selling of cryptocurrency against fiat money may be subject to value-added tax (VAT).[313] This is not the case in the EU, where the Court of Justice has considered Bitcoin a means of payment for tax purposes, thereby exempting its exchange against fiat money from VAT.[314] In other parts of the world, cryptocurrency transactions are also exempt from VAT.[315] That does of course only concern the exchange of cryptocurrencies against fiat money

306 Australia, sub 4; Austria, sub 5; Canada (Québec), sub 3.2; Croatia, sub 5; Czech Republic, sub 4; Denmark, sub 10; Finland, sub 6; France, sub 3.1; Hungary, sub 6; Israel, sub 5; Japan, sub 7; Netherlands, sub 2; New Zealand, sub 5; Poland, sub 3.3; South Korea, sub 9; Sweden, sub 5; Taiwan, sub 5; UK, sub 5; USA, sub 2.4.

307 Canada (Québec), sub 3.2; France, sub 3.1.

308 Australia, sub 4; Czech Republic, sub 4; Finland, sub 6; South Korea, sub 9.1; New Zealand, sub 5.1.3; Poland, sub 3.3; USA, sub 2.4.

309 Czech Republic, sub 4.

310 Denmark, sub 10.

311 Finland, sub 6; France, sub 3.1; Hungary, sub 6.

312 Croatia, sub 5.

313 See Israel, sub 5.4.

314 Czech Republic, sub 3; Hungary, sub 6.

315 South Korea, sub 9; UK, sub 5.

or other cryptocurrencies, not transactions that are paid with crypto-assets, which remain fully taxable.

5.2 *Holding Cryptocurrency*

Tax can also be imposed on the simple holding of crypto-assets, e.g. as trading stock or in financial instruments.[316] It is worth noting that national tax authorities often deviate from the characterisations used in the respective national private law. They may, for instance, consider cryptocurrencies to be "property" for fiscal purposes, even though private law recognises only a "securities entitlement" in their respect.[317]

The tax can be levied, for instance, by calculating the value of the holding at the end of the calendar year.[318] However, determining the precise value may pose considerable problems.[319] One approach to valuation is to use data from public repositories or exchanges.[320] Another approach is to publish a specific end-of-year tax rate for popular cryptocurrencies, such as Bitcoin.[321]

5.3 *Exchanging Cryptocurrency against Another*

Trading one crypto-asset for another is a common practice, particularly in the DeFi space. Some countries do not impose any tax on this activity.[322] This may at least in part be due to the practical difficulties of enforcing such a tax.

5.4 *Paying for Products or Services with Cryptocurrency*

In many countries, paying for products and services using cryptocurrency is permitted, even though the cryptocurrency is not considered legal tender. In this context, the use of cryptocurrencies is usually not taxable.[323] Some countries, however, only exempt the transaction from tax where the products received or services performed are intended for personal use, such as clothes or food.[324]

---

316 New Zealand, sub 5.1.1; Switzerland, sub 6.

317 See e.g. USA, sub 2.4.

318 New Zealand, sub 5.1.1; Switzerland, sub 6.

319 New Zealand, sub 5.1.3; South Korea, sub 9.1; Sweden, sub 5; Switzerland, sub 6; Taiwan, sub 5.

320 New Zealand, sub 5.1.3.

321 Switzerland, sub 6.

322 France, sub 3.1; Poland, sub 3.3.

323 But see Japan, sub 7, which suggests that when a product is purchased with a cryptocurrency, the transfer of the latter will be taxed separately.

324 Australia, sub 4.

5.5 *Providing Crypto-Services*

Gains from providing crypto-services will usually be taxable under ordinary fiscal rules.[325] Such crypto-services may include the operation of a crypto-exchange, a crypto-wallet, or a crypto-ATM.[326] There is nothing surprising about their being submitted to tax.

5.6 *Earning Salaries in Cryptocurrencies*

Undoubtedly, employees who are paid their salary in cryptocurrencies must pay the usual income and related taxes to the state.[327] This also applies to bonuses paid in cryptocurrencies.[328] The reports confirm the applicability of general tax law.

5.7 *Mining*

Income derived from mining is taxable in many jurisdictions.[329] In some countries, this also applies to mining on a non-professional basis;[330] in others, such tax only applies to professional mining activities.[331] Some countries levy some form of tax on hobby mining activities.[332]

Kazakhstan is a particularly interesting case for taxing mining activities: There, the applicable tax rate depends on the source and the amount of energy consumed in the mining process. This may be a suitable step towards making the crypto-industry "greener". However, the Kazak report cautions that the fiscal treatment of mining in Kazakhstan may cause an exodus of miners to other countries.[333] This warning highlights the ineffectiveness of unilateral state action in a global industry.

5.8 *Staking, Lending, Hard Forks, Airdrops*

Staking is the process whereby cryptocurrencies are made available for the "proof-of-stake" consensus algorithm underpinning some decentralised

---

325 New Zealand, sub 5.1.1; Taiwan, sub 5; UK, sub 5.

326 See New Zealand, sub 5.1.1; Taiwan, sub 5.

327 New Zealand, sub 5.1.2; Sweden, sub 5; USA, sub 2.4.

328 New Zealand, sub 5.1.2.

329 Australia, sub 4; Austria, sub 5; Canada, sub 3.2; Croatia, sub 5; Czech Republic, sub 4; Finland, sub 7; Hungary, sub 6; Israel, sub 5.3.; New Zealand, sub 5.1.1; Switzerland, sub 6; UK, sub 5; USA, sub 2.4.

330 See Croatia, sub 5.

331 Australia, sub 4; Israel, sub 5.3.

332 New Zealand, sub 5.1.1; Sweden, sub 5.

333 *Ibid.*

ledgers. Staking can generate financial returns, which may be taxable.[334] Crypto-lending is another way to generate income from cryptocurrencies, which is equally subject to tax in some countries.[335]

Crypto holders can also benefit from hard forks, i.e. where assets multiply through the split of the blockchain into two or more alternative chains. Further gains can be made through airdrops, i.e., where cryptocurrencies are distributed for free or against a minor activity. Some states make these gains subject to (income) tax.[336] In others, there is still some uncertainty about their fiscal treatment.[337]

5.9 *Inheritance and Donations Tax*

Some countries do not levy inheritance tax at all.[338] States that do levy inheritance tax will usually tax any crypto-assets bequeathed by the deceased.[339] An exception is Croatia, where crypto-assets are exempt from inheritance tax.[340]

Donations of cryptocurrencies are taxed in some countries.[341] Czech law exempts donations of cryptocurrencies between spouses and other close family members from tax.[342] Other countries completely exclude donations of cryptocurrency from their fiscal rules.[343]

5.10 *Geographical Scope and Enforcement*

Where a country restricts its tax law geographically, e.g., to income made locally, it must determine where crypto-gains are made. In addition, double-taxation treaties concluded with other countries need to be taken into account.[344]

Enforcing the tax rules in the crypto-context may prove challenging, and different methods have been developed to facilitate tax collection. The U.S. Internal Revenue Service (IRS) requires crypto-exchanges to disclose information on their clients; such as names, addresses, account activity, and account balance.[345] South Korea has adopted an even more radical solution by obliging

334 Austria, sub 5; Finland, sub 7; Switzerland, sub 6.
335 Austria, sub 5; New Zealand, sub 5.1.3; South Korea, sub 9.1; Sweden, sub 5.
336 Austria, sub 5; for airdrops see also UK, sub 5; USA, sub 2.4.
337 Israel, sub 5.5.
338 See e.g. Czech Republic, sub 4.
339 See e.g. Japan, sub 5.1.6; Turkey, sub 7.4.2; UK, sub 5.
340 Croatia, sub 5.
341 Turkey, sub 7.4.2; USA, sub 2.4.
342 Croatia, sub 5.
343 Denmark, sub 10.
344 See Poland, sub 3.3.
345 USA, sub 2.4.

virtual asset service providers, such as crypto-exchanges or wallet providers, to withhold a certain amount from any gains made by their customers.[346] Customers holding accounts with foreign service providers must report to the South Korean tax authorities.[347]

5.11 *No Taxation*

Logically, it is inconsistent for a country to prohibit cryptocurrencies on the one hand, but to tax them on the other. Thus, it is unsurprising that countries banning cryptocurrencies usually do not have any special tax provisions for them.[348]

5.12 *Intermediate Summary*

The fiscal authorities and legislators have been among the first to respond to the emergence of cryptocurrencies. They have generally ensured that the public purse takes a share in the considerable wealth the new technology creates for a select few. The results that taxation authorities around the world have achieved are remarkably consonant, notwithstanding the differences between the means taken to achieve them.

6 Conclusion

We conclude by addressing a provocative question: Is a domestic legal regime for cryptocurrencies impossible? in the title of this book. Our answer is: no. The analysis of a wide range of legal systems demonstrates that legislators, regulators, and courts all over the world have found ways to deal with this new phenomenon. Sometimes, the approach is simply to prohibit them; sometimes, existing legal notions, principles and rules are applied; other times, new rules and legal concepts are created. It remains, thus, a rare occurrence that a legal system has not responded whatsoever to the emergence of digital and decentralised assets recorded on a blockchain. This is testimony to the law's enduring relevance and capability of adaption, even in the face of disruptive innovation; it strongly refutes the popular story that code may eventually replace the law.

Another key conclusion to be drawn from our study is that there is no "one-size-fits-all" solution when it comes to cryptocurrencies. In particular, it seems

346 South Korea, sub 9.1.
347 South Korea, sub 9.3.
348 See China, sub 5.

futile to search for the "true" nature of a cryptocurrency to guide legal treatment; cryptocurrencies may raise very different considerations in different contexts, thereby calling for different characterisations in public, private, criminal, and tax law. While conceptual and terminological rigour are defining virtues for lawyers, they should not forget the policies underpinning legal concepts, principles and rules. Thus, it seems preferable to focus on the broader policies expressed in the law, rather than to engage in endless debates about the boundaries and definitions of a particular legal concept or term. Doubtless, it is important to remain faithful to fundamental principles and avoid reinventing the legal system with each new phenomenon. But it is equally important to further develop and adapt the law in accordance with technological and societal changes. Around an enduring core, the law must evolve.

The analysis has furthermore shown a remarkable variety in how legal systems around the world respond to cryptocurrencies, with the result of an unprecedented level of divergence in the world's legal systems. Such divergence has negative implications, irrespective of one's stance in relation to this new phenomenon. Supporters of cryptocurrencies as a global means of payment and storage of value will be disappointed that the wide range of legislative and regulatory obstacles will constantly inhibit and disrupt the smooth functioning of this global system. Yet opponents of cryptocurrencies will also be concerned that the use of cryptocurrencies cannot be so easily eliminated, whilst the risks they pose remain difficult to address adequately on a national basis. Accordingly, both supporters and opponents of cryptocurrencies must coordinate and cooperate with each other to achieve viable solutions.

To conclude, although a domestic law regime for cryptocurrencies may be possible, any such domestic regime will be far from ideal. By their very design, cryptocurrencies require a global legal framework that will harness their innovative power, while simultaneously curbing potential abuses. If this study has clarified the need for the global harmonisation of cryptocurrency laws, it will have accomplished its objective.

Australia

Andrew Godwin and David Kreltszheim

1 Definition and Legal Qualification

1.1 *How Does the Australian Legal System Currently Provide for or Treat 'Cryptocurrencies'?*

To date, and subject to limited exceptions,[1] Australia has regulated cryptocurrencies and crypto assets (and the underlying blockchain technology) by reference to the existing legal and regulatory framework and has not enacted bespoke laws or legal provisions. As noted by Australia's market conduct regulator, the Australian Securities and Investments Commission (ASIC), the application of regulation is based on the 'rights and features of each individual crypto-asset.'[2] Accordingly:

> whether a crypto asset is within or outside the financial regulatory framework depends on particular characteristics of the crypto-asset offering. This can cause uncertainty for investors and consumers as well as issuers and distributors of these assets. It is a policy matter for government whether or not there should be clarity on this issue.[3]

The Final Report of the Senate Select Committee on Australia as a Technology and Financial Centre (the 'Final Report')[4] considered submissions concerning law reform in relation to the regulation of crypto assets and made various recommendations in this regard.[5] A number of inquiries, reviews and consultations have been undertaken by the Commonwealth Department of the Treasury (the Treasury) and by parliamentary committees. These include the

1 See further in section 1.2 below.

2 The Senate (Australia), Select Committee on Australia as a Technology and Financial Centre, *Second Interim Report* (April 2021), [5.56], available at https://www.aph.gov.au/Parliamentary_Business/Committees/Senate/Financial_Technology_and_Regulatory_Technology/FinancialRegulatoryTech, citing ASIC's answers to questions on notice.

3 Ibid.

4 The Senate (Australia), Select Committee on Australia as a Technology and Financial Centre, *Final Report* (October 2021), For details of this inquiry and copies of the reports, see https://www.aph.gov.au/Parliamentary_Business/Committees/Senate/Financial_Technology_and_Regulatory_Technology/FinancialRegulatoryTech.

5 For potential legal reforms, see further in section 2.5 below.

 | DOI:10.1163/9789004722507_003

inquiry by the Senate referred to above, the Review of the Australian Payments System;[6] the Parliamentary Joint Committee Inquiry into Mobile Payments and Digital Wallets;[7] and consultation on regulating digital asset platforms.[8]

The previous Coalition Government acknowledged the need to modernise the regulatory framework as follows:

> The reviews found new technologies and services are testing our current regulatory definitions, perimeter and powers, and exposing regulatory gaps which could contribute to increased risks of consumer and business harm, possible future systemic instability and impeding private sector investment in innovative products and services.
>
> Failure to modernise our regulatory framework will mean Australian businesses and consumers are increasingly engaging with unregulated parties and the rules governing our systems could be increasingly determined by foreign governments and large multinational companies.[9]

Following its election at the Australian Federal Election in May 2022, the Labor Government confirmed that it 'will improve the way Australia's regulatory system manages crypto assets, to keep up with developments and provide greater protections for consumers.'[10]

At present, cryptocurrencies and crypto assets are governed by the following formal and informal sources of law: the regulatory framework governing financial services and financial products generally, including Chapter 7 of the *Corporations Act 2001* (Cth) (the 'Corporations Act'); legislation governing anti-money laundering and counter-terrorism financing (AML/CTF); legislation governing taxation; and guidance issued by the regulators. The primary regulators that are responsible for supervising this area are as follows: ASIC;

6 Australian Government, *Payments system review – From system to ecosystem* (June 2021). For details of this review, see https://treasury.gov.au/review/review-australian-payments-system.

7 For details of this inquiry, see https://www.aph.gov.au/Parliamentary_Business/Committees/Joint/Corporations_and_Financial_Services/Mobileanddigitalwallet.

8 The Treasury, *Regulating Digital Asset Platforms - Proposal paper* (October 2023), available at https://treasury.gov.au/consultation/c2023-427004.

9 Australian Government, *Transforming Australia's Payments System* (8 December 2021), available at https://treasury.gov.au/publication/p2021-231824, 4.

10 The Treasury, 'Work underway on crypto asset reform' (media release, 22 August 2022), available at https://ministers.treasury.gov.au/ministers/stephen-jones-2022/media-releases/work-underway-crypto-asset-reforms.

the Australian prudential regulator, the Australian Prudential Regulation Authority (APRA); the Australian Transaction Reports and Analysis Centre (AUSTRAC), and the Australia Taxation Office (ATO). Australia's central bank, the Reserve Bank of Australia (RBA), has also issued guidance.

In general, the regulators in Australia have been supportive of innovative areas of business, including cryptocurrency, other blockchain-based business, and financial technology ('Fintech') more broadly.[11] As noted by one of Australia's national law firms, Australia's growth in the area of blockchain and cryptocurrency businesses has been 'driven, in part, by the [Government's] supportive approach for new and innovative financial services and products in the financial technology (fintech) sector.'[12]

The Treasury has stated that the government and the regulators 'continue to monitor developments in cryptocurrencies to ensure that risks are considered and mitigated as appropriate while balancing potential benefits'[13] and that '[i]nter-agency collaboration is ongoing including through the Council of Financial Regulators.'[14]

As noted by ASIC, cryptocurrencies and crypto assets are 'available directly to retail investors in Australia through local digital currency exchanges and overseas based crypto-asset trading platforms.'[15]

---

11 For an outline of the ASIC Innovation Hub and the enhanced regulatory sandbox in Australia, see Gilbert + Tobin, *Global Legal Insights: Blockchain & Cryptocurrency Regulation 2024* (6 November 2023), available at https://www.gtlaw.com.au/knowledge/global-legal-insights-blockchain-cryptocurrency-regulation. See also Lev Bromberg, Andrew Godwin and Ian Ramsay, 'Sandboxes and Bridges – The Impact of Fintech on Regulatory Convergence and Coordination in Asia' in Arner et al (eds), *Research Handbook on Asian Financial Law* (Edward Elgar, 2020).

12 Gilbert + Tobin, Global Legal Insights: Blockchain & Cryptocurrency Regulation 2024 (6 November 2023), available at https://www.gtlaw.com.au/knowledge/global-legal-insights-blockchain-cryptocurrency-regulation.

13 The Senate (Australia), Select Committee on Australia as a Technology and Financial Centre, *Second Interim Report* (October 2021), [5.61], citing the Treasury's answers to questions on notice.

14 Ibid. The Council of Financial Regulators is a coordinating body whose objectives are 'to promote stability of the Australian financial system and support effective and efficient regulation by Australia's financial regulatory agencies.' See the website of the Council of Financial Regulators, 'About', available at https://www.cfr.gov.au/about.html.

15 The Senate (Australia), Select Committee on Australia as a Technology and Financial Centre, *Second Interim Report* (October 2021), [5.56], citing ASIC's answers to questions on notice.

Cryptocurrencies are not considered as legal tender in Australia and are not treated as 'money'. The RBA has outlined its understanding of cryptocurrencies as follows:

> Cryptocurrencies are digital tokens. They are a type of digital currency that allows people to make payments directly to each other through an online system. Cryptocurrencies have no legislated or intrinsic value; they are simply worth what people are willing to pay for them in the market. This is in contrast to national currencies, which get part of their value from being legislated as legal tender. There are a number of cryptocurrencies – the most well-known of these is Bitcoin…while cryptocurrencies can be used to make payments, currently their use as a means of payment is limited and they do not display the key characteristics of money.[16]

Although digital currencies are not defined as 'money' for goods and services tax (GST) purposes in Australia, the law governing GST was amended in 2017 to ensure that payments made using a digital currency receive equivalent treatment to payments made using money.[17]

Cryptocurrencies have been used in Australia as a means of payment and also as an investment class. In June 2021, ASIC issued a consultation paper (Consultation Paper 343) on exchange traded products (ETPs) that invest in, or provide exposure to, crypto-assets, particularly exchange traded funds (ETFs). The consultation paper sought feedback on 'proposed good practices for market operators and product issuers regarding crypto-asset ETPs and other investment vehicles that provide retail investors with exposure to crypto-assets.'[18] The responses to the consultation paper evidenced 'near unanimous support for ETPs and other investment products that provide exposure to crypto-assets being facilitated within the regulatory framework administered by ASIC.

16 Reserve Bank of Australia, 'What are Cryptocurrencies?', available at https://www.rba.gov.au/education/resources/explainers/cryptocurrencies.html.

17 See section 4.1 below. For example see *A New Tax System (Goods and Services Tax) Act 1999* (Cth) sections 9-10(4), 9-85(2), 11-10(3) and 78-10(1). For the definition of 'digital currency' in this context, see the text associated with note 21 below.

18 ASIC, *Crypto-assets as underlying assets for ETPs and other investment products* (Consultation Paper 343, June 2021), available at https://download.asic.gov.au/media/yhbgvq02/cp343-published-30-june-2021.pdf. See also Gilbert + Tobin, Global Legal Insights: Blockchain & Cryptocurrency Regulation 2022 (27 October 2021), available at https://www.gtlaw.com.au/kblockchain-based%20businessnowledge/global-legal-insights-blockchain-cryptocurrency-regulation-2022: 'As well as in payments, there has been a growing expectation that crypto assets (including cryptocurrencies) will become accepted as an investment asset class.'

Furthermore, respondents were largely supportive of [ASIC's] proposals.'[19] In May 2022, cryptocurrency exchange-traded funds commenced trading in Australia.

ASIC has defined stable coins as 'a form of crypto-asset that aim to maintain a stable value relative to a specified unit of account or store of value', including benchmarks such as fiat currencies, commodities and other assets.[20] Stable coins linked to the Australian dollar have been launched by various entities, including two of Australia's major banks.

1.2 *How Is 'Cryptocurrency' Defined in Australia?*

There are definitions of 'digital currency' in both the AML/CTF and tax legislation. The *Anti-Money Laundering and Counter-Terrorism Financing Act 2006* (Cth) (the 'AML/CTF Act') defines 'digital currency' as follows:

> *digital currency* means:
> (a) a digital representation of value that:
>   (i) functions as a medium of exchange, a store of economic value, or a unit of account; and
>   (ii) is not issued by or under the authority of a government body; and
>   (iii) is interchangeable with money (including through the crediting of an account) and may be used as consideration for the supply of goods or services; and
>   (iv) is generally available to members of the public without any restriction on its use as consideration; or
> (b) a means of exchange or digital process or crediting declared to be digital currency by the AML/CTF Rules;
>
> but does not include any right or thing that, under the AML/CTF Rules, is taken not to be digital currency for the purposes of this Act.[21]

---

19 See ASIC, *Response to submissions on CP 343 Crypto-assets as underlying assets for ETPs and other investment products* (Report 705, October 2021), available at https://download.asic.gov.au/media/p3tnevtt/rep705-published-29-october-2021.pdf.

20 The Senate (Australia), Select Committee on Australia as a Technology and Financial Centre, *Final Report* (October 2021, [2.16], citing ASIC.

21 See also the definition of digital currency (or cryptocurrency) provided by AUSTRAC in its glossary at https://www.austrac.gov.au/glossary/digital-currency-or-cryptocurrency: 'A type of currency that only exists in digital rather than physical form (not coins or notes, for example). Digital currency: can be exchanged for goods, services or physical currency; is not issued by or under the authority of a government.'

This definition is similar to the definition published by the Financial Action Task Force (FATF).[22] For a discussion of the AML/CTF legislation, see section 2.6 below.

A definition of a 'digital currency' also appears in the legislation governing the goods and services tax (GST).[23]

For a discussion of the taxation of cryptocurrencies, see section 4.1 below.

In addition, the regulators have adopted general definitions for the terms 'cryptocurrency' and 'crypto assets' for educational purposes. On its financial education website, for example, ASIC defines crypto assets and cryptocurrencies as follows:

> Crypto-assets (crypto) describe an asset class that includes cryptocurrency, digital tokens and coins. It does not exist physically as coins or notes, but as digital tokens stored in a digital 'wallet'. These digital tokens rely on cryptography and technology such as blockchain for security and other features. Crypto may or may not have an actual asset underlying it.[24]

In Consultation Paper 343, ASIC set out its understanding of 'crypto-assets', noting that 'a crypto-asset can be understood to be a digital representation of value or contractual rights that can be transferred, stored or traded electronically, and whose ownership is either determined or otherwise substantially affected by a cryptographic proof,'[25] and that crypto-assets are 'commonly referred to as speculative assets with volatile prices and minimal to no regulatory oversight.'[26]

---

22 Financial Action Task Force, *Report: Virtual Currencies – Key Definitions and Potential AML/CFT Risks* (2014).

23 *A New Tax System (Goods and Services Tax) Act 1999* (Cth), available at https://www.legislation.gov.au/Details/C2021C00398, Part 6.3 (Dictionary). See also ATO, 'GST and digital currency', available at https://www.ato.gov.au/business/gst/in-detail/your-industry/financial-services-and-insurance/gst-and-digital-currency/.

24 ASIC, 'Cryptocurrencies – The risks of investing in crypto', available at https://moneysmart.gov.au/investment-warnings/cryptocurrencies.

25 ASIC, *Crypto-assets as underlying assets for ETPs and other investment products* (Consultation Paper 343, June 2021), available at https://download.asic.gov.au/media/yhbgvq02/cp343-published-30-june-2021.pdf, [8].

26 Ibid, [9]. See also ASIC's submission to the Senate (Australia), Select Committee on Australia as a Technology and Financial Centre, *Final Report* (October 2021), [2.5]: 'A crypto-asset is a digital representation of value or contractual rights that can be transferred, stored or traded electronically. Crypto-assets use cryptography, distributed ledger technology or other technology to provide features such as security and pseudo-anonymity. A crypto-asset may or may not have identifiable economic features that reflect fundamental or intrinsic value.' In its submission, ASIC noted that ASIC noted that this

As noted by the Final Report, ASIC 'uses the term "crypto-asset" as an umbrella term to describe products that are also commonly referred to as "digital assets", "virtual assets" or "digital tokens."'[27]

1.3 *What Definition (if Any) Has Been Retained by the Case-Law or the Legal Doctrine in Australia?*

Courts in Australia have begun to hear cases involving cryptocurrencies. In *Commissioner of Police v Bigatton* [2020] NSWSC 245, for example, the Australian Federal Police sought orders seizing funds and digital currencies in connection with alleged money laundering through a scam called Bitconnect. Although it was not necessary for the court to make a determination on the point, Cavanagh J considered whether dealing in digital currency was dealing in 'money' under the *Corporations Act 2001* (Cth), concluding that cryptocurrencies 'may be considered a form of electronic money'[28] and that there was to date no case that had determined otherwise.[29]

For a further discussion of case law in Australia, see sections 3 and 5 below.

1.4 *What Are the Actual or Potential Legal Relationships between the Different Participants to a Blockchain on Which Cryptocurrencies Are Transferred and Recorded; and under What Conditions May a Participant Have a Claim against Other Participants?*

In Australia, there is no legislation specifically addressing the relationship between any of the participants in transactions relating to a blockchain. This is not to say that the relationship between those participants cannot be regulated by Australian law in some instances. For a further discussion of case law in Australia, see sections 3 and 5 below.

---

definition was adapted from the UK HM Treasury's publication *UK regulatory approach to cryptoassets and stablecoins: Consultation and call for evidence* (January 2021).

27 The Senate (Australia), Select Committee on Australia as a Technology and Financial Centre, *Final Report* (October 2021), [2.4].

28 *Police v Bigatton* [2020] NSWSC 245, [33].

29 *Police v Bigatton* [2020] NSWSC 245, [54]. For a discussion about this case, see Michael Bacina, Louisa Xu and Tom Skevington, 'Blockchain Bites: Bitcoin as money in Australian Courts, Seeking certainty in proof-of-stake tax, Binance launches fiat-to-crypto exchange in Australia, cybersecurity and CBDCs' (Piper Alderman Insight, 7 August 2020), available at https://piperalderman.com.au/insight/blockchain-bites-bitcoin-as-money-in-australian-courts-seeking-certainty-in-proof-of-stake-tax-binance-launches-fiat-to-crypto-exchance-in-australia-cybersecurity-and-cbdcs/.

2 Regulatory Framework

2.1 *Are Cryptocurrencies Explicitly Authorised, or Prohibited or Unregulated in Australia?*

As noted at the beginning, to date Australia has largely regulated cryptocurrencies and crypto assets by reference to the existing legal and regulatory framework and has not enacted bespoke laws or legal provisions. In its submission to the Senate Select Committee on Australia as a Technology and Financial Centre, ASIC summarised its current regulation of digital assets as follows:

> ASIC currently regulates crypto-assets and related products and services to the extent they fall within the existing regulatory perimeter of 'financial products and services'… Crypto-assets that are not financial products and services are generally not regulated by ASIC. They may, however, be subject to other Australian laws – for example, the anti-money laundering and counter-terrorism financing laws regulated by AUSTRAC, consumer protection obligations regulated by the ACCC [Australian Competition and Consumer Commission], and the taxation requirements regulated by the Australian Taxation Office (ATO).[30]

Under the current approach in Australia, the regulation of cryptocurrencies and crypto assets is based on the existing legal and regulatory framework and the 'rights and features of each individual crypto-asset.'[31] The effect of this is that if the activities of an entity (whether a company or an individual) concerning cryptocurrencies and crypto assets fall into the category of providing 'financial services' or issuing, distributing or dealing in 'financial products' (each as defined in Chapter 7 of the Corporations Act), the entity will need to apply to ASIC for an Australian Financial Services (AFS) Licence and will be subject to the various obligations imposed on AFS licensees.[32] These obligations include disclosure obligations and design and distribution obligations.[33]

---

30 The Senate (Australia), Select Committee on Australia as a Technology and Financial Centre, *Final Report* (October 2021), [2.36].

31 The Senate (Australia), Select Committee on Australia as a Technology and Financial Centre, *Second Interim Report* (April 2021), [5.56], citing ASIC's answers to questions on notice.

32 The Senate (Australia), Select Committee on Australia as a Technology and Financial Centre, *Final Report* (October 2021), [2.35].

33 The design and distribution obligations 'are intended to help consumers obtain appropriate financial products by requiring issuers and distributors to have a consumer-centric approach to designing and distributing products.' The process involves undertaking a

In addition, ASIC has certain powers in respect of financial products, including product intervention powers.[34]

2.2 *Are Derivatives Referencing Cryptocurrencies Authorised or Prohibited in Australia?*

Section 761D of the Corporations Act provides a broad definition of a 'derivative'. Derivatives referencing cryptocurrencies are not prohibited in Australia. However, regulatory guidance from ASIC makes it clear that if an issuer of a crypto-asset or an initial coin offering (ICO) is making an offer of a derivative to a retail investor, the issuer will need to prepare a product disclosure statement and comply with other regulatory requirements. In addition, services such as offering, providing financial product advice about, making a market for, and dealing in, derivatives referencing crypto-assets will also require an AFS licence. Further, over-the-counter (OTC) transactions of derivatives, such as contracts-for-difference (CFDs) in crypto-assets and crypto-assets, by AFS licensees and other 'reporting entities' are subject to the transaction reporting requirements under the ASIC Derivative Transaction Rules (Reporting) 2013.[35]

2.3 *Is There a Specific Law or Regulation (Either in Force or in Draft) Dealing with the Regulation of Cryptocurrencies in Australia?*

As noted by Gilbert + Tobin, '[w]hile there have been legislative amendments to accommodate the use of cryptocurrencies, to date these have predominantly focused on the transactional relationships (e.g., the issuing and exchanging process) and activities involving cryptocurrencies, rather than the cryptocurrencies themselves.'[36] Accordingly, other than the AML/CTF Act and the taxation legislation, there is no specific law or regulation that deals with the regulation of cryptocurrencies in Australia. However, '[w]hile there is currently no legislation created to deal with cryptocurrencies as a discrete area of law, this does not prevent them from being captured within existing regimes

'target market determination'. See ASIC, Product design and distribution obligations (Regulatory Guide 274, 10 September 2024), available at https://asic.gov.au/regulatory-resources/find-a-document/regulatory-guides/rg-274-product-design-and-distribution-obligations/.

34 See section 2.7 below for an outline of supervisory enforcement action to date in respect of cryptocurrencies.

35 ASIC, 'Crypto-assets' (Information Sheet 225, INFO 225, reissued in October 2021), available at https://asic.gov.au/regulatory-resources/digital-transformation/crypto-assets/.

36 Gilbert + Tobin, *Global Legal Insights: Blockchain & Cryptocurrency Regulation 2024* (6 November 2023), available at https://www.gtlaw.com.au/knowledge/global-legal-insights-blockchain-cryptocurrency-regulation.

under Australian law.'[37] There is, however, detailed regulatory guidance on cryptocurrencies and crypto assets as outlined below.

2.4 *What Regulatory Guidance Has Been Issued in Australia?*

Regulatory guidance on cryptocurrencies, crypto assets and initial coin offerings is primarily found in ASIC's Information Sheet 225: 'Crypto-assets' (INFO 225).[38] INFO 225 explains how obligations under the Corporations Act and the *Australian Securities and Investments Commission Act 2001* (Cth) (ASIC Act) apply if a business is involved with crypto assets, such as cryptocurrency, tokens or stablecoins (whether there are elements that are decentralised or not), or if an entity is considering raising funds through an ICO.[39]

As previously noted, the obligations that may apply include licensing obligations, disclosure obligations and design and distribution obligations. Failure to comply with any applicable obligations may constitute a criminal offence.

For example, the requirement to hold the relevant licence (such as an AFS licence or a market licence) and to comply with the applicable obligations will apply where an entity:

- issues crypto-assets that fall within the definition of a 'financial product';
- acts as an intermediary in terms of providing advice in respect of crypto-assets that fall within the definition of a 'financial product';
- acts as a miner or transaction processor as part of the clearing and settlement (CS) process for tokens that are 'financial products';
- operates a market for crypto-assets that are 'financial products';
- operates an investment product that offers investors exposure to crypto-assets;
- provides a payment service that involves a 'non-cash payment facility'; or
- acts as a wallet and custody service provider in respect of tokens that fall within the definition of a 'financial product.'[40]

Section 763A of the Corporations Act provides a functional definition of a 'financial product', under which a 'financial product' is defined as 'a facility through which, or through the acquisition of which, a person does one or more of the following: (a) makes a financial investment;[41] (b) manages financial

37 Ibid.

38 ASIC, 'Crypto-assets' (Information Sheet 225, INFO 225, reissued in October 2021), available at https://asic.gov.au/regulatory-resources/digital-transformation/crypto-assets/.

39 Ibid.

40 See ASIC, 'Crypto-assets' (Information Sheet 225, INFO 225, reissued in October 2021), available at https://asic.gov.au/regulatory-resources/digital-transformation/crypto-assets/.

41 See *Corporations Act (2001)* s 763B for when a person makes a financial investment.

risk;[42] (c) makes non-cash payments.'[43] Section 766A of the Corporations Act defines when a person provides a 'financial service' and includes circumstances where a person (a) provides financial product advice;[44] (b) deals in a financial product;[45] (c) makes a market for a financial product;[46] (d) operates a registered scheme; or (e) provides a custodial or depository service.[47]

Activities involving cryptocurrencies and crypto assets will therefore be regulated by Chapter 7 of the Corporations Act if they constitute a 'financial service' or involve a 'financial product' as outlined above.

INFO 225 provides a non-exhaustive list of items that should be considered when crypto-assets are issued or offered, whether through an initial coin offering or through other means. The items include the following:

> **Is the crypto-asset a financial product (or does it involve a financial product)?**
>
> Entities and their advisers need to consider all the rights and features of the proposed crypto-asset, as well as the way in which it will be offered. This analysis is critical to determining whether the crypto-asset is a financial product or involves a financial product. The conclusions of an analysis of the rights and features of the asset [are] more important than how it is named and marketed (e.g. as an ICO).
>
> Our experience suggests that ICOs by their nature seek to raise capital from the public to fund a particular project through the issue of crypto-assets such as tokens. If the crypto-asset issued by the ICO is a financial product (such as an interest in a managed investment scheme or a security), the issuer will need to comply with the relevant capital raising provisions of the Corporations Act, AFS licensing requirements and other regulatory requirements. These regulatory requirements are in place to maintain the integrity of Australia's financial market and ensure consumers are protected.[48]

---

42 See *Corporations Act* (*2001*) s 763C for when a person manages financial risk.

43 See *Corporations Act* (*2001*) s 763D for when a person makes non-cash payments.

44 See *Corporations Act* (*2001*) s 766B for the meaning of 'financial product advice'.

45 See *Corporations Act* (*2001*) s 766C for the meaning of 'dealing'.

46 See *Corporations Act* (*2001*) s 766D for the meaning of 'makes a market for a financial product'.

47 See *Corporations Act* (*2001*) s 766E for the meaning of 'provides a custodial or depository service'.

48 ASIC, 'Crypto-assets' (Information Sheet 225, INFO 225, reissued in October 2021), available at https://asic.gov.au/regulatory-resources/digital-transformation/crypto-assets/.

> **Are you complying with all relevant Australian laws on an ongoing basis?**
>
> Entities need to ensure that they comply with all the relevant Australian laws. This includes ensuring that all the information they provide to consumers, regardless of the media they use, complies with relevant laws including the Corporations Act, ASIC Act and the Australian Consumer Law, as well as anti-money laundering (AML) and know your client (KYC) obligations.
>
> Whether or not a financial product is involved, promoters must always ensure that the ICO does not involve misleading or deceptive conduct or statements. Entities can do so by seeking professional advice (including legal advice) on all the facts and circumstances of the issue or sale of the ICO, not just a part of the sale.[49]

INFO 225 states that '[t]he Corporations Act is likely to apply to a crypto-asset or an ICO that involves a financial product such as a managed investment scheme, security, derivative or non-cash payment (NCP) facility'. It then discusses each of these financial products and notes ASIC's experience that 'some crypto-assets and many ICOs may be, or involve, interests in a managed investment scheme.'[50]

As noted in the above extract from INFO 225, even if crypto assets do not constitute financial products, the general consumer protections under the Australian Consumer Law will still apply, particularly the prohibition against misleading or deceptive conduct in contexts such as advertising and marketing.[51] INFO 225 provides the following inclusive list of conduct that may be misleading or deceptive to consumers:

- stating or conveying the impression that the crypto-assets (such as coins or tokens) or ICO offered are not a financial product if that is not the case;
- stating or conveying the impression that a crypto-asset trading platform does not quote or trade financial products if that is not the case;
- using social media to generate the appearance of a greater level of public interest in a crypto-asset or ICO;

49 Ibid.

50 Ibid.

51 The Australian Consumer Law is contained in Schedule 2 to the *Competition and Consumer Act 2010* (Cth). The Australian Competition and Consumer Commission (ACCC)'s Advertising and selling guide provides guidance on how to ensure advertising complies with the Australian Consumer Law.

- undertaking or arranging for a group to engage in trading strategies to generate the appearance of a greater level of buying and selling activity for an ICO or crypto-asset;
- failing to disclose adequate information about the ICO or crypto-asset, or suggesting that the ICO or crypto-asset is a regulated product or the regulator has approved the ICO or crypto-asset if that is not the case.[52]

INFO 225 notes that ASIC has been delegated powers from the Australian Competition and Consumer Commission [ACCC] 'to, in coordination with the ACCC, respond to potentially misleading or deceptive conduct relating to crypto-assets which affect Australian consumers.'[53] This delegation 'enables ASIC to take action against misleading or deceptive conduct in marketing or selling of ICOs, even if the ICO does not involve a financial product.'[54]

Additionally, if an entity engages in retail lending activities in relation to cryptocurrencies (for example, lending money to consumers to acquire cryptocurrencies), the activities may fall within the scope of the *National Credit Consumer Protection Act 2009* (Cth) and require the relevant entity to hold an Australian credit licence or otherwise be exempt from the requirement to be licensed.[55] ASIC has successfully prosecuted a lender making cryptocurrency-backed loans for falsely claiming that it had an Australian credit licence.[56]

Other ASIC regulatory guidance that is relevant to the regulation of cryptocurrencies includes the following:

- ASIC Regulatory Guide 255: *Providing digital financial product advice to retail clients* (30 August, 2016);[57] and
- ASIC Information Sheet 219: *Evaluating distributed ledger technology* (March, 2017).[58]

---

52 ASIC, 'Crypto-assets' (Information Sheet 225, INFO 225, reissued in October 2021), available at https://asic.gov.au/regulatory-resources/digital-transformation/crypto-assets/.

53 Ibid.

54 See ASIC, 'ASIC takes action on misleading of deceptive conduct in ICOs' (Media Release 18-122, 1 May 2018), available at https://asic.gov.au/about-asic/news-centre/find-a-media-release/2018-releases/18-122mr-asic-takes-action-on-misleading-or-deceptive-conduct-in-icos/.

55 See Gilbert + Tobin, *Global Legal Insights: Blockchain & Cryptocurrency Regulation 2024* (6 November 2023), available at https://www.gtlaw.com.au/knowledge/global-legal-insights-blockchain-cryptocurrency-regulation.

56 ASIC, 'Cryptocurrency lender sentenced for false licence claims' (Media Release 23-223 MR dated 17 August 2023) available at https://asic.gov.au/about-asic/news-centre/find-a-media-release/2023-releases/23-223mr-cryptocurrency-lender-sentenced-for-false-licence-claims/.

57 Available at https://asic.gov.au/regulatory-resources/find-a-document/regulatory-guides/rg-255-providing-digital-financial-product-advice-to-retail-clients/.

58 Available at https://asic.gov.au/regulatory-resources/digital-transformation/evaluating-distributed-ledger-technology/.

2.5 *What Reforms Might Be Adopted in Australia?*

As previously noted above, in its response to various reviews, the Australian Government has acknowledged the need to modernise the regulatory architecture. The Final Report of the Senate Select Committee on Australia as a Technology and Financial Centre considered submissions concerning law reform in relation to the regulation of crypto assets and made various recommendations, some of which continue to be advanced by the Labor Government following its election at the Australian Federal Election in May 2022 as outlined later in this Chapter.

Various reform options were identified in submissions to the Final Report. The reform options include greater regulatory clarity in relation to which crypto assets constitute financial products;[59] temporary regulatory relief in the form of a safe harbour;[60] establishing a market licence regime for digital asset providers[61] or, alternatively, introducing new categories of authorisation under the AFS licensing framework;[62] and incorporating certain crypto assets into the current regulatory framework for 'financial products' (as defined) in Chapter 7 of the Corporations Act.[63]

In any reforms to bring cryptocurrencies or crypto assets expressly within the scope of Chapter 7 of the Corporations Act, the definitions of 'financial product' and 'financial service' will be of critical relevance. As noted by the Australian Law Reform Commission (ALRC), the current definitions are complex for three principal reasons:

- there are extensive lists of inclusions and exclusions for the definitions of the two terms in the *Corporations Act* and the *ASIC Act*, many of which contain further defined terms and create a series of interconnected definitions;
- the definitions vary for the purposes of different provisions, obligations, and prohibitions in Chapter 7 of the *Corporations Act*, and the definitions are different again for the *ASIC Act*; and
- the extent and nature of variations to the definitions are difficult to ascertain as a result of incoherent use of the legislative hierarchy and, in particular,

59 The Senate (Australia), Select Committee on Australia as a Technology and Financial Centre, *Final Report* (October 2021), [3.10].
60 Ibid, [3.16].
61 Ibid, [3.17], [3.23].
62 Ibid, [3.23], [3.69].
63 Ibid, [3.70]–[3.76].

the creation of alternative regulatory retimes and notional amendments to provisions in the *Corporations Act*.[64]

Accordingly, the ALRC has recommended that the definitions be simplified.[65] The extent to which this recommendation accommodates and supports the regulatory treatment of cyptocurrencies and crypto assets will be a litmus test in this regard. A relevant question is whether it will be possible to continue to regulate cryptocurrencies and crypto assets by reference to the existing legal and regulatory framework (and the general definitions), or whether the framework will need to be tailored, including through adopting bespoke provisions and definitions, to achieve fit-for-purpose regulation.

The ALRC has noted the challenges of adopting a new term to describe cryptocurrencies and crypto assets:

> ... it may be appropriate to include a new term in legislation 'if there is no term with an equivalent meaning that is more widely understood'. Such an approach provides a justification for inserting a definition of a 'crypto asset' in financial services legislation. There are, however, a number of questions that should be considered in determining both the label that should be adopted for the concept and the definition used to describe the concept. For example, questions arise as to whether terms such as 'cryptocurrency' or 'digital currency' would be appropriate, given that the concept does not involve a 'currency' as traditionally understood. In addition, the use of terms such as 'stablecoins' may be misleading, particularly given the collapse in May 2022 of a well-known stablecoin, which proved to be anything but stable.[66]

64 Australian Law Reform Commission (ALRC), *Interim Report A – Financial Services Legislation* (ALRC Report 137, November 2021), [7.2]. This interim report was issued as part of the ALRC's inquiry into simplification of the legislative framework for corporations and financial services regulation. For further details of this inquiry and the relevant publications, see the website of the ALRC, available at https://www.alrc.gov.au/inquiry/review-of-the-legislative-framework-for-corporations-and-financial-services-regulation/.

65 ALRC, *Final Report - Confronting Complexity: Reforming Corporations and Financial Services Legislation* (ALRC Report 141, November 2023) Recommendation 31.

66 Australian Law Reform Commission, *New Business Models, Technologies, and Practices* (Backbround Paper FSL7, October 2022), [157], available at https://www.alrc.gov.au/inquiry/review-of-the-legislative-framework-for-corporations-and-financial-services-regulation/consultation-doc/.

In March 2022, the Treasury released a Consultation Paper inviting submissions on the licensing and custody requirements to be imposed on 'crypto asset secondary service providers' (CASSPs).[67] For this purpose, the Consultation Paper proposes that a CASSP be defined as:

> any natural or legal person who, as a business, conducts one or more of the following activities for or on behalf of another natural or legal person:
> – exchange between crypto assets and fiat currencies;
> – exchange between one or more forms of crypto assets;
> – transfer of crypto assets;
> – safekeeping and/or administration of virtual assets or instruments enabling control over crypto assets; and
> – participation in and provision of financial services related to an issuer's offer and/or sale of a crypto asset.

The Consultation Paper focuses on 'secondary' service providers on the basis that a user who directly accesses a distributed network on their own account does not necessarily need the same regulatory recourse as consumers who acquire financial products. This is because 'a crypto asset will do what it is programmed to – mathematically – and in a distributed network changing this programming is at least challenging and at best impossible. Similarly, there is no requirement to trust a central authority to arbitrate transactions.'[68] On the other hand, service providers who facilitate consumer access to crypto assets are centralised actors who introduce the types of regulatory concerns that arise in relation to financial products. In particular, consumers need to trust these 'secondary' service providers who mediate their access to crypto assets.[69]

The Australian Government announced in August 2022 that it would prioritise 'token mapping' as the first step in its reform agenda, resulting in a Consultation Paper that was released in February 2023.[70] It is interesting to note that the Consultation Paper moves away from adopting a granular (or context-specific) definition of crypto assets towards the use of a high-level taxonomy that focuses more on *function* than on the particular label that is used.

67 The Treasury, *Crypto Asset Secondary Service Providers: Licensing and Custody Requirements – Consultation Paper* (21 March 2022). For submissions, see https://treasury.gov.au/consultation/c2022-259046.

68 Ibid, 13.

69 Ibid, 13.

70 The Treasury, *Token Mapping* (Consultation paper, February 2023), available at https://treasury.gov.au/consultation/c2023-341659.

In October 2023, the Treasury released a proposal paper on regulating digital asset platforms.[71] As noted by the Government in a media release:

> [The proposal paper] recommends making crypto exchanges and digital asset platforms subject to existing Australian financial services laws and requiring platform operators to obtain an Australian Financial Services Licence.
>
> In addition, digital asset platforms will need to meet specific obligations that take into account the nature of the platforms. This will include minimum standards for holding tokens, standards for custody software, and standards when transacting in tokens.[72]

The media release noted that further consultation on the draft legislation would take place in 2024.

2.6 *Are Anti-Money Laundering and Counter-Terrorism Financing (AML/CFT) Provisions Applicable in Australia?*

As noted in section 1.2 above, the *Anti-Money Laundering and Counter-Terrorism Financing Act 2006* (Cth) (the 'AML/CTF Act') contains a definition of 'digital currency', which was inserted in 2018. The Department of Home Affairs and AUSTRAC have explained the application of the legislation to digital currency exchanges (DCEs) as follows:

> The regulatory obligations imposed on DCEs under the AML/CTF Act are in line with guidance developed by the FATF [Financial Action Task Force] in 2015. The Act does not regulate cryptocurrency or digital assets, just as it does not regulate fiat currency, such as the Australian dollar. However, following the 2018 amendments, businesses offering DCE services between fiat currency and digital currency (i.e. cryptocurrency), and vice versa are regulated for AML/CTF purposes only. It does not regulate transaction exchanges from digital currency to digital currency.[73]

---

71 The Treasury, *Regulating Digital Asset Platforms - Proposal paper* (October 2023), available at https://treasury.gov.au/consultation/c2023-427004. The proposal papers, at 3, defines a digital asset platform as a 'multi-function platform that holds assets for customers'.

72 The Hon Stephen Jones MP, Assistant Treasurer and Minister for Financial Services, 'Regulation of digital and crypto assets' (Joint media release with The Hon Jim Chalmers MP, Treasurer, 16 October 2023), available at https://ministers.treasury.gov.au/ministers/stephen-jones-2022/media-releases/regulation-digital-and-crypto-assets.

73 The Senate (Australia), Select Committee on Australia as a Technology and Financial Centre, *Final Report* (October 2021), [2.57], citing the submission by the Department of

The effect of the AML/CFT Act is that DCEs that offer the service of exchanging between fiat currency and digital currency are required to register and enrol with AUSTRAC as a reporting entity and are subject to various requirements. These requirements include verifying the identity of their customers through the know-your-customer processes and complying with the ongoing monitoring and reporting obligations, including the requirement to monitor and report suspicious and large transactions.[74]

According to the Final Report, '[t]he committee heard that the current requirement for DCEs to register with the Australian Transaction Reports and Analysis Centre (AUSTRAC) for the purposes of AML/CTF regulation amounts to a very "light touch" regulatory approach to these businesses, and that enhanced regulation is needed.'[75]

In April 2023, the Commonwealth Attorney-General's Department commenced a consultation on modernising Australia's AML/CTF regime.[76] The consultation asks whether the 'travel rule' – broadly, the requirement for sender and recipient information to 'travel' with a transfer of a crypto asset – should be extended to cover DCEs.[77] Additionally, the consultation asks whether Australia should mirror amendments made to the FATF standards in 2018 by extending the AML/CTF regime to cover the following services of DCEs: exchanges between one or more other forms of digital currency, transfers of digital currency on behalf of a customer, safekeeping or administration of digital currency, and provision of financial services related to an issuer's offer and/or sale of a digital currency.[78]

2.7 *What Supervisory Action Has Taken Place to Date in Australia?*

ASIC has issued general information in respect of cryptocurrencies and has warned of their risks.[79] ASIC has also issued a warning in respect of 'an increase

---

Home Affairs and AUSTRAC, 3.

74 See Gilbert + Tobin, *Global Legal Insights: Blockchain & Cryptocurrency Regulation 2024* (6 November 2023), available at https://www.gtlaw.com.au/knowledge/global-legal-insights-blockchain-cryptocurrency-regulation.

75 The Senate (Australia), Select Committee on Australia as a Technology and Financial Centre, *Final Report* (October 2021), [3.26]. Hence the CASSP proposals discussed in section 2.5.

76 Commonwealth Attorney General's Department, *Modernising Australia's Anti-Money Laundering and CounterTerrorism Financing Regime* (April 2023).

77 Ibid, 14–15.

78 Ibid, 13–14.

79 See ASIC, 'Cryptocurrencies – The risks of investing in crypto', available at https://moneysmart.gov.au/investment-warnings/cryptocurrencies; ASIC, 'Warning: Trading crypto-asset related financial products through unlicensed entities' (18 August 2021),

in marketing recommending Australians switch from retail and industry superannuation funds to self-managed superannuation funds (SMSFs) so they can invest in a "high return portfolio."'[80] In a sign that supervisory and enforcement action is likely to increase in this area, ASIC has noted the following:

> In November 2021, ASIC moved to shut down unlicensed financial services business A One Multi Services Pty Ltd, located in Queensland. The Gold Coast – based company appears to be engaging in unlawful activity, with ASIC alleging more than $2.4 million was transferred from A One Multi to buy crypto-assets.
>
> ASIC obtained interim orders and injunctions from the Federal Court in Queensland against A One Multi and its directors Aryn Hala and Heidi Walters to protect investors. Mr Hala appears to represent to investors that he can help them invest their superannuation in an SMSF, and then loan the money in their SMSF to A One Multi. ASIC alleges Mr Hala told investors that they would receive annual investment returns of over 20%.[81]

Additionally, ASIC has warned regulated securities brokers about providing consumers with unregulated cryptoassets alongside shares and other regulated financial products through the brokers' trading apps.[82] ASIC has expressed its concern that the brokers' practices may 'give investors a false sense of security, leading them to believe crypto-assets have the same protections as regulated financial products or they may underestimate the risks.'[83]

---

available at https://asic.gov.au/about-asic/news-centre/news-items/warning-trading-crypto-asset-related-financial-products-through-unlicensed-entities/.

80 ASIC, 'Warning: Self-managed super funds and crypto investments' (17 January 2022), available at https://asic.gov.au/about-asic/news-centre/articles/warning-self-managed-super-funds-and-crypto-investments/.

81 Ibid. See also ASIC, 'ASIC obtains Federal Court orders against unlicensed investment scheme A One Multi Services' (Media Release 21-289MR, 4 November 2021), available at https://asic.gov.au/about-asic/news-centre/find-a-media-release/2021-releases/21-289mr-asic-obtains-federal-court-orders-against-unlicensed-investment-scheme-a-one-multi-services/.

82 ASIC, 'ASIC warns brokers considering high-risk offers to retail investors' (Media Release 22-239 MR, 31 August 2022), available at https://asic.gov.au/about-asic/news-centre/find-a-media-release/2022-releases/22-239mr-asic-warns-brokers-considering-high-risk-offers-to-retail-investors/.

83 Ibid.

Other enforcement action taken by ASIC includes stopping proposed initial coin offerings (ICOs) targeting retail investors[84] and banning individuals from providing financial services.[85]

In October 2022, ASIC commenced civil penalty proceedings for misleading or deceptive representations and engaging in unlicensed conduct in relation to a non-cash payment facility involving a crypto-asset token.[86]

In November 2022, ASIC commenced civil penalty proceedings for unlicensed offerings of fixed-yield 'crypto-asset based' products.[87] On 9 February 2024, the Federal Court found that the defendant had contravened the Corporations Act in relation to its 'earner' product by carrying on an unlicensed financial services business and operating an unregistered managed investment scheme.[88] No similar findings were made in relation to the defendant's 'access' product.

In December 2022, ASIC commenced civil penalty proceedings for unlicensed financial services, breaching product disclosure requirements and failing to comply with design and distribution obligations (DDO) in relation to a cryptoasset 'earn' product.[89] On 14 March 2024, the Federal Court dismissed

84 ASIC, 'ASIC acts against misleading Initial Coin Offerings and crypto-asset funds targeted at retail investors' (Media Release 18-274MR, 20 September 2018), available at https://asic.gov.au/about-asic/news-centre/find-a-media-release/2018-releases/18-274mr-asic-acts-against-misleading-initial-coin-offerings-and-crypto-asset-funds-targeted-at-retail-investors/.

85 ASIC, 'ASIC bans former National Representative of BitConnect cryptocurrency investment scheme from providing financial services for seven years' (Media Release 20-206MR, 3 September 2020), available at https://asic.gov.au/about-asic/news-centre/find-a-media-release/2020-releases/20-206mr-asic-bans-former-national-representative-of-bitconnect-cryptocurrency-investment-scheme-from-providing-financial-services-for-seven-years/.

86 ASIC, 'ASIC sues BPS Financial for alleged misleading statements about crypto-asset Qoin' (Media Release 22-28MR, 25 October 2022), available at https://asic.gov.au/about-asic/news-centre/find-a-media-release/2022-releases/22-287mr-asic-sues-bps-financial-for-alleged-misleading-statements-about-crypto-asset-qoin/.

87 ASIC, 'ASIC sues Block Earner for unlicensed conduct over crypto-asset based products' (media release 22-324MR, 23 November 2022), available at https://asic.gov.au/about-asic/news-centre/find-a-media-release/2022-releases/22-324mr-asic-sues-block-earner-for-unlicensed-conduct-over-crypto-asset-based-products/.

88 *Australian Securities and Investments Commission v Web3 Ventures Pty Ltd* [2024] FCA 64.

89 ASIC, 'Finder Wallet sued for alleged unlicensed conduct and inadequate risk disclosure over Finder Earn product' (Media Release 22-359MR, 15 December 2022), available at https://asic.gov.au/about-asic/news-centre/find-a-media-release/2022-releases/22-359mr-finder-wallet-sued-for-alleged-unlicensed-conduct-and-inadequate-risk-disclosure-over-finder-earn-product/.

those proceedings, finding that ASIC had not made out its pleaded case.[90] ASIC has lodged an appeal against this decision.[91]

On 9 April 2024, ASIC applied for orders in the Federal Court to secure the digital assets of three blockchain mining companies (two incorporated in Australia, one in Hong Kong). ASIC alleged that the companies contravened the Corporations Act by carrying out a financial services business without a licence.[92]

3 Private Law Issues

3.1 *Can Cryptocurrencies Be the Subject of Property Rights?*

Presently the answer to this question is 'yes' for particular purposes only. The particular purposes for which cryptocurrencies may be the subject of property rights are considered elsewhere in this section 3. The approach of providing specific, situational answers to this question[93] is in keeping with the common law that applies in Australian states and territories.

Certain Australian government publications[94] have adopted a general definition of a 'crypto *asset*' – a subset of which is comprised of cryptocurrencies – as 'a digital representation of value that can be transferred, stored or traded electronically… [using] cryptographic proofs to determine *ownership*' (emphasis added). The use of the terms '*asset*' and '*ownership*' in this definition implies that cryptocurrencies may generally be the subject of property rights. Presently this definition purports to be descriptive and is not used to itself constitute or create property rights where none may otherwise be found to exist

---

90 *Australian Securities and Investments Commission v Finder Wallet Pty Ltd* [2024] FCA 228.

91 ASIC, 'ASIC appeals Finder Wallet decision' (Media Release 24-068MR, 6 April 2024) available at https://asic.gov.au/about-asic/news-centre/find-a-media-release/2024-releases/24-068mr-asic-appeals-finder-wallet-decision/.

92 ASIC, 'ASIC obtains Federal Court orders appointing receivers over digital currency assets of blockchain mining companies' (Media Release 24-073MR, 12 April 2024) available at https://asic.gov.au/about-asic/news-centre/find-a-media-release/2024-releases/24-073mr-asic-obtains-federal-court-orders-appointing-receivers-over-digital-currency-assets-of-blockchain-mining-companies/.

93 David Kreltszheim, 'Taking and Enforcing Security Over Cryptocurrency' (2018) 34 *Australian Banking and Finance Law Bulletin* 105, 106; UK Law Tech Delivery Panel UK Jurisdiction Taskforce, *Legal Statement on Cryptoassets and Smart Contracts* (2019) paragraphs 15, 35–41, 85.

94 For example, ASIC, *Consultation Paper 43: Crypto Assets as Underlying Assets for ETPs and Other Investment Products* (June 2021) 7–8; the Treasury, *Crypto Asset Secondary Service Providers: Licensing and Custody Requirements – Consultation Paper* (21 March 2022) 2.

for legal purposes. ASIC has stressed that this is a working definition only and may evolve over time.[95]

If the nature of property rights in cryptocurrencies is to be conceptualised in the abstract, it would be necessary to define that right. The relevant 'property' right of a direct holder of a cryptocurrency (as opposed to somebody who acquires cryptocurrency via an intermediary like an exchange or a custodian) would probably be her/his right to have the public addresses or public keys (associated with the private keys exclusively known and controlled by her/him) appear as the last entry in the blockchain in relation to those amounts.[96] Where a person acquires cryptocurrency via an exchange or custodian and therefore holds it indirectly, the person would usually have contractual rights exercisable against the exchange or custodian. Whether or not that person's contractual rights are supplemented by other rights of a proprietary nature would depend on several variables, including the terms and conditions of the exchange/custodian and its operating procedures.[97]

3.2 *'Transfer' of Ownership of Cryptocurrencies*

Let's say, as a matter of technology, that Alice is able to make cryptocurrency that is directly controlled by her available to Bob on a blockchain by a process that involves applying her private key and using Bob's public key/address. This process results in Bob being given access to cryptocurrency on that blockchain by using the private key that corresponds with his public key/address. As a matter of law, the analysis in section 3.1 would suggest that this process leads to Alice 'transferring' her property rights in that cryptocurrency to Bob. This analysis has not as yet been expressly adopted in Australia but there appears to be no reason why it should not be adopted.[98]

It does not seem to matter whether or not Bob provides something in return to Alice, i.e. whether Bob is simply the recipient of a donation.

---

95 ASIC, above 94, 8.

96 See Kelvin F K Low and Ernie GS Teo, 'Bitcoins and Other Cryptocurrencies as Property?' (2017) 9 (2) *Law, Innovation and Technology* 235, 248, 252–254; David Fox, 'Cryptocurrencies in the Common Law of Property' in David Fox and Sarah Green, *Cryptocurrencies in Public and Private Law* (2019) 139, 143–145; UK Law Tech Delivery Panel Statement, above n 93, paragraphs 63–65. For a more recent analysis addressing additional nuances, see Timothy Chan, 'The Nature of Property in Cryptoassets' (2023) 40 *Legal Studies* 480.

97 See David Kreltszheim, 'What We Know and Don't Know About Cryptocurrency Exchanges: a Summary for Finance and Insolvency Lawyers' (2020) 36 *Australian Banking and Finance Law Bulletin* 7, 10–12.

98 See Timothy Chan, above n 96, at 493–495.

If Bob provides goods to Alice in return for the cryptocurrency, it appears that the transaction will not be regulated under the Australian Sale of Goods legislation. This is because that legislation only applies if Alice pays money to Bob for the goods,[99] and the cryptocurrencies presently available will not constitute money for this purpose. This contrasts with the treatment of the transaction for GST purposes, which reflects that cryptocurrency may function as a method of payment that is an alternative to money.[100]

If Alice holds her cryptocurrency indirectly via an exchange or a custodian, the mechanism for transfer will depend on what the contract between Alice and the exchange/custodian provides for in relation to transfers.

3.3 *Can Cryptocurrencies Be Inherited?*

Yes. Australian commentary suggests that cryptocurrencies may be inherited. In general, the focus of the commentary is on the practical steps to be taken to ensure that the executor is given exclusive control of the private keys needed to access direct holdings.[101] In the case of indirect holdings via an exchange or custodian, the executor would contact the exchange or custodian in the same way as they would contact a bank or any other third party.

3.4 *Can Cryptocurrencies Be Held on Trust?*

Yes. An example is the court order made by the Federal Court of Australia in a dispute between cryptocurrency traders as to their respective entitlements to a fiat currency or in specie distribution by the rehabilitation trustee of Mt Gox Co Pty Ltd. The court order provided for any bitcoin or fiat currency received from the rehabilitation trustee to be held on trust by a professional custodian (holding an Australian Financial Services Licence) to be distributed in due course in accordance with an order by the court.[102] More generally, we consider that the common law approach taken in New Zealand[103] in the *Cryptopia Case* and in Singapore[104] in the first instance judgment in *B2C2 v Quoine* will most likely be adopted in Australia. The effect of adopting this approach is that

---

99 For example, section 6(1) of the *Goods Act 1958* (*Victoria*) and section 6(1) of the *Sale of Goods Act 1923* (*New South Wales*).

100 See section 4.1 below.

101 For example, see the section on digital assets on the website of the Public Trustee in Queensland, Australia: https://www.pt.qld.gov.au/wills/wills-week/digital-legacy/.

102 *Karis v CC Management Pty Ltd* (*No 2*) [2022] FCA 859.

103 *Ruscoe and Moore v Cryptopia Ltd* (*in liquidation*) [2020] NZHC 728 at [69].

104 *B2C2 v Quoine* [2019] SGHC (I) 03l SGCA (I) 02, at [142]. The Court of Appeal left the 'trust' issue open for another day because it found there was no intention to create a trust in any event: at [6] and [144].

cryptocurrency will be taken to be property that is capable of being the subject matter of a trust.[105]

Once it is found that an exchange holds cryptocurrency on trust for users (as was the case in *Cryptopia*, in the insolvency of a cryptocurrency exchange) difficult issues have to be addressed where there is a shortfall in the trust property available for distribution to the entitled trust beneficiaries. How should the losses be apportioned amongst the beneficiaries – rateably or by using a 'first in, first out' approach? Should it make a difference that the exchange had 'earmarked' particular private keys as being held for particular beneficiaries?[106] That is, should the beneficiaries of 'earmarked' private keys bear all of the losses resulting from the compromise of those particular keys? On 1 March 2024, the Court in *Cryptopia* made detailed orders for the distribution of crypto assets to the relevant account holders within each class of crypto assets held by the exchange.[107] It emerged that there was unlikely to be a shortfall in many of the crypto asset classes, because only about 14% of the users had registered their claims and only a sub-set of those users had completed all the steps necessary to qualify themselves for a distribution (including identity verification).[108] On tracing, the Court determined that apportioning the value of a mixed trust fund for each crypto asset class should be based on the contribution of each user to the fund for that class, not on a 'first in, first out' basis.[109]

3.5 *Can Cryptocurrencies Be Subject to Attachment or Otherwise Seized?*

Yes. Set out below are some examples from Australian case law.

- Freezing and disclosure orders in relation to 'Digital Currency', that is, 'property' as defined in section 9 of the Corporations Act that is digital currency, virtual currency, cryptocurrency or similar, including an order for the respondent to deliver to ASIC:
  - the name and address of any Digital Currency exchange at which there is an account in the name of the respondent;
  - all relevant credentials and passwords for access to any Digital Currency held by the respondent including … the public and private access keys

105 Also see Paul Babie, David Brown, Ryan Catterwell and Mark Giancaspro, 'Cryptocurrencies as Property: *Ruscoe and Moore v Cryptopia Limited (In Liquidation)*' [2020] NZHC 728, *University of Adelaide Law Research Paper No 2020-33*, available at https://papers.ssrn.com/sol3/papers.cfm?abstract_id=3578264.

106 See David Kreltszheim, 'Risk Allocation for Hacking and Insolvency of Cryptocurrency Exchanges' (2020) 20 *Insolvency Law Bulletin* 166, 172.

107 *Ruscoe and others v Houchens and others* [2024] NZHC 419.

108 [2024] NZHC 419 at [28]–[29].

109 [2024] NZHC 419 at [11].

  and/or seed, backup or recovery phrase for any software-based or hardware-based wallet and/or storage device;
  - all authentication devices required to facilitate access, operation or control of any Digital Currency held; and
  - any hard wallet device containing Digital Currency held or controlled by the respondent together with that device's access code.[110]
- Orders under the Victorian Supreme Court rules requiring that each of the two signatories to a 'multi-signature wallet' with a specified public address (containing 117.33 Bitcoins) each provide their seed phrase to their respective solicitors for safekeeping, with the intent that the Bitcoins be preserved until the issues between the parties in the proceedings are determined.[111]
- Orders under the *Proceeds of Crime Act 2002* (Cth) restraining the defendants from dealing with specified property, including cryptocurrency, and requiring the defendants to provide information about passwords, passcodes and security accounts relating to the storage of cryptocurrency.[112]
- Orders under the *Proceeds of Crime Act 2002* (Cth) in relation to an account in the name of a defendant that held a cryptocurrency exchange. The Commissioner of the Australian Federal Police contended, and the court accepted, that the terms on which the account was held gave rise to an obligation similar to the position with an ordinary bank account: that is, it gave rise to a chose in action enforceable against the cryptocurrency exchange.[113]
- Freezing orders under the *Criminal Assets Recovery Act 1990* (NSW) restraining any dealings with the property of a named person, including all crypto, digital or virtual currencies (including Bitcoin, Ethereum and Litecoin) held by the named person and seized by police on a particular date following the arrest of the named person.[114]

3.6 *How Would Insolvency Rules Apply to Situations Involving Cryptocurrencies?*

It appears that a user's direct holding of cryptocurrency or indirect holding via an exchange or custodian will be taken to be 'property' for the purposes of the *Bankruptcy Act 1966* (Cth) which applies to individuals.[115] The Australian

110 *ASIC v Remedy Housing* [2021] FCA 671. Also see *ASIC v A One Multi Services Pty Ltd* [2021] FCA 1297 in which similar orders were made.

111 *Chen v Blockchain Global; Abel v Blockchain Global* [2022] VSC 92.

112 *Commissioner of the Australian Federal Police v Kogan* [2019] NSWSC 1866.

113 *Commissioner of the Australian Federal Police v TK* [2022] ACTSC 196.

114 *New South Wales Crime Commission v Ward* [2019] NSWSC 140.

115 Section 5 of the Bankruptcy Act 1966 (Cth) provides that 'property' means real or personal property of every description, whether situate in Australia or elsewhere, and includes any

Inspector General in Bankruptcy has issued a detailed instruction note for trustees in bankruptcy entitled 'Dealing with Cryptocurrency in a Bankrupt Estate.'[116] The basis of the instruction note is that cryptocurrency is property for the purposes of the Bankruptcy Act. Similarly, a company's direct or indirect holding of cryptocurrency would likewise be 'property' for the purposes of section 9 of the Corporations Act and regulated accordingly in the insolvency of the company.[117]

3.7 *Is it Possible to Pledge Cryptocurrencies?*

In Australia, it is possible for a holder of cryptocurrencies to grant security over them, on the basis that they will constitute 'personal property' under the *Personal Property Securities Act 2009* (Cth).[118] However, there is presently no clarity as to the 'collateral classes' in which the registration should be made. Further, given the nature of cryptocurrency – whether directly held or held indirectly via an exchange or custodian – it would be prudent for a secured lender to take practical steps to take control of the cryptocurrency, by transferring it to a wallet exclusively controlled by it and not the security provider. This approach is functionally similar to how a secured lender would take control of (and effectively immobilise) a security provider's interest in an investment instrument like a share or a unit.

3.8 *Is it Possible to 'Lend' Cryptocurrencies?*

Yes. We consider that it is legally possible for a party ('A') to lend cryptocurrency to another party ('B') on condition that B pay interest to A – in cryptocurrency or fiat currency – and return an equivalent amount of cryptocurrency to A at the end of the loan term.[119] This is analogous to certain securities lending arrangements which are utilised in Australia.[120]

---

estate, interest or profit, whether present or future, vested or contingent, arising out of or incident to any such real or personal property.

116 Available at https://www.afsa.gov.au/insolvency/i-am-practitioner/dealing-cryptocurrency-bankrupt-estate.

117 See David Kreltszheim, above n 93, 107–108.

118 See David Kreltszheim, above n 93, 107; Ryan Chan, 'A Break from Bitcoin – Cryptocurrency Collateral on the Ethereum Blockchain' (2021) 32 *Journal of Banking and Finance Law and Practice* 213.

119 Compare *Wang v Darby* [2021] EWHC 3054 which dealt with a different scenario (sale and buyback of cryptocurrency) but in which reference was made to cryptocurrency loan arrangements without disapproval.

120 See the definition of 'non-standard margin lending facilities' in section 761EA(5) of the Corporations Act.

3.9 *Can the Loss of Cryptocurrencies Amount to an Actionable Tort or Other Cause of Action?*

It would appear that the loss of cryptocurrencies cannot be the basis for an action in the tort of conversion in Australia. This is because the tort of conversion is a remedy for a dealing with physical property that is repugnant to the immediate right of possession of another person. There is a limited exception for conversion of physical negotiable instruments. In that case, the physical negotiable instrument is ascribed a value that takes account of the intangible rights embodied in it. Outside of that limited exception, the tort of conversion is confined to a wrongful dealing with physical property. It does not extend to intangible items of property, such as a chose in action.[121]

However, some indirect protection via conversion may be obtained by a plaintiff where a wrongdoer misappropriates cryptocurrency by misappropriating physical property of the plaintiff, such as computer hardware or a written document on which is written the plaintiff's private key.[122]

Further, it would be open to a claimant to initiate:

> ... a proprietary restitutionary action which aimed at the direct enforcement of the claimant's legal title in [cryptocurrency] and awarded the claimant the value of the [cryptocurrency] at the point when the defendant first received [it]. It would not rest on any theory of tortious interference with possession. The claim would commonly be enforced through an action for money had and received [which, despite its name] would not depend on whether [cryptocurrency] was characterised as money.[123]

4 Tax Measures

4.1 *Does Tax Law Apply to Cryptocurrencies, Cryptocurrencies-Related Services or Cryptocurrencies-Originated Value in Australia?*

As noted by the Australian Tax Office (ATO), the tax treatment of cryptocurrencies depends on whether the asset is held as an investment or for other purposes.[124] In March 2022, the former Government released the Terms of

---

121 *William Jingcheng He v Liangping Huang* [2017] VSCA 349 at [103] relying on *OBG Limited v Allen* [2008] AC 1.

122 See David Fox, above n 96, 174–175.

123 Ibid.

124 The Senate (Australia), Select Committee on Australia as a Technology and Financial Centre, *Final Report* (October 2021), [3.111], citing the submission by the Australian Taxation Office.

Reference for a review to be undertaken by the Board of Taxation into the appropriate policy framework for the taxation of crypto assets and transactions in Australia. The Board of Taxation published a Consultation Guide in August 2022, which 'provides an overview of crypto assets and the current taxation treatment within Australia.'[125]

4.1.1 Capital Gains Tax

Where cryptocurrencies are held as an investment, capital gains tax (CGT) rules apply when there is a disposal of these assets. Under the current ATO guidance, disposal of a cryptocurrency asset can occur when someone:

- sells or gifts cryptocurrency;
- trades or exchanges cryptocurrency (including the disposal of one cryptocurrency for another cryptocurrency);
- converts cryptocurrency to fiat currency, such as Australian dollars; or
- uses cryptocurrency to obtain goods or services.[126]

Following various submissions on the issue, including a submission stating that the capital gains tax treatment of token-to token exchanges 'imposes significant and unnecessary uncertainty and regulatory burden on cryptocurrency users, investors and the blockchain industry more generally',[127] the Final Report recommended amendments to the capital gains tax regime.[128]

4.1.2 Income Tax

Cryptocurrency that is used mainly to buy goods and services for personal use (e.g. clothes, food or pay personal bills) is not subject to capital gains tax.[129] For businesses that trade in cryptocurrencies, proceeds from the sale of cryptocurrency held as trading stock are treated as ordinary income, and the cost

125 See Australian Government, The Board of Taxation, 'Review of the Tax Treatment of Digital Assets and Transactions in Australia', available at https://taxboard.gov.au/review/digital-assets-transactions-aus.

126 Ibid, [3.112], citing ATO, 'Transacting with cryptocurrency', https://www.ato.gov.au/general/gen/tax-treatment-of-crypto-currencies-in-australia – specifically-bitcoin/?anchor=Transactingwithcryptocurrency#Transactingwithcryptocurrency. For an outline of the background to assessing cryptocurrencies as CGT assets, see [3.113].

127 The Senate (Australia), Select Committee on Australia as a Technology and Financial Centre, *Second Interim Report* (April 2021), [5.69], citing answers by Dr Bert, Dr Allen and Dr Lane to questions on notice from a public hearing.

128 See section 2.5 above.

129 The Senate (Australia), Select Committee on Australia as a Technology and Financial Centre, *Final Report* (October 2021), [3.114]. citing the submission from the Australian Taxation Office.

of acquiring cryptocurrency that is held as trading stock is tax deductible.[130] Further, payments of cryptocurrency to businesses for goods or services are taxed as regular income based on the value of the cryptocurrency in Australian dollars at the time of the transaction.[131]

4.1.3 Good and Services Tax

As noted above, the legislation governing the GST defines the term 'digital currency.'[132] From 1 July 2017, the supply or acquisition of digital currency has not been subject to GST.[133] This is on the basis that digital currency is a method of payment that operates as an alternative to money.[134] By contrast, a cryptocurrency miner may be subject to GST where it carries on an 'enterprise' for GST purposes.[135]

5 Litigation in Relation to Cryptocurrencies

Given that the jurisdictions in Australia – state, territory and federal – are common law jurisdictions, the courts in Australia will be influenced by decisions of courts in other common law jurisdictions.[136] Case law in Australia has already recognised that cryptocurrencies such as Bitcoin can operate as property to which freezing orders can apply.[137] There appears to be an increasing body of case law in support of the proposition that crypto assets can constitute property

---

130 Ibid, [3.115].

131 Ibid, [3.116].

132 See section 1.2 above.

133 See Gilbert + Tobin, *Global Legal Insights: Blockchain & Cryptocurrency Regulation 2024* (6 November 2023), available at https://www.gtlaw.com.au/knowledge/global-legal-insights-blockchain-cryptocurrency-regulation.

134 Ibid.

135 Ibid: '[a] cryptocurrency miner would generally be required to register for GST if its annual GST turnover is A$75,000 or more, excluding the value of its supplies of digital currencies and other input-taxed supplies.'

136 See, for example, *Wang v Darby* [2021] EWHC 3054 (*obiter* support for the proposition that cryptocurrencies constitute property and can be the subject of a trust); *AA v Persons Unknown & Ors; Re Bitcoin* [2019] EWHC 2556; [2020] WLR (D) 50 (crypto assets treated as property for the purposes of a proprietary injunction); *B2C2 Ltd v Quoine Pte Ltd* [2019] SGHC(I) 03 (held that Bitcoin were personal property that could be the subject of a trust); *Ruscoe v Cryptopia Limited (in liquidation)* [2020] NZHC 728 (cryptocurrencies were property and held on trust).

137 See *Re Blockchain Global (Admins Apptd)* [2021] VSC 762 (19 November 2021).

and be dealt with as such.[138] These include numerous family law disputes in which cryptocurrencies have been mentioned and recognised as relevant to the distribution of assets upon a matrimonial breakdown. For example:

- A subpoena was issued by A for production of a laptop allegedly given to B for safekeeping in August 2015, allegedly containing a cryptocurrency wallet containing cryptocurrency then valued at A$440,000 and A$2,100,000 at the time of the hearing.[139]
- Spousal maintenance payments were increased owing to a husband's lack of candour as to cryptocurrency trading yielding proceeds that plausibly amounted to A$2,685,780.[140]
- Cryptocurrency was expressly mentioned in the property division between a husband and wife.[141]
- A$100,000 worth of bitcoin was supposedly purchased by a husband post-separation. The husband alleged he was caught by a scam. The court held that if that was correct, the husband was in any event responsible for dissipation of joint funds for that purpose. That dissipation of funds was taken into account in the property distribution.[142]
- A husband disclosed spending of A$2,656 on cryptocurrency but alleged that he no longer had any cryptocurrency as of the date of the hearing. That amount was not taken into account for property division purposes.[143]
- A husband admitted to holding A$73,480 in cryptocurrency assets in an application by him for interim property distributions to meet a tax liability. The application was granted despite the cryptocurrency assets not being sold first to meet the tax liability.[144]
- A sentence was confirmed for a husband who breached family proceeding orders by using sums totalling A$180,000 to purchase cryptocurrency. According to the husband, the cryptocurrency was irretrievably lost when his laptop, the ledger Nano wallet containing details of the purchased

138 For a discussion about taking security over cryptocurrency in Australia, see David Kreltszheim, 'Taking and enforcing security over cryptocurrency' *Australian Banking and Finance Law Bulletin* (August, 2018); for a discussion about the treatment of cryptocurrencies in insolvency, see Stacey Steele and Tetsuo Morishita, 'Lessons from Mt Gox: Practical considerations for a virtual currency insolvency' in Arner et al (eds) *Research Handbook on Asian Financial Law* (Edward Elgar, 2020).

139 *Paterson v Hamdy (No 2)* [2022] FedCFamC1F 716.

140 *Rasheem v Rasheen* [2022] FedCFamC1F 248.

141 *Griffiths v Griffiths* [2022] FedCFamC1F 379.

142 *Fallins v Fallins* [2022] FedCFamC1F 495.

143 *Macvean v Manton (No 2)* [2022] FedC FamC1F 689.

144 *Rademaker v Everhart* [2021] FedCFamC2F 171.

cryptocurrency, and the packaging box for the Nano wallet that contained the password to access the cryptocurrency were allegedly stolen.[145]

- A father diverted joint assets, and otherwise purchased cryptocurrency, in 2017. At trial in 2019, the husband asserted that the prevailing value of the cryptocurrency was considerably lower and the lower value should be taken into account for property division and certain other matters. It was found there had been deliberate non-disclosure by the husband and the court held that cryptocurrency should be valued at its purchase price for the purposes of the proceeding.[146]

6 Sources

6.1 *Reports, Legislation, and Regulatory Guidance*

6.1.1 Reports and Consultation Papers

- The Senate (Australia), Select Committee on Australia as a Technology and Financial Centre, Second Interim Report (April 2021)
- Australian Government, *Payments system review – from system to ecosystem* (June 2021)
- The Senate (Australia), Select Committee on Australia as a Technology and Financial Centre, *Final Report* (October 2021)
- Australian Government, *Transforming Australia's Payments System* (8 December 2021)
- Australian Government, *Crypto Asset Secondary Service Providers: Licensing and Custody Requirements – Consultation Paper* (21 March 2022)
- The Treasury, *Token Mapping – Consultation Paper* (February 2023)
- *Commonwealth Attorney General's Department, Modernising Australia's Anti-Money Laundering and Counter Terrorism Financing Regime* (April 2023)
- The Treasury, *Regulating Digital Asset Platforms – Proposal paper* (October 2023)

6.1.2 Legislation

- *A New Tax System (Goods and Services Tax) Act 1999* (Cth)
- *Corporations Act 2001* (Cth)
- *Australian Securities and Investments Act 2001* (Cth)
- The *Anti-Money Laundering and Counter-Terrorism Financing Act 2006* (Cth)
- *National Credit Consumer Protection Act 2009* (Cth)

145 *Lecosky v Durante* [2020] FamCAFC 179.
146 *Powell v Christensen* [2020] FamCA 944.

- *Competition and Consumer Act 2010* (Cth)
- ASIC Derivative Transaction Rules (Reporting) 2013

6.1.3 Regulatory Guidance

- ASIC Regulatory Guide 255: *Providing digital financial product advice to retail clients* (13 August, 2016)
- ASIC Information Sheet 219 (March 2017): *Evaluating distributed ledger technology*
- ASIC, Product design and distribution obligations (Regulatory Guide 274, December 2020)
- ASIC, *Crypto-assets as underlying assets for ETPs and other investment products* (Consultation Paper 343, June 2021)
- ASIC, 'Crypto-assets' (Information Sheet 225, INFO 225, reissued in October 2021)
- ASIC, 'Cryptocurrencies – The risks of investing in crypto'
- ASIC, 'Warning: Self-managed super funds and crypto investments' (17 January 2022)
- Reserve Bank of Australia, 'What are Cryptocurrencies?'

Austria

Martin Miernicki

1 Introduction[1]

1.1 *Development of the Legal Discussion in Austria*

While cryptocurrencies have been present in the Austrian legal literature since at least 2014,[2] the discussion on their legal implication has been in 'full swing' since 2017. Questions of tax and regulatory law were among the first issues to attract attention by legal commentators. In contrast, publications on the classification of cryptocurrencies under private law remained sparse in the beginning of the legal discussion but have developed considerably since then. However, there are still many unresolved questions on the matter.

In the Austrian legal discussion, 'cryptocurrency' (Kryptowährung) is nowadays understood as a subset of the broader term 'crypto-asset' (Kryptowert) that generally refers to all blockchain-/DLT-based assets. The term cryptocurrency is usually used for crypto-assets like bitcoin or ether. Hereinafter, in accordance with the questionnaire provided to the author, the term cryptocurrency 'is used to cover various types of cryptocurrencies, including stable coins. Other crypto assets representing claims or real or personal properties, such as security tokens and utility tokens, are not directly targeted by this Questionnaire. Also, Central Bank Digital Currencies, which are recently attracting attention in many countries, are outside the scope of this [study]'. It should however be noted that stable coins can take various forms. It is possible that they possess characteristics different to 'classic' cryptocurrencies and hence require a separate legal analysis.[3]

1.2 *Statutory Provsions on Cryptocurrencies*

Currently, there are only a few provisions that make explicit reference to cryptocurrency or equivalent terms in Austrian Law. These provisions have been introduced over the course of the last years in response to pressing issues observed in connection with cryptocurrencies but do not provide for a comprehensive legal framework.

1 All websites were last visited on 19 May 2024.

2 H. Eberwein and A. Steiner (eds), *Bitcoins*, Jan Sramek, Vienna 2014.

3 See for more detailed terminological remarks M. Miernicki, *Kryptowerte im Privatrecht*, Manz, Vienna 2023, pp. 15 et seq. [hereinafter: M. Miernicki, *Kryptowerte*].

 | DOI:10.1163/9789004722507_004

One important example can be found in the Act on the Prevention of Money Laundering and Terrorist Financing in the Financial Sector (FM-GwG).[4] Section 2(21) defines 'virtual currencies' (virtuelle Währungen) as 'a digital representation of value that is not issued or guaranteed by a central bank or a public authority, is not necessarily attached to a legally established currency and does not possess a legal status of currency or money, but is accepted by natural or legal persons as a means of exchange and which can be transferred, stored and traded electronically'. Section 2(22) contains a definition of 'service providers with regard to virtual currencies' (Dienstleister in Bezug auf virtuelle Währungen), listing several different services such as safeguarding private cryptographic keys, exchanging virtual currencies for fiat money as well as virtual currencies for other virtual currencies or transferring virtual currencies. These provisions were introduced against the background of the European '5th Anti-Money-Laundering-Directive.'[5]

Section 27b(4)[6] of the Act on the Income Tax (EStG) makes reference to 'cryptocurrencies' (Kryptowährungen) and not to 'virtual currencies'. At the same time, it relies on a definition identical to the FM-GwG. In fact, prior drafts of the provision explicitly referred to the section 2(21) FM-GwG; however, this reference was deleted in the final version of the act. Still, the legislative materials take the FM-GwG into account.[7]

Another important example exists in the realm of the enforcement of private law claims. Section 326[8] of the Austrian Execution Act (Exekutionsordnung) confirms that 'rights arising from virtual currencies' (Rechte aus virtuellen Währungen) are subject to the execution procedure according to sections 326 et seq. While the provision gives no further definition of this term, the legislative materials broadly refer to crypto-assets.[9]

Cryptocurrencies are also referenced in criminal law, as illustrated by section 165(6) of the Austrian Criminal Code (StGB).[10] This provision deals with

---

4 BGBl I 2016/118.

5 Directive (EU) 2018/843 of the European Parliament and of the Council of 30 May 2018 amending Directive (EU) 2015/849 on the prevention of the use of the financial system for the purposes of money laundering or terrorist financing, and amending Directives 2009/138/EC and 2013/36/EU [2018] OJ L156/43.

6 Introduced by BGBl I 2022/10.

7 ErläutRV 1293 BlgNR 27. GP 12.

8 Introduced by BGBl I 2021/86.

9 ErläutRV 770 BlgNR 27. GP 51.

10 BGBl I 1974/60, as amended (BGBl I 2021/159); cf. art. 2(2) Directive (EU) 2018/1673 of the European Parliament and of the Council of 23 October 2018 on combating money laundering by criminal law [2018] OJ L284/22.

money laundering (Geldwäscherei) and specifies that relevant assets include 'units of virtual currencies as well as corresponding gains in value or attached rights' (Einheiten virtueller Währungen und die auf diese entfallenden Wertzuwächse oder durch diese belegte Rechte). In addition, section 74(10) StGB defines 'non-cash payment instrument' as also including 'digital means of exchange' (digitale Tauschmittel); the legislative materials refer to Directive (EU) 2019/713[11] and state that this language also covers 'virtual currency.'[12]

Further provisions that refer to virtual currencies are section 87(2)(19) of the Professional Auditors and Tax Consultants Act 2017 (Wirtschaftstreuhandberufsgesetz 2017)[13] and section 43(2)(19) of the Balance Accountant Act 2014 (Bilanzbuchaltergesetz 2014).[14]

For the time being, the General Civil Code (Allgemeines bürgerliches Gesetzbuch – ABGB)[15] or other sources of private law do not contain an explicit reference to cryptocurrencies.

1.3 *Court Decisions on Cryptocurrencies*

The case law on cryptocurrencies is still developing and decisions of the Austrian supreme courts[16] are currently the exception rather than the rule. The OGH has dealt with a claim to transfer bitcoins on chain from a procedural perspective[17] (international jurisdiction according article 17 Brussels Ia Regulation),[18] bitcoin mining in the context of the Austrian Gambling Act[19] (Glücksspielgesetz),[20] and the deposit of cryptocurrencies in court according

11 Directive (EU) 2019/713 of the European Parliament and of the Council of 17 April 2019 on combating fraud and counterfeiting of non-cash means of payment and replacing Council Framework Decision 2001/413/JHA [2019] OJ L123/18.

12 ErläutRV 1099 27. GP 2.

13 BGBl I 2017/137.

14 BGBl I 2013/191.

15 JGS 1811/946.

16 The Supreme Court (Oberster Gerichtshof – OGH) is the highest court in civil and criminal law matters. For questions of public law, the Administrative Court (Verwaltungsgerichtshof – VwGH) and the Constitutional Court (Verfassungsgerichtshof – VfGH) are the highest courts.

17 OGH 04.11.2020, 3 Ob 95/20x *Zeitschrift für Verbraucherrecht* 2021, 35.

18 Regulation (EU) No 1215/2012 of the European Parliament and of the Council of 12 December 2012 on jurisdiction and the recognition and enforcement of judgments in civil and commercial matters [2012] OJ L351/1.

19 OGH 22.12.2021, 5 Ob 95/21p *Evidenzblatt der Rechtsmittelentscheidungen* 2022/96.

20 BGBl 1991/344.

to section 1425 ABGB.[21] Furthermore, some decisions of lower courts that refer to cryptocurrencies in one way or another are available.[22]

As can be seen, there is no comprehensive case on law on the legal treatment of cryptocurrencies in Austria. Hence, what will be primarily presented in the following are the prevailing views in the legal literature on cryptocurrencies under Austrian law, statements of supervisory authorities and, finally, the author's own opinions.

1.4 *Developments on the European Union Level*

Austrian law is, in several respects, strongly intertwined with the law of the European Union. Within the realm of cryptocurrencies, this concerns, first and foremost, the Market in Crypto-Asset Regulation (MiCAR)[23] that soon will become fully applicable. This regulation will directly apply in Austria and hence develop the legal landscape significantly further. However, as MiCAR puts its focus on regulatory questions, the most important questions of private law will continue to be assessed under Austrian law. At the same time, MiCAR does not resolve all regulatory questions associated with crypto-assets (e.g. their qualification as financial instruments).

The second legislative initiative on the European Union level that will heavily impact the regulatory landscape in Austria is the new legislative framework against money laundering and terrorist financing.[24]

---

21 OGH 20.12.2022, 4 Ob 208/22z. However, the court refrained from clarifying whether cryptocurrency could be subject to a 'deposit' (Hinterlegung) in the first place.

22 See e.g. on questions of private law OLG Linz 26.03.2020, 2 R 31/20x; LG Wels 05.02.2020, 5 Cg 104/19x; see also BVwG 04.04.2022, W107 2233589-1 *Zeitschrift für Finanzmarktrecht* 2022, 457 (on pledges in the regulatory context); on money laundering OLG Linz 30.09.2019 10 Bs 246/19a *Journal für Strafrecht* 2020, 55; see also OGH 29.09.2022, 12 Os 100/22f; (referencing 'bitcoin ATMs' in connection with money laundering); on the registration of virtual asset service providers BVwG 29.06.2021, W148 2235101-1; BVwG 07.09.2021, W158 2235512-1.

23 Regulation (EU) 2023/1114 of the European Parliament and of the Council of 31 May 2023 on markets in crypto-assets, and amending Regulations (EU) No 1093/2010 and (EU) No 1095/2010 and Directives 2013/36/EU and (EU) 2019/1937 [2023] OJ L150/40.

24 European Commission, *Anti-money laundering and countering the financing of terrorism legislative package* https://finance.ec.europa.eu/publications/anti-money-laundering-and-countering-financing-terrorism-legislative-package_en.

2 Regulatory Framework and Supervision

2.1 *Supervision by the Financial Market Authority* (FMA)

The competent authority overseeing and enforcing the most important regulatory laws within the areas of banking and the capital markets in Austria is the Financial Market Authority (Finanzmarktaufsichtsbehörde – FMA). The operations of the authority are based on the Act on the Establishment and the Organization of the Financial Market Authority (Finanzmarktaufsichtsbehördengesetz – FMABG).[25] The FMA generally relies on the well-known 'token-archetypes' to explain its approach towards the various forms of crypto-assets, distinguishing payment/currency tokens, utility tokens, and security/investment tokens.[26] To facilitate the communication between the authority and persons that are interested in operating a business related to FinTech and/or crypot-assets, the FMA provides the FinTech Point of Contact[27] where legal queries about prospective business models can be made.

In 2020, the 'regulatory sandbox' was introduced in section 23a FMABG.[28] Under this rule, innovative business models that are in development can be tested in close cooperation with and legal advice of the FMA. Participation in the regulatory sandbox is limited to a maximum of two years.

As implied above, the regulatory laws relevant for the present purposes do not, with the exception of the FM-GwG, explicitly refer to cryptocurrencies.[29] At the same time, these laws are generally of a technology-neutral nature. Against this background, the FMA assesses crypto-assets and corresponding business models on a case-by-case basis. However, in principle, the FMA deems cryptocurrencies like bitcoin not to be subject to supervision and the mere

---

25 BGBl I 2001/97.

26 FMA, *Fakten, Trends und Strategien 2019*, p. 176 https://www.fma.gv.at/wp-content/plugins/dw-fma/download.php?d=3964&nonce=f25344d6af3c8199.

27 FMA, *FinTech Point of Contact* https://www.fma.gv.at/en/fintech-point-of-contact-sandbox/fintech-navigator/fintech-point-of-contact/.

28 BGBl I 2020/98.

29 See however section 1(7) Securities Supervision Act (WAG 2018 BGBl I 2017/101) stating that the term financial instruments includes instruments issued by means of distributed ledger technology; this language was introduced in connection with article 18 Regulation (EU) 2022/858 of the European Parliament and of the Council of 30 May 2022 on a pilot regime for market infrastructures based on distributed ledger technology, and amending Regulations (EU) No 600/2014 and (EU) No 909/2014 and Directive 2014/65/EU [2022] OJ151/1.

purchase and sale of these assets does not require a license.[30] However, other crypto-assets and/or business models based on cryptocurrencies can require a license or the publication of a prospectus. The most relevant regulatory requirements are summarized below.

2.2 *Regulation of Banking Services, Payment Services and Electronic Money*

The Austrian Banking Act (Bankwesengesetz – BWG)[31] applies to the commercial provision of banking services (gewerbliche Durchführung von Bankgeschäften) which listed in section 1(1). A business model belonging to this list requires a license (section 4 BWG). The BWG distinguishes several different institutions: While 'credit institutions' (Kreditinstitute) provide banking services as defined in section 1(1), 'CRR credit institutions' are those defined in article 4(1)(1) CRR[32] (section 1a BWG). 'Financial institutes' (Finanzinstitute) provide the services listed in section 1(2) BWG as their main focus of operations. These services include, amongst others, payment services according section 1(2) Payment Services Act 2018 (Zahlungsdienstegesetz 2018 – ZaDiG 2018)[33] and the issuance of electronic money according to section 1 E-Money-Act 2010 (E-GeldG 2010).[34]

The following banking services are commonly discussed in connection with cryptocurrencies and crypto-assets:[35]

Deposit business (Einlagengeschäft) according to section 1(1)(1) BWG

The deposit business means the acceptance of third-party money for the purposes of administration or deposit. According to the prevailing opinion, cryptocurrencies and crypto-assets in general do not qualify as money within

30 FMA, *Bitcoin & Co* https://www.fma.gv.at/en/fintech-point-of-contact-sandbox/fintech-navigator/bitcoin-co/ ('The mere buying and selling of tokens similar to Bitcoin in one's own name and on one's own account generally does not trigger the obligation to hold a licence. However, the buying and selling of crypto assets may form part of business models that do require a licence').

31 BGBl 1993/532.

32 Regulation (EU) No 575/2013 of the European Parliament and of the Council of 26 June 2013 on prudential requirements for credit institutions and amending Regulation (EU) No 648/2012 [2013] OJ L176/1.

33 BGBl I 2018/17.

34 BGBl I 2010/107.

35 FMA, *Fakten, Trends und Strategien 2019*, pp. 173-74 https://www.fma.gv.at/wp-content/plugins/dw-fma/download.php?d=3964&nonce=f25344d6af3c8199 (in connection of Initial Coin Offerings).

the present meaning.[36] Hence, exchanging crypto-assets for other crypto-assets, for instance, is generally not considered to qualify as a form of the deposit business.[37] However, if crypto-assets are issued in exchange for money (e.g. legal tender or euro book money), the business model might be considered to fulfil the requirements for the deposit business, especially if the funds are repayable.[38]

Issuing and managing instruments of payment (Ausgabe und Verwaltung von Zahlungsmitteln) according to section (1)(1)(6) BWG

This banking service is, in the present context, primarily relevant for crypto-assets that are issued by a company, e.g. in the context of an ICO.[39] There exists certain doubts about the interpretation of the provision and its application to crypto-assets;[40] the FMA maintains that the provision can apply to crypto-assets (especially if payment tokens are emitted), depending on the business model in question.[41]

Safe custody and administration of securities (Depotgeschäft) according to section (1)(1)(5) BWG

Participation in the emission of a third party and providing corresponding services (Loroemissionsgeschäft) according to section 1(1)(11) BWG

The banking service 'Depotgeschäft' is based on the concept of security (Wertpapier); the same applies to the 'Loroemissionsgeschäft' that additionally refers to several other instruments, like money-market instruments for

---

36 See, e.g., G. Tuder, 'Initial Coin Offerings im Lichte des Bankaufsichtsrechts', in S. Kirchmayr-Schliesselberger, W. Klas, M. Miernicki, S. Rinderle-Ma, A. Weilinger (eds), *Kryptowährungen*, Nomos/facultas, Vienna 2019, pp. 287–288; M. Waldherr, K. Ressnik and T. Schneckenleitner, '§ 1 BWG' in M. Dellinger (ed), *Bankwesengesetz*, LexisNexis, Vienna 8th supp 2016, para 15.

37 A. Schopper/P. Raschner, 'Privat- und aufsichtsrechtliche Rahmenbedingungen für Krypto-Banking' (2022) Österreichisches BankArchiv 262, 265 et seq.; G. Tuder and A. Ahari, 'Die aufsichtsrechtliche Einordnung von Krypto-Assets und Krypto-Assets-Handelsplattformen', in M. Hanzl, H. Pelzmann and M. Schragl (eds), *Handbuch Digitalisierung*, Linde, Vienna 2021, p. 56.

38 FMA, *Fakten, Trends und Strategien 2019*, p. 173 https://www.fma.gv.at/wp-content/plugins/dw-fma/download.php?d=3964&nonce=f25344d6af3c8199; see also C. Steiner, *Krypto-Assets und das Aufsichtsrecht*, finanzverlag, Vienna 2019, pp. 115–16.

39 See, e.g., G. Tuder, 'Initial Coin Offerings im Lichte des Bankaufsichtsrechts', in S. Kirchmayr-Schliesselberger, W. Klas, M. Miernicki, S. Rinderle-Ma, A. Weilinger (eds), *Kryptowährungen*, Nomos/facultas, Vienna 2019, p. 295.

40 See for details C. Steiner, *Krypto-Assets und das Aufsichtsrecht*, finanzverlag, Vienna 2019, pp. 105 et seq.; G. Diwok and D. Gritsch, 'Bitcoin, Geldbegriffe und Zahlungsmittel' (2020) *Zeitschrift für Finanzmarketrecht* 64, 66.

41 FMA, *Fakten, Trends und Strategien 2019*, p. 173 https://www.fma.gv.at/wp-content/plugins/dw-fma/download.php?d=3964&nonce=f25344d6af3c8199.

instance.[42] Cryptocurrencies like bitcoin will generally not qualify as a security or one of the other listed instruments; hence, these banking services are not applicable to crypto-assets of this kind.[43]

Based on the PSD II,[44] the ZaDiG 2018 applies to the commercial provision of the payment services listed in section 1(2) and provides for licensing requirements (section 7 ZaDiG 2018). As far as the listed payment services are directly or indirectly based on the notion of 'funds' (which applies to most payment services), the ZaDiG 2018 does not apply to cryptocurrency transactions.[45] This is because cryptocurrencies generally do not fulfil the definition of funds (section 4(24): banknotes and coins, scriptural money or electronic money):[46] While cryptocurrencies like bitcoin obviously are neither banknotes, coins nor scriptural money, they are generally not considered as electronic money within the meaning of section 1 E-GeldG 2010[47] in Austria.[48] The reason most

42 See section 1(1)(7)(b)–(f) BWG for the complete list.

43 G. Tuder, 'Initial Coin Offerings im Lichte des Bankaufsichtsrechts', in S. Kirchmayr-Schliesselberger, W. Klas, M. Miernicki, S. Rinderle-Ma, A. Weilinger (eds), *Kryptowährungen*, Nomos/facultas, Vienna 2019, p. 304.

44 Directive (EU) 2015/2366 of the European Parliament and of the Council of 25 November 2015 on payment services in the internal market, amending Directives 2002/65/EC, 2009/110/EC and 2013/36/EU and Regulation (EU) No 1093/2010, and repealing Directive 2007/64/EC [2015] OJ L337/35.

45 Crypto-assets emitted in the course of an ICO or a comparable offering might however be regarded as payment Instruments (section 4(14) ZaDiG 2018), FMA, *Fakten, Trends und Strategien 2019*, p. 175 https://www.fma.gv.at/wp-content/plugins/dw-fma/download.php?d=3964&nonce=f25344d6af3c8199. In turn, cryptocurrencies generally do not possess the characteristics of payment instruments, see T. Schneckenleitner, '§ 4 ZaDiG 2018' in A. Weilinger, C. Knauder and M. Miernicki (eds), *Zahlungsdienstegesetz 2018*, Manz, Vienna 30th supp 2022, para 120.

46 B. Kaufmann, '§ 1 ZaDiG 2018' in A. Weilinger, C. Knauder and M. Miernicki (eds), *Zahlungsdienstegesetz 2018*, Manz, Vienna 25th supp 2021, para 105.

47 The act is based on Directive 2009/110/EC of the European Parliament and of the Council of 16 September 2009 on the taking up, pursuit and prudential supervision of the business of electronic money institutions amending Directives 2005/60/EC and 2006/48/EC and repealing Directive 2000/46/EC [2009] OJ 267/7; article 2(2) defines electronic money as 'electronically, including magnetically, stored monetary value as represented by a claim on the issuer which is issued on receipt of funds for the purpose of making payment transactions as defined in point 5 of Article 4 of Directive 2007/64/EC, and which is accepted by a natural or legal person other than the electronic money issuer'.

48 See e.g. C. Steiner, *Krypto-Assets und das Aufsichtsrecht*, finanzverlag, Vienna 2019, pp. 103 et seq.; M. Miernicki, *Kryptowerte* pp. 476 et seq.; T. Schneckenleitner, '§ 4 ZaDiG 2018' in A. Weilinger, C. Knauder and M. Miernicki (eds), *Zahlungsdienstegesetz 2018*, Manz, Vienna 30th supp 2022, para 176. This has recently been confirmed by OGH 26. 4. 2024, 4 Ob 234/23z.

commonly given is that there is no issuer and no corresponding claim.[49] Conversely, other crypto-assets might indeed be regarded as electronic money, depending on the individual case.[50] This also applies to stable coins.[51]

According to the FMA, buying and selling bitcoins by using a bitcoin-ATM (vending machine) does not, as such, require authorization.[52] However, a license might be required in certain situations; for instance, collecting the funds in the ATM and transferring the money to a third party might constitute money remittance (section 1(1)(6) ZaDiG 2018).[53]

Lastly, the FMA highlights that the limited network exclusion (section 3(3)(11) ZaDiG 2018, section 2(3)(1) E-GeldG 2010) can apply to business models based on crypto-assets that fall within the scope of the BWG, ZaDiG 2018 or E-GeldG 2010.[54] As a consequence, the mentioned acts are not applicable.[55]

2.3 *Regulation of Financial Instruments and Prospectus Requirements*

The qualification of a crypto-asset as a financial instrument is of crucial importance in several respects. According to the WAG 2018,[56] an investment firm (Wertpapierfirma) provides investment services and activities (Wertpapierdienstleistungen und Anlagetätigkeiten) that are listed in section 1(3).[57] For

49 See for further details G. Tuder, 'Initial Coin Offerings im Lichte des Bankaufsichtsrechts', in S. Kirchmayr-Schliesselberger, W. Klas, M. Miernicki, S. Rinderle-Ma, A. Weilinger (eds), *Kryptowährungen*, Nomos/facultas, Vienna 2019, pp. 305 et seq.

50 FMA, *Fakten, Trends und Strategien 2019*, pp. 174 https://www.fma.gv.at/wp-content/plugins/dw-fma/download.php?d=3964&nonce=f25344d6af3c8199.

51 T. Schneckenleitner, '§ 4 ZaDiG 2018' in A. Weilinger, C. Knauder and M. Miernicki (eds), *Zahlungsdienstegesetz 2018*, Manz, Vienna 30th supp 2022, para 176.

52 FMA, *Bitcoin & Co* https://www.fma.gv.at/en/fintech-point-of-contact-sandbox/fintech-navigator/bitcoin-co/ ('Due to the fact that there is no issuer, Bitcoins are not subject to supervision by the FMA. The mere buying and selling of Bitcoins using a Bitcoin vending machine is therefore not generally subject to the obligation to hold a licence').

53 Ibid.

54 FMA, *Fakten, Trends und Strategien 2019*, p. 179 https://www.fma.gv.at/wp-content/plugins/dw-fma/download.php?d=3964&nonce=f25344d6af3c8199; on stable coins see FMA, *Fakten, Trends und Strategien 2020*, p. 126 https://www.fma.gv.at/wp-content/plugins/dw-fma/download.php?d=4215&nonce=40e4eaaad87c3c76.

55 However, it should be noted that section 3(4) ZaDiG 2018 contains a reporting obligation.

56 BGBl I 2017/107. The act is based on the Directive 2014/65/EU of the European Parliament and of the Council of 15 May 2014 on markets in financial instruments and amending Directive 2002/92/EC and Directive 2011/61/EU [2014] OJ L173/349.

57 The commercial provision of investment services listed in section 3(3) WAG 2018 requires a license under the regime of the WAG 2018.

these terms, the notion of financial instrument is crucial; this notion is defined in section 1(7) WAG 2018 and covers, amongst others, transferable securities (section 1(5) WAG 2018), money-market instruments (section 1(6) WAG 2018) and derivatives (including DLT-based instruments). The public offering of transferable securities is subject to a prospectus requirement that this based on the Prospectus Regulation (article 3).[58] Being an EU regulation, it directly applies in Austria and the Austrian KMG 2019[59] contains primarily supplementary provisions. Furthermore, the KMG 2019 contains an additional prospectus requirement for the public offering of 'investments' (Veranlagungen) as defined in section (1)(1)(3). The Alternativfinanzierungsgesetz (AltFG)[60] contains special rules for public offerings that are exempted from the obligation to publish a prospectus by virtue of section 3(1)(3), 12(2) KMG 2019. According to what appears to be the prevailing opinion in Austria, cryptocurrencies as such (like bitcoin) generally do not qualify as financial instruments, transferable securities or 'Veranlagungen'.[61] Under this assumption, the WAG 2018 would not, in principle, apply to services related to cryptocurrencies and there would be no prospectus requirement when they are publicly offered.

58 Regulation (EU) 2017/1129 of the European Parliament and of the Council of 14 June 2017 on the prospectus to be published when securities are offered to the public or admitted to trading on a regulated market, and repealing Directive 2003/71/EC [2017] OJ L168/12.

59 BGBl I 2019/62.

60 BGBl I 2015/114.

61 A. Schopper/P. Raschner, 'Die aufsichtsrechtliche Einordnung von Krypto-Börsen in Österreich' (2019) *Österreichisches BankArchiv* 249, 252 et seq.; C. Seggermann, '§ 1 WAG 2018' in E. Brandl and G. Saria (eds), *Wertpapieraufsichtsgesetz 2018*, 2nd ed., Manz, Vienna 1st supp 2018, para 86; C. Steiner, *Krypto-Assets und das Aufsichtsrecht*, finanzverlag, Vienna 2019, pp. 121–122; F. Pekler and R. Rirsch, 'Ausgewählte kapitalmarktrechtliche Aspekte bei der Emission von Crypto-Assets', in S. Kirchmayr-Schliesselberger, W. Klas, M. Miernicki, S. Rinderle-Ma, A. Weilinger (eds), *Kryptowährungen*, Nomos/facultas, Vienna 2019, pp. 358–359; G. Diwok and D. Gritsch, 'Bitcoin, Geldbegriffe und Zahlungsmittel' (2020) *Zeitschrift für Finanzmarketrecht* 64, 66–67; G. Tuder and A. Ahari, 'Die aufsichtsrechtliche Einordnung von Krypto-Assets und Krypto-Assets-Handelsplattformen', in M. Hanzl, H. Pelzmann and M. Schragl (eds), *Handbuch Digitalisierung*, Linde, Vienna 2021, p. 83. See, however, T. Zivny and S. Mock, *EU-Prospektverordnung Kapitalmarktgesetz 2019*, 3rd ed., Manz, Vienna 2022, Art 2 EU-ProspektVO para 19 (deeming not only investment tokens, but also utility tokens and currency tokens to be transferable securities). See also R. Toman, '§ 1 KM 2019' in A. Frössel and R. Toman, *KMG Kapitalmarktgesetz*, Linde, Vienna 2021, § 1 KMG 2019 para 55.

However, certain business models based crypto-assets might qualify as financial instruments,[62] e.g. as derivatives.[63] Cryptocurrencies and other crypto-assets are also discussed as the underlying of a derivative.[64] In this connection, there are different views on whether cryptocurrencies or other crypto-assets can be considered as commodities in the context of capital market law.[65] It should also be noted that security tokens are typically considered as securities within the meaning of the WAG 2018 and the KMG 2019.[66] Furthermore, the FMA highlights that business models related to crypto-assets and/or

---

62 Depending on the individual case, such business models might also involve 'Veranlagungen' within the meaning of the KMG 2019; see e.g. A. Schopper/P. Raschner, 'Privat- und aufsichtsrechtliche Rahmenbedingungen für Krypto-Banking' (2022) *Österreichisches BankArchiv* 262, 267–68 (on platforms that offer 'crypto-accounts'). See also R. Toman, '§ 1 KM 2019' in A. Frössel and R. Toman, *KMG Kapitalmarktgesetz*, Linde, Vienna 2021, § 1 KMG 2019 para 34; T. Zivny and S. Mock, *EU-Prospektverordnung Kapitalmarktgesetz 2019*, 3rd ed., Manz, Vienna 2022, § 1 KMG 2019 para 62 (considering crypto-assets which convey a right as 'Veranlagungen').

63 A. Schopper/P. Raschner, 'Die aufsichtsrechtliche Einordnung von Krypto-Börsen in Österreich' (2019) *Österreichisches BankArchiv* 249, 253–54; F. Pekler and R. Rirsch, 'Ausgewählte kapitalmarktrechtliche Aspekte bei der Emission von Crypto-Assets', in S. Kirchmayr-Schliesselberger, W. Klas, M. Miernicki, S. Rinderle-Ma, A. Weilinger (eds), *Kryptowährungen*, Nomos/facultas, Vienna 2019, pp. 374–375; G. Tuder and A. Ahari, 'Die aufsichtsrechtliche Einordnung von Krypto-Assets und Krypto-Assets-Handelsplattformen', in M. Hanzl, H. Pelzmann and M. Schragl (eds), *Handbuch Digitalisierung*, Linde, Vienna 2021, pp. 84–85.

64 A. Schopper/P. Raschner, 'Die aufsichtsrechtliche Einordnung von Krypto-Börsen in Österreich' (2019) *Österreichisches BankArchiv* 249, 253–54; F. Pekler and R. Rirsch, 'Ausgewählte kapitalmarktrechtliche Aspekte bei der Emission von Crypto-Assets', in S. Kirchmayr-Schliesselberger, W. Klas, M. Miernicki, S. Rinderle-Ma, A. Weilinger (eds), *Kryptowährungen*, Nomos/facultas, Vienna 2019, pp. 374 et seq.

65 See on the issue e.g. A. Schopper/P. Raschner, 'Die aufsichtsrechtliche Einordnung von Krypto-Börsen in Österreich' (2019) *Österreichisches BankArchiv* 249, 253–54; C. Seggermann, '§ 1 WAG 2018' in E. Brandl and G. Saria (eds), Wertpapieraufsichtsgesetz 2018, 2nd ed., Manz, Vienna 1st supp 2018, para 89; F. Pekler and R. Rirsch, 'Ausgewählte kapitalmarktrechtliche Aspekte bei der Emission von Crypto-Assets', in S. Kirchmayr-Schliesselberger, W. Klas, M. Miernicki, S. Rinderle-Ma, A. Weilinger (eds), *Kryptowährungen*, Nomos/facultas, Vienna 2019, pp. 378 et seq.; G. Tuder and A. Ahari, 'Die aufsichtsrechtliche Einordnung von Krypto-Assets und Krypto-Assets-Handelsplattformen', in M. Hanzl, H. Pelzmann and M. Schragl (eds), *Handbuch Digitalisierung*, Linde, Vienna 2021, pp. 86–87.

66 FMA, *Fakten, Trends und Strategien 2019*, pp. 177–78 https://www.fma.gv.at/wp-content/plugins/dw-fma/download.php?d=3964&nonce=f25344d6af3c8199; see also A. Schopper/P. Raschner, 'Die aufsichtsrechtliche Einordnung von Krypto-Börsen in Österreich' (2019) *Österreichisches BankArchiv* 249, 251–52; C. Steiner, *Krypto-Assets und das Aufsichtsrecht*, finanzverlag, Vienna 2019, pp. 34 et seq.

the mining of crypto-assets can require a license under the Alternative Investment Fund Managers Act[67] (Alternative Investmentfonds Manager-Gesetz – AIFMG);[68] details are controversially discussed in the legal literature.[69] In general, however, mining as such is currently not regulated in Austria.[70]

2.4 *Prevention of Money Laudnering and Terrorist Financing*

Similar to other jurisdictions, the use of cryptocurrencies for illicit purposes is a major concern in Austria. In this connection, the FMA regularly publishes reports and guidelines on cryptocurrencies in the context of the prevention of money laundering and terrorist financing.[71]

As noted before, the FM-GwG contains a definition of virtual currencies. While the exact scope of this definition is under debate,[72] there is generally no doubt that cryptocurrencies like bitcoins fall within its scope. Furthermore,

---

67 BGBl I 2013/135; the act is based on Directive 2011/61/EU of the European Parliament and of the Council of 8 June 2011 on Alternative Investment Fund Managers and amending Directives 2003/41/EC and 2009/65/EC and Regulations (EC) No 1060/2009 and (EU) No 1095/2010 o [2011] OJ L174/1.

68 FMA, Bitcoin & Co https://www.fma.gv.at/en/fintech-point-of-contact-sandbox/fintech-navigator/bitcoin-co/; FMA, *Fakten, Trends und Strategien 2019*, pp. 47, 175 https://www.fma.gv.at/wp-content/plugins/dw-fma/download.php?d=3964&nonce=f25344d6af3c8199; FMA, *Frequently Asked Questions zur Anwendung des Alternative Investement-fonds Manager-Gesetz* (AIFMG), updated 2023, p. 16 https://www.fma.gv.at/wp-content/plugins/dw-fma/download.php?d=4879&nonce=7f0e08455d3fddao .

69 See e.g. O. Völkel, 'Mining von virtuellen Währungen als Alternativer Investmentfonds?' (2018) *Zeitschrift für Finanzmarktrecht* 317; S. Tomanek and M. Wintersberger, 'Mining – Geschäftsmodelle im Anwendungsbereich des AIFMG', in S. Kirchmayr-Schliesselberger, W. Klas, M. Miernicki, S. Rinderle-Ma, A. Weilinger (eds), *Kryptowährungen*, Nomos/facultas, Vienna 2019, p. 392.

70 FMA, *Bitcoin & Co* https://www.fma.gv.at/en/fintech-point-of-contact-sandbox/fintech-navigator/bitcoin-co/ ('Generally speaking merely mining Bitcoin in one's own name and on one's own account does not require a licence'); S. Tomanek and M. Wintersberger, 'Mining – Geschäftsmodelle im Anwendungsbereich des AIFMG', in S. Kirchmayr-Schliesselberger, W. Klas, M. Miernicki, S. Rinderle-Ma, A. Weilinger (eds), *Kryptowährungen*, Nomos/facultas, Vienna 2019, p. 405.

71 See e.g. FMA, *Fakten, Trends und Strategien 2023*, pp. 57–59 https://www.fma.gv.at/wp-content/plugins/dw-fma/download.php?d=6153&nonce=a257619302e8ec55; FMA, *Fakten, Trends und Strategien 2021*, 127–130 https://www.fma.gv.at/wp-content/plugins/dw-fma/download.php?d=4967&nonce=75dafefc1750f286; FMA, Rundschreiben Sorgfaltspflichten zur Prävention von Geldwäscherei und Terrorismusfinanzierung (02/2022) paras 363–382 https://www.fma.gv.at/wp-content/plugins/dw-fma/download.php?d=5596&nonce=5ec141b983117df9.

72 See e.g. O. Völkel, 'Zum Begriff „virtuelle Währung"' (2019) *Zeitschrift für Finanzmarktrecht* 346; R. Rirsch, S. Tomanek and T. Weratschnig, 'Der weite Begriff der „virtuellen Währung" im Bereich der Prävention von Geldwäsche und Terrorismusfinanzierung'

section 2(22) FM-GwG contains a list of activities that are provided by 'Dienstleister in Bezug auf virtuelle Währungen' (often called 'VASPs' – virtual asset service providers). Examples of entities that are covered by this wording are trading platforms (both the exchange of cryptocurrencies for other cryptocurrencies and for fiat money) and wallet providers;[73] furthermore, the definition encompasses transfer services and the provision of financial services for issuing and selling virtual currencies.[74]

VASPs are obliged entities under the FM-GwG and must comply with the obligations set forth by the act.[75] According to section 32a FM-GwG, there is a registration requirement for VASPs prior to providing services.[76] Failure to comply with the registration requirement allows the FMA to prohibit business operations (section 32b FM-GwG) and can lead to fines (section 34(4) FM-GwG).

2.5 *Further Questions on the Regulation of Trading Platforms*

According to the FMA, trading platforms for crypto-assets (and wallet providers) are currently only subject to 'limited supervision.'[77] Here, the FMA refers to the rules in the FM-GwG on VASPs mentioned before. Further sources of regulation that can be relevant for 'crypto-exchanges' listing crypto-assets include[78] the rules on regulated markets, multilateral trading facilities (MFTs) and organised trading facilities (OFTs); in Austria, these rules can be found in

(2019) *Zeitschrift für Finanzmarktrecht* 554; see also M. Lindtner, 'Die 5. GeldwäscheRL und ihre Umsetzung im Finanzmarkt-GeldwäscheG' (2019) *ecolex* 949.

73 See on the problem of decentralized exchanges F. Dafinger and M. Hanzl, 'Decentralized Exchanges – (nicht) im Anwendungsbereich des FM-GwG?' (2022) *Zeitschrift für Finanzmarktrecht* 374.

74 FMA, *Fakten, Trends und Strategien 2020*, p. 129 https://www.fma.gv.at/wp-content/plugins/dw-fma/download.php?d=4215&nonce=40e4eaaad87c3c76. See also Lackner, '§ 2 FM-GwG' in M. Dellinger (ed), *Bankwesengesetz*, LexisNexis, Vienna 10th supp 2020, para 61.

75 See for an overview of the different obligations O. Völkel and L. Farahmandnia, 'Registrierungspflicht von Dienstleistern in Bezug auf virtuelle Währungen' (2021) *ecolex* 73.

76 See on the registration requirement especially BVwG 7. 9. 2021, W158 2235512-1.

77 FMA, *Caution: Trading platforms for crypto assets and providers of electronic wallets (wallet providers) are only subject to limited supervision* https://www.fma.gv.at/en/investments/trading-platforms-for-crypto-assets/.

78 See for further relevant rules G. Tuder and A. Ahari, 'Die aufsichtsrechtliche Einordnung von Krypto-Assets und Krypto-Assets-Handelsplattformen', in M. Hanzl, H. Pelzmann and M. Schragl (eds), *Handbuch Digitalisierung*, Linde, Vienna 2021, pp. 88–89.

the Stock Exchange Act 2018 (BörseG 2018)[79] and the WAG 2018.[80] In addition, there is a debate in the legal literature whether exchanges on which cryptocurrencies like bitcoin or other crypto-assets are traded can be considered as commodity exchanges (Warenbörsen) within the meaning of section 1(3) BörseG 2018.[81] Commodity exchanges are not licensed by the FMA, but by the competent Federal Minster (section 3(2) BörseG 2018).

The foregoing refers primarily to the discussion under Austrian law. It should be noted, however, that MiCAR (see 1.4 above) contains a set of rules that apply to crypto-asset service providers, including trading platforms for crypto-assets.

3 Private Law Issues

3.1 *The Legal Concept of 'Sachen' (Things/Assets) under the ABGB and Its Application to Cryptocurrencies*

Austria's central civil law codification is, as mentioned before, the ABGB. The act was published in 1811 and entered into force in 1812. The structure of the ABGB is based on the system of institutions (Institutionensystem), distinguishing the 'law of persons' (Personenrechte, personal rights; sections 15 et seq. ABGB), the 'law of things' (Sachenrecht, property law; section 285 et seq. ABGB) and common provisions (section 1342 et seq.).[82] Thus, the term 'Sache' (that can be translated to 'asset' or 'thing') is of crucial importance for the act. Section 285 ABGB defines a 'Sache' as 'everything that is different from a person and that can be used by humans.'[83] Importantly, 'Sachen' in the legal sense

79 BGBl I 2017/107.

80 FMA, *Fakten, Trends und Strategien 2019*, pp. 178 https://www.fma.gv.at/wp-content/plugins/dw-fma/download.php?d=3964&nonce=f25344d6af3c8199; see also C. Bernsteiner, 'Kryptowährungen und Gewerberecht', in S. Kirchmayr-Schliesselberger, W. Klas, M. Miernicki, S. Rinderle-Ma, A. Weilinger (eds), *Kryptowährungen*, Nomos/facultas, Vienna 2019, pp. 472 et seq.; G. Tuder and A. Ahari, 'Die aufsichtsrechtliche Einordnung von Krypto-Assets und Krypto-Assets-Handelsplattformen', in M. Hanzl, H. Pelzmann and M. Schragl (eds), *Handbuch Digitalisierung*, Linde, Vienna 2021, pp. 90 et seq.

81 See on the issue A. Schopper/P. Raschner, 'Die aufsichtsrechtliche Einordnung von Krypto-Börsen in Österreich' (2019) *Österreichisches BankArchiv* 249, 255; C. Bernsteiner, 'Kryptowährungen und Gewerberecht', in S. Kirchmayr-Schliesselberger, W. Klas, M. Miernicki, S. Rinderle-Ma, A. Weilinger (eds), *Kryptowährungen*, Nomos/facultas, Vienna 2019, pp. 476-467; G. Tuder and A. Ahari, 'Die aufsichtsrechtliche Einordnung von Krypto-Assets und Krypto-Assets-Handelsplattformen', in M. Hanzl, H. Pelzmann and M. Schragl (eds), *Handbuch Digitalisierung*, Linde, Vienna 2021, pp. 92–93.

82 See also section 14 ABGB.

83 This portion of the act was translated by A. Eschig and E. Pircher-Eschig, *Das österreichische ABGB - The Austrian Civil Code*, 2nd ed., LexisNexis, Vienna 2021, section 285 ABGB.

encompass both corporeal and incorporeal assets (section 292 ABGB) and can hence be characterized as a relatively wide concept,[84] especially compared to the German Civil Code's notion of 'Sache' (section 90 BGB).[85] Under the ABGB, corporeal assets are those that 'fall in the [human] senses' ('in die Sinne fallen'; section 292 ABGB), a wording that is not unambiguous;[86] for example, there are different views on whether energy should be considered as a corporeal or an incorporeal asset. Incorporeal assets include rights and data, for instance.[87]

In line with the wide concept of 'Sache', cryptocurrencies are uniformly considered as 'Sachen' within the meaning of section 285 ABGB.[88] Furthermore, cryptocurrencies are generally considered as moveable assets (section 293 ABGB),[89] consumable assets (section 301 ABGB), fungible assets and assets that value of which can be estimated (section 303 ABGB).[90] According to the prevailing opinion, cryptocurrencies are incorporeal assets within the meaning of section 292 ABGB.[91]

3.2 *The Legal Concepts of 'Eigentum' (Property/Ownership) and 'Besitz' (Posession) and Their Application to Cryptocurrencies*

Section 354 ABGB stipulates that the 'Eigentum' (property, ownership) is 'the right to freely enjoy the substance and the benefits of an asset and to exclude

84 However, the notion is not without limits; for instance, the open sea or the free air as such would not qualify as 'Sachen' in the legal sense because they cannot be controlled by humans, see e.g. O. Riss, '§ 285' in P. Bydlinski, S. Perner and M. Spitzer (eds), *Kommentar zum ABGB*, 7th ed., Verlag Österreich, Vienna 2023, para 3.

85 See e.g. C. Wendehorst, 'Rechtsobjekte', in R. Alexy (ed), *Juristische Grundlagenforschung*, Franz Steiner Verlag, Stuttgart 2005, pp. 71–72.

86 See for more details M. Miernicki, *Kryptowerte* pp. 85 et seq.

87 O. Riss, '§ 292' in P. Bydlinski, S. Perner and M. Spitzer (eds), *Kommentar zum ABGB*, 7th ed., Verlag Österreich, Vienna 2023, para 1.

88 See e.g. A. Vonkilch and M. Knoll, 'Bitcoins und das Sachenrecht des ABGB' (2019) *Juristische Blätter* 139, 141; L. Fleißner, 'Eigentum an unkörperlichen Sachen am Beispiel von Bitcoins', (2018), *Österreichische Juristen-Zeitung* 437.

89 However, there are good reasons to question this assumption, since, according to the system of the ABGB, the distinction between moveable and immoveable assets is only made with regard to corporeal assets, see G. Kogler, 'Non Fungible Tokens und Sachenrecht' (2021) *Juristische Blätter* 685, 688–89 (on NFTs); M. Miernicki, *Kryptowerte* pp. 124 et seq.

90 See generally O. Völkel, 'Privatrechtliche Einordnung virtueller Währungen' (2017) *Österreichisches BankArchiv* 385; see also A. Weilinger and M. Miernicki, 'Kryptowährungen im Zivil- und Verbraucherschutzrecht', in S. Kirchmayr-Schliesselberger, W. Klas, M. Miernicki, S. Rinderle-Ma, A. Weilinger (eds), *Kryptowährungen*, Nomos/facultas, Vienna 2019, pp. 93–96.

91 This is confirmed by section 326 EO, M. Miernicki, *Kryptowerte* 168 et seq.

everyone else therefrom.'[92] At the same time, section 353 ABGB stipulates that property refers to both corporeal as well as incorporeal assets ('property in the objective sense'). Since Cryptocurrencies are incorporeal assets within the meaning of section 285 ABGB, a textual analysis of the ABGB might lead to the straightforward conclusion that cryptocurrencies can be the subject of ownership. However, the mere qualification of an assets as an incorporeal thing does not necessarily mean that all provisions belonging to property law apply. This is because, traditionally, despite the ABGB's wording, the prevailing legal opinion in Austria has generally confined the application of property law to corporeal things.[93] However, details are debated and have most extensively been discussed in connection with rights and claims under the property law regime; more recently, the topic of data ownership has been under discussion.[94] With regard to the cryptocurrencies, some authors argue that there is currently no protection under property law and refer to the incorporeal nature of these assets.[95] At the same time, however, many authors are – based on different lines argumentation – of the opinion that cryptocurrencies can be the subject of ownership.[96] The latter result is convincing because cryptocurrencies have characteristics that are different from other incorporeal assets: Unlike data, cryptocurrencies possess a high degree of rivalry and exclusivity; furthermore, unlike claims and rights, cryptocurrencies are not the 'product' of the law but exist independent from a particular jurisdiction. In this light, there is no convincing reason to apply a restrictive reading to sections 353, 354 ABGB; rather, cryptocurrencies can be subject to ownership under Austrian law.[97]

The ABGB defines 'Besitz' (possession) as the (physical) control of a person over an asset (*corpus*) with the intention to keep the assets for her own

---

92 This portion of the act was translated by A. Eschig and E. Pircher-Eschig, *Das österreichische ABGB - The Austrian Civil Code*, 2nd ed., LexisNexis, Vienna 2021, section 354 ABGB.

93 See e.g. R. Welser and A. Kletečka, *Grundriss des bürgerlichen Rechts*, 15th ed., Manz, Vienna 2018, pp. 266, 319–20.

94 See e.g. E. Staudegger, 'Datenhandel – ein Auftakt zur Diskussion' (2014) *Österreichische Juristen-Zeitung*, 107; S. Dürager, 'Sind Daten ein schutzfähiges Gut?' (2018) *Österreichische Blätter für Gewerblichen Rechtsschutz und Urheberrecht*, 260.

95 See e.g. C. Holzner, '§ 353' in A. Kletečka and M. Schauer, *ABGB-ON*, Manz, last updated online 01.01.2023, para 1.

96 See e.g. O. Völkel, 'Vertrauen in die Blockchain und das Sachenrecht' (2020) *Zeitschrift für Finanzmarktrecht* 492, 498. Some authors argue that ownership 'in the wider sense' (Eigentum im weiteren Sinn; Rechtszuständigkeit) is possible, see e.g. A. Vonkilch and M. Knoll, 'Bitcoins und das Sachenrecht des ABGB' (2019) *Juristische Blätter* 139, 141, 142–43.

97 See for a detailed discussion M. Miernicki, *Kryptowerte* pp. 130 et seq., 247 et seq.

(*animus*) (section 309 ABGB).[98] Section 311 ABGB confirms that both corporeal and incorporeal things can, in principle, be subject to possession. Nevertheless, there are different views on whether and to what extent incorporeal assets can be possessed; again, the most extensive debates have been held on rights and claims ('Rechtsbesitz'), while more recent questions concern the capability of data to be subject to possession. The views on cryptocurrencies are divided: While some argue that possession is not possible (at least not in the way corporeal things can be possessed, i.e. 'Sachbesitz'),[99] others deem the rules on possession to apply.[100] In the author's opinion, there are better arguments supporting the latter view because cryptocurrencies can be directly controlled with the private key and are, from this perspective, comparable to corporeal assets; at the same time, the control of a person can unilaterally be interrupted by another person (e.g. by initiating an unauthorized on-chain-transaction). Again, there is no compelling reason to deviate from the language of the ABGB with regard to cryptocurrencies and to deny their capability to be subject to possession.[101]

Example 1 X has 60 bitcoins registered in his/her wallet.

– Has X legal ownership over the 60 bitcoins in his/her wallet? Please provide details.

The fact that somebody has cryptocurrencies 'in' her wallet[102] does not, as such, mean that this person has legal ownership. First and foremost, this person will usually be the possessor of the assets because, in most cases, she will have the intention to keep them for herself as well as direct control. Whether this person is the legal owner of the cryptocurrency is a different question and depends on whether ownership has lawfully been acquired.[103]

---

98 A person that has control over an asset but no will to keep it for his or her own is called the 'Inhaber' (holder) of the asset.

99 See e.g. A. Anderl, M. Aigner and D. Schelling, 'Zivilrechtliche Aspekte' in A. Anderl, *#Blockchain in der Rechtspraxis*, LexisNexis, Vienna 2020, 72; L. Fleißner, 'Eigentum an unkörperlichen Sachen am Beispiel von Bitcoins', (2018), *Österreichische Juristen-Zeitung* 437.

100 See e.g. O. Völkel, 'Vertrauen in die Blockchain und das Sachenrecht' (2020) *Zeitschrift für Finanzmarktrecht* 492, 496. Cf. also G. Kogler, 'Non Fungible Tokens und Sachenrecht' (2021) *Juristische Blätter* 685, 688–89.

101 See for a detailed discussion M. Miernicki, *Kryptowerte* pp. 192 et seq.

102 A wallet is usually understood as a tool for storing and managing (especially private) keys, so that crypto-assets are technically not stored in a wallet. Rather, one could say that the crypto-assets are registered in a person's address in the blockchain network.

103 See on the questions of transfers below.

Example 2 X opened an account with MontC[104] and has 60 bitcoins registered in his/her wallet.

– Has MontC any ownership rights over the 60 bitcoins registered in X's wallet? Please provide details.

There are different service providers that have developed in wake of the emergence of crypto-assets.[105] Assuming that the wallet provider in question merely provides a solution for X to manage her asset – i.e., X has access to and control of the private key –, MontC will normally neither have ownership nor possession of the X's cryptocurrencies. However, if only the wallet service provider has access to the private key, X cannot, for the lack of the *corpus* element, be direct possessor. Instead, MontC can exercise the direct control over the cryptocurrency for X who is thus indirect possessor (mittelbarer Besitzer); in such a case, X would generally still be the owner of the cryptocurrency, since MontC lacks title to acquire the assets. It should be noted that, under Austrian law, the parties can also agree on a third option and stipulate that X has only a claim against the service provider that is in turn owner of the cryptocurrency; this can take the form of a fiduciary arrangement (Treuhandschaft).[106]

Example 3 Assume a hardfork or airdrop of a new cryptocurrency, part of which is registered in a wallet belonging to X.

– Would X or MontC have title to the newly created cryptocurrency?

The solution of the case depends, according to the author's opinion, on the legal relation between X and MontC. Assuming that X receives, in the course of a hardfork, 'new' cryptocurrency because she already has 'old' cryptocurrency and she is the owner of the latter, then she will additionally acquire ownership of the 'new' cryptocurrency. This is because the 'new' cryptocurrency can be legally regarded as a 'fruit' (Frucht) of the 'old' cryptocurrency.[107] If instead MontC is the owner of the 'old' cryptocurrency, the 'new' cryptocurrency would generally be the service provider's property. In principle, however, the parties can agree on a different solution.

Airdrops generally imply a form of a derivative acquisition of property that will in many cases be based on a donation contract (Schenkungsvertrag)

104 MontC is an intermediary that provides wallet services to customers.

105 Cf. also article 3(1)(17) MiCAR that defines 'providing custody and administration of crypto-assets on behalf of clients' as 'the safekeeping or controlling, on behalf of clients, of crypto-assets or of the means of access to such crypto-assets, where applicable in the form of private cryptographic keys'.

106 See for details M. Miernicki, *Kryptowerte* pp. 206–7, 657 et seq.; T. Weidinger, *Kryptowerte in der Insolvenz*, Verlag Österreich, Vienna 2023, pp. 163 et seq., 232 et seq.

107 Methodologically, one would arguably have to base this opinion on the application of section 405 ABGB (by analogy); see for more details M. Miernicki, *Kryptowerte* p. 330 et seq.

according to sections 938 et seq. ABGB.[108] Thus, a crucial question is which persons are parties to such agreement. While this should be assessed on a case-by-case basis, it seems reasonable to assume that the person holding the blockchain-address to which the cryptocurrency is transferred by the company behind the airdrop is party of the contract.

3.3 *Principles of the Transfer of Ownership of Cryptocurrency*

According to the ABGB, the transfer of property rights requires legal title (Titel) and mode of acquisition (Modus) (sections 380, 425 ABGB).[109] The transfer of ownership of cryptocurrency must comply with these conditions. In particular, the title can be a sales contract (section 1053 et seq. ABGB), a barter (section 1045 et seq. ABGB), a donation agreement (section 938 et seq. ABGB) or a loan (section 983 et seq. ABGB).[110] The exchange of money and cryptocurrency is generally considered as a sales contract, while the exchange of cryptocurrency for other crypto-assets is qualified as a barter agreement.[111] As for the modes of acquisition, the ABGB distinguishes physical transfer of an asset (körperliche Übergabe, section 426 ABGB), symbolic transfer of an asset (Übergabe durch Zeichen, section 427 ABGB) and the transfer through agreement (Übergabe durch Erklärung, section 428 ABGB). The on chain transfer of cryptocurrency is generally regarded as a suitable mode for the transfer of ownership, although the legal qualification of this act under section 426 et seq. ABGB diverge.[112] Conversely, it is debated whether providing the private key to a third person is sufficient for the transfer of ownership.[113]

Example 1 X has 60 bitcoins registered in his/her wallet. X wants to give 30 bitcoins to Y.

- Is it legally possible, and under what conditions, for X to make such a transfer?
- What difference would it make if X uses an intermediary (e.g. a wallet provider) to hold and transfer the bitcoins?

---

108 Cf. M. Miernicki, *Kryptowerte* pp. 546 et seq.

109 For the transfer of property rights, the transferor must naturally also have corresponding title or authorization (442 ABGB).

110 See for details M. Miernicki, *Kryptowerte* pp. 531 et seq.

111 A. Schwartze, '§ 1053' in A. Fenyves, F. Kerschner and A. Vonkilch, ABGB §§ 1045–1089, 3rd ed., Verlag Österreich, Vienna 2019, para 12; A. Weilinger and M. Miernicki, 'Kryptowährungen im Zivil- und Verbraucherschutzrecht', in S. Kirchmayr-Schliesselberger, W. Klas, M. Miernicki, S. Rinderle-Ma, A. Weilinger (eds), *Kryptowährungen*, Nomos/facultas, Vienna 2019, pp. 97–99.

112 See e.g. L. Fleißner, 'Eigentum an unkörperlichen Sachen am Beispiel von Bitcoins', (2018), *Österreichische Juristen-Zeitung* 437, 440–41; O. Völkel, 'Vertrauen in die Blockchain und das Sachenrecht' (2020) *Zeitschrift für Finanzmarktrecht* 492, 498–499.

113 See for further details M. Miernicki, *Kryptowerte* pp. 235 et seq.

Under Austrian law, X can transfer 30 bitcoins on chain to an address held by Y to transfer the ownership. According to the author's opinion, providing Y with the keys/passwords to X's wallet/blockchain address would in contrast not suffice for this purpose in the given example.[114] With regard to the title requirement, X and Y can conclude a sales contract, a barter, a donation agreement[115] or a loan, for instance.

If X relies on the services of an intermediary, the legal assessment of the case example is more complex:[116]

If the intermediary is a wallet provider and X has direct control and ownership of the bitcoins, she can directly initiate an on chain transaction to transfer the assets to Y.

If X only has a claim against the intermediary and no ownership of the bitcoins, she can assign this claim according to sections 1392 et seq. ABGB (Zession). The assignment as such does not have an effect on the property rights in the cryptocurrency.

If X is indirect possessor (and owner) of the bitcoins (with the intermediary exercising control for him) X can instruct the intermediary to exercise direct control for Y in the future (Besitzanweisung). As the Besitzanweisung is a valid mode for transferring ownership, Y acquires property in the cryptocurrency.[117] The Besitzanweisung is generally considered as sufficient to satisfy the 'effective transfer' requirement stipulated for donations.[118]

Example 2 X has 60 bitcoins registered in his/her wallet. X wants to sell 5 bitcoins against 10 Ethers.

---

114 However, if X wanted to transfer all the bitcoins as well as the address they are registered in, the transfer is arguably possible; see for details M. Miernicki, *Kryptowerte* pp. 237 et seq.

115 It should be noted that the donation requires (if there is no notary act) the 'effective transfer' (wirkliche Übergabe, section 1(d) NotAktG RGBl 1871/76). According to the author's opinion, the on chain transfer of the cryptocurrency satisfies this requirement; under certain conditions, the same arguably applies to the provision of the private key; see for details M. Miernicki, *Kryptowerte* pp. 546 et seq.

116 See for the following M. Miernicki, *Kryptowerte* pp. 206–7, 240–243, 259–262, 273–4.

117 If cryptocurrency of several customers are registered in the same blockchain address of the service provider, one would have to ask whether X's cryptocurrency can be identified or, at least, whether X's share in the cryptocurreny (in case of co-ownership, section 825 et seq. ABGB) registered in the address can be determined; see for more details Miernicki, *Kryptowerte* pp. 259 et seq., 273–4.

118 R. Bollenberger and P. Bydlinski, '§ 943' in P. Bydlinski, S. Perner and M. Spitzer (eds), *Kommentar zum ABGB*, 7th ed., Verlag Österreich, Vienna 2023, para 5.

- Is it legally possible, and under what conditions, for X to make such a transaction?
- How would such a transaction be classified in your legal system?
- What difference would it make if X uses an intermediary (e.g. a wallet provider) to hold and transfer the bitcoins?

As stated above, an agreement of this kind would be considered as a barter (section 1045 et seq. ABGB). What was said above in connection with intermediaries generally applies also in the present context.

Example 3 X has 60 bitcoins registered in his/her wallet. X wants to sell 5 bitcoins against a legal tender (e.g. Euro, Yen, Dollar).

- Is it legally possible, and under what conditions, for X to make such a transaction?
- How would such a transaction be classified in your legal system?
- What difference would it make, if X uses an intermediary (e.g. a wallet provider) to hold and transfer the bitcoins?

As stated above, an agreement of this kind would be considered as a sales contract (section 1053 et seq. ABGB). What was said above in connection with intermediaries generally applies also in the present context.

Whether Austrian law applies to questions of property and contracts is a question of private international law. With regard to property rights, the legal situation is, for the time being, rather unclear: According to section 31 Act on Private International Law (Gesetz über das Internationale Privatrecht – IPRG),[119] property rights in chattel are assessed according to the rules of the jurisdiction the asset is located in. This rule cannot be easily applied to cryptocurrencies because they are based on decentralized networks and thus lack an exact location.[120] Some authors argue that the location of the private key determines the applicable law[121] which is problematic because the key can be copied and thus be stored on multiple devices or online. Other solutions

119 BGBl 1978/304.

120 See e.g. M. Miernicki and N. Scharl, 'Kollisionsrechtliche Fragen des „digitalen Euro"', *Zeitschrift für Europarecht, internationales Privatrecht und Rechtsvergleichung* 169, 176 et seq.

121 M. Aigner, 'Das internationale Privatrecht und die Blockchain – ein unlösbarer gordischer Knoten?' (2020) *Zeitschrift für Europarecht, internationales Privatrecht und Rechtsvergleichung* 211, 218–19 (also arguing that the principle of closest connection set forth by section 1(1) IPRG leads to the same result).

suggested in the legal literature[122] include the application of section 33a IPRG by analogy, at least in certain situations.[123]

The most important private international rules with regard to contracts are contained in the Rome I Regulation.[124]

3.4 *Cryptocurrencies as Collatoral*

The ABGB provides for rules on the pledging of assets in section 447 et seq. Both incorporeal and corporeal assets can be pledged (cf. section 448 ABGB).[125] As pledges are a group of rights in rem[126] (cf. section 308 ABGB), the acquisition of a pledge requires both title and mode of acquisition. The title can be a corresponding contract (Pfandbestellungsvertrag); the mode is addressed in section 451 et seq. ABGB: To pledge a moveable asset, the creditor must take the assets into custody and for immovable assets, a registration in the land register is required. Section 452 ABGB permits, with regard to moveable assets that do not allow for a physical transfer, the symbolic transfer by way of readily recognizable signs stating that the asset has been pledged. Under Austrian law, the rules on pledged assets are applied by analogy to the transfer of ownership for the purposes of securing an underlying debt (Sicherungsübereignung).[127]

Example 1 Z is a company whose seat is in your legal system. To secure a loan for the financing of a specific project, Z has agreed to pledge 30 bitcoins that are registered in its wallet.

– Would it be possible, and under what conditions, for Z to make such pledge? Is there one or more ways of pledge? What would change if the wallet is kept with an intermediary?

Since pledges under the ABGB can also be incorporeal things, cryptocurrencies are generally considered as being eligible for pledging. According to the

122 A. Anderl, M. Aigner and D. Schelling, 'Zivilrechtliche Aspekte' in A. Anderl, *#Blockchain in der Rechtspraxis*, LexisNexis, Vienna 2020, 77–78; C. Wendehorst, 'Kryptowerte und anwendbares Recht', in R. Welser (ed), 2 *Buchgeld und Bargeld*, Manz, Vienna 2020, p. 11.

123 The provision is based on Art 9 Directive 2002/47/EC of the European Parliament and of the Council of 6 June 2002 on financial collateral arrangements [2002] OJ L167/43.

124 Regulation (EC) No 593/2008 of the European Parliament and of the Council of 17 June 2008 on the law applicable to contractual obligations [2008] OJ L177/6.

125 B. Koch, '§ 448' in P. Bydlinski, S. Perner and M. Spitzer (eds), *Kommentar zum ABGB*, 7th ed., Verlag Österreich, Vienna 2023, para 1.

126 However, when incorporeal things are pledges, one generally does not refer to 'dingliche Rechte', see e.g. E. Helmich, '§ 285' in A. Kletečka and M. Schauer, *ABGB-ON*, Manz, last updated online 01.08.2022, para 2.

127 See e.g. OGH 09.12.2008, 5 Ob 168/08 d *Juristische Blätter* 2009, 437; B. Koch, '§ 451' in P. Bydlinski, S. Perner and M. Spitzer (eds), *Kommentar zum ABGB*, 7th ed., Verlag Österreich, Vienna 2023, para 2.

prevailing opinion, cryptocurrency can be pledged by transferring it to the creditor on chain; conversely, merely providing the private key to the creditor is seen as not meeting the requirements of the ABGB for pledges because the debtor will usually still have de facto access to the cryptocurrency.[128]

If Z's wallet is kept with an intermediary, the solution, again, depends on the legal relation between the intermediary and Z. If Z only has claim, the claim can be pledged; if the intermediary keeps the cryptocurrency for Z, a pledge can be made by instruction (Besitzanweisung).[129]

With regard to the applicable law, similar problems as observed above (section 31 IPRG) occur in connection with pledges.

3.5 *Special Questions on 'Crypto-Lending'*

Example 1 PayB is a company regulated and supervised in its home jurisdiction to provide lending services. Z is a company whose seat is in your legal system. Z intends to borrow 60 bitcoins from PayB, with an interest rate of 5% payable either in a legal tender (e.g. Euro, US Dollar, Yen) or in bitcoins.

– Would it be possible, and under what conditions, for PayB and Z to conclude such a contract? How would such contract be characterised in your legal system? Please provide details.

In a loan agreement, the lender agrees to transfer to the borrower fungible assets that the latter can freely use. At the same time, the borrower undertakes to return the same quantity and quality of the assets to the lender after a certain period of time (section 983 ABGB). The loan can be concluded with or without consideration (entgeltlich/unentgeltlicher Darlehensvertrag); in cases of doubt, the borrower owes reasonable consideration (section 984 ABGB). A loan for consideration that refers to money is called a credit agreement (Kreditvertrag, section 988 ABGB).

The example mentioned above appears to describe a situation where the parties want to conclude a loan agreement within the meaning of section 983 ABGB. This is possible under Austrian law: As mentioned before, cryptocurrency is generally considered as a fungible asset and can hence be subject to a loan agreement.[130] According to the author's opinion, the parties can freely

---

128 See e.g. *F. Dafinger*, 'Bitcoins im Pfandleihgewerbe' (2020) *ecolex* 241, 243; *M. Aigner*, 'Das Pfandrecht und die Blockchain' (2019) *Österreichisches BankArchiv* 816, 822. See for more details M. Miernicki, Kryptowerte pp. 344 et seq. See, however, BVwG 04.04.2022, W107 2233589-1 *Zeitschrift für Finanzmarktrecht* 2022, 457.

129 B. Koch, '§ 451' in P. Bydlinski, S. Perner and M. Spitzer (eds), *Kommentar zum ABGB*, 7th ed., Verlag Österreich, Vienna 2023, para 3.

130 M. Kellner, '§ 984' in P. Rummel, M. Lukas and A. Geroldinger (eds), *ABGB*, 4th ed., Manz, last updated online 01.08. 2022, para 26.

agree on a consideration as set out by the contract mentioned in the example. The contract would not be considered as a credit agreement because cryptocurrency is generally not regarded as money in the legal sense.[131]

In the absence of choice of law, the law applicable to loan agreements is, in principle, determined in accordance with article 4(2) Rome I Regulation. In this connection, one generally refers to the habitual residence (or place of central administration, article 19 Rome I Regulation) of the lender.[132]

Example 2 PayB is a regulated company authorised to provide lending services in your legal system. Z is a company whose seat is in your country. Z intends to borrow 60 bitcoins from PayB, at an interest rate of 5% payable in bitcoins. Z pays back in Bitcoin Cash, which are bitcoin equivalents resulting from a fork in the initial Bitcoin blockchain.

- Would it be possible, and under what conditions, for Z to pay back its loan in Bitcoin Cash instead of bitcoins?
- What difference does it make whether or not the fork took place only after the initial transfer of bitcoin?

According to section 983 ABGB, the borrower is under the obligation to return assets of the same 'type' (Gattung) to the lender. Thus, it is necessary to compare the assets Z pays back with the assets PayB originally transferred under the loan agreement. For this appraisal, it seems necessary to interpret the agreement and ask whether the bitcoin and Bitcoin Cash can be considered as equivalent under this agreement.[133] Most likely, this question has to be answered in the negative.[134] Based on this assumption, one would reach the conclusion that Z cannot lawfully pay back Bitcoin Cash but is under the obligation to transfer bitcoins to PayB. Conversely, the parties could, in principle, agree that Z could settle its debt by transferring forked assets to PayB.

---

131 See for more details M. Miernicki, *Kryptowerte* pp. 540 et seq. See, however, G. Diwok and D. Gritsch, 'Bitcoin, Geldbegriffe und Zahlungsmittel' (2020) *Zeitschrift für Finanzmarkterecht* 64, 71 (applying section 988 ABGB to bitcoins due to reasons of consumer protection). According to the author's opinion, it is more coherent to discuss the application of the rules on consumer protection (and not section 988 ABGB) to 'bitcoin loans'; see also A. Schopper/P. Raschner, 'Privat- und aufsichtsrechtliche Rahmenbedingungen für Krypto-Banking' (2022) *Österreichisches BankArchiv* 262, 74.

132 Cf. G. Musger, 'Art 4 Rom I-VO' in P. Bydlinski, S. Perner and M. Spitzer (eds), *Kommentar zum ABGB*, 7th ed., Verlag Österreich, Vienna 2023, para 9.

133 Cf. M. Kellner, '§ 984' in P. Rummel, M. Lukas and A. Geroldinger (eds), *ABGB*, 4th ed., Manz, last updated online 01.08. 2022, para 46.

134 It is seems likely that one would reach the same conclusion from the perspective of the generally accepted view in commerce (Verkehrsauffassung), cf. M. Kellner, '§ 984' in P. Rummel, M. Lukas and A. Geroldinger (eds), *ABGB*, 4th ed., Manz, last updated online 01.08. 2022, para 46.

3.6 *Law of Succession*

According to section 531 ABGB, the 'rights and obligations of a deceased person are his estate to the extent they are not personal in their nature'.[135] This language covers both corporeal and incorporeal assets[136] and should – although the topic has not been extensively discussed in Austria – also apply to cryptocurrencies[137] as well as claims for cryptocurrencies. Austrian law provides for the option to make a will (Testament, section 552(2) ABGB) to determine the legal succession of a person. To be valid, a will must comply with the conditions set forth in section 564 et seq. ABGB (e.g. formal requirements). It should be noted, however, that the law restricts the freedom of declarations of the last will insofar as it provides for compulsory portions (Pflichtteile) for the deceased person's decedents and her spouse/registered civil partner (sections 756 et seq. ABGB).

Example 1 X has 60 bitcoins registered in his/her wallet. X has a child, Y. X wants to make a will to ensure that the value of his/her wallet is not lost and is passed on to Y. Is it possible, and under what conditions, for X to make such provisions in his/her will?[138]

- If no valid will has been made, how would the rules of your legal system apply to the succession of X in respect of the bitcoins assigned to his/her private key?
- What difference would it make to the assessment of the example case if X holds the bitcoin with an intermediary?

If all conditions for declarations of the will stipulated by the ABGB are met, there appears to be no reason why cryptocurrency should not be capable of being subject to such a declaration.[139] If no valid will has been made, sections 727 et seq. ABGB provide for detailed rules on intestate succession (gesetzliche Erbfolge). In such a case, X's cryptocurrency will ultimately be transferred to the legal heirs (section 730 ABGB).

135 This portion of the act was translated by A. Eschig and E. Pircher-Eschig, *Das österreichische ABGB - The Austrian Civil Code*, 2nd ed., LexisNexis, Vienna 2021, section 531 ABGB.

136 B. Eccher and M. Umlauft, *Erbrecht*, 7th ed. Verlag Österreich, Vienna 2020, p. 1.

137 J. Gebauer, 'Digitale Verlassenschaft' (2015) *Zeitschrift für Informationsrecht* 382, 383; S. Brehm, 'Verlassenschaft 2.0' (2016) *Journal für Erbrecht und Vermögensnachfolge* 159, 164; on NFTs G. Kogler, 'Non Fungible Tokens und Sachenrecht' (2021) *Juristische Blätter* 685, 695; see also M. Miernicki, 'Wann gehören Kunstgegenstände zum gesetzlichen Vorausvermächtnis gem § 745 ABGB? (Teil II)' (2023) *Zeitschrift für Familien- und Erbrecht* 62.

138 It is assumed here that X is the owner of the cryptocurrency.

139 Cf. G. Kogler, 'Non Fungible Tokens und Sachenrecht' (2021) *Juristische Blätter* 685, 695 (on NFTs).

If a service provider is involved it depends, again, on the legal relationship between X and the service provider. If X only has a claim against the provider, the claim can generally be inherited.

The most important rules on private international law are presently set forth by the 'Inheritance Regulation.'[140]

3.7 *Creation of a Trust*

While there are different forms of trusts or foundations (Stiftungen) in Austria, the most relevant form in the present context is the private foundation (Privatstiftung) based on the Private Trust Act (Privatstiftungsgesetz – PSG).[141] Creating a private foundation requires assets worth at least EUR 70.000,– (section 4 PSG). Assets other than money are eligible for this purpose;[142] however, section 11 PSG provides for an audit requirement for all assets that are not domestic currency (e.g. euro). The declaration of the foundation (Stiftungserklärung) can determine a beneficiary (section 9(1)(3) PSG).

Example 1 X has 60 bitcoins registered in his/her wallet. X wants to create a trust over the 60 bitcoins for the benefit of Y. Is this possible, and under what conditions?

While the usage of cryptocurrency for the formation of companies has been discussed in the corporate law context,[143] the creation of private foundations has, to the author's knowledge, not been addressed in the legal literature.[144] Because the PSG permits the creation of a private foundations with assets other than money, there appears to be no reason why cryptocurrencies cannot be used for this purpose. It can be assumed that a formation audit (section 11 PSG) is required; this is implied by the fact that also foreign *currency* (even though cryptocurrency are usually not regarded as currency in the legal sense) is considered to trigger the audit requirement.[145]

---

140 Regulation (EU) No 650/2012 of the European Parliament and of the Council of 4 July 2012 on jurisdiction, applicable law, recognition and enforcement of decisions and acceptance and enforcement of authentic instruments in matters of succession and on the creation of a European Certificate of Succession [2012] OJ L201/107.

141 BGBl 1993/694.

142 N. Arnold, *Privatstiftungsgesetz*, 4th ed., LexisNexis, Vienna 2022, § 4 para 8.

143 M. Miernicki, 'Kryptowährungen und Sachgründung im Gesellschaftsrecht', in S. Kirchmayr-Schliesselberger, W. Klas, M. Miernicki, S. Rinderle-Ma, A. Weilinger (eds), *Kryptowährungen*, Nomos/facultas, Vienna 2019, p. 137.

144 See, however, in the context of accounting B. Arming and G. Wurmhöringer, 'Kryptowährungen in Privatstiftungen (Teil 1)' (2022) *Steuer- und WirtschaftsKartei* 622.

145 N. Arnold, *Privatstiftungsgesetz*, 4th ed., LexisNexis, Vienna 2022, § 4 para 8.

Private Foundations must have their seat in Austria (section 1(1) PSG).[146] Whether Austrian law applies to a foundation is determined according to the seat theory, the seat being the central administration ('tatsächlichen Sitz seiner Hauptverwaltung', section 10 IPRG); however, the incorporation theory can be relevant within the scope of the EU freedom of establishment.[147]

3.8 *Special Questions on Tort Law*

The rules of tort law can be found in sections 1293 et seq. ABGB. A person is generally entitled to compensation for damages if another person has unlawfully caused the damage at her fault. 'Unlawful' behaviour (Rechtswidrigkeit) can be, for instance, derived from the breach of a contractual obligation or the violation of property rights.[148]

Example 1 X opened an account with MontC and has 60 bitcoins registered in his/her wallet. MontC's IT systems have been hacked. As a result, X lost all his/her bitcoins.

- Can X, and under which conditions, bring an action against MontC?
- Can X, and under which conditions, bring an action against the hacker (if he/she is identified)?
- If the hacker has sold the bitcoin to third party Y, could Y be protected as a bona fide purchaser?
- What would be the case if X transferred the bitcoin to the tortfeasor after being misled?

X would have a claim for compensation against MontC if the general conditions set forth in section 1293 et seq. ABGB are fulfilled. In this example, this would most likely require that MontC has caused the damage by neglecting its obligation to protect X's cryptocurrency[149] by employing reasonable measures against unauthorized access by third parties; this obligation will presumably

146 See for further details N. Arnold, *Privatstiftungsgesetz*, 4th ed., LexisNexis, Vienna 2022, § 1 para 22.

147 See generally OGH 19.10.2011, 4 Ob 119/11w Österreichisches *BankArchiv* 2012, 178; see for further details on foundations N. Arnold, *Privatstiftungsgesetz*, 4th ed., LexisNexis, Vienna 2022, Einleitung para 31, § 1 para 23. See in general M. Miernicki, 'Grenzüberschreitende Mobilität nach dem EU-Umgründungsgesetz' (2024) *Österreichisches Juristisches Archiv* 38.

148 See generally e.g. G. Kodek, '§ 1294' in A. Kletečka and M. Schauer, *ABGB-ON*, Manz, last updated online 01.01.2018, para 6 et seq.

149 X's ownership of the cryptocurrency is assumed here. However, questions of tort law can naturally also arise if X and MontC have concluded a fiduciary agreement.

arise from the contract concluded between MontC and X.[150] Under these assumptions, MontC would act unlawfully (in breach of its contract with X).

If X is (still) the owner of the cryptocurrency, she would have claim against the hacker to transfer the cryptocurrency based on her property right (section 366 ABGB; see also 372 ABGB). She could also sue for damages because the hacker violates her property rights.[151] Whether a bona fide purchaser is protected under Austrian law against X's claims is not entirely clear;[152] however, there are good reasons to apply the provisions that allow for an acquisition in good faith (sections 367, 371 ABGB) to cryptocurrency.[153]

If X is misled into transferring the bitcoins to the tortfeasor, X can demand the cryptocurrency to be transferred back based on her property right.[154] Alternatively, (especially in cases in which X has lost ownership),[155] claims can generally also be based on provisions of unjust enrichment and tort law if the corresponding conditions are fulfilled.

The most important rules on the applicable law in the present context are contained in the Rome II Regulation.[156]

It should be noted that hacking and fraud in respect of cryptocurrencies can also be a crime[157] punishable under the Austrian Criminal Code (StGB).[158]

150 The degree of care necessary must be determined on a case-by-case basis; for instance, see in general on the duties of a depositary E. Karner, '§ 961' in A. Kletečka and M. Schauer, *ABGB-ON*, Manz, last updated online 01.07.2018, para 1 et seq. It should be noted that MiCAR contains general rules for crypto-asset service providers as well as special rules for custody and administration services, see article 66 et seq. MiCAR.

151 M. Miernicki, *Kryptowerte* p. 334 et seq. Clearly, this is based on the view that ownership of cryptocurrency is possible; see the discussion above.

152 Arguing against protection e.g. C. Holzner, '§ 367' in A. Kletečka and M. Schauer, *ABGB-ON*, Manz, last updated online 01.01.2023, para 2.

153 See e.g. A. Vonkilch and M. Knoll, 'Bitcoins und das Sachenrecht des ABGB' (2019) *Juristische Blätter* 139, 146–47; see for a detailed discussion M. Miernicki, Kryptowerte pp. 274 et seq.

154 If X was misled into concluding a contract, it might be necessary to void the contract first, e.g. due to deceit (List) or mistake/error (Irrtum) (sections 870 et seq. ABGB).

155 This is conceivable should the hacker acquire property due to 'mixing' (Vermengung, section 371 ABGB); see for details M. Miernicki, *Kryptowerte* pp. 307 et seq.

156 Regulation (EC) No 864/2007 of the European Parliament and of the Council of 11 July 2007 on the law applicable to non-contractual obligations [2007] OJ L199/40.

157 See on these questions e.g. K. Papathanasiou, 'Blockchain und Strafrecht – Herausforderungen und Chancen' (2022) *Zeitschrift für Wirtschafts- und Finanzstrafrecht* 178; S. Glaser, 'Der Bitcoin als staatliche Währung' (2021) *Zeitschrift für Wirtschafts- und Finanzstrafrecht* 264.

158 BGBl 1974/60.

4 Selected Procedural Aspects of Cryptocurrencies

Example 1 X has 60 bitcoins registered in his/her wallet. A creditor of X wants to assert a claim to the bitcoin to satisfy X's debt.

- Is attachment or seizure possible, and under what conditions?
- What difference would it make to the assessment of the example case if X holds the bitcoin with an intermediary?

As stated above, section 326 EO explicitly refers to virtual currencies (virtuelle Währungen). Thus, there can be no doubt that cryptocurrencies like bitcoin are subject to the execution procedure under section 326 et seq. EO.[159] They are legally subject to seizure (Pfändung) when the obliged party receives the prohibition by the court to dispose of or transfer the assets (Verfügungsverbot, section 328(1) EO).[160] To 'physically seize' cryptocurrency, one will have to access the private key; in this connection, the debtor is under the obligation to cooperate (section 27a EO).[161] However, the EO is not unambiguous on this important topic. Commentators suggest the application of section 337 EO on safe deposits (Schrankfach) by analogy to enforce the obliged party's cooperation.[162] Should the private key be stored on a physical device, one can apply section 346 EO on the surrender of chattel.[163] Obviously, identifying and accessing the debtor's cryptocurrency can entail practical problems.[164]

The EO does not contain specific rules on cryptocurrency held with an intermediary. Here, legal seizure can involve the prohibition of performance to the obliged party (Leistungsverbot, section 328(1) EO) directed towards the service provider.[165] Should assistance of the service provider be necessary to access

159 M. Miernicki, *Kryptowerte* pp. 610 et seq.

160 J. Rassi, 'Exekution auf Internetrechte nach der GREx' (2021) *ecolex* 1070, 1073.

161 The legislative materials explicitly refer to the private key, see ErläutRV 770 BlgNR 27. GP 12; for more details see M. Miernicki, *Kryptowerte* pp. 618 et seq.

162 J. Rassi, 'Exekution auf Internetrechte nach der GREx' (2021) *ecolex* 1070, 1073–74 (also referring to section 27a EO and to the administrator's rights based on sections 81, 329 EO); see also M. Trenker, '(Andere) Vermögensrechte nach dem Ministerialentwurf zur Gesamtreform des Exekutionsrechts' (2021) *ecolex* 317, 320.

163 J. Rassi, 'Exekution auf Internetrechte nach der GREx' (2021) *ecolex* 1070, 1074; M. Trenker, '(Andere) Vermögensrechte nach dem Ministerialentwurf zur Gesamtreform des Exekutionsrechts' (2021) *ecolex* 317, 320.

164 Cf. M. Miernicki, *Kryptowerte* pp. 618 et seq.

165 J. Rassi, 'Exekution auf Internetrechte nach der GREx' (2021) *ecolex* 1070, 1073; U. Frauenberger, '§ 326' in A. Deixler-Hübner (ed), *Exekutionsordnung*, LexisNexis, Vienna 36th supp 2022, para 70.

the obliged party's private key, it is suggested that one can rely obliged party's rights vis-à-vis the service provider.[166]

According to section 4(1) EO, the district court competent for the execution procedure is determined by reference to the obliged party's general place of jurisdiction (allgemeiner Gerichtsstand).[167] In cases where the obliged party has no domestic general place of jurisdiction, the court is competent where the assets are located; the location of rights under section 326 et seq. EO is determined according to their closest connection (section 4(2) EO). The legislative materials state that this would be the location of the private key if it is stored on a device or by a service provider.[168] For at least two reasons, this appears to be problematic: First, there is not clarification for cases where the key is stored differently, e.g. online; second, the private key can be stored on multiple devices.[169]

Section 4 EO is also relevant for questions of international jurisdiction (section 27a JN).[170]

Example 2 X opened an account with MontC and has 60 bitcoins registered in his/her account. MontC becomes insolvent.

- Can X, and under what conditions, bring a claim in the insolvency procedure in respect of his/her 60 bitcoins?
- How would the claim of X be classified (proprietary, personal, or other) in the insolvency procedure? Could X claim the return of the deposited bitcoin or only their value in cash?
- What relevance would the specific terms of the agreement between X and MontC have in relation to X's claim?
- Under what conditions would the insolvency rules of your or other legal systems apply (please refer to the relevant private international law rules)?

---

166 J. Rassi, 'Exekution auf Internetrechte nach der GREx' (2021) *ecolex* 1070, 1074 (referring to section 329 EO); M. Trenker, '(Andere) Vermögensrechte nach dem Ministerialentwurf zur Gesamtreform des Exekutionsrechts' (2021) *ecolex* 317, 320 (referring to the rules on safe deposits). See also M. Miernicki, *Kryptowerte* pp. 622 et seq.

167 This is the place of domicile (Wohnsitz), habitual residence (gewöhnlicher Aufenthalt) or seat (section 66, 75 Act on Jurisdiction – Jurisdiktionsnorm RGBl 1895/111).

168 ErläutRV 770 BlgNR 27. GP 6; H. Mini, '§ 4' A. Deixler-Hübner (ed), *Exekutionsordnung*, LexisNexis, Vienna 33th supp 2021, para 15.

169 Cf. J. Rassi, 'Exekution auf Internetrechte nach der GREx' (2021) *ecolex* 1070, 1071–72. See also M. Miernicki, *Kryptowerte* pp. 8 et seq; M. Miernicki and N. Scharl, 'Kollisionsrechtliche Fragen des „digitalen Euro"', *Zeitschrift für Europarecht, internationales Privatrecht und Rechtsvergleichung* 169, 176 et seq.

170 See for further details J. Rassi, 'Exekution auf Internetrechte nach der GREx' (2021) *ecolex* 1070, 1072.

The creditor's options (here: X) depend on the legal relationship between her and MontC; for this purpose, it will be necessary to refer to the agreements concluded between X and MontC.[171] If X has ownership of the cryptocurrency, she is – according to author's opinion – entitled to claim her property and is not restricted by claims of other creditors (dingliche Aussonderung, section 44 Insolvency Act – Insolvenzordnung, IO[172]).[173] A general requirement for the 'Aussonderung' is that the assets can unambiguously be determined.[174]

The situation is more complicated if X only has a claim against the service provider (and no ownership of the cryptocurrency). While some claims (e.g. in connection with fiduciary agreements) might entitle X to claim the cryptocurrency (persönliche Aussonderung, section 44 IO), others do not.[175] Thus, it is necessary to assess the individual case. If X cannot rely on the 'Aussonderung', her claim will, according to the author's opinion, be 'converted' to a monetary claim expressed in euro under section 14 IO to ensure comparability with the other creditors' claims.[176]

Example 3 Z is a company which opened an account with MontC as it accepts payments in bitcoin and other cryptocurrencies. Z's wallet is worth US$200.000 in different cryptocurrencies. Z becomes insolvent.

- How would Z's account be dealt with in the insolvency proceedings? Could some creditors claim priority over the cryptocurrencies registered in Z's account?
- What relevance would the specific terms of the agreement between Z and MontC have in relation to the creditors' claims?

In principle, the insolvency estate consists of all the debtor's assets that are subject to execution (section 2(2) IO). Hence, it is reasonable to assume that cryptocurrency can be part of the insolvency estate if it belongs to the debtor.[177]

---

171 It should be noted that MiCAR protects clients in certain insolvency cases (see esp. article 75(7) MiCAR); see e.g. on this topic M. Miernicki, 'Zum Sonderinsolvenzrecht der Kryptowerte' (2024) *E-Zeitschrift für Wirtschaftsrecht & Digitalisierung* (forthcoming).

172 RGBl 1914/337.

173 M. Miernicki, *Kryptowerte* pp. 650 et seq; T. Weidinger, *Kryptowerte in der Insolvenz*, Verlag Österreich, Vienna 2023, pp. 224 et seq.

174 M. Spitzer, '§ 44' in C. Koller, E. Lovrek and M. Spitzer (eds), *IO*, 2nd ed., Verlag Österreich, Vienna 2023, paras 15–16.

175 See for further details M. Spitzer, '§ 44' in C. Koller, E. Lovrek and M. Spitzer (eds), *IO*, 2nd ed., Verlag Österreich, Vienna 2023, paras 66 et seq.

176 M., Miernicki, Kryptowerte pp. 659 et seq.; see generally G. Musger, '§ 14' in C. Koller, E. Lovrek and M. Spitzer (eds), *IO*, 2nd ed., Verlag Österreich, Vienna 2023, paras 1 et seq.

177 M. Lutschounig, 'Virtuelle Währungen in der Insolvenzmasse' (2022) *Österreichische Juristen-Zeitung* 1179, 1181–82; M. Miernicki, *Kryptowerte* pp. 633 et seq.; T. Weidinger, *Kryptowerte in der Insolvenz*, Verlag Österreich, Vienna 2023, pp. 169 et seq.

As the IO does not contain specific rules on cryptocurrency, the general rules on insolvency proceedings apply. As observed in connection with the EO, identifying and accessing the debtor's cryptocurrency can entail practical problems.[178] Selling the cryptocurrency will often be the most reasonable way to liquidate the cryptocurrency (cf. sections 119 et seq. IO).[179]

It is possible that a creditor claims priority over Z's cryptocurrency if it has been validly pledged. In this case, the creditor has a right to separate satisfaction (Absonderungsrecht, section 48 IO).[180] The same applies to ownership that has been transferred to secure an underlying debt (Sicherungsübereignung, cf. section 10(3) IO).

If Z does not own the cryptocurrency but only has a claim against the MontC, then this claim will form part of the insolvency estate.[181]

The most important rules on international aspects of insolvency proceedings are contained in the 'Insolvency Regulation'.[182]

5 Taxation Principles

As mentioned before, cryptocurrencies are explicitly referred to and defined in the Austrian Act on the Income Tax (section 27b(4) EStG).[183] Income from cryptocurrency is classified as income from capital assets (section 27(1) EStG).[184] Income from cryptocurrency includes current income and income

---

178 Cf. M. Lutschounig, 'Virtuelle Währungen in der Insolvenzmasse' (2022) *Österreichische Juristen-Zeitung* 1179, 1182 et seq.; M. Miernicki, *Kryptowerte* pp. 637 et seq.; T. Weidinger, *Kryptowerte in der Insolvenz*, Verlag Österreich, Vienna 2023, pp. 188 et seq.

179 M. Lutschounig, 'Virtuelle Währungen in der Insolvenzmasse' (2022) *Österreichische Juristen-Zeitung* 1179, 1185; M. Miernicki, *Kryptowerte* pp. 645 et seq.; T. Weidinger, *Kryptowerte in der Insolvenz*, Verlag Österreich, Vienna 2023, pp. 215 et seq.

180 M. Miernicki, *Kryptowerte* pp. 648 seq.; T. Weidinger, *Kryptowerte in der Insolvenz*, Verlag Österreich, Vienna 2023, pp. 244 et seq.

181 M. Miernicki, *Kryptowerte* pp. 635–6.

182 Regulation (EU) 2015/848 of the European Parliament and of the Council of 20 May 2015 on insolvency proceedings [2015] OJ L141/19.

183 See generally, e.g. M. Deichsel, 'Besteuerung von Kryptowährungen gem § 27b EStG – Paradigmenwechsel bei der Besteuerung eines immer mehr an Bedeutung gewinnenden Phänomens' (2022) *Österreichische Steuerzeitung* 31; D. Hohenwarter-Mayr and C. Mittermayer, 'Rechtsbefolgung und Rechtsdurchsetzung bei Kryptowerten im Steuerrecht' (2023) *Zeitschrift für Vergleichende Rechtswissenschaft* 304, 317 et seq.; S. Kirchmayr, 'Zum ertragsteuerlichen Begriff der Kryptowährung', in S. Kirchmayr/M. Miernicki/A. Weilinger/A. Wimmer/A. Wild (eds), Handbuch der Besteuerung von Kryptowährungen, facultas, Vienna 2023, pp. 91 et seq.

184 See on the tax rate and the assessment basis section 27a EStG.

from realized gains (section 27(4a) EStG). Current income includes consideration for the transfer (Überlassung) of cryptocurrency (e.g. loan) or the acquisition of cryptocurrencies through a technical process based on the provision of services for confirming transaction (i.e. mining) (section 27b(2) EStG).[185] At the same time, the act exempts cryptocurrencies acquired in the course of staking, airdrops, bounties or hardforks (section 27b(2) EStG); cryptocurrency so acquired is taxed in accordance with section 27b(3) EStG. The latter provision clarifies the meaning of income from realized gains from cryptocurrencies, including the sale of cryptocurrency and the exchange of cryptocurrency for goods or services. However, exchanging cryptocurrency for other cryptocurrency is no realization within the meaning of the act (section 27b(3)(2) EStG).

6 Conclusions

The overview of the applicable regulatory laws has shown that cryptocurrencies – in contrast to several other forms of crypto-assets – are less often covered by existing Austrian legislation than one might think. However, the MiCAR will soon introduce a comprehensive legislative framework; it remains to be seen how the new rules will impact the European and Austrian crypto scene. However, it is likely that certain grey areas will remain, especially with regard to the qualification of crypto-assets as financial instruments.

With regard to private law, the analysis revealed that the Austrian ABGB is – despite its age – arguably flexible enough to provide reasonable answers to the most pressing issues observed in connection with cryptocurrencies. From this perspective, there is no immediate need for legislative action on the national level, albeit legal uncertainty will subsist to a certain degree until this is confirmed by the OGH. Furthermore, it appears that legislative action is indeed necessary in the area of dematerialized securities[186] but that is a topic for another study.

A delicate question is to what extent international harmonization of the laws on cryptocurrencies (and crypto-assets) is desirable. On the one hand, for instance, as most areas of property remain unharmonized on the EU level, one can ask why exactly crypto-assets require harmonization in this respect.[187]

185 ErläutRV 1293 BlgNR 27. GP 11.

186 See for a detailed account M. Miernicki, *Kryptowerte* pp. 663 et seq.; M. Miernicki, 'Tokenisierung und privates Wertpapierrecht' (2023) *Österreichische Jurist:innenzeitung* 582; M. Miernicki, 'Die Digitalisierung der Wertpapiere als Aufgabe des „Registerrechts"' (2024) *Wirtschaftsrechtliche Blätter* (forthcoming).

187 Cf. M. Miernicki, *Regulation of Initial Coin Offerings in the United States and the European Union*, TTLF Working Papers No. 69, Stanford-Vienna Transatlantic Technology

On the other hand, the pressing issue of private international law is certainly worth considering as a 'candidate' for harmonization (even beyond the borders of the European Union). A further area that might be interest for lawmakers – especially on the European level – might be consumer protection. In this connection, for instance, it should be noted that article 13 MiCAR contains a rule on a withdrawal right for retail holders. At the same time, however, it is unclear why the 'Digital Content Directive'[188] contains an explicit reference to virtual currencies (recital 23), while the 'Sale of Goods Directive'[189] does not provide for a corresponding rule. It is doubtful whether treating cryptocurrencies differently in this context is warranted.[190]

Law Forum, 2020, pp. 41 et seq https://law.stanford.edu/publications/no-69-initial-coin-offerings-in-the-united-states-and-the-european-union-development-status-quo-and-the-path-forward/.

188 Directive (EU) 2019/770 of the European Parliament and of the Council of 20 May 2019 on certain aspects concerning contracts for the supply of digital content and digital service [2019] OJ L 136/1.

189 Directive (EU) 2019/771 of the European Parliament and of the Council of 20 May 2019 on certain aspects concerning contracts for the sale of goods, amending Regulation (EU) 2017/2394 and Directive 2009/22/EC, and repealing Directive 1999/44/EC [2019] OJ L136/28.

190 Cf. for the problems arising in this connection M. Miernicki, *Kryptowerte* pp. 590 et seq.

Canada (Québec)

Pr Patrick Mignault et Pr Arthur Oulaï

1 Introduction

La présente étude porte la situation juridique des cryptomonnaies au Canada dans une perspective essentiellement fédérale et québécoise. Le terme « cryptomonnaie » ou l'expression « monnaie virtuelle » sont utilisés pour désigner des actifs numériques reposant sur la technologie de la chaîne de blocs. Sa définition dans ce texte fera appel à sa perception tant par les autorités canadiennes (tant fédérales que provinciales) que par les auteurs. L'Agence du Revenu du Canada, autorité fédérale chargée de l'application des lois fiscales, définit, pour sa part, la monnaie virtuelle comme « un actif numérique qui peut être utilisé pour acheter ou vendre des biens ou des services. La cryptomonnaie est une monnaie virtuelle fondée sur la chaîne de blocs »[1]. Dans le prolongement des préoccupations fiscales, qui comptent parmi les angles d'analyse des cryptomonnaies les plus explorées au Canada, l'expression cryptomonnaie est vue comme « [faisant] référence à la monnaie numérique, créée par des ordinateurs, stockée électroniquement et disponible à des fins d'investissement ou comme substitut aux monnaies traditionnelles pour l'achat de biens ou de services. [...]. Les transactions en cryptomonnaie se font via une chaîne de blocs »[2].

Au-delà de cette approche qui met en évidence la composante ou la dimension technologique, la définition de la cryptomonnaie ajoute aussi un élément qui porte sur l'organisation de la relation entre les acteurs impliqués dans la transaction, notamment sur l'absence d'intermédiaire. L'un des traits caractéristiques de la cryptomonnaie tient au recours à un mécanisme d'émission décentralisé faisant appel à une certaine désintermédiation financière. Les auteurs Nicole L'Heureux et Marc Lacoursière, prenant l'exemple de la cryptomonnaie Bitcoin, précisent à cet égard: « Le système Bitcoin est décentralisé, ce qui signifie qu'il n'y a pas un émetteur unique de Bitcoin, comme cela est le cas pour les monnaies fiduciaires. Ceci tient de la philosophie de ce concept, inspiré des travaux de l'économiste autrichien Friederich A. Hayek,

---

1 Gouvernement du Canada – Agence du Revenu du Canada, «Monnaie virtuelle» (26 juin 2019), en ligne: https://www.canada.ca/fr/agence-revenu/programmes/a-propos-agence-revenu-canada-arc/observation/monnaie-numerique.html (Date d'accès : 12 septembre 2023).

2 CCH AnswerConnect, « Cryptomonnaie – D'un point de vue fiscal », Wolters Kluwer, 2021, p. 1.

 | DOI:10.1163/9789004722507_005

lequel argumentait que le gouvernement ne devait pas avoir le monopole de l'émission de l'argent »[3]. L'absence d'intermédiaire financier à l'émission concerne dans un premier temps la mise à l'écart de la banque centrale. « Les cryptoactifs sont créés en ligne. Ils s'appuient sur un réseau décentralisé de pair-à-pair. Les « pairs » de ce réseau sont les personnes qui participent aux transactions de cryptoactifs. Leurs ordinateurs constituent le réseau. »[4]. Elle concerne, d'autre part, les institutions financières privées. « Les institutions financières, comme les banques ou les coopératives de crédit, ne participent pas à la gestion ou à la supervision de la monnaie numérique »[5]. Les autorités de la Banque du Canada résument ainsi la particularité des cryptomonnaies : « La principale différence est qu'il n'y a pas d'entité émettrice à l'origine de ces monnaies : ni banque centrale, ni institution financière, ni plateforme Internet. Elles sont émises de manière décentralisée dans un réseau informatique de pair-à-pair, sur lequel personne n'a autorité, et dont les utilisateurs sont en rapport direct les uns avec les autres, un peu comme dans un site de clavardage »[6]. Une fois émise sur le marché, elle devient ensuite sujette à différentes transactions sur le marché secondaire, et alors, des intermédiaires peuvent s'ajouter pour les réaliser.

S'il faut nuancer l'importance accordée à l'absence d'implication des intermédiaires financiers à l'émission, et en particulier des banques centrales, dans une définition pérenne de la cryptomonnaie, l'émission d'une monnaie numérique ne semble pas inscrite pour le moment dans le programme de la banque centrale canadienne[7]. Néanmoins, la Banque du Canada reste à l'écoute de

---

3 Ces deux auteurs poursuivent : « Plus généralement, les partisans de Bitcoin affirment que Bitcoin met un terme au monopole bancaire de l'émission de l'argent, ils critiquent que la réserve obligatoire (fractionnaire) des banques est néfaste et ils favorisent plutôt le concept inspiré de l'ancien étalon-or, qui n'était sous le contrôle exclusif d'aucune autorité ». Nicole L'Heureux et Marc Lacoursière, *Droit bancaire*, 5e édition, Montréal, Éditions Yvon Blais, 2017, p. 876.

4 Gouvernement du Canada – Agence de la consommation en matière financière du Canada, «Monnaie numérique» (3 mai 2021), en ligne : <https://www.canada.ca/fr/agence-consommation-matiere-financiere/services/paiment/monnaie-numerique.html> (Date d'accès: 12 septembre 2023).

5 *Id.*

6 Grahame Johnson et Lukasz Pomorski, « Séance d'information sur les monnaies électroniques » (2014), Banque du Canada, p. 8, en ligne : <https://www.banqueducanada.ca/wp-content/uploads/2014/04/discours_senat.pdf> (Date d'accès : 12 septembre 2023).

7 Marc Lacoursière, « Les enjeux des modes de paiement quant à la pratique notariale », (2020) 2 *Revue du notariat* 274–275.

l'évolution de la situation des cryptomonnaies et n'exclut pas l'émission éventuelle d'une monnaie numérique[8].

Le *Règlement sur la déclaration des opérations douteuses – recyclage des produits de la criminalité et financement des activités terroristes*[9] dans sa définition de l'expression « monnaie virtuelle » à l'article 1(2) met en exergue un élément déjà mentionné plus haut, soit la cryptographie. Cette disposition précise ainsi

> 1(2) *monnaie virtuelle* s'entend :
> a. de la représentation numérique de valeur pouvant être utilisée comme mode de paiement ou à titre de placement, qui n'est pas une monnaie fiduciaire et qui peut être facilement échangée contre des fonds ou contre une autre monnaie virtuelle qui peut être facilement échangée contre des fonds;
> b. de la clé privée d'un système de chiffrement permettant à une personne ou entité d'avoir accès à une telle représentation numérique de valeur. (*virtual currency*)

Le paragraphe (b) de cette disposition fait ainsi ressortir la notion de cryptographie, une des composantes de la cryptologie, cette dernière étant présentée comme la « science des écritures secrètes et des messages chiffrés »[10]. Ce passage rejoint ainsi les différentes définitions précitées dans la mise en évidence de l'importance de la sécurité en matière de cryptomonnaie. Il faut ajouter la dimension de l'anonymat à l'ensemble de ces éléments de définition des cryptomonnaies, car celles-ci «ne sont pas contrôlées par les banques centrales ni par aucun pays; elles peuvent être échangées de manière relativement anonyme »[11].

8 Voir Presse canadienne, « Des implications considérables si la Banque du Canada émet sa propre cryptomonnaie », *Radio-Canada*, 4 janvier 2022, en ligne : <https://ici.radio-canada.ca/nouvelle/1851653/banque-canada-freeland-cryptomonnaie-bitcoin > (Date d'accès: 12 septembre 2023).

9 *Règlement sur la déclaration des opérations douteuses - recyclage des produits de la criminalité et financement des activités terroristes*, DORS 2001-317, art. 1(2).

10 Office Québécois de la langue française, « cryptologie », en ligne : https://www.oqlf.gouv.qc.ca/.

11 Gouvernement du Canada – Agence du Revenu du Canada, «Monnaie virtuelle» (26 juin 2019), en ligne : <https://www.canada.ca/fr/agence-revenu/programmes/a-propos-agence-revenu-canada-arc/observation/monnaie-numerique.html> (Date d'accès: 12 septembre 2023).

2 Aspects de la cryptomonnaie sous l'angle du droit civil québécois

La question de la cryptomonnaie a été peu ou pas étudié en droit civil québécois. L'on peut néanmoins explorer la cryptomonnaie par le prisme de quelques notions civilistes comme celles du bien, du paiement ou encore du contrat de vente ou d'échange.

2.1 *La cryptomonnaie comme un « bien »*

En droit québécois, il n'y a pas d'étude civiliste qui se penche spécifiquement sur la question de la cryptomonnaie comme un bien. Néanmoins, quelques auteurs se sont plus largement intéressés à la propriété virtuelle et se sont interrogés à savoir si la notion de biens incorporels prévue dans le *Code civil du Québec* peut être étendue aux objets dits virtuels. Les auteurs Stéphane Gilker et Charles Lupien, en se basant sur la conception économique de la valeur de l'objet de propriété, soutiennent que la propriété virtuelle est une forme de propriété au sens du Code civil. Ils reconnaissent dans la propriété virtuelle un bien incorporel « dans la mesure où une valeur économique s'attache à ce dernier et, possiblement, où il existe une empreinte matérielle au travers de laquelle cet Objet Virtuel peut être discerné ou appréhendé »[12].

Le *Code civil du Québec* n'offre pas de définition de « biens ». Il précise seulement que les biens, tant corporels qu'incorporels, peuvent être meubles ou immeubles[13]. Lorsqu'un bien ne peut être qualifié d'immeuble selon la loi, il est considéré comme un bien meuble. Face à cette absence de définition de la notion de biens, une vision large est depuis longtemps mise de l'avant par la doctrine :

> « In sum, all things and rights that can constitute the assets of a person's patrimony, all patrimonial assets and rights, are property. This include all rights, whether real or personal, that can be transferred by contract »[14].

---

12 Stéphane Gilker et Charles Lupien, « Le droit de propriété dans les mondes virtuels en droit québécois », Service de la formation continue du Barreau du Québec, *Développements récents en droit du divertissement*, Volume 311, Éditions Yvon Blais, Montréal, 2009, p. 199.

13 *Code civil du Québec*, chapitre CCQ-1991, art. 899 (ci-après, « C.c.Q. »).

14 Voir John B. Claxton, The Corporate Trust Deed under Quebec Law: Article 2692 of the Civil Code of Quebec, (1997) 42 *McGill L.J.* 797, p. 845. L'auteur réfère à Pierre-Basile Mignault, *Droit civil canadien*, vol. 2, Montréal, C. Theoret, 1896, p. 389; André Montpetit et Gaston Taillefer, *Traité de droit civil du Québec*, vol. 3, Montréal, Wilson & Lafleur, 1945, p. 16, Denis-Claude Lamontagne, *Biens et propriété*, 2e édition, Cowansville, Éditions Yvon

Quant à Dobah Carré, elle constate que la thèse de la reconnaissance de la propriété virtuelle en tant que propriété classique pourrait, certes, trouver une pertinence en la matière,[15] mais elle invite à considérer également les règles relatives au droit d'auteur pour mieux traduire la situation juridique des objets virtuels. Elle le précise dans le passage suivant :

> « Puisque l'hypothèse d'admettre en droit interne un droit réel sur un objet virtuel, qui n'existe pas, est très controversée, on s'est alors posé la question de savoir si on peut appréhender la notion de la propriété virtuelle sous l'analyse de la propriété intellectuelle. On a ainsi analysé la définition de l'objet virtuel au regard de celle d'« œuvre de l'esprit » qui est protégée par la loi et la jurisprudence en matière de droit d'auteur. On a pu conclure de cette analyse que les objets virtuels peuvent être qualifiés d'œuvres et se voir protégés par les règles de droit d'auteur si la condition d'originalité de l'œuvre est respectée. Cette condition sera plus ou moins facile à prouver pour l'utilisateur selon le mode de création « traditionnel » ou « moderne » des biens virtuels qu'il aura utilisé dépendamment du monde virtuel *avec* ou *sans* script auquel il sera inscrit »[16].

Cette position ne saurait toutefois constituer une disqualification de la possible existence d'un droit réel ou personnel sur des objets virtuels et par voie de conséquence sur des cryptomonnaies. Autrement dit, l'expression d'une préférence exprimée pour un recours à l'analyse sous l'angle de la propriété intellectuelle n'est pas antinomique de la présence d'un droit réel ou personnel en la matière.

En droit civil québécois, la monnaie virtuelle, actif intangible, devrait recevoir la qualification de bien meuble incorporel pouvant faire l'objet d'un droit de propriété en vertu du *Code civil du Québec* :

> « Ainsi, l'existence de l'objet virtuel en tant que valeur et la vitalité du marché économique de leurs transactions ou «marchandisations»

Blais, 1995, p.1; Madeleine Cantin-Cumyn, « The Trust in a Civilian Context : The Quebec Case », (1994) 3 *Journal of International Trust and Corporate Planning* (U.K.) 69–77, p. 71.

15 Dobah Carré, « La nature juridique de la propriété virtuelle », (2018) 96 *Revue du Barreau Canadien*, p. 239.

16 « Toutefois, en droit civil, la thèse de la reconnaissance de la *propriété virtuelle* en tant que propriété classique n'est pas à bannir. Elle dépend finalement de l'évolution de la notion de propriété qui sera faite par les tribunaux et le législateur dans un sens plus souple, plus moderne, pour s'ouvrir à de nouveaux biens immatériels ». Dobah Carré, « La nature juridique de la propriété virtuelle », (2018) 96 *Revue du Barreau Canadien*, p. 239.

permettent d'inclure les «objets virtuels» dans la catégorie des «biens meubles incorporels», tout comme le droit positif québécois le fait pour les actifs intangibles comme la monnaie, les valeurs mobilières ou le know-how, dès lors qu'ils ont une valeur économique et sont appropriables. De ce fait, puisque les biens virtuels peuvent probablement faire l'objet d'un droit de propriété en vertu du Code civil, il s'agira de comparer les caractéristiques de la propriété virtuelle avec celles de la propriété dite «classique» »[17].

Il en va de même en *common law*, une personne qui fait l'acquisition de cryptomonnaies pour lesquelles elle obtient des certificats de propriété pourrait se voir attribuer ainsi un droit de propriété intangible :

> « [...] the authors have previously shown that an investor who purchases bitcoin directly from a miner, or an exchange, and receives the credentials of ownership upon performance of the contract of purchase, acquires an intangible property right »[18].

2.2 *La cryptomonnaie comme une forme de paiement*

Par ailleurs, le débat sur la qualification juridique des cryptomonnaies en monnaie a eu des échos au Canada. À cet égard, il faut d'abord rappeler les principes généraux en matière de paiement en droit québécois. Selon l'art 1553 du *Code civil du Québec*, par paiement, l'on entend non seulement le versement d'une somme d'argent pour acquitter une obligation, mais aussi l'exécution même de ce qui est l'objet de l'obligation.

Pour sa part, l'art 3(1) de la *Loi sur la monnaie*[19] est sans équivoque : « l'unité monétaire du Canada est le dollar ». Les cryptomonnaies ne sont pas ainsi reconnues comme des unités monétaires au Canada. Plusieurs auteurs se fondent sur cette loi pour dénier toute qualification de monnaie aux unités de cryptomonnaies au Canada[20].

---

17 Dobah Carré, « La nature juridique de la propriété virtuelle », (2018) 96 *Revue du Barreau Canadien*, pp. 207–208; Paul Van Den Bulck, « Le régime juridique des avatars créés dans le cadre des jeux vidéo » (2007) 24 *Propriétés intellectuelles* 279, p. 280; Sylvio Normand, « Les nouveaux biens » (2004) 106 *R Notariat* 177, pp. 189–191.

18 Bradley Crawford, «The Law of Bitcoin» (2017) 59 *Canadian Business Law Journal* p. 408.

19 L.R.C. 1985 c. C-52, art. 3(1).

20 Bradley Crawford, «The Law of Bitcoin» (2017) 59 *Canadian Business Law Journal*, p. 403., Oksana Panova, Yulia Leheza, Andrii Ivanytsia, Volodymyr Marchenko and Vitalii Oliukha, «International Models of Legal Regulation and Ethics of Cryptocurrency Use: Country Review» (2019) 22 *Journal of Legal, Ethical and Regulatory Issues*, p. 3 Matthew P. Ponsford, «A Comparative Analysis of Bitcoin and Other Decentralised Virtual

Quant à la *Loi sur la Banque du Canada*, son article 25(1) accorde le pouvoir exclusif d'émission de billets à la Banque centrale canadienne[21].

Ces dispositions accordent une place exclusive au dollar canadien au détriment de toute autre unité monétaire de même qu'à la Banque du Canada. Des auteurs se fondent sur ces dispositions pour non seulement refuser la qualification de monnaie aux cryptomonnaies[22], mais aussi pour souligner le fait qu'elles n'ont pas cours légal au Canada[23]. Cette dernière position est celle adoptée aussi par des autorités réglementaires au Québec[24].

La question de la qualification des cryptomonnaies à titre de monnaie doit toutefois être distinguée de celle relative à leur pouvoir libératoire envers un débiteur notamment. Même si ces questions entretiennent un lien, elles méritent d'être séparées pour les besoins de l'analyse juridique. En ce qui concerne le pouvoir libératoire, l'article 8 (1) de la *Loi sur la monnaie*[25] prévoit :

> 8 (1) Sous réserve des autres dispositions du présent article, les offres de paiement ont pouvoir libératoire si elles sont effectuées avec :
> a. les pièces qui ont cours légal en vertu de l'article 7;
> b. les billets qui ont cours légal en vertu de l'article 7.1.

Le *Code civil du Québec* s'inscrit, en quelque sorte, dans le sillage de cette disposition de la *Loi sur la monnaie*. Son article 1564 alinéa 1 indique :

> 1564. Le débiteur d'une somme d'argent est libéré par la remise au créancier de la somme nominale prévue, en monnaie ayant cours légal lors du paiement.

Currencies; Legal Regulation in the People's Republic of China, Canada, and the United States» (2015) 9 *Hong Kong Journal of Legal Studies*, p. 34 et p. 41.

21 L.R.C (1985), ch. B-2

22 Prec., note 25.

23 Joncheres souligne ainsi que « [s]i seul le dollar canadien dans son ensemble a une valeur libératoire au Canada, cela implique que seul le dollar canadien a cours légal au Canada. On peut en déduire que le Bitcoin et les autres altcoins n'ont donc pas cours légal au Canada », Erwan Joncheres, *Encadrement juridique des monnaies numériques - Bitcoin et autres cryptomonnaies*, Mémoire de Maîtrise en droit des technologies de l'information, Faculté de droit de l'Université de Montréal, 2015, p. 56. Voir aussi Bradley Crawford, «The Law of Bitcoin» (2017) 59 *Canadian Business Law Journal*, p. 404.

24 Voir Autorité des marchés financiers, «Comment fonctionnent les cryptoactifs?», en ligne: <https://lautorite.qc.ca/grand-public/investissements/les-cryptos/comment-fonctionnent-les-cryptoactifs> et Revenu Québec, «Monnaie virtuelle», en ligne: <https://www.revenuquebec.ca/fr/une-mission-des-actions/vous-aider-a-vous-conformer/quest-ce-que-leconomie-numerique/monnaie-virtuelle/>.

25 L.R.C. 1985 c. C-52, art. 8(1).

> Il est aussi libéré par la remise de la somme prévue au moyen d'un mandat postal, d'un chèque fait à l'ordre du créancier et certifié par un établissement financier exerçant son activité au Québec ou d'un autre effet de paiement offrant les mêmes garanties au créancier, ou, encore, si le créancier est en mesure de l'accepter, au moyen d'une carte de crédit ou d'un virement de fonds à un compte que détient le créancier dans un établissement financier.

Quelques nuances pourraient toutefois être apportées sur la question du caractère libératoire. Déjà en 1938, la Cour suprême du Canada semblait favoriser une approche libérale en la matière[26]. Dans son arrêt *Reference Re Alberta Statutes*, la Cour ne limite pas ce pouvoir libératoire à la seule monnaie ayant cours légal[27]. Un certain esprit libéral semble se dégager aussi de la lecture de l'article 1564 du Code civil du Québec[28]. Une partie de la doctrine paraît souscrire à cette approche libérale[29]. La banque centrale canadienne semble, pour sa part, prendre acte de la diversification des moyens de paiement qui en résulte :

> « Au cours des dernières décennies, au fil des avancées technologiques, les méthodes de paiement des consommateurs ont changé énormément. Elles sont passées essentiellement des supports papier, comme les billets de banque et les chèques, aux supports numériques, comme les cartes de débit ou de crédit, les cartes prépayées, les paiements mobiles (p. ex., Apple Pay et Google Pay) et les transferts électroniques de fonds (p. ex., Virement Interac). On constate même l'utilisation, quoique très limitée, de cryptomonnaies (p. ex., le bitcoin, le litecoin et le Zcash). Le Canada ne fait pas exception à cette tendance mondiale »[30].

---

26 Marc Lacoursière, « Les défis juridiques du paiement virtuel », Service de la formation continue du Barreau du Québec, *Développements récents en droit bancaire*, Volume 427, Éditions Yvon Blais, Montréal, p. 28.

27 *Reference Re Alberta Statutes – The Bank Taxation Act; The Credit of Alberta Regulation Act; And The Accurante News and Information Act*, [1938] R.C.S. 100, p. 116; Voir aussi : M. Lacoursière, *id.*, pp. 28–29

28 Marc Lacoursière, « Les défis juridiques du paiement virtuel », Service de la formation continue du Barreau du Québec, Développements récents en droit bancaire, Volume 427, Éditions Yvon Blais, Montréal, p. 29.

29 Bradley Crawford, « Is Electronic Money Really Money? », (1997) 12 *Banking and Finance Law Review*, p. 402; Guy David, « Money in Canadian Law », (1986) 65 *Revue du Barreau canadien* 192, p. 223; Voir aussi Marc Lacoursière, « Les défis juridiques du paiement virtuel », Service de la formation continue du Barreau du Québec, *Développements récents en droit bancaire*, Volume 427, Éditions Yvon Blais, Montréal, p. 29.

30 Banque du Canada, «Plans de prévoyance concernant une monnaie numérique de banque centrale» (25 février 2020), p. 2, en ligne : < https://www.banqueducanada.ca/2020/02/plans-prevoyance-concernant-monnaie-numerique-banque-centrale/ >.

Enfin, la *Loi sur la monnaie*[31] présente également une ouverture qui mériterait d'être soulignée dans la perspective des développements futurs concernant les cryptomonnaies. Son art 13 (1) prévoit :

> 13 (1) Les actes et opérations, notamment contrats, ventes, paiements, effets, billets, titres et valeurs, relatifs à une somme d'argent ou prévoyant soit le paiement d'une somme d'argent, soit l'obligation d'en payer une, se font d'après la monnaie canadienne, s'ils ne se font pas suivant :
> a. soit la monnaie d'un pays étranger;
> b. soit une unité de compte définie par rapport aux monnaies de plusieurs pays.

Cette disposition a conduit les autorités fiscales canadiennes à sortir les cryptomonnaies de la sphère de la monnaie. Ainsi :

> « Dans l'interprétation technique 2013-0514701I7, *Bitcoins*, datée du 23 décembre 2013, l'ARC a déclaré que les monnaies virtuelles, comme les bitcoins, ne sont pas considérées comme une monnaie émise par un gouvernement d'un pays, comme le dollar américain, pour obtenir ce titre, ils sont généralement traités comme une marchandise aux fins de la *Loi de l'impôt sur le revenu*. Cette position a par la suite été réaffirmée dans l'interprétation technique 2014-0525191E5, *Virtual Currencies* (*bitcoins*) et au paragraphe 1.12 du feuillet S3-F10-C1, *Placements admissibles – REER, REEE, FERR, REEI et CÉLI* »[32].

Ce passage de l'interprétation faite par les autorités fiscales montre toutefois que les développements à l'étranger quant à l'adoption des cryptomonnaies par des gouvernements étrangers pourraient avoir des impacts au Canada. Par ailleurs, la *Loi canadienne sur les paiements*[33] prévoit, à son article 37(1), que:

> 37 (1) Le ministre peut, s'il est d'avis qu'il est dans l'intérêt public de le faire, désigner un système de paiement qui, à son avis :
> a. soit est de portée nationale ou l'est dans une large mesure;
> b. soit joue un rôle important pour favoriser les opérations sur le marché financier canadien ou l'économie canadienne.

---

31 L.R.C. 1985 c. C-52, art. 13(1).

32 CCH AnswerConnect, prec., note 2, pp. 1–2.

33 L.R.C. (1985), ch. C-21, art. 37(1).

L'art 37(2) de la même loi précise aussi que :

> 37 (2) Pour décider s'il est dans l'intérêt public de désigner un système de paiement, les facteurs suivants doivent être pris en compte :
> a. la sécurité financière qu'offre le système de paiement à ses participants et ses usagers;
> b. l'efficacité et la compétitivité des systèmes de paiement au Canada;
> c. l'intérêt du système financier canadien.

L'ensemble de ces dispositions contient les paramètres de développements futurs concernant le régime juridique des cryptomonnaies au Canada.

2.3 *Les transactions sur cryptomonnaie : un contrat de vente ou un contrat d'échange?*

En droit civil, cette qualification juridique de « bien » des cryptomonnaies est la porte d'entrée à l'encadrement de différentes transactions les impliquant. La notion de « bien » est fondamentale à plusieurs actes juridiques ou contrats du *Code civil du Québec* : la fiducie (C.c.Q., art. 1260 et s.), l'administration du bien d'autrui (C.c.Q., art. 1299 et s.), le contrat de vente (C.c.Q., art. 1708 et s.) ou d'échange (C.c.Q., art. 1795 et s.), le contrat de prêt (C.c.Q., art. 2312 et s.) ou les hypothèques (C.c.Q., art. 2660)[34]. Parmi les transactions les plus fréquentes sur les cryptomonnaies entre des utilisateurs, elles pourront constituer des contrats de vente ou d'échange. Le régime juridique applicable à la transaction dépend alors du mode de paiement des cryptomonnaies. Pour qu'une transaction puisse être qualifiée de contrat de vente, la valeur des cryptomonnaies (le bien transigé) doit être payée en argent :

> 1708. La vente est le contrat par lequel une personne, le vendeur, transfère « la propriété d'un bien à une autre personne, l'acheteur, moyennant un prix en argent que cette dernière s'oblige à payer ».

Comme les cryptomonnaies ne constituent pas des monnaies en droit canadien et québécois[35], si l'achat d'une cryptomonnaie se règle en contrepartie d'une autre cryptomonnaie ou qu'une cryptomonnaie est utilisée comme un moyen de paiement, il s'agira plutôt d'un échange (C.c.Q., art. 1795 C.c.Q.). En effet, le

---

34 Voir notamment l'intéressante note publiée par Norton Rose Fulbright sur le cryptoprêt : Xavier Foccorouille-Ménard, « Cryptoprêt : incidences juridiques pour la constitution de sûretés sur des cryptomonnaies », 20 avril 2022.

35 *Loi sur la monnaie*, L.R.C. 1985 c. C-52, art. 3 et 7; *Code civil du Québec*, art. 1564.

contrat d'échange se distingue de la vente en ce que les parties « [...] se transfèrent respectivement la propriété d'un bien, autre qu'une somme d'argent ». L'échange n'implique aucun transfert d'argent comptant en monnaie ayant cours légal. Malgré le fait que le contrat d'échange offre des garanties similaires au contrat de vente (C.c.Q., art. 1798), il s'agit néanmoins d'un régime juridique distinct sur l'obligation de remise (C.c.Q., art. 1796) et de dommages-intérêts (C.c.Q., art. 1797).

Avant de conclure trop rapidement à un contrat de vente ou d'échange, une condition critique pour en appliquer le régime juridique associé à ces contrats est l'exigence d'un transfert de propriété. En l'absence d'un transfert de propriété d'un bien (ou d'un démembrement du droit de propriété), il ne peut y avoir un contrat de vente ou d'échange. Il pourrait alternativement s'agir d'un contrat de prêt ou de louage ou d'un contrat innomé en droit civil[36]. En effet, outre par exemple, dans le cas d'une réserve de propriété lors de la vente, ce transfert de propriété se réalise au moment de l'échange des consentements entre les parties[37].

En matière de cryptomonnaies, ce transfert de propriété s'opèrera par le biais d'un registre d'opération sur la chaîne de blocs :

> Bitcoin est présenté par Nakamoto comme une solution de rechange au « système de paiement traditionnel. Le système traditionnel s'appuie sur des tiers (*trust-based model*) qui agissent comme intermédiaires dans les transactions financières, comme les banques ou les services de traitement de paiements (comme PayPal), afin de garder un registre des transactions et garantir que la partie qui transfère de l'argent a les fonds nécessaires et que le destinataire va recevoir le paiement. Ces tiers imposent souvent des frais pour leurs services, et les transactions sont réversibles. Bitcoin offre une solution permettant d'éviter les frais additionnels et limitant la possibilité d'annuler une transaction. En éliminant l'intermédiaire de la transaction Bitcoin, les participants au réseau poste-à-poste servent de registres et de vérificateurs des transactions[54]. Les transactions Bitcoin sont enregistrées de manière permanente sur le *blockchain* »[55].
>
> « Les transactions sont enregistrées sur le *blockchain* sous forme de blocs, qui se lient les uns aux autres de façon chronologique, c'est-à-dire qui s'ajoutent dans l'ordre dans lequel les transactions ont été effectuées

---

36 *In re St-Pierre : Mière, division détail inc. c. Raymond Chabot inc.*, J.E. 2003-46992 (C.A.), confirmant J.E. 2000-1196, REJB 2000-19438 (C.S.).

37 Jacques Deslauriers, *Vente, louage, contrat d'entreprise ou de service*, 2e édition, Montréal, Wilson & Lafleur, 2013, par. 9, 12 et 27.

> et validées[56]. Chaque bloc contient quatre renseignements en lien avec la transaction : (1) la « signature » du propriétaire original, (2) les détails de la dernière transaction, (3) l'information d'horodatage (*timestamp*) indiquant le moment où le bloc a été créé et (4) la « signature » ou clé publique[57] du nouveau propriétaire ou destinataire»[58,59].

Si la transaction sur la cryptomonnaie implique un transfert effectif de propriété entre des parties, nous pourrons être en présence d'un contrat de vente ou d'échange en fonction du moyen de paiement des cryptomonnaies. Toutefois, il semble bien que différentes transactions sur la cryptomonnaie ne conduisent pas à un transfert de propriété. Dans ces cas d'espèce, nous verrons que les autorités canadiennes en matière de valeurs mobilières peuvent y voir une forme d'investissement soumise au cadre législatif en matière de valeurs mobilières ou encore de produits dérivés. Nous approfondirons cet aspect à la section suivante (3.3. L'encadrement de la cryptomonnaie par le droit des valeurs mobilières).

3 L'émergence d'une réglementation réactive de la cryptomonnaie

Le Canada ne mise actuellement pas sur un cadre réglementaire global pour régir les enjeux juridiques touchant la cryptomonnaie. Toutefois, au cours des dernières années, nous assistons à l'émergence d'une réglementation réactive de la cryptomonnaie à travers différentes lois et règlements pour répondre aux défis qu'elle soulève. Ces dispositions touchent tout particulièrement le recyclage des produits de la criminalité (3.1), la fiscalité (3.2) ainsi que le domaine des valeurs mobilières et des produits financiers dérivés (3.3).

3.1 *Le recyclage des produits de la criminalité*

Mise en place pour contrer le développement des activités criminelles au Canada, la *Loi sur le recyclage des produits de la criminalité et le financement des activités terroristes*[38] (ci-après, la « LRPC ») a été modifiée en 2014 pour répondre à l'émergence des cryptomonnaies et étendre l'application de cette loi aux personnes et entités faisant le commerce de monnaies virtuelles[39] au

---

38 *Loi sur le recyclage des produits de la criminalité et le financement des activités terroristes*, L.C. 2000, ch. 17.

39 Le *Règlement sur le recyclage des produits de la criminalité et le financement des activités terroristes* (DORS/2002-184) définit la monnaie virtuelle à l'article 1(2) comme : (a) de la représentation numérique de valeur pouvant être utilisée comme mode de paiement ou

Canada. La Loi ne s'applique qu'aux entreprises qui négocient des monnaies virtuelles, et non aux crypto-actifs eux-mêmes ou aux interfaces numériques qui permettent la détention de crypto-actifs ou des interactions entre des particuliers[40]. Les dispositions modifiées visaient ainsi à soumettre ces personnes ou entités à des exigences relatives à l'identification des clients, à la tenue de documents, à l'enregistrement des institutions financières et des intermédiaires ainsi qu'à l'information relative aux opérations de cryptomonnaies effectuées[41].

Plus précisément, le champ d'application de la LRPC a été élargi à de nombreuses personnes et entités. Elle vise notamment les banques, les coopératives de crédit, les caisses d'épargne et de crédit, les associations coopératives de crédit, les sociétés d'assurance-vie, les sociétés de fiducie et de prêt, ainsi que les entités autorisées en vertu de la législation provinciale à se livrer au commerce des valeurs mobilières ou d'autres instruments financiers, ou à la fourniture de services de gestion de portefeuille et de conseils en placement. La LRPC touche maintenant aussi les personnes ou entités se livrant au « commerce de monnaie virtuelle » et assujettit les entreprises procédant au transfert de monnaie virtuelle à certaines obligations :

> 5 La présente partie s'applique aux personnes et entités suivantes : [...]
> h) les personnes et entités qui ont un établissement au Canada et qui se livrent à la fourniture de l'un des services suivants : [...]
> (iv) le commerce de monnaie virtuelle, [...]
> h.1) les personnes et entités qui n'ont pas d'établissement au Canada et qui se livrent à la fourniture, à l'intention de personnes ou entités se trouvant au Canada, de l'un des services ci-après et qui les fournissent à leurs clients se trouvant au Canada : [...]
> (iv) le commerce de monnaie virtuelle.

à titre de placement, qui n'est pas une monnaie fiduciaire et qui peut être facilement échangée contre des fonds ou contre une autre monnaie virtuelle qui peut être facilement échangée contre des fonds; (b) de la clé privée d'un système de chiffrement permettant *à* une personne ou entité d'avoir accès *à* une telle représentation numérique de valeur.

40 Ryan Clements et Virginia Torrie, "Crypto Asset Regulation in Canada: Developments and Governance Considerations", (2023) 39 *Banking and Finance Law Review* 345, p. 358.

41 *Loi portant exécution de certaines dispositions du budget déposé au Parlement le 11 février 2014 et mettant en oeuvre d'autres mesures*, Projet de loi C-31, 41e législature, 2e session (sanctionné 19 juin 2014); Russ Marshall, "Bitcoin: Where Two Worlds Collide", (2015) 27 *Bond Law Review* 89, p. 102; Matthew P. Ponsford, "A Comparative Analysis of Bitcoin and Other Decentralised Virtual Currencies; Legal Regulation in the People's Republic of China, Canada, and the United States", (2015) *Journal of Legal Studies* 29, pp. 41–43;. Stephen Small, "Bitcoin; The Napster of Currency", (2015) *Houston Journal of International Law* 581, p. 621.

Cette législation oblige les commerçants de monnaies virtuelles à s'inscrire auprès des autorités à titre d'entreprise de services monétaires (« ESM ») et à se conformer aux exigences en matière de lutte au blanchiment d'argent. Qu'ils agissent à titre de commençants locaux ou étrangers, ils sont ensuite sujets à des exigences de conformité sur la tenue de dossiers ou encore la connaissance du client.

Selon les directives administratives en vigueur, une ESM est considérée « se livrer » au commerce de monnaie virtuelle lorsque l'opération touche (i) un transfert de fonds contre de la monnaie virtuelle; (ii) un transfert de monnaie virtuelle pour des fonds, ou (iii) un transfert d'un type de monnaie virtuelle contre une autre monnaie virtuelle. Il peut également s'agir d'un transfert de monnaie virtuelle à la demande d'un client ou encore de « la réception d'un transfert de monnaie virtuelle à des fins de remise à un bénéficiaire »[42].

Sous la LRPC, une entreprise étrangère « dirige » des services au Canada si elle offre des activités de marketing dirigées à des personnes ou entités au Canada ou encore elle y exploite un nom de domaine du type « .ca ». De même, une entreprise enregistrée dans un registre d'entreprises au Canada, comme le Registraire des entreprises du Québec[43] ou le Répertoire des entreprises canadiennes[44], sera aussi considérée comme dirigeant des services au Canada. Ainsi, une société basée en France qui envoie des courriels à des Canadiens pour faire connaître ses activités de change dirigera des services monétaires au Canada[45]. D'autres facteurs peuvent être notamment pris en compte par les autorités canadiennes :

- décrire ses services comme étant offert au Canada;
- offrir des produits ou services en dollars canadiens;
- offrir un service à la clientèle au Canada;
- demander la rétroaction de ses clients canadiens;
- faire la promotion de ses services au Canada par le biais d'un tiers[46].

---

42 Sur les directrices du Centre d'analyse des opérations et déclarations financières du Canada (CANAFE) : https://fintrac-canafe.canada.ca/msb-esm/msb-fra (Date d'accès: 15 septembre 2023).

43 Voir https://www.quebec.ca/entreprises-et-travailleurs-autonomes/obtenir-renseignements-entreprise/recherche-registre-entreprises/acceder-registre-entreprises (Date d'accès: 15 septembre 2023).

44 Voir https://www.canada.ca/fr/services/entreprises/recherche/repertoiresentreprisescanadiennes.html (Date d'accès: 15 septembre 2023).

45 Sur les directrices du Centre d'analyse des opérations et déclarations financières du Canada (CANAFE) : https://fintrac-canafe.canada.ca/msb-esm/msb-fra (Date d'accès: 15 septembre 2023).

46 Sur les directrices du Centre d'analyse des opérations et déclarations financières du Canada (CANAFE) : https://fintrac-canafe.canada.ca/msb-esm/msb-fra (Date d'accès: 15 septembre 2023).

En 2022, les plateformes de sociofinancement ont été ajoutées aux entités encadrées par la LRPC lorsqu'elles collectent de la monnaie virtuelle pour elles-mêmes, ou pour le compte d'autres personnes ou entités[47].

Sous le *Règlement sur la déclaration des opérations douteuses – recyclage des produits de la criminalité et le financement des activités terroristes* (DORS/2001-317) de la LRPC, il en découle, pour les assujettis, une obligation de transmettre des informations sur les opérations douteuses au Centre d'analyse des opérations et déclarations financières du Canada (CANAFE). Cet organisme a pour mandat « de faciliter la détection, la prévention et la dissuasion du blanchiment d'argent et du financement des activités terroristes, tout en assurant la protection des renseignements personnels qu'il détient »[48].

Face à une opération ou une tentative d'opération douteuse sur des monnaies virtuelles, les commerçants assujettis ont l'obligation de divulguer au CANAFE notamment les informations suivantes :

- les type et montant de chaque monnaie virtuelle en cause;
- les identifiants de l'opération, y compris l'adresse d'envoi et l'adresse de réception;
- l'origine des fonds ou de la monnaie virtuelle en cause;
- le nom des personnes ou entités qui constituent l'origine des fonds ou de la monnaie virtuelle en cause, ainsi que leur numéro de compte ou de police ou à défaut, leur numéro d'identification;
- la manière dont la remise est effectuée;
- les types et montant de chaque monnaie virtuelle en cause
- la valeur de la remise sous certaines conditions
- le nom des personnes ou entités qui constituent l'origine des fonds ou de la monnaie virtuelle en cause,
- leur numéro de compte ou de police ou, à défaut, leur numéro d'identification[49].

Les déclarations pour opérations douteuses sont transmises au CANAFE par voie électronique. Celles-ci peuvent aussi être transmises par support papier dans l'éventualité où une personne ne disposerait pas des moyens techniques nécessaires[50].

---

47 LRPC, art. 5h)(v) et 5h.1)(v); Règlement sur le recyclage des produits de la criminalité et le financement des activités terroristes, DORS/2002-184, art. 29.1.

48 Voir le site institutionnel du CANAFE : https://www.fintrac-canafe.gc.ca/intro-fra (Date d'accès: 15 septembre 2023).

49 *Règlement sur la déclaration des opérations douteuses - recyclage des produits de la criminalité et financement des activités terroristes*, DORS 2001-317, annexes 1 et 2.

50 Gouvernement du Canada, Déclaration d'opérations douteuses à CANAFE, en ligne : https://www.fintrac-canafe.gc.ca/guidance-directives/transaction-operation/Guide3/str-fra. (Date d'accès: 15 septembre 2023).

3.2 *Les aspects fiscaux*

Pour des fins fiscales, comme les cryptomonnaies n'ont pas cours légal au Canada[51], le paiement de biens ou de services au moyen de cryptomonnaies est considéré au Canada comme une opération d'échange (ou de troc), c'est-à-dire une opération économique selon laquelle chaque contractant cède la propriété d'un bien et reçoit, en échange, un autre bien[52]. Cette position rejoint la vision civiliste d'une telle transaction à la section 1.3 Les transactions sur cryptomonnaie : un contrat de vente ou contrat d'échange? Ainsi, la transaction d'une cryptomonnaie contre une autre est aussi considérée comme un échange aux fins de l'impôt fédéral canadien sur le revenu[53]. À la suite d'une telle opération d'échange, la réception de cryptomonnaies implique l'inclusion dans le revenu de la valeur de ce qui est reçu duquel le contribuable peut déduire la valeur du bien transigé, le tout en dollars canadiens[54].

L'achat et la vente de cryptomonnaies sont des opérations imposables au Canada qui, selon le contexte, seront considérées comme un(e) gain (perte) en capital ou un revenu d'entreprise[55]. Si la transaction n'est pas survenue dans un contexte d'entreprise, les opérations sont de nature à créer un(e) gain (perte)

---

51 Voir la section 1.2.

52 Saam Nainifard et Angela Gentile, "Taxation of crypto assets; Country Guides Canada", Wolters Klower, Cheetah, 2021, p. 4; Katsiaryna Ulyanava, "Legal Regulation of the Crypto -Currency Taxation", (2018) 1(1) *Open Journal for Legal Studies* 1, p. 4; Oleg Stratiev, "Cryptocurrency and Blockchain; How to Regulate Something We Do Not Understand" (2018) 33 *Banking and Finance Law Review* 173, p. 203; Stephen Small, "Bitcoin; The Napster of Currency", (2015) *Houston Journal of International Law* 581, p. 620; Oksana Panova et al., "International Models of Legal Regulation and Ethics of Cryptocurrency Use", (2019) 22(2) *Journal of Legal, Ethical and Regulatory Issues* 1, p. 3; Erwan Jonchères, *Encadrement juridique des monnaies numériques - Bitcoin et autres cryptomonnaies*, Mémoire de maîtrise, Université de Montréal, 2015, p. 89; Canada Revenue Agency, 'Barter Transactions", Interpretation Bulletin IT-490, (July 5, 1982) at para 3, online: <https://www.canada.ca/en/revenue-agency/services/forms-publications/publications/it490/archived-barter-transactions.html> [IT-490].

53 Saam Nainifard et Angela Gentile, "Taxation of crypto assets; Country Guides Canada", Wolters Klower, Cheetah, 2021, p. 2.

54 Saam Nainifard et Angela Gentile, "Taxation of crypto assets; Country Guides Canada", Wolters Klower, Cheetah, 2021, p. 4.

55 Katsiaryna Ulyanava, "Legal Regulation of the Crypto-Currency Taxation", (2018) 1(1) *Open Journal for Legal Studies* 1, p. 4; Matthew P. Ponsford, "A Comparative Analysis of Bitcoin and Other Decentralised Virtual Currencies; Legal Regulation in the People's Republic of China, Canada, and the United States", (2015) *Journal of Legal Studies* 29, p. 34; Oksana Panova et al., "International Models of Legal Regulation and Ethics of Cryptocurrency Use", (2019) 22(2) *Journal of Legal, Ethical and Regulatory Issues* 1, p. 3; Saam Nainifard et Angela Gentile, "Taxation of crypto assets; Country Guides Canada", Wolters Klower, Cheetah, 2021, p. 1.

capital en fonction du produit de disposition reçu. Dans ce cas, lorsque le contribuable détient plusieurs cryptomonnaies de même type, elles sont traitées comme des biens identiques en prenant une moyenne des prix de base rajustés pour le calcul du (de la) gain (perte) en capital[56].

S'il s'agit plutôt d'un bien à l'inventaire d'une entreprise, les opérations sont de nature à constituer un revenu d'entreprise[57]. Pour déterminer si les opérations d'un contribuable sont au titre du capital ou du revenu, le critère clé de la jurisprudence est l'intention subjective du contribuable au moment de l'acquisition des biens[58]. À titre informatif, l'Agence de revenu du Canada (ci-après, « ARC ») propose des indices courants et non exhaustifs permettant de qualifier la ligne de conduite d'un contribuable en pareille matière :

> « Vous exercez des activités pour des raisons commerciales et de façon viable sur le plan commercial;
>
> Vous entreprenez des activités de façon professionnelle, ce qui pourrait comprendre la préparation d'un plan d'affaires et l'acquisition d'immobilisations ou d'inventaires;
>
> Vous faites la promotion d'un produit ou d'un service.
>
> Vous démontrez que vous avez l'intention de réaliser un bénéfice, même s'il est peu probable que vous le fassiez à court terme »[59].

56 Saam Nainifard et Angela Gentile, "Taxation of crypto assets; Country Guides Canada", Wolters Klower, Cheetah, 2021, p. 2. Voir aussi Revenu Québec, *Déclaration des revenus relatifs* à la *monnaie virtuelle*, 2021. En ligne : https://www.revenuquebec.ca/fr/une-mission-des-actions/vous-aider-a-vous-conformer/quest-ce-que-leconomie-numerique/monnaie-virtuelle/declaration-des-revenus-relatifs-a-la-monnaie-virtuelle/ (Date d'accès : 15 septembre 2023).

57 Agence du revenu du Canada, *Guide de la monnaie virtuelle pour les utilisateurs de cryptomonnaie et les professionnels de l'impôt,* 26 juin 2021. En ligne : https://www.canada.ca/fr/agence-revenu/programmes/a-propos-agence-revenu-canada-arc/observation/monnaie-numerique/cryptomonnaies-guide.html (Date d'accès: 15 septembre 2023). Voir aussi Oleg Stratiev, "Cryptocurrency and Blockchain; How to Regulate Something We Do Not Understand" (2018) 33 *Banking and Finance Law Review* 173, p. 204; Senate of Canada (Standing Committee on Banking, Trade and Finance), *Study on the Use of Digital Currency*, 41st Parl, 2nd sess, No 13 (June 5, 2014).

58 Saam Nainifard et Angela Gentile, "Taxation of crypto assets; Country Guides Canada", Wolters Klower, Cheetah, 2021, p. 3; *Friesen (J.)* v. *Canada*, [1995] 3 S.C.R. 103, par. 44; *Canada Safeway Ltd.* v. *R*, [2008] 2 CTC 149, par. 43; *Regal Heights* v. *MNR*, [1960] CTC 384; *Happy Valley Farms Ltd.* v. *Minister of National Revenue*, [1986] 2 CTC 259, par. 14.

59 Saam Nainifard et Angela Gentile, "Taxation of crypto assets; Country Guides Canada", Wolters Klower, Cheetah, 2021, p. 3.

Une présomption se développe en jurisprudence à l'effet que l'achat et la vente de cryptomonnaies par une société par actions sont effectués dans le cadre d'une entreprise, ce qui mènerait au traitement du revenu d'entreprise :

> « There is a presumption that the purchase and sale of crypto assets by a corporation is made in the course of a business. The Federal Court of Appeal in *Weaver v. The Queen* and *Ollenberger v. R.* made reference to a corporation only requiring a minimum degree of activity to be considered to be carrying on a business. In *Ollenberger*, the Court used this reference to conclude that most, if not all, corporations are carrying on a business »[60].

Pour ces transactions de biens en inventaire, l'activité est alors considérée comme étant l'exploitation d'une entreprise et le contribuable devra ajouter dans le calcul du revenu tiré de l'entreprise pour l'année d'imposition, le montant des biens figurant à l'inventaire à la fin de l'exercice fiscal (en fonction d'une méthode établie d'évaluation des biens; par exemple l'évaluation de chaque bien au coût d'acquisition ou l'évaluation à la juste valeur marchande)[61].

Enfin, la question de savoir si l'activité particulière de minage constitue une entreprise dans un but lucratif ou un passe-temps est également une question de fait devant être déterminée au cas par cas. Généralement, l'ARC considère l'extraction de cryptomonnaies comme l'activité d'une entreprise compte tenu notamment de « l'énorme puissance de calcul et l'énergie nécessaires pour produire ne serait-ce qu'un seul bitcoin »[62]. Ce faisant, la valeur

60 Saam Nainifard et Angela Gentile, "Taxation of crypto assets; Country Guides Canada", Wolters Klower, Cheetah, 2021, p. 3; *Weaver* v. *Canada*, 2008 FCA 238; *Ollenberger* v. *Canada*, 2013 FCA 74.

61 *Stewart* v. *The Queen*, 2002 SCC 46; Saam Nainifard et Angela Gentile, "Taxation of crypto assets; Country Guides Canada", Wolters Klower, Cheetah, 2021, pp. 2–3. Voir aussi Revenu Québec, *Déclaration des revenus relatifs* à la *monnaie virtuelle*, 2021. En ligne : https://www.revenuquebec.ca/fr/une-mission-des-actions/vous-aider-a-vous-conformer/quest-ce-que-leconomie-numerique/monnaie-virtuelle/declaration-des-revenus-relatifs-a-la-monnaie-virtuelle/ (Date d'accès : 15 septembre 2023).

62 Wolters Kluwer - Cryptomonnaie - D'un point de vue fiscal (2021), p. 2. Oleg Stratiev, "Cryptocurrency and Blockchain; How to Regulate Something We Do Not Understand" (2018) 33 *Banking and Finance Law Review* 173, p. 205; MNP, "The Future Today: Taxing Virtual Currency" (November 10, 2017), online: <http://www.mnp.ca/en/posts/the-future-today-taxing-virtual-currency>, 4. Katsiaryna Ulyanava, "Legal Regulation of the Crypto-Currency Taxation", (2018) 1(1) *Open Journal for Legal Studies* 1, p. 4. Saam Nainifard et Angela Gentile, "Taxation of crypto assets; Country Guides Canada", Wolters Klower, Cheetah, 2021, p. 6; *Stewart* v. *Canada*, 2002 SCC 46.

des cryptomonnaies en dollars canadiens devrait être incluse dans le revenu d'entreprise du contribuable au moment où il a été gagné[63].

3.3 *L'encadrement de la cryptomonnaie comme « valeurs mobilières ou « produits dérivés »*

Au Canada, une transaction impliquant une cryptomonnaie peut, sous différentes conditions, être considérée comme une transaction d'investissement encadrée par la législation en matière de valeurs mobilières ou de produits dérivés. Dans ce secteur d'activité, le cadre règlementaire vise à encourager de saines pratiques commerciales, à favoriser des marchés financiers efficients et à contribuer à la stabilité des marchés.

Il est à noter qu'au Canada chaque province et territoire détient une compétence en valeurs mobilières qui est exercée par une autorité réglementaire distincte. Cependant, pour favoriser des efforts d'harmonisation et de coordination de la réglementation, ces autorités provinciales et territoriales sont regroupées au sein des Autorités canadiennes en valeurs mobilières (« ACVM »)[64]. Plus particulièrement, au Québec, le secteur des valeurs mobilières et des produits dérivés est chapeauté par l'Autorité des marchés financiers (« AMF ») qui fait partie du groupe des ACVM.

Jusqu'à présent, les ACVM traitent le phénomène de la cryptomonnaie sous l'angle plus global des « cryptoactifs » en y intégrant notamment les jetons. Il est néanmoins bien établi que certains cryptoactifs constituant un moyen de paiement ou d'échange, comme le Bitcoin, ne sont pas considérés comme des valeurs mobilières ou des produits dérivés, mais plutôt comme des marchandises tels les devises étrangères ou les métaux précieux[65]. Toutefois, chaque situation demeure un cas d'espèce qu'il faut étudier à partir des critères établis.

Une transaction sur un cryptoactif peut notamment être soumise à la compétence de l'AMF si elle s'intègre sous l'encadrement relatif aux contrats d'investissement (2.3.1.), (2) aux produits dérivés (2.3.2.), ou encore (3) aux plateformes de cryptoactifs (2.3.3.)[66].

---

63 Saam Nainifard et Angela Gentile, "Taxation of crypto assets; Country Guides Canada", Wolters Klower, Cheetah, 2021, p. 6; CRA Document Number 2018-0776661I7. Voir aussi Revenu Québec - Déclaration des revenus relatifs à la monnaie virtuelle (2021), p. 1 (pdf).

64 Pour plus de détails, voir https://www.autorites-valeurs-mobilieres.ca/ (Date d'accès: 15 septembre 2023).

65 ACVM, *Document de consultation conjoint 21-402 des ACVM de l'OCRCVM – Projet d'encadrement des plateformes de négociation de cryptoactifs*, 14 mars 2019, p. 4.

66 Nous ne traitons pas de certains cas particuliers qui impliquent des cryptoactifs comme les fonds d'investissements, les gardiens de valeurs ou encore les bacs à sable réglementaire. À ce sujet, nous référons le lecteur à Ryan Clements et Virginia Torrie, "Crypto Asset

3.3.1 La qualification d'une transaction sur une cryptomonnaie à titre de « contrat d'investissement »

Au Québec, la *Loi sur les valeurs mobilières*[67] (ci-après, « LVM ») définit le contrat d'investissement comme : « [...] un contrat par lequel une personne s'engage, dans l'espérance du bénéfice qu'on lui a fait entrevoir, à participer aux risques d'une affaire par la voie d'un apport ou d'un prêt quelconque, sans posséder les connaissances requises pour la marche de l'affaire ou sans obtenir le droit de participer directement aux décisions concernant la marche de l'affaire »[68]. Suivant les critères établis dans l'arrêt de la Cour suprême du Canada *Pacific Coast Coin Exchange c. Commission des valeurs mobilières de l'Ontario*, une transaction constitue une émission de contrat d'investissement lorsque l'on retrouve les quatre éléments suivants : (1) il y a présence d'un investissement d'une somme d'argent; (2) l'investisseur participe aux risques d'une entreprise commune; (3) l'investisseur s'attend à faire un profit; et (4) le profit proviendra en grande partie des efforts d'autrui[69]. Historiquement, les tribunaux supportent une interprétation large de ces éléments privilégiant une plus grande protection des investisseurs vulnérables[70]. Dans un tel contexte, l'analyse des faits donne aussi préséance à l'objet économique par rapport à la forme juridique de l'opération[71].

Cette approche privilégiant la substance sur la forme est aussi mise de l'avant dans l'application de la qualification de « contrat d'investissement » aux cryptoactifs. Les ACVM se sont notamment intéressés aux émissions de jetons qui peuvent consister dans certaines circonstances à un placement de titres. Pour répondre aux questions de l'industrie sur l'application de la législation en valeurs mobilières aux jetons, les ACVM ont recensé différentes situations ayant « une incidence sur la présence d'un ou de plusieurs éléments d'un

---

Regulation in Canada: Developments and Governance Considerations", (2023) 39 *Banking and Finance Law Review* 345, pp. 353, 354–356.

67 RLRQ, chapitre V-1.1.

68 *Loi sur les valeurs mobilières*, art. 1(9). Sur les notions « d'affaire » et de « marche de l'affaire », voir *Corporation Première Équité A.C.P. Inc.*, Commission des valeurs mobilières du Québec, Montréal, n° 8307, 29 mai 1987, R. Côté, M. Cusson et P. Dussault, p. 12.

69 *Pacific Coast Coin Exchange c. Commission des valeurs mobilières de l'Ontario*, [1978] 2 R.C.S. 112. Voir également Autorités canadiennes en valeurs mobilières, Avis 46-308 du personnel des ACVM – Incidences de la législation en valeurs mobilières sur les émissions de jetons, 2018. Autorités canadiennes en valeurs mobilières, Avis 46-307 du personnel des ACVM – Les émissions de cryptomonnaies, 2017.

70 *Pacific Coast Coin Exchange c. Commission des valeurs mobilières de l'Ontario*, [1978] 2 R.C.S. 112, 128; *Doyon c. Autorité des marchés financiers*, 2017 QCCA 1157, par 46 et 47.

71 *Pacific Coast Coin Exchange c. Commission des valeurs mobilières de l'Ontario*, [1978] 2 R.C.S. 112.

contrat d'investissements »[72]. Bien que ces situations soient proposées à titre illustratif seulement, elles permettent de constater la dimension polyforme des cryptoactifs. Ces situations comprennent notamment les suivantes :

- la chaîne de bloc ou la plateforme de transaction n'est pas encore développée;
- les jetons ne sont pas immédiatement livrés aux acheteurs;
- l'émission vise à recueillir des capitaux qui seront utilisés entre débuter des actions clés qui soutiendront la valeur du jeton;
- l'émetteur a mis en place un programme incitatif pour ceux qui font la promotion de l'émission de jetons;
- la direction conserve un nombre significatif de jetons invendus;
- l'émetteur soutient les jetons qui seront utilisés comme monnaie ou auront une utilité au-delà de la plateforme;
- la direction de l'émetteur déclare qu'elle possède des compétences pouvant hausser la valeur du jeton;
- les jetons ont une valeur fixe qui n'augmente pas automatiquement;
- l'émission est limitée à un certain nombre de jetons ou l'accès futur semble raisonnablement limité;
- l'émetteur permet ou exige que les acheteurs achètent des jetons pour une somme différente de leur prétendue utilité; ou
- la direction fait des déclarations à l'effet que la valeur du jeton augmentera ou compare celui-ci d'autres cryptoactifs s'étant accrus[73].

Le Tribunal administratif des marchés financiers (ci-après, le « TMF ») a reconnu une telle application du contrat d'investissement à une émission de cryptoactifs dans l'affaire *Autorité des marchés financiers c. Plexcorps*[74]. Un regroupement innomé d'une quarantaine de personnes réparties à travers le monde invitait le public à investir dans l'achat de PlexCoin, une monnaie virtuelle offrant un rendement sur l'actif potentiel de 1 354 %. Outre le PlexCoin, le regroupement de Plexcorps proposait une vaste gamme de services par le biais de leur site Internet www.PlexCorps.com. L'AMF a saisi le TMF pour prononcer des interdictions d'opérations sur valeurs et d'autres mesures propres au respect de la LVM[75]. Pour accorder les interdictions demandées, le TMF devait conclure que la proposition de Plexcorps constituait un placement en valeurs mobilières. En s'appuyant sur la définition du « contrat d'investissement », le

72 Autorités canadiennes en valeurs mobilières, Avis 46-308 du personnel des ACVM – Incidences de la législation en valeurs mobilières sur les émissions de jetons, 2018, p. 3.

73 Autorités canadiennes en valeurs mobilières, Avis 46-308 du personnel des ACVM – Incidences de la législation en valeurs mobilières sur les émissions de jetons, 2018, pp. 3–7.

74 2017 QCTMF 88. Voir aussi *Autorité des marchés financiers c. CreUnite*, 2018 QCTMF 8; *Autorité* des *marchés financiers c. Gestion Itradecoins inc.*, 2020 QCTMF 57.

75 *Autorité des marchés financiers* c. *PlexCorps*, 2017 QCTMF 88, p. 2

TMF est venu à la conclusion que l'offre de Plexcoin par le regroupement de PlexCorps répondait à tous les critères établis par la jurisprudence.

Le TMF a conclu qu'il ne s'agissait pas d'une simple transaction sur une cryptomonnaie (le PlexCoin), mais qu'il s'agissait plutôt, par la recherche active de souscripteurs et l'offre de services, d'un placement d'une valeur mobilière qui satisfait tous les critères d'un contrat d'investissement. Notamment, le regroupement invitait le public à participer, par une mise de fonds, au risque de l'affaire en s'en remettant entièrement à l'expertise des créateurs du PlexCoin[76].

Or, lorsqu'il est établi que l'offre de cryptoactif constitue un placement en vertu de la législation en valeurs mobilières, le placement d'une valeur mobilière exige d'établir un prospectus soumis au visa de l'Autorité des marchés financiers:

> 11. Toute personne qui entend procéder au placement d'une valeur est tenue d'établir un prospectus soumis au visa de l'Autorité. La demande de visa est accompagnée des documents prévus par règlement.
>
> Toutefois, dans le cas du placement par un courtier de titres pris ferme, il incombe à l'émetteur d'établir le prospectus[77].

L'article 13 de la LVM précise que le prospectus doit révéler « de façon complète, véridique et claire, tout fait important relatif à un titre émis ou qui fait l'objet du placement »[78]. Lorsque la loi s'applique, à moins de bénéficier d'une dispense de placement privé[79], il faut se conformer au régime de l'appel public à l'épargne. Il importe de mentionner que la notion de titres doit s'interpréter à la lumière de l'article premier de la LVM. Ainsi, le seul fait de solliciter un investisseur sans faire d'opération constitue un placement à l'égard de la Loi[80].

---

76 Stéphane Rousseau, « La règlementation des émissions de cryptomonnaies (ICOs) au Canada; La protection des investisseurs et le bon fonctionnement du marché dans le bac à sable réglementaire », 2018 (1) *Revue internationale des services financiers* 1, p. 3.

77 LVM, art. 11.

78 LVM, art. 13.

79 Différentes options de dispenses de prospectus sont disponibles au Canada dont plusieurs sont harmonisées sous l'Instrument national 45-106 Dispenses de prospectus (ch. V-1.1, r. 21).

80 Stéphane Rousseau, « La règlementation des émissions de cryptomonnaies (ICOs) au Canada; La protection des investisseurs et le bon fonctionnement du marché dans le bac à sable réglementaire », 2018 (1) *Revue internationale des services financiers* 1, p. 4.

De plus, la LVM exige que « [n]ul ne peut agir à titre de courtier, de conseiller ou de gestionnaire de fonds d'investissement, à moins d'être inscrit à ce titre » auprès de l'Autorité des marchés financiers[81].

Le non-respect des dispositions d'ordre public de la LVM constitue des infractions conduisant à des amendes[82] et même des peines d'emprisonnement[83]. Le tribunal peut aussi émettre des interdictions de transiger ou des pénalités administratives ou pénales[84]. Une opération sans prospectus donne ouverture à un recours civil en nullité et en dommages-intérêts[85].

3.3.2 La qualification d'une transaction sur une cryptomonnaie à titre de « produit dérivé »

Dans l'Avis 21-327 des ACVM, le personnel souligne également que la législation pourra s'appliquer lorsqu'un cryptoactif constitue un dérivé[86]. Au Québec, la *Loi sur les instruments dérivés*[87] (ci-après, la « LID ») propose d'ailleurs une définition large de « produit dérivé » :

> « une option, un swap, un contrat à terme, un contrat de différence ou tout autre contrat ou instrument dont le cours, la valeur ou les obligations de livraison ou de paiement sont fonction d'un élément sous-jacent, ainsi que tout autre contrat ou instrument prévu par règlement ou assimilable à un dérivé suivant des critères déterminés par règlement »[88].

À moins de répondre aux critères d'une des diverses exceptions de la LID,[89] une transaction sur un cryptoactif, qui entre dans la définition de « dérivé », pourra aussi être encadrée par l'AMF. Cette piste pour soumettre une transaction impliquant des cryptoactifs à la compétence de l'AMF a été moins utilisée jusqu'à présent dans la jurisprudence que celle du contrat d'investissement. Nous retrouvons toutefois un exemple dans l'affaire *Autorité des marchés*

81 LVM, art. 148.

82 LVM, art. 11, 148, 202, 208.1.

83 LVM, art. 208.1 (placement sans prospectus).

84 LVM, art. 273.1.

85 LVM, art. 214–216.

86 Autorités canadiennes en valeurs mobilières, Avis 21-327 du personnel des ACVM – Indications sur l'application de la législation en valeurs mobilières aux entités facilitant la négociation de cryptoactifs, 2020, p. 2.

87 RLRQ, chapitre I-14.01.

88 *Loi sur les instruments dérivés*, RLRQ, chapitre I-14.01, art. 3.

89 Voir notamment LID, art. 6.

financiers c. Gestion Itradecoins inc[90]. Dans ce cas, le TMF a estimé que les sommes placées dans des jetons ITRC « pourraient par la suite être investies dans des opérations portant sur des dérivés »[91]. Dans cette affaire, Gestion Itradecoins inc. avait sollicité par le biais de sites web et de média sociaux des investisseurs à se procurer des ITRC. En s'appuyant notamment sur le précédent *Autorité des marchés financiers c. Plexcorps*[92], le TMF a conclu que l'acquisition de jetons répondait à la définition d'un contrat d'investissement et faisait de celle-ci un placement de valeurs mobilières. Le TMF a ajouté que :

> « [S]elon la preuve apparente présentée, les sommes placées lors de l'émission initiale des jetons ITRC pourraient par la suite être investies dans des opérations portant sur des dérivés. À cet égard, le site web Itradecoins.sg ferait état de ce qui suit : « Our bots use statistical and specific indicators to take profitable long and short positions even when you sleep ». La version la plus récente du livre blanc mentionnerait ce qui suit : « ltradecoins is using automated & leveraged crypto trading bots to generate daily profit. It uses powerful tools like compound profits, 10 to 20x leverage trades, long and short positions on bybit and binance with BTC futures contracts market. » Or, de telles opérations sur dérivés déclenchent notamment l'application de l'obligation d'inscription au sens de l'article 54 de la LID qui est aussi appliquée par l'Autorité »[93].
>
> Ainsi, au-delà de simples transactions d'achat-vente de cryptomonnaie, des plateformes peuvent proposer par une offre variée des transactions pouvant être assujetties à la compétence de l'Autorité des marchés financiers par LVM ou la LID.

Comme sous la LVM, une personne ou une entité ne peut agir à titre de courtier, de conseiller ou de gestionnaire de produits dérivés, à moins d'être inscrite à ce titre auprès de l'Autorité des marchés financiers[94].

3.3.3 L'enregistrement des plateformes de cryptoactifs

La législation en valeurs mobilières peut enfin s'appliquer à des plateformes facilitant des transactions de cryptoactifs[95]. Sans introduire de nouvelles

---

90 2020 QCTMF 57.

91 *Autorité* des *marchés financiers c. Gestion Itradecoins inc.*, 2020 QCTMF 57.

92 2017 QCTMF 88.

93 *Autorité des marchés financiers c. Gestion Itradecoins inc.*, 2020 QCTMF 57.

94 LID, art. 54.

95 Autorités canadiennes en valeurs mobilières, Avis 21-327 du personnel des ACVM – Indications sur l'application de la législation en valeurs mobilières aux entités facilitant la

règles, les ACVM sont venus indiquer que les plateformes de négociation de cryptoactifs étaient aussi soumises au régime d'enregistrement en place pour assurer la protection des investisseurs. Cette surveillance renforcée découle notamment de l'affaire QuadrigaCX à la fin de 2018 où des investisseurs avaient perdu près de 164 millions de dollars à l'intérieur de la débâcle frauduleuse de la plateforme[96]. À l'intérieur d'un processus rigoureux, les plateformes enregistrées doivent présenter des critères d'aptitude et d'inscription, dont la compétence, la probité et la solvabilité. Elles sont ensuite soumises, notamment, à des exigences concernant leurs opérations, leurs contrôles internes et à une obligation de divulgation à l'égard des clients. Il est à noter qu'en date d'aujourd'hui, seules quelques plateformes de négociation de cryptoactifs ont soumis une demande d'inscription et figurent sur la liste des plateformes enregistrées par l'AMF.

Même si certains cryptoactifs ne constituent pas en soi des contrats d'investissement ou des dérivés, les plateformes ne confèrent parfois à leurs utilisateurs qu'« un droit ou un intérêt contractuel à l'égard d'un cryptoactif sous-jacent, plutôt que de livrer immédiatement celui-ci »[97]. Le droit des valeurs mobilières peut alors trouver application au Canada pour encadrer certaines transactions sur la cryptomonnaie constituant autrement une marchandise lorsqu'elles ne limitent pas à un simple transfert de propriété entre les parties. L'on réfère plus spécifiquement à la notion de livraison immédiate (« *actual delivery* » en anglais)[98] afin de déterminer si la législation en valeurs mobilières trouvera application. Si une transaction sur un cryptoactif n'implique pas une obligation de livraison immédiate, elle peut être soumise la législation en matière de valeurs mobilières. Toutefois, il n'y a pas de critère à proprement parler pour déterminer s'il y a livraison immédiate ou non. La détermination du moment

---

négociation de cryptoactifs, 2020, p. 1. Voir aussi Document de consultation conjoint 21-402 des Autorités canadiennes en valeurs mobilières et de l'Organisme canadien de réglementation du commerce des valeurs mobilières – Projet d'encadrement des plateformes de négociation de cryptoactifs, 14 mars 2019; Autorités canadiennes en valeurs mobilières, Avis 21-3332 du personnel des ACVM – Plateforme de négociation de cryptoactifs : engagements préalables à l'inscription, 22 février 2023.

96 Ontario Securties Commission, QuadrigaCX […].

97 Autorités canadiennes en valeurs mobilières, Avis 21-327 du personnel des ACVM – Indications sur l'application de la législation en valeurs mobilières aux entités facilitant la négociation de cryptoactifs, 2020, p. 2.

98 La notion de "actual delivery" a été inspirée de la *Commodity Exchange Act* (USA), art. 2 (c) (2) (D) (II) (III) (aa) qui exclut "a contract of sale that results in actual delivery within 28 days or such other longer period as the Commission may determine by rule or regulation based upon the typical commercial practice in cash or spot markets for the commodity involved.". Voir https://www.jdsupra.com/legalnews/cftc-final-guidance-on-actual-delivery-42535.

de livraison doit être basée sur les faits et l'ensemble des réalités économiques de la relation[99]. Dans ces cas, c'est le droit contractuel qui suspend la livraison du cryptoactif et qui crée une valeur mobilière ou un dérivé[100].

Pour le personnel des ACVM, l'on considère qu'il y a eu livraison immédiate lorsque les conditions suivantes sont réunies : (1) « [...] la plateforme transfère immédiatement la propriété, la possession et le contrôle du cryptoactif à l'utilisateur, de sorte que celui-ci est libre de l'utiliser, ou de le négocier autrement[101]; (2) après la livraison immédiate du cryptoactif, l'utilisateur de la plateforme n'est pas exposé au risque d'insolvabilité (risque de crédit), au risque de fraude, au risque d'exécution ni au risque d'incompétence de celle-ci.»[102]. D'autres facteurs peuvent également être pris en considération :

- les termes du contrat entre la plateforme et l'utilisateur;
- le règlement immédiat de la transaction;
- la disponibilité de marge ou de levier financier;
- la pratique commerciale sur la livraison immédiate;
- le transfert immédiat dans le portefeuille de l'investisseur; et
- la propriété, la possession ou le contrôle sur le cryptoactif transféré[103].

En somme, les plateformes peuvent se soustraire à la réglementation si le cryptoactif transigé constitue unc marchandise (qu'il n'est pas une valeur mobilière ou un produit dérivé) et les transactions impliquent une livraison immédiate d'un cryptoactif.

99 Autorités canadiennes en valeurs mobilières, Avis 21-327 du personnel des ACVM – Indications sur l'application de la législation en valeurs mobilières aux entités facilitant la négociation de cryptoactifs, 2020, p. 2 : « Il n'existe pas de critère de démarcation précis permettant d'établir si un contrat ou un instrument crée l'obligation, et reflète l'intention, de livrer un cryptoactif ou d'en prendre livraison immédiatement. Toutefois, une opération sur un cryptoactif peut être soumise à la législation en valeurs mobilières si elle n'entraîne pas l'obligation de livrer le cryptoactif visé et d'en prendre livraison immédiatement après ».

100 Ryan Clements et Virginia Torrie, "Crypto Asset Regulation in Canada: Developments and Governance Considerations", (2023) 39 *Banking and Finance Law Review* 345, p. 350.

101 « Une sûreté peut naître dans un certain nombre de cas, notamment l'utilisation d'une marge, d'un effet de levier ou d'un financement en vue de réaliser l'achat. » Autorités canadiennes en valeurs mobilières, Avis 21-327 du personnel des ACVM – Indications sur l'application de la législation en valeurs mobilières aux entités facilitant la négociation de cryptoactifs, 2020, p. 2.

102 Autorités canadiennes en valeurs mobilières, Avis 21-327 du personnel des ACVM – Indications sur l'application de la législation en valeurs mobilières aux entités facilitant la négociation de cryptoactifs,2020, p. 2

103 Alix d'Anglejan-Chatillon et al., "Canada", dans *The Virtual Currency Regulation Review*, 5th Edition, The Law Review, 2022, p. 54.

4 Conclusion

En droit civil québécois, la cryptomonnaie comme un objet de recherche a été peu étudiée par la doctrine. La reconnaissance de la cryptomonnaie à titre de « bien » constitue un point de départ qui mérite plus d'attention. À l'inverse, il est bien établi que la cryptomonnaie, même si elle peut constituer un mode de paiement, ne constitue pas une monnaie ayant cours légal. Selon le mode de paiement, les transferts entre les utilisateurs de cryptomonnaies pourront selon le cas constituer des contrats de vente ou d'échange avec à la clé les enjeux touchant le transfert de propriété qui varient en fonction des spécificités des plateformes de transactions.

Si le droit civil au Québec tarde à s'intéresser de près aux enjeux juridiques des cryptomonnaies, l'on constate en contrepartie une certaine effervescence de la réglementation pour encadrer les transactions impliquant les consommateurs de produits et services financiers canadiens. Le développement de cette réglementation dépendra du futur de la cryptomonnaie : est-elle un effet de mode ou un moyen de paiement en place pour rester? Pour le moment, elle reste au cœur des préoccupations, notamment des régulateurs en valeurs mobilières pour protéger les consommateurs de produits et services financiers contre la fraude et les malversations.

China

Zheli Chen and Dong Yang

1 Introduction

The cryptocurrency industry in Mainland China (hereinafter referred to as China) has experienced a boom to a bust. Due to the low cost of electricity, China once was the center of mining cryptocurrencies. However, since 2017, the Chinese government has taken a series of restrictions on cryptocurrencies, such as banning ICOs, shutting down cryptocurrency exchange platforms, and restricting the mining of cryptocurrencies. These policies are not issued through legislation, but by several administrative organs to jointly promulgate a notice or an announcement, which are departmental regulations in Chinese law.

As a result, cryptocurrencies are less commonly used in China. However, China does not prohibit – and in fact, is not able to prohibit – the possession and trading of cryptocurrencies by individuals. Some people keep cryptocurrencies as a kind of investment. Also, a small number of people use cryptocurrencies for payments, but mainly in criminal acts. Besides, people use stable coins to avoid foreign exchange regulations.

The following three main notices and announcements have been issued by the Chinese government for cryptocurrencies.

2013 Notice on the Prevention of Risk about Bitcoin by People's Bank of China, Ministry of Industry and Information Technology, Banking Regulatory Commission, Securities Regulatory Commission, and Insurance Regulatory Commission (called 'The 2013 Notice') is an earlier document dealing with cryptocurrencies. At that time, cryptocurrencies were not yet diversified, and the only major popular cryptocurrency was Bitcoin. Therefore, the 2013 Notice was also focused only on Bitcoin.

2017 Announcement of the People's Bank of China, the Office of the Central Leading Group for Cyberspace Affairs, the Ministry of Industry and Information Technology, the State Administration for Industry and Commerce, the China Banking Regulatory Commission, the China Securities Regulatory Commission, and the China Insurance Regulatory Commission on Preventing the Financing Risks of Initial Coin Offerings (called 'the 2017 Announcement') was released in 2017, the year of the ICO boom. Its main purpose was to ban ICOs, but it also addressed restrictions and regulations of cryptocurrencies exchange platforms.

2021 Notice on Further Preventing and Resolving the Risks of Virtual Currency Trading and Speculation by People's Bank of China, Office of the Central

 | DOI:10.1163/9789004722507_006

Cyberspace Affairs Commission, The Supreme People's Court, The Supreme People's Procuratorate, Ministry of Industry and Information Technology, Ministry of Public Security, State Administration for Market Regulation, Banking and Insurance Regulatory Commission, Securities Regulatory Commission, and State Administration of Foreign Exchange (called 'the 2021 Notice') is a more stringent restriction on cryptocurrencies. It is worth noting that the issuer of the 2021 Notice also includes the Supreme People's Court, the Supreme People's Procuratorate, and the police department, which means the effectiveness will be different from the 2013 Notice and the 2017 Announcement.

2 Definition of Cryptocurrency in China

2.1 *Definition in Official Notice or Announcement*

Because of China's generally skeptical, restrictive approach to cryptocurrencies, Chinese law does not provide a specific definition of cryptocurrencies. Of course, none of the cryptocurrencies were considered legal tender in China.

It is worth noting that the 2017 Announcement distinguishes 'Virtual Currencies' (in quotation marks) from 'Tokens'. The 2017 Announcement aimed to prohibit ICOs. Therefore, it uses 'Tokens' to refer to the objects issued by the ICO, which are crypto-assets in a broader sense, and uses 'virtual currency' to refer to the cryptocurrency used to pay the tokens' consideration in the ICO process. Since then, official documents in China have been using the term 'virtual currency' to refer to the cryptocurrencies discussed in this article. The 2017 Announcement does not define in detail what 'virtual currencies' are but cites Bitcoin and Ether as two examples.

The 2021 Notice also takes an enumeration approach, citing Tether coin as an example in addition to Bitcoin and Ether. In addition, the 2021 Notice describes several characteristics of virtual currencies as follows:

> ... not issued by a monetary authority, using cryptography and distributed accounts or similar technology, and existing in digital form.

This description of characteristics is not a constituent element in determining whether an object is a virtual currency. However, this description is in fact sufficient to define cryptocurrencies.

2.2 *Definition by Legal Doctrine*

Since China does not have a clear definition of cryptocurrency or virtual currency in its laws, the corresponding academic discussions have failed to reach a consensus. Many scholars have introduced the definitions of virtual currencies in the reports of international organizations such as IMF, CFTF, and the legislation of extraterritorial countries such as the United States (New York State) and Japan, and suggested that Chinese legislation should adopt a similar definition.[1]

Recently, a new concept called 'Coken' that can cover various shared interests on the blockchain, is being discussed in the academic community of China. Coken is a newly coined word with the prefix 'Co-' meaning 'with, together, jointly', combined with the usual word Token. Coken transcend the division between cryptocurrencies and crypto-assets and can function as both a means of payment and a security or other investment vehicle.[2] The aim of the concept of Coken is to establish a new mechanism for collecting and tracking big data based on the existing blockchain mechanism, so as to achieve a real-time and dynamic regulatory system for the blockchain.[3] Coken system is a comprehensive certificate of interest based on data creation, utilizing distributed ledger technology to identify the common threads of multiple subjects in data value creation, with the holders of Coken enjoying the right to receive the distribution of data element revenues based on their contributions.[4] Related research holds important meaning for the future, but a more specific discussion is beyond the scope of this chapter.

3 Regulation and Supervision

The Chinese government has experienced a change in the regulation of cryptocurrencies from permissive to strict. The regulatory objectives and focus of the 2013 Notice, the 2017 Announcement, and the 2021 Notice are different and are described separately below.

1 参见牛馨雨: 《美国纽约州比特币牌照制度研究》, 载《金融法苑》第92辑, 第194页; 杨东、陈哲立:《虚拟货币立法：日本经验与对中国的启示》, 载《证券市场导报》2018 年第 2 期, 第70 页; 漆彤、卓峻帆;《加密货币的法律属性与监管框架——以比较研究为视角》, 载《财经法学》2019 年第 4 期, 第 129–130 页.

2 参见杨东:《“共票”: 区块链治理新维度》, 载《东方法学》2019 年第 3 期, 第 60 页.

3 同前注,第61页;参见杨东:《监管科技:金融科技的监管挑战与维度构建》,载《中国社会科学》2018 年第 5 期, 第 83 页.

4 参见黄尹旭、杨东:《“利益——权利”双元共生:“数据要素×”的价值创造》,载《中国社会科学》2024 年第 2 期.

3.1 *The 2013 Notice*

The 2013 notice was issued in the early days of Bitcoin's introduction into the public eye when few people classified Bitcoin as a "virtual currency", let alone a "cryptocurrency". At the time, Bitcoin was just emerging, and early Bitcoin exchange platforms were already in place where users could buy and sell Bitcoin in legal tender. The main purpose of the 2013 Notice was to prevent the potential money laundering risks associated with Bitcoin, and the main targets were licensed financial institutions and Bitcoin exchange platforms.

First, the 2013 Notice requires "a correct understanding of the nature of bitcoin". The 2013 Notice points out that bitcoin "is not issued by the monetary authority, does not have the monetary nature of legal tender status and compulsory, and is not a real sense of money". Bitcoin "is a specific virtual commodity that does not have the same legal status as currency, and cannot and should not be used as currency in the marketplace".

Second, licensed financial institutions are prohibited from participating in Bitcoin-related businesses. The 2013 Notice requires licensed financial institutions such as banks, security companies, and payment institutions not to price products or services in Bitcoin, not to buy or sell Bitcoin, not to conduct Bitcoin-related insurance business, not to provide Bitcoin clearing, remittance, custody, collateral, and other businesses, and not to invest in Bitcoin.

Third, a very low threshold was set for Bitcoin exchange platforms. The 2013 Notice did not set prudential regulations. Bitcoin exchange platforms only needed to fulfill their filing obligations as websites to operate.

Fourth, anti-money laundering-related regulations are set. The 2013 Notice requires Bitcoin exchange platforms to confirm the identity of users and report suspicious transactions to anti-money laundering authorities.

3.2 *The 2017 Announcement*

The 2017 Announcement came at a time when ICOs were exploding. At that time, ICOs were on the rise and many ICO projects emerged over time, a large part of which belonged to fraudulent projects, also known as air coins, which were hard to distinguish from the real ones and mixed with the pearls.

The Chinese government lacked the ability and legal tools to identify ICO tokens. China's security law still takes an enumerative approach to the definition of securities. The Security Law at that time (amended in 2014) regulated only stocks, corporate bonds, government bonds, investment fund shares, and "other securities as determined by the State Council in accordance with the Law". However, the State Council never exercised this authority to identify other types of securities. 2019 amendments to the Security Law added the categories of depositary receipts, asset-backed securities, and asset management products. In other words, there are no underwriting provisions in China's security law that can define securities as broadly as investment contracts in U.S. law or collective investment schemes in Japanese law.

As a result, Chinese securities law cannot interpret tokens issued by ICOs as securities, making it difficult to impose effective regulation, and thus chooses to prohibit them.[5] Due to the global nature of ICOs, the 2017 Notice directly banned cryptocurrency exchange platforms to block the possibility of Chinese residents investing in overseas ICOs with cryptocurrencies.

First, the 2017 Announcement banned ICOs by administrative means, requiring ICOs that have not yet been implemented to be immediately suspended and ICOs that have been completed to be fully retired.

Second, the 2017 Announcement states that ICOs may be suspected of criminal offenses. However, the subjects of the 2017 Announcement do not include police departments and judicial departments, and accordingly, no ICO participants have been held criminally liable.

Third, the 2017 Announcement outlawed cryptocurrency exchange platforms, banned the exchange business between legal tender and tokens and virtual currencies, prohibited platforms from buying and selling tokens and virtual currencies, and prohibited the provision of pricing and information intermediary services for tokens and virtual currencies. This move led many Chinese cryptocurrency exchange platforms to leave the country and find a stronghold outside of China to continue their business, such as Binance and Huobi, etc.

Fourth, the 2017 Announcement reiterated that licensed financial institutions are not allowed to get involved in any cryptocurrency-related businesses.

3.3 *The 2021 Notice*

After the 2017 Announcement, many cryptocurrency exchange platforms went overseas and still provide services to Chinese residents through multiple channels. In addition, many criminals carry out fraudulent activities and Ponzi schemes in the name of blockchain and virtual currencies. As a result, the 2021 Notice further strengthens the regulation and restrictions on cryptocurrencies.

First, the scope of the prohibited business added a "virtual currency derivatives trading". However, after the 2017 Announcement, derivatives trading in cryptocurrencies was effectively banned. The additional provisions of the 2021 Notice are merely *pro forma*.

5 参见杨东、黄尹旭:《ICO 本质及监管机制变革》, 载《证券法苑》第23 卷, 第307–309 页.

Second, cryptocurrency exchange platforms opened outside of China are explicitly prohibited from providing services to Chinese residents. The Chinese Internet has set up the famous Great Firewall system, which can be used to block the websites of offshore exchange platforms. However, there are still some people who use private VPNs to access offshore exchange platforms to buy and sell cryptocurrencies.

Third, the civil effect of cryptocurrency-related transactions is mentioned. The 2021 Notice states that anyone 'who invests in virtual currencies and related derivatives, contrary to public order and good moral, the relevant civil legal conduct is invalid'. The effect of this provision will be analyzed in the next section.

Fourth, mining of cryptocurrencies, while not banned, is subject to many restrictions. The 2021 Notice calls for monitoring cryptocurrency mining and tracking the flow of new cryptocurrencies. In addition, the National Development and Reform Commission has classified cryptocurrency mining as a "phase-out" industry in its industrial policy, which means cryptocurrency mining farms must pay extra money for electricity.

Fifth, cryptocurrency-related advertising is strictly restricted. 2021 Notice prohibits any form of advertising for cryptocurrency-related business activities and prohibits market entities from using cryptocurrency or related terms in their registered names.

3.4 *Summary*

In general, there are several features of China's public law regulation of cryptocurrencies.

First, the regulatory body of cryptocurrencies is unclear. The 2013 Notice, the 2017 Announcement, and the 2021 Notice were all jointly issued by multiple departments. Among them, the People's Bank of China, as the central bank, has the responsibility of coordinating financial regulation and thus is the lead entity in each case. Since China's financial supervision adopts a separate regulatory system, there is no unified financial regulation authority, resulting in the lack of a clear regulatory body for cryptocurrencies.

Second, the lack of legislation leads to uncertainty in legal effects. The 2013 Notice, the 2017 Announcement, and the 2021 Notice are not formal legislative documents and lack clear legal effect. This problem is especially serious in criminal matters, considering the principle of *nulla poena sine lege*. Although the issuers of the 2021 Announcement include the Supreme People's Court, the Supreme People's Procuratorate, and the Ministry of Public Security, the judiciary will only crackdown on the use of cryptocurrencies as instruments for suspected fraud, money laundering, and other crimes, both before and after the 2021 Announcement.[6]

Third, the cross-border nature of cryptocurrencies has led to instability in the effectiveness of China's regulatory measures. After the 2017 Announcement shutdown of cryptocurrency exchange platforms, cryptocurrency-related businesses have not disappeared in China. There are still many mining sites operating in China. In addition, money laundering crimes using cryptocurrencies are proliferating. Many suspected embezzlers and fraudsters use cryptocurrencies to send their ill-gotten gains overseas.

Fourth, academic discussions related to cryptocurrency regulation remain active. One of the more important discussions is that regulators should use blockchain technology to establish a 'RegChain' which is a blockchain for the purpose of regulation to achieve effective regulation of transactions on the blockchain.[7] The specific implementation relies on the aforementioned concept of Coken combined with big data tools to establish a technology-driven regulatory mechanism.[8]

4 Private Law Issues

4.1 *Abstraction*

The system of property rights provided for in the Chinese Civil Code is similar to that of civil law countries such as Germany and Japan, in that it provides for a number of other types of property rights on the basis of the dichotomy between right *in rem* and claims. Within this system, the Civil Code also provides a declaratory provision on "network virtual property" but does not specify its specific content.

4.1.1 About 'Network Virtual Property'

Considering that the 2013 Notice defines Bitcoin as a virtual commodity, cryptocurrencies should be interpreted as "network virtual property" in similar terms. Civil Code Article 127[9] introduces the concept of network virtual property, but does not specify its nature, and delegates it to other laws.

---

6 Such as 冯桂芬非法吸收公众存款二审案, 辽宁省沈阳市中级人民法院刑事裁定书 (2021) 辽 01 刑终 760 号.

7 参见杨东: 《区块链 + 监管 = 法链》, 人民出版社 2018 年版, 第 5 页.

8 See *supra* note 3.

9 Civil Code Article 127: "Where any laws provide for the protection of data and network virtual property, such laws shall apply."

According to academic discussions, network virtual property initially refers to objects with property value issued by centralized administrators such as online game operators.[10] The nature of network virtual property is controversial between the right *in rem* theory and the claim theory. According to the right *in rem* theory, the holder has the right *in rem* to the network virtual property.[11] The claim theory holds that the holder has a claim on the issuer of the network virtual property.[12] In the case of the network virtual property issued by the centralized manager, the holder cannot enjoy and dispose of the network virtual property without the cooperation of the issuer, so it seems that the claim theory is more reasonable. However, if cryptocurrencies are interpreted as network virtual property, since many cryptocurrencies do not have an issuer, it is obvious that the claim theory cannot be applied.

Article 127 of the Civil Code is inherently open-ended and does not specify the properties of network virtual property. Neither cryptocurrencies nor crypto-assets should be excluded from network virtual property. Therefore, the attributes of network virtual property need to be discussed based on considering cryptocurrencies and crypto-assets, and further legislate accordingly.

4.1.2 Legal Effects of Civil Acts Related to Cryptocurrencies

As mentioned above, the 2021 Notice states that anyone 'who invests in virtual currencies and related derivatives, contrary to public order and good moral, the relevant civil legal conduct are invalid'. From the context, it is not clear whether the meaning is "all investments in cryptocurrencies and their derivatives are invalid because they violate public order and good moral" or "investments in cryptocurrencies and their derivatives are invalid to the extent that they violate public order and good moral".

In theory, the 2021 Notice does not have the power to dismiss all acts involving cryptocurrencies as a violation of public order and good morals. This exceeds the authority of departmental regulations. The main text of Article 153, paragraph 1 of the Civil Code[13] provides that contracts that violate the mandatory provisions of laws and administrative regulations are void,

---

10 参见刘军霞:《首例虚拟财产纠纷案引发的法律思考——兼论虚拟财产的保护》,载《河北法学》2004年第11期,第112–113页.

11 参见杨立新:《民法总则规定网络虚拟财产的含义及重要价值》, 载《东方法学》2017年第3期,第68–69页.

12 参见王雷:《网络虚拟财产权债权说之坚持——兼论网络虚拟财产在我国民法典中的体系位置》,载《江汉论坛》2017年第1期,第125–126页.

13 Civil Code Article 153(1): "A juridical act violating the imperative provisions of any law or administrative regulation shall be void, unless the imperative provisions do not result in the nullity of the juridical act."

while departmental regulations are not included in this scope. Therefore, two approaches exist in judicial practice regarding contracts that violate departmental regulations. The first one is to recognize only the public law effect of departmental regulations, but the departmental regulations cannot cause the contract to be invalid. The second is to invoke paragraph 2 of Article 153 of the Civil Code[14] to indirectly invalidate the contract with the help of the principle of public order and good morals.[15] In 2019, the Supreme Court published the Minutes of the National Courts' Civil and Commercial Trial Work Conference (called "the Minutes"), which formally recognized the second method of treatment. The first sentence of Article 31 of the Minutes provides that "Violation of departmental regulations does not affect the validity of contracts in general, but if the departmental regulations relate to public order and good moral such as financial security, market order, and national macro policies, the contracts shall be determined invalid." Since the Minutes are not formal judicial interpretations, the Supreme Court requires that courts at all levels cannot directly cite the Minutes as the basis for their decisions but can only reason in the reasoning part of the judgment following the ideas of the Minutes. The latter sentence of Article 31 of the Minutes further requires that "When determining whether departmental regulations relate to public order and good moral, people's courts shall prudently consider regulatory intensity, transaction security, social impact, and other aspects, on the basis of examining the subject of the norms, and fully explain reasons in adjudicative instruments."

However, as will be seen from the following analysis,[16] the courts have found almost all transactions involving cryptocurrencies to violate public order and good morals. Indeed, before the 2021 Notice, there were already cases where some courts invoked the public order clause to invalidate civil actions related to cryptocurrencies, although at the same time other courts disagreed with such an approach. Following the 2021 Notice, this practice has largely become commonplace. Almost all transactions involving cryptocurrencies are found to violate public order and good morals and are ruled invalid. Although China recognizes the principle of *lex retro non agit*, interpretations of the law in judicial interpretations or administrative agency documents are usually not

14 Civil Code Article 153(2): "A juridical act contrary to public order and good morals shall be void."

15 参见杜一华、尹鑫鹏:《金融监管规章影响合同效力的公序良俗通道研究》,载《河北法学》2020 年第 11 期, 第 120 页。

16 Some of the cases used in the following analysis involve crypto assets rather than strictly cryptocurrencies. Since there are fewer cases involving only narrowly defined cryptocurrencies, this chapter also examines cases involving crypto-assets and compares them to cryptocurrencies.

considered changes in the law itself, but only changes in interpretation. Therefore, the 2021 Notice has also been applied by Chinese courts to cases that predate the issuance of it.

Some scholars have argued that transactions involving cryptocurrencies necessarily involve cryptocurrency exchange platforms, which have been recognized as illegal. In addition, transactions in virtual currencies, even if they are not directly involved in ICOs, may be briefly involved as part of a "chain of illicit financial activities". Cryptocurrency transactions between individuals are therefore considered to be detrimental to the financial order and the public interest.[17] However, the scholar also pointed out that if the relevant transaction is ruled invalid, it may face a practical difficulty, that is, according to Article 157 of the Civil Code, both parties should return the property after the contract is invalidated, but cryptocurrency is difficult to enforce, which may result in only the party who gave the legal tender be able to reclaim the property, and thus be unfair. Therefore, it was argued that the relevant transaction should not be ruled invalid, but rather the prosecution should be dismissed, or, in special circumstances, the substantive gains and losses of the parties should be balanced through the unjust enrichment system.[18]

4.1.3 Discussion about Private Law Nature of Cryptocurrencies

Chinese academics have two main views on the private law nature of cryptocurrencies.

The first view is that the native assets with the value base provided by blockchain technology have the possibility of exclusive domination, which is consistent with the characteristics of rights *in rem*, and should be regarded as the object of rights *in rem*.[19] For cryptocurrencies that ensure their value based on real-world mechanisms, such as stablecoins, there are two further ideas that can be subdivided. The first idea is to simply define centralized cryptocurrencies as claims on the issuer;[20] the other idea argues that the linking relationship between assets on the blockchain and real-world assets should be examined.[21]

17 参见齐晓丹:《涉虚拟货币合同纠纷的司法裁判路径辨析——以政府监管政策导向与民事法律规范适用的衔接为视角》, 载《法律适用》2022 年第 9 期, 第 112页.

18 同上注, 第 115–116 页.

19 参见司晓:《区块链数字资产物权论》, 载《探索与争鸣》2021 年第 12 期, 第 83–85 页; 韦柳婷、莫初明:《民法视域下数字资产的性质界定和保护路径》, 载《广西政法管理干部学院学报》2022 年第 4 期, 第 89 页.

20 同上注, 韦柳婷、莫初明文, 第 92 页.

21 同前注 19, 司晓文, 第 82 页.

The second view is that cryptocurrencies cannot be the object of rights *in rem*, but only of property rights. The reason for this is that cryptocurrencies are not unique in the sense that the information in their distributed ledgers can be constantly copied. In addition, the private key verification process when transferring cryptocurrencies requires the assistance of miners to complete the bookkeeping. Therefore, the argument goes, cryptocurrencies do not have the same exclusivity as corporeal objects. In contrast, the exclusivity of property rights can require only physical boundaries in the conceptual sense. Therefore, cryptocurrencies can have the exclusivity required of property right objects and can be the object of property rights.[22]

However, discussions on the private law nature of cryptocurrencies have not been able to achieve much consensus due to the precarious state of the private law effects of cryptocurrency-related transactions.

4.2 *Specific Private Law Issues*

4.2.1 Transfer

Before the 2021 Notice, the academic community generally believed that cryptocurrencies were still legal to buy and sell, only that exchange platforms were banned. For example, on the premise of the right *in rem* doctrine, it is argued that the transfer of cryptocurrency becomes effective when the blockchain completes its bookkeeping.[23] This is because the 2017 Announcement only prohibits the buying and selling of cryptocurrencies as a central counterparty, but not all buying and selling. However, the judicial practice appears to be harsher and more uneven, and after the 2021 Notice, this attitude shifts to a more severe trend.

For example, in a case[24] before the 2021 Notice, the party who purchased a crypto-asset SPC argued that the sale contract was invalid, and the court upheld it. However, the decision was made in the absence of the defendant and is currently under retrial proceedings,[25] the effect of which has not yet been determined.

---

22 参见阮神裕:《区块链数字资产的财产意涵》, 载《中国人民大学学报》2023 年第 2 期, 第 148 、 153 页.

23 同前注 19, 司晓文, 第 89 页.

24 杨蒙诉郝泽萱买卖合同纠纷案, 北京市海淀区人民法院民事判决书 (2019) 京 0108 民初 10776 号.

25 杨蒙诉郝泽萱买卖合同纠纷再审案, 北京市第一中级人民法院民事判决书 (2021) 京 01 民申 543 号.

Most cryptocurrency sale and purchase contracts in cases after the 2021 notice will be ruled invalid. In a case[26] involving the purchase and sale of crypto-assets, the court ruled that the sale contract was void and required the seller to return the money paid for the purchase. However, there are a few cases that are different. In another case[27] decided after the 2021 Notice was issued, the court did not invoke the 2021 Notice and instead found the contract of sale to be valid.

Contracts for the purchase and sale of cryptocurrencies between private individuals do not involve financial security or market order, and therefore there is no reason to find that they violate public order and good morals. The current approach of judicial practice interferes excessively with the freedom of trade and seems to be inappropriate.

4.2.2 Trust and Mandate

Since the 2013 Notice, licensed financial institutions have been prohibited from conducting business related to cryptocurrencies. Therefore, financial institutions such as trust companies and investment funds cannot accept cryptocurrencies as trust property. It can be said that there are no commercial trusts for cryptocurrencies in China.

In contrast, the use of civil trusts is very rare in China, and entrusted investments between individuals will hardly be recognized as constructive trusts.[28] Therefore, the legal relationship arising from entrusting others to invest and manage cryptocurrencies is usually dealt with under the framework of contracts of mandate.

After the issuance of the 2021 Notice, contracts of the mandate of investment involving cryptocurrencies are usually found to be invalid by the courts. According to Article 58 of the Contract Law (corresponding to Article 157 of the Civil Code),[29] after a contract is invalidated or revoked, the parties shall

26 彭伟莉诉徐秀慧、张立中买卖合同纠纷二审案，辽宁省沈阳市中级人民法院民事判决书 (2021) 辽 01 民终 19198 号.

27 王雅磊诉吴丽杰买卖合同纠纷二审案，广西壮族自治区防城港市中级人民法院民事判决书 (2021) 桂 06 民终 1365 号.

28 参见赵姿昂:《论推定信托在中国的引入》，载《海南大学学报（人文社会科学版）》2019 年第 5 期, 第 149 页.

29 Civil Code Article 157: "After a juridical act is void, revoked, or determined as having no binding force, the property obtained by the actor as a result of the act shall be restituted; if restitution is impossible or unnecessary, indemnification shall be made at an estimated price. The party at fault shall compensate the other party for any loss suffered as a result of the act; or if both parties are at fault, they shall assume corresponding liabilities respectively, except as otherwise provided for by any law."

return the relevant property; if both parties are at fault, each shall bear the corresponding responsibility. However, the legal effect of invalidity is not uniform in courts across China. Cases can be discussed in two types.

The first type is where the mandator pays legal tender to the mandatary and mandates the mandatary to invest in cryptocurrencies. In one case,[30] the court invoked the 2021 Notice to invalidate the contract of mandate and dismissed the mandator's claim for the return of the principal and the profits due. The case did not accurately apply Article 58 of the Contract Law, resulting in the mandator's blood and money being lost, which was improper. It is worth noting that the first instance decision[31] in the case was made before the 2021 Notice was issued, and instead of declaring the contract invalid, the mandator's claim was upheld.

In another case[32] before the 2021 Notice, the court ruled that the contract of the mandate of investments in crypto-assets was invalid, citing the 2017 Announcement, and applied Article 58 of the Contract Law, finding that the mandator and the mandatary were each at fault and ordering the mandatary to return half of the legal tender paid by the mandator. The decision, in this case, can still be called appropriate.

The second type is where the mandator delivers cryptocurrencies to the mandatary and mandates the mandatary to manage and invest them. Because cryptocurrencies are difficult to discover and enforce, the interests of the mandator in such cases are even more difficult to protect.

In one case,[33] the court invoked the 2021 Notice to rule that the contract of the mandate was void and held that the Bitcoins in the account in question were unaccounted for and that there was no returnable property, thereby ruling that the mandatary was not required to return the Bitcoins or their legal tender equivalent to the mandator.

In another similar case,[34] after the court of first instance ruled that the contract of the mandate was valid and that the mandatary should pay the principal and the agreed profit to the mandator, the court of the second instance, while

30 李凯诉魏锟委托合同纠纷二审案，北京市第三中级人民法院民事判决书（2021）京 03 民终 18277 号.

31 李凯诉魏锟委托合同纠纷案，北京市顺义区人民法院民事判决书（2021）京 0113 民初 11740 号.

32 张丽华诉丛华丰委托合同纠纷二审案，山东省威海市中级人民法院民事判决书（2021）鲁 10 民终 2401 号.

33 刘思宇诉盛林林委托合同纠纷二审案， 北京市第三中级人民法院民事判决书（2021）京 03 民终 14106 号。

34 陆斌诉路昊其他合同纠纷二审案，上海市第一中级人民法院民事判决书（2021）沪 01 民终 16047 号.

invoking the 2021 Notice, ruled that the contract of the mandate was invalid, but recognized the memorandum between the mandator and the mandatary confirming the total amount of principal and profit payable as valid, and thus upheld the conclusion of the first instance judgment in terms of outcome. The logic of the decision, in this case, is questionable. The original contract was ruled invalid while at the same time the memorandum confirming the loss was found valid unless the memorandum was interpreted as an independent gift contract.

In addition, it is not feasible for the mandator to intend to claim the return of the cryptocurrency on the grounds of the return of the original. In a case,[35] the court held that cryptocurrencies lacked a legal way to be priced in China after the cryptocurrency exchange platforms were shut down, and thus were not measurable property, thus ruling that the claim for return of cryptocurrencies was not within the scope of civil litigation and dismissing the suit. Since cryptocurrency is not yet a thing under civil law, it is reasonable that a claim for the return of the original is not possible.

There was a tendency to treat cryptocurrencies and crypto-assets differently until the 2021 Notice is issued. That is, contracts of the mandate of investing in cryptocurrencies were more often ruled valid and contracts of the mandate of investing in crypto-assets were more often ruled invalid. However, after the 2021 Notice, the former is also similarly ruled invalid.

The purpose of the 2017 Announcement and the 2021 Notice is to restrict investments in cryptocurrencies and crypto-assets. After the domestic exchange platforms were thus shut down, those who mandate others to invest in offshore platforms to avoid regulation were found to be invalid for violating public order and good morals, and such interpretation is proper in terms of legal dogmatics.

4.3 *Lending*

Similar to the case of mandating the management of cryptocurrencies, the lending of cryptocurrencies is hardly protected by law in China.

In a case,[36] plaintiff claims to have loaned USDT to the defendant and requests its return. Although the plaintiff did send USDT to the defendant, the court combined with other evidence to find that there was an investment dispute between the plaintiff and the defendant, and it was not sufficient to find

35 孟浩诉郤正华返还原物纠纷二审案,陕西省西安市中级人民法院民事裁定书(2020)陕 01 民终 11210 号.

36 王东诉王涛借用合同纠纷二审案, 浙江省宁波市中级人民法院民事判决书(2021)浙 02 民终 3554 号.

that there was a consensual agreement to lend USDT, and thus dismissed the claim.

In another case,[37] the court ruled outright that Bitcoin was not protected by law and did not fall within the scope of civil actions under the civil procedure law, dismissing the suit. This decision is improper.

The regulatory purpose of the 2017 Announcement and the 2021 Notice suggests that the lending of cryptocurrencies between individuals is not within the scope of the prohibition. Such contracts should also not be found to be invalid. However, courts across China refuse to grant legal protection to lenders of cryptocurrencies on various grounds to avoid the difficulty of discovering and enforcing cryptocurrencies. This phenomenon is highly inappropriate.

4.4 *Loss*

Whether or not a holder can obtain relief after losing a cryptocurrency depends on whether or not it is held through an intermediary such as an exchange platform.

If the holder holds the cryptocurrency directly without an intermediary, a tort law remedy is available. For example, in one case,[38] the defendant used coercion to require the plaintiff to transfer Bitcoin and another crypto-asset, Skycoin (SKY), to himself. The court recognized the plaintiff's claim based on tort liability and ordered the defendant to return the Bitcoin and SKY outright. However, it also allowed the defendant to discount the price, which could not be determined by reference to the oversea exchange platform, but by negotiation. In addition, the parties to the case were foreign and Chinese law was applied following Article 44 of Law on Choice of Law for Foreign-related Civil Relationships.[39]

Conversely, cryptocurrency holders are much less likely to be protected if they are held through an intermediary such as an overseas exchange platform. In one case,[40] the plaintiff opened an account on an overseas exchange platform and held Ripple. After the loss of Ripple, the plaintiff sued the

---

37 徐捷诉林庆星民间借贷纠纷二审案， 江苏省常州市中级人民法院民事裁定书 (2021) 苏 04 民终 4306 号.

38 李圣艳等诉闫向东等财产损害赔偿纠纷二审案，上海市第一中级人民法院民事判决书 (2019) 沪 01 民终 13689 号.

39 Law on Choice of Law for Foreign-related Civil Relationships Article 44: " The laws at the place of tort shall apply to liabilities for tort, but if the parties have a mutual habitual residence, the laws at the mutual habitual residence shall apply. If the parties choose the applicable laws by agreement after any tort takes place, the agreement shall prevail."

40 吴叶飞诉北京火币天下网络技术有限公司网络侵权责任纠纷二审案，北京市第四中级人民法院民事判决书 (2021) 京 04 民终 743 号.

platform's affiliate company in China, claiming that the platform and the affiliate company had conflation of personalities and demanding that the defendant be held liable for the tort. The court found that there was no evidence to prove that a conflation of personalities had occurred, and therefore dismissed the claim. The court also pointed out that opening an account on an overseas exchange platform is contrary to China's financial regulatory policy, and the parties should do so at their own risk.

4.5 *Hard Fork*

Since cryptocurrencies are not explicitly the object of rights *in rem*, new cryptocurrencies generating from hard forks of blockchain of cryptocurrencies cannot be interpreted as *fructus* either. The vesting of new cryptocurrencies generated from hard forks can only be determined by contract.

In one case,[41] the plaintiff opened an account and held Bitcoin on the defendant's cryptocurrency exchange platform. Before the BCC (Bitcoin Cash) hard fork, the defendant announced that it would pay the BCC generated by the hard fork to users. The 2017 Announcement led to the defendant's company phasing out of its business, but the court still ordered the defendant to pay the agreed-upon BCC.

4.6 *Inheritance*

Currently, there are no judicial cases of cryptocurrency inheritance in China. According to the academic discussion, network virtual property belongs to the property that can be legally inherited.[42] Cryptocurrencies are also not an exception.

Discussions on the inheritance of network virtual property have focused on the model of opening an account with an internet service provider (ISP). Scholars pointed out that, in reality, ISPs restrict users' inheritance through user agreements, which should be dealt with by the rules of standard terms (Article 496 Paragraph 2 and Article 497 of the Civil Code),[43] and legislation on matters

41 冯亦然诉北京乐酷达网络科技有限公司合同纠纷案, 北京市海淀区人民法院民事判决书 (2018) 京 0108 民初 24805 号.

42 参见梅夏英、许可; 《虚拟财产继承的理论与立法问题》, 载《法学家》2013 年第 6 期, 第 91–92 页; 李岩:《虚拟财产继承立法问题》, 载《法学》2013 年第 4 期, 第 88 页.

43 Civil Code Article 496(2): "Where standard terms are adopted for contracting, the party furnishing the standard terms shall define the rights and obligations between the parties under the principle of fairness, remind in a reasonable manner the other party to note the terms excluding or limiting the liability of the party furnishing the standard terms or otherwise related to the material interest of the other party, and explain the terms upon

of inheritance of network virtual property is also needed in the future.[44] When applied to cryptocurrencies, such discussions can only be applied to the model of opening an account with an intermediary. However, due to public law prohibitions on cryptocurrency exchange platforms, cryptocurrencies held under this model cannot be inherited as legal property through the judicial process.

The existing discussion of network virtual property is not directly applicable to the situation where cryptocurrencies are held directly without intermediaries. Cryptocurrencies are highly secretive. It is difficult for anyone other than the person directly in possession of the private key to even know about the existence of cryptocurrency. It is also difficult to force the existence of cryptocurrencies to be disclosed by law. Therefore, the inheritance of cryptocurrencies depends on the control of the private key. It is difficult for the law to interfere with and regulate this.

4.7 *Attachment and Pledge*

Due to the secretiveness of cryptocurrencies, attachment and seizure of cryptocurrencies can only be achieved more easily with the help of an intermediary if it is held indirectly through that intermediary. With the ban on cryptocurrency exchange platforms, this is no longer the situation in China.

By contrast, seizing directly held cryptocurrency is very difficult and will likely end up being enforced only with the help of indirect enforcement.

Because of the difficulty of attachment and seizure of cryptocurrencies, cryptocurrencies are also unsuitable for pledges because creditors lack a way to realize their pledges.

4.8 *Insolvency*

When the 2017 Announcement led to the closure of cryptocurrency exchange platforms, each platform delivered cryptocurrencies belonging to its users

---

request of the other party. If the party furnishing the standard terms fails to perform the reminding or explanation obligation, resulting in the other party failing to note or understand the terms in which it has a material interest, the other party may argue that the terms are not a part of the contract."

Article 497: "Under any of the following circumstances, standard terms shall be void: (1) Under the voidness circumstances set forth in Section 3, Chapter VI, Book One of this Code and Article 506 of this Code; (2) The party furnishing the standard terms unreasonably excludes or limits its liability, aggravates the liability of the other party, or restricts the main rights of the other party.; (3) The party furnishing the standard terms excludes the main rights of the other party."

44 同前注 42，梅夏英、许可文, 第 88 页.

after government intervention. A peaceful exit was achieved. Thereafter, as no exchange platforms exist in China, there was no question about the insolvency of exchange platforms or their users.

When the direct holder of a cryptocurrency becomes insolvent, the cryptocurrency is *de facto* difficult to detect and treat as an insolvency estate due to the secretiveness of the cryptocurrency. As a result, there are no relevant judicial cases.

4.9 *Private International Law*

Actions that are not prohibited by public law would be handled by the provisions of the Law on Choice of Law for Foreign-related Civil Relationships. For example, the aforementioned case[45] on tort applies the law at the place of tort by applying Article 44.

In contrast, the acts regulated by the 2017 Announcement and the 2021 Notice involve 'mandatory provisions' (Article 4) or 'public interest' (Article 5) in Law on Choice of Law of Foreign-related Civil Relationships, and Chinese law should be applied. The "public interest" in Article 5 should be interpreted in the same way as "public order and good morals" in Article 153(2) of the Civil Code. Therefore, Chinese law should be applied to all acts involving financial security and market order. In other words, the relevant legal act is likely to be found invalid.

5 Tax

China has no specific provisions on cryptocurrency-related taxes. Cryptocurrencies are subject to income tax on income from the conveyance of property as stipulated in Article 2 of the Individual Income Tax Law and Article 6 of the Enterprise Income Tax Law. However, since the cryptocurrency exchange platform is closed, whether trading on an offshore exchange platform or trading over the counter without going through the platform, the corresponding trading behavior cannot be traced and is difficult to tax. In China, cryptocurrencies are in a *de facto* untaxed state.

45 *Supra* note 34.

6 Cross-Border Issue

6.1 *Cross-Border Issue of Regulation*

China has taken an extremely strict regulatory stance on cryptocurrencies, but there are some problems due to the cross-border nature of cryptocurrencies.

Since cryptocurrency payments cannot be monitored, Chinese residents may use cryptocurrencies to invest in ICO projects overseas, leading to capital outflows. More seriously, criminals who commit crimes such as fraud and embezzlement send their illegal proceeds offshore in cryptocurrency, which is difficult to recover. Due to the presence of cryptocurrency mining factories within China, investors or money launderers can acquire cryptocurrencies within the country and easily send them offshore.

This problem stems from the inherent architecture of cryptocurrencies. The anonymity and cross-border mobility that cryptocurrencies have made it difficult to cope with the existing means of legal regulation.

6.2 *Cross-Border Issue of Litigation*

As mentioned earlier, on the issue of the choice of law, Chinese law adopts a public order and good moral standard, which means cryptocurrency transactions related to financial security and market order should be applied to Chinese law and found invalid.

Similarly, China takes a substantive review approach to the recognition and enforcement of foreign arbitrations and judgments. According to Article 289 of the Civil Procedure Law,[46] not only does it need to comply with the provisions of international treaties and satisfy the principle of reciprocity, but it also needs not to be contrary to the "the sovereignty, security and public interest" before foreign arbitrations and judgments can be recognized and enforced. Similar to the choice of law issue, the "public interest" in this Article should be

46 Civil Procedure Law Article 289: "After examining an application or request for recognition and enforcement of an effective judgment or ruling of a foreign court in accordance with an international treaty concluded or acceded to by the People's Republic of China or under the principle of reciprocity, a people's court shall issue a ruling to recognize the legal force of the judgment or ruling and issue an order for enforcement as needed to enforce the judgment or ruling according to the relevant provisions of this Law if the people's court deems that the judgment or ruling does not violate the basic principles of the laws of the People's Republic of China and the sovereignty, security and public interest of the People's Republic of China. If the judgment or ruling violates the basic principles of the laws of the People's Republic of China or the sovereignty, security or public interest of the People's Republic of China, the people's court shall not grant recognition and enforcement."

interpreted in the same way as "public order and good morals" in Article 153(2) of the Civil Code. Therefore, foreign arbitrations and judgments involving the regulation of cryptocurrencies under public law cannot be recognized and enforced in China.

7 Conclusion

In general, the positioning of cryptocurrencies in Chinese law is not clear. The Chinese government has blocked cryptocurrency exchange platforms and restricted mining of cryptocurrencies by departmental regulations. Although these regulations theoretically do not directly prohibit the private holding and trading of cryptocurrencies, China's judicial practice is still influenced by the relevant regulations. Lower courts across the country have invoked the 'public order and good moral' provisions of the Chinese Civil Code in their decisions, invalidating some of the trading practices related to cryptocurrencies. This has led to a state of confusion in the discussion of legal issues related to cryptocurrencies, failing to reach a stable conclusion.

On the other hand, Chinese academics have engaged in ongoing discussions of cryptocurrency-related issues. The declaratory provisions on network virtual property in the Civil Code provide a wide space for such discussions. With the innovative theory of Coken in practice, it is foreseeable that the application of cryptocurrencies in China will further develop. The legal issues of cryptocurrencies will also increase, pushing for the continuous improvement of cryptocurrency-related laws and regulation.

Croatia

Tomislav Jakšić and Siniša Petrović

1 Legal Qualification

Under Croatian law "cryptocurrencies" are generally not regulated. In other words, the Croatian legislator did not enact legislation that would expressly regulate cryptocurrency transactions, their existence, application, or everyday use. However, this does not mean that the use of cryptocurrencies is forbidden, absent or that they are not circulating in Croatia.

Croatian residents and companies can acquire and transfer any type of cryptocurrency offered by any other person or legal entity.[1] There are no specific restrictions or limitations in this regard. The most popular cryptocurrencies are the ones that also enjoy worldwide attention like Bitcoin (BTC) and Ethereum (ETH). An increase of the public's interest in cryptocurrencies led to the growth of businesses that provide various cryptocurrency-related services (e.g. trading, exchange into other currency, cryptocurrency payment processing, provision of hardware wallets for storage and safekeeping).[2] Commercial entities have also demonstrated interest in other cryptoassets like utility and investment tokens as well as initial coin offerings of new cryptoassets.[3] Furthermore, it is also possible to pay for goods and services with one of the more popular types of cryptocurrencies (e.g. BTC) at some in-person and online stores and also to trade with various types of cryptocurrencies. This growing interest in cryptoassets is further supported by an increasing number of published academic and professional papers as well as various conferences and round tables on related topics.[4] Therefore, interest in cryptocurrencies and other cryptoassets in Croatia seems to be increasing overall.

Although the national legislator decided not to regulate cryptocurrencies and other cryptoassets, the increasing number of cryptocurrency transactions resulted in increased activity of some national regulatory agencies responsible

---

1 For example, residents can register and use foreign apps like Coinbase, Binance, and Revolut to acquire cryptocurrencies.

2 For example, "Bitcoin Store" and "Electrocoin" provide various cryptocurrency services.

3 HANFA Opinion related to the offering of digital assets based on Ethereum blockchain dated 6 April 2020 (available at https://www.hanfa.hr/vijesti/mi%C5%A1ljenje-hanfe-vezano-za-izdavanje-digitalne-imovine-utemeljenoj-na-ethereum-blockchainu/, visited 26 January 2021).

4 For example, see 6. Litigation and Miscellaneous.

 | DOI:10.1163/9789004722507_007

for the supervision of specific markets and services like the Croatian National Bank and the Croatian Financial Services Supervisory Agency. Most importantly, early on interest was especially demonstrated by the national tax authority which has issued opinions on the taxation of income derived from cryptoassets.[5] The tax authority is also doing its best to tax income resulting from the trade of cryptocurrency tokens.

It should be noted that in Croatia it is possible to make domestic payments only in the national currency.[6] Consequently, it comes as no surprise that cryptocurrencies are not recognized as legal tender in Croatia. In 2018 the Croatian National Bank confirmed this by making it clear that cryptocurrencies (it uses a broader term virtual currency) are not considered legal tender in the Republic of Croatia, a foreign currency or a foreign means of payment. It also stated that cryptocurrencies do not qualify as money since they lack some basic functions that are normally attributed to money, namely that it is a measure of value, a means of exchange, and a means of saving.[7] Even though cryptocurrencies have some of these functions, they cannot be relied upon in everyday transactions in the same manner as traditional currencies. Namely, although cryptocurrencies can and some are used as a means of payment, including expression of the numerical value of goods and services, they are generally unable to store a stable value due to their highly volatile nature.[8] This is a result of their dependence on market fluctuations. In other words, participants of a cryptocurrency transaction bear the risk of such volatility which also means that every such transaction results in speculative investment activity. In addition, while traditional (state-backed) currencies are affected by the state's monetary measures, cryptocurrencies are affected solely by the market and its

5 For example, Opinion of the Ministry of Finance Tax Administration No. 410-01/17-08/29 dated 19 March 2018.

6 This does not mean that monetary obligation cannot be agreed in foreign currency, but such obligation shall generally be calculated and then performed in the national currency. For more, see Article 22 Obligations Act (Official Gazette Nos. 35/05, 41/08, 125/11, 78/15, 29/18, 126/21). Between the residents it is possible to make payments in foreign currency only exceptionally. For example, for disbursement of salary to resident employee temporarily working in another country. For more see Article 4 Decision on payments and collections in foreign means of payment in the country (Official Gazette Nos. 111/2005, 16/2015).

7 Position of the Croatian National Bank published as a text under the title "What are virtual currencies?" dated 9 February 2018 (available at https://www.hnb.hr/en/-/sto-su-virtualne-valute-/).

8 R. Siffert, S. Petrović, T. Jakšić, 'Payment of the capital contribution of a company limited by shares in cryptocurrency' 8 (2) 2019 *Zagreb Law Review* 105; I. Parać Vukomanović, 'Pravna priroda virtualnih valuta' 3/2019 *Pravo u gospodarstvu* 414.

stakeholders.[9] In this regard, doubts were also raised concerning the ability of some popular cryptocurrencies (i.e. BTC) to be used as a means of payment as well as the ability of cryptocurrencies to be used as a unit of account.[10] On another note, there are currently no plans to issue a Croatian national currency in the form of cryptocurrency or to issue some sort of stablecoin that is backed up by some other type of asset like the national currency, commodity, or security. However, Croatian residents are free to acquire and trade with existing stablecoins like Tether or Binance USD.

It also comes as no surprise that the Croatian legislator did not define cryptocurrencies. In 2018 the Croatian National Bank concluded that virtual currencies "... are a digital representation of value and they can be considered a specific type of assets which their holders are ready to hold and/or exchange electronically and use them sporadically for mutual payments in line with the belief that such currencies have real value."[11] The term virtual currency was intended to encompass cryptocurrencies, like BTC. In early 2020 for regulatory purposes and implementation of the new rules on the prevention of money laundering and terrorist financing, the Act on the Prevention of Money Laundering and Terrorist Financing determined virtual currency as "... a digital record of value not issued nor guaranteed by the central bank or public authority, which is not necessarily connected to a legally recognized monetary unit and has no legal status of currency or money, but is accepted by natural persons or legal entities as a medium that can be transferred, stored and traded electronically."[12] Although cryptocurrencies have been determined through a broader term of virtual currency, this has been undertaken for narrow regulatory purposes, i.e. mainly for money laundering and terrorist financing prevention. There have also been several definitions of cryptocurrency offered by Croatian academics and experts which generally follow other generally recognized definitions. For example, cryptocurrency is determined as a subset of virtual currency with which it shares specific cryptographic functions for confirmation and verification of transactions.[13] Furthermore, cryptocurrency is

---

9 R. Siffert, S. Petrović, T. Jakšić, 'Payment of the capital contribution of a company limited by shares in cryptocurrency' 8 (2) 2019 *Zagreb Law Review* 105–106.

10 I. Parać Vukomanović, 'Pravna priroda virtualnih valuta' 3/2019 *Pravo u gospodarstvu* 413–414.

11 Position of the Croatian National Bank published as a text under the title "What are virtual currencies?" dated 9 February 2018 (available at https://www.hnb.hr/en/-/sto-su-virtualne-valute-/).

12 Article 4 point 49 Act on the Prevention of Money Laundering and Terrorist Financing (Official Gazette Nos. 108/17, 39/19).

13 I. Parać Vukomanović, 'Pravna priroda virtualnih valuta' 3/2019 *Pravo u gospodarstvu* 408.

also determined more narrowly as a blockchain-based token that holds a book value, which is not necessarily stable but can be used as a means of payment.[14]

The mentioned Act on the Prevention of Money Laundering and Terrorist Financing similarly determined virtual asset as "... a digital record of value that can be digitally traded or digitally transferred and that can be used for payment or investment purposes, not issued nor guaranteed by the central bank or other public authority and not necessarily connected with a legally recognized monetary unit and has no legal status of currency or money."[15] In its position paper from 2021 Croatian National Bank generally determined cryptoassets as "... electronic cryptographic records whose copies are distributed, stored and confirmed in a decentralized manner."[16] It remains unclear whether virtual assets and cryptoassets are considered to be the same or whether the latter is a subset form of the former. Considering that cryptocurrencies are just one of the possible forms of virtual currencies, it is also possible that cryptoassets are just one of the possible forms of virtual assets. However, some doubts remain as to whether cryptocurrencies indeed fall under the scope of cryptoassets.[17] Notwithstanding, it seems that cryptocurrencies are distinguished from cryptoassets. Consequently, de lege ferenda regulation will have to be clear in determining these two terms.

Under Croatian law, it is unclear what are the actual or potential legal relationships between different participants (e.g. miners, wallet providers, customers, and issuers) on the blockchain on which cryptocurrencies are transferred and recorded. It is also unclear what is the legal nature of the cryptocurrency token. Since cryptocurrency tokens are not things nor money, in the current legal vacuum they could qualify as rights.[18] However, this imposes additional questions as to the nature of this right. It should be noted that under Croatian law a right of one person (holder) does not necessarily need to complement an

---

14 T. Jakšić, Smjernice za uređenje kriptovrijednosnih papira u hrvatskom pravu - de lege ferenda, *Zbornik Susreta pravnika u gospodarstvu 2021*, p. 216.

15 Article 4 point 48 Act on the Prevention of Money Laundering and Terrorist Financing.

16 Position of the Croatian National Bank published as a text under the title "Rizici povezani s kriptoimovinom" dated 7 July 2021 (available at https://www.hnb.hr/-/rizici-povezani-s-kriptoimovinom).

17 Some doubts arise from the Position of the Croatian National Bank published as a text under the title "Rizici povezani s kriptoimovinom" dated 7 July 2021 (available at https://www.hnb.hr/-/rizici-povezani-s-kriptoimovinom/). In short, the Croatian National Bank states that it is misleading to refer to cryptoassets as cryptocurrency since that implies the use of cryptoassets for payment purposes or as a money substitute, which is rarely the case.

18 In this direction see R. Siffert, S. Petrović, T. Jakšić, 'Payment of the capital contribution of a company limited by shares in cryptocurrency' 8 (2) 2019 *Zagreb Law Review* 108.

obligation of another person in the specific civil law relationship (like a contract). Since cryptocurrency token is not connected to specific performance or a claim of another but represents a unique electronic entry recorded on the blockchain which is afforded a certain (volatile) market value, right over cryptocurrency token implies the right of disposal with such entry and the corresponding value to new or existing blockchain participants.

One can also argue that between all blockchain participants exists a wide understanding (i.e. a loose form of civil law relationship) by their mere consent to participate in such prearranged blockchain system. The rights formed thus is a recognition between all such participants, including acknowledgment of the right to transfer cryptocurrency tokens to another person.[19] Such a relationship might qualify as a loose form of partnership between persons who participate in the blockchain in predetermined roles (e.g. holders of cryptocurrency tokens, miners, and custodians).[20] Namely, the decentralized (or centralized) algorithm for transferring cryptocurrency tokens recorded on the blockchain operates under predetermined rules which are made known to all participants. Therefore, one could consider that by agreeing to participate in such a system the participant also accepted the rules under which such a system operates. However, the existing rules on partnerships do not fully correspond to the nature of such blockchain systems.[21]

2 Regulatory Framework

As already mentioned, under Croatian law cryptocurrencies are generally unregulated.[22] Their use is only regulated in regard to the prevention of

19 R. Siffert, S. Petrović, T. Jakšić, 'Payment of the capital contribution of a company limited by shares in cryptocurrency' 8 (2) 2019 *Zagreb Law Review* 108–109.

20 According to Article 637 Obligations Act under a contract of partnership, two or more persons mutually undertake to contribute their work and/or property to achieve a common objective. Such partnership is an association of persons and property without legal personality. The Obligations Act enables parties to shape specifics of such partnership to their needs.

21 For example, the rules on the liability of partners to third parties caused by the decentralized system, the ownership over the system, and the joint management of the decentralized system. In this regard see Articles 637 to 660 Obligations Act on partnership.

22 See previously under 1. Legal Qualification. It is yet to be seen what will be the effect of the Regulation (EU) 2023/1114 of the European Parliament and of the Council of 31 May 2023 on markets in crypto-assets, and amending Regulations (EU) No 1093/2010 and (EU) No 1095/2010 and Directives 2013/36/EU and (EU) 2019/1937, OJ L 150, 9.6.2023, pp. 40–205 (MICA Regulation). This report only elaborates on the specific national regulation

money laundering and terrorist financing. The Act on the Prevention of Money Laundering and Terrorist Financing determines measures, operations, and procedures that specific private and regulatory entities shall undertake to prevent and detect money laundering and terrorist financing. This also includes the application of measures aimed to prevent the use of the financial system for such purposes.[23] Pursuant to this act exchange service providers between virtual currencies and recognized national (fiat) currencies, as well as custodian wallet providers are under obligation to undertake prescribed measures, operations, and procedures aimed at the prevention and detection of money laundering and terrorist financing.[24] Such measures, operations, and procedures are applied before and/or during each transaction, as well as during the conclusion of legal acts (contracts) which enable the acquisition or use of assets and enable any other form of disposal with the virtual currency which can be used for money laundering and terrorist financing.[25] This includes, for example, preparation of risk assessment, setting up of policies, controls, and procedures that effectively reduce and manage the risk related to money laundering and terrorist financing, implementation of in-depth client analysis, the appointment of a person who is authorized to implement measures aimed at prevention of money laundering and terrorist financing and performance of a regular internal audit of the system established for the prevention of money laundering and terrorist financing.[26] It can be observed that not all users involved in cryptocurrency transactions are encompassed (e.g. miners or persons responsible for transactions block validation, cryptocurrency issuers, programmers, and coders). The amendments which extended these rules to virtual currencies came into force in mid-2019 and are a result of the transposition of Directive (EU) 2018/843 on the prevention of the use of the financial system for the purposes of money laundering or terrorist financing into Croatian law.[27] The amended Act on the Prevention of Money Laundering and

---

and does not delve into the effects of the EU wide applicable regulations. This is mostly because the MICA Regulation is not yet fully in force and its effects on member state's national laws are yet to be seen.

23 Article 1 para. 1 Act on the Prevention of Money Laundering and Terrorist Financing.

24 Article 9 para. 2 point 17 subpoint. (k) and (l) Act on the Prevention of Money Laundering and Terrorist Financing.

25 Article 9 para. 1 Act on the Prevention of Money Laundering and Terrorist Financing.

26 Article 11 para. 2 Act on the Prevention of Money Laundering and Terrorist Financing.

27 Directive (EU) 2018/843 of the European Parliament and of the Council of 30 May 2018 amending Directive (EU) 2015/849 on the prevention of the use of the financial system for the purposes of money laundering or terrorist financing, and amending Directives 2009/138/EC and 2013/36/EU, OJ L 156, 19.6.2018, pp. 43–74.

Terrorist Financing did not apply retroactively to proceedings already undertaken when the amendments came into force.

Besides this act, the Croatian legislator did not expressly reference cryptocurrencies in any other manner. It was previously mentioned that the Croatian National Bank concluded that cryptocurrencies are not legal tender in Croatia.[28] In addition, it also concluded that cryptocurrency transactions do not represent payment transactions nor can trading and payment in cryptocurrencies be considered a payment service pursuant to the Payment Transactions Act.[29] The Croatian National Bank continued by stating that cryptocurrencies are neither electronic money since they cannot qualify as money. Unlike electronic money, the value for which a specific cryptocurrency can be exchanged for other traditional currencies, goods, or services depends on the market value of such cryptocurrency and not the money invested to acquire it.[30] However, the Croatian National Bank impliedly concluded that the use of cryptocurrencies in Croatia is not illegal by itself.[31]

In this light, derivative referencing cryptocurrencies is not forbidden but so far, no such case has been reported in Croatia. It is yet to be seen whether such derivatives would fall under the scrutiny of the existing capital market regulation which is based on the EU-capital market framework (e.g. the Markets in Financial Instruments Directive and Regulation).[32] Namely, it is still unclear whether derivative referencing cryptocurrencies could qualify as financial instruments. Namely, since cryptocurrencies do not qualify as money or commodity it is unlikely that the reference underlying such derivative can be money or commodity. However, cryptocurrencies as a reference underlying could qualify as a financial index, measure, or an asset and thus fall under the scope of one of the listed financial instruments in Annex I Section C of the Markets in Financial Instruments Directive. In addition, whether derivatives referencing cryptocurrencies could qualify as a financial instrument could

28 See previously under 2. Regulatory framework.

29 Position of the Croatian National Bank published as a text under the title "What are virtual currencies?" dated 9 February 2018 (available at https://www.hnb.hr/en/-/sto-su-virtualne-valute-/).

30 For example, see Article 3 para 1 point 7 and Article 7 para 2 Act on Electronic Money (Official Gazette No. 64/2018).

31 Position of the Croatian National Bank published as a text under the title "What are virtual currencies?" dated 9 February 2018 (available at https://www.hnb.hr/en/-/sto-su-virtualne-valute-/).

32 For example, based on the Directive 2014/65/EU of the European Parliament and of the Council of 15 May 2014 on markets in financial instruments and amending Directive 2002/92/EC and Directive 2011/61/EU, OJ L 173, 12.6.2014, pp. 349–496.

also depend on whether such derivative is exchange-traded and whether such derivatives are cash or physically settled. Therefore, it is generally possible that derivative referencing cryptocurrencies could qualify as swaps, futures, forwards, and options, i.e. as a financial instrument. This means that such derivatives, although not initially contemplated, seem to fall under the scope of the Markets in Financial Instruments Directive. In addition, entities providing various services relating to such derivatives could also qualify as regulated activities that normally require the prior authorization of the supervisory authority (the Croatian Financial Services Supervisory Agency), as well as compliance with subsequent reporting and various other duties.

The lack of any specific legislative framework for cryptocurrencies implies that the Croatian legislator opted for a "wait and see" approach. Since the European Union intended to regulate cryptocurrencies in some manner it might be that the Croatian legislator was relying on the European legislator.[33] Until an EU-wide directive or a regulation enters fully into force it seems that the Croatian legislator relies on the regulatory authorities and the courts to deal with the cryptocurrencies within the scope of existing laws.[34] There are also no specific criminal law provisions that apply to cryptocurrencies or cryptocurrencies-related services.

3 Supervision

In regard to the Act on the Prevention of Money Laundering and Terrorist Financing, the virtual currency exchange service providers and custodian wallet providers are under obligation to notify the Croatian Financial Services Supervisory Agency of their intention to provide such services.[35] The subsequent supervision of obliged entities generally depends on the risk assessment of money laundering and terrorist financing.[36] However, the supervisory authority does not give a license for the provision of exchange or wallet custodian services nor does it supervise the quality of the provided service.[37]

33 For example, the efforts made in regard to the Regulation (EU) 2023/1114 of the European Parliament and of the Council of 31 May 2023 on markets in crypto-assets, and amending Regulations (EU) No 1093/2010 and (EU) No 1095/2010 and Directives 2013/36/EU and (EU) 2019/1937.

34 For more in this regard see under 1. Legal Qualification.

35 Article 9 para. 7 Act on the Prevention of Money Laundering and Terrorist Financing.

36 Article 84 para. 1 Act on the Prevention of Money Laundering and Terrorist Financing.

37 The recently introduced MICA Regulation changes this approach.

With the exception of these anti-money laundering rules, the Croatian National Bank concluded that those who issue cryptocurrencies or provide other related services (e.g. trading service, exchange service, and custodian services) are not regulated nor licensed by the Croatian National Bank or any other public authority in Croatia.[38] Therefore, the provision of services related to cryptocurrencies is unregulated and unsupervised in Croatia. This does not, however, mean that some forms of cryptoassets completely escape supervision. For example, it is yet to be seen whether cryptoassets in the form of investment tokens could qualify as transferrable securities and financial instruments and thus fall under the scope of the existing capital market regulation which is based on the Markets in Financial Instruments Directive and Regulation.[39] In this regard, the Croatian Financial Services Supervisory Agency took an opinion that some crypto tokens could fall under the scope of the existing capital market regulation (e.g. some forms of derivatives). Furthermore, the supervisory authority also concluded that the issuance of crypto tokens could have an investment purpose and could thus be qualified as a regulated investment service.[40]

4 Private Law Issues

In this part, several private law issues will be elaborated. Namely, the property law issues, transfer of cryptocurrencies, their inheritance, possibility to establish a trust based on cryptocurrencies, issues relating to attachment and seizure of cryptocurrencies, the impact of insolvency proceedings on cryptocurrencies, establishing a pledge over cryptocurrencies, lending of cryptocurrencies, and issues relating legal effects of an unjustifiable loss of cryptocurrency through hacking or fraud.

38 Position of the Croatian National Bank published as a text under the title "What are virtual currencies?" dated 9 February 2018 (available at https://www.hnb.hr/en/-/sto-su-virtualne-valute-/).

39 Opinion of the Croatian Financial Services Supervisory Agency relating to the issuance of virtual assets based on the Ethereum blockchain dated 6 April 2020 (available at https:// https://www.hanfa.hr/media/4602/mi%C5%A1ljenje-tokeni.pdf).

40 Opinion of the Croatian Financial Services Supervisory Agency relating to the issuance of virtual assets based on the Ethereum blockchain dated 6 April 2020 (available at https:// https://www.hanfa.hr/media/4602/mi%C5%A1ljenje-tokeni.pdf).

4.1 *Property Law Issues Relating to Cryptocurrency Tokens*

Under the Act on Ownership and Other Property Rights, only moveable (chattels) and immovable things (real estate) may be the subject matter of the right of ownership and other property rights, except for those not having the required capacity.[41] In this regard, things are corporeal parts of nature, different from people and used by people. However, even incorporeal parts are regarded as things if they are expressly recognized as such by law, i.e. when they are extended equal status by the national legislator.[42]

Croatian law generally adopts the corporeality doctrine of things where incorporeality is only exceptionally permitted by law (e.g. the forces of nature when they are subject to human control). Since cryptocurrency tokens have incorporeal (intangible) nature, they cannot be regarded as things based on this requirement of the corporeality of things. Furthermore, in the absence of any specific cryptocurrency regulation which could expressly recognize cryptocurrencies as incorporeal goods, it can only be concluded that cryptocurrencies cannot be regarded as things and are consequently incapable of being subject to property rights like ownership and possession as established by the Act on Ownership and Other Property Rights. It seems very unlikely that de lege ferenda the Croatian legislator is going to give cryptocurrencies equal status as things. This leaves open the question of the legal nature of cryptocurrencies under existing Croatian laws.

4.2 *Transfer of Cryptocurrency Tokens*

If cryptocurrency tokens are qualified as rights under Croatian law, they can be transferred as such. This means that general rules on the assignment of a claim (cession) apply to the transfer of cryptocurrency tokens. Although such assignment is primarily tailored for the transfer of a claim from the creditor to the third party, the rules on assignment represent general rules for the transfer of all rights, not just claims. This means that some of the rules on the assignment of claims are not applicable due to their unsuitability for the transfer of specific rights.[43]

However, it should be noted that the transfer of cryptocurrency tokens has similar characteristics to a transfer by endorsement. Under Croatian law, by

---

41 Article 2 para. 1 Act on Ownership and Other Property Rights (Official Gazette Nos. 91/96, 68/98, 137/99, 22/00, 73/00, 129/00, 114/01, 79/06, 141/06, 146/08, 38/09, 153/09, 143/12, 152/14).

42 Article 2 para. 2 Act on Ownership and Other Property Rights.

43 For example, Article 82 para. 1 Obligations Act provides that the creditor undertakes to notify the debtor of the assignment. This is obviously inapplicable in the context of the transfer of a right like a share in a limited liability company or even a transfer of a cryptocurrency token like BTC.

endorsement can be transferred securities issued in the order form and registered securities but only when expressly permitted by law.[44] Endorsement is just one of the possible ways how security can be transferred.[45] Basically, security is transferred from one person to the other along the chain of endorsements which are entered, usually, on the back of the transferred security. The transferor designates the acquirer as the person upon whose order the performance from the security is to be performed and to whom the transferor hands over such security. This is similar to the transfer of cryptocurrency tokens where the acquirer of such token is chronologically recorded on the blockchain. Namely, the registration of the acquirer as the new holder of the cryptocurrency token, which is based on the transferor's confirmation of the transfer order in the blockchain system, is very reminiscent of the acquirer's registration on the security document as the new holder of such security. Both transfers enable the holder to see who the holders of the transferred item were going back to the initial transferor.

Unlike the assignment, endorsement resolves the issue resulting from the acquisition of cryptocurrency tokens in good faith.[46] Namely, if an unauthorized person (e.g. a hacker who stole another's wallet access information) transfers the cryptocurrency tokens to another person, such acquirer should be considered a legal holder if it was unaware of the transferor's illegitimate holding and disposal over the tokens. In this way, the new legitimate holder of the cryptocurrency tokens is the acquirer that acted in good faith even though the transferor acted in bad faith (i.e. it was aware that the cryptocurrency tokens do not belong to it).

These rules could apply to cases where the legitimate holder uses an intermediary (e.g. a wallet service provider) to hold and transfer the cryptocurrency tokens. For example, such an intermediary could hold cryptocurrency tokens in the name and for the account of the legitimate holder or it could hold them in its own name, but for the account of the legitimate holder. In the first case, the transferor will be the legitimate holder even though the transfer was intermediated, while in the second case, the transferor will be the intermediary who acts for the account of the legitimate holder. This means that the intermediary will not undertake any transfer of the tokens that are formally recorded in its own name without the prior order of the legitimate holder. The relationship

44 Articles 1144 and 1143 para. 2 Obligations Act.

45 The other ways arealready mentioned assignment of claims (cession) and physical delivery.

46 In this regard see Article 15 para. 2 Bill of Exchange Act (Official Gazette Nos. 74/94, 92/10).

between the legitimate holder and the intermediary could generally be based on rules that govern mandate contracts.[47]

Under Croatian law, donation exists when the donor undertakes to transfer to the donee, without expecting anything in return, a thing or an asset right and the donee accepts it.[48] Cryptocurrency tokens can be donated. Therefore, rules on donation apply when the token holder (donor) transfers the token to another person (donee) without any consideration under the condition that the other person accepts such a transfer as a donation. Cryptocurrency tokens can also be exchanged as consideration for some form of counter-performance. The exact rules applicable to such an exchange depend on the nature of the underlying contractual relationship. For example, this can be a sales contract, but also any other contract where some other specific performance was offered in exchange for cryptocurrency tokens. If cryptocurrency tokens are provided in exchange for things or other rights, such a contractual relationship could be understood as a contract of exchange.[49] Generally, there should be no obstacles for the application of various other contract forms where one party generally promises payment in exchange for some specific performance of the other party (e.g. provision of specific work, the performance of specific services, or acts for the account of the mandator, lease or rent of specific thing, carriage of goods). Namely, parties may regulate their mutual obligations in a manner other than according to the provisions of the Obligations Act, unless otherwise indicated by a provision of this law or its meaning (e.g. in case of rare mandatory law provisions).[50] This means that parties can generally agree to provide payment in cryptocurrency tokens instead of money or other traditional means of payment.

As to the application of the private international law rules, Croatian law applies Regulation (EC) No. 593/2008 of the European Parliament and of the Council of 17 June 2008 on the law applicable to contractual obligations (Rome I).[51]

47 See Articles 763 to 784 Obligations Act. A mandate contract is a contract obligating and empowering the mandatary to perform certain acts for the account of the mandator.

48 Article 479 Obligations Act.

49 See Articles 474 to 475 Obligations Act.

50 Article 11 Obligations Act.

51 Article 4 paras. 1 and 2 Regulation (EC) No. 593/2008 of the European Parliament and of the Council of 17 June 2008 on the law applicable to contractual obligations (Rome I) [2008] OJ L 177 6–16. In this regard also see Articles 2 and 25 International Private Law Act (Official Gazette No. 101/17) which refer to the application of the rules of the mentioned Regulation for contractual obligations even though they fall outside of the Regulation's scope of application.

4.3 *Inheritance of Cryptocurrency Tokens*

Under Croatian law, inheritance consists of everything that belongs to the testator (deceased) at the time of his death, except what cannot be inherited due to its legal nature or by law.[52] This means that cryptocurrency tokens, as rights that belonged to the testator at the time of his death, also form part of the testator's estate and thus could be inherited by his heirs. Therefore, general rules on inheritance (succession to the estates) apply. Croatian law generally recognizes succession to the estates based on the law and based on the will.[53]

Therefore, the testator could dispose of his cryptocurrency tokens through a will made in one of the prescribed forms and under observance of the rules provided for its validity. In case the will is invalid, the rules on succession to the estates on the basis of the law apply. This means that heirs inherit the estate of the deceased based on their position in the hereditary order. The heirs of a closer hereditary order shall exclude from the inheritance a person of a further hereditary order.[54] The same applies in the case that the testator did not make a will. Where the testator disposed of his assets in the manner that some of his heirs (e.g. his children and grandchildren as well as his spouse) would not receive a necessary part of the inheritance, the rules on the necessary part of the inheritance apply.[55]

If the testator uses the services of an intermediary, there should generally be no problem since the testator's heirs enter into his legal relationship with such an intermediary. However, a problem might arise if the access information to the wallet is lost with the testator's death and thus his heirs cannot dispose of the value stored in the wallet. It might be prudent to consider de lege ferenda that wallet service providers or other intermediaries are obliged, not only to provide access to the authorized heir determined by the decision on inheritance but also to provide information on the content of the value stored in the wallet upon request of an authorized person (e.g. the court). This might prove problematic if such services are used by a provider resident in another country and especially if such a service provider does not store such information because it uses end-to-end encryption. Besides this issue, it seems that rules applicable to bank accounts held with credit institutions and security depositories could be similarly applied.

52 Article 5 para. 3 Inheritance Act.
53 Articles 8 to 101 Inheritance Act.
54 Article 8 para. 4 Inheritance Act.
55 Articles 69 to 88 Inheritance Act.

4.4 *Trust based on Cryptocurrency Tokens*

Croatian law does not expressly regulate trusts. However, under Croatian law legal effects similar to trusts could be accomplished indirectly through the use of other existing rules. In this light, the owner may generally limit, condition, or term his own rights, and may even encumber them. Furthermore, when the owner prohibits the alienation or encumbrance of his property by a legal transaction, he shall also be obliged to comply with such prohibition. This prohibition also applies to third parties, and is entered in the land register or other corresponding public register. In this way, the owner can also determine other conditions or deadlines that affect his right of ownership.[56] These rules apply to things over which ownership can be established. Since cryptocurrency tokens cannot be regarded as things under Croatian law, these rules cannot apply to them.

However, in regard to rights, similar effects to trust could be established through general contractual rules. For example, a trust could take the form of a partnership which is determined as an association of persons and property without legal personality.[57] However, these rules require that the partnership consists of at least two persons who mutually undertake to contribute work and/or property to achieve a common objective.[58] In this regard, these two or more partners could be trustors that contribute their assets in the form of cryptocurrency tokens for the benefit of the beneficiary. One of the partners could also be a trustee who manages these assets for the benefit of the beneficiary and contributes his work to the partnership.[59] The problem with partnership rules is that they cannot satisfy some of the trust's characteristics (e.g. that trustee is the sole holder of the legal title to trust assets or that the trustor is not liable for debts of the trust). However, it seems that some form of trust could also be established through other contractual means in the form of a third-party beneficiary contract.[60] In any case, such efforts would require a certain amount of contractual creativity. However, it should be noted that such contractual solutions would only have an effect on the parties (inter partes). Furthermore, trusts could be established as a limited liability company where the trustor could contribute the assets into the share capital of the company, and the company through its management would act as the trustee. Other models are also conceivable without the trustor entering the company as a

56 Article 34 Act on Ownership and Other Property Rights.

57 Article 637 para. 2 Obligations Act.

58 Article 637 para. 1 Obligations Act.

59 Articles 638 to 641 Obligations Act.

60 Articles 337 to 340 Obligations Act.

shareholder. In any case, it should be noted that in such situation rules on limited liability companies apply.[61]

4.5 *Attachment and Seizure of Cryptocurrency Tokens*

Under Croatian law, there are no express provisions for attachment of cryptocurrency tokens or their otherwise seizure. It is at least theoretically possible to undertake such measures through the general rules on enforcement. However, the effectiveness of such measures in regard to cryptocurrency tokens is questionable. Under the Enforcement Act attachment is regulated as an interim measure.[62] In general, the court may order an interim measure to secure a claim if the claimant demonstrates that the existence of the claim is probable and that there is a danger that without such a measure the other side will prevent or significantly impede the collection of the claim by transferring, concealing, or otherwise disposing of with his property.[63] Regarding monetary claims, it is considered that the mentioned danger exists if the claim is to be realized abroad.[64] However, the Enforcement Act also provides for a list of measures through which such security (attachment) can be realized. For example, confiscation and deposit of cash, securities, etc. to the court or notary public, an order to the credit institution to deny the opponent of the insurance or a third party the payment from the debtor's account of the amount for which the interim measure has been imposed and prohibition of alienation and encumbrance of other rights to which the claim is directed, with entrusting the administration of these rights to a third party.[65] Listed measures are very specific and only a few of them are directed at the establishment of security over rights. In addition, most of these measures depend on the entry of such interim measures into the public register (e.g. the land register).

Regarding the attachment over cryptocurrency tokens, besides prohibiting its legitimate holder to alienate such tokens or order it to transfer the tokens to another person entrusted with their administration until the interim measure is revoked, there is very little that could be done to protect the claimant's interests. Foremost, it might be difficult to determine whether cryptocurrency tokens even form a part of the opponent's assets so that they can be a target of such interim measures. Furthermore, although a monetary fine

61 Articles 385 to 472.h Companies Act (Official Gazette Nos. 111/93, 34/99, 121/99, 52/00, 118/03, 107/07, 146/08, 137/09, 125/11, 152/11, 111/12, 68/13, 110/15, 40/19).

62 Enforcement Act (Official Gazette Nos. 112/12, 25/13, 93/14, 55/16, 73/17, 131/20).

63 Article 344 para. 1 and Article 346 para. 1 Enforcement Act.

64 Article 344 para. 3 Enforcement Act.

65 Article 345 para. 1 and Article 347 para. 1 Enforcement Act.

or imprisonment can be imposed for breaching duties established by such interim measures, this provides little comfort to the claimant when all of the opponent's assets are stored in cryptocurrency tokens to which he has exclusive access.[66] In case cryptocurrency tokens are held with intermediaries which are seated in Croatia and if access to such tokens is not exclusive to the opponent of an interim measure, e.g. due to the end-to-end encryption of access and stored value data, a court might order such intermediary not to enable the opponent of an interim measure to alienate or dispose of with such tokens or do so itself on behalf of the opponent and for the duration of the measure imposed. However, in all other situations, there seems to be no effective means to ensure the protection of the claimant's interests. This is something that will have to be resolved with future regulation. Regarding cryptocurrency tokens, similar issues are detected regarding other forms of seizure established by the Enforcement Act.

Whether Croatian law applies to attachment and seizure is dependent on international private law rules concerning the recognition and enforcement of foreign court judgments and decisions. Such rules are determined by the International Private Law Act and the Regulation (EU) No. 1215/2012 of the European Parliament and of the Council of 12 December 2012 on jurisdiction and the recognition and enforcement of judgments in civil and commercial matters.[67] In this regard, the International Private Law Act applies only when the recognition and enforcement of foreign court decisions are not covered by the scope of the mentioned Regulation.[68] In other words, attachment and seizure are determined by a foreign court's judgement or decision under the rules of a foreign legal system, dependent on whether such judgement or decision was recognized in Croatia. A judgment given in a member state which is enforceable in that member state is also enforceable in Croatia without any declaration of enforceability being required.[69] Recognition and enforcement can be refused upon application of an interested party and under one of the expressly stipulated grounds (e.g. if recognition is manifestly contrary to

66 Article 16 in connection with Article 345 para. 7 Enforcement Act.

67 International Private Law Act. Regulation (EU) No. 1215/2012 of the European Parliament and of the Council of 12 December 2012 on jurisdiction and the recognition and enforcement of judgments in civil and commercial matters [2012] OJ L 351 1–32.

68 Article 65 International Private Law Act.

69 Article 39 Regulation (EU) No. 1215/2012 of the European Parliament and of the Council of 12 December 2012 on jurisdiction and the recognition and enforcement of judgments in civil and commercial matters [2012] OJ L 351 1–32.

public policy).[70] In other cases, International Private Law Act provides similar grounds for refusal of recognition and enforcement as the Regulation.[71]

4.6 *Impact of Insolvency Proceedings on Cryptocurrency Tokens*

Under Croatian law, the insolvency estate includes all the debtor's assets at the time of the opening of the insolvency proceedings as well as the assets acquired during these proceedings.[72] If one holds cryptocurrency tokens that are registered with an intermediary that became insolvent, it seems that the person will have to demonstrate that such cryptocurrency tokens do not form part of the intermediary's insolvency estate.[73] In that case, the client of an intermediary is not considered an insolvency creditor and can separate such tokens from the insolvency proceedings and seek their transfer to another account of his own choice. Therefore, in the absence of any specific regulation concerning the operation of cryptoasset intermediaries, it is unlikely that cryptocurrency tokens would form part of their insolvency estate. Even if such intermediaries are considered investment companies, the client's cryptocurrency tokens do not form part of the investment company's insolvency estate.[74] However, since cryptoasset intermediaries are unregulated the client will likely have to demonstrate its legal title over the cryptocurrency tokens registered in the account of such intermediary. However, if the intermediary disposed of such cryptocurrency tokens without the client's authorization before the opening of the insolvency proceeding, the client may request a transfer of the counterclaim resulting from such disposal.[75] If such a counterclaim does not exist, the client is entitled to seek damages as one of the creditors of the insolvent intermediary.[76] However, if it was the insolvency manager who disposed of such cryptocurrency tokens, the client may request the transfer of the counterclaim or seek damages as a creditor of the insolvency estate.[77] Creditors of the insolvency estate hold a preferential position compared to other creditors of the insolvent intermediary because their claims are settled before the

70 Article 45 and 46 Regulation (EU) No. 1215/2012 of the European Parliament and of the Council of 12 December 2012 on jurisdiction and the recognition and enforcement of judgments in civil and commercial matters [2012] OJ L 351 1–32.

71 Article 68 to 71 International Private Law Act.

72 Article 134 para. 1 Insolvency Act (Official Gazette Nos. 71/15, 104/17).

73 Article 147 para. 1 Insolvency Act.

74 Article 80 para. 8 Capital Market Act (Official Gazette Nos. 65/2018, 17/2020, 83/2021).

75 Article 148 para. 1 Insolvency Act.

76 Article 148 para. 2 Insolvency Act.

77 Article 148 para. 3 Insolvency Act.

claims of other creditors.[78] In such a situation the client must inform the insolvency manager about their right over the cryptocurrency tokens registered in the account of the insolvent intermediary. Besides the description of the right in question, the client must also provide for the legal grounds of his claim and determine its request.[79]

In the case of the client's insolvency, it is likely that such cryptocurrency tokens would form a part of the client's insolvency estate. After the opening of the insolvency proceedings, the insolvency manager is under obligation to take possession of and manage the entire assets that form part of the insolvency estate.[80] The insolvency manager shall create a list of all items forming the insolvency estate. In doing so, the insolvent client and all persons previously authorized to represent the client (e.g. its management) shall cooperate with the insolvency manager.[81] Normally, when the insolvency manager finds some records referring to the existence of cryptocurrency tokens being held by an intermediary or when such intermediary sends a regular newsletter or contacts the insolvent client in any other way, the insolvency manager will try to take control over the account and accompanying stored value. Whether he will succeed depends on the nature of the relationship with the intermediary similar to what was explained in regard to the inheritance of the cryptocurrency tokens.[82] Some creditors could claim priority over such cryptocurrency tokens if, for example, such tokens were held by the insolvent client on their behalf. This is similar to what was explained previously concerning the right to seek separation of such tokens from the insolvency proceedings and their transfer to another account of the creditor's own choice. It is also possible that such cryptocurrency tokens could be separated from the insolvency estate based on a pledge or other security established for the settlement of a claim.[83]

It should be noted that according to the Insolvency Act, the debtor's mandate relating to the assets which form a part of the insolvency estate is terminated by the opening of insolvency proceedings.[84] The same applies to a work contract where someone has undertaken to perform specific tasks for the debtor.[85] This means that if the contractual relationship between the intermediary and the debtor is qualified as a mandate or work contract, such contract is terminated

78 Article 154 para. 1 Insolvency Act.

79 Article 258 para. 1 Insolvency Act.

80 Article 216 para. 1 Insolvency Act.

81 Article 221 para. 1 Insolvency Act.

82 See previously under 4.3. Inheritance of cryptocurrencies.

83 Articles 149 to 152 Insolvency Act.

84 Article 193 Insolvency Act.

85 Article 195 Insolvency Act.

with the opening of the insolvency proceedings. However, if the intermediary is unaware of this without his own fault, the contract is still active and ongoing.[86] Any contractual provision that in advance excludes or limits the application of this Insolvency Act provision has no legal effect.[87]

According to the Insolvency Act, the law applicable to the insolvency proceedings and their effects is determined by the law of the country in which the insolvency proceedings were opened unless otherwise provided by the provisions of this Act.[88] Regarding the right to request separation of items from the insolvency estate, the law of the country where such items are located, including where the foreign decision to open the insolvency proceedings is recognized, is applicable. Unless at the time of the opening of the insolvency proceedings such items were located in the country where the proceeding was opened.[89] This generally means that legal rules other than Croatian shall apply if the insolvency proceedings were initiated in another country. As to the applicable law to the right to request separation of items, rules of another legal system shall apply if such items are not located in Croatia nor were located in Croatia at the moment when the insolvency proceeding was opened. It is unknown how the court will determine the location of the cryptocurrency tokens since they are generally recorded on a decentralized blockchain that is not located in a specific country or even a specific server. If such tokens are registered in the account of an intermediary, the court might consider using the seat of the intermediary as the location of the tokens. In any case, this is just one of many issues that will have to be resolved with future regulation.

4.7 *Pledge over Cryptocurrency Tokens*

Under Croatian law, it is possible to establish a pledge over an individual right against which the creditor may collect his claim unless provided otherwise by law.[90] This generally means that a pledge over cryptocurrency tokens could be established since such tokens generally store a monetary value and could be converted into money. The basis of such a pledge is a pledge agreement. Under the pledge agreement, the debtor or a third party (pledgor) assumes the obligation to transfer to the creditor a right as security for the purpose of establishing a pledge that is to secure a particular claim of the creditor. The other side assumes the obligation to have the right transferred back to the pledgor as

86 Article 193 para. 2 Insolvency Act.
87 Articles 149 to 152 Insolvency Act.
88 Article 395 Insolvency Act.
89 Article 396 Insolvency Act.
90 Article 298 para. 2 Act on Ownership and Other Property Rights.

soon as the claim terminates.[91] This means that a pledge over cryptocurrency tokens is established by a transfer of such tokens to the creditor solely for the purpose of securing the creditor's claim. Since there is no public register of a pledge which follows the transfer of the cryptocurrency tokens, the transfer of such tokens to the creditor is the only way to ensure the protection of the creditor's security interest. If the wallet is physical (i.e. a USB stick) then a handover of such hardware wallet is required. This is similar to the pledge over bearer security which has to be transferred to the creditor by delivery. In the case of digital wallets and cryptocurrency tokens registered in the accounts of an intermediary, such tokens have to be transferred to the creditor's account. One might consider a transfer of authorizations over the entire account, but this seems unlikely since that would require negotiations with the intermediary and its approval for the changes to the contract or transfer of the contract to the creditor.[92]

With respect to private international law matters, the application of legal rules other than Croatian is determined according to Regulation (EC) No. 593/2008 of the European Parliament and of the Council of 17 June 2008 on the law applicable to contractual obligations (Rome I).[93] According to this Regulation, the relationship between the assignor and the assignee under a voluntary assignment of a claim against another person (the debtor) shall be governed by the law that applies to the contract between the assignor and assignee under this Regulation.[94] The concept of assignment also includes pledges over claims.[95] This means that the application of other legal system's rules will depend on the law applicable to the underlying contract between the assignor and the assignee (e.g. the sales contract). If the underlying contract is

91 Article 307 para. 1 Act on Ownership and Other Property Rights.

92 Article 127 para. 1 Obligations Act according to which each of the parties to a contract may, if the other party consents, transfer the contract to a third person, whereby it becomes the holder of all its rights and obligations arising from that contract.

93 Regulation (EC) No. 593/2008 of the European Parliament and of the Council of 17 June 2008 on the law applicable to contractual obligations (Rome I) [2008] OJ L 177 6–16. In this regard also see Articles 2 and 25 International Private Law Act which refer to the application of the rules of the mentioned Regulation for contractual obligations even though they fall outside of the Regulation's scope of application.

94 Article 14 para. 1 Regulation (EC) No. 593/2008 of the European Parliament and of the Council of 17 June 2008 on the law applicable to contractual obligations (Rome I) [2008] OJ L 177 6–16.

95 Article 14 para. 3 Regulation (EC) No. 593/2008 of the European Parliament and of the Council of 17 June 2008 on the law applicable to contractual obligations (Rome I) [2008] OJ L 177 6–16.

governed by a law other than Croatian, that other law is also applicable to the pledge agreement between the pledgor and the creditor.

4.8 *Lending of Cryptocurrency Tokens*

Under a loan contract a lender undertakes to deliver to a borrower a certain amount of money or quantity of other fungible things, and the borrower undertakes to repay the lender the same amount of money or return the same quantity of a thing equal in kind and quality after a certain time.[96] A borrower may undertake to owe interest in addition to the principal but in commercial contracts, a borrower shall owe interest even where not stipulated.[97] Since the object of a loan contract is either money or fungible things, in the absence of express regulation which qualifies cryptocurrency tokens as either money or a thing it seems that a loan contract could not be concluded for a loan of cryptocurrency tokens.[98] However, as previously mentioned, parties are generally free to regulate their mutual obligations in a manner other than according to the provisions of the Obligations Act.[99] Therefore, there is no reason why parties could not conclude a contract where one party lends a specific amount of cryptocurrency tokens to the other party which in turn promises to return the same amount of tokens and pay the agreed interest rate. Such a contract could completely correspond to the above-described loan contract.

As to the application to laws other than Croatian, under Croatian law, the applicable law for contracts is determined pursuant to the Regulation (EC) No. 593/2008 of the European Parliament and of the Council of 17 June 2008 on the law applicable to contractual obligations (Rome I).[100] This means that the law other than Croatian will apply when parties chose such law to govern their contracts, but in case no such law has been chosen by the parties, the contract shall be governed by the law of the country determined by the Regulation. Since the above-mentioned contract is not covered by the express

96 Article 499 para. 1 Obligations Act.

97 Article 500 Obligations Act.

98 It was previously explained why cryptocurrency tokens are de lege lata not regarded as money or things under Croatian law. See previously under 1. Legal qualification and 4.1. Property law issues relating to cryptocurrency tokens.

99 Article 11 Obligations Act.

100 Regulation (EC) No. 593/2008 of the European Parliament and of the Council of 17 June 2008 on the law applicable to contractual obligations (Rome I) [2008] OJ L 177 6–16. In this regard also see Articles 2 and 25 International Private Law Act which refer to the application of the rules of the mentioned Regulation for contractual obligations even though they fall outside of the Regulation's scope of application.

provisions of the Regulation, the law applicable to the contract is determined as the law of the country where the party required to effect the characteristic performance of the contract has his habitual residence.[101] In other words, this means that the governing law shall be the law of the country in which the lending party has his habitual residence since lending would represent performance that is characteristic of such a loan contract.

Under Croatian law, the provision of financial services, among others, includes granting of loans, including consumer loans and mortgage loans.[102] Such service also represents a mutually recognized financial service.[103] A foreign company that is regulated and supervised in its home jurisdiction for the provision of lending services can provide such services in Croatia under specific conditions. In this regard, Croatian law differentiates between such companies established in another member state of the European Union and companies that are established in third countries. Generally, it is easier for a credit or financial institution established in a member state to provide financial services (lending) in Croatia than for institutions from non-member state countries. It should be noted that in Croatia it is not forbidden for other non-credit or financial institutions to conclude loan contracts with other parties. However, the core business activity of the lender cannot be based on lending or financing third parties.

If one party lends a specific amount of cryptocurrency tokens to the other and the contract expressly provides the loan is repayable in the same cryptocurrency (e.g. BTC), it seems that the loan repayment is only possible in that cryptocurrency. This means that in the case of a hard fork in the blockchain of one cryptocurrency (e.g. BTC), a new type of cryptocurrency comes into existence (e.g. BTC cash) with its own branch of the blockchain which is different from the initial (e.g. the BTC blockchain). Therefore, without the consent of the lender to receive such a new type of cryptocurrency or any other cryptocurrency, the borrower will have to repay the loan in the expressly stipulated cryptocurrency.

---

101 Article 4 para. 2 Regulation (EC) No. 593/2008 of the European Parliament and of the Council of 17 June 2008 on the law applicable to contractual obligations (Rome I) [2008] OJ L 177 6–16.

102 Article 8 para. 1 pp. 2 Credit Institution Act (Official Gazette Nos. 159/13, 19/15, 102/15, 15/18, 70/19, 47/20, 146/20).

103 Article 9 para. 1 p. 2 and para. 3 Credit Institution Act.

4.9 *Legal Effect of Unjustifiable Loss of Cryptocurrency Tokens through Hacking or Fraud*

Under Croatian law, a loss of cryptocurrencies through hacking or fraud amounts to actionable unjust enrichment. Namely, where a portion of the assets of a person is transferred in any manner to the assets of another person and such a transfer is not based on a legal transaction, the decision of a court or another authorized authority or law, the acquirer shall return that portion of assets, or if this is not possible, compensate for the value of the benefit conferred.[104] Transfer of assets shall also imply benefit conferred by the performed act.[105] This means that the legitimate holder of cryptocurrency tokens is entitled to seek the return of the cryptocurrency tokens from the person that has acquired such tokens without any legal ground. However, for such a claim to be made the damaged person must know the identity of the unjustly enriched acquirer. Usually, this is not the case when the tokens were lost due to a hack because a hacker tries to leave as few trails as possible. In addition, stolen tokens are usually immediately transferred to another anonymous user on the blockchain. Although the anonymity of users on the blockchain is a common feature of the technology, that might not necessarily be a design feature of every blockchain-based network. Therefore, future regulation might work towards the reduction of such anonymity.

If the account with cryptocurrency tokens held with an intermediary has been hacked, a client who has been hacked could make a claim against an intermediary only based on a possible breach of a contract. The probability of such a claim depends on the content of a contract between an intermediary and its client. The cause of such an action could be damages caused by a potential breach of obligation by the intermediary. Such a breach might be due to the failure of the intermediary to keep access data secret, encrypted, and confidential. Naturally, such breach of duty does not exist in cases where the loss of access data was the client's fault. In such a situation, action against a hacker can be raised as previously described unjust enrichment claim or even a general and extracontractual claim for damages. If the hacker has sold and transferred the cryptocurrency tokens to another person, based on the rules for unjust enrichment it is also possible to seek the return of such tokens from a person that acquired the tokens in good faith. The rules on unjust enrichment differentiate between a claim towards the acquirer in bad faith and the acquirer in good faith. The difference between these two is whether the acquirer was aware or should have been aware that the assets were initially

104 Article 111 para. 1 Obligations Act.
105 Article 111 para. 2 Obligations Act.

acquired without any legal ground. One of the differences between the two is that the acquirer in good faith must only return the acquired assets and pay the default interest for the use of the assets from the date an application to return such assets was made by the legitimate holder of the tokens. If the acquirer acted in bad faith, the default interest is calculated from the moment the assets were acquired.[106] However, it should be noted that these rules are unsuitable for application in cases where the assets, like cryptocurrency tokens, can and are easily transferred and used for various other activities (e.g. payment for goods or services). That is because such a return could require the unwinding of several previous transactions which would contribute to legal uncertainty. It would be more prudent to accept that in such situations the acquirer in good faith keeps the acquired cryptocurrency tokens and the legitimate holder's right solely lies with the acquirer or acquirers in bad faith in the form of a claim for damages.[107] However, currently, a purchaser of cryptocurrency tokens that acted in good faith in such a situation is not protected.

In case the holder of cryptocurrency tokens was misled by another person to transfer them to that other person, besides the already elaborated upon rules on unjust enrichment, the rules on fraud could also apply. In case such misleading, which can be qualified as fraud, results in the conclusion of a contract, the contract can be annulled and upon annulment, the misled person can seek the return of the cryptocurrency tokens.

In regard to private international law issues, the applicable law to extracontractual obligations is determined based on Regulation (EC) No. 864/2007 of the European Parliament and of the Council of 11 July 2007 on the law applicable to non-contractual obligations (Rome II).[108] Regarding fraud, the applicable law depends on the private international law rules applicable to the contract concluded due to such fraud. As previously mentioned, under Croatian law the applicable law for contracts is determined according to Regulation (EC) No. 593/2008 of the European Parliament and of the Council of 17 June 2008 on the law applicable to contractual obligations (Rome I).[109]

---

106 Article 115 Obligations Act.

107 See previously under 4.2. Transfer of cryptocurrency tokens.

108 Article 10 paras. 1 to 4 Regulation (EC) No. 864/2007 of the European Parliament and of the Council of 11 July 2007 on the law applicable to non-contractual obligations (Rome II) [2007] OJ L 199 40–49. In this regard also see Article 26 International Private Law Act which refers to the application of the rules of the mentioned Regulation for extracontractual obligations.

109 Regulation (EC) No. 593/2008 of the European Parliament and of the Council of 17 June 2008 on the law applicable to contractual obligations (Rome I) [2008] OJ L 177 6–16. In this regard also see Articles 2 and 25 International Private Law Act which refer to the

5 Tax Measures

Under Croatian law, gains realized by trading with cryptocurrency tokens are taxable as an income from capital based on the capital gain.[110] Income from the capital on the basis of capital gains is the difference between the agreed sale price and its purchase value.[111] This means that under Croatian law only the difference between the purchase (invested) and the sale value of the cryptocurrency tokens is taxable (transaction and other fees are deducted from the taxable difference). A taxpayer is under obligation to calculate, suspend and pay the capital income tax by the last day of February of the current year for all capital gains realized in the previous year at the rate of 10%.[112] In case the cryptocurrency token is acquired by mining, the tax is paid as other income or income from self-employment, depending on whether mining is undertaken on a non-continuous basis or a continuous basis.[113] However, capital income on the basis of capital gains is not taxed if the alienation of the cryptocurrency tokens is made between spouses and relatives in the first hereditary line and other close family members, between divorced spouses if the alienation is directly related to divorce, inheritance of financial assets and in the event that the financial assets are alienated two years after such tokens were acquired.[114]

6 Litigation and Miscellaneous

It is unknown whether any litigation or arbitration proceedings were closed or are still pending in Croatia concerning the cryptocurrency tokens. To the best of the authors' knowledge, there are also no class action lawsuits pending or completed. Foreign judgements on cryptocurrency tokens would likely be recognized and enforced in Croatia if they comply with the rules on recognition and enforcement.[115] Even more so if such a judgement was given and

---

application of the rules of the mentioned Regulation for contractual obligations even though they fall outside of the Regulation's scope of application. See previously under 4.2. Transfer of cryptocurrency tokens and 4.8. Lending of cryptocurrency tokens.

110 Opinion of the Ministry of Finance Tax Administration No. 410-01/17-08/29 dated 19 March 2018.

111 Article 67 para. 1 Income Tax Act (Official Gazette Nos. 115/16, 106/18, 121/19, 32/20, 138/20).

112 Article 70 para. 4 Income Tax Act.

113 Articles 30 to 35 and 39 Income Tax Act.

114 Articles 67 para. 8 Income Tax Act.

115 International Private Law Act and Regulation (EU) No. 1215/2012 of the European Parliament and of the Council of 12 December 2012 on jurisdiction and the recognition and enforcement of judgments in civil and commercial matters [2012] OJ L 351 1–32.

is enforceable in another member state of the European Union.[116] It is very unlikely that the public policy exception would play any role in this regard.

There are only several legal academic papers written in regard to cryptocurrencies and other cryptoassets. Several scientific and expert conferences were also held. The published papers are as follows:

B. Moslavac, Bitcoin: Nove perspektive kaznenog djela pranja novca ("Bitcoin: New Perspectives of a Money Laundering Criminal Offence"), *Hrvatska pravna revija*, lipanj 2016, pp. 68–76;

N. Čičin-Šain, Oporezivanje Bitcoina ("Taxing Bitcoin"), *Zbornik Pravnog fakulteta u Zagrebu*, 67, (3–4) 2017, pp. 655–693;

I. Parać Vukomanović, 'Pravna priroda virtualnih valuta ("Legal Nature of Virtual Currencies")' 3/2019 *Pravo u gospodarstvu* 407–425;

R. Siffert, S. Petrović, T. Jakšić, 'Payment of the Capital Contribution of a Company Limited by Shares in Cryptocurrency' 8 (2) 2019 *Zagreb Law Review* 95–114;

T. Jakšić, Smjernice za uređenje kriptovrijednosnih papira u hrvatskom pravu – de lege ferenda ("Guidelines for regulation of cryptosecurities under Croatian law – de lege ferenda"), *Zbornik Susreta pravnika u gospodarstvu 2021*, pp. 211–246.

---

116 Article 39 Regulation (EU) No. 1215/2012 of the European Parliament and of the Council of 12 December 2012 on jurisdiction and the recognition and enforcement of judgments in civil and commercial matters [2012] OJ L 351 1–32.

Czech Republic

Adam Jareš, František Kasl, Pavel Loutocký and Johan Schweigl

1 Definition and Legal Qualification

The Czech community of cryptocurrency users and enthusiasts is highly relevant to the size of population. The Czech start-up scene related to blockchain-based innovation is formidable and with global reach. Probably most famous is the Czech company SatoshiLabs, producing one of the first cryptocurrency hardware wallets Trezor.[1] Also well-known is the Czech company Braiins, which operates SlushPool, the world's first Bitcoin mining pool.[2] Other established names in cryptocurrency environment with Czech origin include Invity,[3] TropicSquare,[4] Tatum[5] or Baserank.[6]

Czech Republic is a member state of the European Union (EU). As such, a significant portion of the legal framework is coordinated through the EU level legislation, regulation or other coordination mechanisms. This was emphasised by Dědek,[7] member of the Bank Board of the Czech National Bank (CNB) during the conference Investiční výhledy (Investment outlooks), which took place on 13 October 2021.[8] He highlighted that among central bankers prevails consensus that cryptocurrencies do not fulfil the definition of 'currency' (in Czech: *měna*), which is the main reason for preferred use of the term 'crypto-asset'. Currency is linked to a set of fundamental indicators of the respective economy, which is principally missing in case of cryptocurrencies. Therefore, cryptocurrencies are to be viewed as investment asset[9] rather

1 See https://satoshilabs.com/.
2 See https://slushpool.com/en/home/.
3 See https://invity.io/.
4 See https://tropicsquare.com/.
5 See https://tatum.io/.
6 See https://content.baserank.io/.
7 For personal profile see https://en.wikipedia.org/wiki/Old%C5%99ich_D%C4%9Bdek.
8 For video feed of this discussion (in Czech, starting at 57:30) see https://www.e15.cz/byznys/finance-a-bankovnictvi/zaznam-z-konference-investicni-vyhledy-kryptomeny-nebo-zlato-do-ceho-investovat-1384369.
9 The term 'investment asset' in this context represents economic qualification of the asset, rather than legal qualification. It should not be confused with 'investment instruments' (in Czech: *investiční nástroje*) as discussed further in the text in the context of Act No. 256/2004 Coll.

 | DOI:10.1163/9789004722507_008

than currency, also from the perspective of the regulator. For this reason, Dědek sees the role of regulation for cryptocurrencies mostly limited to providing adequate transparency for investors about the asset, capital adequacy of service providers and AML/CFT. The asset should be subject to similar regulatory requirements as other comparable investment assets. In reaction to the fact that El Salvador adopted cryptocurrency Bitcoin as a recognised national legal tender, Dědek pointed out that central bank needs to consider, among other aspects, social inclusiveness[10] of the assessed payment instrument (when considering its recognition as legal tender).

Until the end of the year 2020 cryptocurrencies had been regulated only through obligations imposed by the Act No. 253/2008 Coll., on Selected Measures against Legitimisation of Proceeds of Crime and Financing of Terrorism, which defined regulated asset as virtual currencies. This act was since then amended and from 1 November 2021 it is applicable not only to 'virtual currencies', but the scope has been extended to virtual assets. On the same day the amendment of the Act No. 455/1991 Coll., on Licensed Trade, came into force. This amendment implemented new trade without specific qualification requirement called 'Provision of services related to virtual assets' (In Czech: *Poskytování služeb spojených s virtuálním aktivem*).

For the purpose of this chapter, we define a cryptocurrency in the Czech legal context as a type of a crypto asset or a virtual currency:

1. the ownership of which is proven only through cryptography;
2. the ownership is recorded through a decentralized and distributed blockchain database and
3. its users can carry out transactions only electronically through a specific blockchain protocol.[11]

Given the nature of cryptocurrencies, jurisdictional boundaries are easily overcome and transactions involving cryptocurrencies as well as services related to cryptocurrencies commonly involve international element. In similar logic, any internationally available and commonly transferred cryptocurrency is likely to become subject to Czech law, at least in the theoretical perspective of applicable law governing given transaction or specific duties applicable to Czech natural or legal person transacting in given cryptocurrency (e.g., tax obligations). Through this lens, most or all commonly known and transferred cryptocurrencies are likely to circulate in Czech legal system (a reference to specific examples may be derived from databases of most frequented

---

10 In the sense of accessibility of the asset to general public.

11 In Czech legal literature see for similar definition e.g. J. Lánský, *Kryptoměny*. C. H. Beck, Prague 2018, p. 3.

cryptocurrencies worldwide).[12] Due to increasing relevance of stable coins in cryptocurrency uses, in particular in relation to services of decentralised finance, such as DApps, it is more than likely that also these cryptocurrencies often feature in such transactions.[13] We are not aware of any statistics or other data available specifically on cryptocurrencies transferred under Czech law.

As indicated above, no cryptocurrency is regarded as a legal tender under Czech law, but most satisfy the qualification of investment asset. Due to the applicability of property rights to cryptocurrencies, which is explained in more detail further in this chapter, they can potentially serve variety of uses (e.g., as an investment asset, means of payment, collateral asset, object of inheritance rights). Deriving from this set of uses are possible legal relationships between participants to the blockchain on which given cryptocurrency is transferred and recorded. Due to the high versatility of applicable governance rules may wary in crucial details case-by-case. Nevertheless, Czech law or doctrine does not by default exclude any of the commonly recognized roles in cryptocurrency structure (i.e., cryptocurrency owners, wallet holders, block miners etc.) from recognition as party to the respective legal relationship. The legal landscape applicable to cryptocurrencies is multi-layered, with added complexity brought by the limited enforcement of the legal claims by traditional legal means alone; i.e., without relevant knowledge, such as private key, or without cooperation by multiple (often globally-decentralized, i.e., extra-jurisdictional) actors, in case of enforcement through a soft or hard fork on given blockchain. Our aim in the subsequent text is to illuminate the major areas, where application of Czech law to legal relationships linked to cryptocurrencies is relevant or at least can be determined doctrinally. Where necessary, we also aim to highlight the technical limitations or extra-legal preconditions for applicability or enforcement of the (Czech) law in the given context.

2 Regulatory Framework and Supervision

The Czech legal order does not set out the requirements for the granting of authorisations for the use, management or issuance of a cryptocurrency or the provision of cryptocurrency-related services except for a few specifics set out

12 See https://coinmarketcap.com/.

13 See e.g., M. Adachi, A. Born, I. Gschossmann and A. Van der Kraaij, 'The expanding functions and uses of stablecoins.' in European Central Bank, *Financial Stability Review, November 2021*. pp. 54–57. https://www.ecb.europa.eu/pub/financial-stability/fsr/html/ecb.fsr202111~8b0aebc817.en.html.

below. As already mentioned, the Czech National Bank views cryptocurrencies as a subset of crypto assets. It defines them as those, which do not include the rights of the owner against other persons, but nevertheless allow for transfer within its own or another distributed register.[14] The Czech legal order does not recognize cryptocurrencies as money (in Czech: *peníze*) in the legal sense, as they do not have the character of claims in relation to a particular currency.

Thus, cryptocurrencies are not understood as money (in Czech: *platební prostředky*) within the meaning of Section 2(1)(c) of Act No. 370/2017 Coll., on Payment Transactions,[15] nor as electronic money (in Czech: *elektronické peníze*) as defined in Section 4 of the Act.[16] Thus, it is not necessary to obtain authorisation or license in a situation where the purchase or sale of cryptocurrency is made for one's own account, as the definitional features of a payment service pursuant to Section 3 of Act No. 370/2017 Coll. are in such case not fulfilled. Furthermore, no authorisation is required in case of purchase or sale of cryptocurrency for Czech Crowns (CZK) or other currency with forced circulation, as the definitional features of an exchange service pursuant to Section 2 of Act No. 370/2017 Coll. are not fulfilled, in case of making payments solely for the purchase of cryptocurrency between the buyer and the seller or in case of exchange of transfer tokens for goods and services.

Additionally, even though cryptocurrencies are mainly perceived as investment asset, most cryptocurrencies do not qualify as investment instrument regulated under Act No. 256/2004 Coll., on Capital Market Business. The most commonly regarded exception, which nevertheless is not generally applicable, concerns stable coins, which, due to their nature, may fall under the definition of investment instrument provided in Section 3 of the Act No. 256/2004 Coll.

Making any general observation about applicability of the definition of 'investment instrument' is challenging due to the complex multi-layered definition of investment instrument, which we provide in unofficial translation:

'Section 3 Investment instruments

1. Investment instruments are
   a. investment securities,
   b. collective investment securities,
   c. money market instruments,

---

14 See (in Czech) https://www.cnb.cz/cs/dohled-financni-trh/legislativni-zakladna/stanoviska-k-regulaci-financniho-trhu/RS2018-13/.

15 This definition in Section 2(1)(c) of Act reads: '(…) (c) money means banknotes, coins, non-cash funds and electronic money, (…)'.

16 The opinion of the Czech National Bank of 10 February 2014 also commented on this. See https://www.cnb.cz/cs/dohled-financni-trh/legislativni-zakladna/stanoviska-k-regulaci-financniho-trhu/RS2014-02/.

d. options, futures, swaps, forwards and other instruments the value of which is related to the price or value of securities, exchange rates, interest rates or interest yields, greenhouse gas emission allowances, as well as other derivatives, financial indices or financial quantitative indicators, and which give rise to a right to cash settlement or a right to delivery of the thing to which their value relates,
e. instruments allowing the transfer of credit risk,
f. financial contracts for difference,
g. options, futures, swaps, forwards and other instruments whose value relates to commodities and which give rise to a right to cash settlement or to the right of at least one party to elect to be settled in cash if the cash settlement is not due to the default of one of the parties to the derivative or other early termination of the derivative,
h. options, futures, swaps, forwards and other instruments the value of which relates to a commodity (...),
i. options, futures, swaps, forwards and other instruments the value of which relates to a commodity and which give rise to an obligation to deliver that commodity, which are not referred to in point (h), are not for commercial purposes and have the characteristics of other derivative investment instruments,
j. options, futures, swaps, forwards and other instruments the value of which relates to weather indicators, freight rates or inflation rates and other economic indicators published by the official statistics department (...),
k. instruments the value of which relates to assets, rights, debts, indices or quantifiable indicators other than those referred to in points (a) to (j) and which have the characteristics of other derivative investment instruments; in particular those traded on a European regulated market or multilateral trading facility or organised trading facility; and
l. greenhouse gas emission allowances.

2. (...)'

In our opinion, stable coins, due to their link with an underlying reference asset, are likely to be qualified as investment instrument under Section 3(1)(k) of the Act No. 256/2004 Coll., i.e., 'instruments the value of which relates to assets, rights, debts, indices or quantifiable indicators other than those referred to in points (a) to (j) and which have the characteristics of other derivative investment instruments.' In such case issuing and trading in stable coins shall be subject to the regulatory requirements for securities dealers in particular licence, capital adequacy, internal audits and reporting. Nevertheless, the categorization of stable coins as such is currently not clear and would require assessment by the Czech National Bank in a particular case. A significant shift is expected with applicability of the EU-level Regulation 2023/1114 on Markets in Crypto-assets (MICA) in 2024. This harmonizing piece of EU legislation is largely aimed at establishing regulatory framework throughout EU that will apply similar requirements to services related to inter alia stable coins, as apply to services related to investment instruments under the above discussed Czech Act No. 256/2004 Coll. The Czech legislator is reacting to this development by a proposal of an Act on Digital Finances that was approved by Czech government in April 2024 and shall be subject to the ordinary legislative process.[17]

As for now, there is no general requirement under Czech law for the provider of services related to cryptocurrencies to obtain an authorisation or licence. However, under closer look, other potential exception to this statement can be identified, aside from the above-mentioned stable coins.

Authorisation is needed where derivatives on a particular cryptocurrency are traded, as such derivative will meet the definitional characteristics of an investment instrument. For such trading, it is then necessary to obtain the authorisation of a securities dealer, which is defined under Act No. 256/2004 Coll. The entity that trades in this way needs to obtain a securities trader's licence pursuant to Section 4a (and Sections 3 and 5) of Act No. 256/2004 Coll. These are the entities listed in Section 2 of the Act, typically a bank, credit union, securities dealer, insurance company, reinsurance company, investment company, investment fund or pension company. Authorisation is typically granted by the Czech National Bank.

According to Sections 15 and 98 of Act No. 240/2013 Coll., on Investment Companies and Investment Funds, it is necessary to apply for a permit in the case of management of investors' assets (fund) that is invested in cryptocurrency (regardless of whether the fund is offered to the public or only to a limited circle). This authorisation shall be granted to the investment fund or the investment company pursuant to Section 7 et seq. of Act No. 240/2013 Coll. by the Czech National Bank in a procedure pursuant to Section 5 of the Act.

A license must also be applied for when funds are transferred in connection with the organisation of cryptocurrency exchange transactions (this is a payment service pursuant to Section 3 of Act No. 370/2017 Coll.). If customers are allowed, for example, to deposit, withdraw or transfer money, relevant authorisation should be applied for. Both Czech and foreign banks or financial institutions, saving and credit cooperatives, electronic money institutions,

17 See (in Czech) https://www.mfcr.cz/cs/ministerstvo/media/tiskove-zpravy/2024/vlada-schvalila-zakon-o-digitalnich-financich-55549.

small-scale electronic money issuers, payment institutions, small-scale payment service providers, payment account information administrators or postal licence holders apply for an authorisation pursuant to Section 5 of Act No. 370/2017 Coll. This authorisation shall be granted by the Czech National Bank pursuant to Section 7 of the Act.

In the moment when money is exchanged for cryptocurrencies and vice versa, banks, foreign banks and foreign financial institutions, credit unions and money changers are entitled to apply for an authorisation pursuant to Section 3 of Act No. 277/2013 Coll., on Exchange Activities. The Czech National Bank must be applied for an authorisation pursuant to Section 4 of the Act. Furthermore, if the entity has already obtained a licence for another activity from the Czech National Bank (typically the activities of a payment institution pursuant to Section 9 et seq. of Act No. 370/2017 Coll.) and supplements this activity with cryptocurrency business, it is necessary to apply for authorisation. This is also the case for diversification of exchange activities.

The above-mentioned activities are subject to review and authorisation through the Czech National Bank. To our knowledge, the aforementioned legislation sets out exhaustive conditions that must be met if a licence or extension is to be applied for. The conditions for withdrawal or limitation of the licence granted are specifically contained in each of the above-mentioned laws. These provisions also contain the administrative penalties resulting from specific infringements.

In the case of Act No. 256/2004 Coll., the withdrawal of authorisation is defined by Section 145 and it is typically a situation where the assets of the person against whom insolvency has been declared are insufficient to cover the costs of the proceedings and furthermore for a person who has been banned from the activity by a court or administrative authority; a person to whom a permit has been granted has not commenced the authorised activity within 12 months of the permit being granted; a person to whom a permit has been granted has not carried out the activity for which the permit was granted for more than 6 months; or the permit was granted on the basis of false, misleading or incomplete information.

In the case of Act No. 240/2013 Coll., the withdrawal of authorisation is defined in Section 551 and it is typically a situation where the bankruptcy of an investment company (and other entities mentioned in the Act) has been decided and the insolvency petition has been rejected due to the lack of assets of the investment company; where the investment fund has not had a depositary for more than 3 months, etc. The Czech National Bank may then revoke the authorisation pursuant to Section 552 on an optional basis when, for example, the corrective measure imposed has not led to correction; when it is necessary for the protection of investors' interests, etc.

In the case of Act No. 370/2017 Coll., the withdrawal of authorisation is defined in Section 244 et seq., and it is typically a situation where a person has seriously breached an obligation set out in the Act; does not meet the conditions for its granting; the authorisation was granted based on false or incomplete data, etc.

In the case of Act No. 277/2013 Coll., the withdrawal of authorisation is defined in Section 9. However, it only affects exchange agents and not banks or credit unions, as they are subject to more general conditions relating to their overall activities. The licence to operate as a money changer then expires on the death of the money changer or on the dissolution of the money changer, which is a legal person; on the request of the money changer; on the basis of repeated serious breaches of the law; if the money changer ceases to comply with the requirements laid down, etc.

It is obvious from the previous text, that as of now, there is no specific law aimed at regulation of cryptocurrencies in the Czech Republic. The future legislative development in most likely to come from the EU level legislation, in particular directly applicable regulation. This is the case of the Digital finance package[18] as well as the AML/CFT package.[19]

Currently, Czech AML law is the only area with specific provisions dedicated to cryptocurrencies. The Act No. 253/2008 Coll., operates with the term 'virtual asset', as already mentioned in the beginning of the chapter. This in fact is an extensive transposition of the Directive (EU) 2018/843 amending Directive (EU) 2015/849 on the prevention of the use of the financial system for the purposes of money laundering or terrorist financing, and amending Directives 2009/138/EC and 2013/36/EU (so called 5. AML Directive), which operates with the term 'virtual currency'. Interestingly, the recent amendment to Act No. 253/2008 Coll. by Act No. 107/2024 Coll. clarified that for the purpose of this Act, payment in virtual assets is to be deemed as payment in cash. For the purposes of the Act No. 253/2008 Coll., a person providing services related to a virtual asset means a person who, as the object of his or her business, buys, sells, stores, manages, transfers, or arranges the purchase or sale of a virtual asset for another, provides financial services related to the offer or sale of a virtual asset,

---

18 See https://ec.europa.eu/info/publications/200924-digital-finance-proposals_en.

19 See https://ec.europa.eu/info/publications/210720-anti-money-laundering-countering-financing-terrorism_en.

or provides other similar services related to a virtual asset. These persons are required to fulfil proportionate to their business situation the standard AML/CFT regulatory requirements, such as client identification, transaction verification, data retention, reporting of suspicious transaction, risk analysis or transparency measures. For entities not directly subject to the Act No. 253/2008 Coll. are still applicable the provisions in criminal law concerning legalization of proceeds of crime through negligence, as contained in Section 217 of the Act No. 40/2009 Coll., Criminal Code.

There currently is no specific obligation in Czech law to publish a whitepaper or prospectus. Cryptocurrencies, even in cases when considered investment instruments, are not considered securities, thereby not subject to relevant national requirements for prospectus contained in Act No. 256/2004 Coll. or relevant EU-level legislation, in particular Regulation (EU) 2017/1129 on the prospectus to be published when securities are offered to the public or admitted to trading on a regulated market.[20] Change in this regard, at least for certain categories of cryptocurrencies, such as stable coins, comes soon with the above mentioned EU-level Regulation 2023/1114 on Markets in Crypto-assets (MICA). It contains an obligation to publish a whitepaper, however, does not envisage a need for approval of the whitepaper by the regulatory authority, thereby serving merely as a minimal transparency requirement towards investors. Currently, Czech law does not specifically regulate the procedure for publishing a whitepaper or prospectus. In the case of a proposal for the purchase of securities, for example, Act No. 90/2012 Coll., on Commercial Companies and Cooperatives (Act on Commercial Corporations), the Czech National Bank has an option to prohibit a public proposal for a contract. However, there is no similar legislation for cryptocurrencies. As such, there is no obligation to publish a whitepaper or prospectus in relation to cryptocurrencies, yet it is often part of the initial coin offering as a tool for transparency and legitimacy towards potential investors. In case of misleading or false information, the general liability regime under Czech civil law would apply, whereas intentionality of the action needs to be assessed.

Further option is an assessment from the criminal law perspective, as potential crime of fraud, as defined in Section 209 of the Act No. 40/2009 Coll. There is a number of potential crimes, which may be committed in or with the help of cryptocurrencies (e.g., fraud, money laundering, blackmailing, theft, embezzlement), but there are no specific provisions in Czech criminal law aimed at cryptocurrencies or cryptocurrency related services and we are also not aware of any current initiative aiming to introduce any in the legislative

20 See https://www.cnb.cz/cs/dohled-financni-trh/vykon-dohledu/povolovaci-a-schvalovaci-rizeni/povolovaci-a-schvalovaci-rizeni-emitenti/.

process. Most common situation, where cryptocurrencies become relevant from criminal law perspective is likely the loss of cryptocurrencies through hacking or fraud, therefore the value of the affected cryptocurrency units will represent the damage caused by the criminal activity. Due to the international nature of cryptocurrency systems, investigation and successful conclusion of such cases is, however, likely to be complicated. Similarly, any civil law claims by the injured party for the compensation of damages is unlikely to be successful, despite Czech legal system theoretically allowing for such claim. The main obstacles are similar: likely cross-border nature of the case, need for specific expertise and technical limitations inherent for blockchain technology with decentralized administration which obstruct or prevent enforcement of a court order, even if obtained.

As already indicated, in those instances, where authorisation is required, it is granted by the Czech National Bank. Otherwise, there is no specific institution supervising cryptocurrencies and related services. As can be deduced for the position of the Czech National Bank towards cryptocurrencies, which was described in the beginning of this chapter, cryptocurrencies are not viewed as an area, which would require major supervisory measures or actions. We are not aware of any noteworthy regulatory activity by the Czech National Bank concerning cryptocurrencies in the recent past. To our knowledge, the only significant actions against illegal activities connected to cryptocurrencies in the context of Czech law were taken by law enforcement authorities. The most significant in this regard was probably the shutdown of Sheep Marketplace in 2013 and subsequent trail concerning also the seized cryptocurrency. We describe this case in more detail later.

3 Private Law Issues

In order to deal with private law issues related with cryptocurrencies in this section, it is necessary to examine whether it is possible to qualify cryptocurrencies as 'a thing' in the legal sense of its definition in the Czech Civil Code.[21] As Carr states, 'it is axiomatic that for property law rights to exist there must be a legally recognized object over which such right can apply. In civilian

21 Act No. 89/2012 Coll., Civil Code. For more details, please, refer to the translation of the Act provided by Czech Judicial Portal, see http://obcanskyzakonik.justice.cz/images/pdf/Civil-Code.pdf.

terminology such an object is described as a thing or a res.'[22] This statement corresponds with the definition of ownership in Section 1011 of the Civil Code, which reads as follows: 'Everything that belongs to someone, all his corporeal and incorporeal things constitute the person's ownership.'

Under the Civil Code, as a thing in the legal sense is recognized everything that is different from a person and serves the needs of people. There is also stated what is not a thing; human body and its parts as well as living animals. Everything which is not a person and serves the needs of people in objective reality is then a thing in legal sense. Legal doctrine adds one more characteristic feature of a thing, which is to be permissible object of absolute property rights, especially the right of ownership.[23]

Cryptocurrencies meet the conditions for the classification of an object as a thing in the conception of the Czech civil law: they are different from natural and legal persons; serve the need of people as they can, on certain conditions, for example constitute a mean of exchange or represent an investment asset; and can be objects of property rights. They can be held and transferred. The number of transactions performed with cryptocurrencies is the proof of their controllability. Ownership of units of cryptocurrency is proved by cryptography and is registered in blockchain though which transfers are performed.

Since no obligation on the part of the owner or any other person to give, do, suffer or refrain from doing anything is attached to the ownership of a unit of cryptocurrency, it will not be possible to classify cryptocurrency as a right. Some stable coins will be connected with a claim on the issuer to redeem the stable coins for cash or other assets associated with their ownership, nonetheless, everything belonging to someone, all his corporeal and incorporeal things, constitute this persons' ownership. Thus, it would probably be irrelevant, at least from the point of view of a regular owner, whether cryptocurrency is regarded as a right or other thing with incorporeal essence. We therefore conclude that units of cryptocurrencies correspond the legal definition of a (incorporeal) thing in the Czech civil law.

Cryptocurrencies are movable things. But determination of their characteristics as fungible and consumable thing is not that simple. A thing would be considered fungible if it could be altered with another thing of the

---

22 See D. Carr, 'Cryptocurrencies as Property in Civilian and Mixed Legal Systems' in D. Fox, S. Green (eds), *Cryptocurrencies in Public and Private Law*. Oxford University Press, Oxford 2018, p. 179.

23 See O. David and T. Kindl, '§ 489' in J. Švestka, J. Dvořák, J. Fiala (eds), *Občanský zákoník. Komentář*, Wolters Kluwer, Prague 2019.; A. Thöndel, M. Zuklínová, 'Předmět v občanském právu' in J. Dvořák, J. Švestka, M. Zuklínová (eds) *Občanské právo hmotné. Svazek I. Díl první. Obecná* část. 2nd ed., Wolters Kluwer, Prague 2016, p. 377.

same kind. Other things are non-fungible. Money is traditionally regarded as fungible things. Whilst we are able to find many differences between fiat currencies and cryptocurrencies, in our opinion, there is no reason why fiat currencies would be considered as fungible things and cryptocurrencies as non-fungible ones. This is further supported by comparing cryptocurrencies to non-fungible tokens (NFT), which differ mainly in the characteristic that links the unique token with the holder's account as compared to interchangeable tokens of cryptocurrencies. Nonetheless, it is necessary to highlight that Carr, for example, concludes that Bitcoin has elements of exclusivity and control because it consists of digitised information accessed by private keys and proved by the process of mining. In his opinion Bitcoin therefore is only partially fungible because of its cryptographic uniqueness.[24]

If we deem cryptocurrency as a thing, it means that its units would be eligible object of absolute and relative property rights. Therefore, such units would be objects of ownership right. However, it is necessary to admit that this conclusion has its limits due to the nature of cryptocurrencies and possibilities to dispose with them. We also reach the conclusion that according to the wide definition of a thing in the Civil Code a cryptocurrency wallet and an address in a cryptocurrency site should also be separately considered as things in the legal sense. Unlike a cryptocurrency unit, an address is unique and it is not possible to substitute it with different address (even if the same amount of cryptocurrency units is linked with such an address). Therefore, an address should be considered as a non-fungible thing. Similarly, a bank account is considered a thing in a sense of the Czech Civil Code. A bank account itself is not defined by this act and the Civil Code only defines an account contract. Nonetheless, the comparison with a bank account is possible only for the purposes of classification of cryptocurrency address and wallet as a thing. By a deposit to a bank account, the owner loses sole control over the funds. Bank can, according to law, prohibit owner's access to a bank account. That would not be possible with a cryptocurrency address. If an owner knows login data for a bank account or to the internet banking, it does not necessary mean that he will be able to transfer deposited funds. On the other hand, private cryptographic key for a cryptocurrency address provides its owner sole control over the cryptocurrency units linked with a particular address.[25]

24 See D. Carr, 'Cryptocurrencies as Property in Civilian and Mixed Legal Systems' in D. Fox, S. Green (eds), *Cryptocurrencies in Public and Private Law*. Oxford University Press, Oxford 2018, p. 187.

25 See M. Raskin, 'Realm of the Coin: Bitcoin and Civil Procedure' (2015) *Fordham Journal of Corporate & Financial Law*, vol. XX, no. 4, p. 994.

Everything that belongs to a person including corporeal and incorporeal things is considered the person's ownership. Czech Civil Code understands ownership as the owner's right to dispose of his property freely within the limits of the law and also exclude other persons from it. Everyone else is obliged not to disturb an owner. Following individual rights of an owner are usually associated with: right to hold a thing; to use it (or to not use it); to benefit from it; to dispose of it; to destroy it; or to abandon it.[26] Nonetheless, due to the expansive nature of ownership, no explicit enumeration of owner's rights is final.[27] Owner's rights are limited in the blockchain due to its rules and asymmetric cryptography. In general, owner is allowed to treat his possession however he likes, except in a way prohibited by law. In the context of blockchain, rules of the particular cryptocurrency must be taken into consideration. Every disposition with the given cryptocurrency must be performed in accordance with these (technical) rules and limits. Also, a person may be (legally) an owner of certain number of units of cryptocurrency on a particular address, but without the knowledge of private cryptographic key to this address, they will not be able to dispose of them. For example, if the cryptocurrency units are inherited, but the private key is not found in the possession of the testator. Not even a court decision ordering a transfer of such cryptocurrency units will enable the disposition. Without the cooperation of miners and other users of this cryptocurrency or the knowledge of the private key, such restitution is (technically) not possible, despite the law.

If we consider a case example, where X has 60 Bitcoins registered in his/her wallet, we can clearly conclude following the analysis in previous paragraphs that X can have legal ownership not only over the wallet, but also over these Bitcoins as units of cryptocurrency recognised as things in legal sense under Czech law.

If X opened an account with MontC, intermediary providing wallet custody services, the ownership situation is similar to bank account, i.e., subject to specific contractual clauses to the contrary, X retains exclusive ownership over the account and the cryptocurrency units in the account as MontC merely provide a custody service. The fact of technical means for disposition with the account is then legally a matter of possession, which does not establish ownership in itself.

---

26 See J. Spáčil, *Věcná práva. Věcná práva, katastr nemovitostí a správa cizího majetku*. C. H. Beck, Prague 2018, p. 53.

27 See M. Zuklínová, 'Pojem vlastnictví'. in J. Dvořák, J. Švestka, (eds). *Občanské právo hmotné. Svazek 3. Díl třetí: Věcná práva*, Wolters Kluwer, Prague 2015, p. 31.

Following from the nature of ownership, as commonly recognised under continental law, in case of hard fork or airdrop of a new cryptocurrency that would be registered to the wallet owned by X, we find applicable the right to the fruits (usufruct). Thereby ownership of X over the existing units of cryptocurrency, which were the consideration or condition for affiliation of the new units of cryptocurrency to the wallet, would naturally extend to the new units. We see no legal reason, unless specific contractual provisions were part of the contract of custody, for wallet custodial, such as MontC, to claim ownership over these new units under Czech law.

In this context, we searched the answer to the question, under which conditions does the Czech law apply to the issue of ownership right to the cryptocurrency. To our knowledge, the EU law, represented in this context mainly by Regulation Rome II,[28] does not provide collision norms for property rights to intangible things. Furthermore, the Czech Act No. 91/2012 Coll., on Private International Law, provides specific provisions only concerning applicability of the Czech law to the matters of ownership of selected intangible things such as securities or investment instruments, these are, however, not directly applicable to cryptocurrencies. As we established above, that cryptocurrencies, in most cases, do not represent securities[29] or investment instruments. Czech jurisprudence does not provide a clear position on the issue of collision norms for cryptocurrencies,[30] so the issue remains largely unresolved. This fits in the picture described in detail by Fox and Green that the issue of collision norms for cryptocurrencies in the private international law is complex and to a large part no definitive provisions or interpretations are currently established even in other jurisdictions.[31]

An owner will be able to perform a transfer of units of cryptocurrency using any possible method of transfer and such a transfer would be legal in the context of the Czech law. The transfer can be made via transaction on the appropriate blockchain, but also paper wallet or hardware wallet (inclusive the knowledge to unlock and use it) can be handed over physically. To our knowledge, Czech Civil law does not set specific prerequisites or limits on transfer of cryptocurrency.

---

28 Regulation (EC) No 864/2007 of the European Parliament and of the Council of 11 July 2007 on the law applicable to non-contractual obligations (Rome II) [2007] OJ L199/40.

29 J. Dědič, J. Šovar and O. Mikula, 'Proč podle českého soukromého práva nelze uvažovat o (ICO) tokenech jako o cenných papírech' (2018) *Právní rozhledy*, no. 15–16, pp. 554–556.

30 N. Rozehnalová et al., *Czech Private International Law*. 1st ed. Masarykova univerzita, Brno 2015.

31 D. Fox, S. Green, *Cryptocurrencies in Public and Private Law*. Oxford University Press. Oxford 2019.

In this context, we find no specific conditions that need to be met to donate cryptocurrency. The donation tax was cancelled in 2014, but such transfer could be subject to income tax on the part of the receiver, unless specific exceptions applied (in particular donation within closely related persons are exempt). If we considered a case example, where X gives 60 Bitcoins to Y, there are no particular limitations to such transaction. However, as we indicated above, there remains an unresolved uncertainty under private international law, given that the transfer of ownership is directly linked to the provision on creation and extinction of ownership rights.

Transfer through inheritance is closely related to the transfer of ownership by the will of the owner. This relation is expressed in the Article 11 of the Czech Charter of Fundamental Rights and Freedoms which states: 'Everybody has the right to own property. The ownership right of all owners has the same statutory content and enjoys the same protection, inheritance is guaranteed'.[32] Even though inheritance is not expressly mentioned among the ways for acquisition of ownership right in the Czech Civil Code, it is certainly a common and important one.[33] According to the Civil Code, everything that belongs to a person constitutes person's property. The key concept is the 'estate of the deceased'. Units of cryptocurrency as things are eligible to be a part of the estate. However, heir cannot acquire these units without the address they are attached to. The heir must therefore acquire control over the cryptocurrency address. The prerequisite to be able to dispose with the inherited units of cryptocurrency is to possess or acquire the knowledge of the private and public keys they are attached to. The same applies to the situation, when the heir inherits a hardware wallet. In this case, the knowledge of password, passphrase, seed or some other detail that would allow disposition with the stored data is necessary.

The basic principle of the law of succession is the preservation of values. The expression of this principle is the fact that with the death of a person his or her assets will not perish but will be preferably passed to others who had close relationship with the deceased. The law also serves a social function and allows for intergenerational solidarity within family.[34] It also shows respect to a one's efforts to purposefully acquire assets, as these assets will be preserved

32 English translation available at https://www.psp.cz/en/docs/laws/listina.html.

33 J. Dvořák, 'Hlava první: Obecné výklady' in J. Dvořák, J. Švestka, M. Zuklínová (eds), *Občanské právo hmotné. Svazek 4. Díl* čtvrtý: *Dědické právo*. Wolters Kluwer ČR, Prague 2019, p. 20.

34 J. Dvořák, 'Zásady dědického práva' in J. Dvořák, J. Švestka, M. Zuklínová (eds), *Občanské právo hmotné. Svazek 4. Díl* čtvrtý: *Dědické právo*. Wolters Kluwer ČR, Prague 2019, p. 23.

at the greatest possible extend for his descendants.[35] However, as indicated above, by cryptocurrencies this principle could be denied through absence of necessary knowledge passed from the deceased to the heir. The inheritance tax was repealed in the Czech Republic in 2014. Until then a paradox situation could have occurred, when in such a case the heir would not be able to benefit from this part of the estate, which would nevertheless be subject to the inheritance tax. Given the sensitive nature of the knowledge of the private key, most solution for securing smooth inheritance of the units of cryptocurrency simultaneously represent a security vulnerability that can be exploited to the detriment of the owner.

Additionally, apart from the potential frustration of the inheritance through the obstacle for the heir described above, identifying the units of cryptocurrency as part of the estate of the deceased may present similarly challenging obstacle. Due to the pseudonymous decentralized nature of most cryptocurrencies, obtaining information about the addresses in the possession of the deceased from third party may be impossible (in particular in case of paper wallet or hardware wallet). It would therefore be also appropriate for cryptocurrency owners to keep a summary of the cryptocurrency addresses in case of their sudden demise. In more premediated arrangements, as in case of a testament, the above-mentioned knowledge should be included in order to allow effective succession of the ownership to the inheritors.

Considering a case example, where X has 60 Bitcoins in his/her wallet and want to ensure its succession to his/her child Y, we see no particular limits for the wallet (and the necessary knowledge for its effective use) to be included in the will of X. If there is no will, the units of cryptocurrency in the respective wallet will be (if found) included in the estate of X[36] and following the legal regulation of inheritance, the children and spouse of X would inherit it proportionally.[37] Of course, as mentioned above, if the knowledge of the private key would be lost with the demise of X, the effective disposition with the wallet and therein contained cryptocurrency units would become practically impossible, despite legal claim of the heir. If the wallet was in custody of an intermediary, such as MontC, we see no other than procedural modification

---

35 L. Dobešová, 'Dědické právo' in J. Hurdík (eds) *Občanské právo hmotné: obecná část: absolutní majetková práva*. 3rd ed., Aleš Čeněk, Pilsen 2018. p. 194.

36 See Section 1475(2) of the Civil Code: 'The estate shall consist of all assets and debts of the testator, except for rights and obligations attached exclusively to his person, unless they have been recognised as a debt or asserted before a public authority.'

37 See Section 1635(1) of the Civil Code: 'In the first class of heirs, the testator's children and his spouse inherit, each of them equally.'

of the succession in rights. The heir Y would enter into the custody contract instead of the deceased X.

Trust fund (in Czech: *svěřenský fond*) is regulated by Sections 1448 to 1474 of the Civil Code. According to Section 1448(1) of the Civil Code, a trust fund is created by setting aside property from the settlor's ownership by entrusting the trustee with the property for a specific purpose by contract or by acquisition on death. As such, the creation of a trust fund creates a separate and independent ownership right of the trust fund towards the property set aside and the trustee is obliged to take charge of that property and its administration. From contractual perspective the trustee shall exercise the rights of ownership of the property in the trust fund in his own name on behalf of the fund; but the property in the trust fund is neither the property of the trustee, nor the property of the settlor, nor the property of the person to be benefited by the trust fund. In accordance with Section 1451(2) of the Civil Code, the trust fund is established on the day it is registered in the trust fund registry. Units of cryptocurrencies are things in legal sense and therefore part of property of the settlor, which are eligible to set aside and become part of the property of the trust fund. Following our heuristic research of the registry, we identified at least one trust fund, '*Crypto rodinný svěřenský fond*'[38] (In English: Crypto family trust fund) established on 11 January 2022, that is likely to contain cryptocurrencies (the assets that represent the property of the trust fund are for obvious reasons not publicly available information, therefore we have no means of verifying, if this trust fund, or in fact any trust fund actually contains cryptocurrency units as part of its property).

If we considered an example case, where X as the owner of 60 Bitcoins wants to establish a trust fund and put these cryptocurrency units aside as property of the trust fund for the benefit of Y, we see no particular obstacles for him/her in doing so. In our opinion, setting the property aside into the trust fund does not necessarily mean a transfer of the cryptocurrency units, as long as the trustee obtains exclusive control over the property set aside. This could potentially be achieved also through a modification of the custody service with a wallet intermediary, however, given that the settlor is likely to retain access to the wallet by this intermediary, this would commonly not be sufficient, therefore transfer of the funds to a wallet controlled exclusively by the trustee is likely a necessary prerequisite. We are not aware of any specific provision in the applicable private international law, which would apply to trust fund containing cryptocurrencies. Issues of applicable law would therefore probably

---

38 See https://esf.justice.cz/ias/isesf/rejstrik-fond.vysledky?subjektId=1146159&typ=UPLNY.

have to be interpreted and applied in accordance with the general collision norms and pursuant to similar jurisprudence.

In principle, we are not aware of any specific provisions or limitations that would exclude the possibility of seizing an obligation through cryptocurrency units as collateral under the Czech law. Nevertheless, from a practical perspective, this is likely a scenario currently limited to decentralized finance, which is not well developed in the Czech legal environment and therefore remains a regulatory and legal grey zone with lack of any comprehensive jurisprudence. Given the technical prerequisites for the creditor to satisfy the claim from the collateral similar to the prerequisites to effective succession by the heir, the scenario remains largely theoretical in our opinion, at least in the context of Czech law.

Insolvency law applies to all assets in the ownership of the insolvency debtor, therefore also cryptocurrency units. As we mention further in section concerning examples of litigation in relation to cryptocurrencies in the Czech Republic, we were able to identify one case of insolvency proceedings aimed at a cryptocurrency business entity, however, these proceedings were halted pursuant to the petitioning creditor withdrawing the petition. Therefore, the publicly available documentation does not provide any practical guidance about the approach of the insolvency administrator or the insolvency court to the classification and distribution of the cryptocurrency units among the creditors. Czech insolvency law, as contained in the Act No. 182/2006 Coll., on Insolvency, provides only general rules, which in most cases need to be applied to cryptocurrency units by analogy, as they were not formulated with this type of asset in mind. The obvious challenge that we see as specific for dealing with cryptocurrency units in the course of insolvency proceedings is choosing suitable approach to valuation of these assets. Valuation of intangible assets in general, cryptocurrency units in particular, is a broader issue relevant also to tax obligations, business transactions, merger and acquisitions or inheritance proceedings.[39] Certain guidance is provided by the Czech Ministry of Finance in the recommendation concerning accounting treatment of cryptocurrency units.[40]

According to the Czech Civil Code, when a debt is secured by a pledge and debtor fails to fulfil a debt properly and on time, a creditor becomes entitled to

39 For more details on possible approaches see e.g., L. Vomáčka. *Kryptoměny a možnosti jejich oceňování.* Master's thesis, Prague University of Economics and Business, Prague 2018 https://theses.cz/id/vmm3f2/.

40 See https://www.mfcr.cz/assets/cs/media/Ucetnictvi_2018_Sdeleni-MF-k-uctovani-a-vykazovani-digitalnich-men.pdf.

satisfy his claims from the monetization of the pledged thing up to the agreed amount. If the amount is not previously agreed, then up to the amount of the claim with its accessories as of the date on which the pledged thing was sold. A pledge secures a debt and its accessories and, if previously agreed, it may also secure a penalty for a breach of a contract. A pledge is a right in rem, which means that it has effect beyond parties to a contract. Under Czech law, any tradeable thing can serve as a pledge. Even a thing to which the pledgor will acquire the ownership right only in the future is eligible to be a pledge. Units of cryptocurrency represent a thing that is tradeable and as such can serve as a pledge, in particular if the whole cryptocurrency wallet is pledged. Nevertheless, pledging units of cryptocurrency is problematic. The Civil Code states that a pledge of a movable thing is created upon the delivery of such a thing to the pledgee. If the pledged thing is not delivered to the pledgee, it should be marked as pledge so any third person could recognize that it was pledged. We can imagine that hardware wallet with certain amount of a cryptocurrency units would be marked properly as a pledge. It could also be physically delivered to the pledgee. Similarly, units of cryptocurrency can be transferred to the pledgee (or potentially an agreed third party as escrow). However, unless the respective blockchain provides for specific mechanics for marking pledged cryptocurrency, it is not possible to pledge units without transferring them to the pledgee. In case of the pledge of cryptocurrency wallet, another issue arises. The pledgee cannot rely on exclusive control over the pledged assets. Even if a physical storage of the wallet is handed over to the pledgee, the wallet could have been cloned and therefore used also from a different device. Furthermore, disposition with the wallet requires knowledge, which may be not available to the pledgee.

If we focus on the transactional function of cryptocurrencies, we may identify limits to the possibility to pay for products or services with cryptocurrency. The Czech Civil Code requires payment of the purchase price as a conceptual feature of certain contractual relationships. As an example:

- contract of sale, by which the buyer undertakes to take over the object of purchase and pay the purchase price for it,
- tour contract, by which the customer agrees to pay the total price of the tour, or
- contract for work, by which the client undertakes to accept the work and pay the price.

It would seem from Section 492(1) of the Civil Code, which states that '[t]he value of a thing, if it can be expressed in money, is its price', that the price can only be determined in money. This conclusion could mean, for example, that the price of a work could not be paid in a cryptocurrency. Similarly, an online purchase of product or a service would represent a contract of exchange, rather than a contract of sale.

In the case of a contract of sale, the purchase price can be understood as consideration in exchange for the transfer of the ownership to the purchased thing. Similarly, the price represents consideration in exchange for the performance of work by the contract for work. If the purchase price was not expressed in money, it would be a contract of exchange. Nevertheless, cryptocurrency such as Bitcoin was clearly developed with the intention to establish an alternative electronic payment system.[41] As such, it is not dissimilar to vouchers or food stamps. In Czech law, such purchases are considered as based on contract of sale, as long as the purchase price is fixed in a clearly defined payment system.[42]

Similar conclusion can be drawn from the judgment of the Court of Justice of the European Union in the case Skatteverket v. David Hedqvist.[43] This case concerned a preliminary ruling in a dispute between the Swedish Tax Administration and Mr. Hedqvist on whether exchange transactions of traditional currencies for units of Bitcoin provided in the course of a business are subject to value added tax. In the judgment, the Court states that 'the virtual currency with a two-way flow "bitcoin" (…) cannot be regarded as "tangible property" (…) since (…) that virtual currency has no purpose other than that of a means of payment.' The Court then goes on to state that 'since the virtual currency "bitcoin" is a contractual tender, (…) it constitutes a direct means of payment between economic operators who accept it.'

The conclusion that cryptocurrency units can represent purchase price, and therefore that transactions in cryptocurrencies represent contract of sale rather than contract of exchange, also corresponds to the principle of autonomy of the will of the contracting party as enshrined in the Czech Civil Code. Furthermore, there are Czech online e-commerce platforms, such as Alza, that allow for purchase of goods for cryptocurrency units.[44]

---

41 Cf. S. Nakamoto, *Bitcoin: A Peer-to-Peer Electronic Cash System*, 2009, p. 1, https://bitcoin.org/bitcoin.pdf.

42 L. Tichý, P. Pipková, J. Balarin, *Kupní smlouva v novém občanském zákoníku*. 1st ed., C. H. Beck, Prague 2014, p. 32.

43 Case C-264/14, *Skatteverket v. David Hedqvist*, ECLI:EU:C:2015:718.

44 See e.g., https://www.alza.cz/platba-bitcoiny-a-btc-automaty-alza.

4 Tax Measures

The tax law applies to the cryptocurrencies from various perspectives. The most typical is the income tax, which is regulated mainly by the Act No. 586/1992 Coll., on Income Taxes. In general, the tax base is the difference between the costs the tax payers had in connection with obtaining the cryptocurrency and the income they gain from selling or bartering it. The Czech tax law distinguishes between the types of tax payers, i.e., between natural persons who are not engaged in any business activity (such as employees who only trade cryptocurrency on the side, not as their main source of income) and businesses, either in the form of legal persons or sole proprietors. Each of these groups is subject to a different approach. As the regulation of sole proprietors who included cryptocurrencies in their business assets is in many aspects similar to the regulation of legal entities, we will not describe all the differences applying to sole proprietors.

For instance, all the types of tax payers can lower their tax base by subtracting the amount they paid for obtaining the cryptocurrency, as their initial expense. However, much stricter conditions for such a subtraction applies to the natural non-business persons. These non-business tax payers can only count in the costs which were 'substantially' connected with obtaining of the cryptocurrency (aside from the amount for which they had purchased the cryptocurrency, they can count among the costs, for instance, the crypto exchange fees, but they cannot count in, for instance, the fees paid to internet provider). The legal persons, on the other side, are freer to count in various other related expenses (in principle, their tax base is calculated from all sources of its income and various respective expenses, including for instance fees paid to internet provider, electricity bills, etc.).

Another difference between a non-business natural person and a legal person is in the extent in which their losses can be offset against income from trading cryptocurrencies. A non-business natural person can only apply losses from the trading with cryptocurrency, whereas legal entities are again freer in this respect, they can count in losses from a variety of instruments with which the legal entities traded (including, for instance, losses from trading stocks, bonds, etc.). Another difference concerning the count in of losses is in the area of tax year – a non-business natural person can only use losses from the respective year, whereas a legal entity can, to certain extent, apply losses even from the previous five tax years.

From the perspective of income tax, it is very similar whether we sell the cryptocurrency or trade it for another cryptocurrency or a good. If traded, the law provides us with guidance on how to determine the price (income). In principle, the income is in the amount of the product (a good) for which we traded the crypto. Nevertheless, the situation may differ, as in some cases, even if a business accepts certain cryptocurrency for payments, they do not allow to pay for its products directly with given cryptocurrency (i.e. they do not have prices quoted in certain cryptocurrency), but the purchase of a good consists of two transactions, first exchange of the cryptocurrency into fiat money for certain price (cryptocurrency price at a particular cryptocurrency exchange would serve as a benchmark) and then purchase of the good for obtained fiat money. In this case, it would be important for the tax payer (purchaser of the good) to know for how much their cryptocurrency was sold so that they could keep their records.

Similar principles apply to obtaining the cryptocurrency by mining. First, we should emphasize, that under the Czech law, any person (natural or legal), who wants to engage in mining needs to have a licence, a so-called 'trade' (in Czech: *živnost*). It is a type of license, which a person simply gains just upon registering in the Trade Licencing Register.[45] No specific restrictions apply for getting this license. Nevertheless, having such license generally means that a natural person has to register also to health insurance and social security insurance and pay the insurance; the amount is usually calculated based on the profits from previous tax year or for the first year the law prescribes directly the amount. The Czech tax law does not tax the miner in the moment they mined (obtained) the cryptocurrency units, but at the moment of sale or exchange. Expenses connected with mining can be, in principle, used in a similar way as described above in connection to trading cryptocurrencies by business entities.

There are currently few options for tax exemptions under Czech law, when it comes to disposition with cryptocurrencies. The Czech law allows various tax exemptions to investors, these exemptions do not, however, apply to cryptocurrencies. Moreover, there are no special exemptions that would apply to cryptocurrencies. Nevertheless, exemption may apply to derivative securities, providing they have met the requirements put on securities by the Czech law, which value is based on a value of certain cryptocurrency. For instance, if a tax payer holds an investment security issued by an investment fund whose portfolio consists of cryptocurrencies, certain tax exemptions connected with securities apply.

There is also one rather minor tax exemption, which, according to some experts, may apply to trading cryptocurrencies by natural persons. The Act

45 See https://www.rzp.cz/portal/en/.

No. 586/1992 Coll. in Section 10(3) lays down a tax exemption for income up to 30,000 CZK (approximately 1,200 EUR) from 'occasional activities for which no license is needed'. Note that this applies to income, not to profits. There are opinions, that this applies also to income from trading cryptocurrencies in such small volume, whereas others claim that trading in cryptocurrencies is not 'activity', but rather 'administration of ones' own assets' and thus this exemption could only be used for instance for income from activities connected with cryptocurrencies, such as advising someone on how to trade, but not directly on the income from trading cryptocurrencies. The financial administration has not yet issued an official guideline to this issue.

Finally, we should add that the Czech tax law recognizes several types of tax discounts for natural persons. These discounts are simply subtracted from the tax calculated after applying the respective tax rate on a certain tax base. These discounts apply to natural persons, regardless of the type of income to be taxed, i.e., also to income tax on income from trading (or mining) cryptocurrencies.

5 Litigation in Relation to Cryptocurrencies

In general, it should be noted that, at least according to our information, it is rare for Czech courts to deal with issues primarily related to cryptocurrencies. This issue is dealt with typically 'only' as one of the auxiliary issues in the case, most often in the context of criminal proceedings.

One such example is the criminal trial of a perpetrator who was tried for the theft of Bitcoins worth approximately 620,000 EUR, possession of weapons and trafficking in narcotics with a commission of approximately 10,000 EUR. The court of appeal (High Court in Olomouc) set the sentence for such actions to a prison sentence of 9.5 years[46] However, what representative about this case is, that the court focused primarily on the established criminal offences, while the theft of cryptocurrency units was referred to rather secondarily and served mainly as illustration for the overall seriousness of the illegal activity.

The second example is again a criminal case, where three defendants using Bitcoins bought data of more than four thousand payment cards on Russian servers.[47] They were sentenced to imprisonment, but also ordered to forfeit their assets, including the cryptocurrency units, as these were proven to be the

46 See (in Czech) https://www.irozhlas.cz/zpravy-domov/kradez-bitcoinu-soud-olomouc_1805301611_haf.

47 See (in Czech) https://ct24.ceskatelevize.cz/regiony/2644223-za-bitcoiny-nakoupili-udaje-k-platebnim-kartam-poridili-na-ne-zbozi-za-6-milionu.

proceeds of crime. These units of Bitcoin were then auctioned off by the Office for State Representation in Property Matters (In Czech: *Úřad pro zastupování státu ve věcech majetkových*) in a public auction. In this case, the 0.42337268 units of Bitcoin were auctioned for 544,666 CZK (approximately 20,000 EUR).[48]

We also find worth mentioning the case of the pioneer Czech cryptocurrency business company Cryptelo s.r.o.,[49] which issued its own cryptocurrency and raised investments worth near 1 million EUR. However, in 2018 the largest creditor has initiated insolvency proceeding due to the company's inability to keep track of its liabilities.[50] The insolvency court (City Court in Prague) dismissed the bankruptcy petition on 5 February 2019, but the court of appeal (High Court in Prague) annulled the decision and refer the case back for further proceedings. Therefore, on 20 December 2019, the insolvency court declared the company bankrupt and commenced the insolvency proceedings, only for this decision to also be annulled and the case referred back for further proceedings on 19 February 2020. On 20 January 2021 the petitioning creditor withdrew the petition and the debtor approved the withdrawal, which concluded the proceedings.[51] As far as we could research the case, the reason was that the company obtained funds that allowed it to reassure or pay out the concerned creditors.

In the first and second cases mentioned above, it was a public prosecutor who initiated the case as part of criminal proceedings on the basis of documents and evidence obtained by the Police of the Czech Republic. In the third case, it was a private creditor who filed petition for insolvency. The cases described above did not deal with cross-border issues; only in the second case the court mentioned the Russian origin of the stolen payment card data, which, however, did not play significant role.

In 2022, the first judgment directly related to the taxation of cryptocurrencies was issued.[52] This case involved a decision on whether the purchase and subsequent sale of Bitcoin for Czech currency is subject to income tax exemption for an individual taxpayer. The taxpayer argued that Bitcoin constituted a foreign currency and, therefore, that the income from the sale of Bitcoin

48 See (in Czech) https://www.uzsvm.cz/stat-prodal-prvni-zabavene-bitcoiny-a-chysta-dalsi-aukci; see also (in Czech) https://www.e15.cz/kryptomeny/stat-prodal-prvni-zabavene-bitcoiny-a-chysta-dalsi-aukci-1380772.

49 See (in Czech) https://www.linkedin.com/company/cryptelo/.

50 See (in Czech) https://www.e15.cz/kryptomeny/prvni-cesky-kryptokrach-ambiciozni-projekt-cryptelo-je-v-upadku-1366156.

51 See decision of the insolvency court halting the insolvency proceedings, No. MSPH 77 INS 14968/2018-A-122.

52 See the judgment of the Regional Court in Brno, 30 Af 41/2020 of 24 March 2022.

could be regarded as foreign exchange profit arising from exchange activities and, therefore, was subject to the tax exemption. However, according to the Regional Court in Brno, Bitcoin cannot be considered as foreign currency. The court stated that Bitcoin is an unregulated virtual currency, or rather a virtual asset, which is not subject to regulation and supervision by any central bank in the world, and therefore cannot be considered money within the meaning of the Czech Payment Act. Thus, the court considered the sale of bitcoins and other cryptocurrencies to be a sale of an intangible movable asset, which constitutes an increase in property and is thus taxable income to an individual.

As the substance of the four cases discussed above show, cryptocurrencies are currently not a primary focus of court proceedings. In fact, on the basis of the information available to us, we are not aware of any other ongoing proceedings that would be appropriate to be mentioned at this point. This leads us to the opinion that cases concerning cryptocurrencies are still rare in Czech context. Unfortunately, we are not able to commence a thorough research of relevant Czech case law, as only the case law of apex courts and selected case law of lower courts is collected and available in a form of searchable database.[53] As most disputes concerning cryptocurrencies would not yet have reached the stage of decision by an apex court, it is hard to retrieve information about these cases. Awareness to first instance decisions is mostly driven by media coverage, which prefers criminal proceedings.

We are not aware of any pending or completed arbitration proceedings in the Czech Republic involving issues related to cryptocurrencies. There is no special type of proceedings in relation to the issue of cryptocurrencies. There are no specific measures or provisions in Czech law concerning crypto litigation. However, there are current discussions that disputes involving cryptocurrencies could be decided within arbitration, potentially by Arbitration court attached to the Czech Chamber of Commerce and the Agricultural Chamber of the Czech Republic.[54] In general, the conditions for the recognition of foreign arbitral awards must be respected. There is no specific requirement under the Czech legal system in relation to cryptocurrencies, but in the context of public order, it is necessary to respect the regulations related to AML/CFT, consumer protection as well as the legitimate nature of the cryptocurrency issuer (unclear legal status, investor mistrust, etc.).

---

53 For a detailed analysis of the availability of Czech case law see (in Czech) J. Harašta et al. *Citační analýza judikatury*. 1st ed. Wolters Kluwer, Prague 2021 or (in English) also J. Harašta, 'Case Law Retrieval: Critical Evaluation of Czech Legal Information Retrieval Systems'. *Jusletter IT*, Weblaw AG, Bern 2019, vol. 4, no. 21, pp. 1–8.

54 See (in Czech) https://archiv.hn.cz/c7-67287790-psmpu-60ae6e825116b3f.

6 Conclusion

There are very limited sources on Czech law applicable to cryptocurrencies available in other than Czech language. For this reason, we attempted to provide a detailed insight into the relevant aspects of the Czech law discussed in this chapter. Despite obvious limited use for an international reader, we further provided comprehensive references to relevant sources in Czech language and where suitable provided also translated provisions of the relevant law.

In general, Czech law does not present any specific or major obstacles to cryptocurrency transaction, use in private law or provision of related services. However, aside from AML/CFT regulation representing largely a transposition of respective EU directive, it also does not provide for any specific provisions that would comprehensively or in particular issues adjust the legal framework to the particularities of cryptocurrencies. The Czech National Bank, as the regulator of those services related to cryptocurrencies, mostly limits its focus on assets that fulfil the definition of investment instrument (which, as we described above, are most likely certain cryptocurrency derivatives or stable coins).

Despite fairly widespread interest and activities of Czech natural and legal persons in connection to cryptocurrencies, their activities and transaction remain largely elusive to clear legal classification and the applicable law is mostly subject to case-by-case assessment. Even in the area with probably the clearest regulatory requirements for cryptocurrency activities, namely tax law, there remain many specific issues that would need further interpretation. Nevertheless, due to the dynamic nature of the cryptocurrency environment, bringing constantly new features and technical solutions to previously identified limitations or inefficiencies, it is likely that not just the legislation and regulation, but also the jurisprudence will constantly remain attempting and failing to close the ever-increasing gap.

Denmark

René Franz Henschel

1 Introduction and the Legal Qualification of Cryptocurrencies in Danish Law

In Denmark, Bitcoin, Litecoin and similar cryptocurrencies can freely be used as means of exchange, as payment instruments as well as be traded in B2B-, B2C – as well as C2C-transactions.[1] Similarly, derivatives referencing cryptocurrencies and different other investment instruments are allowed. So far, there are no reports on the use of cryptocurrencies in government transactions.

Hundreds of different cryptocurrencies, including stablecoins, pegged to e.g. the US$ or to gold, are offered for trading by Danish as well as international online cryptocurrency exchanges. Danish banks generally do not offer cryptocurrency trading, but one bank offers cryptocurrency trading through a wholly-owned independent subsidiary (LUNAR), and another bank offers investment in more than 15 different cryptocurrencies by way of derivative instruments, i.e. Exchange-Traded Funds (EFT) and Exchange-Traded Notes (ETN) (SAXO BANK). However, this bank does not allow deposits or withdrawal in cryptocurrencies, but only in FIAT.

There are no specific regulations either authorising or prohibiting the issuing of, exchange of, trading of, investment in or use of cryptocurrencies in Denmark, nor are there any other regulations exclusively targeted at cryptocurrencies. No specific domestic regulation is expected in this area in the near future, as the legislators await the final entry into application of the European Commission's Regulation of the European Parliament and of the Council on Markets in Crypto-Assets, and amending Directive (EU) 2019/1937 (COM/2020/593 final) (MiCA). The proposal now awaits the final consulting between the member states and the European Commission, the Council and the European Parliament before entering application.

The new EU-regulation is expected to enter into application late 2024 or early 2025 and will have automatic and direct legal effect in Denmark, without

1 In this report, the term "cryptocurrencies" is used to cover various types of cryptocurrencies, including stable coins. Other crypto assets representing claims or real or personal properties, such as security tokens and utility tokens, are not covered by this report. Also, Central Bank Digital Currencies, which recently attracted attention in many countries, are outside the scope of this report.

 | DOI:10.1163/9789004722507_009

needing to be transposed into national law. However, at present time cryptocurrencies are subject to specific regulation targeting money laundering, see further in the sections below.

Cryptocurrencies are not legal tender in Denmark. Cryptocurrencies are generally considered as a property asset and often compared to commodities or investment assets like gold. Bitcoin is e.g. often referred to as either being a "digital currency" or "digital gold". Cryptocurrencies are on a voluntary basis accepted as a mean of payment (or exchange) in a few number of physical as well as online stores, although the number of stores accepting cryptocurrencies is still very low (according to this author, it is estimated that less than 1% of the stores accept cryptocurrencies).

2 Specific Regulation Relevant for Cryptocurrencies

As mentioned above, no general regulation exclusively targeted at cryptocurrencies has been enacted. However, by the implementation of the European Union's Fifth Money Laundering Directive in the Danish Money Laundering Act, a definition of cryptocurrencies is now found in the Money Laundering Act (Lovbekendtgørelse nr. 807 af 21. juni 2024 om forebyggende foranstaltninger mod hvidvask og finansiering af terrorisme (*hvidvaskloven*)), Sec. 2, no. 16, which defines what is called "Virtual currencies":

> 16) Virtual currency: A digital expression of value that is not issued or guaranteed by a central bank or a public authority, is not necessarily tied to a legally created currency and does not have the same legal status as currency or money, but is accepted by physical and legal entities as a means of exchange, which can be transferred, stored and traded electronically.

This definition in the Money Laundering Act of "virtual currencies" as a "means of exchange, which can be transferred, stored or traded electronically" is so broad that it encompasses not only cryptocurrencies like e.g. Bitcoin and Litecoin, but generally all types of crypto assets, e.g. utility tokens, payment tokens, exchange tokens, security tokens, privacy tokens, DeFi tokens, asset backed tokens, stablecoins, non-fungible tokens etc.

This definition could be said to serve as a *starting point* for the definition of cryptocurrencies in Danish law, but the different authorities – e.g. the financial or tax authorities – are free to apply their own definitions according to the needs in their own specific regulations. Hence, they are not bound by the definition in the Money Laundering Act.

The Danish Authorities often issue information and opinions on cryptocurrencies, e.g. warnings, to investors. As part of this, the authorities may also describe the nature of cryptocurrencies etc., and how cryptocurrencies may or may not fall under their domain or a particular regulation, e.g. as seen on the homepage of The Danish Financial Supervisory Authorities (DFSA) in relation to regulation of financial instruments, quote:

> A cryptocurrency is generally considered as a means of payment, and may also be categorized as a cryptoasset. However, some cryptocurrencies or cryptoassets like Initial Coin Offerings may fall under the Financial Authority definition as a financial instrument, and thus under regulation.[2]

Furthermore, the DFSA mentions tokens:

> Tokens are understood to mean a cryptocurrency with associated properties, which typically gives the right to either the goods or services of the offering company or to the company itself.[3]

Similarly, The Danish Tax Authorities (DTA) apply the laws on taxation on assets to cryptocurrencies. All cryptocurrencies that are considered as "assets" – which presupposes property rights (ownership), cf. further below – are covered by the relevant taxation laws. On their homepage, the DTA notes that holdings of e.g. Bitcoins are covered by the concept of assets, which in principle do not affect the taxable income. However, if, after a specific assessment, it is a question of disposing of assets or property as part of business or speculation, hobby activity or other non-commercial activity, it will be possible to tax the disposal according to the set of rules that apply to these areas. See further on taxation below Sec. 10.

Furthermore, specific regulation may contain other relevant definitions in relation to cryptocurrencies. By the implementation of the Fifth Money Laundering Directive in the Money Laundering Act, not only is the term *cryptoassets* defined; The Act also contains reference to some of the most important *actors* in a cryptocurrency blockchain system, cf. Sec. 1, no. 22–26 and Sec. 2, no. 15, that contain the following descriptions:

---

2 See https://www.finanstilsynet.dk/nyheder-og-presse/sektornyt/2017/orientering-om-ico (last visited 1 June 2024).

3 *Ibid.* See further the Danish National Bank, Kryptoaktiver: Risici, regulering og anvendelse i Danmark, https://www.nationalbanken.dk/media/raqjxz5q/kryptoaktiver-risici-regulering-og-anvendelse-i-danmark.pdf (last visited 1 June 2024).

22) Providers of exchange between virtual currencies and fiat currencies.
23) Virtual Wallet Providers.
24) Providers of exchange between one or more types of virtual currency.
25) Virtual currency transfer providers.
26) Issuers of virtual currency.

As can be seen above, this regulation refers to a whole range of different actors, e.g. providers of exchange, virtual wallet providers, transfer providers and issuers of virtual currencies. Furthermore, a more elaborate definition of a Virtual Wallet Provider is now found in Sec. 2 (15) of the Danish Money Laundering Act:

> 15) Virtual Wallet Provider: An entity that provides services to protect private cryptographic keys on behalf of its customers for the purpose of storing, depositing and transferring virtual currencies.

Thus, Danish law by way of the implementation of the European Union's Fifth Money Laundering Directive in the Danish Money Laundering Act now contains a range of different terms and definitions relevant to a cryptocurrency blockchain system.

Finally, in 2018 the DFSA announced that a particular utility token could not be equated with electronic money in the Danish Payment Act (Lovbekendtgørelse nr. 23 af 18. januar 2023 om betalinger), Sec. 7, subsection 1(6), as the precondition for being covered by the rules for electronic money and hence the rules of registration of issuers etc., cf. the Danish Payment Act Sec. 2, is that the holders of electronic money have a claim against the issuer that is used as a means of payment. However, this does not rule out that future cryptocurrencies may be seen as electronic money covered by the Payment Act, if they represent a claim against the issuer.[4]

3 The Actual or Potential Legal Relationship between the Different Participants in a Blockchain

The actual or potential legal relationship between the different participants in a blockchain on which cryptocurrencies are transferred or recorded are subject both to the specific *public law regulation* as seen above re. the Money Laundering Act as well as to the relevant *private law regulation*, e.g. the Danish

4 See https://www.finanstilsynet.dk/nyheder-og-presse/sektornyt/2018/ft-tagerstilling-ico (last visited 1 June 2024).

Contracts Act (Lovbekendtgørelse nr. 193, af 2. marts 2016 om lov om aftaler og andre retshandler på formuerettens område) that contains the fundamental rules on formation and validity of contracts, and the Danish Sale of Goods Act (Lovbekendtgørelse nr. 1853 af 24. september 2021 om køb).

In principle, the different parties to a blockchain participate in the system based on a voluntary agreement. This agreement may or may not contain governance mechanisms, and may or may not create legally enforceable rights.

In Denmark, a claim that is not based on a legally protected right cannot be subject to litigation. Thus, in order for an actual or potential legal relationship to exist, there has to be legally protectable rights involved, i.e. identifiable as property rights that can be transferred into a monetary amount that can be subject to an enforcement proceeding (e.g. to pay a certain compensation, e.g. a claim equalling the amount of lost cryptocurrencies on an exchange) or subject to a proceeding for recognition (e.g. to recognise that the claimant has a particular right to a certain property, e.g. cryptocurrencies in a wallet on an exchange).

As a starting point, every participant in a blockchain (miners, wallet providers, wallet holders, custodians, customers, issuers etc.) may direct a legal claim towards other participants in the blockchain, or be subject to legal claims from others based on e.g. contract law, sales law, tort law (rules in these areas of the law have generally been developed by court practice), general principles of contract law (*generelle obligationsretlige regler*) or the general principles of associations (*generelle foreningsretlige regler*), or that a certain property right exist, subject to the individual circumstances of the case.

Issuers of cryptocurrencies may be subject to claims based on e.g. contract law and sales of goods law, if the cryptocurrencies are not delivered as agreed, in the right quantity or in the right quality, subject to the normal conditions of a binding contract (offer-acceptance etc.), and the remedies available, cf. the Danish Sale of Goods Act. This is particularly certain for permissioned blockchains that rest on contractual agreements either being embedded in the software code, in the dApp or as other contractual appendixes agreed on as part of joining a permissioned blockchain.

Parties to a permissionless blockchain may also be subject to such claims, potentially also in tort or based on product liability claims. This could be either according to the rules on product liability developed in practice, or according to the Product Liability Act (Lovbekendtgørelse nr. 261 af 20. marts 2007 om produktansvar), which implements the EU Product Liability Directive, and which covers damage to persons and to consumer property. There is, however, still uncertainty as to the extent to which loss or damage to digital assets will be treated. Limitation of liabilities may have effect, mostly in B2B-transactions, as limitation of liability in regard to consumer complaints in product liability cases are not allowed.

Cryptocurrency exchanges, wallet providers, custodians and other intermediaries may be subject to contract law claims based on the individual agreements in permissioned blockchains. Such parties in permissionless blockchains may also be subject to legal claims, potentially both in contract, in tort or based on product liability claims, e.g. in relation to defect software code that causes the loss of cryptocurrencies, keys etc.

It is less likely that holders, investors or other parties who hold, transfer or dispose of cryptocurrencies will be subject to legal claims based in contract, tort or otherwise, but it may be possible to have e.g. a claim for restitution, if, for instance, a holder, investor or other party has erroneously received cryptocurrencies that belong to others or an incorrect amount of cryptocurrencies from a seller, a transmitter, a custodian or other intermediaries into their wallet.

It is less likely that cryptocurrency miners will be subject to claims in contract or tort, but e.g. if they have continued mining although errors have been detected in the software code that cause losses to buyers etc., this cannot be entirely ruled out.

Persons/entities responsible for transactions' block validation may in principle be subject to claims based on contract law, if they validate contrary to the agreements made in permissioned or permissionless blockchains, or if they continue despite knowing that this causes losses to someone.

The law is applicable when Danish law applies as per the relevant choice of law rules, and there is in principle no limitations *ratione personae*. Hence the law may be applied to e.g. programmers and coders associated with the blockchain protocol.

In the absence of an agreement on choice of law, the choice of law will be made according to the Hague Convention of 1955 (implemented in Denmark by lovbekendtgørelse nr. 722 af 24. oktober 1986 om, hvilket lands retsregler der skal anvendes på løsørekøb af international karakter (løsørekøbsloven)) or the EC Choice of Law Convention (Rome Convention) of 1980 (implemented in Denmark by lovbekendtgørelse nr. 139 af 17. februar 2014 om gennemførelse af konvention om, hvilket lands lov der skal anvendes på kontraktlige forpligtelser (kontraktskonventionen).

The choice of law in regard to tort and product liability cases will be decided according to the general principles of choice of law, as there are no specific regulations regulating the choice of law in tort and product liability cases. The general principle applied is a test of "closest connection", see e.g. the Order of the Danish Supreme Court, 31 August 2020 (Case BS-45073/2019-HJR (2. Department) VGH Versicherungen vs. GF Forsikring A/S).

4 Marketing and Advertising of Cryptocurrencies

All types of crypto-related conducts, whether in permissioned or permissionsless blockchains, including marketing, advertising, sale, transfer, disposal, custody or trust-related business of cryptocurrencies are allowed, subject to the marketing regulation, cf. the Danish Marketing Act (Lovbekendtgørelse nr. 866 af 15. juni 2022) – especially Sec. 3 on good marketing practices and Sec. 4 on good business practices, Sec. 5 on misleading practices, Sec. 6 on misleading ommissions and Sec. 7 on aggressive practices.

The Marketing regulation applies to private business as well as to public business, whether they are domiciled in Denmark or not, to the extent that products are offered on the Danish market, cf. Sec. 1 of the Marketing Act.

5 No Specific Criminal Law Provisions are Applicable to Cryptocurrencies

There are no specific criminal law provisions that apply to cryptocurrencies.

6 Anti-Money Laundering and Counter-Terrorism Financing (AML/CFT) Provisions Apply to Cryptocurrencies

As mentioned above, the Money Laundering Act applies to companies engaged in cryptocurrency exchange, e.g. in relation to Customer knowledge procedures (KYC, AML), cf. Section 10, subsection (c) and (d) of the Money Laundering Act, which applies to transactions of the following nature:

> (c) *EUR 500 or more in the case of currency exchange, including exchange between virtual currency and fiat currency, whether the transaction takes place at one time or as several transactions which are or appear to be interconnected; or*
>
> (d) *EUR 1,000 or more by switching between one or more types of virtual currency, the transfer of virtual currency or the issuance of virtual currency, whether the transaction takes place at one time or as several transactions that are or appear to be interconnected;*

According to Sec. 47 of the Money Laundering Act, the DFSA ensures that companies and persons and branches, distributors and agents in Denmark of such foreign companies and persons comply with the law. This includes a duty to register, cf. Sec. 48, subsection 2, and to supply the necessary information, cf. Sec. 49.

According to Sec. 49, subsection 6, the DFSA may obtain certain information pursuant to subsections 1 and 5, for the use of the foreign authorities and bodies mentioned, and according to Sec. 50, the supervisory authorities in an EU or EEA country may, by prior agreement with the DFSA, carry out inspections in the branches, agents and distributors located in Denmark, covered by Sec. 1, subsection. 1, by foreign companies domiciled in the country in question.

The DFSA may participate in the inspection as mentioned in the first sentence. If a company or person, as mentioned in the 1st sentence, opposes inspection by a competent foreign authority, the investigation can only be carried out with the assistance of the Danish FSA.

Furthermore, according to subsection (2), the DFSA may request the competent authorities of an EU or EEA country to assist in ensuring compliance with the Act and the rules issued pursuant to the Act concerning companies and persons covered by section 1 (1). 1, nos. 1–12 and 22–26 (cryptocurrencies), domiciled in another EU or EEA country by supervisory actions, on-the-spot checks or inspections in the territory of another EU or EEA country.

According to Sec. 51, the DFSA may, within a period set by the DFSA, order the companies and persons mentioned in section 1 (1). 1, nos. 1–12, 18 and 22–26 (cryptocurrencies), to take the necessary measures in case of violation of provisions of the Financial Services Regulation, rules issued pursuant thereto, Regulation 2015/847/EU of the European Parliament and of the Council of 20 May 2015 on information to be accompanied by remittances, or regulations containing rules on financial sanctions against countries, persons, groups, legal entities or bodies.

According to Sec. 51 a, the DFSA may order a company covered by § 1, para. 1, nos. 1–8, 9, 10, 18 and 22–26 (cryptocurrencies), except for their branches, distributors and agents in this country to dismiss the person appointed in accordance with § 7, para. 2, within a time limit set by the DFSA, if the person pursuant to Sec. 7, subsection 2, 3rd and 4th sentences, cannot contest the position.

According to Sec. § 51 b, the DFSA may order a company or person covered by § 1, para. 1, nos. 1–8, 9, 10, 18 and 22–26, except for their branches, distributors and agents in this country, that the company or person may temporarily not take on new customer relationships when a serious breach of regulations has been established according to the Act or rules issued pursuant thereto. If the infringement took place in whole or in part in a company's foreign branch, the injunction may be extended to include the branch.

According to Sec. 52, the DFSA may, for companies and persons as mentioned in § 1, subsection 1, nos. 8 and 22–26, lay down detailed rules on notification, registration and publication, including what information must be registered, and which conditions notifiers or others may submit and register electronically in the DFSA's IT system by using digital or corresponding electronic signature, as well as on the use of this system.

According to Sec. 53, The Minister of Business and Industry may for companies as mentioned in Sec. 1, para. 1, nos. 1–12, 18 and 22–26, lay down rules on the obligation of these companies to publish information on the DFSA's assessment of the company, and that the DFSA has the opportunity to publish the information before the company.

According to Sec. 76, decisions made by the DFSA and the Danish Business Authority in accordance with the Financial Services Act and rules issued pursuant to the Act, Regulation 2015/847/EU of the European Parliament and of the Council of 20 May 2015 on information to be enclosed by money transfers and regulations containing rules on financial sanctions against countries, persons, groups, legal entities or bodies may be brought before the Commercial Appeals Board by the person against whom the decision is addressed, no later than 4 weeks after the decision has been notified to the person concerned. Violations of the above said rules may result in fines, unless a higher penalty is due under the rules of the Penal Code. The violation of e.g. Sec. 10 (KYC and AML procedures) may increase to imprisonment for up to 2 years, unless higher punishment is due according Sec. 290 b, subsection 2 of the Penal Code.

7 Supervision of Cryptocurrency-Related Activities

Beside the rules in the Money Laundering Act, referred to above, and the DFSA's role in that regard, there are no other requirements for registration, licenses or authorisations in order to use, manage or issue cryptocurrencies or to provide cryptocurrency-related services as such.

Hence, issuers are not required by law to publish a whitepaper or prospectus. However, if whitepapers or prospectus are misleading, this might be subject to the law on misleading advertising, cf. the Danish Marketing Act, as referred to above, as well as to claims based in contract or tort.

There is no specific supervisory authority for cryptocurrencies and/or cryptocurrency-related services, subject to the rules on the Money Laundering Act above, and subject to the exception that the DFSA has authority to supervise cryptocurrencies that are securities. To the best of this author's knowledge, there has not been any case in which a supervisory authority took action in respect of illegal activities connected to cryptocurrencies, as well as no case in which a supervisory authority had difficulties in taking action in respect of illegal activities connected to cryptocurrencies.

8 Private Law Issues

Cryptocurrencies like e.g. Bitcoin can be subject to property rights (ownership, possession) in Denmark. The ownership to e.g. Bitcoins in a cold wallet or in a hot wallet could be proven by e.g. transaction documents, blockchain data, e-mails, documents proving agreements with wallet providers etc.

If cryptocurrencies are stored in a wallet attached to an account on a cryptocurrency exchange, the question would be, whether the cryptocurrencies are individually identifiable to that particular person or not. The rules on deposits distinguish between *depositum regulare* on the one hand, where specific and individually identifiable objects are to be returned, and *depositum irregulare* on the other hand, where objects of the same kind have to be returned.

In other words, if the cryptocurrencies are not individually identifiable, the owner has a claim for an amount equal to the cryptocurrencies, not necessarily specifically and identifiable cryptocurrencies. The same line of thought can be said to include hardforks or airdrops.

If individually identifiable objects are lost without fault of the depository, the risk is borne by the owner. However, in a *depositum irregulare*, the risk is normally borne by the depository, whether or not a fault has been committed, see further below on hacking.

8.1 *Donation*

Cryptocurrencies can be subject to donation, and are regulated by the Danish Contracts Act. A person owner can freely donate 30 out of his/her 60 Bitcoins to a person Y. It makes no difference, whether X uses an intermediary (*e.g.* a wallet provider) that holds and transfers the Bitcoins.

Cryptocurrencies may also be exchanged as consideration for some form of counter-performance, e.g. if person X transfers 30 Bitcoins to Y, so that Y may deliver a boat to X or Z. This kind of transaction would be regulated by the Danish Contracts Act as well as the Sales of Goods Act.

The rules of private international law, cf. Sec. 3 above, might under the circumstances point towards the application of other legal systems.

8.2 *Transfer*

Ownership to cryptocurrencies may freely be transferred, and an exchange of e.g. a number of Bitcoins against payment of FIAT would normally be considered as a sales transaction covered by the Sales of Goods Act, and an exchange of a number of Bitcoins against a number of Ethers would normally be considered a barter transaction, also subject to the Sales of Goods Act. It makes no difference that the parties may use intermediaries to hold and transfer the cryptocurrencies.

8.3 *Inheritance*

Provided that a particular amount of cryptocurrency as assets can be defined as belonging to the fortune of the deceased, e.g. by presenting the private keys or by presenting ownership to a wallet on an exchange or other intermediary, cryptocurrencies may be inherited according to the normal conditions of inheritance according to the Act on Inheritance (lovbekendtgørelse nr. 1347 af 15. juni 2021 om bekendtgørelse af arveloven (Arveloven)). If a cryptocurrency cannot be identified as belonging to the estate of the deceased (not part of his or hers fortune), the asset will not be included in the estate, see further below Sec. 8 on attachment and seizure and Sec. 9 on insolvency.

A testator/trix may establish a provision in his/her will according to which a child should inherit a particular asset, e.g. a certain number of identifiable Bitcoins, cf. the Danish Act on Death Estate Change, § 13. (Lovbekendtgørelse nr. 1807 af 3. september 2021 om skifte af dødsboer (Dødsboskifteloven)).

If no will is made, the Bitcoins would have to be identified as belonging to the estate of the deceased, cf. Sec. 66 of the Act on Death Estate Change, and then be shared among the heir(s).

The rules on which assets that can be identified as belonging to the testator/trix fortune, follow the same principles as the rules concerning a debtor's fortune in Sec. 32 of the Act on Bankruptcy (Lovbekendtgørelse nr. 775 of 3. maj 2021 om konkursloven).

The Danish Act on Inheritance applies to wills made in Denmark by people domiciled in Denmark. The Act on Death Estate Change applies to deceased domiciled in Denmark.

In case the assets (fortune) of the deceased are located in another territory, if the will is made in another territory, or if the deceased him/herself is domiciled in another territory, complicated choice of law issues occur. The starting point is, that the Danish rules on inheritance and death estate change will apply, but there might be international public law conventions that regulate particular situations.

Denmark is part to the Nordic Death Estate Convention of 19 November 1934, which applies between Denmark, Finland, Iceland, Norway and Sweden. According to this convention, wills established in the participating countries are mutually recognised. The laws on inheritance of the country of domicile will be applied, but the testator/trix may choose the law of another country.

Furthermore, the law on Death Estate Change in the country of the deceased domicile will be applied, unless the deceased has decided otherwise.

If the assets of the deceased are located outside the Nordic countries, if the will is made outside the Nordic countries, or if the deceased was domiciled outside the Nordic countries, the Danish rules will still be applied, but particular rules of the relevant territories may have to be taken into account according to the specific circumstances, e.g. concerning the practical possibility to include Bitcoins on a foreign exchange into the estate of the deceased.

Denmark is not part to Regulation (EU) No 650/2012 of the European Parliament and of the Council of 4 July 2012 on jurisdiction, applicable law, recognition and enforcement of decisions and acceptance and enforcement of authentic instruments in matters of succession and on the creation of a European Certificate of Succession. However, Danish citizens domiciled in other countries, which are parties to this Convention, may call for the application of this convention. Danish citizens in other countries will be subject to the particular inheritance rules of this territory.

Generally, trusts are not allowed according to Danish law, but it is possible to establish charitable foundations in a will, if an irrevocable and effective separation from the person establishing the foundation is established. Furthermore, the foundation must not benefit the founder or the founder's family. However, it is possible to leave cryptocurrencies to an *existing* foundation or charity.

8.4 *Attachment or Seizure*

In principle, cryptocurrencies may be subject to attachment or seizure under the conditions in Sec.s 506 and 507 of the Danish Act on Civil Procedure (Lovbekendt-gørelse nr. 1160 af 5. november 2024 om rettens pleje (Retsplejeloven)).

According to Sec. 507, claims for money are enforced by disbursement in such a large part of the debtor's assets, which in the opinion of the bailiff's court is necessary to cover the claim as well as the costs of the business and the detention's storage until the auction. According to Sec. 508, attachments may be made in cash as well as in real estate, movables, receivables and other assets, the identity of which can be established, but not in future acquisitions.

The problem of the identity of assets can be illustrated by the Order of the Supreme Court in the case 3/2013, 13. august 2013. In this case, the Supreme Court was to issue an order of whether or not it was possible to make an attachment and seizure of a Milk Quota belonging to the insolvent farmer, B. The Supreme Court stated that at the time of the attachment, B could, subject to the rules in the milk quota executive order, transfer the quota to another holding without simultaneously transferring an agricultural area, just as it could be sold on the quota exchange. On that basis, and since the milk quota was not covered by section 38 of the Real Estate Registration Act, the Supreme Court found that the milk quota had to be regarded as an asset that could be seized.

Based on this and similar orders, it is most likely possible for a Danish bailiff to issue an ättachment and to seize cryptocurrencies belonging to a debtor, as long as the cryptocurrencies can be identified as belonging to the assets of the debtor. This is possible whether or not the owner holds the Bitcoin with an intermediary. However, from a practical point of view, the attachment and seizure may be difficult as it presupposes that the bailiff is physically able to seize the cryptocurrencies on the blockchain. Furthermore, a third party that has received the cryptocurrencies belonging to the debtor in good faith may extinguish the rights of the creditors, see also below Sec. 9 on insolvency.

The bailiff has jurisdiction to issue attachment and seizure on assets located in Denmark. This may cause problems re. cryptocurrencies stored on cryptocurrency exchanges etc. in other countries. However, it cannot be ruled out that the bailiff will regard the blockchain as also being located in Denmark, and therefore attachment and seizure may be had as long as the bailiff has access to the private keys of the debtor. However, this remains to be confirmed in practice.

If the cryptocurrencies are situated in a foreign jurisdiction, the rules on attachment or seizure of the other legal systems would apply, as the bailiff only has jurisdiction over property located in Denmark. The bailiff will then ask the bailiff in the foreign country for help.

8.5 *Insolvency Rules*

As a starting point, the Danish rules on insolvency apply to situations involving cryptocurrencies equally as to any other asset that can be said to belong to the debtor's estate, cf. Sec. 32 of the Insolvency Act (Lovbekendtgørelse nr. 775 af 3. maj 2021 om konkursloven). According to Sec. 36, assets in which disbursement of the debtor's debt cannot be made are only included in the bankruptcy estate when this has been specifically determined. This rule makes it clear, that – as a main rule – there is identity between the subject of attachment and seizure, and the rules of insolvency. Hence, if a cryptocurrency cannot be subject of identification, so it can be determined beyond any reasonable doubt that it belongs to the insolvent debtor's estate, the cryptocurrency cannot be part of the bankruptcy estate, cf. also Sec. 82 of the Bankruptcy Act.

Consequently, if cryptocurrencies are owned by others, they are not part of the insolvent debtor's estate and hence not the bankruptcy estate. If a third party claims that cryptocurrencies belong to his or her estate, not the estate of the insolvent debtor, this will be determined by the rules of private law, e.g. at the time an agreement was made on the debtor's sale of the cryptocurrencies to a third party. However, this will depend on the proof of identification of the cryptocurrencies which the third party claims belongs to him or her.

If the debtor has pledged cryptocurrencies, this pledge will as a main rule be upheld, if the lender has the cryptocurrencies in his or her possession.

If e.g. a cryptocurrency exchange goes bankrupt, the owner of the cryptocurrencies may bring forward a claim in the insolvency proceedings. If the deposited Bitcoins etc. can be uniquely identified, the owner may claim return of the Bitcoins. Otherwise, the claim would be for their value in cash, and the claim would thus be reduced to a "simple creditor claim", cf. Sec. 97 in the Bankruptcy Act. The specific terms of the agreement between the cryptocurrency exchange and the owner has as a starting point no relevance in relation to the mandatory insolvency rules, although they may bring proof as to the circumstances of either depositum regulare or irregular, cf. Sec. 5 above.

If a company that has an account with a cryptocurrency exchange goes bankrupt, and this account contains cryptocurrencies, this will be seen as assets belonging to the estate in the insolvency proceedings, subject to the observations above re. identification.

Creditors that have paid with cryptocurrencies for e.g. goods of services that have still not been delivered, would likely not be able to claim priority over the cryptocurrencies in the insolvent companies account, unless the cryptocurrencies are individually identifiable, cf. Sec. 82 in the Insolvency Act. This, however, still remains the be decided in practice.

8.6 *Pledge of Cryptocurrencies*

It is possible to pledge cryptocurrencies, e.g. in relation to secure a loan for the financing of a specific project. The most secure way for the lender to secure his or her right would be to have the cryptocurrencies (the pledge) in his or her possession. If the wallet is kept with an intermediary, the lender may inform the intermediary about the pledge, but the protection towards the borrower's creditors may be difficult. Furthermore, the protection against third party bona fides buyers or lenders may be lost.

If the intermediary, the borrower or the lender are domiciled in another territory, the private international law as described above, Sec. 3, in relation to the effect between creditors, is not governed by the said rules, but by the general principles of choice of law in regard to third party rights (tingsret), which will be *lex rei situs*, i.e. where the pledged property is located. This may lead to the same results as above, re. the "global" nature of the blockchain. Should the cryptocurrencies be determined to be located in Denmark, Danish law will apply, see e.g. the Danish Registration Act (Lovbekendtgørelse nr. 1075 af 30. september 2014 om tinglysning (Tinglysningsloven).

Special problems occur, e.g. concerning the lenders' possibilities to inform third parties and creditors about the pledge, and it is highly likely that the lenders here will face dire difficulties to prove their pledge.

8.7 *Lending Out Cryptocurrencies*

According to Danish law, it is possible to conclude a contract on lending out cryptocurrencies against payment of interest either in FIAT or cryptocurrencies. As a starting point, these contracts will not be subject to financial regulation, if conducted entirely in cryptocurrencies, but if the contract contains reference to FIAT as equivalences, they may be subject to the Act on Financial Services (Lovbekendtgørelse nr. 1731 af 15. december 2023 om finansiel virksomhed).

If the lending services are offered as a professional service by a company domiciled in another jurisdiction, and that company is regulated and supervised in its home country to provide lending services, and the contract can be said to be made in FIAT equivalences, this company may be under the Danish Financial Services Authorities' jurisdiction, if the company conducts business in Denmark (including through a branch or office). If the company has permission to offer lending services in another EU country, or in a country that has an agreement with the European Union, it may be equally allowed to carry out its lending services in Denmark, under supervision of the DFSA, cf. Sec. 30 et seq. of the Law on Financial Services. Otherwise, the company would be required to have a bank license in Denmark, if the lending agreement should be categorised as a lending agreement falling under the rules of the Act on Financial Services.

The law governing the lending contract may be subject to the jurisdiction of another territory according to the choice of law rules in regard to the private law issues, e.g. by a relevant choice of law, cf. above Sec. 3.

If it was assumed that the lending contract called for the borrowing of Bitcoins against the payment of interest in Bitcoins, the contract will most likely fall outside the scope of application of the financial regulation.

A contract that calls for the payment in Bitcoins and/or payment of interest in Bitcoins may as a starting point only be paid back in Bitcoins, not e.g. in Bitcoin Cash or other forks. It does not make any difference whether or not the fork took place only after the initial transfer of Bitcoins.

9 Legal Actions in Case Cryptocurrencies are Lost Due to Hacking or Fraud etc.

If cryptocurrencies are lost due to hacking, e.g. if a cryptocurrency exchange IT system has been hacked, the starting point is that the owner/user may bring an action against the cryptocurrency exchange, if the owner's/user's cryptocurrencies are individually and uniquely identifiable. However, if the cryptocurrency exchange can prove that the hacking took place without any fault on their side (culpa), then the risk is borne by the owner/user him/herself. This follows from the old rule in Sec.s 5-8-14 of Danish Law (Lov nr. 11000 af 15. april 1683 Kong Christian den Femtis Danske Lov), on *depositum regulare*.

If it has been agreed between the cryptocurrency exchange and the owner/user, that the owner/user does not own particular, identifiable and unique coins, i.e. a situation that can be compared to a situation where the owner/user has deposited an amount of money, and does not have a claim to get exactly those specific bills and coins back (*depositum irregulare*), but just the same amount back, then the starting point is, that the risk of hacking is borne by the cryptocurrency exchange, unless agreed otherwise between the parties.

If the hacker is identifiable, the owner/user has a claim based on criminal law and tort law against the hacker. Bona fide buyers are not protected, if the owner/user can prove that the coins sold to the bona fide buyer belong to the owner/user, cf. the rules on vindication in Secs. 6-17-5, 5-8-12 and 5-7-4 of Danish Law.

If the owner has been misled to transfer cryptocurrencies to a tortfeaser, e.g. because the tortfeaser has fraudulently misled the owner, the owner may bring a claim against the tortfeaser based on contract law, cf. Sec. 30 of the Contract Act, as well as a claim for restitution against the tortfeaser. However, bona fide buyers who have the cryptocurrencies in their possession, may be protected from a claim for restitution, cf. the rules on extinction of rights.

10 Taxation of Cryptocurrencies

As mentioned above in Sec. 1, the Danish Tax Authorities (DTA) apply the laws on taxation on assets to cryptocurrencies. There is no special regulation on the taxation of cryptocurrencies, however there is a Commission working on a report as to whether or not there should be a special regulation on the taxation of crypto assets. The Commission is expected to put forward its recommendations in 2025.

All cryptocurrencies that are considered as "assets" – which presupposes property rights (ownership) – are covered by the relevant taxation laws. On their homepage, the DTA notes, that holdings of e.g. Bitcoins are covered by the concept of assets, which in principle do not affect the taxable income, cf. Sec. 5 of the Danish State Taxation Law (Lov nr. 149 af 10. pril 1922 om Indkomst – og Formueskat til Staten (Statsskatteloven)).

However, if a specific assessment is carried out, and it is established that it is a question of disposal of assets or property as part of business activities or speculation, hobby activities or other non-commercial activities, it will be possible to tax the disposal according to the set of rules that apply to these areas.

Buying and selling of cryptocurrency is generally considered to be speculation which means that the intention with the acquisition of cryptocurrency has been to make a profit on a later sale. It is not a condition that the intention of speculation has been the sole purpose of the acquisition, nor is it a condition that speculation is the main purpose of this.

In case the DTA finds that the purpose has been speculation, the profits will be taxed as personal income according to the rules in the Act on Personal Taxation (Lovbekendtgørelse nr. 1284 af 14. juni 2021 om indkomstskat for personer mv. (personskatteloven)), while losses will apply for a tax deduction according to the rules in the Act on Tax Deductions (Lovbekendtgørelse nr. 42 af 13. januar 2023 om påligningen af indkomstskat til staten (Ligningsloven)), see e.g. the decision from the Western High Court, 15 August 2021 (Case of 1. Instance, 15. Department, BS-19699/2020 VLR). Furthermore, in follows from the DTA's practice, that the taxation is made on each and every transaction. Hence, the taxation is asymmetrical, as the tax on personal income might be up to approx. 58%, while the value of tax deductions is below 30%. If e.g. a person sells half of his/her possession of cryptocurrencies with a profit of DKK100,000, and later the same year sells the rest with a loss of DKK100,000, he/she will be subject to a taxation of up to DKK58,000 of the profits, but will only be able to deduct a loss of around DKK30,000. Hence, the tax will amount to DKK28,000, although the net profits are actually zero. This practice has been contested and cases are pending at the Danish Tax Appeal Board.

If a taxpayer has received cryptocurrencies as a gift, there will not be any tax on profits, nor deductables on losses.

The Danish Tax Council has allowed the Tax Authorities to collect information from all Danish domiciled cryptocurrency exchanges etc., to collect information about Danish taxpayers buying and selling cryptocurrencies. It is expected that around 5–10% of the population are now engaged in cryptocurrency trading, compared to less than 1% 5 years ago.

11 Litigation in Relation to Cryptocurrencies

To the best of the author's knowledge, there are currently cases concerning tax issues pending before Danish courts, e.g. concerning the legality of the asymmetrical taxation of profits. There is to the best of the authors knowledge no other pending litigation, arbitration proceeding or class action cases.

There are no special or exclusive heads of jurisdiction available for crypto litigation.

Foreign decisions or arbitral awards involving e.g. ownership to cryptocurrencies would be recognised and enforced to the applicable rules, e.g. (Rome Convention or the New York Convention) without public policy exceptions as a main rule.

Literature

A. Andhov, Relevance of Blockchain for Corporate Lawyers", *Erhvervsjuridisk Tidsskrift* 2020, p. 29 et seq.

J. Enyi, Er bitcoin penge?, *Erhvervsjuridisk Tidsskrift* 2018, p. 127 et seq.

Peter Istrup: Smart contracts – aftaleret og blockchain (Ex Tuto Publishing, 2022), 417 p.

A. Rønne og H. Stevnsborg (red.), Ret SMART – om smart teknologi og regulering (Jurist – og Økonomforbundets Forlag 2018)

L. Nielsen & J. Kristiansen, Kryptoaktiver – Reguleringsudfordringer og reguleringsstrategier, *Erhvervsjuridisk Tidsskrift*, 2021 p. 192 et seq.

Payam Samarghandi, Din grundlæggede guide til MiCA-forordningen (2024), available at https://www.samarlaw.dk/din-grundlaeggende-introduktion-til-mica-forordningen/ (last visited 1 June 2024)

K. Steensgaard & R.F. Henschel, IT-rettens næste generation?, in Festskrift til Mads Bryde Andersen (2018)

J. Trzaskowski (Ed.), Internetretten (3rd edition, Ex Tuto, 2017)

H. Udsen, IT Kontraktret (Ex Tuto, 2020)

H. Udsen, IT-ret (5. Udg., Ex Tuto, 2021)

J. Ullits, Blockchain-baseret sagsbehandling i det offentlige, en farbar vej eller deroute?, *Juristen* 2020, p. 30 et seq.

In Swedish:

Emil Elgebrandt, Kryptovalutor. Särskild rättsverkan vid innehav av bitcoins och andre liknande betalingsmedel (Wolters Kluwer, 2016).

Egypt

Ahmed Elkahwagy

Il est estimé qu'il existe plus de 3 millions de propriétaires de crypto-monnaies en Egypte[1].

Dans le système juridique égyptien, la propriété des crypto-monnaies et les activités liées à celles-ci ne sont pas considérées comme un intérêt juridique à protéger, mais comme un risque à prévenir. Cette vision a incité l'Etat égyptien à utiliser l'arme pénale pour réguler ces actifs, sans considération pour les applications civiles, commerciales ou fiscales. Les crypto-monnaies n'ont pas de cours légal dans le système juridique égyptien.

Malgré la tendance prohibitive prônée par le Gouvernement et le Parlement, et la prolifération d'infractions d'escroquerie très médiatisées[2], les inscriptions d'utilisateurs égyptiens sur CEX.IO, le site d'échange de crypto-monnaie basé au Royaume-Uni, ont augmenté de 250 % en janvier 2021 par rapport au mois précédent[3], avec le site Statista prévoyant une croissance de 10,56% du marché égyptien pour la période 2024–2028[4],

Pour déterminer l'essor des crypto-monnaies à l'aune du système juridique égyptien, cet article analyse la vision globale de ces actifs dans l'espace égyptien, pour essayer de prouver l'existence d'une tendance prohibitive multi-institutionnelle (1). Une fois cette tendance établie, l'analyse portera sur sa consécration dans la nouvelle loi sur la Banque Centrale et le système bancaire n° 194 de l'année 2020 (2). Ensuite, il sera intéressant de discuter de la musculation de la tendance prohibitive par l'extension de la définition des « biens » aux actifs virtuels dans le cadre de la lutte contre le blanchiment d'argent (3). Finalement, l'article pose une conclusion et des perspectives pour le futur (4).

1 https://triple-a.io/cryptocurrency-ownership-egypt-2022/ (consulté le 2 avril 2024).

2 Ahmed Shawkat, « 29 arrested in Egypt after thousands were swept up in Hoggpool cryptocurrency investment scam », CBS NEWS, 9 mars 2023, consulté sur: https://www.cbsnews.com/news/egypt-crypto-investment-scam-hoggpool-arrests/ (consulté le 2 avril 2024).

3 S. Handagama, « Egyptians are buying Bitcoin despite prohibitive new banking laws », 5 mars 2021, consulté en ligne sur: www.coindesk.com. Selon le directeur général de la société, Konstantin Anissimov, les volumes de transactions de bitcoins en Égypte sur CEX.IO ont également augmenté de plus de 400 % de décembre à janvier 2021, reflétant les tendances observées par d'autres plateformes de cryptographie dans le pays.

4 https://www.statista.com/outlook/fmo/digital-assets/cryptocurrencies/egypt (consulté le 2 avril 2024).

 | DOI:10.1163/9789004722507_010

1 La Tendance prohibitive multi-institutionnelle

La Banque centrale d'Égypte (« BCE »), ainsi que l'Autorité de régulation financière (« ARF »)[5], ont tiré les premières sonnettes d'alarme institutionnelles sur les dangers des crypto-monnaies[6], Eu égard à son suivi des nouvelles récemment diffusées sur les crypto-monnaies, tels que Bitcoin et autres, la BCE avait réitéré sa sévère mise en garde contre le commerce de toutes sortes de crypto-monnaies, principalement Bitcoin, en raison du risque extrêmement élevé qui leur est associé. Pour la BCE, les crypto-monnaies se caractérisent généralement par les fluctuations et la volatilité importante des prix. Au regard du fait que leurs marchés sont complètement non réglementés, les investissements en crypto-monnaies sont risqués, hautement spéculatifs et sont susceptibles d'entraîner des pertes soudaines de toute leur valeur. La BCE a rappelé que les crypto-monnaies ne sont émises par aucune banque centrale, ni aucune autorité officielle. De plus, les crypto-monnaies ne sont pas adossées à des actifs corporels et ne sont pas supervisées par aucun régulateur dans le monde, et par conséquent ils n'ont pas le soutien dont bénéficient les autres monnaies officielles émises par les banques[7].

Par conséquent, la BCE a affirmé que le commerce au sein de la République arabe d'Égypte se limite uniquement aux devises officielles approuvées par les autorités. À cet égard, la BCE a appelé tous les acteurs du marché égyptien à faire preuve d'une extrême prudence et d'attention et à ne pas s'engager dans des transactions ayant objet ces devises à haut risque[8].

Le débat sur la légalité des crypto-monnaies a été également enrichi par la position d'instances religieuses. Dar Al-Ifta', l'organisme d'État chargé d'émettre des avis religieux (fatwas), a déclaré que le BTC était une forme de « jeu » interdit en raison de sa nature spéculative.[9] Sa technologie décentralisée sous-jacente constitue une violation du pouvoir régalien de l'État d'émettre de

5 L'Autorité de Régulation Financière (ARF) a été créée conformément à la loi n° 10-2009. L'ARF est chargée de superviser et de réglementer les marchés et instruments financiers non bancaires, y compris le marché des capitaux, les marchés à terme, les activités d'assurance, le prêt hypothécaire, le crédit-bail, l'affacturage et la titrisation.

6 Centre de Presse ARF, Communiqué de presse du 26 mai 2021, consulté en ligne sur : www.fra.gov.eg ; BCE, communiqué de presse du 18 mars 2021, consulté en ligne sur : www.cbe.org.eg.

7 *Ibid.*

8 *Ibid.* La BCE a réitéré sa mise en garde par rapport aux crypto-monnaies en mars 2023, suite au scandale de Hogg Pool. V. BCE, communiqué de presse du 8 mars 2023, consulté en ligne sur: https://www.cbe.org.eg/en/news-publications/news/2023/03/08/warning-statement (consulté le 2 avril 2024).

9 Dar Al-Ifta', Fatwa no. 4205, 28 décembre 2017, consulté en ligne sur: www.dar-alifta.org.

la monnaie puisque cette « monnaie n'est pas reconnue par la plupart des pays et n'est pas soumise à la supervision des institutions bancaires, principalement les banques centrales, qui sont chargées de réglementer la politique monétaire des pays et indiquant si la monnaie est ou non acceptée à la circulation »[10]. Après une présentation exhaustive des opinions des jurisconsultes islamiques sur la question de l'émission de monnaie, Dar Al-Ifta' a conclu que le trafic et l'échange de Bitcoin n'étaient « pas religieusement autorisés ».[11]

2 La Consécration de la tendance prohibitive par la nouvelle loi de la banque centrale

La loi sur la banque centrale et le système bancaire n° 194 de l'année 2020 (« LBCSB »)[12] a adopté l'approche prohibitive issue du « consensus » présenté précédemment. Notre analyse de cette loi est focalisée sur sa définition des crypto-monnaies (2.1), la criminalisation des activités qui leur sont liées (2.2), avant de clore la discussion sur cette loi avec l'exigence de l'agrément du Conseil de la BCE pour légaliser l'exercice de ces activités (2.3).

2.1 *la Définition des crypto-monnaies*

L'article 1 de la LBCSB décrit les « crypto-monnaies » comme des devises stockées électroniquement qui ne sont libellées en aucune des devises émises par les autorités et qui circulent sur Internet. Il s'agit du seul texte juridique égyptien dans lequel figure une définition des crypto-monnaies.

Les crypto-monnaies sont traitées en bloc dans la doctrine égyptienne, sans prise en compte de leurs nuances. A titre d'exemple, la distinction n'est pas établie selon le degré d'anonymat présenté par chacune des crypto-monnaies[13]. Les caractéristiques les plus fréquemment analysées sont l'absence de support matériel et de pouvoir central, le système de minage, le pseudo-anonymat et

---

10 Pour une étude plus détaillée de la légalité des crypto-monnaies en droit musulman, V. B. Fadel, *Al-tanzim Al-qanouni Lel-'omla Al-iftiradiya* (*La regulation juridique du Bitcoin*), Dar al-fikr al-jami'i, Alexandrie, 2021, pp. 89–101.

11 Dar Al-Ifta', Fatwa n° 4205, 28 décembre 2017, *op. cit.*

12 Loi n° 194-2020, *Journal Officiel* n° 37-bis-f, 15 septembre 2020, p. 2.

13 V. A. Tawfiq Chamseddine, *Makhater al-omlat al-iftiradiya fi nazar al-siyasa al-jina'ia* (*Les dangers des monnaies virtuelles à la lumière de la politique criminelle*), Matba'it october al-handasiya, Le Caire, 2019, p. 6.

les risques économiques présentés par la spéculation et la fluctuation de leur cours[14].

2.2 *la Criminalisation des activités liées aux crypto-monnaies*

L'article 206 de la LBCSB stipule qu'il est interdit d'émettre, d'échanger ou de commercialiser des crypto-monnaies, de créer ou d'exploiter des plateformes pour les échanger, ou d'exercer des activités liées à celles-ci, sans obtenir une autorisation du Conseil d'administration de la Banque centrale conformément aux règles et procédures fixées par ce dernier.

La sanction en cas de violation de cette interdiction est l'emprisonnement (de 24 heures à 3 ans selon les principes généraux) et une amende d'au moins un million de livres et n'excédant pas 10 millions de livres égyptiennes (entre 20 et 200 milles euros) (article 225 de la LBCSB).

Un régime procédural spécifique a été prévu pour la poursuite des infractions concernant les crypto-monnaies par les articles 238 et 239 de la LBCSB. Dans les cas autres que le flagrant délit, il n'est pas permis d'engager de poursuites pénales ni d'engager aucune procédure d'enquête dans les infractions prévues par la LBCSB, et notamment les infractions liées aux crypto-monnaies, sauf demande écrite du Gouverneur de la BCE (article 238). Une fois que le Gouverneur reçoit la requête du parquet général, il adresse celle-ci à une administration spécialisée composée par des experts dans les affaires bancaires, économiques et juridiques, qui prépare un rapport pour déterminer l'opportunité des poursuites par rapport à l'affaire présentée (article 239).

Pour bien élucider les différentes activités liées aux crypto-monnaies criminalisées par la LBCSB, nous discutons ci-dessous de l'émission (2.2.1), de l'échange (2.2.2), de la commercialisation (2.2.3), de la création et l'exploitation de plateformes de crypto-monnaies (2.2.4), en renforçant notre démonstration par de faits divers portant sur des affaires liées à ces activités.

2.2.1 L'émission

La doctrine égyptienne interprète le terme « émission » comme l'opération de minage en soi, par la résolution de problèmes mathématiques complexes par les utilisateurs-mêmes du système, en mettant le pouvoir informatique

---

14 B. Fadel, *op. cit.*, p. 35 et s. ; A. Tawfiq Chamseddine, *op. cit.*, p. 18 et s. ; K. Eltabakh, *Al-omlat al-ifiradeya wa dawraha fi tamwil al-irhab wa ghasl al-amwal* (*Les crypto-monnaies et leur rôle dans le financement de terrorisme et le blanchiment d'argent*), Dar al-nahda al-arabeya, Le Caire, 2022, p.69 et s.

de leurs ordinateurs au service de la validation des transactions liées à cette « monnaie »[15].

Avant la promulgation de la loi de 2020, une enquête menée par l'Administration générale des enquêtes sur les fonds publics, en coordination avec le secteur de la sécurité nationale, ont confirmé qu'une personne résidant le Caire utilise son appartement en tant que siège pour la mise en place d'un réseau électronique composé de cartes graphiques d'ordinateurs et cartes mères. Les cartes sont connectées les unes aux autres par des méthodes techniques spéciales en vue d'être utilisées dans l'exploitation minière et l'émission d' « Ethereum ». En le confrontant, l'inculpé a avoué avoir commis les faits et avoir pratiqué cette activité en utilisant les appareils électroniques et le téléphone portable saisis en sa possession[16].

Pour l'instant, la base textuelle sur laquelle est fondée les poursuites pénales n'est pas très claire, surtout que les faits ont été commis avant la promulgation de la loi de 2020.

2.2.2 L'échange

Une affaire qui remonte à 2016 révèle qu'un dentiste a été détenu par les forces de sécurité pour avoir «acheté du Bitcoin», avant l'adoption de l'interdiction générale des activités liées à la crypto-monnaie, sans aucune autre explication quant à son infraction exacte[17].

En octobre 2021, des enquêtes menées par la Direction générale de lutte contre les infractions aux fonds publics, en coordination avec le secteur de la sécurité nationale, ont confirmé qu'une personne, résidant dans le gouvernorat de Buhaira, s'était livrée à une activité criminelle représentée par la vente et l'achat de monnaies virtuelles « Bitcoin » et le marketing électronique pour une entreprise dans un pays étranger via Internet. Les enquêtes ont ajouté que l'inculpé travaille dans la vente de monnaie virtuelle en tant qu'intermédiaire entre l'entreprise et ceux qui souhaitent acheter ces devises via des portefeuilles électroniques établis par l'inculpé à cet effet. L'inculpé a été appréhendé par les forces de sécurité, et en le confrontant, il a avoué son activité criminelle. Il a été constaté que le volume de ses transactions en deux ans s'élevait à 500 000

---

15 M. Gibril Ibrahim, *Al-omlat al-mouchaffara fi manzour al-qanoun al-jina'i* (*Les crypto-monnaies à la lumière du droit pénal*), Dar al-nahda al-arabeya, Le Caire, 2022, pp. 112–113.

16 M. Abdelradi, « La saisie d'un réseau électronique d'émission de monnaies virtuelles », 8 juin 2020, consulté en ligne sur: www.youm7.com.

17 M. Attiya, « La saisie d'un réseau de promotion de crypto-monnaies 'Bitcoin' à Daqahlia », 11 août 2021, consulté sur : www.shorouknews.com.

livres égyptiennes[18]. Dans la même veine, une personne est arrêtée à Souhag le 10 janvier 2022 pour des activités d'achat et de vente de Bitcoins[19].

Si la doctrine égyptienne semble accepter l'interprétation du terme « échange » comme les opérations d'achat et de vente de crypto-monnaies, les limites de ce terme restent cependant floues. Est-ce que les transactions de pair à pair, ainsi que l'achat de produits et de services sur Internet, sont inclus dans la définition de « l'échange »? L'application judiciaire devra éclairer ces points.

2.2.3 La commercialisation

Au regard des actes criminels précédents, l'interdiction de la commercialisation des crypto-monnaies constitue une suite logique de la vision du législateur égyptien en la matière. Ainsi, en février 2021, les forces de sécurité égyptiennes ont appréhendé une personne du gouvernorat de Menoufia (delta du Nil), soupçonnée d'avoir dirigé une page Facebook qui fait la publicité d'une plateforme d'échange de Bitcoin (« BTC »)[20]. En août 2021, le ministère de l'Intérieur a également déclaré l'arrestation de deux citoyens soupçonnés d'avoir créé une société qui travaille dans le minage de BTC et d'avoir commercialisé son utilisation en créant des vidéos et en les publiant sur différents réseaux sociaux[21].

2.2.4 La création et l'exploitation de plateformes de crypto-monnaies

L'article 206 de la LBCSB a également criminalisé la création et l'exploitation de plateformes de crypto-monnaies. Ce verrou national est complété par un blocage sur Internet. Selon des sites spécialisés en crypto-monnaies, les plus grandes plateformes mondiales d'échange comme Binance, Coinbase, Bitfinex, Kraken et Bitstamp, sont bloqués en Egypte[22].

---

18 Y. Albadry, « L'arrestation d'une personne accusée de trafic de monnaies virtuelles Bitcoin à Beheira », 19 octobre 2021, consulté en ligne sur: www.almasryalyoum.com.

19 S. Anwar, « Après l'arrestation d'un chômeur, attention, la circulation de ces monnaies peut conduire à la prison et à une amende d'un million de livres », 10 janvier 2022, consulté en ligne sur: www.elbalad.news.

20 A. Awad, « L'arrestation d'un promoteur de Bitcoin sur Facebook », 24 février 2021, consulté en ligne sur: www.almalnews.com.

21 M. Attiya, « La saisie d'un réseau de promotion de crypto-monnaies 'Bitcoin' à Daqahlia », 11 août 2021, consulté sur : www.shorouknews.com.

22 A. de Candia, « Major exchanges blocked in Egypt », 18 août 2020, consulté sur: www.en.cryptonomist.ch.

2.3 *L'exigence de l'agrément du conseil d'administration de la* BCE

Selon l'article 206 de la LBCSB, les activités mentionnées ci-dessus sont considérées comme criminelles lorsqu'elles sont exercées sans l'autorisation du Conseil d'administration de la BCE et selon les règles et les procédures définies par ce dernier. Néanmoins, plus de trois ans après la promulgation de la loi, le Conseil d'administration de la Banque centrale n'a toujours pas publié les règles déterminant le processus par lequel on peut obtenir une licence pour mener les différentes activités liées aux crypto-monnaies.

Il sera intéressant de comparer l'attitude de la BCE envers les crypto-monnaies avec celle prônée à l'égard des monnaies électroniques, également touchées par l'interdiction générale de l'article 206 de la LBCSB. Selon l'article premier de la LBCSB, une monnaie électronique est définie comme une valeur monétaire libellée en livre égyptienne ou dans l'une des devises émises par les autorités émettrices, due par le titulaire de l'agrément, qui est stockée électroniquement et acceptée comme moyen de paiement. En avril 2021, la BCE a publié les règles régissant la fourniture de services de paiement, 6 mois après la promulgation de la LBCSB. Dans ces règles, les questions de l'émission de monnaies électroniques, ainsi que la licence nécessaire pour le faire, ont été tranchées par la BCE.

La divergence de la BCE dans le traitement des crypto-monnaies et des monnaies électroniques est simple à expliquer, la condition *sine qua non* pour émettre les deuxièmes étant que l'émetteur soit l'une « des banques soumises au contrôle de la BCE »[23].

3 La musculation de la tendance prohibitive : l'Extension de la définition des « biens » aux actifs virtuels dans le cadre de la lutte contre le blanchiment d'argent

Le régime juridique de lutte contre le blanchiment d'argent en Égypte se compose principalement de la loi sur la lutte contre le blanchiment d'argent (loi n° 80 de 2002, telle que modifiée) et de ses règlements d'application, ainsi que d'instructions et de circulaires émises par la Banque centrale d'Égypte, la Cellule de lutte contre le blanchiment d'argent et le financement du terrorisme (EMLCU) et d'autres organismes de réglementation, notamment ceux qui s'appliquent aux banques, aux sociétés de change, aux sociétés de transfert

---

23 BCE, « Règles régissant la fourniture des services de paiement par la téléphonie mobile », avril 2021, p. 10, consulté sur : www.cbe.org.eg.

de fonds, aux compagnies d'assurance et aux entreprises et professions non financières.

Par le biais de la promulgation de la loi n° 17 de l'année 2020 réformant certaines dispositions de la loi sur la lutte contre le blanchiment d'argent n° 80 de l'année 2002[24], le législateur égyptien intervient pour étendre le champ des biens pouvant faire l'objet de l'infraction de blanchiment aux crypto-monnaies en utilisant la terminologie d' « actifs virtuels ». L'Egypte a opté pour le choix de prévoir expressément les crypto-monnaies dans le cadre des infractions de blanchiment, et non pas celui d'interpréter plus largement les textes préexistants comme c'est le cas dans d'autre systèmes juridiques[25].

L'article 1 de la loi de 2002, portant sur la définition des biens, est réécrit ainsi :

« Tous les actifs physiques et *virtuels* et les ressources économiques, y compris le pétrole et les autres ressources naturelles, les biens, les devises nationales ou étrangères, les valeurs mobilières ou les titres commerciaux, et tous les revenus, bénéfices ou autres sources de revenus découlant ou générés par ces fonds ou actifs, ou tout autre actifs préparés en vue de leur utilisation pour obtenir un financement, des produits ou des services, *ainsi que des actifs virtuels ayant une valeur numérique pouvant être échangés, transmis ou transférés numériquement et pouvant être utilisés comme outil de paiement ou d'investissement* (emphase ajoutée) ».

La note explicative relative à la loi de 2020 a clarifié l'objectif des modifications[26], soulignant que celles-ci visent à assurer la conformité du droit égyptien avec les normes internationales dans le domaine de la lutte contre le blanchiment de capitaux. A l'occasion de l'adhésion de l'Égypte au Groupe d'action financière (GAFI) et à la soumission de son système juridique à l'évaluation, les amendements délimitent le périmètre des fonds et des actifs pour inclure tous les actifs virtuels, en accordant aux autorités de contrôle le pouvoir d'adopter des mesures à l'encontre des institutions soumises à leur contrôle, et

---

24 Loi n° 17-2020, *Journal Officiel* n° 10-bis-b, 11 mars 2020, p. 2.

25 V. à titre d'exemple, l'interprétation extensive de l'expression « transaction financière » de l'article 1956 du titre 18 du Code Fédéral américain, faite par la Cour fédérale de New York dans *United States of America v. Ross William Ulbricht*, n° 14-CR-068 (S.D.N.Y. February 4, 2014). Pour une discussion plus détaillée de la question du Bitcoin et le blanchiment d'argent en France et aux Etats-Unis, et plus généralement la réception du Bitcoin en droit pénal, V. A. Elkahwagy, « La délinquance économique à l'heure du numérique: bitcoin, blanchiment et autres observations », Archives de politique criminelle, n° 39, 2017, p. 55 et s.

26 K. Abouzeid, « Le Parlement approuve dans l'ensemble les amendements de la loi sur la lutte contre le blanchiment d'argent », 22 mai 2022, consulté sur: www.dostor.org.

la création de plusieurs règles qui garantissent l'activation de la coopération internationale dans le domaine de la lutte contre le blanchiment d'argent, le financement du terrorisme et les délits connexes.

Les amendements ont également prévu un durcissement des sanctions pénales, infligeant une peine d'emprisonnement n'excédant pas 7 ans et une amende égale au double des fonds en question, pour quiconque commette ou tente de commettre un crime de blanchiment d'argent prévu par la loi. Il a été également décidé de confisquer les fonds ou avoirs saisis résultant du crime de blanchiment de capitaux, ou de prononcer une amende complémentaire équivalente à la valeur des fonds ou avoirs en cas d'impossibilité de les saisir ou en cas de cession à des tiers agissant de bonne foi[27].

4 Conclusion et perspectives

Le système juridique égyptien adopte une approche prohibitive générale à l'égard des crypto-monnaies. La légalité de toute activité liée aux crypto-monnaies dépend de l'agrément d'une autorité centrale. Ce mandat étant confié à la BCE, et non à une autre agence comme l'ARF, est révélateur de la façon dont l'État égyptien aperçoit les crypto-monnaies : plus comme une monnaie concurrente et moins comme des actions ou d'autres instruments financiers[28]. Avec la nouvelle loi de la LBCSB, et l'absence des règles régissant la question de l'agrément, l'Égypte se positionne parmi les pays qui interdisent complètement l'utilisation des crypto-monnaies. La référence aux « activités liées aux crypto-monnaies » est pour le moins ambiguë et pose de multiples obstacles de mise en œuvre quant au principe de légalité : le minage de crypto-monnaies ou le simple fait de créer un porte-monnaie virtuel sont-ils des comportements interdits ? À première vue, la réponse peut être affirmative. Cependant, nous espérons que l'application judiciaire viendra calibrer les confins du texte dans des limites clairement définies.

Malgré la tendance prohibitive, certaines études confirment que les investissements des Egyptiens (surtout âgés de moins de 34 ans) sur le marché des crypto-monnaies ne vont pas ralentir, liant cette tendance à la dévaluation de la livre égyptienne et la hausse exponentielle du taux d'inflation, les actifs

27 Pour discussion, V. K. Eltabakh, *op. cit.*, p. 147 et s.

28 À propos de ce point, V. M. Gordon, 'Bitcoin to Blockchain: how Laws and regulations are conforming to and impacting the use of virtual currency' (2016) 20160428P *NYCBAR* 1.

virtuels présentant ainsi des substituts aux domaines classiques d'investissement et d'épargne[29].

Entre le texte de la loi et la pratique des citoyens, un compromis devra être trouvé. La vague des crypto-monnaies est bien arrivée à la côte égyptienne et la politique législative « devra se résoudre à y surfer en cultivant ses bienfaits, sous peine d'être submergée par son dynamisme »[30].

29 Y. Galal, *Cryptocurrencies Bandwagon...Fad wave or Investment Asset? Firm Level Analysis of Panel Data in Egypt*, Master's Thesis, American University in Cairo, 2022, AUC Knowledge Fountain, p. 75, consulté sur: https://fount.aucegypt.edu/etds/1851

30 A. Elkahwagy, *op. cit.*, p. 66.

Finland

Teemu Juutilainen and Janne Kaisto

1 Introductory Notes

This report answers the Questionnaire 'Cryptocurrencies: the impossible domestic law regime?' for the World Congress of the International Academy of Comparative Law in Asunción 2022. References to statutes are given with their respective numbers in the Statutes of Finland, for example, the 'Act on Virtual Currency Providers (572/2019)'. The statutes can be found in their original form as well as in their amended and consolidated form with the dates of amendment indicated, in the Finlex Data Bank (http://www.finlex.fi/). While Finnish statutes are official only in the Finnish and Swedish languages, Finlex provides some unofficial translations in other languages, mostly in English. These translations have been used in the report (selectively), as have translations found on the websites of relevant public authorities. The reader should note that translated and paraphrased passages of statutes and other legal material in the report may contain inaccuracies. The reader should also take into account that the authors' views on the *lex lata* are often tentative due to the novelty of the topic. Especially in private law questions, views are typically based on general principles or the use of analogies in the absence of cryptocurrency-specific rules. The text was finalised for publication at the end of 2022, and only minor changes have been made since then. Important developments not discussed here include the Markets in Crypto-Assets (MiCA) Regulation,[1] which will become applicable in 2024, and related proposed national legislation.[2]

2 Use, Definition, and Legal Qualification

Cryptocurrencies are receiving increasing attention in Finland, as elsewhere in the world, both enthusiastic and critical. We have no data on the prevalence

1 Parliament and Council Regulation (EU) 2023/1114 of 31 May 2023 on markets in crypto-assets, and amending Regulations (EU) No 1093/2010 and (EU) No 1095/2010 and Directives 2013/36/EU and (EU) 2019/1937 [2023] OJ L150/40.

2 See Government proposal HE 31/2024, issued on 18 April 2024. The proposal puts forward major changes to the legislation discussed in this report. Most importantly, the Act on Virtual Currency Providers would be repealed and replaced by a new Act on Crypto-Asset Service Providers and Markets in Crypto-Assets.

 | DOI:10.1163/9789004722507_011

of specific cryptocurrencies circulating in Finland, but the selection offered by registered 'virtual currency providers' (a category of actors regulated under Finnish law) gives a rough idea. For example, one offers Bitcoin, Ethereum, Litecoin, Chainlink, Aave, Polygon, and USDC (some of these are names of a cryptocurrency, while others are names of a broader system with a cryptocurrency).[3] No cryptocurrency is legal tender in Finland, which is part of the euro area, where only the euro enjoys that status.[4]

A statement in 2019 from the Payment Systems Department of the Bank of Finland to the Economic Committee of the Finnish Parliament notes that cryptocurrencies are used almost exclusively for speculation. The statement describes their use as a means of payment, for example in online shops, in principle possible though very limited, but common in criminal activity, such as trade in illicit goods or extortion.[5] According to the statement, with rare exceptions, traditional financial companies have shown no interest in cryptocurrencies, and neither statistics nor the development of the industry indicate use of cryptocurrencies in retail payments.[6] While the big picture may not have changed much since 2019, the range of cryptocurrency-related services seems to be broadening. For example, one registered virtual currency provider, which is also a licensed payment institution, is offering a cryptocurrency-collateralised credit account and a prepaid debit card, which can be topped up by euros or cryptocurrency and allows spending of euros or cryptocurrency from the client's wallets.[7] We are not aware of stablecoins or cryptocurrencies related to external benchmarks issued in Finland, but those issued elsewhere are traded in Finland as well.[8] One Finnish company says that it is currently developing 'an EU regulated, full-reserve euro stablecoin'.[9]

To date, Finnish law provides no definition of 'cryptocurrency'. However, cryptocurrencies generally fall within the broader definition of 'virtual currency' in the Act on Virtual Currency Providers (572/2019). Under section 2(1)(1) of the Act, 'virtual currency' means value in a digital form which (a) is not

3 See Northcrypto, https://www.northcrypto.com.

4 See European Commission, https://ec.europa.eu/info/business-economy-euro/euro-area/euro/use-euro/euro-legal-tender_en.

5 Suomen Pankki, Maksujärjestelmät-osasto, A. Grym, 'Virtuaalivaluutat', SP 292/C11.2/2019, p. 2, available at https://www.eduskunta.fi/FI/vaski/JulkaisuMetatieto/Documents/EDK-2019-AK-275499.pdf. These observations seem to be based on foreign and international sources.

6 Ibid.

7 See Coinmotion, https://coinmotion.com/credit-account/, https://coinmotion.com/coinmotion-prepaid-debit-card/.

8 E.g., USDC is a stablecoin.

9 See Membrane Finance, https://www.membrane.fi/company.

issued by a central bank or other public authority and is not legal tender, (b) can be used by a person as a means of payment, and (c) can be transferred, saved, and exchanged electronically. Section 2(2) excludes from this definition 'electronic money' as defined in section 5(6a) of the Payment Institutions Act (297/2010).[10]

The category of virtual currencies, as defined in the Act on Virtual Currency Providers, is broader than that of cryptocurrencies in the Questionnaire and in this volume in that virtual currencies may but need not be based on a decentralised system, such as blockchain. Moreover, the use of virtual currencies may but need not be based on cryptographic private and public keys.[11]

Finnish courts and administrative bodies have considered the nature of certain virtual currencies (and cryptocurrencies). The Supreme Court regarded Bitcoin as a 'contractual means of payment' in decision KKO 2020:64, where it held that distraint (attachment) of Bitcoins in an account maintained by a service provider follows the same principles as distraint of funds in a bank account.[12] In turn, the Supreme Administrative Court described Ether (the cryptocurrency of Ethereum) as capable of being used as a 'means of exchange' and 'investment' in decision KHO 2019:42 on income tax.[13]

3 Regulatory Framework

3.1 *Overview*

Cryptocurrencies are neither prohibited nor explicitly authorised under Finnish law. Certain cryptocurrency-related activities are subject to regulation, as described below, but cryptocurrencies themselves are at present unregulated. In particular, the above-mentioned Act on Virtual Currency Providers does not regulate virtual currencies themselves, even though it defines 'virtual currency'. Instead, it regulates business conducted by 'virtual currency providers', defined as virtual currency issuers, virtual currency exchange services and their marketplaces, and wallet service providers (sections 1 and 2(1)

10 S. 5(6a) of the Payment Institutions Act is based on Art. 2(2) of the Parliament and Council Directive 2009/110/EC of 16 September 2009 on the taking up, pursuit and prudential supervision of the business of electronic money institutions amending Directives 2005/60/EC and 2006/48/EC and repealing Directive 2000/46/EC [2009] OJ L267/7.

11 Government proposal HE 167/2018, pp. 84–85.

12 Paras 15–19 of the decision. The Supreme Court draws on Case C-264/14, *Skatteverket v. David Hedqvist*, ECLI:EU:C:2015:718, the Act on Virtual Currency Providers, and Government proposal HE 167/2018.

13 S. 2.2 of the decision.

(2) of the Act). No regulation exists specifically on derivatives referencing cryptocurrencies.

The Act on Virtual Currency Providers is the first piece of statutory law directly addressing cryptocurrencies (as part of the broader category of virtual currencies) and their use in Finland.

3.2 *The Act on Virtual Currency Providers*

3.2.1 Main Purpose

The Act on Virtual Currency Providers is part of a legislative package implementing the EU's 5th Anti-Money Laundering Directive.[14] The Directive requires that Member States register virtual currency exchange services and wallet service providers. The Act goes further than this by including virtual currency issuers in its scope. This inclusion was justified by cryptocurrency-related risks and observed misconduct in connection with initial coin offerings (ICO s).[15] Certain provisions of the Act aim to satisfy requirements derived from the right to work and the freedom to engage in commercial activity in section 18(1) of the Constitution of Finland (731/1999). These concern the obligation of registration, requirements for registration, information recorded in the register, removal from the register, and the consequences of conducting activities without registration. Importantly, the Act aims to address elevated risks of money laundering and terrorist financing related to virtual currencies (pointed out in a national risk assessment) and risks to consumers investing in virtual currencies (warned of by the European Banking Authority and national supervisory authorities).[16] The express objectives of the Act do not include investor protection, but some of its provisions may have effects in that direction.

3.2.2 Temporal Scope

The Act on Virtual Currency Providers was enacted on 26 April 2019 and entered into force on 1 May 2019 (section 18). Those who were conducting activities registrable under the Act at the time of entry into force were allowed to continue unregistered until 1 November 2019 (section 19).

---

14 Government proposal HE 167/2018 pp. 5–6. See Parliament and Council Directive (EU) 2018/843 of 30 May 2018 amending Directive (EU) 2015/849 on the prevention of the use of the financial system for the purposes of money laundering or terrorist financing, and amending Directives 2009/138/EC and 2013/36/EU [2018] OJ L156/43.

15 Government proposal HE 167/2018, p. 84.

16 Ibid., pp. 44–46, 48.

3.2.3 Territorial Scope

Section 1 defines the scope of the Act and contains no exclusion of foreign virtual currency providers. This has been interpreted in legal literature as meaning that the Act applies to both domestic and foreign virtual currency providers that provide services in Finland. The Act has also been understood to apply to domestic virtual currency providers even if they provide services only abroad and not in Finland.[17] The Financial Supervisory Authority (FIN-FSA) has discussed the Act's geographical scope, from the perspective of the obligation of registration, in a press release as follows:

> a trader may provide services related to virtual currencies in Finland only if registered as a virtual currency provider in accordance with the Act. Such services cover, for example, the targeted marketing of a virtual currency or a related service to Finns. … However, the obligation to register does not apply, for example, to situations where a Finnish customer ends up on a foreign service provider's website on his or her own initiative or encounters advertising on international websites that is not targeted specifically at Finnish citizens.[18]

3.2.4 Personal Scope

The personal scope of the Act on Virtual Currency Providers is connected to the definition of 'virtual currency provider'. Under section 1, the Act applies to business conducted by virtual currency providers. Section 2(1)(2) defines 'virtual currency providers' as virtual currency issuers, virtual currency exchange services and their marketplaces, and wallet service providers. These are further defined in section 2(1)(3) to (1)(5), which also makes it clear that virtual currency providers of all three types can be either natural or legal persons. Certain provisions of the Act concern the management and key persons of virtual currency providers (for example, section 7 on trustworthiness criteria).

3.2.5 Material Scope

The Act does not distinguish between cryptocurrencies based on permissioned and permissionless blockchains. Both may fall within the definition of 'virtual currency' in section 2(1)(1).

---

17 J. Hautamäki, M. Atallah and K. Koskikare, *Virtuaalivaluutan tarjoaminen – käsikirja virtuaalivaluuttalain soveltamiseen*, Edita Publishing, Helsinki 2019, p. 28.

18 Financial Supervisory Authority (FIN-FSA), https://www.finanssivalvonta.fi/en/publications-and-press-releases/Press-release/2021/virtual-currencies-may-only-be-marketed-in-finland-by-providers-registered-here/.

The types of cryptocurrency-related conduct covered by the Act can be derived from the definitions of the above-mentioned three types of virtual currency provider in section 2(1)(3) to (1)(5). Thus, the conduct types are: [virtual currency issuer] issuing a virtual currency; [virtual currency exchange service] as a business or professional activity, exchanging a virtual currency as a service for legal tender or another virtual currency, or for another good (or exchanging another good for a virtual currency), or maintaining a marketplace where customers may engage in those activities; [wallet service provider] holding virtual currency on behalf of another person or offering to transfer or store it. Section 2(1)(6) states that 'virtual currency-related service' means issuance of a virtual currency, a virtual currency exchange service, and provision of a wallet service.

In addition to the registration obligation (sections 4 to 9), the Act regulates preservation of service-related documents and information (section 10), safeguarding and holding of client assets (section 11), marketing (section 12), and customer due diligence and risk management systems (section 13).

Virtual currency providers registered under the Act on Virtual Currency Providers are allowed to market virtual currencies and related services. Marketing is regulated in section 12 of the Act. Section 12 also applies to advertising, which forms part of the concept of marketing in this Act as well as in the Consumer Protection Act (38/1978).[19] Section 12(1) requires virtual currency providers to give clients all information on the marketed service that may be relevant for clients in making decisions on the service. Section 12(2) prohibits false or misleading information and other conduct that is inappropriate or unfair from the perspective of clients. As regards consumers, it additionally refers to chapter 2 of the Consumer Protection Act. Under section 12(3), marketing that does not convey information required for the economic security of clients must always be deemed inappropriate. Section 12(4) states that if a virtual currency is a financial instrument as defined in chapter 2, section 2 of the Securities Markets Act (746/2012), then that Act also applies to it.

3.3 *Criminal Law*

No cryptocurrency-specific or cryptocurrency service-specific criminal law provisions exist under Finnish law. Certain provisions of the Criminal Code (39/1889) have been amended to cover acts involving virtual currencies. These are found in chapter 17, section 16c on money collection offences and in chapter 37 on means of payment offences (section 15(3) on definitions).

19 Government proposal HE 167/2018, p. 90.

3.4 *Anti-Money Laundering and Counter-Terrorist Financing*

Section 13 of the Act on Virtual Currency Providers concerns customer due diligence and risk management systems. Under section 13(1), virtual currency providers must know their customers. The beneficial owner of a customer and the person acting on behalf of a customer must be identified and, where necessary, their identity must be verified. Section 13(2) requires virtual currency providers to have in place adequate risk management systems for assessment of risk to their operations caused by customers. Section 13(3) states that customer due diligence is also subject to the Act on Preventing Money Laundering and Terrorist Financing (444/2017, 'AML Act'). Finally, section 13(4) empowers FIN-FSA to issue more detailed regulations on customer due diligence procedures referred to in section 13(1) and risk management referred to in section 13(2).[20]

Virtual currency providers are obliged entities under the AML Act. This entails the following requirements, among other things. Virtual currency providers must prepare a risk assessment on money laundering and terrorist financing and update it regularly (chapter 2, section 3). They must know their customers (chapter 3). They must report suspicious transactions or suspected terrorist financing to the Financial Intelligence Unit (chapter 4, section 1). In addition, they have obligations related to training and protection of their employees and drawing up guidelines to ensure compliance with the AML Act (chapter 9, section 1).[21]

The AML Act requires that customers be identified, and their identity verified, when establishing a regular customer relationship. The same applies to occasional customers where a transaction or the sum of interconnected transactions amounts to at least EUR 10,000, or, for example, where a transaction in a virtual currency-related service as defined in the Act on Virtual Currency Providers amounts to more than EUR 1,000 (chapter 3, section 2).

---

20 See Financial Supervisory Authority (FIN-FSA), Regulations and guidelines 4/2019, Virtual currency providers, p. 12, available at https://www.finanssivalvonta.fi/globalassets/en/regulation/fin-fsa-regulations-and-guidelines/2019/04_2019/2019_04.m1_en.pdf. Customer due diligence is also subject to FIN-FSA Standard 2.4, Customer due diligence – Prevention of money laundering, terrorist financing and market abuse, available at https://www.finanssivalvonta.fi/globalassets/en/regulation/fin-fsa-regulations-and-guidelines/standards/2.4/2.4.std3_en.pdf.

21 See also Financial Supervisory Authority (FIN-FSA), Regulations and guidelines 4/2019, Virtual currency providers, pp. 12–13, available at https://www.finanssivalvonta.fi/globalassets/en/regulation/fin-fsa-regulations-and-guidelines/2019/04_2019/2019_04.m1_en.pdf.

4 Supervision

4.1 *Registration*

Virtual currency providers need not obtain authorisation or licence. However, they may offer services related to virtual currencies only if they are registered as virtual currency providers under the Act on Virtual Currency Providers, which lays down the conditions for registration (section 4). Exempted from the obligation of registration are (1) traders who provide services related to virtual currencies within a limited network and (2) traders who provide services related to virtual currencies occasionally in connection with other professional activity that requires a licence, registration, or prior approval. Others who intend to offer services related to virtual currencies must apply for registration as a virtual currency provider from the Financial Supervisory Authority (FIN-FSA) (section 5).

FIN-FSA must register an applicant who (1) has the right to conduct business in Finland, (2) is not bankrupt and, if a natural person, is of legal age, has not had their capacity to act restricted, and has not had a guardian appointed, and (3) is trustworthy (section 6). In turn, removal from the register follows (1) for not having provided services during the previous six months or having ceased activities, (2) for having been accepted into the register due to incorrect or misleading information, or (3) for no longer meeting the conditions for registration (section 16). Additionally, it follows (4) for serious or repeated negligence after a previously imposed operating ban (section 16).

4.2 *Prospectus*

At present, no cryptocurrency-specific legislation requires cryptocurrency issuers to publish a white paper or prospectus.[22] However, as noted above, under section 12(4) of the Act on Virtual Currency Providers, if a virtual currency is a financial instrument as defined in chapter 2, section 2 of the Securities Markets Act, then that Act also applies to it. In that case, the provisions on prospectus in the Securities Markets Act apply.[23]

4.3 *Supervisory Authority*

Under section 3 of the Act on Virtual Currency Providers, compliance with the Act and the provisions and orders issued pursuant to it are supervised by

---

22 Cf. Commission Proposal for a Regulation of the European Parliament and of the Council on Markets in Crypto-assets, and amending Directive (EU) 2019/1937, COM(2020) 593 final.

23 Government proposal HE 167/2018, p. 90.

the Financial Supervisory Authority as laid down in the Act on the Financial Supervisory Authority (878/2008) and as provided in that Act. The reason stated for this is that virtual currency providers act at the interface of the financial system, while virtual currencies form risks to the financial system and to investors.[24] Sections 15 to 17 of the Act on Virtual Currency Providers deal with FIN-FSA's supervisory and sanctions powers (section 16 on removal from the register was presented above in connection with registration).

Section 15 requires FIN-FSA to prohibit provision of virtual currency-related services carried out in violation of the Act without registration. For a special reason, this prohibition may also be imposed on a person employed by a service provider engaged in such an activity or a person acting on the service provider's behalf. The prohibition must be reinforced by a conditional fine unless this is unnecessary for a special reason (section 15(1)). The right of FIN-FSA to issue a public warning is provided for in the Act on the Financial Supervisory Authority (section 15(2)).[25]

Section 17 of the Act on Virtual Currency Providers lists 'other sanctions against a virtual currency provider'. If a virtual currency provider materially fails to comply with its obligations under sections 8(2), 10, 11, or 13, and the failure is not remedied within a reasonable time set by FIN-FSA, then FIN-FSA may prohibit the virtual currency provider from continuing its activities until the failure is remedied (section 17(1)).[26] FIN-FSA may impose a conditional fine to reinforce the prohibition (17(2)). The right of FIN-FSA to issue a public warning is provided for in the Act on the Financial Supervisory Authority (section 17(3)).[27]

4.4 *Supervisory Measures and Actions*

The information available on the FIN-FSA website suggests that no major supervisory measures or actions have been taken so far. In a press release on 24 November 2021, FIN-FSA noted having 'contacted entities it has found to be engaged in advertising virtual currencies targeted at Finland without proper registration'.[28]

24 Ibid., pp. 48, 85.

25 See s. 39 of the Act on the Financial Supervisory Authority.

26 S. 8(2) concerns notifying FIN-FSA of changes in registered information and of certain other circumstances, s. 10 preservation of documents and information related to services, s. 11 safeguarding and holding of client assets, and s. 13 customer due diligence and risk management systems.

27 See s. 39 of the Act on the Financial Supervisory Authority.

28 Financial Supervisory Authority (FIN-FSA), https://www.finanssivalvonta.fi/en/publications-and-press-releases/Press-release/2021/virtual-currencies-may-only-be-marketed-in-finland-by-providers-registered-here/.

In a press release on 22 November 2017, FIN-FSA issued a warning to consumers about risks associated with cryptocurrencies, including those present in ICO s.[29] In a press release on 17 March 2022, FIN-FSA communicated a warning to consumers issued by the European Supervisory Agencies (EBA, ESMA and EIOPA), according to which 'many crypto-assets are highly risky and speculative' and 'not suited for most retail consumers as an investment or as a means of payment or exchange'.[30]

5 Private Law Issues

5.1 *Ownership*

Cryptocurrencies can be owned under Finnish law. In a case where 60 Bitcoins are registered in X's wallet,[31] X may (or may not) be the owner of the Bitcoins. For X to be the owner, X must have acquired the Bitcoins legally (rather than, say, received them by mistake or through a criminal act). Legislation or case law contains no complete list of the circumstances that constitute acquisition.[32] Rather, this is a matter of general principles of property law. The most typical circumstances involve a disposition aiming to transfer ownership, such as sale, exchange, or gift. In contrast, other circumstances may give rise to an entirely new right of ownership, rather than transfer an existing one. Such circumstances may be said to result in an 'original acquisition'.[33] Examples include cryptocurrency units obtained through mining. At any rate, mere factual control of cryptocurrency has no constitutive effect on its ownership.

In a case where X has opened an account with wallet service provider MontC and 60 Bitcoins are registered in X's wallet, X is likely to be the owner of the

29 Financial Supervisory Authority (FIN-FSA), https://www.finanssivalvonta.fi/en/publications-and-press-releases/Press-release/2017/financial-supervisory-authority-warning-cryptocurrencies-and-icos-initial-coin-offering-are-high-risk-investments/.

30 Financial Supervisory Authority (FIN-FSA), https://www.finanssivalvonta.fi/en/publications-and-press-releases/news-releases/2022/eu-financial-regulators-warn-consumers-on-the-risks-of-crypto-assets/.

31 Speaking of cryptocurrency units registered in a wallet, as in the Questionnaire, may aptly describe the user experience. However, in terms of technology and legal relations, it may be more accurate to speak of cryptocurrency units in addresses (or accounts) as a result of transactions recorded in blockchain.

32 Cf. Real Estate Code (540/1995), ch. 1, s. 1.

33 See generally, A. Saarnilehto et al., *Varallisuusoikeus*, continuously updated online book based on 2nd ed. of the printed version, Alma Talent, Helsinki, chapter VI, section 5, subsection 'Omistusoikeuden saaminen' (cited text by L. Kartio and E. Tammi-Salminen, updated 2011).

Bitcoins, even though MontC holds the private key in custody on X's behalf. If X has acquired the Bitcoins legally, then X is the owner, provided that the wallet is indeed identifiable as belonging to X and the Bitcoins have not been mixed with those owned by MontC, and unless it has been agreed otherwise as part of the arrangement between X and MontC. MontC has no ownership rights in the Bitcoins registered in X's wallet merely as a result of providing wallet services and holding the relevant private key, for these circumstances do not constitute acquisition.

In the case of a hardfork or airdrop of a new cryptocurrency, part of which is registered in a wallet belonging to X at MontC, X is more likely than MontC to be regarded as the owner of the new cryptocurrency units. Again, we should ask whether circumstances constituting acquisition are present. The new cryptocurrency units originating from a hardfork could perhaps be seen as (or comparable to) 'fruits' of the existing units, and as such belonging to the owner of the existing units, in this case most likely to X, by way of original acquisition. As regards airdropped new cryptocurrency units, the purposes of those initiating the airdrop would probably play a role.[34] The usual purposes of marketing a new cryptocurrency and expanding its userbase might be better served by a wider than a narrower distribution of the units, say, to X and other clients of MontC rather than to MontC itself. Be that as it may, it would be within X and MontC's freedom of contract to agree on who will be the owner of new cryptocurrency units in such situations.

The question of the law applicable to acquisition of cryptocurrency is currently unanswered under Finnish private international law. A generalising reading of literature in the field suggests that this law should be determined by applying the relevant 'proprietary' conflict rule at the time when the circumstances that (may) constitute acquisition occur, for example, when a disposition aiming to transfer ownership takes place.[35] However, no such conflict rule exists for cryptocurrencies, unlike, say, for ordinary tangible movables, which are covered by the *lex rei sitae* rule. A conflict rule could be developed based on several alternative connecting factors, and it is possible that one and the same connecting factor would not be suitable or optimal for all cryptocurrencies and situations. So far, Finnish sources of law or legal scholarship have not shed light on the matter.

34 In some circumstances, an airdrop may have the characteristics of a donation (gift). Generally on donation of cryptocurrency, see section 5.2.1 below.

35 See, e.g., R. Koulu, *Kansainvälinen varallisuusoikeus pääpiirteittäin*, WSOY, Helsinki 2005, p. 192.

Despite this uncertainty, it is possible to recognise certain basic situations where Finnish law almost certainly applies because Finland is the only jurisdiction in which the situation has relevant connections. An example could be acquisition through transfer, in Finland, of units of a global decentralised cryptocurrency (with no connection to any particular jurisdiction), such as Bitcoin or Ether, where the transferor, the transferee, and any relevant third parties habitually reside in Finland. The case for Finnish law applying is even clearer if any relevant cold storage wallets are also located in Finland.

5.2 *Transfer of Ownership*

Ownership of cryptocurrencies can be transferred under Finnish law, including through donation, sale, or exchange. Cryptocurrencies can also be inherited and obtained by will.

5.2.1 Donation

Donation of cryptocurrency falls within the scope of the Act on Gift Promises (625/1947), which applies to movable property, both tangible and intangible alike. A central concept in the Act is 'fulfilment' of a gift. Section 1(1) of the Act states that a promise of a gift is ineffective as long as the gift remains unfulfilled, unless the promise is expressed in a promissory note or other document given to the recipient, or unless the circumstances of the promise show that it was meant to become publicly known. Section 1(2) adds that a promise of a gift is ineffective against the promissor's (gift giver's) creditors if the gift remains unfulfilled, even if the promise is made in accordance with section 1(1). The question arises: What constitutes fulfilment of a gift in the case of cryptocurrency? The Act does not offer a direct answer, but sheds light on the matter by defining fulfilment of a gift in terms of certain other types of property in section 3. For example, a gift of a share certificate or a negotiable promissory note is deemed fulfilled once the recipient takes possession of the gifted object (section 3(1)). In turn, a gift of book-entries (e.g., Finnish shares admitted to public trading) is deemed fulfilled once the gifted book-entries are recorded in the recipient's book-entry account (section 3(2)). The principle behind these rules appears to be satisfied once the giver is no longer capable of independently disposing of the gifted object.[36] Accordingly, it should be possible to

36 Under Finnish law, the legal effects of a transfer of possession of an object (e.g., where transfer of possession is required for third-party effects of an agreement or a disposition) can be achieved with less than a 'maximal' transfer of possession from person A to person B. Indeed, it is generally sufficient to put B in a position where A can no longer independently dispose of the object.

fulfil a gift of cryptocurrency by putting the recipient in a position where the giver can no longer dispose of the gifted cryptocurrency.

In a case where 60 Bitcoins are registered in X's wallet and X wants to give 30 Bitcoins to Y, X can legally do so. The Act on Gift Promises applies to this transfer, as described above. If X uses an intermediary, such as a wallet service provider, X could probably fulfil the gift by notifying the intermediary of the gift, provided that the intermediary is an actor independent of X. This would be in accordance with the above articulated principle behind the different property type-specific rules on fulfilment of a gift. Notification is likely to suffice regardless of whether X is the owner of the gifted cryptocurrency or merely holds a personal claim on it (for example in a case where X's cryptocurrency is mixed with that of the intermediary). Section 3(3) and (4) lend support for this view. Section 3(3) states that a gift of an ordinary receivable is fulfilled once the giver (or in certain situations the recipient) has notified the debtor of the transfer. Under section 3(4), a gift of an investment fund unit (other than one falling within the scope of section 3(1) or (2)) is fulfilled once the maintainer of the fund unit register is notified of the transfer.

In terms of private international law, donation of cryptocurrency appears to be a contract covered by the Rome I Regulation.[37] This Regulation allows the parties to choose the applicable law, but also provides rules for situations where the parties have not exercised this choice (Articles 3 and 4). However, any questions of third-party effectiveness in connection with a donation should be covered by a 'proprietary' conflict rule. As explained in the 'Ownership' section (5.1) above, it is currently unclear under Finnish law what that rule should be.

5.2.2 Consideration for Counter-Performance

Exchanging cryptocurrency as consideration for counter-performance is within the freedom of contract of the parties under Finnish law. While cryptocurrencies are not legal tender, they can be used as contractual means of payment, as discussed in section 2 above.

5.2.3 Sale or Exchange against Cryptocurrency

In a case where 60 Bitcoins are registered in X's wallet and X wants to sell 5 Bitcoins against 10 Ethers, X can legally do so (although this would not make

37 Parliament and Council Regulation (EU) No 593/2008 of 17 June 2008 on the law applicable to contractual obligations (Rome I) [2008] OJ L177/6. See J.D. Lüttringhaus, 'Article 1 Material Scope' in F. Ferrari (ed.), *Concise Commentary on the Rome I Regulation*, 2nd ed., Cambridge University Press, Cambridge 2020, p. 24, where donation is regarded as a bilateral contract in which 'the duty to perform lies solely on one party'.

economic sense at current market values, and the legal implications of X's potential error might have to be considered). It is likely that the Sale of Goods Act (355/1987) would provide default rules on the parties' rights and obligations, either directly applied or as expressions of general principles. The transaction could be classified as either sale or exchange, both of which fall within the scope of the Sale of Goods Act, provided that the object is 'movable property' (section 1(1) and (2)).

The transaction is binding between X and the other party based on mere contract, regardless of whether X holds the Bitcoins directly or with an intermediary. In the latter case, X should notify the intermediary of the transaction to fulfil X's obligation towards the other party.[38]

In terms of private international law, sale and exchange of cryptocurrency against cryptocurrency appear to be contracts covered by the Rome I Regulation (see Articles 3 and 4). However, any questions of third-party effectiveness in connection with a sale or an exchange should be covered by a 'proprietary' conflict rule. As explained in the 'Ownership' section (5.1) above, it is currently unclear under Finnish law what that rule should be.

5.2.4 Sale against Legal Tender

In a case where 60 Bitcoins are registered in X's wallet and X wants to sell 5 Bitcoins against a legal tender, X can legally do so. The remarks above on the Sale of Goods Act are relevant here as well. The transaction would be classified as a sale. The remarks above on X holding the Bitcoins with an intermediary apply here, too.

Like sale and exchange of cryptocurrency against cryptocurrency, sale of cryptocurrency against legal tender appears to be a contract covered by the Rome I Regulation. Accordingly, the remarks on private international law in section 5.2.3 above should apply here as well.

5.3 *Inheritance*

Cryptocurrencies can be inherited and acquired by will under Finnish law. No cryptocurrency-specific rules exist, but the general rules of the Inheritance Code (40/1965) apply, since the concept of property in the Code is extensive.

In a case where 60 Bitcoins are registered in X's wallet and X wants to make a will to ensure the passing of the value of the wallet to X's child Y, X can do so by testament (will) under the Inheritance Code.[39] Chapter 10 of the Code sets

38 Third-party effectiveness of the transaction should be assessed as a separate matter.

39 If Y is X's only child, then Y will inherit the Bitcoins even without a will, in line with the order of succession in ch. 2 of the Inheritance Code.

certain formalities that X has to follow to that end. As a starting point, a testament must be made in writing in the simultaneous presence of two witnesses. The Inheritance Code applies similarly regardless of whether X holds the Bitcoins directly or with an intermediary. However, holding the Bitcoins with an intermediary could facilitate Y's access to them. The person who has inherited the Bitcoins is entitled to the private key, and the rights that the deceased had towards the intermediary pass to the heir. If X holds the Bitcoins directly, then X, as the testator, should see to it that practical arrangements are made through which the private key is passed to Y, the heir (and preferably no-one else, although using a trusted middleman is one possible solution).

The general rules on succession in the Inheritance Code apply both in the existence and the absence of a will. Chapter 26 of the Code contains private international law rules, but they apply only if not provided otherwise in the EU Succession Regulation,[40] another act, or an international convention binding on Finland (chapter 26, section 20).

5.4 *Trust*

Trusts cannot be created under Finnish law, at least not in a similar sense as in common law systems. Trust has no direct equivalent among the institutions of Finnish private law. In a case where 60 Bitcoins are registered in X's wallet and X wants to create a trust over the 60 Bitcoins for the benefit of Y, this is generally not possible if Finnish law applies, regardless of whether X holds the Bitcoins directly or with an intermediary. However, some of the legal effects typical of trusts may be achievable by institutions and dispositions available under Finnish law.

Finnish private international law on trusts is unclear.[41] In legal literature, it has been proposed that the law governing the validity of trusts created in a will should be sought from the private international law of inheritance, and the validity of *inter vivos* (or 'living') trusts from the private international law of obligations (in particular, of contracts). The mere fact that trust is an institution unknown to Finnish law has not been regarded as a reason to reject application of foreign law to trusts created abroad due to *ordre public*.[42]

40 Parliament and Council Regulation (EU) No 650/2012 of 4 July 2012 on jurisdiction, applicable law, recognition and enforcement of decisions and acceptance and enforcement of authentic instruments in matters of succession and on the creation of a European Certificate of Succession [2012] OJ L201/107.

41 Finland is not party to the Convention of 1 July 1985 on the Law Applicable to Trusts and on Their Recognition (the Hague Trust Convention).

42 T. Mikkola, 'Trust-instituutio: lainvalintaan ja tunnustamiseen liittyviä näkökohtia' [2002] *Edilex* 1, 10–12.

As for determining the effects of a foreign trust in Finland, a 'comparative method' has been proposed. This would involve investigating the settlor's intentions to discern the purpose of the trust, and then providing the trust with corresponding effects to the extent possible, but without infringing the mandatory provisions of Finnish law. Solutions could be sought from fiduciary obligations, different types of will, agency, and contracts for the benefit of a third party, *stipulatio alteri*. In short, a foreign trust would not be recognised as is, with all its original characteristics but, rather, by adapting it to domestic law. In particular, the effects on insolvency typical of trusts may not be possible in such an adaptation.[43]

5.5 *Enforcement of Debt and Distraint*

Under Finnish law, a debtor's assets can be distrained (attached) and realised by an enforcement officer to enforce a debt under the Enforcement Code (705/2007). As a rule, a creditor must have a receivable established by a court order or judgment to apply for enforcement from the Enforcement Authority.[44] Chapter 4, section 8 of the Enforcement Code states that distraint (attachment) may concern a thing or right belonging to the debtor which can be specified and has economic value, unless distraint of the type of property in question is specifically prohibited by law. This provision is intended to express that, as a starting point, any type of property can be subject to distraint.[45] Therefore, cryptocurrencies, too, can be distrained.

In a case where 60 Bitcoins are registered in X's wallet and a creditor of X wants to assert a claim to the Bitcoins to satisfy X's debt, the creditor may apply for enforcement, as described above. However, X's property would be distrained as part of the enforcement in the order prescribed in chapter 4, sections 24 and 25 of the Enforcement Code, so the distraint could concern X's property other than the Bitcoins.

Finding a debtor's cryptocurrencies and getting access to them may cause practical difficulties in enforcement and distraint. Some solutions offered by the Enforcement Code are found in chapter 3, sections 52 to 63 on the debtor's duty to provide information and chapter 3, sections 64 to 68 on the duty of third parties and authorities to provide information. Where cryptocurrency is held with an intermediary, access can be facilitated by imposing a prohibition

---

43 Ibid., 18–21.

44 See generally, National Enforcement Authority Finland, https://www.ulosottolaitos.fi/en/index.html.

45 Government proposal HE 13/2005, p. 42.

on payments under chapter 4, section 27. Successful distraint of directly held cryptocurrency depends more on the debtor's cooperation.

The Finnish State Treasury has issued guidelines on the treatment of virtual currencies in state agencies and the like units. The most typical situations they cover are supposed to relate to enforcement (distraint) and criminal investigations. The guidelines deal with treatment of virtual currencies in accounting, liability for damages, and the way in which virtual currencies should be held and realised. As for holding, the guidelines recommend off-line wallets instead of relying on third-party service providers or 'exchange services'. Where realisation is needed, public auction is the preferred method.[46]

The Enforcement Code or other Finnish legislation contains no provisions on the international jurisdiction of enforcement officers.[47] In practice, a creditor who is otherwise entitled to apply for enforcement can have enforcement proceedings commenced by informing the Enforcement Authority that the debtor may reside or have property located in Finland. An enforcement officer may only distrain property located in Finland, which gives rise to the question where intangible property should be regarded as being located. It is suggested in legal literature that an enforcement officer can apply the asset location rules of the EU Insolvency Regulation for this purpose, even though the Enforcement Code makes no reference to those rules.[48] They do not address cryptocurrencies or similar assets, but they could perhaps support solutions developed for locating cryptocurrencies held with an intermediary.[49] While defining the location of cryptocurrencies appears problematic, we are not aware of related issues having arisen in enforcement practice.[50]

46 Valtiokonttori, Virtuaalivaluuttojen käsittely kirjanpitoyksiköissä, Ohje 19.02.2018, https://vkazprodwordpressstacc01.blob.core.windows.net/wordpress/uploads/sites/4/2019/03/95443.pdf.

47 On the application of the Enforcement Code on certain other than purely domestic enforcement proceedings, see ch. 1, s. 2.

48 R. Koulu, H. Lindfors and J. Niemi, *Insolvenssioikeus*, continuously updated online book based on 4th ed. of the printed version, Alma Talent, Helsinki, chapter III, section 3, subsections 'Toimivaltainen ulosottomies' > 'Vastaavan ulosottomiehen määräytyminen' > 'Kansainvälinen toimivalta' (cited text by R. Koulu, updated 2020). See Parliament and Council Regulation (EU) 2015/848 of 20 May 2015 on insolvency proceedings (recast) [2015] OJ L141/19, Art. 2(9).

49 See Art. 2(9)(II), (III) and (VIII).

50 E.g., Finnish Supreme Court decision KKO 2020:64 shows that cryptocurrencies have been distrained in Finland. See section 7 below.

5.6 *Insolvency*

In the following, we discuss bankruptcy, that is, collective liquidation-type insolvency proceedings. The relevant rules are found in the Bankruptcy Act (120/2004).[51]

In a case where X has opened an account with MontC and has 60 Bitcoins registered in that account, and where MontC then becomes insolvent and its bankruptcy proceedings begin, X can bring a claim in the proceedings in respect of the Bitcoins. It is possible that X is merely in the position of an unsecured creditor in respect of the Bitcoins, but it is also possible that the Bitcoins are X's property, so that they do not belong to MontC's bankruptcy estate and have to be returned to X under chapter 5, section 6 of the Bankruptcy Act. In other words, X can have a personal or a proprietary claim in respect of the Bitcoins.

For X to have a proprietary claim (and to have the Bitcoins returned), the contract between X and MontC must stipulate that X owns the Bitcoins or that MontC holds them on behalf of X. Additionally, it must be possible to separate X's Bitcoins (or clients' Bitcoins, 60 of which belong to X) from Bitcoins that belong to MontC. This requirement is based on chapter 5, section 6 of the Bankruptcy Act, according to which property of a third party does not belong to the bankruptcy estate insofar as it can be separated from the debtor's property. When fungible objects (such as Bitcoins) mix with other similar objects, they cannot, as a rule, be separated in the sense of chapter 5, section 6 of the Bankruptcy Act. We believe this to mean that X can have a proprietary claim in respect of the 60 Bitcoins only if those Bitcoins (or clients' Bitcoins as a whole) have been held in an address or addresses different from those in which MontC has kept its own Bitcoins.[52] In contrast, X should not lose the proprietary claim on the basis that the 60 Bitcoins have mixed with MontC's other

---

51 Finnish law also provides for collective rehabilitation-type insolvency proceedings. See the Restructuring of Enterprise Act (47/1993) and the Act on the Adjustment of the Debts of a Private Individual (57/1993).

52 See Finnish Supreme Court decision KKO 2020:64, paras 10–14. It could also be argued, based on the Supreme Court's recent decisions in embezzlement cases, that (pre-bankrupt) MontC would acquire ownership of X's Bitcoins immediately if X's Bitcoins are mixed with MontC's Bitcoins. See decisions KKO 2022:46, para. 11; KKO 2021:36, para. 21; KKO 2020:51, para. 23. If this argument holds true, Bitcoins that initially belong to X and become MontC's property as a result of mixing belong to MontC's bankruptcy estate, not because they cannot be separated from the debtor's property (ch. 5, s. 6 of the Bankruptcy Act), but because they are the debtor's property and as such belong to the debtor's bankruptcy estate under the general rule of ch. 5, s. 1 of the Bankruptcy Act. See generally, J. Kaisto and E. Paukku, 'Virtuaalivaluutat, niihin liittyvät palvelut ja asiakasvarojen säilyttäminen' [3/2022] *Liikejuridiikka* 8, 16–20.

clients' Bitcoins, since chapter 5, section 6 of the Bankruptcy Act only requires separability from the debtor's property.

In addition to what has been said above, X's proprietary claim may be at risk if the agreement between X and MontC gives MontC competences that typically only belong to the owner. This could be the case, for example, if MontC has been permitted to dispose of the 60 Bitcoins on the condition that it will replace them with another 60 Bitcoins by an agreed date.

In a case where company Z has opened an account with MontC as it accepts payments in different cryptocurrencies, and where Z then becomes insolvent with a wallet worth USD 200,000 in different cryptocurrencies, those cryptocurrencies belong to Z's bankruptcy estate under the Bankruptcy Act. The Act on the Ranking of Claims (1578/1992) states that the starting point is *pari passu* (section 2), but also lays down exceptions thereto. For example, section 3 deals with the priority afforded to the holders of a right of pledge or a right of retention.

As regards the relevance of the specific terms of the agreement between Z and MontC in relation to creditors' claims, it is possible that the agreement as a whole is such that MontC owes the cryptocurrencies to Z, so that Z's bankruptcy estate now has (personal) claims in those cryptocurrencies. This would give rise to different kinds of questions, including on MontC's potential right of set-off.

Coordination of cross-border insolvency requires a large number of private international law rules. In the case of Finland, these are found in the EU Insolvency Regulation (see especially Article 7 on the applicable law) and in the Nordic Bankruptcy Convention.[53] No cryptocurrency-specific rules exist.

5.7 *Security*

Cryptocurrencies can be pledged under Finnish law. Property is generally capable of being pledged if it can be specified (is a specific object or can be made one) and is transferable, so that realisation by sale is possible if needed.[54] The Finnish law of security distinguishes between creation of a right of pledge in property (pledging the property) and achieving effectiveness against third parties, especially the pledgor's other creditors. Creation occurs by an agreement

53 Convention between Denmark, Finland, Norway, Sweden and Iceland on Bankruptcy, signed at Copenhagen on 7 November 1933 (revised subsequently). On the relationship between the Convention and the Insolvency Regulation, see Art. 85(1)(j) of the latter. See also Bankruptcy Act, ch. 7, s. 1.

54 J. Tepora, J. Kaisto and E. Hakkola, *Esinevakuudet*, 2nd ed., Kauppakamari, Helsinki 2016, pp. 55–56.

between the pledgor and the pledgee or a unilateral disposition by the pledgor to the pledgee.[55] As a rule, third-party effectiveness requires a further step in the name of publicity, although its actual effect in terms of publicity may often be rather limited. The main options for a publicity measure are dispossessing the pledgor of the pledged object, notifying a certain person (such as a third party in possession of the pledged object) of the pledge, and registration. The publicity measure required depends on the pledged object and, sometimes, on the situation.[56]

Creation of a right of pledge in cryptocurrency seems unproblematic. For example, all cryptocurrency units in a certain cryptocurrency address can be regarded as a specific object for this purpose, and cryptocurrencies are generally transferable, as discussed in section 5.2 above.

The question of publicity measures needed for third-party effectiveness is somewhat more difficult. Considering the purposes and effects of the above-mentioned main options, we suggest that third-party effectiveness should be achievable by any measure that prevents the pledgor from independently controlling and disposing of the pledged cryptocurrency units. One way to do this would be to transfer the cryptocurrency units to the pledgee's cryptocurrency address, whose private key is unknown to the pledgor.[57] This address should be empty before transfer, so that the pledgor's cryptocurrency units will not get mixed with those of the pledgee and lose their specificity. Some support for this 'transfer solution' can be drawn from sections 10 and 22 of the Promissory Notes Act (622/1947), according to which a pledge of a negotiable promissory note is ineffective against the pledgor's creditors if the pledgee has not taken possession of the promissory note. Theoretically, it might even be sufficient that the pledgor merely gives the private key to the pledgee and destroys the pledgor's own copy of it, but the question would arise how credible it is that the pledgor no longer knows the private key.

In situations where pledged cryptocurrency units are held with an intermediary, third-party effectiveness should be achievable by notifying the intermediary of the pledge, provided that the intermediary is independent of the pledgor and has not allowed the pledgor's cryptocurrency units to get mixed with its own. In turn, if the pledgor only has a personal claim in cryptocurrency units owned by an intermediary, so that the object of the pledge is that claim rather than the cryptocurrency units, then third-party effectiveness should be

55 Ibid., pp. 82–88.

56 Ibid., pp. 47–53.

57 Another way could involve the use of a multisignature ('multisig') wallet.

achievable by notifying the intermediary (Promissory Notes Act, sections 10 and 31(1)).

In a case where company Z, which has its seat in Finland, has agreed to pledge 30 Bitcoins registered in its wallet to a creditor financing a specific project, Z's options to do so should be assessed in the light of the discussion above. While the state of the law is somewhat unclear, Z should be able to pledge the Bitcoins as agreed, with or without an intermediary keeping the wallet.

Another way to utilise cryptocurrency as security for debt is by way of enterprise mortgage under the Enterprise Mortgage Act (634/1984). In an enterprise mortgage, unlike in a pledge, cryptocurrency units are not used as individual and immediate objects of security. Instead, an enterprise mortgage forms a 'floating security' over, with certain exceptions, the entire movable property of an enterprise (that is, a trader recorded in the Trade Register).[58] The types of mortgageable property are listed in section 3 of the Enterprise Mortgage Act. While the list makes no specific reference to cryptocurrencies, one of its asset categories is 'cash, receivables, securities, book entries, and other financial assets'. It seems clear that 'other financial assets' should be interpreted as inclusive of cryptocurrencies.

For private international law purposes, contractual questions must be distinguished from proprietary questions. Contractual questions, that is, those between a security provider and a secured creditor, are covered by the Rome I Regulation (see Articles 3 and 4). In turn, proprietary questions should be covered by a 'proprietary' conflict rule. However, as explained in the 'Ownership' section (5.1) above, it is currently unclear under Finnish law what that rule should be. Whatever the rule will be, it is supposed to cover the creation of security rights (as a proprietary rather than a contractual matter) and third-party effectiveness of security rights.

5.8 *'Lending'*

In a case where a Finnish company Z intends to borrow 60 Bitcoins from PayB, a company regulated and supervised in its home jurisdiction to provide lending services, at an interest rate of 5 per cent payable either in a legal tender or in Bitcoins, Z and PayB can legally do so. This contract would most likely be characterised as consisting of a full transfer of ownership in the 60 Bitcoins and an obligation to transfer back the same amount (or an agreed larger amount, to include interest) of Bitcoins at an agreed time. In other words, Z would be free to dispose of the originally transferred Bitcoins, while the return obligation

58 See generally, Finnish Patent and Registration Office, https://www.prh.fi/en/yrityskiinnityk set/yleista.html.

(that is, the obligation to transfer back) would not concern exactly the same Bitcoin units. Of course, nothing would prevent Z and PayB from agreeing that the return obligation concerns the originally transferred Bitcoins, rather than any Bitcoin units, but it is difficult to see what purpose this would serve.

The law applicable to these transactions, as between Z and PayB, would be determined by applying the Rome I Regulation (see Articles 3 and 4). In contrast, any questions of third-party effectiveness in connection with the transactions call for a 'proprietary' conflict rule. As explained in the 'Ownership' section (5.1) above, it is currently unclear under Finnish law what that rule should be.

PayB's activities do not qualify PayB as a virtual currency provider under the Act on Virtual Currency Providers.[59] Providing services merely in the shape of the transactions described above does not seem to require PayB to acquire a licence or other authorisation. However, PayB's activities as a whole may be subject to that requirement. In particular, they may fall within the scope of the Act on Credit Institutions (610/2014), which requires authorisation.[60]

In a case where Z intends to borrow 60 Bitcoins from PayB, at an interest rate of 5 per cent payable in Bitcoins, Z could repay its loan in Bitcoin Cash instead of Bitcoins only if Z and PayB have so agreed. Regardless of their common origin, Bitcoin and Bitcoin Cash are two different cryptocurrencies, with both technical and economic differences. Therefore, they cannot be regarded as interchangeable as means of performing a contract. It seems irrelevant in this respect whether the fork that resulted in Bitcoin Cash took place before or after the initial transfer of Bitcoins.[61]

5.9 *Compensation by Way of Damages for Loss, Good Faith Acquisition etc.*

Loss of cryptocurrencies – for example through hacking or fraud – may give rise under Finnish law to liability for damages, and to the right to bring an action for damages. The relevant legal norms differ between situations within and outside of a contractual relationship, that is, between contractual and non-contractual situations.

59 See s. 2(1)(2) of the Act.

60 See chs 1–2 of the Act. On activities of foreign credit institutions in Finland, see chs 16–19.

61 This is not to say that a fork could not pose difficult questions in terms of contractual obligations, e.g., in a situation where the value of the original cryptocurrency changes so dramatically that the purpose of the contract is threatened. Contracts Act (228/1929), s. 36, on the adjustment of contracts, might become relevant in such situations.

In a case where X has opened an account with MontC and 60 Bitcoins are registered in X's wallet until MontC's IT systems are hacked and X loses all 60 Bitcoins, MontC's potential liability to X is of a contractual nature and the (identified) hacker's potential liability to X is of a non-contractual nature.

Assessment of contractual liability follows general principles of contract law. The starting point is what X and MontC have agreed. If they have agreed on limiting (or excluding) MontC's liability for loss of cryptocurrency, then as a rule that limitation applies unless MontC has caused the loss intentionally or through gross negligence. If no such limitation has been agreed, then MontC's liability would probably be assessed as 'exculpatory', meaning that liability for negligence is presumed, but MontC may rebut that presumption by furnishing proof to the contrary.[62]

Assessment of non-contractual liability follows the Tort Liability Act (412/1974) and may have to be done unless the lost Bitcoins are recovered, say, in the course of criminal investigation. Under chapter 5, section 1 of the Act, the loss in question would be treated as so-called 'pure economic loss', that is, economic loss unconnected with personal injury or damage to property (here, 'property' refers to physical objects or 'things'). This kind of damage is compensated if due to an act punishable by law or caused in the exercise of public authority, or in other cases where particularly weighty reasons are present. Hacker's liability could most probably be based either on damage being due to a punishable act or on the presence of particularly weighty reasons.

If the hacker has sold the Bitcoins to third party Y, it is possible that Y is protected as a good faith purchaser and may keep the Bitcoins. The conditions for protection are that Y received the Bitcoins in a way comparable to transfer of possession of a physical object (so that the hacker is no longer capable of independently disposing of the Bitcoins) and that Y was in well-founded good faith at the time of receipt. Here, well-founded good faith means that Y neither knew nor ought to have known that the seller lacked competence to transfer ownership of the Bitcoins due to the absence of legal acquisition. These conditions for protection are based on analogous application of section 14 of the Promissory Notes Act (622/1947), which deals with good faith acquisition. Section 14 applies directly to negotiable promissory notes, but it is applied through statutory reference, for example, to share certificates,[63] and by way of analogy, for example, to banknotes and coins (legal tender), and funds in bank accounts. The characteristics of cryptocurrencies seem similar enough to these

62 This is based on general principles of contract law. Consumer law may include more specific rules.

63 Limited Liability Companies Act (624/2006), ch. 3, s. 13.

assets (especially to funds in bank accounts) to justify extending the analogous application of section 14 to cryptocurrencies.[64] Alternatively, analogy could be based on section 27 of the Act on Book-Entry Accounts (827/1991), which also deals with good faith acquisition. Finally, it should be noted that a situation where hacked Bitcoins are mixed with other Bitcoins held by the hacker would give rise to difficult and thus far unanswered legal questions.

In a case where X voluntarily – but as a result of fraudulent promises or persuasion – transfers the Bitcoins to an address indicated by the fraudulent party, who then spends the Bitcoins for purposes other than those agreed with X, then the initial transfer by X is most likely ineffective as a matter of law. This results from the Contracts Act (228/1929), section 30, on fraudulent inducement. The fraudulent party's liability for damages would be assessed similarly to hacker's liability as noted above, that is, by applying the Tort Liability Act, chapter 5, section 1, on pure economic loss. A potential third-party transferee's position would also be assessed similarly as noted above. Indeed, where the Promissory Notes Act, section 14 (or the Act on Book-Entry Accounts, section 27) applies, good faith acquisition is possible regardless of the specific reason for the transferor's lack of competence to transfer ownership.

As for private international law, the applicable law would be determined by interpreting the Rome I Regulation as regards contractual liability (X v. MontC),[65] and the Rome II Regulation as regards non-contractual liability (X v. hacker or the fraudulent party, assuming that the transfer is ineffective).[66] The question of good faith protection (X v. Y or the fraudulent party's transferee) concerns property law and calls for a 'proprietary' conflict rule. As explained in the 'Ownership' section (5.1) above, it is currently unclear under Finnish law what that rule should be.

6 Tax Measures

Tax law applies to cryptocurrencies, cryptocurrency-related services, and cryptocurrency-originated value in Finland. The Finnish Tax Administration has issued a detailed guide on taxation of virtual currencies. The guide covers

64 In the case of ordinary tangible movables, the conditions for protection as a good faith purchaser are tighter. E.g., protection is excluded if the object in question is obtained from its rightful owner by theft or certain other criminal acts. See Trade Code (3/1734), ch. 11, s. 4, and ch. 12, s. 4; Decree on the Entry into Force of the Penal Code (39B/1889), s. 11.

65 See Arts 3, 4, and 12(1)(c).

66 Parliament and Council Regulation (EU) No 864/2007 of 11 July 2007 on the law applicable to non-contractual obligations (Rome II) [2007] OJ L199/40. See Art. 4.

treatment of virtual currencies in individual income taxation, business and corporate taxation, and value-added taxation.[67]

The leading case on taxation of virtual currencies is Supreme Administrative Court decision KHO 2019:42. Under this decision, virtual currencies are treated as assets referred to in section 45(1) of the Income Tax Act (1535/1992).[68] This means that the rules on capital gains apply to various kinds of transactions involving virtual currency positions. Deductions can be made in the case of a capital loss (section 50(1)), and small capital gains are granted exemption from capital gain tax (section 48(6)).[69]

Since virtual currency units held by a taxpayer are regarded as assets, and not as means of payment, any spending or use of the units results in assessment of taxes. All increases or decreases in the value of a virtual currency position (for example, resulting from selling for a legally established currency, spending to pay for goods or services, or exchanging for another virtual currency) are taxable separately. Acquisition of new virtual currency units through mining is regarded as earned income, and through staking as capital gain.[70]

Under Finnish law, taxable income is calculated by source, namely, business, agriculture, or other activities. Each of the three sources has their own act, each differing from each other in terms of tax treatment (in particular, deductibility of losses). Depending on the circumstances, any of these sources may be relevant in the case of virtual currencies.[71]

The above-mentioned interpretation of virtual currencies as assets for the purposes of income taxation differs from earlier European and national case law on value-added taxation, where virtual currencies are regarded as

67 Verohallinto, Virtuaalivaluuttojen verotus (22.01.2020, VH/5083/00.01.00/2019), https://www.vero.fi/syventavat-vero-ohjeet/ohje-hakusivu/48411/virtuaalivaluuttojen-verotus3/. An unofficial English translation available at https://www.vero.fi/en/detailed-guidance/guidance/48411/taxation-of-virtual-currencies3/.

68 The case concerned a taxpayer's plan to sell Ether units for legally established currency. Apparently, the main question for the taxpayer was whether the calculation rules on capital gains in s. 46(1) of the Income Tax Act apply. The Supreme Administrative Court ruled in the affirmative.

69 Verohallinto, Virtuaalivaluuttojen verotus (22.01.2020, VH/5083/00.01.00/2019), https://www.vero.fi/syventavat-vero-ohjeet/ohje-hakusivu/48411/virtuaalivaluuttojen-verotus3/, 1.2.

70 Ibid., 1.2, 2.5. Cf. K. Keskitalo, 'Virtuaalivaluutan louhiminen: ansio- vai pääomatuloa?' [2022] *Edilex* 1. Keskitalo argues that mining (proof-of-work consensus algorithm) should also be treated as generating capital gain.

71 Verohallinto, Virtuaalivaluuttojen verotus (22.01.2020, VH/5083/00.01.00/2019), https://www.vero.fi/syventavat-vero-ohjeet/ohje-hakusivu/48411/virtuaalivaluuttojen-verotus3/, 1.2.

(contractual) means of payment.[72] The Supreme Administrative Court justified this difference in decision KHO 2019:42, noting that income taxation remains a matter of national law and, unlike value-added taxation, is not harmonised in the European Union.[73]

7 Litigation etc.

We are not aware of concluded or ongoing court proceedings in relation to cryptocurrencies, except for decisions KKO 2020:64 and KHO 2019:42 (and the relevant lower instance decisions) mentioned in sections 2 and 6 above.

The proceedings that resulted in decision KKO 2020:64 started from an appeal by A against distraint (attachment) of Bitcoins.[74] Under an agreement between A and B, B had bought Bitcoins with money provided for that purpose by A and had held those Bitcoins on A's behalf in an account belonging to and controlled by B at a service provider company. The Supreme Court ruled that the Bitcoins on that account could be distrained to repay B's debts, the reason for this being that the Bitcoins bought and held on behalf of A had mixed with B's own Bitcoins in the same account. The Supreme Court reviewed its earlier case law on treatment of mixed funds in a bank account and held that distraint of Bitcoins in an account maintained by a service provider follows the same principles as distraint of funds in a bank account.[75] In turn, the proceedings that resulted in decision KHO 2019:42 started from a taxpayer's request for a Central Tax Board advance ruling on the tax treatment of a (planned) sale of Ether units. The gist of the case is explained in section 6 above.

We are not aware of any arbitration proceedings in relation to cryptocurrencies.

---

72 Case C-264/14, *Skatteverket v. David Hedqvist*, ECLI:EU:C:2015:718; Central Tax Board (Finland) decision KVL 2014/34 (legally binding). In these cases, virtual currency transactions were held exempt from value added tax.

73 S. 2.3 of the decision. See Verohallinto, Virtuaalivaluuttojen verotus (22.01.2020, VH/5083/00.01.00/2019), https://www.vero.fi/syventavat-vero-ohjeet/ohje-hakusivu/48411/virtuaalivaluuttojen-verotus3/, 4.1–4.3.

74 The case description of the Supreme Court leaves it unclear what the immediate object of distraint was, i.e., whether it was Bitcoin units in a certain address or rather the service provider's Bitcoin debt to its client. While the case description refers to 'distraint of Bitcoins' (suggesting that Bitcoins were the immediate object of distraint), the client's account-related rights are not described. See J. Kaisto and E. Paukku, 'Virtuaalivaluutat, niihin liittyvät palvelut ja asiakasvarojen säilyttäminen' [3/2022] *Liikejuridiikka* 8, 15, 18.

75 Paras 14, 19, 22–23.

No cryptocurrency-specific or cryptocurrency service-specific actions exist under Finnish law. However, it seems possible that some cryptocurrency service-related cases could be brought as class actions under the Class Actions Act (444/2007). This Act applies, 'within the limits of the competence of the Consumer Ombudsman, to the hearing of a civil case between a consumer and a business as a class action' (section 1(1)). No cryptocurrency-specific heads of jurisdiction exist under Finnish law.

Recognition and enforcement of foreign decisions in Finland is based on conventions, such as Lugano II,[76] or European Union regulations, such as Brussels Ia.[77] As for arbitral awards, Finland is party to the New York Convention.[78] The relevant conventions and regulations contain no cryptocurrency-related or cryptocurrency service-related provisions. The mere fact that a decision or an arbitral award deals with cryptocurrencies or cryptocurrency services should not give rise to any questions with respect to their application. Accordingly, it is difficult to think of the public policy exception playing any role.

8 Environmental Issues

Awareness is rising on the excessive energy consumption and environmental impact of cryptocurrencies utilising the proof-of-work consensus mechanism. This can be illustrated by a leader of 30 January 2022 in *Helsingin Sanomat*, Finland's largest subscription newspaper, whose title translates as 'Cryptocurrencies would deserve the same reputational damage as other climate-warming activities'. The leader describes the energy consumption of proof of work as 'insane', while 'not aimed at meeting the basic needs of society in the same way as, for example, in industry, transport, or, say, heating homes'. It also suggests that the European Union should move towards banning the most energy-intensive mining of cryptocurrencies.[79]

76 Convention on jurisdiction and the recognition and enforcement of judgments in civil and commercial matters [2007] OJ L339/3.

77 Parliament and Council Regulation (EU) No 1215/2012 of 12 December 2012 on jurisdiction and the recognition and enforcement of judgments in civil and commercial matters [2012] OJ L351/1.

78 United Nations Convention on the Recognition and Enforcement of Foreign Arbitral Awards (New York, 10 June 1958). The domestic rules are included in the Act on Arbitration (967/1992), ss. 51–55.

79 'Kryptovaluutat ansaitsisivat sen mainehaitan, jonka muukin ilmastoa kuumentava toiminta saa', *Helsingin Sanomat* (30.01.2022), https://www.hs.fi/paakirjoitukset/art-2000008550464.html.

9 Publications Relating to the Laws and Regulation of Cryptocurrencies

Grym, A., 'The great illusion of digital currencies', *BoF (Bank of Finland) Economics Review* 1/2018.

Kaisto, J., 'Älykoodi lakina – vai ei sittenkään?' (2020) 118 *Lakimies* 993.

Kaisto, J. and Paukku, E., 'Virtuaalivaluutat, niihin liittyvät palvelut ja asiakasvarojen säilyttäminen' [3/2022] *Liikejuridiikka* 8.

Keskitalo, K., Suomen rahan sääntelyn historia – raha oikeudellisena maksuvälineenä ennen ja nyt, Doctoral thesis, University of Helsinki 2022.

Keskitalo, K., 'Virtuaalivaluutan louhiminen: ansio – vai pääomatuloa?' [2022] *Edilex* 1.

Keskitalo, K. and Väyrynen, J., 'Virtuaalivaluutan tarjoajan asiakkaan tuntemisvelvollisuus – liikkeellelaskijaa koskevat erityiskysymykset' [3/2022] *Liikejuridiikka* 45.

Mattila, J. (ed.), Seppälä, T., Hukkinen, T., Laikari, A., Markkanen, K., Koulu, R. and Jia K., 'Lohkoketjuteknologian hyödyntämismahdollisuudet palkkatulojen verotuksessa', *Valtioneuvoston selvitys – ja tutkimustoiminnan julkaisusarja* 2019:30.

Rahkola, M., 'Katsaus lohkoketjuteknologioiden hyödyntämiseen Suomessa: Raportti tulevaisuusvaliokunnalle', *Eduskunnan tulevaisuusvaliokunnan julkaisu* 1/2019.

France

Hubert de Vauplane

Le droit français en matière d'actifs numériques est en évolution constante. Alors que les premières dispositions législatives datent de 2016, l'entrée en vigueur du Règlement européen MiCA[1] conduit à une refonte assez substantielle des différentes lois existantes, que ce soit pour supprimer des parties entières de la règlementation remplacée par le Règlement MiCA ou pour adapter à ce Règlement certaines dispositions de droit français, ou encore pour créer un régime nouveau en matière de transfert de propriété des crypto-actifs.

A l'heure où ce rapport a été rédigé[2], le projet d'ordonnance devant effectuer toutes ces modifications était en cours d'élaboration. Ce projet s'inspire toutefois assez largement du rapport publié par le Haut Comité Juridique de la Place de Paris[3]. Le présent chapitre mentionne les éléments les plus significatifs de ce rapport qui ont un impact sur le contenu des développements qui suivent.

1 La genèse du régime de la loi pacte

L'introduction au sein du système juridique français de dispositions relatives aux nouvelles technologies liées à la blockchain s'est faite progressivement mais assez tôt.

L'ordonnance n°2016-520 du 28 avril 2016 relative aux bons de caisse introduit, via son article 2, un article L. 223-13 du Code monétaire et financier ouvrant la possibilité d'inscrire l'émission et la cession de « minibons » (des titres de créances négociables) dans un dispositif d'enregistrement électronique partagé (expression française utilisée dans la loi pour faire référence à des systèmes de DLT ou blockchain) permettant l'authentification de ces opérations.

1 Règlement (UE) 2023/1114 du Parlement européen et du Conseil du 31 mai 2023 sur les marchés de crypto-actifs, JOUE L.150/40, 9 juin 2023

2 LE rapport a été rédigé au quatrième trimestre 2023 et à intégré en Mai 2024 les dispositions du projet d'ordonannce relative à l'adaptation du droit français au Règlement MiCA.

3 HCJP, Rapport sur le Règlement MiCA, 27 janvier 2024: https://www.banque-france.fr/fr/system/files/2024-03/Rapport_61_F.pdf.

 | DOI:10.1163/9789004722507_012

Depuis lors, le législateur français a considérablement agrémenté le corpus de ses textes juridiques qui appréhendent la technologie blockchain :

- l'ordonnance n° 2017-1674 du 8 décembre 2017 relative à l'utilisation d'un dispositif d'enregistrement électronique partagé pour la représentation et la transmission de titres financiers ;
- le décret n°2018-1216 du 24 décembre 2018 relatif à l'utilisation d'un dispositif d'enregistrement électronique partagé pour la représentation et la transmission de titres financiers et pour l'émission et la cession de minibons ; et enfin
- la loi n°2019-486 du 22 mai 2019 relative à la croissance et la transformation des entreprises, dite loi PACTE.

La loi PACTE a consacré en droit français une nouvelle catégorie de biens, d'acteurs réglementés et d'opérations financières autour des problématiques juridiques liées au DLT. Cette loi souligne l'implication et la volonté du législateur français dans la réception de la technologie blockchain et plus largement DLT et ses applications diverses.

Dans ce contexte, la loi PACTE introduit dans le système juridique français une nouvelle catégorie de biens incorporels : les actifs numériques. Puis, elle fixe un régime *sui generis* pour les offres au public de jetons (ou *initial coin offerings*, ICO). Enfin, elle instaure une nouvelle catégorie d'acteurs réglementés que sont les prestataires de services sur actifs numériques (PSAN).

Cette loi aura vocation à être remplacée par le futur règlement européen sur le marché des crypto-actifs (MiCA)[4].

1.1 *Actifs numériques*

La loi PACTE a introduit un régime juridique applicable aux « crypto-actifs », qualifiés d'actifs numériques. Cette consécration de la notion d'actif numérique résout avant tout une difficulté terminologique. En effet, la pratique avait tendance à utiliser le terme de jetons pour la majeure partie des actifs numériques. Ce n'est plus le cas, puisque le terme de jeton fait désormais référence à l'une des catégories d'actifs numériques qui en comportent deux.

La notion d'actifs numériques prévue à l'article L. 54-10-1 du Code monétaire et financier recouvre deux catégories d'actifs : les « monnaies virtuelles » et les jetons.

4 COM(2020) 593 final : https://eur-lex.europa.eu/legal-content/FR/TXT/HTML/?uri=CELEX:52020PC0593&from=FR

1.1.1 Les monnaies virtuelles

Au sein de la loi PACTE, la première catégorie d'actifs numériques consacrée est celle des monnaies virtuelles, qui constitue une catégorie « balais » qui recouvre la majorité des crypto-monnaies tels que bitcoin (BTC) ou l'ether (ETH) par exemple.

L'article L. 54-10-1, 2° du Code monétaire et financier en donne une définition. Il s'agit de « toute représentation numérique d'une valeur qui n'est pas émise ou garantie par une banque centrale ou par une autorité publique, qui n'est nécessairement attachée à une monnaie ayant cours légal et qui ne possède pas le statut juridique d'une monnaie, mais qui est acceptée par des personnes physiques ou morales comme un moyen d'échange et qui peut être transférée, stockée ou échangée électroniquement ». Cet actif est défini de façon apophatique par rapport à la monnaie : elle exclut la qualification de monnaie ayant cours légal. En effet, eu égard à l'article L. 111-1 du Code monétaire et financier, seul l'euro a cours légal en France. Une distinction est donc marquée entre d'une part, les monnaies virtuelles et d'autre part, la monnaie légale, représentée soit sous forme de monnaie fiduciaire, soit sous forme de monnaie scripturale. La monnaie virtuelle se distingue aussi de la monnaie électronique. L'article L. 315-1 du Code monétaire et financier définit la monnaie électronique comme « une valeur monétaire qui est stockée sous une forme électronique, y compris magnétique, représentant une créance sur l'émetteur, qui est émise contre la remise de fonds aux fins d'opérations de paiement, et qui est acceptée par une personne physique ou morale autre que l'émetteur de monnaie électronique ». La monnaie électronique désigne à la fois un mode de paiement et un substitut à la monnaie ayant cours légal, permettant d'effectuer des opérations de paiement en ligne au moyen de cartes virtuelles ou encore de porte monnaies électroniques par exemple.

S'agissant du paiement d'une obligation de sommes d'argent, seul le paiement en euros est libératoire, en application de l'article 1343-3 du Code civil. Il existe deux exceptions à ce principe.

En premier lieu, l'article 1343-3, al. 2 permet au débiteur de de se libérer de sa dette en payant celle-ci en devise « si l'obligation (…) procède d'une opération à caractère international ou d'un jugement étranger. Les parties peuvent convenir que le paiement aura lieu en devise s'il intervient entre professionnels, lorsque l'usage d'une monnaie étrangère est communément admis pour l'opération concernée.". Cette exception est limitée, aux termes de l'article précité, aux paiements en "autre monnaie", c'est à dire en monnaie légale étrangère, ce que l'on appelle une devise. Les monnaies virtuelles visées à l'article L. 54-10-1-2° du code monétaire et financier n'étant pas des monnaies légales sou devises, cette exception ne s'applique pas au cas des actifs numériques.

La seconde exception a trait au mécanisme de la dation en paiement de l'article 1342-4 du Code civil qui permet au créancier d'accepter de recevoir autre chose que la somme d'argent qui lui est due, ce qui ouvre la possibilité à un paiement en actifs numériques libératoire, en substitut à de la monnaie ayant cours légal.

Ainsi, si les monnaies virtuelles ne sont pas des monnaies légales et des devises et s'il, sauf le cas de la dation en paiement, elles ne permettent pas de se libérer de sa dette, elle n'en constitue pas moins « *un moyen d'échange* », comme le dispose l'article L. 54-10-1, 2° du Code monétaire et financier, autorisant les parties à un contrat à prévoir le règlement contractuel de leurs dettes sous forme d'un échange.

Outre la fonction de paiement, les monnaies virtuelles et les jetons ont des fonctions plus larges comme celles de moyens d'échange, de réserve de valeur ou encore d'instrument d'investissement[5]. Le traitement qui leur est réservé par le législateur français et européen, ainsi que les régulateurs, notamment en matière de protection des épargnants, témoigne de ces fonctions.

Ce cadre légal permet la circulation de tous les types de crypto-actifs. Néanmoins, en pratique, il convient de souligner que l'Autorité de contrôle prudentiel et de résolution (ACPR) décourage les prestataires de services sur actifs numériques à fournir des services portant sur des actifs numériques favorisant l'anonymat, tels que Monero ou Zcash, en raison d'un risque de blanchiment de capitaux et de financement du terrorisme élevé.

1.1.1.1 *La jurisprudence relative aux crypto-actifs*

Aucune juridiction française n'a abordé la question de la blockchain et des actifs numériques directement. Cependant, il est possible de souligner que deux affaires importantes ont été rendues en relation avec la technologie blockchain.

Premièrement, au niveau européen, la Cour de justice de l'Union européenne a rendu une décision le 22 octobre 2015[6] concernant l'exonération de la TVA sur les échanges de monnaies fiduciaires traditionnelles contre des bitcoins.

Deuxièmement, au niveau national, le tribunal de commerce de Nanterre dans un jugement du 26 février 2020[7] s'est intéressé à la nature juridique du bitcoin et des prêts qui y sont liés. Tout d'abord, concernant la nature juridique du

5 H. de Vauplane, L'analyse juridique du bitcoin, Association d'économie financière, 5 juill. 2014, p. 351.

6 CJUE, 22 oct. 2015, n° C-264/14, Skatteverket c/ David Hedqvist.

7 Tribunal de commerce de Nanterre, 6ème Chambre, 26 février 2020, n° 2018F00466.

bitcoin, le tribunal a estimé que cet actif numérique est fongible et consomptible. Fongible du fait que chaque bitcoin est de « *même nature et qualité* », en ce sens que les bitcoins sont tous issus du même protocole informatique et qu'ils sont équivalents aux autres bitcoins au sens de l'article 1347-1 du Code civil. Consomptible du fait de son utilisation, en ce que chaque bitcoin est « *consommé* » lors de son utilisation, que ce soit pour payer des biens ou des services, pour échanger de la monnaie légale, ou pour prêter. Le différent exposé devant le tribunal traitant justement de la qualification juridique du contrat de prêt de bitcoin, entre prêt de consommation ou prêt à usage. Le tribunal a considéré qu'il s'agissait d'un prêt de consommation au sens de l'article 1892 du Code civil, conduisant à ce que l'obligation de remboursement se réalise par équivalence, et non pas par remise de la chose originelle prêtée, comme dans un prêt à usage pour un corps certain. S'agissant du traitement des bénéfices attachés aux bitcoins prêtés, le tribunal a jugé que ces bénéfices appartenaient à l'emprunteur, conformément aux règles applicables aux prêts à la consommation. En effet, l'article 1893 du Code civil dispose que « *par l'effet de ce prêt, l'emprunteur devient propriétaire de la chose prêtée ; et c'est pour lui qu'elle périt, de quelque manière que cette perte se produise* ». Dans cette affaire, le tribunal n'a pas pris position sur la nature juridique du bitcoin, qui n'était pas la question posée en l'espèce. L'intérêt de cette décision réside dans la qualité attribuée au bitcoin, et par extension, aux actifs numériques : fongibilité et consomptibilité.

1.1.2 Les jetons

La seconde catégorie d'actifs numériques consacrée par la loi PACTE est celle des jetons. Ceux-ci sont définis à l'article L. 552-2 du Code monétaire et financier comme : « *tout bien incorporel représentant, sous forme numérique, un ou plusieurs droits pouvant être émis, inscrits, conservés ou transférés au moyen d'un dispositif d'enregistrement électronique partagé permettant d'identifier, directement ou indirectement, le propriétaire dudit bien* ». L'article L. 54-10-1, 1° du même Code complète cette définition en définissant négativement les jetons par rapport aux instruments financiers et bons de caisse. En effet, l'article L. 54-10-1, 1° du Code monétaire et financier dispose que sont des actifs numériques « *les jetons mentionnés à l'article L. 552-2, à l'exclusion de ceux remplissant les caractéristiques des instruments financiers mentionnés à l'article L. 211-1 et des bons de caisse mentionnées à l'article L. 223-1 du Code monétaire et financier* ». Ainsi, par raisonnement *a contrario*, les jetons – biens incorporels émis, inscrits, conservés ou transférés au moyen d'un dispositif d'enregistrement électronique partagé permettant d'identifier, directement ou indirectement, le titulaire dudit bien – représentant un ou plusieurs droits caractéristiques des instruments financiers ou des bons de caisse sont qualifiés d'instruments financiers ou de bons de caisse.

En vertu du principe de neutralité technologique, les instruments financiers émis, inscrits, conservés et transférés sur un dispositif d'enregistrement électronique partagé restent des instruments financiers soumis au régime applicable aux instruments financiers[8], notamment concernant la fourniture de service d'investissement, la prohibition des abus de marché, ou encore l'offre au public de titres financiers. Finalement, par la notion de jeton, le législateur a entendu encadrer les *utility tokens*, et exclure les *security tokens* du champ de définition des jetons.

Outre la distinction entre *utility* et *security tokens*, s'est posée la question de la qualification des contrats financiers (plus connus sous le nom de produits dérivés) ayant pour sous-jacent des crypto-actifs. A cet égard, l'Autorité des marchés financiers (AMF) a réalisé une analyse juridique des produits dérivés sur crypto-actifs[9] en concluant que ces produits sont des instruments financiers, soumis au monopole des prestataires de services d'investissement. En effet, l'AMF considère que « *l'offre de de dérivés sur crypto-monnaies nécessite un agrément et est interdite à la publicité par voie électronique* »[10].

Depuis la publication de cette analyse, les autorités de régulations françaises publient régulièrement une liste noire des sites internet qui proposent des produits dérivés sur crypto-actifs sans agrément[11]. Outre la publication de cette liste, les autorités de supervision diffusent des mises en garde rappelant les risques de fraude et de blanchiment des capitaux et de financement du terrorisme élevés[12].

1.1.3 Les modifications apportées par le Règlement MiCA

L'article 3.1(5) du règlement MiCA définit un crypto-actif comme « une représentation numé-rique d'une valeur ou d'un droit pouvant être transférée et stockée de manière électronique, au moyen de la technologie des registres distribués ou d'une technologie similaire ». L'article 3.1(9) ajoute qu'un jeton

8 Cf. en ce sens le Rapport du Haut Comité Juridique de la Place de Paris, Titres financiers digitaux ("security token"), 27 novembre 2020 : https://www.banque-france.fr/sites/default/files/rapport_39_f.pdf.

9 https://www.amf-france.org/fr/actualites-publications/actualites/analyse-sur-la-qualification-juridique-des-produits-derives-sur-crypto-monnaies.

10 Communiqué AMF, 22 févr. 2018.

11 Communiqué AMF, 22 févr. 2018. "ACPR", 8 oct. 2019.

12 Communiqué de mise en garde, 26 avr. 2018 : Crypto-monnaies (bitcoin, etc.) : attention aux arnaques !

utilitaire est « un type de crypto-actif destiné uniquement à donner accès à un bien ou à un service fourni par son émetteur ».

Là où le droit français mentionne des actifs numériques, le droit européen préfère utiliser la notion de crypto-actifs. Il ne s'agit pour l'essentiel que d'une différence sémantique.

En effet, les définitions françaises et européennes reposent de façon analogue sur les notions de représentation de droit et de valeur. Pour autant, ces deux notions ne se superposent pas totalement. Dès lors, le rapport du HCJP recommande un alignement des définitions du droit français sur celles du règlement MiCA, ce qui conduira à la suppression des deux définitions de droit français évoquées ci-dessus.

Néanmoins, les définitions du droit français subsisteront pour les besoins de la période transitoire, c'est-à-dire jusqu'au 31 décembre 2025. Dès lors, la notion de crypto-actif au sens du Règlement MiCA constituera un sous-ensemble de la catégorie des actifs numériques.

1.1.4 L'instauration d'un régime sui generis optionnel pour les initial coin offerings

La France a été l'un des premiers pays à adopter un régime juridique spécifique pour les levées de fonds via l'émission de crypto-actifs. Ces offres se sont développées depuis fin 2016, en raison de l'essor de la technologie blockchain et DLT.

En effet, la loi PACTE a introduit un régime spécifique pour les offres au public de jetons, prévoyant le principe d'un visa optionnel délivré par l'Autorité des Marchés Financiers. Selon l'article 552-3 du Code monétaire et financier : « *une offre au public de jetons consiste à proposer au public, sous quelque forme que ce soit, de souscrire à ces jetons* ». Ce nouveau régime, destiné à favoriser le développement des ICO, ne s'applique qu'aux émissions de jetons ayant la qualité d'actifs numériques, et pas aux émissions de jetons assimilables à des titres financiers (*Security Token Offering*, « STO »), qui restent soumises au régime de l'offre au public de titres financiers. Les émetteurs de jetons qualifiés d'actifs numériques ont la faculté (et non l'obligation) de solliciter un visa de l'AMF en vue de réaliser une offre au public de jetons. Le visa de l'AMF n'est pas délivré à un émetteur de jetons mais à une offre de jetons. Il convient de préciser que seules les offres au public de jetons visant plus de 150 personnes agissant pour compte propre peuvent faire l'objet d'un visa de l'AMF. En effet, l'article L. 552-3 du Code monétaire et financier dispose que « *ne constitue pas une offre au public de jetons l'offre de jetons ouverte à la souscription par un nombre limité de personne, fixé par le règlement général de l'AMF, agissant pour compte propre*[13] ». Ce seuil a été fixé à 150 personnes[14].

Le règlement général de l'AMF précise les règles applicables aux émetteurs de jetons. Pour obtenir un visa auprès de l'AMF sur une offre au public de jetons, l'émetteur doit :

- être constitué sous la forme d'une personne morale établie ou immatriculée en France ;
- produire un document d'information (communément appelé « *white paper* ») conformément à l'article 712-2 du règlement général de l'AMF. Ce document d'information, à destination du public doit être concis et compréhensible afin de permettre aux souscripteurs de fonder leur décision d'investissement et de comprendre les risques afférents à l'offre. Il doit être rédigé selon le plan-type défini à l'annexe 2 de l'instruction de l'AMF DOC-2019-06 ;
- mettre en place un procédé permettant le suivi et la sauvegarde des actifs recueillis dans le cadre de l'offre dans le respect de l'article 712-7 du règlement général de l'AMF et à l'instruction de l'AMF précédemment citée ; et
- mettre en place un dispositif permettant de respecter les obligations en matière de lutte contre le blanchiment et le financement du terrorisme prévu aux articles L. 561-2 et suivants du Code monétaire et financier[15].

Le projet de document d'information doit être déposé à l'AMF, accompagné de la documentation listée au paragraphe 3.1 de l'instruction de l'AMF DOC-2019-06. Pareillement, les émetteurs doivent transmettre à l'AMF, préalablement à leur diffusion, les projets de communications à caractère promotionnel de l'offre au public de jetons (sites internet, e-mailing etc). L'AMF vérifie que ces projets sont conformes aux garanties requises par l'article 713-5 du règlement général de l'AMF. À l'issue de l'examen du dossier, l'AMF décide ou non de viser l'offre. Bien que les ICO sans visa demeurent légales, seules les offres au public de jetons ayant reçu le visa de l'AMF pourront faire l'objet en France d'un démarchage ou d'un quasi-démarchage auprès du public.

Ce régime national des ICO a vocation à disparaitre avec l'entrée en vigueur du Règlement MiCA.

---

13 Article L. 552-3 du Code monétaire et financier.

14 Article 711-2 du règlement général de l'AMF.

15 https://www.amf-france.org/sites/default/files/private/2021-07/dispositions-en-matiere-de-lutte-contre-le-blanchiment-des-capitaux-et-le-financement-du-terrorisme.pdf.

1.1.5 Les autorités nationales compétentes

Les institutions financières françaises sont réglementées à la fois par l'AMF et l'ACPR (qui est un organe de supervision instauré au sein de la Banque de France).

L'objectif principal de l'AMF est de protéger les épargnants et investisseurs en assurant le bon fonctionnement des marchés financiers, tandis que l'ACPR est chargée de préserver la stabilité du système financier et de superviser les secteurs de la banque et de l'assurance.

L'intervention de l'AMF et/ou de l'ACPR dépend des services fournis par l'entreprise. Certains acteurs ne traitent qu›avec un seul régulateur (par exemple, une banque ou une compagnie d›assurance serait normalement sous la seule supervision de l›ACPR) mais, en pratique, la plupart des institutions financières traitent avec les deux régulateurs. Par exemple, une compagnie d›assurance serait réglementée par l›ACPR en ce qui concerne ses activités d'assurance, mais son activité de gestion d'actifs serait soumise au contrôle de l'AMF.

L'AMF et l'ACPR peuvent également partager leurs compétences en ce qui concerne le processus d'autorisation. Par exemple, l'ACPR est responsable de l'agrément des prestataires de services d'investissement, mais leur « programme d'activité » (c›est-à-dire la description des activités exercées par l›entité) doit être approuvé au préalable par l›AMF. Une fois que les prestataires de services d›investissement ont obtenu l›agrément, l›ACPR contrôle leur activité et leur situation financière, tandis que l'AMF contrôle le respect du code de conduite applicable.

S'agissant des prestataires sur actifs numériques, la compétence est partagée entre l'AMF et l'ACPR : l'AMF a en charge la procédure d'enregistrement et d'agrément, mais l'ACPR est compétente pour examiner la conformité des aspects liés à la règlementation relatives à la lutte contre le blanchiment et le financement du terrorisme.

1.1.6 Dispositions pénales

Dans l'hypothèse où l'AMF constate que l'offre au public de jetons n'est plus conforme au contenu du document d'information ou ne présente plus les garanties visées à l'article L. 552-5 du Code monétaire et financier, elle peut contraindre l'émetteur disposant d'un visa à mettre fin à toute communication sur l'offre, ou encore retirer le visa à titre définitif ou jusqu'à qu'il satisfasse aux conditions dudit visa. Cette procédure est prévue à l'article L. 552-6 du Code monétaire et financier.

En cas de retrait du visa, l'émetteur de jetons fait l'objet d'une obligation d'information à destination du public. En ce sens, l'émetteur doit mettre à jour son site internet en supprimant toute référence au visa de l'AMF sur son offre de jetons. De même, l'AMF publie sur son site les offre de jetons ayant fait l'objet d'un retrait de visa.

La loi PACTE a insérée une section destinée aux émetteurs de jetons au sein du titre du livre V du Code monétaire et financier relatif aux dispositions pénales.

L'article L. 572-27 du même code, seul article de cette section punit de 6 mois d'emprisonnement et de 7 500 euros d'amende « le fait, pour toute personne procédant à une offre au public de jetons au sens de l'article L. 552-3, de diffuser des informations comportant des indications inexactes ou trompeuses ou d'utiliser une dénomination, une raison sociale, une publicité ou tout autre procédé laissant croire qu'elle a obtenu le visa prévu à l'article L. 552-4 ».

1.1.7 Dispositifs de lutte contre le blanchiment et le financement du terrorisme

Selon l'article L. 561-2 du Code monétaire et financier, l'émetteur de jetons est assujetti, dans le cadre de l'offre, aux obligations de lutte contre le blanchiment des capitaux et le financement du terrorisme prévu aux sections II à VII du premier chapitre du titre VI du livre V du Code monétaire et financier.

Ces contraintes sont limitées aux opérations avec les souscripteurs prenant part à l'offre. Par conséquent, les émetteurs de jetons sont tenus de contrôler l'origine des crypto-actifs ou des fonds recueillis dans le cadre de l'offre afin que les ICO bénéficiant du visa ne soient pas liées à des manœuvres frauduleuses aux fins de blanchiment de capitaux ou de financement du terrorisme.

A l'inverse des autres professionnels listés à l'article L. 561-2 du Code monétaire et financier, les émetteurs de jetons ne sont pas soumis à une surveillance continue. En effet, ceux-ci sont uniquement soumis aux obligations en matière de LCB-FT pour la durée de l'offre de jetons et dans la limite des opérations avec les souscripteurs.

Afin de garantir le respect des obligations en matière de LCB-FT, l'article L. 561-36, 2° du Code monétaire et financier exige que les porteurs de projets mettent en place un dispositif leur permettant de contrôler la provenance des fonds, à l'image des mesures KYC (*know your customer*) s'appliquant aux établissements bancaires et financiers. L'ACPR, l'autorité compétente en matière de surveillance du respect des obligations en matière de LCB-FT, intervient sur ces aspects, en parallèle de l'AMF qui intervient sur les aspects purement liés à l'émission de jetons.

1.1.7.1 *Les mesures relatives à l'évaluation des risques*

L'article L. 561-4-1 du Code monétaire et financier impose aux émetteurs de jetons de mettre en place des dispositifs d'identification et d'évaluation des risques LCB-FT auxquels les souscripteurs sont exposés. Ainsi, l'émetteur de jeton doit être doter d'une organisation, mettre en place des procédures internes et une politique de contrôle adaptées à ces risques mais aussi, une classification des risques en fonction :

- de la nature des produits ou service offerts ;
- des conditions de transactions proposées ;
- des canaux de distribution utilisés ;
- des caractéristiques des clients ;
- du pays ou du territoire d'origine ou de destination des fonds.

1.1.7.2 *Les mesures liées au profil de risque client et le niveau de vigilance*

En fonction de l'approche par les risques retenus dans le cadre de la classification, les émetteurs doivent établir un profil de risque pour chacune de leur relation d'affaires.[16] L'émetteur doit appliquer les mesures de vigilance prévue à cet effet. A ce titre, cinq niveaux de vigilance ont été prévues par le législateur

- des mesures de vigilance simplifies[17] ;
- des mesures de vigilance normales[18] (notamment l'identification du client);
- des mesures de vigilance complémentaires[19] ;
- des mesures de vigilance renforcées[20] ; ct enfin
- la mise en place d'un examen renforcé[21] (détermination de l'origine des fonds).

S'agissant des clients occasionnels, l'article L. 561-5 du Code monétaire et financier prévoit que dans le cadre des mesures de vigilances normales, les mesures d'identification et de vérification d'identité ne sont mises en place que :

- si les personnes visées à l'article L. 561-2 soupçonnent qu'une opération pourrait participer au blanchiment de capitaux ou au financement du terrorisme ;
- lorsque les opérations sont d'une certaine nature ou dépassent un certain montant précisé à l'article R. 561-10 du Code monétaire et financier.

1.1.7.3 *L'obligation de déclaration par les émetteurs auprès de TRACFIN*

Aux termes des articles L. 561-15 et D. 561-32-1 du Code monétaire et financier, les émetteurs de jetons doivent prévoir un processus permettant de déclarer

16 Article L. 561-2-1, alinéa 2 du Code monétaire et financier : la relation d'affaires s'entend de la relation professionnelle ou commerciale avec un client.

17 Article L. 561-9 du Code de commerce.

18 Articles L. 561-5 à L. 561-6 du Code de commerce.

19 Article L. 561-10 du Code de commerce.

20 Article L. 561-10 du Code de commerce.

21 Article L. 561-10-2 du Code de commerce.

à TRACFIN[22] « *les sommes inscrites dans ses livres ou les opérations portant sur des sommes dont il sait, soupçonne ou a de bonnes raisons de soupçonner qu'elles proviennent d'une infraction passible d'une peine privative de liberté supérieure à un an ou sont liées au financement du terrorisme, ainsi que les sommes ou opérations dont il sait, soupçonne ou a de bonnes raisons de soupçonner qu'elles proviennent d'une fraude fiscale, dans certaines conditions définies par décret* ».

D'après l'article L. 561-15-1 du Code monétaire et financier, les émetteurs de jetons doivent adresser à TRACFIN certains éléments relatifs à certaines opérations présentant un risque élevé en matière de LCB-FT. L'article R. 561-31 du même code précise les personnes et opérations concernées, ainsi que les modalités de transmission de l'information.

Enfin, l'article L. 561-8 du Code monétaire et financier dispose que les émetteurs devront rompre les relations d'affaires qu'ils entretiennent avec des acteurs s'ils ne sont pas capables de satisfaire aux obligations prévues aux articles L. 561-5 et L. 561-5-1 du même code.

1.1.7.4 *Les mesures liées aux procédures de contrôle interne*

En considération de l'article L. 561-32 du Code monétaire et financier, les émetteurs doivent désigner, en tenant compte de la taille et de la nature de l'activité, une personne dotée d'une connaissance suffisante des expositions aux risques LCB-FT, comme responsable de la mise en œuvre du dispositif de lutte contre le blanchiment des capitaux et le financement du terrorisme. Il est impératif que cette personne occupe une fonction importante au sein de l'organisation.

Toujours d'après ce même article, les émetteurs devront aussi prendre des « *mesures de contrôle interne* » qui, conformément à l'article R. 561-38-8 du Code monétaire et financier comprend, « *des procédures définissant les activités de contrôle interne relative à la LCB-FT* », un « *contrôle interne permanent* » et un « *contrôle interne périodique* ».

Pour conclure, il est utile de préciser que les émetteurs de jetons sont aussi soumis aux dispositions relatives au gel des avoirs et à l'interdiction de mise à disposition prévue aux articles L. 562-4 et L. 562-4-1 du Code monétaire et financier.

1.2 *Le statut de prestataires sur actifs numériques*

L'enjeu majeur de la loi PACTE a été d'introduire une nouvelle catégorie d'acteurs financiers, celle des prestataires de services sur actifs numériques (PSAN).

---

22 Traitement du renseignement et action contre les circuits financiers clandestins. TRACFIN est un service de renseignement placé sous l'autorité du Ministère de l'Économie, des Finances et de la Souveraineté industrielle et numérique.

Ainsi, la prestation de services portant sur des actifs numériques n'est pas à la portée de tout le monde. Afin de pouvoir y prétendre, il faut respecter les règles établies par ce régime, sous peine de s'exposer à des sanctions.

Pour être considéré comme un PSAN, il faut fournir au moins l'un des services sur actifs numériques prévu à l'article L. 54-10-2 du Code monétaire et financier :

- service de conservation pour le compte de tiers d'actifs numériques ou d'accès à des actifs numériques, le cas échéant sous la forme de clés cryptographiques privées, en vue de détenir, stocker et transférer des actifs numériques ;
- service d'achat ou de vente d'actifs numériques en monnaie ayant cours légal ;
- service d'échange d'actifs numériques contre d'autres actifs numériques ;
- l'exploitation d'une plateforme de négociation d'actifs numériques ;
- la réception et la transmission d'ordres sur actifs numériques pour le compte de tiers ;
- la gestion de portefeuille d'actifs numériques pour le compte de tiers ;
- le conseil aux souscripteurs d'actifs numériques ;
- la prise ferme d'actifs numériques ;
- le placement garanti d'actifs numériques ; et/ou
- le placement non garanti d'actifs numériques.

Le régime du PSAN diffère selon le service fourni par la société. Pour certains services, l'enregistrement auprès de l'AMF est obligatoire tandis que pour d'autres, il s'agit simplement d'un agrément optionnel.

1.2.1 Les prestataires soumis à un enregistrement obligatoire

L'article L. 54-10-3 du Code monétaire et financier prévoit que l'enregistrement est obligatoire pour quatre services sur actifs numériques, dont :

la conservation d'actifs numériques ;
l'achat ou la vente d'actifs numériques en monnaie ayant cours légal ;
l'échange d'actifs numériques contre d'autres actifs numériques ;
l'exploitation d'une plateforme de négociation d'actifs numériques.

Chacun de ces services a été précisément défini à l'article D. 54-10-1 du Code monétaire et financier, issu du décret n° 2019-1213 du 21 novembre 2019.

Dès lors qu'une société fournit un ou plusieurs de ces services en France ou en étant établie en France, la procédure d'enregistrement auprès de l'AMF est obligatoire. Une société est établie en France dès lors que son siège social y est installé. La notion de service sur actifs numériques fourni en France est plus difficile à cerner. L'article L. 54-10-3, alinéa 8 du Code monétaire et financier, dans sa rédaction issue de l'ordonnance n° 2020-15441,[23] renvoie au règlement général de l'AMF pour définir ce qu'il faut comprendre par « *service fourni en France* ».

L'article 721-1-1 du règlement général de l'AMF souligne qu'un service sur actifs numériques est considéré comme fourni en France « *lorsqu'il est fourni par un prestataire de services sur actifs numériques disposant d'installations en France ou lorsqu'il est fourni à l'initiative du prestataire de services sur actifs numériques à des clients résidant ou établis en France* ». Ce même article dispose également de critères non-exhaustifs permettant de considérer si un service sur actifs numériques est fourni ou non en France. Par exemple, un service sur actifs numériques peut être considéré comme fourni en France lorsque « *le prestataire adresse une communication à caractère promotionnel, quel qu'en soit le support, à des clients résidant ou établis en France* » ou lorsque « *le prestataire dispose d'une adresse postale ou de coordonnées téléphoniques en France* ».

Après réception du dossier d'enregistrement, l'AMF procèdera à la vérification de l'honorabilité et de la compétence des dirigeants et bénéficiaires effectifs et sollicitera l'avis conforme de l'ACPR.[24] L'AMF dispose d'un délai de six mois pour instruire la demande d'enregistrement.[25] Le silence gardé par l'AMF vaut décision d'acceptation.

1.2.2 Les prestataires soumis à un agrément optionnel

Que ce soit pour les services soumis à enregistrement obligatoire ou pour ceux qui ne le sont pas, une société peut solliciter l'agrément optionnel de l'AMF. En effet, l'article L. 54-10-5 du Code monétaire et financier souligne que, dès lors qu'une société exerce un ou plusieurs services sur actifs numériques, et à la condition d'être établie en France, il est possible de demander un tel agrément.

Concernant le contenu du dossier d'agrément, les sociétés doivent satisfaire à plusieurs obligations en matière d'organisation, de conduite de l'activité et de ressources financières. A cet égard, le PSAN candidat à l'agrément doit, entre autres :

- disposer d'une assurance responsabilité civile professionnelle ou de fonds propres minimum ;
- avoir au moins un dirigeant effectif ;
- avoir des moyens humains et techniques suffisants ;

23 Ordonnance n° 2020-15441 du 9 décembre 2020 renforçant le cadre de la lutte contre le blanchiment de capitaux et le financement du terrorisme en matière de crypto-actifs.

24 Article L. 54-10-3, alinéa 8 du Code monétaire et financier.

25 Article R. 54-10-4 crée par Décret n° 2019-1248, 28 novembre 2019, art. 1er : JO, 29 nov. 2019.

- avoir un dispositif de contrôle interne ;
- avoir une procédure de traitement des réclamations ;
- avoir des procédures pour lutter contre le blanchiment et le financement du terrorisme ;
- donner une information claire aux clients, signer une convention avec le client ; ou encore
- respecter des exigences spécifiques aux services fournis.

Après l'envoi du dossier d'agrément à l'AMF, celle-ci va alors procéder à son instruction et solliciter l'avis de l'Agence nationale de la sécurité des systèmes d'information (ANSSI) qui devra rendre sa décision dans un délai de deux mois. Enfin, dans un délai de six mois, l'AMF notifie sa décision au demandeur.

1.2.3 Modification du régime de la loi PACTE : de l'enregistrement simple à l'enregistrement renforcé

Le régime d'enregistrement issu de la loi *PACTE* prévoyait un nombre relativement limité d'exigences au moment de l'enregistrement obligatoire par rapport à l'agrément facultatif. Ces exigences ont été renforcées par la loi n° 2023-171 du 9 mars 2023 (loi *DDADUE*) qui a mis en place un enregistrement renforcé obligatoire à compter du 1er janvier 2024 et reprenant en partie les exigences de l'agrément.

La principale différence entre le régime d'enregistrement renforcé obligatoire et le régime d'agrément réside dans l'exigence de fonds propres prudentiels : seuls le régime de l'agrément prévoit un niveau de capital réglemetnaire en fonction des activités exercées.

Cette loi se veut une réponse à la déconfiture de FTX afin de poser des exigences plus importnates aux acteurs français de crypto-actifs. Elle anticipe aussi le Règlement MiCA en ce qu'elle pose des exigences très proches de celles existantes dans ce Règlement.

Avec cette réforme, les PSAN, pour être enregistrés, doivent se conformer aux exigences déclinées aux paragraphes 5° et 6° de l'article L. 54-10-3 nouvellement créé, notamment : disposer d'un dispositif de sécurité et de contrôle interne adéquat, d'un système de gestion des conflits d'intérêts, et d'un système informatique résilient et sécurisé ; communiquer des informations claires exactes et non trompeuses à leurs clients ; publier leur politique tarifaire ; mettre en place une politique de traitement de leurs réclamations.

Afin de clarifier les dispositions transitoires en lien avec ce nouveau régime, l'AMF a mis à jour sa position-recommandation DOC-2020-07 :

- les PSAN ayant finalisé le dépôt d'une demande d'enregistrement considérée comme complète par l'AMF avant le 1er juillet 2023 seront soumis à une procédure d'enregistrement simple. Le caractère complet de la demande est

apprécié au regard de l'exhaustivité des documents fournis mais aussi de la qualité et du degré de précisions des informations ;
- les personnes n'ayant pas déposé un dossier d'enregistrement considéré comme complet par l'AMF avant le 1er juillet 2023 doivent quant à elles compléter et mettre à jour leur dossier pour se conformer aux dispositions de l'enregistrement PSAN renforcé.

Il est également précisé qu'un PSAN déjà enregistré sous un format « simple » demandant une extension à un nouveau service à compter du 1er juillet 2023 est soumis aux dispositions de l'enregistrement renforcé pour l'ensemble des services fournis, y compris ceux pour lesquels il a été préalablement enregistré simple.

Les PSAN ayant déjà obtenu un enregistrement « simple » avant le 1er janvier 2024 bénéficient d'une clause de « grand-père » et continuent de se voir appliquer les exigences de l'enregistrement applicables avant le 1er janvier 2024.

1.2.4 Radiation et retrait d'un PSAN enregistré/agrée

L'AMF peut prendre la décision de radier un PSAN enregistré pour différents motifs[26]. Après un avis conforme de l'ACPR, la radiation peut intervenir dans les cas suivants :
- à la demande du PSAN ;
- d'office, si le PSAN n'a pas exercé son activité pendant douze mois ou n'exerce plus son activité depuis au moins six mois ;
- à l'initiative de l'AMF ou l'ACPR lorsque le PSAN ne respecte plus les conditions de l'enregistrement ou s'il a obtenu celui-ci par de fausses déclarations ou par tout autre moyen irrégulier.

A titre d'exemple, le Collège de l'Autorité des marchés financiers (AMF) a décidé le 27 septembre 2022 de retirer l'enregistrement en qualité de prestataire de services sur actifs numériques (PSAN) à BYKEP SAS, avec effet immédiat. La procédure a été engagée à la suite d'un contrôle sur place réalisé par l'Autorité de contrôle prudentiel et de résolution (ACPR), ayant révélé des faits remettant en cause les conditions de son enregistrement[27].

1.2.5 Dispositions pénales applicable au PSAN

L'article L. 54-10-4 du Code monétaire et financier prohibe la fourniture en France ou en étant établi en France des services sur actifs numériques

---

26 Article D. 54-10-5 et suivants du Code monétaire et financier.

27 Communiqué ACPR-AMF, L'AMF et l'ACPR annoncent la radiation du PSAN BYKEP SAS, 28 septembre 2022.

requérant un enregistrement – à savoir, les services de conservation d'actifs numériques pour le compte de tiers, le service d'échange d'actifs numériques contre d'autres actifs numériques, le service d'achat et de vente d'actifs numériques contre de la monnaie ayant cours légal et le service d'exploitation d'une plateforme de négociation d'actifs numériques –, sans avoir obtenu l'enregistrement de l'AMF. Une situation de monopole a donc été instaurée par le législateur français.

De même, il est aussi interdit d'utiliser utiliser une dénomination, une raison sociale, une publicité ou tout autre procédé laissant croire que la personne est enregistrée auprès de l'AMF. L'article L. 572-23 du Code monétaire et financier précise que le non-respect de ces deux interdictions est sanctionné pénalement. Le contrevenant encourt une peine de prison de deux ans et une amende de 30 000 euros.

En outre, l'AMF publie une liste noire des prestataires non enregistrés qui n'ont pas cessé leur activité, mettre en garde le public et demander la fermeture du site interne de ces prestataires[28].

Dans l'intérêt des utilisateurs, le législateur a introduit deux autres délits en lien avec l'enregistrement des prestataires des services n° 1 à 4. En effet, l'article L. 572-23, alinéa 1er du Code monétaire et financier dispose que tout PSAN qui ne procèderait pas à la déclaration de changement de situation visée à l'article L. 54-10-3 du même code ou qui communiquerait, à l'occasion de cette déclaration des renseignements inexacts à l'AMF s'expose à une peine d'un an d'emprisonnement et une amende de 15 000 euros.

Aussi, les articles L. 572-24 et L. 571-4 du Code monétaire et financier précisent que tout PSAN enregistré qui, après une mise en demeure, ne répondrait pas aux d'informations de l'AMF, qui ferait obstacle de quelque manière que ce soit à l'exercice de sa mission de contrôle ou qui lui communiquerait des renseignements inexacts s'expose à une peine d'un an d'emprisonnement et une amende de 15 000 euros.

1.2.6 Dispositions LCB-FT applicable aux PSAN

Selon l'article L. 54-10-3 du Code monétaire et financier, dans sa version issue de l'ordonnance n° 2020-1544 du 9 décembre 2020, l'obligation d'enregistrement est étendue aux PSAN fournissant les services mentionnés aux 3° et 4° de l'article L. 54-10-2, sans pour autant que l'AMF vérifie s'ils ont mis en place une organisation, des procédures et un dispositif de contrôle interne suivant les

28 Communiqué AMF, 23 novembre 2020.

obligations LCB-FT. Par conséquent, le législateur a fait le choix de dispenser ces acteurs d'ün contrôle *a priori* des dispositifs LCB-FT[29].

Néanmoins, l'article L. 54-10-3, 4° du Code monétaire et financier souligne que pour les services mentionnés aux 1° et 2°, les PSAN doivent être en mesure de se conformer à leurs obligations en matière de LCB-FT, de gel des avoirs et d'interdiction de mise à disposition, par la mise en place d'une organisation et de procédures propres à assurer le respect des dispositions en vigueur en la matière.

En d'autres termes, le contrôle *a priori* s'applique seulement pour les services 1° et 2°, mais le champ des obligations liées à la LCB-FT pour ces services a été modifié afin que l'ACPR et l'AMF ne vérifient que les exigences relatives :
- à la classification des risques ;
- à l'identification ;
- à la vérification d'identité ;
- à la connaissance du client ;
- aux examens renforcés ;
- aux déclarations de soupçons ;
- au gel des avoirs.

En tout état de cause, les vérifications *a priori* sur le contrôle interne, les modalités de formation du personnel, la conservation des documents ou l'externalisation sont exclues. Conformément à l'article L. 561-2, 7° du Code monétaire et financier, les PSAN demeurent assujettis aux obligations des sections 2 à 7 du chapitre relatif aux obligations en matière de LCB-FT. Si un PSAN viendrait manquer à une de ces obligations, les autorités de régulations pourront procéder à un contrôle *a posteriori* pouvant amener une sanction à son égard.

2 Problematiques de droit privé

2.1 *Droit de propriété sur les actifs numériques*

2.1.1 L'Etat du droit positif

En droit français, le droit de propriété est défini par l'article 544 du Code civil, qui dispose que « *la propriété est le droit de jouir et disposer des choses de la manière la plus absolue, pourvu qu'on n'en fasse pas un usage prohibé par les lois ou par les règlements* ». Le droit de propriété est ainsi divisé en trois composantes, à savoir, l'*usus* – c'est-à-dire le droit d'user de la chose dont on est propriétaire –, l'*abusus* – soit le droit de disposer de la chose dont on est

29 Position AMF n° 2020-07, 22 septembre 2020, Questions-réponses relatives au régime des PSAN, point 3.7.

propriétaire – et enfin, le *fructus* – le droit de percevoir les fruits ou produits de la chose dont on est propriétaire.

Le droit français positif avant l'adaptation prévue suite à l'entrée en vigueur du Règlement MiCA n'affirme pas avec force – contrairement aux titres financiers – que les actifs numériques font l'objet d'un droit de propriété. La question ne semble cependant pas faire débat. Celui-ci porte plutôt sur la nature juridique de l'actif : droit réel ou droit personnel.

A cet égard, la qualification juridique des actifs numériques se rapprocherait de celle des titres financiers : l'actif lui-même (titres financier ou actif numérique) n'« est » pas un droit réel en tant que tel, mais le titulaire dispose d'un droit réel sur cet actif, lequel est une créance complexe, à savoir un droit personnel contre l'émetteur au remboursement de son actif.

Se pose alors la question de savoir comment la propriété d'un actif numérique est-elle attribuée ? Ou pour le dire autrement, est-ce que le concept traditionnel de la possession est applicable au cas des actifs numériques dans la mesure où ceux-ci ne sont représentés que par un code dans un protocole informatique ? Le débat, de ce point de vue, se rapproche de celui existant pour les titres financiers numériques, lesquels ne sont plus représentés par une inscription en compte, mais par un code dans la blockchain ou une DLT[30].

Le droit français reconnaît les effets à la possession de biens corporels. La Cour de cassation refusant toutefois l'application de l'article 2276 du Code civil aux biens incorporels, un article L. 211-16 a été inséré en 2009 dans le Code monétaire et financier aux fins d'attribuer à l'inscription en compte des titres financiers, puis à l'inscription dans une blockchain ou une DLT de titres financiers numériques au nom de la personne identifiée par la blockchain ou la DLT, les mêmes effets que la possession[31].

De ce point de vue, un concept nouveau est apparu en matière de titres financiers aux lieu et place de celui de la possession, à savoir la notion de contrôle.

Celle-ci figure dans la directive européenne 2002/47 du Parlement européen et du Conseil du 6 juin 2002 concernant les contrats de garantie financières (« directive Collatéral »), transposée en France aux articles L. 211-36 et s. du Code prévoit que le contrôle donné au bénéficiaire (ou une personne

30 Cf. H. de Vauplane « Des titres papiers aux titres digitaux », Revue d'Economie Financière, 2018/1, n° 129, p. 89.

31 Art. L. 211-16 : « Nul ne peut revendiquer pour quelque cause que ce soit un titre financier dont la propriété a été acquise de bonne foi par le titulaire du compte-titres dans lequel ces titres sont inscrits ou par la personne identifiée par le dispositif d'enregistrement électronique partagé mentionné à l'article L. 211-3 »

désignée par ce dernier). Ce texte organise une technique de constitution et d'opposabilité d'une garantie financière sans transfert de propriété sur des biens (titres, créances sommes d'argent, métaux précieux, etc). L'article 2 (2) de cette directive précise que le contrôle s'acquiert notamment par la livraison, le transfert, la détention ou l'enregistrement de l'actif nanti, sous réserve que les actifs concernés soient clairement identifiés comme étant dans l'assiette de la garantie (article 1 (5) de cette directive).

Les Principes applicables au actifs numériques proposés par UNIDROIT se basent sur la notion de contrôle. Selon ces Principes, et en particulier le Principe 6, la notion de contrôle a pour objet (i) de protéger l'acquéreur de bonne foi d'un actif digital (sans que le contrôle soit l'élément exclusif pour procurer une telle protection) et (ii) d'assurer l'opposabilité d'une sûreté et d'organiser le rang de priorité de ses bénéficiaires.

La notion contrôle est là encore utilisée comme un substitut au concept traditionnel de possession.

Le Principe 6 organise un double effet au contrôle. Le premier, que l'on peut qualifier de « versant positif » désigne la faculté d'utiliser un actif (par exemple, en exerçant un droit de vote qui s'y rattache), ou d'en disposer (par exemple, en procédant à son transfert sur la blockchain) ; et le second effet, que l'on peut qualifier de « versant négatif » a trait au pouvoir de blocage. Lorsqu'il s'agit de régler les conflits entre acquéreurs successifs d'un même actif, c'est *a priori* le premier sens qui paraît le plus adapté, mais lorsqu'il s'agit d'assurer l'opposabilité d'une garantie, c'est plutôt au second que l'on se réfèrera. Ainsi entendu, le contrôle permet d'attribuer au titulaire d'un actif numérique des effets similaires à ceux de la possession.

Cette double fonction existe aussi dans la notion classique de « possession » : celle de l'article 2276 du Code civil[32] n'a pas le même contenu que celle de l'article 2337[33], sans que cela ne pose de difficulté majeure.

C'est donc bien autour de la question du contrôle sur les actifs que la question de propriété se pose.

---

32 Article 2276 : "*En fait de meubles, la possession vaut titre. Néanmoins, celui qui a perdu ou auquel il a* été *volé une chose peut la revendiquer pendant trois ans à compter du jour de la perte ou du vol, contre celui dans les mains duquel il la trouve ; sauf à celui-ci son recours contre celui duquel il la tient*".

33 Article 2337 : « *Le gage est opposable aux tiers par la publicité qui en est faite.*
Il l'est également par la dépossession entre les mains du créancier ou d'un tiers convenu du bien qui en fait l'objet ou du titre qui, tel un connaissement, le représente.
Lorsque le gage a été régulièrement publié, les ayants cause à titre particulier du constituant ne peuvent se prévaloir de l'article 2276 ».

Il semble clair techniquement parlant que la notion de «contrôle» est étroitement liée à la capacité de transférer les actifs numériques sur la blockchain ou DLT. C'est cette faculté de mouvement, de transfert qui caractérise le contrôle. D'où le besoin d'évoquer une « exclusivité » à celui-ci. De ce point de vue, le concept de possession implique lui aussi une exclusivité : une seule et même personne dispose de la possession à l'exclusion de toute autre personne. Cet effet se manifeste naturellement lorsque la possession porte sur un actif tangible, ce qui correspond en effet à la situation factuelle qui sous-tend l'article 2276 al.1 du Code civil. Cette idée d'exclusivité est plus difficile à appréhender s'agissant de biens meubles incorporels ne faisant pas l'objet d'un enregistrement dans un registre officiel (par exemple, certains droits de propriété intellectuelle) ou par une inscription dans un compte unique comme en matière de titres financiers (le compte « pertinent », selon la directive Collatéral).

Cela étant dit, le droit français reconnait à la possession (ou à un équivalent pour les biens incorporels) les mêmes effets que ceux qui sont prévus par les Principes UNIDROIT, même si en l'état actuel des choses, le droit français utilise des termes plus fonctionnels et pratiques telle que la « maîtrise » des moyens d'accès, ou utilise une substitution circonstanciée de la notion de possession par une situation analogue, (art. L. 211-16 du Code) qui résulte d'une inscription dans le compte pertinent.

Ainsi et de façon concrète, un dépositaire / conservateur d'actifs numérique exerce un contrôle sur les actifs numériques de ses clients si :

- le dépositaire est en mesure de transférer les actifs numériques sur la blockchain, en signant une transaction avec les clés privées qui leur sont associées ; et
- le client n'est pas en mesure d'effectuer ce transfert par lui-même, mais peut seulement demander au dépositaire d'effectuer ce transfert en son nom.

De manière concrète, si 60 Bitcoins sont enregistrés dans le portefeuille de X, cela signifie qu'il en détient la clé privée. Par conséquent, X est propriétaire des 60 Bitcoins, et peut par conséquent en disposer, en percevoir les fruits et les utiliser.

A l'inverse, si X ouvre un compte chez MontC – prestataire de service sur actifs numériques enregistré ou agréé par l'Autorité des Marchés Financiers pour la fourniture du service de conservation d'actifs numériques pour le compte de tiers – et dépose 60 Bitcoins sur son compte, alors il n'est plus propriétaire de ces actifs numériques. En effet, MontC détient la clé privée du portefeuille hébergé de X et par conséquent a le contrôle des actifs numériques qui y sont stockés. Finalement, un transfert de propriété des 60 Bitcoins s'opère entre X et MontC, et le droit de propriété de X sur les 60 Bitcoins devient un droit de créance à l'encontre de MontC à hauteur de 60 Bitcoins.

En présence d'un « hardfork » ou d'un « airdrop », deux situations doivent être distinguées : qui de X ou de MontC détient la clé privée ? Si X est détenteur de la clé privée, alors il est propriétaire des actifs numériques obtenus à la suite d'un « hardfork » ou d'un « airdrop », tel qu'expliqué précédemment. Le « fork » ou l'« airdrop » est garanti par un screening effectué par la blockchain effec-tuant le « fork » ou l'entreprise effectuant l'« airdrop » d'actifs numériques.

Inversement, si le portefeuille de X est un portefeuille hébergé par MontC, MontC recevra les actifs numériques issus du « hardfork » ou du « airdrop » pour le compte de X, sauf convention contraire.

Pour autant, le concept de contrôle n'est finalement pas la voie retenue par le droit français qui préfère mettre en place un régime nouveau.

2.1.2 Le projet de définition des crypto-actifs suite à l'adaptation du droit français au Règlement MiCA

Avec le Règlement MiCA, les crypto-actifs sont définis comme des « représentations de valeur ou de droit », laissant entendre que tous les crypto-actifs ne sont pas de même nature : certains représentent une créance contre un émetteur, d'autres représentent une valeur.

Cette différence de nature engendre l'application de régimes patrimoniaux différents. Les crypto-actifs représentant des droits devraient être soumis aux règles régissant la circulation des créances (articles 1321 à 1326 du Code civil), ce qui n'est pas le cas des crypto-actifs représentant des valeurs qui constituent des biens incorporels sui generis.

Dans le cadre du projet d'ordonnance d'adaptation du droit français au Règlement MiCA, il est prévu que les crypto-actifs soient qualifiés de biens meubles incorporels négociables.

Le même projet d'ordonnance prévoit la création d'une régime de transfert de propriété ad hoc pour certains crypto-actifs.

2.2 *Le transfert de propriété sur des actifs numériques*

Le droit français avant sa future modification par l'ordonnance d'adaptation du Règlement MiCA ne prévoit pas de dispositions spécifiques au transfert de propriété des actifs numériques, contrairement aux titres financiers inscrits en compte ou aux titres financiers inscrits dans une blockchain ou une DLT où l'article L. 211-3, alinéa 1 prévoit que : *« Le compte-titres est ouvert ou l'inscription dans un dispositif d'enregistrement électronique partagé est réalisée, au nom d'un ou de plusieurs titulaires, propriétaires des titres financiers qui y sont inscrits. »*

Il convient dès lors de s'en remettre au droit commun.

L'article 1196 al. 1er du Code civil dispose que le transfert de propriété intervient *solo consensu*. Toutefois, il est possible que les crypto-actifs fassent exception à cette règle. En effet, l'alinéa 2 de cet article prévoit que le transfert peut être différé en raison de la nature des choses. Or, les crypto-actifs étant des choses de genre, le transfert de propriété devrait être différé au moment de leur individualisation.

Celle-ci pourrait avoir lieu lors de l'inscription sur la blockchain, c'est-à-dire lors de la délivrance. Il serait aussi possible d'envisager, pour ces biens, une individualisation en les regroupant dans un *wallet* , ce qui permet de les différencier des autres crypto-actifs de même genre. Le procédé serait ainsi équivalent au marquage de marchandises fongibles pour les choses matérielles dans les stocks du vendeur.

Concernant la protection de l'acquéreur de bonne foi, le régime de protection de droit commun contre l'action en revendication du tiers-propriétaire ne devrait pas s'appliquer. En effet, la jurisprudence n'admet pas que l'article 2276 du Code civil, lequel prévoit que la possession vaut titre, soit applicable aux choses incorporelles. L'article L.211-16 du CMF, qui décline ce concept en matière de titres financiers, n'est pas non plus applicable : les crypto-actifs ne sont pas des titres financiers, quand bien même ceux-ci représenteraient des droits. Par conséquent, en application du droit commun, le régime de la possession ne devrait pas être applicable aux crypto-actifs.

Cependant, le projet d'ordonnance d'adaptation du droit français au Règlement MiCA prévoit une disposition spécifique sur la protection du tiers acquéreur de bonne foi, à l'image du régime existant pour les titres financiers.

2.2.1 Dans le cadre de donations

Le régime juridique applicable aux actifs numériques ne prévoit pas de dispositions particulières en matière de donation d'actifs numériques, de sorte que ces donations sont soumises au régime des donations entre vifs de droit commun.

Les dispositions applicables du régime de la donation entre vifs se trouvent essentiellement aux articles du Code Civil (Articles 901 à 911 pour les conditions de fonds ; Articles 931 à 939 pour les conditions de forme).

La pratique tend à faire en sorte que le légataire puisse se voir remettre les clés. On notera toutefois qu'ici, la remise des clés n'est pas tant une condition du transfert de propriété qu'une modalité d'entrée en possession.

2.2.2 Echange contre prestation

Les monnaies virtuelles, telles que définies au 2° de l'article L. 54-10-1 du Code monétaire et financier, sont définies comme pouvant être « *acceptées par des personnes physiques ou morales comme un moyen d'échange* ».

Comme indiqué plus haut, les actifs numériques n'ont pas la qualité de monnaie ayant cours légal en droit français et sur le territoire français. Ainsi, seul le paiement d'une obligation de somme d'argent en euros est libératoire conformément à l'article 1343-3 du Code civil, sous réserve des exception liées à la datation en paiement et aux opérations internationales évoquées plus haut.

2.2.3 Échange d'actifs numériques contre d'autres actifs numériques

Le droit français autorise l'échange d'actifs numériques contre d'autres actifs numériques. Ainsi, un détenteur d'actifs numériques peut légalement réaliser une transaction d'échange d'actifs numériques contre d'autres actifs numériques. L'opération est alors un contrat d'échange, défini par l'article 1702 du Code civil comme « *un contrat par lequel les parties se donnent respectivement une chose pour une autre* ».

De même, le droit français permet de recourir aux services d'un prestataire de services sur actifs numériques pour conserver et transférer des Bitcoins.

Il convient toutefois de préciser que le prestataire de services sur actifs numériques qui propose des services de conservation et d'échange d'actifs numériques en France ou qui les propose en étant établi en France a pour obligation d'être *a minima* enregistré en qualité de prestataire de services sur actifs numériques auprès de l'Autorité des Marchés Financiers.

Quant à l'utilisateur, celui-ci devra respecter les conditions générales d'utilisation du prestataire qui lui fournira les services de conservation et d'échange.

Un prestataire de services sur actifs numériques est soumis au droit français, et notamment à l'obligation d'obtenir un enregistrement auprès de l'AMF, si ce prestataire est établi en France ou s'il est considéré qu'il fournit ses services en France. En application de l'article 721-1-1 du Règlement général de l'AMF, « *un service sur actifs numériques est considéré comme fourni en France lorsqu'il est fourni par un prestataire de services sur actifs numériques disposant d'installations en France ou lorsqu'il est fourni à l'initiative du prestataire de services sur actifs numériques à des clients résidant ou établis en France. Le prestataire de services sur actifs numériques est notamment considéré comme fournissant un service en France lorsqu'au moins l'un des critères suivants est satisfait :(i) le prestataire dispose d'un local commercial ou d'un lieu destiné à la commercialisation d'un service sur actifs numériques en France ; (ii) le prestataire a installé un ou des automates offrant des services sur actifs numériques en France ;(iii) le prestataire adresse une communication à caractère promotionnel, quel qu'en soit le support, à des clients résidant ou établis en France ; (iv) le prestataire organise la distribution de ses produits et services via un ou des réseaux de distribution à destination de clients résidant ou établis en France ; (v) le prestataire dispose d'une adresse postale ou de coordonnées téléphoniques en France ; ou (vi) le prestataire dispose d'un nom de domaine de son site internet en ".fr"* ».

2.2.4 Achat/vente d'actifs numériques contre de la monnaie ayant cours légal

En France, aucune loi n'interdit l'achat ou la vente d'actifs numériques contre une monnaie ayant cours légal. Une telle transaction est donc légalement possible.

Il convient de préciser que la vente d'actifs numériques contre une monnaie ayant cours légal est une opération imposable en droit français, en application du régime fiscal mis en œuvre par la loi Pacte en 2019

En droit français, cette transaction serait qualifiée de contrat de vente, défini par l'article 1582 du Code civil comme « *une convention par laquelle l'un s'oblige à livrer une chose, et l'autre à la payer* ». En l'espèce, la chose serait les actifs numériques, vendus contre de la monnaie ayant cours légal.

Le droit français permet de recourir aux services d'un prestataire de services sur actifs numériques pour conserver et acheter/vendre des actifs numériques contre de la monnaie ayant cours légal.

En revanche, il convient de préciser que le prestataire de services sur actifs numériques qui propose ses services de conservation et d'achat/vente d'actifs numériques contre de la monnaie ayant cours légal en France ou qui les propose en étant établi en France a pour obligation d'être *a minima* enregistré auprès de l'Autorité des Marchés Financiers.

L'utilisateur devra quant à lui respecter les conditions générales d'utilisation fixées par le prestataire.

Un prestataire de services sur actifs numériques est soumis au droit français, et notamment à l'obligation d'obtenir un enregistrement auprès de l'AMF, si ce prestataire est établi en France ou s'il est considéré qu'il fournit ses services en France, selon les dispositions de l'article 721-1-1 du Règlement général de l'AMF évoqué ci-dessus.

2.2.5 Proposition de création d'un régime ad hoc de transfert de propriété des crypto actifs

Le projet d'ordonnance d'adaptation du droit français au Règlement MiCA prévoit la création d'un régime spécifique de transfert de propriété des crypto-actifs.

Ce régime s'inspire largement de celui existant pour les titres financiers, y compris les titres financiers numériques.

Il prend comme principe d'appliquer l'inscription des crypto-actifs dans un registre les effets du transfert de propriété. Selon le projet d'ordonnance, et reprenant la formulation existante pour les titres financiers, le transfert de propriété résulte de l'inscription dans le registre.

Le texte prévoit de distinguer deux situations.

Le principe général, selon lequel le registre dont il est question est la DLT sur laquelle les crypto-actifs en question sont adossés. Dans ce cas, c'est cette inscription dans la blockchain qui constitue le transfert de propriété. La seconde situation est vue comme une exception à la première et ne concerne que les crypto-actifs « intermédiés », c'est-à-dire les crypto-actifs qui font l'objet d'une conservation par un prestataire mentionné au paragraphe 1 de l'article 75 du Règlement MiCA habilité à exercer l'activité de conservation sur crypto-actifs. Dans ce cas-là, ce n'est pas le registre de DLT qui constitue le « lieu » du transfert de propriété, c'est le registre de position tenue par cet intermédiaire mentionné à l'article 75(2) du Règlement MiCA.

Hormis ces deux cas-là, toute autre situation – notamment le cas des transferts *off chain* – conduira à appliquer le régime de droit commun des biens meubles incorporels.

2.3 *Droit de la succession et actifs numériques*

Le régime juridique applicable aux actifs numériques ne prévoit pas de dispositions particulières en matière d'héritage d'actifs numériques, de sorte que l'héritage de ces actifs est soumis au régime de l'héritage de droit commun.

En cas de succession, le transfert opère de plein droit, par l'effet de la loi – sous réserve des règles régissant l'acceptation. A priori, le transfert ne repose pas sur une transaction en blockchain. En pratique, la principale difficulté pour les ayants droit est d'identifier les actifs du *de cujus* et de trouver les clés permettant d'y accéder.

2.4 *Fiducie et actifs numériques*

Le régime juridique applicable aux actifs numériques ne prévoit pas de dispositions particulières en matière de constitution de fiducie pour la gestion d'actifs numériques, de sorte que la constitution d'une fiducie à cette fin est soumise au régime de droit commun de la constitution de fiducie.

La fiducie est définie par l'article 2011 du Code civil comme « *l'opération par laquelle un ou plusieurs constituants transfèrent des biens, des droits ou des sûretés, ou un ensemble de biens, de droits ou de sûretés, présents ou futurs, à un ou plusieurs fiduciaires qui, les tenant séparés de leur patrimoine propre, agissent dans un but déterminé au profit d'un ou plusieurs bénéficiaires* ».

Ainsi, la constitution d'une fiducie pour la gestion d'actifs numériques est conditionnée au transfert par le constituant d'actifs numériques à un fiduciaire pour que ce dernier les gère.

2.5 *Saisie d'actifs numériques*

En droit français, deux régimes entrent en concurrence afin de procéder à la saisie d'actifs numériques.

Le premier régime est celui de la saisie-attribution. Cette dernière permet de saisir exclusivement des créances de « *somme d'argent* » en application de l'article L. 211-1 du Code de procédure civile d'exécution. Or, les actifs numériques n'ont pas la qualité de monnaies ayant cours légal. Ainsi, les actifs numériques ne peuvent pas être qualifiés de sommes d'argent en application de l'article L. 211-1 du CPCE.

Cependant, un régime de la saisie des biens meubles incorporels subsidiaire est prévu à l'article L. 231-1 du CPCE : « *Tout créancier muni d'un titre exécutoire constatant une créance liquide et exigible peut faire procéder à la saisie et à la vente des droits incorporels, autres que les créances de somme d'argent, dont son débiteur est titulaire* ».

Les actifs numériques peuvent ainsi faire l'objet d'une saisie au titre de biens meubles incorporels en application de l'article L. 231-1 du CPCE.

Si ce régime vise la saisie des droits d'associé et des valeurs mobilières, la formulation de l'article L.231-1 du CPCE est suffisamment large pour englober les crypto-actifs représentant des droits. Néanmoins, le dispositif mis en place repose sur la présence d'un tiers (émetteur, mandataire, intermédiaire habilité) qui concourt à la réalisation des opérations de saisie. C'est ce tiers qui est chargé de déclarer les actifs qu'il détient pour le compte du débiteur, et de faire droits aux opérations de transferts qu'implique in fine la mesure de saisie. Lorsque les crypto-actifs sont détenus via un prestataire de service de conservation, ce schéma peut être transposé : le conservateur joue un peu le même rôle que l'intermédiaire habilité. En revanche, lorsque le débiteur détient ses crypto-actifs en propre, leur saisie est impossible sans connaissance de la clé privé. Il existe des dispositions punissant le fait de ne pas révéler des clés cryptographiques, mais elles sont propres à la matière pénale (C. pénal, art. 434-15-2) et ne sont pas applicables pour mener à bien une saisie. Il y a donc là un obstacle, non pas juridique, mais technique : les actifs numériques détenues en propres sans conservateur tiers sont de facto insaisissables.

2.6 *Procédures collectives et actifs numériques*

En droit français, les procédures de sauvegarde, de redressement judiciaire et de liquidation judiciaire sont applicables « à toute personne exerçant une activité commerciale, artisanale ou une activité agricole, et, à toute autre personne physique exerçant une activité professionnelle indépendante, ainsi qu›à toute personne morale de droit privé »[34].

34 Articles L. 620-2, L. 631-2 et L. 640-2 du Code de commerce.

Il convient de préciser que les procédures de sauvegarde, de redressement et de liquidation judiciaire ouvertes à l'encontre d'établissement de crédit, de sociétés de financement, d'établissement de monnaie électronique, d'établissements de paiement et d'entreprises d'investissement sont régies par des règles spéciales qui ne s'appliquent pas aux prestataires de services sur actifs numériques. Ces derniers sont soumis au droit commun des procédures collectives.

En l'absence de mesure de protection spécifique aux titulaires d'actifs numériques déposés chez un conservateur (l'article L. 211-10, al. 2 du Code monétaire et financier prévoit la possibilité pour les clients d'un intermédiaire en faillite de virer ses titres chez un autre dépositaire), et compte tenu de la nature fongible et consomptible de ces actifs, l'analyse en droit de la faillite devrait être la suivante :

Le dépôt par un client d'actifs numériques chez un conservateur constitue un dépôt irrégulier au sens du droit civil. En vertu des règles classiques sur le dépôt irrégulier, le dépositaire acquiert la propriété des actifs déposés, le déposant n'étant plus titulaire que d'une créance de restitution.

Dans ces conditions, les actifs numériques déposés sont intégrés à l'actif général des créanciers. Les titulaires d'actifs numériques déposés en conservation auprès d'un tiers ne sont que des créanciers chirographaires et ne sont remboursés qu'à la fin de la procédure, après le paiement des créanciers privilégiés ou dotés de sûretés.

Ceci étant dit, il pourrait être possible d'appliquer l'alinéa 3 de l'article L.624-16 du Code de commerce qui permet à un créancier d'agir en revendication dans le cadre d'une procédure collective aux fins de récupérer ses crypto-actifs précédemment déposés. Bien sûr, il n'existe pas de jurisprudence à cet égard en droit français pour le cas de faillite d'un conservateur d'actifs numériques.

Deux approches peuvent être soutenues :

– Selon une première approche, l'on pourrait considérer que, bien que les crypto-actifs ne soient pas qualifiés de somme d'argent et de monnaie légale par la loi, ils peuvent y être assimilés dans la mesure où présentent certaines fonctions économiques similaires. Dans cette hypothèse, la jurisprudence française interdit la revendication de sommes d'argent, et dès lors d'actifs numériques.
– Selon une seconde approche, que nous privilégions, la qualification de bien meuble incorporel de nature fongible permet de fonder l'action en revendication portant sur des crypto-actifs précédemment déposés et conservés par un tiers. Selon l'article L.624-16 al. 3 du Code de commerce, « la revendication en nature peut également s'exercer sur des biens fongibles lorsque des biens de même nature et de même qualité se trouvent entre les mains du débiteur ou de toute personne les détenant pour son compte. ».

La question de l'action en revendication sur actifs numériques reste cependant ouverte[35].

MontC est un prestataire de service sur actifs numériques fournissant le service de conservation d'actifs numériques pour le compte de tiers. MontC conserve les actifs numériques de X – autrement dit, X dispose d'un droit de créance à l'encontre de MontC à hauteur des actifs numériques que ce dernier conserve pour le compte de ce premier. MontC est en état de cessation de paiement et est placé en redressement judiciaire, ou en liquidation judiciaire si le redressement s'avère impossible. Dans le cadre de l'une ou l'autre de ces procédures, X peut et doit déclarer sa créance de 60 Bitcoins pour la rendre opposable à MontC et ainsi faire valoir ses droits. La déclaration de créance doit être faite dans un délai de deux mois à compter de la publication du jugement d'ouverture de la procédure collective au Bulletin officiel, sous peine de forclusion.

X n'est qu'un créancier chirographaire et se verra restituer tout ou partie de sa créance, en fonction de l'actif distribuable restant, après le paiement des créanciers privilégiés.

Dans le cas où la relation contractuelle conclue entre X et MontC prévoyait des stipulations particulières en matière de restitution d'actifs numériques pour cause de procédure collective, celles-ci seraient inopérantes à partir de l'ouverture de la procédure collective.

Si MontC était une entité domiciliée dans un pays autre que la France, le droit applicable à la procédure collective serait celui du lieu de la situation de MontC. X, en sa qualité de créancier de MontC, devrait alors procéder à la déclaration de sa créance et, le cas échéant, à d'autres formalités, en conformité avec le droit du lieu de domiciliation de MontC.

Le droit français ne fait pas de distinction entre créancier personne physique et créancier personne morale en procédure collective. Le compte de Z, personne morale, ouvert auprès de MontC recevrait le même traitement que la créance de X.

2.7 *Le nantissement d'actifs numériques*

L'article 2355 du Code civil dispose que le nantissement « est l'affectation, en garantie d'une obligation, d'un bien meuble incorporel ou d'un ensemble de biens meubles incorporels, présents ou futurs. » Les actifs numériques étant

35 H. de Vauplane, "La revendication d'actifs numériques", *RTDF*, 2019/3, p. 56.

des biens meubles incorporels[36], ces derniers peuvent donc faire l'objet d'un nantissement de droit commun.

Le droit français ne présente aucune disposition spécifique en matière de nantissement d'actifs numériques, à l'inverse du nantissement de comptes-titres et de titres financiers.

Le projet d'ordonnance d'adaptation du droit français au Règlement MiCA prévoit la création d'un régime *ad hoc* de nantissement d'actifs numériques s'inspirant du régime du nantissement de compte-titres prévu aux articles L. 211-20 et suivants du CMF.

Le régime du nantissement serait modifié comme suit afin de tenir compte des spécificités des crypto-actifs :

- Comme pour un nantissement de compte-titres, la constitution du nantissement de crypto-actifs est opposable *inter partes* et à l'égard des tiers sans autre formalité que la signature de la déclaration de nantissement. De même, la déclaration doit contenir des mentions obligatoires précisées par décret analogues à celles que contient la déclaration de nantissement de compte-titres. La faculté, pour le créancier, d'obtenir une attestation de nantissement est conservée. Cette attestation sera donnée par le prestataire de services sur crypto-actifs fournissant le service de conservation des crypto-actifs nantis. Dans l'éventualité où les crypto-actifs nantis produiraient des «fruits et produits» en monnaie fiat (à l'instar de titres nantis), l'attestation y relative sera fournie par l'établissement de crédit auprès duquel un compte de fruits et produits devra être ouvert par le constituant. Enfin, il pourrait être prévu par décret que la constitution du nantissement puisse intervenir par *smart contract*.
- A l'instar du nantissement de compte de titres financiers, une clause d'arrosage prévoit que l'adjonction de nouveaux actifs dans l'assiette du nantissement est réputée intervenir à la date du nantissement indiquée dans l'acte, le cas échéant dans le *smart contract*, de manière équivalente à l'inscription de nouveaux titres dans le compte-titres nanti.
- Les crypto-actifs peuvent produire des fruits et produits, notamment dans le cadre de leur immobilisation dans le cadre d'un processus de staking ou encore dans le cadre d'une bifurcation (fork). Dans ce dernier cas, tant les nouveaux crypto-actifs issus d'un fork que les anciens crypto-actifs préexistant au fork (cette situation correspond généralement à celle d'un hard fork, lorsque le fork aboutit à la création d'une nouvelle blockchain et l'attribution aux porteurs d'anciens actifs numériques de nouveau tokens, comme

36 L'article L. 552-2 du Code monétaire et financier définit les jetons comme des biens incorporels.

dans le cas du fork du Bitcoin, BTC/BCH) entrent dans l'assiette du nantissement. Il conviendra donc aux parties de préciser si les anciens crypto-actifs doivent faire, ou non, l'objet d'une mainlevée. L'éventualité de fruits ou produits en toute monnaie ne doit pas être écartée (notamment dans le cas de remboursement d'ART ou d'EMT).

- L'hypothèse de nantissements successifs est envisagée également pour les crypto-actifs. Dans ce cas, l'ordre de nantissements doit être réglé par leurs déclarations initiales.
- Concernant le droit de rétention, il ne semble pas possible de prévoir de manière adéquate dans la loi ou les règlements les modalités techniques/technologiques d'exercice d'un tel droit de rétention. Par conséquent, le projet prévoit de renvoyer aux parties la charge de convenir de telles modalités. Le projet prévoit que le créancier nanti bénéficie en toute hypothèse d'un droit de rétention, qui sera opposable à la procédure collective du constituant.

2.8 *– L'exécution du nantissement pourrait être réalisée, outre par des moyens traditionnels (remise en main propre ou courrier recommandé), par écrit ou par smart contract selon des modalités à fixer par décret le cas échéant. Le prêt d'actifs numériques*

Un an après que le législateur a introduit le régime des prestataires de services sur actifs numériques via la loi PACTE, l'Autorité des Marchés Financiers a publié un guide réglementaire pour aider les prestataires de services d'actifs numériques dans leur procédure d'enregistrement et d'agrément. Le guide se présente sous la forme de questions-réponses dans lesquelles le régulateur fournit des indications sur l'application de la législation[37].

Le régulateur ne cesse de mettre à jour les questions-réponses pour préserver leur pertinence compte tenu de l'évolution constante des pratiques de marché. L'AMF a d'ailleurs modifié sa politique sur le régime des prestataires de services d'actifs numériques pour tenir compte de l'évolution des produits et des modèles d'affaires des acteurs du secteur.

L'AMF reconnait la pratique de prêt d'actifs numériques ou de « *crypto-lending* », qui correspond selon elle « *au fait pour un prestataire de mettre des actifs numériques à la disposition d'une autre personne physique ou morale qui s'engage à les lui restituer à l'issue d'une période déterminée* ».

L'AMF précise que « *selon les modalités que revêtent les services proposés par le prestataire en lien avec ces deux activités, ceux-ci peuvent constituer un service*

37 AMF, Position DOC-2020-07.

sur actifs numériques au sens de l'article L. 54-10-2 du code monétaire et financier et/ou un service de paiement au sens de l'article L. 314-1 du code monétaire et financier et donc requérir un enregistrement ou un agrément respectivement, le cas échéant ».

Des sanctions pénales sont prévues aux articles L. 572-5 (prestataires de service de paiement) et L. 572-23 (prestataires de services sur actifs numériques) du code monétaire et financier en cas d'exercice de l'une ou l'autre des activités sans avoir obtenu d'enregistrement.

Conformément à la décision précitée plus haut et rendue le 26 février 2020 par le tribunal de commerce de Nanterre, le prêt d'actifs numériques est régi par le prêt de consommation prévu par l'article 1892 et suivants du Code civil.

2.9 *La perte d'actifs numériques*

La perte des actifs numériques d'un utilisateur par un prestataire de services sur actifs numériques à la suite d'un piratage ou d'une fraude comporte plusieurs conséquences.

2.9.1 Sur la responsabilité du prestataire de service sur actifs numériques

Dans une telle situation, il convient d'abord de se référer aux conditions générales d'utilisation encadrant la responsabilité du prestataire de services sur actifs numériques en cas de perte des actifs numériques des utilisateurs à la suite d'une fraude ou d'un piratage.

Les stipulations des conditions générales d'utilisation représentent le lien contractuel qui lie l'utilisateur au prestataire de services sur actifs numériques, étant noté que « *les contrats légalement formés tiennent lieu de loi à ceux qui les ont faits* »[38].

Les conditions générales d'utilisation tendent souvent à réduire la responsabilité des prestataires de services sur actifs numériques. Toutefois, certaines clauses pourraient être considérées comme abusives au regard du droit de la consommation. En effet le Code de la consommation prévoit en son article L. 212-1 que « *dans les contrats conclus entre professionnels et consommateurs, sont abusives les clauses qui ont pour objet ou pour effet de créer, au détriment du consommateur, un déséquilibre significatif entre les droits et obligations des parties au contrat* ». Il convient de préciser qu'un consommateur est « *toute personne physique qui agit à des fins qui n'entrent pas dans le cadre de son*

38 Idem.

activité commerciale, industrielle, artisanale, libérale ou agricole » en application de l'article liminaire du Code de la consommation.

En dehors du droit de la consommation, l'article 1171 du Code civil dispose que « *dans un contrat d'adhésion, toute clause non négociable, déterminée à l'avance par l'une des parties, qui crée un déséquilibre significatif entre les droits et obligations des parties au contrat est réputée non écrite* », étant précisé que « *l'appréciation du déséquilibre significatif ne porte ni sur l'objet principal du contrat ni sur l'adéquation du prix à la prestation* ». Ainsi, un utilisateur ayant une qualité autre que celle de consommateur pourrait se prévaloir du caractère réputé non-écrit de la clause limitative de responsabilité stipulée dans les conditions générales d'utilisation.

L'action en responsabilité menée par l'utilisateur à l'encontre du prestataire de service sur actifs numériques serait de nature contractuelle. L'article 1231-1 du Code civil dispose : « *Le débiteur est condamné, s'il y a lieu, au paiement de dommages et intérêts soit à raison de l'inexécution de l'obligation, soit à raison du retard dans l'exécution, s'il ne justifie pas que l'exécution a été empêchée par la force majeure.* »

L'article L. 54-10-5, II, 3° du code monétaire et financier dispose que le PSAN conservateur doit « [*s'assurer*] *de la mise en place des moyens nécessaires à la restitution dans les meilleurs délais des actifs numériques ou d'un accès aux actifs numériques détenus pour le compte de leurs clients* ». Le prestataire de services sur actifs numérique proposant des services de conservation d'actifs numériques a donc une obligation de moyen à respecter.

Le 6° de l'article 722-1 du RGAMF encadre la responsabilité du prestataire de la façon suivant que « *sauf en cas d'événements non imputables, directement ou indirectement, au prestataire de services sur actifs numériques, il effectue la restitution de la maîtrise des moyens d'accès aux actifs numériques au client dans les meilleurs délais. En cas d'impossibilité de restitution de la maîtrise de ces moyens d'accès, le conservateur d'actifs numériques indemnise son client* ».

L'AMF précise dans sa doctrine que les événements non imputables au conservateur d'actifs numériques "*comprennent notamment tout événement dont il pourra démontrer qu'il est indépendant de son fonctionnement, notamment un problème inhérent au fonctionnement du dispositif d'enregistrement électronique partagé ou à un programme informatique automatisé ("smart contract") pouvant reposer sur un dispositif électronique d'enregistrement partagé qu'il ne maîtrise pas*".

A titre d'illustration, la perte des actifs numériques du client conservé pour son compte par le prestataire de services sur actifs numériques du fait du piratage d'un *smart contract* est un évènement non imputable, directement ou indirectement, au PSAN, qui l'exonère de son obligation de restitution ou d'indemnisation, à condition que ce *smart contract* n'ait pas été programmé par le PSAN lui-même.

2.9.2 Sur la responsabilité du pirate informatique

Le droit français permet à l'utilisateur d'agir à l'encontre du pirate informatique ayant causé la perte de ses actifs numériques. L'utilisateur peut faire le choix entre engager la responsabilité pénale ou la responsabilité civile du pirate informatique. Cependant ces responsabilités ne peuvent pas être cumulées sur le même fondement.

En droit pénal, le vol est caractérisé comme étant la soustraction frauduleuse de la chose d'autrui[39] et est puni de trois ans d'emprisonnement et de 45 000 euros d'amende[40]. De plus, le fait d'accéder ou de se maintenir, frauduleusement, dans tout ou partie d'un système de traitement automatisé de données est puni de deux ans d'emprisonnement et de 60 000 € d'amende[41].

En droit civil, l'utilisateur peut engager la responsabilité civile délictuelle du pirate informatique en application des articles 1240 et suivant du code civil.

En pratique, l'engagement de la responsabilité pénale ou civile du pirate informatique n'est pas facile du fait de difficultés d'identification du pirate.

2.9.3 Sur la responsabilité du tiers acquéreur d'actifs numériques

Comme on a vu plus haut, il n'existe pas de disposition propre aux actifs numériques pour protéger les tiers acquéreurs de bonne foi comme il en existe pour les titres financiers.

En droit français, le recel est le fait de dissimuler, de détenir ou de transmettre une chose, ou de faire office d'intermédiaire afin de la transmettre, en sachant que cette chose provient d'un crime ou d'un délit[42].

Au vu de la transparence des transactions sur les dispositifs d'enregistrement électronique partagé (blockchain), et de la facilité d'accès à l'information, il devrait être difficile de prouver la bonne foi du tiers acquéreur des Bitcoins volés.

L'acquéreur risque donc d'engager sa responsabilité pénale sur le fondement du recel de vol.

---

39 Article 311-1 du Code pénal.

40 Article 311-3 du Code pénal.

41 Article 323-1 du Code pénal.

42 Article 321-1 du Code pénal.

2.9.4 Les recours d'un utilisateur induit en erreur pour transférer ses Bitcoins :

En France, est qualifié d'escroquerie le fait, soit par l'usage d'un faux nom ou d'une fausse qualité, soit par l'abus d'une qualité vraie, soit par l'emploi de manœuvres frauduleuses, de tromper une personne physique ou morale et de la déterminer ainsi, à son préjudice ou au préjudice d'un tiers, à remettre des fonds, des valeurs ou un bien quelconque, à fournir un service ou à consentir un acte opérant obligation ou décharge.

L'escroquerie est punie de cinq ans d'emprisonnement et de 375 000 euros d'amende[43].

3 Mesures fiscales

3.1 *Le régime fiscal français*

Il existe un régime fiscal, mis en œuvre par la loi de finances 2019, spécifique aux transferts d'actifs numériques qui peut être résumé comme suit :

Les échanges d'actifs numériques contre d'autres actifs numériques ne constituent pas un événement imposable[44].

Le déclencheur de la taxation peut être le suivant : échange d'un actif numérique contre de la monnaie fiduciaire, échange d'un bien autre qu'un actif numérique ou échange contre la valeur d'un actif numérique ou d'un service.

Le gain net d'une activité non professionnelle est en principe imposable au taux forfaitaire de 30%, dont 12,8% correspondent à l'impôt sur le revenu des personnes physiques et 17,2% aux cotisations de sécurité sociale.

Les activités exercées à titre professionnel sont imposables dans la catégorie des bénéfices industriels et commerciaux (régime des plus-values professionnelles).

Lors de l'ouverture d'un compte d'actifs virtuels dans un établissement étranger, le contribuable doit déclarer les bénéfices tirés de ses comptes étrangers. A défaut, il s'expose à une amende de 750 euros par compte non déclaré.

Ce régime a été complété dans la loi de finances pour 2022. A compter du 1er janvier 2023, les produits de l'achat, de la vente et de l'échange d'actifs numériques réalisés dans des conditions similaires à celles caractérisant une activité d›une personne se livrant à titre professionnel à ce type d›opérations sont imposables en tant que bénéfices non commerciaux[45].

---

43 Article 313-1 du Code pénal.

44 Article 150 VH bis du code général des impôts français.

45 Article 92 du code général des impôts français (CGI).

3.2 *Existe-t-il une quelconque exonération fiscale ?*

Il existe une exonération d'impôt sur la plus-value globale réalisée dans l'année, au sens de l'article 150 VH bis du CGI, si le total des cessions d'actifs numériques est inférieur à 305 euros.

4 Litiges relatifs aux actifs numériques

4.1 *Procédures clôturées*

Un jugement a été rendu le 26 février 2020 par le tribunal de commerce de Nanterre qui a tranché un litige impliquant la société française Paymium qui avait prêté 1000 Bitcoins (BTC) à la société BitSpread entre mai 2014 et juin 2016. Le 1er août 2017 a eu lieu le « *hardfork*[46] » de Bitcoin, BitcoinCash (BCC). Durant ce « *fork* » tout détenteur d'un BTC a reçu un BCC. Dès lors, la société prêteuse a réclamé les 1000 BCC obtenus par BitSpread grâce aux 1000 BTC empruntés.

Le tribunal a estimé que le Bitcoin est de nature fongible et consomptible, de sorte qu'il est consommé lors de son utilisation. Ainsi, le prêt de bitcoins constitue un prêt de consommation au sens de l'article 1892 du Code civil. De cette qualification de prêt de consommation découle le fait que la propriété des Bitcoins prêtés est transférée entre le prêteur et l'emprunteur.

4.2 *Procédures d'arbitrage en lien avec les actifs numériques*

Nous n'avons pas connaissance de procédures d'arbitrage en rapport avec les actifs numériques.

4.3 *Actions de groupe relatives aux actifs numériques*

En France, il est possible des réaliser des actions de groupe en application de l'article L. 623-1 du Code de la consommation. Ces actions de groupe permettent à un groupe de consommateurs ayant subi des dommages similaires, y compris ceux liés aux actifs numériques, de faire valoir leurs droits de manière collective, à travers une association de défense des consommateurs représentative au niveau national et agréée, pouvant agir devant une juridiction civile afin d'obtenir la réparation des préjudices individuels subis.

L'article liminaire du code de la consommation définit le consommateur comme « *toute personne physique qui agit à des fins qui n'entrent pas dans le cadre de son activité commerciale, industrielle, artisanale, libérale ou agricole* ».

46 Scission de la blockchain générant ainsi une nouvelle blockchain et un second actif numérique.

Il n'existe cependant pas de chefs de juridiction spéciaux ou exclusifs aux litiges relatifs aux actifs numériques.

4.4 *Reconnaissance de sentence arbitrale relative aux actifs numériques*

Nous n'avons pas connaissance de sentence arbitrale relative à un litige impliquant des actifs numériques reconnue et exécutée par le tribunal judiciaire.

5 Documentation

Les sources de droit, positions et instructions des régulateurs, ainsi que les principaux articles de doctrine sont notamment :

Loi Pacte du 22 mai 2019 ;

Articles L. 54-10-1 et suivants et D. 54-10-1 et suivants du Code monétaire et financier ;

Articles 721-1 et suivants du Règlement général de l'Autorité des Marchés Financiers ;

Positions de l'Autorité des Marchés Financiers DOC-2020-07, DOC-2019-23, DOC-2019-24.

Germany

Jens-Hinrich Binder

1 Introduction[1]

The legal treatment of cryptocurrencies under German law is a moving target. To date, a consistent framework for the legal qualification of crypto-assets,[2] let alone comprehensive and consistent solutions for the treatment of such assets in areas like contract law, the law of property, inheritance law, IP law, civil procedure (including, for that matter, insolvency law), or tax law are yet to emerge. Although coverage of cryptocurrencies in the academic literature started almost a decade ago,[3] legislative responses to the increasing role of cryptocurrencies within the country have remained piecemeal, with many questions completely unresolved. While a growing number of court decisions addressing virtual currencies in various areas of the law have been reported in recent years, relevant case law continues to be confined to judgments of lower instances, leaving not just many aspects completely uncharted, but also a substantial degree of legal uncertainty. In the area of financial law, however, the situation looks different. Following some initial confusion over the treatment for regulatory purposes, "crypto-assets" (just like, for instance, traditional securities) have been expressly recognised as "financial instruments" for the purposes of the German Banking Act (*"Kreditwesengesetz"*, hereafter: 'KWG'), which prepares the ground for the application of general licensing requirements and for the prudential regulation and supervision of intermediaries dealing in crypto-assets in line with received principles of financial regulation more generally. Significantly, recent legislation has also paved the way for the issuance of so-called crypto securities (*"Kryptowertpapiere"*), *i.e.*, bonds issued electronically

---

1 The author would like to thank Mr Raphael Reiss for valuable research assistance. All remaining errors are his own. The following chapter states the law as of early December 2024.

2 As will be discussed further below, applicable German (regulatory) law is based on the notion of "crypto-assets" rather than "cryptocurrency".

3 For representative early examples, cf. F. Boehm and P. Pesch, 'Bitcoins: Rechtliche Herausforderungen einer virtuellen Währung – Eine erste juristische Einordung', in: *MMR – Multimedia und Recht* (2014), 75–79 and G. Spindler and M. Bille, 'Rechtsprobleme von Bitcoins als virtuelle Währung', in: *WM – Wertpapiermitteilungen. Zeitschrift für Wirtschafts- und Bankrecht* (2014), 1357–1369.

 | DOI:10.1163/9789004722507_013

and registered in a designated registry.[4] While this legislation does not relate to cryptocurrencies and is, therefore, outside the scope of the present report, it is nonetheless illustrative of a more progressive approach to the regulation of crypto-assets in the regulatory realm in recent years. The transactional side of financial services, however, still remains largely uncharted territory, as both conduct-of-business and prospectus requirements yet have to be adapted to the issuance of, and transactions in, cryptocurrencies.

In stark contrast to the regulatory framework, the treatment of crypto-assets under German private law – or, indeed, in other areas – has not yet been addressed in statutory law so far. While it is clear that cryptocurrencies are not recognised as legal tender, their precise qualification has not been addressed in the *Bürgerliches Gesetzbuch* (hereafter "BGB", the Civil Code),[5] resulting in difficulties to qualify relevant transactions in, and the possession of, such assets for the purposes of general principles of private law. In this context, the recognition of crypto-assets in *regulatory* law, which is derived from international and European anti-money laundering standards, is of little use, and does not help to clarify the position of cryptocurrencies in the traditional categories of private property, so that the solution of specific cases rests entirely on the application (and adaptation) of established general principles.

Following a more detailed introduction to the qualification of cryptocurrencies in German regulatory and private law summarised below (*infra*, 2.), the present report examines the applicable regulatory framework in some detail (*infra*, 3.), before turning to the relevant private law issues (*infra*, 4.) and the treatment of cryptocurrencies in tax law (*infra*, 5.) and other areas (*infra*, 6.).

2 The Absence of Common Ground: Definition of Crypto-Assets in Regulatory Law and the Position in Private Law

2.1 *Cryptocurrencies Within Germany – the Current Market*

While detailed statistics on the use of cryptocurrencies within Germany do not appear to exist, it certainly can be said that all relevant known forms, including, in particular *Bitcoin* and *Ethereum*, are also traded between parties in Germany. A country-specific market in such instruments, however, is yet to

4 See Law on electronic securities (*"Gesetz über elektronische Wertpapiere"*) of 3 June 2021, *Bundesgesetzblatt* I, p. 1423.

5 But see section 327(1) sentence 2 BGB (as introduced in 2021), which recognises that 'digital representations of value' may be agreed as a price payable in exchange for 'digital products' or 'digital services'. See, further, infra, 4.1.

emerge,[6] which has been attributed also to the absence of a coherent, reliable legal and regulatory framework that would ensure legal certainty for issuers and investors alike.[7]

2.2 *Statutory Definitions in Regulatory Law*

To date, no reference has been made to (the German language equivalent of) the concept of "cryptocurrencies" – or, for that matter, to "virtual currencies"[8] – in German statutory law. However, the transposition of the 2018 amendment to the EU Anti-Money Laundering Directive (AMLD),[9] in 2019,[10] has led to the recognition of the category of 'crypto-assets' in the KWG, which – as will be discussed further in section 3 below – provides the legal basis for the prudential regulation and supervision of financial intermediaries other than insurance companies within the country. In line with the definition of the term in international standards,[11] section 1(11), sentence 4 KWG now defines the term crypto-asset (*"Kryptowert"*) as

> a digital representation of value that is not issued or guaranteed by a central bank or a public authority and does not possess a legal status of currency or money, but is accepted by natural or legal persons, on the

---

6 For an instructive discussion of the current role of crypto-assets within the country and potential perspectives in this regard, cf., e.g., Deutsche Bundesbank, 'Krypto-Token im Zahlungsverkehr und in der Wertpapierabwicklung', *Monatsbericht* [Monthly Report] July 2019, 39; *id.*, 'Krypto-Token und dezentrale Finanzanwendungen', *Monatsbericht* July 2021, 33; see also V. Brühl, 'Decentralised Finance – wie die Tokenisierung die Finanzindustrie verändert', *Wirtschaftsdienst* 101 (2021), 629.

7 L. Klöhn, N. Parhofer and D. Resas, 'Initial Coin Offerings – Markt, Ökonomik und Regulierung', ZBB – *Zeitschrift für Bankrecht und Bankbetrieb* (2018), 89, at p. 99.

8 E.g., within the meaning defined by Art. 3(18) AMLD: 'a digital representation of value that is not issued or guaranteed by a central bank or a public authority, is not necessarily attached to a legally established currency and does not possess a legal status of currency or money, but is accepted by natural or legal persons as a means of exchange and which can be transferred, stored and traded electronically'. See also EBA, 'EBA Opinion on "virtual currencies"' (EBA/Op/2014/08) (4 July 2014), p. 11.

9 Directive (EU) 2015/849 of the European Parliament and of the Council of 20 May 2015 on the prevention of the use of the financial system for the purposes of money laundering or terrorist financing (…), OJ L 141, p. 73 (as amended by Directive (EU) 2018/843 of the European Parliament and of the Council of 30 May 2018, OJ L 156, p. 43).

10 Law Transposing the Directive Amending the 4th EU Anti-Money Laundering Directive of 12 December 2019, *Bundesgesetzblatt* I, p. 2602.

11 Cf., e.g., Financial Stability Board, 'Crypto-asset markets: Potential channels for future financial stability implications' (10 October 2018), pp. 3–4, referred to in Federal Government, Explanatory Notes to the 2019 legislation, *Bundestags-Drucksache* 19/13827, pp. 48 and 110.

basis of an agreement or otherwise in their current dealings, as a means of exchange or for investment purposes, and which can be transferred, stored and traded electronically.[12]

Sentence 5 of the same provision expressly exempts E-money and other forms of electronic token used exclusively in connection with payments processes from the application of that definition, which has been designed so as to provide a broad, catch-all term covering all relevant virtual assets not confined to virtual currencies in a strict sense.[13] This definition is, broader in scope than the definition of the term "virtual currency" in Art. 3(18) AMLD. Moreover, crypto-assets within the meaning of the KWG now qualify as "financial instruments" (*"Finanzinstrumente"*) for the purposes of the act. The definition thus serves as the basis for the application of general licensing and prudential requirements for intermediaries dealing in crypto-assets in the broadest sense.

Moreover, the definition set out in section 1(11), sentence 4 KWG is also referred to in section 1(29) of the *Geldwäschegesetz* (Money Laundering Act, hereafter: 'GWG') and a statutory instrument complementing the GWG, which stipulates specific duties for the prevention of money laundering in connection with the transfer of crypto-assets.[14]

Upon completion of the present report, German regulatory law thus does not (yet) distinguish between specific forms of crypto-assets, and certainly does not provide for a specific category of cryptocurrencies, but rather treats them as part of a broader phenomenon. The framework summarised above will inevitably change with – and, as far as the licensing and prudential regulation of issuers is concerned, superseded by – the EU Regulation on Markets in Crypto-Assets (MiCAR),[15] which has introduced a similarly broad definition of

12 In the German original: 'digitale Darstellungen eines Wertes, der von keiner Zentralbank oder öffentlichen Stelle emittiert wurde oder garantiert wird und nicht den gesetzlichen Status einer Währung oder von Geld besitzt, aber von natürlichen oder juristischen Personen aufgrund einer Vereinbarung oder tatsächlichen Übung als Tausch- oder Zahlungsmittel akzeptiert wird oder Anlagezwecken dient und der auf elektronischem Wege übertragen, gespeichert und gehandelt werden kann.'

13 Cf. Explanatory Notes to the 2019 Law, *Bundestags-Drucksache* 19/13827, p. 110. On the regulatory position with regard to e-money, see further *infra*, 3.5.

14 See Verordnung über verstärkte Sorgfaltspflichten bei dem Transfer von Kryptowerten (Kryptowertetransferverordnung – KryptoWTransferV) of 24 September 2021, *Bundesgesetzblatt* I, p. 4465.

15 See Commission, Proposal for a Regulation of the European Parliament and of the Council on Markets in Crypto-assets, and amending Directive (EU) 2019/1937 (24 September 2020), COM(2020) 593 final. Upon completion of the present manuscript, the Regulation

crypto-assets,[16] but also differentiate between various forms of assets in terms of the applicable substantive and procedural duties of issuers.

2.3 *The Position in Private Law*

2.3.1 The Starting Point: Cryptocurrencies are Not 'Money'

Importantly, cryptocurrencies (or, indeed, other forms of crypto-assets), just as in any other Member State of the Eurozone, are not recognised as legal tender under German law.[17]

The private law implications of this principle are rather ill-defined, however. Whether cryptocurrencies actually qualify as "money" (or "currency") at all for the purposes of private law, has been debated controversially by scholars in recent years. According to the majority view, this is not the case precisely because they cannot be universally exchanged into "public" currency.[18] The immediate practical consequences of this controversy are rather limited, however. Effectively, the BGB addresses the concept of "money" (or "currency") only in two subsequent provisions on the right to repay non-Euro denominated obligations payable within Germany in Euro (sec. 244 BGB) and on payments on obligations denominated in a currency that no longer exists (sec. 245 BGB). These provisions provide but a poor basis for the treatment of monetary obligations in German private law. Hence, most relevant aspects – for example, the legal consequences of a debtor's inability to pay, or of late payments – have to be derived from more general principles of the law of obligations.[19] As cryptocurrencies are *not* recognised as legal tender, they are not as such, or at least:

---

has been formally endorsed by the European Parliament and the Council, but not yet been published in the Official Journal.

16 Cf. original Commission Draft, Art. 3(1)(2): 'a digital representation of value or rights which may be transferred and stored electronically, using distributed ledger technology or similar technology'. In the final version (now Art. 3(1)(5)), this wording has been changed only slightly ("… representation of *a value* or of *a right*…").

17 Pursuant to Art. 128(1), sentence 3 TFEU, '[t]he banknotes issued by the European Central Bank and the national central banks shall be the only such notes to have the status of legal tender within the Union.'

18 E.g., S. Omlor, 'Geld und Währung als Digitalisate', Juristenzeitung (2017), 754, at pp. 759–60; id., 'Kryptowährungen im Geldrecht', *ZHR – Zeitschrift für das gesamte Handelsrecht und Wirtschaftsrecht* 183 (2019), 294, at 307–08; C. Engelhardt and S. Klein, 'Bitcoins – Geschäfte mit Geld, das keines ist', *MMR – Multimedia und Recht* (2014), 355, at p. 356; G. Spindler and M. Bille, 'Rechtsprobleme von Bitcoins als virtuelle Währung', *WM Wertpapiermitteilungen* (2014), 1357, at 1360-61. But see (supporting a functional interpretation of the concept of "money") also R. Freitag, Commentary to section 244 BGB, in: *BeckOnline-Großkommentar zum BGB* (15 March 2021), para. 31.

19 See, e.g., S. Grundmann, Commentary to section 245 BGB, in: J. Säcker et al. (eds.), *Münchener Kommentar zum Bürgerlichen Gesetzbuch* (9th ed., 2022), paras. 13–22.

not without modifications, subject to the private law principles governing monetary obligations,[20] which will be discussed in more detail below (*infra*, 4.1.1.).

2.3.2 The Classification in Private Law

While it is generally agreed that crypto-currency tokens, as such, cannot be qualified as 'claims' (*"Forderungen"*) under German law, if and to the extent that they do not reflect a bipolar relationship whereby one party (the creditor) has an enforceable right to claim something from the debtor,[21] other alternatives have been discussed rather controversially in recent years.

Some authors have claimed that crypto-assets generally, despite their 'virtual' nature, should be qualified as 'things' (tangible goods, *"Sachen"*) for the purposes of private law.[22] This view is difficult to reconcile with the wording and traditional interpretation of the statutory definition of 'things' in section 90 BGB, however, according to which only tangible (or, in the words of the official translation of the BGB,[23] "corporeal") objects qualify as things. Against this backdrop, most authors have convincingly rejected the qualification of crypto tokens as 'things' within the meaning of section 90 BGB.[24]

---

20 Cf. Grundmann, ibid., para. 34.

21 E.g., K. Langenbucher, 'Digitales Finanzwesen', *AcP – Archiv für die civilistische Praxis* 218 (2018), 385, at p. 406; D. Skauradszun, 'Kryptowerte im Bürgerlichen Recht', in: *AcP – Archiv für die civilistische Praxis* 221 (2021), 353, at pp. 365–66; G. Spindler and M. Bille, 'Rechtsprobleme von Bitcoins als virtuelle Währung', *WM – Wertpapiermitteilungen* (2014), 1357, at p. 1360. It has been debated whether, by these standards, cryptocurrencies issued by a central issuer (*e.g.*, Libra) could qualify as a claim by these standards: see K. Langenbucher, M Hoche and J. Wentz, 'Virtuelle Währungen' in: K. Langenbucher, D. H. Bliesener and G. Spindler (eds.), *Bankrechtskommentar* (3rd ed., 2020), p. 782, at p. 791, para. 37. This is far from settled and not free from doubt, however.

22 See, in particular, D. John, 'Zur Sachqualität und Eigentumsfähigkeit von Kryptotoken', *BKR – Zeitschrift für Bank- und Kapitalmarktrecht* (2020), 76 (arguing that the traditional concept of 'things' as tangible goods should be reinterpreted); see also P. Koch, 'Die "Tokenisierung" von Rechtspositionen als digitale Verbriefung', *ZBB – Zeitschrift für Bankrecht und Bankwirtschaft* (2018), 359, at pp. 362–63); A. Walter, 'Bitcoin, Libra und sonstige Kryptowährungen aus zivilrechtlicher Sicht', *NJW – Neue Juristische Wochenschrift* (2019), 3609, at p. 3613 (both arguing for the application of principles pertaining to tangible goods *per analogiam*).

23 See https://www.gesetze-im-internet.de/englisch_bgb/englisch_bgb.html#p0736.

24 E.g., K. Langenbucher, M Hoche and J. Wentz, 'Virtuelle Währungen' in: K. Langenbucher, D. H. Bliesener and G. Spindler (eds.), *Bankrechtskommentar* (3rd ed., 2020), p. 782, at p. 790 para. 35; J. Schmidt, commentary to § 90 BGB, in: Erman, *BGB* (16th ed., 2020), para. 3; B. Beck and D. König, 'Bitcoin: Der Versuch einer vertragstypologischen Einordnung von kryptographischem Geld', *JZ – Juristenzeitung* (2015), 130, at p. 132; C. Engelhardt and S. Klein, 'Bitcoins – Geschäfte mit Geld, das keines ist', *MMR – Multimedia und Recht* (2014),

If, then, cryptocurrency tokens can neither be qualified as 'claims' nor as 'things' for the purposes of private law, the remaining option would be the qualification as 'other property right', a category whose implications are not as clearly defined. While they cannot be qualified as intellectual property rights for the purposes of German IP law (section 69a in conjunction with section 2(1)(1) *Urheberrechtsgesetz* [Act on Copyrights and Related Rights]),[25] their legal status as an 'other property right' (convincingly) has been acknowledged by many authors, but also remains contested.[26] It should be noted, however, that while this qualification may be helpful in that it clarifies the legal nature of cryptocurrency as such, it certainly does not remove the resulting difficulties to qualify transactions in cryptocurrency for the purposes of contract and property law, which results in a high degree of legal uncertainty that also extends to procedural aspects (see *infra*, 4.1.1., 4.1.2. and 4.2.).

3 Regulatory Framework and Supervision

3.1 *Overview*

As indicated before (*supra*, 2.1.), current German law, which also serves as the legal basis for the supervision of transactions in cryptocurrencies,

---

355, at p. 359; D. Skauradszun, 'Kryptowerte im Bürgerlichen Recht', *AcP – Archiv für die civilistische Praxis* 221 (2021), 353, at pp. 361–63; G. Spindler and M. Bille, 'Rechtsprobleme von Bitcoins als virtuelle Währung', WM – *Wertpapiermitteilungen* (2014), 1357, at 1359.

25 E.g., B. Beck and D. König, 'Bitcoin: Der Versuch einer vertragstypologischen Einordnung von kryptographischem Geld', JZ – *Juristenzeitung* (2015), 130, at p. 131; M.E. Kütük and C. Sorge, 'Bitcoin im deutschen Vollstreckungsrecht', MMR – *Multimedia und Recht* (2014), 643, at p. 644; A. Schlund and H. Pongratz, 'Distributed-Ledger-Technologie und Kryptowährungen – eine rechtliche Betrachtung', *DStR – Deutsches Steuerrecht* (2018), 598, at p. 600; G. Spindler and M. Bille, 'Rechtsprobleme von Bitcoins als virtuelle Währung', WM – *Wertpapiermitteilungen* (2014), 1357, at p. 1360.

26 E.g., K. Langenbucher, 'Digitales Finanzwesen', *AcP – Archiv für die civilistische Praxis* 218 (2018), 385, at p. 407; A. Schlund and H. Pongratz, 'Distributed-Ledger-Technologie und Kryptowährungen – eine rechtliche Betrachtung', *DStR – Deutsches Steuerrecht* (2018), 598, at p. 600; D. Skauradszun, Kryptowerte im Bürgerlichen Recht', *AcP – Archiv für die civilistische Praxis* 221 (2021), 353, at pp. 468–69; G. Spindler and M. Bille, 'Rechtsprobleme von Bitcoins als virtuelle Währung', WM – *Wertpapiermitteilungen* (2014), 1357, at 1360. But see, arguing against the qualification as a property right, also M.E. Kütük and C. Sorge, 'Bitcoin im deutschen Vollstreckungsrecht', MMR – *Multimedia und Recht* (2014), 643, at p. 644; D. Paulus and R. Matzke, 'Smart Contracts und das BGB – Viel Lärm um nichts?', *ZfPW – Zeitschrift für die gesamte Privatrechtswissenschaft* (2018), 431, 451; C. Rückert, 'Vermögensabschöpfung und Sicherstellung bei Bitcoins', MMR – *Multimedia und Recht* (2016), 295, at p. 296.

distinguishes between the regulation of cryptocurrencies for the purposes of prudential financial supervision (*infra*, 3.2.) and the prevention of money laundering (*infra*, 3.5.). In striking contrast to their recognition as "financial instruments" for the purposes of the KWG, however, crypto-assets have not been included in the statutory definition of the same term in the Securities Trading Act (*"Wertpapierhandelsgesetz"*, hereafter 'WpHG') yet, which leaves some uncertainty as to the applicability of the transactions-oriented (conduct-of-business) framework of that act (*infra*, 3.3.). Under the relevant statutory regimes, there is currently no prospectus requirement for the issuance of cryptocurrencies (*infra*, 3.4.).

3.2 *Prudential Regulation of Intermediation in Crypto-Assets*

3.2.1 Scope

As noted before, the definition of crypto-assets as 'financial instruments' for the purposes of the Banking Act (*supra*, 2.1.) prepares the ground for the application of the general licensing requirement for the provision of financial services. Already prior to the legislative amendment to the definition of 'financial instruments' in section 1(11) sentence 1 KWG, the Federal Financial Supervisory Authority (*"Bundesanstalt für Finanzdienstleistungsaufsicht"*, 'BaFin') had treated cryptocurrencies as financial instruments for the purposes of the Act, namely, for want of more specific alternatives, as 'units of account' (*"Rechnungseinheiten"*), within the meaning of section 1(11) sentence 1 no. 7 KWG.[27] The introduction of a more specific definition into the catalogue of 'financial instruments' thus served as a mere clarification of the *status quo ante*.

The current regulatory framework that builds, *inter alia*, on this definition has become rather complex of late. Following a recent overhaul of the applicable EU framework for the licensing and prudential regulation of investment firms, as distinct from banks (or, in technical terms, 'credit institutions'),[28]

---

27 See BaFin, 'Hinweise zu Finanzinstrumenten nach § 1 Abs. 11 Sätze 1 bis 3 KWG' (20 December 2011, as amended), available at https://www.bafin.de/SharedDocs/Veroeffentlichungen/DE/Merkblatt/mb_111220_finanzinstrumente.html. Other forms of 'units of account' within this meaning include, for example, special drawing rights issued by the International Monetary Fund. This interpretation has been rejected in *Kammergericht* (Regional Court of Appeals) Berlin, 25 September 2018 – Case (4) 161 Ss 28/18 (35/18), reported in ZIP – *Zeitschrift für Wirtschaftsrecht* (2018), 2015, at 2017 (a criminal law case). See, for a critical analysis (supporting the BaFin interpretation), G. Lorenz, 'Hält das "alte" Recht noch mit der finanztechnologischen Innovation Schritt?', ZIP – *Zeitschrift für Wirtschaftsrecht* (2019), 1699.

28 See, on the one hand, Directive (EU) 2019/2034 of the European Parliament and of the Council of 27 November 2019 on the prudential supervision of investment firms (...), OJ L 314, p. 64 (Investment Firms Directive, hereafter 'IFD'); on the other hand: Regulation (EU) 2019/2033 of the European Parliament and of the Council of 27 November 2019 on

there are now two separate licensing and regulatory regimes in German law. Universal banks and large providers of financial services other than banks (*"Finanzdienstleistungsinstitute"*, or 'financial services institutions') continue to be regulated by, and supervised according to, a combination of the German KWG and Regulation (EU) 575/2013 (the "Capital Requirements Regulation", hereafter: 'CRR').[29] Investment firms *not* licensed under the KWG, however, are licensed and regulated as *"Wertpapierinstitute"* (translated literally: 'securities [services] institutions') under the newly enacted *"Wertpapierinstitutsgesetz"* (Securities Institutions Act, hereafter: 'WpIG') in conjunction with the EU Investment Firms Regulation.[30] Under the new regime, the licensing and supervision pursuant to the WpIG will be the rule.

The scope *ratione materiae* of both regimes has been, and will be, defined by reference to specific activities for which a license is required ('banking services' or 'financial services' for the purposes of the KWG, and 'securities services' for the purposes of the WpIG). Their provision at a commercial scale triggers the on-going application of specific prudential requirements, as well as their supervision by public authorities.

By contrast, other services related to cryptocurrencies can be carried out both by mere 'financial services institutions', also licensed under section 32 KWG, and by securities institutions licensed and supervised under the WpIG. These include, for instance, the execution of orders for the sale or purchase of cryptocurrencies or the operation of a trading platform for crypto-assets.

Significantly, while the scope *ratione materiae* for both regimes has been defined in largely similar categories, the provision of depositary services in relation to crypto-assets (*"Kryptoverwahrgeschäft"*) remains reserved to financial services institutions licensed pursuant to section 32 KWG.

Other relevant activities, including the issuance of crypto-assets in a wide sense, covering also relevant programming and coding and the block validation of transactions, do not fall within the scope *ratione materiae* under either regime and do not therefore require a license. It should be noted, however, that the provision of loans in cryptocurrency at a commercial scale qualifies as a banking activity by virtue of section 32(1) no. 2 KWG and thus requires a license pursuant to section 32(1) KWG (see further *infra*, 4.1.1.3.). With the full implementation of MiCAR, the framework will change again.

---

the prudential requirements of investment firms (...), OJ L 314, p. 1 (Investment Firms Regulation, herafter 'IFR'), fully in force since 26 June 2021.

29 Regulation (EU) No 575/2013 of the European Parliament and of the Council of 26 June 2013 on prudential requirements for credit institutions and investment firms (...), OJ L 176, p. 1 (as amended).

30 Regulation (EU) 2019/2033 (supra).

Based broadly on parallel criteria delineating the scope *ratione materiae*, the respective scope *ratione personae* of both the KWG and the WpIG regime is defined by the size of the respective institution or, alternatively, of the group of which it is a part. Specifically, the WpIG applies to institutions (a) whose average of monthly total assets, calculated over a period of 12 consecutive months, does not exceed 30 billion Euro or (b) which are not part of a group in which the total value of the consolidated assets, calculated as an average over a period of 12 consecutive months, of all undertakings in the group that individually have total assets of less than EUR 30 billion and that engage in dealing on their own account or in the underwriting and/or placing of financial instruments on a firm commitment basis (cf. section 32(1) sentence 2 KWG). This mirrors the corresponding provisions established by the EU Investment Firm Regulation.[31]

3.2.2 Applicable Prudential Requirements, Licensing Procedure and Sanctions

In order to obtain a license under the respective domestic regime, intermediaries have to provide, along with their application, proof of compliance with qualitative and quantitative minimum criteria which are, to a large extent, defined by European law. Structurally similar requirements will apply for entities licensed under the incoming MiCAR regime.

For *credit institutions* and *financial services institutions* licensed pursuant to section 32 KWG, the relevant criteria are summarised, as negative criteria and largely by way of reference to requirements set out either in the KWG or the CRR, in section 33(1) KWG. They include, in particular:

- minimum quantitative requirements relating to the initial capitalisation ("own funds") of the relevant intermediary, as defined in Art. 26(1) CRR (which are complemented with own funds and liquidity requirements relative to the size and riskiness of on-going business activities);
- minimum qualitative requirements pertaining to the qualification and reputation of senior management and owners of substantial investments in the relevant institution, as defined in sections 2c, 2d, 25c(1) and 25d(1) KWG, and
- minimum requirements relating to the organisation and management of the relevant intermediary, as defined in sections 25a, 25b, 25c(3)-(4b), 25d(4)-(13) KWG.

For *securities institutions* licensed under the WpIG, the relevant requirements are structured similarly, while less restrictive.[32] Minimum quantitative criteria for the initial capitalisation of investment firms regulated thereunder are defined in section 17 WpIG (in conjunction with the IFR), and complemented

31 See Arts. 1(2) and 55 IFR.

32 See, for details, section 16 WpIG in conjunction with Regulation (EU) 2019/2033.

by own funds requirements for the on-going business laid down in Part III (Articles 11–34) of the IFR. Qualitative requirements for senior management and holders of substantial investments are defined in sections 20(1)-(3), 21(1) and (2) and 18(1) no. 3 WpIG, respectively.

Unless the relevant intermediary's size exceeds the threshold defined in section 32(1) sentence 2 KWG and, hence, has to apply for a license under section 32(1) KWG, the application and licensing procedure is defined in sections 15 and 16 WpIG. Applications have to be addressed to BaFin, which will decide in its capacity as national competent authority pursuant to section 5 WpIG.

Under both regimes, licenses can be withdrawn in case the relevant company is found to have breached the applicable prudential requirements summarised above, or, indeed, applicable anti-money laundering law (section 35(2) KWG and section 19(2) WpIG, respectively).

3.2.3 Supervisory Practice and Sanctions

As is the case with all areas of financial supervision, on-going supervisory practice and the imposition of sanctions for the contravention of the licensing requirements are reported individually, on BaFin's website, and in its annual reports (also available from the official website). Judging from these sources, supervisory actions have been rather rare to date, and usually dealt with incidents where individuals or companies engaged in the provision of financial services relating in cryptocurrencies without license.[33] If services are marketed within Germany by providers from other countries, which do not fall within the territorial scope of German financial legislation and supervisory competences, BaFin will nonetheless issue a public warning to that effect.[34]

---

33 E.g., BaFin, 'Crypto.exchange GmbH: BaFin ordnet Einstellung des Finanzkommissionsgeschäfts an' (29 January 2018), https://www.bafin.de/SharedDocs/Veroeffentlichungen/DE/Verbrauchermitteilung/unerlaubte/2018/meldung_180129_Crypto_exchange.html; id., 'Özgün Göcer: BaFin ordnet Einstellung und Abwicklung des Finanzkommissionsgeschäfts an' (26 June 2018), https://www.bafin.de/SharedDocs/Veroeffentlichungen/DE/Verbrauchermitteilung/unerlaubte/2018/meldung_180626_Oezguen_Goecer.html; id., 'Trading-Software „Bitcoin Deutschland" bzw. „Crypto Bank Software": BaFin ermittelt gegen die Verantwortlichen' (1 September 2021), https://www.bafin.de/SharedDocs/Veroeffentlichungen/DE/Verbrauchermitteilung/unerlaubte/2021/meldung_210901_bigtradingeur.html; id., 'Handelsplattform cryptolicht.com: BaFin ermittelt gegen die Smarteek Sp. Z.o.o.' (30 September 2021), https://www.bafin.de/SharedDocs/Veroeffentlichungen/DE/Verbrauchermitteilung/unerlaubte/2021/meldung_210930_cryptolicht.html; id., 'Handelsplattform crypto-brokers.de: BaFin ermittelt gegen die CBROKERS-TECHNOLOGY Ltd.' (23 December 2021), https://www.bafin.de/SharedDocs/Veroeffentlichungen/DE/Verbrauchermitteilung/unerlaubte/2021/meldung_211223_crypto-brokers.html.

34 E.g., BaFin, 'Crypto Code kein nach § 32 KWG zugelassenes Institut' (23 January 2019), https://www.bafin.de/SharedDocs/Veroeffentlichungen/DE/Verbrauchermitteilung/unerlaubte/2019/meldung_190123_Crypto_Code.html.

Pursuant to sections 37 and 38 KWG, in such cases, BaFin can order the relevant individual or company to wind down their activities, appoint a liquidator, and publish the sanctions on its website. It can also report those responsible for criminal prosecution, as the provision of financial services without the required license is an offense punishable pursuant to section 54(1) no. 2 KWG.[35]

3.3 *Regulatory Framework for Transactions in Cryptocurrencies*

In contrast to the institutional (prudential) regulatory treatment of intermediaries involved in transactions in cryptocurrencies, the position with regard to the regulation of transactions as such remains remarkably ill-defined. To some extent, this is part of a broader problem. To date, transactions-oriented regulation of financial services (in a broad sense) – including in the form of organisational and conduct-of-business rules to be followed by intermediaries in their dealings with customers – has remained rather piecemeal, and focuses mainly on traditional securities transactions, while other aspects, including not just traditional banking services but also innovative forms of financial intermediation, have not been addressed in a similarly comprehensive way.[36]

To date, the most detailed transactions-oriented regime for the regulation of financial intermediation can be found in the WpHG, which in turn transposes requirements stipulated by the reformed European Markets in Financial Instruments Directive ('MiFID II').[37] Its scope is largely focused on traditional securities transactions and related business. Specifically, as noted before, crypto-assets, including cryptocurrencies, have not been included in the statutory definition of 'financial instruments' in section 2(4) WpHG (or, for that matter, of 'securities' – *"Wertpapiere"* – as defined in section 2(1) WpHG) so far. Consequently, the applicability of the organisational and conduct-of-business laid down in sections 63 *et seq.* (in particular: sections 63 and 80–83 WpHG) remains, at best, somewhat unclear. The scope of the relevant categories, which are derived from the MiFID II, remains very much focused on traditional forms of traded securities on the one hand and derivatives on the other hand, and is narrower than the corresponding definition of the same terms for the purposes of the KWG. Significantly, 'units of account' (within the meaning of section 1(11) sentence 1 no. 7 KWG, *supra*, 3.2.1) are not covered by the

---

35 See, for a criminal law case involving financial services related to cryptocurrencies without the required license, e.g., Kammergericht (Regional Court of Appeals) Berlin, 25 September 2018 – Case (4) 161 Ss 28/18 (35/18), reported in ZIP – *Zeitschrift für Wirtschaftsrecht* (2018), 2015-18.

36 See, generally, J.-H. Binder, 'Germany', in: D. Busch and C. Van Dam (eds.), *A Bank's Duty of Care* (2017), p. 61.

37 Directive 2014/65/EU of the European Parliament and of the Council of 15 May 2014 on markets in financial instruments (...), OJ L 173, p. 349.

definition of 'financial instruments' laid down in section 2(4) WpHG. While details have been debated controversially, the majority view as to whether cryptocurrencies can be qualified as 'securities' or other 'financial instruments' for the purposes of the WpHG is, understandably, sceptical.[38] While this may be explicable in view of the fact that transactions in cryptocurrencies, to date, appear to occur outside more traditional forms of financial intermediation, the absence of a coherent regulatory framework nonetheless is to be deplored.

3.4 *No Statutory Prospectus Requirements*

Within Germany, prospectus requirements arise under two separate regimes. For securities, the relevant requirements follow directly from the EU Prospectus Regulation of 2017.[39] For a definition of the term 'securities' which, pursuant to Article 1(1), delineates the scope *ratione materiae*, Article 2(a) of that Regulation refers to the definition of the same term in Article 4(1)(44) MiFID II, where 'transferable securities' are defined as:

> '(...) those classes of securities which are negotiable on the capital market, with the exception of instruments of payment, such as:
> a. shares in companies and other securities equivalent to shares in companies, partnerships or other entities, and depositary receipts in respect of shares;
> b. bonds or other forms of securitised debt, including depositary receipts in respect of such securities;
> c. any other securities giving the right to acquire or sell any such transferable securities or giving rise to a cash settlement determined by reference to transferable securities, currencies, interest rates or yields, commodities or other indices or measures'.

Within the German legal literature, it is widely agreed that cryptocurrency token do not fall into this category and that their issuance, consequently, does not trigger a prospectus requirement under Art. 3 of the Prospectus Regulation.[40]

---

38 Cf., e.g., S.M. Bialluch-von Allwörden and S. von Allwörden, 'Initial Coin Offering: Kryptowährungen als Wertpapier oder Vermögensanlage?', *WM – Wertpapiermitteilungen. Zeitschrift für Wirtschafts- und Bankrecht* (2018), 2118, at p. 2123; L. Klöhn, N. Parhofer and D. Resas, 'Initial Coin Offerings – Markt, Ökonomik und Regulierung', *ZBB – Zeitschrift für Bankrecht und Bankbetrieb* (2018), 89, at pp. 100–03.

39 Regulation (EU) 2017/1129 of the European Parliament and of the Council of 14 June 2017 on the prospectus to be published when securities are offered to the public or admitted to trading on a regulated market (...), OJ L 168, p. 12.

40 Cf., e.g., S.M. Bialluch-von Allwörden and S. von Allwörden, 'Initial Coin Offering: Kryptowährungen als Wertpapier oder Vermögensanlage?', *WM – Wertpapiermitteilungen.*

At the same time, cryptocurrencies do not fall within the definition of relevant other investments that would trigger a prospectus requirement under section 6 of the purposes of the Investment Law (*"Vermögensanlagegesetz"*, hereafter: 'VermAnlG').[41]

BaFin does not itself treat cryptocurrency token as falling within either prospectus regime.[42]

Irrespective of the foregoing, it should be noted that, *if* a prospectus has been published in relation to the issuance of cryptocurrency, the issuer will be liable for misleading or inaccurate information therein under principles of private law. These principles had been developed by case law long before the advent of statutory prospectus requirements on the basis of general provisions on pre-contractual liability in the Civil Code and continue to be applied for prospectuses outside the scope of the statutory regimes.[43]

3.5 *Cryptocurrencies as E-Money or Means of Payment for the Purposes of Payment Services Regulation?*

Yet another regime potentially of relevance for the provision of services related to cryptocurrency can be found in the specific framework for the regulation of so-called e-money, as governed by the rules on payment services providers laid

---

Zeitschrift für Wirtschafts- und Bankrecht (2018), 2118, at p. 2123; U. Kleinert and V. Mayer, 'Elektronische Wertpapiere und Krypto-Token', *EuZW – Europäische Zeitschrift für Wirtschaftsrecht* (2019), 857, at p. 860; C. Rennig, 'KWG goes Krypto, Die Aufnahme von Kryptowerten und des Kryptoverwahrgeschäfts in das KWG', *BKR – Zeitschrift für Bank- und Kapitalmarktrecht* (2020), 23, at p. 26, G. Spindler, 'Initial Coin Offerings und Prospektpflicht und -haftung', *WM – Wertpapiermitteilungen. Zeitschrift für Wirtschafts- und Bankrecht* (2018), 2109, at p. 2214; W. Weitnauer, 'Initial Coin Offerings (ICOs): Rechtliche Rahmenbedingungen und regulatorische Grenzen', *BKR – Zeitschrift für Bank- und Kapitalmarktrecht* (2018), 231, at p. 233.

41 See, for a list of relevant instruments, section 1(2) VermAnlG. It is generally agreed that crypto-assets do not fall within the scope of the law, see, e.g., S.M. Bialluch-von Allwörden and S. von Allwörden, 'Initial Coin Offering: Kryptowährungen als Wertpapier oder Vermögensanlage?', *WM – Wertpapiermitteilungen. Zeitschrift für Wirtschafts- und Bankrecht* (2018), 2118, at pp. 2122–23; G. Spindler, 'Initial Coin Offerings und Prospektpflicht und -haftung', *WM – Wertpapiermitteilungen. Zeitschrift für Wirtschafts- und Bankrecht* (2018), 2109, at p. 2214.

42 See BaFin, 'Merkblatt: Zweites Hinweisschreiben zu Prospekt- und Erlaubnispflichten im Zusammenhang mit der Ausgabe sogenannter Krypto-Token' (WA 51-Wp 7100-2019/0011; IF 1-AZB 1505-2019/0003) (16 August 2019), available at https://www.bafin.de/SharedDocs/Downloads/DE/Merkblatt/WA/dl_wa_merkblatt_ICOs.pdf?__blob=publicationFile&v=1.

43 See, for illustration, Landgericht (High Court) Berlin, 27 May 2020 – Case 2 O 322/18, reported in *WM Wertpapiermitteilungen – Zeitschrift für Wirtschafts- und Bankrecht* (2021), 683, at pp. 689–95 (issuer liability for Ether token).

down in the "Zahlungsdiensteaufsichtsgesetz" (Law on the Regulation of Payment Services Providers, hereafter 'ZAG'),[44] which transposes the Second EU Payment Services Directive (hereafter: 'PSD2').[45] Among other things, the law stipulates a specific licensing requirement for providers of payment services (section 10 ZAG) and providers of E-money business (section 11), as defined by section 1(1) and (2) ZAG, respectively, as well as a comprehensive set of prudential (sections 15–18 ZAG) and sector-specific conduct-of-business requirements (sections 45–59 ZAG). While it had been disputed in the past that, at least, Bitcoins could qualify as "e-money" within the meaning of section 1(2) sentence 3 ZAG (transposing Art. 11 PSD2) *a limine*,[46] recent decisions by administrative courts have upheld the classification of certain cryptocurrencies as e-money and/or the object of payment services falling within the scope of the ZAG by BaFin, the competent authority also under that statute.[47] However, in the light of the controversial debate in the academic and judging from the rather special facts of each case, general statements as to the applicability of payment services regulation to issuers of cryptocurrency and providers of related services cannot be made at the present moment in time.

3.6 *Cryptocurrencies and Anti-Money Laundering Regulation*

Anti-money laundering legislation, including measures against the financing of terrorist activities, is laid down in the GWG, which in turn transposes applicable European legislation.[48] As noted before (*supra*, 2.2.), crypto-assets have been included in the list of financial assets covered by the GWG, which now also addresses, as a rule, all types of transfers of such assets (section 1(29) and

---

44 Gesetz über die Beaufsichtigung von Zahlungsdiensten (Zahlungsdienste-Aufsichtsgesetz) of 17 July 2017, *Bundesgesetzblatt* 2017 I, p. 2446.

45 Directive (EU) 2015/2366 of the European Parliament and of the Council of 25 November 2015 on payment services in the internal market (...), OJ L 337, p. 35.

46 E.g., A. Spiegel, *Blockchain-basiertes virtuelles Geld* (2020), pp. 42-45; *J. Mimberg*, commentary on section 1 ZAG, in: F.A. Schäfer, S. Omlor and J. Mimberg (eds.), *ZAG – Zahlungsdiensteaufsichtsgesetz*, para. 219; M. Terlau, commentary on section 1 ZAG, in: M. Casper and M. Terlau (eds.), *ZAG – Zahlungsdiensteaufsichtsgesetz* (2nd. ed, 2020), para. 224. See also Kammergericht (Regional Court of Appeals) Berlin, 25 September 2018 – Case 161 Ss 28/18, reported in *NJW – Neue Juristische Wochenschrift* (2018), 3734, at paras. 18–24.

47 E.g., Hessischer Verwaltungsgerichtshof (Regional Administrative Court of Appeals) Kassel, 13 March 2019 – Case 6 A 2579/18.Z, reported in *Juris* database; id., 28 February 2020 – Case 6 A 1131/19.Z, reported ibid.; Verwaltungsgericht (Administrative Court of first instance) Frankfurt am Main, 4 November 2021 – Case 7 K 1262/20.F, reported in *Juris* database.

48 In particular, Directive (EU) 2015/849 of the European Parliament and of the Council of 20 May 2015 on the prevention of the use of the financial system for the purposes of money laundering or terrorist financing (...), OJ L 141, p. 73 (as amended).

1(30) GWG). In line with the relevant European requirements, the Act stipulates specific organisational duties, including, in particular, requirements for the exploration of customers' identity, as well as reporting requirements in case of suspicious transactions, for financial intermediaries, which now extend also to transactions in cryptocurrencies.

4 Private Law

4.1 *General Private Law*

As for all other transactions between private and/or commercial parties under German law, the applicable rules and principles are to be found in the BGB, the Civil Code. As noted before (*supra*, 2.3.), cryptocurrencies have not been expressly addressed in the BGB. To be sure, the Code, transposing two European Directives,[49] has been amended lately in order to address transactions in "digital products" (in particular, sections 327-327u and 475a). The relevant provisions have been in force from 1 January 2022. However, "digital products", for these purposes, do not include cryptocurrencies,[50] to which the traditional set of provisions governing contracts and property continue to apply. The recognition, in section 327(1), sentence 2 BGB, that 'digital representations' of value may be agreed as a price payable in exchange for 'digital products' or 'digital services' does not itself provide a clear-cut classification of cryptocurrency token for the purposes of contract or property law,[51] and, hence, does not itself create legal certainty as to the treatment of relevant transactions. The following subsections describe the position of cryptocurrencies, first, in the law of obligations (*infra*, 4.1.1.) and, subsequently, the law of property, including, for that matter, the use of cryptocurrency as the object of a pledge (*infra*, 4.1.2.), trust law (*infra*, 4.1.3.) and inheritance law (*infra*, 4.1.4.).

---

49 Directive (EU) 2019/770 of the European Parliament and of the Council of 20 May 2019 on certain aspects concerning contracts for the supply of digital content and digital services, OJ L 136, p. 1 and Directive (EU) 2019/771 of the European Parliament and of the Council of 20 May 2019 on certain aspects concerning contracts for the sale of goods (…), OJ L 136, p. 28.

50 Cf. the statutory definition of the term in section 327(2) BGB.

51 While 'digital representations of value', which include 'virtual currencies' are expressly recognised as a potential 'price' payable for the acquisition of digital services or products (section 327(1), sentence 2 BGB), such currencies do not themselves qualify as digital products or, for that matter, services: cf. Directive [EU] 2019/770, Art. 2(7) and Recital 23.

4.1.1 Law of Obligations

4.1.1.1 *Acquisition of Cryptocurrencies in Exchange for Legal Tender*

Given the comprehensive nature of the German BGB and its abstract nature, designed for application to an indefinite range of transactions relating to an indefinite range of assets, it may appear odd that the legal treatment of transactions in cryptocurrencies, including the simple acquisition of currency tokens against payment of a Euro-denominated amount of money in the technical sense, would present any problems at all. In addition to a "General Part" (*"Allgemeiner Teil"*) defining abstract principles for *all* types of obligations, the BGB lays down – to a large extent non-mandatory – specific rules for individual types of contracts (including, for example, sales contracts, barter contracts, contracts for services, or loan contracts), thus providing different "menus" of provisions that would govern the relevant contractual relationships in the absence of specific individual agreements entered into by the parties. Notwithstanding the abstract form of these principles, which, to a large extent, are *not* designed to govern only transactions in specific asset classes, however, the applicable rules, to a substantial extent, usually are designed in accordance with, and based on, traditional categories of property law. Given the absence of a statutory recognition of crypto-assets generally, and cryptocurrency token in particular, within German property law to date (*supra*, 2.3.2.), the application of established principles of the German law of obligation comes with substantial difficulties,[52] which are also present in the classification of the scenario described in the above case example.

At first sight, the classification of such transactions as sales contracts within the meaning of sections 433 *et seq*. BGB would certainly appear to be the most logical approach, a sales contract, pursuant to section 433(1) and (2) BGB, being defined as a contract for the delivery of a good against payment of a sales price. However, by virtue of section 433(1) sentence 1 BGB, sales contracts are contracts for the delivery of a 'thing' (*"Sache"*) within the meaning of section 90 BGB. As noted before (*supra*, 2.3.2.), crypto token do not fall within the definition of 'things' pursuant to section 90 BGB and, hence, section 433 BGB does not apply.[53]

Against this backdrop, it has been discussed whether the acquisition of cryptocurrency against payment of legal tender could be classified as a barter (*"Tauschvertrag"*) within the meaning of section 480 BGB (which, in turn, refers back to the provisions governing sales contracts, e.g., with regard to the

52 Cf., for an in-depth doctrinal analysis, A. Spiegel, *Blockchain-basiertes virtuelles Geld* (2020), pp. 60–68.

53 Ibid., p. 61; B. Beck and D. König, 'Bitcoin: Der Versuch einer vertragstypologischen Einordnung von kryptographischem Geld', JZ – *Juristenzeitung* (2015), 130, at p. 132.

legal consequences of malperformance).[54] If and where the acquisition of cryptocurrency is made against payment of legal tender, the classification as a barter would be unconvincing, however, since such contracts are meant to cover the mutual exchange of goods or rights other than money.[55]

Moreover, some authors have suggested that the acquisition of cryptocurrency against payment of legal tender could, instead, be classified as a contract for services (*"Werkvertrag"*) within the meaning of section 631 BGB, the service being the execution of the transfer of the relevant amount of cryptocurrency, which requires authorisation through the blockchain.[56] Pursuant to section 631(1) BGB, contracts for services are contracts whereby one party, the "contractor" (*"Unternehmer"*) undertakes to create an agreed 'work' (*i.e.*, any service) on behalf of the customer, against payment of a fee. Given that the relevant transaction focuses on the exchange of cryptocurrency against legal tender, not the mere execution as such, the majority view is, convincingly, that the classification of the transaction as a contract for services does not provide an adequate framework either.[57]

In the absence of more specific alternatives, the acquisition of cryptocurrency against payment of legal tender would thus qualify as a contract for the 'sale of rights and other objects' (other than things within the meaning of section 90 BGB), as defined in section 453(1) BGB.[58] While the acquisition of cryptocurrency does not fall within the standard type of a sales contract (and does not refer to the sale of a 'right'), the application of section 453 BGB, in the form of a sale of 'other objects', nonetheless facilitates the application of sales law and, thus, allows a consistent treatment of the respective obligations for the purposes of contract law.[59]

---

54 See, for an extensive analysis, e.g., A. Spiegel, *Blockchain-basiertes virtuelles Geld* (2020), pp. 62-64. And see C. Engelhardt and S. Klein, 'Bitcoins – Geschäfte mit Geld, das keines ist', MMR – *Multimedia und Recht* (2014), 355, at p. 359.

55 A. Spiegel, *Blockchain-basiertes virtuelles Geld* (2020), at p. 64; Engelhardt and S. Klein, 'Bitcoins – Geschäfte mit Geld, das keines ist', MMR – *Multimedia und Recht* (2014), 355, at p. 359.

56 Cf., for an extensive discussion, A. Spiegel, *Blockchain-basiertes virtuelles Geld* (2020), at pp. 64–65; F. Boehm and P. Pesch, 'Bitcoins: Rechtliche Herausforderungen einer virtuellen Währung', MMR 2014, 75, at p. 78.

57 A. Spiegel, *Blockchain-basiertes virtuelles Geld* (2020), at p. 65; B. Beck and D. König, 'Bitcoin: Der Versuch einer vertragstypologischen Einordnung von kryptographischem Geld', JZ – *Juristenzeitung* (2015), 130, at p. 132; F. Boehm and P. Pesch, 'Bitcoins: Rechtliche Herausforderungen einer virtuellen Währung', MMR 2014, 75, at p. 78;

58 See, e.g., A. Spiegel, *Blockchain-basiertes virtuelles Geld* (2020), at pp. 67–68; B. Beck and D. König, 'Bitcoin: Der Versuch einer vertragstypologischen Einordnung von kryptographischem Geld', JZ – *Juristenzeitung* (2015), 130, at pp. 132–33.

59 E.g., A. Spiegel, *Blockchain-basiertes virtuelles Geld* (2020), at pp. 69–71; B. Beck and D. König, 'Bitcoin: Der Versuch einer vertragstypologischen Einordnung von kryptographischem Geld', JZ – *Juristenzeitung* (2015), 130, at pp. 132–33; L. Shmatenko and St. Möllenkam,

For cross-border scenarios, in accordance with general conflicts-of-laws principles, German law, in the absence of a valid choice-of-law clause, would apply to such transactions if and where the party required to effect the characteristic performance of the contract, *i.e.*, the delivery of cryptocurrency, has its habitual residence within the country. This follows directly from Art. 4(2) of Regulation (EC) 593/2008,[60] while the term 'habitual residence' is defined in Art. 19 of that Regulation.[61]

4.1.1.2 *Acquisition of Cryptocurrency in Exchange for Another Cryptocurrency*

In order to classify the exchange of cryptocurrencies against each other, it is important, first, to note that the use of cryptocurrency as consideration in exchange for goods or services is, at best, unsettled under German private law. If the above transaction were to be classified, just as transactions discussed above (*supra*, 4.1.1.1), as a contract for the 'sale of another object', the performance of the party qualifying as the purchaser would have to be classified as the payment of a 'price' within the meaning of section 433(2) BGB (in conjunction with section 453(1) BGB). Traditionally, however, section 433(2) BGB is generally construed to the effect that payments for sales can only validly be made in legal tender, and only in cash. Again, traditionally, even the (electronic) transfer of money through a financial intermediary is accepted as performance of the purchaser's obligation only if the parties have consented, expressly or impliedly, that such transfer shall be accepted *in lieu* of a payment in cash.[62] As noted before, cryptocurrencies are *not* accepted as legal tender (*supra*, 2.3.1). From this perspective, it is certainly questionable whether payments agreed to be made in cryptocurrency rather than in legal tender should be treated in the same way as electronic transfers. While this has been discussed for obligations other than the price within sales contracts, where the law merely requires

---

'Digitale Zahlungsmittel in einer analog geprägten Rechtsordnung', *MMR – Multimedia und Recht* (2018), 495, at p. 499.

60 Regulation (EC) no. 593/2008 of the European Parliament and of the Council of 17 June 2008 on the law applicable to contractual obligations (Rome I), OJ L 177, p. 1.

61 Pursuant to Art. 19(1), '[f]or the purposes of this Regulation, the habitual residence of companies and other bodies, corporate or unincorporated, shall be the place of central administration.

The habitual residence of a natural person acting in the course of his business activity shall be his principal place of business.'

62 "Leistung an Erfüllungs Statt", as defined by section 364(1) BGB. See, e.g., Bundesgerichtshof (Federal Supreme Court), 17 March 2004, Case VIII ZR 161/03, reported in *ZIP – Zeitschrift für Wirtschaftsrecht* (2004), 1354, at 1355.

payment of a *"Vergütung"* (*i.e.*, a consideration in a broader sense),[63] the majority view remains that the same principle cannot be applied to contracts where the purchaser's obligation refers explicitly to the payment of a 'price'.[64]

It is certainly arguable that this assessment should be reconsidered in view of the recent introduction of section 327(1)(2) to the BGB, which has accepted 'digital representations of value' as a potential price for the acquisition of digital products and services and is inconsistent with the received construction of the purchaser's obligation under section 433(2) BGB. To date, however, the majority view is that, the exchange of a certain amount of token denominated in one particular cryptocurrency against another, unlike the acquisition of cryptocurrency against legal tender can only be qualified as a barter contract within German contract law.[65] All the same, as discussed above, section 480 BGB as the sole provision addressing such contracts in the Civil Code merely refers to the law on sales contracts, so that the parties' rights and obligations effectively follow the same principles as sales. Just as with the acquisition of cryptocurrency against legal tender (*supra*, 4.1.1.1), the parties' rights and obligations do not change if intermediaries are used to hold and transfer the relevant token.

For cross-border barter contracts, the determination of the applicable law is more difficult by comparison with sales contracts, as both parties commit themselves to deliver effectively similar objects of value and, hence, the identification of the 'characteristic performance' for the purposes of Art. 4(2) of the Rome I Regulation (may not be possible merely on the grounds of the respective duties.[66] While case law, in this respect, does not appear to exist, the solution of relevant cases is likely to depend on the circumstances of each particular case. These would be relevant, at least, to determine to which jurisdiction the contract 'is most closely connected' within the meaning of Art. 4(4) of the Rome I Regulation, which applies by default. If, for instance, X has

63 E.g., K. Langenbucher, M. Hoche and J. Wentz, 'Virtuelle Währungen' in: K. Langenbucher, D. H. Bliesener and G. Spindler (eds.), *Bankrechtskommentar* (3rd ed., 2020), p. 782, at p. 787, para. 23; D. Paulus and R. Matzke, 'Smart Contracts und das BGB – Viel Lärm um nichts?', *ZfPW – Zeitschrift für die gesamte Privatrechtswissenschaft* (2018), 431, at p. 450.

64 Ibid. And see, further, e.g., G. Spindler and M. Bille, 'Rechtsprobleme von Bitcoins als virtuelle Währung', in: *WM – Wertpapiermitteilungen. Zeitschrift für Wirtschafts- und Bankrecht* (2014), 1357, at p. 1362.

65 E.g., F. Maultzsch, commentary on section 480 BGB, in: F.J. Säcker et al. (eds.), *Münchener Kommentar zum Bürgerlichen Gesetzbuch* (9th ed., 2024), para. 1.

66 This is usually the case with barter contracts, cf., e.g., D. Martiny, commentary on Art. 4 Regulation (EC) 593/2008, in: F.J. Säcker et al. (eds.), *Münchener Kommentar zum Bürgerlichen Gesetzbuch* (9th ed., 2025), para. 179.

marketed his or her Bitcoins to a broader public from within Germany, and has then been approached by a purchaser from another jurisdiction, it could be argued that the marketing and selling part of the transaction should be qualified either as the dominating and, hence, 'characteristic' performance within the meaning of Art. 4(2), or, at least, as constituting the closest connection to the laws of Germany within the meaning of Art. 4(4) of Regulation (EC) 593/2008.

4.1.1.3 *Loan Relationships*

Just as other aspects relating to the treatment of cryptocurrency under German law, its status in relation to loan contracts remains ill-defined to date. According to section 488(1) BGB, the fundamental provision on traditional loan contracts in the Civil Code, a loan is a contract whereby the lender agrees to pay a certain amount of money to the borrower, whereas the borrower agrees to (a) repay that amount upon maturity and (b) to pay the agreed interest. While it has been argued, convincingly, that the parties can agree to a repayment of value other than money *in lieu* of a repayment denominated in the original currency,[67] it is, at least, dubious whether the provisions on loans in sections 488–90 BGB can be applied also to contractual relationships relating to the lending of cryptocurrency. While it is generally agreed that a lender, under a loan contract within the meaning of sections 488–90 BGB, can, if so agreed, be obliged to provide a loan not just in cash, but also by electronic transfer or in a foreign currency,[68] the classification of 'loans' of cryptocurrency as falling within the scope of these provisions has hardly been discussed so far.[69] Alternatively, such contracts could, in principle, be classified as a *"Sachdarlehen"* (loans of things) within the meaning of section 607 BGB – which is dubious as well, given the wording of that provision, which expressly refers to (tangible) 'things' within the meaning of section 90 BGB. In principle, the respective scope of both regimes can be distinguished with regard to the economic nature of the relevant object: If the object is to provide the borrower with an abstract value rather than a specific good (or other object of value, *e.g.*, an amount of a specific transferable security, the most important practical example of loans

67 S. Omlor, 'Geld und Währung als Digitalisate', *JZ – Juristenzeitung* (2017), 754, at p. 760.

68 E.g., J.-H. Binder, commentary on section 488 BGB, in: *Beck'scher Online-Großkommentar zum BGB* (1 October 2024), para. 207; K.-P. Berger, commentary on section 488 BGB, in: F.J. Säcker et al. (eds.), *Münchener Kommentar zum Bürgerlichen Gesetzbuch* (9th ed., 2023), para. 29.

69 But see, arguing, rather tentatively, in support of the classification as a loan within the meaning of sections 488–90, S. Röß, 'Die Rechtsnatur von Kryptowährungsdarlehen', *NJW – Neue Juristische Wochenschrift* (2021), 3751, at pp. 3752–56.

of things within the meaning of section 607 BGB), the contract should be classified as a loan for the purposes of sections 488–90 BGB. In this light, the classification of loans of cryptocurrency as falling within the scope of sections 488–90 BGB clearly is preferable.[70]

Against this backdrop, notwithstanding the absence of established principles relating to the legal treatment of such loans in German contract law, a transaction whereby cryptocurrencies are borrowed, to the extent that German law is applicable, accordingly should be treated as a valid loan contract under German law.[71] German law, in the absence of a valid choice-of-law clause, would apply to such transactions only if the lender, as the party required to effect the characteristic performance of the contract, has its habitual residence within the country (cf., again, Art. 4(2) of the Rome I Regulation). As discussed before, parties, according to established principles of the law of loans, are free to agree on alternative denominations for the payment of interest in loan contracts, so that this result would apply irrespective of whether interest has to be paid in legal tender or in cryptocurrency.

The question of whether the provision of such loans would require a license under German law is not, in itself, a matter of private law. Generally speaking, the provision of loan contracts (within the meaning of section 488 BGB) at a commercial scale within Germany qualifies as a 'banking business' as defined in section 1(1) no. 2 KWG and, consequently, requires a banking license according to section 32(1) KWG (see further *supra*, 3.2.2). If the relevant intermediary carries out its activities in another EU Member State, and has been duly licensed there, the intermediary may establish branches within Germany pursuant to sections 24a and 53b KWG or, alternatively, may choose to offer its services within the country subject to notification of BaFin pursuant to section 24a(3) KWG. In such cases, the home-country license effectively serves as a "European Passport" facilitating the free entry into foreign markets, as required by Arts. 35–38 and 39–46 of Directive 2013/13/EU.[72]

Problems arise where a loan is repaid in a different cryptocurrency than the one that was borrowed, e.g. in Bitcoin Cash rather than in Bitcoin. In the absence of specific provisions governing transactions in cryptocurrencies in the German Civil code, the acceptability of repayments in token denominated

70 See, e.g., S. Lohsse, commentary on section 607 BGB, in: *Beck'scher Online-Großkommentar zum BGB* (1 August 2023), para. 8.

71 See, for the same conclusion, also S. Röß, 'Die Rechtsnatur von Kryptowährungsdarlehen', *NJW – Neue Juristische Wochenschrift* (2021), 3751, at pp. 3752–56.

72 Directive 2013/36/EU of the European Parliament and of the Council of 26 June 2013 on access to the activity of credit institutions and the prudential supervision of credit institutions and investment firms (...), OJ L 176, p. 338.

in cryptocurrency other than the original cryptocurrency provided to the borrower, according to general principles of contract law, would depend on the parties' agreement. If no express agreement to that effect has been made, the agreement has to be construed according to sections 133, 157 BGB. Applying these provisions, it has to be asked whether the agreement, judging from the perspective of an objective observer in the parties' position, would have covered the substitution of the original amount by an alternative. As the alternative cryptocurrency – in the case example: Bitcoin Cash – may develop in value independently from the original denomination, German courts would not normally presume that this would have been intended, unless there are reasons to assume, in the light of the circumstances of each individual case, that the parties have treated both denominations as equivalent for the purposes of their arrangements. Even if this is not the case, the lender may still accept repayment in another denomination *in lieu* of the original obligation (*"Leistung an Erfüllungs Statt"*, section 364(1) BGB). These principles would apply irrespective of whether or not the fork took place before or after the initial transfer.

4.1.1.4 *Donation of Cryptocurrency; Cryptocurrency Admissible as Consideration*

Donations are possible according to sections 516, 518 BGB, which also apply with regard to 'other objects of value' within the meaning of section 453(1) BGB.[73] As a rule, a donation is only valid and enforceable if the contract has been made before, and documented by, a notary public (section 518(1) in conjunction with section 125 BGB). If, however, the donor has completed the transfer, the contract will be valid even if not so documented pursuant to section 518(2) BGB. German law would apply to the transaction pursuant to Art. 4(4) of Regulation (EC) 593/2008 (as to which, see *supra*, 4.1.1) if the donor has his/her habitual residence within the country. Importantly, German law distinguishes between the donation as such, which provides the legal basis for the transfer, and the transfer as such, just as it distinguishes between the sale of a thing and the actual delivery of the object.

On the acceptability of cryptocurrency as consideration, see *supra*, 4.1.1.2.

4.1.1.5 *Compensation for Loss of Cryptocurrency Due to Tortious Behaviour*

Under German law, the hacking of wallets and similar cases of crypto-theft would be governed by a combination of general principles of contract and of tort law. Suppose X has opened an account with MontC, whose IT system

---

73 E.g., J.D. Harke, commentary on section 516 BGB, in: *Beck'scher Online-Großkommentar zum BGB* (1 October 2024), para. 18.

gets hacked. As far as X's position vis-à-vis MontC is concerned, the relevant action would be for damages arising out of a breach of MontC's obligation to ensure the safekeeping of X's wallet. While the private-law dimension of *Kryptoverwahrgeschäfte* (within the meaning of regulatory law, see *supra*, 3.2.1.) remains ill-defined,[74] and case law does not appear to exist, X, according to general principles, could be entitled to damages pursuant to section 280(1) BGB if and to the extent that he or she can establish to the satisfaction of the court that MontC has failed to apply reasonable protections against violation of its IT systems and that, as a consequence, X has lost his/her Bitcoins stored in the wallet.

By contrast, the hacker (if identified) could be liable in damages under general provisions of tort law. While it is unclear whether tort law, given the virtual nature of cryptocurrencies, would be protected under the general provision of section 823(1) BGB, which protects only a selected range of rights,[75] claims for damages could be based on section 826 BGB, which provides the basis for damages for loss caused by intentional unlawful actions. Moreover, claims could be based on section 823(2) BGB in conjunction with section 202a of the Criminal Code (*"Strafgesetzbuch"*, hereafter 'StGB'), which protects the access to private data.[76] The application of section 303a StGB, which protects the integrity of private data, is however disputed.[77]

If X transferred Bitcoin after having been misled, the tortfeasor would be liable in damages by virtue of section 823(2) BGB in conjunction with section 263 StGB, which penalises fraud.

---

74 It is worth noting, in this context, that there is, to date, no specific legal basis governing liability of a wallet provider for a client's loss of tokens stored in a wallet. This is in contrast to the situation with regard to unauthorised transactions carried out by a payment services provider (cf. sections 675u and 675v BGB). This situation is about to change because of Art. 75(8) of the MiCAR, which provides for a wallet provider's liability for the loss of crypto-assets resulting from a malfunction or hacks.

75 See, for further discussion, e.g., A. Spiegel, *Blockchain-basiertes virtuelles Geld* (2020), at pp. 112-15; L. Shmatenko and St. Möllenkamp, 'Digitale Zahlungsmittel in einer analog geprägten Rechtsordnung', *MMR – Multimedia und Recht* (2018), 495, at p. 498 (both arguing for recognition of cryptocurrencies as a right protected by section 823(1) BGB).

76 L. M. Guntermann, 'Non fungible Token als Herausforderung für das Sachenrecht', *RDI – Recht Digital* (2022), 200, at p. 203.

77 L. M. Guntermann, 'Non fungible Token als Herausforderung für das Sachenrecht', *RDI – Recht Digital* (2022), 200, at p. 203; S. Ludes, 'Der "Kryptodiebstahl" – eine Lücke im deutschen Strafrecht?', *ZdiW – Zeitschrift für das Recht der digitalen Wirtschaft* (2022), 390, at p. 393.

4.1.2 Law of Property

4.1.2.1 *Ownership and Transfer of Cryptocurrency*

As a direct consequence of the uncertain legal nature of cryptocurrencies in German private law (*supra*, 2.3.2.), the treatment of crypto token for the purposes of property law in general and the legal classifications of the transfer of ownership therein in particular remain largely unsettled to date. As noted before, such token neither qualify as 'things' (within the meaning of section 90 BGB) nor as 'rights', which, as such,[78] have not been defined by the Code. As defined by section 903 BGB, the concept of ownership, in a technical sense, applies only to tangible objects (*i.e.*, 'things' within the meaning of section 90 BGB).[79] 'Rights' cannot be owned in that technical sense, while the entitlement of the holder of the right has not been defined as such in the Code.

Thus, the holder's position relating to Bitcoins registered in his/her wallet, under German law, cannot be qualified as 'ownership' in a technical sense. Rather, the position would be perceived as reflecting a claim, namely, as the holder's contractual right against the wallet provider to release the Bitcoin or to transfer them on the holders's order to an acquirer. For the same reason, wallet providers's position to the Bitcoin cannot be qualified as legal 'ownership' in a technical sense.

This fundamental doctrinal problem directly translates into substantial difficulties in terms of the qualification of transfers of cryptocurrency. While 'claims', under the Civil Code, can be the object of an assignment between parties (*"Abtretung"*, sections 398–412 BGB), the legal title in movable 'things' is transferred in accordance with sections 929–31 BGB, while the legal title in real estate follows a specific regime defined by sections 873, 925 BGB. In addition, section 413 BGB provides for the applicability of the law on assignments in relation to rights other than claims. Given that cryptocurrency token qualify as neither 'rights' nor 'things', it is rather obvious that neither regime can be applied directly.

Against this backdrop, a number of authors have argued that the transfer of cryptocurrency should be interpreted by way of an analogy to one of these different statutory means.[80] The majority view appears to be that, as (a) transfers

78 Unlike 'claims', which are defined by a right of one party to demand another party to perform, cf. section 194(1) BGB.

79 Cf. the wording of that provision, which refers expressly to the 'owner of a thing'.

80 E.g., A. Spiegel, *Blockchain-basiertes virtuelles Geld* (2020), at pp. 102–06; Ph. Koch, 'Die „Tokenisierung" von Rechtspositionen als digitale Verbriefung', *ZBB – Zeitschrift für Bankrecht und Bankwirtschaft* (2018), 359, at pp. 362-63 (arguing in support of the application of sections 929–31 BGB by analogy). And see (arguing, unconvincingly, in support of the application of sections 873, 925 BGB [on the transfer of real estate]) Th. Ammann,

of cryptocurrencies require the confirmation of the blockchain and thus follow a different pattern than the typical bilateral relationship characteristic of any of the above statutory models and (b) the "ownership" of cryptocurrency differs from traditional concepts of exclusive rights of ownership, neither category provides a suitable explanation and that, consequently, transfers of cryptocurrency should be treated as a *de facto* shift of legal entitlement based on the parties' actions (*"Realakt"*).[81] Given that neither of the existing statutory modes of transfer actually matches the specific characteristics of transactions in cryptocurrency, this is certainly convincing. It should be noted, however, that both the absence of a satisfactory definition of the legal nature of an "owner's" entitlement *and* the resulting difficulty to classify transactions in cryptocurrency merely highlight the inadequacies of the German law of property as it currently stands. In a nutshell, both the holding and the transfer of cryptocurrency are not addressed by the current Civil Code in a manner that would afford interested parties a degree of legal certainty at least comparable to that traditionally available to the owners of tangible property and their counterparties in related transactions.

4.1.2.2 *Pledges*

Pledges, under German law, are addressed by two distinct regimes: one for pledges relating to 'things' (sections 1204-59 BGB) and another for pledges relating to claims (sections 1273–96 BGB). Moreover, as neither regime fully satisfies practical needs, standard legal practice, over time, has developed alternatives to the statutory regimes, whereby the pledgor, for the duration of the contract, provides the pledgee with the full title in the relevant object of value, and both parties agree that the title will be returned if and when the secured claim is repaid. Depending on the nature of the relevant object of value, the transfer will take either the form of an assignment within the meaning of sections

'Bitcoin als Zahlungsmittel im Internet: Rechtliche Fragestellungen und Lösungsansätze', CR – *Computer und Recht* (2018), 379, at pp. 382–83. See also, for a comprehensive critique of received approaches and a redefinition of transactions, J. Arndt, *Bitcoin-Eigentum* (2021).

81 See, e.g., K. Langenbucher, M. Hoche and J. Wentz, 'Virtuelle Währungen' in: K. Langenbucher, D. H. Bliesener and G. Spindler (eds.), *Bankrechtskommentar* (3rd ed., 2020), p. 782, at p. 792, para. 39; B. Beck and D. König, 'Bitcoin: Der Versuch einer vertragstypologischen Einordnung von kryptographischem Geld', JZ – *Juristenzeitung* (2015), 130, at p. 131; M. Kaulartz and R. Matzke, 'Die Tokenisierung des Rechts', NJW – *Neue Juristische Wochenschrift* (2018), 3278, at p. 3280; S. Omlor, 'Kryptowährungen im Geldrecht', ZHR – *Zeitschrift für das gesamte Handelsrecht und Wirtschaftsrecht* 183 (2019), 294, at 327–29. But see, arguing in support of the application of section 413 in conjunction with sections 398 et seq. BGB, D. Skauradszun, 'Kryptowerte im Bürgerlichen Recht', *AcP – Archiv für die civilistische Praxis* 221 (2021), 353, at pp. 376–379.

398–412 BGB (in the case of claims as security, known as *"Sicherungszession"*) or of a full transfer of ownership of a thing as defined by sections 929–31 BGB (in the case of a 'thing', known as *"Sicherungsübereignung"*).

Within this framework, the feasibility of pledges relating to cryptocurrency faces the same difficulties of classification that have been discussed above with regard to other aspects: As cryptocurrency is neither a tangible 'thing' within the meaning of section 90 BGB nor a 'claim' that could be assigned (see, again, *supra*, 2.3.2. and 4.1.2.1.), it can be pledged neither according to the statutory frameworks defined in sections 1204-59 BGB or 1273–96 BGB, nor can it be pledged under the alternatives thereto developed in legal practice, since these also make use of the respective statutory frameworks developed for the transfer of property.

In a legal environment defined by the principle of freedom of contract, this result is certainly unsatisfactory. In principle, however, it is perfectly conceivable that cryptocurrency can be transferred, subject to conditions similar to those developed for *"Sicherungszessionen"* or *"Sicherungsübereignungen"*, under a functional equivalent of a pledge in property law, and there is nothing to suggest that such an agreement, while certainly not yet common and not as clearly defined as the traditional models, would not be recognised by the courts as valid and enforceable. Such arrangements, however, will, in all likelihood, be treated merely as creating binding obligations between the parties, and will lack the protection in property law that would be associated with the traditional categories of general property law. As a result, their status in the insolvency of a debtor is, at best, uncertain. Given that traditional categories of property law ("rights", or "things" eligible for "ownership" in the technical sense) do not apply, it would certainly be difficult to justify the application of the general principles of security rights and their protection in insolvency in such settings.

4.1.3 Inheritance Law

Under German law, upon the death of a natural person, that person is *ipso iure* succeeded by his/her heir(s) in relation to the legal title in the entire estate pursuant to sections 1922(1) BGB. In the absence of any more specific rules in the Code that would be of relevance to the ownership of 'virtual' property, the same principle also applies in the case of cryptocurrency held by the deceased, so that his/her heir(s) inherit a portfolio of cryptocurrency just as any other asset (or liability) of the deceased.

In technical terms, two scenarios have to be distinguished: If the deceased has access to his/her portfolio through a tangible electronic storage device, *e.g.*, in the case of a wallet stored on his/her personal computer, or a private key stored on an USB storage device, the relevant data, as such, are part of his/her estate and, upon his/her death, are transferred to the heir(s) *ipso iure*.[82] If, by contrast, the relevant cryptocurrency token are stored online in a wallet operated by an intermediary, the heir(s) succeed the deceased in his/her claims against the provider.[83]

4.1.4 Trust

The concept of a trust, as recognised by Common Law jurisdictions, does not, as such, exist in German private law. Technically speaking, it is therefore not possible to create a trust in relation to crypto-assets under German law. As a matter of principle, however, it is possible to hold legal title in relation to property on behalf of another party in a fiduciary capacity, whereby the fiduciary agrees to exercise his/her rights as a full owner only in such ways as directed by, or in the interest of, the beneficiary. It is generally agreed that relationships thus structured, known as "*Vollrechtstreuhand*", constitute a functional equivalent to trusts established in Common Law and offer a similar protection for the legal position of the beneficiary, *e.g.*, in the insolvency of the fiduciary,[84] resulting, effectively, in a specific form of ownership where the exercise of the corresponding rights is restricted in the interest of a person other than the owner. Whether or not a "*Vollrechtstreuhand*" with identical or similar characteristics would be recognised in relation to cryptocurrency is far from settled, however. Given that the regular means of legal transfer of title do not apply with regard to crypto-assets (*supra*, 4.1.2.1.), the doctrinal basis for the structure of such relationships would have to be adjusted substantially. While it is certainly conceivable to structure the relationship between a "beneficiary" and the "fiduciary" in a way that binds the latter, the relationship would be dominated by the corresponding obligations, while the recognition of the arrangement for the purposes of property law would be less clear. Case law in this respect does not appear to exist. Just as with regard to other aspects, the residual difficulties relating to the classification of crypto-assets for the purposes of general

82 E.g., A. Amend-Traut and C.H. Hergenröder, 'Kryptowährungen im Erbrecht', ZEV – *Zeitschrift für Erbrecht und Vermögensnachfolge* (2019), 113, at p. 117; N. Medler, 'Sterben 2.0: Erben und Vererben von Kryptowährungen', ZEV – *Zeitschrift für Erbrecht und Vermögensnachfolge* (2020), 262, at p. 264.

83 Medler, ibid.

84 E.g., Oberlandesgericht Celle, 27.10.2010 – Case 3 U 84/10, reported in *BeckRS* (database) 29670; C. Wendehorst, commentary on Art. 43 EGBGB, in: J. Säcker et al. (eds.), *Münchener Kommentar zum Bürgerlichen Gesetzbuch* (8th ed., 2021), para. 49.

property law translate into a substantial degree of legal uncertainty also in this regard.

4.2 *Procedural Aspects*

4.2.1 Enforcement of Titles

The enforcement of titles against debtors, including the seizure of objects of value owned by the debtor, is governed by Book 8, on "Compulsory enforcement", of the Code of Civil Procedure (*"Zivilprozessordnung"*, hereafter: 'ZPO'). Following general procedural provisions applicable to all enforcement proceedings in Chapter 1 (sections 704–802 ZPO), the Code then lays down special provisions, *inter alia*, for the "enforcement of monetary claims" (*i.e.*, claims for the payment of a certain amount of money, see Chapter 2, sections 802a-63 ZPO). Importantly, the applicable provisions within this chapter then distinguish between enforcement directed against different categories of object of value, such as "physical objects" (sections 808–27 ZPO) on the one hand and "claims and other property rights" (sections 828–63) on the other hand.[85] In order for enforcement actions to be initiated, the relevant creditor must meet a number of general requirements applicable to all enforcement proceedings, as summarised in section 750(1) ZPO, namely: an enforceable legal title (*e.g.*, a judgment by a court), a formal certificate of enforceability (*"Vollstreckungsklausel"*) and, finally, a formal service of that title against the debtor.

With regard to the specific requirements laid down in sections 808–27 and 828–63 ZPO, respectively, the Code follows effectively the categorisation of objects of value characteristic of the Civil Code. In consequence, the difficulties to classify the entitlement of a holder of cryptocurrency within the traditional framework of German property law diagnosed above (*supra*, 4.1.2.) reappear also within the procedural realm. Given that cryptocurrency tokens, for reasons discussed before, cannot be classified as "claims" for the purposes of German law (*supra*, 2.3.2.), the corresponding provisions for enforcement actions directed against "claims" (sections 828–56 ZPO) do not apply directly.[86] Likewise, the regime applicable to the enforcement against "physical objects" (sections 808–27 ZPO) does not fit the purpose, as the relevant provisions are

---

85 In terms of the applicable terminology, this subsection follows the inofficial translation of the Code available at https://www.gesetze-im-internet.de/englisch_zpo/englisch_zpo.html#p2536.

86 E.g., F. Boehm and P. Pesch, 'Bitcoins: Rechtliche Herausforderungen einer virtuellen Währung', MMR – *Multimedia und Recht* (2014), 75, at p. 78; D. Effer-Uhe, 'Kryptowährungen in Zwangsvollstreckung und Insolvenz am Beispiel des Bitcoin', ZZP – *Zeitschrift für Zivilprozess* 131 (2018), 513, at p. 517; M.E. Kütük and Ch. Sorge, 'Bitcoin im deutschen Vollstreckungsrecht', MMR – *Multimedia und Recht* (2014), 643, at p. 644.

tailored to the need to obtain physical possession of the relevant objects.[87] According to the majority view in the academic literature, section 857 ZPO, which provides for a modified application of sections 853–55 ZPO to enforcement actions against "other property rights" cannot be applied either, as that provision, according to prevailing opinion, applies only in relation to such objects of value which are recognised as 'rights' in general property law.[88]

Against this backdrop, it has been discussed whether either the provisions on enforcement actions directed against "physical objects"[89] or those governing enforcement actions against "other property rights"[90] could – and should – be applied by analogy. Given, on the one hand, the structural differences between virtual currency and tangible objects (which sit somewhat squarely with the provisions on the seizure of tangible objects) and, on the other hand, the structural proximity with other objects of value covered by section 857 ZPO, the latter approach is certainly commendable. It should be noted, however, that the usual result of an enforcement action under that provision, *i.e.*, the legal attachment (known as *"Pfändungspfandrecht"*), would not be feasible in relation to cryptocurrency, because, again, such attachment, according to prevailing principles of procedural law, can only arise with regard to recognised "things" or "rights". As a result, owing, again, to the unspecified status of cryptocurrency in general property law, the standard consequences of an enforcement, which safeguard the creditor's right to realise the value of the seized property, cannot arise in the same way with regard to cryptocurrency.[91]

87 E.g., A. Spiegel, *Blockchain-basiertes virtuelles Geld* (2020), at pp. 117–18; Th. Badstuber, 'Bitcoin und andere Kryptowährungen in der Zwangsvollstreckung', *DGVZ – Deutsche Gerichtsvollzieherzeitschrift* (2019), 246, at p. 250; F. Boehm and P. Pesch, 'Bitcoins: Rechtliche Herausforderungen einer virtuellen Währung', *MMR – Multimedia und Recht* (2014), 75, at p. 78; D. Effer-Uhe, 'Kryptowährungen in Zwangsvollstreckung und Insolvenz am Beispiel des Bitcoin', *ZZP – Zeitschrift für Zivilprozess* 131 (2018), 513, at p. 517; M.E. Kütük and Ch. Sorge, 'Bitcoin im deutschen Vollstreckungsrecht', *MMR – Multimedia und Recht* (2014), 643, at p. 644.

88 E.g., A. Spiegel, *Blockchain-basiertes virtuelles Geld* (2020), at p. 118; Th. Badstuber, 'Bitcoin und andere Kryptowährungen in der Zwangsvollstreckung', *DGVZ – Deutsche Gerichtsvollzieherzeitschrift* (2019), 246, at p. 250; M.E. Kütük and Ch. Sorge, 'Bitcoin im deutschen Vollstreckungsrecht', *MMR – Multimedia und Recht* (2014), 643, at pp. 644–45.

89 See, e.g., A. Spiegel, *Blockchain-basiertes virtuelles Geld* (2020), at pp. 118–19.

90 See, e.g., Th. Badstuber, 'Bitcoin und andere Kryptowährungen in der Zwangsvollstreckung', *DGVZ – Deutsche Gerichtsvollzieherzeitschrift* (2019), 246, at pp. 250–51; D. Effer-Uhe, 'Kryptowährungen in Zwangsvollstreckung und Insolvenz am Beispiel des Bitcoin', *ZZP – Zeitschrift für Zivilprozess* 131 (2018), 513, at pp. 524–26.

91 See, for further discussion, D. Effer-Uhe, 'Kryptowährungen in Zwangsvollstreckung und Insolvenz am Beispiel des Bitcoin', *ZZP – Zeitschrift für Zivilprozess* 131 (2018), 513, at pp. 524–25.

As a consequence, even *if* an enforcement directed against (a portfolio of) cryptocurrency token is, in principle, both imaginable and feasible within the framework established by section 857 ZPO, the practical use for the creditor would thus be limited. Specifically, neither regime provides for means for the creditor (or, for that matter, the bailiff carrying out the enforcement) to obtain the relevant keys (public and private) which would be required to realise the value of the tokens at issue.[92]

It should be noted that the situation would be different if the relevant crypto keys are held within an (online) wallet provided by an intermediary. In this case, as noted elsewhere (*supra*, 4.1.3.), the "owner's" position would be characterised by a claim against the intermediary which, as such, would fall directly within the scope of section 857 ZPO.

In summarising the foregoing, the position of cryptocurrency in the German law framework for the enforcement of "monetary claims" can best be described as uncertain.[93] While the initiation of enforcement actions directed against cryptocurrency token is at least conceivable within the received framework, the legal and, hence, the economic consequences of such actions for creditors fall short of those for similar actions directed against traditional categories of property law. Just as diagnosed before with regard to the position of cryptocurrencies in inheritance law (*supra*, 4.1.3.), or with regard to pledges (*supra*, 4.1.1.2.), their uncertain status in property law translates directly into substantial difficulties of classification for the purposes of other areas of substantive or procedural law which, as the procedural framework for the enforcement of claims, effectively build on received categories of property law and are tailored to cater for their respective characteristics. The resulting uncertainty, again: just as diagnosed before, substantially weakens the legal and economic position not just of the "owner" of crypto tokens, but also of other interested parties.

4.2.2 Insolvency Law

There are currently no specific provisions governing the treatment of cryptocurrencies in the insolvency of the "owner" or, indeed, the insolvency of an

---

92 See, for further discussion, ibid., pp. 525–26.

93 It should be noted, in this context, that the situation would be different if a party (*e.g.*, a purchaser of Bitcoin or other crypto token) seeks to enforce a claim for the delivery of cryptocurrency against another party (*e.g.*, the seller). In this case, the enforcement action would be governed by the framework for the enforcement of specific actions, in particular: sections 887 and 888 ZPO (see Oberlandesgericht [Regional Court of Appeals] Düsseldorf, 19 January 2021 – Case 7 W 44/20, reported in ZIP – *Zeitschrift für Wirtschaftsrecht* (2021), 2120–21).

intermediary under German insolvency law. In principle, German law does not distinguish between the insolvency of individuals and corporations and applies in the same way also to licensed financial intermediaries, for which no distinct (administrative or court-based) insolvency regime exists. While BaFin, in its capacity as both supervisory and resolution authority, retains a set of specific administrative powers in relation to insolvent licensed intermediaries, these amount merely to a pre-liquidation administration during which the intermediary's assets are frozen, before the authority then has to apply for the initiation of formal insolvency proceedings under general insolvency law. Hereafter, the firm will then be liquidated by a private-sector insolvency liquidator (*"Insolvenzverwalter"*) under the auspices of the general insolvency court.[94] Against this backdrop, for both scenarios, cryptocurrency token (potentially) affected by the insolvency thus have to be treated in accordance with general principles of insolvency as set down in the Insolvency Code (*"Insolvenzordnung"*, hereafter: 'InsO').

Under the Code, the treatment of claims against the insolvent estate generally depends on the nature of the claim in question. As a rule, *in rem* claims related to assets held by the insolvent debtor but owned by a third party will be enforceable irrespective of the initiation of insolvency proceedings by virtue of section 47 InsO. The scope of that right is restricted to rights *in rem* or *in personam* rights of a similar standing in insolvency. Creditors secured by mortgages, pledges or similar rights in the debtor's assets will, instead, receive a preferential payment out of the proceeds of the liquidation of the relevant assets, but not the assets themselves, as stipulated by sections 49–52 InsO (*"abgesonderte Befriedigung"*).

However, none of these alternatives applies with regard to claims against intermediaries offering safekeeping accounts for cryptocurrency, since these do not qualify as objects which could be "owned" in a legal sense and do not qualify as objects of a pledge.[95] As the relationship between the investor and the intermediary can only be qualified as giving rights to an obligation, the only option for the investor is to assert a claim for damages caused by the unavailability of his/her cryptocurrency against the insolvent estate, which would

94 See, for details, sections 46a and 46b KWG and section 79 WpIG. For a detailed description of the interplay between supervisory law and insolvency in the case of licensed credit institutions, see J.-H. Binder, 'Insolvenzbewältigung bei nicht systemrelevanten Banken', in: id., A. Glos and J. Riepe (eds.), *Handbuch Bankenaufsichtsrecht* (2nd. ed., 2020), Ch. 17.

95 See, e.g., Th. Badstuber, 'Bitcoin und andere Kryptowährungen in der Zwangsvollstreckung', DGVZ – *Deutsche Gerichtsvollzieherzeitschrift* (2019), 246, at p. 253; M.E. Kütük and Ch. Sorge, 'Bitcoin im deutschen Vollstreckungsrecht', MMR – *Multimedia und Recht* (2014), 643, at p. 645.

rank *pari passu* with all other unsecured claims and, hence, be satisfied only *pro rata* out of the proceeds of the liquidation. In this regard, the terms of the contract between the intermediary and the customer would be entirely irrelevant.

To remedy that, the legislator introduced new section 46i(1) KWG, thus only applicable to institutes licensed under the KWG (*supra*, 3.2.2), valid from the 1st of January 2024, whereby the creditor "owns" the cryptocurrencies. This provision makes section 47 InsO (s. above) applicable.[96]

With the bill to digitalise the financial market (*Finanzmarktdigitalisierungsgesetz*) of 2024, a new set of rules for the prudential regulation of crypto markets (*Kryptomärkteaufsichtsgesetz,* hereafter: KMAG) will be introduced. As part of that, regulation under the KWG shall be extended to all intermediaries holding cryptocurrencies for creditors.[97] This would thus generate the right to enforce ones claims irrespective of the insolvency of the intermediary according to section 47 InsO for every cryptocurrency owner.[98]

Similar general considerations apply in case of insolvency of an investor who holds cryptocurrency with a wallet provider or other intermediary. In principle, the treatment of the cryptocurrency portfolios in the investor's insolvency would follow the general principles governing the composition and the liquidation of the insolvent estate, as well as the distribution of the proceeds among the unsecured creditors. The insolvency estate, and thus the scope of the insolvency proceedings in terms of assets covered by the procedure, is defined in sections 35 and 36 of the Insolvency Act, and encompasses, as a rule, all assets of the debtor (section 35(1) InsO). Only assets which cannot be seized by way of an enforcement subject to exemptions in procedural law are excluded (section 36(1) InsO). As 'other objects of value', cryptocurrency token "owned" by the debtor will generally be considered part of the insolvent estate, irrespective of the difficulties of classification for the purposes of general property law.[99]

96 Cf. M. d'Avoine, P. Hamacher, 'Kryptowerte in der Insolvenz', *WM – Zeitschrift für Wirtschaft- und Bankrecht* (2024), 525 at p. 533.

97 Proposed section 44 in conjunction with proposed section 1 KMAG relates back to the scope of MiCAR.

98 Cf. M. d'Avoine, P. Hamacher, 'Kryptowerte in der Insolvenz', *WM – Zeitschrift für Wirtschaft- und Bankrecht* (2024), 525 at pp. 534 seq.

99 E.g., Th. Badstuber, 'Bitcoin und andere Kryptowährungen in der Zwangsvollstreckung', *DGVZ – Deutsche Gerichtsvollzieherzeitschrift* (2019), 246, at p. 253; D. Effer-Uhe, 'Kryptowährungen in Zwangsvollstreckung und Insolvenz am Beispiel des Bitcoin', *ZZP – Zeitschrift für Zivilprozess* 131 (2018), 513, at p. 530; M.E. Kütük and Ch. Sorge, 'Bitcoin im deutschen Vollstreckungsrecht', *MMR – Multimedia und Recht* (2014), 643, at p. 645;

Even though, in principle, cryptocurrencies are thus covered by the general procedural framework for the liquidation of the insolvent estate, it should be noted that the actual realisation of their value for the benefit of the creditors as a whole would meet practical difficulties. In order to get access to the account, and to be able to sell the crypto-assets registered therein, the insolvency liquidator would have to obtain the relevant keys from the debtor. However, unlike the uncertain position in the enforcement process in this regard (*supra*, 4.2.1.), the insolvency liquidator can make use of his general powers to request information from the debtor also in this regard, which should facilitate the effective seizure in the process.[100]

4.3 *Taxation*

There are currently no specific provisions in German tax law addressing the taxation of cryptocurrencies. Upon completion of the present manuscript, the taxation of activities related to cryptocurrencies has been discussed mainly with regard to the treatment of gains generated out of transactions in such assets for the purposes of income tax. Specifically, the applicability of income taxation, in the absence of more specific provisions, rests on the classification of cryptocurrencies as 'other economic assets' ("anderes Wirtschaftsgut") as defined by section 23(1) sentence 1 no. 2 of the Law on Income Tax (*"Einkommensteuergesetz"*, 'EStG'). Following of a number of dissenting decisions by first-instance fiscal courts in this regard,[101] the issue has now been decided by the *Bundesfinanzhof*, the Federal Fiscal Court,[102] which held that crypto assets

J. Schmittmann and Ch. C. Schmidt, 'Elektronische Wertpapiere und Kryptowährungen in Zwangsvollstreckung und Insolvenz', *DZWir – Deutsche Zeitschrift für Wirtschaftsrecht* (2021), 648, at p. 649; D. Skauradszun, 'Kryptowerte im Insolvenzverfahren des Anlegers oder Emittenten', ZIP – *Zeitschrift für Wirtschaftsrecht* (2022), 2610, at pp. 2611–13.

100 See section 97(1) and (2) InsO and, for further discussion of potential scenarios in this regard, M. d'Avoine and Ph. Hamacher, 'Kryptowährungen im Insolvenzverfahren', ZIP – *Zeitschrift für Wirtschaftsrecht* (2022), 6, at pp.10-12; D. Skauradszun, 'Kryptowerte im Insolvenzverfahren des Anlegers oder Emittenten', ZIP – *Zeitschrift für Wirtschaftsrecht* (2022), 2610, at pp. 2615–16.

101 Contrast, e.g., supporting the application, Finanzgericht (Fiscal Court) Berlin-Brandenburg, 20 June 2019 – Case 13 V 13100/19, reported in BB – *Betriebs-Berater* (2020), 176 and Finanzgericht Baden-Württemberg, 11 June 2021 – Case 5 K 1997/19, reported in BB – *Betriebs-Berater* (2021), 2977, with Finanzgericht Nuremberg, 8 April 2020 – Case 3 V 1239/19, reported in *DStR – Deutsches Steuerrecht* (2020), 1243 (expressing doubts in a summary judgment).

102 Bundesfinanzhof, 14 February 2023 – Case IX R 3/22, reported in NJW – *Neue Juristische Wochenschrift* (2023), 867. See, for further discussion, e.g., J. Andres, 'Besteuerung von DLT-Systemen am Beispiel des Bitcoin ohne spezialgesetzliche Grundlage zulässig?', *DStR – Deutsches Steuerrecht* (2021), 1630; O. Ch. Schroen, 'Besteuerungsmöglichkeit von Veräu-

qualify as "other economic assets" and that, consequently, any gains arising from their sale were taxable under that provision.

5 Current Litigation and Arbitration Cases

In the absence of a central register for pending cases before German courts, it is impossible to provide a comprehensive account of relevant pending cases for present purposes. Other than the federal courts, courts generally do not report pending litigation either, so that it is impossible to collect relevant information from decentral sources. Upon completion of the present manuscript, the author is unaware of any major litigation that would have been reported in other sources, *e.g.*, public media.

As far as the recognition of foreign arbitration awards is concerned, despite the difficulties concerning the treatment of cryptocurrencies in various areas of substantive and procedural German law discussed before, there is nothing to suggest that such recognition would be denied on the grounds of public policy concerns, as it is obvious from the foregoing that transactions in cryptocurrencies would not be treated as illegal or conflicting with public policy under German law.

6 Conclusions

In summarising the findings developed above, the treatment of cryptocurrencies in German law, as noted from the start, can best be described as a moving target. As far as the current state of affairs in private law (and, consequently, civil procedure) is concerned, the degree of legal uncertainty, in the absence of specific provisions governing the treatment of such assets for the purposes of property law is remarkable. In this regard, the German Civil Code is illustrative of both the strengths and the weaknesses of a traditional private law codification, which combines abstract principles for application to an unspecified range of objects of value and transactions therein, with more detailed menus for specific types of transactions, in the light of technological developments, which transcend traditional categories. In general, it is particularly the

---

ßerungsgeschäften mit sog. "Krypto-Assets" nach § 23 EStG i.V.m. § 39 AO', Parts I–III, *BB – Betriebs-Berater* (2020), 2133, 2199 and 2263; J. Moritz and J. Strohm, 'Besteuerung von Investitionen in virtuelle Währungen bei privaten Kapitalanlegern', *DB – Der Betrieb* (2018), 3012.

statutory law of obligations that proves sufficiently flexible for adaptation also to virtual assets. It is, in fact, certainly possible to apply general principles of contract law as well as the BGB rules governing specific types of contracts (*e.g.*, sales or loan contracts). However, the absence of a reliable basis for the classification of crypto-assets generally for the purposes of property law comes with wide, and drastic, ramifications that substantially weaken the position of both investors and other interested parties by comparison with owners of tangible property or other recognised rights. As a result, both the legal treatment of transactions related to cryptocurrencies and the treatment of crypto-assets for the purposes of areas of substantive law, such as security interests and inheritance law, and procedural aspects, including the enforcement of titles and insolvency law, remain ill-defined and leave relevant parties with a high degree of legal uncertainty – which inevitably also affects the economic value of such assets to the extent that the relevant position is governed by German law.

By comparison, the development of the regulatory framework for services related to cryptocurrencies – attributable, to a large extent, to incoming EU legislation – is considerably more advanced. Notably, the introduction of the first statutory definition of 'virtual currencies' in the German Banking Act has paved the way for a transparent and predictable application of most existing regulatory frameworks to providers of relevant services. Even in this regard, however, the current state of affairs cannot yet be described as providing a fully comprehensive and consistent framework comparable to the situation with regard to traditional forms (and objects) of financial services. As noted before, residual deficiencies exist, in particular, with regard to the inapplicability of statutory prospectus regimes, to the uncertain classification of cryptocurrencies for the purposes of payment services, and the absence of conduct-of-business rules governing the interactions between intermediaries and investors.

Nonetheless, it is certainly conceivable that the statutory recognition of cryptocurrencies, and, in particular, the introduction of a statutory definition of such assets, in the area of financial law could, over time, reinforce claims for the legislator to follow suit by corresponding adjustments also to the Civil Code. As discussed, the need for a statutory definition that would clarify the treatment in property law, as well as a bespoke regime for the classification of transactions in crypto-assets that would facilitate also a transparent and reliable treatment across other areas of substantive and procedural law, is particularly pressing. Upon completion of the present manuscript, however, the dynamic evolution of the regulatory framework in recent years has yet to disseminate into the area of general private law.

Hungary

István Simon

1 Introductory Observations

Life is changing fundamentally in our age. One of the main driving forces of the changes is technology; the new techniques of information storage, processing and exchange, on a global scale. The rapid exchange of information at global level is not a recent innovation, especially not in the financial industry. However, the previous systems were closed ones. Among the new forms of information exchange systems, there are many open systems in different areas of social and economic life; such as social media, the platform economy and several parts of the crypto ecosystem.

The crypto system, as a globally accessible economic system, raises several questions, especially if we observe cryptocurrencies – as peer-to-peer cash systems – being the term applied in this report.

When discussing the Hungarian legal system, it is important to note that Hungary is a member state of the European Union and therefore EU law applies. A regulation recently issued by the EU Parliament and the Council ("MiCAR") regulates the crypto market in the European Economic Area.[1]

In substance, the MiCAR integrates a part of the crypto ecosystem into the regulated financial market under "the principles of 'same activities, same risks, same rules' and of technology neutrality"[2] and at the same time separates from it as it is discussed in point 3.1.

The Hungarian national report cannot take on the task of explaining the EU rules. These are easily accessible to the interested reader from other sources. However, I briefly summarize the logic of the regulation of the crypto market in point 3.1. below.

What may be relevant in an IACL report for global comparison today is what rules apply under Hungarian law to the crypto market, especially to assets not covered by the MiCAR; Bitcoin is the most important example in this context.

1 Regulation (EU) 2023/1114 of the European Parliament and of the Council of 31 May 2023 on markets in crypto-assets, and amending Regulations (EU) No 1093/2010 and (EU) No 1095/2010 and Directives 2013/36/EU and (EU) 2019/1937 (Hereinafter referred as MiCAR).

2 Recital (9) MiCAR.

 | DOI:10.1163/9789004722507_014

2 Definition and Legal Qualification

2.1 *Cryptocurrencies in the Hungarian Economy*

Cryptocurrencies are present in the Hungarian economy; Bitcoin has existed here since 2011. Although cryptocurrencies are not considered legal tender, a few examples of their usage as means of payment can be found. Beside commercial transactions, cryptocurrencies serve as investment instruments in the Hungarian market. The financial supervisory authority – which is the Magyar Nemzeti Bank ('MNB'), the central bank of the country – has not published official statistics on the cryptocurrency exposures of credit institutions and other licensed financial market service providers. The reason may be that the presence of crypto assets in the regulated market is not significant enough to be detected.

Reliable data on the market share of stable coins in Hungary is not available and the legal system before MiCAR did not provide special rules for them either.

2.2 *Cryptocurrencies in Statute and Case Law*

MiCAR applies directly in Hungary. Article 3 of the MiCAR defines the term crypto-asset and its sub-types, which are specifically regulated in the regulation. Crypto-asset defined as a digital representation of a value or of a right that is able to be transferred and stored electronically using distributed ledger technology or similar technology.[3]

The first subcategory of crypto assets is asset-referenced token which is defined as follows: a type of crypto-asset that is not an electronic money token and that purports to maintain a stable value by referencing another value or right or a combination thereof, including one or more official currencies.[4] For asset-referenced tokens, it is essential that MiCAR keeps the existing market structure of the regulated financial market. One of the prerequisite of the issuance of an asset-referenced token is a legal opinion – and its acceptance by the competent authority – to support that the token does not qualify as e-money token and is not one of the services (products) not covered by MiCAR.[5] Asset-referenced tokens correspond to the concept of a stable coin in "traditional" sense, meaning that the issuer applies reference assets for value preservation. This type of stable coin – in opposite to e-money – does not qualifies as legal tender.

3 Art 3 (5) MiCAR.

4 Art 3 (6) MiCAR.

5 Arts 16 (1) a), 20 (5), 21 (1), 18 (2) e) and 2 (2)-(4) MiCAR.

E-money, the second subcategory, is defined as follows: electronic money token or e-money token means a type of crypto-asset that purports to maintain a stable value by referencing the value of one official currency.[6] The e-money token is in fact a token that makes possible the issuance of electronic money using DLT technology to credit institutions and electronic money issuing institutions. The significance of the definition of e-money token is that it is a new technical form of money creation, and the e-money created this way qualifies as legal tender in the same way as "traditional" e-money.[7]

The third subcategory comprises crypto-assets that are neither asset-referenced tokens nor e-money tokens and meet the criteria set out in the MiCAR including utility tokens. Utility token means a type of crypto asset that is only intended to provide access to a good or a service supplied by its issuer.[8]

In substance, MiCAR defines three categories of crypto assets. It is important to note that MiCAR defines crypto asset types, but an essential element of the regulatory concept – for consumer protection and systemic risk reasons – is control, which requires controlled, supervised, centralised issuance and trading. Therefore, traditional crypto assets, the vast majority of which exist in a decentralized blockchain system, are not covered by MiCAR.

Bitcoin and several other crypto assets will not be covered by MiCAR.

Apart from the new legislative acts crypto-assets have been defined in AML and tax rules – discussed in points 3 and 5 below – for some years in the Hungarian legal system. The only definition of cryptocurrencies in the Hungarian statute law – apart from the global AML standards implemented in the Hungarian law – has been in the Personal Income Tax Act. There has been no distinction made between cryptocurrency and crypto asset in the Hungarian statute law terminology.

Having a look at the case law, one realizes that there only a few published cases in which the expression of Bitcoin or cryptocurrency are included.

2.3 *Cryptocurrencies in the Jurisprudence*

Hungarian jurisprudence has detected the issue and produced publications in the last couple of years. The scholarship has identified the difficulties of including cryptocurrencies in the existing terms of private and public law, such as their classification as property ('thing'), money (currency), securities, right,

6 Art 3 (7) MiCAR.

7 Art 48 MiCAR; Directive 2013/36/EU and Directive 2009/110/EC and their respective implementing legislaton in the legal systems of the Member States. E-money is defined in Article 2, point (2), of Directive 2009/110/EC.

8 Art 3 (9) MiCAR.

and claim. The questions of how cryptocurrency could be defined and integrated into the legal system, or at least handle the challenge it caused, were raised.[9]

Perhaps the first extensive work was Dániel Eszteri's PhD dissertation. He took the position that, according to the features of Bitcoin, it can be defined as a special commodity, and the right of disposal over can be taken as a special intangible of its utilizer. In this definition, it is not the cryptocurrency that is the intangible. The intangible is the right of disposal over the cryptocurrency.[10]

The de lege ferenda responses in substance have two main lines. One of them is to take cryptoassets – including cryptocurrencies – as a sui generis phenomenon and regulate them according to their real properties. The other is to integrate them into the system via extending ownership rights designed for things over cryptocurrencies.

Another issue, beside legislative concepts, is how to manage cryptocurrencies in practice, in the absence of explicit legal norms. The response depends on the nature of the issue to be managed. In the field of international private law, the question on the nature of Bitcoin was raised in connection with CISG.[11] The basic question was whether a contract in which the counter value determined in cryptocurrency falls under CISG – see Art 1 (1) and Art 2 (d) – or not. The author concludes that the position of cryptocurrency under CISG is not clarified; however, it should be taken as money and the contracts as sale of goods contracts.[12] From the perspective of inheritance law, the response of

9 E.g. : Zs. Halász, 'A virtuális pénzeszközökkel összefüggő jogi kérdések az adójog területén' Iustum Aequum Salutare XVI. 2020. 4., 35–44.; Z. Nagy, 'A kriptopénzek helye és szerepe a pénzügyi rendszerben' Miskolci Jogi Szemle 14. évf. (2019) 2.; P. B. Király, 'A kriptovaluták pénzügyi fogyaszóvédelmi aspektusai' Iustum Aequum Salutare XVI. 2020. 4. 45–58.; K. Mezei, 'A kriptovaluták kihívásai a büntető anyagi és eljárási jogban' Pro Futuro 2019/1, 79-98.; L. Rácz, 'A személy és a dolog fogalmának (lehetséges) változásai a mesterséges intelligencia és a kriptovaluták világában', Állam- és Jogtudomány, LXI. évf. 2020/4., 82-107.; Z. Szathmáry, 'Az elektronikus pénz és a bitcoin biztosítása a büntetőeljárásban' Magyar Jog, 2015/11, pp. 644–646.

10 D. Eszteri, A World of Warcraft-tól a Bitcoin-ig: Az egyén, a gazdaság és a tulajdon helyzetének magán- és büntetőjogi elemzése a virtuális közösségekben (From the World of Warcraft until the Bitcoin: the analyses of the civil and crimonal law position of the individual, the economy and the ovenership in virtual communities), PTE Doctoral Dissertation, Pécs, 2015, pp. 187–193.; D. Eszteri, 'Egy bitcoinnal elkövetett vagyon elleni bűncselekmény és az ahhoz kapcsolódó jogi kérdések' Infokommunikáció és jog 2017/1. 25–31., p 29. and 31.

11 United Nations Convention on Contracts for the International Sale of Goods, 1980.

12 M. Király, *A Bécsi Vételi Egyezmény és a Bitcoin* in: Studia in honorem Lajos Vékás (eds: V. Lamm and A. Sajó), HVG-Orac, Budapest, 2019, pp. 154–161, p. 157.

the public notary is to handle cryptocurrencies as personal property (tangible things) by analogy, as will be discussed in point 4.[13]

Criminal law scholarship describes the basic properties of Bitcoin and it concludes that it cannot be subsumed under the existing terms of property (thing), money or means of payment (e.g. credit cards, travelers' cheques). Therefore, the actus reus cannot be established when the object is a property or money; for example in the case of theft. However, it is recognized that cryptocurrency has value. Therefore, for example, the crime of fraud can be established when the asset value is expressed and paid in cryptocurrency.[14]

As to my view on the definition of cryptocurrencies, I consider the best way is to follow the simplest and clearest way of defining cryptocurrency for legal purposes, in both legislative and judicial processes. Cryptocurrency is a data file stored by DLT software connected to a certain address (the public key) the access to which – and its transfer – is only possible by using the private key. Cryptocurrency has an asset value based on the supply and demand in its market. In a private law context, it should be handled as personal property (movable thing) by analogy (see point 4 below). In a public law context – for example, financial regulation – my opinion has been that the distinction between money and currency and between money and legal tender should be clarified. Cryptocurrency may qualify as money but its qualification as currency and legal tender falls within the competence of the legislator (the Parliament). Money is a phenomenon of the economy and society. Money, according to the law, is currency (official money of a country) and legal tender (bank notes and coins denominated in a currency).[15] Therefore, it would be necessary to modify the wording of the discussion. The term cryptocurrency should be used only for instruments issued in the official currency of each state by legally authorized entities, i.e. the central bank and e-token issuing institutions.

MiCAR addresses this problem by keeping e-money token as a new form of electronic money within the banking system and ensures its legal tender status. However, the asset-referenced tokens, as stable coins, are a new form of private money. Stable coins, although considered as money by its users should not be called cryptocurrency. The appropriate term would be crypto asset.

---

13 Á. Mányoki, 'A kriptovaluta mint a hagyatéki eljárás tárgya' KK, 2021/4., pp. 81–99. and 92–93.

14 E.g.: I. Ambrus, *Digitalizáció és büntetőjog*, Wolters Kluver, 2021, pp. 49–51.; K. Mezei, 'A kriptovaluták kihívásai a büntető anyagi és eljárási jogban', Pro Futuro 2019/1, pp. 79–98.

15 For a summary on the legislation over money- see I. Simon, 'Constant and Changing Elements in the Regulation of Money' Annales Universitatis Scientiarum Budapestinensis de Rolando Eötvös Nominatae, Sectio Iuridica. V 51, 2010 https://www.ajk.elte.hu/file/annales_2010_15_Simon.pdf.

2.4 *Legal Relationship between the Participants in the Cryptocurrency System*

The introduction of MiCAR will clarify the legal relationships of crypto market participants in Europe in a certain market segment, but MiCAR rules will not cover a significant part of the market. Therefore, in the following, I will examine how the relationships between crypto market players are currently set up. For future reference, it is important to note that MiCAR does not cover decentralized crypto assets based on blockchain technology, e.g. Bitcoin.

The legal relationships between participants in a blockchain on which cryptocurrencies are transferred are to be built on the functions fulfilled by the participants in the system. The participants discussed here are miners, owners (users), wallet providers and exchanges.

The possible legal relationship between the participants in a block chain is, to a significant extent, determined by the technical basis, the blockchain itself. Cryptocurrency is piece of data stored in a register in the distributed ledger. In a more correct explanation: "The fundamental building block of a bitcoin transaction is an unspent transaction output or UTXO. UTXO are indivisible chunks of bitcoin currency locked to a specific owner, recorded on the blockchain, … ."[16] Thinking in legal relations between participants in the system, the main question is how the different participants relate to cryptocurrency – its existence, storage and transfer – and to each other. The problem is that the system is smart, or at least smarter than to be regulated by law in its core operation. Placing aside those affairs that can destroy it – for example, a majority (51%) miners' attack on the system – the system operates in a predetermined way; there is very little scope for human decision making. The key figures of the system are miners, who verify transactions; however, their job is an automated predetermined process, checking that the technical conditions are met.[17] Since this control is done by computers applying the shared software, to establish a legal relationship between the miners and other participants in the system – as it seems – has no basis. Fraudulent and other similar acts by the miners are out of the scope of this report. Wallet providers are responsible for providing the software, the function of which is to ensure access to the DLT system for the owners of cryptocurrencies and to provide them the capability to execute transactions, sending and receiving cryptocurrencies in a safe manner. The legal relationship between the wallet provider and the owner can be categorized as a software licence contract with the specifics that the context

16 A. M. Antonopoulos, *Mastering Bitcoin,* (revised 1st edn) O'Reilly, 2014, p. 114.

17 K. F. K. Low and E. Mik, ' Pause the Blockchain Legal Revolution' ICLQ vol 69, January 2020 pp. 135–175., p. 142.

requires. In the case of a hardware wallet, the proper operation of the hardware is also an element to be clarified in terms of (product) liability. A special case is the web wallet, in the sense that the wallet provider has an additional, custodial role in the relationship, since holding the keys equals the possession of the cryptocurrencies of the owner. It is important to emphasise that wallet providers are not owners of the cryptocurrencies; they are obliged to separate cryptocurrencies in their custody from their own assets. It has relevance in many respects, especially in cases of liquidation. Cryptocurrency exchanges are organized, concentrated markets of cryptocurrencies that provide the necessary infrastructure for trading, such as connections to the market, correct information on prices, a kind of supervision to combat unfair trade, and connection to currencies. The legal position of the exchange and the legal relationships between the exchange and its clients depends on the regulatory environment – if there exists any – and the general business conditions (terms of use) and other contracts concluded by the parties.[18] The model on the basis of which their legal position can be analysed is a stock exchange and a central securities depository.

3 Regulatory Framework

3.1 *Financial Law*

The financial market in the European Union is governed by regulations with direct effect and directives to be implemented into the domestic legal systems of the member states.

EU law regulates financial market institutions, the services they can provide, their authorization conditions and their supervision. Specific rules apply to different parts of the market, e.g. banking services,[19] investment services.[20]

---

18 For example: https://www.binance.com/en/terms.

19 The governing laws of the operation of credit institutions are the CRR and the CRD: Regulation (EU) No 575/2013 of the European Parliament and of the Council of 26 June 2013 on prudential requirements for credit institutions and investment ('CRR'), Directive 2013/36/EU of the European Parliament and of the Council of 26 June 2013 on access to the activity of credit institutions and the prudential supervision of credit institutions and investment firms ('CRD').

20 The governing laws of the operation of investment service providers are MIFID I–II. and MICAR: Directive 2004/39/EC of the European Parliament and of the Council of 21 April 2004 on markets in financial instruments (MIFID I.); Directive 2014/65/EU of the European Parliament and of the Council of 15 May 2014 on markets in financial instruments (MIFID I.).

Licensed institutions may provide services which are specified in the laws governing them under a license issued by the supervisory authority; in Hungary it is the MNB.

The EU and member state legislator separates financial market sub-markets by applying structural rules. Licensed financial market institutions – e.g. banks, investment service providers, stock exchanges, insurance companies – are allowed to carry out activities in other sub-markets in addition to those provided for in the legislation governing them, only to the extent that the governing legislation allows them to do so. For example, insurance and banking activities cannot be provided by a single legal entity. However, EU rules are based on the universal banking model, credit institutions can provide both financial services and investment services according to the license issued by the supervisory authority. Furthermore, the rules on ownership set out the conditions under which ownership can be acquired in authorized financial market service providers.

The legislator had at least two problems to solve in the context of Distributed Ledger Technology (DLT). One is to integrate the technological development into the regulated financial market, meaning to ensure that authorized institutions can use this technology to provide services and create financial products. The other was to respond to the challenge caused by blockchain based (DeFi) crypto assets. One of the issues in this context is that most traditional crypto assets are based on an encrypted version of DLT, i.e. blockchain. Blockchain-based cryptoassets are difficult to manage – I see them as unmanageable – in terms of safe and sound operation of the financial market and consumer protection, in addition to AML problems.

The legislator has solved the problem of ensuring the usage of DLT technology by explicitly allowing its use. Where this has been very important is the market for investment services. This is because it was necessary to clarify the relationship between financial instrument as defined in capital market law (MIFID) and crypto asset. The solution has been that the legislator has decided that financial instruments – e.g. shares, bonds – can be created and issued using DLT. On the other hand, it stated that products that are financial instruments can only be issued under the legislative acts that govern them, not on a decentralized basis using blockchain technology without license and supervision.[21] Thus, for example, it is not possible under European law to issue shares in decentralized way using blockchain technology.

---

21 The legislative act that regulates that scope of issue is Regulation (EU) 2022/858 of the European Parliament and of the Council of 30 May 2022 on a pilot regime for market

MiCAR applies from 30 December 2024, but parts of it, such as Title III on asset-referenced tokens and Title IV on e-money tokens, applies from 30 June 2024.

If we consider the regulatory concept of MiCAR and the outcome that its rules are supposed to create, we can say that MiCAR keeps the status quo by integrating technical innovation. This means that it defines the cryptoassets, the conditions for their issuance and trading, the conditions for market entry and operation of service providers and provides for supervisory institutions. In the spirit of structural regulation, it specifies that traditional financial market institutions and the services they provide are excluded from the scope of the MiCAR, thus following the solution already mentioned.[22] On the other hand, from a DeFi perspective, it is important to note that traditional cryptoassets, such as Bitcoin, are not covered by MiCAR. NFTs are also not covered by MiCAR, given that value is provided by uniqueness.

To summarize the above, under EU law, traditional financial services institutions can use DLT in their own business when providing services and creating and selling products. According to the regulatory concept, MiCAR seeks to bring the regulation of the crypto market institutions and crypto-assets closer to the traditional centralised regulatory and supervisory structure of the financial market. Crypto assets – based on DLT – can be created and marketed under the MiCAR, but most traditional crypto assets are not covered. Crypto assets are inherently decentralised systems, so MiCAR alone, as a regional legal instrument, is of limited relevance in a global system. As it is expressed in recital (75): "This Regulation should not affect the possibility for persons established in the Union to receive crypto-asset services by a third-country firm on their own initiative." This means that in Europe, only products created/distributed by regulated institutions can be sold, but if European businesses or individuals choose to purchase a crypto asset not covered by MiCAR on their own initiative, i.e. not based on an external offer, they can do it.

On 17 April 2024, the Hungarian Parliament passed an act regulating the crypto assets market, which contains certain implementing rules of the MiCAR.[23] The act entered into force and has applied since 30 June 2024. The Act details the conditions for providing crypto services, contains consumer protection provisions and designates the supervisory authority for the crypto market, which is the Magyar Nemzeti Bank.

---

infrastructures based on distributed ledger technology, and amending Regulations (EU) No 600/2014 and (EU) No 909/2014 and Directive 2014/65/EU.

22 Art 2 (4) MiCAR.

23 Act VII of 2024 on Markets in Crypto-assets ('MiCARHU').

3.2 *Criminal Law and AML*

There are no specific crimes for cryptocurrencies; however, there are rules that are applicable to cryptocurrencies as objects of crimes. The dividing line, in terms of crimes against wealth in Hungarian law is whether the definition of the object of crime is a 'thing' or 'asset value'. Therefore, cryptocurrency cannot be the object of theft since its legislative definition is based on a 'thing' being the object stolen; however, fraud can serve as an example, as its object is a wider category, asset value, as was mentioned above.[24] The significance of transforming legislative definitions can be showed by the crime of money laundering. Effective as of 1 January 2021, the crime of money laundering was redefined and, in accordance with the AML5 Directive, the object of the crime is now asset value, which embraces cryptocurrencies, instead of 'thing', which included only money (legal tender) as it is defined in property law.

Taking a wider look, some other crimes involving attacks on information systems and theft from databases also have been defined or redefined.

FATF global anti-money laundering and counter terrorist financing standards have been followed by the Hungarian legislation via the EU legal harmonization rules and processes. The EU anti money laundering directives have been implemented into domestic law via the amendments of the AML Act.[25]

4 Supervision

The concept of financial supervision is connected to financial regulation.

When discussing the issues of supervision, the structure of the crypto market as described so far should be borne in mind. MiCAR provides for supervision issues and regulates the conditions for the issuance and trading of cryptocurrencies. In Hungary, the Magyar Nemzeti Bank is responsible for the supervision of the crypto market according to the above mentioned MiCARHU.

Under MiCAR licences granted by the supervisory authority are required before the use, management or issuance of a cryptocurrency or the provision of cryptocurrency-related services. Issuers of cryptocurrencies are required to publish a whitepaper or prospectus.

---

24 From a criminal law parspective see: Z. Szathmáry, 'Az elektronikus pénz és a bitcoin biztosítása a büntetőeljárásban' Magyar Jog, 2015/11. pp. 644–646; I. Ambrus, Digitalizáció és büntetőjog, Wolters Kluver, 2021, pp 49–51.; K. Mezei, 'A kriptovaluták kihívásai a büntető anyagi és eljárási jogban', Pro Futuro 2019/1, pp. 79–98.

25 Act LIII of 2017 on the Prevention and Combating of Money Laundering and Terrorist Financing ('AML Act').

However, a significant part of the crypto market, cryptocurrency trading falls outside the regulated market; therefore, it is not supervised in Hungary. It does not mean that this part of the cryptocurrency market is outside the horizon of the MNB as a market supervisor. It only means that the supervisory body only intervenes if the crypto market affects the integrity of the financial market in general. The MNB has kept cautionary notes on its website for investors regarding risky investments not supervised by the Bank. These investments include investment gold, carbon credit, participation rights and cryptocurrencies.[26] Beside this permanent notice, the MNB publishes precautionary notices from time to time, informing investors of the risks of cryptocurrency investments.

To my knowledge, the supervisory authority has not taken any action in respect of illegal activities connected to cryptocurrencies. Actions against illegal activities – such as hacking and fraudulent token issue – belong to the competence of the police and the state prosecutor, not the supervisory authority.

5 Private Law Issues

5.1 *Cryptocurrencies in the Civil Code*

Private law issues are governed in Hungary by Act V of 2013 on the Civil Code ('Civil Code'), promulgated on the 26th of February 2013 and which entered into force on the 15th of March 2014. Cryptocurrencies existed during the last few years of the drafting process; however, their weight in Hungarian and European economic life had not reached such a level that the legislator should have taken them into consideration as a potential phenomenon for civil law legislation. The Civil Code does not contain any explicit rules on cryptocurrencies. As such, I must clarify here that the following are my views; even if they have been formed in the usual academic way of relying on colleagues' previous works of.

When discussing private law questions, it needs to be noted that traditional financial market products created on a DLT basis, such as financial instruments, and the services provided this way qualify in the same way as their traditional technical-based versions. Among the crypto-assets created under MiCAR, e-money tokens, – like non-DLT-based electronic money – is a conditional legal tender. It is conditional in the sense that it requires the technical conditions to be met by the parties to a transaction to make a payment

26 https://www.MNB.hu/felugyelet/piacfelugyelet/befektetoi-figyelmeztetesek/termekekkel-kapcsolatos-tajekozodas/az-MNB-altal-nem-felugyelt-befektetesek (15 02 2022). Although the title refers to initial coin offerings, the content does not differentiate between cryptocurrencies and crypto assets as the questionnaire does.

in this way. It qualifies as money under the Civil Code. Crypto assets that are not asset-referenced tokens and e-money tokens can be classified based on the rights embodied in the token. For example, a utility token is a voucher – i.e. an obligation of the issuer to provide services or sell a product under the prescribed conditions – created in a new technological way, in the form of DLT. Asset-referenced tokens are regulated and supervised stable coins do not qualify as currency (legal tender), however may qualify as money if the participants of the economy accept them. Now, this type of crypto assets is not yet covered by the Civil Code and there is no case law – because there cannot be any. However, I think that in the not-too-distant future there will be an explicit legislative decision on the matter. In my view, it would be appropriate to extend to it the rules of the Civil Code that apply to money and securities.

In the light of the above, I consider the questions posed for the purpose of legal comparison with a view to unregulated crypto assets – e.g. Bitcoin – below.

The first question is whether cryptocurrencies can be subsumed under any categories of the Civil Code by analogy or some other way. To decide on this question, a short summary of some of the basic notions of the Code is necessary.

The definition of property is based on the concept of a 'thing', movable (personal) and immovable. Traditionally, Hungarian civil law stand on the basis – similarly to German private law – that the object of property rights can solely be a 'thing (right in rem)'.[27] The Országgyűlés (the Hungarian Parliament) kept this notion.[28] However, the provisions on things are also to be applied to money, to securities and to natural resources that can be utilized as capital goods.[29] The notion of money in the Civil Code is based on the legal tender concept; banknotes and coins denominated in the Hungarian currency, the forint, qualify as legal tender and therefore as money. Beside the Hungarian Forint, any other currency (legal tender) is recognized as money.[30] It must be added that the Civil Code specifies credit transfer as a payment method that must be accepted for discharging debts; meaning that bank money became legal tender

27 A. Menyhárd, *Dologi jog* (Property Law), ELTE Eötvös Kiadó, Budapest, 2014, p. 7.

28 Sec 5:14 (1) Civil Code; The commentary for the Code explicitly states that Bitcoin is not money since it is not a legal tender. Lajos Vékás – Péter Gárdos (ed): *Commentary to the Civil Code*, sec 5:14, Wolters Kluwer, Electronic legal database (28 01 2022).

29 Sec 5:14 (2) Civil Code.

30 The commentary for the Code explicitly states that Bitcoin is not money since it is not a legal tender. L. Vékás – P. Gárdos (ed), *Commentary to the Civil Code*, sec 5:14, Wolters Kluwer, Electronic legal database (28 01 2022).

in contractual relationships.[31] Any person acquiring money by way of transfer becomes owner of that money, even if the transferor did not own the transferred amount.[32] The same rule applies for securities, provided the transfer met the special conditions of securities transfer. The definition of securities in the Civil Code is as follows: "Securities are unilateral juridical acts which either as a paper-form instrument or a set of data created, recorded, registered and transmitted in another form specified by law (dematerialised securities) represent the entitlement included therein in such a way that the exercise of and disposal over that entitlement is only possible through and in possession of the securities."[33] Contrary to the previous rules, the new Civil Code does not require a statutory basis for instruments to be recognised as types of securities; however, it is important that it must be explicitly stated by the issuer that the issued papers are securities. If a statute prescribes the mandatory terms and conditions of certain types of securities, they will only be recognised as such if they correspond to the prescribed terms and conditions.[34] Shares, bonds and bills of exchange can serve as examples of statute-based securities. Cryptocurrencies do not qualify as money nor securities under the Civil Code.

The question is whether cryptocurrencies qualify as claims also has relevance. The definition of claim requires another party, to whom the entitled party owes something. As such, cryptocurrency cannot be taken as a claim.

Following from the explanation above, cryptocurrencies cannot be subsumed under the existing categories of Hungarian private law. However, they exist in the Hungarian market; investments are made, and cryptocurrency transfers are executed, meaning that cryptocurrency is considered as a phenomenon that carries asset value. The Civil Code gives a rule of interpretation defining the term "vagyontárgy" (in mirror translation: object of asset)[35] that includes: 'thing' (property), right and claim. It seems that "vagyontárgy" means the potential forms of asset. These are partly overlapping categories, and, after a dogmatically sharp analysis, one can state – as István Gárdos did – that all

31 Sec 6:42 Civil Code, I. Gárdos, 'A pénz fogalma' Polgári Jog 2016/1.; I. Simon, *Pénzügyi jog I.* ELTE Eötvös Kiadó, Budapest, 2019, p. 46.

32 Sec 5:40 Civil Code.

33 Sec 6:565 (1) Civil Code.

34 Sec 6:565 (2) Civil Code.

35 Approximately: asset. However this translation is misleading, considering the different versions of the term asset understood in Hungarian law. Private law definitions of asset embrace both the active and the passive side of assets, similarly to those applied in accounting. The net asset positions usually signed by as adjective (net asset, clear asset value) or with an other word, like own capital. The term 'vagyontárgy' defines 3 different legal forms of potential assets, as described above.

the three categories of 'vagyontárgy' can be unified to one: right. It means that the things in law are the object of ownership rights and claims only a special group of rights.[36] The question is now how can acquired asset values – the cryptocurrencies – be protected. It is an important question since, in the lack of statutory law, a solution must be worked out in the judicial practice. I am of the view – not alone in the Hungarian academia, as referred to above – that a rational model of handling cryptocurrencies can be the extension of the rules of thing to them by analogy taking into consideration the special properties of cryptocurrencies. Consequently, cryptocurrencies would similarly be handled like securities, money and natural resources applying the rules of 'thing' as the special context requires. This way ownership rights can be provided and protected by analogy.

Cryptocurrency is not the first phenomenon that exists in the Hungarian market, although outside of positive law. The transfer of rights can be mentioned as an example; it existed for a long time without a clear background in the Civil Code. The lack of regulation carries risk and legal uncertainty. Now, the transfer of rights and contracts are regulated in the new Civil Code.[37]

5.2 *Property Rights in Cryptocurrencies*

When analysing private law issues regarding cryptocurrencies, the first question is the problem of ownership rights. If X has 60 Bitcoins registered in his/her wallet does X have legal ownership of the 60 Bitcoins in his/her wallet?

Since cryptocurrency cannot be found among the objects of ownership defined in the Civil Code, a strict interpretation of it would exclude cryptocurrencies, meaning that ownership rights would not receive legal protection, at least not in this way.

However, taking the lack of an explicit legislative or regulatory ban on crypto business into account and scrutinising the context – for example, the legislation on cryptocurrencies in the EU and in many countries with which Hungary has intensive economic connections, AML rules accepted globally and enacted locally in several countries, the Hungarian legislation on income tax – on more careful examination, one may conclude with good reason that cryptocurrency owners will receive protection of their rights as owners.

Ownership rights are defined and protected at two levels in the Hungarian legal system, at constitutional and at civil law level. At civil law level the

36 I. Gárdos, 'A vagyontárgy és a vagyon fogalma a Ptk.-ban' GJ, 2018/11., pp. 3–10.

37 A. Kisfaludi, 'Transfer of Property, Claims, Rights and Contracts in the New Hungarian Civil Code' ELTE Law Journal 2014/2, pp. 109–122., pp. 109–110.

ownership trias give the core content of rights that are protected.[38] The Fundamental Law of Hungary contains the following basic right: "Everyone shall have the right to property and to succession. The ownership of property shall entail social responsibility."[39] At constitutional law level, ownership rights are protected at their functionality as financial (material) preconditions of the autonomy of the individual's activity; therefore, special in rem rights and social security rights, for example, have been given protection. At constitutional level, it is not the physical reality of the property but the value of that is protected.[40] The quite overt example for the meaning of value protection is the case of expropriation, defined thus in the Fundamental Law: "Expropriation shall only be permitted in exceptional cases, when such action is in the public interest, and only in such cases and in the manner stipulated by an act, under terms of full, unconditional and immediate compensation."[41]

My view is that both the civil law and constitutional law level form a basis for rational argumentation for ownership rights protection and for equity in its classical meaning.

The second question regarding ownership rights is whether the wallet provider who provides custodial services for private keys has ownership rights over the Bitcoins deposited. The question is formulated as follows. X opened an account with MontC. MontC is an intermediary that provides wallet services to customers. X has 60 Bitcoins registered in his/her wallet. Has MontC any ownership rights over them?

MontC does not. The wallet keys and therefore the Bitcoins are deposited at MontC, which acts as custodian. The legal rules for banking services provide a special position to banks as deposit-taking institutions. They take deposits in a way that they acquire ownership rights over the currencies they take, and the depositor has a contractual right to get back the money credited to the bank.[42] MontC is not a bank and the asset in its possession is not currency. From another perspective, it is neither a "money loan" nor a "thing loan", it is

---

38 Sec 5 :13 Civil Code « [Ownership] (1) The owner shall have full and exclusive power of control, subject to limitation by law and by the rights of others, over the object of his ownership. (2) The owner shall in particular be entitled to the right to possess, use, exploit, collect benefits and the right to dispose. (3) The owner may exclude any unauthorised intrusion. "

39 Art XIII (1) Fundamental Law.

40 L. Sólyom, *Az alkotmánybíráskodás kezdetei Magyarországon,* Osiris, Budapest, 2001, p. 626.; e. g.: Constitutional Court decisions 64/1993. (XII. 22.) IV. 1. and 43/1995. (VI. 30.).

41 Art XIII (2) Fundamental Law.

42 I. Gárdos, 'A pénz fogalma' Polgári Jog 2016/1., pp. 1–12.; F. A. Mann, *The Legal Aspects of Money*, (3rd edn.), Clarendon Press, Oxford,1971, p. 6.

a ("safe") custody service. As a custodian, MontC must separate its own assets from the deposited asset.

The third question refers to fruits of and changes in the deposited asset. Assume a hardfork or airdrop of a new cryptocurrency, part of which is registered in a wallet belonging to X. Would X or MontC have ownership rights to the newly created cryptocurrency?

MontC, as a custodian, would not qualify as owner of the created cryptocurrencies in the case of hardfork or airdrop. The owner is X. The owner has the right to decide on which line of cryptocurrency – e.g. Bitcoin or Bitcoin-Cash – he follows. Similarly in the case of airdrops, the increase of the asset value or the fruits it attracted belong to the ownership rights of X, who deposited the bitcoins at MontC. MontC does not become an owner, it is a depository which has to act with due care and collect the proceeds of the deposited cryptocurrency.[43]

Act XXVIII of 2017 on Private International Law ('PIL', or 'PIL Code') gives the legal norms for issues that have international elements. The rules for the example cases discussed in this point are in chapter V of the PIL Code, titled Rights in Rem. The basic rule is as follows: "Unless otherwise provided for by this Act, the law applicable at the place where the thing is situated shall apply to proprietary rights and other rights in rem, as well as to lien and possession."[44] Keeping a consistent line of argumentation of considering cryptocurrencies as personal property ('thing'), by analogy, the next logical step is the statement that cryptocurrencies owned by a Hungarian resident are situated in Hungary. Naturally, several questions arise at this point, but what is to be seen clearly is that, in a "no law field", the most important task is to give legal protection to the owners who have asset values in cryptocurrencies in the context of the legal system with which they are most familiar, and the costs of the judicial procedure are potentially lower than any other solutions. In Hungary several individuals have invested in the crypto market and, the presence of individuals among the investors in the market is significant.

5.3 *Transfer of Cryptocurrencies*

The typical way of transferring property and rights, inter alia, is via contract. The Civil Code states that a contract "is the mutual and concordant juridical

---

43 6:361 Civil Code: « The depository shall collect the proceeds of the deposited thing if, by its nature, it is economically viable. The depositary shall give account to the depositor in relation to the proceeds collected. The depositary shall be entitled to use the proceeds collected to cover his expenses, and shall give the rest to the depositor. »

44 Sec 39 (1) PIL.

act of the parties from which the obligation to perform the service and the entitlement to claim the service arises."[45] The central element of the contract is the agreement of the parties on certain services.[46] The question is whether a valid contract can be concluded on the service of an "object" that does not exist in law. Forming the question in the dichotomy of objective rights (written law) and subjective rights, can an asset value that is not defined in the written law exist and be transferred?[47] I have already answered the first question regarding ownership rights. My answer to the second one is that the economic actors have the subjective right to conclude contracts, meaning that if the contract is not void and if the contract is voidable and they do not do so; the contract is valid. The reasons for invalidity of contracts are defined in the Civil Code.[48] For our purposes, prohibited contracts which breach the statute law or contracts that are concluded by circumventing the statute law must be mentioned.[49] Contracts on cryptocurrencies do not breach the law and I think it requires no further analyses in this context. All the circumstances support this view and administrative bodies are keen on "integrating market innovations". Taking the analyses above into account, it is possible to transfer the ownership rights of cryptocurrencies for consideration or free of charge.

The first example is gift, and the question is whether X, who has 60 Bitcoins registered in his/her wallet, can give 30 Bitcoins to Y without any countervalue.

Gift is governed by the Civil Code, which rules that gift is based on the agreement between the parties involved. The object of gift is a property ('thing'); however, the norms of gift are to be applied to transfer of rights and claims (receivables).[50]

It does not make a difference if X uses a wallet provider to hold and transfer the Bitcoins. X has to make the necessary arrangement to transfer the Bitcoins to Y.

Here we can mention the example of Covid doctors and nurses: a Hungarian resident crypto exchange organized a fund and opened wallets to gather donations in cryptocurrencies.[51]

The second example is barter (exchange contract): X has 60 Bitcoins registered in his/her wallet and wants to sell 5 Bitcoins and receive 10 Ethers.

---

45 Sec 6:58 Civil Code.

46 L. Vékás, *Szerződési jog – Általános rész*, ELTE, Eötvös Kiadó, Budapest, 2016, p. 21.

47 A valuable comparative analyses on the notion of subjective rights: T. Tercsák, *A joggal való visszaélés*, HVG-Orac, Budapest, 2018, pp. 27–124.

48 Sec 6 :88-107 Civil Code.

49 Sec 6:95 Civil Code.

50 Sec 6:235 Civil Code.

51 https://hu.coincash.eu/nagylelku-alapitvanyi-tamogatas-bitcoinban.

As cryptocurrencies do not qualify as money under the Civil Code, these kinds of transactions qualify as barter trade. The Civil Code says, "If the parties undertake obligations for the mutual transfer of ownership of things, other rights or claims then the rules on contract of sale shall apply accordingly. In this case, each party shall be the seller with regard to his own service and shall be the buyer with regard to the other party's service."[52] It would not make a difference if X used an intermediary (e.g. a wallet provider) to hold and transfer the Bitcoins. The exchange contract is concluded between the parties of the exchange. X must make the necessary arrangement to transfer the Bitcoins to Y.

The third example is cryptocurrency purchase for currency: X has 60 Bitcoins registered in his/her wallet and wants to sell 5 Bitcoins against a currency. It is legally possible to do so. Under the Civil Code, it is classified as a sales contract. As the relevant section of the civil Code says "(1) Under a contract of sale, the seller shall transfer the ownership of a thing, and the buyer shall pay the purchase price and take over the thing. ... (3) The rules applicable to the sale and purchase of things shall apply accordingly to contracts giving rise to the obligation of transferring rights or claims reciprocally."[53] It would not make a difference if X used an intermediary (e.g. a wallet provider) to hold and transfer the Bitcoins. X must make the necessary arrangement to transfer the Bitcoins to Y.

In international private contractual relations, the most important source of law in Hungary is the Rome I regulation.[54] If the case covered by this regulation its rules – firstly on the basis of the choice of law by the parties in their contract – channels the case to a legal system that will give the applicable law irrespective whether it is the law of a member state or a third country.[55] If Rome I or international norms do not cover the case the Hungarian international private law norms will give the rules that designate the applicable law. In the case of contracts, the general rule of the PIL Code leaves the choice of law question to the parties. It says, "A contract shall be governed by the law chosen by the parties."[56] If the parties do not stipulate the applicable law in the contract, disputes are governed by the law of the state with which the contract

52 Sec 6:234 Civil Code.

53 Sec 6: 215 Civil Code.

54 Regulation (EC) No 593/2008 of the European Parliament and of the Council of 17 June 2008 on the law applicable to contractual obligations ('Rome I'), OJ L 177, 4.7.2008, pp. 6–16.

55 Art 2 Rome I.

56 Sec 50 (1) PIL Code.

is most closely connected, based on the essential elements of the contract.[57] In the case of transfer of ownership of personal property, the parties have the right to choose the law of either the country in which the thing is currently situated or its destination state for their disputes over rights in rem.[58]

5.4 *Inheritance*

The next example is that of inheritance. X has a child, Y. X has 60 Bitcoins registered in his/her wallet and X wants to make a will to ensure that the value of his/her wallet is not lost and is passed on to Y.

It is possible for X to make such provisions in his/her will. The basic rules of inheritance in the Civil Code are that the estate of a person shall devolve upon an heir in its entirety after the testator's death[59] and inheritance may happen by will or by law.[60] Testators have the right to dispose freely of their property (assets), or a part of it, upon their death by a will.[61]

The notary profession is looking for proper solutions for handling cryptocurrencies as inherited assets. A recent article in their established professional journal concludes – after analysing the position of cryptocurrencies in private law dogmatics, the difficulties of being credibly informed of cryptocurrencies and their registration in the estate inventory (hagyatéki leltár)[62] etc. – that taking cryptocurrencies by analogy as tangible things (personal property) under section 5:14 (2) of the Civil Code, which extends the rules of ownership rights beside things to money, securities and natural energies, is the best alternative solution for handling inheritance in cryptocurrencies. Following from this argumentation, the establishment of the jurisdiction of the public notary assumes that cryptocurrency ("personal property") is located in Hungary. Any other possible way of handling inheritance cases would greatly expand the procedure in terms of administration, time, and money.[63]

It would not make a difference to the assessment of the example if X held the Bitcoin with a custodian. Depending on the certain technical solution for asset transfer, the custodian may be duly notified by grant of probate, if necessary.

57 Sec 51 PIL Code.

58 Sec 45 (1) PIL Code.

59 Sec 7:1 Civil Code.

60 Sec 7:3 Civil Code.

61 Sec 7:10 Civil Code.

62 Sec 20-31/B Act XXXVIII of 2010 on Probate Proceedings.

63 Á. Mányoki, 'A kriptovaluta mint a hagyatéki eljárás tárgya' KK, 2021/4., 81–99., pp. 92–93. and 96–97.

An EU Regulation provides uniform succession rules for all EU member states except Denmark and Ireland.[64] The PIL Code embraces only a few rules relating to oral will and the succession of the state.

5.5 *Trust*

The next example clarifying the position of cryptocurrencies in the legal system is trust. X has 60 Bitcoins registered in his/her wallet and wants to create a trust over the 60 Bitcoins for the benefit of Y.

Although different forms of asset management existed in Hungary, the trust-like institution of asset management is relatively new in the legal system of the country. The Civil Code that entered into force in 2014 has a separate chapter on "A bizalmi vagyonkezelési szerződés"(fiduciary asset management contracts),[65] under which the fiduciary undertakes to manage the assets, rights and receivables entrusted to him by the principal in his own name and on the beneficiary's behalf, and the principal undertakes to pay the fee agreed upon.[66] Hungarian law differentiates between business-like and not business-like asset management. Business-like fiduciary asset management activity is regulated by a separate act[67] and the precondition for entering the market as a service provider is a licence obtained from the MNB. Only one fiduciary asset management contract qualifies as not business-like activity,[68] but the contract concluded with asset manager must be reported to and registered by the MNB.[69]

It would not make a difference to the assessment of the example if X held the Bitcoin with an intermediary. The intermediary is a depository institution tasked with safeguarding the property (cryptocurrency) and giving back it to the owner.[70] X must make the necessary arrangement to transfer the Bitcoins to the fiduciary asset manager.

---

64 Regulation (EU) No 650/2012 of the European Parliament and of the Council of 4 July 2012 on jurisdiction, applicable law, recognition and enforcement of decisions and acceptance and enforcement of authentic instruments in matters of succession and on the creation of a European Certificate of Succession, OJ L 201, 27.7.2012, pp. 107–134.

65 Ch XLIII (sec 6:310 – 330) Civil Code.

66 Sec 310 (1) Civil Code.

67 Act XV of 2014 on Fiduciary Managers and on the Regulations Governing Their Activities (FMRG Act).

68 Sec 3 (1) FMRG Act.

69 Sec 18/A FMRG Act.

70 6:360 Civil Code : « Under a deposit contract, the depositary undertakes to safeguard the movable property to which the contract pertains, and to return it when the contract terminates, and the depositor undertakes to pay the fee agreed upon. »

Fiduciary asset management is a service that is based on a contract between the parties and those Hungarian private international law rules applies that were described above in point 4.3. relating to contracts.

5.6 *Lending*

Cryptocurrency lending is an unregulated activity in Hungary, meaning this activity is not prohibited. The debtor can pay the interest either in cryptocurrencies or in currencies.

Taking the example that PayB is a company regulated and supervised in its home jurisdiction to provide lending services, Z is a company whose seat is in Hungary, Z intends to borrow 60 Bitcoins from PayB, with an interest rate of 5% payable either in legal tender (e.g. Euro, US Dollar, Yen) or in Bitcoins. In this case, PayB can provide cryptocurrency lending to Z, the Hungarian borrower, and Z can pay the interest either in cryptocurrency or in any currency.

The second example for lending where PayB is a regulated company authorised to provide lending services in the Hungarian legal system. Z is a company whose seat is in Hungary. Z intends to borrow 60 Bitcoins from PayB, at an interest rate of 5% payable in Bitcoins. Z pays back in Bitcoin Cash, which are Bitcoin equivalents resulting from a fork in the initial Bitcoin blockchain.

As discussed above, financial services are regulated activities in Hungary and licensed institutions are not allowed to provide lending or any other financial services in cryptocurrency. Therefore, the example contract above cannot be valid in the Hungarian legal system.[71] As discussed above, this applies to services in Bitcoin and in other crypto assets not regulated by European law.

Money lending in any currencies in a business-like manner requires a licence from the financial supervisor. However, outside of the supervised financial market, transactions are governed by the agreements of the parties backed by private law (the Civil Code). Loans given in fungible assets must be paid back in the same kind of asset in the same quantity and quality that was loaned.[72] As such, it is not possible to pay back the Bitcoin loan in Bitcoin Cash without the prior consent of the creditor, meaning that the parties must modify the contract in this respect.

The loan is subject to contract law and those private international law rules that were described above in point 4.3. apply.

---

71 Sec 3 (1) and sec 4 (4) Credit Institutions Act; Sec 6:95 Civil Code.

72 Sec 6:389 Civil Code.

5.7 *Pledge*

The next example concerns the establishment of a security interest over cryptocurrencies. The scenario is that Z is a company whose seat is in Hungary. To secure a loan for financing a specific project, Z has agreed to pledge 30 Bitcoins that are registered in its wallet.

Let's take a hypothetical case that a project finance agreement is concluded and the parties agree to establish security using cryptocurrencies. The basic construction is that both a contract between the parties and the physical transfer of the personal property (possession) is necessary for a valid pledge.[73] There are three ways the cryptocurrencies can be pledged. The first is by way of depositing them at the creditor.[74] The second is using a collateral register if the cryptocurrencies remain in the possession of the owner.[75] The third way – when the cryptocurrency possessed by a third person as custodian – is the agreement between the parties, in which the owner assigns his right to retrieve the cryptocurrencies from the custodian to the creditor if he does not meet his contractual obligations. The owner must notify the custodian.[76]

The case is hypothetical since business-like lending services, together with other financial services, are exclusively for licensed financial institutions, so the possibility of project finance outside the regulated financial market is very limited.

Financial institutions are not allowed to extend loans denominated in cryptocurrencies. The question is whether cryptocurrencies are proper security instruments. The prudential regulations for credit institutions are public law norms. The CRR regulates eligible security instruments for credit risk mitigation[77] and cryptocurrencies are not among them. Due to the large gearing ratio in the operation of credit institutions, and taking the necessity of depositor protection into account, cryptocurrency cannot be accepted as proper security for credit risks. However, the CRR rules referred to only apply in the context of counting the necessary capital.[78]

---

73 Sec 5:88 Civil Code.

74 Sec 5:95 (2) Civil Code.

75 Sec 5:112–117 Civil Code.

76 Sec 5:3 (4), 5:94 (2) Civil Code.

77 Part III Title II Ch 4 section 2 CRR (Regulation (EU) No 575/2013 of the European Parliament and of the Council of 26 June 2013 on prudential requirements for credit institutions and investment firms and amending Regulation (EU) No 648/2012 Text with EEA relevance), OJ L 176, 27.6.2013, pp. 1–337.

78 A Hungarian National Bank 15/2019. (VII.9.) számú ajánlása a hitelkockázat méréséről, kezeléséről és kontrolljáról, point 55.

The PIL Code gives two rules for security in rem. If the security in rem comes into existence upon registration, the law of the state where the security is registered applies. If no registration is required, then the personal law of the provider of security applies.[79]

5.8 *Unlawful Acts against the Cryptocurrency Owner*

The next group of scenarios in the private law section covers illegal acts against the cryptocurrency owner who deposited his cryptocurrency at an institution that offers custody services and a bona fide purchaser who buys "stolen" cryptocurrencies. Four questions wait for answer.

The first question is about contractual liability: X opened an account with MontC and has 60 Bitcoins registered in his/her wallet. MontC's IT systems have been hacked. As a result, X lost all his/her Bitcoins. The question is whether X can, and under what conditions, bring an action against MontC. MontC is an institution; its business is to take cryptocurrency deposits and its duty is to store and safeguard the deposits and to give them back to the owner.[80] Its liability is a contractual one, which means that the custodian is obliged to compensate any damage suffered by the owner (depositor). The Civil Code says, "A person causing damage to the other party by breaching the contract shall be required to compensate for it. He shall be exempted from liability if he proves that the breach of contract was caused by a circumstance that was outside of his control and was not foreseeable at the time of concluding the contract, and he could not be expected to have avoided that circumstance or averted the damage."[81] The liability in the current Civil Code is stricter than it was before. It distributes the risk arising in contractual obligations.[82] The parties have the right to agree on limiting or excluding contractual liability arising from their contract. However, the liability cannot be limited or excluded for intentional breach of contract, or damage to human life, physical integrity and health.[83] In addition, the general rules for contracts in the Civil Code constrain the freedom of contract in terms of limiting or excluding liability for the breach of a consumer contract.[84] These norms relating to consumer contracts are especially important since the vast majority of investors in the Hungarian crypto market are individuals investing their personal – not business – resources,

79 Sec 44 (1)-(2) PIL Code.
80 Sec 6:36 Civil Code.
81 Sec 6:142 Civil Code.
82 L. Vékás - P. Gárdos (ed), *Commentary to the Civil Code*, sec 6:142, Wolters Kluwer, Electronic legal database (31 01 2022).
83 Sec 6:152 Civil Code.
84 Sec 6:100-105 Civil Code.

savings. Although the crypto market is considered a high-risk volatile market, the responsibility of service providers for the proper operation of the technical basis of the market – in my view – cannot however be excluded.

The second question is whether X can, and under what conditions, bring an action against the hacker (if he/she is identified).

X may have a civil law remedy against the person whose illegal act (i.e. hacking or fraud) caused damage to him. The Civil Code formulates the general prohibition of wrongful acts: "Causing damage unlawfully shall be prohibited by law" and it continues with the formulation of the general standard: "A person causing unlawfully damage to another shall compensate for the damage caused. The person causing damage shall be exempted from liability if he proves that he was not at fault."[85] It is a fault-based construction of liability, applying a presumed fault.[86] X has a clear title to enforce his claim for full compensation of damages at the court.

The third problem is the bona fide purchase of Bitcoin. If the hacker has sold the Bitcoin to third party Y, could Y be protected as a bona fide purchaser?

If the hacker sells the stolen bitcoin to a bona fide purchaser, it is more difficult to establish the legal argumentation in favour of either the owner or the bona fide purchaser. The dilemma is not only whether the participants of the unregulated market are entitled to legal protection and if the answer is yes, how. Until this point, the question was how to protect the asset values of owners, whose ownership is based on work (mining) or on consent, embracing a balance of the exchanged values in the event of transfer. Now, the question is how can a balance be struck between the equally equitable interests of the original owner and the bona fide purchaser. How should the law distribute the risk between the two participants in the crypto market? The Hungarian private law stands on the principle of nemo plus iuris and there are only a few exceptions from the general rule. The first exception to be mentioned in this context is buying goods from a vendor at its licensed place of business based on a sales contract.[87] The purpose of this rule is to ensure safety for commercial life. However, the rule is formulated narrowly; only the sale of goods contract falls in the scope of the rule and only the purchase from a licensed/registered trader is acknowledged.[88] The second exception is the transfer of money (i.e.

85 Sec 6:518-519 Civil Code.

86 Á. Funglinszky, 'Risks and Side Effects: Five Questions on the 'New' Hungarian Tort Law' ELTE LAW Journal, 2014/2, 199–221, 200.

87 Sec 5:39 (2)-(4) Civil Code.

88 B. Tőkey, 'A nem tulajdonostól való szerzés, mint harmadik személy érdekeit sértő szerződés' Polgári Jog 2020/7-8., pp. 1–8, 3–8.

currency) and securities transfer. The Civil Code states: "The party to whom money or securities have been transferred, according to the rules on transferring securities, shall acquire ownership even if the transferor was not the owner."[89] The dilemma is that extending the rules devised for money and securities would serve market safety; however, granting this special privilege would harm the interest of the owners and at the same time would give an impetus to the potential alternative money system that would decrease the authorities' room to manoeuvre in terms of monetary and to some extent fiscal policies. Considering the context – a commercial like situation – and recently relatively low level of crypto market capitalization in Hungary, my view is to protect the bona fide purchaser would best serve the interest of the participants in the market. The original owner has the chance to present a claim against both the custodian and the hacker.

The fourth question to be clarified is what the case would be if X transferred the Bitcoin to the tortfeasor after being misled? In the case of misrepresentation or fraud, the contract is voidable.[90] If this occurs then it becomes invalid as of the date on which it was concluded.[91]

Private international law rules govern the problems as follows. In the case of contractual liability, the choice of law by the parties is the main rule, as was written above. The governing law of tort cases is the 864/2007/EC regulation.[92]

5.9 *Insolvency*

When a deposited asset is at stake in the event of insolvency, there are at least two questions. The first is whether the deposited asset forms a part of the assets of the company that takes the deposit or not. The second question is what happens if the deposited asset is not at the disposal of the company that took the deposit.

In the event of insolvency, a distinction between the asset of the insolvent company and the deposited asset must be made. The purpose of the insolvency procedure is to allocate the assets of the insolvent company (those shown in the balance sheet as invested and current assets)[93] to its creditors. The deposited asset is not the asset of the insolvent company; the exact

---

89 Sec 5:40 Civil Code.

90 Sec 6:91 Civil Code.

91 Sec 6:89 Civil Code.

92 Regulation (EC) No 864/2007 of the European Parliament and of the Council of 11 July 2007 on the law applicable to non-contractual obligations (Rome II), OJ L 199, 31.7.2007, pp. 40–49.

93 Sec 3 (1) e) and sec 4 Act XLIX of 1991 on Bankruptcy Proceedings and Liquidation Proceedings ('Bankruptcy Act').

deposited amount of Bitcoin must be given back to the owner. If the deposited cryptocurrency is not at the disposal of the insolvent company for any reason, the depository claim transforms to a monetary claim and the (original) owner of cryptocurrencies becomes a creditor in the liquidation process. Since there is no special rule on this legal case in the Bankruptcy Act, the owner of the cryptocurrency becomes a creditor of the liquidated company and is put into one of the creditor classes.

The example of the individual claimant is as follows: X opened an account with MontC and has 60 Bitcoins registered in his/her account. MontC becomes insolvent. If MontC has the cryptocurrencies then these must be given back to X. If the deposited asset is not at MontC's disposal then X must be put in one of the creditor classes. This type of claim is not prioritized; therefore it qualifies as other claim before the last two classes (managers of MontC etc.).[94]

The second variant of the hypothetical case is related to a corporate claimant: Z is a company which opened an account with MontC as it accepts payments in Bitcoin and other cryptocurrencies. Z's wallet is worth US$200.000 in different cryptocurrencies. Z becomes insolvent. The analysis of the case gives the same result as for the individual claimant above.

According to the EU law that regulates insolvency proceedings, the law of that jurisdiction where the insolvency proceeding is initiated is applicable to the procedure.[95]

5.10 *Enforcement*

The last example is about enforcement. In the example X has 60 Bitcoins registered in his/her wallet. A creditor of X wants to assert a claim to the Bitcoin to satisfy X's debt. The question is whether attachment or seizure is possible, and under what conditions?

All the solutions described below are for enforcing a debt after it falls due. The position of the creditor depends on how his claim is secured.

If the loan contract is a notarial deed, the public notary affixes an enforcement clause on the document after the date the claim become due as specified in the document.[96] The notarial document with an enforcement clause is a proper basis for judicial enforcement; the notary posts it electronically to the central administration of the Hungarian Association of Court Bailiffs

94 Sec 57 (1) f) Bankruptcy Act.

95 Art 7 (1) Regulation (EU) 2015/848 of the European Parliament and of the Council of 20 May 2015 on insolvency proceedings ('Insolvency regulation'), OJ L 141, 5.6.2015, pp. 19–72.

96 Sec 23/C (2) Act LIII of 1994 on Judicial Enforcement ('Judicial Enforcement Act', 'JEA').

and the procedure starts this way.[97] One has to mention here that a recently published article in the professional journal of the bailiffs' profession concluded that, since cryptocurrencies cannot be subsumed to any categories of private law – beside the technical difficulties of grasping them – the legal system does provide a way or method to implement the enforcement.[98] I am of the opposite view. If the cryptocurrency (under a public key), its owner (with a private key) and their relationship are identified at the necessary measure, the enforcement is possible under Hungarian law.

If the loan is collateralized, the Civil Code applies. The Civil Code gives the norms for collateral, specifies the way of establishing pledges and the rights and obligations of the parties who establish security interest, and gives the rules of enforcement.[99]

The Civil Code prescribes the exact time when the right to satisfaction opens; it is when the secured claim falls due.[100] The pledgee has two options to exercise the right to satisfaction, either via judicial enforcement or by another way as defined in the Civil Code.

The Civil Code details three ways of enforcement outside the judicial enforcement process. It is at the pledgee's discretion to select the way of enforcement and he has the right to switch from one form to another. The three ways are the sale or acquisition of the property by the pledgee, and – for the shake of completeness, the third – the enforcement the pledged right or claim.[101] The Civil Code defines the framework of the sale of the collateral by its holder, including the prior notification of the owner, the content of the notification, the potential methods of sale and the rules of settlement and the distribution of sales proceeds. Beside other safeguards, the Civil Code provides a kind of value guarantee for the sale via the principle of reasonable commercial practices, stating "In the course of selling the pledged item, the pledgee shall comply with the requirement of commercial reasonableness, also taking the interests of the pledger and the party personally liable into account."[102] The Civil Code prohibits any contract concluded for transferring ownership of the pledged property to the pledgee at the time when the right to satisfaction

97 Sec 10 b) JEA.

98 E. Lénárd-Hegedűs – S. Udvary, 'Kriptovaluta a vagyonban a végrehajthatóság tükrében' Executio VIII/1. July 2021, 8–14., p. 14.

99 Sec 5:86-144 Civil Code (The rules for enforcement are in sections 5:126–141, and some detailed rules in the 66/2014.(III.13.) Government decree.).

100 Sec 5:126 (1) Civil Code.

101 Sec 5 :127 Civil Code.

102 Sec 5 :133 (1) Civil Code.

opens; it is null and void.[103] The Code sets out the conditions of acquiring the property by the pledgee that safeguards the interests of both the pledgee and owner, as well as any other interested parties.[104]

Pledge provided by consumers can be enforced – with a few exceptions – via the judicial enforcement procedure.[105]

The judicial enforcement path is the other option open for the pledgee. Under the Judicial Enforcement Act, the pledgee has the options to initiate an enforcement process or to initiate a simplified enforcement process for pledgees or to join an enforcement process initiated by others. The precondition for the judicial enforcement is an enforceable document that is issued – in the case of the secured creditor – by the public notary. The notary who prepared the document will attach an enforcement clause to the pledge contract, if the claim falls due as specified in the contract and posts it to the bailiffs' Association as written above.[106]

If the contract is not a deed prepared by the public notary, the pledgee must initiate litigation at court.

If X holds the Bitcoins via an intermediary, the custodian must be properly notified if necessary.

The judicial enforcement under the rules of the Judicial Enforcement Act is possible if the asset is in Hungary.

If the pledgee enforces his claim outside of the judicial enforcement, the Hungarian law applies.[107]

6 Tax Measures

The Hungarian tax law currently in force does not contain any provisions aimed at integrating the changes brought about by MiCAR. It is important to underline again that European law separates the traditional products of the financial market – e.g. financial instruments, like shares, bonds – and traditional services – e.g. financial services, investment services, insurance services – which can now be based on DLT technology, from the "traditional" crypto market and crypto assets, such as Bitcoin. For example, income from shares and bonds issued utilizing DLT technology is not subject to the rules discussed here, but to other rules that already exist for capital income.

103 Sec 5:136 Civil Code.
104 Sec 5:137-138 Civil Code.
105 Sec 5:126 (3) Civil Code.
106 Sec 23/C (3) Judicial Enforcement Act.
107 Sec 39 (1) PIL Code.

In the following, I summarise the current rules aimed at integrating crypto assets into the lawful economy and, more specifically, at generating tax revenues.

Hungarian tax law applies to cryptocurrencies, both in the field of direct and indirect taxes. Although the landscape is not wholly settled yet, it is however clearer than in the past years, which carried more uncertainties as reflected in the literature of the time.[108]

In the scope direct taxes, personal income tax and the corporate tax are discussed in this section. The position of cryptocurrencies in personal income taxation is clarified, in the corporate tax field there are different interpretations, as will be discussed.

Act CXVII of 1995 on Personal Income Tax ('Personal Income Tax Act' or 'PIT') regulates crypto related income taxation. Cryptocurrency dealings – incl. mining – are taxed via a capital gains tax construction defined in a new section 67/C of PIT that entered into force on 1st January 2022. The new section defines cryptocurrencies as follows: "For the purposes of this Section, crypto assets shall mean the digital currency of value or rights, capable of being transferred and stored electronically with the application of distributed ledger or similar technology."[109] This definition does not make a distinction between cryptocurrencies and other crypto assets. The basic concept is that the capital gain, – i.e. the difference between the purchase and the sale price reduced by the costs – defined as the tax base in the act via the "black box" method. There are some conditions prescribed in the act that must be applied.

The first is that the trading environment and the deal itself must be public, accessible to anyone. The second is that the deals are relevant from a taxation perspective when the revenue leaves the crypto ecosystem, meaning it is exchanged for currency of any kind but crypto or for any valuable consideration. The result is the difference between the input and output amount of currencies is the starting point of tax assessment, the tax base calculation. The second step is the calculation of costs and the result is a positive or negative amount which is the tax base. It is important to note that the value spent on the acquisition of a crypto asset can be considered if the taxpayer made this expenditure in the tax year of the sale.[110] However, the tax equalisation scheme

108 Cs. Heinemann, 'Kriptovaluták adózási kérdései, európai megoldások és az erre vonatkozó magyar szabályozás' Manuscript, Kúria, Budapest, 2021; Zs. Halász, ' A virtuális pénzeszközökkel összefüggő jogi kérdések az adójog területén' Iustum Aequum Salutare XVI. 2020. 4., 35–44., 41–43., G. Erdős, 'Bitcoin, a lejárat nélküli követelés' Iustum Aequum Salutare XVI. 2020. 4., 19–33.

109 Sec 67/C (9) PIT.

110 Sec 67/C (4) a) PIT.

mentioned below allows for a three-year period during which the amounts invested can be offset.

The tax base (the income) must be calculated for each ("output") cryptocurrency deal; but an exemption is defined. The taxpayer does not have to establish income if the net positive amount of the income is less than the 10% of the minimum wage – defined in statutory law – provided that the yearly income from crypto deals does not exceed the amount of the minimum wage.

The yearly tax must be calculated in the case of both a positive and negative tax base and the taxpayer must record the tax calculated after either the positive or the negative tax base in his yearly tax return. It is important from the taxpayer's point of view because there is an equalisation mechanism at the level of positive and negative taxes in a three tax years' time horizon, meaning that the positive amount of tax of a given tax year can be reduced by the calculated negative tax of the two previous tax years.

The new rules were introduced with a retroactive effect, meaning that the taxpayer was entitled to assess his tax for the 2021 tax year under the new rules. Moreover, if the taxpayer did not include his income from crypto asset deals in his tax return before, under the new rules, he could do it retrospectively. It is a kind of tax amnesty.

Corporate incomes are taxed under Act LXXXI of 1996 on Corporate Tax and Dividend Tax (Corporate Tax Act, 'CIT'). Since there is no separate accounting regime for taxation purposes, business taxation relies on the general financial accounting rules. The starting point of establishing the corporate income tax base is the income before tax included in the P&L statement of the annual report.[111] The Accounting Act[112] includes the rules that define the connections with the IFRS (International Financial Reporting Standards) based on EU law.[113] Taxpayers manage their accounting and prepare their financial statements either under the rules of the Accounting Act or under IFRS. The Corporate Tax Act must be applied in accordance with the Accounting Act or the IFRS depending on the status of the taxpayer under the above accounting regimes.[114]

The tax position of crypto assets (incl. cryptocurrencies in the terminology of the report) under the CIT raises questions, since the Hungarian tax authority and the IFRS Interpretations Committee (IFRS IC) issued different interpretations on the nature of cryptocurrencies that have a taxation effect.

111 Sec 6 (1) CIT.

112 Act C of 2000 on Accounting.

113 Sec 9/A and 10 Accounting Act; Regulation (EC) No 1606/2002 of the European Parliament and of the Council of 19 July 2002 on the application of international accounting standards, Official Journal L 243 , 11/09/2002 P. 0001 – 0004.

114 Sec 1 (5)-(6) CIT.

In 2017, the National Tax and Customs Authority (Nemzeti Adó – és Vámhivatal, NAV) in one of its interpretive letters – officially not published but available on the taxpayer website[115] – explained its position regarding Bitcoin, i.e., Bitcoin is a promise to pay, with which a payment can be made on the actual rate of exchange, provided it is accepted by the other party. For accounting and corporate tax purposes, it is a claim that must be shown in the balance sheet among the current assets.[116] As Bitcoin has a daily rate, it must be valued at the end of the business year and has to be shown at that value in the balance sheet. This classification has been disputed in the literature.[117]

The IFRS IC agenda decision was issued in June 2019 and states that the Committee is of the view that cryptocurrencies are either intangible assets (IAS 38) or inventories (IAS2). The qualification depends on the purpose for which it is used and, following from this, the envisaged period of holding it. The decision on the classification is at the competence of the taxpayer.

The Court of Justice of the European Union has decided that the services of a Bitcoin exchange in exchanging Bitcoin for currency is exempt from VAT.[118] The Court classified Bitcoin as currency in the context of VAT. Dealings in currencies are exempt transactions in the context of VAT.[119]

7 Litigation in Relation to Cryptocurrencies

To my best knowledge, there have not been any civil litigation or arbitration proceedings relating to cryptocurrencies in the Hungarian judicial and arbitration system.

The response to whether a foreign decision or arbitral award over crypto litigation would be recognised and enforced by Hungarian courts is given partly by international legal norms and partly by the PIL Code.[120] In addition, a decree by the minister of justice gives the rules of reciprocity that exist with

115 https://digitalcash.hu/wp-content/uploads/2017/07/Ad%C3%B32.pdf The interpretive letter – the response to the taxpayer's question on the meaning of a legal norm - is not taken as a source of law, however it guides the practice since it shows the position of the authority is a certain legal issue.

116 The application of the term of 'receivables' could be taken for granted; however here the owner of the cryptocurrency is not a vendor or service provider. The exact Hungarian wording is „vásárolt követelés" which means in a mirror translation "bought claim (receivable)".

117 G. Erdős, 'Bitcoin, a lejárat nélküli követelés' Iustum Aequum Salutare XVI. 2020. 4., 19–33.

118 Case C-264/14 *Hedqvist* point 57, ECLI:EU:C:2015:718.

119 Art 135(1)(e) VAT Directive.

120 Sec 109-123 PIL Code.

three countries, the USA, Germany, and Italy.[121] Special rules apply in the EU context.[122] Concerning arbitration, the New York Convention on recognition and enforcement of foreign arbitration awards[123] was proclaimed in Hungary in 1962.[124] Foreign judgements and arbitration decisions can be recognised and enforced.

Enforcement is not automatic. The competent Hungarian court studies, in a non-contentious procedure, whether the conditions of enforceability of a foreign judgment, arbitration award are met. If yes, it adopts a ruling of confirmation of enforcement for the foreign resolution.[125] The court has no competence to order a retrial and to reconsider the cases on their merits.

On the basis of the views explained above in this report, my view is that a foreign judgment (arbitral decision) on cryptocurrencies that meets the conditions of enforceability would be enforced in Hungary. I cannot see any reason on the basis of which the protection of ownership rights would be denied in usual circumstances. However, under unusual circumstances, issuing a ruling of confirmation of enforcement can be denied for public policy reasons, if it is against the public order.[126] As the Kúria, – the Hungarian Supreme Court – explained in a case concerning the recognition of a foreign arbitration decision, a decision is against the public order if the recognition injures fundamental rights, social value judgements or the basic principles of the legal order. Public order is injured if the decision directly hurts the basis of the economic and social order and, following from this, the domestic sense of justice is injured in an insupportable way.[127] Although there are some issues in the crypto ecosystem from which public policy issues can arise at judicial level, I would not like to engage in speculative forecasts. The technical basis (DLT) that operates on a global scale in itself, and the coexistence of different cultures, including legal cultures, in addition to different positions of wealth that are compounded by the DLT, may touch the public policy threshold in certain cases.

121 Decree of the Minister of Justice 36/2017. (XII. 29.).

122 Regulation (EU) No 1215/2012 of the European Parliament and of the Council of 12 December 2012 on jurisdiction and the recognition and enforcement of judgments in civil and commercial matters, Official Journal L 351, 20.12.2012, pp. 1–32.

123 1958 - Convention on the Recognition and Enforcement of Foreign Arbitral Awards ('New York Convention').

124 Presidential Council Decree 25 of 1962 on the Proclamation of the Convention on the Recognition and Enforcement of Foreign Arbitral Awards signed in New York on the 10th of June 1958.

125 Sec 206 and 208 Act LIII of 1994 on Judicial Enforcement ('Enforcement Act').

126 Sec 109 (4) a) PIL.

127 Kúria Pfvl.21.361/2014/6.

Israel

Ruth Levush

1 Definition and Legal Qualification

Israel is home to many blockchain-related startups.[1] Israel's regulatory scheme, nevertheless, has been criticized for discouraging local business in cryptocurrencies.[2]

Virtual currencies are not recognized as legal currency in Israel,[3] nor are they considered "foreign currency" for the purpose of tax exemption that applies to exchange rate differences.[4]

The Financial Services Supervision (Regulated Financial Services) Law, 5776-2016, however, defines a "virtual currency" as a type of "financial asset," financial services relating to which are subject to licensing requirements.[5]

The Anti-Money Laundering Order (Credit Service Providers' Duties of Identification, Reporting and Registration for the Prevention of Money Laundering and Terrorist Financing) (Amendment), 5781-2021 (AMLO Amendment)[6]

---

1 For a list of some cryptocurrency companies see Tenner Smith, *These are the Top Blockchain Companies in Israel (2021)*, Daily Finance, https://df.media/these-are-the-top-blockchain-companies-in-israel-2021/.

2 Lior Yaffe, *Challenges of Dealing with Cryptocurrencies in Israel*, CoinDesk (updated Sept. 14, 2021), https://www.coindesk.com/markets/2021/08/05/challenges-of-dealing-with-crypto currencies-in-israel/.

3 New Shekel Currency Law, 5745-1985, Sefer HaHukim (SH, Book of Laws, official gazette) No. 1157 p. 216, https://www.gov.il/he/Departments/DynamicCollectors/gazette-official?skip=0&limit=10&FolderType=1&BookletYear=53&BookletNum=1157 (in Hebrew), also available at the Nevo Legal Database, https://www.nevo.co.il/law_html/law01/215_002.htm (all citations from Nevo here and below in Hebrew).

4 TaxA (DC Central Lod) 11503-05-16 Kopel v. Rehovot Tax Assessor (decision by Judge Shmuel Bornstein), paras. 41–45, Nevo (May 19, 2019), https://www.nevo.co.il/psika_html/mechozi/ME-16-05-11503-33.pdf.

5 Financial Services Supervision (Regulated Financial Services) Law, 5776-2016, § 11, SH 5776 No. 2570 p. 1098, consolidated text at Nevo, https://www.nevo.co.il/law_html/law01/501_439.htm.

6 Anti-Money Laundering Order (Credit Service Providers' Duties of Identification, Reporting and Registration for the Prevention of Money Laundering and Terrorist Financing) (Amendment), 5781-2021 (AMLO Amendment), Kovetz Hatakanot (KT, Subsidiary Legislation) 5781 No. 9267, p. 2608 (March 14, 2021), https://www.gov.il/he/Departments/DynamicCollectors/gazette-official?skip=0&limit=10&FolderType=3&BookletNum=9267 (in Hebrew), amending Anti-Money Laundering Order 5778-2018 (AMLO), KT 5778 No. 794 p. 1084; consolidated text of AMLO at Nevo, https://www.nevo.co.il/laws/#/604deb6a0f7d0e7d1f487c95.

 | DOI:10.1163/9789004722507_015

provides a more specific definition.[7] It defines "virtual currency" as "a digital unit of value that can be traded or transferred in a digital manner and be used for payment or investment purposes."[8]

According to media reports, starting 2022, stores and merchants in Israel will be able to receive payments in cryptocurrencies through a new payment terminal provider (Verifone) that is widely used by most stores in the country. The terminal allows payment in Bitcoin, Etherium, Dogecoin, Bitcoin Cash, and Lightcoin. Businesses that choose to receive payments in cryptocurrencies would be able to sign up for the service. Customers could chose to pay in crypto instead of credit, and then a QR code for scanning will appear on the console screen via the customer's crypto wallet app, which will perform the payment operation. The money will go directly from the customer's crypto wallet without conversion to regular currency, but will go to the merchant's account after conversion to regular money.[9]

The actual or potential legal relationships between the different participants to a blockchain on which cryptocurrencies are transferred and recorded do not appear to be regulated at this time. The qualifications for who would qualify as a "participant" or the conditions under which a participant may have a claim against other participants are similarly not yet expressly defined.

2 Regulatory Framework

At the time of writing of this report, no specific comprehensive law or regulation on cryptocurrencies has been enacted or proposed. Instead, activities involving cryptocurrency are regulated under laws and rules governing supervision of financial services and money laundering, as described below.

---

7 Ruth Levush, *Israel: New Order Requiring Identification, Reporting, and Registration of Cryptocurrency Transactions Goes into Effect*, Global Legal Monitor (Nov. 21, 2021), https://www.loc.gov/item/global-legal-monitor/2021-11-21/israel-new-order-requiring-identification-reporting-and-registration-of-cryptocurrency-transactions-goes-into-effect/.

8 AMLO Amendment, § 3 (8).

9 Yair Mor, *The Crypto Revolution on the Way to Israel: You Will Soon Be Able to Pay at the Supermarket in Bitcoin*, ice (Sept. 30, 2021), https://www.ice.co.il/consumerism/news/article/831389 (in Hebrew).

3 Supervision

3.1 *Licensing*

The Financial Services Supervision (Regulated Financial Services) Law, 5776-2016, requires licensing as a condition for provision of financial services. Financial services is defined as engaging in any act other than extending credit that is carried out in the course of practicing a vocation and constitutes either a replacement of one financial asset with another or managing or securing a financial asset.[10]

The Law categorizes virtual currency as a financial asset for purpose of licensing requirements. The Law authorizes the Supervisor of Capital Market, Insurance and Savings to issue a license to persons who provide services in cryptocurrency.[11]

In performing duties and exercising powers under the law, the Supervisor should consider the following objectives:

1. Creating a reliable, secure and stable environment for the provision of financial services by financial service providers, operating in accordance with all laws;
2. Protecting and safeguarding the interest of the customers of the financial service providers as well as promoting their interest;
3. Increasing access to financial services;
4. Increasing the transparency of information and the accessibility of information to customers of financial service providers;
5. Promoting competition in the field of financial services;
6. Encouraging technological and business innovation in the field of financial services;
7. The economic policy of the government;
8. With regard to the provision of deposit and credit services … also the promotion of social goals and mutual assistance.[12]

An applicant may receive a "basic" or an "extended" license, depending on the size of the applicant's available equity as well as additional conditions.[13] The licensee must be at least 18 years of age, a citizen or resident of Israel, and must not have been previously declared legally incapacitated or issued a receivership order in bankruptcy proceedings or been held unfit for provision

---

10 Financial Services Supervision (Regulated Financial Services) Law, 5776-2016, as amended, §§ 11 A & 12.

11 Id.

12 Id. § 3 (translation by author).

13 Id. §§ 15, 16, 37 & 1st supp.

of financial services based on a criminal conviction or other relevant circumstances. A corporation may receive a basic license if it was incorporated and registered in Israel, was not subjected to a judicial order for receivership or for dissolution, and at least one of its officers is a citizen or resident of Israel.[14]

In addition to meeting the conditions for receipt of a basic license, the grant of an extended license requires the Supervisor to consider, among other things, the applicant's business plan and chances of success; the applicant's financial means and sources of funding; as well as public interest considerations.[15]

3.2 *Money Laundering Legislation*

The Prevention of Money Laundering Law, 5760-2000,[16] authorizes the minister of the treasury to establish a "Supervising Authority" for the purpose of managing, processing, and safeguarding security information obtained from reports received under both the Fight against Terrorism Law, 5776-2017,[17] and the Prevention of Money Laundering Law.[18] It further authorizes the minister of the treasury, after consultation with the minister of justice and the minister of internal security, to issue an order specifying the duties of identification, reporting, registration and custody of information for the provision of financial services.[19]

Pursuant to this authority, the minister of the treasury issued the AMLO Amendment on March 14, 2021, which imposes identification and notification requirements on providers of financial services. It defines "provider of financial services" as "a person who is required to have a license to provide a service regarding financial assets in accordance with the Supervision of Regulated Financial Services Law, except for those who provide ATM services."[20]

The AMLOrequires providers of financial services in "virtual currency" to identify, register, and report to the Supervising Authority on both routine and "occasional activities."[21] "Occasional activities" involve the receipt of services

14 Id. § 15.

15 Id. § 16.

16 Prevention of Money Laundering Law, 5760-2000, SH 5760 No. 1753 p. 293, https://www.gov.il/he/Departments/DynamicCollectors/gazette-official?skip=0&limit=10&FolderType=1&BookletYear=68&BookletNum=1753, as amended; consolidated text at Nevo, https://www.nevo.co.il/law_html/law01/017m1_001.htm.

17 Fight Against Terrorism Law, 5776-2017, SH 5776 No. 2556 p. 898, https://www.gov.il/he/Departments/DynamicCollectors/gazette-official?skip=0&limit=10&FolderType=1&BookletYear=84&BookletNum=2556, as amended; consolidated text at Nevo, https://www.nevo.co.il/law_html/law01/501_422.htm.

18 Prevention of Money Laundering Law, § 29.

19 Id. § 7 (b) & 3rd supp.

20 AMLO as amended, § 1. "ATM services" refers to the provision of automatic teller machines.

21 Id. § 2.

in amounts up to 5,000 Israeli shekels (about US$1,615) from the same service provider over a six-month period, or up to 50,000 Israeli shekels for the purpose of requiring service providers to ensure receipt of original signatures from recipients acting on behalf of others, as well as for in-person identification of first-time service recipients under conditions enumerated.[22]

The AMLO provides a detailed list of reporting requirements regarding the identity of service providers and recipients and the particulars of transactions that involve cryptocurrency services. The AMLO also contains instructions on records management and preservation of documents. In addition to in-person identification, the AMLO enables identification by remote visual-identification technology.[23]

The AMLO requires identification of recipients in financial services by presentation of specified documents, depending on the recipients' nationality, corporate status, and legal capacity, among others.[24]

4 Private Law Issues

No case law or discussion was located indicating that cryptocurrencies have been treated differently from other types of property under Israeli private law.

5 Tax Measures

In accordance with Circular No. 05/2018 issued by Israel's Tax Authority on January 17, 2018, virtual currency constitutes an "asset"[25] within its meaning under the Income Tax Ordinance (New Version), 1961.[26]

The tax liability arising from cryptocurrency-related activities depends on their nature, for example depending on whether the virtual currency was

22 Id. § 1.

23 Id. §§ 6, 11–12.

24 Id. §§ 1 & 4.

25 Israel Tax Auth., Circular No. 05/2018: Taxation of Activity by Means of Virtual Payment (Known as "Virtual Currencies") (Jan. 17, 2018), § 3.1, https://www.gov.il/he/departments/policies/income-tax-professional-inst-5-2018 (in Hebrew).

26 Income Tax Ordinance (New Version), 1961, § 88, Dine Medinat Israel [New Version] No. 6, p. 120, as amended, unofficial translation available at Int'l Ctr. for Not-for-Profit Law, https://www.icnl.org/wp-content/uploads/Israel_Ordinance.pdf?_ga=2.109672645.1553357184.1608050241-1365009903.1608050241.

acquired by direct purchase, receiving it in exchange for providing goods and services, mining a new token, or verifying transactions via blockchain.[27]

The Israel Securities Authority has identified three types of cryptoassets:

Currency Tokens: Used as a means of payment, clearing or barter only, do not confer additional rights (such as a yield or ownership of an additional asset) and are not controlled by a central entity. [They] will not be considered a security.

Utility Tokens: Embody a right to a product or service, and are purchased for the purpose of consumption and use only and not for the purpose of investment, will not be considered a security.

Security Tokens: Grant similar rights to securities and will be considered securities.[28]

5.1 *Use of Virtual Currency in Exchange for Goods and Services*

The transfer of a virtual currency as payment for goods and services constitutes a barter. It may therefore subject the receiver to taxation for two taxable events. The first takes place upon the receipt of virtual currency in consideration for the sale of goods or the provision of a service. The second is in respect of the capital or business income, as relevant, upon the sale of the virtual currency, its conversion into local or foreign currency, or the receipt of an asset or other virtual currency as consideration for it.[29]

5.2 *Trade in Virtual Currency*

As noted, virtual currency is recognized by Israel's Tax Authority as an asset. Income derived from the sale of virtual currency by its owner may qualify as a capital gain. The amount received from the trade in excess of the original price, after deduction of inflationary value, will be taxed at a rate of 25% for an individual and 23% for a corporation.[30]

27 Meir Azenkot, *Taxation of Activities in Virtual Currencies* § 3 (Dec. 10, 2020); Knesset (Israel Parliament) Info. & Res. Ctr. (hereinafter KIRK Report), https://fs.knesset.gov.il/globaldocs/MMM/08fa14a9-003a-eb11-811a-00155d0af32a/2_08fa14a9-003a-eb11-811a-00155d0af32a_11_16609.pdf.

28 Id. § 1 (translation by author).

29 Id. § 3.1; Committee for the Examination of Regulation of the Issue of Distributed Ledger Cryptographic Currency to the Public, *Final Report*, at 35-36 (Mar. 2019), https://www.isa.gov.il/%D7%94%D7%95%D7%93%D7%A2%D7%95%D7%AA%20%D7%95%D7%A4%D7%A8%D7%A1%D7%95%D7%9E%D7%99%D7%9D/Reports/177/Documents/CryptoCommitteeFinalReport.pdf (in Hebrew).

30 Income Tax Ordinance § 91.

If, however, the income derived from the sale of virtual currency meets the criteria to deem the recipient a "business" as determined in Israeli case law, it may be subject to a "yielding income tax" (YIT), at a progressive tax rate of 10–50% for an individual, or corporate tax at a rate of 23% for a corporation.[31]

5.3 *Receipt of Virtual Currency through Mining and Blockchain Verification*

Mining of a new virtual currency is performed by utilizing computer technology to verify transactions in the blockchain network. Acceptance of consideration for transaction verification is classified in one of the following two ways:

> Where the consideration is received in the form of virtual currency as part of a business, it will be classified as YIT;
>
> In a situation where the receipt of consideration in virtual currency is not part of the main business income or constitutes private income, for example, by utilizing an individual's personal computer at home for mining or verifying transactions, no tax event occurs upon receiving or creating a new virtual currency. Capital gain, however, will accrue at the time of sale or conversion of the new virtual currency to legal tenders such as new shekels or foreign currency.[32]

According to Israel's Tax Authority, the majority of those who engage in mining and verification of transactions do so as an occupation.[33] Such dealers are subject to YIT as noted above.[34]

For example, mining and verifying of transactions in bitcoin require an investment of working time and in computing equipment with extremely high processing capabilities, as well as electricity consumption, for analyzing and processing a transaction's components and encryption. The reward received for verification of a transaction depends on the speed of processing. For example, the first person who manages to verify the transaction gets the highest reward. The second gets a lower reward, and so on. The last ones to verify the transaction receive a reward that is minimal and may be lower than related

---

31 Id. §§ 2 (1-2), 121, 126; KIRK Report § 3.2; Circular No. 05/2018 § 3.1.4.

32 KIRK Report § 3.3 (translation by author).

33 Id. § 3.3 n. 19, citing a telephone conversation with Michael Asulin, Head of the Department of Encouragement and Capital Investments, Israel Tax Authority (Nov. 26, 2020).

34 See part V.B supra.

expenses, such as electricity and investment costs in equipment and computing, and may even yield a loss.[35]

5.4 *Value-Added Tax Liability for Transactions that Involve Cryptocurrency*

Similar to income tax liability, for the purpose of liability for value-added tax (VAT), virtual currency is viewed as "an asset"[36] and is taxed in accordance with relevant transaction classifications under the Value-Added Tax Law, 5736-1975.[37]

In accordance with Circular No. 05/2018, VAT will apply to income from virtual currencies that derive from a business.[38] Therefore,

> [i]ndividual investors in virtual currencies are not liable for VAT, but anyone who engages in mining will be classified as a dealer and could be subject to VAT. Businesses trading in virtual currencies are classified as financial institutions for tax purposes and are exempt from VAT, so VAT on expenses is not deductible and an additional 17% wage and profit tax applies.[39]

5.5 *Tax Treatment of "Airdrops" and "Hard Forks"*

Official guidance specifically addressing taxation relating to "airdrops" and "hard forks" has not been identified as of this writing.

Israeli experts have suggested, however, that airdrops and hard forks may be characterized as gifts to the recipient, which would constitute a tax event at the time of its conversion and not at the time of its initial receipt. When calculating the taxable profit accrued upon conversion, the base rate of the virtual currency received would be zero, because nothing was paid for it. The

35 KIRK Report § 3.3.

36 Israel Tax Auth., Circular No. 05/2018: Taxation of Activity by Means of Virtual Payment (Known as '"Virtual Currencies"') (Jan. 17, 2018) (hereafter Circular No. 05/2018), § 3.2, https://www.gov.il/he/departments/policies/income-tax-professional-inst-5-2018 (in Hebrew).

37 Value-Added Tax Law (VAT Law), 5736-1975, SH 5733 No. 571 p. 52, https://www.gov.il/he/Departments/DynamicCollectors/gazette-official?skip=0&limit=10&FolderType=1&BookletYear=44&BookletNum=791, consolidated text at Nevo, https://www.nevo.co.il/law_html/law01/271_001.htm.

38 Circular No. 05/2018, § 3.2.3.

39 OECD, *Taxing Virtual Currencies, An Overview of Tax Treatments and Emerging Tax Policy Issues* 38 (2020), https://www.oecd.org/tax/tax-policy/taxing-virtual-currencies-an-overview-of-tax-treatments-and-emerging-tax-policy-issues.pdf; see also KIRK Report § 3.4.

applicable type and tax rate would appear to be determined under the rules that apply to transactions in virtual currencies that are described above.[40]

6 Litigation In Relation to Cryptocurrencies

Israeli courts have entertained a number of cases on the issue of whether banks could legally "sweepingly refuse to accept funds originating in crypto (the answer is no)."[41] On December 28, 2017, for example, the Tel Aviv district court issued an injunction prohibiting the Leumi Bank for Israel from closing an account held by a an international money transfer company based on the bank's stated general concerns regarding its ability to comply with the supervision requirements under the prevention of money laundering and laws.[42]

On February 22, 2021, the Tel Aviv district court issued a temporary injunction in another case against Mercantile Discount Bank. The court ordered the bank to allow the plaintiff to deposit funds originating from trading in Bitcoin-type digital currencies. The Court ruled that in the absence of any concrete concern for unlawful activities on the part of the plaintiffs, the bank could not prevent them from depositing in their account about NIS 2 million (about US$631,772.00) that they had accumulated from the sale of Bitcoin.[43]

The court issued its final decision in the case on November 17, 2021. Recognizing the challenges associated with banks' supervision requirements,[44] Judge Esther Nachlieli-Haaiat opined:

> In fact, the banks have been authorized to be the supervisors of their competitors, and in other words, the current regulatory arrangement allows the "cat to keep the cream" with all the problems associated with it. A situation in which a bank, operating for profit, will be appointed to supervise its competitors [fintech companies] is an unacceptable and in my opinion intolerable situation, regardless of the content of its

40 BLOTAX, *A Guide to Taxing Bitcoin, Crypto and Digital Currencies in Israel* (Aug. 2019), https://www.bloxtax.co.il/blog/bitcoin-tax-guide/.

41 Etti Applalo, *Bank of Israel: We Will Define Rules That Will Help Transfer Customers' Money to Investments in Crypto*, Globes (Dec. 1, 2021), https://www.globes.co.il/news/article.aspx?did=1001392755.

42 Request (DC TA) 32389-02-17 Clearshift (Israel) Ltd. V. Leumi Bank for Israel Ltd., Nevo (Dec. 28, 2017), https://www.nevo.co.il/psika_html/mechozi/ME-17-02-32389-587.htm.

43 CivC (DC TA) 51757-08-18 Roe Arev v. Mercantile Discount Bank, Nevo (Feb. 22, 2021), https://www.nevo.co.il/psika_html/mechozi/ME-18-08-51757-905.htm.

44 For information on supervision requirements see Part III supra.

> requirements from the fintech companies to which it provides its services [...][45]

In Judge Nachlieli-Haaiat's opinion, restricting the activities of Fintech companies by preventing them from accessing banking services based on general money laundering concerns could amount to a violation of freedom of occupation and competition.[46]

She therefore determined that when it comes to the bank closing an account or imposing severe requirements, the greater the severity of the damage involved in refusing to provide a service to a Fintech company, the greater the burden on the bank to present clear, unequivocal and convincing evidence that leaving the account open would cause immediate and tangible damage, in terms of near certainty, to the bank's reputation, the bank's financial stability, and other interests.[47] Accordingly:

> The raising of a red flag by the Bank is not in itself a clear, unequivocal and convincing evidence. The bank must indicate a tangible evidence, such as a concrete suspicious activity or the opinion of the relevant regulator regarding the high degree of risk in the circumstances of the case ... As long as the Fintech company is transparent and responds cooperatively to the bank's requirements, one should not exaggerate the degree of risk posed by financial activity, [an activity that] even if bold, is legitimate.[48]

45 Request (DC TA) 32389-02-17 Clearshift (Israel) Ltd. V. Leumi Bank for Israel Ltd., para. 21, Nevo (Nov. 17, 2021), https://www.nevo.co.il/psika_html/mechozi/ME-17-02-32289-11.htm (translation by author).

46 Id. para. 22.

47 Id. para. 39.

48 Id. (translation by author).

Italy

Ugo Malvagna and Filippo Sartori

1 Definition and Legal Qualification[1]

Until the forthcoming entry into force of a Regulation setting licensing and compliance requirements for platforms providing custody and/or trading services relating to cryptocurrencies, which was issued in February 2022 by the Ministry of Finance (decreto 17 January 2022, on which, see below, para III), individuals based in Italy can freely access virtually all on-line exchange platforms operating transaction on cryptocurrencies, provided that no specific shut-down injunctions have been issued against a specific platform by competent administrative or judicial bodies. In the last few years, quite a number of those orders were issued by the Italian market authority (Commissione Nazionale per le Società e la Borsa: from now on, Consob) *vis-à-vis* platforms that, without being licensed as investment firms under MiFID, would offer, alongside cryptocurrencies, actual investment services (as defined under MiFID and decreto legislativo 24 February 1998 no 58, Testo Unico della Finanza from now on), including derivatives, certificates or contracts for difference having cryptocurrencies as their underpinning. This depends on the Consob's view of cryptocurrencies not qualifying as financial instruments (see below, para 2).

Provided that this general capacity of Italian-based users to trade in cryptocurrencies, the Italian market for cryptocurrencies (on the demand side) appears to be in line with the European average, both in terms of transaction volume per capita and its distribution among different kinds of cryptocurrencies (Bitcoin and Ethereum covering approximately 60% of the market), including so-called stablecoins, *i.e.* cryptocurrencies whose exchange value is – or at least aims at being – correlated to one or more fiat currencies. Apparently, also Italian-based users resort to actual cryptocurrencies moved into them for speculative reasons (in fact, cryptos have increased their market value over time), whereas investment in stablecoins is driven by a less speculative

1 Ugo Malvagna is Associate Professor of Economic and Financial Markets Law in the Law School of the University of Trento and a Member of the Associated Researchers Group at the European Banking Institute. Filippo Sartori is Full Professor of Economic and Financial Markets Law in the Law School of the University of Trento. Parr. 2, 4, and 6 shall be attributed to Ugo Malvagna. Parr. 1, 3, 5 and 7 shall be attributed to Filippo Sartori. Many thanks to Dr. Francesco Petrosino and Dr. Luca Lentini for helping in research and draft review.

 | DOI:10.1163/9789004722507_016

investment objective, being those transactions to which the functional subrogate of the purchase of the fiat currency the stablecoin is referenced. Use of cryptocurrencies and stablecoins as a means of payment seems to be, presently, not significantly developed among consumers; however, no official or accurate data are available in this respect.

In the Italian regulatory landscape, the first legal notion that would include – but is not necessarily limited to[2] – cryptocurrencies, can be traced back to 2017, when decreto legislativo 21 November 2007 no 231, implementing EU-level legislation on the prevention of the use of the financial system for the purposes of money laundering or terrorist financing (AML/CFT), was amended by decreto legislativo 25 May 2017 no 90. *Inter alia*, decreto legislativo no 90/2017, amended article 1 of decreto legislativo no 231/2007 by adding – under para 2, letter qq – a definition of *virtual currency*. According to this provision, a virtual currency is 'the digital representation of value, not issued from a central bank or other public authority, not necessarily linked to a currency which is legal tender, used as a means of exchange in order to purchase goods and services and which can be electronically transferred, recorded and traded'. This notion is instrumental in subjecting to AML duties, as set out by decreto legislativo no 231/2007,[3] any provider of services relating to the utilization of virtual currency

2 Merely referring to a 'digital representation of value ... that can be transferred , stored and traded electronically', the legal definition does not take a specific stance on the nature of the underlying technology. Therefore, from a theoretical standpoint, also electronic digital values not based on a distributed ledger technology (DLT) and/or a blockchain would fall into this definition.In this regard, it is useful to point out that the Italian legal system also has a definition of 'distributed ledger technology' as the IT infrastructure for so-called "smart contracts". Legge 11 February 2019 no 12, converting into law decreto legislativo 14 December 2018 no 135, at Art 8-*ter*, para 1, defines 'technologies based on distributed ledgers' as those 'technologies and informatic protocols which use a shared, distributed, replicable and simultaneously accessible ledger, which is architecturally decentralized on cryptographic basis and allows to record, validate, update and store data both readable and protected by cryptography and verifiable by each participant, nor changeable neither modifiable'. The subsequent paragraph, indeed, defines a smart contract as a 'processor program which operates thanks to technologies based on distributed ledger and whose execution binds two or more parties on the basis of effects previously defined by their self'.

3 Consisting of so-called "customer due diligence", comprising: (a) identifying the customer and verifying the customer's identity on the basis of documents, data or information obtained from a reliable and independent source; (b) identifying the beneficial owner and taking reasonable measures to verify that person's identity, so that the obliged entity is satisfied that it knows who the beneficial owner is, including, as regards legal persons, trusts, companies, foundations and similar legal arrangements, taking reasonable measures to understand the ownership and control.Structure of the customer; (c) assessing and, as appropriate, obtaining information on the purpose and intended nature of the business relationship; (d) conducting ongoing monitoring of the business relationship, including

(that is, 'every natural or legal person who provides to third parties, on a professional basis, and also online, services functional to use, exchange and store virtual currencies and to their converting from or in currencies which are legal tender or digital representation of value, included those convertible in other virtual currencies, as well as services relating to issuing, offering, transfer and compensation services and any others aimed at acquisition, trading and intermediation in the case of exchange of the same currencies').

This stated, it also must be pointed out that the extension of the AML framework to transactions in cryptocurrencies originated spontaneously by the Italian legislator, and later included, in the same terms, in the European Parliament and Council Directive (Eu) 2018/843 of 30 May 2018 amending Directive (Eu) 2015/849 on the prevention of the use of the financial system for purposes of money laundering or terrorist financing, which introduced a common definition of 'virtual currency' at the European level.[4] In parallel, European Parliament and Council Directive (Eu) 2018/843 expanded the subjective scope of AML duties relating to activity in cryptocurrencies, also including a further category of service providers, namely *custodian wallet providers*, *i.e.*, entities 'that provide services to safeguard private cryptographic keys on behalf of its customers, to hold, store and transfer virtual currencies'. This provision has been transposed into Italian legislation (Art 2, para 5, letter I, decreto legislativo no 231/2007) through decreto legislativo 4 October 2019 no 125.

Based on the argument of *sedes materiae*, it might be asserted that such a legal definition was not enacted with a general view of how comprehensively to regulate cryptocurrencies; instead, the only relevant regulatory angle

scrutiny of transactions undertaken throughout the course of that relationship to ensure that the transactions being conducted are consistent with the obliged entity's knowledge of the customer, the business and risk profile, including, where necessary, the source of funds, and ensuring that the documents, data or information held are kept up-to-date (Art 18 of decreto legislativo no 231/2007), and reporting of suspicious transactions (Art 35 para 1 of decreto legislativo no 231/2007). Breach of those duties triggers sanctions, depending on the type of infringement. Art 55 para 1, of decreto legislativo no 231/2007 punishes, with imprisonment from six months to three years and a fine from 10.000 to 30.000 Euros, the lack of adequate due diligence or the communication of false information from the obliged entity.

4 In Art 1 para (2), letter (d), point 18, European Parliament and Council Directive (Eu) 2018/843, virtual currencies are defined as '[...] means a digital representation of value that is not issued or guaranteed by a central bank or a public authority, is not necessarily attached to a legally established currency and does not possess a legal status of currency or money, but is accepted by natural or legal persons as a means of exchange and which can be electronically transferred, stored and traded'.

is AML/CFT. However, this definition is now also embedded in Art 1 para 2, letter f[5] of the above-mentioned decreto del ministero dell'economia e delle finanze 17 January 2022, which, instead, sets a supervision framework regarding the provision of services relating to cryptocurrencies, focusing on custody and/or trading service providers relating to cryptocurrencies (see below, para III).

Against this backdrop, it is suggested that the Italian legislator's attention does not focus on defining and regulating the whole cryptocurrency value chain, including its infrastructural aspects and the mutual relationships between participants to a blockchain; no specific provisions are dedicated to the regulation of so-called mining activity (i.e., processes that would lead to the issuance of further cryptocurrencies), and to a lesser extent. any requirement is laid with reference to the actual content of consensus protocols based on which cryptocurrency ledgers work and are maintained.

Rather, that regulation only insists on the relationships between final users (purchasers and holders of cryptocurrencies) and providers of custody and/or exchange services, the former referring to the keeping of cryptocurrencies deposit accounts, the latter referring to the performing of transactions relating to cryptocurrencies on behalf of clients. In this respect, relevant provisions of decreto del ministero dell'economia e delle finanze 17 January 2022, will be described below, para 3.

2 Regulation

Approaching the issue of cryptocurrency regulation under the Italian legal system, one preliminary distinction has to be drawn. From a regulatory perspective, it is, in fact, necessary to distinguish between financial instruments (as defined under MiFID) involving cryptocurrencies as underlying assets, from actual purchase of cryptocurrencies (either as legal or beneficial owners).

The former category encompasses derivatives, contracts for difference, units of collective investment undertakings, ETFs and ETPs, provided that their underlying is cryptocurrency.[6] Qualifying as transactions relating to financial

5 For the sake of completeness, Art 1 para 2 letter. f) states that virtual currencies consist of 'the digital representation of value nor issued neither guaranteed by a central bank or a public authority, not necessarily linked to a currency which is legal tender, used as a means of exchange in order to purchase goods and services or for investment aims and electronically transferred, stored and negotiated'.

6 On the topic see Esma, *Statement on preparatory work of the European Securities and Markets Authority in relation to CFD s and binary options offered to retail clients*, ESMA71-99-910, 15 December 2017.

instruments, those investment products undoubtedly fall within the objective scope of MiFID and can be offered to the public, provided that compliance with the regulatory framework for investment services in ensured. Thus far, no product intervention or other supervisory powers were exercised by Consob with respect to those instruments.

The latter category appears to be less straightforward. In fact, the question arises about whether or not cryptocurrencies qualify *per se* as financial instruments, namely, as 'transferable securities' under Art 4, para 1, no 44 (bearing the definition: 'those classes of securities which are negotiable on the capital market, with the exception of instruments of payment, such as: (a) shares in companies and other securities equivalent to shares in companies, partnerships or other entities, and depositary receipts in respect of shares; (b) bonds or other forms of securitised debt, including depositary receipts in respect of such securities; (c) any other securities giving the right to acquire or sell any such transferable securities or giving rise to a cash settlement determined by reference to transferable securities, currencies, interest rates or yields, commodities or other indices or measures').

It would be accurate to claim that, among Italian scholars,[7] the prevailing opinion denies that cryptocurrencies would qualify as financial instruments. This seems to be Consob's stance, too; in fact, so far, no sanctions have been imposed against providers of services relating to cryptocurrency under Art 166 of Testo Unico della Finanza (that is, abusive provision of investment services due to the lack of licensing as a bank or investment firm), when online platforms *would only receive and execute orders* relating to the purchase or sale of crypto. On the contrary, Supreme Court caselaw offers one diverging decision,[8] dismissing an appeal against a preventive seizure adopted within a criminal investigation, where the offer of cryptocurrencies was part of a more articulated fraud. In this decision, the Italian Supreme Court (Corte di Cassazione)

---

7 See, among others, N. Vardi, '"Criptovalute" e dintorni: alcune considerazioni sulla natura giuridica dei bitcoin' *Il diritto dell'informazione e dell'informatica*, III, 448–449 (2015); F. Carrière, 'Le "criptovalute" sotto la luce delle nostrane categorie giuridiche di "strumenti finanziari", "valori mobiliari"e "prodotti finanziari": tra tradizione e innovazione' *Rivista di diritto bancario*, 135–136, I (2019); M. Mancini, 'Valute virtuali e Bitcoin' *Analisi giuridica dell'economia*, 125 (2015); A. Caloni, ' "Bitcoin": profili civilistici e tutela dell'investitore' *Rivista di diritto civile*,169 (2019); M. Cian, 'La criptovaluta – alle radici dell'idea giuridica di denaro attraverso la tecnologia: spunti preliminari' *Banca, borsa e titoli di credito*, in part. 331–332 (2019); E. Girino, 'Criptovalute: un problema di legalità funzionale' *Rivista di diritto bancario*, 760, I (2019).

8 Corte di Cassazione, Sezione penale II 25 September 2020 no 26807, *Cassazione penale*, 638 (2021); Corte di Cassazione, Sezione penale II 30 November 2021 no 44337, available at *www.dejure.it*.

stated – but did not sufficiently argue[9] – that all activities carried out by the owner of the website within which the offer was carried out would constitute abusive/illegal financial activity, provided that the offeror was not licensed as a bank or an investment firm.

Indeed, it would be correct to claim that cryptocurrencies would not qualify under Italian law (and perhaps under any other jurisdiction subject to MiFID), as financial instruments. More than one argument supports such a conclusion.

First, the only existing legal definition of cryptocurrency (see above, para 1) explicitly makes reference to their payment/settlement nature ('used as a means of exchange in order to purchase goods and services'), which arguably excludes its qualification in terms of transferable security; Art 1, para 2 of Testo Unico della Finanza expressly states that 'means of payment do not qualify as financial instruments'.

Second, the origination of transferable securities implies the reception of funds by an issuer, thus entailing some form of liability (even if conditional, contingent and/or residual, as in equity or quasi-equity stakes) of the recipient towards the subscriber, whereas cryptocurrencies lack an identifiable issuer.

Finally, proceeds received by issuers of transferable securities are normally financing and undertaking/entrepreneurial activity, on whose outcomes the fair value of the instrument would depend; besides, the entrepreneur's assets (all or part of them) are the guarantee of the underlying liability. However, neither cryptocurrencies refer to any underlying assets, nor do they express or reflect an intrinsic value.

In the spectrum of virtual currencies' tentative legal qualification, it has been suggested[10] that cryptocurrencies could be led back to 'financial

9 In stating grounds for its decision, the Court underlined that 'suitable information was provided in order to make investors capable to evaluate whether adhere or not to the investment'; this was mainly based on the following sentence being on the website of the offeror: 'who has betted on bitcoin within two years has earned more than 97%'.

10 A. Caloni, '"Bitcoin": profili civilistici e tutela dell'investitore' *Rivista di diritto civile*, 169 (2019). On this topic, see also Tribunale di Verona, 24 January 2017. Ruling on a contract between an online platform and a client whose object was an exchange between legal tender and cryptocurrencies (namely, Bitcoin), the Tribunale di Verona has qualified bitcoins as financial instruments and the exchange's activity as a provision of financial services to consumers. Such qualification led to the application of consumer protection regulations (Consumer Code, decreto legislativo 6 September 2005 no 206), which entitles the consumer of a good or service with the right to be informed in a clear and understandable way of the identity of the provider, the main features of the service offered, the risks associated with the characteristics of the product purchased and that do not depend on the professional, as well as remedies provided to the consumer by the law. All information must be provided in written form, the lack of which gives rise to the nullity of the

products', as per in Art 1 para 1, letter u) of Testo Unico della Finanza, whose definition includes 'financial instruments and any other investment form of financial nature'. In the Italian legal system, the existence of such a legal notion, that is not in the MiFID framework, aims at enlarging – beyond activities relating to financial instruments – the perimeter of 'financial activities', which Italian law reserves for licensed banks and investment firms. At the same time, under Italian law (Art 96-*bis* of Testo Unico della Finanza), the offering of a financial product to the public is subject to the duty to publish a prospectus, as well as to all other obligations set out in the European Parliament and Council Regulation (Eu) 2017/1129 of 14 June 2017 on the prospectus to be published when securities are offered to the public or admitted to trading on a regulated market and repealing Directive 2003/17/EC. Finally, distance marketing and promotion of financial products are subject to conduct rules for the provision of investment services, set out by MiFID (Art 32 of Testo Unico della Finanza; Art 125–127 of risoluzione Consob 15 February 2018 no 20307, so-called 'Regolamento Intermediari').

Due to the generic nature of this principle, Corte di Cassazione[11] and Consob[12] tried to draw some more accurate criteria that would guide legal operators in assessing if a certain transaction would fall into the category of financial products. Specifically, a financial product requires three elements to be met: (a) a capital contribution from one party to another; (b) the expectation of a financial performance; (c) the taking of a risk which is directly linked to the capital outlay.

In this regard, however, it is submitted that, if one should not rule out that articulated/complex transactions involving the offering cryptocurrencies can be qualified as financial products when all three of the above requirements concur,[13] it should now be taken into account that the newly-adopted decreto

---

contract with relative legitimation in favor of the consumer. Since the contract was not complying with those provisions, it was declared null and void.

11 Corte di Cassazione, 5 February 2013 no 2736, available at *www.dejure.it.*

12 Consob deliberations on this matter are several; see, particularly, comunicazioni Consob 30 November 1995 no DAL/RM/95010201; 10 July 1997 no DAL97006082; 22 October 1998 no DIS/98082979; 28 January 1999 no DIS/99006197; 12 May 2000 no DIS/36167; 1 June 2001 no DEM/1043775; 4 October 2012 no DIN/12079227; 6 May 2013 no DTC/13038246. All available at *www.consob.it.* In the same terms have expressed the last communications by Consob that had as object such operations in cryptocurrencies and these are deliberation no 19866/2017 and no 20660/2018.

13 In fact, Consob has stepped in and exercised its supervisory and sanctioning powers when structured products or investment plans involving – but not limited to – cryptocurrencies were being offered (for instance, so-called 'mining packages'), and also when the offeror of cryptocurrencies would also commit to purchase them back over a period

del ministero dell'economia e della finanza (below, para 3) tips the 'qualification' scale in favor of cryptocurrencies not being regulated and supervised as financial products, but rather as currencies.[14] This implies that exchanges which would only receive and execute orders relating to the purchase or sale of crypto, as well as other intermediaries receiving those orders and transmitting them to exchanges, would neither qualify as offerors of financial products, nor as subjects carrying out the activities of distance marketing and promotion of financial products.[15] This being so, one may wonder if activities relating to cryptocurrencies storage and transfer should then be considered, and to what extent, as provision of payment services under PSD2 (European Parliament and Council Directive (Eu) 2015/2366 of 25 November 2015 on payment services in the internal market, amending Directives 2002/65/Ec, 2009/110/Ec and 2013/36/Eu and Regulation (Eu) no 1093/2010 and repealing Directive 2007/64/Ec). This begs the question as to whether or not cryptocurrencies, when conceived as means of payments, fall into the category of 'funds', for purposes of qualifying cryptocurrency-related service providers as providers of payment services under no 2 of Annex I of PSD2 ('execution of payment transactions, including transfers of funds on a payment account with the user's payment service provider or with another payment service provider', wherein 'payment account' means – according to article 4(12) of PSD2 – 'an account held in the name of one or more payment service users which is used for the execution of payment transactions').[16]

of time. In those cases, Consob has qualified the whole product or service as a 'financial product' (other than a financial instrument), and issued orders of temporary suspension of the offer due to the lack of a prospectus (Art 99 para 1 letter b of Testo Unico della Finanza: deliberations 20901/2019 and 20878/2019, available at *www.consob.it*), *or definitively shut the offering down (Art 99 para 1 letter c of Testo Unico della Finanza: deliberations 20845/2019; 20858/2019, available at www.consob.it)*.

14 Despite that, *in practice*, they are purchased and traded due to a speculative intent, much more than they are purchased in order for them to be used as means of payment.

15 It is indeed controversial whether or not a contract according to which an intermediary would purchase crpytos on behalf of clients but maintain legal ownership over those assets would qualify as a derivative contract having cryptos as its underlying asset (i.e., a financial instrument).

16 It is noted that Recital 10 to European Parliament and Council Directive (Eu) 2018/843 rules out that hypothesis.

3 Supervision

As already set out, the bulk of the Italian supervision framework on cryptocurrencies is currently provided by decreto del ministero dell'economia e delle finanze 13 January 2022. This Regulation inscribes supervision on exchanges and e-wallet (custody) service providers within the existing framework on professional currency-exchangers, whose activity is reserved for registered firms, provided that abusive currency-exchanger activity carries a pecuniary fine. In particular, according to Art 17-*bis*, para 1 of decreto legislativo 13 August 2010 no 141, 'professional currency-exchange activity, consisting of the negotiation of currency means of payments with immediate settlement, is reserved for subjects registered in a specific book held by the Body referred to in Art 128-*undecies* of the Italian Banking Act [i.e., the Institution of Financial Agents and Credit Brokers, Organismo degli agenti in attività finanziaria e dei mediatori creditizi: from now on, OAM]'. Registration is subject to requirements set out in para 3 of the same article and triggers the obligation to report all transactions to the OAM which, in turn, is subject to supervision by the Ministry of Finance.

Implementing provisions of Art 17-*bis*, paras 8-*bis* and 8-*ter* of decreto legislativo no 141/2010, Ministry of Finance decree 13 January 2022 establishes a further section of the above-cited book, dedicated to 'providers of services relating to the utilization of virtual currency' ('every natural or legal person who provides to third parties, on a professional basis, online or not, services functional to use, exchange and store virtual currencies and to their conversion from or in currencies which are legal tender or digital representations of value, including those convertible in other virtual currencies, as well as services relating to issuing, offering, transferring and offsetting and any other service aiming at acquiring, trading and intermediating of exchanges of the same currencies') and 'digital portfolio service providers' ('every natural or legal person provides to third parties, on a professional basis, online or not, services consisting of the safeguard of private cryptographic keys on behalf of its customers, in order to hold, store and transfer virtual currencies').

Registration enables firms to provide services relating to the utilization of virtual currency and digital portfolio services in favor of Italian-based users (whereas provision of those services without being registered constitutes an administrative offense) and is conditional upon particular requirements which also include the location of both the legal and real seat in Italy or, in the sole case of service providers incorporated in the UE, a stable organization in Italy. Registration requests must also carry the information about which services are provided, as well as about how those services are provided (Arts 3 and 4).

Reporting obligations imposed on cryptocurrency-related service providers must be complied with through standards which include (a) identity of clients using services and (b) aggregate data – to be transmitted to OAM on a quarterly basis – relating to the overall activity of each service provider *vis-à-vis* each client (Art 5).

Finally, the decree expressly entrusts the Tax Inspectorate with inquiry and control powers (Art 6).

4 Private Law Issues

4.1 *Cryptocurrencies as 'Goods' under Article 810 of the Italian Civil Code*

The issue as to whether holders of cryptocurrencies are entitled to real (i.e., proprietary) rights or, rather, credit/obligation rights *vis-à-vis* specific subjects (namely, transferor and transferees, custodians and other service providers) naturally raises the question on the nature of cryptocurrencies, under a strict private-law perspective.

The current state of the debate among Italian scholars shows that it is commonly considered that cryptocurrencies would fall into the notion of 'good' under Art 810 of the Italian Civil Code, according to which 'goods are all those things that can be the subject of rights'. In fact, the qualification of cryptocurrencies as goods is the *necessary and sufficient* prerequisite in order to qualify them as ownership.

The main obstacle to such conclusion would lie in their incorporeal nature. According to traditional doctrines, in fact, the concept of 'thing' would, *per se*, imply the asset's physical existence, save specific exceptions provided for by the law (i.e., energy, according to Art 814 of Civil Code), which would form an exhaustive list.[17]

However, a counter argument has been put forward,[18] based on the observation that technological and social evolution has made such principle obsolete, provided that it would leave without *erga omnes* enforcement all

17 M. Comporti, 'Diritti reali in generale', in A. Cicu, F. Messineo, L. Mengoni eds., *Trattato di diritto civile e commerciale*, (Milano: Giuffrè, 2011) 125; V. Zeno Zencovich, '*Cosa*', in R. Sacco eds., *Digesto delle discipline privatistiche/Sezione civile*, (Torino: Utet giuridica, 1988) IV 438.

18 C. Camardi, 'Cose, beni e nuovi beni, tra diritto europeo e diritto interno' *Europa e diritto privato*, 955 (2018); M. Giuliano, 'Le risorse digitali nel paradigma dell'art. 810 cod. civ. ai tempi della blockchain' *Nuova giurisprudenza civile commentata*, 1214, II, (2021).

those immaterial entitlements which – according to the characteristics of its subject – would require such protection.[19]

Such a guiding principle supports the qualification of cryptocurrencies in terms of goods. It goes without saying that the *spending power* which is inherent to cryptocurrencies needs to be protected through enforcement means, characterized by 'exclusivity' and 'absoluteness' (*ius alios excludendi*).

In light of the above, it seems fair to agree that cryptocurrencies are to be qualified as digital ownership – namely, immaterial and fungible goods protected by a proprietary right.[20]

4.2 *Ownership of Cryptocurrencies Stored in a 'Cold Wallet' or in a 'Hot Wallet'*

Having regard to the above, the question arises as to who is the actual *legal owner* of cryptocurrencies, when token keys are stored in electronic wallets,[21] as happens in the vast majority of cases.

In this regard, some opinions[22] suggest that a distinction should be drawn between software-based wallets which are *not connected to the web* (so-called 'cold wallets'), and wallets where private keys are stored in the custodian's

---

19 O. T. Scozzafava, 'Dei beni', in P. Schlesinger eds., *Il codice civile. Commentario*, (Milano: Giuffrè, 1999) 28; see also Id., *Goods and legal forms of property* (Milan, 1982), 39 ff.

20 D. Masi, 'Le criptoattività: proposte di qualificazione giuridica e primi approcci regolatori' *Banca, impresa, società*, 247 (2021); G.M. Nori, 'Bitcoin, tra moneta e investimento' *Banca, impresa, società*, 173 (2021); E. Calzolaio, 'La qualificazione del bitcoin: appunti di comparazione giuridica' *Danno e responsabilità*, 188 (2021); D. Fauceglia, 'La moneta privata, le situazioni giuridiche di appartenenza e i fenomeni contrattuali' *Contratto e impresa*, 1253, III (2020) 1253.

21 Indeed, it seems clear that no such doubts can arise when private keys are kept in a physical hardware device or printed on paper.

22 See the decision by Tribunale di Firenze 21 January 2019 no 18, *Giurisprudenza commerciale*, 1073 (2020), and, among academics, the opinion of V. De Stasio, *Prestazione di servizi di portafoglio digitale relativi alla valuta virtuale "Nanocoin" e qualificazione del rapporto tra prestatore e utente' Banca, borsa e titoli di credito*, 399, II, (2021). In the above-cited decision, the Court of Florence has opined on how depositors of cryptocurrencies (in that case, Nanocoin) should be treated within the bankruptcy procedure of a defaulted wallet service provider, which was performing custodian activity through a 'hot wallet'. Particularly, provided that the custodian was systematically transferring deposited cryptos to its own blockchain address, the Court stated that it had become the owner of all deposited cryptos, so that the depositor would not be able to recover them as owners (through a reivindicatio). Instead, they were to be treated as creditors and subject to par condicio creditorum, meaning that the judicial liquidator was required to sell all remaining cryptocurrencies and distribute the proceeds among all creditors pari passu.

servers so that crypto holders, in order to spend their tokens, need to access an account via an internet connection (so-called 'hot wallets').

With reference to the first case, it is argued that cryptocurrency holders maintain ownership over cryptos, insofar as the custodian does not apprehend or control private keys, so that it would be technically impossible for the custodian to spend a token without the owner's consent, which maintains exclusive control over private keys.

The case of 'hot wallets' is more complex. Since in this case, private keys are actually controlled by the custody service provider, owners of cryptocurrencies stored in a 'hot wallet' can only spend their tokens by accessing their wallet through the internet and instructing the custodian to perform a certain transaction. Thus, an agency relationship is in place between crypto-holders and custodians.

In this context, the question arises as to whether or not transmission of private keys to the custodian automatically triggers the transfer of cryptocurrencies' ownership to the depositary, so that the depositor's entitlement would change into a mere restitution credit of the same quantity and quality of cryptocurrencies (*tantundem eiusdem generis*) *vis-à-vis* the depositary; assuming this perspective, such contractual structure would fall into the notion of 'irregular deposit contract' on the basis of Art 1782 of the Civil Code, according to which 'when the object of the deposit contract is money or other fungible assets, and the depositary is entitled to freely use them, then the depositary becomes owner of those goods and is obliged to restitute to the depositor the same quantity and quality of those goods'.

It is apparent that this qualification issue is crucial in determining the legal treatment of several aspects, including those relating to regulation of insolvency and seizure/foreclosure of those assets.

In this regard, it is submitted that a further distinction should be made, when assessing whether or not custodians (through a 'hot wallet') become the owners of deposited cryptocurrencies. Indeed, according to the Italian legal system, the mere *traditio* of a fungible thing to the custodian does not itself convey ownership over the asset, provided that such an effect depends exclusively on the fact that the parties have agreed to entitle the depositary with the right to use and dispose of the assets (Art 1782 of the Civil Code). If the existence of such a provision is not *per se* impossible, this should arguably *not be the case* with most common e-wallet contracts. Conversely, if – as it should ordinarily happen – the parties have agreed that the depositor shall not dispose of cryptos if not in execution of the depositor's instructions, no transfer of ownership rights will have occurred and, consequently, the depositor is obliged to *separate* (*in accounting terms*) those assets from its own assets and from assets received by other depositors. At the same time, it might be argued that if the custodian's activity is limited to storing depositors' private keys without transferring deposited cryptos to its own blockchain address, *as far at the deposit contract is concerned*, cryptocurrencies should be treated as non-fungible assets, provided that it is always possible to trace to which client any act of disposal relates (so-called de-fungibilization, 'defungibilizzazione').

Given this situation, the type of contract that best reflects the parties' underlying interests is the 'regular deposit' contract (Art 1766 of the Civil Code), whereby delivery of private keys to the depositor neither implies the transfer of ownership over cryptocurrencies, which remain the depositor's,[23] nor transfers possession of cryptocurrencies from the owner to the custodian; in fact, when a 'regular deposit' contract is in place, the depositary only has 'custody' or 'detention' ('*detenzione*') of the contract's object, while possession is still the depositor's (so-called 'indirect' possession, meaning that it is exercised *through another subject, i.e.*, the custodian: Art 1140, para 2 of the Civil Code).

4.3 *Purchase, Acquisition and Transfer of Cryptocurrencies*

Before considering how cryptocurrencies are transferred through *inter vivos* deeds, as well as *mortis causa*, a few words are required about how events occurring on the blockchain would affect proprietary entitlements of holders of private keys.

In this regard, should be stressed that the existence of a ledger, keeping track of transactions relating to tokens, does not imply that cryptocurrencies qualify, under Italian law, as 'movable property entered into public registers' according to Art 815 of the Civil Code (which states that 'movable goods entered into public registers are subject to special provisions established for them or, in the absence of such provisions, to provisions relating to movable property'). In fact, it would not be possible to claim that distributed ledgers

23 In the case examined by the Tribunale di Firenze 21 January 2019 no 18, it was found that the owner of the platform had full availability of the cryptocurrencies (nanocoin) contained in his wallet, provided that all deposited cryptos were immediately transferred to the wallet service provider's address. Therefore, according to the Court of Florence, the relationship had to be qualified in terms of irregular deposit (Art 1782 of the Civil Code), implying the conveyance of property in favor of the recipient.On this topic, see also, D. Fauceglia, 'Il deposito e la restituzione delle criptovalute' *Contratti*, 669 (2019). The opinion of A. Caloni 'Deposito di criptoattività presso una piattaforma exchange: disciplina e attività riservate' *Giurisprudenza commerciale*, 1073 (2020), according to which, the trading function underlying the relationship would result in the lack of the power of disposal of the platform manager and the qualification of the deposit as regular pursuant to Art 1766 of the Italian Civil Code.

(including permissionless ones) can *ipso facto* – that is, without a domestic or foreign dedicated legal provision – qualify as 'public registers', also considering the absence of a national authority in charge of regulating and overseeing the register.

It follows from this assumption that the loss of the 'spending power' associated with the possession of certain private keys, due to events occurring on the blockchain (for instance, a hard fork which would invalidate the blocks through which a certain token was acquired) needs to be conceived as destruction or loss of movable property (*amissio vel interitus rei*), implying the extinction of the related proprietary entitlement. Conversely, the acquisition of a new 'spending power', as a result of an airdrop of cryptocurrencies or a hard fork that would make what were previously invalid blocks valid, should be considered – from a legal standpoint – as an *ex lege* purchase of a chattel without owner ('*occupazione*' according to Art 923 of Civil Code), which would stem from the mere possession (direct or indirect, *i.e.*, through a 'hot wallet') of private keys, enabling a newly-originated 'spending power'.

As to the analysis of *inter vivos* transfer of cryptocurrencies, provided that cryptocurrencies qualify as digital fungible property, it follows that owners of cryptos can dispose of them for consideration[24] (including exchanges

24 It is argued that legal qualification as a sale contract, rather than a barter/trade-in contract, of any contract by which cryptocurrencies are transferred as a consideration for a counterperformance, does not depend on the issue of cryptos qualifying, or not, as actual (foreign) currencies. On the issue of cryptocurrencies being, or not, 'money' from a private-law perspective, see M. Passaretta, 'Virtual currencies in a private law perspective: between payment instruments, alternative forms of investment and improper securities, in Cryptoactivity, currencies and bitcoin', in S. Cerrato, R . Morone, P. Dal Checco eds., (Milan, 2021) 101; see also N. Vardi, '"Criptovalute" e dintorni: alcune considerazioni sulla natura giuridica dei Bitcoin' *Diritto dell'informazione e dell'informatica*, 445(2015); G.L. Greco, 'Monete complementari e valute virtuali', in M.T. Paracampo eds., *Fintech* (Torino: Giapichelli, 2017) 210; R. Bocchini, 'The development of virtual currency: first attempts at framing and discipline between economic and legal perspectives' in *Diritto dell'informazione e dell'informatica*, 27 (2017); G. Lemme, S. Peluso, 'Cryptocurrency and detachment from legal money: the bitcoin case' *Rivista di diritto bancario*, 407, I (2016); V. De Stasio, 'Verso un concetto europeo di moneta legale: valute virtuali, monete complementari e regole di adempimento'*Banca, borsa e titoli di credito*,747, I (2018); M. Krogh, 'Transazioni in valute virtuali e rischi riciclaggio. Ruolo e responsabilità del Notaio' in *Notaries*, 157 (2018); M. Cian, 'La criptovaluta – Alle radici dell'idea giuridica di denaro attraverso la tecnologia spunti preliminari' *Banca, borsa e titoli di credito*, 315, I, (2019). In fact, when parties agree that an asset (namely, cryptocurrencies) would be accepted as a means of payment (so-called conventional money), this is sufficient to treat that contract as a sale rather than a barter. Of course, this would not imply that those assets would qualify as legal tender (either domestic or foreign). On this topic, see M. Semeraro,

from a cryptocurrency to another cryptocurrency) or without consideration (i.e., donation, on which see below), according to Italian general rules on contracts,[25] when Italian *lex contractus* applies according to European Parliament and Council Regulation (EC) 593/2008 of 17 June 2008 on the law applicable to contractual obligations, the so-called Rome I Regulation (which is also applicable to donations, except so far as aspects relating to family and succession law are concerned, when legge 31 May 1995 no 218 applies: see below). According to Art 1378 of the Civil Code, property over generic/fungible assets is transferred from one party to another when those assets are made 'specific' (so-called '*individuazione*'), typically by way of their delivery to the recipient.[26] Such provision is applicable to all kind of contracts involving the conveyance of property over generic goods, including donations.

With reference to cryptocurrencies, delivery consists of the purchaser being put in control of the 'spending power' associated with a certain token. This can occur via both with respect to an *on-chain* and an *off-chain* transfer. The former case implies a valid transaction taking place on the chain, through which one or more tokens are sent from the seller's address (i.e., a hash identifying the public key associated with the seller's private keys) to the purchaser's address. In the latter case, actual possession over *private keys* is handed over to the purchaser, while nothing happens *on-chain* and tokens remain registered under the same *public keys*. Such a handover can occur in several forms, according to how private keys are stored. In a case in which private keys are kept in a hardware device or printed on paper, physical delivery is required (and sufficient), whereas in a case in which tokens are stored in a software-based wallet, a distinction has to be drawn between software-based 'cold wallets' and 'hot wallets'; in the case of a software-based 'cold wallet', it is required that private

---

'Moneta legale, moneta virtuale e rilevanza dei conflitti' *Rivista di diritto bancario,* 137, II (2019).

25 Including contracts relating to the subscription of corporation shares. In this respect, see Corte d'Appello di Brescia, 30 October 2018, which dealt with the issue of whether or not cryptocurrencies (in that case, OneCoin) are apt to form the object of contribution for purposes of increasing the legal capital of a limited liability company. The Court denied that, based on the assumption that OneCoin does not have a liquid secondary market enabling the formation of that crypto's market valuesee: see M. Natale, 'Dal "cripto-conferimento" al "cripto-capitale"' Banca, borsa e titoli di credito, 741, II (2019); C. Flaim, 'Nuove frontiere del conferimento in società a responsabilità limitata: il caso delle criptovalute' Giurisprudenza commerciale, 900, II (2020).; R. Battaglini, 'Conferimento di criptovalute in sede di aumento del capitale sociale' Giurisprudenza commerciale, 913, II (2020).

26 This is also the moment at which the risk of accidental loss shifts to the recipient (*res perit domino*).

keys be extracted from the wallet and delivered to the recepient, or that off-line wallets' credentials are delivered to the recipient; in the case of 'hot wallets', delivery is executed when the seller's custodian transfers private keys to the recipient's custodian (when this is the same as the seller's, it is sufficient that the seller's account is charged and the recipient's account is credited).

From an Italian international private law perspective, it should be made clear that Italian courts will apply Art 1378 of the Italian Civil Code, insofar as the relevant movable property is located in Italy (*lex rei sitae*). In fact, according to Art 51 of the Italian private international law (legge no 218/1995), rules regarding the actual transfer of ownership (*modus adquirendi*) are not governed by the *lex contractus*, which only governs the contract as a precondition of the property conveyance (*titulus adquirendi*). Besides, Art 52 states that 'as far as goods in transit are involved, the applicable law is the place of destination'.

One might then wonder as to when a cryptocurrency token can be deemed to be located in Italy. On this point, it is argued that the criterion of *rex lei sitae* fits the case of physical property better than 'virtual' property. However, it is submitted that the case of cryptocurrency needs to be approached commencing with the assumption that tokens cannot be 'enjoyed', as a thing, but just disposed of; therefore, tokens are nothing more than a 'spending power'. Consequently, tokens should be deemed to be located where private keys associated with a certain token (that is, private keys enabling the token's 'spending power') are stored. Of course, in case of an on-chain transfer, the relevant private keys are the recipient ones.

Based on the principle of freedom of contract, there is no reason to rule out that cryptocurrencies can be donated. According to Art 782 of the Civil Code, the solemn form of the notarial public deed is prescribed, including the presence of two witnesses at the moment at which the deed is signed before the notary (Art 48 of the notarial law, regio decreto 16 February 1913 no 89), under penalty of nullity of the deed.

If the donation concerns movable things, in addition to the formal requirements cited above, the deed of donation (or a separate note signed by the donor, the recipient and the notary) must specifically include details of the things donated, and their value (Art 782, para 1, of the Civil Code). However, if the donated property is of 'modest value', the form of the public deed is not required *ad substantiam actus* (i.e., under penalty of nullity), so long as there is actual delivery of the donation's object (Art 783 of the Civil Code).

As regards applicable law, the Rome I Regulation and Italian private international law must be applied in a coordinated manner. In fact, the deed's existence and validity, as well as the content of obligations arising from donations, fall within the scope of application of Rome I, with the exception of obligations arising from family and succession law (Art 1, para 2, letter b and letter c, European Parliament and Council Regulation (EC) 593/2008). When this is the case, Art 56 of legge no 218/1995) applies, establishing that donations are governed by the national law of the donor at the time of the donation. However, the donor can opt-in (through a declaration called *professio iuris*) for the law of the State of his/her residence at the time of the donation to be applicable. Eventually, the third paragraph of Art 56 specifically deals with formal validity, establishing that the donation is valid in this respect when it complies with the relevant provisions of *either* the law applicable to the donation *or* the law of the State in which the deed of donation is made.

Having regard to inheritance law issues, it should first be noted that the Italian system is based on the principle of the general transferability *successionis causa* of all assets, rights and relationships which belonged to the deceased person (*de cuius*). This is stated in law in order to ensure the continuity of relationships with creditors and counterparties.

Over the last few years, Italian scholars focused on the *mortis causa* succession of so-called digital assets, that is, the heterogeneous set of assets having computer-based origin, including accounts and files, which can be contained both in off-line devices and in online storage systems.[27] Cryptocurrencies certainly fall into this category.

With reference to *mortis causa* transfer of digital assets, the question arises regarding testators as to what meaning should be attributed to testamentary provisions assigning certain credentials (in case of cryptocurrencies, private keys associated to public keys which enable cryptocurrencies to be spent) to specific persons.

In this regard, learned Italian academics[28] make it clear that a difference exists between situations in which the testator aims to assign to the beneficiary

---

27 C. Camardi, 'L'eredità digitale. Tra reale e virtuale' *Diritto dell'informazione e dell'informatica.*, 65, 1 (2018); M. Palazzo, 'La successione nei rapporti digitali' *Vita notarile*,1309 (2019); M. Cinque, 'L'eredità digitale alla prova delle riforme' *Rivista di diritto civile*, 72 (2020); S. Delle Monache, '*Successione* mortis causa *e patrimonio digitale' Nuova giurisprudenza civile commentata*, 460 (2020).

28 U. Bechini, 'Password, credenziali e successione mortis causa' *Studio CNN* n. 6-2007/IG, available at http://www.notariato.it/wp-content/uploads/6-07-IG; V.D. Greco, 'Il diritto alla trasmissione dei dati digitali post mortem: il problema della disposizione mortis causa delle credenziali di accesso a risorse digitali', in M. Bianca, A. Gambino, R. Messinetti eds, *Libertà di manifestazione del pensiero e diritti fondamentali* (Milano: Giuffrè, 2016) 195; F. Mastroberardino, *Il patrimonio digitale* (Napoli: Edizioni Scientifiche Italiane, 2019) 204; M. Palazzo, 'La successione nei rapporti digitali' *Vita notarile*, 1321, 1329 (2019); A. D'Arminio Monforte, *La successione nel patrimonio digitale* (Pisa: Pacini giuridica, 2019)

the ownership of the digital asset which credentials protect (in such a case, the assignment of passwords means the assignment of the digital asset) and those in which the assignment of a password to someone is instrumental in the execution of a certain task in favour of another subject, for whose performance the assignee is appointed (in such case, a *post mortem exequendum* mandate occurs).

If the deceased person has not disposed of his/her estate through the act of making a valid will (succession *ab intestato*), so-called legitimate succession (successione legittima) will take place (Art 457 of the Civil Code), meaning that the entire inheritance will be devolved to legitimate heirs (member of the deceased subject's family, according to specific law provisions based on a proximity criterion: see Arts 565 ff. of the Civil Code). Legitimate succession concerns the entire assets of the deceased (so-called *universum ius defuncti*), therefore including any cryptocurrencies possibly owned by the *de cuius*. In this case, heirs will become joint owners of all assets of the estate.

Finally, it should be stressed that the answer to the issue of *mortis causa* transferability of cryptocurrencies does not change depending on how private keys are stored. However, when they are stored in 'hot wallets', it is also necessary to deal with the succession in the contractual relationship between the *de cuius* and the intermediary. In principle, according to the aforementioned standard of general transmissibility of relations upon death, the contractual relationship with the intermediary should also be included in the estate.

As regards the relevant private international law issues, European Parliament and Council Regulation (Eu) 650/2012 of 4 July 2012 on jurisdiction, applicable law, recognition and enforcement of decisions and acceptance and enforcement of authentic instruments in matters of succession and on creation of European Certificate of Succession, states that the succession will be subject to Italian law if the deceased subject had his habitual residence in the territory of the Italian Republic at the time of his death (Art 21) or if the testator, despite having his habitual residence in another State, possesses Italian citizenship, and opt-in the application of Italian law through a declaration (*professio iuris*) contained in the act of will.

135; A. Magnani, *Il trasferimento* mortis causa *del patrimonio digitale, Atti e* quaestiones *notarili nell'era contemporanea e digitale* (Bari: Cacucci editore, 2020) 100; V. Putortì, 'Patrimonio digitale e successione mortis causa' *Giustizia civile,* 173 (2021); L. Di Lorenzo, 'L'eredità digitale' *Notariato,* 146 (2021).

4.4 *Insolvency-Related Matters*

Assuming, based on the arguments set out above, that cryptocurrencies can form the object of ownership (qualifying as 'goods' under Art to 810 of the Civil Code), it follows that creditors are able to seize their debtors' cryptocurrencies in cases of non-performance of an obligation (according to Art 2740, para 1, of the Civil Code, 'the debtor is liable towards its creditors with all its present and future property'). Procedural aspects of the foreclosure procedure change slightly, according to whether private keys can be recovered directly from the debtor, in which case rules on garnishment of movable goods apply ('pignoramento mobiliare', Arts 513 ff of the Code of Civil Procedure), or their recovery requires some form of cooperation from a third party currently keeping the debtor's property, in which case rules on third-party garnishment apply (*'pignoramento presso terzi'*, Arts 543 ff of the Code of Civil Procedure).

Limited to situations in which the debtor is an entrepreneur, their insolvency can trigger bankruptcy, as a procedurally consolidated foreclosure of all the debtor assets, in order to satisfy creditors who have lodged their claims. Bankruptcy procedures are regulated by decreto legislativo 12 January 2019 no 14.

When private keys are digitally stored with a third party through a 'hot wallet', the question arises as to how token-holders' claims may be treated, should the custodian go bankrupt. The answer to this question very much depends on the issue, as discussed above, as to whether or not depositing cryptocurrencies in a e-wallet implies conveyance of the deposited assets' property in favor of the custodian.

As has already been argued, it is submitted that, according to Italian law (see Art 1782 of the Civil Code), delivery of fungible movables to a custodian does not, *per se,* make the recipient the owner of those assets, to the extent that the recipient is contractually bound not to dispose of cryptos if not in the execution of the depositor's instructions. Further, it may be useful to repeat (see above) that if the custodian's activity is limited to storing depositors' private keys without transferring deposited cryptos to its own blockchain address, it is argued that, *as far as the deposit contract is concerned*, cryptocurrencies should be treated as non-fungible assets, provided that it is always possible to trace to which client any act of disposal relates.

From the position of the custodian's insolvency procedure, this means that depositors will maintain a proprietary entitlement over deposited assets, which remain separated from the bankrupt's assets and cannot be seized by the custodian's general creditors, *insofar as they can be traced.* Thus, the procedure's receiver/liquidator is not entitled to liquidate those assets in order to satisfy creditors, but must restitute those assets to depositors, provided that they have lodged their proprietary claim (*rei vindicatio*) according to Art 210 of the Insolvency Code (decreto legislativo no 14/2019).

4.5 *Liens on Cryptocurrencies (Including Trust)*

According to Art 2786 of the Civil Code, a pledge is a security entitlement, originating from an agreement between the creditor and the pledged property's owner, which is effective only on condition that the owner of the pledged property is dispossessed of it. Furthermore, the law also requires a written deed with a 'certain date' under article 2704 of the civil code, in which the pledged subject, the claim protected by the lien and its amount are specified (Art 2787, no 3 of the Civil Code).

With respect to cryptocurrencies, dispossession implies delivery of private keys to the creditor or to a custodian jointly appointed by the parties, so that the owner of the lien's subject cannot dispose of the pledged property without the consent of the creditor or the third-party custodian.

Having regard to the creation of trusts over cryptocurrencies, it should be noted that the Italian legal system does not have a legal tool featuring the same characters as a common-law trust. However, in its legal framework, Italy subscribed to and implemented the Hague Convention on the Law Applicable to Trusts and on their Recognition, of 1 July 1985 (legge 16 October 1989 no 364).

Based on this instrument, foreign trusts' effects must be recognized by Italian courts. Of course, the actual effects of a foreign-law trust will depend on the applicable law.

Traditionally, a debate had been conducted, among Italian legal academics and courts, about the recognizability of a trust in which all connecting factors would point to Italy, and whose only international element would be the choice of a regulating foreign law (so-called 'domestic trust'). Caselaw has settled ruling in favor of it,[29] while this hypothesis is a matter around which academics remain skeptical.[30]

4.6 *Loan of Cryptocurrencies*

Pursuant to Art 1813 of the Italian Civil Code, the loan is the contract by which one party (lender) delivers to another (borrower) a certain amount of money or other fungible things and the other commits to return, at a particular future date (in one or more instalments, as the case may be), as many things of the same kind and quality (*tantuntem eiusdem generis*). Thereafter,

---

29 See, among others, Corte di Cassazione 9 May 2014 no 10105, *Banca, borsa e titoli di credito*, 251 (2016).

30 P. Spolaore, *Garanzia patrimoniale e trust nella crisi d'impresa* (Milano: Giuffrè, 2018).

in consequence of delivery, ownership of the borrowed things passes into the property of the borrower (Art 1813 of the Civil Code). Normally, the loan is an onerous contract; the lender's attribution is compensated by accruing interest, whose rate must necessarily be agreed in writing, otherwise the legal rate applies (Arts 1815, para 1 and 1284, para 3 of the Civil Code). As a general rule, accrued interest are paid in Euros, as legal tender (Art 1277 of the Civil Code), but parties can agree that the debtor can either perform its obligation in legal tender or with other goods. In this case, a so-called 'alternative obligation' would arise (Art 1285 of the Civil Code).

Having already pointed out that cryptocurrencies qualify as fungible movables, it is argued that a loan agreement might also have them as its object. Based on the principle of private autonomy (Art 1322, para 1 of the Civil Code), any private individual can lend or borrow cryptocurrencies. One might wonder what would happen, should a hard fork occur on the blockchain. In this case, in fact, two different types of cryptocurrencies might co-exist with reference to the same blockchain (the one based on the 'amended' version of the protocol, which would not recognize as valid any transaction based on the original version of the protocol, and the others based on the original version of the protocol, which would not recognize as valid any transaction based on the new version of the protocol). In this regard, it is submitted that the fungible nature of those assets requires an inquiry to be carried out as to whether or not there is fungibility between them (*i.e.*, whether or not it might be argued that they belong to the same *genus*, and differ only in terms of their respective quality; in this regard, Art 1178 of the Civil Code states that 'when the obligation's object is a fungible asset, the debtor has to provide things whose quality is not below average'). Moreover, it should also be ascertained as to whether or not the ante-fork cryptocurrencies still exist and are exchangeable on the market. Should it not be the case, then an alternative scenario arises. Either post-fork cryptocurrencies are deemed to belong to the same *genus* as the pre-fork cryptocurrencies, so that the debtor can perform its obligation delivering them, or they are not, in which case Art 1818 of the Civil Code would apply, according to which, if restitution of the borrowed assets becomes impossible or grossly burdensome due to a supervening cause that is not attributable to the borrower, then the debtor has to perform its obligation in domestic legal tender, based on its market value at the moment when the obligation is due. It should be stressed that this provision would only apply in a case of supervening impossibility, by which the original impossibility would make the contract invalid.

With reference to the lending party, it should be noted that entering in such contracts must not give rise to an economic activity carried out on a professional basis. In fact, moving from the assumption that, *from a regulatory and supervisory perspective*, cryptocurrencies are treated by the Italian legal system as foreign currencies (see above, paras 2 and 3); it might be argued that the undertaking of granting cryptocurrency loans constitutes a financing activity. Consequently, such activity is subject to licensing (in Italy or in any other EU Member States), according to Arts 14 and 106 of decreto legislativo 1 September 1993 no 385, the consolidated act on banking regulations. Furthermore, authorization is required if the lender has a non-EU banking license.

Accordingly, *de facto* exercise of a professional activity of granting cryptocurrency loans gives rise to the phenomenon of 'abusive banking', which triggers both private law and criminal law consequences. With reference to the former, caselaw has consistently ruled that each single loan agreement entered into by an unauthorized credit undertaking is null and void. In some cases, general rules on nullity (Arts 1418 ff of the Civil Code) were applied. In other cases – and, it is argued, more correctly – it was ruled that so-called 'protective nullity' (Art 127, para 2 of the decreto legislativo no 385/1993) would apply, meaning that only the borrower is granted the legal standing to promote the nullity claim, and *ex officio* declaration by the judge is only possible insofar as the borrower has an actual benefit from the nullity been declared.[31] With reference to the latter, Art 132 of the consolidated act on banking regulations, decreto legislativo no 385/1993, prescribes the punishment of imprisonment for between six months to four years, as well as a fine of between € 2,065 and € 10,329.

4.7 *Liability Due to Loss of Cryptocurrencies*

As regards the consequences of the loss (e.g., through hacking or fraud) of cryptocurrencies, this issue seems especially relevant where private keys are stored in a 'hot wallet'.[32]

Generally speaking, a custodian's liability under a deposit contract is set out by Arts 1218 and 1768 of the Civil Code, according to which the custodian is liable for loss of deposited assets if it did not diligently perform its custody activity. Provided that the custodian carries out its activity on a professional basis, the assessment as to whether or not it complied with the due standard of diligence must be based on 'the nature of the undertaking' (Art 1176, para 2 of the Civil Code, so-called professional diligence).

31 In the first sense, Corte di Cassazione 28 February 2018 no 4760, available at www.dejure.it; in the second, Corte di Cassazione 23 September 2019 no 23611, *Banca, borsa e titoli di credito*, 123 (2021).

32 And perhaps also in a software-based cold wallet enabling crypto-holders to recover wallet's credentials.

However, Italian caselaw has often ruled that when custody refers to money or securities received by clients, which can be disposed of through the internet (namely, in the case of an online bank account), then a stricter standard of liability would apply, by reason of the inherently hazardous nature of such activity. From a positive standpoint, this would call for an application, by analogy, of Art 2050 of the Civil Code (referring to tort liability), according to which 'whoever causes a damage to other when carrying out a hazardous activity, due to its nature or to the nature of the means it is carried out with, is liable unless it shows proof that it adopted all appropriate measures to avert the damage'.[33] Moreover, to be taken into account is that the hacking of a 'hot wallet' by a fraudulent third party also implies an occurrence of a data breach; from this standpoint, it is noted that failure of the data controller (in this case, the wallet service provider) to ensure integrity and confidentiality of data makes it liable for consequential damage, other than 'if it proves that it is not in any way responsible for the event giving rise to the damage' (Art 82, para 3 of the European Parliament and Council Regulation (Eu) 2016/679 on the protection of natural persons with the regard to the processing of personal data and on the free movement of such data, and repealing Directive 95/46/Ec, also known as GDPR).

Of course, should the hacker be identified, the owner of stolen cryptocurrencies would be able recover its property, provided that this can be traced to the hacker hands (which would generally be possible also if stolen property has already been mixed with other goods belonging to the same *genus*: Art 939 of the Civil Code). With reference to third parties purchasing stolen cryptos from the hacker, their purchase is protected by the law according to Art 1153 of the Civil Code, that is if: (*i*) it is a *bona fide* purchaser of a movable good; (*ii*) the sale's object has been delivered to it; (*iii*) the sale contract is valid if not for its object not being the seller's.

Eventually, one may want to consider the hypothesis of the holder of the cryptocurrencies making the transfer in favor of a counterparty, as a consequence of being misled by the recipient. Apparently, provisions on contract annulment for fraud and deceit are going to be applied. In order for annulment of the contract to be granted by a court, it is necessary to show proof that deceptions perpetrated by the counterparty were such that, without them, the

33 Other authors believed that, under Italian law, a strict liability regime applies whenever breach of contract stems from the materialization of a risk which normally connected to the nature of the business activity exercised by the debtor. References in U. Malvagna, *Clausola di "riaddebito" e servizi di pagamento. Una ricerca sul rischio d'impresa* (Milano: Giuffrè, 2018).

deceived subject would not have entered into that contract (Art 1439 of the Civil Code). Annulment implies that all that was given in performing the contract can be recovered from the recipient through a restitution claim (*condictio indebiti*). Conversely, if the deceptions were not so serious for it to be essential to have the deceived subject's consent, the contract remains valid, but the deceiver must pay compensatory damages (Art 1440 of the Civil Code).

5 Tax Measures

The fiscal framework of cryptocurrencies in the Italian system is aligned with EU law, since domestic legislation depends on EU-level regulation of Value Added Tax (VAT) Directive.

As it is known, the European Court of Justice (C-264/144 of 22 October 2015) stated that «*i) Article 135(1)(e) of the VAT Directive must be interpreted as meaning that the supply of services such as those at issue in the main proceedings, which consist of the exchange of traditional currencies for units of the 'bitcoin' virtual currency and vice versa, performed in return for payment of a sum equal to the difference between, on the one hand, the price paid by the operator to purchase the currency and, on the other hand, the price at which he sells that currency to his clients, are transactions exempt from VAT, within the meaning of that provision; ii) Article 135(1) (d) and (f) of the VAT Directive must be interpreted as meaning that such a supply of services does not fall within the scope of application of those provisions*».

The European Court of Justice's opinion has been later confirmed by the Italian Revenue Agency (Risp. AE n. 72 E, September 2nd 2016), which confirmed the VAT exemption. However, scholars believe that principles stated in that decision cannot be automatically applied to all crypto exchanges, so that this issue is still open to further discussion.[34]

6 Litigation in Relation to Cryptocurrencies

Hereinafter, the few cases relating to cryptocurrencies already decided by Italian courts are briefly described.

6.1 *Verona Local Court, January 24th, 2017*

Ruling on a contract between an online platform and a client whose object was an exchange between legal tender and crypto-currencies (namely, Bitcoin),

34 See, S. Capaccioli, *Diritto Tributario*, in S. Capaccioli (edited by), *Criptoattività, criptovalute e bitcoin*, Milan, 2021, 347 ff.

the Court of Verona has qualified bitcoins as financial instruments and the exchange's activity as a provision of financial services to consumers. Such qualification led to the application of consumer protection regulations (Consumer Code, Legislative Decree no. 205/2006), which entitles the consumer of a good or service with the right to be informed in a clear and understandable way of the identity of the provider, the main features of the service offered, the risks associated with the characteristics of the product purchased and that do not depend on the professional, as well as remedies provided to the consumer by the law. All information must be provided in written form, the lack of which gives rise to the nullity of the contract with relative legitimation in favor of the consumer. Since the contract was not complying with those provisions, it was declared null and void.

6.2 *Brescia Court of Appeal, October 30th, 2018*

The Court of Appeal of Brescia dealt with the issue of whether cryptocurrencies (in that case, OneCoin) are apt to form object of contribution for the purposes of increasing the legal capital of a limited liability company. The Court denied that, based on the assumption that OneCoin does not have a liquid secondary market enabling the formation of that crypto's market value.[35]

6.3 *Florence Local Court, January 21st, 2019*

As outlined above (*supra*, no. 4), the Court of Florence has stated on how depositors of cryptocurrencies (in that case, Nanocoin) should be treated within the bankruptcy procedure of a defaulted wallet service provider, which was performing custodian activity through a «hot wallet». Particularly, provided that the custodian was systematically transferring deposited cryptos to its own blockchain address, the Court stated that it had become the owner of all deposited cryptos, so that depositor would not be able to recover them as owners (through a *reivindicatio*). Instead, they were to be treated as creditors and subject to *par condicio creditorum*, meaning that the judicial liquidator was required to sell all remaining cryptocurrencies and distribute the proceeds among all creditors *pari passu*.

35 On this topic, see M. Natale, *Dal "cripto-conferimento" al "cripto-capitale"*, in *Banca borsa tit. cred.*, (6, II) 2019, 741 ff.; C. Flaim, *Nuove frontiere del conferimento in società a responsabilità limitata: il caso delle criptovalute*, in *Giur. Comm.* (4, II), 2020, 900 ff.; R. Battaglini, *Conferimento di criptovalute in sede di aumento del capitale sociale*, in *Giur. Comm.* (4, II), 2020, 913 ff.

7 Conclusions

In conclusion, the analysis carried out above shows the actual peculiarity of cryptocurrencies to be the impossibility of referring that asset class to traditional concepts and categories underpinning financial regulation.

At the same time, cryptocurrencies constitute the paradigm of «tokens», as a form of fully-digitally originated goods, whose underlying technologies (blockchain-DLT) enable the enforceability erga omnes of the digital asset's inherent entitlements.

One final remark should be made with reference to the issue of decentralization. As is known, the main promise of blockchain is to enable platforms, where assets can be originated and traded on a "peer-to-peer" basis (meaning without any intermediation of institutional actors such as commercial banks, central security depositories, central banks). However, earlier analysis was able to highlight that multiple forms of intermediaries are present in this field, especially with reference to wallet-related and exchange-related services. This being so, it is submitted that we are experi-encing an era of new and more complex intermediation, rather than of disintermediation. So, the question arises as to whether or not those new service providers can guarantee customers an ade-quate level of protection, and of how regulation would foster widespread trust in these new digital markets.

Japan

Tetsuo Morishita

1 Introduction

1.1 *Overview of Cryptoassets in Japan*

Japan is a country that has a substantial volume of transactions of cryptoassets,[1] and a comprehensive regulatory framework for cryptoassets. Though there are no available statistics, it is presumed that most of cryptoassets transactions in Japan are for investment and speculation purposes and most of investors hold and transact cryptoassets through cryptoassets exchanges. To provide crypto asset brokerage, exchange, and custody services as a business, one must be registered with the Prime Minister as a 'crypto asset exchange.' Supervision relating to crypto assets is conducted by the Financial Services Agency (FSA), the sole financial regulator in Japan. Recently, issuance of security tokens for investment in real estates have been increased.[2]

As discussed in more detail below, regulation of crypto assets in Japan consists of (1) regulation under the Payment Services Act ('PSA') (*Shikin Kessai ni kansuru Horitsu*) for cryptoassets such as Bitcoin, (2) regulation under the Financial Instruments and Exchange Act ('FIEA') (*Kinyu Shohin Torihiki Ho*) for security tokens used for investment purposes such as ICOs and STOs, and (3) regulation under the Banking Act ('BA') (*Ginko Ho*) and PSA for stablecoins that are issued at prices linked to a fiat currency and promise redemption at the same amount as the fiat currency. There are other digital assets not regulated by financial laws, but such digital assets are beyond the scope of this report.

While legislation has been developed for the regulation of cryptoassets, there is no special legislation for private law issues of cryptoassets, and case law is not well developed, so many unclear private law issues remain.

1 According to the Japan Virtual and Crypto assets Exchange Association, the spot transactions amounting to about 141.7 billion yen was handled by 32 regulated cryptoasset exchanges in February 2024 (https://jvcea.or.jp/about/statistics/).

2 According to Boostry, a Japanese company which provide platform service for security tokens, the issuance of security tokens in Japan in 2023 amounted to 97.6 billion yen, which is 5.6 times of 2022 (https://boostry.co.jp/blog/st-market-fy2023e).

 | DOI:10.1163/9789004722507_017

1.2 *Definition of Cryptoassets*

1.2.1 Cryptoasset under PSA

In Japan, PSA, which is the statute that has a chapter on the regulation of cryptoassets exchanges, defines cryptoassets. When Japan first introduced the regulation on cryptoassets in 2016, PSA used the term 'virtual currencies' (*kaso tsuka*).[3] In response to the occurrence of hacking incidents and the emergence of ICOs, the government amended PSA and other laws in 2019 to strengthen and expand regulations on virtual currencies.[4] At that time, it was considered misleading to refer to 'virtual currency' considering that it did not serve the function as currency, and following the 2018 G20 Finance Ministers and Central bank Governors Meeting wherein the term 'cryptoassets' was used instead of 'virtual currencies,' the term 'virtual currencies' was replaced by 'cryptoassets (*ango shisan*).' In 2022, PSA was amended again to address stablecoins.

Article 2(14) of PSA defines 'Cryptoassets' as (i) property value (limited to that which is recorded on an electronic device or any other object by electronic means, and excluding the Japanese currency, foreign currencies, and currency-denominated assets and electronic payment instruments (*denshi kessai syudan*)…) which can be used in relation to unspecified persons for the purpose of paying consideration for the purchase or leasing of goods or the receipt of provision of services and can also be purchased from and sold to unspecified persons acting as counterparties, and which can be transferred by means of an electronic data processing system; and (ii) property value which can be mutually exchanged with what is set forth in the preceding item with unspecified persons acting as counterparties, and which can be transferred by means of an electronic data processing system.[5] This definition of PSA is referred by other statutes such as FIEA.

'Property value (limited to that which is recorded on an electronic device or any other object by electronic means), 'which can be transferred by means of an electronic data processing system,' in this definition is what corresponds to so-called 'digital assets' or 'digital tokens.' According to this definition, 'cryptoassets' are digital assets/digital tokens that can be used to pay for goods or services to unspecified persons and can be purchased or sold to an unspecified person, or can be exchanged for cryptoassets with unspecified persons,

3 Regarding the regulation of virtual currencies as of 2016, see Tetsuo Morishita, 'Recent development of Japanese laws' in D. Arner, W. Wan, A. Godwin, W. Shen and E. Gibson (eds), *Research Handbook on Asian Financial Law*, Edward Elgar 2020, pp. 465–469.

4 Ibid, pp. 469–474.

5 English translations of Japanese legislation in this article are based as far as possible on translations available at 'Japanese Law Translation', a website operated by the Ministry of Justice (https://www.japaneselawtranslation.go.jp/).

and that are not a currency-denominated asset or electronic payment instrument. Bitcoin and Ethereum are typical cryptoassets under this definition. If the electronic property value can be used for payment only to a specific person, then it may be regulated as a funds transfer or prepaid payment instrument, not as a cryptoasset.

1.2.2 Electronic Payment Instruments

If electronic property value, which can be transferred by an electronic data processing system and can be used for payment to unspecified persons, is denominated in Japanese or foreign currency, such value may be regulated as a funds transfer (*kawase torihiki*) under BA, funds transfer under PSA (*shikin ido*), or as an electronic payment instrument under PSA (*denshi kessai syudan*).[6] 'electronic payment instrument' is the category that is newly introduced to address stablecoin in the 2022 amendment of PSA. Article 2(5) of PSA defines 'electronic payment instrument' as one of the following: (i) property value that can be used to pay for the purchase or lease of goods, etc. or the provision of services to an unspecified person, and that can be purchased from and sold to an unspecified person (limited to a currency-denominated asset which is recorded on an electronic device or any other object by electronic means and excluding securities, electronically recorded claim, prepaid payment instruments and other items designated by cabinet order), and which can be transferred by means of an electronic data processing system;[7] (ii) property value which can be mutually exchanged with what is set forth in the preceding item with unspecified persons acting as counterparties, and which can be transferred by means of an electronic data processing system; (iii) specified beneficial interest in trust; and (iv) other items designated by cabinet order as being equivalent to what is set forth in the preceding three items.[8]

---

6 To provide fund transfers as business, one must either obtain a banking license to operate unlimited funds transfer business or register as a fund transfer service provider that can provide a more limited service of fund transfers.

7 According to the Cabinet Order on Electronic Payment Instrument Handling Service Providers, property value which is issued without consideration and can be used only by persons specified by the issuer will be excluded from this item (Article 2(1)), and certain types of prepaid payment instruments that have high liquidity are included in this item (Article 2(2)).

8 The Cabinet Order on Electronic Payment Instrument Handling Service Providers stipulates that the commissioner of the FSA may designate specific cryptoassets as electronic payment instruments, taking into consideration circumstances such as the extent to which they may be used for the payment of consideration and the status of their use. This is a catch-all provision to regulate digital assets that have the same functions and risks as stablecoins, but no item has been designated by FSA so far.

1.2.3 Electronically Recorded Transferable Rights to Be Indicated on Securities, etc.

FIEA regulates so-called security tokens and apply regulations that are similar to those applied to shares and bonds. This regulation on security tokens was introduced in the 2019 amendment to address ICOs and STOs. Cabinet Office Order on Financial Instruments Business has introduced the new category, 'Electronically Recorded Transferable Rights to Be Indicated on Securities, etc.' (*denshikirokuiten yukasyoken hyojikenrito*) as what corresponds to so-called security tokens. 'Electronically Recorded Transferable Rights to Be Indicated on Securities, etc.' is defined as either (i) securities for which no paper certificates are issued,[9] (ii) 'specified electronically recorded monetary claims,'[10] or (iii) 'electronically recorded transferable rights,' (*denshikiroku itenkenri*)[11]

---

9 Typically, shares, bonds and notes for which no paper certificates are issued.

10 Electronically recorded monetary claims are claims issued under the Electronically Recorded Monetary Claim Act. Electronically recorded monetary claims are issued and transferred based on the electronic record managed by Electronic Monetary Claim Recording Institutions that are designated by the Prime Minister. At present, no electronically recorded monetary claims are specifically designated as securities under FIEA.

11 'Electronically recorded transferable rights' is the category introduced in the 2019 amendment to address ICOs. 'Electronically recorded transferable rights' are (i) beneficial interests in trust (including similar rights against a foreign party), (ii) membership rights of a general partnership company or limited partnership company (including similar rights against a foreign entity), or (iii) interests in certain types of collective investment schemes,.which are indicated on property value that is recorded on an electronic device or any other such object by electronic means and that can be transferred by using an electronic data processing system.

The criteria for determining whether rights are indicated on property value recorded on an electronic device, in other words, whether rights are represented on tokens, is not stipulated in law and remains unclear. Whether or not a right is 'Electronically recorded transferrable right' under FIEA, FSA expressed its view as follows: When the change of records on a ledger, which is managed by issuer, etc. and records the holder and quantity of rights, and the transfer of rights are carried out as a series of actions, then such rights will fall under the category of Electronically recorded transferrable rights. FSA also opines, when a blockchain that records the quantity of tokens transferred from one address to another is used, then the recorded quantity of tokens is considered as 'property value' in the above definition (FSA, Notes on the Financial Instruments and Exchange Act, etc. (Financial Instruments and Exchange Act Guidelines), 2-2-2.)

Electronically recorded transferrable rights are treated as Type I securities (securities with high liquidity and are subject to stricter regulations) under FIEA (FIEA distinguishes Type I and Type II securities). However, if (i) technical measures making it impossible to have persons other than some specifically listed investors such as qualified institutional investors acquire the relevant property value or to transfer that property value to such persons, or (ii) technical measures making impossible to transfer the relevant property value without an application from a person who holds said right and consent of the issuer of said right on each occasion, have been taken, such rights are excluded from 'electrically recorded and that are indicated on property value which can be transferred by using an electronic data processing system (limited to that which is recorded on an electronic device or any other object by electronic means.)[12] The basic idea of the regulation is such tokenized securities or rights should be subject to more strict regulation, because they may have more liquidity among many investors by using blockchain technology.[13]

1.2.4 Relationship among Categories

If a token meets the requirements of both cryptoassets and electronic payment instruments, then it is regulated as electronic payment instruments not as cryptoassets.[14] If a token meets the requirements of both cryptoassets and electronically recorded transferable rights to be indicated on securities, etc., then it is regulated as the latter.[15]

---

transferable rights.' (this is because liquidity of such rights is low so that strict regulation is considered unnecessary). The rights excluded from 'electronically recorded transferable rights' under the above exception are regulated as Type II securities (securities with lower liquidity and are subject to lighter regulation than that for Type I securities).

12 Article 6-3 of the Cabinet Order on Financial Instruments Business.

13 Report from the Study Group on Virtual Currency Exchange Services established in FSA (December 2018), 22–24 (in English translation available at https://www.fsa.go.jp/en/refer/councils/virtual-currency/20181221-1.pdf.).

14 Article 2(14)(i) of PSA.

15 Article 2(14) of PSA. On March 24, 2023, to respond to the requests from industries, FSA amended its Operational Guideline relating to Cryptoasset Exchanges, and added descriptions to clarify the interpretation regarding whether various tokens issued on the blockchain fall under the category of cryptoassets under PSA. Note ① in I-1-1 (i) of the Guideline explains tokens would not meet the definition of cryptoassets if the issuer has made it clear that the tokens are not intended to be used in relation to unspecified persons for the purpose of paying consideration or if, considering the price, quantity, technical characteristics, etc. of the tokens, their use for paying consideration to unspecified persons, if any, should be limited. The Operational Guideline is an internal guideline for staff members of FSA to perform administrative functions and is not legally binding. However, it has the nature of de facto regulatory code. The English translation of the Guideline is available at https://www.fsa.go.jp/common/law/guide/kaisya/e016.pdf (however, as of April 23, 2024, the newest available English translation is the June 2021 version and does not reflects the recent amendments.).

2 Regulatory Framework

2.1 *Overview of Regulations of Digital Assets*

Although there are no laws or regulations in Japan that generally prohibit the issuance or trading of cryptocurrencies in a broad sense, in order to provide services related to cryptoassets as business, they are subject to regulation as either 'cryptoassets' or 'electronic payment instruments' under PSA, or as security tokens under FIEA. In addition, businesses dealing with derivatives of cryptoassets are regulated under FIEA in a similar way as other financial derivatives, and wrongful acts and market manipulations of the cryptoassets market are prohibited under FIEA.

2.2 *Regulation of Cryptocurrencies*

2.2.1 History of the Development of Regulations

It was May 2016 that Japan first introduced the regulation of cryptocurrency.[16] The scope of the first version of the regulation was limited to the regulation of cryptocurrency exchanges for AML/CTF purpose to address global concerns on the use of cryptocurrencies for illegal activities and for customer protection purposes based on the experience of the bankruptcy of Mt. Gox in 2014. However, a serious hacking event of a cryptocurrency exchange occurred in January 2018, and the FSA set up the Study Group on Virtual Currency Exchange Services to address various issues relating to cryptocurrencies, such as the increase of speculative transactions in cryptocurrencies, the demands for higher customer protection and the emergence of ICOs and STOs. The Study Group published its Report in December 2018.[17]

Following the recommendations in the Report, in May 2019, substantial reforms of the regulations on cryptocurrencies was made, including: (i) the term 'virtual currencies' used in PSA was changed to 'cryptoassets;' (ii) regulation of cryptoasset exchanges was strengthened; (iii) new regulation on cryptoasset custodians was introduced; (iv) new regulation under FIEA on issuers and intermediaries of security tokens was introduced; (v) cryptoasset derivatives and margin transactions became subject to securities regulation and

---

16 About the regulation of cryptocurrencies introduced in May 2016, see Tetsuo Morishita, Recent Developments of Japanese laws and regulations on FinTech, in D. Arner, W. Wan, A. Godwin, W. Shen and E. Gibson (eds), *Research Handbook on Asian Financial Law*, Edward Elgar 2020, pp. 465–469.

17 The Report from the Study Group on Virtual Currency Exchange Services (December 2018) English translation of the Report is available at https://www.fsa.go.jp/en/refer/councils/virtual-currency/20181228.html.

margin regulation under FIEA; and (vi) the regulation of unfair transactions such as market manipulation became applicable to cryptoassets.

Further, in 2022, Japan introduced a new regulation of so-called 'stablecoin.' The regulation of cryptoassets was also amended to clarify the relationship between regulations on cryptoassets and regulations on stablecoins.

From October to December 2024, the Financial System Council's Working Group on Payment Systems at FSA discussed the revision of the legal system for cryptoassets and published its report in January 2025.[18]

2.2.2 Regulation of Crypto Exchanges

PSA defines 'cryptoassets exchange service' as carrying out one or more of the following four categories in the course of its trade: (i) purchase and sale of cryptoassets or exchange with other cryptoassets; (ii) intermediary, brokerage or agency services for the purchase/sale/exchange of cryptoassets; (iii) management of user's money in connection with (i) and (ii); and (iv) management of cryptoassets on behalf of other persons. No person may provide a cryptoassets exchange service without registration to the Prime Minister.[19] As the above definitions indicate, cryptoasset exchanges may themselves act as counterparties to their customers' transactions to buy and sell cryptoassets ((i) above), act as intermediaries in transactions between customers (ii) above), and provide custody services ((iv) above).FSA has expressed its view that a service provider is considered as providing custody services when it is in a position to transfer customers' cryptoassets without customers' involvement, for example by holding private keys sufficing to transfer the cryptoassets by itself.[20]

18 The Report from the Working Group on Payment Systems (January 2025) (in Japanese) is available at https://www.fsa.go.jp/singi/singi_kinyu/tosin/20250122.html. In the report, some improvements of the current regulation are proposed, such as (i) enabling FSA to order the holding of assets in Japan in the event of the insolvency of a cryptocurrency exchange or electronic payment service provider, etc., (ii) establishing a new regulatory category of brokerage business that only acts as an intermediary for cryptocurrency transactions without holding customer assets, and making it subject to lighter regulations than cryptoasset exchanges, for example, the minimum capital is not required, (iii) when issuing stablecoins using a trust, allowing a certain percentage of the trust assets to be invested in government bonds rather than deposits (see, 4.2), and (iv) continuing its policy of not allowing banks to issue stablecoins that can be transferred to unspecified parties (4.2).

19 Article 63-2 of PSA.

20 FSA, Operational Guideline for Crypto-assets Exchanges, I-1-2-2③. Under such interpretation, if a service provider and its customer each have a key, and if both keys are necessary to transfer cryptoassets (i.e. multisig), the service provider is not considered as conducting 'management of cryptoassets on behalf of another person.' In this case, the customer faces the risk that, if the service provider does not manage the private key in accordance with the customer's instructions, the customer will not be able to transfer its cryptoassets.

In the application for registration, the names of cryptoassets that an applicant plans to handle must be specified.[21] FSA checks if the cryptoassets listed in the application are appropriate from the perspective of AML/CFT, protection of customers and proper execution of services.[22] With this, FSA has the de facto power to control the cryptoassets that may be dealt with by cryptoasset exchanges in Japan, and there are cryptoassets that FSA has refused to permit handling by cryptoassets exchanges in Japan.

The minimum capital requirement for the application for registration is 10 million yen and the amount of net assets is not below zero.[23] While there is no restriction of other businesses that may be conducted by cryptoasset exchanges, there are various conduct regulations. Cryptoasset exchanges must take measures to securely manage their data processing system and customer information.[24] Advertisements by cryptoasset exchanges are required to clearly and accurately indicate the risk of price fluctuations, etc., in order to deter their customers from misperceiving risks and to discourage speculative transactions.[25] The cryptoasset exchanges are prohibited from making false or misleading representations when soliciting and entering into contracts, making misleading advertisements, making unsolicited and unsuitable promotions. Also, they are prohibited from transacting with their customers knowing that the customers will engage in unfair dealings or market manipulation.[26] Cryptoasset exchanges must explain the characteristics of cryptoassets and provide other important information before it enters into transactions with their customers.[27]

To protect customers' assets, cryptoasset exchanges must manage customers' cryptoassets and money separately from its own cryptoassets and money.[28] Customers' cryptoassets must be managed in separate wallets from the wallets

---

21 Article 63-3(VII) of PSA. When a cryptoasset exchange wants to handle a new cryptoasset, it is required to give prior notice to the Prime Minister.

22 FSA, Operational Guideline for Cryptoasset Exchanges, I-1-2-3.

23 Article 63-5(iii) of PSA, Article 9 (1) of the Cabinet Office Order on Cryptoasset Exchange Service Providers.

24 Article 63-8 of PSA.

25 Article 63-9-2 of PSA, Article 18 of the Cabinet Office Order on Cryptoasset Exchange Service Providers.

26 Article 63-9-3 of PSA, Article 19 and 20 of the Cabinet Office Order on Cryptoasset Exchange Service Providers.

27 Article 63-10 of PSA, Article 21 and 22 of the Cabinet Office Order on Cryptoasset Exchange Service Providers.

28 Article 63-11 of PSA, Article 26 and 27(1) of the Cabinet Office Order on Cryptoasset Exchange Service Providers.

where the exchanges' own cryptoassets are managed.[29] Customers' cryptoassets must be managed in mediums that are not constantly connected to the internet (cold-wallets), except to the minimum extent necessary for the smooth operation of the business (at most 5% of the total value).[30] To protect customers from the risk of hacking, cryptoasset exchanges must hold the cryptoasset of the same type and the same volume as the customer's cryptoassets held in a medium that is constantly connected to the internet (hot-wallet), and such cryptoassets shall be kept as their own cryptoassets but in separate cold-wallets from the wallets where their own cryptoassets are kept (such crypto-assets are called 'performance-guarantee cryptoassets', because they are kept to ensure the performance by cryptoasset exchanges even when cryptoassets kept in a hot-wallet are stolen by hackers).[31] Customers have a lien (right to receive payment in priority) over the cryptoassets segregated for customers and the performance guarantee cryptoassets to secure their claim for the transfer of cryptoassets against their cryptoasset exchanges.[32] Cryptoasset exchanges must reconcile the balance of cryptoassets deposited by customers and performance guarantee cryptoassets on their books with the amount of cryptoassets on the blockchain or other network every business day. If the balance of cryptoassets on the blockchain is less than the balance of cryptoassets on the books, they must analyze the cause of the deficiency and the deficiency must be resolved within five business days.[33]

In the regulation of cryptoasset exchanges, self-regulatory organizations play important roles by stipulating detailed self-regulatory rules, monitoring of members, providing guidance and recommendations, etc.[34] Japan Virtual and Crypto assets Exchanges Association is certified as a self-regulatory organization relating to cryptoasset exchanges business, and has enacted various regulations and guidelines, such as the regulation and guideline on handling of cryptoassets, the regulation and guideline on solicitation and advertisement

29 FSA, Operational Guideline for Cryptoasset Exchanges, II-2-3-2(3)①②.

30 Article 27 (2)(3) of Cabinet Office Order on Cryptoasset Exchange Service Providers.

31 Article 63-11-2 of PSA, Article 29 of the Cabinet Office Order on Crypto-asset Exchange Service Providers.

32 Article 63-19(2) of PSA.

33 FSA, Operational Guideline for Cryptoasset Exchanges, II-2-3-2(3)④.

34 Article 87 and 88 of PSA stipulate that the prime minister may certify an association as a self-regulatory organization ('certified association for payment service providers') that conduct various listed activities to ensure proper operation of cryptoassets exchange business by members and customer protection.

in cryptoasset exchange business, the regulation and guideline on AML/CFT in cryptoasset exchange business.[35]

Article 63-22 of PSA stipulates that foreign cryptoasset exchanges not registered in Japan must not conduct solicitation of people in Japan.[36] The administrative guidelines of FSA mention that the act of foreign cryptoasset exchanges posting advertisements on their website regarding cryptoasset exchange services constitutes the act of 'solicitation' in principle, except in cases where the website clearly shows that the service is not provided to persons in Japan or where the exchanges take necessary measures not to transact with persons in Japan, such as by checking the location of their customers.[37] Though there are no penalties for violations of Article 63-22, if a person provide cryptoasset exchange services without registration in Japan, the person who has committed the violation is subject to imprisonment for not more than three years or a fine of not more than three million yen, or both.[38] It is envisaged that if Japanese customers are actually solicited by a foreign entity, the effectiveness of the regulation will be ensured by FSA's notifying the home country authorities that the service provider is engaged in illegal activity in Japan, encouraging them to supervise the service provider. Even if Japan's regulations are applied to foreign service providers, it is not easy to make the regulations effective against foreign service providers that do not have a base in Japan. From February 2018 to November 2024, FSA has issued warnings to 21 foreign businesses for conducting cryptoasset exchange services to Japanese residents via the Internet without registering as Cryptoasset Exchange Service Providers in Japan,[39] but it seems to be difficult to get them to get meaningful responses.

---

35 Japan Virtual and Crypto assets Exchanges Association is certified also as a certified financial instruments business association under the FIEA relating to businesses relating to investment tokens.

36 Foreign cryptoasset exchanges in PSA are parties who have made registrations under foreign laws that are similar to PSA. So, a foreign party who has not made such registration is out of the scope of this provision. The reason why this provision limits the scope in this way is that, for those who are registered in a foreign country, there is room to correct illegal activities by approaching foreign authorities when they conduct illegal solicitation, but for those who are not under the supervision of foreign authorities, there is no way to actually stop illegal activities even if they conduct illegal activities under Japanese law, and such regulation is practically ineffective.

37 FSA, Operational Guideline for Cryptoasset Exchanges II-5-2.

38 Article 107 (XII) of PSA.

39 The list of foreign service providers to which FSA has issued warnings is available at https://www.fsa.go.jp/policy/virtual_currency/kasoutsuka_mutouroku.pdf.

2.2.3 Regulation of Cryptoasset Derivatives

Cryptoassets are listed as 'financial instruments' under FIEA,[40] and registration as a Type 1 Financial Instruments Business is required to engage in over-the-counter derivatives trading of cryptoassets as a business.[41]

Margin transactions of cryptoassets are regulated to avoid the situation that customers take excessive risks, and in the case of individual customers, the maximum leverage ratio is twice.[42]

2.2.4 Prohibition of Wrongful Acts and Market Manipulations, etc.

As in the case of transactions in other securities, FIEA prohibits (i) using wrongful means, schemes, or techniques in cryptoasset transactions, (ii) spreading rumors, using fraudulent means, committing assault, or using intimidation for the purpose of carrying out crypotasset transactions or for the purpose of causing a fluctuation in the market price of a cryptoasset, (iii) engaging in acts with the aim of misleading others into believing that cryptoasset transactions are thriving, or otherwise misleading others about the state of such transactions.[43] However, prohibition of insider trading is not applicable to cryptoasset transactions, because it was considered that what constitutes material facts having a significant influence on investors' decisions is unclear in relation to cryptoassets because of their variety and flexibility of product design.[44]

3 Regulation of Security Tokens

3.1 *Overview*

As mentioned in 1.2.3 above, the new regulation on security tokens was introduced in the amendment of FIEA in 2019. Electronically Recorded Transferable Rights to Be Indicated on Securities, etc' (*denshikirokuiten yukasyoken hyojikenrito*) ('ERTRBIS'). In essence, ERTRBIS refers to securities or interests in collective investment schemes that are represented by tokens recorded on

40 Article 2 (24) (III)-2 of FIEA.

41 Article 28 (1) (II) of FIEA. Operators of Type I Financial Instruments Business, who typically handle securities with high liquidity, are subject to stricter rules than operators of Type II Financial Instruments Business (Hiroyuki Kansau et.al, *Japanese Financial Instruments and Exchange Act*, Zaikeisohosha, 2018, at 634ff.).

42 Article 38(9) of FIEA, Article 117(1)(XXXXVII) and 117(41) of Cabinet Office Order on Financial Instruments Business.

43 Article 185-22, 23, 24 of FIEA.

44 The Report from the Study Group on Virtual Currency Exchange Services (December 2018), at 26.

a blockchain, etc. The new regulation does not regulate tokens, but the rights represented on tokens, and applies the same rules to the issuance and distribution of ERTRBIS as are applied to stocks and bonds.

3.2 *Regulation on Issuance of Security Token*

When offering ERTRBIS to the public, the same disclosure regulations apply as for public offerings of stocks and bonds. Additional disclosures are required to reflect the fact that they are represented by tokens, such as the technology used to record and transfer the tokens, the platform used, and the unique risks associated with the use of electronic tokens, such as hacking.[45] Also, when a white paper is used for solicitation, the white paper must be disclosed.[46]

3.3 *Regulation of Intermediaries Handling Security Tokens*

Regarding ERTRBIS, only Type I Financial Instruments Business Operators may provide intermediary services such as solicitation, sales and custody.[47] FIEA stipulates various regulations applied to Financial Instruments Business Operators such as establishment of an appropriate operational control system, duty of sincerity to customers, regulation of advertisements, delivery of documents explaining the transactions, making an alternative dispute resolution mechanism available to customers, prohibition of misleading explanations, prohibition of compensation for customers' losses, the principle of suitability, and segregation of customers' assets.[48] In addition, security tokens deposited by customers shall be kept in cold wallets except to the minimum extent necessary for the smooth operation of the business.[49]

In addition to such laws and regulations, Japan Security Token Offering Association, as a certified self-regulatory organization, stipulates various rules relating to handling of ERTRBIS by member companies.

---

45 Form 6-5, Note (5)c, (26)c etc., Cabinet Office Order on Disclosure of Information on Regulated Securities.

46 Article 12 (1)(I)(f) of the Cabinet Office Order on Disclosure of Information on Regulated Securities.

47 Hiroyuki Kansaku et.al, Japanese Financial Instruments and Exchange Act (Zaikeisyohosha, 2018), at 634ff.

48 From Article 35-3 to 40-3 of FIEA.

49 Article 136 (1) (V) (VI) of the Cabinet Office Order on Financial Instruments Business. IV-3-6 of Comprehensive Guidelines for Supervision of Financial Instruments Business Operators, etc. stipulates points to check appropriateness of the business of Financial Instruments Business Operators that are dealing with ERTRBIS. English translation of the Guideline is available at https://www.fsa.go.jp/common/law/guide/kinyushohin_eng.pdf. See, at 208ff.

4 Regulation of Stablecoins

4.1 *Overview*

As mentioned in 1.2.1, stablecoins linked to fiat currencies are excluded from the definition of cryptoassets in PSA, and not regulated as cryptoassets under PSA. Prior to the amendment of BA and PSA in 2022, the issuance of such stablecoins were considered to fall under the category of fund transfers. In Japan, only banks licensed under BA and fund transfer service providers registered under PSA, may provide fund transfer services. Therefore, only banks and fund transfer service providers were allowed to issue such stablecoins linked to fiat currencies under the Japanese law. Regarding the intermediaries handling such stablecoins linked to fiat currencies, it was unclear how they would be regulated.

To develop the regulations on stablecoins, as mentioned in 1.2.2, the 2022 amendment of PSA introduced a new concept of 'electronic payment instruments', which corresponds stablecoins, and added the third type of issuing stablecoin, with which other parties than banks and fund transfer service providers may issue stablecoins by using a special trust scheme. Also, the 2022 amendment has introduced the regulatory framework for intermediaries dealing with stablecoins.

4.2 *Regulation of Issuance of Stablecoins*

Theoretically, electronic payment instruments may be issued by banks, fund transfer service providers and special trust companies[50] When a bank or a fund transfer service provider issues stablecoin to its customers, the customers' monetary claims on its bank deposit or on the funds provided by the customer to fund transfer service providers for the purpose of fund transfer is considered represented by the stablecoins. So, it is assumed that such monetary claim on the deposit or the fund kept by the fund transfer service provider will be transferred linked to the transfer of the stablecoin. In principle, redemption is ensured even if the issuer fails, when issued by banks, through bank prudential regulations and a deposit insurance system for deposits, and when issued by fund transfer service providers, through the requirement that

50 Digital moneys issued by banks or fund transfer service providers, for which technical measures are taken to allow transfers only to persons who have been checked by the issuer for AML/CFT purpose, and to require the issuer's consent or other involvement each time it is transferred, are not regulated as electronic payment instruments, because they cannot be used against unspecified persons (Operational Guideline for Electronic Payment Instrument Business Providers, I-1-1② note 1.).

fund transfer service providers must deposit to the official depository or trust the full amount of funds received from customers but not used for transfers in accordance with PSA or enter into a guarantee agreement for such amount with banks.[51] However, FSA has expressed a negative view on banks issuing permissionless type stablecoins because it means banks may owe debts to unspecified and unknown persons and such a situation may be incompatible with the sound and proper management of banks' business.[52]

The 2022 amendment of PSA introduced the third category of issuing stablecoin using trusts by introducing a new provision about 'specified trust beneficial interests'.[53] A specified trust beneficial interest is a beneficial interest in a money trust that is indicated on a property value that can be transferred using an electronic data processing system (i.e. token), and in which the entire amount of money accepted by the trustee under the trust agreement is managed by a savings account.[54] This specified trust beneficial interest corresponds to a claim on fund kept by a fund transfer service provider in the case of stablecoins issued by fund transfer service providers. The company issuing such specified trust beneficiary rights is called a specified trust company, and a specified trust company can issue stablecoins using the specified trust beneficiary rights mechanism without a banking license or fund transfer business registration. Unless the specified trust company receives special permission, the amount of a stablecoin issued for one customer cannot exceed 1 million yen.[55]

---

51 Article 43-45 of PSA.

52 FSA's Response to the Public Consultation concerning electronic payment instruments on May 26, 2023, Response No. 8 (https://www.fsa.go.jp/news/r4/sonota/20230526/01.pdf). Regarding bank deposit, FSA expressed its view that deposit claims that can be transferred electronically are not considered as electronic payment instruments if the necessary check under the Act on Prevention of Transfer of Criminal Proceeds is conducted in each transfer and if the issuer's consent is required in each transfer, because such deposit can't be purchased from and sold to an unspecified person. FSA, Operational Guideline for Electronic Payment Instrument Handling Service Providers, note on 1-1-1 ②.

53 Article 2(9) of PSA.

54 Article 3 of the Cabinet Order on Electronic Payment Instruments Business Operators stipulates that all trust assets need to be kept in an account such that a beneficiary can demand repayment at any time. As mentioned in footnote 18, the Report from the Working Group on Payment Systems in January 2025 propose to relax this regulation and allow a part of the money be invested in government bonds.

55 Article 36-2(1)(2), 37-2(2), 40-2(1) of PSA and Article 12-2(1) of Order for Enforcement of the Payment Services Act.

4.3 *Regulation of Intermediaries of Stablecoins*

The 2022 amendment introduced regulations on intermediaries of stablecoins. Such intermediaries are called *'denshi kessaito toriatsukaigyo'* (electronic payment handling service provider) (EPHSP) in BA,[56] and '*denshi kessaisyudanto torihikigyo*' (electronic payment instruments handling service provider) ('EPIHSP) in PSA.

According to Article 2(10) of PSA, EPIHSP is a party who carries out one of the following businesses:

a. purchase and sale of electronic payment instruments or exchange of an electronic payment instrument with another electronic payment instrument;
b. intermediary, brokerage or agency services for above (a);
c. management of electronic payment instruments on behalf of another person; or
d. at the request of a fund transfer service provider, to enter into an agreement with a customer who has entered into a contract for continuous use of the fund transfer services with the fund transfer service provider about the following operations relating to the fund that the fund transfer service provider has received from the customer on behalf of the fund transfer service provider by means of an electronic data processing system; (a) to transfer the fund, and to decrease the amount of the claim relating to the fund transfer service equivalent to the amount of the fund transfer; and (b) to increase the amount of the claim equivalent to the amount of funds received through a fund transfer.

Article 2(17) of BA has the definition of EPHSP, whose content is similar to above (d). These provisions are complicated, but in essence, they divide the business of intermediaries regarding stablecoins into (i) the business of buying, selling, brokering, and custody of stablecoins as in the cryptoasset exchange business, and (ii) providing operation of transferring stablecoins on behalf of the issuer by decreasing the amount of sender's claims represented by the stablecoin and increasing the amount of recipient's claim represented by the stablecoin.[57]

---

56 Article 2(17) of BA. However, as mentioned in 4.2, FSA has not allowed banks to issue stablecoins.

57 This is based on the same legal concept that when remitting money using a bank deposit, the amount of the deposit claim is reduced by debiting funds from the remitter's deposit account, and the amount of the deposit claim is increased by crediting the receiver's deposit account.

Similar regulations as applied to crypto asset exchanges are applied to EPIHSP.[58] EPIHSP is prohibited from accepting money deposits from customers, and it must enter into a contract with the issuer of electronic payment instruments that stipulates how to share their liability to compensate for damage incurred by users of the electronic payment instruments, etc.[59]

As in the case of cryptoassets exchanges, applications for registration need to specify names of electronic payment instruments they would like to handle.[60]

One of the hot issues in the 2022 amendment was how to handle stablecoins issued by parties in foreign countries. Before the 2022 amendment, it had been the practice that Japanese cryptoasset exchanges could not handle foreign stablecoins, because FSA didn't allow cryptoasset exchanges to handle stablecoins issued by issuers in foreign countries, for concerns about the risk of AML/CFT and to protect users in the event of the issuer's insolvency. However, in response to the voices of industries arguing that the handling of stablecoin issued by foreign operators should be allowed, after the 2022 amendment, Japanese EPIHSPs may handle foreign stablecoins, which are equivalent to electronic payment instruments issued under foreign laws, under the following conditions: (i) the issuer of the foreign stablecoin must have made the necessary registrations in the relevant foreign country; (ii) the issuer must properly manage the assets necessary for the redemption of the foreign stablecoin in accordance with the relevant foreign law; (iii) the issuer can suspend trading of the foreign stablecoin if the foreign stablecoin is suspected of being used for a crime; (iv) the EPIHSP promises to redeem the foreign stablecoin from the customer in the amount of the redemption obligation if the issuer is unable to fulfil the redemption obligation, etc., and the EPIHSP preserves the funds necessary for such redemption; and (v) the EPIHSP must ensure that both the amount of foreign stablecoin that will transfer in each fund transfer and the amount of the same that it will manage for a customer but not be used for immediate fund transfer will not exceed 1 million yen.[61]

---

58 Article 62-10 (management of information security), 62-11 (guidance of entrusted parties), 62-12 (measure of customers protection), 62-14 (management of users' property), 62-16 (contract with ADR service provider) of PSA.

59 Article 62-13 and 62-16 of PSA.

60 Article 62-4(8) of PSA.

61 Article 30(v)–(vi) of the Cabinet Order on Electronic Payment Instruments Business Operators. 1 million yen is the maximum amount that type II fund transfer service providers may handle. Under PSA, there are three types of fund transfer service providers. Type I has no limitation of the amount that it may handle but is subject to strict regulations. Type II is the standard type that can handle up to 1 million yen. Type III can handle 50 thousand yen or less and is subject to lighter regulations.

5 Private Law on Cryptoassets

5.1 *Legal Nature of Cryptoassets*

Unlike regulatory law, which has detailed provisions in place, the current state of private law regarding cryptoassets remains unclear. Various views have been expressed on the private law nature of cryptoassets and transactions of cryptoassets in court cases and by academics and practitioners.

5.1.1 Court Cases on Cryptoassets

First, there are several court decisions relating to legal nature of cryptoassets and cryptoasset transactions.

(1) Judgment of Tokyo District Court, August 5, 2015 (LEX/DB25541521)[62]

In this case, upon the bankruptcy of Mt. Gox, a cryptocurrency exchange incorporated under Japanese laws, a customer who had deposited bitcoins with Mt. Gox brought a suit against the bankruptcy trustee, claiming that the deposited bitcoins were owned by him and seeking restitution based on a right of segregation.[63] The judgement stated that in order to be the object of ownership, it must be a tangible object as well as exclusively controllable. The court denied the right of restitution based on ownership, stating that bitcoin is not a tangible object and is not exclusively controllable. The court opined that considering the mechanism of bitcoin, that is, no specific amount of the holder is recorded on the blockchain, but the amount held by a party is calculated from the record of all transactions, and such records are created with the contribution of miners, the holder of private key does not have the exclusive control of bitcoin.

(2) Judgment of Tokyo District Court, January 31, 2018, Hanrei Jiho No. 2387, p. 108[64] In the bankruptcy proceeding of Mt. Gox, a customer filed an action to oppose the assessment of its bankruptcy claim by the trustee. The court stated, 'although the legal nature of the rights of holders of bitcoins (electromagnetic

62 The author discussed this judgement in Stacy Steele and Tetsuo Morishita, Lessons from Mt Gox: practical considerations for a virtual currency insolvency, in D.Arner, W. Wan, A. Godwin, W. Shen and E. Gibson (eds), *Research Handbook on Asian Financial Law*, Edward Elgar 2020, 490ff.

63 Article 62 of the Bankruptcy Act stipulates, 'the commencement of bankruptcy proceedings shall not affect a right to segregate, from the bankruptcy estate, property that does not belong to the bankrupt.'

64 The author discussed this case in Stacy Steele and Tetsuo Morishita, Lessons from Mt Gox: practical considerations for a virtual currency insolvency, in in D.Arner, W. Wan, A. Godwin, W. Shen and E. Gibson (eds), *Research Handbook on Asian Financial Law*, Edward Elgar 2020, 479, 488ff.

records) is not necessarily clear, at least when bitcoins are recognized as virtual currency, it is understood that they have aspects as claims that require the similar treatment as currency,' and such claims were understood to be transferred when bitcoins (electromagnetic records) were transferred using an electronic data processing system, by their nature.[65]

(3) Judgment of Tokyo District Court, December 26, 2018 LEX/DB25558193

A sales agreement for bitcoin was concluded between a dining bar and an individual, and the buyer sought cancellation of the sales agreement and return of the purchase price because the seller did not deliver bitcoin despite the buyer had paid for it. The court held that, although the sales agreement for bitcoin was concluded, the purchase agreement was cancelled due to the seller's delay in performance and ordered the return of the purchase price as the fulfilment of the obligation of each party to restore the other party to its original condition.[66]

(4) Judgment of Tokyo District Court, December 20, 2019, Kinyu Shoji Hanrei No. 1590, p. 41

A customer who had deposited bitcoin with a virtual currency exchange claimed that the contract between the customer and the exchange was a contract for deposit of fungibles or a contract equivalent thereto, and that Bitcoin Gold that branched off from bitcoin as a result of the hard fork belonged to the customer because it was the same deposited property or the fruit of the same deposit as the original bitcoin, and requested to transfer Bitcoin Gold to the customer. The court didn't mention the legal nature of bitcoin, but rejected the customer's claim stating that there was no express agreement between the customer and the exchange regarding how cryptoassets generated as a result of hard fork should be treated, and Bitcoin Gold was not listed as the cryptoassets that the exchange would deal with. Also, the judgment opined that there was no implied agreement that Bitcoin Gold should be allocated to the customer, considering the following facts: the exchange had not developed necessary system to deal with Bitcoin Gold, it had not made necessary registration under PSA to deal with Bitcoin Gold, it had announced that Bitcoin Gold might not be allocated to customers when risk management was insufficient, and it was the exchange who had made decisions regarding the allocation of cryptoassets

65 Under Japanese law, in order to ensure the high level of liquidity of cash, the legal principle that the person in possession of cash is treated as the owner has been recognised.

66 Article 545 (1) of the Civil Code stipulates 'if one of the parties exercises the right to cancel, each party assumes an obligation to restore the other party to that other party's original state[...]'.

created as a result of hard fork in the previous cases such as Ethereum Classic and Bitcoin Cash. .

(5) Judgement of Tokyo District Court, February 21, 2020 (LEX/DB 25584768)

This is a case in which the plaintiff, alleging that he was defrauded of bitcoin by being deceived into investing in an ICO, sought damages based on torts. The defendant argued that 'bitcoin is not an object of ownership and does not constitute a property right other than ownership, as it is merely a property value that is convertible into cash. As bitcoins are identified through the distributed management of transaction data by blockchain technology and there is no specific management body, there is no concrete agreement between the parties concerned, and they do not constitute a claim by a person against another person. Furthermore, bitcoin only has the possibility of exchange with currency, it does not realize any value in itself, and it cannot be considered a legally protected interest.' The judgment held that 'according to the provisions on 'cryptoassets' in PSA, virtual currency is defined as a property value that serves as a means of payment, and is understood to have the nature of exchangeability with legal tender and to be traded with others, such as buying, selling or exchanging. Therefore, rights to demand the return of virtual currency from virtual currency exchanges are understood to be rights or legal interests with property value, and those whose rights are infringed may claim damages in tort against the infringer.'

(6) Judgment of Tokyo District Court, March 2, 2020, Kinyu Shoji Hanrei No. 1598, p. 42

A customer who had deposited Bitcoins with a virtual currency exchange claimed that the bitcoins were stolen due to unauthorized access and sought damages for breach of a contract for bailment of bitcoins. The court ruled that a bailment is a contract to keep a certain thing in custody,[67] and since bitcoin is not a tangible thing, no contract for bailment was formed.

(7) Judgment of Tokyo District Court, July 31, 2020, Kinyu Shoji Hanrei No. 1605, p. 40

A customer who had an account at a cryptoasset exchange sent bitcoin from his bitcoin address to its account at the cryptoasset exchange. The account agreement said that users hold all responsibility for sending cryptoassets that are not dealt with by the exchange to users' accounts. The customer sent bitcoin from his bitcoin address to his account at the exchange, but that information to send the bitcoin also contained the transfer of USD Tether to its account.

67 Article 657 of the Civil Code stipulates, 'a bailment becomes effective if one of the parties asks the other party to keep a certain thing in custody, and the other party gives consent to keeping it in custody.'

Because the exchange did not have a system to handle Tether, the customer was not able to withdraw or transfer the Tether unless the exchange made a system improvement, which the exchange refused. The customer requested the return of the Tether arguing that there was a quasi-bailment agreement for Tether or benevolent intervention in another's business,[68] or unjust enrichment. The court dismissed the customer's claim and mentioned that there is no quasi-bailment agreement or benevolent intervention in another's business considering the exchange did not list Tether as one of the cryptoassets it was handling, and that it was not able to handle it unless it made the necessary system improvement. Also, the judgment opined that, considering that the exchange itself was not able to dispose of Tether without the system improvement, no unjust enrichment existed for the exchange.

(8) Judgment of Tokyo District Court, June 28, 2021 (LEX/DB25601053)

A person lent 200 bitcoins to two individuals agreeing that the bitcoin must be returned by the specified dates, but the two persons failed to return the bitcoin. The lender demanded the return of the bitcoin arguing that there was a loan for consumption contract.[69] The court opined, 'bitcoin, which is a virtual currency, is an intangible information, but it has property value and can be transferred under the control of a private key. Since loan for consumption contracts under the Civil Code are understood to transfer ownership of things by delivering the subjects 'money or other thing' (Civil Code Article 587), it cannot be said that bitcoin, which is an intangible object and not a subject of ownership, falls under 'money or other things' as defined in this article. However, in light of the above-mentioned nature of bitcoin, when the bitcoin lending agreement is concluded and the transfer of bitcoin has been made, ..., there are no grounds to deny legally binding effect to the agreement by restricting the principle of private autonomy.... PSA does not define the private legal nature of virtual currency (cryptoassets), but Article 2, Paragraph 5, Item 1 of PSA is understood to naturally assume that a contract of sale and purchase can be validly concluded for virtual currency (cryptoassets), including bitcoin.'[70]

(9) Judgment of Tokyo District Court, August 24, 2023 (LEX/DB25612386)

---

68 Article 697 of the Civil Code stipulates that a person that has begun to manage a business for another person without being obligated to do so must manage that business, in accordance with the nature of the business, in the way that best suits the interests of the principal.

69 Article 587 of Civil Code stipulates 'a loan for consumption becomes effective when a first party receives money or any other thing from a second party, having promised to return a thing of the same type, quality, and quantity.'

70 In conclusion, the court dismissed the claim of the lender because it was delivered for illegal cause (Article 708 of Civil Code).

As a result of the cancellation of the business transfer agreement, it was disputed whether the defendant had an obligation to return the cryptoasset called TAVITTCOIN, which had been transferred from the plaintiff to the defendant based on the business transfer agreement, to the plaintiff as part of the obligation to restore the original state. The defendant argued that, due to the nature of cryptocurrency, it was impossible to return the crypto asset itself, but the court rejected the defendant's argument, stating that it was contradictory to claim that it was impossible to return the crypto asset itself while also accepting that it had property value, and ordered the defendant to return the TAVITTCOIN. The plaintiff also argued that the defendant should pay compensation if he was unable to return the TAVITTCOIN, but the court ruled that the amount of compensation should be calculated based on the market price at the time of the conclusion of the oral proceedings, and as the TAVITTCOIN had no market value at the time of the conclusion of the oral proceedings and had already lost its property value, the claim for compensation was not granted.

None of these cases made the legal nature of cryptoassets clear. However, instead of saying that cryptoassets are not entitled to any legal protection, their basic stance is to recognise that cryptoassets have property value, and to protect the rights and safety of transactions related to cryptoassets in the same way as transactions of other property. Then, in cases where a solution that takes into account the unique characteristics of crypto assets, which presuppose a certain technical mechanism, is required, it seems that the terms and conditions set by the crypto asset exchange operator are respected. For example, case (4) and case (7) did not enter into the legal nature of cryptoassets but dealt the cases as a matter of contract rather than a matter of property law.

5.1.2 Private Law Analysis under Japanese Law

Currently, most individuals who own cryptoassets do not own their own wallets and manage their own private keys, but rather open accounts with intermediaries such as cryptoasset exchanges, and these exchanges manage the private keys for their individual (or collective) customers. When considering the rights to cryptoassets, those directly participating in blockchain network (in which case the legal nature of cryptoassets and the rights of holders become issues) and those holding cryptoassets through exchanges (in which case, in addition to the legal nature of cryptoassets and the rights of holders, contractual relationships between the holders and the exchanges become issues) should be distinguished. In the latter scenario, even if a customer and an exchange understand that there is a sales contract or an exchange holds cryptoassets in bailment on behalf of its customer, if the cryptoassets cannot be the object of ownership, then the customer can have no ownership in the cryptoassets.

On the other hand, even if cryptoassets can be the object of ownership, if the relationship between the customer and the exchange is like a bank deposit, where the exchanges are allowed to invest the deposited cryptoassets and is only required to return the same quantity of cryptoassets to the customer, the customer only has a personal claim against the exchange for the return of the quantity of cryptoassets, but not the ownership of the cryptoasset.

The majority view in Japan on the legal character of cryptoassets starts from the basic understanding that, under Japanese law, the subject matter of property rights is limited to things, and, under Japanese law, things are limited to tangible objects;[71] therefore, cryptoassets that are not tangible objects cannot be subject to property rights such as ownership rights.

Some typical approaches of academics and practitioners are as follows: (i) Fact Approach: The possession of cryptoassets is nothing more than a factual situation in which a person has exclusive control over the ability to transfer cryptoassets associated with an address to another address through exclusive control of the private key, and does not entail any rights or legal relationships; (ii) Property Law Approach: Although cryptoassets are not things, they are property with proprietary value, and the legal principles of property rights that are applied to tangible properties should be applied mutatis mutandis to their attribution and transfer; (iii) Network Approach: Transaction rules for cryptoassets should be primarily governed by the rules agreed upon by the participants in the network, typically implemented by codes and programs.

In the author's view, the fact that cryptoassets are traded as property in real world should be respected and, it is not appropriate to apply a legal treatment that deviates from the common sense of business dealings. From such a perspective, the above judgments (3) (5) and (8) make sense. Even if it is difficult to treat intangible information and data in general in the same way as tangible things, unlike information in general, the exclusive control of cryptoassets is practically possible through the use of a private key. Thus, although cryptoassets are not things, they should be treated as property with economic value, and the legal principles of property rights that apply to tangible property should be applied mutatis mutandis to the attribution and transfer of cryptoassets. Blockchain records are important evidence when considering the attribution and transfer of rights. Although the rules of property law should be applied to the attribution and transfer of cryptoassets, the concrete rules of property law differ depending on the nature and function of the tangible objects (property law applied to bank notes and coins, security certificates and

71 Such opinions rely on Article 86 of the Civil Code stipulating, 'the term 'things' as used in this Code means tangible objects.'

general goods may differ reflecting their nature and function). Currently, most transactions of cryptoassets are for investment purposes, and in such situations the property law as applied to the attribution and transfer of certificates (immaterial or dematerialised) of investment securities should be applied to the attribution and transfer of cryptoassets. On the other hand, if cryptoassets perform the same function as currency, it is desirable to apply the property law as applied to bank notes and coins, i.e. that the person in possession of the object (a banknote) always has ownership rights over the object. The above judgment (2) seems to imply this idea. However, considering that bitcoin are usually used for investment purposes, it was basically inappropriate to apply the rules of property law for currencies to bitcoin.

5.1.3 Trust of Cryptoassets

Notwithstanding the above-mentioned uncertainty as to the legal character of cryptoassets, there is no dispute that cryptoassets can be subject to a trust. It is widely accepted that, under Japanese Trust Act, property may be subject to a trust if it meets the following four requirements: (i) can be estimated to monetary value; (ii) has positive value; (iii) can be transferable from the settlor; and (iv) can be identifiable.[72] Cryptoassets are considered to satisfy these requirements.

5.1.4 Collateralization of Cryptoassets

Because of the unclarity regarding the legal nature of cryptoassets, it is also unclear whether a legally valid pledge can be established over cryptoassets.[73] There are services that provide loans to individuals and corporations by using cryptoassets as collateral. Although it is not clear what kind of contracts are concluded and what kind of legal structure is adopted in such services, in many cases users are required to send cryptoassets to an address specified by the service provider as a method of collateral taking.[74] It seems to be the typical legal arrangement that a secured creditor accepts the deposit of cryptoassets from a party granting security interest and assume the obligation to return the cryptoassets to the party granting security interest, and when executing

72 Hiroto Dogauchi, Shintaku Ho (Trust Law, 2nd ed., Yuhikaku 2022, 35 (in Japanese)

73 Regardless of such unclarity of legal nature of cryptoassets, holders of cryptoassets through intermediaries may pledge claims against cryptoasset exchanges.

74 Tetsuo Morishita, Angoshisan no Tanpo (Collateralization of Cryptoassets) in Dogauchi et al. (eds), *Gendai no Tanpoho* (Law on Collateral in the modern age) (Yuhikaku, 2022) (in Japanese).

the security interest is necessary, the secured creditor offsetting the obligation to return the deposited cryptoassets against their secured claim.[75]

5.1.5 Attachment of Cryptoassets

There are two types of attachment of cryptoassets: attachment of cryptoassets held in un-hosted wallets by those who manage cryptoassets themselves, and attachment of cryptoassets deposited with cryptoasset exchanges by those who hold cryptoassets through cryptoasset exchanges.

Though there are no reported cases or express statutory provisions, it is considered that the cryptoassets in un-hosted wallets may be attached through the procedure of 'Compulsory Execution against any Other Property Right' (Article 167) under the Civil Execution Act.[76] Even if an order of seizure is issued on a cryptoasset, if the private key information is not available, the cryptoasset cannot be transferred or changed into cash. It is argued that attachment creditors may request a debtor to deliver secret keys based on the legal principle regarding the delivery of deed in the case of attachment of personal claims.[77]

For cryptoassets deposited with cryptoasset exchanges, it is usual to seize claims that customers have against exchanges for the transfer of the cryptoassets, and there are cases that have allowed such seizure.[78]

5.1.6 Inheritance of Cryptoassets

Under Article 896 of the Civil Code, from the time of commencement of inheritance, an heir shall succeed blanket rights and duties attached to the property of the decedent. There is no dispute that cryptoassets are subject to

---

75 Fumiaki Sano, *Shokai Dejitaru Kinyu Homu* (Detailed Digital Financial Law) (Kinyu Zaisei Jijo Kenkyukai, 2021), p. 369 (in Japanese).

76 Article 167(1) of Civil Execution Act stipulates that compulsory execution against a property right other than real property, a vessel, movables or a claim shall be governed by the rules of execution against a claim, except as otherwise provided. In case of execution against a claim, execution is conducted by issuing an order of seizure, prohibiting the obligor from collecting or otherwise disposing the claim and prohibit the third party obligor from providing performance to the obligor (Article 145 (1) of Civil Execution Act).

77 Article 148 of Civil Execution Act stipulates, 'when a deed exists for a claim pertaining to a seizure, the obligor shall deliver such deed to the obligee effecting a seizure.'

78 On the attachment of cryptoassets, Yukinao Takamatsu, Minjishikko niokeru Angoshisan no Toriatsukai to Gutaiteki Taio (Handling and Practice in Civil Execution on Cryptoassets) in Amane Hori ed, *Angoshisan no Hoteki Seithitsu to Jitsumu* (Legal Issues and Practice of Cryptocurrency) (2021) (in Japanese), at 53–56.

inheritance.[79] The National Tax Agency has announced that inheritance tax is imposed when cryptoassets are acquired from a decedent by inheritance.[80]

5.1.7 Contractual Duties of Cryptoasset Exchanges

The relationship between cryptoasset exchanges and customers depends on the contract between the two parties. In January 26, 2018, a cryptoasset exchange CoinCheck was hacked and cryptoasset NEM that was worth 58 billion yen was stolen. In March, the exchange announced that it would make monetary compensation to all customers who held NEM in their account based on the quantity so held.[81] The exchange suspended its operation of various cryptoassets more than a month and customers were not able to transfer/dispose of their cryptoasset for that period. There are several court cases in which customers claimed damages, etc.

For example, in the judgement of Tokyo District Court, December 21, 2020, Kinyu Shoji Hanrei No. 1612, p. 42, customers argued that the exchange breached its duty to keep customers' NEM by using cold wallets and multi-sig. The judgement ruled that, even if the defendant owed a duty of care to securely manage the cryptoasset, the defendant did not owe a duty to the plaintiffs to manage NEMs in cold wallets and use multi-sig setting at the time of hacking considering the market practice and the standard of the technologies of the time of hacking.[82]

In the judgment of Tokyo District Court, February 4, 2019, Kinyu Homujijo No. 2128, p.88, a customer argued that the suspension of the operation was a breach of contract. The court rejected this argument, for such suspension was allowed according to the provisions in the term of use stipulating, 'in the event of theft of its assets by hacking or other means, the exchange may suspend or discontinue providing all or part of the service without prior notice to each

79 Hiroyuki Fujitake, Sozokuji niokeru Angoshisan no Toriatukai to Gutaiteki Taio (Handling and Practice in Inheritance of Cryptoassets) in Amane Hori ed, *Angoshisan no Hoteki Seithitsu to Jitsumu* (Legal Issues and Practice of Cryptocurrency) (2021) (in Japanese), at 59.

80 National Tax Agency, Angoshisan nikansuru Toriatukai nitsuite (Joho) (Handling of Cryptoassets) (December 22, 2022) (in Japanese) (https://www.nta.go.jp/publication/pamph/pdf/virtual_currency_faq_03.pdf) at 38.

81 https://corporate.coincheck.com/press/dG-nDV-c.

82 There are some cases that made the same ruling such as Tokyo District Court, October 30, 2020 (LEX/DB25586315), Tokyo District Court, March 8, 2021 (LEX/DB25588916),Tokyo District Court, March 11, 2021 (LEX/DB25588624), Tokyo District Court, August 24, 2021 (LEX/DB25601386). However, as mentioned above, the current regulation requests exchanges to use cold wallets as far as possible.

customer. The exchange shall not be liable for any loss or damage incurred by each customer as a result of this action.'

In the judgement of Tokyo District Court, April 27, 2022, LEX/DB25605502, some customers who received the compensation from the exchange filed a lawsuit against the exchange, demanding that the cryptoassets held in their accounts at the time of the hacking be sent to other accounts. The exchange argued that the above compensation extinguished its obligation to transmit the customers' cryptoassets in accordance with the customers' instructions. The court ruled that the above compensation was made unilaterally by the exchange without the customer's consent, and that the compensation did not extinguish the obligation to transmit the cryptographic assets.

Though it is not a case concerning cryptoasset exchanges, there is a case in which how damages should be calculated. In the judgement of Tokyo District Court on June 22, 2022 (LEX/DB25606388), a person who entrusted cryptoassets instructed a person who was entrusted the cryptoassets to dispose the cryptoassets, but the latter person did not follow the instruction of the former and was liable for breach of contract. The plaintiff argued that the damages should be calculated at the highest value of the cryptoassets since the plaintiff gave the instruction and up to the date of the conclusion of the oral argument of the litigation. However, the judgment used the market price on the date of the conclusion of the oral argument to calculate the amount of damages. It reasoned that to award damages at the interim maximum amount, there must be circumstances in which the plaintiff certainly was able to obtain the equivalent of the conversion at the interim maximum amount and the foreseeability of the defendant with regard to this, but there was neither such circumstances nor the foreseeability.

5.1.8 Insolvency of Cryptoasset Exchanges

Cryptoasset exchanges are subject to ordinary insolvency proceedings such as bankruptcy and civil rehabilitation. One specific example is the bankruptcy proceedings initiated on April 24, 2014 with respect to Mt. Gox.[83] In the Mt. Gox bankruptcy proceedings, one of the important issues was the conversion rate of the claim for bitcoin into Japanese yen and high volatility of the price of bitcoin. Under Japanese law, the amount of non-monetary claims such as claims for the return of bitcoin shall be evaluated at the commencement of

83 Various issues relating to the Mt. Gox Insolvency Proceeding were discussed in Stacy Steele and Tetsuo Morishita, Lessons from Mt Gox: practical considerations for a virtual currency insolvency, in D. Arner, W. Wan, A. Godwin, W. Shen and E. Gibson (eds), *Research Handbook on Asian Financial Law*, Edward Elgar 2020, 479.

insolvency proceedings. While there was a huge increase in the value of the bankruptcy estate because of the rise of the price of bitcoin, the amount of the bankruptcy claims was fixed with the conversion rate at the time of the commencement of the bankruptcy proceeding, and creditors would have been received only a monetary dividend evaluated at the very low price of bitcoin. As a result, it was expected that substantial assets would have remained even after the bankruptcy claims had been fully repaid. If so, such assets would have been received by the CEO of Mt Gox, who substantially held a large portion of Mt Gox shares. Therefore, some creditors filed a petition for the commencement of civil rehabilitation proceeding, which was granted by the court on June 22, 2018, and the case was transferred from bankruptcy to civil rehabilitation. Because the conversion rate at the time of the commencement of civil rehabilitation was much higher, the amount of the creditors' claims in Japanese yen substantially increased.

Another important issue was whether customers would be entitled to receive dividend in bitcoins not in cash. While there are divergent views on whether it is possible to pay dividends in non-monetary form in insolvency proceedings, it is generally considered it possible if creditors agree to receive dividends in non-monetary form and the court approves. In fact, in Mt Gox"s civil rehabilitation proceedings, creditors can choose whether to be paid in Japanese Yen, in bitcoin or in Bitcoin Cash. Although there are legal difficulties in calculating the dividend in crypto assets and paying out dividends in cryptoassets, it should be permissible to calculate the dividend in money and then pay out cryptoassets to creditors who wish to receive cryptoassets instead of money as substitute performance (In this case, from the perspective of creditors' equality, it is desirable that all creditors, not only creditors who have deposited cryptoassets, can equally wish to be repaid in cryptoassets). [84]

5.1.9 Private Law Issues on Security Tokens

5.1.9.1 *Security Tokens as Negotiable Instruments*

For security tokens, it is desirable to create a situation where the rights represented by the token (e.g., monetary claims, trust beneficiary interests) belong to the holder of the token recorded on the blockchain, and when the token is transferred, the rights are also transferred. This is because the use of tokens would be meaningless if the holder of a token cannot claim that the rights

84 N Kobayashi and N Takeuchi, 'Tosanji niokeru Angoshisan no Toriatsukai to Gutaitekitaio' (Treatment of crypto assets in insolvencies and concrete ways of handling), Kinsyu Shoji Hanrei, No 1611, 71ff. (2021) (in Japanese). Information about the insolvency proceeding of Mt. Gox is available at https://www.mtgox.com/.

belong to him or her, or if the rights are not transferred when the token is transferred and a separate procedure must be followed to duly assert the transfer of the rights to other third parties.

If tokens can be treated in the same way as security certificates/negotiable instruments (*yukashoken*), such result may be achieved. In this regard, there is a view that the rules on securities (*yukashoken hori*) should be applied to security tokens *mutatis mutandis* if (1) it is necessary and reasonable to apply the rules on securities , (2) the representation on the token is not inconsistent with the right represented, and (3) the token is generally recognized as having claims and rights embodied on it, and it is also generally recognized that the attribution and transfer of claims and rights embodied on the token should be determined in accordance with the holdings and transfer of tokens.[85] The author agrees. There are two issues in this regard: (1) the question of whether an instrument can be securities without a express statutory basis, such as a bill of exchange or bill of lading, and (2) even if the answer to (1) is "yes," the question of whether an instrument can be securities without a paper certificate. On issue (1), the prevailing view in Japan is, if it is accepted as securities by commercial practice or the public's general belief, the express statutory basis is not essential to treat an item as securities.[86] Issue (2) is the same question as whether the property law rules can be applied to cryptoassets and paperless securities. In this regard, electronic records that meet certain conditions, such as being able to accurately record the attribution and transfer of rights in a form that is externally recognizable and free from the risk of tampering and double transfer, should be provided the same legal meaning as possession of papers. Applying the property law rules mutatis mutandis to situations without papers would provide a common theoretical foundation for the various digital assets. Even if we were to apply (mutatis mutandis) the property law rules, the rules for money, for securities, and for movable property may differ.[87]

5.1.9.2 *Special Rule on Notice of the Assignment of a Claim under Act on Strengthening Industrial Competitiveness*

The most troubling aspect of security tokens not being treated as securities is the need to notify the debtor and obtain a certified date when transferring the

---

85 Yuto Okoshi, 'Denshikiroku Itenkenri (Token Hyoji Kenri) no Daiikko Yukashoken Gaitosei nitsuite (Eligibility of Electrically Recorded Transferrable Rights (Rights represented on tokens) to Type 1 Securities), Shojihomu No. 2206, 109 (2019).

86 Judgement of Supreme Court, June 24, 1969, Mishu Vol. 23, No. 7, 1143.

87 I discussed more details of this issue in Tetsuo Morishita, Application Of Property Law To Data As Property, Tsinghua China L. Rev., 14(S) 45, 2023.

claim represented by the token, which is a general requirement for the duly assertion of transfers of claims against third parties under Article 467 of Civil Code.[88] It is impractical if such procedures have to be carried out separately in the digital setting using blockchain.

To address this difficulty, in 2021, a special rule on notice of the assignment of claim was introduced in the Act on Strengthening Industrial Competitiveness. Article 11-2 (1) of the Act stipulates, if a notice of or consent to the assignment of a claim is given by using an information system provided by an approved implementer of new business activities in accordance with an approved plan for new business activities, the notice, etc. of the assignment of a claim using that system is deemed to be the notice or consent that is made using an instrument bearing a certified date prescribed in Article 467, if the system allow the person that gives the notice, etc. of the assignment of a claim and the person that receives it to easily check the time, date, and details of the notice of the assignment of a claim and the system stores a record of the notice in such manner as necessary for preventing alteration of the record. This is a sand-box framework to test new technologies and 3 companies is approved under this framework as of October 2024. However, none seem to have reached practical use.[89]

5.1.9.3 *Security Tokens Using Trust with Certificates of Beneficial Interest*

The most commonly used legal structure for security tokens so far is the use of trust with certificate of beneficial interest under the Trust Act, and this legal structure has been used in security token products representing interest in real estate. A trust with certificate of beneficial interest is created making real property and relevant funds the trust assets, and the terms of trust stipulates that no certificate will be issued for beneficial interest.

Then, two ideas are used to create legal link between the beneficial interest and the security tokens recorded on the blockchain. The first is a mechanism that enables the transfer of beneficial interests in a trust to be duly asserted against third parties by transferring the security token. Article 185 (1) of the

88 Article 467 of Civil Code stipulates the assignment of a claim may not be duly asserted against the obligor or any other third party, unless the assignor gives notice thereof to the obligor or the obligor has consented to the same, and such notice or consent may not be duly asserted against a third party other than the obligor unless the notice or the consent is made using an instrument bearing a certified date.

89 Koichi Hirata, 'Security Token nikansuru Genjo nitsuite' (Current situation of Security Tokens), the material presented by the Japan Security Token Offering Association at the 11th meeting of the Study Group on Digital and Decentralized Finance at FSA (June 6, 2023) (https://www.fsa.go.jp/singi/digital/siryou/20230606/2jstoa.pdf) at 19.

Trust Act stipulates the term of trust may provide that a certificate indicating beneficial interests is to be issued, and Article 185(2) stipulates that the provisions of the preceding paragraph do not preclude the terms of trust from providing that a beneficiary certificate will not be issued for a beneficial interest with a specific content.[90] According to Article 195 of the Act, transfer of a beneficial interest in a trust with certificates of beneficial interest may not be asserted against the trustee and other third party unless the name and address of the person who has acquired the beneficial interest has been entered or recorded in the beneficial interest register. Based on these articles, the system using the record of blockchain as the beneficial interest register is incorporated in the scheme and the assignment of the beneficial interest may be duly asserted against third party based on the record of the blockchain, i.e., the record of the holder and transfer of the security tokens.

The second is a mechanism to prevent the transfer of rights by means other than the transfer of security tokens. Beneficial interests for which no certificates are issued may be transferred by the agreement of parties. However, article 93(2) of the Trust Act stipulates the clause of the terms of trust that prohibits or restricts the transfer of a beneficial interest may be asserted against a transferee or other third party who knew or was grossly negligent in failing to know that the clause of restriction on transfer was provided. So, in the term of trust, it is stipulated that the consent of the debtor is required to transfer of beneficial interest and the record of transfer of security token on the blockchain is deemed to be the consent of the debtor.[91] With this arrangement, transfer of security token becomes only way to transfer the beneficial interest.

Although this mechanism is an innovative effort that uses various provisions of trust law, and has been used in practice, the author cannot deny the impression that it is too technical. The development of a more general, legal theory on the attribution and the transfer of digital assets needs to be developed.

---

90 From the sense of words, it seems a bit strange to allow no issuance of certificate in the special category of trust with certificates of beneficial interest, but Takahito Kato, 'Tokun to Tokunka sareta Kenri no Kyori' (The distance between tokens and tokenized rights) in Hideki Kanda ed, Kigyo Hosei no Syorai Tenbo (Future Prospects of Corporate laws) (Shihonshijo Kenkyukai, 2022),349, at 378 opines that it does not conflict with the basic structure of the Trust Act, considering that stock companies may choose if they issue certificate or not.

91 Tatsuya Saito, Token kaga motarasu Kinyu Shisutemu no Mirai to Kiseki (The future and history of financial system brought by tokenization), SBI Research Review, Vol. 5 (2024) 35, at 37ff.

5.1.10 Private Law Issues on Stablecoins

The private law status of the attribution and transfer of stablecoins is also still unclear. As mentioned in 4.1 above, stablecoins may be issued by banks, fund transfer service providers, and special trust companies.

As examined in relation to security tokens, it is necessary to realize the situation where the monetary claim represented by tokens belong to holders of the tokens recorded on the blockchain, and when the tokens are transferred, the claims linked to the tokens need to be also transferred. Claims for funds deposited for fund transfer in the case of fund transfer service providers and specific trust beneficiary interest in the case of specified trust companies are the claims linked to the tokens.[92] It is necessary to legally ensure that these claims are transferred in conjunction with the transfer of the tokens recorded on the blockchain, and avoid the situation where the transfer of claims must be made with procedure outside of the blockchain, that is, assignment of claims by notice with certified dates to debtors.

The legal structure that is currently considered attractive by academics and practitioners is the "extinguishment/creation structure," in which, with the transfer of token, the previous holder's claim against the issuer is extinguished and the new holder's claim against the issuer is newly created. When a fund transfer is made from one bank account to another bank account, it is not considered an assignment of a deposit claim, but rather the deposit claim in the sender's bank account is extinguished and the deposit claim in the receiver's bank account is newly created. This legal structure makes it unnecessary to notify the debtor for the assignment of claims. It is being discussed whether the same legal structure could be used for stablecoin.[93] The author believes that rather than this legal structure, it would be more appropriate to consider that monetary claims are represented by tokens, and then apply property law (the same property law that applies to banknotes) to the attribution and transfer of the tokens.

5.1.11 Private International Law on Cryptoassets

There are no special provisions or court decisions regarding the governing laws for cryptoassets.

92 Ditigal Money no Shihojono Seishitsu womeguru Horitsumondai Kenkyuukai, 'Ditigal Money no Kenri to Iten' (Rights and Transfer of Digital Money), Kinyu Kenkyu Vol 43, No.1, 1 (2024) discusses the nature of claims and possible legal structures in three types of stable coins.

93 For more details, Id. at 25ff.

Regarding the contractual issues, the governing law will be determined in accordance with the Act on General Rules for the Application of Laws, including the provisions of Article 7 (parties may choose the applicable law to contracts), Article 8 (in the absence of choice by parties, the law of the place that is most closely connected is applied, and the location of business of the party that provides a characteristic performance is presumed as the place that is the most closely connected), and Article 11 (in the case of a consumer contract, consumers may invoke the application of mandatory law of its habitual residence). With regard to transactions on the blockchain, there may be cases where it is difficult to determine whether there is an agreement on the governing law.

Regarding torts, Article 17 of the Act on General Rules for the Application of Laws stipulates, 'the formation and effect of a claim arising from a tort are governed by the law of the place where the result of the wrongful act occurred; provided, however, that if the occurrence of the result at the relevant place was ordinarily unforeseeable, the law of the place where the wrongful act was committed governs.' Though how to determine the place where the result of the wrongful act occurred may be challenging, in this author's view, if a foreign hacker steals someone's cryptoassets, the place where the result occurred should be the location of the holder of the cryptoassets.

A particular difficulty arises regarding property law issues relating to property recorded on the blockchain. Article 13 of the Act on General Rules Law for the Application of Laws provides that '(A) real right to movables or immovables and any other right requiring registration are governed by the law of the place.' It is not easy to identify a physical location concerning cryptoassets. In this author's view, where the participants in the blockchain choose the governing law, that law should govern the property law issues. In cases where there is no choice of governing law by the parties, if it is clear that there is an administrator who plays a central role, such as having a certain authority in the system, it may be appropriate to use the location of the administrator as the connecting factor. If neither of the above two linkages can be found, then the law of the location of the person holding the cryptoassets in dispute, or, in the case of a person who holds cryptoassets through an intermediary, the law of the location of that intermediary should govern.[94]

94 The author discussed private international law issues on virtual currencies in Tetsuo Morishita, Blockchain and Japanese Private International Law, in Andrea Bonomi, Matthias Lehmann, and Shaheeza Lalani ed., Blockchain and Private International Law (Brill, 2023), 765.

6 Criminal Law on Cryptoassets

6.1 *AML/CTF*

The Act on Prevention of Transfer of Proceeds of Crime obliges certain entities specified in the Act to check the identity of customers in specified transactions, keep records of such transactions and report suspicious transactions to the relevant administrative authorities. Banks, cryptoasset exchanges, financial instruments business operators, EPHSP, and EPIHSP are listed as the specified entities.[95]

The so-called 'travel rule', the rule that cryptoasset exchanges who send cryptoassets at the request of customers must notify the recipient's cryptoasset exchanges of certain matters concerning the sender and the recipient, has been adopted by Japan Virtual and Crypto assets Exchanges Association as a self-regulatory rule since April 2022. Article 10-3 of Act on Prevention of Transfer of Proceeds of Crime apply the same travel rule to the specified entities.

6.2 *Theft of Cryptoassets*

As explained above, the majority of court cases in Japan do not recognize cryptoassets as things that could be subject to ownership or possession. Reflecting this current state of civil law, the prevailing view is that the stealing of cryptoassets is not subject to the crimes of theft or embezzlement, which presuppose the existence of a tangible object.[96] However, the fact that it is not a tangible object does not mean that it is not subject to legal protection under criminal law. Some court precedents have held that it is subject to the crime of computer fraud.[97]

In the judgement of Tokyo District Court, July 8, 2021 (LEX/DB25590771), a person who caused NEM, a virtual currency illegally stolen from a virtual currency exchange through unauthorized access, to be sent to his own NEM address, knowing that the NEM had been illegally stolen, was charged with a crime under Article 11 of the Act on Punishment of Organized Crimes and Control of Criminal Proceeds (crime of receiving proceeds of crime, etc.). The issue was whether the acquisition of NEM constituted to 'illegally obtain a profit by creating a false electronic or magnetic record' as defined in the criminal offense

95 Article 2(2) of Act on Prevention of Transfer of Proceeds of Crime. Specified transactions are designated regarding each type of entity. In the case of cryptoasset exchanges, the specified transactions are cryptoasset exchange services as defined in PSA (see 2.2.2).

96 Ryosuke Terunuma, Crypto-assets and Property Right, 66-1,2,3 Sophia Law Review 1, 12ff (2022) (in Japanese).

97 Tokyo District Court, July 8, 2021 (LEX/DB25590771) (Reiwa 2 nen (toku (wa) No. 884, No. 1158, No. 1373, No. 1661, No. 2199, No. 2456) and Tokyo District Court, March 24, 2021 (LEX/DB25590382) (Reiwa 2 nen (toku wa) No. 885 (Tokuwa), No. 1565, No. 2168).

of computer fraud under Article 246-2 of the Penal Code,[98] and whether NEM constituted proceeds of crime under the Act on Punishment of Organized Crimes and Control of Criminal Proceeds. The court stated that NEM constitutes a 'cryptoasset' under the PSA and is a property value that can be used to reimburse an unspecified person for the purchase or borrowing of goods or the provision of services, and can also be used to exchange (buy or sell) such cryptoassets with an unspecified person as the other party. Then it continued to state that the private key associated with the NEM address is required to transfer the NEM recorded on the blockchain, and ... only the holder of the private key can transfer the NEM. Furthermore, PSA provides various regulations for cryptoassets to prevent them from being used for money laundering and crime financing and to protect users, based on the premise that they can be used as a new means of payment. The judgment held that, according to the above analysis, NEM is a property value, and has the nature of a right considering the form of control and the mode of protection, etc., and falls under the category of 'property right' as defined in Article 246-2 of the Penal Code. The defence counsel argued that cryptoassets did not fall under the category of 'property rights,' citing theories on the nature of cryptoassets under private law and pointing out that cryptoassets are not subject to property rights. But the judgment concluded that a 'property right' in the above article of the Penal Code is satisfied if the right has monetary value and is not limited to proprietary rights on things or personal claims. The court also stated that the fact that the legal nature of cryptoassets under private law has not yet been established does not immediately lead to the conclusion that cryptoassets are not subject to protection under the crime of computer fraud, which was established to punish illegal gain of property through fraudulent acts.

The judgments of Tokyo District Court, March 24, 2021 (LEX/DB25590382) and Tokyo High Court, March 22, 2022 (LEX/DB25596696) are criminal cases similar to the above Tokyo District court case, and the courts held that NEM is to be recognized as a 'property right' under Article 246-2 of the Penal Code.

In order for the crime of computer fraud to be established, 'false information' must be input into the computer.[99] The judgment of the Supreme Court,

---

98 Article 246-2 of Penal Code stipulates, '... a person who illegally obtains or causes another person to illegally obtain a profit by creating a false electronic or magnetic record relating to acquisition, loss or alteration of property rights by inputting false data or giving unauthorized commands to a computer utilized for the business processes of another person, or by putting a false electronic or magnetic record relating to acquisition, loss or alteration of property rights into use for the business processes of another person, is punished by imprisonment for not more than 10 years.'

99 See the text of Article 246-2 of Penal Code as shown in footnote 98.

July 16, 2024 (Saibansho Jiho, No.1843, p25) held that sending transaction information to the blockchain network of crypto assets after signing it with an illegally obtained private key constitutes the crime of computer fraud, as it provides the computers that comprise the network with 'false information' that the transaction was carried out by a genuine authorised person.

6.3 *Confiscation of Cryptoassets*

Article 13 (1) of the Act on Punishment of Organized Crimes and Control of Proceeds of Crime stipulates that proceeds of crime may be confiscated provided that they are real property, movables, or monetary claims. In addition, Article 16 (1) of the Act stipulates that, if proceeds of crime is neither real property, movable, nor monetary claims, a sum of equivalent value to the property may be collected from the criminal.

In the Tokyo High Court Judgment on June 23, 2022 (Koto Saibansyo Keiji Saiban Sokuhosyu, 2022, at 188), it was disputed if rights of criminals against a cryptoasset exchange to request transfer of cryptoassets may be confiscated. It was held that cryptoassets have no compulsory acceptability as Bank of Japan notes have, so rights to request transfer of cryptoassets do not constitute 'monetary claims.' The judgment mentioned, 'it is difficult to determine the level to which such cryptoassets must be accepted by society as a means of payment to become a confiscable monetary claim, and the boundary between monetary and non-monetary claims, and thus the determination of whether confiscation is possible, may become ambiguous and unstable.' It also mentioned that such conclusion would not cause any injustice because proceeds of crime may be deprived from criminals under Article 16 (1) even when cryptoassets may not be confiscated.

6.4 *Use of Others' Computer Power for Mining*

In the Supreme Court Judgment on January 20, 2022, Saiko Saibansyo Keiji Hanreisyu, Vol. 76, No. 1, at 1, it was disputed whether the act of using part of the computer capabilities of website visitors without the visitors' consents to mine cryptoassets by using a programme whereby when a visitor browses a website, program code is provided to the visitor's computer such that the mining operation is automatically carried out using the visitor's computer while the visitor is browsing., and sharing income from the mining with website visitors, constitutes the offence of making electronic records containing unauthorized commands. The court sentenced not guilty for the following reasons: The impact on the computer's functions and information processing by the computer was limited and the degree of the impact was such that viewers wouldn't notice it. In addition, the system by which website operators gain profit through website browsing is important for the distribution of information via websites, and when compared with advertising display programs that are socially accepted as such a system, the program code in this case does not have any significant difference in terms of the impact on the functions of the viewer's computer or information processing by the computer.

7 Taxation of Cryptoassets

Currently, income earned from the sale or use of cryptoassets is classified as 'miscellaneous income,' and the amount of income tax is calculated by combining it with other income such as salaries. As a result, the higher the total income, the higher the tax rate. In contrast, income earned from the sale and purchase of stocks and other financial products is taxed separately from other income and is subject to a fixed tax rate regardless of the amount of total income. Although there have been requests from the business community and others to change the tax treatment to be the same as that for financial products, this has not been realized.

The National Tax Authority releases detailed Q&A on the tax treatment of cryptocurrencies on its website.[100] For example, when a person purchases a product with the cryptoasset it holds, it means that the person transferred the cryptoasset, and the amount of income related to this transfer is the difference between the transfer price of the cryptoasset and the cost the person has spent to get that cryptoasset.[101]

---

100 National Tax Agency, *Angoshisan nikansuru Zeimujo no Toriatsukai nitsuite* (Tax treatment of cryptoassets) (Q&A), (December 25, 2023 version) (https://www.nta.go.jp/publication/pamph/pdf/virtual_currency_faq_03.pdf).

101 Ibid, p. 5.

Kazakhstan

Farkhad Karagussov

Kazakhstan's legislative system does not operate the notion of cryptocurrency as a legal term. However, the legal framework exists for certain objects which in essence fall under the common understanding of cryptocurrencies.

Respective legal regime for cryptocurrencies in Kazakhstan has been introduced recently. Three stages of its development until now can be identified.

The first stage represented efforts, first operational and later regulatory, of the National Bank of the Republic of Kazakhstan (the "NB RK"). In February 2018 the NB RK circulated a letter to local financial organisations insisting to abstain from any transactions with cryptocurrencies.[1] Further, in 2018 the NB RK prohibited banks and banks' employees to engage into any transactions with cryptocurrencies, restricted cryptocurrencies payments for shares and prohibited financial intermediaries from dealing with financial instruments which value is defined in cryptocurrencies.

The second stage was associated with the legislative introduction (in 2020) of the notion of digital assets and prohibition of circulation of cryptocurrencies in Kazakhstan.

And finally, in 2023 a new taxation regime for digital miners and licensing requirements for digital mining have been introduced, as well as transactions involving cryptocurrencies became allowed within digital assets' exchanges which operate in a jurisdiction other than the one of Kazakhstan.

1 Definition and Legal Qualification

Neither regulations of the NB RK nor a legislative act of the Republic of Kazakhstan (the "RK") have used and defined the term "cryptocurrency". However, this term is widely used in daily life and informal communications.

In relation to cryptocurrencies the NB RK regulations operate two notions. The first one is a term "digital (virtual) units" [*tsifrovaya* (*virtual'naya*)

1 Воротилов А. Нацбанк РК уведомил банки: операции с криптовалютами запрещены (*A. Vorotilov, The National Bank of the RK Notified Banks: cryptocurrencies operations are prohibited*) [15.02.2018], https://forbes.kz/finances/finance/natsbank_rk_uvedomil_banki_operatsii_s_kriptovalyutami_zapreschenyi/.

 | DOI:10.1163/9789004722507_018

yedinitsa].[2] The second notion can be named "value units."[3] Both of the terms are similarly defined as "digital records created and recorded in a decentralised information system with application of cryptography methods and (or) computer calculations", but the second one has been clearly recognised as not being financial instruments or financial assets and not representing someone's entitlement to a property claim under the RK law.

At the same time, the RK Civil Code operates the term "digital assets."[4] Until February 2023, the same term was also used in the Law on Informatisation, which also classified digital assets into two categories: "secured digital assets" and "unsecured digital assets."[5]

Now the same terms and classification of digital assets are established in Article 1 of the Law on Digital Assets which has defined a "digital asset" as "a property created in electronic digital form with the assignment of a digital code, including the use of cryptography and computer computing, registered and secured by unchangeability of information based on distributed data platform technology.[6]

Secured digital assets represent a digital legal form (certification method) of certain type of property rights with respect to goods and provision of services. Their legal regime can be compared with the one of certified securities which are considered as both a type of certain property and a qualified form of certification of respective property rights.

Cryptocurrencies, like Bitcoin, cannot be recognised as secured digital assets under the RK law. Therefore, no consideration of a legal framework of secured digital assets is included in this chapter.

Unsecured digital assets are defined as "digital assets received in an information system in the form of a reward for participation in maintaining consensus in the blockchain and not expressing anyone's monetary obligations,

---

2 The Rules of the State Registration of Non-State Bonds Issuance … approved by the Resolution of the Management Board of the National Bank of the Republic of Kazakhstan dated 29.10.2018 No. 248, Paragraph 17, https://adilet.zan.kz/rus/docs/V1800017884.

3 The Rules to Conduct Activity on Management of Investment Portfolio approved by the Resolution of the Management Board of the National Bank of the Republic of Kazakhstan dated 03.02.2014 No. 10, Paragraph 33-1, https://adilet.zan.kz/rus/docs/V1400009248.

4 The Code of the Republic of Kazakhstan dated 27.12.1994 No.268-XIII "The Civil Code of the Republic of Kazakhstan (General Part)" (as amended), paragraph 2 of Article 115, https://adilet.zan.kz/rus/docs/K940001000.

5 The Law of the Republic of Kazakhstan dated 24.11.2015 No. 418-V "On Informatisation" (as amended), Article 33-1, https://online.zakon.kz/Document/?doc_id=33885902 (its English version, not updated, at: https://adilet.zan.kz/eng/docs/Z1500000418).

6 The Law of the Republic of Kazakhstan dated 06.02.2023 No. 193-VII "On Digital Assets", Article 1, https://adilet.zan.kz/rus/docs/Z2300000193.

which can be traded digitally on a digital asset exchange" (Article 1 (3) of the Law on Digital Assets).

Obviously, the aforementioned NB RK regulations and the Law on Digital Assets define both terms, the digital (virtual) units or value units, on the one hand, and unsecured digital assets, on the other hand, similarly in essence. Both definitions relate to cryptocurrencies, because they generally correspond to a global understanding of cryptocurrencies as tokens which are rewarded to a person for participation in consensus algorithms.[7]

Therefore, under the RK law cryptocurrencies are subject to the legal regime of unsecured digital assets, and not of secured digital assets.

No cryptocurrency has been legislatively recognised to circulate as the legal tender in Kazakhstan.

In addition, cryptocurrency has not been defined to be a mean of payment or a payment instrument. Moreover, according to Article 11 (4) of the Law on Digital Assets, unsecured digital assets also have been qualified as not being financial instruments or financial assets, and therefore, cryptocurrencies cannot be considered being money, national or foreign currency, securities and derivative instruments as well as any other objects of property rights which would fall under definitions of "financial instruments" and "financial assets" set out in Article 128-1 of the RK Civil Code.

In general, a legal significance of cryptocurrency (as well as its economic nature) remain unrecognised in Kazakhstan's legal and economic theories. It is obvious though that, from the standpoint of classical political economy, cryptocurrency does not have a use value (in German – *Gebrauchswert*) and its appearance in active turnover as an object of civil (property) rights has not been the result of human labor (which used to be considered as a true 'measure of value' of goods) but rather of, in essence, a misuse of produced electrical energy and computing equipment.

2 Regulatory Framework

The regulatory framework for cryptocurrencies existing in the RK has been based on the understanding that cryptocurrencies such as Bitcoin and all of

---

7 Coinbase, What is "proof of work" or "proof of stake"?, https://www.coinbase.com/ru/learn/crypto-basics/what-is-proof-of-work-or-proof-of-stake; R. Houben and A. Snyers, Crypto currencies and Blockchain. Legal context and implications for financial crime, money laundering and tax evasion [July 2018], p.19, https://www.europarl.europa.eu/cmsdata/150761/TAX3%20Study%20on%20cryptocurrencies%20and%20blockchain.pdf.

the alternative digital coins (ETH, LTC, BCH and etc.) as well as stable coins (USDT, BUSD, USDC and etc.) represent high-risk and unwelcomed investment opportunities and instruments which may threat and harm the financial well-being of the RK citizens.

Therefore, the RK law concerning cryptocurrencies has been developed based on two pillars: (i) allowed mining of cryptocurrencies and (ii) prohibited issuance and circulation of unsecured assets (cryptocurrencies and cryptocurrency-based derivatives). Such regulation and the prohibition are of common nature and had to apply with respect to any person whether it is a resident or non-resident of the RK, individual or legal entity and etc.

Initially there no exceptions from the legislative prohibition were clearly formulated. But one could assume that certain reservations were initially made in the Law on Informatisation for a business involving operations with cryptocurrencies within the Astana International Financial Centre (the "AIFC").[8] However, a regulatory framework established within the AIFC is not a part of the RK legal system and Kazakh law. The AIFC is an independent entity within the allocated territory of the RK which is excluded from the RK's civil, financial and judicial legal frameworks and self-governed "based on principles of laws of England and Wales."[9] Due to its such specific status the AIFC cannot be considered as the RK jurisdiction, though it is located in the territory of Kazakhstan.[10]

The prohibition of issuance and circulation of unsecured digital assets on the territory of Kazakhstan has remained existing with adoption of the Law on Digital Assets in 2023. However, the exception has clearly been provided for. Particularly, digital miners are now allowed to sell cryptocurrencies they obtained in result of digital mining. But, such sale can happen only through a digital assets' exchange created and functioning in the AIFC and within the AIFC regulatory framework only, *i.e.* not under the RK law (Article 11 of the Law on Digital Assets).

8 Бекназаров А. О регулировании цифровых активов в Республике Казахстан и МФЦА (*A. Beknazarov, On regulation of the digital assets in the Republic of Kazakhstan and the AIFC*), [29.07.2021], https://online.zakon.kz/Document/?doc_id=36513764.

9 The Constitutional Law of the Republic of Kazakhstan dated 07.12.2015 No. 438-V "On Astana International Financial Centre" (as amended), https://online.zakon.kz/Document/?doc_id=39635390.

10 Карагусов Ф. О конвергенции права, привлечении инвестиций в Казахстан и функционировании Международного финансового центра «Астана» как exorbitant jurisdiction (*F. Karagussov, On convergence of law, attracting investments to Kazakhstan and functioning of the Astana International Financial Center as an exorbitant jurisdiction*), [23.01.2023], https://katpartners.kz/Articles/MFCA_exorbitant_jurisdiction.pdf.

Article 8 (4) of the Law on Digital Assets has also established the mandatory sell threshold. During the period from 1 January and 31 December 2024 such sale must be made in an amount of at least fifty percent of digital assets owned by digital miners, and after 1 January 2025 the minimum sale amount shall increase to at least seventy-five percent. It appears that the rest of their cryptocurrencies digital miners can hold in possession or also sell through digital assets' exchanges licensed by the AIFC.

Even with such new regulation, the ban for circulation of cryptocurrencies looks controversial because in the digital era any prohibition of issuance and circulation of anything having digital form is extremely ineffective without creation of relevant prevention mechanisms.[11]

A plenty of digital methods exist which allow both issuance and circulation of cryptocurrencies regardless such legislative prohibitions. All existing online services, such as launchpads (BSCPad, BullPerks, TrustSwap and etc.), cryptocurrency exchanges (Binance, Coinbase, Kraken and etc.), digital currency exchangers (BitMEX, EXX, OKEx and etc.), cryptocurrency wallets (MetaMask, BitGO, XAPO and etc.), in general can combine all of the methods.[12]

Another controversy (though not in law, but in practice) could be found in the fact that there were no attempts undertook to block in the RK any use of such digital methods as mentioned above. Even Binance cryptocurrency exchange which caused legal problems in many jurisdictions throughout 2021 has been always accessible in Kazakhstan.[13] Moreover, for unclear reasons Binance have been presented in the AIFC,[14] and the NB RK has considered to integrate the RK's CBDC (digital Tenge) on Binance's blockchain network BNB Chain.[15]

---

11 The only effective mechanism ensuring such prohibitions has appeared to be created by China where they are able to effectively block access to any use of available methods through internet. But they also established and enforced legislative prohibitions for industrial mining of cryptocurrencies.

12 Existing legislative prohibition of issuance and circulation of cryptocurrencies in the RK (apart from operation within the AIFC's exorbitant jurisdiction) means that all of the abovementioned online services could not be recognised legal in Kazakhstan.

13 T. Geron, Protocol: Here's everything going wrong at Binance, the world's biggest crypto exchange. [22.09.2021], https://www.protocol.com/fintech/binance-regulation-crypto.

14 AIFC: Binance obtains In-Principle Approval from AFSA to operate a Digital Asset Trading Facility and Provide Custody in the Astana International Financial Centre [15.08.2022], https://aifc.kz/press-relizy/binance-obtains-in-principal-approval-from-afsa-to-operate-a-digital-asset-trading-facility-and-provide-custody-in-the-astana-international-financial-centre/.

15 S. Handagama, Kazakhstan to Test National Digital Currency on BNB Chain, Binance CEO Zhao Says [27.10.2022], https://www.coindesk.com/policy/2022/10/27/kazakhstan-to-test-national-digital-currency-on-bnb-chain-binance-ceo-zhao-says/.

It appears that (when an access to internet and blockchain is not physically blocked) blockchain technology does not allow any national law to effectively control circulation of cryptocurrencies within the national legal system, including control of compliance with any ban of such circulations. Cryptocurrencies' ledgers are not regulated by any national law and, therefore, any operations recorded in those ledgers cannot be regulated by national legal and administrative regimes which would allow neither control of operations nor any enforcement of the national legislation related to cryptocurrencies.

Unlike the existing ban for issuance and circulation of cryptocurrencies, since 2020 the law has allowed their mining.

In Article 1 (8) of the Law on Digital Assets digital mining is defined similarly as it was earlier defined in the Law on Informatisation, *i.e* as "a process of conveying of calculating operations with use of computers, power supplies according to established algorithms of encryption and data processing ensuring validation of data blocks integrality in the informatisation objects by methods of blockchain".

In addition, the Law on Digital Assets introduced a concept of a "digital mining pool" which means "a legal entity accredited in accordance with the legislation of the Republic of Kazakhstan on digital assets to provide the service of combining a capacity of a hardware and software complex for digital mining [by] digital miners [and] distributing digital assets among digital miners [which digital assets were] obtained in result of their joint activities" (Article 1 (10)).

Introduction of the notion of "digital mining pool" has been made because since 2023 digital mining activities can be carried out by digital miners only through a digital mining pool using its digital mining data center (Article 8 (2) of the Law on Digital Assets).

Specific anti-money laundering and counter-terrorism financing (AML/CTF) provisions applicable to operations with digital assets have been also introduced into the legislation of the RK. Since January 2022 those entities who issue digital assets, organise trades with digital assets or engage in digital assets' exchange into money, other values and property are recognised as subject of financial monitoring.[16] As such they are obliged to conduct know-your-client procedures on their clients and report on respective suspicious operations. Currently respective provisions relate to operations with only secured digital

16 The Law of the Republic of Kazakhstan dated 28.08.2009 No. 191-IV "On Anti-money Laundering and Combating Financing of Terrorism" (as amended), sub-paragraph 20 of paragraph 1 of Article 3, https://adilet.zan.kz/rus/docs/Z090000191.

assets because issuance and circulation of unsecured digital assets (cryptocurrencies) are prohibited in the RK.

3 Supervision

Since 2023 a state control in the field of digital assets has been provided in the RK legislation. Particularly, in accordance with Article 12 of the Law on Digital Assets the state control in the sphere of digital assets shall be carried out in the form of inspections and preventive controls in accordance with the RK Entrepreneurial Code.[17]

Before the Law on Digital Assets introduced the requirement of state control over the mining and circulation of digital assets in 2023, there no supervisory measures / actions were regulated by law with the exception of some notification regime for those who intended to be involved into digital mining (until 2022) or providing mining equipment and some other activities involving cryptocurrencies (starting from 2022). But all those measures cannot be considered as implementation of supervisory, control or even truly monitoring powers by the State.

Except for existence of such notification requirement, no state or other public measures were taken against any of those entities involved in cryptocurrencies mining and operations. As the only exception, numerous raids can be mentioned which were undertaken by law-enforcement agencies and prosecutors in 2022 to reveal those miners who failed to notify relevant authority about start of their activity and which raids resulted in seizure of mining equipment.

In 2023 the Law on Digital Assets has established that the RK Ministry of Digital Development, Innovations and Aerospace Industry (the "Ministry") is the authorised governmental body in the sphere of digital assets.

In accordance with Article 4 of the Law on Digital Assets, the Ministry has been vested with the following authorities concerning cryptocurrencies: (i) ensures the implementation of state policy in the field of digital assets and exercises state control in the field of digital assets, as well as carries out intersectoral coordination in the field of digital assets; (ii) issues licenses to carry out digital mining activities; (iii) approves the rules for reporting information on the income of digital miners and digital mining pools for tax purposes, the rules for accreditation of digital mining pools; rules for licensing digital

17 The Code of the Republic of Kazakhstan dated 29.10.2015 No.375-V "The Entrepreneurial Code of the Republic of Kazakhstan" (as amended), https://adilet.zan.kz/rus/docs/K1500000375.

mining activities; rules for accounting and maintaining a register of hardware and software complex for digital mining; (iv) accredits digital mining pools; (v) maintains a register of hardware and software complex for digital mining; (vi) exercises other powers provided for by laws and acts of the RK President and the RK Government.

In addition to establishing such competence of the Ministry, Article 4 (2) of the Law on Digital Assets has also provided for specific powers and responsibilities of a governmental body exercising state management in the field of electric power industry (which is the RK Ministry of Energy). Such powers include the following: (i) to set out requirements for connecting digital miners to electrical networks; (ii) to approve a mechanism for determining the electricity quota for digital miners, and (iii) to exercise some other powers provided for in the RK legislation.

Besides, in accordance with Article 11 of the Law on Digital Assets, requirements applicable to digital assets' exchanges and procedures for licensing their activity shall be established by acts of the AIFC (which are not a part of the RK law though). However, it is also established that the AIFC shall agree with the NB RK such of the AIFC's acts as: (i) a procedure and mechanisms for interaction of the RK commercial banks and the AIFC's resident participants concerning opening bank accounts for the AIFC's participants (they must be also agreed with the RK Financial Market's Regulator), and (ii) a list, terms and procedure for reporting by digital assets' exchanges.

In 2023 the Law on Digital Assets has established that digital mining business is subject to be licensed (Article 8 (1)). According to Article 9 of the Law respective type of the licenses shall be granted to a digital miner for the duration of three years.

Two kinds of digital mining licenses can be granted to digital miners which depends on whether a digital miner: (i) owns a digital mining data processing center or possesses it on another legal ground, or (ii) does not own such data processing center but operates using its own hardware-software complex for digital mining hosted in a data processing center. The Ministry approves the rules and procedures for granting such licenses and it is empowered to grant them to those digital miners who applied for the licenses.

The applicants must pay the licensing fee in the amount and procedures regulated by the RK Tax Code.[18]

The Law on Digital Assets provides for that granted digital mining licenses can be suspended and resumed in its effect (Article 9). Particularly, the licenses'

18 The Code of the Republic of Kazakhstan dated 25.12.2017 No. 120-VI "The Code On Taxes And Other Mandatory Payments To the Budget (The Tax Code)" (as amended), Article 550, https://adilet.zan.kz/rus/docs/K1700000120.

effect can be suspended when: (i) a false information for obtaining the license was presented by an applicant; (ii) the digital miner failed to complied with requirements of the RK legislation; (iii) within the prescribed period the digital miner failed to eliminate violations revealed in result of an unscheduled inspection by the authorized body; (iv) within the time limits established by the RK legislation on digital assets, the digital miner failed to inform the authorized body in time about changes happened in earlier submitted information; (v) when the digital miner files an application on suspension of the license. Other cases when the licenses can be suspended can also be regulated by the RK legislation.

While suspension and renewal of the license for digital mining can be carried out by the Ministry, deprivation of the license can be made by the RK court only.

In turn, an activity of digital mining pools is subject to accreditation. According to Article 10 of the Law on Digital Assets, accreditation of a digital mining pool represents a procedure for a digital mining pool to acquire official recognition of the compliance of its activities with the requirements established by the RK legislation. All costs associated with obtaining the accreditation shall be at the digital mining pool's own expense.

Article 10 of the Law on Digital Assets has established mandatory conditions which must be met to obtain the accreditation by a digital mining pool. The following such conditions shall apply: (i) the hardware and software complex of the digital mining pool must be located in the RK territory; (ii) test protocols with positive test results confirming compliance with information security requirements shall exist and be available; (iii) other requirements set out in the Ministry's rules of accreditation of digital mining pools shall be complied with.

Once a digital mining pool obtains accreditation it shall provide the Ministry and tax authorities with information about the income of the digital mining pool and digital miners participating in it. Such reports shall be made in accordance with the reporting rules approved by the Ministry and it is made for the digital mining taxation purpose.

Finally, as said above, Article 11 of the Law on Digital Assets sets out that functioning of digital assets' exchanges is licensed and regulated by acts of the AIFC (which is not part of the RK jurisdiction), some of which must be agreed with the NB RK and the RK Financial Market's Regulator.

4 Private Law Issues

Circulation of any assets/property is regulated by law based on general provisions of the RK Civil Code according to which civil/property rights' objects may be freely disposed or transferred to any person in order of the universal succession (e.g. in case of inheritance or reorganization of a company), as well as property titles and objects can be transferred in any other way provided that they are not excluded from the circulation or not limited in circulation (Article 116 (1)).

Digital mining may not be attributed to circulation of digital assets. It can be considered only as a ground of emerging of civil rights to certain types of objects/assets (Article 7 of the RK Civil Code). Particularly, according to Article 8 (3) of the Law on Digital Assets, a digital miner becomes an owner of cryptocurrency originated in result of digital mining.

However, the digital miner's does not obtain the ownership right to such cryptocurrency directly. All cryptocurrency obtained in result of digital mining shall be distributed among participating digital miners by respective digital mining pool. For this case Article 10 (4) of the Law on Digital Assets has reserved that such distribution of digital assets does not represent an issuance or circulation of digital assets.

But such reservation is controversial as long as it means that an individual digital miner becomes an owner of unsecured digital assets originated in result of his activity only after the assets were distributed to the miner by the digital mining pool (as a separate legal personality). And the Law does not explain what is a legal ground tor one independent person (a digital mining pool) to possess assets originated by efforts and at expense of other persons (individual digital miners). It is also unclear what could be a nature of a property right the digital mining pool would obtain in respect to cryptocurrencies originated by other persons' efforts in order to distribute them among participating digital miners for the last mentioned to become recognised owners of the cryptocurrency. The Law also failed to set out the principle of such distribution of unsecured digital assets among digital miners. These factors make respective legal regime poorly grounded and leading to infringement of the digital miners' property rights to cryptocurrencies they have obtained in result of digital mining.

Prohibition of the unsecured assets' circulation in the RK jurisdiction entails that cryptocurrency cannot be contractually acquired, sold, gifted, otherwise transferred, be subject to attachment, be pledged or lent, as well as a trust or management arrangements with respect to cryptocurrencies cannot be created. In addition, insolvency proceedings and actionable tort regarding loss of cryptocurrencies cannot be established and apply. Besides, because of the legislative prohibition of cryptocurrencies' circulation, it is unclear whether Kazakh courts would recognise unsecured digital assets to be a property possible for inheritance.

This means that the established constitutional guarantee of the ownership right (Article 6 and 26 of the RK Constitution detailed in Article 188 (1) of the

Civil Code) does not work with respect to cryptocurrency owned in the result of mining. And such inconsistency with the RK Constitution can serve as a ground to challenging the constitutionality and applicability (at least in this part of the regulation) of the respective provision in the Law on Digital Assets.

The possibility (and the mandatory sale requirements) to sell cryptocurrencies mined on the territory of Kazakhstan through digital assets' exchanges which operate under a legal regime different from the RK law causes two other private-law issues.

The first one is the question of how the cryptocurrency originated by digital miners under the RK law can be placed for trading at a digital assets' exchange which is created in an exorbitant jurisdiction (which is not the part of the RK legal system) and is subject to a foreign legal regime (which is not the RK law). From the legal stand-point such transfer of cryptocurrency is prohibited by the RK law.

Another issue relates to the question of whether a Kazakh-resident digital miner can sell the cryptocurrency he or she owns in the amount exceeding the mandatory sell threshold. From one hand, such sell can be effective by a transfer in the blockchain legers which do not belong to the RK jurisdiction and cannot be controlled by the RK system. Therefore, such transfers would be made not in the territory of the RK, and one can assume that respective ban for circulation of cryptocurrencies in the RK should not apply.

From the other hand, the question remains unclear if the cryptocurrencies (even obtained in result of digital mining on the territory of the RK) can be considered as a property originated under the RK Law, provided that the cryptocurrencies ledgers are located outside of the RK system and the RK law cannot serve as a ground or framework for emerging and implementation of property rights with respect to the cryptocurrency.

From the more theoretical point of view, there also a common problem exists in the RK private law doctrine according to which the right of ownership can be recognized with respect to a thing (i.e. material object of property). A system of property rights to intangible property (such as money on bank accounts, non-documentary securities, cryptocurrencies, etc.) as well as a legal regime of various financial accounts still remains insufficiently developed in the RK private law theory and legislation.

5 Tax Measures

Until 2022 there no any tax regime existed to apply to origination of cryptocurrencies and property right to them, as well as to any operation with them.

Since 1 January 2022 the RK Tax Code has provided for taxation of digital mining activity (Articles 606-1–606-5). Special fee is charged based on a volume of electrical energy consumed for digital mining.

Digital miners and service providers of complex computing infrastructure for performing computing operations and data processing for digital miners have be recognised as payers of the mining fee.

As the basic rate, the amount of the fee shall be calculated at the rate of 2 Tenge per 1 kilowatt-hour of consumed electrical energy during the respective reporting period (which is a calendar quarter).

However, the fee shall be calculated at the rate of 1 Tenge per 1 kilowatt-hour of consumed electrical energy if a digital miner consumes electricity produced by renewable sources of electrical energy at his own power plants on the RK territory or uses its own power-generating equipment which is not connected to the RK unified electrical power system.

In case if a digital miner or respective service provider fails to having control devices for measurement of volume of electricity consumption and/or such devices are in a faulty state, the volume of consumed electricity shall be calculated based on the round-the-clock consumption of the maximum power of electrical energy.

The fee shall be paid quarterly to the state budget at place of location of a taxpayer.

In addition to the fee for mining, an income tax is payable on the income received in result of operations with (sale of) cryptocurrencies. The taxation regime in this case is the general one. However, deficiency of the RK tax administration system, as well as lack of efficient system to control operation with cryptocurrencies outside digital assets' exchanges may lead to ineffectiveness of application of such income tax regime.

6 Litigation in Relation to Cryptocurrencies

Since circulation of cryptocurrencies is prohibited in Kazakhstan, no disputes and litigations within regulated civil procedures can objectively take place with respect to cryptocurrencies under existing legal regime. As the only exception a claim for recognition or protection of the ownership right to cryptocurrencies emerged in result of their mining could be possible under existing legal regime.

However, no specific actions or class actions in disputes relating to cryptocurrencies have been known yet. Neither special or exclusive heads of jurisdiction can be mentioned available for cryptocurrencies-related litigation.

But breach of the prohibition for operations with cryptocurrencies should lead to criminal or at least administrative prosecutions. However, this prohibition does not constitute a legally defined crime or administrative violation and there no specific liability for breach of the prohibition has been provided for by the RK legislation at this point.

Nevertheless, we are aware of two criminal proceeding involving cryptocurrencies which took place in 2017 and 2022. First one was initiated by the State against a RK-resident individual who scammed other RK-resident individuals by imitating selling of Bitcoins to them for a low price. The scammer reimbursed losses (approx. USD 15,000) of his victims and was sentenced to three years of probation.[19] The second one has a similar context but the amount of reimbursed losses comprised approx. USD 280,000.[20] Given that not all of the judicial and arbitration cases are publicly available in Kazakhstan we cannot confirm that the mentioned cases are the only ones taken place in the RK by these days.

As a general rule, as established in the RK Code on Civil Procedures, decisions of foreign courts and arbitral rewards can be enforceable by the RK courts if recognition and enforcement of such decisions and arbitral rewards is provided by law and (or) international treaty ratified by the RK and or on the basis of reciprocity.[21]

Kazakhstan is a party to the 1958 New York Arbitration Convention and also it is a party to numerous bilateral and multilateral international treaties concerning recognition and enforcement of foreign courts decisions.

However, the RK courts may reject recognition and enforcement of such decision and arbitral rewards if it results in breach of public order of the RK. Since circulation of cryptocurrencies is prohibited in the RK such recognition and/or enforcement by the RK courts shall likely be impossible.

---

19 Sentence of the District Court № 2 of the Yessiliskii District of Astana dated 15.01.2018 No. 7135-17-00-1/616, The "Paragraph" Information System: https://online.zakon.kz/Document/?doc_id=35213965.

20 Press release regarding sentence of the District Court № 2 of the Yessiliskii District of Astana, [28.10.2022], https://astana.sud.kz/rus/news/sudom-rassmotreno-delo-o-kriptomoshennichestve.

21 The Code of the Republic of Kazakhstan dated 31 October 2015 # 377-V "The Civil Procedure Code of the Republic of Kazakhstan" (as amended), Article 501, https://adilet.zan.kz/rus/docs/K1500000377.

7 Miscellaneous

A legal theory of cryptocurrency is merely developed in the RK. Only very few publications can be noticed to be valuable for development of theoretical basis of legal regime for cryptocurrencies and, in general, digital assets. In his article concerning recently introduced concept of digital assets M. Suleimenov opined that digital assets (without any references to their acknowledged types) represent a form of existence of property rights.[22]

In their publication F. Karagussov and A. Bondarev proposed explanation of the term "cryptocurrency", compared it with concepts of money and electronic money, stressed out specific features of cryptocurrencies which are different from those of fiat money, collated money circulation and cryptocurrencies market, described situation related to use and regulation of cryptocurrencies in Kazakhstan as of beginning of 2020, and concluded that the cryptocurrencies' circulation cannot be under, at least, full control of the State.[23]

Lack of well-developed theoretical considerations of legal nature of cryptocurrencies and neglectfulness of the legislator and regulators to the existing scientific elaborations led to creation of unclear and ineffective legal framework for cryptocurrencies in thc RK.

Nevertheless, the following three fields can be identified as directions of current and further development of crypto industry in Kazakhstan: (i) improvement of the existing legal framework for digital assets in the RK, (ii) understanding of significance and impact on the RK jurisdiction of the existing legal environment for circulation of cryptocurrencies and other digital assets within the AIFC and (iii) elaboration of relevant pilot project and introduction of Digital Tenge as the RK national currency.

7.1 *Legal Framework for Crypto Industry in Kazakhstan: Background and Current State of Affairs*

For a long time since crypto industry appeared and substantially evolved in the RK the State did not try to legally allow or forbid individuals and companies

---

22 Сулейменов М.К. Цифровизация и совершенствование гражданского законодательства (*M. Suleimenov, Digitalization and improvement of the civil legislation*), [26.02.2020], https://online.zakon.kz/Document/?doc_id=39931835.

23 Карагусов Ф., Бондарев А. *Ценные бумаги и деньги как объекты гражданских прав. Электронные деньги и платежные системы. Учебное пособие.* (*F. Karagussov and A. Bondarev, Securities and Money as Objects of Civil Rights. E-money and Payment Systems: Tutorials*), Almaty: Caspian Social University, 2020, pp. 112–118, (electronic version at: https://katpartners.kz/Edu_files/Sec_money.pdf).

to participate in this industry. First signs of the State's concern in cryptocurrencies appeared in 2018 and coincided with the rise of Bitcoin in December of 2017.

Particularly, in February 2018 the NB RK, in absence of respective legal framework, started with recommendations to abstain from any transactions with cryptocurrencies which were addressed only to financial institutions functioning in the RK. Despite of a recommendatory nature of this position of the NB RK no any case of financial institutions ignored the recommendations is known.

That position of the NB RK was based on the recognition of Kazakhstani Tenge as the only legal tender in the RK. However, under the RK currency regulation, foreign currencies can also serve as legal tender in Kazakhstan under specific and very limited circumstances (for example, settlements between resident and non-residents of the RK can be made in foreign currency). But such exceptions allow use of foreign currency and not any of a legal tender recognized in foreign jurisdictions. That means that Bitcoin (accountable only on digital wallets) which was recognised by El Salvador as its legal tender cannot be available for settlements in Kazakhstan because it is not a foreign currency according to the established legal definition of this term under the RK law.

In October 2018 the NB RK amended its previous Rules on risk management system and internal control in banks,[24] and later replaced them with new Rules,[25] both of which set forth the prohibition to banks and their employees to engage in any transactions with cryptocurrencies.

In 2018 the NB RK also prohibited payments for shares made in any digital (virtual) units and derivatives with underlying digital (virtual) units / asset. The same prohibition was established with respect to indexation in digital

24 The Rules of Forming of Risk Management System and Internal Control of Second-tier Banks approved by the Resolution of the Management Board of the National Bank of the Republic of Kazakhstan dated 26.02.2014 No. 29 (ceased to be in force), Paragraph 8, https://adilet.zan.kz/rus/docs/V1400009322.

25 The Rules on Creation of the Risk Management System and Internal Control in Second-tier Banks and Branches of Non-resident Banks approved by the Resolution of the Management Board of the National Bank of the Republic of Kazakhstan dated 29.11.2019 No. 188 (as amended on 30.12.2021), Paragraphs 33 (12), 33 (10) and 98 (4), https://adilet.zan.kz/rus/archive/docs/V1900019632/30.12.2021.

assets of bonds' nominal value and interest rates,[26] as well as circulation of financial instruments which price depends on cryptocurrency's price.[27]

Besides, since 2018 securities brokers and dealers as well as managers of investment portfolios have been prohibited to enter into transactions involving derivatives where the transaction price would depend on the values created and recorder in decentralized systems.[28]

Obviously, in absence of any clear conceptual approaches for a legal framework of cryptocurrency the NB RK took a position of prevention of crypto industry's invasion to the financial market of the RK. Such approach allowed the RK to postpone a development of a legal framework for cryptocurrencies and to mitigate the risk of massive involving of the unqualified private investors into the high volatility assets.

Later, in 2020 the RK introduced first set of national regulation for cryptocurrencies having amended the RK Civil Code and the Law on Informatisation as well as approved some supportive regulations.[29] In result, the broader term "digital assets" has now used as the basic concept of the new legal framework instead of use of the notion "cryptocurrencies".

Generally, all the legal terms and basic provisions regarding digital assets are now set forth in the Law on Digital Assets. Definitions of such terms as "digital assets", "unsecured digital assets", "digital mining" and "digital mining

---

26 The Rules of the State Registration of Non-State Bonds Issuance ... approved by the Resolution of the Management Board the National Bank of the Republic of Kazakhstan dated 29.10.2018 No. 248, Paragraph 17, https://adilet.zan.kz/rus/docs/V1800017884.

27 Requirements Concerning Issuers and their Securities Eligible for (Admitted to) Circulation at the Stock-Exchange [...] approved by the Resolution of the Management Board of the National Bank of the Republic of Kazakhstan dated 27.03.2017 No. 248 (as amended), Paragraph 3, https://adilet.zan.kz/rus/docs/V1700015175.

28 The Rules to Conduct Activity on Management of Investment Portfolio approved by the Resolution of the Management Board of the National Bank of the Republic of Kazakhstan dated 03.02.2014 No. 10, Paragraph 33-1, https://adilet.zan.kz/rus/docs/V1400009248 (as applicable to portfolio managers); and The Rules of Broker and (or) Dealer Activity on Securities Market and on Procedures for Banking Operations Performed by Broker and (or) Dealer approved by the Resolution of the Management Board of the National Bank of the Republic of Kazakhstan dated 03.02.2014 No. 9 (as amended), Paragraph 53-1, https://adilet.zan.kz/rus/docs/V1400009249 (as applicable to brokers / dealers).

29 The Rules of Informing regarding Activity on Digital Mining approved by the Order of the Minister of Digital Development, Innovations and Aerospace Industry of the Republic of Kazakhstan dated 13.10.2020 No. 384/НҚ, https://adilet.zan.kz/rus/docs/V2000021445; and The Rules of Issuance and Circulation of Secured Digital Assets approved by the Order of Minister of Digital Development, Innovations and Aerospace Industry of the Republic of Kazakhstan dated 29.10.2020 No. 407/НҚ, https://adilet.zan.kz/rus/docs /V2000021546.

pool" have been reproduced above in this chapter. In addition to those terms, the Law defined the following three other notions which relate to cryptocurrencies regulation in the RK:

> "digital assets' exchange" meaning "a digital platform that provides organizational and technical support for trading, issuance, circulation and storage of digital assets" (Article 1(5));
>
> "digital miner" meaning "an individual entrepreneur or legal entity of the Republic of Kazakhstan carrying out digital mining activities" (Article 1 (7)), and
>
> "data processing center [of] digital mining" means "an information and communication infrastructure facility consisting of a hardware and software complex for digital mining and a production building located outside the residential area, using electrical energy in accordance with the Law of the Republic of Kazakhstan "On Electric Power Industry" (Article 1 (11)).

Besides, the Law on Informatisation defines the following legal terms:

> "blockchain" meaning an information and communication technology ensuring permanence of information in the distributed platform of data on the base of interdependent data blocks chain, established algorithms of integrality validation and cryptography methods (Article 1 (38-2));
>
> "distributed platform of data" meaning a technological platform, which components are interconnected with the established algorithms, placed on the various nodes of network, may have one or more possessors and may have varying level of identical data (Article 1 (39-1)).

However, definitions of "blockchain" and "distributed platform of data" are purely technical with no any legal content and, in general, there no practical sense in defining technological terms by legislative acts can be found. But definitions of "digital assets" and "digital mining" have certain legal significance and deserves a legal consideration.

The RK legislator has tried to establish a broader definition of "digital asset" to cover all the diversity of instruments presented in the crypto market. Such approach seems reasonable because, as of today, existing cryptocurrencies coexist with other digital assets like non-fungible tokens and tokenized assets (securities, metals, goods and raw materials). Besides, the definition can include potential new instruments emerging from time to time on the rapidly evolving crypto market.

At the same time, the Law on Digital Assets creates more detailed regulations for secured digital assets, but pays much less attention to creation of a sound legal regime for unsecured digital assets having been limited to a certain legal framework for digital mining only.

However, regardless of their type, digital assets shall not ensure rights on the financial instruments and they shall not provide their owners / possessors with rights in relation to a legal entity (obviously, the law means shareholder or participants rights in a company). It appears that such restriction was introduced as the RK's response to at least the following two issues.

The first one relates to the well-known "US Securities and Exchange Commission vs. Ripple" case where Ripple is alleged in unregistered securities offering and the court has to decide whether the XRP cryptocurrency is a security or not. In that context, under the RK law Ripple's XRP could be qualified as unsecured digital asset.

The second problem which the RK legislator obviously intended to resolve was the exclusion of the situation where tokenized securities could be treated as traditional investment securities such as shares, corporate bonds and, probably, treasury notes.

In April 2022 the NB RK cancelled the abovementioned prohibition regarding banks' operations with cryptocurrencies which previously existed in the Rules of risk-management and internal control in banks. Instead the NB RK introduced the provision which requires banks to reject operations with high-risk of money laundering and terrorist financing. In addition, those Rules were amended with strict and precise AML/CFT provisions concerning banks' interaction with the AIFC participating companies in case when such companies provide services on management of a digital assets' platform, as well as concerning banks' clients operations involving the clients' interaction with the AIFC participating companies.[30]

Thus, the NB RK demonstrates a cautious approach by allowing only banks to process corresponding transactions, keeping previous prohibitions for the indexation of nominal value and interest rate of bonds in digital assets, as well as the circulation of financial instruments which price depends on cryptocurrency price as well as for brokers, dealers and managers of investment portfolios.

Finally, in 2023 the Law on Digital Assets was passed. The purpose of that Law was to codify the most of the regulations concerning digital assets,

---

30 The Rules on Creation of the Risk Management System and Internal Control in Second-tier Banks and Branches of Non-resident Banks approved by the Resolution of the Management Board of the National Bank of the Republic of Kazakhstan dated 29.11.2019 No. 188, (as amended), Paragraphs 33 (12), 33 (10) and 98 (4), https://adilet.zan.kz/rus/docs/V1900019632.

determine characteristics of secured digital assets, introduce licensing regime for mining data-centers' activity, as well as to restrict circulation of unsecured digital assets (including their issuance and mining, crypto exchanges' activity) to allow it only within the jurisdiction of the AIFC (which is not the jurisdiction of the RK). The main provisions of the Law on Digital Assets applicable to cryptocurrencies have been described in this chapter above.

7.2 *The Astana International Financial Center (AIFC) Framework*

The AIFC regulations allow functioning of cryptocurrencies' exchanges within its regulatory framework and its activity can considerably affect business practice in the RK jurisdiction.

Although the AIFC regulatory framework is not recognised to be a part of the RK law, since 15 November 2020 participants of the AIFC (i.e., companies registered under the AIFC regulations) which perform specified types of activities determined by the AIFC Financial Service Authority have been recognised as subjects of financial monitoring by the RK law.

The financial monitoring under the RK law was established with respect to operations of the AIFC participants involving use of digital assets trading facility. Such facility functions regularly and brings together multiple parties (whether as principal or agent) with a view to the entering into contracts to buy, sell or exchange digital assets for a fiat currency; and/or to exchange one digital asset for another digital asset, in its facility, in accordance with its non-discretionary rules.

The AIFC regulations also chose the term "digital assets" instead of cryptocurrency. The AIFC Glossary defines "digital assets" as a "digital representation of value that can be digitally traded and functions as a medium of exchange; or a unit of account; or a store of value; can be exchanged back-and-forth for fiat currency, but is neither issued nor guaranteed by the government of any jurisdiction, and fulfils the above functions only by agreement within the community of users of the digital asset and accordingly is to be distinguished from fiat currency and e-money."[31]

Obviously, the AIFC Glossary: (i) does not classify digital assets into secured and unsecured types like the RK law does and (ii) it considers digital assets as cryptocurrency only.

Since 26 October 2021 the AIFC has set forth certain limits on purchasing digital assets by retail investors. Particularly, AIFC Rules provides that an "authorised digital asset trading facility must maintain effective systems and

31 The AIFC Glossary, the AIFC Act No. FR0017 of 29.04.2018 (as amended), p. 30, https://aifc.kz/files/legals/40/file/glo_v13_fr0017_01.07.2022.pdf.

controls to ensure that a retail client using its service does not invest, in respect of all digital assets in aggregate calculated over a period of one month, an amount which exceeds the greater of: USD 1,000; or the lesser of 10 percent of the annual income; or 5 percent of the net worth of such retail client (excluding the value of the primary residence), up to a maximum aggregate amount of USD 100,000."[32]

According to mass media, the AIFC's participants (who obviously freely deal with the digital assets within the AIFC) were expected to "start working with local banks allowing their clients the opportunity to officially and openly work with cryptocurrency."[33] And in September 2022 one of the RK's major bank has completed its first purchase of crypto for fiat[34] involving the AIFC based cryptocurrency exchange. The purchase was performed within the framework of crypto exchange – client – bank.[35]

Implementation of the mentioned purchase operation certainly violated the RK law which prohibits circulation of cryptocurrencies in Kazakhstan. Since circulation of cryptocurrency is not prohibited within AIFC, such of their intention means an unreasonable attempt to extend the exterritorial influence on the RK individuals and companies who are prohibited from dealing with cryptocurrencies.

It looks like the RK regulators try to restrict circulation of cryptocurrencies among the RK's residents only to the investing purposes. But the access to the cryptocurrencies stored on the digital wallets of the AIFC-based crypto exchanges granted to the an RK's resident banks will create a high risk of transition of payment operations from national currency (Kazakhstan Tenge) to the cryptocurrencies.

Even if such operations would be performed within the AIFC's framework, the result of them (for example, transfer of goods, works and services) will take

---

32 AIFC Authorised Market Institution (AMI), the AIFC Rules No. FR0002 of 2017, p. 45, https://aifc.kz/files/legals/57/file/ami_v6_fr0002_23.11.2020-final.pdf and https://afsa.orderly.kz/articles/6.7.-clients-of-an-authorised-digital-asset-trading-facility-and-investment-limits.

33 A. Arystanbek, Bank Accounts for Cryptocurrency Will Be Available in Kazakhstan As Country Expands Its Crypto Mining to Global Market, [27.07.2021], https://astanatimes.com/2021/07/bank-accounts-for-cryptocurrency-will-be-available-in-kazakhstan-as-country-expands-its-crypto-mining-to-global-market/.

34 H. Partz, Kazakhstan ready to legalize crypto as Russians flock to the country, [29.09.2022], https://cointelegraph.com/news/kazakhstan-ready-to-legalize-crypto-as-russians-flock-to-the-country.

35 Press release of the Eurasian Bank: Kazakhstan citizens to legally buy and sell cryptocurrency, [28.09.2022], https://eubank.kz/kazakhstantsy-smogut-legal-no-pokupat-i-prodavat-kriptovalyutu-28-09-2022/.

place on the territory of the RK. Thus, the established prohibition of cryptocurrencies' circulation in the RK territory (which is restated in the draft of the Law on Digital assets) obviously shall be ineffective. We can already observe announcement of a payment instrument (bank crypto card) to be issued by the end of 2022 which will cause indirect circulation of cryptocurrencies in the RK's territory.[36]

7.3 *The RK Central Bank's Digital Currency Pilot Project*

In December 2021 the National Bank of the RK published the Report on its pilot project concerning development of Digital Tenge (the "DT") as a central bank's digital currency (the "CBDC").[37]

The main objectives of the pilot project for 2021 included the test of the feasibility of the DT concept through the experimental confirmation of the technological realisation based on distributed ledger technology as well as the definition of the core CBDC model parameters for the RK together with all stakeholders.

There no CBDC have been introduced in the RK yet. But we share the position that a legal tender cannot be issued by any person except for the State. The CBDC has to represents a form of fiat money backed by the State and, as in Kazakhstan, secured, at least, by all assets of the NB RK.

Tragic events which took place in the RK (especially in Almaty) in the beginning of January of 2022 showed that the payment infrastructure based on internet connectivity can be useless during the public emergency. Therefore, it is highly positive sign that the RK's DT project considers the possibility of offline circulation of Digital Tenge.

8 Conclusions

The RK law has provided for a legal regime for cryptocurrencies which requires further development and improvements. For example, unification of legal terminology related to digital assets remains urgent and advisable.

Until digital mining is regulated in the RK, it is expected that the State will ensure responsible conduct of its authorised bodies and organisations, not only when establishing a legal regime and legislative prohibitions concerning

36 Ibid; as well as the current announcement on the web-site of the International Bitcoin Exchange, https://intebix.kz/ru.

37 The National Bank of the Republic of Kazakhstan: Digital Tenge (pilot project), [15.12.2021], https://nationalbank.kz/en/page/cifrovoy-tenge-pilotnyy-proekt.

cryptocurrencies, but also when allocating national resources for the implementation of one or another business activity of private entities in general. And the State continues to create legal mechanisms focused on better protection of public good and national security.

Among important directions of such efforts the State has already undertook some extremely important steps to prevent making national backup power stations available to digital miners. The reason for such steps is that those reserves cannot be used by digital miners for their narrow material interests thereby creating risks for the well-being of citizens and the continuity of other (and much more significant) economic activities in the country. The cryptocurrency industry may not ignore and hamper world-wide efforts to ensure a cleaner and more favorable ecology and the environment in general.

Certain measures to protect the national energy system from unregulated mining have been provided for by new laws passed in December 2022. Among them the following can be mentioned: (i) limiting availability of sources of electricity which can be used for mining (allowing the use of renewable energy, own generation and imported electricity only), and (ii) placing significant restrictions on consumption of electricity directly from the general energy system (where such consumption can be available for miners only with a surplus of electricity and through its purchase exclusively at a specialised exchange of the Kazakhstan's operator of the electricity and capacity). But, despite the Laws proposed better protection for the national system, it is difficult to confirm that these legislative amendments have already brought to a notable positive development.

However, the key contradiction of the existing legal framework will remain as long as allowed digital mining continues to exist despite of the existing ban of issuance and circulation of cryptocurrencies in the RK. Today such contradiction has already provided legal grounds for digital miners owning cryptocurrencies to claim an unconstitutionality of existing restrictions of their ownership rights. But it is more important to publicly recognise that digital mining can be seriously harmful for the national economy and wellbeing of our people. Therefore, digital mining on the territory of Kazakhstan should be also prohibited by law.

In addition, while the AIFC remains to function as an exorbitant jurisdiction, a clear state policy is needed to insist that the AIFC's regulations either also clearly prohibit operations with cryptocurrencies within its jurisdiction or, at least, prevent involvement of the RK citizens and companies in cryptocurrency operations sourced in the AIFC.

It should also be understood that regulation of digital assets in the AIFC and consequences for retail clients and the national economy heavily depend on a bona fide performance of the officers responsible for the AML/CFT. Therefore, both a legislative policy of the RK and regulatory policy of the AIFC should include effective measures to ensure appropriate implementation of functionalities by respective officers of those two jurisdictions. Moreover, regulators should provide for an effective mechanism protecting the RK's economy from the indirect circulation of the cryptocurrency which is potentially caused by the cooperation of the RK banks and the AIFC-based crypto exchanges.

9 Perspectives

In a mid-term perspective no grounds for existence and circulation of any cryptocurrency in Kazakhstan can be seen unless it is issued by the State and its circulation as a legal tender is fully controlled by the State. Once the State introduces a national digital currency (the DT as the RK's CBDC) we see no reason for circulation of privately created and promoted cryptocurrencies.

It appears that steps to introduce the CBDC all over the world is just an initial stage for the greater changes. The future of circulation of property rights objects is in a transition from traditional contracts to self-executable smart-contracts, which is recognised by many different States and powered by a state-recognised blockchains (though, in theory, CBDC may not be necessarily based on blockchain).

In these circumstances, introduction of the DT in the RK shall be considered as a positive development for the automation and digitalization of the circulation of different types of various assets (the most of objects of civil rights) in the RK. As soon as the NB RK decides on introduction of the DT as a third form of national currency (in addition to cash and bank account balances), property rights and some of non-property rights which are currently certified in various centralized state ledgers may be tokenized to allow more effective and secured transfers and circulation.

This is where the legal practice will evolve and probably will require local lawyers to learn coding of smart-contacts which will become a day-to-day necessity either smart-contracts will be a standalone form of agreement or an instrument for implementation of traditional written agreement.

Macau SAR (China)

Alexandr Svetlicinii and Celia Filipa Ferreira Matias

1 Definition and Legal Qualification

Under the "one country, two systems" principle embedded in the Constitution of the People's Republic of China (PRC) and implemented in the Macau Basic Law, the Macau Special Administrative Region (SAR) enjoys a high degree of autonomy in the exercise of the executive, legislative and judicial powers.[1] The Basic Law of the Macau SAR designates *Macau pataca* (MOP) as the legal tender of the region, which is issued by the Macau SAR Government.[2] Macau does not apply exchange control policies and its currency remains freely convertible.[3] The government has granted authorization to two commercial banks, Banco Nacional Ultramarino SA and Bank of China (Macau) Ltd to issue banknotes.[4] Currently, Macau does not have its own digital currency. The 2023 law on legal framework of currency issuance allows for the MOP to be issued in a digital form.[5] The law does not, however, cover 'traditional' decentralized cryptocurrencies, which leaves the current *status quo* unaltered, as described below.

The current regulatory policy of Macau SAR in relation to cryptocurrencies is based on the prevention of money laundering and other financial offenses, the protection of consumers from risks related to cryptocurrencies, as well as supporting the regulatory policies of the PRC Central Government. Macau's economy relies primarily on gambling and tourism industries while the overwhelming majority of tourists enter the SAR from Mainland China. The PRC applies currency controls by limiting the amounts of cash that can be taken out of Mainland China as well as the amounts that Mainland residents are allowed to withdraw from the ATMs outside Mainland China. As a result, the currency control policies implemented by the Mainland China authorities restrict the amounts that can be used for gambling in Macau.

In order to avoid currency controls, Mainland residents frequently resort to pawn shop services in Macau: after paying for the purchase of jewellery or

1 See Alexandr Svetlicinii, "Introduction to Macao Law" In *Legal Systems of Asia: A Short Guide* (Korea Legislation Research Institute, 2016), 39–51.

2 Macau Basic Law, Article 108.

3 Macau Basic Law, Article 109.

4 See AMCM, Currency in Circulation in Macao, https://www.amcm.gov.mo/en/currency/currency-in-circulation-in-macao.

5 Law 10/2023 (Legal Framework of Currency Issuance), Article 3.

 | DOI:10.1163/9789004722507_019

other luxury items with their credit cards, Mainland residents then pledge these items in pawn shops and thus obtain cash for gambling in Macau casinos. Since 2014, the Mainland China authorities have attempted to curtail these practices that were frequently used for money laundering and strengthened their cooperation with the relevant Macau authorities.[6] Adjusting to the new realities, several businesses in Macau started to operate "Bitcoin ATMs", which allowed Mainland residents to exchange their Bitcoins for cash while in Macau.[7]

In 2014, prompted by the consumers' inquiries and media reports on the operation of the "Bitcoin ATMs" in Macau, the Monetary Authority of Macau (AMCM) emphasized that "Bitcoin is a type of virtual commodity which is neither a legal tender nor a financial instrument subject to the supervision of the AMCM."[8] Therefore, the AMCM considered the use of terms such as "Bitcoin ATM" or other expressions implying the provision of financial services as misleading. It has warned the public that Bitcoin "virtual commodities" may entail risks related to money laundering and terrorist financing. The "Bitcoin ATMs" were subsequently renamed into "Bitcoin Vending Kiosks" and continued operations without using regular know-your-customer features such as fingerprint authentication, ID card reading, confirming messages and photographing. As a result, users could withdraw money anonymously, which increased the risk of money laundering. The courts in Mainland China have heard several criminal cases where the offenders transferred the money obtained from various scams and other illegal activities to a cryptocurrency exchange platform, bought Bitcoin, transferred the cryptocurrency to digital wallets and then exchanged it for cash in Macau.[9]

In 2018, the company Dragon Coin Group launched the initial coin offering (ICO) for Dragon Coins (DRG), which would allow investors to exchange their

6 See Mainland and Macau reach agreement on signing a memorandum of cooperation on anti-money laundering supervision (21 July 2014), https://www.yicai.com/news/3996516.html.

7 See How to exchange bitcoins for cash using bitcoin ATMs in Macau? (15 May 2019), http://www.120btc.com/baike/btc/2832.html.

8 AMCM, Caution against Engagement in Bitcoin Transactions (2 December 2015), https://www.amcm.gov.mo/en/news-notice/statement/detail/caution-against-engagement-in-bitcoin-transactions/30.

9 See Beijing Lekuda Internet Technology Ltd, Co. v. Suihua Huachen Commerce and Trade Ltd, Co. and Peng Quanquan (29 July 2016), http://wenshu.court.gov.cn/website/wenshu/181107ANFZ0BXSK4/index.html?docId=ce26a59964e944ab96fdb04617d482b4.

tokens for physical casino chips that can then be used for gambling.[10] As the cryptocurrency remained unregulated in Macau, the AMCM reacted by issuing another press release,[11] where it explicitly excluded the qualification of "virtual currencies" as legal tender or financial assets, ascribing to them, instead, the *prima facie* qualification of "digital commodities."[12]

Since cryptocurrencies are not subjected to supervision or regulation in the Macau SAR, there are no statutory or codified provisions dealing with the legal definition of "cryptocurrencies" in public or private law. In its press releases, which are not binding for the public authorities or courts, the AMCM has referred to cryptocurrencies as "type of virtual commodity" that is not recognized neither as "legal tender" nor as "financial instrument."[13] On another occasion, the AMCM referred to cryptocurrencies as "tokens and virtual currencies", which can be "traded", albeit outside the financial regulation framework.[14] The AMCM also acknowledged that "virtual currencies or virtual commodities" can be used as means of payment, but such payment services cannot be provided in Macau by the financial institutions regulated under the Financial System Act enforced by the AMCM.[15]

In the absence of statutory regulation of the transactions with cryptocurrencies, the legal relationships between the different participants (*e.g.* miners, wallet providers, wallet holders, custodians, customers, issuers, *etc.*) to a blockchain on which cryptocurrencies are transferred and recorded will be governed by private law rules concerning property rights and contracts. This allows the participants to a blockchain to arrange their relationships as

---

10 See Dragon Coin won't face any issues with Macau regulators – CEO (Macau Business, 29 May 2018), https://www.macaubusiness.com/dragon-coin-wont-face-any-issues-with-macau-regulators-ceo/.

11 AMCM, AMCM reiterates virtual currencies are not legal tenders Public is urged to be vigilant against potential fraud (6 August 2018), https://www.amcm.gov.mo/en/news-notice/statement/detail/virtual-coin/525.

12 See also Macau issues cryptocurrency crime warning after link to former triad boss emerges (South China Morning Post, 20 April 2018), https://www.scmp.com/news/hong-kong/economy/article/2142562/macau-monetary-bosses-issue-warning-over-cryptocurrency-links?module=perpetual_scroll_0&pgtype=article&campaign=2142562.

13 AMCM, Caution against Engagement in Bitcoin Transactions (2 December 2015), https://www.amcm.gov.mo/en/news-notice/statement/detail/caution-against-engagement-in-bitcoin-transactions/30.

14 AMCM, Alert to Risks of Virtual Commodities and Tokens (27 September 2017), https://www.amcm.gov.mo/en/news-notice/statement/detail/alert-to-risks-of-virtual-commodities-and-tokens/642.

15 AMCM, AMCM reiterates virtual currencies are not legal tenders. Public is urged to be vigilant against potential fraud (6 August 2018), https://www.amcm.gov.mo/en/news-notice/statement/detail/virtual-coin/525.

provision of services subjected to the concrete terms of any agreements governing these services. Under the principles of private autonomy and contractual freedom, such contracts may contain any lawful clauses, not being subject to a *numerus clausus* rule, as is the case of rights *in rem*. The Macau Civil Code specifically regulates several contracts ("typical contracts"), setting out rules regarding the obligations of the parties, effects, and other aspects of the contract in question. These rules can assist in determining the applicable legal framework in case of atypical contracts.

A wallet is an electronic means of "storage" of cryptocurrencies within the blockchain,[16] which involves the custody by the wallet provider of a private key giving access to the tokens "owned" by a certain participant. Exchanges are platforms for converting and trading cryptocurrencies.[17] Users "deposit" their tokens in a wallet provided by the exchange and grant access to their private keys, allowing it to perform certain operations on their account, such as conversion and negotiation of cryptocurrencies, for which it charges a commission. These arrangements may, subject to the terms agreed between the parties, be deemed to correspond to a contract of mandate, by which "one of the parties promises to perform one or more legal actions on account of another".[18] In certain cases, provided the relevant intermediaries are engaged in a commercial activity, the legal framework of the contract of agency, by which "one of the parties promises to enter into contracts on account of another, in an autonomous and stable manner, for remuneration"[19] may apply.

2 Regulatory Framework

The Financial System Act provides for licensing of the following types of financial institutions: (1) "non-bank credit institution" that engages in investment or use of clients' funds maintained at the same institution; (2) "other financial institution" that does not engage in investment or use of clients' funds maintained at the same institution but provides payment services.[20] None of the above categories covers operations with cryptocurrencies, which leads

16 Kuo Chuen, David Lee, and Robert H. Deng (eds), *Handbook of Blockchain, Digital Finance, and Inclusion, Volume 1: Cryptocurrency, FinTech, InsurTech, and Regulation*, Elsevier Science & Technology, 2017, p. 215.

17 Ibid, p. 210.

18 Commercial Code, approved by Decree-Law no. 40/99/M, of 3 August 1999, Article 1083.

19 Commercial Code, approved by Decree-Law no. 40/99/M, of 3 August 1999, Article 622.

20 Decree-Law no. 32/93/M of 5th July, Approves the Legal Regime of the Financial System of the Territory of Macau, https://bo.io.gov.mo/bo/i/93/27/declei32.asp#32, Article 1.

to a situation where cryptocurrencies appear outside the legal framework for financial services in Macau. However, the provision of financial services in relation to asset management, as well as currency exchange or funds transfer are covered by the above-mentioned sector-specific legislation. In the absence of the dedicated regulatory framework for cryptocurrencies, the region's financial regulator, the AMCM, has routinely resorted to soft law and advocacy to mitigate potential risks related to cryptocurrency transactions.

AMCM has repeatedly warned banks, other financial institutions and the general public of various risks related to cryptocurrency transactions and called upon the regulated entities to abstain from such transactions. In a 2017 press release, the AMCM defined cryptocurrency as a virtual commodity, which is "neither a legal tender nor a financial instrument subject to supervision."[21] The AMCM has warned the public of considerable risks related to trading of cryptocurrencies such as money laundering and terrorism financing. In 2018, AMCM has explicitly required all banks and payment services institutions in Macau SAR "not to participate in or provide, directly or indirectly, any financial services that involve the use of virtual currencies or virtual commodities as the means of payment."[22] In 2022, the AMCM further reiterated that virtual currencies are characterized by a high level of speculation and fall outside the scope of its supervision, which leaves residents vulnerable to fraud or even to being involved in criminal activities.[23]

Currently, Macau does not have any specific law or regulation (either in force or in draft) dealing with the regulation of cryptocurrencies. At the same time, the regulatory approach taken by the AMCM, which, through advocacy and supervision of the financial institutions, discourages all types of operations with cryptocurrencies, makes it practically impossible for intermediary wallet services providers to be registered and operate within the jurisdiction of Macau. For example, an e-wallet operator will find it impossible to carry out its activities in connection to the financial institutions in Macau, which have been instructed by the AMCM not to support any cryptocurrency-related transactions.

21 AMCM, Alert to Risks of Virtual Commodities and Tokens (27 September 2017), https://www.amcm.gov.mo/en/news-notice/statement/detail/alert-to-risks-of-virtual-commodities-and-tokens/642.

22 AMCM, AMCM reiterates virtual currencies are not legal tenders Public is urged to be vigilant against potential fraud (6 August 2018), https://www.amcm.gov.mo/en/news-notice/statement/detail/virtual-coin/525.

23 AMCM, AMCM urges residents in general to be cautious regarding possible risks arising from the fact that virtual currencies are not legal tender (6 January 2022), https://www.gov.mo/pt/noticias/580320/.

3 Private Law Issues

3.1 *General Traits of Macau Private Law*

The private law of the Macau SAR is influenced by Continental European law, via the Portuguese legal system and, therefore, it can be classified as a civil law legal system. As such, the main sources of private law are the Civil Code[24] (CC), the Commercial Code[25] (ComC) and the Civil Procedure Code[26] (CPC).

The CC regulates the main areas of general private law, including obligations, property, family and succession law. The ComC regulates various aspects of the commercial activity, including, *inter alia*, commercial companies, commercial contracts, and securities. The CPC regulates judicial proceedings in private law matters, serving, in addition, as the subsidiary procedural framework for unregulated matters from other branches of procedural law.

The interpretation of legal provisions is guided by the CC, which directs the interpreter to go beyond the letter of the law (albeit without entirely abandoning it) and to "reconstitute, based on the legal texts, the legal thought, considering in particular the unity of the legal system, the circumstances in which the law was created and the specific conditions of the time in which it is applied."[27] This allows the interpreter to apply old laws to new situations, even when the legislator could not have envisioned those situations. All the above-mentioned texts (CC, ComC and CPC) were enacted in 1999, after the Internet had become a reality but before the legislator could have considered the emergence of cryptocurrencies.

As a civil law legal system, Macau law does not contemplate the rule of precedent. Therefore, aside from those resulting from a specific type of appeal set out in the CPC, court decisions hold merely interpretative value, which may be deemed equivalent to that of legal doctrine. In this regard, it must be noted that, given the relatively recent establishment of the Macau SAR (in 1999), many legal issues are yet to be the subject of local court decisions and legal doctrine (although great effort on the latter has been made in recent years, notably with the publication of annotated codes and textbooks). Considering the historical relationship with the Portuguese legal system, Portuguese scholarly opinions and court decisions are still considered of some persuasion in the practice of local courts and public authorities. There is, however, a need for careful consideration of any textual variations and differences in context.

24 Civil Code, approved by Decree-Law no. 39/99/M of 3 August 1999.

25 Commercial Code, approved by Decree-Law no. 40/99/M, of 3 August 1999.

26 Civil Procedure Code, approved by Decree-Law 55/99/M, of 8 October 1999.

27 CC, Article 8.

3.2 *Property Rights*

In the context of private law, the legal qualification of cryptocurrencies has extensive implications. For instance, from the standpoint of property law (or "the law of things", as per the terminology adopted in the CC), the qualification of tokens as "things" determines whether they may be deemed the subject of rights of ownership or other rights *in rem*, and the applicability of the corresponding legal protection (e.g. the action to recognize and enforce ownership rights).

The CC sets out that "only *things* can be the subject of the right of ownership regulated in this Code."[28] Ownership is one among several rights *in rem* regulated by the CC. Rights *in rem* are considered to be subject to a *numerus clausus* rule, i.e. only those set forth by law can be deemed to have that quality. From among that catalogue of *in rem* rights, ownership is considered the widest in terms of the powers that can be exercised over a thing.

Another aspect worth noting is that article 1226 of the Macau CC differs from the corresponding provision of the Portuguese Civil Code[29] in that it does not require things to be corporeal to be the subject of ownership rights regulated by the Code. Both codes, however, exclude author's rights (copyright) and industrial property from their scope.[30]

This exclusion should be understood as merely systematic, meaning that both codes admit the existence of non-corporeal things (such as intellectual creations inventions and trademarks), which are the subject of exclusive rights regulated elsewhere. Therefore, both Codes admit the possibility that non-corporeal things can be the subject of ownership rights.

Considering that cryptocurrency tokens cannot be qualified as intellectual property,[31] and, consequently, the intellectual property legal framework is not directly applicable (although it might apply by analogy in certain cases), one must revert to the CC in search for a workable legal framework for cryptocurrencies. In this regard, the first step is to determine if cryptocurrencies may be qualified as things.

---

28 CC, Article 1226.

29 Approved by Decree-Law no. 47344/66, of 25 November 1966.

30 António Menezes Cordeiro, *Tratado de Direito Civil Português, I Parte Geral, Tomo II Coisas* (*Treaty of Portuguese Civil Law, I General Part, Tome II Things*), *2nd Ed*, Almedina 2002, pp. 108–113.

31 Whereas the underlying code may be protected by copyright, what is at stake in this context is the token itself as a unit representative of value and not that of intellectual creation.

"Thing" is defined by CC as an "autonomous reality, external to the person, endowed with utility and susceptible of being *the object* of legal relationships of dominion."[32]

As per the first criterion, a thing is autonomous if it does not depend on another reality to exist. For instance, body parts (e.g. a hand) are considered non – autonomous for these purposes. One might ask if, having an underlying computer code, the tokens may be deemed separate from it. Reasoning by analogy, tokens may be said to be autonomous in the same way that a literary work is independent from its carrier (e.g. a book, printed in paper or in electronic format).

Second, tokens are "external to a person" as they are neither physical parts of a person, nor rights of personality or family rights.[33]

Third, cryptocurrencies have been characterized as having multiple functions, with tokens classified as currency, commodity, asset, etc.[34] Their utility can be deemed correspondent to either of these functions (or a combination thereof, as in the case of hybrid tokens).

A possible (albeit unlikely) qualification of tokens as legal tender would not exclude their qualification as things. Money has, in fact, been qualified by scholars as a movable (corporeal) thing representative of value.[35]

Finally, things must be susceptible of being individually appropriated. This requirement has been said to exclude the qualification as a thing for realities like the Sun, the oceans or the planet Earth. Tokens may be digitally appropriated and such dominion is recorded in the blockchain and the digital wallet.

Therefore, there is at least a theoretical possibility of cryptocurrencies being qualified as "things". However, besides establishing such theoretical qualification, it is of the utmost importance to determine the applicable legal framework.

As mentioned above, the most widely accepted example of non-corporeal things are intellectual creations, which have been regulated separately. In the absence of special legislation on cryptocurrencies, it must be inquired if the provisions of the CC on matters of property can apply. A possible answer may

32 CC, Article 193/1.

33 João Gil de Oliveira, João Cândido de Pinho, *Código Civil de Macau: anotado e comentado: jurisprudência, Livro 1 Parte Geral* (*Macau Civil Code: annotation and commentary, Case Law, Book 1, General Part*), Centro de Formação Jurídica e Judiciária, 2018, p. 111.

34 José Engrácia Antunes, 'As Criptomoedas' ('Cryptocurrencies'), (2021) I/II Revista da Ordem dos Advogados 119.

35 António Menezas Cordeiro, *Tratado de Direito Civil Português, I Parte Geral, Tomo II Coisas* (*Treaty of Portuguese Civil Law, I General Part, Tome II Things*), *2nd Ed*, Almedina 2002, pp. 149–150.

be found in article 1227/2, which prescribes that such provisions may apply subsidiarily to the intellectual property provisions (copyright and industrial property), if they are in *harmony* with the nature of such institutes and do not contradict their specific legal frameworks. It could then be said that property law rules may apply to cryptocurrencies to the extent that such rules (or a particular rule) are in harmony with their nature.

For example, if X has 60 Bitcoins registered in her wallet, there is room to argue that X has legal ownership over those tokens. In accordance with article 1229 of the CC, she has the full and exclusive right of possession, use, and disposition of the things. This corresponds to the abilities granted to blockchain users by way of code, which mimics physical possession.

The CC provides that the transfer of property rights over a specific thing takes place as a mere effect of the conclusion of a contract. In this regard, the possession of the private key may affect the assignment of the property rights over the tokens.[36] If X has 60 Bitcoins registered in her wallet and the wallet is a decentralized wallet, which means X is the one who manages the private key to the 60 Bitcoins, then X has legal ownership over the 60 Bitcoins in her wallet. Suppose X has 60 Bitcoins registered in her wallet and the wallet is a centralized wallet, which means the wallet provider is the one who manages the unique private key to the 60 Bitcoins. In that case, X does not have the legal ownership over the 60 Bitcoins in her wallet. In such a case, one can argue that X has a creditor's right against the wallet service provider for the 60 Bitcoins.

On the contrary, if X opens an account with MontC, an intermediary that provides wallet services, MontC would be a mere holder as it merely has "custody" of the private keys, holding them in X's name and not being externally perceived by others as owner.[37]

Airdrop of new tokens to X's wallet, as a result of a hardfork, would be deemed a form of primary acquisition, as the token did not have a prior owner. The CC allows for the "occupation" of "animals and movable things" with the mentioned characteristic of never having had an owner. The provisions in the section dedicated to this form of acquisition are not easily adapted to a non-corporeal reality, which underscores the difficulties in applying a set of rules to cryptocurrencies that did not envisage their emergence.[38] Besides this rule, new tokens may be seen as "future things" from the parties' perspective when entering into a contract. For instance, MontC's conditions of service

36 CC, Article 402.

37 CC, Article 1177.

38 CC, Articles 1243 ff.

may stipulate the ownership of new tokens airdropped to X's wallet.[39] In the absence of such stipulation, for the above-stated reasons, attributing ownership to X would be correct.

Based on the above discussion concerning the differences between decentralized (off-chain) and centralized (on-chain) wallets, the ownership over new tokens generated by the hardfork will also depend on the access to private keys. At the same time, one can argue that the new token is a "natural fruit" that comes directly from the on-chain wallet,[40] and therefore, X should automatically acquire property rights over these newly created "fruits".

The decentralized nature of blockchain technology makes cross-border relationships common. The CC is also the main source of conflict of laws rules in Macau. Articles 45 and 46 use the criterion *lex rei sitae* (place where the thing is located) for property law cases. For things in transit, article 45 applies the law of the place of destination. Neither criterion seems adequate to the reality of cryptocurrencies. A more suitable solution is prescribed by article 47 in case of author's rights, related rights and industrial property – the applicable law is the law of the place where protection of the right is sought. The above rule could be applied to tokens by analogy. If this interpretation was accepted, a claim before a Macau court relating to cryptocurrency tokens, based on property law would be decided in accordance with the laws of Macau. Conversely, foreign law might apply if protection were sought elsewhere.

3.2 *Transfer of Ownership*

The following sections consider, with reference to hypothetical scenarios, the solutions that Macau law might offer in relation to problems arising from several types of transactions with tokens, namely transfer, loan and pledge.

3.3.1 Gratuitous Transfer

The contract of gift, whereby someone transfers a thing or right, or assumes an obligation in favor of another person, at the cost of one's own property, with a charitable spirit is regulated by the CC. As a matter of principle, there is no apparent legal obstacle to the gifting of tokens. The main requirement for the conclusion of the contract is the acceptance by the beneficiary,[41] which, regarding movable things, is understood as the material transfer of the thing or a representative title thereof. By analogy, the acceptance of a gift of tokens occurs with the electronic transfer of tokens, in accordance to technical processes

39 CC, Article 202.

40 CC, Articles 204 and 205.

41 CC, Article 939.

of the blockchain. If the transfer is not immediate, the gift may be concluded through written agreement.[42]

Other general aspects to take into consideration are the prohibition of gift *mortis causa*;[43] the prohibition of gift of future goods;[44] and the personal character of the gift,[45] which entails that, in principle, a person cannot appoint another, by way of mandate, to designate the beneficiary or to determine the object of the gift. This last aspect is particularly relevant when the intervention of intermediaries is considered. On one hand, it seems to imply that certain aspects of a gift may be carried out by intermediaries (e.g. the physical – or electronic – transfer of the thing), but two essential aspects of the contract – the beneficiary and the object – cannot be determined by the intermediary. This limitation applies to both wallet and exchange providers.

The gratuitous transfer of tokens can be also viewed as a transfer of information (private key) from one person to another directly, or using a wallet provider as an intermediary. In this regard, there is no need to consider the provisions regulating the contract of gift as the relationship between the transferor and the wallet provider is governed by the terms of the services contract concluded between them.

In a cross-border situation, the laws of another jurisdiction could apply, depending on the location of certain elements of the legal relationship and the determinations made by the parties. The general rule applicable to the substantial contractual regime is the law chosen or envisaged by the parties,[46] subject to the existence of a "serious interest" of the parties in the application of that law, or a connection with any of the relevant elements of the legal relationship.[47] The validity and interpretation of the contractual declaration follows the law determined according to these criteria.[48] However, in terms of validity, it may be sufficient to comply with the requirements of form set out by the laws of the place where the declaration is made.[49]

---

42 According to article 3 of Law no. 5/2005, an electronic document satisfies the requirements of written form for the purposes of Macau law if its content can be represented as a written declaration and its integrity can be demonstrated.

43 CC, Article 940.

44 CC, Article 936/1.

45 CC, Article 943.

46 CC, Article 40/1.

47 CC, Article 40/2.

48 CC, Article 34.

49 CC, Article 35.

3.3.2 Transfer for Consideration

The qualification of a transfer of tokens for consideration depends on the terms of that transfer, the nature of the consideration in each transaction, and the fundamental issue of whether tokens can be viewed as legal tender (as previously discussed).

The sale and purchase contract is regulated by the CC and defined as a "contract whereby the property of a thing or other right is transferred for a price".[50] The payment of "price" is understood as a pecuniary obligation, which is discharged through the delivery of currency with legal tender in Macau.[51]

Therefore, in a scenario where X has 60 Bitcoins registered in her wallet, and wants to sell 5 Bitcoins for a certain amount expressed in MOP, this amount is considered a price.[52] The 5 Bitcoins are, as argued above, non-corporeal things, which can be the object of legal relationships, in this case, the sale and purchase for a pecuniary consideration set in MOP.

Several conditions applicable to the sale and purchase of cryptocurrency tokens are set out in the CC:

1. The prohibition of selling goods owned by another person without authorization.[53] Such sales shall be deemed null and void. Still, the seller cannot enforce the invalidity against a good faith buyer, and a buyer who intentionally enters into such contract cannot enforce the invalidity thereof against a good faith seller.
2. The contract of sale and purchase results in the transfer of ownership over a thing (*in rem* effect) or right, the creation of an obligation to pay the price, and, where applicable, an obligation to deliver the thing. Along with ownership over the thing or right, the contract causes the risk of destruction or deterioration of the thing to be transferred to the buyer. This effect can, however, be delayed or modified by agreement between the parties.[54]
3. Except for the sale and purchase of immovable things, the sale and purchase agreement can generally be concluded in any form, including oral.
4. The contract of sale can be entered into by a third party on account or on behalf of the parties. In the case of an exchange or other intermediary in the context of cryptocurrency transactions, the rules governing agency may apply.

---

50 CC, Article 865.
51 CC, Article 543.
52 CC, Article 865.
53 CC, Article 882.
54 CC, Article 795.

For example, if X has 60 Bitcoins registered in her wallet and wants to sell 5 Bitcoins against 10 Ethers. In this case, considering the position expressed by the Macau authorities, both cryptocurrencies are unlikely to be considered legal tender and, consequently, a "price". Therefore, the contract cannot be qualified as sale and purchase. Instead, it is considered an atypical contract, publicly known as a contract of exchange, but not specifically regulated in the CC. As it entails the transfer of a thing for consideration, the contract of exchange follows the legal framework of the contract of sale and purchase, to the extent that such provisions are compatible with the nature and framework of the agreement.[55] Therefore, many of the conditions set out in respect of the contract of sale and purchase also apply to the contract of exchange.

The transfer of tokens for consideration may involve the transfer of legal tender (currency) between the seller and buyer. As discussed above, the commercial banks and other financial institutions in Macau are discouraged by the AMCM to support any transactions involving cryptocurrencies. Therefore, the transfer of funds related for the cryptocurrency trading can be refused by the financial institutions in Macau and could be reported to the regulatory authorities as "suspicious transactions" pursuant to the anti-money laundering regulations.[56]

3.4 *Loan*

The contract of loan is defined by the CC as a "contract whereby a party lends money or another fungible thing to another, and the other party shall return the same amount of the same kind and quantity."[57] Fungible things are those which can be understood as perfectly replaceable items. Thus, irrespective of the qualification of tokens as money (which, as mentioned, is bound to face opposition of local authorities), it is still legally possible to enter into a loan of cryptocurrency tokens. However, significant uncertainties arise as to the applicable legal framework, due to a lack of specific legal provisions in the Macau legal system.

One of such uncertainties is the determination and payment of interest. To illustrate the issue, the following hypothetical scenario is considered: PayB is a company regulated and supervised in its home jurisdiction to provide lending services. Z is a company whose seat is in Macau. Z intends to borrow 60

55 CC, Article 933.

56 Administrative Regulation No. 7/2006 Approves measures of a preventive nature against money laundering and terrorist financing crimes, https://bo.io.gov.mo/bo/i/2006/20/regadm07.asp, Article 7.

57 CC, Article 1070.

bitcoins from PayB, with an interest rate of 5% payable either in MOP or in Bitcoins. Further to what was said, the contract would be qualified as a loan of a fungible thing (the Bitcoins). Pursuant to the CC,[58] the lender can be remunerated by the stipulation of interest, which cannot, however, exceed three times the legal interest rate.[59]

The above case has two options for determining the interest rate: in Bitcoin and in MOP. The first hypothesis seems less problematic, as both principal and interest would be units or subunits of the same kind. If, however, it is stipulated that interest shall be payable in MOP, the parties must determine the moment of conversion, which may have significant consequences, considering the fluctuation of the value of cryptocurrencies against legal tender. Moreover, as cryptocurrencies are not deemed legal tender, the rules on obligations in specific legal tender other than MOP do not apply.[60]

The parties may select the laws of Macau to regulate their contractual relationship or the laws of any other jurisdiction to which the transaction has a relevant connection, or which corresponds to a serious interest of the parties.[61] Issues related to the interpretation of the contractual declarations shall follow the law determined as per article 40 of the CC, and matters of form shall follow the same rule, subject to a *favor negotii* clause.[62]

In another scenario, PayB is a regulated company authorised to provide lending services in Macau and Z is a company whose seat is in Macau. Z intends to borrow 60 Bitcoins from PayB,[63] at an interest rate of 5% payable in Bitcoins. Z pays back in Bitcoin Cash.[64] In this case, it must be inquired whether this payment of Bitcoin Cash liberated Z from its obligation to repay the principal. As previously noted, a loan presupposes the return of fungible things of the same kind and quantity as the initially borrowed. Macau courts have not decided any cases of cryptocurrency loans up to the time of writing and, therefore, the interpretation of applicable legal provisions[65] in this scenario remains unpredictable. If Bitcoin and Bitcoin Cash are deemed to be things of different kinds,

58 CC, Article 1072.

59 CC, Article 1073/1. Pursuant to Executive Order no. 29/2006 on legal and stipulated interest rates without determining the rate or quantity, the current legal interest rate is 9.75%.

60 CC, Article 545.

61 CC, Article 40.

62 CC, Article 35.

63 This hypothesis is, at present, merely theoretical, considering AMCM's instructions to local financial institutions to not engage in "virtual currency" operations or transactions.

64 Bitcoin equivalents resulting from a fork in the initial Bitcoin blockchain.

65 CC, Article 1070.

then Z's obligation to repay shall only be deemed performed if PayB consents to such payment.[66]

3.5 *Pledge*

The Macau legal system does not prohibit the use of cryptocurrencies to secure the repayment of loans or performance of other obligations. Indeed, the use of intellectual property rights, which are also considered as non-corporeal things to secure obligations is a fairly established practice in our jurisdiction.

The applicable legal framework depends on the terms of the agreement between the parties and whether the secured obligations arise from the performance of a commercial activity. The CC regulates pledge in two different forms: the pledge over things and the pledge over rights. Although the qualification of tokens as things has been proposed throughout this report, the application of the rules on the pledge of rights appears as more consistent with the practice and scholarship that applies this legal framework to intellectual property rights.[67]

Exclusively for commercial debts, the ComC sets out an additional form of security – the floating charge, which is defined as "a security over all or some of the goods, except immovable goods, that are allocated to a commercial enterprise, the effects of which shall be suspended until the moment when the creditor calls for the consolidation [*crystallization*] of the security, provided the legally or contractually provided conditions have taken place."[68] This form of security has been understood in legal practice to be applicable to intellectual property rights, namely trademarks. This security is subject to written form requirement with witnessed signatures, and registration with the Commercial and Movable Assets Registry.[69] In view of the foregoing if, for instance, Z, a company whose seat is in Macau, has agreed to pledge 30 Bitcoins registered in its wallet to secure a loan for the financing of a specific project, it may grant both a pledge of rights and a floating charge (assuming the 'project' is of commercial nature) or either of them.

If Z's Bitcoin wallet is kept by an intermediary, there is a risk that, when enforcement is sought, the wallet provider fails to release the Bitcoins. Therefore, it is likely that creditors would seek further assurance that such enforcement will be feasible, such as some form of commitment on the part of the

66 CC, Article 828.

67 Mário Júlio de Almeida Costa, *Direito das Obrigações* (*Law of Obligations*), 9th Ed, Almedina 2004, p. 861.

68 ComC, Article 928.

69 ComC, Article 931.

wallet provider. In addition, this security may be understood as referring to creditor's right towards the wallet provider. To ensure the efficacy of the pledge (even though doubts remain on this interpretation), prudence would dictate the notification of the pledge to the relevant intermediary.[70]

As stated in previous subsections, the law applicable to contractual obligations shall be the law chosen by the parties, with the already mentioned restrictions and exceptions regarding validity requirements. In addition, as the pledge is considered an *in rem* security, the issue of whether *lex rei sitae* is applicable should be considered. As suggested above, the application by analogy of legal provisions related to intellectual property is considered appropriate, given the nature of cryptocurrencies.[71] Consequently, the law of the place where protection of the right is sought would apply.

Finally, one should note that due to the regulatory approach of the AMCM, the commercial banks and other financial institutions in Macau are prohibited from supporting any cryptocurrency-related transactions. As a result, these institutions will be unlikely to accept tokens as a security for loans or to support any payments related to such arrangements.

3.6 *Trust*

Macau enacted its Trusts Law in 2022.[72] The new law is parsimonious in its provisions and makes no mention of specific types of assets other than those subject to registration. Therefore, whether a trust of cryptocurrencies can be created is a matter for interpretation – which currently relies only on the text of the law, considering that the courts are yet to apply it in practice.

As a rule, any assets that at the time of the establishment of the trust are determined or determinable can be trust property.[73] In cases involving cryptocurrencies, a scenario of indeterminacy is plausible, especially if the trust was created by will and came into effect after the death of the founder.[74] If the trust property is not determinable, the trust is considered null and void.[75]

Another possible cause of invalidity of the trust is to have a purpose contrary to law or public order or in case of unlawful trust property. Despite the lack of regulation on cryptocurrencies in Macau, there is currently no reason

70 CC, Article 677/2.

71 CC, Article 47.

72 Law no. 15/2022, published on the 13 November 2022 ("Trusts Law").

73 Trusts Law, Article 10.1.

74 According to Article 3 of the Trusts Law, a trust can be constituted either by contract or by will.

75 Trusts Law, Article 8(2).

to believe that cryptocurrencies will be considered contrary to law or public order for the purposes of this provision.

Among the duties of the trustees is that of managing the trust by oneself (i.e. without sub-contracting or otherwise fully assigning the relevant functions). However, provided that the constitutive act of the trust so allows or in case of just cause, the trustee may appoint third parties to perform one or more acts or functions within the purpose of the trust.[76] This may allow trustees to use intermediary services, such as exchanges. If these intermediaries are already engaged at the time of the establishment of the trust, that circumstance should be regulated in the constitutive act (be it contractual or testamentary).

3.7 *Seizure and Attachment*

Macau civil procedural law allows both seizure and attachment (in the sense of temporary seizure) of goods within judicial proceedings. The procedure of attachment follows the rules regulating the seizure and, therefore, this analysis will focus on the latter.

Pursuant to CPC, seizure may be applied to any assets of the debtor.[77] The CPC distinguishes between seizure of immovable goods, movable goods and rights. As proposed earlier, cryptocurrency tokens may be qualified as non-corporeal things, which does not strictly correspond to any of the mentioned categories. Although, conceptually, this might come across as contradictory, in order to identify a workable legal framework, it may be necessary to apply by analogy provisions on the seizure of rights and, whenever the tokens are held in a wallet, rules on the seizure of bank deposits.[78]

Thus, in a case where X has 60 bitcoins registered in her wallet and a creditor wants to enforce a claim against the Bitcoin, the creditor has to initiate enforcement proceedings. Assuming that the requirements for the enforcement are met, the court then notifies the debtor about the assets to be seized, which must be seizable and sufficient for the payment of the total debt and charges.[79] Thus, if the debtor identifies other assets the value of which is sufficient to repay the debt, the creditor cannot demand seizure of the Bitcoins. The right to identify the assets to be seized is, however, transferred to the creditor if the debtor did not identify any alternative assets, or the value of the identified assets is not sufficient to repay the debt.[80]

76 Trusts Law, Article 20.
77 CPC, Article 704.
78 CPC, Article 749.
79 CPC, Article 717.
80 CPC, Article 720.

If the Bitcoins are held in a wallet, as mentioned, the rules on seizure of bank deposits may apply by analogy.[81] In this case, the court requests the wallet provider to disclose the balance of X's account on the date of the seizure and X is notified that those amounts shall remain unavailable henceforth. Certain operations may, however, still be carried out, namely those initiated before the seizure.

Following the initial phases of enforcement proceedings, repayment of the debt may be conducted through (1) delivery of cash, (2) assignment of attached assets, (3) assignment of income from the attached assets, and/or (4) the proceeds of the sale of attached assets.[82] Macau procedural laws apply to any court proceedings taking place in Macau. Substantive aspects of the dispute are decided in accordance with the relevant private international law rules, as described in the preceding sections. Enforcement proceedings based on judgements issued by Macau courts are referred to the court that decided the case in the first instance. Enforcement proceedings based on arbitral awards are referred to the court of first instance.[83] Enforcement proceedings based on decisions of foreign courts or arbitrators are processed in conjunction with the proceedings for the recognition of the foreign judgement or arbitral award.[84]

3.8 *Insolvency*

Insolvency proceedings are regulated by CPC, which provides the procedural framework in which creditors' rights may be satisfied. Cryptocurrency tokens may appear within these procedures as assets held by the bankrupt entity, but their legal treatment shall depend on the circumstances.

In a hypothetical scenario X has 60 Bitcoins registered in her account with wallet provider, MontC.[85] In what terms can X recover those tokens if MontC becomes insolvent? The previous qualification of tokens as things warrants, in our view, their treatment as assets not belonging to the insolvent entity.

Under the substantive framework of the contract of agency, it is a duty of the agent to return to the principal any things in her possession.[86] However,

81 CPC, Article 749.

82 CPC, Article 765.

83 CPC, Article 21.

84 CPC, Article 24.

85 Assumed, for the purposes of this work, to be duly licensed to provide wallet services in Macau. However, this hypothetical status does not correspond to the regulatory reality in Macau at present, as there are no specific licensing requirements for the provision of such services.

86 CC, Article 1087.

the mere fact that agency does not imply the transfer of ownership of those things to the agent would determine, on its own, that restitution.

If the terms of the arrangement between X and MontC differ from this paradigm, a different conclusion might be reached. For instance, if there is a transfer of ownership from X to MontC, then X's right to receive the Bitcoins will be a creditor's right, to be claimed together with the others within the bankruptcy proceedings. The difference in consequences is substantial. Whereas creditors only have a right to have their claims satisfied through the sale of MontC's assets, the owners of assets held by MontC on their account have a right to have those assets returned to them.

In procedural terms, if those assets (in this hypothesis, X's Bitcoins) are erroneously included in MontC's assets during insolvency proceedings,[87] X has several opportunities to request the return of those assets. After the declaration of insolvency by the court, within the deadline set out in such decision, the owners of assets of which the insolvent was a mere "possessor on another person's behalf" can request the return of such assets.[88] No such assets can be sold within the insolvency proceedings until that request has reached a final decision without the possibility of appeal.

In another scenario, Z is a company which opened an account with MontC as it accepts payments in Bitcoin and other cryptocurrencies. Z's wallet is worth USD 200,000 in different cryptocurrencies. Z becomes insolvent. In this hypothesis, Z's creditors would seek to obtain satisfaction of their claims through the assets held by MontC on Z's account. These actions may involve court proceedings against MontC in case of failure to surrender Z's crypto assets. Once the deadline for opposition has elapsed, the bankruptcy administrator lists all claims to be recognized or verified.[89] The final decision ranks all such claims, either in relation to the estate of the insolvent entity, or, in the case of secured claims, in relation to the specific assets (including the cryptocurrency tokens). At the end of the proceedings, the assets are sold for the satisfaction of the creditors' rights.

If, however, the arrangement between Z and MontC involved the transfer of property over the tokens to MontC, this transfer can only be invalidated under certain circumstances. Otherwise, the tokens would not be included into the debtor's assets subjected to insolvency proceedings.

---

87 CPC, Article 1095.

88 CPC, Article 1153.

89 CPC, Article 1144 CPC.

Macau courts hold exclusive jurisdiction over proceedings leading to the insolvency of legal entities registered in Macau. Macau law applies to any proceedings taking place in Macau courts.[90]

3.9 *Inheritance*

Aside from practical issues related to the transfer of private keys, there is no legal obstacle to the inheritance of cryptocurrency assets, which would be integrated in the deceased's estate upon his/her passing. A portion of the person's assets is reserved for the mandatory succession and inherited by certain classes of successors defined by law, such as the spouse and descendants. The remaining part will go to the beneficiary(ies) according to the person's will. If a person dies without a will, that portion of assets is also allocated to the classes of successors defined and ranked by law.[91]

The administrator of the estate is responsible for identifying all of the deceased's assets and, whenever necessary, request the delivery of assets held by third parties, both judicially and extra-judicially.[92] In the case of cryptocurrencies, if the deceased never revealed her private key, it may be impossible, in practice, to access those assets. If, however, they are held by an intermediary who holds the private key, such intermediary may be required by court to surrender the assets to the heirs.

The law applicable to succession shall be the law of the place of residence of the deceased at the time of passing.[93] However, the capacity to create, modify or revoke a will is determined by the law of the place of residence at the time of making the will.[94]

3.10 *Civil Liability*

The Macau legal system distinguishes between contractual and extra-contractual civil liability. Extra-contractual liability is regulated through a general clause in the CC, which refers to liability for unlawful actions.[95] There are specific provisions for strict liability, which shall not be considered in this report.

The requisite elements of extra-contractual liability include: (1) an action (or omission), (2) wrongfulness ("unlawful violation of someone's right or any

90 CPC, Article 20.
91 CC, Article 1973.
92 CC, Article 1926.
93 CC, Article 59.
94 CC, Article 60.
95 CC, Article 477.

legal provision aimed at protecting someone's interests"), (3) fault, (4) damage, and (5) causality. The loss of cryptocurrencies, for instance, because of a hacking or fraud, can, in principle meet these criteria, provided that the victim can adduce necessary evidence in a given case.

Contractual liability is based on the breach of obligations assumed towards the other party.[96] The debtor is presumed to be at fault for the failure to perform or defective performance of the respective obligations.[97]

In a hypothetical case, X opened an account with MontC and has 60 Bitcoins registered in her wallet. MontC's IT systems have been hacked. As a result, X lost all her Bitcoins. MontC's liability towards X is, under Macau law, considered to be of contractual nature if MontC failed to perform its obligations towards X as a result of the hack. As it is an obligation of MontC to return the cryptocurrencies to X, if it fails to do so, it shall be presumed to be at fault. X can then demand the performance of the obligation (i.e., return of 60 Bitcoins to X at the expense of MontC or the corresponding amount) and possible damages for late performance.

The hacker's liability, on the other hand, would be of extra-contractual nature, as the latter has no pre-existing contractual relationship with X. In case the hacker is identifiable and actionable, X can bring a lawsuit for the compensation of her damage against both MontC and the hacker, invoking the most favourable rules of both frameworks, while no duplication of damages is allowed.[98]

A transfer by the hacker of any appropriated tokens belonging to X would constitute a "sale of goods owned by another", which is null and void.[99] The said provision protects the *bona fide* purchaser from any attempts of invalidating the sale on the part of the seller, but not of the original owner. The *bona fide* purchaser is entitled to be compensated by the seller for damages.[100]

In another scenario, X might have been misled by another person to transfer her Bitcoins to that person. In this case, there is a possibility for X to invalidate the transfer by invoking malice.[101] Malice for these purposes is defined as "any suggestion or artifice used with the intention or awareness of causing or maintaining an error on the part of the author of a [contractual] declaration, or the

96 CC, Article 787.

97 CC, Article 788.

98 Manuel Trigo, *Lições de Direito das Obrigações* (*Lessons on the Law of Obligations*), Faculdade de Direito da Universidade de Macau 2014, pp. 238–240.

99 CC, Article 882.

100 CC, Article 889.

101 CC, Articles 246 and 247.

dissimulation of an error thereof."[102] An action is not deemed to be "suggestion or artifice" when it is deemed legitimate in accordance with the prevailing trade usages and compatible with good faith. The actions of a person who uses malice may also fall within the elements of extra-contractual liability, which might allow for compensation of other damages besides the restitution of Bitcoins by way of annulment of the transfer.

Generally, extra-contractual liability shall be regulated by the law of the place where the main activity that caused the damage took place (or, in case of omission, ought to have occurred).[103]

4 Litigation in Relation to Cryptocurrencies

Litigation in relation to cryptocurrencies in Macau has been limited to a small number of criminal cases involving crypto mining and investment frauds. In a 2020 case,[104] an individual convinced several others to invest in three companies that would, allegedly, pursue the business of speculation in cryptocurrencies, with the promise of high returns. Each of the three victims gave the defendant amounts that ranged from MOP100,000 to MOP300,000. Those amounts were used for personal spending, gambling and repayment of gambling debts, and the victims did not receive any return of their purported investment. The court of first instance convicted the defendant for fraud, a decision which was later confirmed by the court of second instance.

In another recent case, two businessmen – one from Hong Kong and another from Macau – promoted a cryptocurrency mining business to potential investors in Macau. This resulted in MOP 14.2 million of investment by 71 persons. According to media reports, of the two defendants, the Hong Kong-based businessman and major shareholder was found guilty of fraud and sentenced to ten years imprisonment, whereas Macau businessman was found not guilty, but deemed to have acted negligently while promoting the investment business and, consequently, liable to compensate the victims.[105]

102 CC, Articles 246 and 247.

103 CC, Article 44.

104 Second Instance Court case 367/2020, of 13 May 2020.

105 Nelson Moura, Court clears local businessman of criminal intent in crypto mining trial, hands HK defendant 10-year prison sentence (Macau Business, 22 April 2022), https://www.macaubusiness.com/court-clears-local-businessman-of-criminal-intent-in-crypto-mining-trial-hands-hk-defendant-10-year-prison-sentence/.

The recognition and enforcement of foreign judgments in Macau depends on the fulfilment of six requirements:

- Absence of doubts on the authenticity of the document in which the decision is contained, or on the clarity of the decision;
- *Res judicata* status in accordance with the place of issuance;
- Originating from a court the jurisdiction of which was not fraudulently established and not covering any subject matter of the exclusive jurisdiction of Macau courts;
- Not corresponding to a subject matter that is the subject of ongoing litigation or a *res judicata* decision in Macau;
- Proper service of process to the defendant, in accordance with the laws of the place of the court of origin, and compliance with the principle of *contractictoire* and equality of the parties;
- Confirmation of the decision not leading to a result manifestly contrary to public order.[106]

The above requirements apply, to the extent possible, to arbitral awards. However, recognition of arbitral awards issued by the tribunals in member states of the New York Convention on the Recognition and Enforcement of Foreign Arbitral Awards[107] shall follow the requirements set out therein.

As regards the legal requirements listed above, their fulfilment generally depends on a case-by-case analysis of the circumstances. However, the last requirement (the confirmation not leading to a result manifestly contrary to public order) may pose potential difficulties in cases related to cryptocurrencies, considering the current position of the Macau authorities vis-à-vis these virtual assets. In this context, a decision that qualifies cryptocurrencies as legal tender and attaches relevant legal consequences to that qualification might meet opposition based on the said requirement. It must be noted however, that the law qualifies this exception with the words "manifestly contrary", which seems to limit cases of refusal of confirmation to only the most egregious violations of public order. Therefore, it is plausible to say (although the absence of prior cases prevents a more assertive answer) that, except for situations of clear violation of public policy, decisions relating to cryptocurrencies can be recognized and enforced in Macau.

106 CPC, Article 1200.

107 The New York Convention was published in the Official Gazette as an attachment to the Chief Executive's Notice 3/2007 of 22 March 2007. The reservations formulated by the People's Republic of China are also applicable in Macau.

Netherlands

Jasper Verstappen

1 Cryptocurrencies in Dutch Law

Within the Dutch legal system, no officially recognized cryptocurrencies exist. Moreover, in case law it has been held that bitcoin cannot be recognized as legal tender.[1] Whilst these cases focus mostly on bitcoin, the reasoning adopted by the courts is *mutatis mutandis* applicable to alternative cryptocurrencies. This contribution will maintain that any conclusions regarding bitcoin, unless explicitly stated otherwise, will apply equally to cryptocurrencies in general. These cases will be considered later.

The Dutch Central Bank (DNB) and the Netherlands Authority for the Financial Markets (AFM) follow the definition given by the fifth anti-money laundering directive, which defines virtual currencies as:

> a digital representation of value that is not issued or guaranteed by a central bank or a public authority, is not necessarily attached to a legally established currency and does not possess a legal status of currency or money, but is accepted by natural or legal persons as a means of exchange and which can be transferred, stored and traded electronically.[2]

The DNB and the AFM take a functional approach and, within the above-mentioned definition, recognize three overlapping categories of cryptos. Firstly, there are the transaction cryptos. This type of cryptos is meant for general transactions or value transfers. Users of such cryptos can engage in global peer-to-peer transactions without relying on a third party. Bitcoin, Litecoin, and Dash are mentioned as examples of transaction cryptos. A second category is that of utility cryptos. Utility cryptos are used as an entitlement to the use of, or access to, a specific application or service offered by or through a platform. Examples of utility coins are ether and filecoin, which give the user the right

1 Rb. Overijssel 14 May 2014, ECLI:NL:RBOVE:2014:2667; Gerechtshof Arnhem-Leeuwarden, 31 May 2016, ECLI:NL:GHARL:2016:4219.

2 See Article 1(1) of the Dutch Money Laundering and Terrorist Financing Prevention Act, implementing Article 1(2) d of Directive (EU) 2018/843 of the European Parliament and of the Council of 30 May 2018 amending Directive (EU) 2015/849 on the prevention of the use of the financial system for the purposes of money laundering or terrorist financing, and amending Directives 2009/138/EC and 2013/36/EU.

 | DOI:10.1163/9789004722507_020

to use or access services running on the underlying ethereum network or to purchase decentralised cloud storage from another respectively. Lastly, there are the investment cryptos which are used as an alternative for, or an addition to, existing financial instruments.[3]

Whilst some attention has been devoted to adoption and application of cryptocurrencies within The Netherlands by the Dutch authorities, no cryptocurrencies or stable currencies feature within the Dutch system. Noteworthy in this context is the announcement made by the DNB in its 2015 Annual Report that by 2016 it would have developed a prototype cryptocurrency (‘*DNBcoin*’) in order to investigate the potential offered by blockchain technology in ensuring an accessible, available and safe payments system.[4] In a speech at the Dutch Blockchain Conference in 2016, Ron Berndsen, Head of the Market Infrastructures Policy Department at the DNB, explained that the purpose of this experiment was to gain a deeper understanding of the actual implementation of this technology. Moreover, he affirmed that this experiment was exclusively meant for internal test purposes and that the goal was never to create any coin that would be put in circulation.[5] Following this experiment, the DNB continued to look into implementations of blockchain technology and distributed ledger technology under the heading of the *Dukaton*-project. With the exception of a bulletin dated 7 June 2018, very limited information on this project is available.[6] It is however known that the DNB developed four prototypes with different variations of a consensus algorithm. It identified capacity shortages, inefficiency caused by high energy consumption, and a lack of full certainty that a payment is completed, as the principal limitations. Additionally, it noted that blockchain could be leveraged to improve financial market infrastructural resilience to external attacks, at the expense of its capacity and efficiency. Altogether the DNB concluded that, as of yet, the technology ‘fails to meet the very high demands of a financial market infrastructure.[7]

---

3 De Nederlandsche Bank and Autoriteit Financiele Markten, ‘Cryptos: Recommendations for a Regulatory Framework’ (December 2018), p. 3. Available at: www.afm.nl/~/profmedia/files/rapporten/2019/adviesrapport-crypto-eng.pdf?la=en (accessed on 09 April 2024).

4 De Nederlandsche Bank, ‘Jaarverslag 2015’ 23 March 2016, p. 194. Available at: https://www.dnb.nl/media/ja2fdpec/2015-anual-report.pdf (accessed on 09 April 2024).

5 Ron Berndsen, ‘If blockchain is the answer, what is the question?’ Speech at the Dutch Blockchain Conference (20 June 2016). Note that this speech is no longer available in publication or online. A copy of this speech is in possession of the author and available upon request

6 De Nederlandsche Bank, ‘DNB Experimenteert met blockchain’ (7 June 2018). Available at: https://www.dnb.nl/actueel/algemeen-nieuws/dnbulletin-2018/dnb-experimenteert-met-blockchain/ (accessed on 09 April 2024).

7 Ibid; see also T. Zhang and Z. Huang, ‘Blockchain and central Bank Digital Currency’ (2022) 8 *ICT Express* 2, 266.

At the time of writing, based on the very limited amount of information available, it would seem that these experiments have been concluded. Moreover, the goals of these experiments were never to create the foundation for a Dutch cryptocurrency or a stablecoin suitable for circulation. Hence, the Dutch system features no stable coins nor cryptocurrencies related to external benchmarks nor do there seem to be any plans for the creation of such cryptocurrencies in the near future.

2 Definitions

The Dutch Tax Authority defines cryptocurrencies as 'possessions'[8] and therefore consider it to be a taxable asset.[9] From a definitional point of view, the Dutch Tax Authority makes no distinction between cryptocurrencies and crypto-assets. All crypto-assets, including cryptocurrencies, seem to be treated as 'possessions'. It has been suggested that, for the purposes of valuation, a distinction must be made between cryptocurrencies, tokens, and crypto-futures.[10]

The position of the Dutch Government has evolved over the years. In response to questions from Parliament, the Dutch Minister of Finance stated in 2013 that bitcoin does not meet the requirements included in the Financial Supervision Act and can therefore not be regarded as 'money' or a 'financial product.'[11] This is in line with what is suggested by literature.[12] No clear definition was given by the Minister in 2013.[13] In 2018, in another response to questions from Parliament, the Minister of Finance states that cryptocurrency might be a 'source of income', which would render it taxable within Box 1. According to the Minister, whether this is indeed the case should be decided by the Tax Authority on the basis of the facts and circumstances of a concrete situation. In this communication, the Minister also considered that a Box 3

8 According to the Dutch Tax Authorities cryptocurrencies fall within the 'other possessions' (*overige bezittingen*) and are therefore taxable as capital income other than income derived from a dwelling, dividends, or shares ('box 3 income').

9 A. Bal, 'Developing a Regulatory Framework for the Taxation of Virtual Currencies' 47 *Intertax* (2019) 219, 223; T. Spaans and M. van Roey, 'Quo Vadis bitcoin' (2015) 84 *Computerrecht* 113, 118–119.

10 M. de Reus and E. van Nijnatten, 'Belastingheffing over cryptobezittingen in box 3' (2018) 34 *NJB* 2520, 2523–2524.

11 See article 1:1 Financial Supervision Act; Aanhangsel Handelingen II 2012/13, nr. 2508, 3.

12 T. Spaans and M. van Roey, 'Quo Vadis bitcoin' (2015) 84 *Computerrecht* 113, 118; F.H.J. Mijnssen, *Verbintenissen tot betaling van een Geldsom*, Wolters Kluwer, Deventer 2017, pp. 4–6.

13 Aanhangsel Handelingen II 2012/13, nr. 2508, 3.

definition of 'possessions' is also a possibility. It is this latter definition which has become the standard for the Tax Authority over the years.[14]

Hence, the definition of cryptocurrencies has been developing over the past years. A clear-cut and concrete definition cannot be given, as it is dependent on the context. Different regulatory agencies maintain different definitions.

3 Case Law on Cryptocurrencies

A relevant case came before the court of Overijssel in August 2012. Parties agreed on the sale of 2750 bitcoins at a price of 8,05 Euro per bitcoin, for a grand total of 22,137.50 Euro. Claimant has transferred this sum to the defendant, after which the defendant transferred 990 bitcoins to the claimant. The remaining 1760 bitcoins have never been transferred to the claimant. In response the claimant seeks to annul the agreement, as well as damages for the 1760 bitcoins that were not delivered and damages he suffered as a result of the value of bitcoin increasing from the moment the defendant was in breach of his obligation.[15] Article 6:125 Dutch Civil Code holds that a creditor has a right to claim compensation for damages he has suffered as a result of a change in exchange rate after the moment the defendant was in default.[16] The defendant holds that, whilst he was in default, the damages the claimant has suffered as a result of the change in exchange rate are not subject to compensation, as bitcoin should not be considered 'money'.[17]

In order to come to a qualification of bitcoin in the context of the Dutch Civil Code, the court first considers whether bitcoins might be considered scriptural money (*giraal geld*)[18] as defined by article 6:114 Dutch Civil Code. This category concerns money held and managed by a banking institution on

14 Aanhangsel Handelingen I 2017/18, nr. 34 775, 6–7.

15 Rb. Overijssel 14 May 2014, ECLI:NL:RBOVE:2014:2667, no. 2.1-3.2.

16 This is known as '*koerswijzigingsschade*' in Dutch law.

17 Rb. Overijssel 14 May 2014, ECLI:NL:RBOVE:2014:2667, no. 3.3.

18 This contribution follows the translation for *giraal geld* employed by official European Union documentation. See, for example, Commission Decision of December 2009 on State aid C 21/05 (ex PL 45/04) which Poland plans to implement for Poczta Polska as compensation of universal postal service obligations or Opinion of the European Central Bank of 5 December 2008 on a proposal for a Directive on the taking up, pursuit and prudential supervision of the business of electronic money institutions which translate this term as 'scriptural money'.

behalf of clients.[19] This relationship is contractual rather than proprietary.[20] The court holds that crypto wallets are fundamentally different from financial accounts, even though they fulfil the same functions. The fact that wallets are managed by the users themselves, rather than third parties, causes the court to conclude that bitcoins cannot be scriptural money.

Following this, the court considers whether bitcoin might be considered as currency (*chartaal geld*). Currency payments are covered by article 6:112 Dutch Civil Code, which holds that the money that is paid to settle an obligation must be accepted in the country in whose currency the payment is made. In reference to an explanatory memorandum published in 1981 during the preparatory phase of the New Dutch Civil Code, the court notes that the legislature has opted to use the word currency rather than legal tender to prevent arguments based on the theory that currency must always derive that capacity from a state.[21] The court therefore concludes that, whilst determining whether a certain means of payment should be considered a currency is first and foremost, but not exclusively, to be determined on the basis of whether it could be considered as legal tender.[22]

The court, in reference to the Council Regulation On the Introduction of the Euro and a statement made by the Minister of Finance, concludes that the Euro is the exclusive means of payment in the Netherlands, and that, for this reason, bitcoin cannot be considered currency in this context.[23] This decision by the court has been criticised for establishing that currency, in the context of the Dutch Civil Code, can derive that capacity from both state, as well as non-state sources (e.g. common societal use), but neglecting to consider whether bitcoin might be considered a currency through being used as such in society and common economic conduct.[24] It seems likely though that, considering

---

19 F.H.J. Mijnssen, *Verbintenissen tot betaling van een Geldsom*, Wolters Kluwer, Deventer 2017, p. 3.

20 HR 26 January 2007, ECLI:NL:HR:2007:AZ0614.

21 C.J. van Zeben, J.W. du Pon and M.M. Olthof, *Parlementaire geschiedenis van het nieuwe Burgerlijk Wetboek. Boek 6, Algemeen gedeelte van het verbintenissenrecht*, Kluwer, Deventer 1981, p. 459.

22 Rb. Overijssel 14 May 2014, ECLI:NL:RBOVE:2014:2667, no. 4.8.

23 Council Regulation (EC) No 974/98 of 3 May 1998 on the introduction of the euro; Aanhangsel Handelingen II 2013/14 nr. 830.

24 W.A.K. Rank, 'Betaling in bitcoins: geld of ruilmiddel, betaling of inbetalinggeving' *Ars Aequi* 2015, 177, 180; W.A.K. Rank, 'bitcoins: Civielrechtelijke en toezichtrechtelijke aspecten' in R.A. Wolf (ed.) *bitcoins: Civiele en fiscale aspecten in beeld*, Wolters Kluwer, Deventer 2015; M. Zeegers, 'bitcoin: juridische en fiscale aspecten inbeeld' 7087 *Weekblad Fiscaal Recht* 329; R. Koolhoven, 'Over geldvoorwerpschulden en de betaling met bitcoins' in R.J.C. Flach (ed.) *Dwingend privaatrecht op maat*, Boom, Den Haag 2015, pp. 89–90.

the limited use of bitcoin in day-to-day economic conduct, especially in 2015, and the tendency of bitcoin buyers to consider their purchase as a speculative investment rather than the acquisition of a means of payment, the court would have concluded that bitcoin was not a currency. Regardless of that likely outcome, it is a missed opportunity to not engage in this exercise whilst having created the opportunity to do so.

Upon appeal, the claim for damages as a result of a change in exchange rate on the basis of article 6:125 Dutch Civil Code is rejected.[25] The court of appeal observes that, in light of the facts and circumstances of this case, article 6:125 of the Dutch Civil Code is not open for the claimant to rely on directly, nor, as the claimant attempted upon appeal, to rely on indirectly.[26] With this avenue being definitively closed, the court observed that it is no longer necessary to investigate the different potential qualifications of bitcoin.[27]

All qualifications explored by the courts in this case are governed through the law of obligations. Money, regardless in which of the variations that have been elaborated upon previously, represents a claim and is therefore subject to the law of obligations.[28] This does not hold true as far as the rights to coins or banknotes are concerned. Rights with respect to such objects are instantiations of the claims they represent and as such are governed through the law of property.[29] Whilst questions on proprietary claims with regard to coins and banknotes are of no concern to the case at hand, nor to this contribution in general, it does pose an interesting follow-up question.

Having closed the door to a qualification within the law of obligations, the court seems to open the door to a proprietary qualification. By stating that 'in this case, the object concerned 2,750 bitcoins [..]' and 'since the present case concerns the termination of a contract of sale, the bitcoin ought to be equated to a thing with a "daily price".'[30] Additionally, the court holds that 'in this case

25 Gerechtshof Arnhem-Leeuwarden, 31 May 2016, ECLI:NL:GHARL:2016:4219.

26 Ibid, no. 4.6.

27 Ibid, no. 4.7.

28 W.A.K. Rank, 'Commentary on section 6.1.11 of the Dutch Civil Code', in H.B. Krans, C.J.J.M. Stolker, W.L. Valk and M.H. Wissink, *Tekst & Commentaar: Vermogensrecht*, Wolters Kluwer, Deventer 2021, pp. 856 *et seq*; B. Bierens, 'Juridische en economische perspectieven op geld: Een verkenning van de samenhang tussen geld, economie en recht naar aanleiding van W.W. Boonstra, 'geld. Wat is het, wat doet het, waar komt het vandaar?' VU University Press, Amsterdam, 2018' 3 *Tijdschrift voor Financieel recht* (2019) 102.

29 J. Hijma and M.M. Olthof, *Compendium van het Nederlandse Vermogensrecht*, Wolters Kluwer, Deventer 2020, pp. 12–13.

30 Gerechtshof Arnhem-Leeuwarden, 31 May 2016, ECLI:NL:GHARL:2016:4219, no. 4.6.

bitcoins could be considered as things that have been bought in accordance with article 7:36 Dutch Civil Code.'[31]

This phrasing by the court strongly suggests a proprietary qualification, rather than a qualification based on the law of obligations. The Dutch Civil Code defines the scope of the law of property in article 3:1 Dutch Civil Code as 'all things and all patrimonial rights and interests.' In light of the wording chosen, the court seems to be willing to accept a proprietary qualification of bitcoin. The court has been heavily criticised for doing so. Two main points of criticism should be distinguished.

Firstly it has been suggested that the court fails to give due considerations to the Hedqvist-judgment of the Court of Justice of the European Union.[32] Even though the area of law that this case concerns is different (the Hedqivist case concerns matters of tax law, while the case under investigation here concerns matters of private law), literature has nonetheless argued that observations parallel to the Court of Justice in Hedqvist should have been made.[33] In the Hedqvist case the Court of Justice observes that the 'virtual currency has no purpose other than to be a means of payment' and 'currencies other than those that are legal tender in one or more countries, in so far as those currencies have been accepted by the parties to a transaction as an alternative to legal tender and have no purpose other than to be a means of payment, are financial transactions'.[34] This would bring one to conclude that a bitcoin cannot be considered to be an object in the eyes of the Dutch civil code.[35]

A second point of criticism is limited to the realm of Dutch private law and relates to an alleged failure of the court to not only identify the correct proprietary qualification of bitcoin, but also its failure to explore a potentially much more suitable qualification that is readily available. This second point of critique centres on articles 3:1 and 3:2 of the Dutch Civil Code. These articles outline the objects that are subject to the law of property within the Dutch legal system. Article 3:1 of the Dutch Civil Code holds that 'property is composed of all things and all patrimonial rights and interests', whilst article 3:2 defines 'things' as 'corporeal objects which can be subject to human control'. The requirements imposed by Dutch law on patrimonial rights and interests are given by article 3:6 Civil Code and includes 'any rights of a proprietary

31 Ibid, no. 4.8.

32 CJEU 22 october 2015, Case C-264/14, *Skatteverket v David Hedqvist* ECLI:EU:C:2015:718.

33 W.F. Dammers, 'bitcoins: een vreemde zaak? Noot bij Hof Arnhem-Leeuwarden 31 mei 2016, ECLI:NL:GHARL:2016:4219' 3 *Tijdschrift voor Internetrecht* (2016) 110, 111.

34 Case C-264/14, *Skatteverket v David Hedqvist* ECLI:EU:C:2015:718, 24 and 49.

35 W.F. Dammers, 'bitcoins: een vreemde zaak? Noot bij Hof Arnhem-Leeuwarden 31 mei 2016, ECLI:NL:GHARL:2016:4219'3 *Tijdschrift voor Internetrecht* (2016) 110, 111.

nature which, either separately or together with another right, are transferable, rights which are intended to procure a tangible benefit to their holder, or rights which have been acquired in exchange for actual or expected tangible benefit.' There is consensus amongst authors that bitcoins cannot be considered corporeal objects susceptible to human control.[36] However, the observation of the court that bitcoin might be considered a 'thing' in the context of Dutch law is not necessarily irreconcilable with this idea, as property includes both things as well as patrimonial rights. However, the court states that bitcoins might be considered things for the purposes of the Dutch Civil Code. When confronted with the claim by the defendant that article 7:36 Dutch Civil Code is not applicable because, according to the defendant, a bitcoin is not a thing, the court makes the following observation:

> Article 7:47 Dutch Civil Code determines that a patrimonial right can be subject to a sale and that, in such a case, articles 7:36 *et seq* Dutch Civil Code apply equally insofar as this is in conformity with the right in question. The fact that a bitcoin is a patrimonial right is not disputed by the parties, [..] and therefore the applicability of article 7:36 Dutch Civil Code can be considered consistent with the nature of that article.[37]

The court of appeal therefore takes a pragmatic approach. In order to resolve the case before it, the observation that a proprietary qualification is suitable suffices. A clear and precise determination is, for the purposes of the court of appeal, not necessary.

A subsequent case concerns ether, another cryptocurrency.[38] The relevant facts of this case are as follows. The claimant has bought mining-rigs, powerful computers that run mathematical processes through which cryptocurrencies can potentially be gained, from the defendant. These rigs remain in

36 W.A.K. Rank, 'bitcoins: civielrechtelijke en toezichtrechtelijke aspecten' in R.A. Wolf (ed.) *bitcoins: Civiele en fiscale aspecten in beeld*, Wolters Kluwer, Deventer 2015, 35; W.A.K. Rank, 'Betaling in bitcoins: geld of ruilmiddel, betaling of inbetalinggeving' *Ars Aequi* 2015, 177, 183; V. Tweehuysen, ‚Goederenrechtelijk puzzelen met bitcoins', Ars Aequi 2018, 602, 606; J. Hijma, *Mr. C. Assers Handleiding tot de beoefening van het Nederlands Burgerlijk Recht. 7. Bijzondere overeenkomsten. Deel I. Koop en ruil*, Deventer: Wolters Kluwer 2019, no. 210; J. L. Snijders and Y.C. Tonino, 'Goederenrechtelijke status van bitcoin (kapitaalkracht)' 6 *Financiering, Zekerheden & Insolventierechtpraktijk* (2018) 46, 51; R. Koolhoven, 'Over geldvoorwerpschulden en de betaling met bitcoins' in R.J.C. Flach (ed.) *Dwingend privaatrecht op maat*, Boom, Den Haag 2015, p. 88.

37 Gerechtshof Arnhem-Leeuwarden, 31 May 2016, ECLI:NL:GHARL:2016:4219, no. 4.8.

38 Rb. Midden-Nederland 07 December 2017, ECLI:NL:RBMNE:2017:6646.

the possession of the defendant who will use these rigs to mine ether on behalf of the claimant. In exchange for this service, the defendant will receive a 10% commission. At a certain point in time, the defendant stops transferring ether to the claimant, after which the claimant files for preliminary relief with the court of Midden-Nederland. Like the previously discussed case, the court is called upon to give a private law qualification of cryptocurrency. The court of Midden-Nederland follows the same approach as the previously discussed court of Overijssel. It should be noted that, because this case concerns preliminary relief proceedings, the motivation by the court is much more concise. First the court observes that, in reference to the Hedqvist case of the Court of Justice, ether cannot be considered money. With regard to the private law qualification of ether, the case simply concludes that:

> The judge in preliminary relief proceedings therefore assumes that ether is property, so that a transfer of ether can be ordered subject to a penalty.[39]

This case, in line with the case previously discussed, seems to suggest that a proprietary qualification of cryptocurrencies is possible within the Dutch private law legal framework. However, this court, due to the nature of preliminary relief proceedings, was not in a position to provide a complete and comprehensive overview on why such a qualification is appropriate.[40]

A final case that deserves mention here is slightly different from the previous cases as it concerns an insolvency case.[41] The court in this case is confronted with a request to declare the bankruptcy of Koinz Trading. It follows from article 1 of the Dutch Insolvency Act that a creditor can be declared bankrupt, either on their own request or on request of their debtors, if they cease debt payments. A debtor is any legal or natural person that has a claim on that creditor, provided that claim, in case of non-payment, entitles the holder thereof to recourse against the estate of the debtor in case of his insolvency, provided the claim arises from a relationship that exists at the time the bankruptcy was ordered.[42] It follows from this that claims need to be open to validation (*verifieerbare vordering*). In the case at hand, the debtor has a claim in bitcoin. The question therefore is whether a claim in bitcoin is open

39 Ibid., no. 4.6.

40 W. Weij and M.C. Landerbarthold, 'Ruis in de ether en de juridische kwalificatie(s) van cryptovaluta: noot bij rechtbank Midden-Nederland 7 December 2017, ECLI:NL:RBMNE:2017:6646, 2 *Tijdschrift voor Internetrecht* (2018) 66, 68.

41 Rb. Amsterdam 14 February 2018, ECLI:NL:RBAM:2018:869 (*Koinz Trading*).

42 HR 19 april 2013, ECLI:NL:2013:BY6108.

to validation. Whether or not a claim in bitcoin fulfils this requirement is dependent on the factual analysis of the characteristics of the cryptocurrency in question[43]

This qualification is more than a mere teleological interpretation made by the court in order to declare the bankruptcy of Koinz Trading. The fact that the report of the trustee in bankruptcy makes no mention of any bitcoins in the bankrupt estate and the fact that cryptocurrencies are absent from the financial report of the trustee in bankruptcy, suggests that this proprietary qualification kept the cryptocurrency out of the bankrupt estate.[44] This case therefore illustrates the importance of a clear, precise, and thorough qualification of cryptocurrencies in a legal system by indicating the consequences of such a qualification. It shows that this is more than merely an academic exercise.

4 Regulatory Framework

4.1 *Cryptocurrencies, AML & CFT Requirements, and Supervision*

The Dutch Money Laundering and Terrorism Financing Prevention Act (*Wet ter voorkoming van witwassen en financiering terrorisme*) has limited applicability in relation to cryptocurrency. Cryptocurrencies in general are not covered by the Dutch Money Laundering and Terrorism Financing Prevention Act since cryptocurrencies cannot be classified as legal tender nor as financial products.[45]

The scope of the Dutch Money Laundering and Terrorism Financing Prevention Act was broadened with the implementation of the fifth anti-money laundering Directive.[46] Article 47 (1) of this Directive explicitly includes providers of exchange services between virtual currencies and fiat currencies and

43 Rb. Amsterdam 14 February 2018, ECLI:NL:RBAM:2018:869 (*Koinz Trading*).

44 See 'Verslag 22-01-2021', identifier: 16_18_69_F_V_23 and 'financieel verslag 22-01-2021', identifier: 16_mne_18_69_F_V_22_B, both available via: https://insolventies.rechtspraak.nl/#!/details/16.mne.18.69.F.1316.1.21 (accessed 09 April 2024); see also B. Bierens, 'Noot bij rechtbank Amsterdam 14 februari 2018, ECLI:NL:RBAMS:2018:869' 6 *Jurisprudentie Onderneming & Recht* (2018) 154.

45 M.R. Hoekstra and B.N. Schep, 'beleggingsinstellingen en icbe's' in B. Snijder-kuipers and A.T.A. Tilleman, *Handboek WWFT*, Wolters Kluwer, Deventer 2019, p. 129; D. Busch, 'Kroniek financieel recht: financieel recht in onzekere tijden' 16 *NJB* (2021) 1270, 1282.

46 Directive (EU) 2018/843 of the European Parliament and of the Council of 30 May 2018 amending Directive (EU) 2015/849 on the prevention of the use of the financial system for the purposes of money laundering or terrorist financing, and amending Directives 2009/138/EC and 2013/36/EU.

custodian wallet providers within its scope.[47] With the implementation of the fifth anti-money laundering Directive into the Dutch Money Laundering and Terrorism Financing Prevention Act, the Act now includes article 23b which holds that

> (1) Any person who [..] offers professional or commercial exchange services between virtual and fiat currencies shall register with the Dutch Central Bank. (2) any person who [..] offers, professionally or commercially, custodian wallets must register with the Dutch Central Bank.'

This approach aims to place crypto-service providers in a gatekeeping-role. The intended effect of requiring crypto-service providers to act as gatekeepers was to counter the anonymity that is inherently connected to transactions of cryptocurrency and to reduce the opportunities for persons transacting with cryptocurrencies to hide such transactions.[48] A registered party is subject to the requirements of the Dutch Money Laundering and Terrorism Financing Prevention Act, which includes the duty to identify a client and verify their identity, certain risk-assessment duties, transaction monitoring-duties, and the duty to report unusual transactions to the DNB. Additionally, the registered person is obliged to part with clients with whom they identify unacceptable risks.

In order to register, a crypto-service provider has to provide the following. Firstly, the crypto-service provider must produce a business plan with at least a schematic overview of the activities that the service provider currently undertakes and the transaction streams, as well as the strategy of the company. Secondly, the crypto-service provider must produce a registration form for all policymakers (administrators, supervisors, etc.). Thirdly, the crypto-service provider must produce a clear overview of its governance structure. Fourthly, the crypto-service provider must produce an overview of its risk – and control-structure. Additionally, the crypto-service provider must produce a risk-assessment that covers integrity risks, risks regarding conflicts of interests, and monitoring of clients and transactions.[49]

---

47 J. Baukema, 'Concept implementatiewet AMLD V: eerste crypto-regulering in aantocht' 4 *Tijdschrift voor Financieel Recht* (2019) 197, 201.

48 A.G. Silonero, 'Heimelijke transacties met cryptocurrencies: een grijs gebied tussen witwaspraktijken en verstandige praktijken' 1 *Computerrecht* (2021) 3, 15; Kamerstukken II 2018/19, 35245, 3.

49 DNB, 'Toelichting bij registratie ten behoeve van een aanbieder van cryptodiensten' May 2020, available at: https://www.dnb.nl/media/g4ipdf4t/toelichting-registratieformier-cryptodiensten.pdf (accessed on 09 April 2024).

Following article 23d(1) and (3) of the Dutch Money Laundering and Terrorism Financing Prevention Act, the DNB can decide to not register or remove the registration in case the information provided proves to be incorrect. If, following the moment of registration, information becomes available to the DNB on the basis of which the crypto-service provider would not have been granted registration, had the information been available at the moment of registration, the DNB can decide to remove the registration.[50] The DNB can decide to remove the registration if the crypto-service provider fails to meet the requirements stipulated by the Sanctions Act, fails to meet its financial registration obligations, has failed to provide any services within six months following the registration, has ceased to provide services or has discontinued the service for more than six months, or if the company that provides the service is transferred.[51]

Recently the DNB was challenged in the way in which they fulfilled their supervisory role in this respect. The DNB, in their interpretation of the Dutch Money Laundering and Terrorism Financing Prevention Act, had determined that a registered person who offers custodian wallets, must, every time that wallet is used, verify that it is the client himself who uses that wallet. The preliminary relief judge notes that

> The law includes a registration duty, rather than a licensing duty [and] the regulating of such providers in the Netherlands is not stricter than in other Member States. With this Act, the Netherlands complies with the (minimum) level of harmonisation required by the Directive. The interpretation of the Dutch Central Bank of this registration regime [..] appears to have characteristics of a licensing regime, now that the interpretation of the registration requirement is subject to a quite far-reaching preliminary assessment.[52]

The preliminary relief judge ordered the DNB to respond to the claimants objections, thereby reconsidering its interpretation. Following this case, the DNB has adjusted its interpretation and thereby the way in which it exercises its supervisory role in this respect.[53]

---

50 Article 23d(3) subs b-c of the Dutch Money Laundering and Terrorist Financing Prevention Act.

51 Ibid subs d-h.

52 Rb. Rotterdam 07 April 2021, ECLI:NL:RBROT:2021:2968, no. 6.4.

53 DNB, 'Het screenen van een relatie bij een (inkomende en uitgaande) transactie' 19 May 2021, available at: https://www.dnb.nl/voor-de-sector/open-boek-toezicht/sectoren/aanbieders-cryptodiensten/integriteitstoezicht-op-aanbieders-van-cryptodiensten

5 Private Law Issues

5.1 *Proprietary Qualifications of Cryptocurrencies*

Section 1 of this contribution has outlined the landmark cases in which the fundamental characteristics of cryptocurrencies are analysed against foundational aspects of the Dutch system of private law. These landmark cases have sparked a rich academic debate amongst Dutch scholars. This section will provide a literature review of what was written in the context of this debate, parallel to the line of case law that was explored previously. This literature review will be organised chronologically. However, before outlining the different positions that have been taken in the context of that debate through this literature review, a short reminder of the different proprietary qualifications is in place.

5.2 *A Chronological Overview of a Growing Recognition: General Remarks*

The scope of the Dutch law of property is outlined in article 3:1 of the Dutch Civil Code. This article holds that property includes all things and all proprietary rights and interests. Two potential qualifications therefore follow: that of 'thing' and that of 'patrimonial right'. The former of these is defined by article 3:2 Dutch Civil Code as 'all corporeal objects which can be subjected to human control' while the requirements for the latter are given by article 3:6 Dutch Civil Code: 'any right of a proprietary nature which either separately or together with another right is transferable, is intended to procure a tangible benefit to their holder, or has been acquired in exchange for actual or expected tangible benefit.' While this might seem like a dogmatic difference, Akkermans points out that this distinction is relevant in light of the definition of ownership given by article 5:1 of the Dutch Civil Code, which defines the right of ownership as 'the most extensive right a person can have over a corporeal object'. He points out that, in light of this article, the right of ownership is restricted to corporeal objects. However, the Dutch Civil Code does recognise 'entitlement' as an alternative relation a person might have with respect to non-corporeal objects. Entitlement, as a legal qualification, is comparable to ownership under Dutch law. The distinction between rights in respect to corporeal objects and rights in respect of incorporeal objects is a result of the Dutch legislature intending to reflect the idea that in the former it is not the ownership in the object that is sold, but the object itself. In short, while it is actually the right of ownership that is transferred to the acquirer, the word 'thing' is used to denote the

/sanctiewet-1977/het-screenen-van-een-relatie-bij-een-inkomende-en-uitgaande-transactie/ (accessed on 09 April 2024).

object. Effectively, the right of ownership could be regarded as a proprietary right itself, or patrimonial rights could be considered a consequence of the right of ownership.[54]

Regardless of the perspective one takes, two different variations of such patrimonial rights exist. Firstly, there are the relative patrimonial rights. Which includes those rights that can be effectuated against a particular counterparty, including claims created through contract or tort. Secondly, there are the absolute patrimonial rights, which include those rights that have their foundation in the right of ownership, and therefore have effect against third persons.[55]

This bird's-eye view provides an overview of the instruments available in the proprietary toolbox provided by the Dutch Civil Code. The next sections will show that the debate amongst Dutch scholars on the qualification of cryptocurrencies in Dutch law has focussed predominantly on these instruments, with an emphasis on the 'patrimonial right' as an appropriate qualification.

5.3 *A Growing Recognition: Responses in 2015 to the First Bitcoin Case*

In the 2014 judgment of the Overijssel court,[56] which was extensively discussed in section 3, the first case in which a Dutch judge was asked to consider bitcoin from a private law point of view, two questions were central. Firstly, was the court correct in determining that bitcoin could not be considered a currency? The second question, more importantly, focused on alternative qualifications: if bitcoin indeed cannot be considered a currency, what is the appropriate legal qualification?

---

54 B. Akkermans, *The principle of numerus clausus in European property law,* Intersantia, Cambridge 2008, pp. 257–258; J.C. Van der Steur, *Grenzen van rechtsobjecten; een onderzoek naar de grenzen van objecten van eigendomsrechten en intellectuele eigendomsrechten,* Kluwer, Deventer 2003, p. 15; see also J.H.M. van Erp and B. Akkermans, *Cases, Materials and Tekst on Property Law,* Hart Publishing, Oxford 2012, p. 382. It should be noted that the question whether or not the right of ownership can be regarded as a property right is a hotly debated topic, a discussion of which is beyond the scope of this contribution, see for example; W. Snijders, ' T.F. De Jong, De structuur van het goederenrecht, diss. Groningen, 2006' 6689 *Weekblad voor privaatrecht, Notariaat en Registratie* (2006) 831; R.W.E. van Leuken, M.M.C. van de Moosdijk and V. Tweehuysen, *Hartkamps Compendium van het vermogensrecht,* Wolters Kluwer, Deventer 2017, no. 36; T.H.D. Struycken, *De numerus clausus in het goederenrecht,* Kluwer, Deventer 2007, pp. 95–100.

55 S.E. Bartels and A.I.M. van Mierlo, *Mr. C. Assers handleiding tot de beoefening van het Nederlands Burgerlijk Recht. 3. Vermogensrecht algemeen. Deel IV. Algemeen goederenrecht,* Wolters Kluwer, Deventer 2021, no. 1; E.F. Verheul, 'Bescherming van de huurder van een roerende zaak' in F. Verstijlen, F.J. Beekhoven van den Boezem, and G. Bergervoet, *Groninger Zekerheid,* Kluwer, Deventer, 2014, pp. 426-427; J.H.M. van Erp and B. Akkermans, *Cases, Materials and Tekst on Property Law,* Hart Publishing, Oxford 2012, p. 90.

56 Rb. Overijssel 14 May 2014, ECLI:NL:RBOVE:2014:2667.

This first question was extensively analysed by Rank and Koolhoven.[57] Both authors, in separate publications, follow the same line of reasoning as the court. Rank points out that, whilst the reasoning of the court might be slightly unsatisfactory, the court's conclusion is likely to be correct. In support of the conclusion of the court, he refers to article 1:1 of the Dutch Financial Supervision Act, which determines that one of the criteria of 'electronic currency' is that it represents a 'claim on the issuer'. Bitcoin is explicitly *not* a claim on a specific issuer, neither are they issued in exchange for (fiat) currency. It is therefore concluded that bitcoin, according to Dutch law, cannot be consider scriptural money, currency, or legal tender, but the reasoning of the court in order to reach that conclusion leaves room for improvement.[58]

Koolhoven, while reaching a similar conclusion, takes a different approach. She observes that money, be it scriptural money, currency, or legal tender, is first and foremost a medium of exchange. Within that broad category of money, a distinction has to be made between corporeal objects of monetary value (such as coins or bills) and incorporeal objects of monetary value, such as claims on a bank. Bitcoin, just like money, is a medium of exchange. It seems very similar to scriptural money, as both are incorporeal, transferrable, and can be used to procure a tangible benefit to the holder. However, Koolhoven also concludes that bitcoin cannot be considered scriptural money as it does not represent a claim on a bank.[59]

Regarding the second question on an alternative and more appropriate qualification of bitcoin, Koolhoven states that, in light of its incorporeal nature and the fact that a bitcoin does not represent a claim on a bank or a specifically identifiable person, it is more likely to be an absolute patrimonial right.[60] Rank

57 W.A.K. Rank, 'bitcoins: Civielrechtelijke en toezichtrechtelijke aspecten' in R.A. Wolf (ed.) *bitcoins: Civiele en fiscale aspecten in beeld*, Wolters Kluwer, Deventer 2015; W.A.K. Rank, 'Betaling in bitcoins: geld of ruilmiddel, betaling of inbetalinggeving' *Ars Aequi* 2015, 177; R. Koolhoven, 'Over geldvoorwerpschulden en de betaling met bitcoins' in R.J.C. Flach (ed.) *Dwingend privaatrecht op maat*, Boom, Den Haag 2015.

58 W.A.K. Rank, 'bitcoins: Civielrechtelijke en toezichtrechtelijke aspecten' in R.A. Wolf (ed.) *bitcoins: Civiele en fiscale aspecten in beeld*, Wolters Kluwer, Deventer 2015, p. 33; W.A.K. Rank, 'Betaling in bitcoins: geld of ruilmiddel, betaling of inbetalinggeving' *Ars Aequi* 2015, 177, 179-181; see also, on electronic currency, E.D.C. Neppelenbroek, *Elektronisch Contractenrecht*, Boom, Den Haag 2019, pp. 259–260; B. Bierens, *Geld in het vermogensrecht*, Wolters Kluwer, Deventer 2020, pp. 20 *et seq.*

59 R. Koolhoven, 'Over geldvoorwerpschulden en de betaling met bitcoins' in R.J.C. Flach (ed.) *Dwingend privaatrecht op maat*, Boom, Den Haag 2015, p. 89.

60 Ibid, p. 94.

takes an even more cautious approach. He observes that the scope of Dutch property law is limited to things on the one hand, and patrimonial rights and interests on the other hand. In light of the fact that article 3:2 Dutch Civil Code defines things as corporeal objects, he concludes that a bitcoin cannot be a thing. Therefore, the qualification of a patrimonial right could be an alternative qualification. The Dutch Civil Code does not define patrimonial rights, but does include certain requirements in article 3:6 Dutch Civil Code. Patrimonial rights, according to this article, are transferable, aim to provide the recipient a material advantage, or have been acquired in exchange for an actual or expected tangible benefit. Even though bitcoins are transferable and aim to provide a benefit to the holder, Rank writes that qualifying bitcoins as a patrimonial right is 'somewhat problematic'. A patrimonial right is part of a person's patrimony. A relative right forms the active side of an obligation. This can never be the case for bitcoin. In order for a particular right to qualify as a relative patrimonial right, it ought to have a corresponding passive side in another person's patrimony: i.e. a debt. It is the very nature of bitcoin that opposes this. With bitcoin there is no issuer, no debtor, and therefore no debt. Rank therefore observes that, in light of this, placing bitcoin within the Dutch proprietary framework might be done by qualifying it as an absolute patrimonial right. Absolute patrimonial rights have *erga omnes* effect and therefore do not require a corresponding 'passive side' to be part of a specific person's patrimony. In order to do so, Rank draws parallel with proprietary qualifications of software. He observes that the question whether software can be qualified as property is a contested topic, but concludes that, even if it cannot by itself, a roundabout approach has been expected through intellectual property. Copyright is a patrimonial right in Dutch law.[61]

5.4 *A Growing Recognition: a Response in 2016 to the Bitcoin Appeal*

Following Koolhoven's and Rank's reaction to the 2014 case regarding the qualification of bitcoin, that decision was appealed. The decision on appeal was discussed in section 3 of this contribution. Like the decision in first instance, this decision was not free from criticism either. The judge on appeal strongly suggests that bitcoin should be regarded as property.[62] Dammers, in

61 W.A.K. Rank, 'bitcoins: Civielrechtelijke en toezichtrechtelijke aspecten' in R.A. Wolf (ed.) *bitcoins: Civiele en fiscale aspecten in beeld*, Wolters Kluwer, Deventer 2015, pp. 35–36; W.A.K. Rank, 'Betaling in bitcoins: geld of ruilmiddel, betaling of inbetalinggeving' *Ars Aequi* 2015, 177, 183–184; see also F.H.J. Mijnssen, *Verbintenissen tot betaling van een Geldsom*, Wolters Kluwer, Deventer 2017, pp. 4-6.

62 Gerechtshof Arnhem-Leeuwarden, 31 May 2016, ECLI:NL:GHARL:2016:4219, no. 4.6.

his response to the decision on appeal, makes several observations. First, he refers back to the Hedqvist-case by the Court of Justice of the European Union and asks the question whether the Appellant court has given due consideration to this decision.[63] This line of reasoning has been explored in section 3 of this contribution and will therefore not be repeated here.

A second point of critique raised in this response revolves around the standard used by the court in deciding that bitcoin cannot be currency. Referring back to Koolhoven, it is argued that the qualification of currency, in light of the Dutch Civil Code, can be based on it being recognized as such by a state (*wettig betaalmiddel*) or through its use as such (*gangbaar geld*). This latter possibility is not explored by the courts.[64] While this criticism seems valid, it seems doubtful whether the limited actual use of bitcoin would be sufficient for it to be qualified as currency.

Following this observation, Dammers applies the reasoning laid out by Koolhoven with respect to the decision in first instance to the decision of the appellant judge and comes to the same conclusion. He holds that, in light of this case, bitcoin is more likely to be an absolute patrimonial right rather than a relative patrimonial right.[65]

5.5 *A Growing Recognition: Legal Thinking Following the 2018 Ether Case*

A relevant case, following the 2014 bitcoin case and its appeal, is the ether case. The preliminary relief judge in this case held that ether is property. The court, referring to the Hedqvist judgment, concludes that bitcoin is not currency and 'therefore' is property.[66] Exploring whether bitcoin falls within the scope of article 3:1 of the Dutch Civil Code, from the perspective of the case at hand, it is submitted that bitcoins are incorporeal, non-individual, nor subject to human control. Hence, it cannot meet the requirements stipulated by article 3:2 Dutch Civil Code and therefore not be a thing. This leaves, as has been extensively

---

63 W.F. Dammers, 'bitcoins: een vreemde zaak? Noot bij Hof Arnhem-Leeuwarden 31 mei 2016, ECLI:NL:GHARL:2016:4219'3 *Tijdschrift voor Internetrecht* (2016) 110, 111; Case C-264/14, *Skatteverket v David Hedqvist* ECLI:EU:C:2015:718.

64 W.F. Dammers, 'bitcoins: een vreemde zaak? Noot bij Hof Arnhem-Leeuwarden 31 mei 2016, ECLI:NL:GHARL:2016:4219'3 *Tijdschrift voor Internetrecht* (2016) 110, 111; R. Koolhoven, 'Over geldvoorwerpschulden en de betaling met bitcoins' in R.J.C. Flach (ed.) *Dwingend privaatrecht op maat*, Boom, Den Haag 2015, pp. 89–91.

65 W.F. Dammers, 'bitcoins: een vreemde zaak? Noot bij Hof Arnhem-Leeuwarden 31 mei 2016, ECLI:NL:GHARL:2016:4219'3 *Tijdschrift voor Internetrecht* (2016) 110, 112.

66 W. Weij and M.C. Landerbarthold, 'Ruis in de ether en de juridische kwalificatie(s) van cryptovaluta: noot bij rechtbank Midden-Nederland 7 December 2017, ECLI:NL:RBMNE:2017:6646, 2 *Tijdschrift voor Internetrecht* (2018) 66, 66.

discussed in the context of the previously explored bitcoin case, only the qualification of 'patrimonial right'. Weij and Landerbarthold note that Dammers wrote that qualifying a bitcoin as an absolute patrimonial right might be appropriate. However, they suggest that, in light of the broad wording of article 3:6 Dutch Civil Code an alternative qualification might be appropriate. They believe that a cryptocurrency, given the broad nature of article 3:6 Dutch Civil Code, could be defined as a claim from the holder on the entire crypto community on the blockchain. They conclude that the reasoning by the court provides little certainty and adds to the confusion by simply stating that ether is property, while neglecting to define it more precisely as a patrimonial right.[67]

A different reaction to this case is given by Tweehuysen, who considers this case, in conjunction with the Koinz-Trading case discussed previously, proof of judges being willing to accept a new patrimonial right.[68] In an elaborate analysis, she describes that whether or not bitcoin might be qualified as an absolute patrimonial right is dependent on the openness of the Dutch system of property law. The system is not fully closed, as patrimonial rights (not being things or claims) exist that do not have their legal basis in the Dutch Civil Code. These include certain licenses and intellectual patrimonial rights. These are created by statute: the same cannot be said for bitcoin.[69]

The question therefore is whether a *numerus clausus* of absolute patrimonial rights exists in Dutch private law. This is a contested topic. Looking at the system of law, the existence of *numerus clausus* of absolute patrimonial rights has been assumed.[70] Looking at the memorandum of reply of article 3:6 Dutch Civil Code, it should be noted that the definition chosen by the legislature is not exhaustive.[71] However, Struycken argues, in light of an analysis of Meijers writing (the architect of the New Dutch Civil Code), that whilst the list might not be limitative, recognition of new patrimonial rights is primacy of the legislature.[72] Tweehuysen shows that this line of reasoning is by no means the generally accepted line of reasoning, even referring back to Meijers himself who has stated that recognizing a new patrimonial right is dependent on the efficient

67 W. Weij and M.C. Landerbarthold, 'Ruis in de ether en de juridische kwalificatie(s) van cryptovaluta: noot bij rechtbank Midden-Nederland 7 December 2017, ECLI:NL:RBMNE:2017:6646, 2 *Tijdschrift voor Internetrecht* (2018) 66, 67–68.

68 V. Tweehuysen, ‚Goederenrechtelijk puzzelen met bitcoins', *Ars Aequi* 2018, 602, 607.

69 Ibid.

70 T.H.D. Struycken, *De numerus clausus in het goederenrecht*, Kluwer, Deventer 2007, p. 114.

71 *Kamerstukken II* 1970/71, 3770, nr. 5, pp. 9–10.

72 T.H.D. Struycken, *De numerus clausus in het goederenrecht*, Kluwer, Deventer 2007, p. 488.

design of the system of private law.[73] Additionally, she refers to Snijders and Bartels who argue in favour of a broad interpretation of the landmark case *Quint/Te Poel.* In this case, which concerns the law of obligations, the Dutch Supreme Court held that obligations that do not have their basis in a legal agreement, do not necessarily have to arise from a statutory provision either. Instead, in situations in which no statutory provisions are provided, a solution should be sought that fits in the system of law and aligns with the situations for which statutory provisions are available.[74] Those who argue for a broad interpretation of this case do so with a view of applying the rule formulated by the Supreme Court not exclusively in the area of the law of obligations, but expanding its scope to the law of property.[75]

5.6 *A Growing Recognition: an Alternative Perspective*

The previously mentioned authors have taken the legal system as their starting point. An alternative perspective is taken by Snijders and Tonino, who provide a thorough technical foundation and take this technical foundation as the starting point for their legal analysis. What distinguishes their perspective from that of the previous authors, is that rather than attempting to provide a private law qualification for the bitcoin-token, they argue that the appropriate object deserving of a proprietary qualification is 'bitcoin spending power' (*bitcoin kapitaalkracht*).

The transaction-system within the bitcoin-blockchain functions on the basis of unspent transaction outputs. A person attempting to make a transaction, will reference unspent transaction outputs (which result from transactions made by others to them). Such unspent transaction outputs have no intrinsic value. A person who is active on the bitcoin-network has a wallet and a private key. This wallet is connected to his address, on which the transactions that generate unspent transaction outputs are received. The position of the user on such a network, they argue, is capable of being expressed in monetary

---

73 F.M.J. Verstijlen, 'Goederenrecht 2.0?', in E. Koops et al, *Digitaal privaatrecht*, Boom, Den Haag 2014; W. Snijders, 'Ongeregeldheden in het vermogensrecht (I)' 6607 *Weekblad voor privaatrecht, Notariaat en Registratie* (2005) 79; E.M. Meijers, *De algemene begrippen van het burgerlijk recht,* Universitaire Pers Leiden, Leiden 1948, p. 86; V. Tweehuysen, Goederenrechtelijk puzzelen met bitcoins', *Ars Aequi* 2018, 602, 607.

74 C.H. Sieburgh, *Mr. C. Assers Handleiding tot de beoefening van het Nederlands Burgerlijk Recht. 6. Verbintenissenrecht. Deel I. De verbintenis in het algemeen, eerste gedeelte,* Wolters Kluwer, Deventer 2020, no 52; HR 30 January 1959, ECLI:NL:HR:1959:AI1600 (*Quint/Te Poel*).

75 S. Bartels, ‚20 jaar Nieuw BW en het goederenrecht: er is in die tijd veel/weinig gebeurd', *Ars Aequi* (2012) 478, 486; W Snijders, ‚Twintig jaar nieuw BW', *Ars Aequi* (2012) 946, 947.

terms, since the wallet, and the private key that gives the user access to that wallet, can be used to make bitcoin transactions with the aforementioned unspent transaction outputs. It is the position itself, rather than the unspent transaction outputs, that are capable of being expressed in monetary terms. This position is what the authors define as '*bitcoin kapitaalkracht*'.[76] In light of the fact that such *kapitaalkracht* is determined by the position an individual holds with respect to the network as a whole which, in turn, determined the number of bitcoins one can spend, this contribution will translate this as 'bitcoin spending power'.

After having established that 'bitcoin spending power', for the same reasons as why the previously discussed authors concluded that bitcoin is not a thing, they explore the question whether it might be a patrimonial right. Elaborating on the potential for 'bitcoin spending power' to be a relative patrimonial right, the observation is made that at the core of such a right is an obligation. Such obligations require a passive side (the debt) and an active side (the claim). Snijders and Tonino suggest, in opposition to some of the previous authors, that a relative patrimonial right is an appropriate qualification. Whilst there is no central issuing body that can be identified as the person in whose patrimony the passive side of the obligations falls, the notion that participants to the bitcoin-network stand in a certain relation to each other is key. By acquiring access to the bitcoin-network, a participant implicitly accepts the rules that govern the network as well as the expectation that other users will accept a bitcoin-transfer as performance for future agreements. The authors note however that this is an expectation rather than an obligation, and therefore it is very doubtful whether 'bitcoin spending power' can be qualified as a claim: it seems insufficient.[77]

Rather than attempting to qualify bitcoin (spending power) as an absolute patrimonial right, they draw parallels with a bartering system, which was the topic of a Supreme Court judgment.[78] In such a system, participants are seen as members. Only members can enter into agreements which are fully or partially executed using bartering-units. Administration of transactions amongst members is done by a service-organisation. Transactions are settled in current accounts, expressed in bartering-units. Such bartering units cannot be exchanged for a value in fiat currency. The Supreme Court, when confronted

76 J. L. Snijders and Y.C. Tonino, 'Goederenrechtelijke status van bitcoin (kapitaalkracht)' 6 *Financiering, Zekerheden & Insolventierechtpraktijk* (2018) 46, 49–50.

77 Ibid, 52.

78 HR 05 November 1993, ECLI:NL:HR:1993:ZC1128.

with the question whether such bartering-units could be considered patrimonial rights, agreed with the appellant court when it held that:

> [..]Bartering-units can be equated to money, not as money that is part of a persons' patrimony as a thing, but instead as money that can be effectuated by the holder thereof as a claim against, for example, a bank. The facts that members are unable to withdraw the Bartering-units for cash or are able to use these Bartering-units outside of the Bartering-organisation does not affect this conclusion.[79]

Suggesting strong parallels between this Bartering-system and 'bitcoin spending power', Snijders and Tonino suggest that the relevant difference between the bitcoin system and the Bartering-system lies in the fact that transactions in the bitcoin system are administered in a transparent ledger, which is maintained by the network as a whole rather than a closed administration maintained by a central service-organisation. In light of this observation, the authors reason that this qualification can be applied *mutatis mutandis* to 'bitcoin spending power'.[80] While they do not make this explicit, their reasoning seems to suggest that bitcoin (spending power) should be qualified as a relative patrimonial right against the bitcoin-network.

5.7 *A Growing Recognition: a Contractual Foundation for a Proprietary Qualification*

The bitcoin-system as a whole might be viewed as a multi-party agreement. The initial participation of a user, a member, or a node to that system should be considered as the implicit acceptance of a third-party clause. It follows from article 6:253 (1) Dutch Civil Code that a contract creates the right for a third party to claim performance of a party to that contract if the contract itself contains a term to that effect and the third party has accepted this term. It could be argued that the bitcoin-system meets these conditions. The third-party clause, as part of the multi-party agreement, is included for the sole benefit of anyone wishing to participate as a member, miner, or node to the system. Moreover, it follows from article 6:254 (1) Dutch Civil Code that a third party, following acceptance of the third-party clause, will be considered a party to that agreement. In the case of the bitcoin-network, acceptance takes place through participation in the network, in accordance with article 6:253(3)

79 HR 05 November 1993, ECLI:NL:HR:1993:ZC1128, no. 3.2.

80 J. L. Snijders and Y.C. Tonino, 'Goederenrechtelijke status van bitcoin (kapitaalkracht)' 6 *Financiering, Zekerheden & Insolventierechtpraktijk* (2018) 46, 52–53.

Dutch Civil Code in conjunction with Article 3:37 (3) Dutch Civil Code. This person, now a full member to the agreement (i.e. the bitcoin-system), is subject to all the general rights and obligations contained in the agreement. The agreement takes the form of a framework agreement that contains not only all the rights and obligations of persons within the bitcoin-system, but also the rights and obligations with respect to individual transactions. De Graaf notes that the content of this framework agreement, rather than being provided through writing, is provided through the technical functioning of the blockchain. Individuals that are, or want to be, party to that agreement have the option to acquaint themselves with the exact nature of the rights and obligations stipulated therein by consulting the source-code and documentation. The open-source nature of the software allows for this.[81] This approach and interpretation seems to align well with the, in crypto-communities popular, creed that 'code is law'.[82]

Having established the contractual nature of the bitcoin-system as a whole, De Graaf brings to mind the bitcoin block reward. The technology underlying bitcoin, and, in light of the reasoning above, the framework agreement that is the bitcoin-network, enforces a block reward for the miner that proposes the next correct block.[83] In light of the contractual nature of the bitcoin-network, the rights of users with respect to other users, miners, and nodes should be considered as claims.[84]

Furthermore, prior to engaging in the proprietary analysis, he makes one preliminary observation that sets him apart from the previous authors:

> 'Practically speaking, focussing the qualification of (the registration of) a bitcoin and the bitcoin transactions that are in the bitcoin-ledger and stored in the bitcoin-file is futile. After all, this file is stored in a decentralized manner all over the world on all nodes [...]. It is for this reason that no singular unique files exist. Additionally, disposing, charging, seizing, or recovering of most or all files is a practical impossibility.'[85]

---

81 T. de Graaf, 'De kwalificatie van bitcoins' 94 *NJB* (2019) 6, 10.

82 See L. Lessig, *Code is Law V2.0*, Basic Books, New York 2006.

83 A full technological exploration of the functioning of the network is beyond the scope of this contribution. Those interested are referred to A.M. Antonopoulos, *Mastering bitcoin*, O'Reilly Media USA, Sebastopol 2017.

84 T. de Graaf, 'De kwalificatie van bitcoins' 94 *NJB* (2019) 6, 11.

85 Ibid, 12.

He therefore posits that the proprietary qualification of bitcoin should be focussed on the private key, the wallet in which the private key is stored, as well as the carrier on which the wallet is stored. Transferring a bitcoin from a certain bitcoin-address can only be done by using the private key that relates to that bitcoin-address. In order to transfer that bitcoin, the transferor makes use of the claims that he has *vis-à-vis* the miners and the nodes in order to perform their control – and verification-obligations. As part of these control – and verification-obligations, the network will check whether the transfer is initiated by the correct private key (i.e. the private key that relates to the wallet used).[86] The control – and verification-obligations do not see to the holder of the private key. Pseudonymity is sometimes presented as a feature of the network.[87] The network can guarantee pseudonymity by not checking whether the person using a certain private key has a right to do so.[88]

In order to reflect this technical reality in law, the claim that an individual has against the miners and nodes should be converted to a bearer instrument as soon as possible. De Graaf argues for a legal fiction in order to qualify the technical reality presented by bitcoin: the exact moment when the bitcoin is mined (or, to use his words, 'one legal Planck-second later')[89], the claims *vis-à-vis* miners and nodes are converted into bearer claims (*vorderingen aan toonder*). It is worth noting that this qualification would circumvent the arguments based on the *numerus clausus* raised against qualifying bitcoin as a patrimonial right, as Dutch securities law is free of such a *numerus clausus*.[90] The author assumes that, part of the framework-agreement (i.e. the bitcoin-network), is the obligation that any bitcoins that are mined are immediately converted to bearer instruments, more specifically; bearer claims representing a claim payable to bearer, i.e. the holder of the private key.[91]

86 Ibid. p. 13.

87 See for example A.M. Antonopoulos, *Mastering bitcoin*, O'Reilly Media USA, Sebastopol 2017, pp. 57–76.

88 Whether this would be technically feasible or even possible is a different question and well-outside the scope of this contribution.

89 'Planck time' represents the time required for light to travel a distance of 1 Planck length (the shortest possible measurable distance in physics) in a vacuum. In particle physics, Planck time represents the shortest possible unit of time. The author seems to suggest that a 'legal Planck second' represents the shortest possible unit of time in legal sciences.

90 T. de Graaf, 'De kwalificatie van bitcoins' 94 *NJB* (2019) 6, 13; R. Zwitser, *order en toonderpapieren*, Wolters Kluwer, Deventer 2017, pp. 10–11.

91 T. de Graaf, 'De kwalificatie van bitcoins' 94 *NJB* (2019) 6, 13.

In this construction, the private key is stored in the wallet. This private key enables a holder to mine new bitcoins, but also allows a person to access and dispose of previously mined bitcoins. The wallet itself can either exist in physical form (i.e. a paper wallet)[92] or be stored on a physical device. In that latter situation, two variations exist: dedicated devices (such as a Ledger Nano X Hardware Wallet) or a non-dedicated device (such as a smartphone or a computer). The difference between the two is that the former is meant to store the wallet and the wallet alone, while the latter will generally store other files as well. The claims have been converted to bearer instruments, payable to the holder of the private key. The private key is contained in the wallet, which, in turn, exists either physically or is stored on a physical device. Effectively this means that the claims are represented by the device or the physical form of the wallet. De Graaf refers to this as the physical carrier of the claims.[93]

6 Final Remarks

Following the judgment in the first bitcoin case in the Netherlands in 2014, a concise but rich body of literature has developed. This body of literature reflects a growing recognition of cryptocurrencies within the Dutch system of private law. This literature review has given a chronological overview of this growing recognition, thereby providing a background against which the case law following the 2014 bitcoin-case can be analysed. It seems that no clear qualification has arisen at this time. Looking at the case law in conjunction with the body of literature that has been developed parallel to this line of cases, three things become clear.

Firstly, there is no reason, at least not from the case law nor from the accompanying literature, to distinguish between different cryptocurrencies. While it is conceivable that, at some point, a particular implementation of blockchain technology takes root, and results in a particularly unique cryptocurrency, that requires a revaluation of the appropriate qualification in light of that implementation and potentially a deviation from the standard.

92 Such paper wallets are effectively private keys printed, or written, on paper. These can be generated offline and therefore provide additional security as these wallets have never 'touched' the internet, see A.M. Antonopoulos, *Mastering bitcoin*, O'Reilly Media USA, Sebastopol 2017, pp. 88 *et seq* for more information.

93 T. de Graaf, 'De kwalificatie van bitcoins' 94 *NJB* (2019) 6, 14.

In order to do so, a generally applicable standard for cryptocurrencies is required first. The case law and literature suggest that patterns are emerging, which might, over time, result in a general standard. This general standard could be applicable to cryptocurrencies. Following this, over time we might see the development of a *lex specialis* applicable to specific (types of) cryptocurrencies. However, at the time of writing, at least with respect to Dutch law, it would be bold to even recognize a general standard, let alone specific standards that deviate therefrom. Regardless, patterns are slowly emerging from case law and literature that are shaping towards a general standard. To put it short; the conclusions drawn with respect to bitcoin or, in the case of the 2017 case before the court of Midden-Nederland, ethereum, seem to be applicable to cryptocurrencies as a whole, rather than exclusively to bitcoin or ether.

Secondly, the cases considered, as well as the literature review, suggests consensus on the monetary nature of cryptocurrency in the Netherlands. The Dutch legal system does not, and cannot, recognize cryptocurrencies as currency, legal tender, or scriptural money. While it could be argued that the judges confronted with bitcoin adopted a practical and pragmatic stance in order to provide a just result, and therefore had no choice but to qualify bitcoin proprietarily rather than monetarily. In the cases considered previously, this qualification provided a more just result, a result that could not have been reached had the judge concluded that the more appropriate qualification for cryptocurrencies was that of a currency, legal tender, or scriptural money. Additionally, the literature review shows that the Dutch legal system leaves no room for such a monetary qualification. This aligns with the role of the Dutch supervisory authorities, as outlined in section 4. Only in very specific situations do activities related to cryptocurrencies fall within the full scope of the supervisory authorities. Apart from these specific situations, the supervisory authorities have a limited role to play.

Thirdly, a strong movement can be observed that recognizes cryptocurrencies as representing an absolute patrimonial right. This holds true both for case law, as well as in scholarly writing. A preliminary observation made by those who argue this point is that the law of property includes things and patrimonial rights. Things are limited to corporeal objects, which is a requirement that cryptocurrencies are unable to meet. Following this preliminary observation, two follow-up points are made in order to establish that cryptocurrencies are absolute patrimonial rights. First, it is noted that for a relative patrimonial right to exist, an active side (a claim) and a passive side (debt) is required. The decentralized nature of the cryptocurrency network makes that a cryptocurrency cannot represent a claim that corresponds to a debt in a specific persons' patrimony. For this reason, cryptocurrencies cannot be qualified as relative patrimonial rights. Hence, the only qualification available in private law, for reasonsons outlined in the previous section, is that of absolute patrimonial rights.

New Zealand

Kelly Buchanan

1 Introduction

1.1 *Current Status of Cryptocurrencies*

There is currently no specific law regulating cryptocurrencies in New Zealand.[1] However, certain technology-neutral laws may apply to those who conduct cryptocurrency activities, including those governing registration and supervision of financial service providers, consumer protection, anti-money laundering requirements, and taxes.

The New Zealand Parliament's Finance and Expenditure Committee (FEC) commenced an inquiry into "the current and future nature, impact, and risks of cryptocurrencies" on June 30, 2021. In addition to examining how cryptocurrencies are created and traded, and the risks to users, traders, the monetary system, and financial stability, the committee was tasked with establishing "whether means exist to regulate crypto-currencies, either by sovereign states, central banks, or multi-lateral cooperation."[2]

Also in 2021, the Reserve Bank of New Zealand developed discussion documents to

> look at the potential for a Central Bank Digital Currency (CBDC) to work alongside cash as government-backed money, issues arising from new electronic money forms including crypto assets (such as BitCoin) and stable coins (such as proposed by a Facebook-led consortium), and how the cash system might need to change to continue to meet the needs of users.[3]

1 This chapter was completed in early 2022 and reflects the status of the law, guidance, and discussions in New Zealand at that time.

2 *Inquiry into the Current and Future Nature, Impact, and Risks of Cryptocurrencies*, New Zealand Parliament, https://www.parliament.nz/en/pb/sc/make-a-submission/document/53SCFE_SCF_INQ_111968/inquiry-into-the-current-and-future-nature-impact-and. See also Diana Clement, *Lawyers Urged to Upskill on "Virtual Assets,"* 31 ADLS Law News (Sept. 10, 2021, republished at https://www.stacehammond.co.nz/lawyers-urged-to-upskill-on-vitual-assets/; Gary Hughes, *Complex Cryptocurrencies Sector Features in Two Parliamentary Inquiries in Trans-Tasman Region*, Thomson Reuters, Legal Insight (Sept. 22, 2021), https://insight.thomsonreuters.co.nz/legal/posts/complex-cryptocurrencies-sector-features-in-two-parliamentary-inquiries-in-trans-tasman-region.

3 Press Release, Reserve Bank of New Zealand, Reserve Bank Confirms Consultations "Key to the Future of How New Zealanders Pay and Save" (July 7, 2021), https://www.rbnz.govt.nz

 | DOI:10.1163/9789004722507_021

The Reserve Bank also undertook "a regulatory gap analysis to assess whether the current (cross agency) regulatory framework remains fit for purpose and to identify what further measures may be needed in collaboration with other agencies."[4] It stated that "it is likely that New Zealand regulators, including the Reserve Bank, will need enhanced regulatory toolkits to manage the risks posed by some forms of crypto-assets."[5]

In addition, the Ministry of Justice, which administers the Anti-Money Laundering and Countering Financing of Terrorism Act 2009 (AML/CFT Act), commenced a review of that legislation in 2021, looking "generally at where things are not working and could be improved, including in areas involving cryptocurrencies, virtual assets, and virtual asset service providers."[6] A consultation document was published in October 2021.[7]

Cryptocurrencies are not considered legal tender in New Zealand, but may be used for payments. The Reserve Bank noted in its submission to the FEC that "there does not appear to be broad acceptance among businesses for crypto-assets as a means of payment. According to one survey, less than 100 New Zealand companies are currently accepting crypto-assets as a means of payment."[8]

New Zealand investors do appear to be buying various types of cryptocurrencies: according to a survey of retail investors conducted by the Financial Markets Authority (FMA) in June 2021, "six per cent of investors said they intend to invest in cryptocurrency in the next 12 months, lifting the proportion of surveyed investors with an investment in cryptocurrency to 34 per cent."[9]

/news/2021/07/reserve-bank-confirms-consultations-key-to-the-future-of-how-new-zealanders-pay-and-save.

4 Reserve Bank of New Zealand, Submission, Inquiry into the Current and Future Nature, Impact, and Risks of Cryptocurrencies ¶ 1.8 (Sept. 2, 2021), https://www.parliament.nz/resource/en-NZ/53SCFE_EVI_111968_FE2044/e638a91cd4342b9777637d4f81bcd9ef99d4a47d.

5 Id. ¶ 5.5.

6 Ministry of Justice, Submission, Inquiry into the Current and Future Nature, Impact, and Risks of Cryptocurrencies ¶ 4 (Nov. 14, 2021), https://www.parliament.nz/resource/en-NZ/53SCFE_EVI_111968_FE2622/98384ff1174d11d04074c700530a17dd8d45cd40.

7 Ministry of Justice, *Review of the AML/CFT Act: Consultation Document* (Oct. 2021), https://consultations.justice.govt.nz/policy/aml-cft-review/user_uploads/amlcft-statutory-review-consultation-document.pdf.

8 Reserve Bank of New Zealand, Submission, supra note 3, ¶ 4.2.

9 Press Release, Financial Markets Authority (FMA), Online Investing Platforms Transform Attitudes to Investing (Aug. 5, 2021), https://www.fma.govt.nz/news-and-resources/media-releases/online-platforms-transform-attitudes/. See also FMA, *Retail Investor Platforms Research,* slide 18 (July 27, 2021), https://www.fma.govt.nz/assets/Reports/FMA-Retail-Investor-Platforms-Research.pdf.

In March 2021, a New Zealand-based company, Techemynt, launched "NZDS," a "stablecoin backed 1:1 by the New Zealand Dollar."[10] Previously, there had been several attempts to create a stablecoin backed by the dollar, including the NZDT issued in May 2017 by cryptocurrency exchange Cryptopia.[11] The Reserve Bank stated that it

> has a particular interest in so-called stablecoins, a subset of cryptoassets. These stablecoins have the most potential to crowd out existing forms of money. As such, stablecoins pose particular risks, including to monetary sovereignty and financial stability, which are central to the Reserve Bank's mandate, in addition to market integrity, money laundering and other risks.[12]

1.2 *Definitions*

Government agencies have provided the following explanations of cryptocurrency and related terms:

- The FMA states that "[c]ryptocurrencies are a type of cryptoasset. They use encryption technology to control the amount of currency issued and to record ownership and payments."[13]
- Inland Revenue uses the term cryptoassets, which it states are "cryptographically secured digital representations of value that can be transferred, stored or traded electronically. They use some form of distributed ledger technology such as blockchain."[14]
- The Reserve Bank also prefers the term cryptoassets, stating in its FEC submission that [t]he term 'crypto-currencies' is used to describe a wide range of digital assets that claim to be alternative forms of money, Bitcoin being the most well-known. However, the Reserve Bank prefers not to use the term 'crypto-currency' as it implies attributes – a safe store of value, a stable medium of exchange and a reliable unit of account – associated with conventional

10 *Welcome to Techemynt*, Techemynt, https://www.techemynt.com/.

11 Sebastian Sinclair, *Compliant Stablecoin Launches in New Zealand*, Nasdaq (Mar. 10, 2021), https://www.nasdaq.com/articles/compliant-stablecoin-launches-in-new-zealand-2021-03-10.

12 Reserve Bank of New Zealand, Submission, supra note 3, ¶ 1.3.

13 *Cryptocurrencies*, FMA (last updated Sept. 17, 2021), https://www.fma.govt.nz/investors/ways-to-invest/cryptocurrencies/.

14 *What Cryptoassets Are*, Inland Revenue, https://www.ird.govt.nz/cryptoassets/about.

currencies that 'crypto-currencies' do not have. The Reserve Bank considers 'crypto-assets' a more appropriate term than 'cryptocurrencies'.[15]

- The Department of Internal Affairs (DIA), which supervises a range of entities under the AML/CFT Act,[16] uses the terms "virtual assets" and "Virtual Asset Service Providers" (VASPs), which appears to be based on the approach of the Financial Action Task Force (FATF).[17] The DIA explains that "[a] virtual asset is a digital representation of value that can be digitally traded or transferred, and can be used for payment or investment purposes. One example is Bitcoin, which is a virtual currency."[18]

A bill introduced in the Parliament in September 2021 proposed to amend the Goods and Services Tax Act 1985 (GST Act) to establish a GST exemption for cryptoassets.[19] The bill included the following definition of cryptoasset:

> cryptoasset means a digital representation of value that –
> a. exists in –
>   i. a database that is secured cryptographically and contains ledgers, recording transactions and contracts involving digital representations of value, that are maintained in decentralised form and shared across different locations and persons; or
>   ii. another application of the same technology performing an equivalent function; and
> b. is designed to be fungible[20]

15 Reserve Bank of New Zealand, Submission, supra note 3, ¶ 3.1.

16 *Anti-Money Laundering and Countering Financing of Terrorism: Information for the Public*, Department of Internal Affairs (DIA), https://www.dia.govt.nz/AML-CFT-Information-for-public.

17 See *Regulation of Virtual Assets*, FATF, http://www.fatf-gafi.org/publications/fatfrecommendations/documents/regulation-virtual-assets.html.

18 *Virtual Asset Service Providers*, DIA (Nov. 2019), https://www.dia.govt.nz/AML-CFT-Virtual-Asset-Service-Providers.

19 *Taxation (Annual Rates for 2021-22, GST, and Remedial Matters) Bill*, New Zealand Parliament, https://www.parliament.nz/en/pb/bills-and-laws/bills-proposed-laws/document/BILL_115767/taxation-annual-rates-for-2021-22-gst-and-remedial-matters. See also *Taxation (Annual Rates for 2021-22, GST, and Remedial Matters) Bill*, Inland Revenue, https://taxpolicy.ird.govt.nz/bills/53-65; Campbell Pentney et al., *Crypto Clarity? New Tax Bill Proposes Tax Exemptions for Cryptoassets, GST on NFTs and More*, Bell Gully (Sept. 16, 2021), https://www.bellgully.com/insights/crypto-clarity-new-tax-bill-proposes-tax-exemptions-for-cryptoassets-gst-on-nfts-and-more/.

20 Taxation (Annual Rates for 2021-22, GST, and Remedial Matters) Bill (65–1) cl 5, https://legislation.govt.nz/bill/government/2021/0065/12.0/whole.html.

In its April 2020 decision in the case of *Ruscoe v Cryptopia Limited (in liquidation)*, the New Zealand High Court (the third highest court in the country) sought to "identify and describe, in general terms, the features of cryptoassets that may be regarded as genuinely novel or distinctive, as compared with conventional assets, so that we can then consider whether and how those features might be relevant to issues of legal and proprietary status."[21] It concluded that

> [a]lthough not all systems possess all of them, we can therefore identify the principal novel and characteristic features of cryptoassets as being:
> a. intangibility;
> b. cryptographic authentication;
> c. use of a distributed transaction ledger;
> d. decentralisation; and
> e. ruled by consensus.[22]

1.3 *Relationships between Participants*

In *Ruscoe v Cryptopia*, the High Court found that Cryptopia, a New Zealand custodial cryptocurrency exchange that became insolvent after it was hacked and cryptocurrencies were stolen from its wallets, held digital assets on trust for accountholders. The judge considered that "at law cryptocurrencies are 'property' and are able to form the subject of a trust."[23] In addition to finding the cryptocurrencies are property under the Companies Act 1993,[24] the judge stated:

> I am satisfied that cryptocurrencies meet the standard criteria outlined by Lord Wilberforce to be considered a species of "property" [being: identifiable subject-matter; identifiable by third parties; capable of assumption by third parties; some degree of permanence or stability[25]]. They are a type of intangible property as a result of the combination of three

---

21 *Ruscoe v Cryptopia Limited (in liquidation)* [2020] NZHC 728 at [27], http://www.nzlii.org/nz/cases/NZHC/2020/728.html.

22 Id. at [28]–[31].

23 Id. at [141].

24 Companies Act 1993 s 2(1) (definition of "property"), https://www.legislation.govt.nz/act/public/1993/0105/latest/whole.html. The definition reads: "property means property of every kind whether tangible or intangible, real or personal, corporeal or incorporeal, and includes rights, interests, and claims of every kind in relation to property however they arise."

25 Jack Pembroke-Birss & Michael Sinclair, *Cryptocurrencies are Property Capable of Being Held of Being Held on Trust, New Zealand High Court Holds*, Norton Rose Fulbright (May 2020), https://www.nortonrosefulbright.com/en/knowledge/publications/d6ea37bd/cryptocurrencies-are-property-capable-of-being-held-on-trust-new-zealand-high-court-holds.

> interdependent features. They obtain their definition as a result of the public key recording the unit of currency. The control and stability necessary to ownership and for creating a market in the coins are provided by the other two features – the private key attached to the corresponding public key and the generation of a fresh private key upon a transfer of the relevant coin.[26]

The judge then turned to whether the requirements for a valid express trust – certainty of subject matter, objects, and intention – were present, and ruled in the affirmative. The judge stated that "in the current circumstances it appears all cryptocurrency holdings were held on trust by Cryptopia, although Cryptopia was itself one of the beneficiaries of some trusts relating to cryptocurrency which the company had itself introduced."[27]

In terms of intent, the judge was

> satisfied that Cryptopia manifested its intent through its conduct in creating the exchange without allocating to accountholders public and private keys for the digital assets it commenced to hold for them. The SQL database that Cryptopia created showed that the company was a custodian and trustee of the digital assets and effect needs to be given to this.[28]

Furthermore, "Cryptopia did not intend to and did not trade in the digital assets in its own right according to the evidence before me except to the extent that it too was a beneficiary of the trusts established."[29] The judge found that "a trust came into existence for each of the cryptocurrencies as soon as Cryptopia came each time to hold a new currency for accountholders."[30] With respect to the terms of the trusts, the judge stated that

> Cryptopia essentially fulfilled the role of a bare trustee in relation to the accountholders. Cryptopia's trust duties therefore were somewhat confined. Its principal role was to hold each group of digital assets as trustee for the accountholders, to follow their instructions, and to let individual accountholders then increase or reduce their beneficial interest in the relevant trusts in accordance with the system Cryptopia had created for that purpose.[31]

---

26 *Ruscoe v Cryptopia Limited (in liquidation)* [2020] NZHC 728 at [120].
27 Id. at [144].
28 Id. at [153].
29 Id. at [154].
30 Id. at [155].
31 Id. at [196].

Legal commentators have noted that the decision "is one of only a few currently in the common law world to address expressly the question, in a fully reasoned judgment, as to whether digital assets such as cryptocurrencies constitute property and can be the subject of a trust."[32]

2 Regulatory Framework

Different laws may apply to cryptocurrency activities depending on the context and entities involved, including the following:

- Financial Markets Conduct Act 2013 (FMCA)[33]
- Financial Service Providers (Registration and Dispute Resolution) Act 2008 (FSP Act)[34]
- Fair Trading Act 1986[35]
- Companies Act 1993
- AML/CFT Act 2009[36]
- Income Tax Act 2007[37]
- GST Act 1985[38]
- Crimes Act 1961[39]
- Criminal Proceeds (Recovery) Act 2009[40]

---

32 Pembroke-Birss & Sinclair, supra note 24. For further discussion, see Matteo Solinas, *Investors' Rights in (Crypto) Custodial Holdings:* Ruscoe v Cryptopia Ltd (in Liquidation), 84(1) MLR 155 (2021), https://onlinelibrary.wiley.com/doi/epdf/10.1111/1468-2230.12588; Paul T. Babie et al., *Cryptocurrencies as Property: Ruscoe and Moore v Cryptopia Limited (in Liquidation)* [2020] *NZHC 728* (U. of Adelaide Law Research Paper No. 2020-33, Apr. 17, 2020), https://papers.ssrn.com/sol3/papers.cfm?abstract_id=3578264.

33 Financial Markets Conduct Act 2013, https://www.legislation.govt.nz/act/public/2013/0069/latest/whole.html.

34 Financial Service Providers (Registration and Dispute Resolution) Act 2008 (FSP Act 2008), https://www.legislation.govt.nz/act/public/2008/0097/latest/whole.html.

35 Fair Trading Act 1986, https://www.legislation.govt.nz/act/public/1986/0121/latest/whole.html.

36 Anti-Money Laundering and Countering Financing of Terrorism Act 2009, https://www.legislation.govt.nz/act/public/2009/0035/latest/whole.html.

37 Income Tax Act 2007, https://www.legislation.govt.nz/act/public/2007/0097/latest/whole.html.

38 Goods and Services Tax Act 1985, https://www.legislation.govt.nz/act/public/1985/0141/latest/whole.html.

39 Crimes Act 1961, https://www.legislation.govt.nz/act/public/1961/0043/latest/whole.html.

40 Criminal Proceeds (Recovery) Act 2009, https://www.legislation.govt.nz/act/public/2009/0008/latest/whole.html.

Several government agencies have produced guidance on the application of these existing laws to cryptocurrencies and related activities, including the FMA, Inland Revenue, and the Department of Internal Affairs (DIA).

2.1 *AML/CFT Law*

The DIA is the lead AML/CFT contact for VASPs. VASPs that provide financial services "fall within the existing definition of a 'financial institution' in the AML/CFT Act 2009."[41] While it will be the AML/CFT supervisor for most VASPs, the DIA notes that the FMA may be the supervisor depending on the services provided by a particular VASP. In particular, if a VASP's activities involve a virtual asset that is a "financial product" under the FMCA, or providing investment opportunities in virtual assets, it will likely be supervised by the FMA.[42]

The DIA sets out five relevant categories of VASPs that are recognized for the purposes of AML/CFT law, along with the types of virtual asset activities undertaken by such entities: Virtual Asset Exchanges, Virtual Asset Wallet Providers, Virtual Asset Broking, Initial Coin Offering (ICO) Providers, and providing investment opportunities in virtual assets.[43]

In March 2020, the DIA published guidelines for VASPs[44] along with a fact sheet.[45] Various other information relevant to VASPs and their AML/CFT responsibilities is also provided on a dedicated page on the DIA's website.[46] The guidelines provide examples of potential "capture points," where a business offers services that fit under the definitions specified in section 5(1) of the AML/CFT Act.[47] If an entity is involved in capture points as part of its "ordinary course of business," it will have compliance obligations under the Act.[48] In addition, in order to by captured by the Act, "one or more of the business's activities must be carried on within New Zealand in the ordinary course of

41 *Virtual Asset Service Providers*, DIA, supra note 17. The definition of "financial services" is set out in section 5(1) of the AML/CFT Act.

42 DIA, *Guidelines: Virtual Asset Service Providers – Complying with the Anti-Money Laundering and Countering Financing of Terrorism Act 2009*, at 9–10 (Mar. 2020) (Guidelines), https://www.dia.govt.nz/diawebsite.nsf/Files/AML-CFT-2020/$file/AML-CFT-VASP-Guideline.pdf.

43 Id.

44 Id.

45 DIA, *Factsheet – Virtual Asset Service Providers* (2020) (Factsheet), https://www.dia.govt.nz/diawebsite.nsf/Files/AML-CFT-2020/$file/AML-CFT-VASP-Factsheet.pdf.

46 *Information for Virtual Asset Service Providers*, DIA, https://www.dia.govt.nz/Information-for-Virtual-Asset-Service-Providers.

47 Guidelines, supra note 41, at 4.

48 Id. at 5.

business."[49] In essence, "VASPs have the same obligations as other reporting entities under the Act," including appointing a compliance officer, undertaking a risk assessment, and developing an AML/CFT program, and then submitting annual reports, having independent audits, and meeting record keeping requirements,[50] as well as responsibilities to conduct customer due diligence[51] and to report suspicious activities and transactions.[52]

The fact sheet highlights that "[w]ire transfers are an especially important captured activity for VASPs. In New Zealand, the definition of wire transfer is set out in section 5 of the [AML/CFT] Act."[53] The DIA states that the definition covers

- Transactions from fiat currency to virtual assets, and
- Transactions from virtual assets to fiat currency,
- But does not include virtual asset to virtual asset transactions.

> VASPs must be particularly aware of their wire transfer obligations as described in sections 27 and 28 of the Act, as well as the associated PTR [prescribed transaction reporting] obligations. These obligations apply to any transaction that is over NZD$1,000.
>
> VASPs should, in addition, be aware of the FATF recommendations in relation to wire transfers, which include virtual asset to virtual asset transactions. VASPs should be aware that other international jurisdictions they deal with (and other VASPs based in those jurisdictions) may require this, and consequently, it would be considered 'best practice' for VASPs to include virtual asset to virtual asset transactions in their wire transfer procedures.[54]

The Ministry of Justice consultation document produced as part of the review of the AML/CFT Act discussed the need to include all types of VASPs in order to fully comply with binding standards issued by FATF in 2019. In particular, it stated that while the existing definition of financial institution in the AML/CFT Act is sufficiently broad to cover four of the five virtual asset activities identified by FATF, there is a need to extend obligations to wallet providers "to ensure all virtual asset service providers are clearly captured."[55]

---

49 Id.

50 Id. at 12.

51 Id. at 21–27.

52 Id. at 19–20.

53 Factsheet, supra note 44, at 2.

54 Id. at 2; Guidelines, supra note 41, at 18–19.

55 Ministry of Justice, *Review of the AML/CFT Act: Consultation Document*, supra note 6, at 27.

Furthermore, the document asked for comments on whether there are any obligations that need to be tailored for VASPs; whether there is any further support that should be provided to assist them with complying with their obligations; whether specific thresholds for occasional transactions should be set for VASPs; and whether regulations should be issued to declare that transfers of virtual assets are cross-border wire transfers.[56]

The document also discussed the potential introduction of registration and licensing frameworks under the AML/CFT Act. With respect to the registration of reporting entities, the document stated that some "high-risk businesses," including VASPs, "are only subject to limited fit-and-proper checks before being able to offer the services," and "there is a greater risk of these businesses being owned or controlled by criminals or their associates."[57] A registration system could include sufficient fit-and-proper checks as part of the process.

With respect to additional licensing requirements for reporting entities, the document stated that such a regime would "only be used for businesses which are at high risk of being misused for money laundering and terrorism financing and are not currently required to be licensed" under another system.[58] Certain entities, including VASPs, could be required to be licensed instead of only being registered, allowing agencies to "further mitigate the risks for those businesses and the sector overall."[59]

2.2 *Criminal Law*

The AML/CFT guideline for VASPs advises that "it is a criminal offence to knowingly and intentionally engage in, or facilitate any other person to engage in, money laundering or the financing of terrorism. The New Zealand Police are responsible for investigating and prosecuting ML/TF offences, as well as forfeiture proceedings relating to the proceeds of crime."[60]

The AML/CFT law, as well as provisions of the Crimes Act 1961 and Criminal Proceeds (Recovery) Act 2009, may be used by the New Zealand Police in investigating and prosecuting activities involving cryptocurrencies and to seize cryptocurrencies. According to two authors,

> [t]he New Zealand courts have held that intangible property is capable of being property for the purposes of criminal law. Accordingly, under

56 Id. at 81–82.
57 Id. at 15–16.
58 Id. at 16.
59 Id. at 17.
60 Guidelines, supra note 41, at 11.

> the Crimes Act 1961 (the Crimes Act) – the primary piece of legislation that prescribes criminal offences in New Zealand – there are a number of criminal offences that could apply to the use of virtual currencies. These include theft, obtaining property or causing loss by deception, as well as crimes involving computers.
>
> It is an offence to obtain property or valuable consideration by deception, or cause loss to another person by deception. This could cover circumstances in which a person is scammed by a malicious issuer of an ICO (where the issuer purports to raise money for a project by issuing virtual currency in an ICO with no intention of honouring its obligation to deliver certain products or services to the investor who purchased the virtual currency). […]
>
> It is possible that the general offence of theft could also apply to virtual currencies. However, if that theft was procured by a person hacking another's computer or accounts, prosecution as a crime involving computers may also apply. These include accessing a computer system for dishonest purposes and accessing a computer system without authorisation. This could cover the recent trend of viruses that hijack a target computer's processing power for the purposes of mining virtual currencies. As with other parts of New Zealand law, this crime is not concerned specifically with virtual currencies, but is drafted broadly enough that the kind of activity above would be covered.[61]

For example, the Police investigated the loss of a significant amount of cryptocurrency from Cryptopia in January 2019. The Police noted that "[a] priority for police is to identify and, if possible, recover missing funds for Cryptopia customers; however there are likely to be many challenges to achieving this."[62]

In November 2019, the Police announced that NZ$6.2 million in cryptocurrency and NZ$800,000 in banked funds had been restrained, under the Criminal (Proceeds) Recovery Act 2009, from a man based in New Zealand who

---

61 Deemple Budhia & Tom Hunt, *New Zealand, in* The Virtual Currency Regulation Review 210, 217 (Mark S. Sackheim & Nathan A. Howell eds., 2nd ed. 2019), available at https://www.russellmcveagh.com/getmedia/8079c77d-15de-4f3d-8308-910ff5b67520/New-Zealand-chapter-in-The-Virtual-Currency-Regulation-Review/. Cybercrime offenses are contained in sections 249 to 252 of the Crimes Act 1961. See *Cybercrime*, New Zealand Police, https://www.police.govt.nz/advice-services/cybercrime-and-internet/cybercrime.

62 Press Release, New Zealand Police, Update: Investigation Involving Cryptocurrency Company (Jan. 16, 2019), https://www.police.govt.nz/news/release/update-investigation-involving-cryptocurrency-company.

operated a website that allegedly distributed a large number of copyrighted films, and who laundered the proceeds.[63]

In July 2021, it was reported that the Police had confiscated nearly NZ$32 million worth of cryptocurrency in the previous six years, with the vast majority seized in the 2019–2020 fiscal year. Almost all of the seizures had related to money laundering, with smaller amounts related to drug offending also seized.[64]

3 Supervision of Providers of Cryptocurrency Services

3.1 *Registration Requirements*

Where an individual or entity's cryptocurrency activities involve the provision of "financial services" to persons in New Zealand, the FSP Act applies, requiring such providers to be registered on the Financial Service Providers Register (FSPR).[65] If the financial services are offered to retail clients, the provider must belong to an approved dispute resolution scheme.[66]

According to the FMA, cryptocurrency activities considered to be financial services, as defined in section 5 of the FSP Act, include exchanges, wallets, deposits, broking, and ICOs.[67] Certain persons are disqualified from registering as a financial service provider, including an undischarged bankrupt; a person prohibited from being a director of a body under the specified legislation; a person subject to a management banning order under relevant legislation; a person prohibited from being a director of a body under the laws of another country; a person convicted of certain offenses or who is subject to a forfeiture order; and a person who has been deregistered within the past year.[68] In addition, the FMA may prevent a person from registering as a financial services provider where such registration could give a misleading impression that the

63 Press Release, New Zealand Police, Police Restrain Cryptocurrency Following Investigation into Streaming Service (Nov. 23, 2019), https://www.police.govt.nz/news/release/police-restrain-cryptocurrency-following-investigation-streaming-service.

64 Jason Walls, *Revealed: Govt Sells $30m of Seized Criminal Cryptocurrency*, NewstalkZB (July 9, 2021), https://www.newstalkzb.co.nz/news/crime/documents-reveal-the-government-sold-30-million-of-seized-criminal-cryptocurrency/.

65 *Cryptocurrencies – Cryptocurrency/Cryptoasset Services*, FMA (last updated Mar. 15, 2021), https://www.fma.govt.nz/compliance/role/cryptocurrencies/. See also *Spotlight on Crypto: Using New Zealand Based Cryptocurrency Trading Platforms*, FMA (updated Sept. 3, 2021), https://www.fma.govt.nz/news-and-resources/fma-stories/spotlight-on-cryptocurrency/.

66 FSP Act 2008 ss 11 & 48.

67 *Cryptocurrencies – Cryptocurrency/Cryptoasset Services*, FMA, supra note 64.

68 FSP Act 2008 s 14(2).

provider is operating or regulated in New Zealand, or could damage the integrity or reputation of New Zealand's financial services markets or its regulation thereof.[69]

A registered financial service provider can also be deregistered for these reasons.[70]

Registered trading platforms "are prohibited from engaging in misleading conduct or making false, deceptive, or unsubstantiated statements," and are required to meet AML/CFT obligations, as discussed above.[71] The relevant fair dealing provisions applicable to providers of financial services are contained in part 2 of the FMCA. Providers are advised to "ensure messaging about risks and rewards of buying or trading cryptoassets is balanced. Do not cherry-pick or omit key information, or bury key messages about risk in the fine print."[72]

3.2 *Requirements for Providers of Financial Products*

If the activity involves cryptoassets that may be financial products under the FMCA, additional regulatory requirements apply. The FMCA sets out four types of regulated financial products: debt securities, equity securities, managed investment products, and derivatives. The FMA explains that, while each ICO must be considered on a case-by-case basis, different types of cryptoassets may be considered to be one of these four types of financial products:[73]

- A cryptoasset will be a debt security "if investors have a right to be repaid money or paid interest on money lent to, deposited with, or owed by a person, company, or unincorporated entity making a cryptoasset offer." Asset-backed tokens, which give investors a right to redeem the token in exchange for the asset, "are not considered debt securities (unless the asset is cash)."
- A cryptoasset will be an equity security "if investors buy, or have the option to buy, for example, a share in a New Zealand incorporated company or a body corporate incorporated outside New Zealand. A cryptoasset that provides an option to buy a share is an offer of both the cryptoasset and the equity share."
- With respect to managed investment products, these would involve situations where persons
  - contribute money or cryptoassets to receive interests (cryptoassets) in a scheme (a structure or project that allows investors to pool their money)

69 Id. s 15A.
70 Id. ss 18A & 18B.
71 Id.
72 *Cryptocurrencies – Cryptocurrency/Cryptoasset Services*, FMA, supra note 64.
73 Id.

  - have a 'right to receive a financial benefit' (as defined in the FMC Act) from the scheme – such as money, rights to a share in profits, cryptoassets, additional cryptoassets, or changes in the cryptoassets' value and these benefits are principally produced by someone else, and
  - do not have day-to-day control over the project or business (even if they have the right to be consulted or to give directions).
- Utility tokens "are not considered managed investment products simply because they can be traded on a cryptoasset exchange or other secondary market. This is because any profits an investor receives by trading those utility tokens on a cryptoasset exchange are not 'rights to receive a financial benefit' under a managed investment scheme."
- A cryptoasset may be a derivative
  if, under the terms of the cryptoasset, the issuer or holder may be required to pay an amount or provide something else in the future, and the amount to be paid or the value of the cryptoasset is derived from the value or amount of something else, such as a commodity or asset.

Furthermore, the FMA "can designate cryptoassets to be a particular financial product if, based on their economic substance, this is necessary to promote fair and efficient financial markets in New Zealand or any of the other purposes of the FMC Act."[74] The FMA also has the power to "exempt any person or class of persons, or any transaction or class of transactions, from compliance with certain obligations imposed under the FMCA."[75]

The FMA also explains some of the ways in which other activities related to cryptocurrencies may involve the provision of financial products.[76] For example, an exchange that allows trading of cryptoassets that are financial products will need to consider whether it is operating a financial product market, and therefore if it needs to be licensed. Wallets that hold money for depositors may be offering debt securities, unless depositor funds are held in trust. Providers of transaction services related to cryptoassets that are financial products may have obligations as a provider of a regulated client money or property service. Entities that provide investment opportunities in cryptoassets "will be regulated in the same way as if you were providing investment opportunities in traditional assets or financial products."

The FMA advises that, in order for an ICO to make regulated offers of different financial products, licensing requirements must be met. For example, to make a regulated offer of debt securities to retail investors in New Zealand, an

74 Id.

75 Budhia & Hunt, supra note 60, at 213.

76 *Cryptocurrencies – Cryptocurrency/Cryptoasset Services*, FMA, supra note 64.

entity must appoint a licensed supervisor; for a managed investment scheme, the manager must be licensed and a licensed supervisor must be appointed; and for derivatives, the issuer must be licensed.[77]

In addition, for ICOs involving any of the four types of financial product, the issuer must register a product disclosure statement (PDS), meet fair dealing requirements, and meet financial reporting obligations. To offer managed investment products, the entity must also have a trust deed that sets out investor rights and the supervisor's role.[78]

The FMA provides further guidance on the application of fair dealing requirements to ICOs:

> If your ICO is providing a financial product or financial service, all promotional material – including your white paper, website and on social media posts – must comply with the fair dealing provisions in Part 2 of the FMC Act. The provisions prohibit you from engaging in misleading conduct and making false, deceptive or unsubstantiated statements about the financial product or service, irrespective of the type of investor you are offering to, or where they are located.
>
> Even if your ICO is not providing a financial service or financial product, 'fair dealing' requirements still apply to white papers and other communications about your ICO under the Fair Trading Act 1986. This prohibits misleading and deceptive conduct, and applies to the trading of assets, commodities and other goods and services.
>
> The Commerce Commission is responsible for ensuring you comply with this Act.
>
> Other general consumer protection laws also apply to ICOs, including laws preventing fraudulent and other criminal conduct – like obtaining money by deception.[79]

The FMA is empowered to enforce the fair dealing requirements by issuing "orders requiring ICO issuers in New Zealand to comply with the law, including amending or taking down non-compliant promotional material."[80] Such

77 Id. For further information on the regulation of cryptocurrency activities under the FMCA and the FSP Act, see Jared Cotton, *Sending a Bit More Coin Home? An Analysis of Retail User Protection in Bitcoin Remittance Markets*, 49 VUWLR 107, 118–126 (2018), http://www.nzlii.org/nz/journals/VUWLawRw/2018/5.html; Budhia & Hunt, supra note 60, at 210–217.

78 *Cryptocurrencies – Cryptocurrency/Cryptoasset Services*, FMA, supra note 64.

79 *Fair Dealing and Initial Coin Offers*, FMA, https://www.fma.govt.nz/compliance/role/cryptocurrencies/fair-dealing-and-initial-coin-offers/.

80 Id.

orders may be published. Furthermore, "[a] breach of the fair dealing requirements is also a civil liability offence with a potential pecuniary penalty. ICO issuers can also be ordered to pay compensation to people who have suffered a loss as a consequence of a breach of the fair dealing requirements."[81]

3.3 *Actions Related to Cryptocurrency Activities*

The FMA has issued various warnings with respect to specific entities and their cryptocurrency activities, stating for example that an entity or website is not a registered financial service provider, may be operating in breach of the FMCA, and/or may be operating a scam.[82] In addition, it was reported in 2017 that an e-commerce site had withdrawn its ICO due to hacking and "concerns expressed by the FMA about the accuracy of some of the statements" within its offering disclosure.[83] However, no references to major formal actions against cryptocurrency entities by the FMA were located.

4 Private Law Issues

Ruscoe v Cryptopia related to the rights of accountholders in the event of the insolvency of a cryptocurrency exchange.[84] The finding that the cryptocurrency held in Cryptopia's digital wallets were property that could be held on trust for users meant that "cryptocurrencies were beneficially owned by the account holders, and were therefore not part of the pool of assets capable of being distributed to unsecured creditors in the liquidation."[85]

This ruling could also have broader private law implications, with the decision showing "the courts are willing to apply established legal principles to

---

81 Id.

82 See, e.g. *crypto-boosts.com*, FMA (Aug. 18, 2021), https://www.fma.govt.nz/news-and-resources/warnings-and-alerts/crypto-boosts-com/; *Crypto Currency Trading Group*, FMA (Mar. 2, 2021), https://www.fma.govt.nz/news-and-resources/warnings-and-alerts/crypto-currency-trading-group/; *Cryptominingnz*, FMA (Sept. 21, 2021), https://www.fma.govt.nz/news-and-resources/warnings-and-alerts/cryptominingnz/; *Mido Finance Limited*, FMA (Nov. 11, 2021), https://www.fma.govt.nz/news-and-resources/warnings-and-alerts/mido-finance-limited/.

83 Matt Nippert, *Teen's Under-Fire Cryptocurrency Offer Withdrawn*, NZ Herald (Nov. 27, 2017), https://www.nzherald.co.nz/business/teens-under-fire-cryptocurrency-offer withdrawn/4XSHKGGPUKSU6Q6TIVVIWVLVD4/.

84 See discussion supra, parts I.B, I.C.

85 Glen Holm-Hansen et al., *High Court Recognized "Property" in Cryptocurrency*, Hesketh Henry (Apr. 16, 2020), https://www.heskethhenry.co.nz/insights-opinion/high-court-recognizes-property-in-cryptocurrency/.

cryptocurrencies."[86] However, "there is still uncertainty for cryptocurrency owners … partly due to cryptocurrency exchanges not yet clearly establishing how they hold cryptocurrencies for their users,"[87] and ambiguity regarding application of the principles governing express trusts in different situations.[88] From January 30, 2021, the Trusts Act 2019[89] now applies to all express trusts that are governed by New Zealand law, as well as to "statutory trusts such as intestate estates, and to other trusts recognised at common law or in equity, if a court deems it appropriate."[90]

In terms of possible actions regarding stolen cryptocurrencies, one author argues that

> [t]he *nemo dat quod non habet* ["no one can give what they do not have," i.e., a transferor of property cannot pass title it does not possess] principle should apply if cryptocurrencies are continued to be viewed as property. This may put victims of cryptocurrency theft in a position to expand the tort of conversion in New Zealand. Although, if cryptocurrency is classified as money, then innocent purchasers could take legal title to stolen cryptocurrency. While this is unlikely, the technical theoretical debate further evidences that cryptocurrencies legal status in New Zealand is far from certain. This may only be from test cases if Parliament does not want to regulate.[91]

He further explains that, under current precedent, the tort of conversion does not apply to intangible property. As cryptocurrencies were found to be an intangible in *Cryptopia*, a claim in conversion against an innocent third party recipient would fail. However, "there is an increasingly persuasive argument for New Zealand to depart from this precedent. The courts would be directly faced with this decision if a victim of cryptocurrency [theft] brought an action against someone found to possess their cryptocurrency."[92]

---

86 Fraser Aitken, *Trusting Cryptocurrencies: Aspects of the Common Law and Equity Affecting Cryptocurrency Owners* 5 (LLB(Hons) dissertation, University of Otago, Oct. 2020), https://www.otago.ac.nz/law/research/journals/otago828533.pdf.

87 Id. at 6.

88 Id. at 16.

89 Trusts Act 2019, https://www.legislation.govt.nz/act/public/2019/0038/latest/whole.html.

90 Rhonda Powell, *The New Trusts Act 2019: Key Changes to Consider*, LawTalk (Nov. 29, 2019), https://www.lawsociety.org.nz/news/lawtalk/lawtalk-issue-935/the-new-trusts-act-2019/.

91 Aitken, supra note 85, at 6.

92 Id. at 39.

A New Zealand law firm has also stated that "[a] general finding that cryptocurrency is property could lead to liability for conversion, or claims for knowing receipt, restitution of property or unjust enrichment," and that the comprehensive treatment of this question by the judge in *Cryptopia* "will be useful for later courts in New Zealand and elsewhere."[93] Furthermore, recognition of cryptocurrency as property could mean that it could potentially have other uses, such as security collateral.[94]

5 Tax Law

Inland Revenue treats cryptoassets as "a form of property for tax purposes."[95] Furthermore, "the tax treatment depends on the characteristics and use of the cryptoassets. It does not depend on what they are called."[96] New Zealand does not have a general capital gains tax, thus the only taxes that potentially apply are income tax and GST.

5.1 *Income Tax*

Inland Revenue's website provides cryptoasset tax guidance for both individuals and businesses.

5.1.1 Individuals

In terms of individuals buying and selling cryptoassets, the guidance states that persons may have to pay tax because they are

- acquiring cryptoassets for the purpose of disposal (for example to sell or exchange)
- trading in cryptoassets
- using cryptoassets for a profit-making scheme.[97]

---

93 Matt Kersey et al., *Insolvency Case Recognises Trusts Over Cryptocurrency in Ruscoe v Cryptopia*, Russell McVeagh (Apr. 15, 2020), https://www.russellmcveagh.com/insights/april-2020/insolvency-case-recognises-trusts-over-cryptocurre.

94 Id.

95 *Cryptoassets*, Inland Revenue, https://www.ird.govt.nz/cryptoassets.

96 Id. For further background and analysis, see James Cochrane, *NZ Tax Treatment of Crypto-Assets (For Investors)*, Stace Hammond (May 14, 2021), https://www.stacehammond.co.nz/new-zealand-tax-treatment-of-crypto-assets/; Simon Akozu & Zoe Barnes, *INSIGHT: New Zealand Proposing to Remove Tax Barriers to Cryptoasset Investment*, Bloomberg Tax (Mar. 19, 202), https://news.bloombergtax.com/daily-tax-report-international/insight-new-zealand-proposing-to-remove-tax-barriers-to-cryptoasset-investment.

97 *Buying and Selling Cryptoassets*, Inland Revenue, https://www.ird.govt.nz/cryptoassets/individual/buying-selling.

The relevant purpose is that which occurred at the time a person acquired the cryptoassets. Inland Revenue states that "[i]f you plan on selling or exchanging your cryptoassets at some point in the future, then you have a purpose of disposal. It does not matter how long you plan to hold onto your cryptoassets for before selling or exchanging them."[98]

If a person's cryptoasset activities amount to their being in the business of trading, or dealing, in cryptoassets, income tax is payable on the profits.[99] Inland Revenue states that the main way to tell if a person is in such a business is to look at the frequency of their transactions and how much time and effort is put into buying, selling, or exchanging cryptoassets. If a person is in the business of trading cryptoassets, their cryptoassets are likely to be "trading stock."[100]

A person's cryptoasset activity may be a profit-making scheme if "there is a coherent plan of action (a scheme)" and the person enters into the plan for the purpose of making a profit.[101] A general plan is all that is needed for the amounts received from the scheme to be taxable.

In terms of mining cryptoassets, Inland Revenue states that, in most cases, cryptoassets received from mining (such as transaction fees and block rewards) are taxable.[102] A person may also need to pay income tax on any profit made from subsequently selling or exchanging the mined assets.[103] People who mine cryptoassets may have to pay tax because they

- are in the business of mining cryptoassets
- carry on a profit-making scheme
- earn ordinary income from providing mining services
- mine cryptoassets for the purpose of disposal (to sell or exchange).[104]

Various factors are looked at in determining whether a person's cryptoasset mining is a business. Inland Revenue states that such mining is "generally an activity aimed at making a profit, not a hobby. The longer you mine, the larger the size of your operation, and the more time, money and effort you put in,

---

98 *Acquiring Cryptoassets to Sell or Exchange*, Inland Revenue, https://www.ird.govt.nz/cryptoassets/individual/buying-selling/acquiring-sell-exchange.

99 *Trading in Cryptoassets*, Inland Revenue, https://www.ird.govt.nz/cryptoassets/individual/buying-selling/trading.

100 Id.

101 *Using Cryptoassets for a Profit-Making Scheme*, Inland Revenue, https://www.ird.govt.nz/cryptoassets/individual/buying-selling/profit-making-scheme.

102 *Mining Cryptoassets*, Inland Revenue, https://www.ird.govt.nz/cryptoassets/individual/mining.

103 Id.

104 Id.

the more likely it is that you are in business. Your financial results are also relevant."[105]

If a person's mining activity falls short of being a business, they may still be considered to be using cryptoassets for a profit-making scheme if the main purpose of a person's cryptoasset mining is to make a profit. In that case, "[a]ll amounts you get from the profit-making scheme are included as your income. This includes cryptoassets and money."[106] In other cases, where the mining is neither a business nor a profit-making scheme, a person may have ordinary income from providing a service, and income tax would be payable on their mining rewards when these are received, as well as tax being payable when the mining rewards are sold or exchanged (if this was the purpose of the mining).[107] Inland Revenue states that cryptoasset mining activity will be considered as purely a hobby "[i]n very limited circumstances."[108] Even if it is a hobby, a person may still need to pay tax when they receive cryptoassets as ordinary income from providing a service, or sell cryptoassets that were mined for the purpose of selling them.[109]

5.1.2 Businesses

Inland Revenue states that a business "needs to pay tax on cryptoassets it receives as payment, or that it sells or exchanges."[110] How tax applies depends on the type of business involved.

A person or entity might be in a cryptoasset business if it does one of more of the following activities: cryptoasset mining, cryptoasset trading (or dealing), have a cryptoasset exchange business (including crypo ATMs).[111] Any amounts received by a cryptoasset business from selling or exchanging cryptoassets is considered business income, and the cost of acquiring those cryptoassets can be deducted from the income. Furthermore, the trading stock rules apply

---

105 *Mining Cryptoassets as a Business*, Inland Revenue, https://www.ird.govt.nz/cryptoassets/individual/mining/business.

106 *Mining Cryptoassets for a Profit-Making Scheme*, Inland Revenue, https://www.ird.govt.nz/cryptoassets/individual/mining/profit-making-scheme.

107 *Mining Cryptoassets for Ordinary Income*, Inland Revenue, https://www.ird.govt.nz/cryptoassets/individual/mining/ordinary-income.

108 *Mining Cryptoassets as a Hobby*, Inland Revenue, https://www.ird.govt.nz/cryptoassets/individual/mining/hobby.

109 Id.

110 *Cryptoassets for Businesses*, Inland Revenue, https://www.ird.govt.nz/cryptoassets/business.

111 *Cryptoasset Businesses*, Inland Revenue, https://www.ird.govt.nz/cryptoassets/business/businesses.

because a cryptoasset business "generally holds cryptoassets for the purpose of selling them in the ordinary course of that business."[112]

Even where a business is not a cryptoasset business, it will need to account for any cryptoassets that it uses in the same way it would for any other business asset.[113] If a business accepts cryptoassets as payment for goods or services it provides, this is considered a barter transaction and the cryptoassets received are part of its business income. If the cryptoassets are subsequently sold or exchanged, this is also considered business income. In this case, a deduction can be claimed for the cost equal to the value of the cryptoassets when they were received, which is the same value the business paid tax on – meaning the income earned from the barter transaction is not taxed twice.[114]

Inland Revenue has issued rulings on situations where a business pays an employee salary or wages in cryptoassets, pays bonuses in cryptoassets, or provides cryptoassets issued by an employer to an employee. In these cases, the business will need to account for "pay as you earn" or fringe benefit taxes. An additional ruling considers "whether the employee share scheme rules apply to some types of employer-issued cryptoassets provided to employees."[115]

5.1.3 Calculating the Tax Payable

Both individuals and businesses need to file a tax return if they have taxable income from their cryptoasset activity. In order to enter their cryptoasset tax (or loss), they need to calculate the New Zealand dollar value of the cryptoasset transactions, and work out cryptoasset income and expenses.[116]

Cryptoasset income might include income from mining, staking, lending cryptoassets to another person, selling or exchanging cryptoassets, or getting paid in cryptoassets for goods and services. In addition, if cryptoassets are held as trading stock, a business's income also includes the closing value of the trading stock at the end of the income year.[117] Cryptoasset expenses that a business may deduct include the amount paid for the cryptoasset (including any transaction fees), depreciation of relevant capital assets (such as computer hardware or software), interest charged on money borrowed to buy

112 Id.

113 *Using Cryptoassets for Business Transactions*, Inland Revenue, https://www.ird.govt.nz/cryptoassets/business/transactions.

114 Id.

115 *Providing Cryptoassets to Employees*, Inland Revenue, https://www.ird.govt.nz/cryptoassets/business/employees.

116 *Taxing Cryptoasset Income*, Inland Revenue, https://www.ird.govt.nz/cryptoassets/taxing.

117 *Working Out Your Cryptoasset Income and Expenses*, Inland Revenue, https://www.ird.govt.nz/cryptoassets/taxing/income-expenses.

cryptoassets (if any profit from their sale is taxable), and other expenses such a miner's electricity or rental costs. For trading stock, a business's expenses also include the opening value of the trading stock.[118]

In terms of calculating the New Zealand dollar value, the individual or business will need to use "an appropriate conversion rate at the relevant date," such as through the use of centralized data repository sites or from a public exchange.[119]

Inland Revenue states that if a person held cryptoassets that were stolen, they may be able to claim a deduction for the loss.[120] The amount that can be claimed is the cost that the person initially paid to acquire the cryptoassets. A loss can only be claimed if the cryptoassets would have been taxable if the person had sold them or if they were trading stock.[121]

5.2 *2021 Tax Bill*

In February 2020, Inland Revenue published an issues paper on GST policy, which included a chapter on cryptocurrencies. A key issue identified was that cryptocurrencies have "an unfavourable GST treatment compared to money or other investment products," with the resulting proposal to "[e]xclude cryptocurrencies from GST and the financial arrangements rules," while still applying income tax to profits made when cryptocurrencies are sold or traded.[122] This proposal was subsequently included in the taxation bill introduced in September 2021, with Inland Revenue explaining that

> [t]he current position is that cryptoassets likely fall within the scope of existing GST rules (although this position is unclear). Under current law, the application of GST to cryptoassets would vary depending on the facts, the features of the cryptoasset and the residency of the parties to the transaction. The supply of a cryptoasset could be subject to GST at 15%, an exempt financial service, or a zero-rated supply to a non-resident.[123]

---

118 Id.

119 *Calculating the New Zealand Dollar Value of Cryptoassets*, Inland Revenue, https://www.ird.govt.nz/cryptoassets/taxing/convert-currency.

120 *Taxing Cryptoasset Income*, supra note 115.

121 *Stolen Cryptoassets*, Inland Revenue, https://www.ird.govt.nz/cryptoassets/taxing/income-expenses/stolen.

122 Inland Revenue, *GST Policy Issues: An Officials' Issues Paper* 5 (Feb. 2020), https://taxpolicy.ird.govt.nz/-/media/project/ir/tp/publications/2020/2020-ip-gst-issues/2020-ip-gst-issues-pdf.pdf?modified=20210420042736&modified=20210420042736.

123 Inland Revenue, *Taxation (Annual Rates for 2021–22, GST, and Remedial Matters) Bill: Commentary on the Bill* 13 (Sept. 2021), https://taxpolicy.ird.govt.nz/-/media/project/ir/tp

This situation created issues with respect to potentially disincentivizing purchasing of cryptoassets by residents; double taxation when an asset is purchased with cryptocurrency and that cryptocurrency is converted back to fiat currency; and compliance costs for taxpayers, since the GST treatment of a cryptocurrency would vary depending on the classification of the asset.[124] Furthermore, in terms of the rules governing accounting for "financial arrangements" involving deferral of giving or receiving consideration, under which financial arrangements are broadly defined, these rules were likely to apply to some types of cryptoassets, which could

> lead to accrual-based taxation on large unrealised gains and losses from cryptoasset values, which can be very volatile. This would require a taxpayer to convert their cryptoassets value into NZD, spread income and expenditure over the time of the arrangement and undertake a base price adjustment on maturity. In addition to these compliance costs, applying the financial arrangements rules to cryptoassets could bias a taxpayer's investment decision towards cryptoassets not subject to these rules.[125]

In order to exclude cryptoassets from GST and the financial arrangements rules, the bill included a definition of "cryptoassets" that would be inserted into both the GST Act and the Income Tax Act 2007.[126] The definitions of both "goods" and "services" in the GST Act would be amended to expressly exclude cryptoassets,[127] and the Income Tax Act would be amended to include cryptoassets as an excepted financial arrangement.[128] All of these changes would have an application date of January 1, 2009, "the date that the first cryptoasset, bitcoin, was launched."[129]

/publications/2021/2021-commentary-argrm-bill/2021-commentary-argrm-bill-pdf.pdf ?modified=20210906231753&modified=20210906231753.

124 Id.

125 Id. at 14.

126 Id. at 15.

127 Id. at 16.

128 Id. at 19.

129 Id. at 15, 16 & 19.

Poland

Przemysław Katner

1 Development of the Polish Cryptocurrency Market

1.1 *Polish Cryptocurrency Market in Practice*

Considering that the world's first Bitcoin transfer transaction was carried out in January 2009, Polish experience with cryptocurrencies and their trading is quite long. The first Polish cryptocurrency exchange ('Bitomat') was established already in 2011 and others followed shortly thereafter.[1] In turn, at the beginning of 2014, the first Polish cryptocurrencies were issued – Polcoin (PLC), PolishCoin (PCC) and PLNcoin (PLNC).[2] In the same year, one of the Polish 'mines' of cryptocurrencies was ranked fifth in the world in terms of computing power.[3] In March 2019, the Polish currency was the fifth most popular currency used for Bitcoin trading. However, the distance between the leading currencies and the PLN was huge.[4]

Currently, purchasing any cryptocurrency in Poland, including stable coins (e.g. Bitcoin (BTC), Etherum (ETH), USD Tether (USDT), USD Coin (USDC), Ripple XRP (XRP), Litecoin (LTC), Dogecoin (DOGE), Bitcoin Cash (BCH), Dash (DASH), Binance Coin (BNB)) is not a problem.[5] In fact, due to the principle of freedom of contract indicated in Article 353[1] of the Polish Civil Code[6] it never

---

1 E.g. Bitchange, BitMarket.eu and Bidextreme.

2 See Ł. Woźnicki, 'PolishCoin, PolCoin i PLNC. W Polsce są już aż trzy narodowe kryptowaluty. Dlaczego?' [PolishCoin, PolCoin i PLNC. There are already three national cryptocurrencies in Poland. Why?], https://wyborcza.pl/7,75398,15707096,polishcoin-polcoin-i-plnc-w-polsce-sa-juz-az-trzy-narodowe.html; I. Miciuła and M. Różycka, 'Stan rynku kryptowalut w Polsce na tle światowego rozwoju' [The state of the cryptocurrency market in Poland against the backdrop of global development], *Finanse, Rynki Finansowe, Ubezpieczenia* 2018, No. 4, part 2, p. 55.

3 See 'Krajowa ocena ryzyka prania pieniędzy oraz finansowania terroryzmu' [National money laundering and terrorist financing risk assessment], Ministry of Finanse, Warszawa 2019, p. 131.

4 See K. Włosik, 'Liquidity of bitcoin – insights from Polish and global markets', *Ruch Prawniczy, Ekonomiczny i Socjologiczny* 2019, No. 3, p. 181, who took data from the webside bitcoincharts.com.

5 The article of 26.10.2023, available at https://cryps.pl/artykul/jak-wygladaly-poczatki-rynku-kryptowalut-w-polsce/ indicates that according to current Triple-A statistics, 3% of the population in Poland, i.e. about 1.2 million people, have cryptocurrencies.

6 Act of 23.04.1964 Civil Code, uniform text, Journal of Laws 2024, item 1061 as amended, hereinafter referred to as 'PCC'. According to Article 353[1] PCC 'Parties entering into a contract

 DOI:10.1163/9789004722507_022

was. However, the easiest is to buy BTC and ETH, due to the wide availability of these cryptocurrencies. One can also invest in cryptocurrencies using EFTs or CFDs, which are offered, for example, by forex brokers.[7]

The most popular way to purchase/sell cryptocurrencies is the use of cryptocurrency exchanges, both Polish and foreign (e.g. Binance, BitMEX). At the moment, the largest and most liquid Polish (or actually of Polish roots, i.e. founded and managed by Poles) cryptocurrency exchange is zondacrypto (previously Zonda and BitBay), established in 2014, where nearly 180,000 transactions are made per day with the possibility of buying or selling around 70 different cryptocurrencies.[8] In order to buy/sell cryptocurrencies, one can also use Internet (online) exchange offices, in which the payment in exchange for the purchased/sold cryptocurrency can be made by bank transfer, with a debit/credit card, and even with BLIK,[9] or stationary exchange offices (not that common) that trade in cryptocurrencies with available cash payments. Another option is to use a bitomat, which is a type of ATM, with which one can exchange cryptocurrency for cash or cash for cryptocurrency. This possibility mostly applies to Bitcoin, Ethereum and Tether, but in number of bitomats it is also possible to purchase (sell) other cryptocurrencies (e.g. USDC, LTC or DASH). Currently, there are around 200 bitomats in Poland.[10] Finally, one can buy cryptocurrency directly from another cryptocurrency holder.[11]

The purchase of cryptocurrencies in Poland usually serves investment purposes, or rather and more precisely – due to the high volatility of rates – speculative purposes. On the one hand, this is due to the possibility of a rapid increase in their value, on the other hand, it is because the number of stationery points where one can pay with them is relatively small. The fact is that initially this number was increasing. Thus, in 2017, it was estimated that BTC

---

may determine the legal relation at their own discretion, provided that its content or purpose do not prejudice the nature of the relation, a statute or the principles of community coexistence'.

7 See e.g. https://moneteo.com/artykuly/gdzie-i-jak-kupic-kryptowalute; see also 'Odpowiedź podsekretarza stanu w Ministerstwie Finansów - z upoważnienia ministra - na interpelację nr 25661 w sprawie zapisów ustawy o obrocie instrumentami finansowymi' [Reply of the Undersecretary of State in the Ministry of Finance - on behalf of the Minister - to interpellation No. 25661 on the provisions of the Act on Trading in Financial Instruments], 15.05.2014, https://www.sejm.gov.pl/sejm7.nsf/InterpelacjaTresc.xsp?key=5810D51A.

8 See https://spidersweb.pl/2021/11/bitbay-zonda-zmiany.html; https://zondacrypto.com/pl/home.

9 E.g. www.bitcan.pl.

10 See https://coinatmradar.com/bitcoin-atm-near-me/; different numbers can be found at https://bitomaty.info/#lista-bitomatow, but this list of bitomats is not exhaustive.

11 See https://bitcoin.pl/bitcoin-jak-zaczac.

was accepted by approximately 130 commercial and service outlets,[12] and in 2021 there were about 250 of them.[13] However, at the moment the number is smaller.[14]

1.2 *Obstacles Affecting Development*

As in many other places, the development of the cryptocurrency market in Poland was not free from certain shocks. Already in July 2011 – in the same year in which it was established – allegedly due to an administrator error (although it is also said that there was a hack) the Bitomat.pl cryptocurrency exchange lost the BTC server wallet, and with it the cryptocurrency of people using its services. In this case 17,000 BTC were lost.[15] Ultimately, the website was put up for sale, it was bought by the MtGox cryptocurrency exchange and the lost BTC were returned to the website users.[16] In turn, in the case of the BitMarket.eu cryptocurrency exchange, its users' BTC were deposited on the foreign cryptocurrency exchange Bitcoinica. The latter was hacked in July 2012 and this led to the closure of the BitMarket.eu website.[17]

As another example, in November 2013, cryptocurrencies were stolen from the online wallet of the bidextreme.pl cryptocurrency exchange, which resulted in the loss of users' BTC and LTC stored on it.[18] In 2016, hacker attack hit the Polish Bitcurex cryptocurrency exchange and led to its closure (initially problems with the operation of the exchange were claimed to be a result of an update of the Bitcoin client).[19] The case is still under investigation of the District Prosecutor's Office.[20] In 2019, the Coinroom cryptocurrency exchange,

12 See 'Krajowa ocena ryzyka prania pieniędzy oraz finansowania terroryzmu' [National money laundering and terrorist financing risk assessment], Ministry of Finance, Warszawa 2019, p. 131.

13 See https://coinmap.org/ (accessed 10.12.2021).

14 See https://coinmap.org/, that lists about 80 available venues, although not all places where one can pay with cryptocurrencies are listed there. An example can be an online computer store SuperTech, where one can pay with 12 cryptocurrencies, incl. Bitcoin, Etherum, Lisk, Ripple.

15 See https://niebezpiecznik.pl/post/awaria-bitomat-pl-polacy-stracili-swoje-bitcoiny/.

16 See https://niebezpiecznik.pl/post/polska-gielda-bitcoinow-bidextreme-pl-zaatakowana-i-okradziona/?similarpost; https://gieldykryptowalut.pl/krotka-historia-upadlych-polskich-gield-kryptowalut/; https://bitcointalk.org/index.php?topic=83794.0.

17 See https://gieldykryptowalut.pl/krotka-historia-upadlych-polskich-gield-kryptowalut/.

18 See https://niebezpiecznik.pl/post/polska-gielda-bitcoinow-bidextreme-pl-zaatakowana-i-okradziona/?similarpost.

19 See https://gieldykryptowalut.pl/krotka-historia-upadlych-polskich-gield-kryptowalut/. The website also contains a list of Polish cryptocurrency exchanges and exchange offices that have ceased their activities.

20 See https://bitcoin.pl/bitcurex-prokuratura.

that was previously entered on the Polish Financial Supervision Authority ('the KNF') list of public warnings, declared bankruptcy. In the same 2019, a large Polish cryptocurrency exchange Bitmarket ceased to operate. The exchange was supposed to be used by approximately 60,000 users, whose deposits covered a total of approximately 2,300 BTC. In a related criminal case there is a charge of fraud amounting to approximately PLN 100 million.[21]

1.3 *Position Of State Authorities towards Cryptocurrencies*

For a long time the development of the cryptocurrency market took place despite the lack of Polish legal regulations specifically dedicated to cryptocurrencies. This raised doubts about the legality of cryptocurrency trading, even raised in the Senate of the Republic of Poland.[22] At the same time, as in many other countries, the financial market regulatory authorities approached (and are still approaching) cryptocurrencies with caution. A special example in this respect may be the Announcement of the National Bank of Poland ('the NBP') and the Financial Supervision Authority ('the KNF') on virtual currencies[23] of 7 July 2017 that warned against buying and investing in virtual currencies due to various types of risk related to their trading, such as the lack of guarantees of funds kept in virtual currencies by the Bank Guarantee Fund, the lack of universal acceptability, the possibility of loss due to theft (e.g. as a result of a cyberattack on an entity conducting the exchange of virtual currencies or the user's infrastructure), the risk of fraud, in particular as a result of creating a financial pyramid, and at the same time a problem in pursuing claims and high volatility of prices. As a result, the NBP and the KNF concluded that:

> buying, holding and selling virtual currencies by entities supervised by the Financial Supervision Authority would be burdened with high risk and would not ensure stable and prudent management of the financial institution. The National Bank of Poland and the Financial Supervision Authority also point out that financial institutions should exercise

---

21 See https://bitcoin.pl/upadek-bitmarket-historia-polskiego-mt-gox-po-roku; https://www.money.pl/pieniadze/upadek-bitmarket-prokuratura-wszczela-sledztwo-w-sprawie-gieldy-kryptowalut-6401455347251329a.html.

22 See statement of Senator M. Klima at the 30th session of the Senate on April 4, 2013, https://www.senat.gov.pl/gfx/senat/userfiles/_public/k8/dokumenty/stenogram/odpow30an.pdf, p. 45.

23 It should be noted that the terms 'virtual currency' and 'cryptocurrency' are not synonyms. Each cryptocurrency is considered a virtual currency, but not every virtual currency is a cryptocurrency. In this article the term 'virtual currency' is used when it is used by the cited source or law provision.

> particular caution in establishing and cooperating with entities trading in virtual currencies, in particular with regard to the risk of using these entities for money laundering and terrorist financing.[24]

This view was upheld, among others, by the Position of the Office of the Financial Supervision Authority on the issuance and trading of crypto-assets of 10 December 2020, which additionally raised the risk of losing access to the purchased crypto-assets and emphasized that the fact of using only the IT environment and innovative technology in the issuance and trading of crypto-assets does not exclude the application of financial market law. In particular, 'the digitization of the process cannot be used to introduce solutions that intentionally serve to commonly raise capital from non-professional investors.'[25] This position was also recently confirmed in 2023 in the KNF statements 'The Polish Financial Supervision Authority reminds about the principles of operation of cryptocurrency exchanges and cryptocurrency exchange offices in Poland and warns about the risks' and 'The regulatory situation on the crypto-assets market.'[26]

---

24 See 'Komunikat Narodowego Banku Polskiego i Komisji Nadzoru Finansowego w sprawie „walut" wirtualnych z dnia 7 lipca 2017 r.' [Announcement of the National Bank of Poland and the Polish Financial Supervision Authority on virtual currencies of 07.07.2017], https://www.knf.gov.pl/knf/pl/komponenty/img/Komunikat_NBP_KNF_w_sprawie_walut_wirtualnych_7_07_2017_57361.pdf; see also https://nbp.pl/uwazaj-na-kryptowaluty/ indicating other authorities that issued warnings related to cryptocurrencies, incl. General Inspector of Financial Information, Office of Competition and Consumer Protection.

25 See 'Stanowisko Urzędu Komisji Nadzoru Finansowego w sprawie wydawania i obrotu kryptoaktywami' [Position of the Office of the Financial Supervision Authority on the issuance and trading of crypto-assets], 10.12.2020, https://www.knf.gov.pl/knf/pl/komponenty/img/Stanowisko_UKNF_ws_wydawania_i_obrotu_kryptoaktywami_71794.pdf, pp. 2-3; see also 'Ostrzeżenie urzędu KNF o ryzykach związanych z nabywaniem oraz z obrotem kryptoaktywami (w tym walutami wirtualnymi oraz kryptowalutami)'[Warning from the Polish Financial Supervision Authority about the risks associated with the purchase and trade of crypto-assets (including virtual currencies and cryptocurrencies)], 12.01.2021, https://www.knf.gov.pl/knf/pl/komponenty/img/Ostrzezenie_UKNF_o_ryzykach_zwiazanych_z_nabywaniem_oraz_z_obrotem_kryptoaktywami_72241.pdf.

26 See 'UKNF przypomina o zasadach działalności giełd i kantorów kryptowalut w Polsce i ostrzega o ryzykach' ['The Polish Financial Supervision Authority reminds about the principles of operation of cryptocurrency exchanges and cryptocurrency exchange offices in Poland and warns about the risks], 27.01.2023, https://www.knf.gov.pl/knf/pl/komponenty/img/UKNF_przypomina_o_zasadach_dzialalnosci_gild_i_kantorow_kryptowalut_w_Polsce%20_i_ostrzega_o_ryzykach.pdf and 'Sytuacja regulacyjna na rynku kryptoaktywów' ['The regulatory situation on the crypto-assets market], 11.09.2023, https://www.knf.gov.pl/komunikacja/komunikaty?articleId=83761&p_id=18.

The KNF also entered some platforms and entities enabling cryptocurrency trading on the list of public warnings. The list contains, among others, information on notifications submitted by the KNF on suspicion of committing a crime.[27]

However, the above-mentioned announcement of 2017, confirmed by the subsequent warning and statements, also clearly stated that the mere trading of virtual currencies in Poland does not violate national or European Union law. This position was consistent with the position of the Minister of Finance expressed several years earlier on June 28, 2013, that 'the operation and trade in virtual currencies in the territory of the Republic of Poland does not violate Polish or EU law.'[28]

2 Definition and Legal Qualification

2.1 *What Cryptocurrency Is Not*

Although cryptocurrencies can be seen as money in the economic sense[29] or as private money,[30] there is a fairly unanimous opinion in Polish doctrine, both in private and in public law, that cryptocurrency does not constitute money in the legal sense, as this concept is reserved for means of payment issued within the legal system of countries.[31] It is even pointed out that nothing in this respect will change if any country in the world recognizes cryptocurrency as an official means of payment on its territory or if the central bank of the country announces of the official rate against its currency.[32] Cryptocurrency

27 See https://www.knf.gov.pl/dla_konsumenta/ostrzezenia_publiczne?warningName=bitbay&warningTypeId=all.

28 See https://www.senat.gov.pl/gfx/senat/userfiles/_public/k8/dokumenty/stenogram/odpow30an.pdf, p. 46.

29 See e.g. M. Michna, *Bitcoin jako przedmiot stosunków cywilnoprawnych* [Bitcoin as an object of civil law relations], Legalis, Warszawa 2018, Ch. 1, §2.

30 See e.g. M. Lemkowski in M. Gutowski (ed.) *Kodeks cywilny. Tom II. Komentarz* [Civil Code. Volume II. Commentary], Legalis, Warszawa 2022, commentary to Article 358, point 5.

31 See e.g. F. Zoll in A. Olejniczak (ed.), *System Prawa Prywatnego. Tom 6. Prawo zobowiązań – część ogólna* [System of Private Law. Vol. 6. Obligations – general part], Warszawa 2023, p. 1144; T. Dybowski and A. Pyrzyńska in K. Osajda (ed.), *System Prawa Prywatnego. Tom 5. Prawo zobowiązań – część ogólna* [System of Private Law. Vol. 5. Obligations – general part], Warszawa 2019, p. 271.

32 See e.g. M. Lemkowski in M. Gutowski (ed.) *Kodeks cywilny. Tom II. Komentarz* [Civil Code. Volume II. Commentary], Legalis, Warszawa 2022, commentary to Article 358, point 5.

is not also a currency,[33] means of payment[34] or electronic money.[35] It is not a financial instrument.[36] In the judgment of 22 February 2024, the Provincial Administrative Court in Poznań stated that 'virtual currencies cannot be

---

33 See e.g. M. Grabowski, *Ustawa o usługach płatniczych. Komentarz* [Act on Payment Services. Commentary], Legalis, Warszawa 2020, commentary to Article 34, point 1; judgment of the Supreme Administrative Court of 27.04.2022, II FSK 2181/19, https://orzeczenia.nsa.gov.pl/doc/DC967F7AE0.

34 See e.g. W. Srokosz, 'Legalna definicja kryptowaluty' [Legal definition of cryptocurrency] in W. Rogowski (ed.), *Regulacje finansowe. Fintech – nowe instrumenty finansowe – resolution* [Financial regulations. Fintech - new financial instruments - resolution], Legalis, Warszawa 2017; 'Komunikat Narodowego Banku Polskiego i Komisji Nadzoru Finansowego w sprawie „walut" wirtualnych z dnia 7 lipca 2017 r.' [Announcement of the National Bank of Poland and the Polish Financial Supervision Authority on virtual currencies of 07.07.2017], https://www.knf.gov.pl/knf/pl/komponenty/img/Komunikat_NBP_KNF_w_sprawie_walut_wirtualnych_7_07_2017_57361.pdf, p. 1.

35 See e.g. 'Komunikat Narodowego Banku Polskiego i Komisji Nadzoru Finansowego w sprawie „walut" wirtualnych z dnia 7 lipca 2017 r.' [Announcement of the National Bank of Poland and the Polish Financial Supervision Authority on virtual currencies of 07.07.2017], https://www.knf.gov.pl/knf/pl/komponenty/img/Komunikat_NBP_KNF_w_sprawie_walut_wirtualnych_7_07_2017_57361.pdf, p. 1; K. Górniak, 'Prawo własności jednostek waluty kryptograficznej' [Ownership of cryptocurrency units], *Kwartalnik Prawa Prywatnego* 2019, No. 3, p. 567; however, the document 'Ostrzeżenie Urzędu KNF o ryzykach związanych z nabywaniem oraz z obrotem kryptoaktywami (w tym walutami wirtualnymi oraz kryptowalutami)' [Warning of the KNF Office on the risks related to the acquisition and trading of crypto-assets (including virtual currencies and cryptocurrencies)], https://www.knf.gov.pl/knf/pl/komponenty/img/Ostrzezenie_UKNF_o_ryzykach_zwiazanych_z_nabywaniem_oraz_z_obrotem_kryptoaktywami_72241.pdf, pp. 7–8, indicates that, if additional conditions are met, stable coins may meet the definition of electronic money.

36 See e.g. A. Kruszewski, 'Polskie regulacje dotyczące walut cyfrowych' [Polish regulations on digital currencies] in W. Rogowski (ed.), *Regulacje finansowe. Fintech – nowe instrumenty finansowe – resolution* [Financial regulations. Fintech - new financial instruments - resolution], Legalis, Warszawa 2017; K. Zacharzewski, 'Praktyczne znaczenie bitcoina na wybranych obszarach prawa prywatnego' [The practical significance of Bitcoin in selected areas of private law], *Monitor Prawniczy* 2015, No. 4, p. 193; 'Komunikat Narodowego Banku Polskiego i Komisji Nadzoru Finansowego w sprawie „walut" wirtualnych z dnia 7 lipca 2017 r.' [Announcement of the National Bank of Poland and the Polish Financial Supervision Authority on virtual currencies of 07.07.2017], https://www.knf.gov.pl/knf/pl/komponenty/img/Komunikat_NBP_KNF_w_sprawie_walut_wirtuanych_7_07_2017_57361.pdf, p. 1.

considered rights of a similar nature to securities and derivatives.'[37] It is also not subject to the provisions of the Payment Services Act.[38]

However, there is still a discussion as to what cryptocurrency exactly is and what civil law rights are associated with it (e.g. ownership, relative right, possession).

2.2 *Definition of Cryptocurrency in Public Law*

As previously indicated, for a long period of time Polish law did not have any legal regulations directly related to cryptocurrencies. Trading in them – admissible due to the lack of the ban – caused in particular tax problems related to the taxation of income, and this led to the formation of official tax interpretations and court cases. In the documents of the tax chambers, Bitcoin was referred to, inter alia, as a digital certificate, electronic certificate, payment instrument, virtual currency, digital currency, electronic currency, alternative means of payment, electronic entitlement instrument, money voucher, electronic money voucher, etc.[39]

In 2017, the KNF and the NBP adopted, in accordance with the definition proposed by the European Banking Authority, that 'virtual currencies are a digital representation of value, not necessarily issued by a central bank or public authority, not necessarily related to the currency of a specific country, but recognized by natural and legal persons as means of payment that can be transmitted, stored or traded electronically.'[40]

The first attempt to define the virtual currency by law was made in the draft Act on the Central Accounts Base of 2016. According to the wording of Article 2 point 6 of the draft, it was meant to mean 'a transferable property right, the subject of which is the digital representation of value, having its equivalent in

37 See judgment of the Voivodship Administrative Court in Poznań of 22.02.2024, I SA/Po 895/23, https://orzeczenia.nsa.gov.pl/doc/C59FF5C3D8.

38 See e.g. K. Zacharzewski, 'Praktyczne znaczenie bitcoina na wybranych obszarach prawa prywatnego' [The practical significance of Bitcoin in selected areas of private law], *Monitor Prawniczy* 2015, No. 4, p. 194.

39 See K. Zacharzewski, 'Bitcoin jako przedmiot stosunków prawa prywatnego' [Bitcoin as an object of private law relations], *Monitor Prawniczy* 2014, No. 21, p. 1133.

40 'Komunikat Narodowego Banku Polskiego i Komisji Nadzoru Finansowego w sprawie „walut" wirtualnych z dnia 7 lipca 2017 r.' [Announcement of the National Bank of Poland and the Polish Financial Supervision Authority on virtual currencies of 07.07.2017], https://www.knf.gov.pl/knf/pl/komponenty/img/Komunikat_NBP_KNF_w_sprawie_walut_wirtualnych_7_07_2017_57361.pdf, p. 1.

a means of payment, treated as a medium of exchange and a unit of account, not having the status of legal tender and not being electronic money within the meaning of the Act of 19 August 2011 on Payment Services that may be transferred, stored or sold for the means of payment by electronic means'.[41] However, the act was not adopted.

The definition, however, appeared in the Act on Combating Money Laundering and the Financing of Terrorism of 2018.[42] Pursuant to Article 2 section 2 point 26 of the act:

virtual currency – shall be understood as digital representation of a value which is not:

a) a legal tender issued by NBP, foreign central banks or other public administration authorities;
b) an international clearing unit established by an international organization and accepted by individual countries belonging to or cooperating with such organization;
c) electronic money within the meaning of the Act of 19 August 2011 on Payment Services;
d) a financial instrument within the meaning of the Act of 29 July 2005 on Trading in Financial Instruments;
e) a bill of exchange, a promissory note or a cheque

– and is convertible in business dealings for legal tenders and accepted as the means of exchange and also may be electronically stored or transferred or may be the object of electronic trade.[43]

Under the act, virtual currencies belong to a wider category of property values that contains i.a. property rights or other movable property or immovable

41 See the draft Act on the Central Accounts Base of 14.12.2016, https://legislacja.rcl.gov.pl/docs//2/12293403/12400901/12400902/dokument264390.pdf.

42 Act on Combating Money Laundering and the Financing of Terrorism of 01.03.2018, uniform text, Dziennik Ustaw [Journal of Laws - 'J. of L.'] 2023, item 1124 as amended.

43 In the draft Act on the Crypto-assets Market of 09.08.2024, hereinafter referred to as 'the draft Act on the Crypto-assets Market', the definition of a virtual currency in the Act on Combating Money Laundering and the Financing of Terrorism will be replaced by a definition of a crypto-asset that refers to Article 3 point 14 of Regulation (EU) 2023/1113 of the European Parliament and of the Council of 31 May 2023 on information accompanying transfers of funds and certain crypto-assets and amending Directive (EU) 2015/849 [2023] OJ L 150/1, hereinafter referred to as 'Regulation 2023/1113' and the notion 'virtual currencies' is used in the act no more; the draft Act on the Crypto-assets Market is available at https://legislacja.rcl.gov.pl/projekt/12382311/katalog/13040399#13040399.

properties, means of payment, financial instruments within the meaning of the Act of 29 July 2005 on Trading in Financial Instruments, other securities, and foreign exchange values (Article 2 section 2 point 27 of the act).[44]

The presented definition does not distinguish between different types of virtual currencies (e.g. cryptocurrencies) and does not recognize varied types of cryptocurrencies (like stable coins or cryptocurrencies related to external benchmarks). It also includes centralized virtual currencies, which have a single central administrator who manages their issuance and distribution, and maintains a central payment register and is authorized to redeem units of a given virtual currency.[45] Nevertheless, it does not cover options or futures contracts based on cryptocurrencies (e.g. BTC) as the underlying instrument, as these are financial instruments.[46] This act – due to its normative scope – treats also the issues related to the trading of cryptocurrencies a bit incidentally.

The indicated definition is referred to by tax law, e.g. Article 5a point 33a of the Natural Persons' Income Tax Act[47] and Article 4a point 22a of the Legal Persons' Income Tax Act.[48] It was also referred to by, inter alia, Regulation of the Minister of Finance on the cessation of the collection of tax on civil law transactions on the contract of sale or conversion of the virtual currency.[49]

---

44 In the draft Act on the Crypto-assets Market the Article 2 section 2 point 27 of the Act on Combating Money Laundering and the Financing of Terrorism includes in this category crypto-assets that take place of virtual currencies.

45 https://sip.legalis.pl/document-full.seam?documentId=mjuwelrsgyydenbyge3ti&refSource=guide.

46 See e.g. 'Odpowiedź podsekretarza stanu w Ministerstwie Finansów - z upoważnienia ministra - na interpelację nr 25661 w sprawie zapisów ustawy o obrocie instrumentami finansowymi' [Reply of the Undersecretary of State in the Ministry of Finance - on behalf of the Minister - to interpellation No. 25661 on the provisions of the Act on Trading in Financial Instruments], 15.05.2014, https://www.sejm.gov.pl/sejm7.nsf/InterpelacjaTresc.xsp?key=5810D51A.

47 Natural Persons' Income Tax Act of 26.07.1991, uniform text, J. of L. 2024, item 226 as amended; in the draft Act on the Crypto-assets Market the amended Article 5a point 33a of the Natural Persons' Income Tax Act is to contain the current definition of virtual currency from Article 2 section 2 point 26 of the Act on Combating Money Laundering and the Financing of Terrorism.

48 Legal Persons' Income Tax Act of 15.02.1992, uniform text, J. of L. 2023, item 2805 as amended; in the draft Act on the Crypto-assets Market the amended Article 4a point 22a of the Legal Persons' Income Tax Act is to contain the current content of Article 2 section 2 point 26 of the Act on Combating Money Laundering and the Financing of Terrorism.

49 Regulation of the Minister of Finance on the cessation of the collection of tax on civil law transactions on the contract of sale or conversion of the virtual currency of 11.07.2018, uniform text, J. of L. 2020, item 793 as amended.

However, the definition is not universal in Polish law, and its wording is criticized in civil law doctrine.[50] It also does not explain the legal nature of cryptocurrencies. As a result, in the judgment of the Supreme Administrative Court of 27 April 2022 the court found cryptocurrencies as intangible property rights.[51] And in the judgment of the Voivodship Administrative Court in Wrocław of 6 December 2023 the court stated that the position that under the Natural Persons' Income Tax Act virtual currencies (cryptocurrencies) are considered property rights is incorrect.[52] In turn, in the doctrine of criminal law one can find the position from 2023 that 'in the current form of Article 115 para. 9 of the Criminal Code the view that bitcoin is not a movable item' (movable property) 'within the meaning of criminal law (...) seems to be out of date, and it is justified to include bitcoin in the cash recorded in the account and thus grant it legal protection, as it undoubtedly performs a payment function and it constitutes a measurable property value, which means that it may be subject to, for example, theft or appropriation.'[53]

2.3 *Definition and Legal Qualification in Private Law*

In the doctrine of civil law, from the very beginning, there has been no consensus on what a cryptocurrency is. The positions to a large extent were related to Bitcoin as the most popular cryptocurrency. It can be pointed out that K. Zacharzewski found cryptocurrency (or more precisely – Bitcoin) as a type of property, not being a thing, constituting a transferable relative property right, which cannot, in the technical and legal sense, be an object of ownership and

50 See e.g. m.in. J. Szewczyk, 'O cywilnoprawnych aspektach bitcoina' [On the civil law aspects of Bitcoin], *Monitor Prawniczy* 2018, No. 5, pp. 248–49.

51 See judgment of the Supreme Administrative Court of 27.04.2022, II FSK 2181/19, https://orzeczenia.nsa.gov.pl/doc/DC967F7AE0.

52 See judgment of the Voivodship Administrative Court in Wrocław of 06.12.2023, I SA/Wr 413/23, https://orzeczenia.nsa.gov.pl/doc/137C4B1CAC; see also point 3.2, where is the justification of such statement under that act.

53 A. Barczak in B. Gadecki (ed.), *Kodeks karny. Art. 1-316. Komentarz* [Criminal Code. Articles 1-316. Commentary], Warszawa 2023, comment to Article 115, point 53; the author is a judge of the District Court in Olsztyn and a chairman of the 2nd Criminal Department; such view finds some support in the draft Act on the Crypto-assets Market which proposes to amend the Code of Criminal Procedure by specifying in Article 236b of this Code that 'an item or object within the meaning of the provisions of this Chapter also includes funds in an account or crypto-assets' within the meaning of Regulation 2023/1114.

may be a part of property of a person entitled only as a claim (receivable).[54] In turn, K. Górniak assumed that 'cryptocurrencies are an intangible good (object), and its holders have absolute property rights to such a good. The existence and content of the right to digital currency should be derived from the analogous application of the provisions on things to cryptocurrencies, which leads to the conclusion that cryptocurrencies are the object of ownership (Article 140 PCC per analogiam).'[55] Marcin Michna finds that 'Bitcoin is only the object of performance in the obligation relationship – it is therefore a self-existent (independent) object of performance. In this case, we are dealing with an intangible good that is not subject to protection of absolute rights'.[56] Similarly Jarosław Szewczyk argues that Bitcoin is not a component of property (within the meaning of Article 44 PCC),[57] but having a specific public address and a private key that allows the use of Bitcoin undoubtedly constitutes a favorable factual situation with a measurable property value and may be recognized as a component of property.[58] In 2017, W. Srokosz assumed that so far a legal definition of cryptocurrencies was generally not needed in the area of civil law regulation. Civil law, thanks to the extensive tools of interpretation and the principle of freedom of contracts combined with the principle of equality of the parties in the civil law relationship, copes with technological novelties, including blockchain technology.[59] Finally, in 2019, T. Dybowski and A. Pyrzyńska concluded that due to the function of money in legal transactions, the definition of cryptocurrencies (virtual currencies) adopted in the

---

54 K. Zacharzewski, 'Bitcoin jako przedmiot stosunków prawa prywatnego' [Bitcoin as an object of private law relations], *Monitor Prawniczy* 2014, No. 21, p. 1133.

55 K. Górniak, 'Prawo własności jednostek waluty kryptograficznej' [Ownership of cryptocurrency units], *Kwartalnik Prawa Prywatnego* 2019, No. 3, pp. 566–567. Similarly, P. Machnikowski in E. Gniewek (ed.) *System Prawa Prywatnego. Tom 3. Prawo rzeczowe* [System of Private Law. Vol. 3. Property law], Warszawa 2020, on p. 30 assumes that cryptocurrencies should be approached similarly to energy, which makes it possible to apply to them provisions on ownership with the necessary modifications.

56 M. Michna, *Bitcoin jako przedmiot stosunków cywilnoprawnych* [Bitcoin as an object of civil law relations], Legalis, Warszawa 2018, Ch. II, §6.

57 Article 44 PCC: 'Property shall include ownership and other property rights'.

58 J. Szewczyk, 'O cywilnoprawnych aspektach bitcoina' [On the civil law aspects of Bitcoin], *Monitor Prawniczy* 2018, No. 5, p. 247.

59 W. Srokosz, 'Legalna definicja kryptowaluty' [Legal definition of cryptocurrency] in W. Rogowski (ed.), *Regulacje finansowe. Fintech – nowe instrumenty finansowe – resolution* [Financial regulations. Fintech - new financial instruments - resolution], Legalis, Warszawa 2017, p. 3.

Act on Combating Money Laundering and the Financing of Terrorism of 2018 should be used in the private law system.[60]

3 Regulatory Framework

3.1 *Introduction*

From the presented comments, including the position of the Polish Financial Supervision Authority and the National Bank of Poland and the actual functioning of Polish cryptocurrency exchange offices and exchanges, it can be concluded that trading in cryptocurrencies has generally been allowed in Poland from the very beginning. Still, there are no specific laws dealing with the regulation of cryptocurrencies in Polish legal system. For this reason, among others in the areas of civil, financial and criminal law, cryptocurrency issues are generally resolved on the basis of pre-existing regulations, i.e. before the advent of cryptocurrencies, or adopted irrespective of their existence. There are, however, certain provisions in the Act on Combating Money Laundering and the Financing of the Terrorism of 2018 and tax law referring to cryptocurrencies.

The situation will change upon date of effect of Regulation (EU) 2023/1114 of the European Parliament and of the Council of 31 May 2023 on markets in crypto-assets, and amending Regulations (EU) No 1093/2010 and (EU) No 1095/2010 and Directives 2013/36/EU and (EU) 2019/1937,[61] which covers cryptocurrencies, as well as Regulation 2023/1113[62] and the Polish Act on the Crypto-assets Market, the draft of which is available on the website of the Government Legislation Center and is currently in the review phase. The planned date of adoption of the draft of the act by the Council of Ministers is the fourth quarter of 2024, after which the project should be submitted to the Parliament. It is assumed (Article 157 of the draft) that the act will enter into force on 30 December 2024 (which is rather doubtful).

60 T. Dybowski and A. Pyrzyńska in K. Osajda (ed.), *System Prawa Prywatnego. Tom 5. Prawo zobowiązań – część ogólna* [System of Private Law. Vol. 5. Obligations – general part], Warszawa 2019, p. 271.

61 Regulation (EU) 2023/1114 of the European Parliament and of the Council of 31 May 2023 on markets in crypto-assets, and amending Regulations (EU) No 1093/2010 and (EU) No 1095/2010 and Directives 2013/36/EU and (EU) 2019/1937 [2023] OJ L 150/40, hereinafter referred to as 'Regulation 2023/1114'; as to the date of effect see Article 149 section 2-4 of the Regulation 2023/1114.

62 See Article 40 of the Regulation 2023/1113, which points to 30.12.2024.

3.2 *Act on Combating Money Laundering and the Financing of Terrorism*

The Act on Combating Money Laundering and the Financing of Terrorism not only defines virtual currencies, but also imposes certain obligations on a group of entities carrying out business activity connected with cryptocurrencies. It implements the European Union's anti-money laundering and countering the financing of terrorism (AML/CFT) rules. As a result, from 31 October 2021 it implements the 5th anti money laundering Directive (AML V).[63]

In this respect, it should be noted that in accordance with Article 2 section 1 point 12 of the act, the entities carrying out business activity consisting in the provision of services in the scope of (a) exchange between virtual currencies and means of payment, (b) exchange between virtual currencies, (c) intermediation in the exchange referred above or (d) maintenance of accounts understood as a collection, maintained in electronic form, of identifying data enabling the entitled persons to use virtual currency units, including the conduct of transactions of their exchange, are called obliged institutions.[64] It had been so even before the AML V was adopted due to FATF recommendations and the existence of the draft of AML V at the time the Act on Combating Money Laundering and the Financing of Terrorism was adopted in 2018. Such institutions shall apply the financial security measures as regards their customers (e.g. customer identification and verification of his/her identity) in specified cases like i.a. establishment of business relationships, conducting an occasional transaction with the use of a virtual currency equivalent to the amount of EUR 1,000 or higher (since 31 October 2021),[65] or a suspicion of money laundering or terrorist financing (Article 35 section 1 of the act). They are also obliged i.a. to provide to certain organ (the General Inspector) varied

---

63 Directive (EU) 2018/843 of the European Parliament and of the Council of 30.05.2018 amending Directive (EU) 2015/849 on the prevention of the use of the financial system for the purposes of money laundering or terrorist financing, and amending Directives 2009/138/EC and 2013/36/EU OJ L 156/43; see also https://ec.europa.eu/info/publications/anti-money-laundering-directive-5-transposition-status_en.

64 In the draft Act on the Crypto-assets Market the amended Article 2 section 1 point 12 of the Act on Combating Money Laundering and the Financing of Terrorism, instead of the entities mentioned, refers to crypto-asset service providers within the meaning of Article 3 section 1 point 15 of Regulation 2023/1114, providing at least one of the crypto-asset services referred to in Article 3 section 1 point 16 of this regulation, with the exception of service of providing advice on crypto-assets referred to in Article 3 section 1 point 16 letter h of this regulation.

65 In the draft Act on the Crypto-assets Market it refers to transaction with the use of a crypto-assets (in place of virtual currency) and regardless of whether the transaction is carried out as a single operation or several operations that appear to be related to each other.

information and notify certain circumstances that are related to money laundering or terrorist financing.[66]

3.3 *Tax Law*

Initially, the tax law in Poland had no provisions that strictly referred to cryptocurrencies. The jurisprudence basically assumed that the income from the sale of the purchased cryptocurrency is considered to be taxable income from property rights.[67] However, doubts referred to i.a. the case of exchanging one cryptocurrency into another, because in such a situation it was sometimes assumed that there was revenue subject to income tax,[68] and in other cases – tax neutrality.[69]

From 1 January 2019, the problem of taxing cryptocurrencies is regulated in tax laws, although there are still various issues that raise doubts.[70] Among other things, it has been resolved that an exchange between virtual currencies (crypto-crypto), whether or not made on a cryptocurrency exchange, remains neutral for income tax purposes.

According to art. 7b section 1 point 6 letter f of the Legal Persons' Income Tax Act of 15 February 1992 r.[71] revenues from the exchange of virtual currency for a legal tender, goods, service or property right other than the virtual currency or from the payment of other liabilities by the virtual currency shall be considered revenues from capital gains. The exception is in case of taxpayers carrying

---

66 The draft Act on the Crypto-assets Market provides for additional, new duties in the drafted Article 45 section 3 and 4 and in Article 45a of the Act on Combating Money Laundering and the Financing of Terrorism.

67 See e.g. judgment of the Supreme Administrative Court of 06.03.2018, II FSK 488/16, *Monitor Prawniczy* 2018, No. 7, p. 338, where the court clearly stated that in civil law relations bitcoin is a type of property within the meaning of Article 44 of Polish civil code; see also judgment of the Supreme Administrative Court of 27.04.2022, II FSK 2181/19, https://orzeczenia.nsa.gov.pl/doc/DC967F7AE0.

68 See e.g. judgment of the Voivodship Administrative Court in Gliwice of 11.04.2018, I SA/Gl 248/18, https://orzeczenia.nsa.gov.pl/doc/29DBB6617D.

69 See e.g. judgment of the Voivodship Administrative Court in Olsztyn of 09.05.2018, I SA/OL 201/18, https://orzeczenia.nsa.gov.pl/doc/63EA59051B; see also M. Michna, *Bitcoin jako przedmiot stosunków cywilnoprawnych* [Bitcoin as an object of civil law relations], Legalis, Warszawa 2018, Ch I, §3.

70 See e.g. judgment of the Voivodship Administrative Court in Gliwice of 02.02.2023, I SA/Gl 812/22, https://orzeczenia.nsa.gov.pl/doc/7D2409566F; of the Supreme Administrative Court of 06.06.2023, II FSK 2963/20, https://orzeczenia.nsa.gov.pl/doc/D27434B023; of the Voivodship Administrative Court in Gdańsk of 11.07.2023, I SA/Gd 342/23, https://orzeczenia.nsa.gov.pl/doc/1B9B0E0D7C.

71 Uniform text, J. of L. 2023, item 2805 as amended.

out business activity consisting in the provision of services in the scope of (a) exchange between virtual currencies and means of payment, (b) exchange between virtual currencies, (c) intermediation in the exchange referred above or (d) maintenance of accounts understood as a collection, maintained in electronic form, of identifying data enabling the entitled persons to use virtual currency units, including the conduct of transactions of their exchange. In their case such revenues shall be included in the revenues other than revenues from capital gains. Such entities account for revenues and costs under the source of non-agricultural economic activity. And under Article 12 section 4 point 27 of the act the value of virtual currency obtained in exchange for other virtual currency is not considered the revenue.

Article 22d of the Legal Persons' Income Tax Act provides further, that the incomes earned from transfer of virtual currencies against consideration shall be taxable at 19 per cent rate of the income earned. This provision shall apply taking into account the double taxation avoidance agreements to which the Republic of Poland is a party. However, application of the tax rate resulting from a relevant double taxation avoidance agreement or non-payment of the tax pursuant to such agreement shall be possible provided that the taxpayer's seat location for tax purposes is documented by a certificate of residence obtained from the taxpayer. The abovementioned income shall be the difference gained in a given tax year between the total revenues (as defined above) and the revenue earning costs determined under certain provisions.[72]

Similar approach is taken under Natural Persons' Income Tax Act of 26 July 1991 r.[73] Article 17 section 1 point 11 and section 1f of the act provides that revenues from transfer of virtual currency against consideration (the exchange of virtual currency for a legal tender, goods, service or property right other than the virtual currency or payment of other liabilities by the virtual currency) is seen as revenues from money capital.[74] And according to article 30b section 1a of the act, the incomes earned from transfer against consideration of virtual currency is subject to 19 per cent income tax of the income earned. Such income shall be the difference gained in a given tax year between the total

72 See A. Obońska in K. Gil, A. Obońska, A. Wacławczyk and A. Walter (eds), *Podatek dochodowy od osób prawnych. Komentarz* [Income tax from legal persons. Commentary], Legalis, Warszawa 2019, comment to Article 22 d, points 1-8.

73 Uniform text, J. of L. 2024, item 226 as amended.

74 Article 17 para 1g of the act provides the same exception as in the case of the Legal Persons' Income Tax Act.

revenues earned from transfer of virtual currencies against consideration and the revenue earning costs determined under relevant provisions (Article 22 sections 14 to 16 of the act).

Taking into account the current version of the draft Act on the Crypto-assets Market, its entry into force will not affect the taxation. The changes it proposes in tax acts concern the adoption by these acts of terms previously defined in the Act on Combating Money Laundering and the Financing of Terrorism. Therefore, the way of taxation will continue to refer to, among others, the current concept of virtual currency.

3.4 *Criminal Law*

In the field of criminal law there are no specific provisions that apply directly to cryptocurrencies and (or) cryptocurrencies-related services. However, it is indicated that provisions of a broader scope may apply to them. Some authors also classify (and some don't) cryptocurrencies as information, property, material benefit, or even movable property.[75] For these reasons, e.g., an Article 287 of the Criminal Code[76] could be used in a situation of obtaining someone else's cryptocurrencies with the use of the private key of the injured party and without his consent. It states in para. 1 that 'whoever, with the purpose of gaining a material benefit or inflicting damage upon another person, without authorization affects automatic processing, collecting or transmitting of computer data, alters or deletes a computer data record, or enters a new computer data record, is subject to the penalty of deprivation of liberty for between 3 months and 5 years'.[77] If such an offence is committed with regard to an object of significant value[78] the perpetrator is subject

75 See e.g. A. Petrys, 'Bitcoin – współczesna alternatywa wobec pieniądza fiducjarnego w aspekcie prawnokarnym' [Bitcoin - a contemporary alternative to fiat money in the criminal law aspect], *Palestra* 2021, No. 9, pp. 69–73; A. Barczak in B. Gadecki (ed.), *Kodeks karny. Art. 1-316. Komentarz* [Criminal Code. Articles 1-316. Commentary], Warszawa 2023, comment to Article 115, point 53; A. Behan, *Waluty wirtualne jako przedmiot przestępstwa* [Virtual currencies as a subject of crime], Kraków 2022.

76 Act of 06.06.1997 Criminal Code, uniform text, J. of L. 2024, item 17 as amended, hereinafter referred to as 'CC'.

77 Under para. 2, in a case of lesser gravity, the perpetrator is subject to a fine, the penalty of limitation of liberty or the penalty of deprivation of liberty for up to one year. And if the fraud has been committed against an immediate family member, it is prosecuted upon the harmed party's motion (para. 3).

78 According to Article 115 para. 5 CC 'Properly of significant value means property with a value at the time when the prohibited act is committed, exceeding 200,000 PLN.'

to the penalty of deprivation of liberty for between one year and 10 years (Article 294 para. 1 of the CC).

Among other provisions of Criminal Code that could be used in case of crimes connected with cryptocurrencies there are also, inter alia, Article 267 CC (para. 1: 'Whoever without authorization gains access to information not intended for him by opening a sealed letter, plugging into a telecommunications network, or by breaching or bypassing an electronic, magnetic, computer or other special protection of such information, is subject to a fine, the penalty of limitation of liberty or the penalty of deprivation of liberty for up to 2 years'. Para. 2: 'Whoever without authorization gains access to a whole computer system or a part of it, is subject to the same penalty'. Para. 3: 'Whoever, with the purpose of gaining unauthorized access to information, installs or employs a wire-tapping or visual device, or other device or software, is subject to the same penalty'. Para. 4: 'Whoever discloses to another person information obtained in the manner referred to in para. 1–3, is subject to the same penalty'), Article 269b para. 1 ('Whoever produces, obtains, sells or makes available to other persons ... computer passwords, access codes or other data enabling unauthorized access to information stored in a computer system, telecomputer system or telecomputer network, is subject to the penalty of deprivation of liberty for between 3 months and 5 years') and Article 284 para. 1 ('Whoever appropriates someone else's movable item or property right, is subject to the penalty of deprivation of liberty for up to 3 years').[79]

It should also be noted that under Article 153b of the Act on Combating Money Laundering and the Financing of Terrorism, an entity conducting activity in the field of virtual currencies which conducts this activity having not obtained an entry into the register of activity in the field of virtual currencies shall be subject to a pecuniary penalty of up to PLN 100,000. The act provides also certain criminal law consequences in case such an entity violates its obligations as an obliged institution under that act.

79 See e.g. M. Michna, *Bitcoin jako przedmiot stosunków cywilnoprawnych* [Bitcoin as an object of civil law relations], Legalis, Warszawa 2018, Ch. 1, §3; K. Zacharzewski, 'Praktyczne znaczenie bitcoina na wybranych obszarach prawa prywatnego' [The practical significance of Bitcoin in selected areas of private law], *Monitor Prawniczy* 2015, No. 4, p. 195, who points out also other articles in the Polish Criminal Code that might be used; the translation of the articles by W. Wróbel (ed.), A. Wojtaszczyk and W. Zontek, www.lex.pl; see also P. Opitek, 'Kryptowaluty jako przedmiot zabezpieczenia i poręczenia majątkowego' [Cryptocurrencies as an object of collateral and bail], *Prokuratura i Prawo* 2017, No. 6, p. 49.

The above-mentioned Article 153b will be repealed with the entry into force of the Act on the Crypto-assets Market, if the present draft Act on the Crypto-assets Market in this regard is adopted. However, the draft contains Articles 109–119 containing new criminal provisions. They concern, among others:

- making an offer to the public of a crypto-asset, other than an asset-referenced token or e-money token, or seeking admission to trading of such a crypto-asset without required by Regulation 2023/1114 drawing up, notifying the Financial Supervision Authority or publishing its white paper,
- unauthorised activities referred to in Article 59 and 60 of Regulation 2023/1114 related to provision of crypto-asset services,
- not providing information and explanations required by the Financial Supervision Authority (under Article 32 of the draft) and not preparing or submitting copies of documents and other information media in certain situations,
- obstructing or thwarting the inspection by the Financial Supervision Authority of activities of specific entities in order to determine the compliance of their activities with the provisions of the act and Regulation 2023/1114 and the delegated and implementing regulations issued on its basis.

4 Supervision

4.1 *Supervision under the Act on Combating Money Laundering and the Financing of Terrorism*

From 31 October 2021 an Article 129m of the Act on Combating Money Laundering and the Financing of Terrorism provides that business activity covering provision of the services mentioned in Chapter 3.2., called "activity in the field of virtual currencies', is the activity regulated within the provisions of the Act of 6 March 2018 – Entrepreneurs' Law[80] and may be performed after obtaining an entry into the register of activity in the field of virtual currencies. Such an activity may be conducted by a natural person, legal person or an organizational unit without legal personality. In the first case it can only be a natural person who wasn't validly sentenced for a certain types of crimes like an intentional offence against operations of state institutions and territorial self-government, against justice system, against credibility of documents, against

80 Act of 06.03.2018 Entrepreneurs' Law, uniform text, J. of L. 2024, item 236.

property, against economic trading and property interests in trading under civil law, against trading in money and securities, an offence committed to obtain a material or personal benefit or an intentional fiscal offence. In case of a legal person or an organizational unit without legal personality – the shareholders entrusted with managing the company's affairs or authorized to represent the company or members of the governing bodies may have not been convicted for the offence referred to above. The clean criminal record requirement also applies to the persons in charge of the activities related to performing activity in the field of virtual currencies and to the beneficial owner of the entity carrying out such activity (Article 129n). The abovementioned natural persons shall have knowledge or experience related to the activity in the field of virtual currencies. This condition is fulfilled in the case of completion of training or a course covering legal or practical issues connected with activity in the field of virtual currencies, or performance, for at least one year, the acts related to such an activity, in both cases confirmed by relevant documents.

The authority competent for the matters of the register of activity in the field of virtual currencies is the minister competent for public finance.[81] His tasks include (1) maintaining this register and determining the organizational conditions and technical manners of its maintenance; (2) processing information about the entities entered into this register; (3) examining applications for entry into this register, updating the entries and removing entities from the register; (4) imposing the pecuniary penalties referred to in the act (in Article 153b) upon the entities conducting activity in the field of virtual currencies, which entities failed to fulfill the obligation to obtain an entry into this register. He is also the controller of the data processed in this register. An entry into the register of activity in the field of virtual currencies is made based on an entrepreneur's application submitted in electronic form and containing i.a. indication of the services provided and certain declaration. The minister should make an entry into this register within 14 days from the day of receipt of the application. He may refuse to do so, by a decision, where the application is incomplete and has not been supplemented within the set time limit or the data contained in the application is contrary to the state of fact. He shall also remove, by a decision, an entity performing activity in the field of virtual currencies from this register i.a. in the case of determining that the entity fails to satisfy the conditions required by law to carry out activity in the field of virtual

81 He may appoint, by a regulation, an authority of the National Revenue Administration to perform the tasks of the authority competent for maintaining the register of activity in the field of virtual currencies, determining the scope of those tasks having regard to the technical and organizational background of the office supporting this authority.

currencies or that the entity submitted the declaration contrary to the state of fact.

The above-mentioned solutions regarding entry into the register of activity in the field of virtual currencies will disappear (the provisions of Article 129m-x of the act will be repealed) with the entry into force of the act on the crypto-assets market, if the present draft Act on the Crypto-assets Market in this regard is adopted. This is due to the introduction by Regulation 2023/1114 of a new system for conducting and regulating activities in the field of crypto-assets, which renders the existing provisions on such activities redundant as establishing a parallel restriction on the same matter.

However, according to the draft Act on the Crypto-assets Market, in the period from the date of entry into force of the act on the crypto-assets market until the date of obtaining the authorisation referred to in Article 59 section 1 letter a of Regulation 2023/1114, or refusal to grant this authorisation, no longer than until 30 June 2025, an entity entered into the register of activities in the field of virtual currencies on the date of entry into force of the act on the crypto-assets market carries out activities in the field of virtual currencies in accordance with the provisions of the Act on Combating Money Laundering and the Financing of Terrorism in its current wording (with some changes).

4.2 *Supervision – Current Situation*

Except for the register of activity in the field of virtual currencies run by the minister competent for public finance, in force from 31 October 2021 after the amendment of the Act on Combating Money Laundering and the Financing of Terrorism as described above, so far there are no other special licenses or authorizations required before the use, management or issuance of a cryptocurrency or the provision of a cryptocurrency-related services and no other specific supervisory authority.[82]

As a result, the issuers of cryptocurrency are not required to publish a white paper or prospectus, although in fact they usually do so. It does not mean that in case such white paper or prospectus is published there are no civil or

---

82 See i.a. 'Ostrzeżenie Urzędu KNF o ryzykach związanych z nabywaniem oraz z obrotem kryptoaktywami (w tym walutami wirtualnymi oraz kryptowalutami)' [Warning of the KNF Office on the risks related to the acquisition and trading of crypto-assets (including virtual currencies and cryptocurrencies)], 12.01.2021, https://www.knf.gov.pl/knf/pl/komponenty/img/Ostrzezenie_UKNF_o_ryzykach_zwiazanych_z_nabywaniem_oraz_z_obrotem_kryptoaktywami_72241.pdf, pp. 2–3.

criminal law consequences if it is incorrect or misleading. However, these consequences will be based on general provisions i.a. Article 286 CC and 294 para. 1 CC that concern fraud, Article 415 PCC being a general rule dealing with torts or Article 471 PCC containing general rule in case of nonperformance of obligation. The first two provide that whoever, with the purpose of gaining a material benefit, induces another person to disadvantageously dispose of personal or someone else's property by misleading this person or by exploiting this person's error or incapability to duly understand the undertaken action, is subject to the penalty of deprivation of liberty for between 6 months and 8 years, in case of an act of lesser gravity – to a fine, the penalty of limitation of liberty or the penalty of deprivation of liberty for up to 2 years and if the crime is committed with regard to a property of substantial value – to the penalty of deprivation of liberty for between one year and 10 years. The Article 415 PCC states that whoever by his fault caused a damage to another person shall be obliged to redress it. And Article 471 PCC stipulates that the debtor shall be obliged to redress the damage resulting from the nonperformance or improper performance of the obligation unless non-performance or improper performance were due to circumstances for which the debtor is not liable.

As it is essentially an unregulated market, there are also no detailed and systemic solutions ensuring the safety of investors and facilitating their possible pursuit of claims from unreliable entrepreneurs (including, among others, specific actions and class actions). There are also no special or exclusive heads of jurisdiction available in case of crypto litigation. A foreign decision or arbitral award over crypto litigation would be recognized and enforced by Polish courts based on general rules of recognition of foreign decisions or awards specified in Part four of the Code of Civil Procedure.[83]

In any case, the use, management or issuance of a cryptocurrency or the provision of a cryptocurrency-related services by certain institution may be subject to supervision by certain supervisory authority if such an institution is under supervision due to its other activity. Example of this is the Financial Supervisory Authority ('the KNF') that supervises the financial market,

83 Act of 17.11.1964 Code of Civil Procedure, uniform text, J. of L. 2024, item 1568 as amended. The general rule from Article 1145 provides that 'judgments of foreign state courts issued in civil matters shall be recognized by operation of law unless there are obstacles listed in Article 1146', i.a. it is not final and non-revisable in the state where it was issued, it was issued in a case which falls under the exclusive jurisdiction of Polish courts, a party was deprived of the possibility to defend during the proceedings. One of such obstacles is that such recognition would be contrary to the fundamental principles of the legal order of the Republic of Poland (public policy clause) but in case of crypto litigations it wouldn't rather play any role.

covering i.a. banking activity and payment institutions. Hence, in the case of cryptocurrency exchanges and cryptocurrency exchange offices, the KNF exercises supervision over the activities consisting in the provision of payment services by these entities in accordance with the provisions of the Act of 19 August 2011 on Payment Services. That's also why it issued in the past varied warnings that concerned the activity of a number of Polish cryptocurrency exchanges, i.a. BitBay or Coinroom, mentioned above. The KNF presents also information about warnings issued by supervisory authorities in other countries (i.e. concerning Binance Market Limited).[84] However, at no stage can we speak of a direct supervision of the KNF over activities related directly to the issue and trading of cryptocurrencies and, more broadly, crypto-assets.[85]

4.3 *Supervision – Upcoming Changes*

The situation regarding supervision will change quite significantly with the entry into force of Regulation 2023/1114 and the Act on the Crypto-assets Market. Licensing, organizational, prudential and information obligations will be imposed on professional market participants, including issuers and intermediaries.

The Regulation 2023/1114 is intended to improve investors' access to information about products, services and risks of the crypto-asset market, increase the reliability and fairness of trading, including the quality and security of using services, as well as the stability and resilience of professional participants of this market. Regulation establishes in particular:

- transparency and disclosure requirements for the issuance, offer to the public and admission of crypto-assets to trading on a trading platform for crypto-assets;
- requirements for the authorisation and supervision of crypto-asset service providers, issuers of asset-referenced tokens and issuers of e-money tokens, as well as for their operation, organisation and governance;
- requirements for the protection of holders of crypto-assets in the issuance, offer to the public and admission to trading of crypto-assets;
- requirements for the protection of clients of crypto-asset service providers;

---

84 See https://www.knf.gov.pl/komunikacja/komunikaty?articleId=74107&p_id=18.

85 See i.a. 'Ostrzeżenie Urzędu KNF o ryzykach związanych z nabywaniem oraz z obrotem kryptoaktywami (w tym walutami wirtualnymi oraz kryptowalutami)' [Warning of the KNF Office on the risks related to the acquisition and trading of crypto-assets (including virtual currencies and cryptocurrencies)] of 12.01.2021, https://www.knf.gov.pl/knf/pl/komponenty/img/Ostrzezenie_UKNF_o_ryzykach_zwiazanych_z_nabywaniem_oraz_z_obrotem_kryptoaktywami_72241.pdf, pp. 2–3; 'Sytuacja regulacyjna na rynku kryptoaktywów' ['The regulatory situation on the crypto-assets market], 11.09.2023, https://www.knf.gov.pl/komunikacja/komunikaty?articleId=83761&p_id=18, pp. 1–3.

- measures to prevent insider dealing, unlawful disclosure of inside information and market manipulation related to crypto-assets, in order to ensure the integrity of markets in crypto-assets.

However, the Polish Financial Supervision Authority indicates that the solutions adopted in the regulation will not eliminate the risks characteristic of crypto-assets, and the standard of investor protection will remain significantly lower than the level of protection offered to investors of traditional financial market assets. And although the regulation will apply, with certain exceptions, from 30 December 2024, a transition period may last until 1 July 2026, during which crypto-asset service providers will be able to continue providing services in a largely unregulated manner.[86]

The draft Act on the Crypto-assets Market serves the application of Regulation 2023/1114 and 2023/1113, by specifying the organization and exercise of supervision over offerors, persons applying for the admission of crypto-assets to trading, issuers of asset-referenced tokens and e-money tokens, crypto-asset service providers and issuers of crypto-assets other than asset-referenced tokens and e-money tokens. Therefore, the act is to include, among others, provisions regarding:

- various types of obligations imposed on such entities, e.g. in the field of professional secrecy,
- information obligations towards the Polish Financial Supervision Authority,
- civil liability in connection with the crypto-asset white paper,
- the method and scope of supervision over the crypto-assets market (competent authority within the meaning of Article 93 section 1 of Regulation 2023/1114 is to be the Polish Financial Supervision Authority),
- numerous supervisory measures and administrative sanctions, including the possibility of blocking the crypto-asset or money account, suspending transaction and maintaining the register of Internet domains used to operate in the field of cryptocurrencies without the required authorisation or entitlement and the consequences of entering them in the register,
- criminal liability (Articles 109–119).

Currently, the draft Act on the Crypto-assets Market is in the review phase, and its final content remains uncertain, especially since various reservations have been raised against it by the consulting bodies.[87]

86 Sytuacja regulacyjna na rynku kryptoaktywów' ['The regulatory situation on the crypto-assets market], 11.09.2023, https://www.knf.gov.pl/komunikacja/komunikaty?articleId=83761&p_id=18, pp. 1–3.

87 See https://legislacja.rcl.gov.pl/projekt/12382311/katalog/13040399#13040399.

5 Private Law Issues

5.1 *Introduction*

Following the comments made while defining and discussing legal qualification of cryptocurrencies, there is no uniform approach to them under Polish private law. The problem is not solved by the definition from the Act on Combating Money Laundering and the Financing of Terrorism and rather won't be solved by the Regulation 2023/1114. As a result, there is also no uniform position as to whether cryptocurrencies can be subject matter of property rights – and if, than to what extent. This, in turn, is important for legal constructions and regulations that can be applied in the case of, for example, trading in them, establishing security, conducting execution, inheritance, civil law protection, etc.[88]

5.2 *If Cryptocurrency Is Subject Matter of Ownership Right*

The author who adopts the analogous application of the provisions on things (i.e. Article 45 PCC) to cryptocurrencies and recognizes them by analogy as the subject matter of ownership right also concludes that the person entitled to them has the right of ownership. The ownership of cryptocurrencies would be a property right, transferable, absolute (*erga omnes* effective). In his opinion, cryptocurrencies can also be the subject matter of de facto dominance (control), and thus by analogy – possession, with the *corpus* (*corpus possessionis*) element consisting in access to the public key by disposing of the private key.[89]

In this approach, the transfer of ownership of cryptocurrencies takes place, as a rule, on the basis of the provisions on the transfer of ownership of things specified only as to their kind (Article 155 para. 2 PCC; only exceptionally Article 155 para. 1 PCC in the case of cryptocurrencies specified as to their identity),[90]

---

88 See e.g. P. Sobański, 'Kryptowaluty a regulacje prawa spadkowego. Rozważania de lege lata' [Cryptocurrencies and the regulations of inheritance law. De lege lata considerations], *Monitor Prawniczy* 2019, No. 8, pp. 443–50, who is trying to solve the cryptocurrency inheritance problem.

89 See K. Górniak, 'Prawo własności jednostek waluty kryptograficznej' [Ownership of cryptocurrency units], *Kwartalnik Prawa Prywatnego* 2019, No. 3, pp. 586–614.

90 Article 155 PCC provides in para. 1: 'A contract of sale, exchange, donation, conveyance of immovable property or another contract obliging to transfer the ownership of a thing defined as to its identity shall transfer the ownership to an acquirer unless a special provision or the parties have decided otherwise'. In para. 2: 'If the object of a contract obliging to transfer the ownership are things designated only as to their kind, the transfer of the ownership shall require the transfer of the possession of those things. The same shall

where the transfer of possession requirement is fulfilled by the registration of transfer in the distributed ledger of transactions operating within the blockchain and the attribution of cryptocurrency units to an address constituting the public key of the acquiring party. In case when a cryptocurrency unit is mined, the ownership right to it originates and is obtained by primary acquisition. The ownership can also be obtained from an unauthorized person in cases where it is possible with regard to movable things (e.g. under Article 169 PCC), and also by acquisitive prescription (Article 174 PCC). This right may be the subject matter of universal succession, in particular, it can be inherited as a part of an estate. It may also be the subject matter of an ordinary legacy.[91]

K. Górniak points out that the entitled person, depending on the situation, would theoretically be protected by *rei vindicatio* (of greater importance only in bankruptcy proceedings), *actio negatoria* and possessory claim. However, protection under the provisions on tort and unjust enrichment would be of greater importance. One could also carry out execution from cryptocurrency units, but this would have to be done in accordance with Article 1050 of the Code of Civil Procedure, i.e. in the manner applicable to nonpecuniary performances consisting in activities that another person cannot perform for the debtor and the performance of which depends solely on his will. This is due to technological issues making it impossible to physically take back the cryptocurrency.[92]

5.3 *If Cryptocurrency Is a Claim*

In turn, the author who assumes that Bitcoin is a claim (receivable) indicates that it is a transferable relative property right, the transfer of which cannot take place under Article 155 PCC (that refers to transfer of ownership), but by way of assignment under Article 510 para. 1 PCC and an additional activity consisting in using the private key.[93] Based on his theorems it can be indicated that the obligation to transfer a cryptocurrency (an assignment is a causal legal action) may result from a contract of sale (the object of which, in accordance with Article 555 PCC, may also be – apart from things – a right)[94]

---

apply to the case in which the object of the contract obliging to transfer the ownership are future things'.

91 See K. Górniak, 'Prawo własności jednostek waluty kryptograficznej' [Ownership of cryptocurrency units], *Kwartalnik Prawa Prywatnego* 2019, No. 3, pp. 614–42.

92 Ibid.

93 Under Article 510 para. 1 PCC: 'A contract of sale, exchange, donation or other contract obliging to transfer the receivable, shall transfer the receivable to the acquiring party, unless a specific provision provides otherwise or the parties have decided otherwise'.

94 Article 555 PCC provides that: 'The provisions on the sale of a thing shall apply respectively to the sale of energy, rights and water'.

or a contract of exchange (in a situation where in exchange for cryptocurrency we receive a transfer of property), where the provisions on the contract of sale are applied accordingly. In his opinion, cryptocurrency gives the entitled person the right to use it and dispose of it, which is the result of a broad analogy with Article 140 PCC governing the right of ownership. The debtor with respect to Bitcoin is a group consisting of all – on a global scale – people involved in the obtaining of Bitcoin. The author also assumes that beyond all doubt the transfer of the title to Bitcoin is not the transfer of possession, although the factual control may be exercised over the private key and the subjective right of the entitled person in this respect is exclusive (and effective *erga omnes*). Thus, *rei vindicatio* can be used by the owner of a private key deprived of its possession against a non-owner who has it, but no longer than until the key is used.[95] Bitcoins can be borrowed, you can also agree on interest rate in Bitcoins. They may also be a component of the spouses' joint property, being the subject of its division in the event of divorce. Bitcoins are also a part of the estate in case of inheritance.[96]

5.4 *If There Is No Subjective Right to Cryptocurrency*

Next, the authors who claim that there is no subjective right (neither absolute nor relative) with respect to Bitcoin recognize that it constitutes an intangible good being an object of performance in the obligation relationship. Based on their concepts, cryptocurrency would be a self-existent (independent) object of performance, as is in case of know-how.[97] However, having a specific public address and a private key that allows the use of cryptocurrency constitutes a favorable factual situation of the holder of relevant keys with a measurable property value and constitutes a component of property.[98] The very transfer of a cryptocurrency is usually a purely actual activity consisting in the use of a

95 See K. Zacharzewski, 'Bitcoin jako przedmiot stosunków prawa prywatnego' [Bitcoin as an object of private law relations], *Monitor Prawniczy* 2014, No. 21, pp. 1132–39.

96 See K. Zacharzewski, 'Praktyczne znaczenie bitcoina na wybranych obszarach prawa prywatnego' [The practical significance of Bitcoin in selected areas of private law], *Monitor Prawniczy* 2015, No. 4, pp. 187–91.

97 See M. Michna, *Bitcoin jako przedmiot stosunków cywilnoprawnych* [Bitcoin as an object of civil law relations], Legalis, Warszawa 2018, Ch. II, §6. In Poland, know-how is traditionally denied to be protected by a subjective right. It should be noted, however, that there are also positions in the doctrine that assume the existence of such a right to know-how. For views on this matter, see i.e. U. Promińska in W.J. Katner (ed.), *System Prawa Prywatnego. Tom 9. Prawo zobowiązań – umowy nienazwane* [System of Private Law. Vol. 9. Law of obligations – innominate contracts], Warszawa 2018, pp. 1011–12.

98 See J. Szewczyk, 'O cywilnoprawnych aspektach bitcoina' [On the civil law aspects of Bitcoin], *Monitor Prawniczy* 2018, No. 5, p. 247.

private key.[99] A contract in which one of the parties, in exchange for the transfer of ownership of things or rights, undertakes to transfer the cryptocurrency does not constitute a sale contract (regulated under Articles 535 et seq. PCC) or an exchange contract (Articles 603–604 PCC), as cryptocurrency is neither a thing, right, nor money,[100] but it is an innominate contract,[101] the economic purpose of which, however, is very similar to the purpose of the sale contract. Therefore, by analogy legis, the statutory provisions on sale should be applied accordingly. On the other hand, if the payment in cryptocurrency was made in exchange for a service, the provisions on the contract of mandate should be applied accordingly (Article 750 PCC).[102] One can also directly apply the provisions on the lease contract (in which the rent will be set in cryptocurrency) and on the contract of donation in the event of a free transfer of cryptocurrency units to another person. In the case of borrowing cryptocurrency units, we will not be dealing with a loan contract (due to its object specified in Article 720 para. 1 PCC that defines this contract), but with another innominate contract, with respect to which we will apply *per analogiam* the provisions of the loan contract.[103]

5.5 *Position of the Courts*

Against this background, the situation in the jurisprudence looks interesting. It seems that courts assume that in case of cryptocurrency we are dealing with a subjective property right relating to it (without specifying its nature), which is a component of property and may also be traded. For example, in the judgment of 10 February 2021, II FSK 2870/18, the Supreme Administrative Court indicated that 'the exchange of cryptocurrencies, i.e. one intangible property right for another such right, constitutes an exchange contract within the meaning of Article 603 in connection with Article 555 of the Act of 23 April 1964 Civil

---

99 Although it can also be done by a transfer of private key to a new information carrier owned by another person or by the transfer of ownership of the key carrier.

100 Article 535 para. 1 PCC provides that 'By the contract of sale the seller undertakes to transfer the ownership of a thing to the buyer and to release the thing to him and the buyer undertakes to collect the thing and to pay the price to the seller'. And Article 603 PCC: 'By the contract of exchange each party undertakes to transfer to the other party the ownership of a thing in exchange for an obligation to transfer the ownership of the other thing'.

101 On the concept of innominate contracts see i.a. W.J. Katner in W.J. Katner (ed.), *System Prawa Prywatnego. Tom 9. Prawo zobowiązań – umowy nienazwane* [System of Private Law. Vol. 9. Law of obligations – innominate contracts], Warszawa 2018, pp. 1–23.

102 Article 750 PCC: 'The provisions on mandate shall apply accordingly to contracts for services, which are not governed by other provisions'.

103 See M. Michna, *Bitcoin jako przedmiot stosunków cywilnoprawnych* [Bitcoin as an object of civil law relations], Legalis, Warszawa 2018, Ch. IV, §1–2.

Code'.[104] This position was also taken by the Supreme Administrative Court in the judgment of 27 April 2022.[105]

5.6 *First, Second or Third View – Which One Is Proper?*

If we look at what the cryptocurrencies actually are (although there are also varied approaches to this extent), it is rather doubtful – despite some support for such a view in the doctrine[106] – that in the current legal state they can be considered as the object of ownership right (its object under Article 140 PCC are things), even though it would certainly facilitate many legal issues. At most, one can consider the application of sole Article 140 PCC per analogiam to the extent it indicates the content of the ownership right. One shouldn't also confuse the cryptocurrency with a tangible carrier containing a private key that enables its use, as some authors seem to do, and with the private key itself. It is worth mentioning here that there may be many tangible carriers containing the same key (copies of it), or such a carrier may not exist at all (e.g. assuming that someone would memorize the key). Yet, when we talk about the absolute right to cryptocurrency, one could consider a solution within the field of intellectual property law, as cryptocurrency units are created as an effect of an operation of a computer program created by a man (people).

At the same time, the view that with respect to cryptocurrency we are dealing with a subjective right in a form of a claim (receivable) is rather rejected in the doctrine, i.a. due to problems with identifying the debtor. In this respect, however, it could be indicated that there are various cryptocurrencies (not only Bitcoin), hence one could consider the existence of claims against the

---

104 Judgment of the Supreme Administrative Court of 10.02.2021, II FSK 2870/18, https://orzeczenia.nsa.gov.pl/doc/8889489BE0; see also the judgment of the Voivodship Administrative Court in Gliwice of 11.04.2018, I SA/GL 248/18, https://orzeczenia.nsa.gov.pl/doc/29DBB6617D.

105 Judgment of the Supreme Administrative Court of 27.04.2022, II FSK 2181/19, https://orzeczenia.nsa.gov.pl/doc/DC967F7AE0.

106 See P. Machnikowski in E. Gniewek (ed.), *System Prawa Prywatnego. Tom 3. Prawo rzeczowe* [System of Private Law. Vol. 3. Property law], Warszawa 2020, p. 30; A. Weber-Elżanowska, 'Zapłata w bitcoinach za przeniesienie własności rzeczy lub praw – uwagi na tle wybranych instytucji prawa obligacyjnego' [Payment in Bitcoins for the transfer of ownership of things or rights - comments against the background of selected institutions of law of obligations] in K. Bilewska, W.J. Kocot, D. Krekora-Zając (eds), *Wykonywanie zobowiązań. Księga jubileuszowa dedykowana profesorowi Adamowi Brzozowskiemu* [Performance of obligations. Jubilee book dedicated to professor Adam Brzozowski], Warszawa 2021, p. 586.

person (people) creating software for a given cryptocurrency (that may be known),[107] as well as against entities that are participants in the system (in particular against these that manage nodes),[108] at least in the form of duty to accept (*pati*) the existence of a given address (public key) and the association of cryptocurrency units with it resulting from the blockchain register.

However, while acquiring a cryptocurrency unit we are certainly dealing at least with the emergence of a favorable factual situation on our side, in which we obtain an actual control over the cryptocurrency unit consisting in the possibility of disposing of it, that has certain value and legal significance, resembling possession (although not being a possession due to the subject matter of possession specified by law). Indeed, in a way, the situation is similar to legal qualification under Polish law of, e.g., know-how.

Notwithstanding, regardless of whether we adopt the first, second or third of the approaches presented above, the cryptocurrency itself or – which seems to be more correct – the related subjective right to cryptocurrency or the favorable factual situation consisting in attributing the cryptocurrency units to a specific public address (public key) at the disposal of a given person shall constitute a component of property that is understood as distinguishable set of assets (sometimes also liabilities) which are the subject matter of inheritance, trading, securing receivables, the basis for liability, etc.[109] In this way, cryptocurrencies are also treated by jurisprudence, where the courts, for example, divide the joint property of the spouses taking into account, inter alia, such assets as cryptocurrencies associated with a specific public and private key.[110]

Based on the above, it can also be indicated that – regardless of the approach to the existence of the subjective right to cryptocurrencies – in the case of acquisition of cryptocurrencies in exchange for cash, we are dealing with a contract where statutory provisions on sale from PCC are applied at least by

---

107 Another question is whether the problem (or present impossibility) with identifying the debtor negates the existence of the claim.

108 As to the civil law relationships between the participants in the system (e.g. the cryptocurrency software developer, the miners, custodians) see i.a. D. Szostek, *Blockchain a prawo* [Blockchain and law], Legalis, Warszawa 2018, Ch. III, para. 4 point II.

109 See i.a. W.J. Katner in M. Safjan (ed.), *System Prawa Prywatnego. Tom 1. Prawo cywilne – cześć ogólna* [System of Private Law. Vol. 1. Civil law – general part], Warszawa 2012, pp. 1297–98 as to the concept of property.

110 See P. Katner, 'Cryptocurrencies: The Impossible Domestic Law Regime?' in B. Lewaszkiewicz-Petrykowska, D. Skupień (eds), *Rapports polonais, XXI Congrès international de droit compare, Asunción 23–28 X 2022*, Łódź 2022, p. 177.

analogy. It is similar in a situation where, in return for the cryptocurrency, the other party undertakes to transfer the ownership of things or a right,[111] and also (or in this – depending on the adopted solution) in the case of exchanging one cryptocurrency for another. At least by analogy the provisions on the loan contract are applied while borrowing cryptocurrencies.[112] In turn, in the case of a free transfer of cryptocurrency to another entity by contract as a rule we shall apply directly the provisions on the contract of donation, as in most cases it will be simply a contract of donation.[113] Being a component of property, cryptocurrencies can also be inherited (or subject to ordinary legacy)[114] based on general rules of law of succession (in the same way as other components of property),[115] although to be able to dispose of them the heir should have access to the relevant private key.

5.7 *Possibility of Applying Provisions on Pecuniary Obligations to Cryptocurrencies*

From the point of view of Polish private law, it is also important to answer the question whether general provisions regulating pecuniary obligations apply to the obligation of an amount expressed in cryptocurrency, e.g. Article 358 PCC (currency principle), Article 358[1] PCC (principle of nominalism and scope of possible valorization), Article 359 PCC (possibility to demand capital interest on a sum of money and its scope), Article 481 PCC (possibility

111 See i.a. A. Weber-Elżanowska, 'Zapłata w bitcoinach za przeniesienie własności rzeczy lub praw – uwagi na tle wybranych instytucji prawa obligacyjnego' [Payment in Bitcoins for the transfer of ownership of things or rights - comments against the background of selected institutions of law of obligations] in K. Bilewska, W.J. Kocot, D. Krekora-Zając (eds), *Wykonywanie zobowiązań. Księga jubileuszowa dedykowana profesorowi Adamowi Brzozowskiemu* [Performance of obligations. Jubilee book dedicated to professor Adam Brzozowski], Warszawa 2021, pp. 586–88.

112 Under Article 720 para. 1 PCC 'By a contract of loan, the lender shall assume the obligation to transfer to the borrower the ownership of a specified sum of money or a specified amount of things designated only as to their kind, and the borrower shall assume the obligation to return the same sum of money or the same amount of things of the same kind and the same quality'.

113 In accordance with Article 888 PCC 'by a contract of donation the donor shall assume the obligation to make a gratuitous performance for the benefit of the donee at the expense of his property'.

114 Or perhaps even subject to vindication legacy, as under Article 981[1] PCC in a testament drawn up in the form of a notarial deed, the testator can decide that a specified person shall acquire the object of legacy, e.g. transferable property right, upon opening of the inheritance (vindication legacy).

115 Book four of the Civil Code contains provisions on inheritance.

to demand interest for delay and its scope) or Article 454 para. 1 PCC (place of fulfillment of the pecuniary obligation). The answer to this question is not obvious, despite the previously made comments that cryptocurrencies are not considered money or currency in the legal sense in Polish law.[116] It is indicated, among others, that it cannot be given abstractly for all cases and it is necessary to analyze individual regulations and their functions and evaluate them from the point of view of cryptocurrencies.[117] For example, the dominant position is that Article 358 PCC[118] does not apply to cryptocurrencies.[119] But with regard to the possibility and scope of application of Article 481 PCC, opinions are divided.[120]

5.8 *Bunkruptcy and Enforcement Issue*

With respect to cryptocurrency, general bankruptcy and enforcement rules apply. It is however difficult to clearly indicate the appropriate mode of their conduct. By way of example, a recent publication on the subject presents that the execution conducted by a court bailiff seems permissible under Article 909 *et seq.* of the Code of Civil Procedure, which regulate the case of execution against other property rights (other than e.g. receivables, movable property) or, assuming that we are dealing with a quasi-debt collection claim, under provisions on execution of non-pecuniary performances.[121] On the other hand, one

116 However, see Ł. Mazur, 'Kryptowaluty jako środek umarzania zobowiązań' [Cryptocurrencies as a means of performing obligations] in J. Gołaczyński (ed.), *Prawo umów elektornicznych. Zarys systemu* [Electronic contract law. System outline], Warszawa 2024, Chapter VIII, §3.V, 5§.

117 See F. Zoll in A. Olejniczak (ed.), *System Prawa Prywatnego. Tom 6. Prawo zobowiązań – część ogólna* [System of Private Law. Vol. 6. Obligations – general part], Warszawa 2023, p. 1144.

118 Under Article 358 para. 1 PCC 'If the object of the obligation to be fulfilled within the territory of the Republic of Poland is a sum of money denominated in foreign currency, the debtor may fulfill the performance in the Polish currency, unless the Act, court pronouncement which forms the source of the obligation, or an act in law reserves the fulfillment of the performance exclusively in foreign currency'.

119 See e.g. K. Zagrobelny in P. Machnikowski (ed.), *Zobowiązania. Tom I. Przepisy ogólne i powiązane przepisy Księgi I KC. Komentarz* [Obligations. Volume I. General provisions and related provisions of Book I of the Civil Code. Commentary], Warszawa 2022, comment to Article 358, points 12–13.

120 See F. Zoll in A. Olejniczak (ed.), *System Prawa Prywatnego. Tom 6. Prawo zobowiązań – część ogólna* [System of Private Law. Vol. 6. Obligations – general part], Warszawa 2023, p. 1145.

121 See M. Marcinkowska, 'Egzekucja komornicza z kryptowalut' [Court bailiffs conducting execution against cryptocurrencies], *Przegląd Prawa Handlowego* 2021, No. 6, pp. 12–16.

can find information on successful execution conducted under provisions on enforcement against other receivables (under Articles 895–908 of the Code). In this case the bailiff turned to the Polish cryptocurrency exchange where the debtor had stored cryptocurrency and conducted enforcement against the claim to get it back from the exchange. As a result, the exchange transferred the stored cryptocurrencies to the given public address and they were sold.[122]

5.9 *Impact of the Regulation 2023/1114 and Act on the Crypto-Assets Market*

The above-mentioned comments will not be significantly affected by the entry into application of Regulation 2023/1114 and the Act on the Crypto-assets Market. In principle, they do not deal with private law issues. It is worth noting, however, that they provide for civil liability for the information given in a crypto-asset white paper (the draft Act on the Crypto-assets Market extends its scope in relation to Regulation 2023/1114). In addition, imposing various requirements on crypto-asset service providers may make it easier to prove their liability in the event of damage and to pursue claims.

122 See https://jakodzyskacpieniadze.pl/2019/02/19/bitcoin-zajety-przez-komornika-case-study-vindicat-pl/.

Singapore

Christian Hofmann, Lisa-Marie Ross and Ryan Chan-Wei

1 Introduction[1]

Similar to previous waves of technological advancement, cryptoassets offer the potential to revolutionise the delivery of financial services. Cryptoassets could facilitate more efficient transactions, enhance financial inclusion, and unlock large swathes of previously untapped economic value. They even carry the capacity to redefine fundamental finance concepts, including store of value, transfer of value, and the establishment and transference of asset rights.

Notwithstanding the tremendous promise of cryptoassets, there has been increasing clarity in recent years concerning the risks that they can pose, not least due to the collapse of the FTX exchange and the death spiral of the TerraUSD stablecoin. In light of this, many financial regulatory agencies have realised that there is a need to ensure that appropriate regulatory frameworks are in place that can mitigate the risks posed by cryptoassets while still preserving the benefits that they can offer.

Singapore mirrors this worldwide trend. Guided by a national economic strategy to attract foreign investment and anchor Singapore as a global hub for innovation, the Monetary Authority of Singapore (MAS) has strived to adopt a measured approach towards the regulation of cryptoassets. Regulatory measures have been implemented in a way that aims to strike a balance between promoting a responsible and innovative digital asset ecosystem, while also protecting consumers and discouraging speculation in cryptoassets.

This chapter provides a summary of the measures that have been adopted and highlights the likely future trajectory for regulatory developments. However, it is important to first understand the broader context of how Singapore's technology-neutral and risk-based regulatory approach has evolved over time.

As cryptoassets started to gain wider acceptance amongst the retail public, MAS responded by issuing general cautions about the risks tied to digital token

1 The authors are grateful for comments from many colleagues and for funding from the Centre for Asian Legal Studies (CALS) at National University of Singapore, Faculty of Law.

 | DOI:10.1163/9789004722507_023

investments[2] and emphasising that these investments were excluded from traditional regulatory safeguards if they fell "outside of the remit of MAS' rules."[3]

At this point, MAS had not introduced any bespoke regulatory frameworks targeting the unique risks posed by cryptoassets, and justified this approach on the basis that digital token transactions had not gained widespread acceptance.[4] For example, in 2017, only 20 retailers accepted Bitcoin in Singapore, and volumes of trades in digital coins were also low, with trades primarily executed for speculative purposes.[5] Even in 2020, the combined peak daily trading volumes of Bitcoin, Ether, and XRP was only 2% of the average daily trading volume of securities on SGX.[6] Furthermore, only a fraction of the over 60 recognised market operators in Singapore (regulated under the Securities and Futures Act) offered trades in securities tokens,[7] and trading volumes were generally very small.[8]

---

2 Ravi Menon, "Crypto-Tokens: the Good, The Bad, and The Ugly" (*MAS*, 15 Mar 2018) at 'investor protection', https://www.mas.gov.sg/news/speeches/2018/crypto-tokens-the-good-the-bad-and-the-ugly (accessed 5 May 2024).

3 MAS, MAS warns Digital Token Exchanges and ICO Issuers (*MAS*, 24 May 2018) at 5, https://www.mas.gov.sg/news/media-releases/2018/mas-warns-digital-token-exchanges-and-ico-issuer (accessed 29 Sep 2024); MAS, Reply to Parliamentary Question on Crypto Asset Market, Question No 869 Notice Paper 348 of 2021 (*MAS* 5 Apr 2021) at 10, https://www.mas.gov.sg/news/parliamentary-replies/2021/reply-to-parliamentary-question-on-crypto-asset-market (accessed 5 May 2024).

4 MAS, *Consultation Paper P021-2017 Proposed Payment Services Bill* (21 Nov 2017) 3.19; Ong Ye Kung, "Payment Services (Amendment) Bill" (*MAS*, 4 Jan 2021) at 13, https://www.mas.gov.sg/news/speeches/2021/payment-services-amendment-bill (accessed 5 May 2024); MAS, Reply to Parliamentary Question on Crypto Asset Market, Question No 869 Notice Paper 348 of 2021 (*MAS* 5 Apr 2021) at 4–5, https://www.mas.gov.sg/news/parliamentary-replies/2021/reply-to-parliamentary-question-on-crypto-asset-market (accessed 5 May 2024); Ravi Menon, "The Future of Money, Finance and the Internet" (MAS, 9 Nov 2021) at 'cryptocurrencies', https://www.mas.gov.sg/news/speeches/2021/the-future-of-money-finance-and-the-internet (accessed 5 May 2024).

5 MAS, Reply to Parliamentary Question on the prevalence use of cryptocurrency in Singapore and measures to regulate cryptocurrency and Initial Coin Offerings, Questions no 1494 Notice Paper 869 of 2017 (*MAS*, 2 Oct 2017) at 3, https://www.mas.gov.sg/news/parliamentary-replies/2017/prevalence-use-of-cryptocurrency-in-singapore (accessed 5 May 2024).

6 MAS, Reply to Parliamentary Question on Crypto Asset Market, Question No 869 Notice Paper 348 of 2021 (*MAS* 5 Apr 2021) at 4, https://www.mas.gov.sg/news/parliamentary-replies/2021/reply-to-parliamentary-question-on-crypto-asset-market (accessed 5 May 2024).

7 Asia Pacific Exchange Pte. Ltd., ICE Futures Singapore Pte. Ltd., Singapore Exchange Derivatives Trading Limited, Singapore Exchange Securities Trading Limited, see under MAS, https://eservices.mas.gov.sg/fid/institution?sector=Capital%20Markets&category=Approved%20Exchange (accessed 5 May 2024).

8 MAS, Reply to Parliamentary Question on Crypto Asset Market, Question No 869 Notice Paper 348 of 2021 (*MAS* 5 Apr 2021) at 6, https://www.mas.gov.sg/news/parliamentary-replies/2021/reply-to-parliamentary-question-on-crypto-asset-market (accessed 5 May 2024).

However, as the risks posed by cryptoassets started to crystallise, MAS recognised that it was necessary to introduce a tailored regulatory framework for cryptoassets that were intended to be used as a means of payment by the general public, and to that end the Payment Services Act (PS Act) came into force in early 2020, which focused initially on regulating technology (e.g. security vulnerabilities) and money laundering risks.

The PS Act has evolved significantly since then and the next section will provide more details about its current scope. It has moved beyond its early focus on technology and money laundering risks to address consumer protection risks as well, and its regulatory perimeter has been expanded substantially to align with international standards.

Although the PS Act has served as the main vehicle through which MAS regulates cryptoasset service providers, the Securities and Futures Act (SFA) and Financial Services and Markets Act (FSMA) are also important components of MAS' technology-neutral and risk-based approach towards regulating cryptoassets.

This chapter will offer a detailed analysis of the existing regulatory landscape and recent updates in Section 2, followed by a discussion of case law in Section 3. Lastly, Section 4 will address the anticipated future trajectory for regulatory developments, considering the persistent challenges posed by cryptoassets.

2 Existing Regulatory Landscape

Singapore's legislation does not define the concept of 'cryptocurrency' and 'cryptoasset', but instead relies on broader terms such as 'digital token' and 'digital payment token.'[9] It is not necessary for a token to utilise distributed ledger technology (DLT) to be classified as a 'digital token' or 'digital payment token' since it is sufficient that tokens are able to be 'transferred, stored or traded electronically.'[10]

Cryptoassets can come under the ambit of one of three legislative acts in Singapore, depending on their characteristics. The SFA would apply when a cryptoasset performs the same functions as a capital markets product, such as a security or unit in a collective investment scheme. This is consistent with MAS' technology-neutral approach towards regulating cryptoassets.[11] The PS

9 PS Act s2 at 'digital payment token'; FSMA s136 at 'digital token'.

10 PS Act s2 at 'digital payment token' at (d); FSMA s136 at 'digital token' at (b).

11 MAS, Reply to Parliamentary Question on Crypto Asset Market, Question No 869 Notice Paper 348 of 2021 (*MAS* 5 Apr 2021) at 6, https://www.mas.gov.sg/news/parliamentary-

Act would apply when a cryptoasset displays the characteristics of a digital payment token, which is the case for most cryptocurrencies.[12] Finally, the Commodity Trading Act (CTA) might apply when a cryptoasset is backed by commodities.[13]

Most cryptoassets in Singapore will fall within the regulatory perimeter of either the PS Act or SFA – they are therefore the most salient sources of law and will be discussed in more detail below. Compliance with these two Acts is monitored and enforced by MAS, while compliance with the CTA is monitored and enforced by Enterprise Singapore (a statutory board under the Ministry of Trade and Industry).

2.1 *Security Tokens*

MAS has noted that some digital tokens may 'represent ownership or a security interest over an issuer's assets or property', and the offers of such digital tokens would be a regulated activity that is subject to the requirements that apply to capital market products such as 'securities, units in a collective investment scheme, derivatives contracts and spot foreign exchange contracts for the purposes of leveraged foreign exchange trading.'[14] Depending on their envisaged purpose, digital tokens might therefore be characterised as shares, debentures, units in business trusts, security-based derivatives contracts, or units in collective investment schemes.[15] However, the mere fact that digital tokens are tradeable on the secondary market would not affect whether they are categorised as capital markets products under the SFA.[16]

Unless specifically exempted, offerors of security tokens must comply with retail investor protection measures, especially the requirement to lodge and register a prospectus with MAS prior to the offer of the tokens.[17] However, providers of digital token services generally seek to avoid the prospectus

---

replies/2021/reply-to-parliamentary-question-on-crypto-asset-market (accessed 5 May 2024).

12 See also below at 2.2.

13 Legal definition of a commodity within the meaning of the CTA, see CTA s 2; See in more detail in regard to the qualification of asset-backed cryptocurrencies: J. Koh, 'Crypto Conundrum Part I: Navigating Singapore's Regulatory Regime' (2020) *SAL* Prac 3, at 17–9.

14 MAS clarifies regulatory position on the offer of digital tokens in Singapore (*MAS*, 1 Aug 2017) at 4, https://www.mas.gov.sg/news/media-releases/2017/mas-clarifies-regulatory-position-on-the-offer-of-digital-tokens-in-singapore (accessed 5 May 2024); MAS, *A Guide to Digital Token Offerings* (26 May 2020) at 2.1. For the definition of capital market products, see SFA s 2(1).

15 MAS, *A Guide to Digital Token Offerings* (26 May 2020) at 2.4.

16 Ibid., at case study 7.

17 For all of the above points see MAS, MAS clarifies regulatory position on the offer of digital tokens in Singapore (*MAS*, 1 Aug 2017) at 4–5, https://www.mas.gov.sg/news/media-releases/2017/mas-clarifies-regulatory-position-on-the-offer-of-digital-tokens-in

requirement due to its high costs and the risk of liability for misinformation or failure to disclose relevant information to which the issuer, its directors, all underwriters, and any person who has made a statement and consented to being named in the prospectus is subject.[18] Such avoidance is possible even if MAS classifies digital tokens as securities that fall within the SFA's regulatory ambit, because Singapore law follows global principles and exempts certain types of offers of securities from the prospectus requirement: for instance, digital token issuers could rely on the exemptions for small offers[19] or private placements,[20] or restrict their offers to institutional and accredited investors.[21]

To benefit from the aforementioned exemptions, the following conditions must be met: for small offers, the total amount raised with all digital tokens over a period of 12 months must not exceed SGD 5 million;[22] and for private placements, the offers should have been made to no more than 50 persons within any 12-month period.[23] Offers to institutional investors are generally exempted,[24] and offers to accredited investors, defined as wealthy individuals with net personal assets exceeding SGD 2 million or an income in the past 12 months of at least SGD 300,000 (as well as corporations with net assets exceeding SGD 10 million in value), are also exempted.[25] In addition, the law treats persons who acquire digital tokens for at least SGD 200,000 per transaction like accredited investors and exempts such transactions from the prospectus requirement.[26]

-singapore (accessed 5 May 2024). The requirement to register a prospectus stems from SFA ss 240, 239(3). On the information a prospectus must contain, see s 43.

18 The issuer of securities is 'the entity that issued or will be issuing the securities being offered', SFA s239(1). For the full list of persons subject to criminal liability, s253(4). For those subject to civil liability, s254(3).

19 SFA s272A.

20 SFA s272B.

21 SFA s275.

22 SFA s272A(1)(a). The amount is calculated in accordance with s272A(4).

23 SFA s272B (1)(a)-(b). To address circumvention attempts, entities and trustees are counted as one person if 'the entity or trust is not formed primarily for the purpose of acquiring the securities which are the subject of the offer' whereas in the opposite case, every member of the entity or beneficiary of the trust is counted individually, and entities and trustees are counted as one person if 'the entity or trust is not formed primarily for the purpose of acquiring the securities which are the subject of the offer' whereas in the opposite case, every member of the entity or beneficiary of the trust is counted individually, see s272B(5)(b). For consecutive sales in secondary markets see s272B(5)(g).

24 SFA s274. For the definition of institutional investors, see s4A(1)(c).

25 SFA s275.

26 SFA s 275(1A). MAS has explicitly confirmed that these exemptions from the prospectus requirement apply to offers of securities provided via crowdfunding platforms. See MAS, *Response to Feedback Received – Facilitating Securities-Based Crowdfunding* (8 Jun 2016) 5.

In addition to the specific requirements that apply to particular types of exemptions (e.g. maximum number of investors), further requirements apply generally to all categories of exemptions: all investors must be properly informed about the exemption to the prospectus requirement[27] and about restrictions that apply to sales of the tokens in secondary markets when they are issued under an exemption to the prospectus requirement.[28] For instance, exempted offers must not be advertised,[29] but instead directly addressed to a person in the target group (for institutional or accredited investors) or to specific persons who might be interested in the offer (for small offers and private placements).[30] These requirements are strictly enforced, and MAS has halted offerings because of noncompliance.[31] In one case, the issuer relied on the accredited investor exemption but failed to comply with the advertising prohibition when it posted about a security token offering on LinkedIn, and MAS consequently halted the offering.[32]

Numerous additional regulatory obligations arise if digital tokens fall within the SFA's scope. For example, corporations or persons offering services related to securities must hold a capital markets services licence,[33] and exchanges that facilitate trades in digital tokens must be authorised as approved exchanges or market operators by MAS if the tokens constitute securities or futures contracts.[34]

2.2 *Digital Payment Tokens*

The PS Act is the most important regulatory instrument for cryptoassets in Singapore. This is because most cryptocurrencies fall within the definition of a "digital payment token", which is defined in the PS Act as "any digital representation of value" that "(a) is expressed as a unit"; "(b) is not denominated in any currency, and is not pegged by its issuer to any currency"; "(c) is, or is intended to be, a medium of exchange accepted by the public, or a section of the public,

27 SFA s272A(1)(b)(i) and s275(1)(c).

28 On the restrictions that apply to the resale of the securities, see SFA ss272A(1)(b)(ii), (3), (8).

29 SFA s272A(1)(c), s272B (1)(a)-(b) and s275(1)(a).

30 SFA s272A(3).

31 MAS, MAS halts securities token offering for regulatory breach (*MAS*, 24 Jan 2019), https://www.mas.gov.sg/news/media-releases/2019/mas-halts-securities-token-offering-for-regulatory-breach (accessed 5 May 2024).

32 Ibid.

33 SFA ss7, 82 and Second Schedule.

34 MAS, MAS warns Digital Token Exchanges and ICO Issuers (*MAS*, 24 May 2018) at 2, https://www.mas.gov.sg/news/media-releases/2018/mas-warns-digital-token-exchanges-and-ico-issuer (accessed 5 May 2024).

as payment for goods or services or for the discharge of a debt"; and "(d) can be transferred, stored or traded electronically".

The position that most cryptocurrencies fulfil the statutory definition of a 'digital payment token' is reflected in several statements from courts and government authorities, including Singapore's highest court, the Court of Appeal. The Inland Revenue Authority of Singapore (IRAS) has clarified that even though payment tokens do not constitute fiat currency or legal tender,[35] they nevertheless serve as a mode of payment in Singapore.[36] The High Court has stated that "(w)hile the word 'currency' connotes a medium of exchange, a cryptocurrency is not associated with any physical object (unlike how a currency such as the US Dollar is),"[37] and defined cryptocurrencies somewhat circuitously as virtual currencies such as Bitcoin and Ethereum.[38] The Court of Appeal has also described cryptocurrency usage as 'computer-generated, high-frequency transactions in digital quasi-currencies.'[39] Finally, MAS has stated in the Frequently Asked Questions (FAQs) on the PS Act that digital payment tokens are "what we commonly call cryptocurrencies."[40] Examples of cryptocurrencies traded in Singapore include Bitcoin, Ether, and XRP.[41]

However, although the PS Act is the core regulatory instrument that MAS relies on for regulating and supervising cryptoasset service providers in Singapore, it is important to note that its scope also extends to the broader payments sector in Singapore. Other regulated payment services under the PS Act include, inter alia, cross-border money transfer and merchant acquisition.

When the PS Act took effect in early 2020, it replaced prior legislation applicable to payment services,[42] and widened the scope of regulated payment services to keep pace with technological changes, such as by introducing the new category of a "digital payment token service". Some of the primary risks that the PS Act seeks to mitigate include consumer protection risks, technology

35 Which is in line with the interpretation in the Currency Act s13(1) and the PS Act s2(1).

36 IRAS, *IRAS e-Tax Guide Income Tax Treatment of Digital Tokens* (09.10.2020) 5.1.

37 *CLM v CLN and others* [2022] SGHC 46, at 10.

38 Ibid.; see also *B2C2 Ltd v Quoine Pte Ltd* [2019] SGHC(I) 03, at 1.

39 *Quoine Pte Ltd v B2C2 Ltd* [2020] SGCA(I) 02, at 1.

40 MAS, *Frequently Asked Questions on the Payment Services Act* (19Apr 2024) at 12.1.

41 MAS, Reply to Parliamentary Question on Crypto Asset Market, Question No 869 Notice Paper 348 of 2021 (*MAS* 5 Apr 2021) at 4, https://www.mas.gov.sg/news/parliamentary-replies/2021/reply-to-parliamentary-question-on-crypto-asset-market (accessed 5 May 2024); IRAS, *IRAS e-Tax Guide GST: Digital Payment Tokens* (*Second Edition*) (3 Aug 2022) 5.2.

42 The PS Act consolidates pre-existing legislation for payment services in a new Act with a wider regulatory scope. This pre-existing legislation is the Payment Systems (Oversight) Act, Cap 222A, 2007 Rev Ed, and the Money-changing and Remittance Businesses Act, Cap 187, 2008 Rev Ed.

risks, and anti-money laundering and combating the financing of terrorism (AML/CFT) risks.[43]

In addition, the PS Act seeks to promote and protect competition in the market for payment services. To that end, the PS Act gives MAS the authority to 'designate' a payment system if it impacts the operations of other payment systems and stifles competition.[44] Such a designation requires that 'the payment system may have an impact on the operations of one or more other payment systems in Singapore, and the designation is necessary to ensure efficiency or competitiveness in any of the services provided by the operator of the payment system.'[45] It allows MAS to restrict the operations of the dominant payment system or impose conditions on its operations.[46] In particular, it authorises MAS to force designated payment systems into compliance with common technical standards, thereby facilitating interoperability with other payment systems and forestalling discriminatory market practices.[47]

This pursues objectives that are similar to those envisaged under the EU Payment Services Directive[48] that orders EU Member States to ensure that 'payment institutions have access to credit institutions' payment accounts services on an objective, non-discriminatory and proportionate basis' and that the access shall be 'sufficiently extensive as to allow payment institutions to provide payment services in an unhindered and efficient manner.'[49]

The designation mechanism arguably serves to challenge the predominant role of banks in payment services, which stems from banks' unique authority to accept deposits. Among retail depositors, checking accounts serve as the primary conduit for cashless transactions. The EU regulations address this by granting alternative payment service providers access to customers' bank accounts, thereby facilitating the operational model of e-money issuers through seamless transfers between bank accounts and e-money storage

43 MAS, Explanatory Brief on the Payment Services Bill (*MAS*, 19 Nov 2018), https://www.mas.gov.sg/news/speeches/2018/explanatory-brief-on-the-payment-services-bill (accessed 5 May 2024).

44 Ong Ye Kung, "Payment Services Bill" (*MAS*, 14 Jan 2019) at 8 and 13, https://www.mas.gov.sg/news/speeches/2019/payment-services-bill (accessed 5 May 2024).

45 PS Act s42(1)(b). For other reasons see (a) and (c).

46 PS Act s44(3).

47 Ong Ye Kung, "Payment Services Bill" (*MAS*, 14 Jan 2019) at 29, https://www.mas.gov.sg/news/speeches/2019/payment-services-bill (accessed 5 May 2024).

48 Directive (EU) 2015/2366 of the European Parliament and of the Council of 25 November 2015 on payment services in the internal market, amending Directives 2002/65/EC, 2009/110/EC and 2013/36/EU and Regulation (EU) No 1093/2010, and repealing Directive 2007/64/EC [2015] OJ EU L 337/35.

49 Ibid., art 36.

facilities, like chip-enabled cards or smartphone applications. Although the designation mechanism does not explicitly target banks, its implications appear to be directed toward the banking sector because Singapore's payments infrastructure, much like Europe and other global regions, relies heavily on banks.

The core regulatory mechanism of the PS Act is the framework it provides for the licensing of payment service providers, which stipulates that any payment service provider must obtain a license from MAS prior to commencing operations. This enables MAS to dictate the standards that it expects of payment service providers and to exercise supervisory control over the activities of payment service providers.[50] Most licensed payment service providers hold either a Standard Payment Institution (SPI) licence or a Major Payment Institution (MPI) licence.[51] The criterion that distinguishes SPI and MPI licences is the volume of payment transactions. If the monthly average of the aggregated amount of all payment transactions exceeds SGD 3 million for one payment service or SGD 6 million for two of them, an MPI licence is mandatory.[52] An MPI licence is also required when the payment service provider issues e-money accounts[53] and large sums of e-money are stored in these accounts[54] or issued by the licensee[55] on a daily basis.

According to MAS, when reviewing licence applications, they place a strong emphasis on the quality of an applicant's leadership team and risk governance culture,[56] and assess an applicant's AML/CFT controls against stringent benchmarks.[57] This robust approach to issuing licences has drawn global attention,

50 Unless one of the narrow exemptions apply, see PS Act s5(1)(a),(b).

51 PS Act s6(4)(a)(VI). The PS Act also covers a third licence, the money changer licence which covers an entirely different area of financial services and is of no relevance for payment transactions. See for all three licences PS Act s6(2)(a)–(c).

52 PS Act s 6(5)(a)(II)(A) and (B). See also P. Yuen, 'Payment Systems' in D. Neo, H. Tjio and L. Luh Luh (eds), *Financial Services Law & Regulation*, (SAL Academy Publishing 2019).

53 A service provider engages in an 'emoney account issuance service' when 'each payment account issued stores emoney', PS Act s 6(17).

54 For the detailed list of criteria see PS Act s6(5)(b)(I) and (II) (A) or (B).

55 PS Act s6(5)(c)(I) and (II).

56 Factors recently highlighted in the licence review are: (i) formalised risk assessment of new products and technologies, (ii) customer due diligence for all transactions, (iii) ongoing monitoring of customer behaviour and risk profiles, (iv) compliance to value transfer rules and (v) technology risk management, see Ravi Menon, "MAS' Approach to the Crypto Ecosystem" (*MAS*, 27 Apr 2022) at 'MAS' Expectations of crypto service licensees', https://www.mas.gov.sg/news/speeches/2022/mas-approach-to-the-crypto-ecosystem (accessed 5 May 2024).

57 Ibid.

with Singapore becoming renowned for its 'vigorous licensing regime.'[58] As an example of how the licensing requirement has served to weed out errant market actors, the global crypto exchange 'Binance.com' was placed on the MAS Investor Alert List in September 2021, and prohibited from offering payment token services to Singapore residents.[59] In light of that development, 'Binance Asia Services Pte Ltd' (Binance's Singapore subsidiary) withdrew its application for a payment token service licence shortly thereafter, in December 2021.[60]

Holders of certain other licences are exempted from the licensing requirement under the PS Act, principally because these licences subject their holders to comparable or stricter regulatory requirements than PS Act licences, and it would therefore be redundant to impose a double licensing regime. Examples include commercial banks licensed under the Banking Act, merchant banks licensed as financial institutions under MAS Act, and finance companies licensed under the Finance Companies Act. Holders of a licence to issue credit or charge cards under the Banking Act are also exempted from the licensing requirement.[61] However, it is important to note that these exemptions only apply to the licensing requirement. All exempted financial intermediaries are still required to comply with the conduct of business obligations that apply to holders of PS Act licences.[62]

Although exempted entities are authorised to provide the services listed in the PS Act in addition to the services for which they are primarily licensed, the exact opposite applies to PS Act licence holders, who may only engage in the specific payment services for which they are licensed, and activities falling outside of this predefined scope are explicitly forbidden.[63] In so doing, the PS Act makes clear that holders of payment services licences are prohibited from conducting the transformation services that form the core of the traditional banking business. Since PS Act licence holders fulfil a distinct role and are subject to regulatory requirements that are substantially different from banks,

58 Douglas W. Arner et al., "The Financialization of Crypto: Lessons from FTX and the Crypto Winter of 2022–2023" (2023) University of Hong Kong Faculty of Law Research Paper No. 2023/19.

59 MAS, Investor Alert List, https://www.mas.gov.sg/investor-alert-list?q=&sort=date_dt%20desc&page=7 (accessed 5 May 2024).

60 The licence withdrawal was announced on 13.12.2021 and Binance.sg closed down its digital payment token services in Singapore on 13 Feb 2022, see under Binance Singapore, https://binancesingapore.zendesk.com/hc/en-us/articles/4416402912525-Announcement-to-all-Binance-sg-users (accessed 5 May 2024).

61 For the full list of exemptions see PS Act s13(1).

62 These obligations are found in PS Act ss15-19, 20(2), (4) and (5), 23, 24 and Part 2 Division 5.

63 PS Act s20(1). For the definition of lending see s20(5).

they are not allowed to collect money from the public to finance a wide range of financial services.[64] Instead, they are limited to accepting the funds needed to execute payment services for their customers.

Another important nuance about the PS Act is that it does not actually regulate the issuance or creation of digital payment tokens, but instead focuses on the activities and services that underpin the transfers of those tokens – such as furnishing 'gateways to the regulated financial system and nodes through which value may be moved'.[65] The PS Act is unique in only regulating cryptoassets when they are intended to be used as or are suitable for usage as means of payment – not only is there a potential regulatory lacuna with respect to the issuance of such tokens, but the PS Act also appears to view transfers of digital payment tokens as being the same type of regulated activity as conventional payments in fiat currency, even though they are in fact fundamentally different.

2.3 *Recent Developments*

MAS adopts a nimble and adaptive approach towards financial regulation, and this is reflected in how Singapore's regulatory policies on cryptoassets have evolved significantly since the PS Act was introduced. This section will highlight how this has occurred in three salient areas: first, the enactment of the FSMA which addresses gaps in the regulation of 'digital tokens'; second, the expansion of the regulatory scope of a digital payment token service under the PS Act; and third, the introduction of heightened consumer protection measures in light of significant volatility in cryptoasset markets during the 'crypto winter' of 2022.

2.3.1 Regulatory Gaps Filled by the FSMA

The FSMA, which was passed on 5 April 2022, was designed as an omnibus bill that aimed to achieve a broad spectrum of regulatory objectives. Its goals included the consolidation and harmonisation of regulatory requirements

64 Arguing in this direction, MAS, Explanatory Brief on the Payment Services Bill (*MAS*, 19 Nov 2018) at 12, https://www.mas.gov.sg/news/speeches/2018/explanatory-brief-on-the-payment-services-bill (accessed 5 May 2024).

65 Based on Singapore's explicit policy decision, see Ravi Menon, "Singapore FinTech: Innovation, Inclusion, Inspiration" (*MAS* 12 Nov 2018), https://www.mas.gov.sg/news/speeches/2018/singapore-fintech (accessed 5 May 2024); MAS, *Consultation Paper P021-2017 Proposed Payment Services Bill* (21 Nov 2017) 3.19.

throughout the entire financial sector to avoid regulatory arbitrage, and the enhancement of regulation of digital token services provided overseas.[66]

The FSMA has addressed an important regulatory lacuna where digital token service providers did not face significant supervisory oversight if they were based in Singapore but provided their services exclusively outside of Singapore.[67] Following the recommendations of the Financial Action Task Force (FATF),[68] MAS subjects digital token service providers based in Singapore to the licensing requirements under the newly introduced FSMA, even if they provide their services exclusively outside of Singapore.[69] Digital token services include payment tokens as defined in s2(1) of the PS Act, and securities tokens as defined in s2(1) of the SFA.[70]

Similar to the regulatory approach adopted by the PS Act, the requirement for digital token service providers to obtain a license is a key pillar of the FSMA.[71] Both Acts pursue similar objectives, such as supporting the growth and innovation of digital products and services while ensuring that money laundering and terrorism financing risks are adequately addressed,[72] and service providers therefore face comparable regulatory requirements under both Acts.[73]

It is worth noting that non-fungible tokens (NFTs)[74] and utility tokens are currently not included within the regulatory ambit of the FSMA (nor the

---

66 Alvin Tan, "Financial Services and Markets Bill" (*MAS*, 4 Apr 2022) at 3, https://www.mas.gov.sg/news/speeches/2022/financial-services-and-markets-bill-second-reading-speech-on-4-april-2022 (accessed 5 May 2024); MAS, Explanatory Brief for Financial Services and Markets Bill 2022 (*MAS*, 14 Feb 2022) at 3, https://www.mas.gov.sg/news/speeches/2022/explanatory-brief-for-financial-services-and-markets-bill-2022 (accessed 5 May 2024).

67 Alvin Tan, "Financial Services and Markets Bill" (*MAS*, 4 Apr 2022) at 20–21, https://www.mas.gov.sg/news/speeches/2022/financial-services-and-markets-bill-second-reading-speech-on-4-april-2022 (accessed 5 May 2024); MAS, Explanatory Brief for Financial Services and Markets Bill 2022 (*MAS*, 14.02.2022) at 9, https://www.mas.gov.sg/news/speeches/2022/explanatory-brief-for-financial-services-and-markets-bill-2022 (accessed 5 May 2024).

68 FATF, *International Standards on Combating Money Laundering and the Financing of Terrorism & Proliferation* (*The FATF Recommendations*) (Updated March 2022) p. 17 and p. 76.

69 FSM Act s136 et seqq.

70 FSM Act Part 9 Division 1.

71 FSM Act s137.

72 Alvin Tan, "Financial Services and Markets Bill" (*MAS*, 4 Apr 2022) at 3 and 8, https://www.mas.gov.sg/news/speeches/2022/financial-services-and-markets-bill-second-reading-speech-on-4-april-2022 (accessed 5 May 2024).

73 Ibid., at 23–4, MAS, Explanatory Brief for Financial Services and Markets Bill 2022 (*MAS*, 14 Feb 2022) at 11–2, https://www.mas.gov.sg/news/speeches/2022/explanatory-brief-for-financial-services-and-markets-bill-2022 (accessed 5 May 2024).

74 Defined by MAS as 'form of digital token, where each token has distinct and unique features that are verified and secured by blockchain technology. … NFTs can be used to

PS Act), since MAS presently does not regard NFTs as financial products.[75] However, if an NFT were to possess characteristics of regulated digital tokens (e.g. securities tokens), then compliance with the full slate of regulatory requirements (e.g. SFA rules) would be required.[76] Additionally, enhancements to the regulation of NFTs are on the horizon. For example, there are plans to include NFTs in the scope of the reporting duties under the Organisation for Economic Cooperation and Development's (OECD) prospective Crypto-Asset Reporting Framework (CARF).[77] CARF would very likely be applicable in Singapore because it is adapted from the Common Reporting Standards (CRS), which is an internationally agreed standard that Singapore has committed to implement in order to better combat tax evasion.[78] CARF aims to establish a similar reporting framework for transactions in digital assets, and it stands to reason that Singapore would probably subscribe to CARF in the same way that it has adopted CRS.[79]

Finally, the FSM (Amendment) Act, which was passed on 9 May 2023, also established the legislative framework for a new information platform: 'Collaborative Sharing of ML/FT Information & Cases' (COSMIC).[80] COSMIC, which was officially launched on 1 April 2024, is a trusted and secure digital platform for financial institutions to share about unusual activities involving their customers in order to detect and deter criminal activity.[81] The legislative amendments provide a legal framework that allows for the sharing of information in

represent any underlying asset, they have for now been mainly used to tokenise digital art and other collectibles', MAS, Reply to Parliamentary Question on Regulation of NFT Activities, Question No 1567 Notice Paper 963 of 2022 (*MAS*, 15 Feb 2022) at 1, https://www.mas.gov.sg/news/parliamentary-replies/2022/reply-to-parliamentary-question-on-regulation-of-nft-activities (accessed 5 May 2024).

75 Ibid., at 2.

76 Ibid., at 3.

77 OECD, *Crypto-Asset Reporting Framework and Amendments to the Common Reporting Standard* (10.10.2022) 11 and 48.

78 IRAS, 'CRS Overview and Latest Developments', https://www.iras.gov.sg/taxes/international-tax/common-reporting-standard-(crs)/crs-overview-and-latest-developments (accessed 5 May 2024).

79 OECD, *Crypto-Asset Reporting Framework and Amendments to the Common Reporting Standard* (10 Oct 2022) 3.

80 Alvin Tan, "Financial Services and Markets (Amendment) Bill" (MAS 9 May 2023) at 4, https://www.mas.gov.sg/news/speeches/2023/financial-services-and-markets-amendment-bill-2023 (accessed 5 May 2024).

81 Ibid., also see MAS, 'MAS Launches COSMIC Platform to Strengthen the Financial System's Defence Against Money Laundering and Terrorism Financing' (*MAS*, 1 Apr 2024), https://www.mas.gov.sg/news/media-releases/2024/mas-launches-cosmic-platform (accessed 5 May 2024).

a way that is appropriately safeguarded and does not infringe on the duties of confidentiality that financial institutions owe to their customers.[82]

2.3.2 Expansion of Scope of Digital Payment Token Service

The regulatory scope of the PS Act has evolved in response to rapidly evolving developments in the payments space. The PS (Amendment) Act, which came into force on 4 April 2024,[83] contains a variety of new provisions empowering MAS to impose measures on payment service providers in areas ranging from consumer protection to financial stability.[84] For example, a new section 21A(2) confers a broad authority upon MAS to impose any measures on digital payment token service providers that it deems necessary or expedient in the interest of the public (or section of the public), financial stability, or monetary policy efficacy.[85]

The most significant change introduced by the PS (Amendment) Act is the broadening of the scope of what constitutes a regulated digital payment token service. By expanding its regulatory perimeter to enhance its ability to regulate and supervise digital payment token service providers for AML/CFT risks, MAS appears to be aligning itself with international best practices on the regulation of cryptoassets, such as the FATF's updated guidance on mitigating AML/CFT risks in the cryptoasset sector.[86]

Prior to the amendments taking effect in April 2024, the provision of a digital payment token service comprised the activities of "dealing in digital payment tokens" and "facilitating the exchange of digital payment tokens,"[87] both of which implicitly required the service provider to come into possession of the digital payment tokens in question.[88]

---

82 Ibid., at 3 and 5.

83 MAS, 'MAS Expands Scope of Regulated Payment Services; Introduces User Protection Requirements for Digital Payment Token Service Providers' (*MAS*, 02Apr 2024), https://www.mas.gov.sg/news/media-releases/2024/mas-expands-scope-of-regulated-payment-services (accessed 5 May 2024).

84 These new powers will stem from s21A(1), (2) of the reformed PS Act, see MAS, Reply to Parliamentary Question on Crypto Asset Market, Question No 869 Notice Paper 348 of 2021 (*MAS* 5 Apr 2021) at 5, https://www.mas.gov.sg/news/parliamentary-replies/2021/reply-to-parliamentary-question-on-crypto-asset-market (accessed 5 May 2024).

85 PS (Amendment) Act s3.

86 FATF, 'Updated Guidance for a Risk-Based Approach to Virtual Assets and Virtual Asset Service Providers' (*FATF*, 28 Oct 2021), https://www.fatf-gafi.org/en/publications/Fatfrecommendations/Guidance-rba-virtual-assets-2021.html (accessed 5 May 2024).

87 PS Act, Part 3 of First Schedule.

88 PS Act First Schedule, Part 3; Ong Ye Kung, "Payment Services (Amendment) Bill" (*MAS*, 4 Jan 2021) at 7, https://www.mas.gov.sg/news/speeches/2021/payment-services-amendment-bill (accessed 5 May 2024).

However, 'possession' appears to be an inadequate yardstick, because digital tokens are inherently intangible[89] and consequently cannot be possessed.[90] Instead of 'possession', 'control' might be more suitable and legally accurate in the context of digital tokens, as it is a broader term that does not only connote physical possession of a tangible item.[91] To fall within the regulatory perimeter of the PS Act, it should now suffice for service providers to have some form of control over the digital tokens in question.

The recognition by MAS of the fact that possession is an inadequate term in the digital sphere also shows in the expansion of the regulatory scope of digital payment token services via the PS (Amendment) Act to also include 'service providers of [digital payment tokens (DPTs)] that facilitate the use of DPTs for payments, and may not possess the moneys or DPTs involved.'[92]

As part of this expansion, the regulatory scope of a digital payment token service now includes seven additional services, which aim to address the unique and heightened AML/CFT risks posed by cryptoassets.[93] Four of the new services pertain to custody activities, and these services leverage on the notion of 'control' raised earlier.[94] For example, the new services include "safeguarding a digital payment token, where the service provider has control over the digital payment token" and "any service of carrying out for a customer an instruction relating to a digital payment token, where the service provider has control over the digital payment token."[95]

However, two of the new services adopt an even broader approach towards determining the existence of a regulatory nexus by not even requiring a form of control, but instead regarding it sufficient that a service provider simply plays a facilitative role in the process of a digital payment token transaction. These are the services of "arranging (whether as principal or agent) for the transmission of digital payment tokens from one digital payment token account (whether in

89 UK Jurisdictional Taskforce, *Legal Statement on Cryptoassets and Smart Contracts* (November 2019) at 31.

90 Ibid., at 67; analysing the property aspect of cryptoassets in common law in detail: K. Low, 'Trusts of Cryptoassets' (2020) Trust Law International and Trusts and Private Wealth Management: Developments and Directions CUP https://papers.ssrn.com/sol3/papers.cfm?abstract_id=3749040 (accessed 5 May 2024).

91 UK Jurisdictional Taskforce, *Legal Statement on Cryptoassets and Smart Contracts* (November 2019) at 67.

92 Ong Ye Kung, "Payment Services (Amendment) Bill" (*MAS*, 04.01.2021) at 8, https://www.mas.gov.sg/news/speeches/2021/payment-services-amendment-bill (accessed 5 May 2024).

93 PS (Amendment) Act s7; MAS, Explanatory Brief for Payment Services (Amendment) Bill (*MAS*, 2 Nov 2020) at 3, https://www.mas.gov.sg/news/speeches/2020/explanatory-brief-for-payment-services-amendment-bill (accessed 5 May 2024).

94 PS (Amendment) Act s7(e).

95 Ibid.

Singapore or elsewhere) to another digital payment token account (whether in Singapore or elsewhere)" and "inducing or attempting to induce any person to enter into or to offer to enter into any agreement for or with a view to buying or selling any digital payment token in exchange for any money or any other digital payment token (whether of the same or a different type)."[96]

Only one of the new services appears to invoke the need for 'possession' to occur, and that is the service of "accepting (whether as principal or agent) digital payment tokens from one digital payment token account (whether in Singapore or elsewhere), for the purposes of transmitting, or arranging for the transmission of, the digital payment tokens to another digital payment token account (whether in Singapore or elsewhere)."[97] However, even though it has been established earlier that 'possession' may be an inadequate yardstick of whether a service provider is engaging in a regulated activity, it is important to view this activity within the broader context of the newly expanded list of digital payment token services. Only three of the nine activities make any reference to 'possession', with the remaining six only requiring 'control' or some form of facilitation (e.g. 'inducement'). Additionally, the activities are not mutually exclusive, in that a service provider may be caught for multiple activities simultaneously, such as by providing a custodial service (which only requires 'control') that also offers the service of transmitting digital payment tokens from one account to another. Considering this, it is arguable that the regulatory perimeter of a "digital payment token service" is now broad enough to nullify the deficiencies of using 'possession' as an indicium of whether an activity is caught for regulation.

In this context, it is instructive to refer to the guidance that MAS has provided in the FAQs on the PS Act.[98] The FAQs not only support the foregoing analysis that 'possession' is no longer of much importance for the new regulatory framework of digital payment token services, but also offer further clarification about how 'inducement' and 'control' might be defined.[99]

With respect to 'inducement', the FAQs state that a service provider would be engaging in the service of "inducing (...) any person to enter into (...) any agreement for or with a view to buying or selling any digital payment token in exchange for any money or any other digital payment token (...)" even if the service provider only acted as a "conduit through which a customer may enter into an agreement to buy or sell [digital payment tokens] in exchange for

---

96 Ibid.

97 Ibid.

98 MAS, *Frequently Asked Questions on the Payment Services Act* (19 Apr 2024).

99 Ibid., at 24.1 to 26.4.

money or any other [digital payment tokens]."[100] To illustrate how this interpretation might be applied in practice, the FAQs provide a case study which explains that 'inducement' would be made out if a service provider (Company X) offered an option on its mobile application interface for customers to utilise digital payment tokens to top up value in their e-wallet, even if the actual process of effecting the transfer of value (e.g. conversion of digital payment tokens to fiat currency) was undertaken by a separate service provider (Company Y) and Company X did not in fact come into 'possession' (and it could be added: or evident control) of any digital payment tokens during the course of the transaction.[101]

The FAQs also shed light on the meaning of 'control' in the context of custodial wallet services, by explaining that it would entail a service provider having the ability to manage "access" or "execute transactions" involving the digital payment tokens stored within its custodial wallets.[102] Importantly, such 'control' need not be "absolute or exclusive" and the span of 'control' would also extend to digital payment token instruments, such as by control over the "private cryptographic keys."[103]

2.3.3 Heightened Consumer Protection Measures

One of the first business conduct restrictions that MAS imposed on digital payment token service providers was the prohibition from targeting the public in Singapore with the promotion of their digital payment token services (e.g. advertisements), which was introduced in January 2022. However, such service providers were still permitted to use their corporate websites, mobile applications, and official social media accounts for these promotional activities, as long as they did so without trivialising the risks of trading in digital payment tokens.[104] This restriction meant that, in effect, digital payment token service providers were only allowed to promote themselves to prospective customers who had known of their existence and specifically sought their services.

Although this was an important first step, the events of the 'crypto winter' of 2022, such as the collapse of FTX, showed that bolder action was needed to protect consumers from the risks posed by malignant actors in the cryptoasset sector. It was therefore timely that MAS signalled its intention in October 2022 to introduce significantly enhanced business conduct and consumer

100 Ibid., at 25.2.
101 Ibid., at Case Study 2.
102 Ibid., at 26.1.
103 Ibid.
104 MAS, *Guidelines on Provision of Digital Payment Token Services to the Public* (17 Jan 2022) at 2.

access measures.[105] To this end, MAS engaged in a public consultation and subsequently published response papers in July 2023 and November 2023 to announce the finalised policy positions.[106] These measures, which will be explained below, are slated to take effect in stages from October 2024 and MAS released a first tranche of guidelines in April 2024 to provide additional clarity about how the measures should be implemented.[107]

The business conduct measures, which aim to ensure that customers of digital payment token service providers are treated "fairly and properly,"[108] introduce rigorous segregation and custody requirements.[109] Under these new measures, digital payment token service providers are required to segregate customers' assets from their own assets, and place those assets on trust for the benefit of their customers.[110] The intent of this measure is to facilitate the return of customers' assets in the event that the digital payment token service provider goes into insolvency.[111]

Digital payment token service providers are additionally required to maintain proper records and conduct daily reconciliation of customers' assets checks,[112] and implement robust risk management controls to protect customers' assets that include storing of at least 90% of customers' digital payment tokens in cold wallets.[113]

Digital payment token service providers would also need to establish an operationally independent custody function, to mitigate the risk of loss of customers' assets due to internal fraud.[114] Finally, digital payment token service providers would be prohibited from facilitating the lending or staking of retail

---

105 MAS, *Consultation Paper P008-2022, Consultation Paper on Proposed Regulatory Measures for Digital Payment Token Services* (26 Oct 2022).

106 MAS, *Response to Public Consultation on Proposed Regulatory Measures for Digital Payment Token Services (Part 1)* (3 Jul 2023); MAS, *Response to Public Consultation on Proposed Regulatory Measures for Digital Payment Token Services (Part 2)* (23 Nov 2023).

107 MAS, 'MAS Expands Scope of Regulated Payment Services; Introduces User Protection Requirements for Digital Payment Token Service Providers' (*MAS*, 2 Apr 2024), https://www.mas.gov.sg/news/media-releases/2024/mas-expands-scope-of-regulated-payment-services (accessed 5 May 2024); MAS, *Guidelines on Consumer Protection Measures by DPT Service Providers* (2 Apr 2024).

108 MAS, *Consultation Paper P008-2022, Proposed Regulatory Measures for Digital Payment Token Services* (28 Oct 2022) at 4.1.

109 Ibid., at 4.5 to 4.14.

110 MAS, *Response to Public Consultation on Proposed Regulatory Measures for Digital Payment Token Services (Part 1)* (3 Jul 2023) at 2.1 to 2.6.

111 Ibid.

112 Ibid., at 2.12 to 2.14.

113 Ibid., at 2.22 to 2.28.

114 Ibid., at 2.33 to 2.37.

customers' digital payment tokens, because of the high levels of risk inherent in these activities.[115]

In addition to the segregation and custody requirements mentioned above, digital payment service providers should establish an effective framework for resolving customer complaints[116] and mitigate potential conflicts of interest.[117] On the latter, the measures proposed by MAS are consistent with the proposals set out in the Final Report on Policy Recommendations for Crypto and Digital Asset Markets that the International Organisation of Securities Commissions (IOSCO) published in November 2023.[118] For example, as recommended by IOSCO, if a digital payment token service provider conducts a combination of activities that may give rise to a conflict of interest (e.g. operating a market while also acting as a broker), it should ensure that comprehensive functional segregation is established and transparent disclosures are provided to its customers.[119]

Measures introduced for the protection of retail customers aim predominantly at raising their awareness of the hazards of trading in cryptoassets and discouraging them from speculating on cryptoasset prices.[120] These measures include a requirement for digital payment token service providers to conduct a thorough assessment of whether prospective retail customers are fully cognisant of the risks involved in trading in cryptoassets, before onboarding them as customers.[121] Additionally, digital payment token service providers are prohibited from extending incentives (e.g. referral bonuses) to retail customers, so as not to inordinately impact a customer's decision-making calculus about whether to trade in cryptoassets.[122] MAS also restricts digital payment token service providers from accepting any payments for digital payment token services that may be financed by debt and supplying retail customers with access to leverage for the purposes of engaging in digital payment token transactions (e.g. margin trading).[123]

---

115 Ibid., at 3.8 to 3.15.

116 MAS, *Response to Public Consultation on Proposed Regulatory Measures for Digital Payment Token Services (Part 2)* (23 Nov 2023) at 3.27 to 3.28.

117 Ibid., at 3.7 to 3.14.

118 IOSCO, *Policy Recommendations for Crypto and Digital Asset Markets: Final Report* (16 Nov 2023).

119 MAS, *Response to Public Consultation on Proposed Regulatory Measures for Digital Payment Token Services (Part 2)* (23 Nov 2023) at 3.10.

120 Ibid., at 2.16 to 2.20 and 2.23 to 2.25.

121 Ibid., at 2.16 to 2.20.

122 Ibid., at 2.23 to 2.25.

123 Ibid., at 2.29 to 2.31.

3 Singapore's Case Law on Cryptoassets

Cryptoassets are increasingly becoming the subject of litigation in Singapore. The existing case law includes decisions examining (1) whether cryptoassets may be treated as property that may be held on trust and (2) whether stolen cryptoassets could be the subject of a proprietary injunction.

In landmark rulings, the Singapore International Commercial Court and the Court of Appeal applied common law principles of contract and property law to digital payment tokens in *B2C2 Ltd v Quoine Pte Ltd*[124] (*B2C2 v Quoine*) and *Quoine Pte Ltd v B2C2 Ltd* (*Quoine v B2C2*).[125]

B2C2 v Quoine, in particular, contributed considerably to the discussion about the legal characterisation and treatment of digital payment tokens by disentangling and defining the contractual relationships between the various parties and intermediaries involved in trades of such tokens. The Singapore International Commercial Court grouped the contractual relationships between currency exchange platforms and traders (whether buyers or sellers) of digital payment tokens into three categories: platform contracts, margin contracts, and trading contracts.[126] According to the Court, platform contracts exist between currency exchange platforms and their users, and govern the use of the platforms' services.[127] Margin contracts for lending relationships constitute a separate group of contracts agreed between borrowers and lenders when margin traders participate in the token trades.[128] Finally, trading contracts were held to exist directly between the counterparties of the executed trades (namely the sellers and buyers of the digital payment tokens),[129] with the rights of the counterparties *inter se* determined by the platform's terms and conditions.[130]

On the issue of whether conventional property rights could be applied to digital payment tokens, the Court provided valuable guidance by applying the classic definition of a property right (as set out in *National Provincial Bank Ltd*

124 *B2C2 Ltd v Quoine Pte Ltd* [2019] SGHC(I) 03.

125 *Quoine Pte Ltd v B2C2 Ltd* [2020] SGCA(I) 02.

126 *B2C2 Ltd v Quoine Pte Ltd* [2019] SGHC(I) 03, at 126.

127 *Quoine Pte Ltd v B2C2 Ltd* [2020] SGCA(I) 02, at 50.

128 The lender of the margin contract is financing the transactions of the margin trader and becomes the direct counterpart in case of trade execution, *B2C2 Ltd v Quoine Pte Ltd* [2019] SGHC(I) 03, at 126.

129 Ibid.

130 Ibid., at 131.

v Ainsworth)[131] to digital payment tokens – ultimately affirming their property status as well as the subsequent creation of a trust between the parties.[132]

However, it is important to note that while both decisions (*B2C2 v Quoine* and *Quoine v B2C2*) affirmed the treatment of digital payment tokens as property in a general sense, they did not elaborate further on the specifics of this property right. Additionally, although the Singapore International Commercial Court had affirmed the creation of a trust between the parties, the Court of Appeal reversed that judgment, holding that at least one condition for the creation of a trust had not been fulfilled. The Court of Appeal applied the yardstick established in *Vintage Bullion DMCC v Chay Fook Yuen*[133] for the affirmation of the certainty of intention to create a trust and ruled that no express trust arose to that effect.[134] The Court of Appeal argued that the practised segregation of customer and company accounts constituted a necessary but insufficient condition for establishing intention to create a trust.[135] In particular, the Court highlighted that the amount of digital payment tokens in the cold wallet did not necessarily match the customer account balances as reflected in Quoine's databases, which meant that the arrangement in question corresponded more with the model of deposits in a bank account and did not evince the strict segregation required to establish that the digital payment tokens were being held on trust.[136]

B2C2 v Quoine and *Quoine v B2C2* were followed by *CLM v CLN and others*,[137] in which the High Court considered whether stolen cryptocurrency assets "were capable of giving rise to proprietary rights which could be protected via a proprietary injunction."[138] The Court ultimately decided in the affirmative

---

131 Conditions property right: (i) definable, (ii) identifiable by third parties, (iii) capable of assumption by third parties, (iv) some degree of permanence or stability, *see National Provincial Bank Ltd v Ainsworth* [1965] UKHL1, at 1248. However, the court did not assess the conditions individually since the question of property was not disputed, *B2C2 Ltd v Quoine Pte Ltd* [2019] SGHC(I) 03, at 142.

132 Conditions for the creation of a trust: (i) certainty of intention, (ii) certainty of subject matter, (iii) certainty of objects, see *B2C2 Ltd v Quoine Pte Ltd* [2019] SGHC(I) 03, at 141.

133 *Vintage Bullion DMCC* (*in its own capacity and as representative of the customers of MF Global Singapore Pte Ltd* (*in creditors' voluntary liquidation*)) *v Chay Fook Yuen* (*in his capacity as joint and several liquidator of MF Global Singapore Pte Ltd* (*in creditors' voluntary liquidation*)) *and others and other appeals* [2016] SGCA49, at 61.

134 *Quoine Pte Ltd v B2C2 Ltd* [2020] SGCA(I) 02, at 145–49.

135 Ibid., at 145.

136 Ibid., at 147.

137 *CLM v CLN and others* [2022] SGHC 46.

138 Ibid., at 40.

and granted the proprietary injunction,[139] although the judgment did not offer further clarity on the precise property status of digital payment tokens. However, in examining how the *Ainsworth* requirements would successfully apply to such tokens, it helpfully characterised them as follows: (i) definable computer-readable strings of characters, (ii) identifiable by third parties through the allocation of a private key to the owner by a computer software, (iii) capable of assumption by third parties through vivid activity at trading markets, and (iv) having some degree of stability through being recorded on the blockchain.[140]

Not long after *CLM v CLN and others* was decided, the High Court addressed similar issues in *Janesh s/o Rajkumar v Unknown Person* (*CHEFPIERRE*),[141] where it ruled that the 'Bored Ape Yacht Club' NFT could be the subject of a proprietary injunction.[142] The procedural aspects of that case were remarkable in the extent to which they reflected the unique context of the case: the Court allowed for the court papers to be delivered digitally through the messaging function of the defendant's cryptoasset wallet address as well as the digital platforms Twitter and Discord.[143]

Perhaps the most recent milestone case was *ByBit Fintech Ltd v Ho Kai Xin*,[144] which concerned the question of whether cryptoassets were "property capable of being held on trust and, if so, what type of property they are."[145] The cryptoasset at issue was the USDT stablecoin. Significantly, the High Court found that the stablecoin constituted a 'chose in action' and was capable of being held on trust – specifically, a constructive trust.[146]

It seems clear from the case law thus far that cryptoassets (including NFTs)[147] are recognised as being a form of property. Cryptoassets would therefore be capable of being held on trust and the subject of proprietary injunctions, although the exact contours of the property rights and remedies attached to cryptoassets are still being refined. This is particularly salient for

---

139 Ibid., at 46.

140 Ibid., at 45.

141 *Janesh s/o Rajkumar v Unknown Person* (*"CHEFPIERRE"*) [2022] SGHC 264.

142 Ibid., at 81.

143 Ibid., at 25.

144 *ByBit Fintech Ltd v Ho Kai Xin and others* [2023] SGHC 199.

145 Ibid., at 3.

146 Ibid., at 29 to 39 and 42 to 44.

147 On this, see e.g. Kelvin FK Low, "The Emperor's New Art: Cryptomania, Art & Property" (2022) 86 CPLJ 378; Juliet M Moringiello & Christopher K Odinet, "The Property Law of Tokens" (2022) 74 Fla L Rev 607; A. Zaid Hamzah, "Recognising Cryptocurrencies as Property?" (2022) Sing JLS 474 at 477.

holders of NFTs, because they will have to rely on the common law for protection of their ownership rights in the absence of a formal regulatory framework targeted at NFTs. It will be important to pay close attention to the evolution of the common law in this space, and it seems likely that courts in Singapore will continue to make meaningful strides towards developing the jurisprudence surrounding the proprietary nature of cryptoassets.

4 Looking Forward

Developing a regulatory framework for stablecoins is likely to be a core pillar of MAS' evolving approach towards the regulation of cryptoassets, due to the unique regulatory challenges posed by stablecoins and their foundational role in the cryptoasset ecosystem.[148] Retail investors may perceive stablecoins as being safer than cryptocurrencies that do not possess value-stabilising mechanisms, but regulators must ensure that stablecoins are indeed deserving of the higher levels of trust that retail investors vest in them.

The absence of regulatory oversight of stablecoins could be problematic because retail investors may not understand the technological and financial nuances underpinning stablecoins, such as the fact that algorithmic stablecoins are not actually backed by reserve assets, making them especially vulnerable to risks. The TerraUSD crash in May 2022 serves as a stark example of this.[149] In addition to harming large swathes of retail customers, contagion from the crash led to significant repercussions in the broader crypto ecosystem, as exposure to TerraUSD was a contributory factor in the bankruptcies of major cryptoasset players such as Three Arrows Capital and Celsius Network.[150]

Furthermore, even reserve-backed stablecoins do not offer a panacea – some stablecoins are purportedly backed by sound asset reserves, but a regulatory

---

148 In detail on regulatory considerations for stablecoins, Financial Stability Board (FSB), 'Regulation, Supervision and Oversight of "Global Stablecoin" Arrangements - Final Report and High-Level Recommendations' (last modified October 2020), online (pdf): *FSB* https://www.fsb.org/wp-content/uploads/P131020-3.pdf; European Central Bank (ECB), Stablecoins' role in crypto and beyond: functions, risks and policy (last visited 17 May 2023), online: *ECB* https://www.ecb.europa.eu/pub/financial-stability/macroprudential-bulletin/html/ecb.mpbu202207_2~836f682ed7.en.html; International Organisation of Securities Commissions and Bank for International Settlements' Committee on Payments and Market Infrastructures, Application of the Principles for Financial Market Infrastructures to stablecoin arrangements (last modified July 2022), online (pdf): *BIS* https://www.bis.org/cpmi/publ/d206.pdf.

149 Ibid., at 82 [Box A].

150 Ibid., at 81–2.

lacuna surrounding stablecoins (in particular, inadequate disclosure rules and lack of mandatory audits) could engender significant information asymmetries between stablecoin providers and consumers. Some unscrupulous stablecoin providers may exploit such opportunities to represent their stablecoins as being fully collateralised by safe reserve assets, when in fact they have eroded their collateral by tapping into it for inordinately risky commercial purposes (e.g. lending to third parties).[151] However, if consumer confidence is shaken by an exogenous shock, the lack of transparency about the quality of collateral could instigate a vicious cycle, where consumers assume the worst and a run on the stablecoin ensues. En masse redemptions would almost certainly devastate stablecoin providers who have exposed their supposedly risk-free liquid collateral to excessive amounts of third-party solvency and liquidity risk. In the absence of adequate collateral, redemption at par would no longer be possible, and it is highly likely that secondary market trading would also break down completely.[152]

Ultimately, as the popularity of stablecoins mounts, regulators must ensure that they are held to standards that adequately reflect the risks to which they expose retail investors. Mandatory disclosure to investors and markets, supervisory oversight from a competent financial authority, and a robust regime that holds natural and legal persons responsible in the event of intentional and negligent misconduct are elements that appear necessary in the interest of investor protection and market integrity. Moreover, the asset reserves from which stablecoin schemes derive their claims of price stability must be stringently regulated. Managers of those reserves must inform the competent authorities, token holders, and future investors about the general principles that govern their administration of the reserves; and any unforeseen incidents, liquidity issues, or value write-downs must be immediately disclosed.[153] Some regulators are additionally planning to subject asset-backed stablecoins to minimum capitalisation requirements, and this should be welcomed.[154]

---

151 D. Arner, R. Auer and J. Frost, 'Stablecoins: risks, potential and regulation' (2020) *BIS Working Papers* No 905, 15, https://www.bis.org/publ/work905.pdf (accessed 5 May 2024).

152 These theoretical risks are reflected in central banks' statements on central bank digital currency (CBDC) projects, see A. N. Didenko et al., 'After Libra, Digital Yuan, and COVID-19: Central Bank Digital Currencies and the New World of Money and Payment Systems' [2020] UNSWLRP No. 20/59, 28; Bank of Canada et al., 'Central bank digital currencies: foundational principles and core features' (2020) Bank for International Settlements Report no 1 in a series of collaborations from a group of central banks) at para 2.3.2.

153 Some of these proposals and several more requirements are reflected in the European Union's Markets in Crypto-Assets Regulation (MICA-R) proposal, art 32.

154 Ibid., art 31.

MAS is at the forefront of global regulatory thinking on stablecoins, and first communicated its readiness to enhance regulatory oversight of stablecoins via a public consultation in October 2022.[155] Following a rigorous assessment of the feedback received from the consultation, MAS published its finalised policy positions in August 2023.[156] Although the details of the regime are still being developed, it is clear from publicly available materials that MAS envisions a twofold regime where stablecoins that fall within the regulatory perimeter of the new framework would receive the label of an "MAS-Regulated Stablecoin" upon fulfilling all stipulated requirements, while all other stablecoins would remain regulated as digital payment tokens.[157]

The central pillars of MAS' proposed stablecoin regulatory framework are: (1) value stability, (2) capital standards, (3) redemption at par, and (4) transparent disclosure.[158] To protect value stability and mitigate the risks of a run, MAS will subject reserve assets to requirements with respect to composition, valuation, custody, and audit.[159] Capital standards refer to a buffer of minimum base capital and liquid assets that stablecoin issuers must hold to "enable an orderly wind-down of business if necessary."[160] Redemption at par means that stablecoin issuers must honour all requests for redemption at par value within five business days – this is crucial to ensuring that the stablecoin will also trade at par in secondary markets.[161] Finally, transparent disclosure entails publishing complete and timely information about the key aspects of the stablecoin arrangement, such as the value-stabilising mechanism and audits of the reserve assets.[162]

The scope of MAS' proposed regulatory framework would include all single-currency stablecoins issued out of Singapore that are pegged to the Singapore Dollar or any G10 currency, and MAS hopes that this framework will

---

155 MAS, *Consultation Paper P009-2022, Consultation Paper on Proposed Regulatory Approach for Stablecoin-related Activities* (26.10.2022); MAS, 'MAS Finalises Stablecoin Regulatory Framework' (*MAS*, 15.08.2023), https://www.mas.gov.sg/news/media-releases/2023/mas-finalises-stablecoin-regulatory-framework (accessed 5 May 2024).

156 MAS, *Response to Public Consultation on Proposed Regulatory Approach for Stablecoin-related Activities* (15.08.2023).

157 Ibid., at 2.18.

158 MAS, 'MAS Finalises Stablecoin Regulatory Framework' (*MAS*, 15.08.2023), https://www.mas.gov.sg/news/media-releases/2023/mas-finalises-stablecoin-regulatory-framework (accessed 5 May 2024).

159 Ibid., at 3.

160 Ibid.

161 Ibid.

162 Ibid.

"facilitate the use of stablecoins as a credible digital medium of exchange, and as a bridge between the fiat and digital asset ecosystems".[163]

5 Conclusion

Singapore has adopted a measured approach towards addressing the risks posed by cryptoassets. It strives to protect retail customers while also seeking to promote innovation, and does so by implementing a robust licensing regime that targets specific risks (e.g. AML/CFT) in a calibrated manner without creating an unduly onerous regulatory burden. In response to the events of the 'crypto winter' of 2022, not least the collapse of FTX, MAS expanded its regulatory perimeter and enhanced consumer protection by introducing a range of new business conduct and consumer access measures.

Recent case law has placed a spotlight on the proprietary nature of cryptoassets and it will be instructive to observe how the jurisprudence will continue to develop. In the years ahead, it will also be essential to pay attention to further regulatory guidance from MAS, particularly in emerging areas such as stablecoin regulation, because MAS' approach towards cryptoasset regulation will keep evolving to adapt to new challenges posed by cryptoassets. Finally, it is important to note that MAS is an active participant at multilateral fora where best practices on cryptoasset regulation are discussed, and consequently its policies are aligned with international standards and norms.

163 Ibid., at 3 and 5.

South Korea

Changmin Chun, Sung Yun Kang, Seung Jae (SJ) Yoo and Joon-Young Kim

1 Overview

The Act on Reporting and Use of Certain Financial Transaction Information (the "AML Act"), which was amended and took effect as of 25 March 2021, was the only Korean statutory regulation which is designed to regulate virtual assets, including cryptocurrencies until the Act for Protection of Virtual Asset Users (the "Virtual Asset User Protection Act") was passed by the National Assembly and enacted on 18 July 2023. The Virtual Asset User Protection Act, which is designed to regulate the virtual asset service industry from consumer/investor protection perspectives, is scheduled to take effect from 19 July 2024. Before the AML Act took effect, the Korean regulators had taken a number of different measures to directly or indirectly regulate cryptocurrency related businesses and activities. There have been active discussions among Korean regulators as to how newly emerging virtual assets and virtual asset related businesses and services may be regulated on the basis that certain existing legal regimes, such as the Financial Investment Services and Capital Markets Act (the "FSCMA") and the Foreign Exchange Transaction Law (the "FETL") may apply depending on specific nature and type of individual virtual asset or business or service involving virtual asset. In addition, there have been ongoing discussions on how to regulate virtual assets under the general legal regimes, such as civil laws, criminal laws and tax laws.

Accordingly, in order to understand how virtual assets are regulated under the Korean legal regimes, it is important to understand how conventional regulatory frameworks, in addition to the AML Act and the Virtual Asset User Protection Act, may apply depending on how a particular virtual asset may legally be classified (*see more details in Chapter 2*). In this Chapter 1, we discuss (i) a brief history of regulatory environments of virtual assets in Korea, (ii) certain Korean laws and regulations commonly used for analyzing issues involving virtual assets and governmental authorities supervising virtual assets and virtual asset related businesses, (iii) how virtual assets are defined or classified under applicable Korean laws (including the AML Act) and (iv) how virtual assets and virtual asset related businesses are regulated under the current regulatory regimes in Korea through certain precedents and examples.

 | DOI:10.1163/9789004722507_024

2 History of Legal and Regulatory Environment

Fully-fledged studies and researches on cryptocurrencies were first started in Korea in early 2013 when the Bank of Korea issued a report[1] on Bitcoin.

Discussions on institutionalization of cryptocurrency in Korea began at the end of 2016, led by the Financial Services Commission (the "FSC"), which is in charge of financial policies in Korea. On 24 October 2016, the FSC announced that it would pursue the institutionalization of digital currencies based on the trend of such institutionalization in other jurisdictions such as the U.S. and Japan.[2] On 17 November 2016, the FSC, the Financial Supervisory Service (the "FSS"), and the Bank of Korea formed a task force team (the "Cryptocurrency TFT") to review digital currency-related issues.[3]

In 2017, however, trading price of cryptocurrencies, especially that of Bitcoin and Ether, fluctuated significantly and, as a result, speculative investments in cryptocurrencies and drastic increase in cross-border capital movements arising out of price arbitrage of cryptocurrencies between Korea and other jurisdictions (which is also known as "*kimchi premium*")[4] became social issues in Korea, which led the Korean regulators to shift their speed and direction of regulating cryptocurrencies.

In order to prevent illegal activities involving cryptocurrency, the Cryptocurrency TFT was expanded by adding the National Tax Service, the Korea Fair Trade Commission (the "KFTC") and the Prosecutors' Office as new members to the task force.[5] At the Cryptocurrency TFT meeting held on 1 September 2017, the Korean government decided to take action against cryptocurrency related activities based on its determination that while cryptocurrencies may not be considered as fiat currencies or financial products, they may negatively affect the financial system.[6]

---

1 D.G. Lee, 'Current Status and Implications of Bitcoin (in Korean)' [2013] 2013-2 *Payment and Settlement Survey of Bank of Korea* http://www.bok.or.kr/portal/bbs/B0000232/view.do?ntId=195888&menuNo=200706.

2 FSC, 'Announcement of Basic Direction of 2nd Phase of the Fintech Development Roadmap (in Korean),' *FSC Press Release*, 24.10.2016. https://www.fsc.go.kr/no010101/72407.

3 FSC, 'First Conference on T/F for Digital Currency Institutionalization (in Korean),' *FSC Press Release*, 17.11.2016. https://www.fsc.go.kr/no010101/72440.

4 W.R. Kim, 'Bitcoin and Ether, Why 'Premium' Occurred. ... Understanding the Arbitrage Transaction (in Korean),' *Etoday*, 31.05.2017. https://www.etoday.co.kr/news/view/1497653.

5 Ministry of Science and ICT, 'Virtual Asset Transaction Management Plan (in Korean),' *Joint Press Release by Relevant Ministries*, 28.05.2021. https://www.korea.kr/news/pressReleaseView.do?newsId=156454245.

6 FSC, 'Holding of the "Joint TF by Virtual Currency-Related Agencies" Current Status of Virtual Currency and Countermeasures (in Korean),' *FSC Press Release*, 04.09.2017. https://www.fsc.go.kr/no010101/72809.

According to media reports, the price of Bitcoin plunged by about 40% from KRW 24.99 million on 8 December 2017 to KRW 13.91 million on 10 December 2017.[7] Shortly thereafter, on 13 December 2017, the Korean government announced emergency measures regarding cryptocurrency.[8] In the absence of any laws or regulations in Korea which are designed to directly regulate cryptocurrency, such government measures were intended to indirectly regulate cryptocurrency by regulating licensed financial institutions. The cryptocurrency market in Korea had experienced a cooling-off period.

With the support from G20, the FATF amended Recommendation 15 in October 2018 to newly add the definition of "virtual asset" and "virtual asset service provider" and issued Interpretive Note to Recommendation 15 and Guidance for a Risk-Based Approach for Virtual Assets and Virtual Asset Service Providers.[9]

In order to reflect such international standards for anti-money laundering and anti-terrorism financing ("AML/CFT") in Korean laws, the AML Act, which stipulates certain AML/CFT related requirements of, among others, financial companies, was amended on 24 March 2020 and such amended AML Act took effect on 25 March 2021.[10]

2.1 *Main Laws and Regulations Applicable to Virtual Assets*

While the aforementioned amendment to the AML Act and the Virtual Asset User Protection Act is explicitly designed to regulate virtual assets and virtual asset related services and businesses, certain requirements and restrictions under the FSCMA and the FETL may be applicable to such topics depending on characteristics and nature of virtual assets.

The FSCMA may apply to virtual assets which are deemed "security-type tokens" and any sale thereof as well as services and businesses involving virtual assets similar to those, which the FSCMA is intended to regulate, such as margin trading and derivative instruments (*see Section 1.5.2 below for more details*).

7 Korea Herald Business, 'Controversy over Fraud due to Price Crash…Bitcoin (in Korean),' *Korea Herald Business*, 11.12.2017. http://news.heraldcorp.com/view.php?ud=20171211000043.

8 Office for Government Policy Coordination, Prime Minister's Secretariat, 'Emergency Meeting on Virtual Currency (in Korean),' *Joint Press Release by Relevant Ministries*, 13.12.2017. https://www.korea.kr/news/pressReleaseView.do?newsId=156243146.

9 FATF, Guidance for a Risk-Based Approach to Virtual Assets and Virtual Asset Service Providers [2019] https://www.fatf-gafi.org/media/fatf/documents/recommendations/RBA-VA-VASPs.pdf.

10 Bill Information of National Assembly, 'Proposed Partial Amendment to the Act on Reporting and Using Specified Financial Transaction Information (No. 2024776) (in Korean)' [2020] https://likms.assembly.go.kr/bill/billDetail.do?billId=PRC_S1W9V1R1K2Y5J1A5K3V1Z0L4X1H3W9.

In particular, in case a virtual asset is considered as a "investment contract security" under the FSCMA, which is similar to "investment contract" under the "Howey test" in the U.S., certain requirements and restrictions for public offering of securities under the FSCMA may apply. The Korean government, in its announcement on 3 May 2023, revealed its plan to regulate "security-type tokens" based on the FSCMA. The FSC announced a guideline on the issuance and distribution of certain types of security-type tokens. Under this guideline, certain existing laws and regulations would be amended so that the token security in the form of electronic securities based on distributed ledger technology may be issued and distributed. Certain legal systems would also be newly established for, among other things, managing token security issuers' accounts and over-the-counter brokerage service providers. As a result, certain proposed amendments to the FSCMA and the Act on Electronic Registration of Stocks and Bonds, etc. (the "ESA") for the above purpose are currently pending at the National Assembly.

Similar to some other jurisdictions, such as China, Korea has stringent foreign exchange rules and regulations (including the FETL). Accordingly, to the extent any virtual asset transaction is consummated on a cross-border basis, the FETL may apply. In particular, in the case of "stablecoins" (especially, those which grant a right to collect certain fiat currency), such stablecoins may be regarded as foreign exchange which is regulated under the FETL.

In addition to the FSCMA and the FETL, certain general laws such as civil laws, criminal laws and tax laws may apply to virtual assets and virtual assets involved businesses and services.

2.2 *Regulatory Authorities Supervising Virtual Assets*

Currently, the following government agencies have direct supervisory authorities over virtual assets: (i) the FSC, which is in charge of setting policies on virtual assets, (ii) the Korean Financial Intelligence Unit (the "KoFIU") of the FSC, which is in charge of reviewing reports filed by virtual asset service providers (the "VASPs") and supervising matters relating to AML/CFT involving virtual assets and (iii) the FSS, which is delegated with authority to review the VASP application. In addition, to the extent any virtual asset involved transaction is considered to involve cross-border foreign exchange transactions for the purpose of the FETL, the Ministry of Economy and Finance and/or the Bank of Korea may supervise matters relating to such transactions. Depending on type and nature of issues involving virtual assets, the KFTC (overseeing matters relating to, among others, advertisements and standard contractual terms and conditions to/for consumers), the Ministry of Science and ICT (overseeing blockchain related policies), the Ministry of Economy and Finance and the National Tax Service (overseeing tax matters) and the Prosecutors' Offices and police departments (overseeing criminal matters) may act as supervisory authorities in regards to virtual asset related matters.

3 Virtual Asset Classification and Definition

3.1 *Virtual Asset Classification*

There is no statute or guidance from the Korean regulatory authorities that provides a coherent insight on how virtual assets would be classified under Korean law, other than the definition of virtual asset under the AML Act or the Virtual Asset User Protection Act.

The FSS issued a press release on 23 June 2017 where it announced its views on what cryptocurrencies would "not" be classified from financial regulatory perspectives.[11] Namely, the FSS's position was that cryptocurrencies would not be classified as: (i) fiat currencies; (ii) prepaid electronic means or electronic currencies under the Electronic Financial Transactions Act (the "EFTA"); or (iii) financial investment instruments under the FSCMA. Unfortunately, the FSS's such press release did not provide clear guidance on how cryptocurrencies may be classified. Subsequently, the FSS took the position that it would be difficult to generalize the classification of cryptocurrency as each cryptocurrency has its own unique nature and characteristics and, depending on details, such each cryptocurrency may be classified as financial investment products regulated under the FSCMA or prepaid electronic means regulated under the EFTA. However, the Korean financial regulators are understood to have a position that certain cryptocurrencies such as Bitcoin and Ether may not be classified as financial investment products under the FSCMA or prepaid electronic means under the EFTA.

As "legal tender" is defined as "the Bank of Korea notes and coins issued by the Bank of Korea" under the Bank of Korea Act, it is clear that cryptocurrency may not be regarded as legal tender under the Bank of Korea Act and such interpretation has been confirmed by the Korean financial and foreign exchange regulators through their public announcements[12] while whether any

---

11 FSS, 'Matters to be Noted for Virtual Currency Investment (in Korean),' *FSS Press Release*, 23.06.2017. https://www.fss.or.kr/fss/bbs/B0000188/view.do?nttId=13497&menuNo=200218.

12 FSC, 'Holding of the "Joint TF by Virtual Currency-Related Agencies" - Current Status of Virtual Currency and Countermeasures (in Korean),' *FSC Press Release*, 04.09.2017. https://www.fsc.go.kr/no010101/72809; FSC, 'Government's position on virtual currency (in Korean),' *FSC Press Release*, 15.01.2018. https://www.fsc.go.kr/no010101/72983; FSC,

central bank digital currency ("CBDC") may be classified as legal tender would be a separate issue.

Currently, depending on how a cryptocurrency is characterised and treated, different set(s) of Korean laws and regulations would apply. For example, to the extent such cryptocurrencies are treated as "securities" (as defined under the FSCMA), they would be subject to the FSCMA. If the cryptocurrencies are considered as "virtual assets" (as defined under the AML Act), they would be subject to the AML Act and the Virtual Asset User Protection Act. Once the Virtual Asset User Protection Act takes effect, however, the AML Act will be amended, so that the definitions of "virtual assets" and "virtual asset service providers" (VASPs) under the AML Act follow the definitions under the Virtual Asset User Protection Act.

Cryptocurrencies that fall under the definition of electronic currency or prepaid electronic payment means (PEPM) under the EFTA would be subject to the EFTA, which is intended to regulate electronic payments and settlements.

3.2 *Definition of Virtual Asset under the AML Act*

Before the amended AML Act took effect on 25 March 2021, there was no specific legal definition of "cryptocurrency" or "virtual asset" in Korea. Under the AML Act, a "virtual asset" is defined as "an electronic representation with economic value that is tradable or transferrable electronically (including any rights thereto)" which excludes the following:

(a) token or information about a token that may not be exchanged by monies, commodities, or goods and services and the use and place of which has been restricted by the issuer;
(b) tangible and intangible items acquired through game products as provided under Article 32(1)(7) of the Gaming Industry Promotion Act (the "GIPA");
(c) electronic prepaid means and electronic currency under Article 2(15) and Article 2(5), respectively, of the EFTA;
(d) electronically registered stock, etc. (Electronic Security), under Article 2(4) of the Act on the ESA;
(e) electronic bills under Article 2(2) of the Issuance and Distribution of Electronic Bills Act;
(f) electronic bills of ladings under Article 862 of the Commercial Act;
(g) electronic bond under Article 2(16) of the EFTA;

'Results of meetings with relevant ministries on virtual currency (in Korean),' *FSC Press Release*, 28.05.2019. https://www.fsc.go.kr/no010101/73709.

(h) gift certificates stored and used on mobile devices such as mobile phones in which the issuer sets the amount of money or the quantity of usable goods; or
(i) other items that are equivalent to those specified in Article 1 and Article 2 of the Presidential Decree of the AML Act that the commissioner of the KoFIU announces to be excluded as a virtual asset in consideration of the type and characteristics of the transaction (none have yet been announced).

The Virtual Asset User Protection Act defines "virtual asset" (excluding CBDC) and "VASP" substantially the same way as they are defined under the AML Act.

4 Issues Involving Usage of Virtual Assets or Services Involving Virtual Assets

4.1 *Service Providers Regulated under the AML Act*

Currently, the AML Act regulates "virtual asset service providers," which generally include cryptocurrency exchanges, cryptocurrency wallet providers and custodians as well as other cryptocurrency intermediaries (*see Section 5.1 for more details for definition of "virtual asset service provider" under the AML Act*). While the AML Act defines "virtual asset service provider" quite broadly, the financial regulators, in practice, have regulated and supervised cryptocurrency exchange, cryptocurrency wallet service providers and cryptocurrency custody service providers only.

Accordingly, certain participants in cryptocurrency and blockchain markets such as programmers and coders associated with the blockchain protocol, cryptocurrency miners and issuers, holders and investors of cryptocurrency have not been regulated under the AML Act to date in practice (while certain general laws such as criminal laws, civil laws and tax laws and, depending on nature and type of virtual assets or actions associated therewith, the FSCMA and the FETL may apply). However, please note that the Korean financial regulators have recently shown some tendencies to more broadly apply the definition of "virtual asset service provider." (*see Section 5.1.2 for more details*).

4.2 *Financial Transactions Involving Virtual Assets*

4.2.1 Cryptocurrency Derivatives

Under the FSCMA, a person engaging in the business of trading, dealing and/or brokering "derivatives" is required to obtain a relevant license from the FSC.

The legal question is whether cryptocurrency may be considered an "underlying asset" for the purpose of the definition of "derivative" under the FSCMA. In response to a local securities company's query as to whether it would be permitted to conduct marketing activities in respect of Bitcoin futures products based on their financial investment business license, the Korean financial regulators have shared their unofficial views to the effect that Bitcoin futures may not be considered as "derivative" under the FSCMA as Bitcoin would not fall under any of the above categories of "underlying assets." However, we believe the financial regulators had expressed such views, which was made over Bitcoin futures only, mainly to discourage such local securities company from engaging in any activities involving cryptocurrency without having sufficiently considered any implications thereof under the FSCMA. Based on applicable regulations (including the FSCMA) and the regulators' interpretative rulings thereof, the financial regulators appear to have shown tendency to broadly define "underlying assets" for the purpose of the FSCMA and they are reasonably expected to take similar stance in the case of cryptocurrency derivative and futures products.

4.2.2 Margin Trading Involving Cryptocurrency

In September 2017, the FSC announced a ban on margin trading, prohibiting individuals from borrowing funds or cryptocurrencies from cryptocurrency exchanges in order to sell them.[13] The FSC declared that such practice violates the existing Korean lending and credit laws and directed financial institutions to halt all transactions and partnerships that enable margin trading.

4.2.3 Services of Lending and Borrowing Cryptocurrencies

Under the AML Act, lending and borrowing service is not explicitly included in the scope of virtual asset services. In particular, it is unclear whether services of lending and borrowing virtual assets may substantively fall under any of the categories, which would constitute "virtual asset service" under the AML Act.

However, it is theoretically possible for the regulators to apply laws and regulations applicable to general lending and borrowing services on services of lending and borrowing virtual assets. Services of borrowing virtual assets may be subject to the Act on the Regulation of Conducting Fundraising Business without Permission (the "Fundraising Act") if the regulators view such borrowing services as engaging in the business of receiving "money" on the pretext of savings, installment savings, or installments or deposits made pursuant to an agreement to pay the whole of the principal thereof or an amount exceeding such principal in the future. In such cases, a person may not provide such

13 FSC, 'Joint TF of Virtual Currency-Related Agencies is held to check the progress status of each agency (in Korean),' *FSC Press Release*, 29.09.2017. https://www.fsc.go.kr/po010102/72848?srchCtgry=2&curPage=20&srchKey=&srchText=&srchBeginDt=&srchEndDt.

borrowing services without having obtained relevant license under the Baking Act and other applicable regulations.

Services of lending victual assets may be subject to the Act on Registration of Credit Business and Protection of Finance Users (the "Credit Act"). Under the Credit Act, "credit business" is defined as the business of lending "money" or the business of collecting claims that have arisen under loan agreements and have been transferred by a credit service provider or a credit financial institution. A person who intends to engage in lending services or loan brokerage business must register each of its business offices with the applicable city mayor or regional governor. There have not been any governmental guidelines or court precedents which address whether virtual assets would constitute "money" for the purpose of the above requirement under the Fundraising Act and the Credit Act.

4.2.4 Cryptocurrency Fund (Collective Investment Schemes)

The FSC ruled on 24 October 2018 to the effect that a cryptocurrency fund which manages cryptocurrencies collected from a multiple number of unspecified investors and distribute profits realized from such asset management is in violation of the public fund regulation sunder the FSCMA.[14]

4.2.5 DeFi Services

Based on the Updated Guidance for a Risk-Based Approach to Virtual Assets and Virtual Asset Service Providers, which was released in October 2021, the FATF highlighted necessity to regulate DeFi applications.[15] As of September, 2023, the Korean financial regulators had not officially released any guidelines or announcement regarding whether/how DeFi applications should be regulated.

4.2.6 Cryptocurrency Payment

Under the EFTA, a person who intends to provide settlement services for e-commerce transactions is required to be registered as payment gateway. Due to the Korean government's policy announced in 2017 which would prohibit a finance company from engaging in cryptocurrency related business, a question

14 FSC, 'Investors' Notes for the Virtual Currency Fund (in Korean),' *FSC Press Release*, 24.10.2018. https://www.fsc.go.kr/no010101/73376?srchCtgry=&curPage=159&srchKey=&srchText=&srchBeginDt=&srchEndDt.

15 FATF, Updated Guidance for a Risk-Based Approach to Virtual Assets and Virtual Asset Service Providers [2021] p. 27 https://www.fatf-gafi.org/media/fatf/documents/recommendations/pdfs/FATF%20Recommendations%202012.pdf.

has arisen as to whether such a person may use cryptocurrency for such settlements and, if so, whether such person must be registered with KoFIU as a VASP in accordance with the AML Act. In reviewing the settlement service using PayProtocol AG's "PayCoin (PCI)," the KoFIU determined in 2022 that such settlement services would be considered as virtual asset services as prescribed under the AML Act.

5 Regulatory Framework

5.1 *Overview of the AML Act*

5.1.1 Background

In this Chapter, we discuss in further detail of the AML Act which is currently the only law directly regulating virtual assets in Korea. The AML Act was amended on 25 March 2021 in Korea to newly adopt virtual asset related regulations which require VASPs and financial companies to comply with certain obligations for efficiently preventing money laundering and fighting against terrorism financing.

5.1.2 Definition of VASP and "Major VASP"

The AML Act imposes certain anti-money laundering requirements on a VASP "doing business in or towards Korea," including the requirement to file a report (a "VASP Report") with the Commissioner of the KoFIU.

If a person engages in virtual asset service businesses in Korea with having failed a VASP Report with the KoFIU, such a person may be subject to an imprisonment of up to five (5) years or a criminal fine of up to KRW 50 million. The term "virtual asset service provider" under the AML Act is broadly defined as a person who conducts any of the following businesses with virtual assets:

(a) selling or purchasing virtual assets;
(b) exchanging virtual assets for other virtual assets;
(c) transferring virtual assets for sale and purchase, exchange, storage, and management of virtual assets at the request of clients;
(d) storing or managing virtual assets;
(e) brokering, intermediating or acting as an agent with regard to any of the activities in (a) and (b) above; and
(f) other categories of business as may be prescribed in the Presidential Decree of the AML Act.

The financial regulators' guideline for filing of a VASP Report and press releases with respect to the amended AML Act indicate that the requirements to file a VASP Report under the AML Act would apply to the following so-called "major

VASPs":[16] (i) virtual asset exchanges that engage in operating a platform that brokers or facilitates virtual asset exchanges and sales, (ii) custody service providers that engage in the business of taking custody of or managing virtual assets on behalf of customers and (iii) wallet service providers that engage in the business of taking custody of, managing or transferring virtual assets on behalf of third parties by, for example, providing centralized or trustee wallet services.

As VASP is quite broadly defined under the AML Act, depending on the change of financial regulators' interpretation on major VASP, such persons may become subject to the VASP Report obligation in future. The Korean financial regulators have recently shown some tendencies to more broadly apply the definition of "virtual asset service provider." For example, the FSC issued an interpretative ruling on 30 August 2023 to the effect that where a person engages in sale and purchase of virtual assets, such person may be considered "virtual asset service provider" based on all facts and circumstances, including such person engages in such activities for its business purpose.

5.1.3 AML Requirements for VASP and Financial Companies

As with other financial companies, "VASPs" are subject to various AML requirements, including suspicious transaction report under the AML Act, and customer due diligence ("CDD") and, for such purpose, are required to develop and implement its own internal control system to satisfy such requirements.

In addition to the existing CDD requirement, a financial company, which intends to enter into any transaction with a VASP, is required to ensure that, among others, such a VASP has complied with the VASP Report obligation and separately manage deposits from customers from its own property. Furthermore, such a financial company is required not to elect or to terminate such transactions with such VASP if it is found that such a VASP has failed to comply with applicable conditions and requirements under the AML Act, such as maintaining the validity of its VASP Report and the information security management system ("ISMS") certification.

16 Nonetheless, it is difficult to conclude that the requirement to file a VASP Report under the AML Act will only apply to "major VASPs" discussed in the regulatory guidelines referred to above going forward on the basis that such regulatory guidelines which was released back in February 2021 only intended to illustrate examples for the VASP Report filing requirement.

5.1.4 "Doing Business in Korea" Test

If a person (located outside Korea) is deemed "doing business in Korea" as a result of provision of its goods or services in Korea, certain Korean laws and regulations may apply (despite such person's principal place of business being outside Korea). However, no bright-line test has been established by the Korean courts to determine under what circumstances it would be appropriate for the Korean regulators or the Korean courts to exercise jurisdiction over such person domiciled or located outside Korea. As such, a Korean court would take into account all surrounding facts and circumstances to make such determination.

Article 6(2) of the AML Act provides that the AML Act shall apply to any financial transactions undertaken offshore by a VASP to the extent such transactions have any effect in Korea. Based on Article 6(2) of the AML Act, the Korean financial regulators issued a statement on 22 July 2021 that any foreign virtual asset exchanges (i) providing transactions and payment services in KRW, (ii) offering Korean language services on their platforms or websites and/or (iii) implementing marketing activities targeting Korean users, including those being conducted online (such as YouTube, blog, or other social media platforms which may be accessible by Korean users) would be deemed as "doing business in Korea" and, as a result, must file a VASP Report with the KoFIU in accordance with the AML Act.[17]

5.2 *VASP Report Requirement*

In order to file a VASP Report with the KoFIU, a VASP must satisfy the requirements set forth below:

(a) The VASP shall have obtained an ISMS certification by the Korea Internet & Security Agency;

(b) The VASP shall have obtained real name verification account services from a local bank if the VASP intends to facilitate fiat-crypto transactions;

(c) The VASP shall not have been subject to, in the past five (5) years, (i) a criminal fine or a heavier punishment or (ii) a violation of certain finance-related laws and regulations set forth in the Presidential Decree, including but not limited to the AML Act, the Act on Regulation and Punishment of Criminal Proceeds Concealment, the Act on Prohibition against the Financing of Terrorism and Proliferation of Weapons of Mass Destruction, the FETL, and the FSCMA; provided that if the VASP is a

17 KoFIU, 'The KoFIU notifies foreign VASPs of their obligation to report,' *KoFIU Press Release*, 22.07.2021. https://kofiu.go.kr/cmn/file/downloadBoard.do?seCd=0001&ordrNo=289&fileOrdrNo=2.

corporate entity, this requirement applies to such VASP's representatives and executives; and

(d) There shall be no record within the past five (5) years that VASP's report has been rejected due to its failure to satisfy certain requirements of VASP.

If the VASP fails to maintain its compliance to the requirements set forth in sub-paragraphs (a) to (d) above subsequent to its original filing of the VASP Report with the KoFIU, the KoFIU may cancel its VASP Report which has been previously accepted. There is no foreign ownership restriction for VASPs. A foreign entity may also file a VASP Report as a foreign VASP.

6 Supervision on Cryptocurrency Businesses

6.1 *Supervisory Authority Actions on Cryptocurrency Related Activities*

Under the AML Act, the KoFIU has investigative and supervisory authority over VASP s and may delegate its investigative authority to the FSS. The Virtual Asset User Protection Act allows the FSC to delegate some of its duties to the FSS. Therefore, it is expected that upon the implementation of this law, the FSC will entrust its supervisory duties to the FSS.

In order to publish a game application or program in Korea, a game rating must be obtained from the Game Rating and Administration Committee (the "GRAC") unless there are certain exceptions. Recently, a question has arisen as to whether blockchain-based games, through which users may acquire cryptocurrency and/or NFT s, would fall under "speculative games" in respect of which GRAC may refuse to grant such game rating or cancel its previously granted game rating under the GIPA. For example, the GRAC has recently revoked the rating of, and refused to further review and rate, "Five Stars for Klaytn" and other similar games that allowed NFT minting of game items. In fact, there is an ongoing administrative litigation over such revocation/refusal by the GRAC to rate "Five Stars for Klaytn."[18] On 28 January 2022, the GRAC publicly released its position that if any free gifts, such as cryptocurrency, token and NFT, are offered in a game or any goods or certificates collected from such game may be converted into cash or other similar currencies, there is a high chance that such features are in violation of the GIPA.[19]

---

18 E.S. Choi, 'GRAC - Korea Creative Content Agency ... Will blockchain games take a breath? (in Korean),' *Dailian Newspaper*, 26.10.2021. https://m.dailian.co.kr/news/view/1045599.

19 GRAC, 'Guidance on Independent Rating Criteria for Speculation and Sexuality No.2022-5 (in Korean),' *Public Notice by GRAC*, 28.01.2022. https://www.grac.or.kr/board/Inform.aspx?bno=741&type=view.

6.2 *Supervisory Authority on Cryptocurrency Issuance*

Currently, there are no laws or regulations which are designed to regulate issuance of cryptocurrency. The FSC, however, announced in 2017 that all initial coin offerings (ICOs) would be prohibited, regardless of whether a given coin would be regarded as security-type token.[20] In light of the above, there are no rules or regulations in Korea which would require a person intending to issue cryptocurrency to be subject to any disclosure obligations for purposes of protecting investors or users' interests. A number of proposed laws intended to regulate virtual asset business industry, which are pending at the National Assembly, are known to call for such public disclosure obligations for issuing virtual assets.

While there are no Korean laws or regulations which directly regulate issuance of cryptocurrency, certain existing Korean laws may nonetheless apply depending on type and nature of cryptocurrency or activities associated with cryptocurrency. If an issuance of cryptocurrency is regarded as a "public offering" of "securities" (in case of security-type tokens) under the FSCMA (i.e., solicitation vis-a-vis 50 or more potential investors to subscribe/acquire securities to be newly issued) or an unauthorized fund-raising activity under the Fundraising Act, the FSC and the FSS may exercise their authority to supervise such issuance of cryptocurrency, and the Prosecutor's office may prosecute through criminal investigation. In addition, depending on the contents of disclosures made in any whitepaper for such cryptocurrency issuance, the issuer of such cryptocurrency may be found to have committed fraud under the criminal laws of Korea or violated certain advertisement laws and regulations of Korea based on any false or overstated advertisements.

7 Private Law Issues

7.1 *Overview of Civil Law Aspects of Cryptoassets*

When it comes to the civil law issues of cryptoassets, cryptoasset transactions can be compared with securities transactions. Shares and bonds themselves are not securities in Korean civil law but they are rights *in personam* if not materialised in certificates.[21] Only after are they embodied in certificates

---

20 Office for Government Policy Coordination, Prime Minister's Secretariat, 'Emergency Meeting on Virtual Currency (in Korean),' *Joint Press Release by Relevant Ministries*, 13.12.2017. https://www.korea.kr/news/pressReleaseView.do?newsId=156243146.

21 However, shares or bonds, etc. are treated similar to materialized securities when they are registered on the electronic register under the ESA.

they become securities, i.e. *Yugajeungkweon* (*Wertpapiere*) which can be the object of rights *in rem*. Likewise, cryptoassets are mere rights if they are not materialised in any tangibles, even though there are some opinions that cryptoassets could be things under the Korean Civil Code (the "KCC") because the capability of exclusive control can be identified even in cryptoassets, based on the fact that private key holders can have functionally the same exclusive control vis-à-vis the cryptoassets. These opinions are, however, not the prevailing view. According to the prevailing view of the civil law scholars, cryptoassets are intangibles; thus, they are not things under the KCC. The Corollary of the prevailing view is that cryptoassets themselves are mere rights and cannot be the object of ownership rights under the KCC. In addition, the protection rule of innocent acquirers cannot be applicable to cryptoassets because they are not things. However, cryptoassets can be the objects of pledge because asset rights (*Jaesankweon*; *Vermögensrecht*)[22] can be the object of a pledge under the KCC (Art. 345) even if they are mere rights. Besides the rights pledge under the Article 345 of the KCC, cryptoassets can be used as collaterals by means of the title transfer collateral regime that has been recognised by the Korean court for a long time.

Specific methods for transfer or pledge of cryptoassets depend on the nature of specific cryptoassets. Cryptoassets such as Bitcoin or Ether is not a claim enforceable against someone. There is no specific rule for transfer or pledge of such types of cryptoassets. This may mean that there could be two (2) options for transfer or pledge of cryptoassets: First, Bitcoin or Ether which provides the holders with no claim can be transferred or pledged by any agreed method between the parties; and second, no requirement for transfer or pledge of Bitcoin or Ether suggests that such transfer of pledge actions cannot be recognised as legal ones. Additionally, the *erga omnes* effect of such a transfer or pledge cannot be provided even though it is possible to take the first opinion that the requirement for transfer or pledge of Bitcoin or Ether can be specified by the parties to the relevant contract. However, such cryptoassets as utility tokens that provides the holders with certain rights against the token issuers can be classified as nominative claims. In this case, transfer and pledge methods should follow the one provided in Article 450 of the KCC, and such transfer and pledge can be exercised vis-à-vis third parties if the requirements of the KCC are met. However, it is not as convenient as securities transfer or pledge

---

22 The concept of *Jaesankweon* is not defined in the KCC. According to the German term, *Jaesankweon* can be translated into *Vermögensrecht* which is usually translated as property rights in English. In order to avoid any confusion, the term 'asset rights' is employed hereafter.

and the innocent acquisition protection is not available in this case as cryptoassets are by no means tangibles.

The Korean private international law (the "PIL") Act was enacted on 15 January 1962 and the Act was fully revised and came into effect on 1 July 2001. The current PIL Act, *Gukjesabeop* was again revised in January 2022 and became effective on 5 July 2022. This new PIL Act includes detailed specific international adjudicatory jurisdiction rules.[23] Under the new Korean PIL Act, cryptoassets may not be subject to the rules for rights *in rem* except for the rights pledge. Thus, new rules and theoretical development are required for the proprietary issues of cryptoassets and transactions thereof. However, contractual issues are expected to be overcome by the party autonomy rule under Article 45 and the objective connecting factors provided in Article 46 with some theoretical adjustments for the characteristics of cryptoasset transactions.

7.2 *Proprietary Issues of Cryptoasset Transactions*

7.2.1 Ownership to Cryptoassets

As mentioned above, ownership cannot be created for cryptoassets because they are intangibles; however, cryptoassets are asset rights. This means that X, as an asset right holder, may not be protected by the rules for rights *in rem* under the KCC, even if X can enjoy some degree of property rights. In the case where X holds her cryptoassets with Intermediary MontC and X loses her capability to directly access the cryptoassets because MontC manages the private keys to the cryptoassets, X's right is changed to be a mere contractual right to return her cryptoassets vis-à-vis MontC. X can, however, directly hold her asset rights if X still can manage her private keys to the cryptoassets.[24] There is no clear rule for transformed cryptoassets resulting from a hardfork but such cryptoassets are kinds of surrogated cryptoassets of the original cryptoassets. Thus, X, by analogy, could assert her asset rights to the transformed cryptoassets. Similarly, airdropped cryptoassets can, by analogy, be viewed as fruits under Article 101 of the KCC; or they can be regarded gifts according to gift contracts under Article 553 of the KCC. Therefore, it seems that X has a legitimate position to take the hardforked or airdropped cryptoassets.

23 The previous PIL Act that was enforced on 1 July 2001 has only one general provision for international jurisdiction. Due to the inclusion of a number of new provisions for specific rules for international adjudicatory jurisdiction and change of composition of the PIL rules, the numbering of the all provisions under the new PIL Act was also changed. In this section, the provision number of the Korean PIL Act follows the new one. For your information, however, the substance of the main provisions with regard to this analysis is the same.

24 See FSC, Legal Interpretation No.210227 (in Korean), 21.12.2021.

Currently, there is no specific court decision that deals with the issue of ownership rights to cryptoassets. However, several civil law cases presuppose that cryptoassets are at least asset rights.

7.2.2 Pledge of Cryptoassets

Cryptoassets as asset rights could be objects of pledge and title transfer for the collateral purpose. The former is a rights pledge under Article 345 of the KCC and the latter is a collateralisation method recognised by the case law. A rights pledge can be established by the assignment method of a normative claim if cryptoassets are characterised as nominative claims. However, security interests in cryptoassets could be created only by the parties' agreement if they are not classified as nominative claims. However, there is not only no authoritative opinion on this issue, but also no specific discussion on this issue in Korea.

Therefore, if Korean company Z wants to pledge its 30 Bitcoins that are in its wallet, Z may pledge them by mere agreement with the collateral taker; however, it is not clear that such a method could be recognised in the court. However, Z may pledge its 30 Bitcoins by assigning its right to return them to the collateral taker in accordance with Article 450 of the KCC if the 30 Bitcoins are kept with an intermediary.

7.2.3 Cryptoassets in Insolvency Situations

Articles 70 and 407 of the Korean Insolvency Act, i.e. Debtor Rehabilitation and Insolvency Act (the "DRIA")[25] provide with legitimate owner's rights of revendication (*hwanchuikweon, Aussonderungsrecht*) of their assets out of the rehabilitation or insolvency estate. It is ownership to properties that can be the objects of such rights of revendication, but some rights such as intangible property or otherwise can be the object of the rights of revendication.[26]

It is, however, highly unclear that cryptoassets can be classified as such rights that could be an eligible object for the rights of revendication. Currently, there is no case where a trading platform for cryptoassets entered into an insolvency proceedings in a Korean court, thereby leaving this issue all up in the air. It

---

25 *Chaemooja Hwoesaeng Mit Pasane Kwoanhan Beopryul*, Act No. 7428 of 31 March 2005 as amended. DRIA is an Act consolidating previous insolvency related laws. For details on DRIA, see S.G. Oh, ed., *Korean Bankruptcy Law Symposium* [2008] Korean L vol. 7:2; and Yong-Seok Park, "Unified Insolvency Law of Korea" [2003] 3:2 J. Korean L. 161 (providing a detailed overview of the draft DRIA in comparison with the U.S. federal bankruptcy law.).

26 See C.Y. Rim, 'Consignment Sales and Rights to Revendication (in Korean),' [2019] Rehabilatation L.J. vol. 19, 6–19; and S.D. Park, 'Rights to Revendication in Corpoate Rehabilatation Procedure (in Korean)' [2018] Management L.J. vol. 29:2.

would, however, be likely that the clients (i.e. mandators) of the trading platform could not exercise such rights of revendication because they could be classified as mere claimholders (holders of contractual rights to return) even though it would be unreasonable. An opposite opinion could be also possible, especially when the clients of the platform have an exclusive control over their private keys while the platform operator provides a mere wallet application service. Even in this, it is unclear that clients could exercise the rights of revendication, given that the concept of ownership or similar rights thereon cannot be established in the case of cryptoassets.

In the case that a client company Z of the platform becomes insolvent with United States Dollars ("USD") 200,000 worth of cryptoassets in its account, the cryptoassets in the Z's account may be included in the insolvency estate. Therefore, all general creditors of Z can claim no priority over the cryptoassets. They can enjoy their claims in accordance with the *pari passu* principle in the insolvency proceeding of Z. This result would not change by the fact that Z and the platform agreed certain specific terms such as close-out netting on this issue. Article 120(3) of the DRIA sets out the eligible financial transactions[27] that can be effective in spite of the opening of the insolvency of one of the transaction parties. This is because cryptoasset transactions are not included in the objects of the eligible financial transactions under Article 120(3) of the DRIA and Article 14 of the Enforce Decree of the DRIA, which specifies financial investment instruments, currencies, credit risk, etc., with no interpretive room for cryptoassets.

7.3 *Contract, Inheritance, Trust and Tort law Issues of Cryptoasset Transactions*

7.3.1 Exchange and Sale Contract

In terms of sale contracts and exchange contracts, a key element to distinguish them is whether cryptoassets are involved as the object of the counter performance in cryptoasset transactions. Let's assume that X wants 10 Bitcoins. Further assume that X receives 5 Bitcoins from Y by delivering her 10 Ethers to Y; and X again receives 5 Bitcoins from Z by paying USD 100,000 to Z. The former transaction is characterised as an exchange contract; and the latter transaction is classified as sale contract. Whether X uses an intermediary does not matter under the KCC in characterising the transactions above. It is also possible that the former transaction is characterised as sale with accord and satisfaction if

27 For the special provision, see Y.K. Lee, 'Critical Study on the Special Provision of the Debtor Rehabilitation and Bankruptcy Act Relating to Qualified Financial Transactions (in Korean)' [2019] Seoul L.J. vol. 60:2, 254–264.

the parties' intention was to enter into a sale contract with USD 100,000 but later Y pays X with 10 Ethers as substitution.

7.3.2 Inheritance of Cryptoassets

According to Article 1005 of the KCC, an inheritor universally succeeds, from the time of the commencement of the inheritance, to all of the rights and obligations pertaining to the inheritee's assets. The inheritee's assets mean any of positive or negative assets of the inheritee without regard to the fact that they are tangibles, intangibles or mere claims or not; provided that the assets that are entirely personal to the inheritee are excluded. Accordingly, cryptoassets can be inherited by inheritors. A Will can also be employed if a person wants to dispose of her propertics. Finally, existence of an intermediary does not have an effect on inheritance.

7.3.3 Trust of Cryptoassets

According to the prevailing opinion, a wide range of assets can be eligible for being included in the trust property if the assets are disposable and transferrable.[28] Therefore, it is highly likely that cryptoassets can be eligible assets for establishing a trust. The creation and effectiveness of a will trust and a self trust come into being at the moment when the will have been effective and the declaration has been made. Besides, for the purpose of ensuring enforceability of a trust vis-a-vis the third party, the trust is required to be disclosed (Art. 4 of the Trust Act). Such disclosure can be made by registering the trust property on the relevant books, such as shareholders' book, securities account book, building registry, etc. When such kinds of books, etc. do not exist, separate management of the property is required. The separate management of the asset must be objectively discernible for other's recognition. If there is no method for such objective recognition by a third party, the asset cannot be asserted as a trust property.[29]

In this regard, it is likely that cryptoassets can be transferred to the trustee X for the purpose of establishing a trust. However, practically it would be hard to meet the requirement of disclosure in the case that X is not an intermediary. If X is an intermediary, it would be relatively easy to meet the disclosure requirement by booking on the X's account that certain amount of specific cryptoassets are trust property. However, there is no settled practice on this issue in Korea and legally speaking, cryptoassets might not be an eligible asset which

28 For details of the discussion, see S.S. Jung, *Trust Law*, Jiwon Publishing, Seoul 2021, pp. 244–258.

29 S.S. Jung, supra note, p. 298.

licensed trust service providers can take as trust property under Article 103 of the FSCMA. Article 103(1)(7) mentions intangible asset rights but it is unclear that such intangible assets include cryptoassets.

7.3.4 Lending of Cryptoassets

A loan contract is one of the typical contacts that the KCC provides for. The KCC specifies two (2) kinds of loan contacts: loan contract for consumption (*Darlehn*) (Art. 598 of the KCC) and loan contract for use (*Leihe*) (Art. 609 of the KCC). The object of the loan contract is overwhelmingly money, but any other substitution is also possible (Art. 606 of the KCC). In the case of this kind of substitution loan, the loan amount is determined at the time of delivery. This is a mandatory rule for the protection of the loan taker, i.e. the borrower. Not to mention it, it is possible for the parties to agree more favourable terms of the loan amount determination for the loan taker in such a substation loan. Finally, the parties to the loan contract for consumption may agree in advance that the loan taker may return different kinds of assets (Art. 607 of the KCC). In this case, the estimated amount of the assets at the time of the agreement shall not be over the amount of the loan and interests. This is also a mandatory rule for the protection of the loan taker.

Accordingly, if Korean company Z borrows 60 Bitcoins from PayB, that is incorporated under X law and seated in X, with a 5% interest rate payable in KRW or USD or in Bitcoins, this contract can be seen as a substitution loan contract under Article 606 of the KCC. Currently, Korea has no specific license regime for the cryptoassets lending services; but if PayB actively provides its lending services towards Koreans, it could be subject to the AML Act[30] in accordance with Article 6(2)[31] of the AML Act even if it is located in X. In the case of illegal service provision without a legitimate license, PayB shall be subject to criminal penalties of imprisonment with labour for up to five (5) years or a fine not exceeding KRW 50 million (Arts. 7(1) and 17(1) of the AML Act).

In another scenario that PayB is licensed for such a lending service in Korea and Z borrows 60 Bitcoins from PayB, at a 5% interest rate payable in Bitcoins. In addition, Z pays back Bitcoin Cashes that are Bitcoin equivalents resulting from a fork. According to Article 607, PayB and Z agreed in advance

30 Under the AML Act, there is no specific entry regulation for lending services; however, such service providers could be viewed as cryptoasset dealers.

31 Article 6 (2) specifies an extraterritorial effect as follows: with respect to the financial transactions, etc. of the VASP, the activities of the VASP shall be subject to this Act even if such activities have been made outside Korea, provided that the activities have an effect on Korea.

that Bitcoin equivalents can be returned. It would, however, be possible for Z to perform its obligation by Bitcoin Cash under Article 466 if PayB takes it as substitutes although there is no such a prior agreement between them. In this case it can be viewed that PayB implicitly agreed substitute performance by Z. If there is no prior agreement with, or consent of PayB to the substitute performance, Z could be in breach of the contract. In terms of the breach, it does not matter whether the hardfork took place only after the initial transfer of Bitcoin or not because this is viewed as a contractual issue.

7.4 *Tort Issues*

Currently, there are no special remedy rules for the cryptoasset services as are financial services providers under the FSCMA. In the situation that an intermediary MontC's IT system has been hacked and its client X lost all of her Bitcoins in her wallet managed by MontC, X may sue MontC for the breach of their contract and the unlawful act of MontC, if MontC provides its services in Korea. X also may sue the hacker for the hacker's unlawful act, based upon Article 750 of the KCC. If the hacker has sold some of the hacked Bitcoins to Y and if it is identifiable that Y bought 'the' Bitcoins from the hacker, X may claim the right to return the Bitcoins against Y, meaning that Y is not protected by the innocent acquisition rule, given that Bitcoin is not a thing that is subject to the rules of rights *in rem*. In this case, Y may have a compensatory claim to the hacker based on the breach of their sale contract and the hacker's unlawful act. However, it may be practically hard to identify specific sellers and buyers in some cases of the transactions on an exchange. Therefore, in practice it would be a difficult work for X to find the buyers. If X transferred her Bitcoins to Y via MontC, due to the fraud of Z, X may not claim against MontC but has a tort claim to Z and a claim to Y due to the unjust enrichment,[32] in that MontC has no reason to know the fraud situation and properly acted in accordance with the instruction of X.[33]

7.5 *Attachment and Provisional Measures to Cryptoassets*

Broadly speaking, the Korean Civil Execution Act (the "CEA") categorises the objects of civil enforcement measures into the following three (3)

32 See S. Ct. Decision 16.12.2021, 2020Do9789.

33 Facts are different but there are two (2) district court cases that denied a trading platform's liability for hacking. See Seoul Central District Court Decision, 10.01.2019, 2018GaDan5048171; Seoul Central District Court Decision, 20.12.2018, 2017GaHap585293 (Higher court's decision being the same. See Seoul High Court Decision, 10.09.2020, 2019Na2004142). See Section 4.2 for further details.

types: (1) movables, (2) real estates, and (3) claims and other asset rights. Third ones are any valuable assets or rights that are not tangible movables or realties.[34] Cryptoassets could fall into the last type of other asset rights. Thus, the parties to cryptoasset transactions had a dispute and the court's decision was to award the plaintiff a monetary claim or to deliver or return certain cryptoassets to the plaintiff, the plaintiff may ask the execution court to attach the cryptoassets. No specific method is specified in the CEA but such attachment could be made by delivering the cryptoassets to the wallet of the executor (*Gerichtsvollzieher*) or the executor's account open with an intermediary analogically to the attachment methods of monetary claims under Articles 223 through 227 (Art. 251 of the CEA). Simply taking the relevant private keys to the cryptoassets would not be a proper way, given that private keys could have already been copied to others. Where compulsory execution is impossible, it is a usual practice of courts to order payment of the amount calculated by the market price on the closing date of pleading. Where cryptoassets are managed by an intermediary, it is also a possible way to order for the intermediary to lock up certain amount of cryptoassets in the relevant accounts so that such cryptoassets cannot be disposed of.

7.6 *Conflict of Laws Issues in Relation to Cryptoasset Transactions*

7.6.1 Introduction and Proprietary Issues

The Korean PIL Act (the "KPILA") comes into play when there is a foreign element in legal relations (Art. 1 of the KPILA). As is the European PIL methodology, the first step of a PIL analysis is to characterise the legal relations in issue. According to such qualification process of the legal relations, connecting factors are determined. For instance, if a legal relation is characterised as real rights relation, relevant connecting rules under the KPILA such as Articles 33 through 37 apply. More specifically, when transfer of cryptoassets and the rights to the cryptoassets came to be the issues between the parties, Article 33, which is applicable to the issue of movables or realties' rights *in rem* or rights that can be registered, cannot be applicable because, as discussed earlier, cryptoassets are neither movables nor real properties under the interpretation of the KPILA, too. Also, Application of Article 33 is not desirable even if cryptoassets can be viewed as movables because the connecting factor under Article 33 is the *lex rei sitae or lex situs*, i.e. the location of the things, and cryptoassets have no physical location as are intangibles. In this regard, the issue of to whom cryptoassets belong could be solved by analogy of Article 37 that provides

34 See Art. 251 of the CEA.

that contractual security interests in claims, shares, or other rights or securities certificates that materialise them are governed by the law of the rights that are the object of the security interests; provided however that, security interests in bearer securities are governed by Article 35 (the *lex cartae sitae*). If then, another issue that which law is the law of cryptoassets arises. Currently, there is no clear answer to this but the law applicable to claims could govern such cryptoassets as utility tokens that provides for right to claim to someone. However, no reasonable answer can be found for the law applicable to such cryptoassets as Bitcoin or Ether that provides no claims to someone. Arguably, the habitual residence of the private key holder or the law of the blockchain system, i.e. quasi-party autonomy could be a reasonable solution. In the case of security interest issues, the same analysis above can be applicable.

7.6.2 Contractual Issues

The KPILA allows a full party autonomy in the case of contractual issues with respect to the contracts for sales, exchanges, loans, etc. More specifically, Article 45 of the KPILA provides that contracts shall be governed by the law expressly or implicitly chosen by the parties, provided that the implicit choice can be acknowledged only in the case where it is reasonable to do so out of the contents of the contract or of all other circumstances. Where no explicit or implicit choice has been made by the parties under Article 45 of the KPILA, the law applicable to the contracts is the law of the country that has the closest connection with the contract (Art. 46(1) of the KPILA). The closest connection with the contract is presumed to exist in the country where the habitual residence of the party who has to perform its obligation is located at the time of conclusion of the contract (in the case where the contract is concluded in the course of the party's occupation or business activities, the place where the party's business is located) (Art. 46(2) of the KPILA).[35] Therefore, where X who has 10 Bitcoins entered into a sale contract with Y without any explicit or implicit choice of law for the contract, the objective connecting factor is the habitual residence of X because X has to perform her obligation to transfer 10 Bitcoins. It does not matter whether X holds 10 Bitcoins through an intermediary because the issue is the contractual one between X and Y, not with an intermediary (let's say Z). If the issues are any contractual matter with Z, the contract is a mandate contract; thus, the objective connecting factor is the place of Z where it provides its mandate services. Where Z has multiple

35 In the case of contract of which object is the rights to real estates, however, the place where the real estate is located is presumed to have the closest connection to the contract (Art. 46(3) of the KPILA).

business places, the relevant place is the place of the business which has the closest connection to the contract.[36] As a special connecting rule, Art. 47 of the KPILA provides for a special connection for consumer contracts. This special rule is for the consumers' protection as is Article 6 of Rome I. This author has the opinion that cryptoasset transactions can be subject to this special rule. If this rule is applicable to cryptoasset transactions, X, a natural person, may claim Intermediary Z for its breach of the contract and the mandatory rules of X's habitual residence. This means that the protection afforded to X under the law of X's habitual residence can be asserted, although X and Z chose Law α for their contract (Art. 47(1) of the KPILA). It should be noted that Article 47 protects only passive consumers. The protection under Article 47 cannot be asserted if Z made no effort of marketing towards Korea but X voluntarily opened her account with Z.

The KPILA sets out no rules on trust. Korea is not a contracting State of the Hague Trust Convention. As for a testamentary trust a persuasive opinion is that the issue is characterised as inheritance issues; thus, the law applicable to inheritance addresses the issue,[37] as specified in Article 77. With regard to *inter vivos* trust, there are serval opinions of how to characterise such living trust as follows: (1) a stand-alone single legal relation as is the Hague Trust Convention, (2) bifurcating contractual and proprietary issues, (3) an organization or entity, and (4) contracts. It seems that a persuasive view among them is the second one, thereby, applying Articles 45 and 46 of the KPILA for the contractual issues of trust and Article 33 of the KPILA for the proprietary issues of trust.[38]

7.6.3 Tort Issues

In relation to tort issues, the connecting factor under Article 52 of the KPILA is the law of the place of the tort (*lex loci delicti commissi*) or the law of the place of the damage (*lex loci damni*). The victims may choose one of the places that is advantageous to them.[39] In a number of cases, however, it might be difficult to localise the places of tort because of the characteristics of the cryptoasset transactions that are made on the cyber space. Especially, the transactions

36 K.H. Suk, *Commentary on Korean Private International Law* (in Korean), Seoul, Parkyoungsa, 2013, p. 309.

37 K.H. Suk, 'Trust and Private International Law (in Korean)' in S.S. Jung & H.J. Rho ed., *Issues of Trust Law*, vol. 2 Seoul, Sohwa, 2015, p. 372.

38 See K.H. Suk, supra note, pp. 372–381.

39 See S. Ct. Decisions, 24.05.2012, 2009Da22549 and 2009Da68620. These are the first Supreme Court decisions that allowed the victims' choice between the place of tort and the damage in favour of the victims.

made on a DeFi exchange (DEX) may make this issue more complicated. With respect to tort PIL issues of the DEX, no specific discussion has been made yet in Korea. Thus, theoretical developments are required in this PIL area in the near future.

7.6.4 Insolvency

The DRIA[40] and the KPILA have no conflict of laws rules for international insolvency issues. In principle the cross-border insolvency issues are governed by the *lex fori concursus*, i.e. the law applicable to the insolvency proceedings, given that the fundamental conflict of laws principle is to connect the legal relations to the place where the closest connection is located.[41] The *lex fori concursus* governs both procedural and substantive issues with regard to the cross-border insolvency.

Therefore, if the Korean intermediary X located in Seoul commences its insolvency proceedings in Seoul, the following issues are governed by the DRIA of (1) whether X's assets located abroad are included in the insolvency estate, (2) whether security interests created under a foreign law and of which objects are located abroad can be enforced, (3) whether set-off can be allowed, (4) whether avoidance be can exercised, and (5) what is the effect of the insolvency proceeding on the non-executory contracts.[42] Conversely, where a foreign intermediary Y located in Hamburg commences its insolvency proceedings in Hamburg, German insolvency law governs the issues of (1) whether Y's assets located in Seoul is included in the insolvency estate, (2) whether the German insolvency administrator has a position to manage the assets in Seoul and (3) whether enforcement of security interests in the assets in Korea are restricted by the German insolvency proceeding, provided that the German insolvency proceeding should be recognised in Korea under Articles 631 and 632 and the assistance decision has to be made in accordance with Article 636.[43]

---

40 However, Part 5 (Articles 628 through 642) of the DRIA provides some rules in relation to international insolvency, which somewhat modelled the UNCITRAL Model Law on Cross-Border Insolvency of 23.05.1997. For details of Part 5 of the DRIA, see, Y.S. Kim, 'Korean Practice of the UNCITRAL Model Law on Cross-Border Insolvency and the Improvement Plan (in Korean)' [2021] Korea PIL J, vol. 27:2, 6–28.

41 K.H. Suk, supra note, pp. 630–631.

42 Ibid., p. 630.

43 Ibid.

8 Litigation

8.1 *Litigation Related to Criminal Laws Issues*

The Korean Criminal Code does not explicitly regulate cryptocurrency. However, if a person commits a criminal act, such as fraud or breach of fiduciary duty, as stipulated in the Criminal Code using cryptocurrency or takes any action which would be subject to a criminal sanction under any special law or act, such person may be subject to a criminal punishment in Korea. For example, if a person operates a multilevel sales distribution business without being registered under the Door-to-Door Sales Act or engages in any illegal fundraising activities in violation of the Fundraising Act, he/she may be subject to a criminal punishment as prescribed under such special law.

So far, there are several criminal litigations involving cryptocurrency in Korea where cryptocurrency was used for committing fraud, illegally raising funds or conducting multilevel sales distribution activity as well as those involving cryptocurrency exchange operators.

In May 2018, which was before the AML Act was enacted, the Supreme Court recognized the property value of cryptocurrency for the first time in 2018.[44] In Supreme Court case in August 2020, the Supreme Court held that a cryptocurrency exchange's entry of KRW points in a borrowed name account established with such cryptocurrency exchange without having received any cash at such cryptocurrency exchange's bank account constituted "forgery" under the Criminal Code.[45] In November 2021, the Korean Supreme Court ruled that Bitcoin, which was the object of fraudulent act, would be recognized as "proprietary benefit" received by the wrongdoer.[46]

In December 2021, in a case where a person's virtual assets were transferred to a third party's electronic wallet without any specific reason or ground and such person argued that such third party owed a fiduciary duty to maintain/manage such virtual assets, the Supreme Court held that no such fiduciary duty would be established on the basis that, while virtual asset may be recognized as proprietary benefit of such person, virtual assets are not regulated as much as legal tender under the current laws and regulations and they do not entertain the same level of protection as such protection granted to legal tender under the Criminal Code.[47]

44 See S. Ct. Decision, 30.05.2018, 2018Do3619.
45 See S. Ct. Decision, 27.08.2020, 2019Do11294.
46 See S. Ct. Decision, 11.11.2021, 2021Do9855.
47 See S. Ct. Decision, 16.12.2021, 2020Do9789.

In a court case where a person received certain number of Bitcoins from its investors at an electronic wallet and, in return, paid investors 1% of such deposited Bitcoins on daily basis while the principal and interest thereof may be withdrawn by the investors, the court found that (i) such action of having an investor send and deposit such number of Bitcoins to its electronic wallet would constitute a fund-raising activity in violation of the Fundraising Act and (ii) such arrangement would constitute a monetary transaction without any sale and purchase of goods or services or based on a disguised sale and purchase of goods or services, which would be in violation of the Door-to-Door Sales Act.[48]

8.2 *Litigation Related to Cryptocurrency Trading Exchange's Service*

Litigations involving services of cryptocurrency exchanges have mainly been damage claim or tort claim lawsuits based on, among others, hacking, deposit by mistake and system error. The Korean courts' rulings on such cases differed based on facts and circumstances specific to each case and whether any burden of proof is satisfied.

In a damage claim lawsuit filed against a cryptocurrency exchange by its user for his/her loss allegedly resulted from extortion of cash points due to system hacking against the exchange, the Seoul High Court dismissed the plaintiff's claim and ruled in favour of such cryptocurrency exchange as such user did not satisfy the burden of proof by failing to sufficiently establish the causal relationship between his/her loss with the exchange's default.[49] In another damage claim lawsuit filed against a cryptocurrency exchange by its user for his/her loss allegedly resulted from the exchange's failure to return his/her virtual assets due to system hacking which had led the exchange to shut down its entire system, the Seoul Central District Court ruled in favour of the user recognizing his/her loss.[50]

In late 2017, there were a number of damage claim lawsuits brought against cryptocurrency exchanges for losses allegedly resulted from trading suspension caused by system error which took place while cryptocurrency prices

48 See S. Ct. Decision, 01.12.2020, 2020Do11088(Dismissal of appeal) and its lower courts' decision(Seoul Central District Court Decision, 24.07.2020, 2020No389 and Seoul Central District Court Decision, 16.01.2020, 2019GoDan1432).

49 See Seoul High Court Decision, 10.09.2020, 2019Na2004142.

50 See Seoul Central District Court Decision, 05.11.2021, 2018GaHap567582; D.Y. Kim, 'Court's First Judgment: "Coin Exchange Should Compensate Victims from the Hacking" (in Korean),' *The JoongAng*, 10.11.2021. https://www.joongang.co.kr/article/25022703.

drastically plunged.[51] However, the court had dismissed one of such lawsuits filed by approximately 600 cryptocurrency investors against a major cryptocurrency exchange.[52] The Seoul High Court recognized the loss incurred by certain users to a cryptocurrency exchange which resulted from certain restrictions to log-in to their system (preventing such users from trading cryptocurrencies for certain period of time).[53]

According to a news report on 2 June 2021, there was an unjust enrichment lawsuit brought against a cryptocurrency exchange by its user for mistakenly depositing approximately KRW 600 million in total into the cryptocurrency exchange's electronic wallet.[54]

During the course of adopting a new government policy to require cryptocurrency exchanges to subscribe real name verification account service from a local bank, certain banks suspended cash deposits into cryptocurrency exchanges' collection accounts. In response, such cryptocurrency exchanges applied to the court for a preliminary injunction against such suspension made by the banks. Depending on specific facts and circumstances for each of such cases, the courts had granted such application in some cases and dismissed such applications in some cases.[55] For the purpose of having their VASP Report "accepted" by the KoFIU, a number of cryptocurrency exchanges were forced to delist cryptocurrencies with low liquidity or credibility and, as a result, the issuers of such delisted cryptocurrencies had applied to the court for a

---

51 J.Y. Won, 'the investors are not indemnified from the damages caused by computer failure on the virtual asset exchange (in Korean),' *PaxNet News*, 06.08.2020. https://paxnetnews.com/articles/63773/094046; S.K. Lee, '[Court Decision] "Damage Caused by Connection Disruption of the Exchange"...Cryptocurrency Investor Lawsuit, "Defeated" (in Korean),' *Lawltimes*, 22.01.2018. https://www.lawtimes.co.kr/Legal-News/Legal-News-View?serial=139584.

52 J.H. Hwang, 'Court's Decision "No Intention or Negligence on Bithumb's IT Failure" ... Investors Lost' (in Korean), *Yonhapnews*, 26.07.2020. https://www.yna.co.kr/view/AKR20200725025100004.

53 See Seoul High Court Decision, 28.05.2021, 2020Na2034712, Seoul Central District Court Decision, 04.09.2020, 2019GaHap567183.

54 M.H. Lee, '[Exclusive] Virtual Currency Investors "Please Return the Deposit" ... class action towards Upbit worth hundreds of millions of won (in Korean),' *Chosun Ilbo*, 03.06.2021. https://biz.chosun.com/topics/law_firm/2021/06/03/VW7HLKKVENEFZKV-V4KKIPCXJHQ/.

55 M.K. Park, 'Court Hearing "Unfair Suspension of Deposit of Cryptocurrency between Nonghyup and Shinhan Bank" (in Korean),' *The Korea Economic Daily*, 14.08.2019. https://www.hankyung.com/it/article/201908145846v.

preliminary injunction to invalidate the delisting of their cryptocurrencies but most of such applications were dismissed by the courts.[56]

9 Taxation on Cryptocurrencies

Until the amendments of the tax laws in December 2020, there was no specific statute under the Korean tax law that expressly provided for the taxation on gains from virtual asset transactions. For domestic corporations, however, the Korean tax authority relied on the generally applicable corporate income tax principle which provides for the taxation on increases in the net asset value of domestic corporations.

The amended tax law, which was promulgated in December 2020 and is scheduled to take effect on 1 January 2025, sets forth the tax rules concerning gains realized by resident and non-resident individual investors and foreign corporate investors from virtual asset transactions. The amended provisions also provide reporting obligations for overseas accounts held for purposes of trading virtual assets. Meanwhile, pursuant to the relevant tax rulings, a Value Added Tax shall not be imposed on a supply of virtual assets.

9.1 *Individual Income Tax Law*

Under the amended Individual Income Tax Law (the "IITL"), income generated from a transfer or lending of virtual assets ("virtual asset gains") by a Korean resident individual will be subject to taxation as "other income" starting from 1 January 2025.[57] Such "virtual asset gains" over the amount of KRW 2.5 millions (per tax year) will be subject to taxation as "Other Income" (Art. 21 of the IITL) at the rate of 22% (including local tax). When calculating the taxable amount, taxpayers are allowed to deduct certain necessary expenses, including the acquisition cost of the virtual asset and other directly associated expenses.

In the case of non-resident individuals, any gains realized from a transfer or lending transaction of virtual assets (including a withdrawal of virtual assets

---

56 S.H. Lee, H.J. Hong and S.H. Han, 'The court ruled "an exchange has the authority to delist the coins" (in Korean),' *Maeil Business Newspaper*, 10.08.2021. https://www.mk.co.kr/news/economy/view/2021/08/775445/.

57 The taxation on virtual asset gains has been postponed for two (2) years with the effective date delayed from 1 January 2023 to 1 January 2025. Note that information reporting rules on overseas virtual asset accounts took effect from 1 January 2022.

from a virtual asset service provider as defined under the AML Act) on or after 1 January 2023 is subject to withholding tax as domestic source 'other income.'[58]

A non-resident individual eligible for the benefits of a tax treaty may be subject to non-taxation or exemption with respect to such other income, depending on the provisions of the treaty.

In the case of non-resident individuals, income taxes are collected by means of withholding. The withholding amount shall be an amount equivalent to 10% of the consideration received for the transfer of a virtual asset or an amount equivalent to 20% of the consideration after deducting the necessary expenses (e.g., the acquisition cost and other directly associated expenses), whichever is lesser. However, in the event that the necessary expenses cannot be substantiated, the withholding amount shall be 10% of the consideration. Local income tax, which is 10% of the aforementioned withholding tax, may be levied in addition depending on any applicable treaty.

A withholding agent must withhold any requisite withholding tax amount (including local income tax, if applicable) from the proceeds payable to non-resident individual and pay such withheld taxes by the 10th day of the following month to the relevant tax authority in Korea. In the event that the virtual asset transaction is made through a VASP, the VASP shall be the withholding agent and be required to withhold such tax amount at the time of a non-resident individual accountholder's withdrawal of any virtual asset from such VASP (Art. 156 of the IITL).

9.2 *Corporate Income Tax Law*

As discussed above, even prior to the 2020 amendments to the Korean tax laws, any gains from virtual asset transactions realized by a domestic corporation were subject to taxation based on the general corporate income tax principle that imposes taxes on increases in the net asset value of a domestic corporation. The amended Corporate Income Tax Law (the "CITL") further provides a detailed valuation method for virtual assets. Beginning from 1 January 2022, virtual assets are defined as assets subject to valuation, such as inventory or securities, and will be valued based on the FIFO (first in, first out) method (Arts. 73 and 77 of the Enforcement Decree of the CITL).

Foreign corporations are subject to the same taxation rules on virtual asset gains as in the case of non-resident individuals (Arts. 92, 93 and 98 of the CITL).

58 Note, however, there are ongoing tax appeals on the issue of whether an non-resident individual's virtual asset gains realized on or before the end of 2024 can be subject to taxation as domestic source 'other income' pursuant to other sub-categories of 'other income' stipulated in Article 119 of the IITL.

9.3 *Reporting Obligations on Overseas Virtual Asset Accounts by Residents*

According to the International Tax Coordination Law, overseas virtual asset accounts and VASPs have been recently added to the scope of the overseas financial account reporting regime. Therefore, if the balance of the foreign financial account held by a resident individual or a domestic corporation exceeds KRW 500 million for any of the last day of each calendar month in a year, starting 1 January 2022, such account holder shall report the information of its overseas financial account to the National Tax Service between June 1 and June 30 of the following year.

Sweden

Kelly Chen

1 Introduction

Prior to the EU regulation on markets in crypto-assets (MiCA Regulation or MiCAR), cryptocurrencies were not prohibited but unregulated in Sweden.[1] This unregulated state was highly problematic. The Swedish financial supervisory authority, Finansinspektionen (FI), has for example explicitly warned consumers against trading with cryptocurrencies. A main issue identified was the lack of consumer protection. Even with the upcoming EU legislation, FI remains concerned with the high risks associated with investing in cryptocurrencies for consumers.

This chapter takes a closer look at the legal framework of cryptocurrencies in Sweden as of 2023. The MiCA Regulation, which Sweden as a member state of the EU must adhere to, entered into force in June 2023. It will however start to apply in December 2024.[2] This chapter reflects on whether the MiCA Regulation could address the issues with cryptocurrencies in the Swedish market. Moreover, the chapter explores the private law regime governing cryptocurrencies. It shows that cryptocurrencies are granted a rather high level of protection under private law, which could be attributed to a fairly pragmatic view on the notion of property in Sweden. Lastly, the chapter points out that the upcoming EU regulation will not only reform the regulatory framework of cryptocurrencies in Sweden but have a substantial impact on the private law one as well.

The chapter is organized as follows. First, it will provide an overview of the circulation of cryptocurrencies in the Swedish market, including whether they can function as means as payment or held for investment purposes. Second, it examines the regulatory framework of cryptocurrencies, including the MiCA Regulation and whether it will fill the existing regulatory gap in Sweden. Third, the chapter discusses the subject of cryptocurrencies from a private law perspective. Fourth, the relevant tax measures are presented in brief. Lastly, the chapter concludes with a few remarks on, among others, the potential

1 Regulation (EU) 2023/1114 of the European Parliament and of the Council of 31 May 2023 on markets in crypto-assets, and amending Regulations (EU) No 1093/2010 and (EU) No 1095/2010 and Directives 2013/36/EU and (EU) 2019/1937 [hereafter the MiCA Regulation].

2 Title III and IV will however apply from June 2024, see Article 149 the MiCA Regulation.

 | DOI:10.1163/9789004722507_025

interplay of private and public law in the field once the MiCA Regulation has entered into application.

2 The Circulation of Cryptocurrencies

It is generally acknowledged that Bitcoin is the most well-known cryptocurrency. This is the case in the Swedish market as well. Examples of other cryptocurrencies that have gained recognition are Ethereum and Litecoin.[3] While cryptocurrencies can be used as means of payment, they are not recognized as legal tenders. The Swedish central bank, Riksbanken, has stated that albeit bitcoins and other similar types of cryptocurrencies were created for payment uses, they are often bought and held for investment purposes.[4] In 2022, Riksbanken concluded that most cryptocurrencies have been used as speculative investments rather than means of payment. They have not been widely accepted as payments and cannot retain their value over time. Thus, cryptocurrencies have insofar not functioned well for payment purposes.[5]

In 2020, the Swedish financial supervisory authority FI conducted a thematic review of the market for financial instruments with crypto-assets as underlying asset. It showed that the most common financial instrument linked to crypto-assets was tracker certificates that had bitcoins as underlying assets.[6] Riksbanken as well as FI have expressed concerns over crypto-assets. FI has deemed instruments with cryptocurrencies as the underlying asset as unsuitable investments products for consumers.[7] As further developed below, a main reason stated is the lack of adequate consumer protection regulation of the underlying crypto-asset.

In addition, stable coins are categorized as a subgroup of cryptocurrencies and can be used as a means of payment in Sweden. The Swedish central bank

3 Söderberg, Gabriel, Are Bitcoin and Other Crypto-assets Money? [Sw. Är Bitcoin och andra kryptotillgångar pengar?], Economic Commentary, Riksbanken, No. 5 2018, available at https://www.riksbank.se/globalassets/media/rapporter/ekonomiska-kommentarer/svenska/2018/ar-bitcoin-och-andra-kryptotillgangar-pengar.pdf [last viewed 30 April 2024] (hereafter Söderberg 2018).

4 Differences between E-kronor, Cryptocurrencies and Crypto-Assets, Riksbanken, last updated August 2023, available at https://www.riksbank.se/en-gb/payments--cash/e-krona/difference-between-e-krona-and-crypto-assets/ [last viewed 30 April 2024].

5 Payments Report 2022 [Sw. Betalningsrapport 2022], Riksbanken, p. 12.

6 Financial Instruments with Crypto-assets as Underlying Asset, FI Supervision Report, Finansinspektionen, No. 21, 22 February 2021 [hereafter FI Supervision Report 2021].

7 FI Supervision Report 2021, p. 10.

has recognized stable coins that are pegged to other assets, e.g., national currencies and other financial assets, to be more stable than cryptocurrencies such as bitcoins. Two areas of concern were however identified. The first one is that a wide application of stable coins could pose risks to financial stability and the financial system in general. Here, Riksbanken made comparisons to risks generally associated with money market funds.[8]

The second concern is from a policy perspective. As explicated by Riksbanken, if stable coins that are backed by another country's currency, for example US dollars, gain a strong foothold in the Swedish market, it could come to constrain the government's possibility to take measures of monetary policy nature or intervene when there is a financial crisis.[9]

3 The Regulatory Framework

3.1 *Defining Cryptocurrencies*

There was no legal definition of cryptocurrencies in Sweden prior to the MiCA Regulation. The terms often used included cryptocurrencies and crypto-assets, and Swedish public authorities have showed a preference towards the latter. Since cryptocurrencies are more often held for investment purposes, Riksbanken has viewed crypto-assets to be a more appropriate term. It has also been emphasized that there are crypto-assets that are not created for payment uses.[10] Moreover, both FI and the Swedish tax authority, Skatteverket (SKV), use the term crypto-assets. SKV has explained that crypto-assets that function as a means of payment can also be called cryptocurrencies, virtual currencies or digital currencies.

It could be argued that while crypto-assets and cryptocurrencies are often used interchangeably, a distinction between the two is emerging. The key determining factor is the function. The term crypto-assets can be used in a wide as well as narrow sense. The former encompasses all cryptocurrencies, which can function as means of payment or for investment purposes, and the latter refers to cryptocurrencies that are created solely for payment uses. The term cryptocurrencies, on the other hand, has a more specific meaning, referring only

8 Payment Report 2021 [Sw. Betalningsrapport 2021], Riksbanken, p. 11 (hereafter Riksbanken Payment Report 2021).

9 Riksbanken Payment Report 2021, p. 12.

10 Differences between E-kronor, Cryptocurrencies and Crypto-Assets, Riksbanken, last updated August 2023, available at https://www.riksbank.se/en-gb/payments--cash/e-krona/difference-between-e-krona-and-crypto-assets/ [last viewed 30 April 2024].

to those cryptocurrencies that seek to serve as means of payment. Possibly, for the sake of clarity, crypto-assets, only in its narrow sense, should be used interchangeably with cryptocurrencies. In the following sections of this chapter, crypto-assets will be used in its wide scope, and cryptocurrencies to refer to the payment function only.

Riksbanken has defined crypto-assets as "digital units that are created and transferred between users through the use of cryptographic calculations". Cryptography, in turn, is understood as "the study of methods used to transfer information between a sender and a receiver without a third party being able to access it. This encrypts the information. Only those that have the right to take part of the information can have the key to enable the information."[11]

Under the MiCA Regulation, crypto-assets are defined as "a digital representation of a value or of a right that is able to be transferred and stored electronically using distributed ledger technology or similar technology."[12] FI opted to follow the EU definition at an early stage, before the provisional agreement was reached.[13] It should be noted that the EU, especially in the aftermath of the financial crisis of 2008, has increasingly enhanced the regulation of the internal financial market. From a Swedish perspective, it could be argued that FI has demonstrated a fairly high level of willingness to adapt to new EU financial regulations. In areas where the EU policy aligns with the Swedish one, FI has encouraged market participants to be at the forefront of applying new regulations.[14] In some cases, Sweden has also refrained from legislating at the national level due to potential EU regulatory frameworks.[15]

3.2 *The Framework Pre-MiCA*

Prior to the MiCA Regulation, crypto-assets were subject to limited authorization and financial supervision in Sweden. Compared to some other jurisdictions, the Swedish regulation of crypto-assets was rather scarce. Depending on how the crypto-asset was constructed, it could be regulated by legislations such as the Electronic Money Act (2011:755) and the Financial Instruments Trading Act (1991:980). The competent authority would be the financial supervisory authority FI. The majority of crypto-assets did however not fall within

11 Söderberg 2018.
12 Article 3(5) the MiCA Regulation.
13 See e.g. FI Supervision Report 2021, p. 4.
14 See Chen, K., Sustainable Finance in Sweden: A State-of-Art Overview, Juridisk tidskrift, 2023–24 nr 2 [hereafter Chen 2023].
15 Such as in the field of green bonds, see Chen 2023. See also Governmental Report, To Promote Green Bonds [Att främja gröna obligationer] SOU 2017:155.

the scope of the regulations. As a result, crypto-assets were generally considered as unregulated in Sweden.[16]

As seen above, financial instruments that have crypto-assets as the underlying asset are permitted in the Swedish market. While the instruments are subject to the relevant regulations, the underlying crypto-assets remained outside of the remit of financial supervision. Moreover, trading platforms for crypto-assets are subject to registration but not supervision in Sweden.[17] It has been empathized that price manipulation is common in these unregulated marketplaces.[18] In essence, it could be argued that there was a considerable regulatory gap with regard to crypto-assets in Sweden pre-MiCAR.

Financial instruments with crypto-assets as the underlying asset are governed by the Securities Market Act (2007:528), which implements the Markets in Financial Instruments Directive (MiFID II). Firms that distribute these instruments are thus subject to authorization, operating and organizational requirements. Moreover, since the instruments are complex and primarily sold without investment advice, the firms must conduct an appropriateness test when distributing them.[19] There are also product governance requirements, especially with regard to the identified target market, that the firms must comply with.[20] Further, firms that offer these instruments should regularly review the products to ensure, inter alia, that the identified target market and the chosen distribution strategy remain be appropriate.[21]

As stressed by FI, persons who produce or disseminate investment recommendations on these instruments must take reasonable care to ensure that the information is objectively presented. This is of particular importance if an instrument is complex and difficult to value, such as where the underlying asset is linked to a high level of uncertainty and there is a lack of transparency. Market abuse regulations are also applicable to the tracker certificates and other listed products with crypto-assets as the underlying asset. Insider trading and market manipulation are thus prohibited.[22]

It should however be noted that this framework does not cover all aspects. It has for example been emphasized that issuers of tracker certificates, which

16 FI Supervision Report 2021, p. 5.
17 See section 3.4. below.
18 FI Supervision Report 2021, p. 11.
19 Sec. 9:24 and 9:25 Securities Market Law.
20 Sec. 8:13 and 8:14 Securities Market Law.
21 Sec. 5:22 FI Regulation FFFS 2017:2.
22 FI Supervision Report 2021, p. 15.

is the most common financial instrument with crypto-assets as the underlying asset in Sweden, were not regulated.[23]

3.3 *The MiCA Regulation and Sweden*

Most likely, the MiCA Regulation will be investigated in-depth elsewhere. The following section will thus discuss the regulation briefly. It will focus on the Swedish perspective. The Swedish financial supervisory authority FI has stated that it is necessary with new regulations that are better equipped to manage the risks associated with crypto-assets. FI has expressed three main concerns with crypto-assets. The first one is the lack of proper consumer protection and the second one the risks of crypto-assets being used for money laundering or other criminal purposes. Third, there is the environmental impact of crypto-assets. Well-known crypto-assets such as Bitcoin requires for example extremely high electricity usage, and the electricity is generally sourced from fossil fuels such as coal and oil. FI has together with the Swedish environmental agency recommended the EU to consider whether banning energy-intensive crypto production could be justified, sending a clear signal of Sweden's view on these types of crypto-assets from a sustainability point of view.[24] However, the Director General of FI has emphasized that crypto-assets that use proof-of-stake rather than proof-of-work as consensus mechanism need significantly less energy.[25]

FI has noted that the lack of proper consumer protection could be partially rectified by the MiCA Regulation, which includes, inter alia, consumer protection rules for the issuance, trading, exchange and custody of crypto-assets. In essence, the MiCA Regulation will establish a bespoke regime for all crypto-assets that are not covered elsewhere in EU financial services legislation and crypto-asset service providers. The regulation lays down uniform rules for (i) transparency and disclosure requirements for the issuance, offer to the public and admission of crypto-assets to trading on a trading platform; (ii) the authorisation and supervision of crypto-asset service providers, issuers of

23 FI Supervision Report 2021, p. 5.

24 Crypto-assets are a Threat to the Climate Transition – Energy-intensive Mining Should be Banned, Speech by Erik Thedéen, Director General of Finansinspektionen, and Björn Risinger, Director General of the Swedish Environmental Protection Agency, available at.https://www.fi.se/en/published/presentations/2021/crypto-assets-are-a-threat-to-the-climate-transition--energy-intensive-mining-should-be-banned/ [last viewed 30 April 2024].

25 Crypto-Assets: Risks and Opportunities, Speech by Erik Thedéen, Director General of Finansinspektionen, FI dnr 21-348, 16 June 2021, available at https://www.fi.se/contentassets/0727d79ddf8e44df82013b8912e125ae/tal-finansanalytikerforen-16juni-eng.pdf [last viewed 30 April 2024].

asset-referenced tokens and issuers of e-money tokens, as well as their operation, organization and governance; (iii) the protection of holders of crypto-assets in the issuance, offer to the public and admission to trading; (iv) the protection of clients of crypto-assets service providers; (v) measures to prevent insider dealing, unlawful disclosure of inside information and market manipulation to ensure the integrity of crypto-asset markets.[26]

As seen above, crypto-assets are defined broadly in the MiCA Regulation and encompasses stable coins. It has been noted that stable coins have been subject to extensive regulation under the MiCA regime.[27] It is however specified that the regulation does not apply to crypto-assets that qualify as e.g. financial instruments, deposits including structured deposits and securitization positions as defined in relevant EU financial legislation.[28] In this regard, changes to major regulatory frameworks are needed to encompass crypto-assets. It is for example necessary that MIFID II clarifies that financial instruments include those issued by means of distributed ledger technology.[29]

Moreover, in terms of providers of crypto-asset services, they will be subject to comprehensive authorization, operating and organizational requirements. Under the MiCA Regulation, crypto-asset services are custody and admission of crypto-assets on behalf of clients; operation of a trading platform; exchange (crypto for funds and crypto for crypto); execution of orders on behalf of clients; placing of crypto-assets; reception and transmission of orders on behalf of clients; advice on crypto-assets; and portfolio management; transfer services for crypto-assets on behalf of clients.[30] All service providers that seek to operate in the EU must have a registered office in a member state and obtain authorization from the relevant national competent authority.[31] The service providers must act honestly, fairly and professionally in accordance with the best interests of their clients and prospective clients. The information,

26 Article 1 the MiCA Regulation. It should be noted that compared to the Commission Draft of MiCA, the protection of clients of crypto-related services was further clarified.

27 Zetzsche, D., Annunziata, F., Arner, D. and Buckley, R., The Markets in Crypto-Assets Regulation (MICA) and the EU Digital Finance Strategy, European Banking Institute Working Paper Series No. 2020/77, 5 November 2020 (hereafter Zetzsche et al. 2020).

28 Article 2(4) the MiCA Regulation. The scope was extended in comparison to the Commission Draft of MiCA. It also included that the MiCA Regulation does not apply to non-fungible tokens (NFTS), see article 2(3) the MiCA Regulation.

29 See Proposal for a Directive of the European Parliament and of the Council amending Directives 2006/43/EC, 2009/65/EC, 2009/138/EU, 2011/61/EU, EU/2013/36, 2014/65/EU, (EU) 2015/2366 and EU/2016/2341.

30 Article 3(16) the MiCA Regulation. Compared to the Commission Draft, the list was extended with transfer services and portfolio management of crypto-assets.

31 Article 59 the MiCA Regulation.

including marketing communications, provided to clients must be fair, clear and not misleading. Service providers must not, deliberately or negligently, mislead a client in relation to the real or perceived advantages of any crypto-assets. They must also warn clients of the risks associated with transactions in crypto-assets.[32] In addition to these general conditions, the regulation sets out specific requirements by type of service.[33] It has been argued that the most stringent rules are related to custody services.[34]

Once adopted, the regulation will apply directly in all member states and effectively harmonize the regulation of crypto-assets across the EU. Under the MiCA framework, passporting, i.e., authorization in one member state will provide the access to the entire internal market, will be possible.[35] In terms of third country entities, offerors should notify their crypto-asset white paper and marketing communications to the competent authority of the member state where the crypto-assets are intended to be offered.[36] Moreover, a third country firm that provides crypto-asset services would need EU authorization if it seeks to solicit clients or potential clients in the EU, as well as if it wishes to promote or advertise its services in the internal market.[37]

From a Swedish perspective, the MiCA Regulation could be a welcomed initiative. In 2021, the Director General of FI stated that he was pleased that MiCA was undergoing negotiations at the EU level.[38] Moreover, the regulation of stable coins could address the Swedish central bank's concerns regarding financial stability. Under the MiCA regime, the lack of proper of consumer protection would be, at least partially, rectified. In addition, as further developed below, the risks of crypto-assets being used for money laundering activities falls under EU's anti-money laundering framework. As for the environmental issues, although the MiCA Regulation has not provided a solution as far-reaching as the proposal of FI and the Swedish environmental agency, it has not overlooked the significance of the environmental impact of crypto-assets. It is prescribed that actors in the crypto market are required to declare information on their environmental and climate footprint. Draft regulatory technical

32 Article 66 the MiCA Regulation.

33 Articles 75–82 the MiCA Regulation.

34 Zetzsche et al. 2020, p. 20.

35 Article 59(7) the MiCA Regulation.

36 Recital 31 the MiCA Regulation.

37 Article 61 the MiCA Regulation.

38 Crypto-assets Today and in the Future, Speech by Erik Thedéen, Director General of Finansinspektionen, p. 4, available at https://www.fi.se/contentassets/0dbda3ac99ba46248c92de5f4261f591/tal-crypto-assets-today-future-erik-thedeen-13dec21-eng.pdf [last viewed 30 April 2024].

standards will be developed by the European Securities and Markets Authority (ESMA) and European Banking Authority (EBA).[39]

3.4 *Anti-Money Laundering and Criminal Provisions*

Crypto-assets were addressed in EU's directive on the prevention of the use of the financial system for the purposes of money laundering or terrorist financing (AMLD V).[40] The directive extended the scope to include providers of exchange services between virtual currencies and fiat currencies as well as custodian wallet providers.[41] The Swedish implementation of AMLD V included changes to the Act on Currency Exchange and Certain Financial Operations (1996:1006). Under the Act, legal and natural persons that seek to carry out currency trading on a large scale or other financial operations, such as the management of or trade with virtual currencies, must register with the financial supervisory authority.[42] They must, inter alia, comply with the anti-money laundering framework including the Swedish Money Laundering and Terrorist Financing Prevention Act and related regulations.

Under Swedish law, custodian wallet providers are entities that safeguard private cryptographic keys on behalf of their clients, to hold, store and transfer virtual currencies.[43] The definition of providers of virtual currency exchange services goes however beyond AMLD V. As noted in the preparatory work, the scope of AMLD V does not encompass providers of exchange services between different virtual currencies, the Swedish government established however that it was necessary to include these providers. As a result, in Sweden, providers of virtual currency exchange services are those engaged in the exchange between virtual currencies and fiat currencies, electronic money, or other virtual currencies.[44]

---

39 See e.g. Recital 7 the MiCA Regulation.

40 Article 1(2)(d)(19) of Directive (EU) 2018/843 of the European Parliament and of the Council of 30 May 2018 amending Directive (EU) 2015/849 on the prevention of the use of the financial system for the purposes of money laundering or terrorist financing, and amending Directives 2009/138/EC and 2013/36/EU [hereafter AMLD V]. It should be noted that the Commission adopted a new anti-money laundering and countering the financing of terrorism (AML/CFT) legislative package, including a proposal for AMLD VI, in 2021. The Council and Parliament reached a provisional agreement on the directive in January 2024, and it was passed in the Parliament in April 2024.

41 Recital 8 of AMLD V.

42 Sec. 1(2) of the Act on Currency Exchange and Certain Financial Operations.

43 Legislative Proposal, Enhanced Measures against Money Laundering and Terrorism Financing [Sw. Skärpta åtgärder mot penningtvätt och finansiering av terrorism], Prop. 2018/19:150, p. 94 (hereafter Prop. 2018/19:150).

44 Prop. 2018/19:150, p. 38.

Money laundering is criminalized in Sweden, the Act on Penalties for Money Offences applies to all persons and entities that must comply with anti-money laundering regulations. Further, Sweden has implemented the Directive on Combating Fraud and Counterfeiting of Non-cash Means of Payment by amending the Penal Code.[45] Moreover, general criminal law provisions on, inter alia, fraud are applicable since virtual currencies are considered property under Swedish law.

It should also be noted that the revised Transfer of Funds Regulation, along with certain parts of the MiCA Regulation, entered into force in June 2023.[46] The regulation gives effect to the recommendations of the Financial Action Task Force (FATF) on virtual assets and wire transfers.[47] Under the revised framework, the obligation of payment service providers is extended to accompany transfers of funds with information on the payer and payee to crypto-assets. The regulation will apply from December 2024.

4 Private Law Issues

4.1 *General Departure Points*

Evaluating crypto-assets from a private law perspective is not an easy task. In the Swedish legal system, while certain issues can be solved by existing statutory provisions and legal principles, others remain problematic. As developed below, crypto-assets are recognized as property under Swedish law. Crypto-assets are not especially regulated, it is thus necessary to apply general principles of private law. The Sale of Goods Act (1990:931) and the Funds Accounting Act (1944:181) could be applied analogously. In terms of the relationships between the different participants in a blockchain, they are essentially regulated by a patchwork of private law provisions. Issues arising between the participants would be determined on the basis of the particular circumstances and whether they fall under the scope of a specific area of law.

In terms of legal sources, since crypto-assets are not regulated by a specific private law statute, there is no preparatory work, which is an important legal

45 Legislative Proposal, A New Criminal Provision that Protects Means of Payment [Sw. En ny straffbestämmelse som skyddar betalningsverktyg], Prop. 2020/21:73.

46 Regulation (EU) 2023/1113 of the European Parliament and of the Council of 31 May 2023 on Information Accompanying Transfers of Funds and Certain Crypto-Assets and Amending Directive (EU) 2015/849.

47 See Recommendations 15 and 16, the International Standards on Combating Money Laundering and the Financing of Terrorism and Proliferation, the FATF Recommendations, updated November 2023.

source in Swedish law, available. Neither has the Supreme Court provided any guidance on the subject matter. The taxation of crypto-assets has been reviewed by the Supreme Administrative Court.[48] The findings are however not very helpful from a private law perspective. While crypto-assets have been subject to scholarly debate, legal doctrine in the field remains rather scarce.[49] In 2021, a governmental research report was issued regarding Riksbanken's initiative to introduce a central bank digital currency (CBDC). The report did not only examine CBDC but cryptocurrencies as well, shedding some light on the understanding of crypto-assets from a private law perspective.[50]

4.2 *Ownership and Transfer of Ownership*

Although the question has been disputed, it could be argued that crypto-assets are recognized as property under Swedish law. An important aspect to take into account is that they are considered fungible. In general, it is possible for intangibles to be recognized as property without a specific legislation deeming it so in the Swedish legal system. They must however be recognized as property by the parties and the general public. Under such circumstances, crypto-assets can be legally owned.[51]

As discussed above, the regulatory framework in Sweden pre-MiCA prescribed that custodian wallet providers were subject to registration but not supervision. The relationship between such a provider and its clients was not specifically regulated. In order to determine the relationship between the two, it is necessary to take a closer look at the functioning of the service provider. The Swedish Prosecution Authority issued a legal guidance on cryptocurrencies in 2021.[52] It explicated that transfers of cryptocurrencies require private cryptographic keys, which can be stored in different manners. If they are in a wallet held by another party, it is referred to as custodial wallet. The legal guidance describes the functioning of such wallets as a client of a custodian wallet

48 See section 5 below.

49 See e.g. Elgebrant, Emil, Kryptovalutor: Särskild rättsverkan vid innehav av bitcoins och andra liknande betalningsmedel, Wolters Kluwer, Stockholm, 2016 (hereafter Elgebrant 2016).

50 Elgebrant, Emil, Forskningsrapport om juridiska aspekter av digitala valutor – En förmögenhetsrättslig studie, Betalningsutredningen, Fi 2020:12 (hereafter Elgebrant 2020).

51 Elgebrant 2016, p. 31 f. For the discussion on the level of recognition by the general public, see also Lindskog, Stefan, Betalning, 3 ed., Norstedts Juridik, 2022, p. 79 ff.

52 Kryptovalutor, Rättslig vägledning 2021:11, Åklagarmyndigheten, August 2021, available at https://www.aklagare.se/globalassets/dokument/rattspromemorior-och-rattslig-vagledning/rav-202111-kryptovalutor.pdf [last viewed 31 January 2022] (hereafter Swedish Prosecution Authority Legal Guidance on Cryptocurrencies 2021).

provider would generally register an account with the latter. By logging into the account, the client will be able to manage her bitcoins. However, this does not necessarily mean that the keys to the crypto-assets are at the disposal of the client. The keys could be known to the wallet provider only. It is also possible that the means of the client could be mixed up with others' at the same address and the wallet provider keeps track of the means of different clients by internal bookkeeping or other similar systems. Hence, albeit the client can view the balance of her account and manage the account freely, she is essentially dependent on the wallet provider to make a transaction in the blockchain. Under such circumstances, it has been viewed that the functioning of the wallet provider would be similar to a bank's, and the client would owe a claim on the wallet provider.[53]

If such a comparison could be made, it would evoke the question of whether the bank or the client owns the money in the latter's account. Under Swedish law, it is generally viewed that the money would become the bank's property and the client holding a claim on the bank.[54]

If new means, i.e., crypto-assets, are created through an airdrop and appear in a client's account, it would be viewed as a donation.[55] The client would be the original owner. Donation is a contract under Swedish law and acknowledgement from the receiving party is required. The threshold is however low, the receiver of a gift does for example not need to contact the donator. In this case, it could be sufficient that the client logs into her account and see the new funds (and do not reject them thereafter).

Under Swedish law, since crypto-assets are recognized as property, they could be protected by the legal order as other types of properties. Private ownership of property is a fundamental premise in Sweden.[56] Owners have the right to transfer ownership rather freely. It is thus possible to transfer the ownership of crypto-assets. They can for example be sold, exchanged, or donated as gifts. However, due to the particular characteristics of crypto-assets, it raises the difficult question of how ownership can be manifested to an external party.[57]

---

53 The Swedish Prosecution Authority Legal Guidance on Cryptocurrencies 2021, p. 8.

54 See e.g. Wallin-Norman, Karin, Finansiella instrument, Jure, Stockholm, 2011, p. 18. Elgebrant considers the client to hold a claim on the bank as well, but argues that the claim is the object of ownership, see Elgebrant 2020, p. 19, 29 and 46.

55 Elgebrant 2016.

56 Certain statutory incursions do however exist in relation to for example land leases and landlord/tenant law.

57 Elgebrant 2016, p. 77 ff.

As for donation, the general principles on donation would apply. Most likely, a donation of crypto-assets would be comparable to donating other properties that are fungible such as (traditional) money. If an intermediary, such as a custodian wallet provider, is used to perform the transfer of the gift from one client's account to another account, and the wallet provider functions as a traditional bank as described above, an agent-principal relationship between the wallet provider and the client would arise. The wallet provider would be subject to the general obligations of an agent in performing the transfer. From a law of obligations perspective, the use of an intermediary will not have an impact on the relationship between the giving and receiving part of a gift. However, as further explicated below, it could have relevance in determining when a donation has been completed.

In principle, crypto-assets could be exchanged as consideration for some form of counter performance as long as their value is recognized by the parties and by the general public. It is legally possible to sell and buy crypto-assets. It can also be traded with fiat currencies and other crypto-assets. As seen above, virtual currency exchanges between virtual and fiat currencies as well as between different virtual currencies are accepted in Sweden.[58]

In a sale of crypto-assets, it is necessary to determine when the sale has been completed. As discussed by Elgebrant, the Act on Sale of Goods could apply analogously. It should be noted that a crypto transaction would involve several steps. The question is whether all the measures or only some of them must be taken in order to complete a sale. The Sales Act would require all the measures to be taken, a registration in a wallet is for example not sufficient. The wallet provider needs to execute the order and a transaction in the blockchain must have taken place.[59] This line reasoning can be applied to donation as well, the donation is completed when all the steps to make a crypto transaction have been taken.

Crypto-assets can be inherited and included in a will. They would be considered assets belonging to the estate in a similar fashion as other types of assets. The estate would distribute the inheritance among the heirs according to the will, if there is a valid one, and the general rules under the Inheritance Code. Most likely, if the keys are held in a custodial wallet, it would be necessary to specify that it is the crypto-assets that one wishes to pass on as they are the ones that are recognized as property.[60]

---

58 See section 3.4. above.

59 Elgebrant 2016, p. 80.

60 The private keys would for example be viewed as technical means to administrating the crypto-assets, see e.g. Elgebrant 2020, p. 31 ff and The Swedish Prosecution Authority Legal Guidance on Cryptocurrencies 2021.

4.3 *Property Rights and Insolvency Law*

It has been emphasized that the term 'property right' can be used in more than one sense in Swedish legal writing. It may refer the powers that the owner of a property possesses in relation to any other person, such as receiving yield from the property. This is usually called static property right or static third-party protection. The other aspect is so-called dynamic property rights or dynamic third-party protection, which includes all issues that may arise between one of the parties in a contract and a third party, when a property is assigned or when limited right in the property is granted to another person. If one of the parties to the contract is awarded third party protection, she is said to have a proprietary right and an obligatory (contractual) right.[61]

In terms of crypto-assets, first of all, recognized as property, they could be subject to attachment or otherwise seized. They could, under certain circumstances, also be pledged or used as security in a loan (as long as agreed upon by the parties).[62] As for attachment, crypto-assets could be subject to attachment under the Enforcement Code (1981:774), which prescribes that personal property (movables) can be taken in execution if the property belongs to the debtor or if it can be presumed that the property belongs to her.[63] In terms of presumption of ownership, the Code states that presumption is made if the property is in the debtor's possession, unless the property belongs to another.[64] In this regard, presumption of ownership cannot be assumed since crypto-assets cannot be possessed.[65]

In terms of seizure, the matter was discussed in the Swedish Prosecution Authority's legal guidance. Crypto-assets can be seized, but only as monetary seizure.[66] In Sweden, it is possible to seize money, claims of a right to payment or other rights. While crypto-assets are not money or claims of a right to payment, they fall under the scope of other rights.[67]

Further, under Swedish insolvency law, if one party holds crypto-assets for another, it could be possible for the latter to obtain protection in the former's bankruptcy. As mentioned above, crypto-assets are viewed as fungible properties in Sweden. Elgebrant has noted that the Funds Accounting Act could be applied analogously to fungible properties, including crypto-assets. The Act

61 Håstad, Torgny, Property Rights regarding Movables, in Bogdan, Michael (eds.), Swedish Legal System, Norstedts Juridik, 2010, p. 419.

62 For an in-depth analysis on this matter, see Elgebrant 2016, pp. 106–112.

63 Sec. 4:17 of the Enforcement Code.

64 Sec. 4:18 of the Enforcement Code.

65 Elgebrant 2016, p. 88.

66 The Swedish Prosecution Authority Legal Guidance 2021, p. 22.

67 Legislative Proposal, A More Effective Criminalization of Money Laundering [Sw. En effektivare kriminalisering av penningtvätt], Prop. 2013/14:121, p. 119.

prescribes that the right to separation is granted if one party is holding means for another based on an assignment, such as in a commission relationship, an agreement between the parties, or due to obligations specified in legislation. Under such circumstances, the party holding crypto-assets would be obligated to separate the means of another from her own.[68]

4.4 *Loss of Crypto-Assets: Liability and Compensation*

In Sweden, someone that loses crypto-assets due to hacking or fraud would generally be protected by the legal order. In the case of hacking, it would be possible to bring a criminal action against the hacker if she is identified as hacking is a criminal offense in Sweden.[69] One would thus be able to receive compensation for the loss. As discussed below, a question that can arise is how to determine the value of crypto-assets.[70] However, if the hacker sells the crypto-assets to a third party, the buyer would not be protected as a bona fide purchaser under the Good Faith Acquisition of Personal Property Act (1986:796) since the scope of the act is limited to chattels. Neither could the Act on Promissory Notes (1936:81), which prescribes protection for bona fide acquisition after double disposition, i.e., when the owner has assigned or pledged her property twice, be applied analogously.[71]

Further, if someone was misled to agree to transfer her crypto-assets to another, the agreement could be found void based on the provision on fraud under the Contracts Act (1915:218).[72] Fraud is also a criminal offence under the Penal Code (962:700).[73] A criminal action would thus be possible.

4.5 *Litigation in Relation to Crypto-Assets*

Insofar, there have been no rulings from the Swedish Supreme Court, only the Supreme Administrative Court, that are related to crypto-assets. A number of crypto-related disputes have however been brought to the lower courts. Although rulings by the Court of Appeal and District Court hold no precedence in Swedish law, they could provide some insights into often disputed issues with crypto-assets.

Possibly, a ruling from Nedre Norrland Court of Appeal could be used to illustrate the various aspects of crypto-related disputes.[74] The case was a criminal action against a Swedish person that hacked into the computer of a

68 Elgebrant 2016, pp. 96–99.
69 Sec. 4:9c of the Penal Code. See also sec. 9:1 of the Penal Code.
70 See section 4.5. below.
71 Elgebrant 2016, pp. 82–83.
72 Sec. 30 of the Contracts Act.
73 Sec. 9:1 of the Penal Code.
74 Hovrätten för nedre Norrland mål B 377–18.

Slovenian person. The hacker had transferred the plaintiff's LEOcoins to himself without permission.

The defendant claimed that no economic loss was incurred since LEOcoins have no recognized value under the legal order. The Court of Appeal stated however that virtual currencies are now an established notion in the Swedish legal order, notwithstanding some currencies such as Bitcoin is more well-known than others. The court further stated that it should be generally acknowledged that virtual currencies can be sold on digital trading platforms and in some contexts be used as means of payment instead of payments made through traditional bank systems. In this regard, the court confirmed that crypto-assets should be considered as property and its value being generally acknowledged.

Another aspect that was raised concerned the value of virtual currencies. In the case, it could be established that at the point of the transfer, the LEOcoins were listed on coinmarkecap.com. The prosecutor stated that the LEOcoins at hand had a value of 190 579 SEK, supported by among others information from coinmarketcap.com. The court concluded however that in the absence of proof of, for example, how virtual currencies are listed and the regulation thereof, and if possible, the sale of the LEOcoins at the exact time of the transfer, it could not be sufficiently proved that the value of the LEOcoins in question was equivalent to 190 579 SEK. It could however be established that the bitcoins that the claimant bought with the LEOcoins for had a value between 20 000–30 000 SEK. It could thus be established that the LEOcoins were worth at least 20 000 SEK.

This was indeed only one of the crypto-related cases in the appellate courts and more studies are needed to draw any conclusive analysis. However, an aspect that could be discussed is the valuation of crypto-assets. As mentioned above, the financial supervisory authority FI has expressed concerns with the unregulated state of crypto marketplaces. In this regard, the upcoming regulations on the operation of trading platforms for crypto-assets could address the regulatory gap and provide some clarity for the courts as well.

5 Tax Measures

Crypto-assets and miners are subject to taxation in Sweden. In 2018, the Swedish Supreme Administrative Court provided guidance on the taxation of bitcoins.[75] The case involved an individual who had purchased, sold and exchanged with bitcoins. He had also used bitcoins to buy goods. The question raised was which

---

75 HFD 2018 ref. 72.

category of assets bitcoins should belong to. In this regard, it should be noted that in Sweden, individuals are liable to tax on capital income, including capital gains, and the rate is flat. The methods for computing the taxable capital gain from different types of assets differ however significantly. In terms of bitcoins, the court concluded that they are not equivalent to transferable securities such as shares, or a foreign currency. Neither do they fall under the category of personal property. Bitcoins were thus considered as "other assets" under the Income Tax Act (1999:1229).[76] As a result, the capital gains tax on crypto-assets is calculated using the so-called average basis cost method (Sw. genomsnittsmetoden).[77]

The scope of capital gains tax on crypto-assets has been explicated in a legal guidance from the Swedish tax authority, Skatteverket. It includes the sale, exchange and use of crypto-assets to pay for goods and services.[78] Lending activities involving bitcoins and other fungible crypto-assets are subject to capital gains tax as well if the debtor can sell or otherwise freely dispose over the assets. The tax authority has issued a statement regarding crypto-related lending activities, including lending to decentralized trading platforms, lending to decentralized loan platforms, lending via centralized loan platforms and decentralized loan of crypto-assets.[79] Using crypto-assets as security in a loan is however excluded from the remit of capital gains taxation as the ownership of the assets has not be transferred. Giving or receiving, as well as inheriting, crypto-assets are not subject to taxation since there is no gift or inheritance taxes in Sweden.

Further, for individuals, if crypto-assets are received as payment for work, it will be taxed as employment income. If the assets are later on sold or otherwise exchanged, they will be subject to capital gains tax. In terms of mining, in accordance with the statement of the tax authority, bitcoins and other crypto-assets gained by mining would generally fall under the scope of employment income, as income from a hobby. However, depending on the circumstances, the assets could be taxed as business income. Factors that the tax authority would take into account are whether the activities are conducted regularly in a professional and cost-effective manner over a longer period with appropriate equipment. Another aspect is whether a surplus can be expected from the activities over the entire financial calculation period. Lastly, if the computing

76 Sec. 52:3 sub-paragraph 1 of the Income Tax Act.

77 Sec. 48:7 of the Income Tax Act.

78 Rättslig vägledning, Kryptotillgångar, Skatteverket, available at https://www4.skatteverket.se/rattsligvagledning/2832.html?q=BITCOIN#h-Kryptotillgangar [last viewed 30 April 2024].

79 Kapitalvinstbeskattning vid överföring av kryptotillgång till en plattform för utlåning, byte eller förvaring, Ställningstagande av Skatteverket, Dnr: 8-1302842, 9 November 2021, available at https://www4.skatteverket.se/rattsligvagledning/398415.html [last viewed 30 April 2024].

capacity of the equipment can be assumed to generate more than 25 bitcoins annually (or the equivalent value in transaction fees or other virtual currency). However, if the operation is small-scale and no surplus is expected over the calculation period, it is not considered a business operation.[80]

6 Conclusion

In the past decades, especially in the aftermath of the financial crisis of 2008, EU has increasingly enhanced the regulation and supervision of the financial markets. A development that has substantially altered the legal landscape in the member states. Sweden is no exemption in this regard.[81] In terms of the regulation of crypto-assets, as seen above, the MiCA Regulation seems to be a welcomed initiative. Considering the state of play in Sweden pre-MiCA, it could be argued that the EU regulation may serve as a missing puzzle in the regulatory landscape. Undoubtfully, questions will arise when the regulation enters in application.

However, while crypto-assets will fall under the remit of financial regulation and supervision in the EU, the risks of crypto-assets being used for illegitimated and illegal purposes will most likely continue to exist. This is no surprise considering the anonymous nature of crypto-assets. In this regard, it is crucial to have proper anti-money laundering and terrorism financing framework in place. However, given the original vision of crypto-assets such as Bitcoin, i.e., creating a peer-to-peer electronic cash system that is decentralized and anonymous, it cannot be excluded that there will be crypto-assets that aim to operate outside of the traditional constraints of nation borders. Here, as long as they do not serve illegitimate and illegal purposes, the a-national character of crypto-assets could, and perhaps should, be left intact.

In terms of the significant carbon footprints left by some crypto-assets, although discussed at an initial stage, a ban has insofar not been introduced at the EU level. In this regard, in addition to any regulatory initiative, it is necessary to follow the developments on the market. Ethereum, which is one of the largest cryptocurrencies based on market cap in the world, switched for example from the proof-of-work to proof-of-stake mechanism in September 2022. It is indeed too early to draw any conclusive assumptions, the crypto market will

80 Beskattning vid mining av bitcoin och andra virtuella valutor m.m., Ställningstagande av Skatteverket, Dnr: 131 191846-15/111, 24 April 2015, available at https://www4.skatteverket.se/rattsligvagledning/338713.html?date=2015-04-24&q=mining [last viewed 30 April 2024].

81 For more about the impact of EU financial markets law on Sweden, see Chen, K., Legal Aspects of Conflicts of Interest in the Financial Services Sector in the EU and China – the XYZ of Norm-making, Doctoral Dissertation, Stockholm University, June 2018 (hereafter Chen 2018).

most likely undergo a number of changes during the coming years, to prepare for upcoming regulations as well as seeking to correct itself in order to avoid further regulations.

Lastly, while EU legislations in the financial markets are often viewed as of a public law nature, the private/public law divide is not a guiding principle in EU law. Although the private/public law divide is deeply entrenched in the legal system of many member states, EU law operates on different terms. As seen in other areas of EU financial services law, legislations from the EU have not only reshaped the member states' public regulation of the financial markets but have had a significant impact of the private law framework as well. The duty of loyalty prescribed upon financial advisors and portfolio managers is merely one example.[82]

Evidently, the field of crypto-assets is following this development. As discussed above, in addition to authorization requirements, issuers and service providers of crypto-assets are subject to various organizational and conduct of business rules under the MiCA Regulation. Crypto-asset service providers are for example obligated to act in the best interests of the clients, which can be recognized as the duty of loyalty in many national private law regimes.[83] The contractual relationship between a crypto-related service provider and a client would thus no longer only be governed by the private law of the member states, it will be regulated at the EU level as well. This could be viewed as another example of EU financial regulation influencing the development of contract law in the financial markets.[84] It could be argued that the introduction of MiCA will give rise to a rather intricate interplay between private and public law in the field of crypto-assets in the EU. The potential effects of the upcoming EU regulation on the private law framework of crypto-assets in the member states could thus be an interesting, especially from a comparative perspective, topic to explore.

Acknowledgement

I would like to thank Emil Elgebrant for all his insightful comments about cryptocurrency. I would also like to thank Jori Munukka and Johan Sandstedt for their valuable comments on earlier drafts of this chapter. All errors and omissions remain my own.

---

82 For more about the duty of loyalty owed by investment firms towards their clients, see Chen 2018, p. 196 f.

83 Article 66 the MiCA Regulation. See also Articles 14 and 27 the MiCA Regulation for offerors and issuers. It should however be noted once a private law principle has been transformed to a regulatory requirement, it is necessary to apply and interpret it in conformity with the new regulatory context, see Chen 2018, p. 176 f.

84 For further discussion on this interplay, see Chen 2018, p. 182.

Switzerland

Rolf H. Weber and Rainer Baisch

1 Introduction

1.1 *Historical Developments*

Already in 2014, the Federal Council published a Report assessing the legal environment of virtual currencies and the potential risks of loss and misuse on the new decentralized and cross-border infrastructures.[1] Notwithstanding this Report, subsequently a definition of cryptocurrencies has not been implemented in Swiss law; there is no specific statutory provision related to cryptocurrencies (except the surrender right of Art. 242*a* Bankruptcy Act applying to all crypto assets).

In December 2018, the Federal Council adopted a general Report[2] on the legal framework for blockchain and distributed ledger technology (DLT), especially addressing regulatory needs regarding the financial sector. On the one hand, the Report stated that Switzerland's legal framework is suitable for dealing with new technologies, including blockchain; on the other, the Report analyzed the need for selective legal adjustments. In parallel to this Report an analysis of an interdepartmental working group on money laundering and terrorist financing risks was published.[3] This analysis describes potential threats caused by crypto assets due to the anonymity of token transactions and their direct execution without a financial intermediary. Not only the potential of the criminal exploitation of design errors in cryptocurrencies but also investor fraud, particularly in the case of Initial Coin Offerings (ICOs), is addressed, as well as crime patterns like terrorist financing, laundering of funds from the sale of illegal services and products, phishing scams, or drug trafficking.

---

1 Federal Council report on virtual currencies in response to the Schwaab (13.3687) and Weibel (13.4070) postulates of June 25, 2014; <https://www.newsd.admin.ch/newsd/message/attachments/35355.pdf >.

2 Federal Council report: Legal framework for distributed ledger technology and blockchain in Switzerland. An overview with a focus on the financial sector, Bern, 14 December 2018; <https://www.newsd.admin.ch/newsd/message/attachments/55153.pdf>.

3 National Risk Assessment (NRA): Risk of money laundering and terrorist financing posed by crypto assets and crowdfunding Report of the interdepartmental coordinating group on combating money laundering and the financing of terrorism (CGMF), October 2018; <https://www.newsd.admin.ch/newsd/message/attachments/56166.pdf>.

 | DOI:10.1163/9789004722507_026

Considering the potential for innovation and enhanced efficiency both in the financial sector and in other sectors of the economy the Federal Council was interested in the opportunities offered by the distributed ledger technology for Switzerland. Therefore, framework conditions were developed that support the establishment of an innovative and sustainable place for fintech and blockchain companies, while combating abuses and ensuring the integrity and good reputation of Switzerland as a financial centre and business location.

Regarding Blockchain and distributed ledger technology, Switzerland has taken a pioneering role in the crypto-community with the home of the «Crypto Valley» in the Canton of Zug, the FINMA Guidelines related to the token issuance,[4] the technology-neutral DLT Act of September 2020[5] (in force since February and August 2021, respectively)[6] and the FINMA-approved SIX Digital Exchange (SDX).[7] In practice, all common cryptocurrencies are available for the broader public.

The welcoming Swiss crypto laws attracted some important players in the crypto universe; therefore, based on the positive approach towards blockchain solutions, many crypto companies are located in Switzerland. For example, the company behind the Ether, Ethereum Foundation, has its domicile in Zug;[8] its decentralized, open-source blockchain runs smart contract functionalities; Ether is the cryptocurrency generated by the Ethereum protocol being now based on a proof-of-stake system for adding more blocks to the blockchain.[9]

---

4 FINMA, ICO Guidelines, 16 February 2018; <https://www.finma.ch/en/news/2018/02/20180216-mm-ico-wegleitung>.

5 Bundesgesetz zur Anpassung des Bundesrechts an Entwicklungen der Technik verteilter elektronischer Register, BBl 2020 7801; Loi fédérale sur l'adaptation du droit fédéral aux développements de la technologie des registres électroniques distribués, FF 2020 7559.

6 Federal Council, Federal Council brings DLT Act fully into force and issues ordinance, 18 June 2021; <https://www.admin.ch/gov/en/start/documentation/media-releases.msg-id-84035.html>.

7 FINMA, FINMA issues first-ever approval for a stock exchange and a central securities depository for the trading of tokens, 10 September 2021; <https://www.finma.ch/en/news/2021/09/finma-issues-first-ever-approval-for-a-stock-exchange-and-a-central-securities-depository-for-the-trading-of-tokens/>.

8 See <https://ethereum.org/en/>.

9 Proof-of-stake validation uses pre-defined consensus mechanisms to achieve distributed consensus. The proof-of-work validation is based on miners expending energy. Ethereum uses now proof-of-stake, where validators explicitly stake capital in the form of ETH into a smart contract on Ethereum. This staked ETH then acts as collateral that can be destroyed if the validator behaves dishonestly or lazily. The validator is responsible for checking that new blocks propagated over the network are valid and for occasionally creating and propagating new blocks themselves (<https://ethereum.org/en/developers/docs/consensus-mechanisms/pos/>).

Solana, a high-performance open-source blockchain, having one of the ten biggest values regarding market capitalization, is a leading blockchain for NFTs.[10] Also Tezos, a self-upgradable and energy-efficient proof of stake blockchain, was established in Switzerland.[11] Bitcoin Suisse, a regulated Swiss financial intermediary (but not licensed as a bank), provides trading, prime brokerage, custody, lending, staking, and other crypto-financial services for private and institutional clients.[12] Since 2021, in the Canton of Zug taxes can be paid with cryptocurrencies which are daily exchanged to fiat money by Bitcoin Suisse.[13]

1.2 *Act on Distributed Ledger Technology*

Based on the idea that there is no need for fundamental adjustments to the Swiss legal framework, the DLT Act (Federal Act on the Adaptation of Federal Laws to Developments in Distributed Electronic Register Technology)[14] and the associated Ordinance[15] with specific adjustments concretizing the relevant topics came into force in 2021. The DLT Act sets provisions that are intended to make the legal framework applicable to tokens; however, the DLT Act is not a separate legal instrument; the DLT Act adapted ten relevant laws in the DLT field. The following changes in the legal framework have mainly been introduced:

- In civil law, increase of legal certainty for the transfer of rights by means of digital registers;
- In insolvency law, further clarification of the segregation of crypto-based assets in the event of bankruptcy;
- In financial market law, introduction of a new and flexible authorization category for blockchain-based financial market infrastructures;
- In banking law, reconciliation of the bank insolvency law provisions with the adjustments in general insolvency law;

---

10 See <https://solana.com/de>.

11 See <https://tezos.com/>.

12 See <https://www.bitcoinsuisse.com/>.

13 See <https://www.zg.ch/behoerden/finanzdirektion/steuerverwaltung/tax-payment-with-cryptocourrencies>.

14 DLT Act, Bundesgesetz zur Anpassung des Bundesrechts an Entwicklungen der Technik verteilter elektronischer Register, BBl 2020 7801; < https://www.fedlex.admin.ch/eli/fga/2020/2007/de>.

15 Verordnung vom 18. Juni 2021 zur Anpassung des Bundesrechts an Entwicklungen der Technik verteilter elektronischer Register, AS 2021 400; Ordonnance du 18 juin 2021 sur l'adaptation du droit fédéral aux développements de la technologie des registres électroniques distribués, RO 2021 400.

- In anti-money laundering law, more explicit anchoring of the current practice of making decentralized trading platforms subject to the Anti-Money Laundering Act.

The Swiss financial market regulations generally are principles-based and as far as possible technology-neutral.[16] Thereby, the legal framework intends to reflect the nature of tokens while the focus is set on the economic function ("substance over form"). In consequence, the legal system allows for some flexibility to explore innovative business models; however, the financial market authority (FINMA) requires that projects be assessed on a case-by-case basis by applying the principle «same risks, same rules».

2 Definition and Legal Qualification

2.1 *Crypto Assets and Cryptocurrencies*

Like the legislation in most other countries, Swiss law does not contain a definition of the term "cryptocurrency" or "virtual currency". Generally, a cryptocurrency is defined as a digital non-governmental asset based on a combination of cryptographic algorithms; its existence is confirmed and recorded on a ledger being distributed on a network of independent computers.[17] In 2012, the European Central Bank defined cryptocurrencies as a type of unregulated currency which is issued and often controlled by its developers.[18]

Swiss legal doctrine contains definitions for cryptocurrencies (or virtual currencies, respectively),[19] which are partly based on the «ICO Guidelines» published in 2018 by FINMA: "*Payment tokens are synonymous with cryptocurrencies and have no further functions or links to other development projects. Tokens may in some cases only develop the necessary functionality and become accepted as a means of payment over a period of time.*"

16 The reader should also be aware that the authors' views on the *lex lata* are partially tentative due to the nature of the topic as a moving target. Therefore, questions in private law can only be addressed based on general principles or the use of analogies when there are no cryptocurrency-specific rules in place or relevant case law available.

17 World Economic Forum (WEF), Navigating Cryptocurrency Regulation: An Industry Perspective on the Insights and Tools Needed to Shape Balanced Crypto Regulation, 2021, 5; <https://www3.weforum.org/docs/WEF_Navigating_Cryptocurrency_Regulation_2021.pdf>.

18 European Central Bank, Virtual Currency Schemes, Frankfurt am Main 2012; <https://www.ecb.europa.eu/pub/pdf/other/virtualcurrencyschemes201210en.pdf>.

19 See C. Zellweger-Gutknecht and R. H. Weber (2022) 6 *EuZ*, G10 and G18/19; <https://eizpublishing.ch/wp-content/uploads/2022/09/EuZ-2022-06-Zellweger-Weber-Horst-V1_01-korr-20220601.pdf> see also R. H. Weber and R. Baisch (2023) 39 *B.F.L.R.*, 473/74; M. Brogli and G. Loderer (2024) Kryptowährungen, Stablecoins und CBDC, in: C. Stengel and T. Weber (eds.), Digitale und mobile Zahlungssysteme, 2 ed. Zurich, 85-94.

2.2 *Legal Qualification*

Switzerland is a crypto-friendly country based on a progressive and positive attitude towards cryptocurrencies; however, no cryptocurrency is legal tender in Switzerland.

Due to the lack of regulatory requirements, FINMA as the Swiss supervisory authority decided, also in the interest of the DLT community, to publish a basic token classification scheme encompassing three groups, thereby acknowledging that hybrid forms and transformations are possible; consequently, any project related to the issuance, trading, or custody of tokens, must be evaluated against these criteria:[20]

- *Payment tokens* (*cryptocurrencies*) are intended to be means of payment and do not give the holder any claims against the issuer. Payment tokens do not qualify as legal tender under Swiss law, but they can be used as a private means of payment (e.g., Bitcoin, Ether, Tezos).
- *Utility tokens* give access to a digital utility or service provided by the issuer on an already operational blockchain (e.g., Ethereum).
- *Asset/security tokens* are tokens that secure legal claims to dividends, interest payments, membership rights, etc., or can represent shares in a company comparable to conventional financial assets.

Based on the FINMA ICO Guidelines cryptocurrencies are classified as "payment tokens". In a decision from January 2024, the Swiss Federal Administrative Court (Bundesverwaltungsgericht) addressed the question whether a specific blockchain-based token, which was distributed to several thousand investors resulting in received funds amounting to millions, must be considered as a security. The classification as a security leads to the need of a respective FINMA license because anyone who trades in securities needs a permit. The court qualified the token in question including the value rights embodied in it as security within the meaning of the Swiss law.[21]

After having received an enquiry from the Geneva-based Libra Association, FINMA published a Supplement to its ICO Guidelines in September 2019 outlining the approach towards stable coins under Swiss supervisory law, to be mainly applied in respect of the Libra/Diem/Facebook project.[22] Equally for the classification of stable coins, FINMA follows the existing approach applied

---

20 ICO Guidelines of February 2018; <https://www.finma.ch/en/~/media/finma/dokumente/dokumentencenter/myfinma/1bewilligung/fintech/wegleitung-ico.pdf?la=en>.

21 Swiss Federal Administrative Court (Bundesverwaltungsgericht), Judgment number B-4185/2020, 16.01.2024.

22 See D. A. Zetzsche, R. P. Buckley, and D. W. Arner, 'Regulating Libra' (2021) 41:1 *Oxford Journal of Legal Studies*, 80.

to DLT-based tokens and focuses on the economic function and the purpose of a token according to a principles-based and technology-neutral understanding. Therefore, when assessing concrete projects, FINMA applies the «same risks, same rules» principle targeted to the specific features of each case.[23] Because stable coins can vary greatly, the requirements under supervisory law may differ depending on which assets (e.g., currencies, commodities, real estate, or securities) the individual token is backed and on the legal rights of its holders. Money laundering, securities trading, banking, fund management and financial infrastructure regulations are all of relevance.[24]

The new Article 5a para. 1 Banking Ordinance[25] defines crypto-based assets as assets that actually or according to the intention of the organizer or issuer serve to a significant extent as a means of payment for the purchase of goods or services or the transfer of money or value. In consequence, the Federal Council is authorized to classify those crypto assets which justify a license requirement analogously to the acceptance of classic deposits.

3 Regulatory Framework

3.1 *General Remarks*

Cryptocurrencies are neither explicitly authorized nor prohibited. In principle, the given and only slightly adapted laws are in place. Consequently, the issuance of a cryptocurrency is not subject to any license or authorization requirement. Cryptocurrencies are largely unregulated; only a few legal provisions exist, for example the requirement to comply with anti-money laundering (AML)-regulations in case of issuance and trade of cryptocurrencies or the right of surrender of cryptocurrencies from the bankruptcy estate of a third person (Article 242a of the Swiss Debt Enforcement and Bankruptcy

---

23 FINMA: "*FINMA utilises the following approaches: (i) FINMA applies the existing rules to DeFi applications and in doing so abstracts from the use of specific technologies or procedures (principle of technology neutrality); (ii) if a DeFi application offers the same service and poses the same risks as intermediaries in the traditional financial market, FINMA also applies the same rules (same risks, same rules); (iii) if, from an economic perspective, a DeFi application offers an activity under financial market law that would require licensing, FINMA also assumes a licensing requirement in the case of new types of technical or legal implementation (substance over form).*"; see <https://www.finma.ch/en/documentation/dossier/dossier-fintech/decentralized-finance-defi/>.

24 See FINMA Supplement; <https://www.finma.ch/en/news/2019/09/20190911-mm-stable-coins/>.

25 Banking Ordinance: <https://www.fedlex.admin.ch/eli/cc/2014/273/de>.

Law [Bankruptcy Act – SchKG]).[26] Derivatives referencing cryptocurrencies can also be issued in Switzerland. The only restriction concerns the trade of derivatives on DLT platforms (Article 73d para. 3 of the Financial Market Infrastructure Act [FinMIA]).[27]

The already referenced FINMA Guidelines regulating payment tokens (i.e., cryptocurrencies) initially shaped the handling of crypto assets. Article 242a Bankruptcy Act introduced the segregation right. The bankruptcy administration can order the release of crypto-based assets over which the bankruptee has the power of disposal at the time when the bankruptcy is declared. An enforceable claim requires, on the one hand, that the debtor has undertaken everything necessary to keep the crypto-based assets available for the entitled beneficiary at all times. On the other, the crypto-based assets must be assigned either to the beneficiary individually or to a community with a clear allocation of shares to the different entitled individuals.

The provision in the Bankruptcy Act protects the "owner" of cryptocurrencies in case of bankruptcy of the service provider physically controlling them. Insofar, cryptocurrencies enjoy even a better legal treatment than fiat money which cannot be surrendered in case of bankruptcy. As far as the application *ratione temporis* and the application *ratione loci* is concerned, the general legal principles apply, no specialities are given. In respect of the application *ratione personae*, programmers, coders, and cryptocurrency miners are not subject to the regulations. Cryptocurrency issuers, exchanges, wallets providers, custodians or other intermediaries do have to comply with AML. Holders of cryptocurrencies can exercise the surrender right.

The applicable regulations relate to cryptocurrencies based on permissioned and permissionless blockchains. Sale, transfer, or disposal of cryptocurrencies is allowed, no restrictions are imposed (except compliance with AML-regulations by financial intermediaries).[28] The same assessment applies to the custody or trust business, to the marketing of cryptocurrencies, to the advertising of cryptocurrencies and to similar business activities.

3.2 *Legal Framework of DLT Act*

Already in 2018, the Swiss Federal Council published a legal analysis addressing Blockchain and DLT which identified certain legal aspects in private, financial

26 Bankruptcy Act: <https://www.fedlex.admin.ch/eli/cc/11/529_488_529/de>.

27 FinMIA: <https://www.fedlex.admin.ch/eli/cc/2015/853/en>.

28 See also R. H. Weber and S. Iacangelo, 'Legal Issues in relation to the Transfer of Tokens' (2018) *CapLaw-2018-30*; <https://caplaw.ch/2018/legal-issues-in-relation-to-the-transfer-of-tokens/>.

market and insolvency law that need to be addressed.[29] The main focus of the following DLT Act is not directed to cryptocurrencies but DLT securities mirroring the tokenization of assets. The two further addressed main areas are DLT trading venues and the segregation of DLT assets in insolvency proceedings.

With the DLT Act the Banking Act[30] was modified: Anyone who accepts certain crypto-based assets must apply for a license in accordance with Article 1b Banking Act.[31] This normative adjustment takes account of the fact that crypto-based assets have some similarities to deposits in the Banking Act. Correspondingly, tokens held in collective custody can now also be separated or segregated, if it is clear what share of the joint assets the custody account customer is entitled to (see above the explanations to Article 242a Bankruptcy Act). This provision is also reflected in the modified Article 16 Banking Act that expanded the definition of custody assets. Now custody assets according to Article 37d Banking Act are no longer only movable property and securities of the custodian, but also crypto-based assets if the bank has undertaken the necessary steps to keep these available for the custodian in the described sufficiently segregated way.

3.3 *Swiss Banking and FinTech License*

All banks, private bankers and saving banks (thrifts) are subject to application of the Banking Act.[32] Deposits from the public may only be accepted on a "commercial basis" if a natural or legal person has obtained a banking license (Article 6 Banking Act).[33] Acting commercially within the meaning of the Banking Act is everybody who continuously accepts more than 20 collectively held crypto-based assets or publicly announces to accept crypto-based assets held in collective custody, even if fewer than 20 crypto-based assets are subsequently received.

---

29 Federal Council report, Legal framework for distributed ledger technology and blockchain in Switzerland, An overview with a focus on the financial sector, Bern, 14 December 2018, <https://www.newsd.admin.ch/newsd/message/attachments/55153.pdf >.

30 Banking Act: <https://www.fedlex.admin.ch/eli/cc/51/117_121_129/de>.

31 Art. 1b Banking Act: The provisions of this law apply mutatis mutandis to persons who are mainly active in the financial sector and: (a) accept public deposits of up to CHF 100 million or crypto-based assets designated by the Federal Council on a commercial basis or publicly recommend them; and (b) neither invest nor earn interest on these public deposits or assets.

32 See <https://www.finma.ch/en/documentation/legal-basis/laws-and-ordinances/banks/>.

33 Unofficial translation: KPMG; <https://assets.kpmg/content/dam/kpmg/ch/pdf/ch-banking-act-en.pdf>.

In principle, separable assets do not constitute liabilities under Article 6 para. 1 Banking Ordinance and are therefore not regarded as deposits from the public; thus, their custody does not require a banking license (Article 1a let. a and b Banking Act).

As a result of the developments in the fintech sector, Switzerland has adapted its Banking Act to promote innovation. The very strict requirements of the Banking Act only apply analogously to a limited extent if deposits from the public of more than CHF 1 million and of less than CHF 100 million or if only crypto-based assets are accepted under the conditions that the deposits are not invested. Thus, the limit of CHF 100 million for public deposits contained in Article 1b Banking Act does not apply to separable crypto-based assets held off the balance sheet from numerous investors in unlimited amounts for safekeeping.

This assessment applies in particular to payment tokens, which in terms of their function can be comparable to fiat money and for which unequal supervisory treatment in custody does not appear to be justified. If, during the custody of crypto-based assets, the assets of the investors and those of the bank are not mixed and no lending business is conducted, the acceptance of such crypto-based assets held in collective custody should only be subject to the recently created fintech license (Article 1b Banking Act).[34] The Federal Council message stated that the acceptance of crypto-based assets, incl. the payment tokens, due to their comparability with fiat money, should trigger an authorization requirement.[35] This treatment seems justified due to the fact that the acceptance of classic public deposits in state currency generally requires a license under the Banking Act and the acceptance of payment tokens has a similar function if they are used as a means of payment. The Swiss legislator assumed that when depositors of payment tokens are not protected by deposit insurance, the risk of losing their assets should be countered by an authorization requirement and the associated regulatory requirements.

3.4 *Classification of Cryptocurrencies under the Revised Banking Act*

The Federal Council formulated in the revised Banking Ordinance the specific requirements for the safekeeping of collectively held crypto-based assets (incl. Cryptocurrencies). The Banking Ordinance also defines the license requirements pursuant to Article 1b Banking Act (acceptance of crypto-based assets). Due to their comparability with fiat money, payment tokens being held in collective custody are concerned. The minimum capital requirements specified in the Banking Ordinance for enterprises under Article 1b Banking Act are based

34 See FINMA <https://www.finma.ch/en/authorisation/fintech/fintech-bewilligung/>.

35 BBL 2020 233, 302.

on the deposits received from the public (Article 17a Banking Ordinance). FINMA can impose higher minimum capital requirements in individual cases (Article 17a para. 2 Banking Ordinance) if the risk associated with the business is high (e.g., operational risks).

For the sake of clarity, Article 1b para. 4 let. d Banking Act states that the crypto-based assets under this regime are not covered by the deposit guarantee. This is appropriate because the said crypto-based assets are generally separable under Article 16 Banking Act.

Article 5a para. 1 Banking Ordinance defines crypto-based assets within the meaning of Article 1b para. 1 let. a Banking Act. Collectively held crypto-based assets that actually or with the intention of the organizer or issuer to a significant extent serve as a means of payment for the purchase of goods or services or the transfer of money or value are captured. Thus, if such crypto-based assets are accepted, a license pursuant to Article 1b Banking Act is required.

Regarding the customization of the crypto-based assets, the authorization requirement for their acceptance applies if the assets in question correspond to custody account values in accordance with Article 16 para. 1bis let. b Banking Act. If the assets are not segregated in the event of bankruptcy (Article 37d Banking Act), they qualify as public deposits and the general licensing requirements under Articles 1a or 1b para. 1 let. a Banking Act apply.

In a nutshell, in can be said that the acceptance of crypto-based assets constituting securities that are suitable to be segregated, require a license if they are held in collective custody. If custody is carried out in such a way that the assets are individually assigned to a customer in a custody account and if the crypto-based assets can be separated according to Article 16 para. 1bis let. a Banking Act,[36] no difference to non-crypto-based (individually held) custody account assets and accordingly no reason for a new authorization requirement is given.[37]

3.5 *Public Deposit vs. Safekeeping Account*

The new approach based on the DLT Act, which changes the classification as a public deposit according to FINMA practice to a classification as a safekeeping account, raises regulatory questions. While for the interest-bearing acceptance of deposits from the public in the amount of CHF 100 million, which are invested or interest-bearing, an ordinary banking license pursuant to Article

36 This provision corresponds to the general rule of Art. 242a of the Debt Enforcement and Bankruptcy Law as introduced by the DLT Act; see also below chapter 5.5.

37 See also S. Kramer and S. Chabbey, 'New DLT Regulation – latest developments and perspectives' (2018) *CapLaw-2021-50*; <https://caplaw.ch/2021/new-dlt-regulation-latest-developments-and-perspectives/>.

1a let. b Banking Act is required, there is no corresponding regulation for the interest-bearing acceptance of crypto-based assets, i.e., no approval is required. However, Article 16 para. 1bis Banking Act excludes a respective investment because the definition as a custody account value means that the crypto-based asset must be kept available at all times which excludes the possibility to invest it or lend it to third parties.

According to Article 1 para. 2 Banking Act, the Federal Council can provide for exceptions to the ban on accepting deposits from the public, provided that the protection of depositors is guaranteed. The potential exceptions are stated in Article 5 Banking Ordinance. But since the acceptance of crypto-based assets is no longer treated as accepting deposits from the public, the applicability of these exceptions to avoid the authorization requirement also lapses.

The risk of loss appears lower for utility tokens, which allow the crypto-based access to a utility or service, and for asset tokens, which are economically like stocks, bonds, or derivatives, since these tokens contain concrete claims that are easier to trace in the real world. Accordingly, the acceptance of utility and asset tokens does not trigger any banking law approval requirements.[38]

3.6 *Wallet Provider and Staking*

Because pursuant to Article 5a para. 1 Banking Ordinance, only the collective storage of crypto assets is subject to a license, the safekeeping of crypto values, which are held directly on the blockchain in a wallet made available for the customer individually, would not require a license if the wallet provider undertakes everything to keep them available at all times. Therefore, the question arises whether crypto assets which are assigned to generate staking rewards are always really available.

"Staking" means using cryptocurrencies or other crypto-based assets as collateral to actively participate in the validation of transactions in a blockchain-based system with a decentralized organization.[39] Due to the technical complexity, holders often do not "stake" their crypto-based assets themselves, but instead transfer them to an intermediary who has the necessary operational expertise. Staking is like posting a security, with the effect that the crypto value is blocked for the duration of the staking period. When offering staking services, it must be checked whether it is guaranteed that the preferential rights of the owners of the staked crypto-based assets are enforceable at any time.

38 Utility Token are designed to be used for a specific purpose; they offer holders benefits like the access to products and services.

39 See L. Cong, Z. He and K. Tang, 'Staking, Token Pricing, and Crypto Carry' (2022) SSRN; <https://papers.ssrn.com/sol3/papers.cfm?abstract_id=4059460>.

The contractual obligations entered into during the staking must not endanger the ability to segregate the deposited crypto-based assets at any time.

However, if a service provider makes a mistake when staking for its customers, stored crypto values can be lost (slashing); in principle, this does not constitute a legal issue insofar as the service provider is liable to the customer for such errors. Although the slashing risk is an operational risk and not a classic investment risk, it cannot be ruled out that the prohibition on investments could be violated because rewards are earned like interest. The individual custody of crypto assets by a staking service provider requires at least affiliation with a self-regulatory organization under the Swiss AML Act.[40] Undoubtedly, a fintech or banking license is required to offer staking services for collectively held cryptocurrencies. If crypto-based assets are received in a non-segregated manner, this qualifies as public deposit, so staking under a fintech public deposit concession constitutes a prohibited investment. In principle, staking crypto assets from customer deposits would require a banking license; however, if the crypto deposits are secured by a default guarantee (Article 5 para. 3 let. f Banking Ordinance),[41] they are not considered a deposit; then only an affiliation to a self-regulatory organisation as a financial intermediary is required.

During the year 2023, FINMA developed a very restrictive (and not published) practice in the regulatory treatment of staking; most providers were confronted with the requirement to apply for a banking license. Legal academics and practitioners reacted negatively by publishing papers discussing the legal framework. Subsequently, in December 2023, FINMA released a supervisory notice providing Guidance on staking services.[42] Unlike FINMA Ordinances and Circulars, the content of such "FINMA Guidance" is not legally binding but rather a supervisory tool to inform market participants about its supervisory practice and aims to assist in the proper application of the rules. The focus of this Guidance lays on customers protection when a staking service provider falls into bankruptcy. FINMA states how staking services will be

40 AML Act (Federal Act on Combating Money Laundering and Terrorist Financing): <https://www.fedlex.admin.ch/eli/cc/1998/892_892_892/en>.

41 In the event of the bankruptcy of an issuer, each customer must have an own claim against the Swiss bank issuing the default guarantee, at least covering the total of all public; see FINMA Guidance 06/2024, Stablecoins: risks and challenges for issuers of stablecoins and banks providing guarantees, 26 July 2024; <https://www.finma.ch/en/~/media/finma/dokumente/dokumentencenter/myfinma/4dokumentation/finma-aufsichtsmitteilungen/20240726-finma-aufsichtsmitteilung-06-2024.pdf?sc_lang=en&hash=03D675C1247EAFAE0C391363A2F18B9A>.

42 FINMA Guidance 08/2023, Staking, 20 December 2023 <https://www.finma.ch/en/~/media/finma/dokumente/dokumentencenter/myfinma/4dokumentation/finma-aufsichtsmitteilungen/20231220-finma-aufsichtsmitteilung-08-2023.pdf?sc_lang=en&hash=C3A637EC142F1A521AD1F88FCC4124F2>.

treated and which proactive care for the segregation of staked cryptoassets is needed in view of insolvency risks.[43]

Without clear information to its customers and the proper implementation of risk-mitigating measures, staking services might cause risks, being subject to capital requirements. The Guidance describes the different forms and the inherent risks of staking cryptoassets as well as risk-mitigating steps that need to be implemented. The specific technical design of the staking services, which in turn depend on the proof-of-stake-system of the blockchain storing an asset could lead to a situation in which the requirements of the DLT Act are not met and assets are not protected in the event of the custodian's bankruptcy. The supervisory treatment of staking services distinguishes between custody assets that are protected in the event of bankruptcy and deposits exposed to insolvency risks; in consequence, licensing obligations and capital requirements for authorized institutions could be affected. The central criterion for bankruptcy protection can be seen in the requirement, that the cryptoassets are available for the customer "at all times"; however, this is not possible, if the custodian carries out staking on its own account. Anyhow, the segregation when staking on behalf of the customer depends on the staking mechanism of the respective blockchain. In bankruptcy proceedings, blockchains that do have a lock-up period or sanctions mechanism (slashing) for staking are problematic.

The legal rules in place were designed with simple custody services in mind rather than any kind of complex staking mechanism. In practice, often a certain amount of cryptoassets is needed for staking, thereby setting a level which requires the collection of cryptoassets of various customers at a single staking address to reach this amount. The offer of such staking services requires a banking license when payment tokens are held in collective custody.

3.7 *Criminal Law and AML Provisions*

Swiss criminal law does not contain any specific provisions applicable to cryptocurrencies and/or cryptocurrencies-related services. However, the Swiss Criminal Code[44] contains several provisions which eventually could be relevant in the cryptocurrencies context: As "ordinary" crimes, theft (hacking), fraud and misappropriation/unlawful appropriation (embezzlement) need to be considered. Furthermore, specific computer crimes could be relevant, namely illegal procurement of data (unauthorized obtaining of data), computer fraud, unauthorized access to a data processing system or damage to data.

43 The Swiss Blockchain Federation published a staking circular (only in German): <https://blockchainfederation.ch/wp-content/uploads/2024/04/SBF-Zirkular-2023_01_Staking-Updated-Version_Final.pdf>.

44 Swiss Criminal Code: <https://www.fedlex.admin.ch/eli/cc/54/757_781_799/en>.

FINMA is of the opinion that money laundering and securities regulations are most relevant in respect of crypto values because money laundering risks are especially high in a decentralized blockchain-based system, in which assets can be transferred anonymously and without any regulated intermediaries.[45] The AML Act (AMLA) contains requirements for financial intermediaries including, for example, the need to establish the identity of beneficial owners.[46] In addition, the AML Ordinance (AMLO)[47] sets out the requirements for the professional practice of financial intermediation and the due diligence obligations and reporting duties which traders must fulfil, while the FINMA Ordinance (AMLO-FINMA)[48] describes how the financial intermediaries have to implement their obligations to prevent money laundering and terrorist financing. Swiss law closely follows the FATF Recommendations[49] and is partly even stricter. In particular, the so-called "travel rule" is applicable, i.e., providers of cryptocurrencies-related services are obliged to do the KYC identification of the customers and need to apply for the affiliation with an AML self-regulatory authority (being established as private association in Switzerland). FINMA's rather strict approach is leading to the assumption that based on a payment claim against the issuer at any time, also the identity of all persons holding such a token must be adequately verified by the issuing institution or by appropriately supervised financial intermediaries.[50]

Several provisions in the AMLO-FINMA affect the offering of services regarding virtual currencies. In general, the contracting party must identify the ultimate beneficiary according to the KYC rules imposed on the service providers when single or connected crypto-related transactions exceed the threshold of 1,000 Swiss Francs within a period of 30 days; therefore, respective technical precautions need to be in place to detect such transactions. Since cryptocurrencies do not qualify as cash in Switzerland (AMLO), since "*or other anonymous means of payments*" was added in the AMLO-FINMA to clarify that all

45 See FINMA: <https://www.finma.ch/en/news/2018/02/20180216-mm-ico-wegleitung/>.

46 Federal Act on Combating Money Laundering and Terrorist Financing (Anti-Money Laundering Act, AMLA): <https://www.fedlex.admin.ch/eli/cc/1998/892_892_892/en>.

47 Verordnung über die Bekämpfung der Geldwäscherei und der Terrorismusfinanzierung (Geldwäschereiverordnung, GwV) <https://www.fedlex.admin.ch/eli/cc/2015/791/de>.

48 Verordnung der Eidgenössischen Finanzmarktaufsicht über die Bekämpfung von Geldwäscherei und Terrorismusfinanzierung im Finanzsektor (Geldwäschereiverordnung-FINMA, GwV-FINMA) <https://www.fedlex.admin.ch/eli/cc/2015/390/de>; for a general overview see C. Stengel and L. Ruckstuhl (2024) Finanzmarktrecht Schweiz, in: C. Stengel and T. Weber (Fn 19), 182–187.

49 FATF, Updated Guidance for a Risk-Based Approach to Virtual Assets and Virtual Asset Service Providers, FATF, Paris 2021; <https://www.fatf-gafi.org/media/fatf/documents/recommendations/Updated-Guidance-VA-VASP.pdf>.

50 See FINMA Guidance 06/2024 (Fn 41).

cryptocurrencies are in scope of that provision (Art. 51*a* Abs. 1bis). This affects not only crypto-ATM-providers and any virtual asset service providers (VASPs) but also any kind of exchange services offered by DLT trading facilities.

4 Supervision

4.1 *Licensing Requirements*

So far, no Swiss court decision dealing with the applicability of Swiss laws to cryptocurrencies has become known; however, FINMA has clarified based on its principles-based approach that the existing laws – e.g., the Swiss financial market laws – are applicable to new technologies as well. In consequence, the issuance of a cryptocurrency is not subject to any license or authorization. In case of professional custody services, particularly the offering of wallets for cryptocurrencies, a FINMA license is required according to the new provision of Article 1b Banking Act. This license is called "light", however, in practice the required obligations and provisions are not very "light".[51]

There is no specific supervisory authority for cryptocurrencies and/or cryptocurrencies-related services; however, FINMA has full supervisory and sanction power. To the extent that the provider of cryptocurrencies-related services is licenced (for example in accordance with Article 1b Banking Act), FINMA strictly exercises the supervisory functions. FINMA has sanctions powers like other supervisory authorities (such as BaFin) and FINMA is also applying sanctions in practice.

4.2 *Licensing of DLT Trading Facilities*

In connection with trading facilities, next to the various FINMA Guidelines the following legal provisions are relevant:
- Financial Market Infrastructure Act (FinMIA)[52]
- Financial Market Infrastructure Ordinance (FinMIO)[53]
- FINMA Financial Market Infrastructure Ordinance (FinMIO-FINMA)[54]

According to Chapter 4*a* (Articles 73*a* et seqq.) of the Financial Market Infrastructure Act (FinMIA), DLT trading facilities are permitted to operate a facility for multilateral trading of DLT securities whose purpose is the simultaneous exchange of bids between several participants and the conclusion of contracts based on non-discretionary rules and which (i) either admits participants in accordance with Article 73*c* para. 1 let. e FinMIA ("retail customers"), or (ii)

51 See above chapter 3.3.

52 FinMIA: <https://www.fedlex.admin.ch/eli/cc/2015/854/en>.

53 FinMIO: <https://www.fedlex.admin.ch/eli/cc/2015/854/en>.

54 FinMIO-FINMA: <https://www.fedlex.admin.ch/eli/cc/2015/855/en>.

holds DLT securities in central custody based on uniform rules and procedures, or (iii) clears and settles transactions in DLT securities based on uniform rules and procedures. At least one of these three conditions must be satisfied to trigger a licensing requirement as a DLT trading facility. The DLT trading facility must be structured as a legal entity under Swiss law and have its registered office and head office in Switzerland.

FINMA as the regulatory authority is responsible for granting the license to the provider of a DLT trading facility. Upon filing of an application, FINMA assesses whether the intended business activities require a DLT trading facility license and whether the planned business activities are possible under the applicable licensing provisions. To simplify the application process, FINMA has published Guidelines.[55] Interested parties can also present their project to FINMA prior to submitting the application.

The Guidelines also define the minimum structure for the legally required audit firm test report to be submitted with the license application. Among other things, FINMA expects the audit firm to provide a certificate with a clear audit opinion on compliance with regulatory provisions like (i) compliance with capital and liquidity requirements, (ii) documentation and staffing of risk management, (iii) appropriateness of the IT application landscape and IT security, (iv) guarantee of impeccable business activity and (v) staffing of internal controls. In consequence, an applicant must have a personal structure in place even before it is clear how long the application process will last and whether it will be successful; these requirements set high market entry barriers.[56]

After receiving the application, FINMA will inform the applicant which FINMA staff member is responsible for the licensing procedure and whether any additional information or documents need to be submitted. The duration of the licensing procedure depends on the complexity of the project and the quality and completeness of the application. So far, no DLT-license has been granted by FINMA to an applicant.

---

55 FINMA, Guidelines for applications concerning licensing as a DLT trading facility according to Article 73a ff. of the Financial Market Infrastructure Act; <https://www.finma.ch/en/authorisation/fintech/dlt-handelssystem>.

56 FINMA: "*After receiving the application, FINMA will inform the applicant which FINMA staff member is responsible for the licensing procedure and whether any additional information or documents need to be submitted. Before a license is granted as a DLT trading facility, FINMA requires an audit to be carried out by an audit firm. The duration of the licensing procedure depends on the complexity of the project and the quality and completeness of the application*"; <https://www.finma.ch/en/authorisation/fintech/dlt-handelssystem>.

4.3 *Whitepaper Prospectus Requirements*

Issuers of cryptocurrencies are not required by law to publish a whitepaper/ prospectus.[57] However, in practice, a whitepaper is usually published. If the issuer of cryptocurrencies combines a payment token with other functions in a specific project, it might also be advisable to ask FINMA for a so-called "No-Action-Letter" (in order to be legally safe); in such case, a detailed Questionnaire attached to the ICO Guidelines must be filled out and the respective information comes close to a whitepaper.

The FINMA ICO Guidelines set out how the authority applies financial market legislation in handling enquiries from ICO organizers. The Guidelines define the information FINMA requires to deal with such enquiries and the principles upon which it will base its responses, creating clarity for market participants. However, financial market law and regulations are not applicable to all ICOs. Depending on the way ICOs are designed, they may not in all cases be subject to regulatory requirements. Circumstances must be considered on a case-by-case basis because there is not enough relevant case law or consistent legal doctrine.

4.4 *Major Supervisory Measures/Actions*

FINMA investigated many ICOs and as well several cases related to secondary crypto market activities.[58] FINMA identified violations of the AML Act and other illegal conduct regarding ICOs; there is also a FINMA warning list. In several cases enforcement proceedings were initiated when e.g., companies ignored FINMA's regulatory pre-assessment or breached the Swiss Banking Act. FINMA consistently takes enforcement actions against non-compliant business models violating or circumventing supervisory laws, such as the banking, securities, or anti-money laundering regulations. The ultimate action is that a company is being liquidated by FINMA.

Apart from the usual criminal sanctions and the closure of business, FINMA is mandated to initiate legal action against any individual not complying with financial market laws (for example non-compliance with good and proper business conduct); the sanction consists in the prohibition to further work in financial markets.

There are cases in Switzerland in which FINMA acted in respect of illegal activities related to cryptocurrencies. One case concerned Envion AG having

57 A white paper is just an informational document issued by a company or organization to promote or highlight the features of a solution, product, or service that it offers or plans to offer.

58 Already in 2018 FINMA issued a related Press: FINMA is investigating ICO procedures, 29 September 2017; <https://www.finma.ch/en/news/2017/09/20170929-mm-ico>.

issued asset tokens.[59] In another decision a specific blockchain-based token was qualified as a security.[60]

We assume that the extraterritoriality of activities hampered enforcement action in several cases. But we are not aware of any case in which FINMA had difficulties in taking any actions in respect of illegal activities connected to cryptocurrencies in Switzerland.

5 Private Law Issues

5.1 *Technology Neutral Private Law*

For all transactions between private and/or commercial parties under Swiss law, the applicable rules and relevant principles are enacted in the Civil Code (CC)[61] or in the Code of Obligations (CO).[62] Cryptocurrencies are not expressly mentioned in these legal acts. In principle, cryptocurrencies are legal in Switzerland and there is no regulation in place regarding the purchase and sale of virtual currency units or their use as a means of payment for goods and services. However, the principles-based and technology-neutral approach of the Swiss regulatory framework results in the legal handling of cryptocurrencies like other goods that may have a certain value.

The term crypto asset is regularly used as overarching term and includes cryptocurrencies. In consequence of the principles-based and technology-neutral approach, the traditional private law provisions are to be also applied to crypto assets.[63]

---

59 An important example of enforcement actions are FINMA's actions against Envion AG: FINMA initiated the enforcement proceedings against Envion AG in March 2019 and found that (i) Envion AG unlawfully took deposits from the public on a commercial basis for which it should have obtained a (banking) license in advance, (ii) the repayment obligation of Envion AG, vis-à-vis the token owners, who made payments in US dollars, Bitcoins and Ethers to receive Envion tokens, was qualified as taking deposits from the public, (iii) the conditions for the Envion tokens issued in a bond-like form during an initial coin offering (ICO) were not equal for all investors and the prospectuses did not meet the minimum statutory requirements and (iv) there was no internal audit unit as required by law. In principle, the company Envion AG having issued asset tokens (not cryptocurrencies) being subject to a FINMA license was closed down with immediate effect and then liquidated.

60 Swiss Federal Administrative Court (Bundesverwaltungsgericht), Judgment number B-4185/2020, 16.01.2024.

61 CC: <https://www.fedlex.admin.ch/eli/cc/24/233_245_233/en>.

62 CO: <https://www.fedlex.admin.ch/eli/cc/27/317_321_377/en>.

63 See also S. Kramer and S. Chabbey, 'New Swiss DLT Regulation: Status Update and Outlook' (2021) *CapLaw-2021-18*; <https://caplaw.ch/2021/new-swiss-dlt-regulation-status-update-and-outlook/>.

5.2 *Property Law and Law of Obligations*

Property law in a narrow sense is not applicable to cryptocurrencies since tokens are not of a physical nature. If no specific provision is available (as for example in case of the transfer of ledger-based securities or the right to surrender), ownership rules could be considered to be applicable by analogy.[64] In consequence, the given legal rules are applied to cryptocurrencies in the Swiss legal system, i.e., the CC and the CO provide the relevant legal provisions.

Case example (1)

X has 60 Bitcoins registered in his/her wallet.

X wants to sell 5 Bitcoins against a legal tender (e.g., Euro, Yen, Dollar).

X has 60 Bitcoins registered in his/her wallet.

X wants to sell 5 Bitcoins against 10 Ethers.

- Has X legal ownership over the 60 Bitcoins in his/her wallet?
- Is it legally possible, and under what conditions, for X to make such a transaction?
- How would such a transaction be classified in your legal system?
- What difference would it make if X uses an intermediary (e.g., a wallet provider) to hold and transfer the Bitcoins?
- X opened an account with MontC and has 60 Bitcoins registered in his/her wallet.
- Has MontC any ownership rights over the 60 Bitcoins registered in X's wallet?

Under what conditions would the rules of your or other legal systems apply (please refer to the relevant private international law rules)?

According to the prevailing doctrine, the CC is based on a narrow technical term, which only includes impersonal, three-dimensional, demarcated, existing, and physically tangible objects that can be subjected to human possession. Therefore, the view that cryptocurrencies (native tokens) or data in general are to be considered as things (Article 713 CC)[65] which would allow the

64 Dissenting opinion: Crypto-based assets as such do not constitute property within the meaning of the Swiss Civil Code and the provisions of property law are not applicable to them by analogy; see S. Zogg, 'Bitcoin als Rechtsobjekt – eine zivilrechtliche Einordnung' (2019) *recht*, 100 seq.; BSK ZGB II-Ernst/Zogg, Vor Art. 919 ff. N 20c.

65 Article 713 CC: "Chattel ownership relates to movable physical objects and to forces of nature that may be the subject of legal rights and which do not form part of any immovable property."

establishment of direct, subjective, real, and absolute rights is controversially discussed. Because the technical term is not explicitly defined in the law, interpretations come into play. In an economic sense the criterion of controllability based on the technical design of cryptocurrencies is relevant, i.e., the possession of the public and private key by the holder. In summary, cryptocurrencies are neither things in the legal sense nor equivalent legal objects due to the lack of physicality and the lack of a legal basis that would extend the scope of property law to such immaterial goods.

The first and best-known example of a token – Bitcoin – as well as other cryptocurrencies represent a special case in terms of legal qualification.[66] Unlike in ICOs, there is no issuer who offers tokens for capital. Accordingly, there is no legal relationship between the issuer and the acquirers of tokens that could qualify as a claim or membership relationship. Consequently, the value of such tokens cannot be measured according to a legal position conveyed to them. It is also questionable whether the rules of ownership can actually be interpreted digitally and thus the element of physicality can be dispensed.

A token is an entry in a decentralized register and has no legal effect on its own. However, such an entry can be based on a right that was established in a legal transaction and can exist independently of the link with a token. Therefore, the question of the legal effects of the transfer of tokens is closely linked to the interpretation of legal transactions. The cases in which the parties want a right to be transferred by disposing of a token can only be answered by way of interpreting the legal transactions on which the corresponding right and its transfer are based.

Cryptocurrencies are assets sui generis. As mentioned, the qualification as a thing fails due to the lack of physicality, which is a mandatory prerequisite for the qualification de lege lata. Intellectual property law does not apply due to the numerus clausus of its forms. The qualification as a claim is also not possible since cryptocurrencies do not contain any claim against a third party. The holder of a payment token is merely the holder of a value which results from supply and demand being held by the envelope in the form of the token.

During the preparation of the DLT Act, it was assumed that cryptocurrencies, which primarily represent value within the blockchain context, are purely factual, intangible assets which is in line with the prevailing academic view; civil law does not impose any requirements for their transfer – and accordingly no obstacles.[67]

---

66 For further information :<https://bitcoin.org/en/>.

67 Federal Department of Finance, Bundesgesetz zur Anpassung des Bundesrechts an Entwicklungen der Technik verteilter elektronischer Register Erläuternder, Bericht zur Vernehmlassungsvorlage, Bern, 22 March 2019, 8 and 29; <https://www.newsd.admin.ch

The Federal Council's message on the DLT Act also made it clear that a distributed ledger as a decentralized register, which makes the tokenized assets tradable, is subject to application of securities laws. The securitization of rights combines book-entry rights with paper forms meaning that they can be traded on the capital market. These rules for the attestation of rights in certificates were used to develop rules for the electronic registration of rights. However, it is explicitly clarified that the term DLT uncertificated security ("DLT-Wertrecht") only includes tokens that represent a legal position (claim, membership); therefore, cryptocurrencies are excluded.[68]

The CO contains specific rules for individual types of contracts (e.g., sales contracts, contracts for services, or loan contracts). Due to the absence of specific legal rules, any contractual relationships regarding cryptocurrencies must be assessed based on the individual agreements entered into by the parties. The DLT Act introduced "DLT-Wertrechte" but not cryptocurrencies. Since cryptocurrency tokens are not explicitly recognized in a statute, the application of established principles of the CO bears some challenges. A sales or barter contract would require an object. Some authors argue that the acquisition of a cryptocurrency against payment of legal tender should be classified as a service contract. Thereby, the execution of the transfer of the relevant amount of cryptocurrency could be seen as service.

But such a classification does not seem to be adequate. Agreements on the exchange of cryptocurrencies and legal tender cannot be assigned to any conventional type of contract. Moreover, Swiss law classifies such a contract as innominate contract.[69] The rights and obligations of the parties are to be derived from the agreement itself.[70] In the absence of any contractual rulemaking, the provisions of the sales law are to be applied mutatis mutandis. Therefore, any non-sufficient performance by one of the parties falls under those sales law provisions that deal with non-fulfillment by the debtor.

Within the contract law framework, the involvement of any kind of intermediary does not change the legal structure of such a contract; thus, the rights and obligations between the parties are not principally touched. Any cross-border scenarios must be solved according to general conflicts-of-laws principles. In

/newsd/message/attachments/56192.pdf> and press release: <https://www.admin.ch/gov/en/start/documentation/media-releases.msg-id-74420.html>.

68 BBl 2020 258.

69 Innominate contract can be defined in a negative way as contracts which are not a typical contract addressed in the CC.

70 One of the important features in Swiss contract law is that the parties' original intent usually prevails over statutory provisions; therefore, the primary source of contractual obligations is the contract itself.

principle, the acquisition of cryptocurrency in exchange for another cryptocurrency can be assessed in a similar way. In the case example, depending on the type of wallet the position of X relating to the Bitcoins registered in his/her wallet, does not constitute ownership in its classical meaning but rather a contractual right against the wallet provider to release/transfer the Bitcoins.

MontC's position to the Bitcoin is to be qualified similarly. Due to the fact, that any transfer of cryptocurrencies requires the confirmation of the DLT network, a third party comes into play. Consequently, the typical bilateral nature of classical contract models is inadequate. In the absence of the characteristic feature of traditional ownership in cryptocurrency holdings and transactions just a legal entitlement based on the physical actions of the involved parties can be assumed.

Regarding the above question under what conditions the rules of other legal systems apply, it can be said, that when it comes to cross-border transactions and the respective contracts, international private law comes into play. Next to the determination of the applicable law the legal analysis of relevant cases would mainly depend on the circumstances of the particular case.

5.3 *Lending and Pledge*

Case example (2)

PayB is a company regulated and supervised in its home jurisdiction to provide lending services. Z is a company whose seat is in your legal system. Z intends to borrow 60 Bitcoins from PayB, with an interest rate of 5% payable either in a legal tender (e.g., Euro, US Dollar, Yen) or in Bitcoins.

- Would it be possible, and under what conditions, for PayB and Z to conclude such a contract? How would such contract be characterised in your legal system? Please provide details.
- Under what conditions would the relevant rules of your or other legal systems apply (please refer to the relevant private international law rules)?
- Please also detail whether, and under what conditions, as per your legal system, the lending services provided by PayB would require a bank licence or other authorisation, and what would be the legal consequences in case of infringement of such requirement.
- PayB is a regulated company authorised to provide lending services in your legal system. Z is a company whose seat is in your country. Z intends to borrow 60 Bitcoins from PayB, at an interest rate of 5%

payable in Bitcoins. Z pays back in Bitcoin Cash, which are Bitcoin equivalents resulting from a fork in the initial Bitcoin blockchain.

- Would it be possible, and under what conditions, for Z to pay back its loan in Bitcoin Cash instead of Bitcoins?
- What difference does it make whether or not the fork took place only after the initial transfer of Bitcoin?

The above mentioned and already discussed legal concerns regarding the legal qualification of cryptocurrencies should not be disregarded also when it comes to a loan contract.

PayB and Z could conclude a loan contract according to general contract law. Such contract would be characterised in the Swiss legal system as a private law contract. Because Swiss law is applied in a principles-based and technology neutral way, the relevant rules of the Swiss legal system are to be applied. The lending services provided by PayB would require a bank licence depending on the design of the concrete project if the service is actively promoted in Switzerland. No license is required in case of reverse solicitation.

While specific provisions governing transactions in cryptocurrencies are missing in the CC, the case examples must be analysed according to the general principles of Swiss contract law; therefore, the legal qualification depends on the individual agreement between the parties. Consequently, the option of a repayment in a token which is denominated in another cryptocurrency than the original cryptocurrency provided to the borrower depends on the individual contract. If the alternative (e.g., Bitcoin Cash in the case example) performs value-wise independently and differently from the original denomination and there is no respective contractual agreement, it is unlikely that a Swiss court would presume that the parties had a corresponding intention.

Case example (3)

Z is a company whose seat is in your legal system. To secure a loan for the financing of a specific project, Z has agreed to pledge 30 Bitcoins that are registered in its wallet.

- Would it be possible, and under what conditions, for Z to make such pledge? Is there one or more ways of pledge?
- What would change if the wallet were kept with an intermediary?
- Under what conditions would the relevant rules of your or other legal systems apply (please refer to the relevant private international law rules)?

In Switzerland a pledge also is a common form of security over tangible property which entitles the secured party to realise the secured asset in case of a default of the debtor; such an agreement is not subject to any formal requirements. The common form when using a tangible movable property as a security requires that the possession of the movable property is transferred to the secured party meaning that the security provider fully gives up possession. Therefore, the creation of a security interest is anyhow not very practical under Swiss law. In the case of a pledge referring to cryptocurrencies, a potential intermediary and the security provider could enter into an account control agreement (wallet). In such a framework, the feasibility of pledges relating to cryptocurrency faces the above discussed difficulties regarding tangibility and the traditional rules for the transfer of property; especially when it comes to insolvency proceedings, legal risks will arise. Looking at the case it would be possible for Z to make a pledge and the legal conditions according to contract law would apply while there is, in principle, no difference when using an intermediary.

5.4 *Inheritance, Donation and Trust*

Case example (4)

X has 60 Bitcoins registered in his/her wallet. X has a child, Y. X wants to make a will to ensure that the value of his/her wallet is not lost and is passed on to Y.

- Is it possible, and under what conditions, for X to make such provisions in his/her will?
- If no valid will has been made, how would the rules of your legal system apply to the succession of X in respect of the Bitcoins assigned to his/her private key?
- What difference would it make to the assessment of the example case if X holds the Bitcoin with an intermediary?
- Under what conditions would the succession rules of your or other legal systems apply, both in presence and in absence of a will (please refer to the relevant private international law rules)?

Under Swiss law, upon the death of a natural person, that person is succeeded by the heirs in relation to any legal title; therefore, such a succession would also occur in case of cryptocurrencies. The major problem is the access to a wallet by the private key. X can make provisions in his/her will because Swiss law is applied principles-based and technology neutral. If no valid will has been made, the Swiss legal system does not apply special rules to the succession of X in respect of the Bitcoins assigned to his/her private key. Identical to all other assets, the inheritance law is applied principles-based and technology neutral. When X holds the Bitcoin with an intermediary, there is no difference to the real world if X can properly prove his/her entitlement. In any case, the Swiss succession rules would apply, both in presence and in absence of a will.

Case example (5)
Under what conditions would the rules on donation of your or other legal systems apply (please refer to the relevant private international law rules)?

Because Swiss law is applied principles-based and technology neutral, cryptocurrencies can be donated. The provisions governing the donation in the CO are applicable.

Case example (6)
X has 60 Bitcoins registered in his/her wallet. X wants to create a trust over the 60 Bitcoins for the benefit of Y.

- Is this legally possible, and under what conditions?
- What difference would it make to the assessment of the example case if X holds the Bitcoin with an intermediary?

To date, in Switzerland there is no "own" trust law in place. But since the Hague Trust Convention came into force, foreign trusts have been recognized in Switzerland. The Federal Council was commissioned by the parliament to create the legal basis for a Swiss trust. In January 2022, the Federal Council opened a consultation on changing the Code of Obligations. In the future, it should be possible to set up a trust under Swiss law. But for the time being, it is not possible to create a trust in relation to cryptocurrencies under Swiss law. However, its legally feasible to hold asset titles on behalf of another party as a fiduciary; details depend on the contractual relationship between a beneficiary and the fiduciary.

Because Swiss law is applied principles-based and technology neutral, the provisions of the CO and of financial market law are eventually applicable. Thereby, it is legally possible to develop a legal construct for the benefit of others. It will make no difference to the assessment of the example case if X holds the Bitcoin with an intermediary.

5.5 *Insolvency Law*

Case example (7)

X opened an account with MontC and has 60 Bitcoins registered in his/her account. MontC becomes insolvent.

- Can X, and under what conditions, bring a claim in the insolvency procedure in respect of his/her 60 Bitcoins?
- How would the claim of X be classified (proprietary, personal, or other) in the insolvency procedure?
- Could X claim the return of the deposited Bitcoin or only their value in cash?
- What relevance would the specific terms of the agreement between X and MontC have in relation to X's claim?
- Under what conditions would the insolvency rules of your or other legal systems apply (please refer to the relevant private international law rules)?

Z is a company which opened an account with MontC as it accepts payments in Bitcoin and other cryptocurrencies. Z's wallet is worth US$200.000 in different cryptocurrencies. Z becomes insolvent.

- How would Z's account be dealt with in the insolvency proceedings?
- Could some creditors claim priority over the cryptocurrencies registered in Z's account?
- What relevance would the specific terms of the agreement between Z and MontC have in relation to the creditors' claims?

Due to the changes in the Swiss Federal Act on Debt Enforcement and Bankruptcy as well as in banking regulations introduced by the DLT Act, the treatment of digital assets in a bankruptcy event of a custodian is clarified in favor of the depositor. When the respective requirements are fulfilled, the adapted provisions allow the segregation of the digital assets for the benefit of the relevant creditors.

When MontC becomes insolvent and holds a FINMA license, the insolvency proceedings are executed by an administrator authorized by FINMA; the same happens when FINMA is of the opinion that MontC has no license but should have one. FINMA will act in its capacity as both supervisory and resolution authority. Based on the already discussed new provisions in the Swiss DLT Act, X is entitled to bring a claim in the insolvency procedure in respect of his/her

60 Bitcoins; in consequence, X can claim segregation in the insolvency proceedings. Thereby, the specific terms of the agreement between X and MontC must be in line with the Swiss law. Under any conditions the Swiss insolvency rules would apply.

When Z who owns a wallet worth US$200.000 in different cryptocurrencies becomes insolvent, in principle, Z's account would be dealt with in the insolvency proceedings as all other assets. The treatment of cryptocurrency portfolios in insolvency proceedings follows the general principles governing the liquidation of the insolvent debtor. Even if the law allows the segregation of cryptocurrencies, the actual realization comes with practical difficulties because the liquidator needs access to the relevant keys from the debtor. A creditor could claim priority over the cryptocurrencies registered in Z's account only when a valid and enforceable contract is in place granting such a right.

5.6 *Fraud*

Case example (8)

In your legal system, would the loss (*e.g.*, through hacking or fraud) of cryptocurrencies amount to an actionable tort or other cause of action? Which laws or cases would be applied to address these issues in your legal system? Case example: X opened an account with MontC and has 60 Bitcoins registered in his/her wallet. MontC's IT systems have been hacked. As a result, X lost all his/her Bitcoins.

- Can X, and under which conditions, bring an action against MontC?
- Can X, and under which conditions, bring an action against the hacker (if he/she is identified)?
- If the hacker has sold the Bitcoin to third party Y, could Y be protected as a bona fide purchaser?
- What would be the case if X transferred the Bitcoin to the tortfeasor after being misled?

Under Swiss law in such a case the individual contractual provisions, the general principles of contract law and of the relevant tort law are applicable. X can bring an action against MontC if this is not excluded in the individual contract. X can also start legal action (under general provisions of tort law) against the hacker because the law is applied principles-based and technology neutral. If the hacker has sold the Bitcoin to the third-party Y, then Y could be protected as a bona fide purchaser based on Article 933 CC, but court precedents are not yet available. Dissenting opinion: If tokens on a blockchain cannot be classified as items within the meaning of the Swiss Civil Code, Articles 933 et seq. would not be applicable to them either; see BSK ZGB II-Ernst/Zogg, Art. 933 N 8b. If X transferred the Bitcoin to the tortfeasor after being misled (fraud), in principle, the contractual transfer can be challenged (Article 24 or Article 28 CO). X has a claim for damages arising out of a breach of MontC's obligation to ensure the safekeeping of the wallet. Much depends on MontC's provable arguments that a reasonable protection was in place to avoid the violation of its IT systems. Again, the virtual nature of cryptocurrencies can cause some difficulties.

6 Tax Measures

Swiss tax law is fully applicable to cryptocurrencies, cryptocurrencies-related services, or cryptocurrencies-originated values; there are no exemptions available. Assets in cryptocurrencies are also subject to wealth tax (§ 38 StG Zurich).[71] All cantons and communes levy a mainly progressive tax on the assets of individuals based on the taxpayer's total assets usually assessed at market value. For reasons of simplicity, these are to be declared in the list of securities and credit balances as "other credit balances", stating the designation of the cryptocurrency. Proof must be provided by means of a printout of the digital wallet (wallet) as of the end of the tax period. The Federal Tax Authority publishes a year-end tax rate for Bitcoin. Other cryptocurrencies are to be declared at the year-end price of the most common exchange platform for this currency.

Capital gains from movable private assets are tax-free (§ 16 (3) StG Zurich) and capital losses are irrelevant for tax purposes. If cryptocurrencies are part of the business assets, the tax regulations on self-employment apply being mainly relevant for commercial trading in cryptocurrencies. The practice for commercial securities trading[72] is applied mutatis mutandis to distinguish it from private asset management. The mining and staking of cryptocurrencies by providing computing power for a fee by a natural person leads to taxable income from self-employment for this person.

---

71 See <https://www.zh.ch/de/politik-staat/gesetze-beschluesse/gesetzessammlung/zhlex-ls/erlass-631_1-1997_06_08-1999_01_01-111.html>.

72 Circular No. 36 of the Swiss Federal Tax Administration of July 27, 2012; <https://www.estv.admin.ch/estv/de/home/direkte-bundessteuer/fachinformationen-dbst/dbst-kreisschreiben.html>.

7 Outlook

The DLT Act only removed some obstacles regarding "DLT-Wertrechte" but not for cryptocurrencies like Bitcoin. Swiss law established a legal basis for issuing and trading rights represented by tokens on a blockchain. The existing discrepancy between an innovation-friendly legislator and a cautious financial market supervisory authority that pays attention to investor protection and market stability means that although many activities could be principally permitted, the hurdles to obtaining a corresponding license are quite high. The ambivalent status of cryptocurrencies, which are neither a legal tender nor a "thing" under Swiss law, leads to some legal uncertainty and, consequently, to legal risks.

Bibliography

H. Bärtschi and C. Meisser, 'Virtuelle Währungen aus finanzmarkt – und zivilrechtlicher Sicht' in R. H. Weber and F. Thouvenin (eds.), *Rechtliche Herausforderungen durch webbasierte und mobile Zahlungssysteme*, Zurich/Basel/Genf 2015, pp. 113–160

H. Bärtschi, N. Jaquemart and S. Meyer, 'Zahlung und Verzug bei virtuellen Währungen' in S. Emmenegger (ed.), *Zahlungsverkehr*, Basel 2018, pp. 177–248.

M. Eggen, 'Chain of Contracts' (2017) *AJP*, 3

M. Eggen, 'Verträge über digitale Währungen' (2017) *Jusletter*, 4 December 2017

M. Eggen and C. Sillaber, 'DLT-Handelssysteme' (2020) *Jusletter*, 11 May 2020

B. V. Enz, 'Erfüllung und Vollstreckung von Kryptowährungsforderungen' (2021) 117 *SJZ*, 583

P. Favrod-Coune and K. Belet, 'Conflict of Laws and Tokens in Swiss Private International Law' in A. Bonomi, M. Lehmann and S. Lalani (eds.), *Blockchain and Private International Law*, Leiden/Boston 2023, 673–708

W. Ernst and S. Zogg in BSK ZGB II (Basler Kommentar, Zivilgesetzbuch II), 7th ed., Basel 2023

A. Geiger and S. Keller, 'Kryptowährungen in der Nachlassplanung und -abwicklung', *SJZ* 2022, 203

B. Graham-Siegenthaler and A. Furrer, 'The Position of Blockchain Technology and Bitcoin in Swiss Law' (2017) *Jusletter*, 8 May 2017

B. Maurenbrecher and U. Meier, 'Insolvenzrechtlicher Schutz der Nutzer virtueller Währungen' (2017) *Jusletter*, 4 December 2017

C. Meisser, L. Meisser and R. Kogens, 'Verfügungsmacht und Verfügungsrecht an Bitcoins im Konkurs' (2018) *Jusletter IT*, 24 May 2018

L. Meisser, 'Kryptowährungen: Geschichte, Funktionsweise, Potential', in R. H. Weber and F. Thouvenin (eds.), *Rechtliche Herausforderungen durch webbasierte und mobile Zahlungssysteme*, ZIK Bd. 61, Zurich 2015, 73–92.

G. Molo and M. Brunone, 'Kryptowährungen im Visier der staatlichen Kontrolle' (2022) *sic!*, 299

L. Müller and M. Ong, 'Aktuelles zum Recht der Kryptowährungen' (2022) *AJP*, 198

L. Müller, M. Reutlinger and P. J. A. Kaiser, '*Entwicklungen in der Regulierung von virtuellen Währungen in der Schweiz und der Europäischen Union*' (2018) *EuZ*, 80

F. Piller, 'Virtuelle Währungen – Reale Rechtsprobleme?, Eine zivil – und vollstreckungsrechtliche Untersuchung aus der Sicht der Bitcoin-Nutzer' (2017) *AJP*, 1426

M. Pydar and C. Zellweger-Gutknecht, 'Ist Bitcoin eine Währung im Sinne von Art. 147 IPRG?' (2022) *Jusletter*, 9 May 2022

A. Schurr and A. Layr, 'Emission und Übertragung von DLT-Wertrechten im internationalen Privatrecht Liechtensteins und der Schweiz' (2022) *ZVglRWiss*, 32

C. Stengel and T. Weber (eds.), *Digitale und mobile Zahlungssysteme*, 2 ed. Zurich 2024

H.-C. von der Crone, F. J. Kessler and L. Angstmann, 'Token in der Blockchain – privatrechtliche Aspekte der Distributed Ledger Technologie' (2018) *SJZ*, 337

R. H. Weber, 'Zivilrechtliche Aspekte von Geschäftsabwicklungen auf DLT-Handelsformen' (2021) *SZW*, 450

R. H. Weber, 'Haftungsfragen beim Handel von digitalen Vermögenswerten' (2021) *SJZ*, 679

R. H. Weber and R. Baisch, 'Crowdinvesting mittels Initial Coin Offering – Regulierungsaufgaben im Token-Universum' (2019) *SZW*, 135

R. H. Weber and R. Baisch, 'DLT-basierte Finanzprodukte' (2022) *SZW*, 683

R. H. Weber and R. Baisch, 'Cryptoassets: Taxonomy and Regulatory Approaches' (2023) *B.F.L.R.*, 467

R. H. Weber and S. Iacangelo, 'Rechtsfragen bei der Übertragung von Token' (2018) *Jusletter IT*, 24 May 2018

R. H. Weber and H. Kuhn (eds.), *Entwicklungen im Schweizer Blockchain-Recht*, Zurich 2021

C. Zellweger-Gutknecht, D Tschudi and K. MacCabe (eds.), *Kryptowerte*, Basel 2024

C. Zellweger-Gutknecht and R. H. Weber, 'Digital Money – Taxonomy and Regulatory Approaches' (2022) *EuZ* 6, G 1

S. Zogg, 'Zwangsvollstreckungsrechtliche Behandlung von Kryptowährungen' (2020) *recht*, 1

S. Zogg, 'Bitcoin als Rechtsobjekt – eine zivilrechtliche Einordnung' (2019) *recht*, 95

Taiwan

Christopher Chao-hung Chen and Wang-Ruu Tseng

1 Introduction

In the past decade, there has been much hype regarding crypto-currencies, which broadly could refer to various forms of crypto-assets or tokens no matter they are based on distributed ledger technology (DLT) or not. With crypto-currencies gaining popularity in the market, new legal problems also arise globally. Taiwan is not exempted to the trend. This report focuses on the current state of Taiwan law regarding crypto-currencies.

In the remainder of this report, Part 2 considers legal definitions related to crypto-currencies under existing Taiwan law. Part 3 focuses on regulations of crypto-currencies for fund-raising and payment purposes, especially from the angle of securities regulations, banking law and regulations of payment services firms. Part 3 also updates the status of so-called central bank digital currencies (CBDCs) in Taiwan. Part 4 shifts to private law issues related to crypto-currencies. The report will examine the contractual or proprietary nature of crypto-currencies based on a limited number of case laws and academic discussion in Taiwan. Part 5 briefly introduces tax law issues related to crypto-currencies. Part 6 concludes this report.

2 Legal Definition and Nature of Crypto-Currencies under Taiwan Law

At the time of writing, there is no dedicated law in Taiwan governing crypto-currencies directly. The government has not designated bitcoins, Ethers or any other crypto-currencies as a kind of legal tender. Hence, none of them acquires the status of 'currency' under Taiwan law. At the time of writing, the government has not issued or recognised any form of stablecoins as a kind of legal tender or currency.

There is no uniform legal definition regarding crypto-currencies in Taiwan yet. The closest reference to crypto-currencies is through anti-money laundering laws.[1] In the 'Regulations Governing Anti-Money Laundering and

1 See section 3.4.5 below for more discussion of anti-money laundering issues.

 | DOI:10.1163/9789004722507_027

Countering the Financing of Terrorism for Enterprises Handling Virtual Currency Platform or Transaction' (Virtual Currency AML/CFT Regulations) issued in 2021, the Financial Supervisory Commission (FSC) provides the first legal definition of 'virtual currency' in Taiwan.[2]

There are some key points to the definition. First, a 'virtual currency' means a 'digital representation of value' recorded digitally by using cryptography and distributed ledger technology. The definition limits its scope to 'crypto-currencies' on a blockchain. But it does not cover other forms of digital representation of money (such as monetary value stored in an electronic wallet or stored value card). It is also clear from the second sentence of the definition that the FSC does not mean to apply the Virtual Currency AML/CFT Regulations to other forms of electronic money or digital representation of money, to which there is a separate set of AML\CFR rules that are applicable.

Second, the definition limits the scope of virtual currencies to those for 'payment or investment purposes.' It does not cover crypto-assets not used for payment or investment purposes (e.g. some non-fungible tokens representing anything other than money or monetary value). In short, the FSC limits the Virtual Currency AML/CFT Regulations to crypto-currencies used for financial purposes. This is in line with the FSC's mission to regulate financial services.

In summary, at the time of writing, there is only one formal legal definition of 'virtual currency' under Taiwan law. However, the definition is specifically drafted for anti-money laundering practices for virtual currency businesses. Thus, the wordings of the definition should be put into the context. Otherwise, there is no definition of crypto-currencies (or virtual currencies) given in other laws and regulations or developed by judiciaries. Whether the definition could be expanded to other areas or for general purpose will be up for debate in the future.

3 Regulation of Crypto-Currencies in Taiwan

From the regulatory perspective, the threshold issue is whether fund-raising or trading activities of crypto-currencies fall within the ambit of Taiwan's financial regulations. If the answer is affirmative, the follow-up question is how Taiwan law currently deals with crypto-currencies under financial regulations. This part first introduces Taiwan's financial regulatory framework and the considers regulatory directives issued by Taiwan's financial regulators regarding

2 Regulations Governing Anti-Money Laundering and Countering the Financing of Terrorism for Enterprises Handling Virtual Currency Platform or Transaction reg 2(1)(2).

crypto-currencies and the implications in practice. It worth noting that Taiwan thus far does not outrightly ban crypto-currencies for any purpose. Hence, any regulatory issue related to crypto-currencies must be carefully analysed under existing regulations. To clarify, this report analyses whether crypto-currencies are regulated under the existing regulatory framework in Taiwan; but this report does not consider further whether and how crypto-currencies should be regulated in the future.

In the following sections, Section 3.1 first introduces Taiwan's financial regulatory framework. Section 3.2 examines the legal status of crypto-currencies under securities regulations. Section 3.3 further considers legal issues under Taiwan's Banking Act. Section 3.4 shifts attention to payment regulations, including an update on central bank digital currencies. Section 3.5 turns to the impact of anti-money laundering regulations on crypto-currencies.

3.1 *Introduction to Taiwan's Financial Regulatory Framework*

In general, Taiwan's financial regulatory framework is based on sectoral regulations with a universal regulator. The structure affects how crypto-currencies are or could be regulated under Taiwan law. This section provides a broad introduction to Taiwan's financial regulatory framework for further discussion in this part.

First, the FSC is the primary financial regulator governing financial institutions and the financial market. The Central Bank of the Republic of China (Central Bank) is in charge of matters related to currency, foreign exchange, and monetary policies (e.g. market interests rate, loan portfolio and housing prices).

Second, despite a universal regulator, Taiwan's financial regulatory framework is still based on sectoral regulations divided into three major sectors: capital market, banking, and insurance. The division is also reflected in the internal structure of the FSC under which there are three major bureaus – the Securities and Futures Bureau, Banking Bureau, and Insurance Bureau – in addition to the Financial Examination Bureau. The main piece of legislation governing the capital market is the Securities and Exchange Act. Regarding mutual funds and investment trust, there is also the Securities Investment Trust and Consulting Act. There is also the Futures Trading Act governing the futures market. For the banking sector, the FSC has power to regulate banks under the Banking Act. The Banking Bureau is also in charge of regulating financial holding companies, credit cooperatives and new payment services providers. Third, regulations of insurance companies and brokers are based on the Insurance Act. Based on relevant laws, the FSC has issued many subsidiary regulations and regulatory orders or guidance for further regulations.

Furthermore, the Central Bank has the legal mandate to promote financial stability, guide sound banking operation, maintain the stability of value of currency, and foster economic development.[3] The Central Bank has power over issuance and regulation of Taiwan's legal tender and any issue related to currency rate and foreign exchange. The Central Bank also sets the benchmark interest rates in Taiwan.

Taiwan's financial regulatory framework affects how crypto-currencies may be regulated now or in the future. If crypto-currencies are used as a fund-raising vehicle, it could fall within the scope of securities regulations or even banking regulations. If they are used as a payment instrument, it might trigger issues related to payment services regulations and foreign exchange that is under the jurisdiction of the Central Bank. Further, if banks or insurers in Taiwan invests or uses crypto-currencies in their businesses, it might be regulated under banking and insurance regulations respectively, notably with regarding anti-money laundering and countering of finance of terrorism practices.

3.2 *Crypto-Currencies under Taiwan's Securities Regulations*

Regarding securities regulations, the preliminary issue is whether crypto-currencies are a kind of securities defined under the Securities and Exchange Act (SEA). Pursuant to the SEA, the term 'securities" refers to "government bonds, corporate stocks, corporate bonds and other securities approved by the competent authority'.[4] The term could also include 'stock warrant certificate, certificate of entitlement to new shares, and certificate of payment or document of title to any of the securities" referred above.[5] Based on the authorisation by the SEA, the FSC has issued regulatory guidance over the years to clarify the scope of the term 'securities'.

Regarding crypto-currencies, the underlying difficulty is that they do not look like (at least on the face of it) traditional corporate shares, government or corporate funds, units in investment funds or other warrants or certificates that are commonly deemed as securities. However, there is no denial that crypto-currencies could be used to raise funds from the public through the so-called initial coin offerings (ICOs) or under the sexy label of 'decentralised finance' (DeFi) recently. In other words, the practical legal question is whether a person or an entity issuing crypto-currencies to raise funds from the public should apply for approval from the FSC before such issuance and consequentially

3 Central Bank of the Republic of China (Taiwan) Act article 2.

4 Securities and Exchange Act article 6(1) (Taiwan).

5 Securities and Exchange Act article 6(2) (Taiwan).

subject to additional regulatory requirements such as prospectus, continuous transparency requirements and corporate governance standards, etc.

On 3 July 2019, the FSC has clarified the issue with a regulatory order based on the power given by article 6(1) of the SEA. Under the order, a crypto-currency that carries the features of 'securities' is deemed to be a kind of 'securities' under the SEA.[6] The FSC generally describes a crypto-currency as an instrument that could be circulated and digitally represents transferable value based on cryptography, distributed ledger technology or other similar technology.[7] Largely, the description looks similar to the legal definition in AML/CFT regulations discussed in Section 2 above. However, to qualify as 'securities', the crypto-currencies also need to possess the following features: soliciting investors to provide funds invested in a common enterprise (or project) with the expectation to receive future profits arising from the efforts by the issuer or a third party.[8]

In other words, the FSC designated crypto-currencies as kind of 'investment contract' following the definition and framework laid out in the US case of *SEC v. W.J. Howey Co.*[9] The standards provided by the FSC in the new regulatory order clearly followed what the US court has defined as the *Howey* test. However, one should note that, unlike the US law, Taiwan's SEA does not expressly include the term 'investment contract' in statutory wordings. Taiwan's financial regulator simply borrows from what they have seen under the US law to be part of Taiwan law. Hence, the FSC's approach could be seen as a kind of cheap shot to bring crypto-currencies under the ambit of Taiwan's securities regulations through statutory interpretation based on the FSC's statutory power to designate 'securities'.

At the time of writing, there is no actual case of an issuer applying to the FSC to issue crypto-currencies as an investment contract in Taiwan. This report reckons that Taiwan's securities regulator has taken steps to regulate issuance of crypto-currencies as a fund-raising tool by including crypto-currencies as a kind of 'securities'. However, it is unclear whether there will be different rules

---

6 Financial Supervisory Commission letter *gin-guan-cheng-fa* No. 10803211643 dated 3 July 2019 (金融監督管理委員會金管證發字第 10803211643 號函 (3 July 2019)), https://law.fsc.gov.tw/LawContent.aspx?id=GL002732#lawmenu (last accessed 20 January 2022).

7 Financial Supervisory Commission Order *gin-guan-cheng-fa* No. 10803221164 dated 3 July 2019 (金融監督管理委員會金管證發字第 1080321164 號令 (3 July 2019)) item 2, https://www.fsc.gov.tw/ch/home.jsp?id=128&parentpath=0,3&mcustomize=lawnew_view.jsp&dataserno=201907030002&aplistdn=ou=newlaw,ou=chlaw,ou=ap_root,o=fsc,c=tw&dtable=NewsLaw (last accessed 20 January 2022).

8 *Id.*

9 328 U.S. 293 (1946).

for crypto-currencies in terms of prospectus, issuance, transparency, corporate governance, and other aspect of regulations at the time of writing.

Moreover, without changing any law, the FSC clarified in June 2019 with a media release regarding regulations of securities token offering (STO).[10] Assuming a crypto-currency is a kind of security token (i.e. tokens carrying the features of securities), the FSC stated that the token would be considered 'exempted securities' (that are exempted from the registration requirement)[11] if the total amount raised from the offering of STOs is below NT$30 million.[12] However, if the amount is over NT$30 million, an issuer should apply for a sandbox experiment under the Financial Technology Development and Innovative Experimentation Act.[13]

In addition, in the same media release, the FSC stated its regulatory intention to restrict issuers of STOs that qualify as exempted securities to be an unlisted company incorporated in Taiwan. Investors of those STOs are limited to be professional investors only.[14] Moreover, an issuer of STOs should prepare for prospectus and a platform that facilitates the issuance of STOs should apply for a licence to be securities dealers.[15] In other words, as exempted securities, the FSC seems to be prepared to allow issuance of STOs within the existing regulatory framework and market infrastructure of securities brokers/dealers.

However, FSC has thus far not put the above-mentioned points into blackletter regulations. It is also unclear whether the FSC treat STOs and crypto-currencies carrying the features of investment contracts to be the same kinds of securities. There is no further guidance on whether a prospectus is required for initial coin offering (ICO) in Taiwan if it is not a kind of STO. Nor is it clear whether a white paper drafted for an ICO would satisfy the prospectus requirement under Taiwan's securities regulations. In theory, the same requirements with other conventional securities (such as shares) should be applicable to crypto-currencies if they qualify as securities. However, whether existing requirements are suitable for crypto-currencies and ICOs is a debatable issue.

Last, if crypto-currencies for fund-raising purpose could be deemed as a form of 'investment contract' regulated under the SEA, it seems that brokers

---

10 FSC media release on 27 June 2019, https://www.fsc.gov.tw/ch/home.jsp?id=96&parentpath=0,2&mcustomize=news_view.jsp&dataserno=201906270004&aplistdn=ou=news,ou=multisite,ou=chinese,ou=ap_root,o=fsc,c=tw&dtable=News (last accessed 5 January 2022).

11 Securities and Exchange Act article 22-1.

12 See above n 10.

13 *Id.*

14 *Id.*

15 *Id.*

or dealers handling crypto-currencies (e.g. a crypto-exchange) might require a licence under the SEA. However, at this moment, there is no further regulation or guidance issued by the FSC regarding whether crypto-exchanges require to be licensed under the SEA.

In addition, for securities firms licensed under the SEA, the FSC allows securities dealer to make proprietary trading of security tokens, being virtual currencies that have the nature of securities.[16] If a firm solely deals with security tokens, the minimum capital requirement is reduced from NT$40 million to NT$10 million.[17] A securities dealer making proprietary trading of security tokens should also establish proper internal control systems complying with rules published by the Taipei Exchange.[18]

In summary, the FSC has clarified the matter by designating crypto-currencies as 'securities' as a form of 'investment contract', assuming the crypto-currencies satisfy the criteria. There is also limited regulatory guidance about securities token offering. There is also no further guidance on the consequence on such decision such as prospectus or other regulatory requirements. It is also unclear whether a crypto-exchange requires to be licensed as a securities broker/dealer as a result. It requires the financial regulator to further clarify the matters and complete the full regulatory structure regarding crypto-currencies. How regulators should regulate the market of initial coins offering or issuance of crypto-currencies in Taiwan is a separate question that is subject to further policy debates.[19]

In the end, it worth noting that at the time of writing the Taiwan Futures Exchange, the sole futures market in Taiwan, has not offered any futures or options contracts related to crypto-currencies. Hence, there is no developed derivatives market regarding crypto-currencies in Taiwan. Nor is there a known market of over-the-counter derivatives market for crypto-currencies in Taiwan

16 Standards Governing the Establishment of Securities Firms article 3(1)(2).

17 *Id.*

18 *Id.* article 11(2). See also Regulations Governing Securities Firms reg 45-1.

19 See Yueh-Ping Alex Yang, *Initial Coin Offerings and Securities Regulation: Focusing on the Definition of "Securities" under Taiwan's Securities Exchange Act* (2018) 43 Financial and Economic Law Review 135; Ting-Hsien Cheng, *Discussions on the Security Token under Taiwan's Securities Regulation and Compliance with Securities Supervision* (2021) 3(1) Taiwan Financial and Economic Law Review 149; Huang-Chih Sung and Jie-Hua Wu, *Legal Theories and Supervision Norms of Cryptocurrency* (2021) 117 Taipei University Law Review 133; Chao-Tsung Huang, *A Brave New World for ICO? On Taiwan's Regulatory Framework of STO* (2020) 6 NCTU Law Review 151.

yet. The FSC did announce its intention to regulate crypto-exchanges in March 2023,[20] but there is no legislative draft made in public yet at the time of writing.

3.3 *Crypto-Currencies and Illegal Banking Activities*

Another significant legal risk presented to issuers of crypto-currencies is the application of the Banking Act. The main concern comes from the crime of illegal collection of deposits or funds from the public under the Banking Act.

Article 29 of the Banking Act provides that '[u]nless otherwise provided by law, any person other than a Bank shall not accept deposits, manage trust funds or public property under mandate or handle domestic or foreign remittances.'[21] The Banking Act further provides that "[u]sing borrowed money, accepting investments, making the depositor a shareholder or using other classifications in order to accept deposits or obtain capital from the general public by agreeing to pay or paying a bonus, interest, share dividend interest or other reward in an excessive amount, shall be deemed the act of accepting deposits.'[22] Breaching article 29 might result in imprisonment for a term between 3 and 10 years in addition to fines not more than NT$200 million.[23]

The provision has been applied not only to illegal collection of deposits but also some schemes soliciting money from the public in the name of investment or other purposes, including some multi-level marketing schemes.[24] The legislative purpose is not only to penalise people who accepts deposits without acquiring a banking licence but also to sanction schemes that attract people to place money with the operator in return for a promise of unsustainable high profits.[25] In other words, the provision is against some forms of Ponzi schemes.

The issue then is whether issuing crypto-currencies to solicit funds from the public may breach Taiwan's Banking Act. In a decision delivered in November 2021, the defendant was sentenced to 3.5 years in prison for operating an illegal banking scheme to attract people to give them money to invest in

20 See the media release of Financial Supervisory Commission on 30 March 2023 in https://www.fsc.gov.tw/ch/home.jsp?id=2&parentpath=0&mcustomize=news_view.jsp&dataserno=202303300001&dtable=News (last accessed 22 August 2023).

21 English translation of statutory texts is provided by the Ministry of Justice in https://law.moj.gov.tw/ENG/LawClass/LawAll.aspx?pcode=G0380001 (last accessed 8 December 2021).

22 Banking Act of the Republic of China article 29-1.

23 Banking Act of the Republic of China article 125(1).

24 E.g. Supreme Court Criminal Judgment 110 *tai-shan* No. 1910; Supreme Court Criminal Judgment 110 *tai-shan* 4521.

25 See reasoning of Supreme Court Criminal Judgment 110 *tai-shan* No. 3277.

crypto-currencies.[26] In another case, the accused was found breaching the Banking Act by operating a Ponzi scheme to solicit victims to put in money to invest in mining machines and mining of crypto-currencies such as bitcoins[27] or Cube Coins.[28] Hence, it seems to be clear that the Banking Act is applicable if there is a Ponzi scheme claiming to draw investment proceeds from crypto-currencies.

However, it is unclear whether the issuance of crypto-currencies alone to investors in exchange for money may amount to a breach of the Banking Act. The cases mentioned in the previous paragraph are all schemes under which a person solicit people to invest in crypto-currencies in return for lucrative proceeds. In a criminal charge filed in 2017, the court faced a situation where a person was accused of breaching article 29 of the Banking Act by operating a scheme that invited people to put in their bitcoins in return for proceeds from more bitcoins in the future.[29] On the face of it, this was a Ponzi-like scheme other than the fact that investors place bitcoins rather than money. Both the District Court and the Taiwan High Court decided that the accused committed the crime of general fraudulence by cheating victims to place bitcoins into a fraudulent scheme. However, both courts decided that the scheme did not breach the Banking Act. The underlying rationale behind the District Court is that the term 'obtaining funds or capital from the public' should be limited to situations where the operator of an illegal scheme receives 'money or funds' that could be deposited into a lawful bank.[30] Since crypto-currencies are not treated as currencies yet and banks certainly do not accept them as deposits, a Ponzi scheme accepting bitcoins from the public does not breach the Banking Act. The position was affirmed by the Taiwan High Court upon appeal.[31]

However, later court decisions in 2022 seems to suggest that it could amount to an illegal Ponzi scheme under the Banking Act by soliciting bitcoins as investments in return for a promise of lucrative profits.[32] It worth noting that

---

26 Taichung District Court Criminal Judgment 108 *jin-su* No. 263 (2021). See also Kaohsiung District Court Criminal Judgment 110 *jin-chong-su* No. 8 (2022)(defendants held guilty for a similar scheme).

27 Supreme Court Criminal Judgment 110 *tai-shan* No. 5315; Supreme Court Criminal Judgment 110 *tai-shan* No. 5314.

28 Taiwan High Court (Taichung Brach) Criminal Judgment 110 *jin-shan-su* No. 1729 (2022).

29 Taiwan High Court Judgment 107 *jin-shan-su* No. 83 (2019), appealed from New Taipei District Court Judgment 106 *jin-su* No. 8 (2018).

30 New Taipei District Court Judgment 106 *jin-su* No. 8 (2018).

31 Taiwan High Court Judgment 107 *jin-shan-su* No. 83 (2019).

32 Taiwan High Court Criminal Judgment 109 *jin-shan-su* No. 59 (2022) and Taiwan High Court Criminal Judgment 109 *jin-shan-chong-su* No. 27 (2022)(both judgments relating to same scheme).

the defendants in the 2022 case accepted not only bitcoins as investment but also an equivalent value of cash in lieu of bitcoins. Hence, it is unclear whether accepting crypto-currencies alone as investment would still amount to breach of the Banking Act as an illegal Ponzi scheme. Nevertheless, the latest decisions open the door to penalize illegal Ponzi scheme by accepting crypto-currencies in lieu of cash.

It is clear that the Banking Act were made well before the advent of crypto-currencies. Hence, from a historical perspective, it is hard to fault some courts' decision to exclude crypto-currencies from the application of the Banking Act when one operates a crypto Ponzi scheme. Given the potential criminal sanctions, it is understandable that some courts are reluctant to expand the scope of the provisions mentioned above. But whether this is correct decision may be up to debate. The case was also a rare situation where courts affirmed the position that crypto-currencies were not legal currencies under existing Taiwan law. This report will offer more analysis on this point in Part 4 below.

In short, it seems clear that merely issuing crypto-currencies may not be sufficient to be a scheme breaching the Banking Act. If crypto-currencies are rewarded on the basis of mining (e.g. bitcoins) or other kinds of proof of work, this report argues that it is much less likely to become a kind of Ponzi scheme as it lacks a centralised structure to issue tokens and to manage funds (where proceeds might come from). However, if there is a single or centralised issuer of a crypto-currency, it is not wholly impossible to be a Ponzi-like scheme if an issuer boasts unusually high profits to investors of the crypto-currencies and other features. Courts would look for other factors such as the intention or parties and whether there is a promise to give usually high proceeds and the intention of parties.

3.4 *Regulation of Crypto-Currencies for Payment Services*

3.4.1 Regulatory Framework of Payment Services in Taiwan

At the time of writing, there is no uniform legislation governing payment services in Taiwan. Instead, regulations of payment services in Taiwan are split into several pieces of legislation.

First, the Central Bank oversees Taiwan's monetary system and issuance of currencies. Under the Central Bank of the Republic of Taiwan Act (Central Bank Act), the Central Bank is empowered to issue currencies in Taiwan as legal tender.[33] It is also in charge of printing and minting of cash notes and coins.[34] The Central Bank also has the obligation to maintain reserves to support New

33 Central Bank of the Republic of Taiwan Act article 13(1) and (2).

34 *Id.* article 13(3).

Taiwan Dollars.[35] In short, the Central Bank in Taiwan monopolize the issuance of money. Naturally, it has power to regulate foreign exchange.[36]

Second, traditionally payment services are dominated by banks and naturally banking regulations govern the provision of payment services. Under Taiwan's Banking Act. a bank can provide not only services related to deposit and loans but also some payment services involving negotiable instruments, letters of credit and commercial bank drafts.[37]

Third, in addition to banking laws and traditional payment instruments that pass through the banking system (e.g. cash, bank drafts or credit cards), Taiwan also has specialized laws governing electronic stored value cards (SVCs) and non-bank electronic payment services providers (PSPs). On the one hand, the Act Governing Issuance of Electronic Stored Value Cards (ESVC Act) was first issued in 2009 (and significantly revised in 2015) to regulate the issuance of SVCs, such as the EasyCard used for mass rapid transport system in Taipei. The ESVC Act focuses on issuers and the issuance of SVCs which appear in physical forms or in electronical format.[38] On the other hand, the Act Governing Electronic Payment Institution (EPI Act) was first promulgated in 2015 and later significantly revised in 2020 (with effect from 1 July 2021) to regulate electronic payment services providers. The EPI broadens the scope of regulation from SVCs to other kinds of electronic PSPs, including electronic wallet providers or even small currency exchanges.[39] The ESVC Act and EPI Act grant the FSC a power to regulate issuers of SVCs and electronic PSPs. Since the EPI Act and ESVC Act overlaps in their scope, the ESVA Act was repealed on 27 January 2022. The discussion below will then focus on provisions in the EPI Act.

Whether the regulations mentioned above can apply to crypto-currencies if they are used as a payment vehicle? The underlying legal risk is that criminal sanctions may apply if an issuer of a payment token is found to breach the Central Bank Act, the Banking Act, and EPI Act. For instance, the EPI Act provides criminal penalties against those who conduct illegal payment services.[40]

In the following sections, this report first considers whether issuers of a crypto-currency could fall within the jurisdiction of the EPI Act as electronic SVCs. The report then considers possibilities of regulating crypto-currencies and crypto-exchanges under the EPI Act. The discussion below will be based

---

35 *Id.* article 16.

36 *Id.* articles 18 and 33.

37 Banking Act s 3.

38 Act Governing Issuance of Electronic Stored Value Cards article 3(1).

39 Act Governing Electronic Payment Institutions article 4.

40 Act Governing Issuance of Electronic Stored Value Cards article 30; Act Governing Electronic Payment Institutions article 46.

on the former ESVC Act and EPI Act, though some cases mentioned below applied the previous versions of the Acts. This part also introduces the current state of central bank digital currencies in Taiwan. For clarification, this report does not analyse further whether the two Acts are sufficient to regulate the market for electronic payments outside the banking sector. The discussion in this section assumes that a crypto-currency is used for payment purposes for simplicity of discussion.

3.4.2 Crypto-Currencies and Electronic Stored Value Card

One legal issue is whether crypto-currencies as payment tokens was a kind of electronic SVC under Taiwan's EPI Act (formerly under the ESVC Act). A licence from the FSC is required if the answer is affirmative.[41] Otherwise the issuer could be subject to heavy criminal sanction.[42]

The scope of the regulation hinges upon the definition of 'electronic stored value cards'. The term is defined as 'an IC chip, card, certificate or other forms of debt obligation that uses electronic, magnetic or optical means to store monetary value and performs the function of data storage or computing and is used for multiple payment purposes.'[43] The term 'use for multiple payment purposes' means 'using an electronic stored value card to pay for products and services provided by contracted merchants, or to pay for government fees and other fees', but excluding payment for transportation services or services used to 'accept, through a network or electronic payment platform, the registration and opening of an electronic payment account by users and to accept the deposit of stored value funds from users using electronic equipment to convey the receipt/payment information via connection.'[44]

The critical issue is whether a crypto-currency is a kind of instrument using electronic means to store monetary value and performing the function of data storage or computing. A litigation in 2014 shed some light on the issue. The case was regarding a company called Addcn Technology (AT), which operated some online platforms for people to search for rented houses or used cars, etc. One platform was about an exchange of points earned or virtual treasures used in online games. The platform provided a service called 'T-points'. Members of the platform could purchase T-points upfront, check balance on their accounts, and use the T-points to pay other parties when they trade for virtual

41 Act Governing Electronic Payment Institutions articles 3 and 4.

42 Act Governing Electronic Payment Institutions article 46(1).

43 Act Governing Electronic Payment Institutions article 3(5).

44 Act Governing Electronic Payment Institutions article 3(10).

assets from online games. The company also allowed members to exchange T-points to New Taiwan dollars on a 1:1 ratio.

AT's chief executive officer was then charged with an offence of carrying illegal stored value card businesses. The main problem was that the T-points looked like a replacement for legal currencies on the platform by allowing members to deposit New Taiwan dollars into T-points accounts and use T-points to pay in exchange for virtual assets. Public prosecutors argued that AT was an issuer of SVCs under the then ESVC Act.[45] The defendant argued that the T-points could only be used on the specific platform and could not be used anywhere else.

The New Taipei District Court held that the defendant was not guilty.[46] The judge decided that T-points did not qualify as an 'SVC' because T-points did not provide a function to store and calculate monetary value. In addition, T-points were not in the format of 'chips, card, certificates or other forms'. The court recounted the legislative history and decided that 'other forms' included only instruments in physical formats (i.e., a physical stored value card). In contrast, T-points were purely electronic records. Therefore, T-points did not qualify as an 'SVC' under the ESVC Act at the time. Moreover, the court also decided that T-points were not used for 'multiple payment purpose since they could only be used in one single platform. Hence, the defendant was acquitted. When reaching this conclusion, the court heavily relied on the legislative history of the then ESVC Act for the interpretation of relevant statutory wordings. Public prosecutors naturally appeal against the district court's decision to the Taiwan High Court, which in 2018 dismissed prosecutors' appeal based on the same reasoning.[47]

In short, the courts refused to broaden the scope of the legislation when the technology and market environment was much different from when the ESVC Act was promulgated in 2009. In the AT case, it seems that the courts find it difficult to treat a limited form of electronic wallet like T-points as an SVC for 'multiple payment purpose'. It is perhaps fair to argue that Taiwan's then ESVC Act was initially designed to regulate the issuance of physical SVCs like Taipei's EasyCard or iPass in Kaohsiung (both initially issued for public transport). On this basis. it is reasonable to restrict the regulatory scope of electronic SVCs given that a breach of the then ESVC Act (currently under the EPI Act) may result in criminal penalties.

---

45 The alleged facts occurred before the promulgation of the EPI Act. Hence, the case fell within the jurisdiction of the ESVC Act.

46 New Taipei District Court Judgment 103 *gin-chong-su* No. 6.

47 Taiwan High Court Criminal Judgment 106 *gin-shan-chong-su* No. 24.

How does the AT case affect crypto-currencies for payment services? This report argues that it is less likely that a typical crypto-currency would fall within the regulatory scope of electronic SVCs. On the one hand, a crypto-currency does not function like a physical SVC which can deducted value stored in the card or facility when a user taps the card for payment. Although a crypto-currency may represent some monetary value, it is more like an alternative to cash (as a medium of exchange) rather than an instrument in which carries monetary value stored by a user to be used in shops or public transport. On the other hand, crypto-currencies have not reached the stage where people widely use them to pay for goods or services in the market. As the court in the AT case took a narrow interpretation of the term 'multiple purpose payment', there is a fair chance to argue that a crypto-currency is not an SVC since it has not been used for 'multiple purpose payment'.

3.4.3 Crypto-Currencies and the Electronic Payment Institution Regulations

In 2015, the EPI Act was passed to 'promote and sound operations and development of payment institutions.'[48] The EPI Act was amended significantly in December 2020 (with effect from 1 July 2021). The discussion below is based on current version of the EPI Act after the amendment.

In general, an electronic payment institution (EPI) is defined as "an institution approved by the [FSC] to operate businesses specified in [the Act].'[49] The types of businesses that an EPI could operate include 'collecting and making payments for real transactions as an agent', 'receiving stored funds', 'engaging in domestic foreign small-amount remittances business', and 'engaging in buying and selling foreign currencies and currencies issued by Mainland China, Hong Kong, or Macao.'[50] In addition, an EPI may also engage in some services associated with the main businesses above (such as providing integrated services of payment related information communication), subject to regulatory approval.[51] In short, the EPI regulates non-bank PSPs that collect payments from users and receive money stored in payment accounts as well as domestic remittance services.

The legal issue then is whether an issuer of crypto-currencies or a crypto-wallet operator could fall within the jurisdiction of the EPI Act. If the answer is affirmative, then the issuer or provider must acquire a licence under the EPI

48 Act Governing Electronic Payment Institutions article 1.
49 Act Governing Electronic Payment Institutions article 3(1).
50 Act Governing Electronic Payment Institutions article 4(1).
51 Act Governing Electronic Payment Institutions article 4(2).

Act and otherwise it may be penalised with criminal sanctions.[52] So far, there is not yet any case law on the application of the EPI Act to crypto-currencies or operators of crypto-wallets.

Regarding an issuer or miner of crypto-currencies, it is arguable that the issuer does not 'collect and making payments' for other transactions. Nor does it receive and store funds for users like an electronic wallet. An issuer simply generates crypto-currencies into the market. Hence, the mere action of mining or issuing crypto-currencies should be outside the scope of the EPI Act.

A more contentious issue is whether a crypto-wallet operator fall within the ambit of the EPI Act if the crypto-wallet allows users to transfer value by exchanging crypto-currencies. Based on statutory wordings, the critical question is whether the funds stored in the wallet and transfer of funds must be represented in legitimate currencies rather than something that carries value such crypto-currencies. The EPI Act only generally refers to terms such as 'funds' or 'payments'. It does not specifically refer to 'money' or 'currency'. Hence, there could be a room for interpretation regarding whether crypto-currencies stored in or transferred through a crypto-wallet amounts to 'funds' as defined in the EPI Act.

As discussed in section 3.3 above, Taiwan courts have taken a rather narrow view when applying the Banking Act to treat a crypto Ponzi scheme as illegal banking activities. Thus, there is a possibility that courts may interpret the terms in the EPI Act in a similarly narrow manner. The general intention of legislators seems to target electronic wallet providers or other non-bank PSPs. However, the ambiguity of statutory language does not preclude the possibility of regulating crypto-wallet operators under the EPI Act.

So far, the FSC is silent on whether it intends to regulate crypto-wallets in Taiwan other than for issues related to money laundering (see section 3.5 below). It remains to be seen whether the FSC will make further clarification or regulatory guidance under the EPI Act regarding crypto-currencies.

3.4.4 Current Development of Central Bank Digital Currencies in Taiwan

The Central Bank is also exploring the application of central bank digital currencies (CBDCs). At the time of writing, the government has not introduced any law to provide any legal mandate to the Central Bank to issue CBDCs. Nor does the Central Bank has offered any official regulatory guidance regarding CBDCs even if issuing digital currency is already within the mandate of the

52 Act Governing Electronic Payment Institutions articles 4, 5 and 46.

Central Bank. However, the Central Bank is conducting ongoing experiments and proof of concepts privately. Some information was briefly revealed in a report by the Central Bank to the Legislative Yuan (Taiwan's legislative body) on 1 November 2021.[53]

There are a few key points to note regarding the current state of CBDCs in Taiwan. First, the Central Bank and the government has no intention to rush to issue CBDCs for the sake of issuing CBDCs or to be a leader in their issuance in the world. The Central Bank's stance is to ensure that there is a sufficient demand domestically for CBDCs in Taiwan before rolling out CBDCs to the market.[54] Second, the Central Bank follows the three general principles indicated by the Bank for International Settlement regarding CBDCs: 'do no harm', 'co-existence' and 'innovation and efficiency.'[55] Third, the Central Bank declared in the report that it has concluded a pilot stage of study on the feasibility of CBDCs on the wholesale level in June 2020. Currently, the Central Bank is conducting the second stage of experiment regarding general or retail CBDCs. This stage is projected to conclude in September 2022. The Central Bank and the government will most likely consider whether to issue CBDCs after the conclusion of the second stage of testing. At the time of writing this report, there is no clear clue on how CBDCs will be issued and managed in the future.

3.5 *Regulating Crypto-Currencies for Anti-Money Laundering Purposes*

In Taiwan, the Money Laundering Control Act was amended in 2018 to apply AML/CFT laws to platforms of virtual assets.[56] In June 2021, the FSC published the Virtual Currency AML/CFT Regulations. The Regulations clarify the obligation of crypto-exchanges in relation to money laundering and the financing of terrorism. A breach of the Regulations may result in criminal penalties.[57]

Under the Virtual Currency AML/CFT Regulations, an 'enterprises handling virtual currency platform or transaction' is defined to include businesses that provide services related to an exchange between a crypto-currency and New Taiwan Dollars (or any foreign currencies) or another kind of crypto-currency, transfer of crypto-currencies, custodian and administration of crypto-currencies, and other financial services related to an offer or sale of

53 See Central Bank's report to the Legislative Yuan dated 1 November 2021, in https://www.cbc.gov.tw/tw/lp-2169-1.html (last accessed 6 January 2022).

54 *Id.* at 9.

55 *Id.* at 2-3.

56 Money Laundering Control Act article 5(2).

57 Money Laundering Control Act article 2 and 14 *et seq.*

crypto-currencies.[58] The Regulations expect an 'enterprises handling virtual currency platform or transaction' to conduct customer due diligence.[59] An 'enterprises handling virtual currency platform or transaction' should also conduct continuous transaction monitoring[60] and should decline a transaction if it is a suspicious.[61]

Although the Virtual Currency AML/CFT Regulations have an impact on shaping the crypto-currency market. For instance, crypto-wallets must establish proper internal control and audit systems as well as policies and measures to address potential money laundering.[62] The demand for consumer due diligence and transaction monitoring also imply that customers need to provide more personal information and leave more trails of the flows of crypto-currencies and associated monetary flow. This may be against the characteristic of anonymity of crypto-currencies.

4 Private Law Issues of Crypto-Currencies

This part turns to private law relationship regarding a crypto-currency or blockchain. This report notes that there is no legislative attempt to define relevant contractual rights regarding and proprietary nature of crypto-currencies under Taiwan's Civil Code. Despite there is only a limited number of judicial authorities visiting the issue, this report attempts to paint a picture of private law issues regarding crypto-currencies under Taiwan law, based on existing case law and interpretation of the Civil Code and some other statutes.

In the remainder of this part, Section 4.1 first considers the nature of contractual relationship on a blockchain and between a user and a crypto-wallet. Section 4.2 then examines property rights related to crypto-currencies under Taiwan and how they might affect other transactions or circumstances such as sale, donation, loan, inheritance, trust, security interests and insolvency, etc. A reader should note that some arguments are tentatively made based on the prominent views expressed by limited case laws. The legal position may not be conclusive under Taiwan law.

58 Regulations Governing Anti-Money Laundering and Countering the Financing of Terrorism for Enterprises Handling Virtual Currency Platform or Transaction reg 2(1).

59 *Id.* regs 3 and 5.

60 *Id.* reg 12.

61 *Id.* reg 4.

62 *Id.* reg 15.

4.1 *Contractual Relationship regarding Crypto-Currencies*

It is important to examine the underlying legal relationship among relevant parties involving the crypto-currencies. There are two perspectives to examine the ways a person can hold crypto-currencies. One is when a holder (i.e. a miner or node) of a crypto-currency has direct access to the blockchain regarding the crypto-currency. The other situation is where a person holds crypto-currencies through a crypto-wallet. Therefore, largely we can identify two basic contractual relationship: the contract(s) governing the blockchain regarding a particular crypto-currency and the contracts(s) governing the relationship between a holder and a crypto-wallet or crypto-exchange.

First, is a blockchain a contract (or contracts) among miners or nodes? It seems reasonable to argue that their relationship must be of a contractual nature, given that miners and nodes have to follow the protocol underlining the creation and management of a particular crypto-currency. However, so far there is no legislation or judicial decision examining the nature of relationship among miners or nodes on a blockchain in Taiwan. Hence, the contractual nature of a blockchain remains unclear at the time.

Second, there must be a contract between a user and an operator of a crypto-wallet when the user opens an account with the operator. For instance, BitoPro, a crypto-wallet operated in Taiwan, has a user agreement stated in its website.[63] A person who opens an account with BitoPro in principle should have agreed to the user agreement (the BitoPro agreement). The services provided by BitoPro include the provision of trading services of crypto-currencies and allowing users to view real-time market prices and transaction status as well as transferring crypto-currencies.[64] BitoPro also provides the basic trading rules in the user agreement.[65] It worth noting that the BitoPro user agreement (as it is in the end of December 2021) is quite short. It may be a sign that the laws and contracts in this area still have room for development in the future. It also worth noting that the BitoPro user agreement contains some clauses that are heavily favourable to the crypto-wallet (e.g. a user's liability to compensate losses of the operator, 'its shareholders, employees, agents, and associated companies')[66]. Whether this exclusion provision may sustain challenges in civil courts will be an interesting question.

---

63 BitoPro website: https://www.bitopro.com/terms (last accessed 27 December 2021). (BitoPro User Agreement).

64 BitoPro User Agreement Chapter 1 Section 3 provisions 1 and 2.

65 BitoPfo User Agreement Chapter 1 Section 7.

66 BitoPro User Agreement Chapter 4.

4.2 *Property Rights Regarding Crypto-Currencies*

At the time of writing, there is no legislation defining the nature of crypto-currencies under Taiwan law. It is debatable whether crypto-currencies are a kind of property or they mere represent a contractual obligation between relevant parties.[67] The proprietary nature of crypto-currencies will then determine various legal issues related to crypto-currencies, such as donation, sale, inheritance, trust, attachment and seizure, lending and insolvency. There have been different views expressed by courts and scholars in the past few years. Through a limited number of judicial decisions, courts have clarified a bit on the nature of crypto-currencies, despite there is no settled view yet. In the following section, this report first draws discussion from some judicial decisions that have considered the proprietary nature of crypto-currencies in different contexts. Then, this report will consider some issues related to crypto-currencies when they are used in various transactions.

4.2.1 The Nature of Crypto-Currencies under Property Law

First, Taiwan courts and the government so far do not treat crypto-currencies as a kind of legal tender. In a judgment delivered in 2019 regarding a Ponzi scheme operating based on accepting and delivering bitcoins,[68] the Taiwan High Court first affirmed that crypto-currencies are not legal currencies. Hence, a fraudulent scheme tricking victims to put in bitcoins with the expectation of receiving more bitcoins in the future was not an illegal banking activity under Taiwan's Banking Act.[69] The court further mentioned that bitcoins are more akin to 'crypto-assets' than money.[70] However, it was unclear what the court referred to as 'crypto-assets' and whether it implies that owners of crypto-currencies enjoy some kind of property rights recognised in the Civil Code. Thus, Taiwan courts have so far clarified that crypto-currencies are not legally-speaking 'money' or currencies, but they also leave the door open as to the nature of crypto-currencies in private law.

Second, some courts view crypto-currencies as a kind of fungible property. This affects how courts would enforce an obligation requiring a delivery of crypto-currencies. In a case about enforcing a contractual obligation to deliver bitcoins, the court decides that bitcoins are a kind of fungible property that

---

67 Yueh-Ping Yang, *The Legal Nature of Virtual Currencies* (2020) 301 Taiwan Law Review 43, 48 (楊岳平, 論虛擬通貨之法律定性, 月旦法學雜誌, 301 期, 2020 年 6 月, 頁 48).

68 See above Section 3.3.

69 Banking Act articles 29 and 29-1.

70 Taiwan High Court Judgment 107 *jin-shan-su* No. 83 (2019).

carried certain value.[71] Since they are fungible properties, the court decided against compelling the defendant to deliver specific bitcoins to the plaintiff when the defendant breached his contractual obligation. Instead, in line with the common practice of enforcing an obligation to deliver fungible properties (e.g. rice), the court would order the defendant to pay the costs to acquire the fungible properties rather than specific properties (i.e. bitcoins in this case). If the defendant fails to pay the amount to the plaintiff, the court will then seize the defendant's properties to enforce an unsatisfied judgment.[72] However, the court will not order the defendant to transfer specific bitcoins in an enforcement action. If we follow this view, crypto-currencies are properties and therefore the holder of a crypto-currency should enjoy ownership rights.

The next issue is who the owner is regarding a crypto-currency. It is relatively clear if a holder of crypto-currency directly owns the token on a blockchain. However, it is unclear whether the real 'owner' of a crypto-currency is a crypto-wallet operator or a user claiming to hold the crypto-currencies if the tokens are stored in a crypto-wallet. It is debatable whether the legal title of crypto-currencies lies exclusively with the alleged holder of crypto-currencies or with the crypto-wallet operator in which the tokens are stored.

The identity of real owner of crypto-currencies is essential to determine the legal relationship among parties in other contexts. Since Taiwan is a civil law jurisdiction and does not recognize 'equitable ownership' as in many common law countries, the legal title of crypto-currencies must lie with either the real owner or the wallet operator (but not both). The issue has not been visited by Taiwan court yet. It may partly depend on the contractual arrangements between a holder and a crypto-wallet provider. However, for instance, the BitoPro agreement mentioned earlier fails define the ownership of crypto-currencies. It will require legislators or courts to clarify in the future when a proper case enters the judicial system.

Third, there are also courts arguing that bitcoins represent a form of intangible proprietary interest in a criminal case regarding a fraudulent scam tricking victims to transfer bitcoins.[73] Therefore, a person defrauding a victim to transfer bitcoins may still constitute the crime of general fraudulence.[74] The view taken by the criminal court is necessary to penalise fraudsters under the

71 Taiwan High Court (Tainan Branch) Judgment 108 *kan* No. 123.

72 *Id.* See also Tainan District Court Judgment 106 *su* No. 1907 (regarding a case about lending bitcoins).

73 Taiwan High Court Judgment 107 *jin-shan-su* No. 83. See also Taiwan High Court (Taichung Branch) Judgment 106 *shan-su* No. 1014.

74 See Criminal Code of the Republic of China article 339.

Criminal Code. Otherwise, there could be a loophole if a fraudster is sanctioned for a fraudulent scam inducing victims to pay money, but another fraudster is acquitted if he cheats another victim to transfer bitcoins instead of cash.

Fourth, another theory is to treat crypto-currencies as a kind of security or negotiable instrument. As mentioned above, some kinds of crypto-currencies carrying the feature of 'investment contract' may be deemed as a kind of 'securities' under Taiwan's securities regulation. Beyond the scope of securities regulations, some also argue that crypto-currencies may constitute 'negotiable instruments' under the Civil Code, i.e., an instrument that represents certain rights carrying value.[75] The concept under the Civil Code is wider than 'securities". Under this view, some propose that crypto-currencies could be deemed as intangible negotiable instruments that exist in the form of electronic records.[76] The instrument may then represent property rights or obligations depending on the substance of a crypto-currency.[77] Nevertheless, so far there is no judicial authority adopting this approach.

There are also diverging academic views regarding the nature of crypto-currencies. There are commentators who prefer to treat crypto-currencies as properties outrightly, despite they exist only in digital format.[78] However, there are also commentators who arguing that bitcoins or other crypto-currencies are just intangible things that are neither chattel nor real estate.[79] Moreover, there are also scholars who propose crypto-currencies to be a kind of obligation[80] or simply a kind of financial instruments.[81]

The diversity of views simply reflects the fact that crypto-currencies could be used for different purposes. The legal treatment should vary depending on their purpose and function in the market or in a transaction. Hence, there is no consensus yet on how property law should deal with crypto-currencies. It is up to legislators and courts in the future to further develop the issue on the nature of crypto-currencies.

To facilitate the discussion below, this report adopts the Civil Court's approach to treat crypto-currencies as fungible properties without examining further the nature of ownership right attached to the crypto-currencies.

---

75 Yang (n 67) 51.

76 *Id.*

77 Yang (n 67) 54–55.

78 Yang (n 67) 49.

79 Yang (n 67) 50.

80 Yang (n 67) 50.

81 Huang-Chih Sung and Jie-Hua Wu, *Legal Theories and Supervision Norms of Cryptocurrency* (2021) 117 Taipei University Law Review 133, 157–8.

Recognizing that there is no clear legal authority regarding when a person holding crypto-currencies is not a miner or node on a blockchain recording the crypto-currencies, this report will proceed on the basis that the person is the holder of legal title of crypto-currencies if they are deposited in a crypto-wallet.

4.2.2 Sale, Donation, Barter or Lending of Crypto-Currencies

If crypto-currencies are fungible properties, then people should be able to sell their crypto-currencies in exchange for cash. Pursuant to the Civil Code, a contract of sale is 'a contract whereby the parties agree that one of them shall transfer to the other his rights over property and the latter shall pay a price for it.'[82] Hence, one can sell crypto-currencies to another. However, as mentioned above, since crypto-currencies are treated as fungible properties, civil courts would not order specific performance and instead order a buyer to compensate for damage suffered by the seller if the buyer fails to meet his obligation.

Furthermore, there seems to be no reason to argue that one cannot donate or give away crypto-currencies to another person for no consideration.[83] There is no law in Taiwan yet prohibiting a person donating crypto-currencies to another person. How to transfer a crypto-currency to another person with or without consideration should depend on the protocol of a blockchain or rules governing a crypto-wallet.

Similarly, there is no reason to suggest that it is impossible to transfer a certain number of crypto-currencies (e.g. bitcoins) in exchange for a certain number of another crypto-currencies (e.g. Ethers). The bottom line is that Taiwan law recognises barter.[84]

Last, is it possible to lend crypto-currencies to another person? Under Taiwan law, there are two forms of 'lending'. First, there is a contract of loan for consumption, which is defined as 'a contract whereby one of the parties shall transfer to the other the ownership of money or other fungible things, and the parties agree that the latter shall return things of the same kind, quality and quantity.'[85] A contract of loan for consumption typically refers to a loan or money or fungible properties so that a borrower does not have to return the exact properties to the lender (and instead, properties of the same nature). Assuming that we accept crypto-currencies as a kind of fungible properties, it seems to be possible to lend crypto-currencies to another person much like a

82 Civil Code article 345(1).

83 See Civil Code article 400.

84 Civil Code article 398.

85 Civil Code article 474(1).

loan of money as long as it is allowed to happen on a blockchain or through a crypto-wallet.

Second, there is a contract of a loan for use. Under the Civil Code, it is defined as 'a contract whereby one of parties shall deliver a thing to the other and agrees that the latter shall return the thing after gratuitously using it.'[86] Unlike a contract of loan for consumption, a contract of a loan for use requires a borrower to return the exact property to the lender. In the case of crypto-currencies, it means that the borrower has to return the exact same crypto-currency (with same serial number or specification, etc.) to the lender. How this is possible depends on the protocol of a blockchain and a crypto-wallet.

4.2.3 Crypto-Currencies and Inheritance

The Civil Code provides that "[unless] otherwise provided for in this Code, an heir assumes all the rights and obligations pertaining to the estate of the decedent at the time of the commencement of the succession, except those rights and obligations which exclusively belong to the decedent."[87] Following the same reasoning stated above, holdings of crypto-currencies should be able to be inherited if the holder/owner passes away no matter the law treats crypto-currencies as fungible properties, intangible proprietary interests, or mere contractual rights. Under Taiwan law, receivables could be inherited (subject to the contract and the nature of the obligation). Hence, crypto-currencies (or the value represented thereby) should be able to be inherited by proper heirs of a deceased person.

So far there is no law or reported case against a person using a will to manage the crypto-currencies one holds. In theory, even if crypto-currencies do not carry property rights and represent only a contractual claim of monetary value, there is no law prohibiting a deceased person from allocating the contractual claim to heirs or other third parties. However, how exactly inheritance and a will can work in the case of transferring crypto-currencies when an owner passes away should depend on the protocol of a blockchain (if the owner is a miner) or the contract between the ownership and a crypto-wallet in which the coins are deposited. It also requires clarification from market participants or future courts regarding verification (of public and private keys) when a holder of a crypto-currency is deceased.

---

86 Civil Code article 464.

87 Civil Code article 1148(1).

4.2.4 Crypto-Currencies and Trust

Regarding crypto-currencies and trust, whether one can create a trust comprising of crypto-currencies must depend on whether they are considered 'right of property' under Taiwan law, as the definition of trust under Taiwan law requires the transfer or disposal of "a right of property."[88] If we take the view that crypto-currencies could be deemed as fungible properties, one should be able to create a trust with crypto-currencies comprising all or part of the trust assets. The conclusion should be the same even if we treat crypto-currencies as a kind of contractual claim on monetary value. However, it still requires future courts to clarify the matter.

It is also possible that the relationship between a user and a crypto-wallet is one of trust of which the user is a beneficiary and/or settlor and the crypto-wallet operator is a trustee. Whether there is a trust created over the holdings of crypto-currencies regarding a crypto-wallet should depend on the agreement between the user and a crypto-wallet. Although the example provided in Section 4.1 above does not indicate it is a trust relationship for BitoPro, it remains a possibility to use trust as a vehicle to manage crypto-currencies.

4.2.5 Attachment and Seizure

In theory it seems possible to create security interests over crypto-currencies under Taiwan law. What is unclear is the nature of such security interest. It then would affect how it might be enforced by courts. First, it is certain that any security interest attached to holdings of crypto-currencies is not a kind of mortgage, which is defined as 'a preferential right of a creditor to receive satisfaction of a claim from the proceeds from sale of real property that a debtor or a third party has provided, without transferring possession, as security for the claim.'[89] It is clear that crypto-currencies are not real properties. Hence, there is no argument that crypto-currencies could be subject to mortgage.

Second, whether crypto-currencies could be subject to a pledge? There are two kinds of pledges under Taiwan law. On the one hand, there is a pledge of personal property, defined as 'a preferential right of a creditor to receive satisfaction of a claim from the proceeds from sale of personal property the possession of which has been transferred by a debtor or a third party as security for the claim.'[90] To qualify as a pledge of personal property, the premise is that crypto-currencies are a kind of personal properties. As discussed in Section 4.2.1 above, there have been courts considering crypto-currencies to

88 Trust Law article 1.

89 Civil Code article 860.

90 Civil Code article 884.

be fungible properties or at least a form of proprietary interests, though no court expressly claims crypto-currencies to be personal properties yet. If one holds crypto-currencies directly on a blockchain, at least it is arguable that the holdings of crypto-currencies may be akin to other traditional personal properties. If one holds crypto-currencies through a crypto-wallet, the issue becomes more complicated as the rights of a user must depend on the agreement between the parties. If a holder does not enjoy direct proper rights over crypto-currencies stored in a crypto-wallet, there should be little chance of creating a pledge. It requires future courts to clarify the matter.

On the other hand, Taiwan law also recognises a pledge of rights. A pledge of rights is defined as 'a pledge the subject of which is a transferable claim or other transferable right.'[91] It seems much more likely to treat any security interest created over crypto-currencies to be a pledge of rights. No matter one is a miner or simply holds crypto-currencies through a crypto-wallet, there is no denial that the person enjoys a claim over the crypto-currencies (or the value represented by the coins), regardless whether we frame such claim as proprietary or contractual rights. The situation may be similar to a pledge created over securities (e.g. shares or debentures). While it still requires future courts to confirm, it is reasonable to assume that one can create a pledge over crypto-currencies under Taiwan law. Then, how such pledge could be attached, seized or enforced could follow the same rules about a pledge created over securities or negotiable instruments.

4.2.6 Insolvency Law and Crypto-Currencies

There is no specific legislation and case laws explaining how insolvency law in Taiwan may apply to holdings of crypto-currencies. In Taiwan, there is the Insolvency Act published since 1935 and the law remains largely unchanged since then. Without going into details of how insolvency law may interact with crypto-currencies, there could be three different scenarios that courts have to consider in the future.

The first scenario is when a miner or node is bankrupt. In this situation, it is reasonable to assume that the person is a direct owner of the crypto-currencies registered on the chain. Therefore, there is no reason to exclude the holdings of crypto-currencies held by the person from his list of assets if the crypto-currencies carry monetary value and could be converted into cash. Hence, in principle, other creditors should be able to tap those virtual assets. However,

91 Civil Code article 900.

how creditors or the court-appointed liquidator could deal with those assets is unclear under Taiwan law.

The second scenario is when a bankrupt person has crypto-currencies deposited in a crypto-wallet. If we take the civil court's view that crypto-currencies are fungible properties, it follows that there is no reason to exclude holdings of crypto-currencies in a crypto-wallet from the bankrupt person's assets. How creditors and liquidators can deal with those holdings of crypto-currencies partly depend on the agreement with a crypto-wallet operator and partly it might depend on the protocol governing a crypto-currency. Again, it is unclear how Taiwan court will deal with those assets under Taiwan's Insolvency Act.

The third scenario is where a crypto-wallet operator goes bust. This situation is untested in Taiwan yet. If a crypto-wallet operator puts crypto-currencies that it holds for customers into a segregated trust account, it is perhaps possible to argue that those crypto-currencies under trust are not properties of the crypto-wallet operator. Nevertheless, when there is no trust account created, it opens the door for a crypto-wallet operator's creditors to tap those virtual assets for value. The answer goes back to the root of the problem: who owns the crypto-currencies in a crypto-wallet, the user or crypto-wallet operator? There is no clear case law yet in Taiwan in this regard. Any solution also depends on the nature of crypto-currencies under Taiwan to clearly define the nature and scope of ownership rights regarding crypto-currencies.

5 Tax and Crypto-Currencies

There is no specific tax law governing crypto-currencies in Taiwan, but it does not mean there is no tax issues for transactions with crypto-currencies. Since crypto-currencies are not treated as a legal tender or a kind of currency recognized by the Central Bank, Taiwan's tax authorities likely would treat a trade of crypto-currencies or using crypto-currencies to pay for goods as a form of barter.[92] On this basis, tax authorities have clarified in 2019 that fees collected by a crypto-exchange for processing crypto-currencies transactions should be subject to sales tax.[93] However, how to calculate income and profits may vary depending on the transaction structure of a crypto-exchange.[94] Likewise, if a

92 Tony Tsai, *Long-awaited for the Official Explanation: Analyze the MOF Explanation Regarding Cryptocurrency Transaction* (2019) 15 Angle Accounting Magazine 103, 103 (2019).

93 *Id.* at 104.

94 Cindy Huang and Yi-Siang Sia, *The Current Situation and Taxation Issues of Virtual Currency: From the Perspective of Natural Person's Transaction* (2021) 41 Angle Accounting Magazine 54, 60.

firm earns profits due from mining or trading of crypto-currencies, it is subject to corporate income tax.[95] Similarly, an individual should in principle pay for personal income tax.[96]

For securities tokens, a transaction may be subject to the securities transaction tax levied on transactions involving a transfer of securities.[97] Since some crypto-currencies may be designated as a form of investment contract and henceforth be classified as "securities", it is highly likely that trading activities of those securities-like crypto-currencies should be subject to the securities transaction tax.

6 Conclusion

In conclusion, this report explores the current state of law governing crypto-currencies in Taiwan. There are some key findings. First, Taiwan law clearly dismisses the idea of treating crypto-currencies as currencies, but there are limited judicial authorities recognizing crypto-currencies to be fungible properties or to at least represent some proprietary interests. However, legislators and courts are silent on the nature of ownership of crypto-currencies. This may potentially affect some legal issues in the future such as creating security interests over crypto-currencies stored in a crypto-wallet or the situation where a crypto-wallet operator is bankrupt. Second, from regulatory perspective, Taiwan's financial regulator officially recognises crypto-currencies as a kind of securities governed by capital market regulations if the crypto-currencies carry the features of an investment contract. However, the regulatory status of crypto-currencies which are not securities is much less certain. On the one hand, the court has clarified that a crypto Ponzi scheme may not fall fault of the Banking Act as illegal banking activities. It is also likely that crypto-currencies are not stored-value cards. Nevertheless, it remains to be seen whether an issuer of crypto-currencies or a crypto-wallet operator should be considered an electronic payment institution. Last, the Central Bank in Taiwan is experimenting and testing central bank digital currencies (CBDCs) at the time of writing. But it remains to be seen how the central bank will handle CBDCs in the future.

95 Tsai (n 92) 104.

96 *Id.*

97 See media report in the Economic Times in https://money.udn.com/money/story/122229/5859508 (last accessed 6 January 2022).

Turkey

Meliha Sermin Paksoy

1 Introduction

Turkey's cryptocurrency market is among the top five in the world with nearly 5 million cryptocurrency service provider accounts.[1] Turkish Lira ranks fourth in the list of most traded national currencies for Bitcoin.[2] The market volume for cryptocurrencies in Turkey corresponds to 900 million dollars.[3] The Central Bank of Republic of Turkey's announcement of a ban on the use of the cryptocurrencies in payments caused Bitcoin to lose 4.6% of its value.[4] Ethereum and XRP fell between 6% and 12% after this ban.[5] The reasons given for the high interest in the crypto markets are the high inflation and the depreciation of the Turkish Lira.[6] However, it is believed that the chance of a quick and easy profit is also tempting for the Turkish citizens to invest in cryptocurrencies.[7]

There are five local[8] and more than 30 cryptocurrency platforms which base their operations in Turkey.[9] Most investors prefer Bitcoin. Ripple, Digibyte, Bitcoin Cash and Stellar are next most invested cryptocurrencies.[10] Stable

---

1 Hurriyet Daily News, 8.1.2022, https://www.hurriyetdailynews.com/turkey-aims-at-safe-financial-base-for-cryptocurrency-market-170636#:~:text=Turkey's%20cryptocurrency%20market%20is%20among,cryptocurrency%20platform%20by%20a%20watchdog;DailySabah,25.4.2021,https://www.dailysabah.com/business/finance/collapses-of-exchanges-vs-turkish-crypto-boom.

2 Coinhills, 31.01.2022, https://www.coinhills.com/market/currency/.

3 CNNTurk, 02.12.2021, https://www.cnnturk.com/dunya/turkiyedeki-hacmi-ne-kadar-iste-rakamlarla-kripto-para?page=1.

4 Reuters, 16.04.2021, https://www.reuters.com/technology/turkey-bans-use-cryptocurrencies-payments-sends-bitcoin-down-2021-04-16/.

5 Ibid.

6 Ibid.

7 The Times of India, 6.1.2022, https://timesofindia.indiatimes.com/business/cryptocurrency/blockchain/use-of-stablecoins-rises-hugely-in-turkey-as-inflation-touches-all-time-high/articleshow/88731029.cms.

8 CoinGecko, 31.01.2022, https://www.coingecko.com/tr/borsalar?country=TR.

9 Hurriyet Daily News, 8.01.2022, https://www.hurriyetdailynews.com/turkey-aims-at-safe-financial-base-for-cryptocurrency-market-170636#:~:text=Turkey's%20cryptocurrency%20market%20is%20among,cryptocurrency%20platform%20by%20a%20watchdog.

10 Bilgi Teknolojileri ve İletişim Kurumu *Kripto Para Araştırma Raporu,* https://www.btk.gov.tr/uploads/pages/arastirma-raporlari/kripto-para-raporu-5f11dfe709c25.pdf.

 | DOI:10.1163/9789004722507_028

coins are also very popular in Turkey. According to the reports, the new Turkish Lira accounted for 28.96 percent of all trades that are paired with Tether. For Binance's stablecoin BUSD, this rate is 7.20 percent.[11] Neither of these nor other cryptocurrencies traded in Turkey are accepted as legal tender. Cryptocurrencies are also not accepted as foreign currency.[12] Since use of cryptocurrencies in payments is prohibited in Turkey, cryptocurrencies only have investment values.

2 Definition of the Cryptocurrency

There is no separate legal definition of cryptocurrency in Turkey. Article 3 of the Regulation On the Disuse of Crypto Assets in Payments defines crypto assets as intangible assets that are created virtually using distributed ledger technology or a similar technology and distributed via digital networks, but are not classed as fiat money, deposit money, electronic money, payment instrument, securities, or other capital market instruments.[13] On July 2, 2024, long-awaited cryptocurrency regulations come into effect by adding various articles to the Capital Markets Law. Also in article 3 of the Capital Markets Law, crypto assets are defined, but there is no separate definition for cryptocurrencies.[14] According to this definition, crypto assets are intangible assets that can be created and stored electronically using distributed ledger technology or similar technology, distributed over digital networks, and can represent value or rights. So far, Turkish lawmakers have opted not to distinguish crypto assets from cryptocurrencies.

---

11 The Times of India, 6.1.2022, https://timesofindia.indiatimes.com/business/cryptocurrency/blockchain/use-of-stablecoins-rises-hugely-in-turkey-as-inflation-touches-all-time-high/articleshow/88731029.cms.

12 T.E Yardimci, 'Icra Takibi Yoluyla Bitcoin Alacağinin Ileri Sürülmesi ve Borçlunun Bitcoininin Haczedilmesi', *Ankara Hacı Bayram Veli Üniversitesi Hukuk Fakültesi Dergisi,* 2019, XXIII, 2019, 3, 1, p. 102; F. Bilgili and F. Cengil, 'Bitcoin Özelinde Kripto Paralarin Ticaret Şirketlerine Sermaye Olarak Getirilmesi' *Ankara Hacı Bayram Veli Üniversitesi Hukuk Fakültesi Dergisi,* 2019, XXIII, 3, p. 140; E. Balikci, 'Dava Ve Takip Konusu Olabilmesi Bakimindan Kripto Paralar', *ERÜHFD,* 2021, XVI, 2, p. 287.

13 Official English translation is available at https://www.tcmb.gov.tr/wps/wcm/connect/c241af16-e730-45b5-bb0d31d3af28884e/Regulation+on+the+Disuse+of+Crypto+Assets+in+Payments.pdf?MOD=AJPERES&CACHE=NONE&CONTENTCACHE=NONE.

14 Bağımsız Denetim, https://bdturkeycom.teimg.com/bdturkey-com/uploads/2024/01/kripto-varlik-kanun-taslagi-yeni.pdf.

According to one definition in the legal doctrine, cryptocurrency is a currency taken from virtual wallets and spent with a password.[15] Another author defines cryptocurrency as an individual asset based on special knowledge/data just like know-how, trade secret, customer circle.[16] The author of this article would define cryptocurrency a cryptographic intangible and fungible asset which can be transferred peer-to-peer through blockchain technology.

So far, there are two main court decisions related to the definition of cryptocurrencies. The Istanbul Enforcement Law Court ruled that cryptocurrencies are like commodities, securities, digital and virtual money and therefore can be attached.[17] Antalya District Court of Appeal accepted cryptocurrencies as part of the digital estate and defined cryptocurrencies as a digital system used even in international payments.[18]

3 Regulation of Cryptocurrencies in Turkey

3.1 *Regulation on the Disuse of Crypto Assets in Payments*

On 16 April 2021, Central Bank of the Republic of Turkey (CBRT) issued a regulation prohibiting the use of crypto assets in payments for goods and services, which was published in the Official Gazette.[19] Regulation on the Disuse of Crypto Assets in Payments (Regulation) came into force on 30 April 2021.

In Article 3 of this Regulation, crypto assets are defined as intangible assets as explained under previous title. Though crypto asset is a broader term that includes not only cryptocurrencies but also utility and security tokens, this definition indicates that Turkish lawmakers consider cryptocurrencies to be intangible assets. Turkish lawmakers do not want cryptocurrencies to be an

---

15 D.A. Imamoglu, *Kripto Para Birimleri ve Türk Hukukunda Düzenlenmesi*, Seckin, Ankara 2021, p. 37.

16 K.B. Kapanci, 'Özel Hukuk Penceresinden Blokzincir: "Sanal Para" Değerleri ve "Akıllı Sözleşmeler" Üzerine Değerlendirmeler', E. Aksoy Retornaz and O. G. Güçlütürk (eds), *Gelişen Teknolojiler ve Hukuk I - Blokzincir ve Hukuk*, Onikilevha, Istanbul 2021, p. 173.

17 A. Erdem and I. Duranoglu, 'Turkey: Latest Developments On Crypto Assets In Turkey: How The Recent Regulations Going To Effect Taxation And Enforcement Of Crypto Currencies?', 2021, https://www.mondaq.com/turkey/fin-tech/1138378/latest-developments-on-crypto-assets-in-turkey-how-the-recent-regulations-going-to-effect-taxation-and-enforcement-of-crypto-currencies, N.6.

18 Antalya BAM 6. HD, 13.11.2020, E.2020/1149, K.2020/90, https://www.batur.av.tr/dijital-miras-ve-kripto-paralar-konusunda-emsal-karar.html.

19 Also available in English https://www.tcmb.gov.tr/wps/wcm/connect/c241af16-e730-45b5-bbod-31d3af28884e/Regulation+on+the+Disuse+of+Crypto+Assets+in+Payments.pdf?MOD=AJPERES&CACHE=NONE&CONTENTCACHE=NONE.

alternative payment instrument to the Turkish Lira. Therefore, they intentionally refrain from using the phrase 'cryptocurrency'.

According to this Regulation, crypto assets cannot be used directly or indirectly as a means of payment. Services that enable direct or indirect use of crypto assets in payments are also prohibited. Payment service providers cannot develop business models that use crypto assets directly or indirectly in the provision of payment services and issuance of electronic money, and they cannot provide any services related to such business models. Moreover, payment and electronic money institutions cannot act as intermediaries for platforms that offer trading, custody, transfer, or issue services related to crypto assets, or for fund transfers to be made by these platforms.

In short, the Regulation prohibits payments using crypto assets, but does not prohibit investing in crypto assets. Before this ban, the use of the crypto assets, especially cryptocurrencies, in payments was not a common practice. Just days before the Regulation was published, Royal Motors, which distributes Rolls-Royce and Lotus cars in Turkey, became the first in the country to declare accepting payments in cryptocurrencies.[20]

On the date of publication, CBRT shared a press release and explained why the Regulation was enacted. According to the CBRT, 'Crypto assets entail significant risks to the relevant parties due to the following reasons: (i) they are neither subject to any regulation and supervision mechanisms nor a central regulatory authority, (ii) their market values can be excessively volatile, (iii) they may be used in illegal actions due to their anonymous structures, (iv) wallets can be stolen or used unlawfully without the authorization of their holders, and (v) transactions are irrevocable. Recently, some initiatives have emerged regarding the use of these assets in payments. It is considered that their use in payments may cause non-recoverable losses for the parties to the transactions due to the above-listed factors and they include elements that may undermine the confidence in methods and instruments used currently in payments.' The last sentence of this press release indicates that one of the reasons for enacting this regulation was to protect the value of the Turkish Lira. The other reasons given don't explain much why investing in cryptocurrencies is not banned, even though payments with crypto assets have been banned.

Following the Regulation, it was signaled that Turkish lawmakers were working on a cryptocurrency law in cooperation with the Central Bank (CBRT), the Turkish Banking Regulatory and Supervisory Authority (BDDK) and the Capital Markets Board (SPK). This process took more than three years, and the

20 Daily Sabah, 16.04.2021, https://www.dailysabah.com/business/finance/turkey-to-ban-use-of-cryptocurrencies-for-buying-goods-services.

recent amendments to the Capital Market Law regulating cryptocurrencies entered into force on July 2, 2024, as explained in detail in the next section.

3.2 *Newly Minted Regulations of Crypto Assets: "Crypto-Asset Code"*

Although there is no separate code regulating crypto assets in Turkey, certain amendments have been made to the Capital Markets Law (CML), which are also referred to as the new Crypto Asset Code. The Capital Markets Board of Turkey (the Board) will be responsible for overseeing and implementing these new regulations, and the Board will also have the authority to enact secondary legislation.

One very positive development is that the new amendments define the concepts of crypto wallet, crypto asset, crypto asset trading platform, crypto asset custody service, and crypto asset service provider.

The segregation of customers' assets from those of the crypto asset service provider is also crucial for protecting customers against the insolvency of the service provider. Requiring customer assets to be held in separate legal entities such as banks is also a well-considered move, especially following the collapse of several local cryptocurrency exchange platforms, which will be discussed in more detail in subsequent sections.

Taxation is deliberately not addressed in these amendments; authorities have expressed that issues related to taxation will be further studied and regulated separately.

Government authorities state that these regulations will create a conducive financial environment for the healthy growth of blockchain-based businesses. After a long period of lack of supervision and ambiguity regarding definitions and liabilities, these amendments are seen as a very positive development to prevent abuse and clarify matters in the cryptocurrency ecosystem.

3.2.1 Requirements for Crypto Asset Service Providers

According to the new law, it is mandatory to obtain permission from the Board for the establishment and commencement of operations of crypto asset service providers, and they shall exclusively perform the activities determined by the Board. (Art. 35/ B (1) CML) New amendments defines crypto asset service providers as platforms, entities providing crypto asset custody services, and other entities designated to provide services related to crypto assets, including the initial sale or distribution of crypto assets (Art. 3 CML).

Crypto asset service providers are obligated to make the necessary arrangements, take precautions, and establish the necessary internal control units and systems to manage their systems securely. The technical criteria that crypto asset service providers applying for a license under the law must meet will be determined by Scientific and Technological Research Council of Turkey (TUBITAK) (Art. 35 B (11) CML).

Under the recent amendments, platforms based abroad that target individuals residing in Turkey or engage in prohibited activities related to crypto assets are considered unauthorized crypto asset service providers (Art. 99/A 1 CML). Consequently, foreign-based crypto asset service providers must halt their activities directed at Turkish residents within three months from the effective date of these amendments (Temporary Article 11 CML).

Shareholders, board members, and representatives of these service providers must also adhere to the conditions set by the Board.

Individuals and legal representatives of entities found operating as crypto asset service providers without permission may face imprisonment for three to five years and fines ranging from five thousand to ten thousand days (Art. 109 A CML).

Lastly, it is crucial to note that authorization by the Board for crypto asset platforms does not imply that transactions are guaranteed by the public funds (Art. 35 C (4) CML)

3.2.2 Operational Standards for Crypto Asset Platforms and Wallet Providers

Contracts signed between crypto asset trading platforms and customers who intend to trade on these platforms may be established remotely, either in written form or through the use of remote communication tools, regardless of whether the communication is remote or not, provided that it is determined by the Board to replace the written form, and through methods that will be conducted via a computer or electronic communication device and allow for the verification of customer identity. (Art. 35 C (1) CML)Any contractual provision that eliminates or limits the responsibilities of crypto asset service providers to their customers is invalid. (Art. 35 C (1) CML).

Platforms are required to establish a written listing procedure for determining which crypto assets will be traded or initially sold or distributed on their platforms and for terminating the trading of these assets. (Art. 35 C (2) CML).

It is essential that the crypto assets of customers on the platforms be kept in the customers' own wallets. Custody services for crypto assets that customers prefer not to hold in their own wallets must be provided by banks authorized under regulations to be issued by the Board and approved by the Banking Regulation and Supervision Board, or by other entities authorized by the Board to provide crypto asset custody services. Cash belonging to customers must be kept in banks. (Art 35/C (6) CML). However, it is important to emphasize that crypto assets held in banks and the cash of customers within this scope are not subject to the deposit and participation fund insurance provisions.

(Art. 35 C 6 CML)Funds and crypto assets of the customers will be segregated from the crypto asset service providers' assets and therefore customer funds and assets will not be attached due to the insolvency of the crypto asset service provider. –

3.2.3 Audit and Financial Strengthening Measures for Crypto Asset Service Providers

The financial audits and information systems independent audits of crypto asset service providers shall be conducted by independent audit firms (Art.99/B 2).

The Board has the authority, upon determining that crypto asset service providers are unable to meet their obligations for cash payments or crypto asset deliveries arising from their activities, or that their financial structure has significantly weakened, to request them to strengthen their financial position within a period not exceeding three months. Additionally, the Board may temporarily suspend the activities of crypto asset service providers immediately and without prior notice, revoke their operating licenses, or restrict the signing authority of responsible managers and employees whose duties have been identified (Art. 99/A (2) CML).

4 Criminal Law Liability of Hackers, Service Providers and Money Launderers

The legal doctrine thinks that if the cryptocurrency-related services become involved in fraudulent behavior, Article 157 of the Turkish Penal Code (TPC) will be applied.[21] According to this article, a person who deceives a person

21 T. Tomrukcu, 'Kripto Varlıkların Konu Oldukları Dolandırıcılık Sucları', Y. Unver and K. Oz (eds), *Krıpto Para Ve Ceza Hukuku,* Seckin, Ankara 2022, p. 271; M. Balcı and K. Cakir, 'Kripto Para Dolandırıcılığı', *Terazi Hukuk Dergisi,* 2021, 16, 181, p. 1686; Z.E. TARAKCIOĞLU, 'Kripto Varlıklar ve Ceza Hukuku Sorumluluğu', *AkdHFD,* 2021, 11, 2, p. 336; E. Retornaz Aksoy, 'Ceza Hukuku Perspektifinden Blokzincir', Aksoy Retornaz and O. G. Güçlütürk (eds), Gelişen Teknolojiler ve Hukuk I - Blokzincir ve Hukuk, Onikilevha, Istanbul 2021, p. 303; Kapanci, p. 176; E. Şen, 'Bitcoin Çalınır Mı?', 2016, N.17, https://www.haber7.com/yazarlar/prof-dr-ersan-sen/1948163-bitcoin-calinir-mi#:~:text=Maddi%20de%C4%9Fer%20ifade%20eden%20bitcoinin,su%C3%A7un%20kapsam%C4%B1na%20girdi%C4%9Fi%20tespit%20edilmelidir.&text=Bu%20su%C3%A7lar%3B%20TCK%20m.142,m.245'de%20

with fraudulent acts and provides a benefit to herself or someone else at the expense of her or someone else is sentenced to imprisonment from one year to five years and a judicial fine up to five thousand days. Use of an information system in the fraudulent act is a reason to increase the envisaged punishment (Art. 158 1-f). Since most cryptocurrency fraud cases involve the use of information systems, this paragraph will normally apply.[22] If this fraud was committed by taking advantage of the facilities provided by the press and media, this constitutes an aggravating circumstance.

On 20 April 2021, Thodex, one of the top crypto currency exchange platforms in Turkey, abruptly ceased trading. After multiple complaints from 391,000 registered users of this platform, on 22 April 2021, the Chief Prosecutor of Istanbul Anatolia launched an investigation for establishing an organization with intent to commit a crime and qualified fraud by using information systems as a tool.[23] Police detained 62 people and issued detention warrants for 16 people. However, the owner and founder, Faruk Fatih Ozer, fled the country allegedly scamming $2 billion in investments.[24] It was found that Thodex and Faruk Fatih Ozer had transferred funds to Binance, public prosecuter's office asked Binance to block the relevant accounts.[25] Thodex's bank account was also seized.[26] In 2002, these persons got caught and the court sentenced the detained defendants to 11,196 years, 10 months, and 15 days of imprisonment each for 'establishing and leading a criminal organization,' 'aggravated fraud,' 'money laundering,' and 'committing fraud through the use of information systems.[27]

Very shortly after this incident, on 23 April 2021, Vebitcoin, another local crypto exchange platform, halted operations after citing deteriorating financial conditions. Following this development, authorities arrested four people linked with this exchange, who were accused of fraud.[28] In addition,

d%C3%BCzenlenmi%C5%9Ftir.; S. Sarıkaya, Kripto Para Dolandırıcılığı, AndHD, 2023, 9, 2, pp. 555–556.

22 Tarakcioglu, p. 336; Sarikaya, pp. 555–556.

23 Anadolu Ajansı, 19.05.2021, https://www.aa.com.tr/tr/turkiye/thodex-sorusturmasinda-firari-olan-faruk-fatih-ozerin-yengesi-yakalandi/2246681.

24 Cointelegraph, 23.04.2021, https://cointelegraph.com/news/turkish-police-detain-62-over-alleged-2b-thodex-crypto-exchange-fraud.

25 Sabah, 13.9.2021, https://www.sabah.com.tr/ekonomi/2021/09/13/thodex-sorusturmasinda-son-dakika-sinirlarini-asti.

26 Ibid.

27 BBC News Türkçe, 22.1.2024, https://www.bbc.com/turkce/articles/cjl32gl45w8o.

28 Ibid.

the Financial Crimes Investigation Board blocked Vebitcoin's accounts and launched an investigation.[29]

Prevailing legal opinion is that cryptocurrencies cannot be stolen, as Art. 141 of the TPC defines theft as removing someone else's moveable property without the consent of the possessor for the benefit of oneself or someone else.[30] As explained below, since cryptocurrency isn't a moveable property, articles sanctioning theft cannot be applied where the control of the cryptocurrency is lost due to the intentional intervention of a third party. In one case, the Turkish Court of Cassation ruled that act of unlawful capture the character of the Knight Online game participant doesn't constitute theft but a violation of Article 244 of the TPC.[31] Only if there is a cold wallet, the storage medium can be stolen.[32] Similar to the capture of the character, the authority of the private key holder over the record of cryptocurrency can be protected by the legal order within the framework of Article 244 of the Turkish Penal Code.[33]

If crypto currency service provider is hacked, then Article 244 of the TPC can be applied.[34] According to this article, anyone who hinders or disrupts the operation of an information system is penalized. A person who corrupts, destroys, changes, or makes inaccessible data in an information system, places data on the system, sends existing data to another place, is also punished.

Crypto currencies can be used for money laundering. According to the Art. 282 of the TPC, a person who transfers abroad the proceeds obtained from an offence requiring a minimum penalty of six months or more imprisonment or processes such proceeds in various ways in order to conceal the illicit source of such proceeds or to give the impression that they have been legitimately acquired shall be sentenced to imprisonment from three years up to seven years and a judicial fine up to twenty thousand days.

A person who, without participating in the commitment of the offence mentioned previously, purchases, acquires, possesses, or uses the proceeds

---

29 Bloomberg, 26.04.2021, https://www.bloomberg.com/news/articles/2021-04-26/losses-arrests-and-a-manhunt-cryptomania-hits-home-in-turkey.

30 Sen, N.17 ; Aksoy Retornaz, p. 301; Tarakcioglu, p. 328; Kapanci, p. 175.

31 Y. 2. CD. 13.1.2020, E. 2019/11010, K. 2020/568, www. emsal.yargitay.gov.tr.

32 Aksoy Retornaz, p. 301; Kapanci, p. 175.

33 M. S. Cekin, 'Kripto Varlıklar Üzerinde Gerçekleştirilen İşlemlerin Borçlar Hukuku ve Eşya Hukuku Açısından Değerlendirilmesi', İstanbul Medipol Üniversitesi Hukuk Fakültesi Dergisi, 2022, 9, 1, p. 11.

34 U. Balcı, 'Kripto Paraların Ceza Hukuku Boyutu ve Türk Mevzuatındaki Muhtemel Düzenleme Yeri', *Türkiye Baralor Birliği Dergisi*, 2021, 34, 155, p. 245; A. Altunkas, '5237 sayılı Türk Ceza Kanunu Kapsamında Parada Sahtecilik Suçu (TCK m.197)', *Terazi Hukuk Dergisi*, 2021, 16, 174, p. 214; Aksoy Retornaz, p. 309; Tarakcioglu, p. 332.

which is the subject of that offence knowing the nature of the proceeds shall be sentenced to imprisonment from two years up to five years. Art. 282 of the TPC is not the only measure to prevent the money laundering. There is a separate Law on Prevention of Laundering Proceeds of Crime. Relevant measures of this law, which is implemented by Financial Crimes Investigation Board, are explained in more detail in the next section.

According to the recent amendments in the Capital Markets Law regulating crypto assets, members of the board of directors and other members of a crypto asset service provider who, due to their duties, misappropriate or embezzle money or negotiable instruments, other property, or crypto assets entrusted to them for custody, protection, or surveillance, shall be punished with imprisonment from eight to fourteen years and a judicial fine of up to five thousand days. They shall also be liable to compensate for the damages caused to the crypto asset service provider (Article 110/A (1) CML).

5 Anti-Money Laundering and Counter Terrorism Measures to Be Followed by the Crypto Asset Service Providers

In many countries there are financial intelligence units to combat money laundering and terrorism financing. In Turkey, this fight is essentially waged by Financial Crimes Investigation Board (MASAK), which is directly attached to Ministry of Finance.

On 1 May 2021, Regulation on Measures to Prevent Money Laundering and Terrorism Financing[35] was amended and 'Crypto Asset Service Providers' became an obliged party. According to the Law No. 5549 on Prevention of Laundering Proceeds of Crime,[36] an obliged party, in this context, crypto asset service provider must identify the customer, report suspicious transactions, provide information and documents, store the relevant information and documents, and report every transaction, which is above a threshold set by the ministry of finance (Art.3-9A of the Law No.5549). For every breach of these obligations, obliged party must pay an administrative fine imposed by MASAK.

On 4 May 2021, the MASAK released a guideline for the cryptocurrency service providers to help comply with anti-money laundering anti-terrorism measures. This guide explains suspicious transactions, reporting and identification

35 Not amended English version available at https://ms.hmb.gov.tr/uploads/sites/2/2019/04/R_RoM-1.pdf.

36 Not amended English version available at https://ms.hmb.gov.tr/uploads/sites/2/2019/04/Law-No_5549-on-Prevention-of-Laundering-Proceeds-of-Crime-1.pdf.

processes in detail. Several examples are given for suspicious transactions. For example, if customers who appear to be acting independently share the same address, phone number and similar contact, information, this is considered a suspicious transaction.[37]

In practice, to prevent money laundering, crypto currency service providers allow the customers to make cash transfers only from and to their own bank accounts in Turkey.[38]

On 27 December 2021, MASAK fined Binance, or BN Teknoloji, 8 million Turkish Liras (nearly $ 634,000) for the violations that came out during the liability check carried out under the Law On Prevention Of Laundering Proceeds Of Crime.[39] Similarly, administrative fines were decided to be imposed on the local service providers Bitci Teknoloji AŞ, Icrypex Bilişim AŞ, Paribu Teknoloji AŞ, and BTC Türk for the breaches of obligations committed in 2021.[40] In 2002, MASAK suspended transactions of the global cryptocurrency trading platform operating under the trade name FTX.com because it has been determined that customer deposits were not properly safeguarded, suspicion of strong criminal activity has been reached concerning the transfer or exportation of customer deposits to other persons or entities through false transactions and it has been determined that customers were induced to buy and sell non-existent cryptocurrencies, and the market supply and demand were managed in a fictitious manner contrary to normal market operations.[41]

Additionally, recent amendments to the Capital Markets Law regarding the regulation of crypto assets state once more that crypto asset service providers are obliged to verify the identities of their customers in accordance with Law on the Prevention of Laundering Proceeds of Crime, and other relevant legislative provisions (Art. 35 C (1) CML).

---

37 MASAK, *Kripto Varlık Hizmet Sağlayıcılar Rehberi,* p.16, https://ms.hmb.gov.tr/uploads/sites/12/2021/05/Kripto-Varlik-Hizmet-Saglayicilar-Rehberi.pdf.

38 Gurses, p. 110.

39 Hurriyet Daily News, 8.01.2022, https://www.hurriyetdailynews.com/turkey-aims-at-safe-financial-base-for-cryptocurrency-market-170636#:~:text=Turkey's%20cryptocurrency%20market%20is%20among,cryptocurrency%20platform%20by%20a%20watchdog.

40 Mynet, 17.2.2022, https://finans.mynet.com/haber/detay/kripto-para/masak-tan-btc-turk-paribu-bitci-ve-icrypex-e-18-8-milyon-liralik-ceza/436899/.

41 TC Maliye ve Hazine Bakanlığı Mali Suçlar Araştırma Kurumu, 23.10.2022, https://masak.hmb.gov.tr/duyuru/ftx-com-ticari-unvaniyla-faaliyet-gosteren-kripto-varlik-alim-satim-platformu-hk.

6 Property Law Discussions Regarding the Nature of the Cryptocurrencies

6.1 *Are Cryptocurrencies Movable Properties?*

Objects of the rights in rem such as ownership and limited rights in rem are properties in Turkish property law. However, property is not defined by law. Although there is no legal definition, legal doctrine unanimously defines property as tangible asset other than individuals, on which individual dominance can be achieved, and which has economic value.[42] Cryptocurrencies can be limited and controlled and have a material value, however, since cryptocurrencies are intangible, especially not having a three-dimensional physical existence, the prevailing opinion in Turkey is that cryptocurrencies cannot be defined as property.[43]

However, another view claims that since there is no explicit definition of property in Turkish property law, a broader approach could be accepted and cryptocurrency can be defined as property without being tangible.[44] In Article 762 of the Turkish Civil Code (TCC), natural forces such as electricity are legally recognized as movable property by law. According to the above-mentioned view, this article testifies to the willingness of the lawmaker to adapt to the requirements of modern times. Therefore, this view claims that cryptocurrencies can be defined as movable property.

The author is of the opinion that things without a physical dimension cannot be defined as property unless there is an explicit rule like Art. 762 of the TCC. Since rights in rem presuppose the physical three-dimensional existence of things, intellectual property rights cannot be the subject of property rights and are regulated separately. These rules fit the nature of intellectual property rights better than the rights in rem regime. Additionally, since cryptocurrencies are very different from traditional moveable properties, accepting cryptocurrencies as moveable will most likely lead to incompatibility issues. Most remedies in property law require the physical existence of the object to be enforceable. For example, the restitution of cryptocurrency through a rei

42 K. Oguzman and O. Selici and S. Oktay Özdemir, *Eşya Hukuku,* Filiz, Istanbul 2021, N.19.

43 A. Turanboy, 'Kripto Paraların Ortaya Çıkmaları ve Hukuki Nitelikleri', *Banka ve Ticaret Hukuku Dergisi,* 2019, 35, 3, p. 57; Imamoglu, p. 92; Yardimci, p. 104; Balikci, p. 283; Kapanci, p. 171; Gurses and et al, p. 80; Cekin, p. 8.

44 Bilgili and Cengil, p. 101; G. Ozdemir, 'Kripto Paraların Eşya Niteliği', *SDÜHFD*, 2021, 11, 1, p. 302; F. Bilgili and F. Cengil, 'Bitcoin Özelinde Kripto Paraların Eşya Niteliği Sorunu', *Hukuk Kitapligi,* 2019, p. 12; Hinted in P. Çağlayan Aksoy,'The applicability of property law rules for crypto assets: considerations from civil law and common law perspectives', *Law, Innovation and Technology,* 2023, 15, 1, pp. 220–221.

vindicatio claim against the will of the cryptocurrency holder will mostly not work. On the other hand, it is stated that adhering to a conventional interpretation of property law principles results in transactions being governed by technology-encoded rules rather than legal systems. Qualification of property is also believed to be important in solving problems such as hacking, theft, fraud, and deletion.[45] In author's opinion, the necessity of regulation is evident, but the solution does not lie within property law. For problems such as hacking, theft and fraud, Turkish criminal law and tort law provide various solutions, as stated above.

Indeed, while there is a tendency to categorize cryptocurrencies as property in common law countries, it is increasingly recognized that creating a separate asset class for these currencies and subjecting them to rules tailored to their nature is being advocated more and more.[46] In short, in Turkish law, cryptocurrency cannot be defined as property.

6.2 *Ownership from the Perspective of Constitutional Law*

Art. 683 (1) of the TCC states that object of the ownership right can only be properties. Since cryptocurrencies cannot be defined as a property, cryptocurrencies cannot be object of ownership from the perspective of the property law. Therefore, for example, X has no legal ownership of the 60 Bitcoins in his private wallet. The result does not change when opening an account with an intermediary that offers wallet services. In the latter case, X only has a contractual claim to the value of 60 Bitcoins from the wallet provider.

At this point, however, it should be noted that ownership is defined differently in Turkish constitutional law. In Turkish constitutional law, all rights with material value are constitutionally protected under the umbrella of the term 'ownership'.[47] In short, even if cryptocurrencies cannot be defined as a property from a property law perspective, they are constitutionally protected within the scope of constitutional ownership. According to Art. 35 of the Turkish Constitution (TC) ownership right can only be restricted by law for reasons of public interest. Additionally, restriction of ownership as a fundamental right is subjected to certain limitations (Art. 13 of TC).

45 Caglayan Aksoy, pp. 220–221.

46 P. Caglayan Aksoy, 'Anglo-Sakson Ülkelerinde Gelişmeler' 28.8.2023, https://blog.arksigner.com/blokzinciri-teknolojisi/anglo-sakson-hukuku-ulkelerinde-gelismeler.

47 S. Simsek, 'Mülkiyet Hakkinin Kapsami, Sinirlandirma Nedenleri ve Şartlari Acisindan 1982 Anayasasi ve Avrupa İnsan Haklari Sözleşmesi: Karşilaştirmali Bir Analiz -I', *TBB Dergisi*, 2010, 91, p. 188.

6.3 *Possession on Cryptocurrencies*

In Turkish property law, possession is defined as 'effective control over a thing' (Art. 973 (1) of the TCC). On the other hand, according to paragraph 2, the effective exercise of the right also counts as possession in the case of easements and real burdens.

Possession, like ownership, depends on the existence of a thing, unless there is a legal exception. As stated above, only three-dimensional physical objects can be accepted as property. Since cryptocurrencies are not accepted as a thing/property, possession on cryptocurrencies is also not possible. Therefore, the use of force in self-defense against unlawful interference, restitution and trespassing lawsuits, and other remedies granted to possessors to protect their possession cannot be used for the protection of cryptocurrencies. Additionally, the protections afforded by possessory remedies in property law would be unlikely to offer effective protection in cases of interference with cryptocurrencies.

7 Legal Relationships between the Actors of the Cryptocurrency System

7.1 *Classification of Relationships between the Parties*

Crypto currency holders are participants in a blockchain on which cryptocurrencies are transferred and recorded, and do not have a central authority as a respondent. Participants are not a party to a contract. The relationship between the participants is also not considered to be a simple partnership. In Art. 620 of the Turkish Code of Obligations (TCO), a simple partnership is defined as a contractual relationship in which two or more persons agree to combine their efforts or resources to achieve a common goal. In simple partnership, each partner must contribute, which may be money, objects, claims or labor. The participants in a blockchain have no common goal and they don't make contributions.

Within the system it is possible to transfer the cryptocurrency peer-to-peer, but cryptocurrency holders also choose to use intermediaries to purchase or sell their cryptocurrencies. In the guideline of the MASAK, cryptocurrency service providers are defined as organizations that mediate crypto asset purchases and sales via electronic trading platforms.[48] The main income of these service providers are the commissions collected for each transaction. There are

48 MASAK, Kripto Varlık Hizmet Sağlayıcılar Rehberi, p.6, https://ms.hmb.gov.tr/uploads/sites/12/2021/05/Kripto-Varlik-Hizmet-Saglayicilar-Rehberi.pdf.

different types of cryptocurrency service providers. As some of the cryptocurrency service providers only sell cryptocurrencies, some of them sell and purchase cryptocurrencies and some of the platforms only act as an intermediary between the people who wants to sell and buy cryptocurrencies.[49] If the cryptocurrency service provider only sells cryptocurrencies, the contract between the cryptocurrency service provider and buyer is a sui generis contract to which articles of sales contract can be applied *per analogiam.*[50] In the Turkish Code of Obligations, a contract of sale requires the transfer of possession and property against payment of a price. Cryptocurrency transfers occur through the sharing of information indicating that a specific cryptocurrency will now be moved to the wallet of another cryptocurrency holder.[51] Here, it is a matter of making a change in the data recording system.[52] If the cryptocurrency service provider itself does not have cryptocurrencies, the sale and purchase of cryptocurrencies can also be considered a contract to which the rules of the commission contract are applied.[53] Pursuant to Art. 532 of the TCO, a buying or selling commission agent is a person who, for a commission, buys or sells movable property or securities in his own name but on behalf of another (the customer). Art. 546 of the TCO states that the provisions of the commission contract are also applicable to the purchase and sale broker who undertakes the works that are not considered as buying and selling brokerage, in return for a fee, on his own behalf and for the account of the person giving the proxy. Therefore, if cryptocurrency service provider buys or sells cryptocurrencies in his own name but for the account of the user, to the contract provisions of commission contract will be applied.

If the cryptocurrency service provider only acts as an intermediary between the sellers and buyers, there is a brokerage contract. Pursuant to Art. 520 of the TCO, a brokerage contract is a contract whereby the broker is instructed to alert the principal to an opportunity to conclude a contract or to facilitate the conclusion of a contract in exchange for a fee. The broker's fee is due upon conclusion of the contract.

If a customer opens an account in these cryptocurrency service providers, customer usually automatically will have a wallet that is usually managed by

49 F. Bilgili and F. Cengil, 'Bıtcoın Özelinde Kripto Paraların Ticaret Şirketlerine Sermaye Olarak Getirilmesi', *Ankara Hacı Bayram Veli Üniversitesi Hukuk Fakültesi Dergisi*, 2019, XXIII, 3, p. 6; There are also centralized and decentralized cryptocurrency platfroms Tomrukcu, p. 266.

50 Kapanci, p. 185; Cekin, p. 18.

51 Kapanci, p. 179.

52 Cekin, p. 4.

53 Gurses, pp. 106–107.

the respective service provider and in these cases the cryptocurrency service provider has the private key of the wallet. Since the platform holds the private key, these service providers have control over the wallet and the cryptocurrencies in the wallet. Only the person who has the wallet's private key can be considered the holder of the cryptocurrency. This relationship between the cryptocurrency service provider and customer is like opening a bank account, where the bank owns the money, but the account holder only has a contractual claim.[54] Some authors also argue that provisions of the bailment agreement could be applied to the wallet provider services by analogy.[55]

7.2 *Civil Liability of the Hackers and Cryptocurrency Service Providers*

In Turkish legal system, the loss (through hacking or fraud) of cryptocurrencies can amount to an actionable tort. Art. 49 of the TCO regulates general tort liability in Turkey. Pursuant to the paragraph 1 of this article, any person who unlawfully causes damage to another, whether willfully or negligently, is obliged to provide compensation. Only violation of an absolute right or any other asset protected with a special norm will fulfil the condition of unlawfulness. If there is no absolute right or special norm, paragraph 2 may be also a ground for tort liability. According to the second paragraph, a person who willfully causes damage to another in an immoral manner is likewise obliged to provide compensation.

Although there is no special norm protecting cryptocurrencies, Art. 157 of the TPC protects all the assets of a person as mentioned above. From the perspective of the tort law, this article qualifies as a special norm protecting cryptocurrencies.[56] Therefore, cryptocurrency fraud also leads to tortious liability for the fraudulent person.[57] For instance, if X transferred the Bitcoin to the tortfeasor after being misled by Y, Y would face both criminal and tort liability.

The same explanation applies to hacking as well, hacking a cryptocurrency service provider constitutes a violation of Art. 244 of TPC.[58] For example, X opened an account with MontC and registered 60 Bitcoins in his wallet and then MontC's IT systems were hacked. As a result, X lost all his/her Bitcoins. In this case, the hacked company MontC, may bring up a tort lawsuit against the hacker if he is identified. X can assert a contractual claim against MontC, since MontC is contractually obliged to prevent hacking. Unless MontC

54 Bilgili and Cengil, Sermaye Olarak Koyulması, p. 6; Gurses, p. 119.
55 Gurses, p. 107.
56 Kapanci, p. 176
57 Kapanci, p. 176.
58 Kapanci, p. 177.

proves that he was not negligent, MontC must pay X 60 Bitcoins. Author believes that X can bring a tort case against the hacker, because Art. 244 aims not only to protect the information system but also the account holders. Therefore, it can be qualified as a special norm protecting the claims of the customer too. Thus, MontC and hacker will be jointly liable for the losses of X.

Recent amendments stipulate that crypto asset service providers bear responsibility for damages resulting from their unlawful activities and their inability to meet cash payment and/or crypto asset delivery obligations. They are also liable for losses of crypto assets due to issues such as operational failures in their information systems, cyber-attacks, breaches in information security, or actions of their personnel, in accordance with Article 71 of Law No. 6098, which governs strict liability for residual risks of hazardous activities.[59]

Additionally, if it is found that the chairman, board members, other personnel, or any real person partners who legally or practically control the management of a crypto asset service provider have engaged in actions considered as embezzlement under article 110/A of the Capital Markets Law, they can be held personally liable to cover the amount embezzled, limited to the damages caused to customers. This personal liability can be enforced through a court ruling for their direct personal bankruptcy, upon the request of the Board. If these actions were carried out to benefit third parties, the same provisions apply to those who benefited, based on the advantages they gained (Art. 110 B (1) CML).

7.3 *Bona Fide Acquisitions of Cryptocurrencies*

There are no legal norms regarding bona fide buyers of cryptocurrencies or intangible assets. According to Art. 990 of the Turkish Civil Code, cash and bearer securities cannot be reclaimed from a recipient in good faith, even if the possessor was dispossessed of them against his or her will. An analogous application of this article to bona fide acquisitions of cryptocurrencies might not be possible because, under Turkish law, bona fide acquisitions are only protected when there is explicit regulation enabling it.

Therefore, if a hacker sells the hacked Bitcoins to a third party, Y, Y cannot be protected as a bona fide buyer. This would also be the case if the Bitcoin holder had transferred the Bitcoin to the tortfeasor after being misled, and Y

59 III. Liability for Dangerous Activities and Compensation ARTICLE 71- If damage arises from the activities of an enterprise that poses a significant danger, the owner of the enterprise and, if any, the operator shall be jointly and severally liable for this damage. TCO https://www.mevzuat.gov.tr/mevzuatmetin/1.5.6098.pdf.

had acquired the Bitcoins from the tortfeasor. Since the transfers of cryptocurrencies are not reversible and there is no central authority, it would be very difficult to compel these recipients to return the relevant Bitcoins in kind.

7.4 *Transfer Of Cryptocurrencies*

7.4.1 Inter Vivos Transfers

In Turkish private law, freedom of contract is the basic principle and under the umbrella of this basic principle, transfers of cryptocurrencies are also possible. According to Article 35/C (5) of the CML, crypto asset service providers must maintain records of customer crypto asset transfers and fund transfers in a secure, accessible, and traceable manner. They are responsible for maintaining the integrity, accuracy, and confidentiality of all transaction records.

The transfer of cryptocurrencies may be based on various types of contracts. For example, donations of cryptocurrencies re also permissible under Turkish law, which could be a reason for such transfers. According to Art. 285 of the TCO, a donation is any inter vivos disposition in which a person uses his assets to enrich another without receiving an equivalent consideration. Assets include everything that has a material value. Thus, since cryptocurrencies also have material value. They can also be subject of donation. Art. 288 of the TCO rules that the promise of a donation is only valid if it is in writing. However, if the promise of donation is fulfilled, even if written form is not observed in promise of donation, transfer is valid when the assets are handed over to the recipient.

Within this overview it is possible that X donates 30 Bitcoins to Y. Before the performance validity of the promise of donation of 30 Bitcoins depends on the fulfillment of the written from. However, upon the successful transfer of 30 Bitcoins, non-observance of the written form is no matter an issue. In this example X is supposed to have capacity to act, and Y's legal representative should not forbid him from obtaining 30 Bitcoins if Y has capacity to consent but no legal capacity to act.

In Turkish law, investment in cryptocurrencies is not restricted. Therefore, if X has 60 Bitcoins registered in his/ her wallet. He may sell for example 5 Bitcoins against Turkish Lira. This is an innominate contract and X is free to find the buyer B. In this case, first X and B will agree on the number of the Bitcoins and Turkish Lira to be paid in exchange and then they can fulfill their obligations. Usually, however, buyer and seller meet in a cryptocurrency exchange platform.

International cryptocurrency exchange markets operating in Turkey enable its users to buy cryptocurrency with certain other cryptocurrencies. For example, X can sell 5 Bitcoins against 10 Ethers. There are cross exchange rates for BTC/ETH and XRP/BTC.[60] With or without intermediaries, this transaction is classified as an innominate contract to which provisions of barter and sales contract can *per analogiam* apply.[61] If one of the parties is foreign and the parties have not explicitly designated any law, the relation arising from the contract will be governed by the most connected law to the contract (Art. 24 (4) of Turkish Private International and Procedural Law).[62] At this point, it is important to emphasize that the operation of foreign cryptocurrency exchange markets is limited by the recent amendments. Foreign cryptocurrency exchange markets should stop their activity in Turkey within three months starting from 2nd July 2024.

7.4.2 Transfer of Cryptocurrencies by Inheritance

Pursuant to Turkish Inheritance and Gift Tax Act article 1, passing of the goods belonging to persons who are citizens of the Republic of Turkey and goods in Turkey to other persons through succession or any other gratuitous way is subject to Inheritance and Gift Tax.[63] In article 2, goods are defined as immovables, movables, and any other assets. On 23 September 2020, upon the request of heirs, Edirne Tax Office issued an opinion on whether Bitcoins of the deceased are subject to inheritance and gift tax.[64] In this opinion, tax office stated that the heirs must pay inheritance and gift tax to receive the Bitcoins of the deceased, which are in account of a wallet provider. The tax office also clarified that before transferring cryptocurrencies to the heirs, the crypto service providers must either check whether the heir has paid inheritance and gift tax or deduct inheritance and gift tax from the customer's account.

60 Imamoglu, p. 69.

61 Kapanci, p. 185.

62 If the parties have not explicitly designated any law, the relation arising from the contract will be governed by the most connected law to the contract. This law is accepted to be the law of the habitual residence (at the moment of the conclusion of contract) of the debtor of the characteristic performance; the law of the workplace or (in absence of a workplace) the law of the residence of the abovementioned debtor in case the contract is concluded as a result of commercial and professional activities; in case that the debtor has multiple workplaces, the law of the workplace which is the most tightly related to the contract. Nevertheless, considering the state of all affairs if there is a law more tightly related to the contract, that particular law shall govern. Art. 24 (4) of the TPIL.

63 However, if a Turkish citizen has estate abroad but his heir or gratuitous successor is neither a citizen or resident of Turkey, then this person is exempt from inheritance and gift tax (Art. 1 p. 3).

64 Gelir Idaresi Baskanligi, https://www.gib.gov.tr/node/146488/pdf.

On 9 July 2020, the 6th Chamber of Antalya District Court of Appeal ruled that cryptocurrencies constitute a part of the estate.[65] Additionally, cryptocurrency platforms declare to their customers that the crypto assets are subject to inheritance law and cryptocurrencies pass to the heirs in the event of the customer's death.[66]

However, the issue of inheritance is much more complex because of the cryptographic nature of the crypto currencies. For example, X has 60 Bitcoins registered in his wallet and X has a child Y. If X is the only person who knows the private key, then to inherit the 60 Bitcoins, Y must have access to the private key. In this case, X could write his will and include the private key in the will. It would then be better if X submitted this will in a closed form to the notary for safekeeping. After the submission of closed wills, the notary informs the Civil Registry Office of the existence of the will and when X dies Civil Registry Office informs the notary and notary submits the will to the court of first instance and judge of that court opens and reads this will in a meeting of heirs. Unless other heirs with reserved portions bring an action for a reduction, X's testament will be executed accordingly.

According to the author, in case of cryptocurrencies which enabling smart contracts, it would be better for X to formulate a contract according to which relevant cryptocurrencies will be transferred to Y's account upon his death. In this case X must ensure Y knows about this smart contract.

If X dies without a valid will and without sharing the private key with anyone else, Y and other legal heirs will inherit 60 Bitcoins, but heirs won't not be able to access and control the Bitcoins unless they somehow learn the private key. If X had a wallet in crypto service provider, then provider would have the private key, then the heirs would pay the inheritance and gift tax and ask the crypto service provider to transfer them 60 Bitcoins.

According to Article 20 (1) of the Turkish International Private and Procedural Law No. 5718 (TPIL), the inheritance is governed by the national law of the deceased. Therefore, even if a Turkish heir holds cryptocurrencies through intermediaries operating in other countries, the inheritance will be governed by Turkish law. However, according to the second paragraph of the same article the provisions regarding the reasons for the opening of the inheritance, its

---

65 Antalya BAM 6. HD, 13.11.2020, E.2020/1149, K.2020/90 (https://www.batur.av.tr/dijital-miras-ve-kripto-paralar-konusunda-emsal-karar.html, 23.01.2022).

66 PARIBU, 26.10.2020, https://www.paribu.com/blog/en/paribu-guide/the-digital-assets-on-paribu-are-subject-to-the-law-of-inheritance-attorney-mehmet-turkarslan/?__cf_chl_jschl_tk__=AZL79HExbo83X5Kfvpgc94lVH.Rs14yVjRLjLAme2L8-1643285621-0-gaNycGzNCLo.

acquisition and partition are subject to the law of the country where the estate is located.

7.5 *Pledge of the Cryptocurrencies*

In cryptocurrency exchange platforms or custody service providers, customers typically have what are known as 'wallets'. In this scenario, cryptocurrency exchange platforms and custody service providers act as holders of the cryptocurrencies, as they are the only ones holding the private keys. Therefore, the customer has only a claim against the cryptocurrency service provider, and the provider is obligated to supply the customer with the same amount of cryptocurrencies. In Turkish property law, transferable claims and other rights can be pledged (Art. 954 of the TCC). Contracts of cryptocurrency exchange platforms usually state that account (wallet) cannot be transferred to others. However, transfer of the account differs from the transfer of the claim arising from the account ownership. Therefore, account owner's claim can be pledged by fulfilling the requirements for pledging claims. Unless otherwise specified, pledging of claims and other rights is regulated by the provisions governing the pledging of moveable properties. To pledge a claim not evidenced in writing or for which only a borrower's note exists, the pledge agreement must be executed in writing and, where applicable, the borrower's note transferred. The pledgee and the pledger may inform the debtor of the pledge (Art. 954/ 955 of the TCC). Additionally, claims can be pledged under the Law on Pledges over Movable Property in Commercial Transactions as explained below.

In Turkey, there is also a special Law on Pledges over Movable Property in Commercial Transactions. Article 5 paragraph 1 of this Law defines movable property very widely including assignable claims and other similar rights. This Law only applies to pledges between credit institutions and merchants, artisans, farmers, producers' organizations, real and legal persons who are self-employed, between merchants and/or tradesmen. For the pledge to be effective, the pledge agreement must be in writing or signed with secure electronic signature and entered in the Register of Pledged Movables. Even though it might be disputed[67] if cryptocurrencies qualify as 'other rights', in the draft recent cryptocurrency amendments explicitly stat that cryptocurrencies cannot be pledged according to this law.[68]

On the other hand, if the cryptocurrency holder continues to have the private key, pledge does not offer much security to the pledgee, because without the consent of the private key holder cryptocurrency cannot be exchanged

67 In favor of the inclusion Tevetoglu, p. 121.

68 Draft Art.35/B (21).

with fiat money. Therefore, there will be problems with enforcement. On the other hand, it is also stated that smart contracts can be used for bypassing this problem, and pledge of cryptocrrencies can be widely utilized.[69]

7.6 *Lending of Cryptocurrencies*

Pursuant to Art. 241 of the TPC, the person who lends money to someone else to gain profit commits usury and is sentenced to imprisonment from two to six years and a judicial fine from five hundred days to five thousand days. However, since cryptocurrencies are not classified as money, lending of cryptocurrencies to gain profit does not meet the legal definition of this crime. In Turkish penal law, broad interpretation of the rules is strictly forbidden.

In Turkey, companies and real persons authorized to provide money lending services are limited by law (Banking Law, Decree on Money Lending Transactions, etc), and crypto currency service providers are not included among those companies or natural persons. However, crypto currencies are not considered money, but rather accepted as intangible and fungible assets.

Although authorized money lending institutions don't lend loans as cryptocurrencies, lending and borrowing of cryptocurrencies are practiced in Turkey. Some crypto currency service providers lend and borrow cryptocurrency.[70] This practice constitutes a fixed-term loan contract. A fixed-term loan contract is an agreement whereby the lender undertakes to transfer the ownership of a sum of money or of other fungible goods to the borrower, who in return undertakes to return objects of the same quantity and quality to him (Art. 386 I). Although cryptocurrency is not money, it is a fungible asset. Unless parties agree otherwise, borrower must return fungible objects of the same quantity and quality. For example, if the subject of the fixed-term loan is Bitcoins, the lender must not accept repayment in Bitcoin Cash. Even though Bitcoin Cash is a Bitcoin equivalents resulting from a fork in the initial Bitcoin blockchain, Bitcoin Cash and Bitcoin are not the same fungible asset with the same quantity and quality. All in all, it is a different cryptocurrency with a different value and technical qualities. It doesn't matter that the fork took place before or after the initial transfer of cryptocurrencies.

It is also possible for Turkish companies or citizens to lend a crypto loan from an authorized foreign crypto lending institution. Normally, in this case, the parties agree on the applicable law. If the parties have not expressly specified a

69 Tevetoglu, p. 121.

70 Investing, 24.02.2009, https://tr.investing.com/news/cryptocurrency-news/binance-deposit-kriptolarnz-faizle-dunc-verin-lending-558027.

right, the contractual relationship is governed by the law most closely related to the contract, which is mostly lender's law (Art. 24 IV of the TPIL).

8 Other Private Law Issues

8.1 *Cryptocurrencies as Capital*

In Turkish commercial law, legal doctrine is in opinion that cryptocurrencies can be brought into commercial companies as capital.[71] Article 127 of the Turkish Commercial Code states that money, receivables (paragraph 1a) and transferable and financially valuable assets (paragraph 1j) can be brought into the companies as capital, unless otherwise provided by law. There is a limitation of this general rule in Article 342 of the Turkish Commercial Code, which relates to cryptocurrencies. According to the paragraph 1, there shall be no limited right in rem, attachment, and measure on the transferable and financially valuable assets, that are brought to the company as capital.

To be a capital in a commercial company, the value of the cryptocurrencies should be determined. In collective partnerships and commendams, the value of the cryptocurrencies can be ascertained by the founders/partners (Art. 213 1e, 305, 307). In limited and joint stock corporations an expert appointed by the court of first instance will be in charge of this determination (Art. 343 – 578).

8.2 *Trust and Segregation of Customer Assets*

Trust is foreign legal institution under Turkish Law. In Turkish property law, division of ownership as legal and equitable title is not an option.[72] On the other hand, investor funds cannot be segregated from the assets of investment management companies unless there is a specific law.[73] However, new amendments in CML stipulate that customers' crypto assets and cash will be segregated from the assets of the respective crypto assets service provider. This ensures that customer assets are not subject to any attachment, pledge or interim measure, or included in the crypto currency service provider's insolvency estate and vice versa.

71 Bilgili and Cengil, Sermaye Olarak Getirilmesi, pp. 8–9.

72 G. Kurtulan Guner, *Trust ve Türk Hukuku Açısından Değerlendirilmesi*, Onikilevha, Istanbul 2020, p. 357.

73 Kurtulan Guner, p. 358.

8.3 *Advertisement Of Cryptocurrencies*

Until recently, there were no specific restrictions regarding cryptocurrency advertising. In 2020, one of the local crypto service providers became the main sponsor of the Turkish Football Federation, men's, and women's national football teams and many football teams in the Super League. Thodex, the bankrupt local cryptocurrency exchange platform, used to have a lot of advertisements featuring famous models. Social media is often used in cryptocurrency advertising. Some social media platforms and tech giants like Facebook and Google have their own cryptocurrency advertising policies.[74] In the new amendments concerning cryptocurrencies, it is stated that cryptocurrency trading platforms shall comply with the principles determined by the Capital Markets Board regarding their publications, announcements, advertisements, and notices (Art. 35 C 9 CML)) The details of these regulations are not yet clear.

9 Enforcement and Bankruptcy Law Issues

9.1 *Enforcement of a Cryptocurrency Obligation*

If a party obliges himself to give a sum of certain cryptocurrency contractually, is the other party able to initiate an enforcement proceeding to obtain the agreed sum of the relevant cryptocurrency? More specifically what will happen if X owns 10 Bitcoins to Y, but doesn't transfer the relevant amount? Is it possible to enforce this transfer?

In Turkish law of enforcement, there are two main ways to enforce a claim: an enforcement proceeding without a judgment and an enforcement proceeding initiated by a creditor holding a judgment against the debtor.

9.1.1 An Enforcement Proceeding without a Judgment

It is possible to enforce a monetary and collateral claim without obtaining a judgement first. Although cryptocurrencies are not local or foreign currency, prevailing opinion thinks that the creditor may initiate the general attachment procedure to enforce a cryptocurrency claim without a judgement,[75] because Turkish doctrine and jurisdiction holds that gold also can be subject of general attachment procedure.[76] This acceptance should also be valid for

74 Facebook, 31.01.2022, https://www.facebook.com/business/help/438252513416690?id=595195347635322; Google, 31.01.2022, https://support.google.com/adspolicy/answer/2464998?hl=tr.

75 Bilgili and Cengil, p. 102.

76 Y. 12.HD, 12.3.2014, E. 2014/4346, K.2014/7087 (www.hukukturk.com, 18.01.2022).

cryptocurrencies, because cryptocurrencies can be converted to Turkish Lira as easily as gold. This means that the creditor can demand the Bitcoin equivalent in Turkish Lira at the time the enforcement proceedings are initiated (Art.58 (1–3) of the Turkish Enforcement and Bankruptcy Law).[77]

9.1.2 An Enforcement Proceeding Initiated by a Creditor Holding a Judgment against the Debtor

To use this enforcement option, the creditor should first obtain a judgment on the specific performance of the cryptocurrency obligation. If a specific performance is not impossible, according to Turkish law, the creditor can demand a specific performance of the obligation in question.

In Turkish enforcement law, enforcement of the judgements is regulated in two sections: enforcement of the judgements regarding monetary and collateral claims and enforcement of the judgements other than the monetary and collateral claims.

Since cryptocurrencies are not defined as property, money or a mean of security, the obligation to transfer certain number of cryptocurrencies should be subject to the latter, which are regulated in Articles 24–31a of the Turkish Enforcement and Bankruptcy Law (TEBL). Article 30 on enforcements of judgments regarding the performance or non-performance of an ac will be applied. According to the first paragraph of this article, the enforcement authority will order the debtor to transfer the appropriate number of cryptocurrencies at the time determined by the court. This order will also contain a warning that the debtor may be imprisoned for three months (Art. 343 of the TEBL) if he fails to comply with this order. In this case, if the debtor does not transfer the cryptocurrencies, the creditor can wait until an attachment is made on the debtor's property and the corresponding amount is received after the sale of the attached property. The creditor can also request that the court (Art. 113 of the TCO) or the Enforcement Office (Art. 30 II of the TEBL) grant him the right to receive the same amount of cryptocurrency from someone else and charge the debtor for these costs.

9.2 *Attachment of the Cryptocurrencies for the Monetary Debt*

Until very recently, there was no specific regulation on the attachment of cryptocurrencies in Turkish law. After recent amendments, now, Art. 99 par.7 of Capital Market Law regulates measures, attachment, and all kinds of administrative and judicial requests related to clients' cash and crypto assets are

77 Bilgili and Cengil, p. 101; Yardimci, p. 107; dissenting Balikci, p. 298.

exclusively carried out by crypto asset service providers. Within the framework of this law, it will be possible to query cash and crypto assets through information systems and to attach them electronically. Additionally, under Turkish Enforcement and Bankruptcy Law, any asset that has a financial value can be attached unless otherwise stated, and cryptocurrencies are not among the exceptions. Therefore, cryptocurrencies can be attached.[78] However, the decentralized structure of cryptocurrencies should be considered when attaching them.

The debtor must make a declaration of assets sufficient to cover the creditor's claim (Art.74–75 of the TEBL). If the debtor does not properly declare his assets, for example if he does not declare that he has cryptocurrencies, he might face imprisonment punishment according to the Art. 338 of the TEBL.

However, the decentralized structure of cryptocurrencies should be considered when attaching them. If there is a private wallet and the private key is unknown to others, attachment procedures cannot be used against the will of the wallet owner.[79] However, if cryptocurrency is stored in the wallet of the cryptocurrency custody service provider, the customer's account will be suspended upon the enforcement office's attachment order.[80]

In April 2021, Istanbul Enforcement Court decided that debtor's crypto currencies can be subject to attachment. In this case, the court ruled: 'Although the plaintiff filed a complaint alleging that cryptocurrencies can't be attached, it was decided to dismiss the complaint as it was understood that cryptocurrencies should be considered within the scope of commodities and securities, it was considered as a kind of digital currency or virtual currency, and therefore could be attached'.[81] Even though the court did not clearly explain the nature of cryptocurrencies, it did clarify that cryptocurrencies can be attached. In this lawsuit, the debtor had Bitcoins his account/wallet in a cryptocurrency exchange platform and following the attachment order of the enforcement office, the platform blocked the debtor's access to his account/wallet.

9.3 *Bankruptcy of the Crypto Service Providers or Customers*

The bankruptcy of the crypto service providers poses the biggest problem for the customers of these services. For example, X opens an account with MontC,

78 M. Tevetoglu, *Hukuki Yönleriyle Kripto Varlıklar ve Kripto Varlıkların İlk Arzı*, Aristo, 2021, p. 117.

79 Imamoglu, p. 155; İ.M, Ozsoy, *Kripto Para Haczi*, Seckin, Istanbul 2021. p. 82. Bilgili and Cengil, p. 103.

80 Imamoglu, p. 156.

81 Erdem and Duranoglu, N. 6.

a local crypto service provider, and registers 60 Bitcoins in his/her account. If MontC becomes insolvent, X can only make a personal claim in the insolvency proceedings in relation to his 60 Bitcoin. Therefore, X must form the insolvency estate of MontC with all other creditors to obtain his claim. X can only demand 60 Bitcoin's value in cash (Art. 198 (1) of the TEBL). However, bankruptcy administration can opt for specific performance of 60 Bitcoins (Art. 198 (2) of the TEBL. The specific terms of the agreement between X and MontC make no difference unless X's claim is secured with a right in rem.

Art. 35 C 7 of Capital Markets Law protects customers in the event of the crypto service provider's insolvency. According to this article, cash and crypto assets belonging to customers are separate from the assets of crypto asset service providers, and records are kept in accordance with this provision. Under no circumstances can customers' cash and crypto assets held by crypto asset service providers be seized, pledged, included in the bankruptcy estate, or subjected to precautionary measures due to the debts of the crypto asset service providers, even for public receivables. It is also important to emphasize that according to the new law, wallet providers and exchange platforms must be separate legal entities. Customers' crypto assets must be kept in their own wallets, as a principle. Additionally, customers' crypto assets and cash will be segregated from the wallet provider's assets. Any asset of the customer will not be subject to any attachment, pledge or interim measure for the insolvency of the wallet provider. Likewise, the assets of the crypto asset service providers cannot be seized, pledged, included in the bankruptcy estate, or subjected to precautionary measures due to the debts of the customers. (Art. 35 C (7) CML)

For example, Z as a company opens an account with MontC as it accepts payments in Bitcoin and other cryptocurrencies. Z's wallet is worth $200,000 in various cryptocurrencies. Z becomes insolvent. As explained above, in this case Z only has a contractual claim against MontC. Z's account with MontC is treated like a bank account during the attachment procedure. Only the creditors whose claims are secured with rights in rem have priority over the cryptocurrencies registered in Z's account (Art. 206 of the TEBL).

10 Taxation of Cryptocurrency Investors and Cryptocurrency Service Providers

To date of the submission, there is no specific legislation in Turkey on the taxation of cryptocurrencies or related services. However, it is highly expected that lawmaker will soon introduce specific tax regulations. On the other hand, it is also envisaged that a possible high tax rate will result in investors remaining unregistered and anonymous.[82]

So far, it has been undisputed that the income of the cryptocurrency exchange platforms and wallet providers is commercial income within the meaning of Article 37 of the Income Tax Act.[83] These cryptocurrency service providers must pay corporate/ income taxes.[84] Value Added Tax (VAT) issues have so far been very unclear. However, since cryptocurrency exchange platforms issue an invoice, customers must pay VAT when buying and selling cryptocurrencies.[85]

There are ongoing discussions regarding VAT. There is a tendency to exempt the purchase and sale of cryptocurrencies from VAT, citing the ECJ ruling.[86] However, it is also argued that there can be no exemption where the buying and selling of cryptocurrencies constitutes commercial income.[87]

The ambiguity surrounding the nature of cryptocurrencies also makes it very difficult to determine the subject of earnings on which earnings are taxed. This creates more confusion when it comes to the value derived from cryptocurrencies. A distinction must be made between continuous activities and incidental gains of the people. If a person does not continuously buy and sell cryptocurrency, their earnings from the sale of cryptocurrency constitute an incidental income.[88] For 2022, TRY 58,000 of incidental gains are tax-exempt. However, if the incidental gain exceeds this threshold, the excess profit is subject to income tax. Furthermore, if the person does not sell cryptocurrency, only the increase in value of the cryptocurrency does not constitute income

---

82 M. Yuce, 'Kripto Paraya Vergi Gelecek mi?', *Kriter Dergi*, 2021, 6, 60, N.7, https://kriterdergi.com/ekonomi/kripto-paraya-vergi-gelecek-mi#:~:text=Kripto%20paran%C4%B1n%20para%20birimi%20olarak,kurum%20kazanc%C4%B1%20kapsam%C4%B1nda%20vergilendirilmesi%20gerekmektedir.

83 A. Mert, 'Deniz Kabuğundan Kripto Paraya:Bitcoin'in Vergisel Boyutu', A. Aşçı Akıncı and S. Ovalıoglu (eds), *VIII Genç Vergi Hukukçuları Sempozyumu*, Onikievha, Istanbul 2018, p. 339; L. Ates, 'Bitcoin: Sanal Para ve Vergileme', *Vergi Sorunları Dergisi*, 2018, 37, 308, p. 137; O .G, Yalcin, Taxation of cryptocurrencies and initial coin offerings, 2021, Unpublished Master Thesis, https://tez.yok.gov.tr/UlusalTezMerkezi/tezSorguSonucYeni.jsp#top2, p. 86.

84 Yalcin, p. 87 ; Ates, p. 137; Gurses, p. 129.

85 Imamoglu, p. 152; BTCturk, 31.1.2022, https://www.btcturk.com/yasal-bilgiler/kullanici-bilgilendirme.

86 Mert p. 343; Yuce, N.12.

87 H.F. Gunay and V. Kargi, 'Kripto Paranın Vergilendirilmesi Fikrinin Mali Yönden Değerlendirilmesi', *Journal of Life Economics*, 2018,5, 3, *pp. 71–72; Yuce*, N. 12.

88 Yuce, N.12, Mert, p. 339.

and the person does not have to pay any taxes.[89] If the buying and selling of the cryptocurrencies is carried out continuously to profit from the rising exchange rate of the cryptocurrency, the profit constitutes a commercial gain.[90]

Taxation of the mining is less disputed. If a person is involved in mining as a self-employed[91] and continuous entrepreneur, his income will be taxed as self-employment earnings according to the Art. 65 and following of the Income Tax Law. If mining is not a continuous occupation, then mining constitutes incidental gain.[92] If mining is done as a corporate activity, then income is commercial income pursuant to Art. 37 of Income Tax Law.[93] Then mining company must pay corporate/ income tax.[94]

11 Public Policy Exception in Enforcement and Recognition of Foreign Court Decisions and Arbitral Awards

There is no automatic enforcement and execution of foreign decisions or arbitral awards rendered in foreign jurisdiction. To achieve enforcement and execution, the applicant must go through an enforcement procedure in the form of a court action as described in Art. 50–63 of the TPIL.[95] Turkey is also a party to United Nations Convention on the Recognition and Enforcement of Foreign Arbitral Awards dated June 10, 1958 (New York Convention). Rules of New York Convention and Law No. 5718 on enforcement of foreign arbitral awards are very similar to each other, especially the grounds for refusal of enforcement of arbitral awards.[96] So, through the procedures stated in the convention or law, it should be also possible to enforce and execute a foreign decision and arbitral award over a crypto litigation in Turkey. However, would the public policy exception play a role here? Because, as explained above, payments with cryptocurrencies are banned in Turkey.

89 Ates, p. 137.
90 Gunay and Kargi, p. 71; Yuce, N. 13.
91 Self-employed is a person who provides a service or involved in an income generating occupation based on his expertise and personal skills.
92 Mert, p. 337.
93 Yalcın, p. 87; Yuce, N.12.; Gurses and et al, p. 127.
94 Yalcın, p. 87; Ates, p. 137.
95 English translation of the code available at http://jafbase.fr/docAsie/Turquie/Private%20international%20law%20Turkey.pdf.
96 A.B. Erkan, 'Turkish Courts' Approach to Public Policy as a Ground for Refusal of Enforcement of Foreign Arbitral Awards', 24.6.2016, https://turkishlawblog.com/read/article/132/turkish-courts-approach-to-public-policy-as-a-ground-for-refusal-of-enforcement-of-foreign-arbitral-awards.

Turkish legal doctrine thinks public policy exception should be used rarely.[97] Even incompatibility with the constitution because of recognition of the unfounded court decisions wasn't enough to consult to public policy exception.[98] Therefore, the author believes that the ban introduced by a regulation protecting the value of the Turkish lira is not sufficient to invoke the exception of public policy.

12 Conclusion

Turkish investors play an important role in the cryptocurrency market. However, until recently there was no supervision for cryptocurrency service providers. The collapse of two local cryptocurrency exchange platforms proved that regulatory legislation and supervision is very much needed in this field. The new 'Crypto Asset Code' provides several well-thought-out solutions for the security of the system. Although Turkish lawmakers have banned cryptocurrency payments, a total ban is undesirable. It is obvious that lawmakers do not want the cryptocurrencies to compete with the Turkish lira. It is therefore highly unlikely that the payment ban will be lifted soon.

---

97 A. Dolunay, 'Yabanci Mahkeme Kararlarinin Taninmasi Ve Tenfizinde Kamu Düzeni', *Prof. Dr. Yıldırım Uler'e Armağan*, Yakın Doğu Üniversitesi Yayınları, Lefkosa 2014, p. 49.

98 Y. İBK, 10.2.2012, E. 2010/1, K. 2012/1 (www.hukukturk.com , 31.12.2022).

United Kingdom (UK) (England and Wales)

Amy Held, Alisdair MacPherson and Burcu Yüksel Ripley

1 Definition and Legal Qualification[1]

1.1 *Legal Treatment*

Cryptocurrencies are not legal tender in the UK. Legal tender has a narrow technical meaning, and the classification of what constitutes legal tender varies across the three jurisdictions of the UK (i.e., England and Wales, Scotland, and Northern Ireland).[2] In England and Wales, Royal Mint coins and Bank of England banknotes constitute legal tender. One reason why cryptocurrencies are not considered as money or currency is because "they are too volatile to be a good store of value, they are not widely-accepted as means of exchange, and they are not used as a unit of account."[3]

1.2 *Legal Definition*

There is no general legal definition of 'cryptocurrency' either in regulatory or private laws in the UK. The term tends to be avoided in these contexts, probably for policy reasons to avoid any confusion with fiat currencies. Cryptocurrencies are usually referred to as 'exchange tokens', as one type of cryptoasset, along with security and utility tokens, under the broader umbrella term 'cryptoassets'.

The term 'cryptoasset', on the other hand, has been defined for certain legal purposes. For example, the Financial Services and Markets Act (FSMA) 2023 introduces a definition of cryptoassets into the FSMA 2000 as: "any cryptographically secured digital representation of value or contractual rights that (a) can be transferred, stored or traded electronically, and (b) that uses technology supporting the recording or storage of data (which may include distributed ledger technology)."[4] A similar definition, albeit referring to distributed ledger technology (DLT) as the underlying technology, is found in the Money

1 The law is stated generally as at 30.09.2023.
2 Bank of England, 'What is legal tender?' https://www.bankofengland.co.uk/knowledgebank/what-is-legal-tender.
3 Cryptoassets Taskforce, *Final Report* (2018) https://assets.publishing.service.gov.uk/government/uploads/system/uploads/attachment_data/file/752070/cryptoassets_taskforce_final_report_final_web.pdf, para 2.13.
4 See section 69 of the FSMA 2023 which also states that this definition may be amended by the Treasury by regulations.

 | DOI:10.1163/9789004722507_029

Laundering and Terrorist Financing and Transfer of Funds (Information on the Payer) Regulations 2017 (SI 2017/692).[5]

In its Legal Statement on Cryptoassets and Smart Contracts, the UK Jurisdiction Taskforce pointed out that formulating a precise definition in this area is difficult and unlikely to be useful given the great diversity of systems and assets in existence and rapid technological development.[6]

1.3 *Other Definitions*

The Cryptoasset Taskforce Final Report considers 'exchange tokens' as a type of cryptoasset that "do not provide the types of rights or access provided by security or utility tokens, but are used as a means of exchange or for investment."[7] HM Treasury views them as a type of cryptoasset too,[8] based on the Financial Conduct Authority (FCA)'s Guidance on Cryptoassets.[9]

These definitions and taxonomy are also adopted by the Cryptoassets Manual of HM Revenue & Customs (HMRC), with the addition of stablecoins as another type of cryptoasset which are tokens that "minimise volatility as they may be pegged to something that is considered to have a stable value such as a fiat currency (government-backed, for example US dollars) or precious metals such as gold."[10]

---

5 See Regulation 14A(3)(a) inserted by Regulation 4(7) of the Money Laundering and Terrorist Financing (Amendment) Regulations 2019 (SI 2019/1511) and further Part 2.4 below.

6 UK Jurisdiction Taskforce, *Legal statement on cryptoassets and smart contracts* (2019) https://35z8e83m1ih83drye28009d1-wpengine.netdna-ssl.com/wp-content/uploads/2019/11/6.6056_JO_Cryptocurrencies_Statement_FINAL_WEB_111119-1.pdf, para 26.

7 Cryptoassets Taskforce, *Final Report* (2018) https://assets.publishing.service.gov.uk/government/uploads/system/uploads/attachment_data/file/752070/cryptoassets_taskforce_final_report_final_web.pdf, pp. 11–14 and p. 17, para 2.11.

8 e.g. HM Treasury, *UK regulatory approach to cryptoassets and stablecoins: Consultation and call for evidence* (2021) https://assets.publishing.service.gov.uk/government/uploads/system/uploads/attachment_data/file/950206/HM_Treasury_Cryptoasset_and_Stablecoin_consultation.pdf, para 1.12.

9 FCA, *Guidance on Cryptoassets*, Consultation Paper CP 19/3 (2019) https://www.fca.org.uk/publication/consultation/cp19-03.pdf, paras 2.4 and 2.5, and FCA, *Feedback and Final Guidance to CP 19/3*, Policy Statement PS19/22 (2019) https://www.fca.org.uk/publication/policy/ps19-22.pdf, para 2.2.

10 HMRC, *Cryptoassets Manual* (2021), CRYPTO10100 - Introduction to cryptoassets: what are cryptoassets https://www.gov.uk/hmrc-internal-manuals/cryptoassets-manual/crypto10100.

2 Regulatory Framework

2.1 *Regulatory Status*

There is presently no specific regulatory regime that applies to cryptoassets and related activities. The prevailing general approach is to consider whether any given cryptoasset or related activity falls within the scope of existing regulatory regimes. The most relevant of these are those implemented in the context of financial services, markets, and instruments.

Cryptoassets and related activities may be 'regulated' either: (i) if they come within scope of; or (ii) pursuant to an express provision in, an existing regulatory regime. The financial regulatory authorities have thus far generally focussed on the first approach. Derivatives, exchanges, custody, and promotions are the main areas where the second approach has been taken.

Any cryptoasset or related activity that does not fall within the existing regimes thus is 'unregulated'. Many cryptocurrencies will be so classified.

2.1.1 Financial Conduct Authority (FCA)

Of the two key regulatory authorities for the UK's financial services sector, the FCA has been the more active in respect of cryptoassets and related activities. Broadly, it adopts the 'same risk, same regulatory outcomes' approach, which emphasises substantive similarity to products and activities already within the regulatory perimeter, irrespective of designation by market participants.

In its Policy Statement of July 2019,[11] the FCA identified four main points at which cryptoassets and related activities are likely to fall within the regulatory perimeter:

- 'Specified Investments' under the Financial Services and Markets Act 2000 and the associated 'Regulated Activities' Order 2001[12]
- 'Financial Instruments' under the MiFID regime[13]

---

11 FCA, 'Feedback and Final Guidance to Consultation Paper CP 19/3', Policy Statement PS19/22, 07.2019 https://www.fca.org.uk/publication/policy/ps19-22.pdf.

12 FSMA 2000 and FSMA (Regulated Activities) Order 2001 (SI 2001/544).

13 FSMA 2000 (Markets in Financial Instruments) Regulations 2017 (SI 2017/701), implementing Directive 2014/65/EU of the European Parliament and of the Council of 15 May 2014 on markets in financial instruments and amending Directive 2002/92/EC and Directive 2011/61/EU.

– 'E-Money' under the Electronic Money Regulations 2011[14]
– Activities falling within the scope of the Payment Services Regulations 2017.[15]
In June 2023, the FCA published a Policy Statement[16] setting out the anticipated rules on financial promotion for cryptoassets[17] that will come into force on 8 October 2023. Broadly, a 'qualifying cryptoasset' is defined as any cryptographically secured digital representation of value or contractual rights that is transferable and fungible, but does not include cryptoassets which meet the definition of electronic money or an existing controlled investment.[18] The Statement sets out four rules for legally promoting cryptoassets to consumers.

2.1.2 The Prudential Regulation Authority (PRA)

There are currently no prohibitions on financial institutions regulated by the PRA from gaining exposure to or holding cryptoassets. To date, the PRA has gone no further than to issue 'Dear CEO' letters in 2018[19] and 2022[20] in respect of existing or planned exposures to cryptoassets. The letters remind firms of their obligations under the PRA rules[21] and highlight aspects of the existing framework that the PRA would expect firms to consider when measuring and mitigating risks resulting from crypto activities.

---

14 SI 2011/99, implementing Directive 2009/110/EC of the European Parliament and of the Council of 16 September 2009 on the taking up, pursuit and prudential supervision of the business of electronic money institutions amending Directives 2005/60/EC and 2006/48/EC and repealing Directive 2000/46/EC.

15 SI 2017/752, implementing Directive (EU) 2015/2366 of the European Parliament and of the Council of 25 November 2015 on payment services in the internal market, amending Directives 2002/65/EC, 2009/110/EC and 2013/36/EU and Regulation (EU) No 1093/2010, and repealing Directive 2007/64/EC.

16 FCA, 'Policy Statement PS23/6: Financial Promotion Rules for Cryptoassets' 06.2023 https://www.fca.org.uk/publication/policy/ps23-6.pdf.

17 Made under the FSMA 2000 (Financial Promotion) (Amendment) Order 2023 (SI 2023/612) ('FPO 2023').

18 Schedule 1 para 26F, FPO 2023.

19 'Dear CEO' Letter from Sam Woods, 28.06.2018 https://www.bankofengland.co.uk/-/media/boe/files/prudential-regulation/letter/2018/existing-or-planned-exposure-to-crypto-assets.pdf.

20 'Dear CEO' Letter from Sam Woods, 24.03.2022 https://www.bankofengland.co.uk/-/media/boe/files/prudential-regulation/letter/2022/march/existing-or-planned-exposure-to-cryptoassets.pdf.

21 PRA Fundamental Rules 3, 5, and 7.

2.2 *Derivatives*

The FCA Conduct of Business Sourcebook (COBS) contains certain prohibitions against the selling, distribution or marketing of cryptoasset derivatives and of cryptoasset exchange traded notes to retail clients.[22] By the relevant definitions of 'cryptoasset derivatives' and 'cryptoasset exchange traded notes',[23] it is clear the FCA does not necessarily consider that the underlying cryptoasset will in all cases be regulated.

The FCA is further of the view[24] that although cryptocurrencies *per se* are not regulated, cryptocurrency derivatives are capable of being financial instruments under MIFID II. The FCA has further identified in particular cryptocurrency futures; cryptocurrency contracts for differences; and cryptocurrency options as likely requiring authorisation.

2.3 *Criminal Law*

There are no criminal offences specific to cryptocurrencies and related activities. However, in *R v West*,[25] cryptocurrencies were treated and confiscated[26] as 'criminal property' and 'proceeds of criminal conduct' within the scope of s 372(1) of the Proceeds of Crime Act 2002.

2.4 *AML/CTF*

The Money Laundering and Terrorist Financing (Amendment) Regulations 2019 implement the fifth iteration of the European Union (EU)'s Anti-Money Laundering Directive[27] and amend several of the UK's anti-money laundering and counter terrorist-financing legislation. Broadly, the amendments define[28]

---

22 COBS 22.6.5R. See https://www.handbook.fca.org.uk/handbook/COBS/22/6.html. See also FCA, 'Prohibiting the sale to retail clients of investment products that reference cryptoassets', Policy Statement PS20/10, 10.2020 https://www.fca.org.uk/publication/policy/ps20-10.pdf.

23 See the parallel Definitions.

24 FCA, 'Cryptocurrency Derivatives: FCA statement on the requirement for firms offering cryptocurrency derivatives to be authorised', 06.04.2018 https://www.fca.org.uk/news/statements/cryptocurrency-derivatives.

25 *R v West*, Southwark Crown Court (14 December 2017, Unreported).

26 M. Busby, 'Bitcoin worth £900,000 seized from hacker to compensate victims' *The Guardian*, 23.08.2019 https://www.theguardian.com/technology/2019/aug/23/bitcoin-seized-hacker-grant-west-uk-compensate-victims.

27 SI 2019/1511; implementing Directive (EU) 2015/849 on the prevention of the use of the financial system for the purposes of money laundering or terrorist financing, and amending Directives 2009/138/EC and 2013/36/EU.

28 Regulations 4(7), 14(12) and (13), 15(12) and (13) of the Money Laundering and Terrorist Financing (Amendment) Regulations 2019 (SI 2019/1511).

and bring 'cryptoasset exchange providers' and 'custodian wallet providers' within the scope of the UK's existing AML/CTF Regulations.[29] In addition, new provisions for cryptoasset transfers and for changes in control of registered cryptoasset businesses came into force on 1 September 2023 pursuant to the Money Laundering and Terrorist Financing (Amendment) (No. 2) Regulations 2022 (SI 2022/860).[30]

3 Supervision

3.1 *Licences and Authorisation*

Businesses carrying on cryptoasset activities (including in relation to cryptocurrencies) are required to register with the FCA.[31] To successfully register with the FCA, information regarding the business and associated individuals needs to be provided. The FCA must refuse registration if the applicant or any 'officer, manager, or beneficial owner' of the applicant is not a 'fit and proper person' to carry on the business of a cryptoasset exchange provider or custodian wallet provider.[32]

In addition, there are restrictions on the financial promotion of investment activities including in relation to cryptoassets. Such assets can only be promoted to consumers in the UK if: (i) the promotion is communicated by an authorised person: (ii) the promotion is made by an unauthorised person but approved by an authorised person; (iii) the promotion is communicated by or on behalf of a cryptoasset business registered with the FCA; or (iv) the promotion is communicated in accordance with another exemption.[33]

29 Regulations 2-13 Money Laundering, Terrorist Financing and Transfer of Funds (Information on the Payer) Regulations 2017; Regulation 14 Terrorism Act 2000; and Regulation 15 Proceeds of Crime Act 2002.

30 See Money Laundering, Terrorist Financing and Transfer of Funds (Information on the Payer) Regulations 2017 (SI 2017/692), Part 7A.

31 To comply with the Money Laundering, Terrorist Financing and Transfer of Funds (Information on the Payer) Regulations 2017 (SI 2017/692) (as amended by the Money Laundering and Terrorist Financing (Amendment) Regulations 2019 (SI 2019/1511)).

32 See Money Laundering, Terrorist Financing and Transfer of Funds (Information on the Payer) Regulations 2017, Regulation 58A and Schedule 3.

33 FSMA 2000, section 21 (as amended by the Financial Services and Markets Act 2023, section 69); Financial Services and Markets Act 2000 (Financial Promotion) Order 2005 (SI 2005/1529), especially Regulation 73ZA, as amended by the Financial Services and Markets Act 2000 (Financial Promotion) (Amendment) Order 2023 (SI 2023/612); and see Schedule 1, para 26F of the 2005 Order for the meaning of 'qualifying cryptoasset' in this context. See also FCA, *Policy Statement PS23/6 on Financial Promotion Rules for*

Beyond these circumstances, licences or authorisations from an authority are not generally required before cryptocurrencies are used/managed/issued or before cryptocurrency-related services are provided, unless the activities undertaken constitute 'regulated activities'.[34] Only authorised or exempt persons may carry on a regulated activity in the UK.[35] If the cryptoassets business involves regulated activity, then authorisation will be required from the FCA (and in some circumstances the PRA), which consists of receiving permission to carry on regulated activities.[36] Security tokens and e-money tokens are the forms of cryptoasset which will fall into the regulated category and can be considered 'specified investments' under legislation.[37] Other forms of cryptoassets, including exchange tokens and utility tokens, are (broadly) unregulated cryptoassets.[38] Given the changing landscape in this area, it is possible that the regulatory regime could be expanded to include additional types of cryptoasset in the future.

Regarding the authorisation needed for certain types of cryptoasset business noted above, there are various requirements outlined in legislation.[39] It must be clear that a business is able to comply with the rules regarding the relevant activity (or activities) being undertaken. Firms seeking to engage in regulated activities and applying for permission to do so from the FCA need to meet the FCA's 'threshold conditions'.[40]

3.1.1 Scope of Authorisation and Licencing Requirements

'Cryptoasset exchange providers' and 'custodian wallet providers' carrying on cryptoasset activities falling under the relevant legislation (noted above) need

---

Cryptoassets (2023), available at https://www.fca.org.uk/publications/policy-statements/ps23-6-financial-promotion-rules-cryptoassets. Section 25 of FSMA 2000 provides that it is a criminal offence to breach the restrictions on financial promotion in section 21.

34 See FSMA 2000, section 22 and the FSMA 2000 (Regulated Activities) Order 2001, Articles 73 ff.

35 FSMA 2000, sections 19 and 31.

36 See FSMA 2000, Part 4A.

37 See FSMA 2000, section 22 and FSMA 2000 (Regulated Activities) Order 2001/544. The FSMA 2023, section 69 has amended section 22 of the 2000 Act, so that investment in section 22(4) expressly includes "where an asset, right or interest is, or comprises or represents, a cryptoasset". See also e.g., Electronic Money Regulations 2011 (SI 2011/99).

38 For further details about which cryptoassets fall within the regime requiring authorisation and those which do not, see the FCA's Guidance on Cryptoassets (PS19/22, 2019) – https://www.fca.org.uk/publication/policy/ps19-22.pdf. And for the legal consequences of breaching the prohibition on an unauthorised person carrying out a regulated activity, see FSMA 2000, s 23, which outlines criminal penalties.

39 FSMA 2000, Part 4A.

40 FSMA 2000, section 55B and Schedule 6.

to register with the FCA.[41] A party must not act as a cryptoasset exchange provider or custodian wallet provider if they have not been registered.[42]

The FCA can suspend or cancel the registration of a cryptoasset exchange provider or custodian wallet provider if, at any time after registration takes place, it is satisfied that the provider does not meet the fit and proper person requirements.[43] The providers are required to provide to the FCA such information that it directs in relation to compliance by the business with the requirements under the legislation,[44] and the FCA can, if it reasonably considers, require a report by a 'skilled person' regarding a provider.[45] The FCA may also exercise powers of direction with respect to a cryptoasset business.[46]

As well as being the supervisory authority for credit and financial institutions, the FCA is the supervisory authority for 'cryptoasset exchange providers' and 'custodian wallet providers.'[47] The registration discussed above is with the FCA, which must maintain a register of cryptoasset providers and custodian wallet providers.[48] The FCA also keeps a list of unregistered cryptoassets businesses (of which it is aware) and these may subsequently be the subject of enforcement action.[49]

A further requirement is that a cryptoasset exchange provider or custodian wallet provider who establishes a business relationship, or enters into a transaction, with a customer arising out of the activities of the cryptoassets business must, before establishing the relationship or entering the transaction, inform the customer if the activity is not within the scope of the Financial

41 Money Laundering, Terrorist Financing and Transfer of Funds (Information on the Payer) Regulations 2017, Regulations 8 and 14A.

42 Money Laundering, Terrorist Financing and Transfer of Funds (Information on the Payer) Regulations 2017, Regulation 56(1).

43 In reg 58A(2) of the Money Laundering, Terrorist Financing and Transfer of Funds (Information on the Payer) Regulations 2017 – see Regulation 60(2A).

44 See Money Laundering, Terrorist Financing and Transfer of Funds (Information on the Payer) Regulations 2017, Regulation 74A.

45 Money Laundering, Terrorist Financing and Transfer of Funds (Information on the Payer) Regulations 2017, Regulation 74B.

46 Money Laundering, Terrorist Financing and Transfer of Funds (Information on the Payer) Regulations 2017, Regulation 74C.

47 See Money Laundering, Terrorist Financing and Transfer of Funds (Information on the Payer) Regulations 2017, Regulation 7.

48 Money Laundering, Terrorist Financing and Transfer of Funds (Information on the Payer) Regulations 2017, Regulation 54(1A). For the FCA's register of cryptoassets businesses, see https://register.fca.org.uk/s/search?predefined=CA.

49 Details are provided here https://register.fca.org.uk/s/search?predefined=U.

Ombudsman Service's jurisdiction and/or is not subject to protection under the Financial Services Compensation Scheme.[50]

Parties undertaking regulated activities will require authorisation from the FCA for doing so (see above), but only certain types of cryptoasset activities fall into the regulated category and need such authorisation.

3.2 *Prospectuses*

Depending on the type of token in question, issuers of cryptocurrencies may, in some circumstances, be required to publish a prospectus (and may be subject to other disclosure requirements too). There is no special regime for cryptocurrencies in this area but the issuance of a cryptocurrency may fall within the general rules requiring a prospectus.[51] A prospectus is necessary if a token is a transferable security and is to be offered to the public or admitted to trading on a regulated market; however, a prospectus is not required if an exemption applies.[52]

Where a prospectus is required, it must be approved by the FCA.[53] It will only be approved if it contains the 'necessary information' which is material to an investor for making an informed assessment of: (a) the assets and liabilities, profits and losses, financial position and prospects of the issuer and any guarantor; (b) the rights attaching to the securities; and (c) the reasons for the issuance and its impact on the issuer.[54]

There are various rules regarding the application for approval of a prospectus to the FCA and the FCA's decision regarding the application.[55]

---

50 Money Laundering, Terrorist Financing and Transfer of Funds (Information on the Payer) Regulations 2017, Regulation 60A.

51 For discussion of prospectus requirements, see e.g., L. Gullifer and J. Payne, *Corporate Finance Law: Principles and Policy*, 3rd ed., Hart, Oxford 2020, pp. 510 ff.

52 See Guidance on Cryptoassets Feedback and Final Guidance to CP 19/3, Policy Statement PS19/22 (July 2019), p. 50; Regulation (EU) 2017/1129 (Prospectus Regulation) art 3 and FCA Handbook, Prospectus Regulation Rules Sourcebook (PRR) 1.2.1; FSMA 2000, s 85. The Prospectus Regulation is retained EU law, with some amendments – see Prospectus (Amendment etc.) (EU Exit) Regulations 2019 (SI 2019/1234). For the exemptions, see Prospectus Regulation, art 1(4) and PRR, 1.2.3; and see the discussion at Gullifer and Payne, *Corporate Finance Law: Principles and Policy*, pp. 512–513.

53 FSMA 2000, section 85(7).

54 FSMA 2000, section 87A; Prospectus Regulation, Art 6(1) and PRR, 2.1.1. And see the rest of PRR, 2.1.1 and Prospectus Regulation, Arts 6 and 7 for further details of the requirements. See also the discussion in Gullifer and Payne, *Corporate Finance Law: Principles and Policy*, pp. 513 ff.

55 For further information, see e.g., FSMA 2000, sections 87C and 87D; Regulation (EU) 2019/980, Chapter V; PRR, 3.1.

There is the possibility of liability in respect of an incorrect or misleading prospectus. For a party making a claim, there are various avenues available. The FSMA 2000, s 90, offers specific liability for prospectuses. Under this, any person responsible for a prospectus is liable to pay compensation to a person who has acquired securities to which the prospectus applies, if the claimant has suffered loss as regards those securities due to any untrue or misleading statement in the prospectus or an omission of any matter that was required to be included in the prospectus.[56] The legislation provides exemptions (defences) to such a claim,[57] including that there was a reasonable belief that the statement was true or that the claimant acquired securities with knowledge that the statement was false or misleading or the matter was omitted.

While a s 90 claim is likely to be the most appealing course in the majority of circumstances, there are other routes available for claims. At common law, if there have been intentionally fraudulent misrepresentations, then the tort of deceit allows for liability.[58] There can also be liability for a negligent misstatement in a prospectus, but because the loss will involve pure economic loss, the law is rather restrictive.[59] A successful claim will depend upon meeting the requirements of foreseeability, proximity of relationship and that it is fair, just and reasonable to impose a duty.[60] In relation to proximity, the defendant will need to have assumed responsibility to the claimant in the matter: it will need to be shown that the defendant knew the information would be provided to the claimant and that the claimant would rely on it.[61] In the context of a statement in a prospectus, this is a test that can certainly be met, particularly where initial investors are purchasing on the strength of statements in the prospectus. Depending on the circumstances, there could also be successful contractual claims (e.g., between the issuer of the securities and initial purchasers),[62] and claims under the Misrepresentation Act 1967, ss 1–2.[63]

56 FSMA 2000, section 90(1).

57 Under FSMA 2000, Schedule 10.

58 See e.g., *Derry v Peek* (1889) 14 App Cas 337; *Clerk & Lindsell on Torts*, 23rd ed., Sweet & Maxwell, London 2020, ch 17.

59 *Clerk & Lindsell on Torts*, para 7–103.

60 *Caparo Industries plc v Dickman* [1990] 2 AC 605.

61 See *Hedley Byrne & Co Ltd v Heller & Partners Ltd* [1964] AC 465; *Henderson v Merrett Syndicates* [1995] 2 AC 145; and *Clerk & Lindsell on Torts*, paras 7-104 onwards, for discussion.

62 By virtue of the statement being considered incorporated into the contract.

63 For some discussion of the various civil law remedies, see Gullifer and Payne, *Corporate Finance Law: Principles and Policy*, pp. 522 onwards.

Furthermore, there are administrative sanctions available to the FCA.[64] As well as the role they have in approving or not approving a prospectus, they can, for example, suspend or prohibit an offer of securities to the public, suspend or prohibit admission to trading, publicly censure an issuer (or other relevant party) or impose monetary penalties on them.[65]

There may also be criminal liability in some circumstances, such as where there has been behaviour constituting criminal fraud or where the prospectus has been used for market manipulation.[66]

With respect to enforcement of securities law (including prospectus liability), while there are some signs of improvement, the levels of public enforcement (by the FCA) and private enforcement are relatively low in the UK, particularly compared to the USA.[67]

4 Private Law Issues

There are broad similarities between the private law of Northern Ireland and the private law of England and Wales, both of which are common law systems. Scots private law is markedly distinct as a mixed jurisdiction with considerable civilian influences. This part of the Report focuses on the law of England and Wales. Regarding private law, it draws primarily upon the Recommendations and Conclusions of the Final Report on Digital Assets of the LCEW[68] published on 28 June 2023. Although these do not, strictly speaking, have the force of law, the LCEW's position is indicative of how the courts might develop the common law. It is, however, worth noting that property law is an area in which the law of England and Wales is increasingly fragmented; and that there is a school of thought that takes a fundamentally different approach to both the ontological orientation of property law as well as the property status of

64 FSMA 2000, sections 87J–87O.

65 See FSMA 2000, sections 87K–87M and 91. See Gullifer and Payne, *Corporate Finance Law: Principles and Policy*, pp. 534–535 for discussion.

66 On the latter point, Gullifer and Payne, *Corporate Finance Law: Principles and Policy*, p. 533, suggest that sections. 89–90 of the Financial Services Act 2012 could be relevant. Regarding fraud, see Fraud Act 2006.

67 See Gullifer and Payne, *Corporate Finance Law: Principles and Policy*, pp. 535–537, and the sources cited there.

68 The 'Final Report' and 'Summary of Final Report' are both available at https://www.lawcom.gov.uk/project/digital-assets/.

cryptoassets.[69] Regarding private international law, the LCEW's project on 'Digital Assets and Electronic Trade Documents (ETDs) in private international law: which law, which court?' is currently at the pre-consultation stage.[70]

4.1 *Private Law*

4.1.1 Cryptocurrencies as Objects of Property Rights

The LCEW recommends statutory confirmation of the common law position[71] that things will not be deprived of legal status as objects of personal property rights, merely because they do not fall within either of the two established categories of personal property, i.e., things in action and things in possession.[72] As such, the LCEW recommends a third category of personal property, but does not consider it appropriate nor necessary to define in the statute the hard boundaries of such a third category of thing.[73] Rather, the LCEW considers the common law to be the better vehicle for this purpose,[74] but is clear that a variety of digital assets, including crypto-tokens, may fall within this third category.[75]

Notwithstanding the view that the substantive law of third category objects is best developed by the courts, the LCEW concludes that factual control (plus intention) can found a legal proprietary interest in a digital object; and that in certain circumstances, such a control-based legal proprietary interest can be separated from (and be inferior to or short of) a superior legal title.[76] This clearly draws upon the principle that, in respect of things in possession,

69 The basic division is between those who conceptualise property law as 'thing-based' in the civilian sense, and 'rights-based' in the traditional sense of the common law; see A. Held, '(Digital) Things as Objects of Property Rights: What Can Crypto Learn from Comparative Law?' (2024) XX OJLS 1-27 (online advance publication at https://doi.org/10.1093/ojls/gqae034) and the treatment of the common law in C. von Bar (trans JG Allen) *Things as Objects of Property Rights* (OUP 2023). For a recent example of the two opposing views, see R. Goode, 'What is Property?' (2023) 139 LQR 1 and R. Stevens, 'Crypto is Not Property' (2023) 139 LQR 615. See also William Swadling's review of the first edition of M. Bridge et al (eds), *The Law of Personal Property* (2013) in (2015) LMCLQ 595.

70 https://lawcom.gov.uk/project/digital-assets-and-etds-in-private-international-law-which-court-which-law/. See generally B. Yüksel Ripley, 'Law Commission of England and Wales's New Project on Conflict of Laws and Emerging Technology', EAPIL Blog https://eapil.org/2021/11/30/law-commission-of-england-and-waless-new-project-on-conflict-of-laws-and-emerging-technology/.

71 LCEW, 'Digital Assets: Summary of Final Report', (June 2023), p 8.

72 LCEW, 'Digital Assets' (June 2023), Recommendation 1 (Summary of Final Report, pp. 7–9 and 18).

73 LCEW, 'Digital Assets: Summary of Final Report', (June 2023), pp. 8–9.

74 ibid., p 8.

75 ibid.

76 LCEW, 'Digital Assets' (June 2023), Conclusion 1 (Summary of Final Report, pp. 10 and 19).

possession itself confers a (relative) title valid against all but those who assert a superior title;[77] which underpins both title (which is roughly comparable to civilian notions of 'ownership') and the custodial technique of bailment.[78] Accordingly, it seems more likely that the courts will draw upon the principles applicable to things in possession and apply them by analogy to objects of the third category to determine proprietary entitlements and relationships based on control, as opposed to those applicable to things in action.

Thus, where X has 60 Bitcoins registered in a non-intermediated wallet, factual control conferred by the private keys, plus intention would likely suffice to found a legal proprietary interest in the 60 Bitcoins by an analogy to possession conferring a relative legal title to a thing in possession.

Where X opens an account with MontC, such intermediated holding arrangements could be characterised in two ways based on the LCEW's analysis. First, applying the LCEW's trust characterisation,[79] legal title to the 60 Bitcoins would be vested in MontC, who holds for X and other accountholders on a consolidated unallocated basis as equitable tenants in common. Second, applying the LCEW's control-based structure,[80] which is clearly analogous to a bailment of things in possession, X would retain a superior legal title relative to MontC who would hold a lesser control-based proprietary entitlement.

One core consideration for the control-based structure is that, normally, a bailment cannot arise where a common depository receives fungible goods from multiple depositors and commingles them such that the original deposits are unidentifiable.[81] Where, however, the depositors agree amongst themselves that they will be tenants in common over the whole and that intention is clearly evinced, a bailment may still arise.[82] A tenancy in common may also arise under statute upon certain sales of bulk goods.[83] This requirement in

---

77 The position is well established at common law; a standard authority cited is Lord Hoffmann in *Alan Wibberley Building Ltd v Insley* [1999] 1 WLR 894 (HL), 898: "possession is in itself a good title against anyone who cannot show a prior and therefore better right to possession".

78 See generally N. Palmer, 'Bailment', in A. Burrows (ed), *English Private Law*, 3rd ed., OUP, Oxford 2013.

79 LCEW, 'Digital Assets' (June 2023), Conclusion 4 (Summary of Final Report, pp 12-13 and 20).

80 ibid., Conclusion 5 (pp. 13 and 20).

81 *South Australian Insurance Co Ltd v Randell* (1869) LR 3 PC 101, PC; *Chapman Bros Ltd v Verco Bros Ltd* (1933) 49 CLR 306; cf *Mercer v Craven Grain Storage Ltd* [1994] CLC 328, HL; *Coleman v Harvey* [1989] 1 NZLR 723.

82 *Mercer v Craven Grain Storage Ltd* [1994] CLC 328 (HL); *Re Stapylton Fletcher Ltd* [1994] 1 WLR 1181; cf *Gill and Duffus (Liverpool) Ltd v Scruttons Ltd* [1953] 1 WLR 1407; *Glencore International AG v Metro Trading International Inc* [2001] 1 Lloyd's Rep 2000.

83 Section 20A Sale of Goods Act 1979.

the law of bailment may be problematic for intermediated holdings on a consolidated unallocated basis, but it seems that the courts will be free to develop the rules around intermediated control of third category objects as a distinct concept to bailments of things in possession.

The division of property rights between X and MontC would remain as above in respect of new cryptocurrencies resulting from a hardfork or airdrop, save for where the parties clearly intend otherwise.

4.1.2 Transfer of Ownership

The LCEW concludes that it is possible (with the requisite intention) to effect a legal transfer of a crypto-token off-chain by a change of control, or on-chain by a transfer operation that effects a state of change on the blockchain.[84]

The LCEW further concludes that a special defence of good faith purchaser for value without notice applicable to crypto-tokens can be recognised and developed by the courts through incremental development; and the reasoning can be extended to other third category objects.[85] The availability of this defence draws upon an analogy with money in the form of cash and negotiable instruments,[86] but it is worth noting that these objects have their origins in the *lex mercatoria*, not the common law of property,[87] where the *nemo dat* rule applies strictly to things in possession.[88] The position is further different in equity,[89] and under certain statutory exceptions for the sale of goods.[90]

---

84 LCEW, 'Digital Assets' (June 2023), Conclusion 2 (Summary of Final Report, pp. 11 and 19).

85 ibid., Conclusion 3 (pp. 12 and 19).

86 LCEW, 'Digital Assets: Final Report' (June 2023), [6.53]–[6.54]. It is worth noting that the authority cited, *Miller v Race* (1758) 1 Burr 452, 97 ER 398, concerned promissory notes of the Bank of England.

87 See A. Held, 'Crypto-Financial Assets in a DLT-Based Market Infrastructure: Legal Principles of Ownership and Obligation' (2019), p. 5, fn 11-15 http://hdl.handle.net/11343/274809. For the changing value of coins from use value as metal to exchange value as money, and for the reception of *lex mercatoria* into the common law, see P.S. Atiyah, *The Rise and Fall of Freedom of Contract* (Clarendon Press, Oxford 1979), pp. 104–105; 137. See also W. Swadling, 'Property,' in A. Burrows (ed), *English Private Law*, 3rd ed., OUP, Oxford 2013, who notes the common law 'exception' for money relates to commercial necessity: [4.487]–[4.499].

88 *Farquharson Bros & Co v King & Co* [1902] AC 325 (HL). There are some limited exceptions, see W. Swadling, 'Property,' in A. Burrows (ed), English Private Law, 3rd ed., OUP, Oxford 2013, [4.487]–[4.499].

89 *Pilcher v Rawlins* (1871) 7 Ch App 259; W. Swadling, 'Property', in A. Burrows (ed), English Private Law, 3rd ed., OUP, Oxford 2013, [4.496].

90 Sections 21-26 Sale of Goods Act 1979. There was an old doctrine of sale in the market overt protecting bona fide purchasers, which has since been abolished. See W. Swadling, 'Property', in A. Burrows (ed), *English Private Law*, 3rd ed., OUP, Oxford 2013, [4.490].

Where X wishes to transfer property rights in some of the Bitcoins in his/her wallet to Y, generally, it makes no difference whether the transfer from X to Y is by way of donation or by way of mutual exchange pursuant to a contract. Given the LCEW's position on the special defence, whether Y gave valuable consideration will have implications should a competing interest said to pre-exist the transfer to Y be asserted by a third party.

In the commercial context, the common law of contract accords primacy to the principle of freedom of contract. As such, an agreement between X and Y that X will transfer 5 Bitcoin to Y in consideration of some counter-performance, be it another 10 Ether or £1,000, will be enforceable under the law of contract. The types of remedy for breach of such contract available, however, will differ, depending on how the transaction is characterised.[91]

4.1.3 Succession

As with the law of contract, a key principle of the English law of succession is testamentary freedom.[92] As such, there is, in principle, no reason why X could not include the 60 Bitcoins in a will to be distributed to Y upon X's death.

Following the LCEW's Conclusions, it would seem that a gift of the private key as pure data in itself would be possible as the transfer of a third category object by an off-chain change of control.[93]

It has been written that a legacy in a will of a device (e.g., a laptop) will carry all of the device's transistors and magnetic disks in which all digital records (including a private key) are stored. Accordingly, a testator, X, wishing to give a gift of a private key to Y should ensure it is stored on a device owned by him[94] and ensure that medium is expressly made subject to the gift to Y. This is broadly consistent with the 'documentary intangibles' fiction applied to choses in actions recorded or evidenced on paper.[95]

---

91 The default English remedy for breach of contract is damages and/or debt, i.e., an action for the agreed sum of the price. Given that neither Bitcoin nor Ether are 'money', such remedy would only be available for the £1,000 in legal tender as the 'price'.

92 See, e.g., section 3 of the Wills Act 1837, which provides statutory confirmation that all property may be disposed of by will.

93 LCEW, 'Digital Assets' (June 2023), Conclusion 2 (Summary of Final Report, pp. 11 and 19).

94 L. Sagar, *The Digital Estate*, Sweet & Maxwell, London 2018, [8.10].

95 E. McKendrick (ed), *Goode and McKendrick on Commercial Law*, 6th ed., Penguin, London 2020, [2.16] and [2.53] et seq. For the consequences of this characterisation, see S. Dromgoole and Y. Baatz, 'The Bill of Lading as a Document of Title', in N. Palmer and E. McKendrick (eds), *Interests in Goods*, 2nd ed., 1998, in M. Bridge *et al* (eds), *The Law of Personal Property*, 3rd ed., Sweet & Maxwell, London 2021, [1-026], footnote 120.

Where a will has not been made, the 60 Bitcoins will fall under the rules of intestacy, as set out in the Administration of Estates Act 1925. Where X is survived only by issue (assume Y is X's only child), the matter is straightforward: Y will take the entire estate. Where, however, X is survived by both Y and a spouse or civil partner, Y and the spouse/civil partner take the entire estate between them. Classification under the English property taxonomy is important here, because the spouse first takes X's personal chattels absolutely. Section 55(1)(x) of the Administration of Estates Act 1925 defines 'personal chattels' as 'tangible movable property' with some qualifications relating to money, securities/ investments, and business use.

Prima facie, characterising the 60 Bitcoins as a third category of personal property would not fall within the definition of 'personal chattels', given its intangible form as a matter of fact. By contrast, a cold hardware wallet or piece of paper on which the private key is recorded may well fall within the definition of 'personal chattels' for the purposes of the Administration of Estates Act 1925.

4.1.4 Trusts

There are three traditional requirements for the creation of an express trust.[96] Of these, only one is potentially problematic where X wishes to create a trust over the 60 Bitcoins in his wallet in favour of Y: the requirement that the subject matter of the trust (i.e., the 60 Bitcoins) is sufficiently certain.

In some commercial contexts, the requirement of certainty has been attenuated in line with the concept of fungibility. Traditionally, neither the common law nor equity recognised proprietary interests in commingled fungible assets.[97] This position was reversed in the trust context in *Hunter v Moss*[98] in respect of shares, which was subsequently applied to intermediated securities held in omnibus securities accounts in the cases arising from the Lehman insolvency[99] and generally remains authoritative.

The LCEW concludes that crypto-token intermediated holding arrangements can be characterised and structured as trusts, with the intermediary holding as trustee on a consolidated unallocated basis for equitable tenants

96 See generally W. Swadling, 'Property', in A. Burrows (ed), *English Private Law*, 3rd ed., OUP, Oxford 2013, [4.166] et seq.

97 *Re Goldcorp Exchange Ltd* [1995] 1 AC 74, PC. This applied both to bailments and to trusts.

98 [1994] 1 WLR 452 (CA).

99 *Re Lehman Brothers International (Europe)* [2010] EWHC 2914 (Ch); *Re Lehman Brothers International (Europe)* [2009] EWHC 2545 (Ch).

in common.[100] This position is consistent with the reasoning of the *Hunter v Moss* line of authority.

Outside this specific commercial context, where the cryptoassets purportedly impressed with trust are held on a consolidated unallocated basis, it is unclear whether the requirement that the subject matter of the trust is certain would be fulfilled. Here, *Wang v Darby*[101] is of interest as a fully defended application inviting the judge to determine whether the claim that certain cryptoassets were impressed with a trust had a real prospect of success for the purpose of a summary judgment application. Following *Hunter v Moss,* it was common ground between the parties that, as a matter of English law, a unit of Tez constitutes an asset which can, in principle, be the subject of a trust. The judge, however, appeared to express some misgivings by observing that this was so, "notwithstanding [a unit of Tez's] entirely fungible character and non-identifiable status: no single unit bears any unique serial number or means of identification."[102]

4.1.5 Attachment and Seizure

4.1.5.1 *Civil Freezing Orders*

The freezing order formerly known as the '*Mareva* injunction' is not a true attachment order; nor is, strictly speaking, concerned with execution. However, given that such orders have featured heavily in the cryptoasset litigation before the English courts, they warrant a brief mention.

The freezing order differs from a true attachment order in that they operate *in personam;* i.e., they are directed to the Respondent personally and have no proprietary effects. As they are neither premised on any definition of 'property', the fact that cryptocurrencies have been considered 'assets' for the purpose of the standard form freezing order[103] does not have any broader property law significance.

Freezing orders are typically sought at an interim stage and require the Respondent to refrain from dealing with the assets listed in the order to a specified financial threshold to ensure that he cannot improperly frustrate any judgment ultimately entered against him following trial.

The effects of a freezing order have limited reach beyond the enjoined Respondent: third parties notified of the order – typically the Respondent's

100 LCEW, 'Digital Assets' (June 2023), Conclusion 4 (Summary of Final Report, pp. 12–13 and 20).

101 [2021] EWHC 3054 (Comm). See further Part 6.1.1 below.

102 [2021] EWHC 3054 (Comm), [8].

103 Annexed to CPR PD25A.

bank or, indeed, the cryptocurrency exchange at which the Respondent holds cryptocurrencies – may find themselves in contempt of court if they act inconsistently with the terms of the freezing order. This is of particular relevance in the case where the Respondent holds 60 Bitcoins with an intermediary: not only will the applicant typically have brought the intermediary on notice of the freezing order but also the intermediary may well have been named as a co-Respondent in the application for the purposes of the disclosure orders typically sought alongside a freezing order.

4.1.5.2 *Final Civil Judgments*

A judgment creditor with a final judgment of a money award is entitled to use any method of enforcement to satisfy the judgment debt. Of present relevance is the writ and/or warrant of control,[104] which allow the judgment creditor to take possession of the judgment debtor's assets, sell them, and apply the proceeds of the sale to the satisfaction of the debt.

Although, prima facie, the procedure may seem limited to tangible goods, the relevant statutory (asset-based) definition[105] is wider than that at common law: 'goods' means 'property of any description, other than land.' In any event, given that the procedure is available in respect of intangibles such as securities,[106] it does not seem in principle that the procedure is limited to tangible goods.[107]

Another option for the judgment creditor is to apply to the court for the appointment of a receiver by way of equitable execution,[108] which has traditionally been sought where the usual methods of execution have not been possible; either owing to the nature of the asset itself or the nature of the judgment debtor's interest in the asset. The effect of the receivership order is that the judgment debtor is personally ordered not to receive any asset that would otherwise be owed and delivered to him; which is, instead, diverted to the appointed receiver to be applied to the satisfaction of the judgment debt.[109]

In all cases, applications may be made for orders summoning the judgment debtor to attend court to "provide information about his means or any other matter about which information is needed to enforce a judgment."[110] The order

---

104 CPR Parts 83 and 84.

105 Schedule 12, Part 3, Tribunals, Courts, and Enforcement Act 2007.

106 Part 4 Taking Control of Goods Regulations 2013 (SI 2013/1894).

107 Given the uncertainty as to who is entitled to the rights of owner, the procedure is not without risk for the creditor.

108 Section 37 Senior Courts Act 1981.

109 *Masri v Consolidated Contractors International Co* SAL [2008] EWCA Civ 303, [52]–[59].

110 CPR Rule 71.2(1).

may require the judgment debtor to produce relevant documents within his control,[111] and will require him to answer questions on oath.[112] Disclosure of any crypto-asset holdings will fall within these terms, and will be usually effective through contempt proceedings.[113]

A final requirement is that the relevant assets to be attached are situate within the jurisdiction.[114]

4.1.5.3 *Criminal Proceedings*

The Proceeds of Crime Act 2002 adopts a wide, non-exhaustive (asset-based) definition of 'property'[115] that is, in line with many criminal statutes, wider than the definitions in the common law of property.[116] Cryptoassets have been seized as criminal property or proceeds of crime under the 2002 Act.[117]

4.1.6 Insolvency

The Insolvency Act 1986 is underpinned by a very wide and non-exhaustive (asset-based) definition of property.[118] As such, there is no reason to suggest that cryptocurrencies cannot form part of an insolvency estate.

Where X has opened an account with MontC, the intermediated holding structure will determine the rights X has. Under the LCEW's trust characterisation,[119] X, as a beneficiary equitable tenant in common, will be entitled along with the co-tenants to the Bitcoins, which will be removed from the insolvency estate and transferred to a new trustee. Under the LCEW's control-based characterisation,[120] an analogy with bailment would lead to X being

111 CPR Rule 71.2(6)(b).
112 CPR Rule 71.2(6)(c) and Rule 71.6(1).
113 PD70A paragraph 1.2(a) and CPR Part 81 (Applications and Proceedings in Relation to Contempt of Court).
114 See further Part 4.2 below.
115 Sections 84(1), 232(1), 316(4), 340(9).
116 Under section 4(1) Theft Act 1968, property is defined as including "money and all other property, real or personal, including things in action and other intangible property".
117 *R v West*, Southwark Crown Court (14 December 2017, Unreported).
118 Section 436(1): '"property" includes money, goods, things in action, land and every description of property wherever situated and also obligations and every description of interest, whether present or future or vested or contingent, arising out of, or incidental to, property.'
119 LCEW, 'Digital Assets' (June 2023), Conclusion 4 (Summary of Final Report, pp. 12–13 and 20).
120 ibid., Conclusion 5 (pp. 13 and 20).

entitled to immediate control over the Bitcoin based on the superior proprietary title based on control.[121]

Where Company Z has opened an account with MontC and Company Z subsequently becomes insolvent, the wide definition of property under section 436(1) of the Insolvency Act 1986 will likely bring the value of Z's wallet within Z's insolvency estate; irrespective of whether Z's claims against MontC are proprietary[122] or personal.[123] Hence, having excluded proprietary claims to any of the cryptocurrencies in Z's wallet, the question of whether any of Z's creditors rank ahead in priority to other creditors will depend on their contracts with Z.

In the cases of insolvencies of both MontC and Z, the rights conferred by contracts between the relevant parties, as well as the intermediated holding structure, are of paramount significance in determining the types of claims a creditor may bring.

4.1.7 Pledge and Other Security

English law only recognises four kinds of consensual security: pledge, contractual lien, equitable charge and mortgage.[124] Technically speaking, pledge (as well as lien) can only be created over assets in respect of which it is possible to transfer possession.

However, given that the LCEW considers control analogous to possession such that proprietary interests may be founded by control, which may be relative in control-based intermediated structures in a manner similar to bailment, there seems to be no reason why the requirement of possession for pledges of things in possession will not be similarly adapted. As such, it seems unlikely that the courts will have difficulty in recognising a security interest in a cryptocurrency comparable to the pledge based on control. Such interest would be analogous, but distinct to pledge of things in possession.

Accordingly, where Company Z has agreed to 'pledge' 30 Bitcoins that are registered in its wallet to secure a loan, the courts will likely recognise some security interest analogous to the pledge. Z could also offer some other, non-possessory, form of security interest in the 30 Bitcoins, such as a charge.

---

121 ibid., Conclusion 1 (pp. 10, 13 and 19).

122 This would fall within 'money, goods, things in action, land and every description of property wherever situated'.

123 This would fall within 'obligations and every description of interest, whether present or future or vested or contingent, arising out of, or incidental to, property'.

124 See generally L. Smith, 'Security', in A. Burrows (ed), *English Private Law*, 3rd ed., OUP, Oxford 2013.

4.1.8 Loans

In principle, contracts of loan, lease, and hire are subject to the same principle of freedom of contract as any other contract governed by English law. On this view, where Company Z intends to borrow 60 Bitcoins from company PayB with an interest rate of 5% payable either in legal tender or Bitcoins, there is, in principle, no reason why the parties could not do so as a matter of contract. The precise characterisations of the transaction and of the Bitcoins, however, give rise to various different considerations and legal effects.

Both gratuitous loans and contracts of hire of things in possession take legal effect as a bailment.[125] Accordingly, they require the return *in specie* of the asset loaned or hired, and the 'lender' does not part with the superior right of 'general property' in the asset. Strictly speaking, therefore, if it were possible to classify Bitcoin as an asset in respect which the parties have entered into a contract for hire in consideration of a '5% interest rate,' by analogy to bailment and things in possession, Z would not be entitled to 'pay the loan back' in Bitcoin Cash, nor any other 'Bitcoins,' but could only discharge its obligation to return by delivering the exact same 60 Bitcoins back to PayB. Again, the issues of fungibility seen above in the context of trusts and bailments arise.

In this respect, loans of cash/money, differ in that the obligation to return is not generally in respect of the specific coins and banknotes advanced, but an equivalent sum; as such, the parties do not stand in a relationship of bailment, but in one of creditor and debtor.[126] It is against this background that the Regulated Activities Order (RAO) 2001 captures the provision of certain types of 'credit agreements'[127] as a 'lender' as a specified activity,[128] where 'credit' is defined as including cash loans and 'any other form of financial accommodation'.[129]

It follows that whether PayB's loan of 60 Bitcoins is a regulated activity turns on whether the provision of Bitcoin is a 'form of financial accommodation'. Since cryptocurrencies are not legal tender, cash, banknotes, nor finance

---

125 See generally N. Palmer, 'Bailment', in A. Burrows (ed), *English Private Law*, 3rd ed., OUP, Oxford 2013, especially [16.45] and [16.61]; H.G. Beale *et al* (eds) *Chitty on Contracts*, 34th ed., Sweet & Maxwell, London 2021, Vol II [35-066] et seq.

126 N. Palmer, 'Bailment', in A. Burrows (ed), *English Private Law*, 3rd ed., OUP, Oxford 2013, [16.15].

127 Article 60B(3) FSMA 2000 (Regulated Activities) Order 2001.

128 See Chapter 14A FSMA 2000 (Regulated Activities) Order 2001 for 'Regulated Credit Agreements'.

129 Article 60L, FSMA 2000 (Regulated Activities) Order 2001.

within the central banking system, it is unlikely that loans of Bitcoin will fall within the meaning of a 'credit agreement' under the RAO 2001.

This would mean that PayB, if established in the UK, would not require any authorisations to provide Z with a 'loan' of 60 Bitcoins, however, there would be significant difficulty in characterising such 'loan' in the financial sense of the provision of 'credit'. If the alternative analogy to bailment is drawn, the constraints upon Z to return the 60 Bitcoins *in specie* as a bailee under a contract of hire would limit the commercial utility of the transaction.

In this respect, it is worth noting the practice of securities 'lending' in prime brokerage. Such 'loans' which are not strictly loans, but generally agreements to return equivalent securities under sale and repurchase agreements. Thus, in *Wang v Darby*,[130] the parties characterised their transaction as a 'sale and buyback', expressly avoiding a loan characterisation for accounting purposes.[131] No issue was taken with whether such transaction was possible as a matter of law. The only comment by the judge was that the facts did not strictly align with a repo transaction, but the specific characterisation of the transaction was immaterial to the issues for determination.[132]

In sum, an arrangement under which Company Z intends to 'borrow' 60 Bitcoins from company PayB with an 'interest rate of 5% payable either in legal tender or Bitcoins' could be properly characterised under English law as a loan or hire of a third category property object by analogy; but not as a loan of cash/money. Otherwise, it could be characterised as a kind of sale and repurchase agreement, with the 'interest rate' further characterised as simple contractual consideration rather than in the familiar sense associated with traditional finance.

4.1.9 Tort and Hacking[133]

Where X opened an account with MontC and lost all the Bitcoins in his digital wallet due to MontC's IT systems being hacked, the nature of the claims X may bring against MontC will depend on the contractual terms upon which X opened the relevant account. In addition to the contractual causes of action, X could also potentially sue in tort and for breach of fiduciary duty. All claims,

130 [2021] EWHC 3054 (Comm). See further Part 6.1.1 below and A. Held, 'Baking, Staking, Tezos, and Trusts: Crypto Sale and Repurchase Agreements Analysed by the High Court' (2022) 2 JIBFL 96.

131 [2021] EWHC 3054 (Comm), [29]–[31].

132 Ibid., [78]; [89].

133 This Part addresses tort, whilst recognising other non-contractual causes of action, such as unjust enrichment and fiduciary duty, may be available. Consumer protection issues may also arise.

however, would depend on the precise scope of MontC's duties to X, as undertaken expressly or impliedly in the agreement between them.

In order for X to bring a property claim against any third parties to whom the hacker conveys the 'stolen' Bitcoins, or indeed the hacker himself, X could only plausibly bring a claim based on a property or proprietary interest.

If an action analogous to conversion based on control were available, the LCEW's special defence of bona fide purchaser[134] would likely apply in some form. Accordingly, whilst the property claim against the hacker would prevail, if the hacker sold the Bitcoin to a third-party Y, who paid in good faith without notice of X's interest, Y would be able to avail himself of the special defence.

The position is effectively the same in equity. Should X bring a property claim as, for example, the beneficiary under a trust created or implied by X's arrangements with MontC, X's interest in equity will not bind Y as a *bona fide* purchaser for value of MontC's title at law without notice of X's interest.

Where the hacker has fraudulently induced X to part with the Bitcoin, additional causes of action under the law of obligations – notably fraud and misrepresentation at common law and under the Misrepresentation Act 1967 – will be available (see further Part 6.1 below).

4.2 *Private International Law*

There is currently no specific provision concerning conflict of laws aspects of cryptocurrencies. The Rome I and Rome II Regulations[135] and pre-existing common law rules are applicable as appropriate.

It has been argued that cryptocurrencies are a form of intangible property in English private international law.[136] Questions of proprietary rights regarding moveable property are predominantly governed by the *lex situs* (i.e., the law of the place where the property is situated) and the general practice for intangible movables with no physical location (such as money debts, shares, rights of action, intellectual property) has been to ascribe them to an artificial or fictional legal situs where they can be pursued or enforced.[137] However, the

134 LCEW, 'Digital Assets' (June 2023), Conclusion 3 (Summary of Final Report, pp. 12 and 19).

135 The Law Applicable to Contractual Obligations and Non-Contractual Obligations (Amendment etc.) (EU Exit) Regulations 2019 (SI 2019/834) as amended by the Jurisdiction, Judgments and Applicable Law (Amendment) (EU Exit) Regulations (SI 2020/1574). They are 'assimilated law' after the end of 2023, as per section 5 of the Retained EU Law (Revocation and Reform) Act 2023.

136 A. Dickinson, 'Cryptocurrencies and the Conflict of Laws' in D. Fox and S. Green (eds), *Cryptocurrencies in Public and Private Law*, OUP, Oxford 2019, para 5.97.

137 Lord Collins of Mapesbury and others (eds), *Dicey, Morris & Collins on the Conflict of Laws*, 16th ed., Sweet & Maxwell, London 2022, para 23-025.

identification of the *lex situs* for cryptocurrencies poses difficulties as, in addition to not having a physical location, they are underpinned by DLT. In *Ion Science v Persons Unknown*,[138] *Fetch.AI Ltd v Persons Unknown*[139] and *D'Aloia v Persons Unknown*,[140] English courts took the view, based on Professor Dickinson's proposal, that the location of a cryptoasset (Bitcoin in the first two cases, and USD Tether (USDT) and USD Coin (USDC), so-called stablecoins, in the third case) is the place where the person or company who owned the coin or token is domiciled.[141] In *Tulip Trading Ltd v Bitcoin Association For BSV & Ors*,[142] however, the English High Court suggested that the situs is the place of residence or business of the owner, not their domicile.[143]

There are various important questions subject to the *lex situs* concerning e.g., ownership, types of enforcement of debts against property by a creditor,[144] or the creation of security interests.[145] Clarity on the determination of the situs for cryptocurrencies is still needed as the matter has not been settled by authority yet.[146] Digital location[147] is one of the issues that the LCEW will be considering as part of its ongoing project.

Where the transfer of title to a cryptocurrency does not involve physical objects, this blurs the boundaries between proprietary and obligatory rights.[148] Article 14 of Rome I, which governs various issues regarding the transfer of

---

138 Unreported, 21.12.2020.

139 [2021] EWHC 2254 (Comm).

140 [2022] EWHC 1723 (Ch).

141 For Professor Dickinson's proposal involving an analogy to goodwill, see Dickinson, 'Cryptocurrencies and the Conflict of Laws', paras 5.97 and 5.119. On this solution, see also Collins and others, *Dicey, Morris & Collins on the Conflict of Laws*, para 23-050.

142 [2022] EWHC 667 (Ch).

143 This was because Professor Dickinson's proposal referred to the law of the place of residence or business, not domicile. For the discussion on the *lex situs*, see [141]–[158] of the judgment. See also Collins and others, *Dicey, Morris & Collins on the Conflict of Laws*, para 23-050, who assess that a habitual residence or place of business test would be preferable to a domicile test given the uncertainties around identifying domicile in difficult cases.

144 P. Torremans (ed), *Cheshire, North & Fawcett: Private International Law*, OUP, Oxford 2017, p. 1275.

145 P. Beaumont and P.E. McEleavy, *Anton's Private International Law*, 3rd ed., W. Green, Edinburgh 2011, para 21.66.

146 See also A. Held, 'Does Situs Actually Matter When Ownership to Bitcoin is in Dispute?' (2021) 4 JIBFL 269.

147 LCEW, Smart legal contracts: Advice to Government (2021) https://s3-eu-west-2.amazonaws.com/lawcom-prod-storage-11jsxou24uy7q/uploads/2021/11/Smart-legal-contracts-accessible.pdf, para 7.145.

148 See B. Yüksel Ripley and F. Heindler, 'The Law Applicable to Crypto Assets: What Policy Choices are Ahead of Us?' in A. Bonomi, M. Lehmann and S. Lalani (eds), *Blockchain and Private International Law*, Brill, Leiden 2023, p. 270.

intangible movables and which is materially in similar terms to Rule 143 in Dicey, Morris & Collins at common law,[149] is argued to be of limited relevance to cryptocurrency transactions as they frequently do not involve a claim in the sense of a legally enforceable right arising under the law applicable to the relationship between participants in the system.[150] Therefore, it has been suggested that the proprietary effect of a cryptocurrency transfer can be governed by the law of the participant's residence[151] and, if the dispute arises solely between the parties to the transaction, the effects (contractual and proprietary) as between the parties to the transaction could plausibly be governed by its applicable law.[152]

Cryptocurrencies may give rise to other questions as to how they fit in the existing rules of private law in different fields. For example, in succession, a question might arise whether cryptocurrencies in a legacy should be paid in the same cryptocurrency or converted to and paid in sterling. In the past, the answer regarding legacy in a foreign currency seemed to have depended on whether the legatee resides abroad (in which case no conversion is necessary) or in the UK (in which case there will be a conversion unless the will indicates otherwise).[153] Based on the modern authorities on foreign currency obligations, it is now argued that the legacy should be paid in the foreign currency even where the legatee resides in the UK.[154] Given that the UK currently does not regard cryptocurrencies as money or legal tender, it is not clear whether or to what extent this argument would apply to cryptocurrencies.

For trusts over cryptocurrencies, the weight to be given to the situs is a matter to consider in determining the law with which the trust is most closely

149 See Collins and others, *Dicey, Morris & Collins on the Conflict of Laws*, para 25R-057.

150 Dickinson, 'Cryptocurrencies and the Conflict of Laws', paras 5.101 and 5.106; Collins and others, *Dicey, Morris & Collins on the Conflict of Laws*, para 25-080.

151 See Dickinson, 'Cryptocurrencies and the Conflict of Laws', para 5.109. There is some recognition for this by the English courts as noted above.

152 See ibid. However, legal issues concerning effects within a cryptocurrency system of the transactions whose subject matter is or includes cryptocurrencies are argued to be governed by the consensus rules of the given system and any rules of law applicable to the relationships between system participants. For this argument and the underlying analysis, see Dickinson, 'Cryptocurrencies and the Conflict of Laws', paras 5-15-5.72; Collins and others, *Dicey, Morris & Collins on the Conflict of Laws*, para 25-080; B. Yüksel Ripley, 'Cryptocurrency Transfers in Distributed Ledger Technology-Based Systems and their Characterisation in Conflict of Laws' in J. Borg-Barthet, K. Trimmings, B. Yüksel Ripley and P. Živković (eds), *From Theory to Practice in Private International Law: Gedächtnisschrift for Professor Jonathan Fitchen*, Hart Publishing, Oxford 2024, pp. 118-119.

153 Collins and others, *Dicey, Morris & Collins on the Conflict of Laws*, para 28–071.

154 ibid.

connected under the 1985 Hague Convention on the Law Applicable to Trusts and on their Recognition whose provisions were given effect in the UK by the Recognition of Trusts Act 1987 not only in relation to the trusts described in Articles 2 and 3 of the Convention but also in relation to any other trusts of property arising under the law of any part of the UK or by virtue of a judicial decision whether in the UK or elsewhere.[155]

Concerning insolvency, a question might arise if cryptocurrencies fall into the scope of the definition of 'establishment' in the 2006 Cross-Border Insolvency Regulations[156] which implemented the 1997 UNCITRAL Model Law on Cross-Border Insolvency for Great Britain (i.e., England and Wales, and Scotland) with certain modifications, including the extension of this definition to cover intangible assets by the replacement of the Model Law term 'goods' with 'assets' in Schedule 1, Article 2(e).[157] This is important to determine for the foreign non-main proceedings as they are taking place in a State where the debtor has an establishment based on that definition.[158]

Further contractual and non-contractual questions can arise concerning cryptocurrencies under Rome I and Rome II. One example concerns the type of a contract for lending cryptocurrencies and potential impact of mandatory rules or public policy under Rome I if such contract is illegal under the law of the borrower's country. Another example relates to non-contractual liability arising from hacked crypto accounts under Rome II. In *Fetch.AI*, the English court considered that in determining the law of the country in which the damage occurs under Article 4(1), the first and decisive question is where a cryptocurrency is to be regarded as being located and that this is in the place where its owner is domiciled (in this case England, resulting in the application of English law).[159]

---

155 Section 1(2) of the Act. It is assessed that the situs of intangible moveable property may be given little weight in this determination as it is fictional. See D. McClean and V. Ruiz Abou-Nigm, *Morris: The Conflict of Laws*, Sweet & Maxwell, London 2021, para 19-004; Collins and others, *Dicey, Morris & Collins on the Conflict of Laws*, para 29-022.

156 SI 2006/1030.

157 Beaumont and McEleavy, *Anton's Private International Law*, para 25.148.

158 See Schedule 1, Article 2(f) of the 2006 Regulations.

159 See further Part 6.1 below. For a criticism of the judgment for adopting an approach localising loss based on the owner's domicile, see A. Held and M. Lehmann, 'Hacked crypto-accounts, the English tort of breach of confidence and localising financial loss under Rome II' (2021) 10 JIBFL 708. See also *LMN v Bitflyer Holdings Inc* [2022] EWHC 2954 (Comm), [20].

5 Tax Measures

There is currently no specific and dedicated legislation concerning the tax treatment of cryptocurrencies in the UK. The UK's tax authority, HMRC, has produced a 'Cryptoassets Manual' regarding the treatment of cryptocurrencies and other cryptoassets for tax purposes.[160] As noted by HMRC, when individuals dispose of cryptoassets, they will be liable to pay Capital Gains Tax.[161] If an individual receives cryptoassets from their employer, or via 'mining, transaction confirmation or airdrops', they will be liable to pay Income Tax and National Insurance contributions.[162] Cryptocurrencies in this context will count as benefits in 'money's worth' and therefore as a form of earnings.[163] In addition, cryptoassets will be considered property for the purposes of Inheritance Tax.[164] There is a possibility too that cryptoassets could create liability for Stamp Duty and Stamp Duty Reserve Tax; however, HMRC does not consider that existing exchange tokens would be likely to meet the requirements for falling within this regime.[165]

If a company or other type of business is carrying out activities involving exchange tokens, they are liable to pay tax. As noted by HMRC, the relevant activities include: buying and selling exchange tokens; exchanging tokens for other assets (including other types of cryptoassets); 'mining'; and providing

---

160 HMRC, *Cryptoassets Manual* (2021) https://www.gov.uk/hmrc-internal-manuals/cryptoassets-manual.

161 HMRC, *Cryptoassets Manual* (2021), CRYPTO20050 – Cryptoassets for individuals: which taxes apply https://www.gov.uk/hmrc-internal-manuals/cryptoassets-manual/crypto20050.

162 ibid. If airdrops are received "without doing anything in return (for example, not related to any service or other conditions)" or "not as part of a trade or business involving cryptoasset exchange tokens or mining", Income Tax may not apply to them. See HMRC, CRYPTO21250 - Cryptoassets for individuals: Income Tax: airdrops https://www.gov.uk/hmrc-internal-manuals/cryptoassets-manual/crypto21250.

163 See Income Tax (Earnings and Pensions) Act 2003, for the meaning of earnings. HMRC also view exchange tokens like Bitcoin as 'Readily Convertible Assets' – see HMRC, *Cryptoassets Manual* (2021), CRYPTO21100 – Cryptoassets for individuals: Income Tax: earnings from employment – readily convertible assets https://www.gov.uk/hmrc-internal-manuals/cryptoassets-manual/crypto21100; and 2003 Act, section 702.

164 HMRC, *Cryptoassets Manual* (2021), CRYPTO25000 – Cryptoassets for individuals: Inheritance Tax https://www.gov.uk/hmrc-internal-manuals/cryptoassets-manual/crypto25000. See Inheritance Tax Act 1984, ss 1-6 for definitions relating to the inheritance tax regime, including the meaning of 'estate' (section 5).

165 HMRC, *Cryptoassets Manual* (2021), CRYPTO24000 – Cryptoassets for individuals: Stamp Duty, Stamp Duty Reserve Tax and Stamp Duty Land Tax https://www.gov.uk/hmrc-internal-manuals/cryptoassets-manual/crypto24000.

goods or services in return for exchange tokens.[166] If a business has engaged in these activities, they will likely be liable to pay one or more forms of tax (dependent in part on the type of business involved), namely Capital Gains Tax, Corporation Tax, Corporation Tax on Chargeable Gains, Income Tax, National Insurance Contributions, Stamp Taxes and VAT.[167] For example, '[a] ll forms of property' are considered assets for the purposes of Capital Gains Tax and Chargeable Gains, and this expressly includes 'incorporeal property generally'.[168]

In terms of VAT, HMRC provides that it is "due in the normal way on any goods or services sold in exchange for cryptoasset exchange tokens" and the due value will be "the pound sterling value of the exchange tokens at the point the transaction takes place."[169] Services supplied by exchanges (exchanging exchange tokens for legal tender/or other exchange tokens and vice versa), are exempt from VAT, which is also in line with the CJEU's decision in C-264/14 *Skatteverket v David Hedqvist*.[170]

6 Cryptocurrency Litigation

6.1 *Court Proceedings*

Several cases have come before the English courts, which have predominantly concerned interim *ex parte* applications for permission to serve proceedings out of the jurisdiction and interim relief. As such, they are neither binding nor persuasive authority on the substantive private law. Nevertheless, they give interesting insights into commercial practice and the nature of disputes that are likely to arise.

166 HMRC, *Cryptoassets Manual* (2021), CRYPTO40050 – Cryptoassets for businesses: which taxes apply https://www.gov.uk/hmrc-internal-manuals/cryptoassets-manual/crypto40050.

167 ibid.

168 Taxation of Chargeable Gains Act 1992, section 21(1); HMRC, *Capital Gains Manual* (2016; updated2022),Chargeableassets:intangibleassets:rightshttps://www.gov.uk/hmrc-internal-manuals/capital-gains-manual/cg12010. And see also the 1992 Act, section 8, regarding the company's total profits for Corporation Tax purposes including 'chargeable gains'.

169 HMRC, *Cryptoassets Manual* (2021), CRYPTO45000 - Cryptoassets for businesses: Value Added Tax (VAT) https://www.gov.uk/hmrc-internal-manuals/cryptoassets-manual/crypto45000.

170 Judgment of the Court (Fifth Chamber) of 22 October 2015.

6.1.1 *Wright v BTC Core (Rev1)* [2023] EWCA Civ 868 and [2023] EWHC 222 (Ch)

The First Claimant, Dr Craig Wright, claimed, as alleged creator of the bitcoin system and author of the Bitcoin Whitepaper, to be the owner of certain database rights subsisting in three blockchain databases. He also claimed the Claimants own the copyright which subsist in the White Paper and related software.

Dr Wright brought the claim in objection to two airdrops, each of which allegedly effected 'significant' changes to the bitcoin system by creating forks in the blockchain. The result was that from block 478,558 created on 1 August 2017, the original Bitcoin blockchain and a new 'BTC' blockchain ran in parallel; and from 15 November 2018, a new parallel 'BCH' blockchain was created.

Dr Wright's case was that the Claimants' database rights and copyrights entitle them to prevent the further operation of the BTC Blockchain and the BCH Blockchain without their consent.

In the Claimants' application to serve proceedings out of the jurisdiction, the High Court held that the claims in database right and of infringement of copyright in the White Paper raise serious issues to be tried; and, the other relevant requirements being met, service out of the jurisdiction should be permitted.

Permission was refused in relation to the software on the basis that, because it was not 'recorded, in writing or otherwise' in accordance with section 3(2) of the Copyright, Designs and Patents Act 1988 (known in international IP law as 'fixation'), the Claimant had no realistic prospect of establishing a copyright subsisted in it. This decision was reversed by the Court of Appeal on the basis that the fixation requirement could be met.

The question of Dr Wright's identity will likely be tried as a separate preliminary issue in *Crypto Open Patent Alliance v Wright* [2021] EWHC 3440 (Ch) (see below).

6.1.2 *Tulip Trading Limited v Bitcoin Association for BSV* [2023] EWCA Civ 83 and [2022] EWHC 667 (Ch)

The Claimant alleged it had been deprived of access to some US$4.5 billion worth of Bitcoin that it owned, following a hack that had compromised the corresponding private keys. The Claimant further alleged that the Defendants, who were open-source software developers who maintain the bitcoin source code on a non-commercial basis, owe fiduciary and tortious duties to the Claimant to re-write or amend the underlying software code to enable it to regain access to the Bitcoin.

As the Defendants had refused to do so, the Claimants sought and obtained permission to serve the Defendants out of the jurisdiction on the basis of claims in tort[171] and claims relating principally to property.[172]

On the Defendants' challenge to the jurisdiction, the High Court set aside permission to serve out on the basis that the Claimant had no realistic prospect of establishing the facts pleaded amounted to a breach of fiduciary duty. The Court of Appeal reversed the decision, holding that the appropriate time to determine the existence of these duties in the circumstances pleaded would be after the facts are established at trial.

Related cases include two interim applications for security for costs made by various Defendants in respect of the Claimant's application to serve proceedings out of the jurisdiction in [2022] EWHC 2 (Ch), followed by consequential matters in [2022] EWHC 141. In the latter case, it was held that Bitcoin is unsuitable as a form of security, owing to its high level of volatility.

6.1.3 *Piroozzadeh v Persons Unknown Category A & Ors* [2023] EWHC 1024 (Ch)

The Claimant had fallen victim to a fraud whereby he was induced to transfer, *inter alia*, some 879,818 Tether to four separate cryptocurrency wallets held by the Third Defendant. These were transferred on and ultimately traced to five wallets held at the 8th and 9th Defendant cryptocurrency exchanges.

The Claimant obtained *ex parte* interim orders requiring the 8th and 9th Defendants to preserve the Claimant's Tether or its traceable proceeds, together with ancillary orders and for service out of the jurisdiction. The Claimant further made claims against the 8th and 9th Defendants as constructive trustees of the Tether based on receipt of property obtained by wrongdoing.

On the 8th Defendant's application, the proprietary injunction was discharged on the basis that the Claimant had failed in its duty of fair presentation by, *inter alia,* failing to draw attention to the equitable defence of *bona fide* purchaser for value of a legal title without notice of an equitable interest. Such defence would extinguish any equitable interest of the Claimant under the alleged constructive trust.

Of particular note is the uncontested evidence of the 8th Defendant as to its operational model: its users do not retain any property in the Tether deposited in their accounts but are credited with the amount of the deposit

171 CPR PD6B para 3.1(9).

172 CPR PD6B para 3.1(11).

and permitted to draw against any credit balance as in a conventional banking arrangement. Such deposits are then swept into a central unsegregated pool address where they are treated as part of the 8th Defendant's general assets. As such, the Judge considered that the injunction would serve no useful purpose in the absence of any explanation as to how it would be practicable for the 8th Defendant to preserve the Claimant's deposited Tether.

6.1.4 *D'Aloia v Person Unknown & Ors* [2022] EWHC 1723 (Ch)

The Claimant alleged he was the victim of a fraudulent misappropriation of approximately 2.1 million USDT, and 230,000 USDC by the 1st Defendant Persons Unknown using a website representing that it was connected with a legitimate US-regulated business. The Claimant, having traced the assets to various addresses operated by the 2nd – 7th Defendant Exchanges, made an application for interim injunctive relief, disclosure, and ancillary orders.

The Judge found there were serious issues to be tried relating to the claims against the 1st Defendant in fraudulent misrepresentation and deceit, unlawful means conspiracy, unjust enrichment, and constructive trust. Permission for alternative service by NFT on the 1st Defendant was further granted.

6.1.5 *Danisz v Persons Unknown and Huobi Global Ltd (t/a Huobi)* [2022] EWHC 280 (QB)

The Claimant was induced by a website known as 'Matic Markets Ltd' to invest sums totalling approximately £27,000 to acquire certain Bitcoin. When she sought to withdraw the Bitcoin and the profit she was led to believe had accrued, her request was refused. Upon investigations, it became apparent that the Matic operation was likely wholly fraudulent and run by organised criminals; not only engineered to misappropriate funds invested in it by investors, but also with the capacity to interfere with banking and other online transactions.

Accordingly, the Claimant sought an *ex parte* interim application for: an interim proprietary injunction against both Defendants; a worldwide freezing order against Persons Unknown; and a *Banker's Trust* disclosure order against the Second Defendant.

Permission was granted to serve proceedings out of the jurisdiction on the basis of a claim in tort committed or where damage was sustained in the jurisdiction.[173]

173 CPR PD6B para 3.1(9)(a).

6.1.6 *Wang v Darby* [2021] EWHC 3054 (Comm)

The dispute concerned two related contracts pursuant to which the Claimant and Defendant exchanged specified quantities of Tez and Bitcoin with one another, on terms as to reciprocal restoration of the same amounts of each currency upon an agreed period.

The parties were diametrically opposed on the key issues of legal characterisation of the transactions; and the proprietary consequences of the Claimant transferring Tez to the Defendant.

The Claimant applied to continue a worldwide freezing order and proprietary injunction granted *ex parte*; and the Defendant applied for strike-out/reverse summary judgment in respect of the 'proprietary claims' pleaded against him in the action.

6.1.7 *Ion Science Limited v Persons Unknown* (Unreported)

The Claimants alleged that they had been induced by one 'Ms Black,' purportedly a senior associate of a Swiss entity called 'Neo Capital', to invest in cryptocurrency products. Giving 'Ms Black' remote control over his laptop, the Second Claimant enabled commission payments of approximately 64.36 Bitcoin (GBP 577,002). It then allegedly transpired that 'Neo Capital' did not appear on the Swiss register of companies; had received a warning from the Swiss regulatory authorities for providing unauthorised financial services; and had no online presence, save for a website.

The Claimants brought proceedings in deceit, unlawful means conspiracy, and equitable claims in property; and issued an *ex parte* interim application for a proprietary injunction, a worldwide freezing order, and an ancillary disclosure order against Persons Unknown.

Permission to serve proceedings out of the jurisdiction was granted on the bases of claims in tort,[174] and constructive/resulting trusts relating to property in the jurisdiction.[175]

6.1.8 *Fetch.AI Limited v Persons Unknown* [2021] EWHC 2254 (Comm)

The First Claimant alleged a fraud in which Persons Unknown had obtained access to the First Claimant's trading accounts with the Binance exchange, and then traded the cryptocurrencies credited therein at a massive undervalue. The losses were alleged to be over US$2.6 million.

The Claimant sought: an interim proprietary injunction, worldwide freezing order and ancillary information disclosure against the Persons Unknown; an

174 CPR PD6B para 3.1(9).

175 CPR PD6B para 3.1(15).

interim disclosure order, either in *Bankers Trust* and/or pursuant to CPR 25.1(1)(g) and/or under *Norwich Pharmacal*, against Binance Markets Limited; and an interim order using the *Bankers Trust* jurisdiction and/or CPR rule 25.1(1)(g) against Binance Holdings Limited. The intended causes of action were breach of confidence, unjust enrichment, and constructive trust.

Permission to serve out of the jurisdiction was granted on the bases of claims for breach of confidence;[176] relating to property within the jurisdiction;[177] restitution;[178] and constructive/resulting trusts relating to assets within the jurisdiction.[179]

English law was held to apply under the Rome II Regulation as: the place where the damage occurs in a claim made in tort/delict within the meaning of Article 4(1); an equitable proprietary claim within the meaning of Articles 3, 10, and possibly 11; and a claim in restitution/unjust enrichment within the meaning of Article 10.

6.1.9 *Lubin Betancourt Reyes v Persons Unknown* [2021] EWHC 1938 (Comm)

The Claimant attempted to make a payment of $105,458 in US Dollar Tethers to a contractual counterparty in the Philippines. To do so, the Claimant had to enter the destination wallet for the payment into his account with the Binance exchange.

The Claimant alleged that he entered the destination wallet by its relevant address, but before clicking on the 'send' button to complete the payment, a malware program on his computer near-instantaneously substituted a near-exact replica of the Binance platform page with a different public address in the destination box.

Thus, when the Claimant clicked 'send', the payment went, not to the Claimant's counterparty, but to a wallet operated by the First Defendant Person Unknown, a phishing fraudster. The evidence suggested that the proceeds were not merely the sum the Claimant wished to send to his counterparty but, in effect, the whole of his account.

Some Tethers transferred to the First Defendant's wallet were sent to a wallet of the Second Defendant Person Unknown and the remainder to a wallet of the Third Defendant Persons Unknown.

---

176 CPR PD6B para 3.1(21).
177 CPR PD6B para 3.1(11).
178 CPR PD6B para 3.1(16).
179 CPR PD6B para 3.1(15).

Accordingly, the Claimant issued an interim application *ex parte* for a worldwide freezing order coupled with ancillary disclosure; a proprietary injunction on the basis of knowing receipt of the proceeds of fraud; a disclosure order under either the *Bankers Trust* jurisdiction and/or the *Norwich Pharmacal* jurisdiction; and applications for permission to serve out of the jurisdiction and to serve by an alternative means.

Permission to serve out of the jurisdiction was refused as against: the First Defendant on the basis of a claim in conversion because Tether is not susceptible to possession, but were granted in respect of the claims in tort[180] and constructive trust.[181] Permission was granted against Binance as a necessary or proper party to the claim.[182]

6.1.10 *AA v Persons Unknown and Ors* [2019] EWHC 3556 (Comm)

A hacker had infiltrated the firewall of a Canadian insurance company and installed malware, which bypassed the system's anti-virus software and then encrypted all of the company's computer systems. The company then received notes from the First Defendant Person Unknown, demanding a ransom for decryption.

The Applicant was the company's insurer and agreed to pay the ransom of 109.25 Bitcoin (USD 950,000). The Applicant then tracked the Bitcoin it paid, 96 of which were tracked to a public address linked to the Bitfinex exchange.

The Claim Form raised proprietary claims in restitution and/or constructive trust, or for the tort of intimidation and/or fraud and/or conversion. The Applicant then issued an interim application for: a *Bankers Trust* order and/or a *Norwich Pharmacal* order requiring the Bitfinex exchange to provide specified information in relation to a cryptocurrency account owned or controlled by the Second Defendant Person Unknown who own/control specified Bitcoin; a proprietary injunction in respect of the Bitcoin held at the relevant Bitfinex account; a freezing injunction in respect of Bitcoin held at the specified Bitfinex account; and consequential orders, including alternative service and service out of the jurisdiction.

Permission to serve out of the jurisdiction was granted for the claims in tort[183] and for an interim remedy under section 25(1) of the Civil Jurisdiction and Judgments Act.[184]

---

180 CPR PD6B para 3.1(9).
181 CPR PD6B para 3.1(15).
182 CPR PD6B para 3.1(3).
183 CPR PD6B para 3.1(9).
184 CPR PD6B para 3.1(5).

6.1.11 *Crypto Open Patent Alliance v Wright* [2021] EWHC 3440 (Ch); [2023] EWHC 1894 (ChD)

This was a claim for declaratory relief that the Defendant is not Satoshi Nakamoto/the author of the Bitcoin Whitepaper, nor the owner of the copyright in the Whitepaper, and any use by the Claimant of the Whitepaper will not infringe any copyright owned by the Defendant.

This issue of identity is common to three further cases pending in the English courts: the two actions in *Wright v Coinbase & Kraken* [2023] EWHC 1893 (Ch); and *Wright v BTC Core (Rev1)* [2023] EWCA Civ 868 and [2023] EWHC 222 (Ch).

Following the most recent case management decision for all four cases in *Crypto Open Patent Alliance v Wright (Rev1)* [2023] EWHC 1894 (Ch), it is likely that the issue will be tried as a hybrid preliminary issue in the *Crypto Open Patent Alliance* case, to which parties in the other three cases will ultimately be effectively bound.

6.2 *Arbitration*

The authors are not aware of any arbitration proceedings concerning cryptocurrencies in England and Wales.

The UK Jurisdiction Taskforce published the Digital Dispute Resolution Rules in 2021 'to be used for and incorporated into on-chain digital relationships and smart contracts'.[185] They are considered ground-breaking in allowing for arbitral decisions to be implemented directly on-chain using a private key[186] and the optional anonymity of the parties.[187] A model dispute resolution clause[188] and governing law provisions are included.[189]

6.3 *Recognition and Enforcement of Foreign Court Judgments and Arbitral Awards*

The recognition and enforcement in the UK of foreign judgments or arbitral awards given in relation to crypto disputes is subject to the existing recognition and enforcement regimes in place, some of which are considered below.

---

185 UK Jurisdiction Taskforce, Digital Dispute Resolution Rules, Version 1.0, 2021, https://technationio.wpenginepowered.com/wp-content/uploads/2021/04/Lawtech_DDRR_Final.pdf.

186 Rule 12.

187 Rule 13.

188 Rule 3.

189 Rule 16.

6.3.1 Foreign Court Judgments

The UK is a party to the 2005 Hague Convention on Choice of Court Agreements.[190] Whether the Convention applies to the forum selection clauses embedded in a blockchain protocol or smart contract is one of the questions raised by the Permanent Bureau of the Hague Conference on Private International Law.[191]

The recognition and enforcement in the UK of judgments given in relation to crypto disputes by a court in an EU Member State or in Switzerland, Norway and Iceland in cases commenced but not concluded before the end of the Brexit transition period would be subject to the provisions of the Brussels-Lugano regime.[192]

The Administration of Justice Act 1920 (Part II) and the Foreign Judgments (Reciprocal Enforcement) Act 1933 provide for the enforcement in the UK of certain judgments from certain countries. A foreign judgment under which a sum of money is payable may be enforceable in the UK by registration under these Acts. In relation to foreign judgments awarded in cryptocurrencies (which may or may not be from a country that recognises and/or adopts cryptocurrencies as money or legal tender), a question may arise whether such judgments would be considered as judgments for the payment of a sum of money under these Acts.[193]

Both Acts set out certain grounds on which no judgment may be registered[194] or the registration must or may be set aside respectively.[195] One of these grounds is that the original court had no jurisdiction in the circumstance

---

190 The Convention was given effect in domestic law by the Private International Law (Implementation Agreements) Act 2020 which amended the Civil Jurisdiction and Judgments (Hague Convention on Choice of Court Agreements 2005) (EU Exit) Regulations 2018 (SI 2018/1124).

191 See the 'Proposal for the Allocation of Resources to Follow Private International Law Implications relating to Developments in the Field of Distributed Ledger Technology, in particular in relation to Financial Technology', (Prel. Doc. 28.02.2020) https://assets.hcch.net/docs/f787749d-9512-4a9e-ad4a-cbc585bddd2e.pdf, para 15. This needs to be interpreted uniformly, by considering the Convention's international character as per Article 26, among the Contracting States.

192 See the Withdrawal Agreement and the Civil Jurisdiction and Judgments (Amendment) (EU Exit) Regulations 2019 as amended by the Jurisdiction, Judgments and Applicable Law (Amendment) (EU Exit) Regulations (SI 2020/1574).

193 See section 12(1) of the Administration of Justice Act 1920 and section 1(2) of the Foreign Judgments (Reciprocal Enforcement) Act 1933. On whether the remedial powers available to English courts include the power to give a judgment in a cryptocurrency, see Dickinson, 'Cryptocurrencies and the Conflict of Laws', paras 5.89–5.92.

194 See section 9(2) of the Administration of Justice Act 1920.

195 See section 4(1)(a) the Foreign Judgments (Reciprocal Enforcement) Act 1933.

of the case. The application of the grounds of competence (e.g., section 4(2)(b) of the Act 1933) for enforcement of judgments relating to cryptocurrencies can raise the determination of the situs of cryptocurrencies in a given case. If the original court, based on that determination, is found to have had no jurisdiction, the judgment will not be registered or registration shall be set aside in the UK.

Another ground on which no judgment may be registered or the registration must be set aside under the Acts is public policy. Given the exceptional nature of public policy and generally no review of merits at the recognition and enforcement stage, it would likely be rare, particularly in commercial contexts, for a public policy plea to be successful regarding recognition and enforcement in the UK of foreign judgments relating to crypto disputes. It is argued that the status of cryptocurrencies as property would grant them a degree of recognition and protection under international law, most notably under the European Convention on Human Rights.[196] Depending on the circumstances of the case, a foreign judgment infringing this protection under international law may cause the judgment not to be registered or registration may be set aside in the UK on the ground of public policy.[197]

If the recognition and enforcement of a foreign judgment does not fall within the scope of a bilateral or multilateral regime to which the UK is a party or of the 1920 or 1933 Acts, the judgment may be recognised or enforced at common law.[198]

In England and Wales, it is a general principle that a foreign court judgment will not be recognised or enforced unless the foreign court is regarded as one

196 C. Proctor, 'Cryptocurrencies in International and Public Law Conceptions of Money' in D. Fox and S. Green (eds), *Cryptocurrencies in Public and Private Law*, OUP, Oxford 2019, paras 3.21 and 3.59.

197 In a broader context, refusal of the recognition or enforcement of a foreign judgment which is contrary to the European Convention on Human Rights (given the force of law in the UK by the Human Rights Act 1998) could be rather seen as a result that primary legislation produces. See Collins and others, *Dicey, Morris & Collins on the Conflict of Laws*, para 14-155.

198 For England and Wales, see generally Ministry of Justice, Cross-border civil and commercial legal cases: guidance for legal professionals, 2020 https://www.gov.uk/government/publications/cross-border-civil-and-commercial-legal-cases-guidance-for-legal-professionals/cross-border-civil-and-commercial-legal-cases-guidance-for-legal-professionals#jurisdiction-and-recognition-and-enforcement-of-judgments. However, a foreign judgment cannot be enforced in the UK under the 1920 or 1933 Acts or at common law if the enforcement would be contrary to section 5 of the Protection of Trading Interests Act 1980. See Collins and others, *Dicey, Morris & Collins on the Conflict of Laws*, para 14-220.

having international competence in the given case. For judgments *in rem*, the situation of the property, at the time of the proceedings, within the jurisdiction of the foreign court is recognised as a ground of competence.[199] If cryptocurrencies are regarded as property, this ground would raise the determination of the situs of cryptocurrencies in a given case and, based on where the situs is, the foreign court might be deemed to have or lack jurisdiction, affecting the enforcement of the judgment in the UK. For judgments *in personam*, jurisdiction is less problematic in this context. The foreign court is deemed to have jurisdiction if the person against whom the judgment was given was present in that country at the time of the commencement of the proceedings, or appeared as claimant or counterclaimant in the proceedings in the foreign court, or submitted to the jurisdiction of that court by voluntarily appearing in the proceedings, or had agreed to submit to the jurisdiction of that court or of the court of that country.[200] Additional requirements include that the judgment is final and conclusive on the merits;[201] and is unimpeachable[202] on the grounds of fraud,[203] public policy[204] or breach of natural justice.[205] There is no strong reason to think that recognition and enforcement of a foreign judgment will be refused on fraud, public policy, or breach of natural justice grounds just because the debt or sum of money owing relates to cryptoassets. This is particularly so, given that the UK continues to position itself as a 'pro-cryptoasset' country.

6.3.2 Foreign Arbitral Awards

The UK is a party to the 1927 Geneva Convention on the Execution of Foreign Arbitral Awards and the 1958 New York Convention on the Recognition and Enforcement of Foreign Arbitral Awards.

England and Wales prides itself on being an arbitration-friendly jurisdiction. Recognition and enforcement of arbitral awards in England and Wales (and Northern Ireland) is governed by the Arbitration Act 1996. Under section 66(1) of the Arbitration Act 1996, an arbitral award may, by leave of the court, be enforced in the same manner as a judgment or order of the court to the same effect. The only ground for refusing leave is where, pursuant to section

199 Collins and others, *Dicey, Morris & Collins on the Conflict of Laws*, Rule 50, paras 14R-108-14-114.
200 ibid., Rule 46(1); Rule 47, para 14R-024 onwards.
201 ibid., Rule 46(1)(b), para 14R-024 onwards.
202 ibid., Rule 46(1), para 14R-024 onwards.
203 ibid., Rule 46(1); Rule 53, para 14R-024 onwards.
204 ibid., Rule 46(1); Rule 54, para 14R-024 onwards.
205 ibid., Rule 46(1); Rule 55, para 14R-024 onwards.

66(3), the person against whom it is sought to be enforced shows that the tribunal lacked substantive jurisdiction to make the award.

Part III of the Act deals with the recognition and enforcement of (certain) foreign awards. A New York Convention award is recognised and enforced in England and Wales as per sections 100–104. It may be enforced by leave of the court in the same manner as a judgment or order of the court under section 101(2). As per section 103, there are limited grounds for refusal of recognition and enforcement. One of them is public policy. In *Payward Inc v Chechetkin*,[206] the Commercial Court refused to enforce a foreign arbitration award concerning a crypto dispute between a cryptocurrency trading platform and its customer on public policy grounds as the court found that Mr Chechetkin, a British citizen resident in England, was a consumer for the purposes of the Consumer Rights Act (CRA) 2015 and that both the CRA and the FSMA 2000 were expressions of English/UK public policy and therefore enforcement would be contrary to public policy.

206 [2023] EWHC 1780 (Comm).

United States of America

Frank Emmert

1 Introduction[1]

As new technologies emerge, they offer various opportunities for businesses, and solutions to real-world problems. In such cases, business developers, app developers, and investors need guidance from regulators. This guidance should not only provide a snapshot of what is currently allowed but also reliable information on what will be allowed in the foreseeable future. This is particularly important for technologies that require investment of significant time and money and have the potential to create revolutionary changes, which could potentially make existing solutions and business models redundant.

Blockchain or distributed ledger technology (DLT) is a prime example of a technology that promises to revolutionize everything we have been doing on the internet. While we have been able to perform financial transactions on our smartphones, such as checking our bank balances, making payments via PayPal or Venmo, and ordering stuff on Amazon and Doordash, these were evolutionary or incremental improvements to existing technologies and business models. They did not require new or special regulations for the most part. The risks associated with those innovations – occasional fraudulent activities by misrepresenting "vendors" and "buyers" – were largely absorbed within the existing systems of customer protection in the credit card market, with banks and other centralized institutions serving as trusted intermediaries.

The emerging applications of Blockchain and DLT will be very different. The technology is creating a trustless environment, which means that the financial system of the future can operate without the need for trusted intermediaries. In the brave new world of cryptocurrencies, there is no need for commercial banks to facilitate funds transfers, nor for central banks to issue currency and control interest and exchange rates. There also are currently no authorities with clearly defined supervisory powers, no guarantees by institutions or insurers, and not even clear, let alone comprehensive rules of the road enacted by legislators or courts.

---

1 An earlier version of this text was published in the American Journal of Comparative Law in 2023. That article, together with my other publications, is available free of charge on ResearchGate (https://www.researchgate.net/profile/Frank-Emmert). The present chapter reflects the evolution of the law up to December 2024. For comments or questions, please e-mail femmert@iu.edu.

 | DOI:10.1163/9789004722507_030

Despite this, in late 2024, the equivalent of US$ 3.7 Trillion[2] was held by millions of individuals in the form of more than 10,000 new digital currencies in more than 200 million cryptocurrency wallets, completely disconnected from traditional bank accounts and credit cards. Moreover, the daily transaction volume in crypto markets regularly exceeded US$ 300 Billion in late 2024.[3] This sum is even more astonishing given the fact that every one of those "virtual currencies"[4] is privately created and managed, and none of the user wallets are protected by the Federal Deposit Insurance Corporation (FDIC) or any equivalent mechanisms in other countries.[5] Further, other than holding value and transferring value from one wallet to another, there is presently still not very much that can be done with all the crypto money since there are not a lot of goods or services that can be bought with crypto. More importantly, there are hardly any reliable smart contract[6] applications available that deliver innovative and sophisticated business

2 By comparison, the entire U.S. GDP in 2024 was around US$ 27.9 Trillion, "only" about 7 times the value of the crypto market, while the market capitalization of Apple, whose iPhone alone has sold more than 1.5 Billion times, making it the most valuable company in the world, was also US$ 3.7 Trillion, about the same as the crypto market.

3 The numbers are from Coinbase, https://www.coinbase.com/explore.

4 "Virtual currencies" are "a digital representation of value that can be digitally traded and functions as: (1) a medium of exchange; and/or (2) a unit of account; and/or (3) a store of value, but does not have legal tender status (i.e., when tendered to a creditor, is a valid and legal offer of payment) in any jurisdiction. It is not issued or guaranteed by any jurisdiction and hence fulfils the above functions only by agreement within the community of users of the virtual currency. Virtual currency is distinguished from fiat currency (a.k.a. 'real currency,' 'real money,' or 'national currency'), which is the coin and paper money of a country that is designated as its legal tender; circulates and is customarily used and accepted as a medium of exchange in the issuing country. It is distinct from e-money, which is a digital representation of fiat currency used to electronically transfer value denominated in fiat currency." FATF Report, *Virtual Currencies, Key Definitions and Potential AML/CFT Risks*, Financial Action Task Force (June 2014), http://www.fatf-gafi.org/media/fatf/documents/reports/Virtual-currency-key-definitions-and-potential-aml-cft-risks.pdf.

5 In the U.S., the FDIC's deposit insurance automatically protects funds in traditional bank accounts at licensed banks up to US$ 250,000 per depositor. In case a bank fails, the government agency steps in, and compensates the bank customers.

6 A smart contract is a piece of software running on a Blockchain that automatically executes a function like a funds transfer when certain conditions are met. The fact that the smart contract is stored on a Blockchain makes it immutable. As an example, a buyer and a seller could agree on a sale of goods where the buyer locks the funds into a smart contract, and the program automatically releases the purchase price to the seller the moment a third party like a customs office or carrier confirms the shipment of the goods. If the goods are not shipped by a certain date, the contract can be programmed to automatically return the funds to the buyer. For more details, see Larry A. DiMatteo, Michel Cannarsa & Cristina Poncibò, *The Cambridge Handbook of Smart Contracts, Blockchain Technology and Digital Platforms*, Cambridge Univ. Press 2020.

solutions actually desired by the market.[7] Last but not least, the entire market is characterized by extreme volatility where a single coin – and to some extent the entire market cap – could jump up or down by 10% or more in a single day.[8]

DLT technology has yet to prove its potential in practice and is facing challenges in scaling up.[9] However, it is highly unlikely that Blockchain and DLT will turn out to be bubbles that will eventually burst and be forgotten. This is because a large number of companies from various industries have invested and are continuing to invest significant amounts of money in the development of smart contract applications running on Blockchain.

Since 2020, this sustained investment has averaged almost US$1 billion every single month, and it keeps going up.[10] As the technology celebrates its 15th birthday in 2024, we may safely say that the investors who continue to pour ever more money into the development of actual business models and solutions – "use cases" for cryptocurrencies – have a pretty good understanding of what the technology can and cannot achieve and what they are buying with all this money.[11]

What is far less clear, however, is the guidance provided by the regulators in different jurisdictions. The inventors of digital money were partly motivated by a rejection of traditional government control over money and money

---

7 Merely buying and selling goods and services is not enough to justify the creation of digital money. This can already be done using our existing structures, such as online banking, and credit- and debit cards. Unless distributed ledger technology (DLT) can offer significant advantages in terms of speed, cost, or safety, there is no reason to switch from fiat money to crypto. Ultimately, the usefulness of cryptocurrencies will arise from new applications that provide business solutions that are unattainable with fiat money and traditional financial services.

8 Bitcoin, the most widely known digital currency, was launched in January 2009, and started trading in July 2010 at US$ 0.0008. At its peak in November 2021, it reached more than US$ 68,000. By September 2023, it had dropped back to around US$ 28,000. Most recently, the valuation exceeded US$ 100,000 for the first time. An investor who put US$ 1,000 into Bitcoin in the early days and held onto it would be looking at a fortune of about US$ 125 Billion right now.

9 On the Ethereum Blockchain, for example, the wait times for the confirmation of a transaction have sometimes been in the range of tens of minutes, and the processing fees can go into tens of dollars during peak hours. Checking out in the supermarket with a crypto app on a smart phone will not happen if the confirmation of the transaction takes several minutes, while a credit card swipe is confirmed in just a few seconds *and* costs less in fees. To be fair, Ethereum switched from Proof-of-Work (PoW) to Proof-of-Stake (PoS) on 15 September 2022, reducing the computing effort needed to confirm transactions on the chain and, thereby, the energy consumption, wait times, and fees.

10 https://www.statista.com/statistics/800426/worldwide-blockchain-solutions-spending/.

11 For examples of potential use cases see Sam Daley, *Blockchain Applications and Real-World Use Cases Disrupting the Status Quo* (16 December 2021), available at https://builtin.com/blockchain/blockchain-applications.

supply.[12] When Satoshi Nakamoto published his famous white paper in 2009,[13] the world was trying to climb out of the 2007/08 Financial Crisis, and the U.S. Federal government had just bailed out the financial sector with over US$ 1 Trillion in funds that were essentially newly printed money, diluting the existing money supply and, therefore, the value of assets and savings in the hands of corporations and private citizens.[14]

Traditional fiat currencies are controlled by central banks who are overseen, whether they are nominally independent or not, by governments and legislators and subject to political pressures and exigencies. Cryptocurrencies, by contrast, are either controlled by pre-determined mathematical algorithms (for example, the cap on the total supply of Bitcoin, or by consensus mechanisms potentially involving all those who use and own the currency (miners, app developers, exchanges, wallet providers, node operators, end users, etc.). The decentralization of control, wrestling the currency out of the hands of politicians seeking re-election, and giving it to stakeholders seeking preservation of value, is one of the key features of cryptocurrencies. Unsurprisingly, however, the political establishment and the established financial industry are not willing to give up control over currencies without a fight. In this regard, it did not help that a variety of less benevolent uses of cryptocurrencies were also introduced, such as entrepreneurs with impressive websites and not-so-impressive business models absconding with the money of retail investors, wealthy people avoiding income taxes by relying on the anonymity supposedly offered by cryptocurrencies,[15] as well as willing and unwilling parties making financial transfers to and from organized crime and terrorist organizations.[16]

---

12 A good introduction to the cypherpunk movement by some of its core members is Julian Assange, Jacob Applebaum, Andy Müller-Maguhn & Jérémie Zimmermann, *Cypherpunks: Freedom and the Future of the Internet*, OR Books 2016. See also Craig Jarvis, *Cypherpunk Ideology: Objectives, Profiles, and Influences (1992-1998)*, Internet Histories - Digital Technology, Culture and Society 2022, Vol. 6, No. 3, pp. 315-342, https://doi.org/10.1080/24701475.2021.1935547.

13 Satoshi Nakamoto, *Bitcoin: A Peer-to-Peer Electronic Cash System*, https://bitcoin.org/bitcoin.pdf.

14 Since 2009, things have gotten worse. To prevent a downturn in the economy as a consequence of the Covid19 pandemic, the U.S. Federal Government, including the U.S. Federal Reserve, has injected more than US$ 11 Trillion of newly printed or borrowed money into the U.S. economy. For details see Frank Emmert, *Chapter 52: United States of America*, in Marc Bungenberg (ed.), *International Subsidies*, NOMOS Verlag, Baden-Baden, in print.

15 For information how cryptocurrency transactions can be traced to the parties doing them see Andy Greenberg, *Tracers in the Dark – The Global Hunt for the Crime Lords of Cryptocurrency*, Vintage Books, New York 2022.

16 What is also clear, however, is the fact that illicit activity involving cryptocurrencies, such as money laundering, tax evasion, and the financing of crime, remains below the comparable illicit activity using traditional fiat currencies by an order of magnitude. The relative lower significance of cryptocurrencies in illicit global markets has been confirmed

This report will provide an overview of official responses, regulatory guidance, and legislative mandates created for DLT and cryptocurrencies at the U.S. Federal level and at the level of the individual states in the United States.

2 Federal Laws

The United States Constitution provides for a federal structure of government and grants to the Federal Government only the powers enumerated in the Constitution itself. Unsurprisingly, the 1787 Constitution does not mention cryptocurrencies. Nevertheless, the Federal Government would have the power to regulate cryptocurrencies based on the interstate commerce clause.[17] So far, it has not done so, and it is unlikely that specific legislation will be developed at the Federal level in the foreseeable future. This does not mean that there are no Federal laws of concern to developers, traders, and users of cryptocurrencies.

2.1 *Banking and Financial Services Regulation*

Federal laws regulating banking and other money services businesses, as well as protecting consumers of financial services, can impact businesses dealing in cryptocurrencies.

A highly important law in this area is the *Dodd-Frank Wall Street Reform and Consumer Protection Act* of 2010 (Dodd-Frank),[18] enacted in response to the financial crisis of 2007/08. Although controversial, complex, not exactly a

---

by FinCEN and many others. They have corroborated time and again that illicit transactions in fiat currencies have to be counted in Trillions, whereas illicit transactions in cryptocurrencies are still counted "only" in Billions. At least for now, even the biggest crooks would rather entrust their hard-stolen money to the safe havens of the U.S. dollar. Gilmour and Hicks conclude that "[f]or many criminals, the new technologies are needlessly risky when compared to tried and trusted transfers by banks." See Nicholas Gilmour & Tristram Hicks, *The War on Dirty Money*, Policy Press 2023, at p. 86. For data see, inter alia, Jim Richards, *Crypto vs Fiat: Is One or the Other More of a Haven for Illicit Finance?*, RegTech Consulting LLC 12 Nov. 2021, https://regtechconsulting.net/crypto-blockchain/crypto-vs-fiat-is-one-or-the-other-more-of-a-haven-for-illicit-financing/. See also Europol Spotlight, *Cryptocurrencies: Tracing the Evolution of Criminal Finances*, Luxembourg 2021, https://www.europol.europa.eu/cms/sites/default/files/documents/Europol%20Spotlight%20-%20Cryptocurrencies%20-%20Tracing%20the%20evolution%20of%20criminal%20finances.pdf.

17 U.S. Constitution, Article 1, Section 8, Clause 3. For detailed analysis see Erwin Chemerinsky, Constitutional Law, Wolters Kluwer, 6th ed. 2019, in particular Chapter 2.C., as well as William Eskridge & John Ferejohn, *The Elastic Commerce Clause: A Political Theory of American Federalism*, 47 Vand. L. Rev. 1355 (1994).

18 Public Law 111–203, 124 Stat. 1376.

model of high-quality legislative drafting, and with many provisions requiring administrative action to implement, it pursues three important objectives.

The first goal of Dodd-Frank is to reign in the riskiest activities of banks and financial service providers. The "Volcker Rule" prevents banks from proprietary speculative trading in securities, futures, options, and other derivatives.[19] Dodd-Frank charges the Securities and Exchange Commission with regulating derivative trading[20] as part of a broader push to better manage the risks emanating from the shadow banking system and the creation of ever more artificial money in the form of derivatives. This goal is pursued, inter alia, by a requirement that derivatives be cleared and traded on exchanges, effectively guaranteeing the performance of both sides via clearinghouses.[21] If a smart contract "incorporates software code to automate aspects of the derivative transaction and operates on a distributed ledger, such as a blockchain",[22] it is called a "smart derivatives contract" and subject to the provisions of Dodd-Frank. This explains why Coinbase, the largest U.S.-based crypto exchange, acquired the crypto futures exchange FairX in 2022, in order to be able to offer crypto derivatives in the U.S.[23]

Second, Dodd-Frank creates a system to oversee financial institutions of sufficient size, i.e. systemically important institutions whose failure can cause significant damage to the overall financial system, and to limit the damage caused

19 *Id* at § 619.

20 *Id* at Tit. VI, VII, I. Derivatives are financial contracts between two parties speculating on or hedging against future price movements of underlying assets like stocks, bonds, currencies, or commodities. Neither of the parties actually has to own the underlying asset. Derivatives come in the form of futures, options, forwards, and swaps. They can be traded "over-the-counter" as privately negotiated contracts in unregulated markets, or they can be traded on regulated platforms like the Chicago Mercantile Exchange (CME). The purpose is to make money from speculative trading. Since the contracts can be highly leveraged, they allow large positions with small amounts of capital and are seen as very risky. The leverage also triggers credit expansion and even multiplication, which has similar effects to an expansion of the money supply by the Federal Reserve. See, inter alia, Erik F. Gerding, *Credit Derivatives, Leverage, and Financial Regulation's Missing Macroeconomic Dimension*, 8 Berkeley Bus. L.J. 29 (2011), available at https://scholar.law.colorado.edu/faculty-articles/165.

21 *Id* at Tit. VIII.

22 Perkins Coie LLP, *Derivatives & Repo Report* (December 21, 2020), https://www.derivativesandreporeport.com/2020/12/isda-continues-guidelines-for-smart-derivatives-contracts-series-with-credit-and-fx-guidelines/.

23 FairX was regulated by the Commodity Futures Trading Commission (CFTC) as a licensed Designated Contract Market. See Reuters, *Coinbase Buys Crypto Futures Exchanges, Plans to Sell Derivatives in U.S.* (13 January 2022), https://www.reuters.com/technology/coinbase-buys-crypto-futures-exchanges-plans-sell-derivatives-us-2022-01-13/.

by their potential failure. In essence, this part of Dodd-Frank is intended to keep banks and other financial service providers from overly risky business conduct and from becoming too big to fail.[24] This section is increasingly relevant for the distributed ledger technology or DLT financial service industry since some providers are already meeting the thresholds or could be deemed systemically important companies and so subject to this oversight.

Dodd-Frank pursued its third central goal through the creation of the Consumer Financial Protection Bureau (CFPB). The CFPB is a powerful new Federal agency "that makes sure banks, lenders, and other financial companies treat [consumers] fairly."[25] The CFPB has the power to order "restitution, disgorgement, injunctive relief, and significant civil penalties for violations of the 19 federal statutes under its purview."[26] While some of these statutes do not easily apply to transactions involving DLT and cryptocurrencies, some do.

For example, the *Consumer Credit Protection Act*, and in particular its Subchapters I (*Truth in Lending Act TILA*), II (Restrictions on Garnishments), IV (*Equal Credit Opportunity Act*), V (*Fair Debt Collection Practices Act FDCPA*), and VI (*Electronic Funds Transfer Act EFTA*) are broadly construed and cover any natural or legal persons regularly extending credit to consumers "in connection with loans, sales of property or services, or otherwise", including credit card issuers.[27] These rules are not limited to conventional banks but are also applicable to any form of consumer credit provided by technology companies in the area of Decentralized Finance or DeFi, utilizing digital wallets and smart

24 There are several components of the Act in pursuit of this goal. The *Federal Reserve* now has to conduct annual stress tests for the largest banks and financial institutions (Title I). Title II provides rules and authorities for the *Securities Investor Corporation* (*SPIC*) for the orderly liquidation of troubled financial companies. The insurance industry is being supervised by the *Federal Insurance Office* (*FIO*) at the Treasury Department (Title V). Hedge Funds have to register with the SEC and provide information about their trades and portfolios (Title IV). Title I Section 112 of the Act on the authority of the *Financial Stability Oversight Council* (*FSOC*) includes the goal "to promote market discipline, by eliminating expectations on the part of shareholders, creditors, and counterparties of [large, interconnected bank holding companies or nonbank financial companies] that the Government will shield them from losses in the event of failure", the so-called moral hazard. For additional analysis *see*, e.g. Charles Goodhart, The Regulatory Response to the Financial Crisis (2009); Elisa Kao, *Moral Hazard During the Savings and Loan Crisis and the Financial Crisis of 2008-09: Implications for Reform and the Regulation of Systemic Risk through Disincentive Structures to Manage Firm Size and Interconnectedness*, 67 N.Y.U. Ann. Surv. Am. L. 817 (2011–2012); Karl S. Okamoto, *After the Bailout: Regulating Systemic Moral Hazard*, 57 UCLA L. Rev. 183 (2009–2010).

25 See https://www.consumerfinance.gov/.

26 *Seila Law LLC v. Consumer Fin. Prot. Bureau*, 140 S. Ct. 2183 (2020), at 2187.

27 15 U.S. Code § 1602(g).

contracts instead of banks, bank accounts, and wire transfers.[28] It does not matter whether or not the technology company or financial service provider has a bank charter or a securities license, although it is increasingly unlikely that a larger financial services company can operate without such.[29] Similarly, while protection by the Federal Deposit Insurance Corporation (FDIC) traditionally insures only bank deposits against losses up to US$ 250,000, there is no reason, in principle, why a DeFi corporation could not become a member of the FDIC and obtain deposit insurance.

Along the same lines, other Federal consumer protection laws" on matters such as data protection and privacy,[30] as well as deceptive advertising,[31] are fully applicable to financial service providers in the Blockchain space.

In addition to Dodd-Frank and consumer protection laws", financial services providers must comply with transparency rules regarding their customer base. The provision of "money transmission services" is among the ways "money services business" is defined by the Financial Crimes Enforcement Network (FinCEN), a bureau of the U.S. Department of the Treasury charged with combating money laundering, terrorism financing, and other major financial crimes.[32] Banks, money services businesses, casinos, brokers or dealers in securities, loan or finance companies, and a number of similar enterprises are subject to registration and reporting requirements, as well as the implementation of

28 *See, e.g.*, Campbell Harvey, Ashwin Ramachandran & Joey Santoro, DeFi and the Future of Finance (2021).

29 See, for example, Jack Malich, *My Unfair Lady: An Analysis of The CFPB's Authority to Prosecute Discriminatory Conduct Under Dodd-Frank's UDAAP Standard in the Age of the Major Questions Doctrine*, Columbia Business Law Review 2024, https://dx.doi.org/10.52214/cblr.v2023i2.12483. For international comparative analysis see Tsai-Jyh Chen, An International Comparison of Financial Consumer Protection (2018).

30 At the Federal level, "financial institutions", defined as "any institution the business of which is engaging in financial activities", are subject to the privacy rules of 15 U.S.C. §§6801-6827 and, in particular, the *Gramm-Leach-Bliley Act on Disclosure of Nonpublic Personal Information* (§§6801–6809).

31 At the Federal level, individuals and corporations are subject to the *Federal Trade Commission Act* (15 U.S.C. §§41–58). 15 U.S.C. §45 is the older Unfair or Deceptive Acts or Practices (UDAP) provision of Sec. 5 of the Federal Trade Commission Act, giving oversight powers to the FTC. However, since Dodd-Frank, there is also the Federal Unfair, Deceptive, or Abusive Acts or Practices (UDAAP) law (12 U.S.C. §§ 5531, 5536), giving oversight powers to the CFPB. The two acts have some similarities but also different scopes of application and different enforcement authorities.

32 See, e.g., FinCEN, *Application of FinCEN's Regulations to Certain Business Models Involving Convertible Virtual Currencies*, FIN-2019-G001 (May 9, 2019), https://www.fincen.gov/resources/statutes-regulations/guidance/application-fincens-regulations-certain-business-models.

Know Your Customer (KYC) and Anti-Money Laundering (AML) procedures.[33] Even those technology companies that do not provide money transmission services are considered "virtual asset service providers" by the Financial Action Task Force (FATF) and, therefore, "have the same full set of obligations as financial institutions and [certain] designated non-financial businesses and professions."[34] Based on the Bank Secrecy Act (BSA),[35] FinCEN has the power to issue injunctions and temporary restraining orders for ongoing violations and to sanction those violations with civil and criminal penalties, including imprisonment.

2.2 *Commodities Regulation*

Rules and regulations for the crypto industry have been produced for years by the Commodities Futures Trading Commission (CFTC). Originally created to supervise futures contracts for agricultural commodities, the mission of the CFTC is "to promote the integrity, resilience, and vibrancy of the U.S. derivatives markets through sound regulation."[36]

---

33 31 C.F.R. Ch. X, Parts 1000-1060. On 18 March 2013, FinCEN issued an "interpretive guidance to clarify the applicability of the regulations implementing the Bank Secrecy Act ('BSA') to persons creating, obtaining, distributing, exchanging, accepting, or transmitting virtual currencies. [...] A user is a person that obtains virtual currency to purchase goods or services. An exchanger is a person engaged as a business in the exchange of virtual currency for real currency, funds, or other virtual currency. An administrator is a person engaged as a business in issuing (putting into circulation) a virtual currency, and who has the authority to redeem (to withdraw from circulation) such virtual currency. [...] A user who obtains convertible virtual currency and uses it to purchase real or virtual goods or services is not an MSB under FinCEN's regulations. Such activity, in and of itself, does not fit within the definition of 'money transmission services' and therefore is not subject to FinCEN's registration, reporting, and recordkeeping regulations for MSBs. [...] An administrator or exchanger that (1) accepts and transmits a convertible virtual currency or (2) buys or sells convertible virtual currency for any reason is a money transmitter under FinCEN's regulations [...]." FinCEN, *Application of FinCEN's Regulations to Persons Administering, Exchanging, or Using Virtual Currencies*, https://www.fincen.gov/resources/statutes-regulations/guidance/application-fincens-regulations-persons-administering.

34 See Financial Action Task Force (FATF), Virtual Assets and Virtual Asset Service Providers – Updated Guidance for a Risk-Based Approach 4 (2021). See also the Joint Statement on Activities Involving Digital Assets issued by the Leaders of the Commodity Futures Trading Commission (CFTC), Financial Crimes Enforcement Network (FinCEN), and Securities and Exchange Commission (SEC) on 11 October 2019, https://www.bipc.com/assets/PDFs/U.S.%20Joint%20Statement%20on%20Activities%20Involving%20Digital%20Assets.pdf.

35 12 U.S.C. § 21.

36 https://www.cftc.gov/About/AboutTheCommission.

With few exceptions, the *Commodity Exchange Act* makes it unlawful to enter into or execute a transaction "for the purchase or sale of a commodity for future delivery" unless the transaction is conducted on a registered exchange and "evidenced by a record in writing which shows the date, the parties to such contract and their addresses, the property covered and its price, and the terms of delivery."[37] The supervisory powers of the CFTC extend even to foreign boards of trade if they provide access to traders located in the U.S.[38]

In order to assert its authority to regulate cryptocurrencies, the CFTC announced that "virtual currencies, such as Bitcoin, have been determined to be commodities under the Commodity Exchange Act."[39] A Federal Court upheld this view in *CFTC v. McDonnell and CabbageTech, Corp. d/b/a Coin Drop Market*.[40] As a result, cryptocurrency businesses may need licenses or registration as Derivatives Clearing Organization (DCO), Designated Contract Market (DCM), Swap Execution Facility (SEF), Swap Data Repository (SDR), Commodity Pool Operator (CPO), Commodity Trading Advisor (CTA), Futures Commission Merchant (FCM), Introducing Broker (IB), Swap Dealer (SD), and/or Foreign Boards of Trade.

The application of the *Commodity Exchange Act* to cryptocurrencies means that any person found in violation of the Act is subject to civil liability for actual damages and/or enforcement of the respective contract (specific performance) pursuant to 7 U.S. Code § 25 – Private Rights of Action. If a registered entity is violating the provisions of the Act, it can be suspended from trading.[41] Furthermore, the CFTC can impose monetary penalties of up to US$1 Million or "triple the monetary gain to the person for each such violation," whichever is greater, as well as "restitution to customers of damages proximately caused by violations of the person."[42]

37 7 U.S.C. § 6.

38 7 U.S.C. § 2(a)(1)(E).

39 https://www.cftc.gov/sites/default/files/2019-12/oceo_bitcoinbasics0218.pdf. Commodities are normally "defined broadly to include not only 'physical commodities,' such as cotton or gold, but also currencies or interest rates. The definition also includes 'all services, rights, and interests ... in which contracts for future delivery are presently or in the future dealt in.' 7 U.S.C. §1(a)(9). As a general matter, the CFTC has oversight over futures, options, and derivatives contracts. [It] also has jurisdiction where there is fraud or manipulation involving commodities trade in interstate commerce". See Daniel Stabile, Kimberly Prior & Andrew Hinkes, Digital Assets and Blockchain Technology – US Law and Regulation (2020), at p. 68.

40 287 F.Supp.3d 213 (E.D.N.Y. 2018).

41 7 U.S.C. § 7b.

42 7 U.S.C. § 9(10).

2.3 *Securities Regulation*

The Securities and Exchange Commission (SEC) was created by the *Securities Exchange Act* of 1934 (Exchange Act)[43] and is charged with administering that statute, the *Securities Act* of 1933 (Securities Act),[44] and certain other investor protection laws. The SEC can adopt rules having the force of Federal law. The *Securities Act* requires companies to register securities[45] in order to provide thorough and accurate financial information before they can offer or sell such securities to the public. The *Exchange Act* covers a wide variety of topics, including, for example, making it "unlawful for any person to effect transactions in security futures products that are not listed on a national securities exchange or a national securities association registered pursuant to [the Exchange Act]."[46]

The regulatory authority of the SEC and the CFTC overlap. While the CFTC is focused on futures, i.e. contracts for the delivery of a commodity at a set price at some future time, futures contracts might call for the delivery of a security at a set price sometime in the future. Firms trading in such securities futures must comply with both the *Exchange Act* and the *Commodity Exchange Act* and register with both the SEC and the CFTC.[47] This overlap is especially pronounced for businesses in the cryptocurrency markets because the CFTC decided that cryptocurrencies are commodities and subject to CFTC regulatory oversight, while, as discussed below, the SEC has decided that cryptocurrencies, for the most part, are securities and subject to SEC regulatory oversight. The overlap is not complete, however, because CFTC regulation only applies to *futures* contracts involving crypto, not an exchange of fiat for crypto or crypto for (other) crypto, or a purchase of goods or services paid with crypto, so long as such transactions are executed immediately. By contrast, SEC regulation applies to sales of both securities and securities futures.

The application of SEC regulations depends on whether the digital asset constitutes a "security." Section 2(a)(1) of the *Securities Act* defines a "security" to encompass a host of items, including – of particular significance to crypto – an "investment contract."

An early application of this definition to cryptocurrency transactions came in 2013, when the SEC launched a securities fraud civil enforcement

---

43 15 U.S.C. § 78.

44 *Id* at § 77.

45 *Id* at § 77e(a), (c).

46 *Id* at § 78f(h)(1).

47 *E.g.*, American Bar Association, White Paper on Digital and Digitized Assets: Federal and State Jurisdictional Issues 243–275 (2020), available at https://www.americanbar.org/con-tent/dam/aba/administrative/business law/idpps_whitepaper.pdf.

action against Bitcoin Savings and Trust (BTCST), an unincorporated Texas venture, and its owner/operator, Mr. Trendon Shavers.[48] From February 2011 to August 2012, Shavers solicited investments in BTCST over the internet and promised returns of up to 1% per day or 7% weekly, based on Shaver's success at trading Bitcoin. Shavers used the majority of the funds to build a Bitcoin mining operation and held only a smaller portion in a "reserve fund" for investors seeking to cash out. After Shavers reduced the interest payments on the common accounts from 7% to 3.9% per week, too many investors demanded their money back, and Shavers had to shut down since he could not honour all demands. The SEC determined that Shavers was operating a Ponzi scheme. He used at least 150,000 BTC for personal expenses, and the Court eventually found that "[d]efendants' illicit gains obtained as a result of their fraud (bitcoins received from BTCST investors less bitcoins returned to them) total 180,819 bitcoins, or more than $101 million based on currently available bitcoin exchange rates."[49] Shavers also admitted that neither his trading nor his mining activities would have supported the interest payments he promised to the investors. Although Shavers claimed that securities laws simply did not apply to cryptocurrency investments and, therefore, that the Federal Court lacked jurisdiction, the Court entered an order regarding its subject-matter jurisdiction, holding that "BTCST investments in this case were investment contracts, and, thus, securities."[50]

The court's finding that the BTCST investments were investment contracts and, hence, securities stems from applying the so-called *Howey* Test. In *SEC v W.J. Howey Co.*,[51] the U.S. Supreme Court held in 1946 that

> an investment contract for purposes of the Securities Act means a contract, transaction or scheme whereby a person invests his money in a common enterprise and is led to expect profits solely from the efforts of the promoter or a third party.

BTCST, like Ponzi schemes generally, involved an investment of "money" (in this case, in the form of Bitcoin) into a common enterprise with the promoter (Shaver) and the other investors, and with the expectation of profits solely from the efforts of the promoter (Shaver's trading, investing or mining). These features are not necessarily found in every sale of cryptocurrency by a creator

48 *S.E.C. v. Shavers*, No. 4:13-CV-416 (E.D. Tex. Sep. 18, 2014).

49 *Id*, at 9–10.

50 *Id*, at 12.

51 328 U.S. 293, 298–99 (1946).

or developer, raising the question of whether the decision in BTCST is more about Ponzi schemes than it is about crypto. Indeed, perhaps the main thing this decision stands for is to prevent fraudsters from avoiding the reach of the securities laws by having investors give them crypto rather than fiat currency.

Of potentially broader impact, the SEC ruled in July 2017 that the creators of The DAO tokens were in violation of the Securities Act when they were using "a Decentralized Autonomous Organization ('DAO Entity')."[52] From April to May 2016, the creators of The DAO, based in Germany, sold over 1 Billion DAO Tokens for a total of around 12 Million Ether, equivalent at the time to about US$ 150 Million. Among more than 11,000 buyers were several hundred individuals in the United States. The White Paper published by the creators described a "crowd-funding contract" for the creation of a new type of company entirely in the crypto space, i.e. without a physical address or incorporation, created to invest in other Blockchain projects.

Among the innovative elements was a promise that the governance of The DAO would be fully decentralized and automated, without any corporate officers, instead giving all token holders proposal- and voting rights in the selection of projects for investment. Furthermore, "the constitution" of The DAO would be a smart contract on the Ethereum Blockchain and, therefore, immutable. Token holders would earn profits from the return on their investments[53] and benefit from increases in the value of the DAO Token, as it was going to be trading on several major exchanges.

The SEC, however, primarily saw an initial coin offering (ICO) for fundraising purposes – similar to an initial public offering (IPO) in the stock markets – in violation of Section 5 of the Securities Act's prohibition on the sale of unregistered securities. The DAO had neither registered with the SEC nor delivered "a statutory prospectus containing information necessary to enable prospective purchasers to make an informed investment decision."[54] However, since The DAO had already been delisted by major exchanges after a security vulnerability, the SEC did not consider it necessary to pursue an enforcement action.

In 2018, the SEC issued a cease-and-desist order against Zachary Coburn, founder and owner of the EtherDelta online platform. EtherDelta was launched in July 2016 and enabled users to buy and sell Ethereum, as well as ERC20 tokens, i.e. cryptocurrencies secured on the Ethereum Blockchain. The SEC concluded that "EtherDelta meets the criteria of an 'exchange' as defined

52 S.E.C. Release No. 81207, 2 (July 25, 2017).

53 Slockit, Slock.it DAO demo at Devcon1: IoT + Blockchain, YOUTUBE (Nov. 13, 2015), https://www.youtube.com/watch?v=49wHQoJxYPo.

54 S.E.C. Release No. 81207, *supra* note 42, at 10.

by Section 3(a)(1) of the Exchange Act and Rule 3b-16 thereunder", yet was neither registered with the SEC nor had an exemption from registration.[55] This placed EtherDelta in violation of Section 5 of the Securities Exchange Act "as a market place for bringing together the orders of multiple buyers and sellers in tokens that included securities as defined by Section 3(a)(10) of the Exchange Act."[56] Coburn saved EtherDelta by selling it to a foreign buyer rather than seeking SEC registration for it.

Since July 2013, the SEC has brought several enforcement actions against crypto exchanges and many against companies and individuals involved in unregistered ICOs.[57] Well-known targets of the SEC were Consensys Software (MetaMask, 2024), Kraken (2023), Stoner Cats 2 (NFTs, 2023), Impact Theory (NFTs, 2023), Celsius Network (2023), Coinbase (2023), Binance (2023), Bittrex (2023), Terraform Labs and Do Kwon (2023), FTX and Sam Bankman-Fried (2022), Kim Kardashian (social media promotion), Forsage and Vladimir Okhotnikov (2022), BlockFi (crypto lending, 2022), BitConnect (2021), Poloniex (2021), Ripple Labs (2020), and McAfee (2020). An interesting and particularly high-profile ICO case was the SEC's emergency action against Telegram's pre-sale of Grams, a token intended to run on Telegram's own blockchain platform TON. The case was brought in Federal court in New York, although Telegram is incorporated in the UK and operates out of Dubai. The SEC forced Telegram to return the equivalent of US$ 1.4 Billion it had collected from retail investors in the pre-sale of Grams.[58] Another example involving a non-U.S. entity is the enforcement actions against UK-based Blotics Ltd. f/d/b/a Coinschedule Ltd. for publicizing current and upcoming ICOs by third parties on a website that was accessible in the United States.[59]

Although many SEC actions involve ICOs classified as unregistered securities offerings, there are numerous cases not connected to coin or token sales or fundraising. While the current and the former chairman of the SEC seem to agree "that cryptocurrency tokens [and coins?] are 'largely' used to raise money for entrepreneurs and, *as such*, meet 'the time-tested definitions of an investment contract and are thus under the securities laws,'"[60] the more interesting

---

55 S.E.C. Release No. 84553, 3 (November 8, 2018).

56 *Id.*, at 9.

57 While the SEC brought between 17 and 25 crypto-related enforcement actions to court per year between 2018 and 2022, there were 42 in 2023, as a result of a targeted crackdown by Gary Gensler, who was appointed to the chair in 2021. For a comprehensive list see https://www.sec.gov/spotlight/cybersecurity-enforcement-actions.

58 *S.E.C. v. Telegram Group*, No. 19 Civ. 9439, (S.D.N.Y. Oct. 11, 2019). For discussion, see, inter alia, Frank Emmert, *The Long Arm of the SEC in the Regulation of Digital Currencies*, 33 Ind. Int'l & Comp. L. Rev. 1 (2023), at 28–30.

59 S.E.C. Release No. 10956 (July 14, 2021).

60 Ephrat Livni, *S.E.C. Chiefs From Left and Right Agree: Regulate Crypto*, N.Y. Times (Dec. 3, 2021), at B3, emphasis added.

question is to what extent entrepreneurs can do *other business* with cryptocurrencies without falling afoul of the securities laws and regulations. The SEC's 2019 guidance document, *Framework for "Investment Contract" Analysis of Digital Assets*,[61] is of limited help in this regard.

In this document, the SEC purports to "provide a framework for analysing whether a digital asset is an investment contract and whether offers and sales of a digital asset are securities transactions." Yet, the SEC really does not go beyond the *Howey* criteria of investment of money, common enterprise, and reasonable expectation of profits derived from the efforts of others. Beyond that, "[w]hether a particular digital asset at the time of its offer or sale satisfies the *Howey* test depends on the specific facts and circumstances." The only useful section of the guidance document lists some characteristics that make it *unlikely* that the *Howey* test is met:

- The distributed ledger network and digital asset are fully developed and operational.
- Holders of the digital asset are immediately able to use it for its intended functionality on the network, [...].
- The digital assets' creation and structure is designed and implemented to meet the needs of its users, rather than to feed speculation as to its value or development of its network. For example, the digital asset can only be used on the network and generally can be held or transferred only in amounts that correspond to a purchaser's expected use.
- Prospects for appreciation in the value of the digital asset are limited. For example, the design of the digital asset provides that its value will remain constant or even degrade over time, and, therefore, a reasonable purchaser would not be expected to hold the digital asset for extended periods as an investment.
- With respect to a digital asset referred to as a virtual currency, it can immediately be used to make payments in a wide variety of contexts, or acts as a substitute for real (or fiat) currency.
- This means that it is possible to pay for goods or services with the digital asset without first having to convert it to another digital asset or real currency.
- If it is characterized as a virtual currency, the digital asset actually operates as a store of value that can be saved, retrieved, and exchanged for something of value at a later time.
- With respect to a digital asset that represents rights to a good or service, it currently can be redeemed within a developed network or platform to acquire or otherwise use those goods or services. [...]

61 https://www.sec.gov/corpfin/framework-investment-contract-analysis-digital-assets.

- The digital asset is marketed in a manner that emphasizes the functionality of the digital asset, and not the potential for the increase in market value of the digital asset. [...]
- Restrictions on the transferability of the digital asset are consistent with the asset's use and not facilitating a speculative market.
- If the AP facilitates the creation of a secondary market, transfers of the digital asset may only be made by and among users of the platform.[62]

The SEC continues that "[d]igital assets with these types of use or consumption characteristics are *less likely* to be investment contracts."[63] This will hardly be comforting for anyone seeking to develop a DLT or cryptocurrency business with activities in the United States. A good example is the SEC's cease and desist order against TokenLot. The SEC did not make a distinction between coins or tokens that are securities and others that are not and ordered all coins and all tokens in all wallets of the corporation to be destroyed.[64] Similarly, when Munchee Inc. announced an ICO for MUN utility tokens, the white paper stated that the company had done a "*Howey* analysis" pursuant to the SEC's DAO report and that "as currently designed, the sale of MUN utility tokens does not pose a significant risk of implicating federal securities laws."[65] Since the token supply was limited and an increase in value was expected, the SEC disagreed with Munchee's analysis and stated that even if the tokens "had a practical use at the time of the offering, it would not preclude the token from being a security."[66] In the 2021 case of the DeFi company Blockchain Credit Partners, the SEC treated interest-bearing asset tokens and governance tokens equally as unregistered securities, forced the business to shut down and return the funds raised in the sale, and fined the owners.[67] The list goes on.

The status quo may be summarized as follows: Digital coins offered for fundraising purposes or likely to increase in value because of limited supply and broadening use options can be referred to as investment coins. At present, an ICO or any other sale of such coins is likely to be classified as an investment contract by the SEC and needs to be registered. An issuance of utility

62 *Id.*

63 *Id.*, emphasis added.

64 S.E.C. Release No. 10543, 6 (Sep. 11, 2018). It is not entirely clear, however, whether the SEC demanded that all coins and tokens are to be treated equally or whether the unregistered broker-dealer was poorly advised and voluntarily agreed to go beyond what might have been required by law.

65 S.E.C. Release No. 10445, 3–4 (Dec. 11, 2017).

66 *Id.*, at 9.

67 S.E.C. Release No. 10961 (Aug. 6, 2021).

tokens *not intended* as currency[68] is still likely to be classified as an investment contract by the SEC if the token supply is limited, the tokens are traded on exchanges, and there may be an expectation of an increase in value. The same is true for non-fungible tokens (NFTs) if they are easily traded, and there is an expectation of increasing value.[69] The situation is different mainly for coins or tokens that cannot increase in value, making them unsuitable for speculative investments. The main examples are stablecoins,[70] as well as coins or tokens with unlimited supply or fixed prices that function more like gift cards or prepaid vouchers.

The SEC's approach to treating sales of cryptocurrencies with the potential to increase in value as investment contracts is not unproblematic. This same analysis would turn the sales of artworks by a budding artist into the sale of securities if the purchasers were betting that the later works of the artist would make the early works they purchased more valuable.[71]

---

68 Different definitions have been offered for coins and tokens. Some definitions rely on differences in technology, namely that a coin is running on its own Blockchain (Bitcoin, Ether, etc.), while a token is running on another Blockchain, e.g. ERC-20 tokens running on the Ethereum Blockchain. Other definitions look at the functionality, where coins are intended to have much of the functionality of a currency, i.e. a widely accepted medium of exchange and store of value, while tokens are application-specific for a particular business and can be traded only for goods and services of that business. However, the terminology has not been consistently used and many of the buyers of cryptocurrencies are either unaware of or indifferent to these distinctions.

69 Until recently, there had not been a decision by the SEC about the sale of non-fungible tokens or NFTs, including whether a trading platform for NFTs would need to be registered with the SEC. However, a Forbes article, *Digital Art May Be Next in the SEC's Crosshairs*, available at https://www.forbes.com/sites/insider/2021/07/15/digital-art-may-be-next-in-the-secs-crosshairs/?sh=698f690a32df predicted that "[w]here financial innovation goes, the SEC is bound to follow." Sure enough, on 28 August 2023, the SEC "charged Impact Theory, LLC, a media and entertainment company headquartered in Los Angeles, with conducting an unregistered offering of crypto asset securities in the form of purported non-fungible tokens (NFTs). [...] The order finds that the NFTs offered and sold to investors were investment contracts and therefore securities." Impact Theory accepted a cease-and-desist order and was obliged to pay more than US$ 6.1 million "in disgorgement, prejudgment interest, and a civil penalty." See https://www.sec.gov/news/press-release/2023-163.

70 For examples, with further analysis, see Frank Emmert, *Smart Money for the People: Using Financial Innovation and Technology to Promote ESG*, Duke Law and Technology Review 2023, Vol. 22, No. 1, pp. 21-70; as well as Frank Emmert, *Can Cryptocurrency Save Islamic Finance?*, Manchester Journal of Transnational Islamic Law & Practice 2024, Vol. 20, No. 3, pp. 317-345.

71 See Frank Emmert, *The Regulation of Cryptocurrencies in the United States of America*, European Journal of Law Reform 2023, Vol. 25, No. 1/2, pp. 27-122, at pp. 67-68.

Entrepreneurs planning to sell goods or services for cryptocurrency and unsure whether they need to register with the SEC can ask for a "No-Action Letter" from the Commission.[72] The applicants need to provide a detailed description of their business model and arguments why it would not be in violation of the securities laws and regulations. However, "[t]he no-action process can be time consuming, and the SEC staff has no obligation to consider every no-action request. The no-action relief [if any] is provided only to the requester [and only] based on the specific facts and circumstances detailed in the request letter."[73] If the business model evolves during the implementation, the letter is worthless. Furthermore, "the SEC staff reserves the right to change the positions reflected in prior no-action letters."[74]

The SEC registration process required before selling a security – the details of which are beyond the scope of this report – is complex, time-consuming, and expensive. While various exemptions exist, allowing sales of securities without registration – for example, sales only to so-called accredited investors[75] – these exemptions have seen little use by cryptocurrency businesses. Even the exemption for crowdfunding authorized by the JOBS Act requires such fundraising to be "conducted through a broker or funding portal" registered with the SEC,[76] and the issuer must comply with a half dozen conditions, including making a complex filing with the SEC.[77]

Securities law obligations are not limited simply to registration but include mandates designed to ensure the accuracy of disclosure and sanctions on inaccurate disclosure. Hence, the SEC has gone after registered issuers whose public

72 https://www.investor.gov/introduction-investing/investing-basics/glossary/no-action-letters. For a practical example, see the no-action letter issued to Turnkey Jet Inc. of Palm Beach, Florida on 2 April 2019. Turnkey "propose[d] to offer and sell blockchain-based digital assets in the form of 'tokenized' jet cards ('Tokens'). [...Turnkey] propose[d] to launch a Token membership program [...] and develop a Token platform [...] to facilitate Token sales for air charter services via a private blockchain network [...]."; see https://www.sec.gov/divisions/corpfin/cf-noaction/2019/turnkey-jet-040219-2a1-incoming.pdf. Importantly, Turnkey promised to always only sell and redeem the tokens at the price of US$ 1, making the tokens analogous to pre-paid vouchers or gift cards.

73 Stabile, Prior & Hinkes, *supra* note 39, at 175.

74 *Id.*

75 While there are a number of categories of persons who are accredited investors, the one with the broadest significance are natural persons with specified high levels of income or wealth. 17 CFR § 230.501(a).

76 15 U.S.C. § 77a et seq.

77 *Id.*, § 77f. Anyone wishing to register a planned coin or token issue is highly recommended to get in touch with Oscar Jofre at KoreConX (https://koreconx.com/), one of the few service providers willing and able to shepherd an ICO through the entire regulatory framework and quite possibly the only one offering to do so at a manageable price point.

disclosures about the development of their cryptocurrency platforms were inaccurate.[78] More broadly, Congress reacted to major accounting scandals involving Enron, Worldcom, and other companies by enacting the *Sarbanes-Oxley Act* of 2002 (SOX).[79] SOX mandates potentially burdensome actions by companies subject to its reach, which are designed to promote more accurate *continuous* financial disclosures.

SOX applies to all publicly traded companies in the U.S., as well as foreign companies if they are publicly traded and doing business in the U.S. This includes cryptocurrency businesses if the *shares* are traded on public exchanges. However, what has not yet been definitively resolved is the question of whether the SOX Act applies to companies *merely because their proprietary coins or tokens are publicly traded on crypto exchanges*. On the one hand, this was clearly not envisaged by the legislature when the Act was first conceived. On the other hand, the SOX Act refers to "issuers" of securities[80] and the SEC, which administers SOX, has classified most cryptocurrencies as securities.[81] Bitcoin (BTC) and Ether (ETH) are exceptions in this regard since they have never been offered by an original issuer in anything that could resemble an investment contract.[82] Nevertheless, as discussed above, businesses trading in BTC or ETH may be offering investment contracts.[83]

All told, the current approach makes it almost impossible to develop any kind of legitimate business dealing with cryptocurrency and smart contracts and soliciting partners and investors in the U.S. for anyone without massive financial resources. As a result, the SEC's oversight of the crypto markets has

---

78 As an example, an order pursuant to Sec. 12(k) of the Securities Exchange Act of 1934 was entered against IBITX Software Inc., see S.E.C. Release No. 83084 (April 20, 2018).

79 Pub. L. 107–204.

80 15 U.S. Code 7201, § 2(7).

81 The view that SOX applies to businesses if their digital coins or tokens are publicly traded in the U.S. is shared by Megan Knab, *Does SOX Suck for Crypto: What Sarbanes-Oxley Is (and Isn't)*, VeriLedger 6 May 2019, https://medium.com/veriledger/does-sox-suck-for-crypto-what-sarbanes-oxley-is-and-isnt-687a4459bd01. The opposite view was taken by The Institute of Internal Auditors in an open letter of 5 December 2022 "calling for Congress to establish [stricter] requirements designed to bolster corporate governance at cryptocurrency exchanges operating in the United States [...] since [unfortunately] most cryptocurrency exchanges are not subject to SOX compliance." See https://www.theiia.org/en/content/communications/press-releases/2022/december/the-iia-calls-upon-congress-to-require-cryptocurrency-exchanges/.

82 Both BTC and ETH are still commodities, however, and subject to oversight by the CFTC, as discussed above.

83 For more detailed analysis and a recommendation to ensure SOX compliance see Fortris, *SOX Compliance for Digital Asset Treasury Management*, 14 March 2023, https://fortris.com/blog/sox-compliance-digital-assets.

mainly achieved one thing: The respective businesses are largely unable to operate legally in U.S. markets. Instead, they move offshore or into the shadows. Some do and some do not exclude U.S. buyers from coin sales and other transactions. However, in pretty much all the cases, the U.S. has lost the ability of providing actual oversight and meaningful investor protection. Any companies remaining in the U.S. and trying to be in full compliance struggle under the weight of overlapping regulation of limited usefulness. President-elect Donald Trump, however, has promised to make the United States the "crypto capital of the planet" and, to that end, create a more favourable regulatory environment. Trump has his own crypto project in the form of World Liberty Financial,[84] and is well-known to look after his personal financial interests. This makes it at least possible that the U.S. Federal Government will take a more permissive approach to cryptocurrencies going forward.

2.4 *Taxation*

After the CFTC classified cryptocurrencies as *commodities*, and the SEC classified them as *securities*, the Treasury Department, more specifically its Financial Crimes Enforcement Network (FinCEN), classified them as monetary instruments, akin to *currency*.[85] By contrast, the United States Internal Revenue Service (IRS) , also part of the Treasury Department, decided that cryptocurrencies are *not currency* for taxation purposes but are *property* instead.[86] This has significant consequences for the tax treatment of cryptocurrencies and Blockchain businesses. First, anybody buying and selling crypto is liable for capital gains taxes on an increase in value at the time the crypto is sold. For example, if a person buys Bitcoin at US$ 20,000 and sells it at US$ 30,000, she has realized a capital gain of US$ 10,000 per coin. The tax rate depends on

84 https://www.worldlibertyfinancial.com/.

85 The *Anti-Money Laundering Act* of 2020 (Division F of Pub. L. 116–283) entered into force on 1 January 2021. It defines "monetary instruments" as used in the *Bank Secrecy Act* (BSA), as United States coins and currency. However, the Secretary of the Treasury "may prescribe by regulation, coins and currency of a foreign country, travelers' checks, bearer negotiable instruments, bearer investment securities, bearer securities, stock on which title is passed on delivery, and similar material" to also be monetary instruments. FinCEN proposed by regulation that convertible virtual currencies (CVC s) and digital assets with legal tender status (LTDA s) are "similar material." FinCEN elaborated that "pursuant to 31 U.S.C. 5312(a)(3)(D), CVC and LTDA are both value that substitute for currency and are therefore 'monetary instruments' under the BSA." (https://www.federalregister.gov/documents/2021/01/15/2021-01016/require-ments-for-certain-transactions-involving-convertible-virtual-currency-or-digital-assets).

86 IRS Notice 2014-2.

whether the crypto was held for over a year or not. The long-term capital gains rate is generally more favourable. While the IRS should be very happy with its classification during times like now, when most cryptocurrencies experience strong appreciation in value, the corollary to the classification as property is that a decline in value between the acquisition and the sale can also be deducted from taxes as a loss and can be used to offset gains in other crypto transactions during the same tax year.[87]

Furthermore, direct cost related to the transactions, in particular gas fees and potentially fees related to the wallet and registration on an exchange, are also deductible expenses. Importantly, losses in crypto trading can also offset gains in *other property transactions*, for example, in real estate, stocks and bonds, and mutual funds or ETFs, and vice verse. This can open up interesting perspectives for tax planning purposes.

In addition to capital gains tax on sales of crypto, the acquisition of crypto currency may be taxable as income. If a wallet owner acquires digital assets for free, for example, in an airdrop or after a hard fork, she must report the transaction as income.[88] If an employee is partially paid in crypto, she must report this as income, and the employer may have to withhold Federal income tax and report the income on Form W2.[89] If an individual or a company is selling goods or services in exchange for crypto, they must account for the income and can deduct their expenses.[90] The same is true for miners, who must report

87 The IRS also confirmed that a wallet owner who purchased different amounts of a particular coin at different times for different prices can determine which of those are sold at a subsequent sales transaction. See the answer to Question 39 in the Frequently Asked Questions on Virtual Currency Transactions, https://www.irs.gov/individuals/inter-national-taxpayers/frequently-asked-questions-on-virtual-currency-transactions. In other words, the IRS does not insist on the principle of First-In, First-Out for calculating capital gains on cryptocurrency transactions. While FIFO is the default accounting method, the IRS allows crypto owners to specifically identify which coins and tokens they are selling. This makes sense, since they are identifyable on the blockchain. As a result, an investor who needs to access some of the money tied up in crypto does not have to liquidate the earliest purchases with the highest capital gains but can manage the transaction to lower the tax burden. For more information see Trevor English, 6 Things Tax Professionals Need to Know About Cryptocurrency Taxes, ThomsonReuters, 17 October 2023, https://www.thomsonreuters.com/en-us/posts/tax-and-accounting/cryptocurrency-taxes/.

88 I.R.S. Revenue Ruling 2019-24, interpreting 26 C.F.R. 1.61-1.

89 I.R.S. Revenue Ruling 2014-21. As a separate matter, the individual will also have to report the income for State income tax in their State of residence, unless they live in Alaska, Florida, Nevada, New Hampshire, South Dakota, Tennessee, Texas, Washington, or Wyoming, i.e. one of the nine States of the U.S. that do not impose personal income taxes.

90 *Id.*

the fair market value of the income at the time when the mining is successful and the crypto is credited. Of course, the miner can also deduct her expenses, in particular, the cost of acquiring and operating the computers used in the mining efforts.[91]

Finally, the funds raised in an ICO are subject to income tax since the sale is considered a sale of property.[92] This is not the case for the sale of corporate stock in an IPO or otherwise, or of interests in entities (such as most LLCs) treated as partnerships for income tax purposes. If revenue from IPOs is not subject to income tax because the buyers are getting equity and voting rights and not just tokens or coins, the same should apply to an ICO involving a DAO. Federal income tax law provides tax-free treatment for IPOs of stock or partnership interests in order to promote business formation and financing. Although Federal securities law treats an ICO as a sale of securities the same as IPOs of stock or limited partnership or LLC interests (which, like ICOs, can be investment contracts), a standard ICO does not create a business partnership between the issuers and the buyers of the coins or tokens. This is different for a DAO, however.[93]

The value of the digital assets must be reported in US dollars at the time when the capital gains were realized or when the income was credited. This can cause a variety of challenges. First, the value of a particular coin or token can vary significantly over a single day. A declaration is relatively straightforward if a transaction involves the purchase or sale of crypto in exchange for fiat, in particular, US dollars. Ether purchased at US$3,500 is entered at that price into the taxpayer's records. Things are less clear if there is no direct fiat transaction, for example, if the digital asset is acquired by mining or in an airdrop, or if the transaction involves the exchange of one coin for another (e.g., the purchase of ADA with ETH). The IRS speaks of "fair market value," but I doubt that it can expect the taxpayer to account for the exact time when the decisive block is confirmed on the respective day for the determination of the value of the cryptocurrency. Second, there are plenty of digital assets for which there is no generally accepted "exchange rate" determined by major exchanges.

---

91 *Id.*

92 The I.R.S. publication *Frequently Asked Questions on Virtual Currency Transactions* simply refers to I.R.S. Publication 544, *Sales and Other Disposition of Assets*, without distinction of the procedure or reasons for a sale of cryptocurrency. See https://www.irs.gov/individuals/international-taxpayers/frequently-asked-questions-on-virtual-currency-transactions. This should also mean that operating expenses incurred *prior to the ICO* can be offset against income from the ICO.

93 For further analysis see Zac McClure & Arthur Teller, *Guide to DAO Taxes in 2024*, TokenTax, 1 October 2024, https://tokentax.co/blog/crypto-taxes-for-daos.

The IRS enforcement action against Coinbase may provide some direction for the approach that the IRS will likely take in the foreseeable future in order to police tax compliance by those trading in cryptocurrencies. Coinbase was incorporated in California and, at least at the relevant time, was the largest cryptocurrency exchange serving U.S. customers. In 2017, it was active in 33 countries and had 5.9 million customers with transactions of over US$ 6 Billion. In 2016, the IRS requested nine categories of documents, including complete user profiles, know-your-customer due diligence, documents regarding third-party access, transaction logs, records of payments processed, correspondence between Coinbase and Coinbase users, account or invoice statements, records of payments, and exception records produced by Coinbase's AML system for all transactions in the years 2013–2015 involving United States persons.[94] Coinbase refused to comply with the summons, and the IRS agreed to narrow the request to accounts 'with at least the equivalent of $20,000 in any one transaction type (buy, sell, send, or receive) in any one year during the 2013–2015 period.' [...] The Narrowed Summons 'do[es] not include users: (a) who only bought and held bitcoin during the 2013–15 period; or (b) for which Coinbase filed Forms 1099-K during the 2013–15 period.'[95]

Nevertheless, even the narrowed summons, according to Coinbase, covered about 8.9 million transactions of some 14,355 account holders. Since Coinbase continued to refuse the broad request by the IRS, the court had to decide, inter alia, which pieces of information would have to be disclosed as "relevant" for the legitimate purpose of "ascertaining the correctness of any return, making a return where none has been made, determining the liability of any person for any internal revenue tax or ... collecting any such liability..."[96] In the end, the court agreed that Coinbase had to disclose some but not all of the requested information. Specifically, Coinbase was ordered to disclose,

> for accounts with at least the equivalent of $20,000 in any one transaction type (buy, sell, send, or receive) in any one year during the 2013 to 2015 period: (1) the taxpayer ID number, (2) name, (3) birth date, (3) address, (4) records of account activity including transaction logs or other records identifying the date, amount, and type of transaction (purchase/sale/exchange), the post transaction balance, and the names

94 *U.S. v. Coinbase, Inc.*, No.17-cv-01431-JSC, 2017 WL 5890052 (N.D. Cal., Nov. 28, 2017).

95 *Id.*

96 *Id.*, the court referred to I.R.C. § 7602.

of counterparties to the transaction, and (5) all periodic statements of account or invoices (or the equivalent).[97]

By contrast, the court found that "account opening records, copies of passports and driver's licenses, all wallet addresses, all public keys for all accounts/wallets/vaults," as well as "records of know-your-customer diligence, agreements or instructions granting a third-party access, control, or transaction approval authority, and correspondence between Coinbase and the user or any third party with access to the account/wallet/vault pertaining to the account/wallet/vault opening, closing, or transaction activity" were not relevant at the preliminary stage of the investigation. However, the court did not rule out IRS access to this information at later stages of investigations into account holders.[98]

What we can learn from the Coinbase case is the difficulty of anyone – whether it is a large crypto exchange or the IRS – to police millions of small transactions. In theory, "[u]nder Notice 2014–21, every time a US taxpayer buys a cup of coffee with virtual currency, that act constitutes a 'selling of property' that causes a gain or loss for tax purposes."[99] In practice, the IRS will have to focus on larger transactions. However, the inability of our tax authorities to apply their own definitions consistently and their inevitable focus on major tax cheaters is just another example of the failure of our legislators and regulators to provide clear, comprehensive, consistent, and practical guidance for businesses in the blockchain space, their users, and all taxpayers.

3 State Laws

A wide variety of existing State laws might impact cryptocurrencies. For example, shady business practices by anyone promoting or selling cryptocurrency could run afoul of general State laws on Unfair or Deceptive Acts or Practices (UDAP).[100] UDAP claims are important in the context of cryptocurrencies

---

97 *Id.*
98 *Id.*
99 Stabile, Prior & Hinkes, *supra* note 39, at 268.
100 For example, under Sec. 1780 of the *California Consumer Legal Remedies Act*, "[a]ny consumer who suffers a damage as a result of the use or employment by any person of a method, act, or practice declared to be unlawful by Section 1770 may bring an action against that person to recover or obtain any of the following:
(1) Actual damages, […]
(2) An order enjoining the methods, acts, or practices.
(3) Restitution of property.

because they provide private remedies, as well as remedies for consumer protection agencies and State Attorneys General.[101] They may allow the aggregation of private claims in class action lawsuits,[102] they typically provide for substantial monetary liability and other sanctions, and they often have a lower standard of proof compared to securities law claims. While the Private Securities Litigation Reform Act (PSLRA) of 1995[103] allows securities fraud class actions, it imposes heightened pleading standards. Plaintiffs must allege facts giving rise to a strong inference of scienter (wrongful state of mind), the alleged misstatements or omissions must have been material, plaintiffs must prove reliance on the alleged material misrepresentations or omissions, and they usually need to show how and why the alleged fraud cause their economic losses. By contrast, in UDAP cases, the standard of proof is the preponderance of evidence, i.e. it has to be more likely than not that the claim is true, intent is not required, meaning that even innocent or inadvertent misrepresentations along the lines of overly optimistic profit or growth projections can be actionable, and reliance by the investor on the alleged unfair or deceptive acts does not have to be proven. In other words, even investors that were suspicious of

---

(4) Punitive damages.

(5) Any other relief that the court deems proper.

Sec. 1770 prohibits, inter alia, "(5) Representing that goods or services have sponsorship, approval, characteristics, ingredients, uses, benefits, or quantities that they do not have or that a person has a sponsorship, approval, status, affiliation, or connection that the person does not have." I am surprised that to the best of my knowledge, nobody has yet tried to recover damages from persons who sold unregistered coins or tokens in an ICO and then did not deliver a successful business model that caused the coins or tokens to go up in value, in particular since class actions are possible under these kinds of statutes.

101 See, for example, O'Melveny & Myers LLP, *State UDAP Enforcement Poses New Risk for Crypto Companies*, 27 January 2023, https://www.omm.com/insights/alerts-publications/state-udap-enforcement-poses-new-risk-for-crypto-companies/.

102 As an example, after the Tezos ICO in July 2017, a group of investors filed a class action lawsuit against the Swiss-based Tezos Foundation, Dynamic Ledger Solutions Inc., and the owners Arthur and Kathleen Breitman for violating Federal securities law, as well as California's UDAP law. Plaintiffs alleged that the Tezos ICO was an unregistered securities offering, violating Sections 5, 12, and 15 of the Securities Act of 1933, and that the defendants had violated California's UDAP law by exaggerating the progress of the Tezos network, misrepresenting the ownership of the network, and making false statements how the ICO revenue would be spent. After three years of litigation, Tezos settled the claims in 2020 for US$ 25 Million plus attorney fees. See In Re Tezos Securities Litigation, Case No. 3:17-cv-06779-RS (N.D. Cal.).

103 Private Securities Litigation Reform Act of 1995, Pub. L. 104-67, 109 Stat. 737 (codified as amended in scattered sections of 15 U.S.C.).

or did not believe the profit or growth projections can bring damage claims.[104] The National Consumer Law Center (NCLC) maintains an online treatise on the UDAP statutes of all 50 States of the U.S.[105]

In addition, many states, unlike the Federal Government, have adopted specific legislation dealing with DLT technology and cryptocurrencies. In general, the U.S. Several States have two competing approaches to addressing any new regulatory challenge. They can adopt different approaches independent of each other and thereby serve as "laboratories of democracy."[106] Alternatively, they can seek to avoid conflicting rules by adopting uniform legislation promulgated by the Uniform Law Commission (ULC). A well-known example would be the Uniform Commercial Code (UCC), which all 50 States have largely adopted.

3.1 *Uniform Acts*

Regarding DLT and cryptocurrencies, the ULC has so far only had a limited impact. The 2017 Uniform Regulation of Virtual-Currency Business Act (URVCBA)[107] was designed to provide a uniform statutory framework "for the regulation of companies engaging in 'virtual-currency business activity,' such as exchanging, transferring, or storing virtual currency; holding electronic precious metals or certificates of electronic precious metals; or exchanging digital representations of value within online games for virtual currency or legal tender."[108]

Depending on the type of services offered, individuals or companies are either exempt from the URVCBA, must register, or must obtain a license. The URVCB was developed at the request of various stakeholders, including non-bank financial service providers interested in DLT and digital money, who seek

104 See, for example, Andrew C. Glass, Gregory N. Blase & Jeremy M. McLaughlin, *Lurking Beneath the Surface: UDAP Claims in ICO Litigation*, K&L Gates, 12 March 2018, https://www.klgates.com/Lurking-Beneath-the-Surface-UDAP-Claims-in-ICO-Litigation-03-12-2018. See also Shaen Corbet (ed.), *Understanding Cryptocurrency Fraud – The Challenges and Headwinds to Regulate Digital Currencies*, De Gruyter 2022, in particular the chapter on ICO fraud and regulation by Thomas Conlon and Richard J. McGee (pp. 43-54).

105 See https://library.nclc.org/book/unfair-and-deceptive-acts-and-practices. Unfortunately, the book is not free.

106 For a rather critical view of the feasibility of the concept, see Charles W. Tyler & Heather K. Gerken, *The Myth of the Laboratories of Democracy*, 122 Colum. L. Rev. 2187 (2022).

107 https://www.uniformlaws.org/viewdocument/final-act-154?CommunityKey=e104aaa8-c10f-45a7-a34a-0423c2106778&tab=librarydocuments.

108 https://www.uniformlaws.org/committees/community-home?communitykey=e104aaa8-c10f-45a7-a34a-0423c2106778&tab=groupdetails.

legal certainty for their business models. Several provisions for the protection of consumers were included.[109] The URVCB does not define virtual currency and is intended to cover all forms of digital assets. Although approved by the ULC and supported by the American Bar Association (ABA), it has so far only been enacted by California, Louisiana, and Rhode Island.[110]

The ULC's 2018 Supplemental Commercial Law for the Uniform Regulation of Virtual-Currency Businesses Act ("Supplemental Act")[111] was designed to incorporate UCC Article 8 on Investment Securities into agreements made between virtual currency businesses and the users of their services and to avoid State legislation of cryptocurrencies that would be incompatible with UCC Article 9 on Secured Transactions.[112] It was only adopted by Rhode Island[113] and has, meanwhile, been largely superseded by recent reforms to UCC Article 9 and the introduction of UCC Article 12 (see below).

By contrast to the URVCBA, the ULC's 2019 Revised Fiduciary Access to Digital Assets Act (RUFADAA) was adopted widely by the states.[114] However, its scope and coverage is extremely limited. The RUFADAA governs access to a person's online accounts when the account owner dies or loses the ability to manage the account. A fiduciary is a person appointed to manage the property of another person, subject to strict duties to act in the other person's best interest. The act allows fiduciaries to manage digital property like computer files, web domains, and virtual currency.[115]

By far the most important work done by the ULC is the Uniform Commercial Code (UCC). The question of whether the UCC applies to smart contracts and other business transactions made electronically and secured on a Blockchain and/or involving a transfer of cryptocurrency is a question of State law. To the extent the UCC does not provide clear answers, State law has to be

---

109 *Id.*

110 *See* Rhode Island Bill HB 5847/SB 753 of 2019.

111 https://www.uniformlaws.org/viewdocument/final-act-with-comments-86?CommunityKey=fc398fb5-2885-4efb-a3bb-50865010 6f95&tab=librarydocuments.

112 *See* Anita Ramasastry, President of the Uniform Law Commission, January 29, 2019 letter to Representative Tyler Lindholm expressing the ULC's concerns about Wyoming's draft law SF 125, available at https://www.uniformlaws.org/viewdocument/communications-with-wyoming-1?CommunityKey=e104aaa8-c10f-45a7-a34a-0423c2106778&tab=librarydocuments.

113 See Rhode Island Bill HB 5847/SB 753 of 2019.

114 As of 15 December 2024, the RUFADAA was enacted by 49 States and territories, excluding only Delaware, Louisiana, and Puerto Rico. Legislation has been introduced but not yet adopted in Massachusetts.

115 https://www.uniformlaws.org/committees/community-home?communitykey=f7237fc4-74c2-4728-81c6-b39 a91ecdf22&tab=groupdetails.

interpreted by State courts, and those interpretations would invariably differ. Therefore, the ULC created a *Joint Study Committee on the Uniform Commercial Code and Emerging Technologies* and adopted a set of amendments to the UCC on 26 July 2022.[116] A new *UCC Article 12 UCC Controllable Electronic Records* defines certain electronic records like those secured on a Blockchain to supplement the concept of a written record. This allows contracts to be concluded and security interests to be perfected via transactions on a Blockchain. Corresponding amendments have been incorporated into the other Articles of the UCC. For example, *UCC Article 2 on Sales* was amended to expressly cover contract formation through electronic agents/autonomous algorithms, sales of digital assets, transfer of digital currency, integration of the Uniform Electronic Transactions Act (UETA) and the Electronic Signatures in Global and National Commerce Act (E-SIGN), as well as ownership and transfer of goods subject to Blockchain or DLT registration or identification.[117] Functionally similar amendments were made in UCC Article 2a on Leases.

As the Study Committee explained, *UCC Article 3 on Negotiable Instruments* should be updated for "an environment in which treatment of written instruments is increasingly automated" and to clarify whether concepts of transfer, negotiation, holder in due course, note, and draft, can apply without modification to electronically recorded instruments, and whether Article 3 needs to be explicitly extended to cover payment in private currency.[118]

Similar questions were raised with regard to *UCC Article 4 Bank Deposits and Collections*. Specifically, the Study Committee was looking at collection by non-bank payment-service providers, collection of electronically created items, and to what extent Article 4 should be "pruned back … [to cover] only those matters not covered by federal law".[119] Arguably, most cryptocurrency exchanges, and certainly the providers of DeFi services, are "non-bank payment service providers" if they don't qualify directly as banks.

116 The text of the 2022 amendments, with prefatory note and comments, is available at https://www.uniformlaws.org/viewdocument/final-act-164?CommunityKey=1457c422-ddb7-40b0-8c76-39a1991651ac&tab=librarydocuments.

117 For a discussion of the issues see Larry di Matteo, et al, The Cambridge Handbook of Smart Contracts, Blockchain Technology and Digital Platforms, 59–140 (2020).

118 ULC Joint Study Committee on the Uniform Commercial Code and Emerging Technologies – Suggested Approach to the Study Committee's Work – Significant Issues that the Study Committee Might Consider, at pp. 2-3, available at https://www.uniformlaws.org/HigherLogic/System/DownloadDocumentFile.ashx?DocumentFileKey=0bac4fae-3e0f-c7de-93e6-4a621e3608f1&forceDialog=0.

119 *Id.*, at 3.

The Study Committee was also considering whether *UCC Article 4A Funds Transfers* was "satisfactory given new and emerging AI/processing applications" and, specifically, whether the Article's provisions "can accommodate the use of distributed-ledger-based token transactions to clear and settle funds transfers."[120] What may be of specific interest is the question of "whether the security-procedure and loss-allocation provisions (§§ 4A-201 through 4A-203) are satisfactory given cybersecurity and increasing interloper fraud risks." Under § 4A-201, banks can establish a "security procedure" to verify "that a payment order [...] is that of the customer". The bank is largely protected if it followed the agreed-upon security procedure and made the transfer in good faith, i.e. before it was notified of a data breach or that the payment order was otherwise made by an unauthorized third party. §4A-105, however, defines "bank" as "a person engaged in the business of banking and includes a savings bank, savings and loan association, credit union, and trust company." This definition would not cover enterprises merely selling goods or services in exchange for cryptocurrency, nor most currently existing crypto exchanges. It would only cover those DeFi operators that are actually engaged in "the business of banking." The amendments to UCC Article 4A did not change the scope of application, which remains limited to actual banks. However, they clarify that security procedures may rely on "the use of algorithms or other codes, identifying words, numbers, symbols, sounds, biometrics, encryption, callback procedures, or similar security devices." The question whether non-banks are similarly protected if they follow the agreed-upon security procedures remains outside of the scope of UCC Article 4A and, therefore, subject to (other) State law, including case law.

The charge of the Study Committee with regard to *UCC Article 5 Letters of Credit* was limited to questions of presentation of electronic drafts and other electronic documents relevant in the context of Smart Contracts on a Blockchain that may be used in ways analogous to letters of credit. Similar considerations apply to *UCC Article 7 Documents of Title.*

The work of the Study Committee was most interesting and most difficult regarding the remaining provisions of the UCC. *UCC Article 8 Investment Securities* governs the ownership and transfer of securities. UCC § 8-103 stipulates that

"(a) [a] share or similar equity interest issued by a corporation, business trust, joint stock company, or similar entity is a security. [...] (c) [an] interest in a partnership or limited liability company is not a security unless it is dealt in

120 *Id.*

or traded on securities exchanges or in securities markets, its terms expressly provide that it is a security governed by this Article, [...]. However, an interest in a partnership or limited liability company is a financial asset if it is held in a securities account."

Since cryptocurrencies are typically held and transferred differently from traditional securities, amendments to the UCC were necessary to accommodate crypto transactions. UCC § 8-103, in combination with UCC § 8-102(a)(9)(iii), now stipulates that "a controllable account, controllable electronic record, or controllable payment intangible" is only a financial asset akin to a security if the parties have agreed that "the property is to be treated as a financial asset under this Article." As a result, the UCC avoids the conflation of crypto assets in controllable accounts with securities but enables the parties to agree on the application of the rules on investment securities.

UCC Article 9 Secured Transactions deals with transactions in which one party extends credit, in particular for the purchase of goods or services, and obtains a security interest in collateral owned by the other party. The concept is attractive in the crypto space because it allows holders of coins or tokens to monetize their assets by borrowing against them while continuing to benefit from increases in value. By contrast to a sale of crypto assets, the loan is also not subject to capital gains tax. Article 9 provides for a two-step procedure. First, the parties enter into a loan agreement that provides for security and is called a "security agreement." Second, the security interests must be perfected to be enforceable against third parties. Specifically, if the debtor falls into insolvency or pledges the same collateral again, the first secured creditor will only prevail if the security interest is perfected. Depending on the type of collateral and security interest, perfection may be achieved by taking physical possession or control of the collateral, or by filing a financing statement with a designated state authority maintaining a public record of security interests outstanding for a named debtor.[121]

Article 9 specifies the types of collateral that can be used for a secured transaction. In addition to tangible goods, these include "(A) proceeds to which a security interest attaches; (B) accounts, chattel paper, payment intangibles, and promissory notes that have been sold [...]."[122] Securities and commodities, including futures contracts, are frequently used as collateral for secured transactions. Since the SEC defines most cryptocurrencies as securities and the CFTC has declared all of them to be commodities, Article 9 should be applicable to transactions using cryptocurrencies as collateral. Alternatively,

---

121 U.C.C. §§ 9-308–9-316.

122 *Id.* at § 9-102(a)(12).

cryptocurrencies could be relied upon as (intangible) property based on the definition of the IRS.

The ULC Committee, however, chose a different approach that does not depend on the definitions of the SEC, CFTC, or IRS. First, the amendments stipulate that "electronic money" only includes cryptocurrencies that are adopted as legal tender in at least one country. If this is indeed the case, a security interest can be perfected by obtaining control pursuant to Article 9 UCC.[123]

In addition, and specifically for all other digital assets, the Committee developed the new *UCC Article 12 Controllable Electronic Records*, which enables the perfection of a security interest using Blockchain technology. The Committee explicitly states that Article 12 does not cover only those "electronic (intangible) assets that are created using existing technologies such as distributed ledger technology (DLT), including blockchain technology" but also "aspires to apply to electronic assets that may be created using technologies that have yet to be developed, or even imagined."[124] A controllable electronic record for the purposes of the UCC has to grant some benefit, be stored in an electronic medium, and provide the owner the *exclusive* power to use or transfer the record, hence the control over the benefit.[125] Like with Article 9 UCC, a qualifying purchaser under Article 12 acquires the controllable record free from third-party rights.

---

123 While the Joint Committee expanded the definition of money to any cryptocurrencies adopted by at least one country, the final version of the 2022 amendments, as adopted by National Conference of Commissioners on Uniform State Laws in August 2022, added the following language: "The term does not include an electronic record that is a medium of exchange recorded and transferable in a system that existed and operated for the medium of exchange before the medium of exchange was authorized or adopted by the government." This somewhat cryptic phrase has rather far-reaching consequences. Under the Committee Draft, Bitcoin would already qualify as "money" because it has been adopted as legal tender by El Salvador. Other cryptocurrencies would join the "money" definition as soon as at least one country accepts them as legal tender. However, under the final version of the 2022 amendments, Bitcoin is not money because it was created before it was adopted by El Salvador. In effect, this permanently eliminates all known cryptocurrencies from the definition of "money" in the UCC. The only cryptocurrencies that will qualify as "money" under the UCC will be those that are adopted as such by a country and then created *afterward*. At least, in my opinion, this can only be achieved by central bank issued e-money or central bank digital currencies (CBDCs).

124 UNIFORM COMMERCIAL CODE AMENDMENTS (2022), *supra* note 116, at 229.

125 "Exclusive power" is further defined to exist "even if (1) the electronic copy or a system in which the electronic copy is recorded limits the use of the electronic record or has a protocol programmed to transfer control; or (2) the secured party has agreed to share the power with another person" (Draft § 9-105(d)). This accommodates smart contracts with conditionalities, as well as multi-signature wallets. *Id.*, at 246.

The question of how a security interest in crypto should be perfected, i.e. how *control* over a controllable electronic record needs to be established, is addressed in § 12-105:

A person has control of a controllable electronic record[126] if the electronic record, a record attached to or logically associated with the electronic record, or a system in which the electronic record is recorded:

1. gives the person:
   A. the power to avail itself of substantially all the benefit from the electronic record; and
   B. exclusive power, subject to subsection (b), to:
      i. prevent others from availing themselves of substantially all the benefit from the electronic record; and
      ii. transfer control of the electronic record to another person or cause another person to obtain control of another controllable electronic record as a result of the transfer of the electronic record; and
2. enables the person readily to identify itself in any way, including by name, identifying number, cryptographic key, office, or account number, as having the powers specified in paragraph (1).

Control can also be exercised through another person pursuant to § 12-105(b).

Control and transfer of control are relatively straightforward for sales transactions and merely require transfer from one wallet with its public/private key combination to another wallet. Matters are slightly more complicated if the ownership of the digital assets is not transferred but used in a secured transaction. Once Articles 9 or 12 UCC apply, a lender secured by crypto would benefit from a variety of protections. An obvious solution for the control of the record could be the use of so-called multi-signature wallets restricting the debtor from disposing of the crypto without the consent of the creditor. However, in the absence of such an arrangement, and if at least one controlling private key has not been transferred to the creditor, perfection may not have been achieved.[127]

---

126 Control of an electronic copy of a record evidencing chattel paper, by contrast, is dealt with in § 9-105.

127 As Professor Comizio points out, without the 2022 amendments, "secured lenders [would] find that financing arrangements that list virtual currency as collateral lack the U.C.C.'s well-established enforcement protections. Uncertainty regarding collateral [would cast] a shadow over digital asset transactions that increases transaction costs, reduces efficiencies, and leaves market participants vulnerable." See Gerard Comizio, Virtual Currency Law, 157 (Wolters Kluwer 2022). This problem has been largely resolved.

All told, the ULC's Joint Committee did some heavy lifting to clarify issues that were not self-evident and had created considerable legal uncertainty for businesses and users in the crypto and DLT sectors in the U.S. The final draft was jointly sponsored by the Uniform Law Commission and the American Law Institute and adopted by the ULC in July 2022 and recommended for enactment by the Several States. As of 15 December 2024, the 2022 amendments have already been implemented by Alabama, California, Colorado, Delaware, the District of Columbia, Georgia, Hawaii, Illinois, Indiana, Iowa, Kentucky, Louisiana, Maine, Minnesota, Nebraska, Nevada, New Hampshire, New Mexico, North Dakota, Oklahoma, Pennsylvania, Rhode Island, South Dakota, Virginia, and Washington. Corresponding legislation has been introduced in Massachusetts, Missouri, New York, Tennessee, and West Virginia. The remaining 23 States and Territories have so far not initiated the adoption of the 2022 amendments, but the issues do not seem controversial, and it is to be expected that the 2022 amendments will be fully implemented by all 53 States and Territories in the coming years.

The most important changes to the UCC can be summarized as follows:

- The definition of "money" in § 1-201 is limited to include only those cryptocurrencies that are created at the behest of at least one sovereign government.[128]
- The criteria for a "security procedure" under § 4A-201 are clarified to exclude merely "requiring a payment order to be sent from a known email address, IP address or phone number" since it has become too easy "to make a payment order from a different origin appear to have been sent from such an address of phone number."[129]
- Authorized and verified payment orders according to § 4A-202 must be based on a recorded agreement with the client, not necessarily a written agreement.
- Payment orders for the purposes of §§ 4A-207 and 208 can be "evidenced by a record." This will be equally valid as a signature.
- The same concept is introduced for the "signing" of letters of credit in § 5-104.
- In § 7-106, control over a document of title is expanded from a single authoritative copy to "one or more authoritative electronic copies" if it is possible to distinguish authoritative and non-authoritative copies, for example, with a cryptographic key.

128 See *supra*, note 123.

129 Uniform Commercial Code Amendments (2022), *supra* note 116, at 58-59.

- § 8-102 imports the concept and definition of "controllable account," "controllable electronic record," and "controllable payment intangible" from §§ 9-102 and 12-102.[130] Previously, under § 8-102(9)(A) a "financial asset" could be "(i) A security; (ii) An obligation of a person or a share, participation, or other interest in a person or in property or an enterprise of a person, which is, or is of a type, dealt in or traded on financial markets, or which is recognized in any area in which it is issued or dealt in as a medium for investment; or (iii) Any property that is held by a securities intermediary for another person in a securities account if the securities intermediary has expressly agreed with the other person that the property is to be treated as a financial asset under this article. (B) As context requires, the term "financial asset" means either the interest itself or the means by which a person's claim to it is evidenced, including a certificated or uncertificated security, a security certificate, or a security entitlement."[131]

With the amendment, if the parties agree to treat a digital asset as a financial asset under Article 8 and the digital asset is, in fact, held in a securities account for an entitlement holder, the rules applicable to "controllable electronic records" under Article 12 would not apply to the entitlement holder's security entitlement related to the financial asset. If the financial asset itself is a controllable electronic record, however, then the rules in Article 12 would apply to the securities intermediary's rights with respect to the controllable electronic record.

Unsurprisingly, a number of amendments were made to UCC Article 9 to ensure compatibility with the new technology and the new UCC Article 12,.

- The definition of "chattel paper" is revised from "a record evidencing a right to payment" to simply "a right to payment" (§ 9-102(a)(11). However, the record evidencing the right to payment is still needed for the perfection of the security. Perfection can be achieved in the traditional way by filing a financing statement with the respective state authority or by obtaining control of the controllable electronic record, for example, the private key to a crypto wallet (§ 9-107A).
- Pursuant to § 9-317(h) and (i), buyers of controllable electronic records and buyers of controllable electronic accounts and controllable payment intangibles are put on an equal footing with buyers of traditional chattel paper and/or electronic documents. That means that a security interest in a controllable electronic record, controllable account, or controllable payment

130 Uniform Commercial Code Amendments (2022), *supra* note 116, at 81.

131 See, for example, https://code.dccouncil.gov/us/dc/council/code/sections/28:8-102.

intangible that is perfected *by control*, as defined in § 9-314, has priority over a conflicting security interest that is perfected by another method.

- § 9-203 on attachment and enforceability of security interests is expanded to clarify that "a security interest is enforceable against the debtor and third parties with respect to the collateral" if the following conditions are met:
  1. value has been given;
  2. the debtor has rights in the collateral or the power to transfer rights in the collateral to a secured party; and
  3. one of the following conditions is met: [...]

  (C) the collateral is a certificated security in registered form, and the security certificate has been delivered to the secured party under Section 8-301 pursuant to the debtor's security agreement; or

  (D) the collateral is controllable accounts, controllable electronic records, controllable payment intangibles, deposit accounts, electronic documents, electronic money, investment property, or letter-of-credit rights, and the secured party has control under Section 7-106, 9-104, 9-105A, 9-106, 9-107, or 9-107A pursuant to the debtor's security agreement; or

  (E) the collateral is chattel paper, and the secured party has possession and control under Section 9-314A pursuant to the debtor's security agreement.
- Nevertheless, pursuant to § 9-332(a), a "transferee of tangible money takes the money free of a security interest if the transferee receives possession of the money without acting in collusion with the debtor in violating the rights of the secured party." Pursuant to § 9-332(c), the same is true for a transferee obtaining control of electronic money.

As stated in the Prefatory Note to Article 12, the amendment to the UCC is intended not only to provide rules for current emanations of DLT and Blockchain technology, but also for "technologies ... that may be developed in the future."[132] The Joint Committee of the Uniform Law Commission (U.L.C.) and the American Law Institute (ALI) Joint Committee explained the purpose of Article 12 as follows:

> The adoption of DLT has underscored two important trends in electronic commerce. First, people have begun to assign economic value to some electronic records that bear no relationship to extrinsic rights and interests. For example, without any law or binding agreement, people around the world have agreed to treat virtual currencies such as bitcoin [...] as

132 https://www.uniformlaws.org/viewdocument/final-act-164?CommunityKey=1457c422-ddb7-40b0-8c76-39a1991651ac&tab=librarydocuments, at 231.

> a medium of exchange and store of value. Second, people are using the creation or transfer of electronic records to transfer rights to receive payment, rights to receive performance of other obligations (e.g., services or delivery of goods), and other interests in personal and real property.
>
> These trends will inevitably result in disputes among claimants to electronic records and their related rights and other benefits. Uncertainty as to the criteria for resolving these claims creates commercial risk. The magnitude of these risks will grow as these trends continue.
>
> [...] Article 12 is designed to reduce these risks by providing the legal rules governing the transfer – both outright and for security – of interests in [... controllable electronic records]. These rules specify the rights in a controllable electronic record that a purchaser would acquire. Many systems for transferring controllable electronic records are pseudonymous, so that the transferee of a controllable electronic record is unable to verify the identity of the transferor or the source of the transferor's title. Accordingly, the Article 12 rules would make controllable electronic records negotiable, in the sense that a good faith purchaser for value would take a controllable electronic record free of third-party claims of a property interest in the controllable electronic record.[133]

Once the updates to the UCC are implemented by all or nearly all of the States and Territories, the revised UCC will be well prepared to handle a variety of transactions involving digital assets, including various forms of smart contracts for the transfer of rights and value. Until then, however, the situation is still in flux in some States and Territories and State may have to fill the gaps in the unamended UCC. However, it seems highly likely that the even the judges in States that have not yet implemented the changes will refer to the work of the Joint Committee in their quest to find equitable rules and solutions for disputes.

133 Prefatory Note to Article 12, https://www.uniformlaws.org/viewdocument/final-act-164?CommunityKey=1457c422-ddb7-40b0-8c76-39a1991651ac, at 229. The U.L.C. provides the specific example of a sale of Bitcoin. If seller S is the lawful owner, Article 12 provides that buyer B acquires "whatever rights S had or had power to transfer" (*Id.* at 232). However, even if S is a hacker who acquired the Bitcoin illegally from the real owner O, if "B obtains control of the bitcoin for value, in good faith, and without notice of any claim of a property interest, B would be a *qualifying purchaser*" and protected against claims by O (*Id.* at 233, emphasis added). This is commonly referred to as the "take-free rule."

3.2 *Overview of Individual State Approaches*

Beyond the efforts of the ULC, State legislative and regulatory activity regarding cryptocurrencies has been dynamic and diverse. Just since 2021, more than 100 pieces of legislation dealing with digital or virtual currencies were adopted by the Several State. The National Conference of State Legislatures (NCSL) maintains a website with links to all cryptocurrency-related legislation introduced, pending, and adopted by any of the 50 States, as well as the District of Columbia, Guam, the Mariana Islands, Puerto Rico, and the U.S. Virgin Islands.[134] The website's organization, however, makes it somewhat of a challenge to navigate.

Overall, the states can be divided into four groups when it comes to legislation in this area. The first group consists of States like Alaska, Arizona, Colorado, Florida, Nevada, New Hampshire, Tennessee, Texas, South Dakota, Washington, and Wyoming, actively encouraging or at least facilitating the development of Blockchain-based businesses. Puerto Rico, although not a State, falls into this category as well. These States and Territories have pretty much concluded that the technology is here to stay and can be harnessed for good. States in the first group are seeking advantages as welcoming jurisdictions attracting investment and jobs.

Most of the other States have adopted some legislation but do not consider themselves as actively promoting the development or use of digital currencies or seeking to attract cryptocurrency developers or exchanges. Most of them have adopted some guidance and some limits, essentially trying to find a middle ground based on the idea that Blockchain can be a legitimate and valuable industry as long as it complies with a number of restrictive rules and regulations.

Finally, a few states are widely considered hostile to cryptocurrency businesses. This includes New York,[135] California,[136] and Hawaii.[137]

A superficial look at the distribution of States into the three groups would suggest that their relative openness, indifference, or hostility to cryptocurrencies

---

134 For the current year, see https://www.ncsl.org/financial-services/cryptocurrency-digital-or-virtual-currency-and-digital-assets-2024-legislation.

135 New York requires crypto businesses to obtain a BitLicense, see below, and has some of the highest State income taxes in the country, plus additional New York City taxes.

136 California has the highest State income taxes in the U.S. and recently adopted crypto regulation comparable to New York's BitLicense, which will go into effect in July 2026. See https://dfpi.ca.gov/regulated-industries/digital-financial-assets/.

137 Hawaii also has comparably high State income taxes and a burdensome Money Transmitter License with strict fiat reserve requirements. See https://cca.hawaii.gov/dfi/learn-more-about-money-transmitters/.

is independent of their geographic location, geographic and population size, and political orientation.

Space does not permit this report to address the relevant laws in all the States. Instead, this report will address New York as an example of a restrictive approach in a State that is a financial center, and Wyoming as an example of a State promoting itself as a friendly jurisdiction to cryptocurrency and related developers and service providers.

3.2.1 New York

Pursuant to the New York Financial Services Law, the Department of Financial Services (NYDFS) issued virtual currency regulation 23 NYCRR Part 200, commonly known as "the BitLicense."[138] Under this regulation, the NYDFS has granted a number of virtual currency licenses and charters and claims that "New Yorkers have a well-regulated way to access the virtual currency marketplace and that New York remains at the center of technological innovation and forward-looking regulation."[139] A BitLicense is required for anyone engaging in virtual currency business activity "involving New York or a New York Resident,"[140] i.e. not just for businesses based in New York. Virtual currency business activity includes

1. receiving or transmitting virtual currency,
2. storing, holding, or maintaining custody or control of virtual currency on behalf of others;
3. buying and selling virtual currency as a customer business;
4. performing exchange services as a customer business; or
5. controlling, administering, or issuing a virtual currency.[141]

The only natural or legal persons involved with virtual currencies exempt from the licensing requirement are

---

138 See Official Compilation of Codes, Rules and Regulations of the State of New York, Title 23. Financial Services, Chapter I. Regulations of the Superintendent of Financial Services, Part 200. Virtual Currencies, available online at https://govt.westlaw.com/nycrr/Browse/Home/NewYork/NewYorkCodesRulesandRegulations?guid=I7444ce80169611e594630000845b8d3e&originationContext=documenttoc&transitionType=Default&contextData=(sc.Default).

139 New York State Department of Financial Services, *Virtual Currency Businesses*, available at https://www.dfs.ny.gov/virtual_currency_businesses.

140 § 200.2(q).

141 *Id.* An exemption applies for "digital units" used exclusively within online gaming platforms and have no market or application otherwise, digital units that can only be redeemed as part of a customer loyalty program, as well as digital units used like prepaid cards; § 200.2(p).

1. persons that are chartered under the New York Banking Law and are approved by the superintendent to engage in virtual currency business activity; and
2. merchants and consumers that utilize virtual currency solely for the purchase or sale of goods or services or for investment purposes.[142]

Anyone else engaged in virtual currency business requires a license from the NYDFS. Applicants must provide extensive information about themselves, including a background report – including a full set of fingerprints and photos – prepared by an independent investigatory agency acceptable to the superintendent for each individual applicant, each principal officer, principal stockholder, and principal beneficiary of the applicant, as well as "all individuals to be employed by the applicant who have access to customer funds." Among the many requirements is also "an explanation of the methodology used to calculate the value of virtual currency." It will be interesting to see whether this will lead to the development of standards for the valuation of coins and tokens that are not traded widely on exchanges.

The superintendent generally has 90 days after a filing and payment of the US$ 5,000 application fee to "investigate the financial condition and responsibility, financial and business experience, and character and general fitness of the applicant" and either approve or deny the license.[143] Once approved, a license is generally not limited in time and remains valid unless it is surrendered by the licensee.[144] However, any license can be suspended or revoked by the superintendent at any time "on any ground on which the superintendent might refuse to issue an original license, for a violation of any provision of this [regulation], for good cause shown [...]."[145]

Among the requirements imposed on licensees is to:

> maintain and enforce written compliance policies, including policies with respect to anti-fraud, anti-money laundering, cyber security, privacy and information security, and any other policy required under this [regulation], which must be reviewed and approved by the licensee's board of directors or an equivalent governing body [... and] designate a qualified individual or individuals responsible for coordinating and monitoring

142 § 200.3(c).
143 § 200.6(a).
144 § 200.6(b).
145 § 200.6(c).

> compliance with this Part and all other applicable Federal and State laws, rules, and regulations.[146]

They must also "maintain at all times such capital in an amount and form as the superintendent determines is sufficient to ensure the financial integrity of the licensee and its ongoing operations based on an assessment of the specific risks applicable to each licensee"[147] as well as "maintain a surety bond or trust account in United States dollars for the benefit of its customers in such form and amount as is acceptable to the superintendent for the protection of the licensee's customers."[148] Further, "[t]o the extent a licensee stores, holds, or maintains custody or control of virtual currency on behalf of another person, such licensee shall hold virtual currency of the same type and amount as that which is owed or obligated to such other person."[149]

There are also extensive recordkeeping requirements,[150] required reports and financial disclosures,[151] as well as disclosure requirements for consumer protection,[152] which are largely comparable to those applying to publicly traded companies. The superintendent also has expansive examination powers,[153] and there are the usual anti-money laundering obligations for larger transactions over US$ 3,000.[154] New York has also adopted specific cybersecurity requirements for financial services companies,[155] as well as specific transaction monitoring requirements for the enforcement of Know-Your-Customer (KYC) and Anti-Money Laundering (AML) requirements.[156]

---

146 § 200.7.

147 § 200.8(a).

148 § 200.9(a).

149 § 200.9.

150 § 200.12.

151 § 200.14.

152 § 200.19.

153 § 200.13.

154 § 200.15.

155 See Official Compilation of Codes, Rules and Regulations of the State of New York, Title 23. Financial Services, Chapter 1. Regulations of the Superintendent of Financial Services, Part 500. Cybersecurity Requirements for Financial Services Companies, available online at https://govt.westlaw.com/nycrr/Document/I60c61d250d5f11e79781d30ba488e782?viewType=FullText&originationContext=documenttoc&transitionType=CategoryPageItem&contextData=(sc.Default).

156 See Official Compilation of Codes, Rules and Regulations of the State of New York, Title 23. Financial Services, Chapter 1. Regulations of the Superintendent of Financial Services, Part 504. Banking Division Transaction Monitoring and Filtering Program Requirements and Certifications, available at https://govt.westlaw.com/nycrr/Document/If190167558ac

To its credit, it must be said that the BitLicense regulation is one of the most clearly written pieces of legislation or regulation applicable to cryptocurrency businesses in the United States, eliminating the need for specialized lawyers, which are normally required when dealing with securities law. That said, the BitLicense regulation "is generally regarded as the most onerous regulation of virtual currency businesses in the United States."[157] Alex Adelman and Aubrey Strobel have complained that

> New York, generally regarded as the financial capital of the world, has clung to regulations that make it immensely difficult for crypto companies, especially smaller startups, to operate in the state. [...] The [BitLicense] has staved off grassroots innovation in the city by ensuring that only companies with abundant disposable capital can shoulder its notoriously time and capital-intensive application and compliance measures.[158]

According to their information, "the time allocation, legal fees and other costs drive the total cost of pursuing a BitLicense to more than $100,000, surpassing the means of most early-stage startups."[159] The result, Adelman and Strobel argue, is to push many startups either to more welcoming states like Wyoming or entirely offshore. As a possible motive, they point to financial service providers and institutional banks serving as the primary source of revenue for the NYDFS.[160]

3.2.2 Wyoming

Long-dominated by mining and agriculture, Wyoming was looking for opportunities to grow and diversify its economy and found them in the crypto space. In 2016, Wyoming declared digital currencies to be permissible investments[161] and exempted "the transmission of monetary value and digital currency from

---

11e6806bc9321b10fb4e?viewType=FullText&originationContext=documenttoc&transitionType=CategoryPageItem&contextData=(sc.Default).

157 Stabile, Prior & Hinkes, *supra* note 39, at 108.

158 Alex Adelman & Aubrey Strobel, Opinion: *Kill the BitLicense – The State's Regulatory Regime Has Been Bad for New York and Bad for Crypto*, https://www.coindesk.com/policy/2021/10/19/kill-the-bitlicense/.

159 *Id.*

160 *Id.*

161 Wyoming Money Transmitter Act – Investments, HB0026 (2016), available at https://www.wyoleg.gov/Legislation/2016/HB0026.

the Wyoming Money Transmitter Act licensure requirements".[162] In 2018, Wyoming made explicit that "a person who develops, sells or facilitates the exchange of an open blockchain token is not subject to specified securities and money transmission laws" as long as the token is for consumptive purposes – i.e. a utility token – and not marketed as an investment.[163] Going further, Wyoming exempted virtual currencies from Wyoming property taxes.[164] The State also updated its Business Corporations Act "authorizing corporations to use electronic networks or databases for the creation or maintenance of corporate records; authorizing the use of a data address to identify a corporation's shareholder; authorizing corporations to accept shareholder votes if signed by a network signature that corresponds to a data address; [and] specifying requirements for use of electronic networks or databases;"[165] and it made it easier for limited liability companies (LLCs) "to establish series of members, managers, transferable interests or assets as specified; specifying powers; providing for limitations on liabilities; providing for management, termination and dissolution; authorizing distributions to members".[166] Series LLCs can be used to hold different assets – like different blockchains or cryptocurrency wallets – in separate LLCs, with separate rules about distributions, and segregated liability. In 2019, Wyoming clarified that digital assets are property for the purposes of the UCC, and provided a welcoming framework for custodial services for digital assets. In effect, this bill authorizes banks to provide custodial

162 Wyoming Money Transmitter Act – Digital Currency Amendments, HB0062 (2016), available at https://www.wyoleg.gov/Legislation/2016/HB0062.

163 Open Blockchain Tokens – Exemptions, HB0070 (2018), available at https://www.wyoleg.gov/Legislation/2018/HB0070. See Erik Kuebler, Wyoming House Unanimously Approves Two Pro-Blockchain Bills, Yahoo Finance, 20 February 2018, https://finance.yahoo.com/news/wyoming-house-unanimously-approves-two-164211109.html?guccounter=1&guce_referrer=aHR0cHM6Ly93d3cuYmluZy5jb20v&guce_referrer_sig=AQAAACcsmKCEAVtidx_MOO9QqE3XYaP2Nbt2Rom_eBq5qq5qRSP5qImvh4D0a8O2pA_oIZd_g9vfynhnTyW9jfB2wgmg_exj4D5kbddQnqkj16YjxBbSRtzRx2zzWgLBMcr8Wp784Z_KneLqvpd2xYGX8hJFGuvaMfnwHMsS5L102M5A. For additional analysis see Jennifer Post, Wyoming Signs Cryptocurrency Bills Into Law, ThompsonCoburn LLP 11 April 2018, https://www.thompsoncoburn.com/insights/publications/item/2018-04-11/wyoming-signs-cryptocurrency-bills-into-law.

164 Property Taxation – Digital Currencies, SF0111 (2018), available at https://www.wyoleg.gov/Legislation/2018/SF0111. The state generally does not charge state income taxes.

165 HB0101 (2018), commonly referred to as "the Blockchain Filings Bill" because it allows the use of blockchain records for corporate record-keeping and filings with the Secretary of State; the bill is available at https://www.wyoleg.gov/Legislation/2018/HB0101. In 2019, Wyoming added HB0185 (2019) "authorizing authorizing corporations to issue certificate tokens in lieu of stock certificates"; see https://www.wyoleg.gov/Legislation/2019/HB0185.

166 HB0126 (2018) has been referred to as "the Series LLC Bill" and is available at https://www.wyoleg.gov/Legislation/2018/HB0126.

services for crypto.[167] Issuers of utility tokens can do so in Wyoming by filing a "notice of intent."[168] The fees for the notice amount to a comparably modest US$ 1,000. In 2020, Wyoming clarified how UCC Article 9 would apply to virtual currencies used as collateral in secured transactions.[169] As a result, Wyoming has largely accomplished already in 2020, what the ULC Joint Study Committee and the 2022 amendments to the UCC are achieving only now, namely to define "control" and "possession" for purposes of perfecting a security interest and determining priority among several perfected interests when dealing with cryptocurrencies.[170]

With its open-for-crypto-businesses attitude, Wyoming not only attracted unicorns like the crypto exchange Kraken, the Blockchain platform Cardano, and the payment protocol company Ripple Labs to move to the State; thousands of DLT startups have incorporated in the State. In 2020, Wyoming created the Special Purpose Depository Institution Bank Charter (SPDI), specifically for banks seeking to deal both in fiat and cryptocurrencies.[171] Since then, Kraken Bank,[172] as well as Caitlin Long's Avanti Bank and Trust,[173] have obtained crypto banking charters.

In July 2021, the State went further by creating "a supplement to the Wyoming Limited Liability Company Act to provide law controlling the creation and management of a DAO."[174] The summary explains that "[a] decentralized autonomous organization (DAO) is a limited liability company with special provisions allowing the company to be algorithmically run or managed (in whole or in part) through smart contracts executed by computers."[175] As the

---

167 Digital Assets – Existing Law, SF0125 (2019), available at https://www.wyoleg.gov/Legislation/2019/SF0125.

168 Wyoming Utility Token Act – Property Amendments, HB0062 (2019), available at https://www.wyoleg.gov/Legislation/2019/HB0062.

169 Digital Assets – Statutory Amendments, SF0047 (2020), available at https://www.wyoleg.gov/Legislation/2020/SF0047.

170 https://wyoleg.gov/2020/Summaries/SF0047.pdf. See also Digital Representation Tokens, HB 0043 (2020), available at https://www.wyoleg.gov/Legislation/2020/HB0043.

171 State of Wyoming, Division of Banking, *Special Purpose Depositary Institutions*, available at https://wyomingbankingdivision.wyo.gov/banks-and-trust-companies/special-purpose-depository-institutions.

172 https://www.kraken.com/en-us/bank.

173 Maria Aspan, *How Caitlin Long Turned Wyoming into Crypto Country*, Fortune (29 July 2021), available at https://fortune.com/2021/07/29/caitlin-long-wyoming-crypto/.

174 Decentralized Autonomous Organizations, SF0038 (2021), available at https://www.wyoleg.gov/Legislation/2021/SF0038.

175 Select Committee on Blockchain, Financial Technology and Digital Innovation Technology, *Decentralized Autonomous Organizations, Summary/Major Elements*, LSO No. 21LSO-0263, SEA No. 0073, Chapter 162, available at https://wyoleg.gov/2021/Summaries/SF0038.pdf.

high-level summary explains, the bill also "establishes baseline requirements for member managed or algorithmically managed DAO's and provides definitions and regulations for DAO formation, articles of organization, operating agreements, smart contracts, management, standards of conduct, membership interests, voting rights, the withdrawal of members and dissolution."[176] This new law not only makes Wyoming the first jurisdiction anywhere in the world to explicitly provide a legal basis for a DAO; it also provides the details that make the operation of such an organization predictable and transparent. In 2024, Wyoming added a law specifically providing for "the formation and management of decentralized unincorporated nonprofit associations".[177] Although it is too soon to tell how many DAOs will be created in Wyoming pursuant to this legislation – especially since the Federal SEC and CFTC regulations are also still applicable – a quick online search brings up dozens of law firms offering their services for the incorporation of such organizations. Last but not least, after already creating the Wyoming Stable Token Act in 2023,[178] Wyoming added SF0052 (2024), which basically authorizes the State to create the first government-issued stablecoin in the U.S.[179] Altogether, Wyoming has adopted more than 30 crypto-friendly legislative acts, clearly positioning the State as the most welcoming jurisdiction in the U.S.[180]

4 Conclusions on the Current Legal Regime Provided for Cryptocurrencies in the United States of America

If the long-term investments necessary for new technologies, particularly technologies with disruptive potential, require clear regulatory guidance and

176 *Id.*

177 SF0050 (2024) is available at https://www.wyoleg.gov/Legislation/2024/SF0050.

178 SF0127 (2023) is available at https://wyoleg.gov/Legislation/2023/SF0127.

179 See https://www.wyoleg.gov/Legislation/2024/SF0052.

180 For additional analysis see, inter alia, Zachary Miller, *The Right Side of the Coin: State Approaches in Regulating Virtual Currencies*, 45 Seton Hall Legis. J. 809 (2021); Kelly Mahoney, *Cryptocurrency: Regulate or Facilitate? How States' Approaches to Cryptocurrency Can Be Applied on a Federal Level*, 43 J. Nat'l Ass'n Admin. L. Judiciary Iss. 2 (2023), available at: https://digitalcommons.pepperdine.edu/naalj/vol43/iss2/3; Pawan Jain, *From Crypto Wild West to Regulated Frontier: Unleashing the Potential of Blockchain Technology*, 126 W. Va. L. Rev. 239 (2023-2024); as well as Max Padilla, *Governor Mark Gordon on Wyoming's Economy, Disconnect from Washington, and Cryptocurrency*, Chicago Policy Review 2024, retrieved from https://library.indianapolis.iu.edu/cgi-bin/proxy.pl?url=https://www.proquest.com/scholarly-journals/governor-mark-gordon-on-wyoming-s-economy/docview/2917868901/se-2.

a stable regulatory environment, then U.S. regulators deserve a failing grade. This report shows a U.S. legal regime for cryptocurrency developers, issuers, traders, service providers, and exchanges, full of conflicting answers and unduly burdensome requirements imposed by different regulators. Even forward-looking States like Wyoming are hamstrung by overly restrictive and at least partly conflicting rules and regulations issued by Federal agencies like the SEC and the CFTC. In addition, if State-level regimes like the New York BitLicense are applied not only to businesses incorporated in New York but to anyone who sells crypto to anyone living there, each and every State in the U.S. can, at least in theory, de facto impose their version of crypto law on the entire industry. Since the SEC, in particular, is not shy to impose its decisions on crypto businesses from around the world, regardless of their place of incorporation or domicile, as long as they provide services (also) to U.S. citizens and entities, we all have to put up with this complex and frustrating legal situation. Moreover, the approach taken by U.S. legislators and regulators is in flux and rapidly evolving. This means, unfortunately, that crypto businesses that cannot or do not want to comprehensively and effectively exclude any U.S. parties from their activities will have to continuously monitor U.S. law with the help of qualified and expensive U.S. attorneys and experts.

President-elect Trump has campaigned in part on a promise that the U.S. is going to do "something great with crypto"[181] and that he would fire the SEC Chairman Gary Gensler on his first day in office.[182] Whether the new administration in Washington will be able to cut this Gordian knot remains to be seen.

---

181 See, e.g., Tanaya Macheel, *Trump Says the U.S. Is Going to Do 'Something Great with Crypto'*, CNBC 12 December 2024, https://www.cnbc.com/2024/12/12/trump-says-the-us-is-going-to-do-something-great-with-crypto.html.

182 See, e.g., Marco Quiroz-Gutierrez, *Trump Vowed to Oust SEC Chairman Gary Gensler, and These Crypto Advocates Could Take His Place*, Yahoo Finance, 10 November 2024, https://finance.yahoo.com/news/trump-vowed-oust-sec-chairman-093300465.html?guccounter=1&guce_referrer=aHR0cHM6Ly93d3cuZ29vZ2xlLmNvbS8&guce_referrer_sig=AQAAAFO8Dq-zAOv5coCetZoDaoKV2naAK1mQpYdvE9ETICIbg9v4v6zcJfGhjQykYZEZwUgxhCS10HDT6_XXZoRDEyoWfMdoWC5EzS8J_NrOJ2ml84I3rBA_HLnoWL99PTTWE5zahe33SSPODvla8zyTwNTYCSUkoBwCes4ti8NuWMTQ.

Index

www.ingramcontent.com/pod-product-compliance
Lightning Source LLC
LaVergne TN
LVHW090000031026
849161LV00019B/8